THE HUMAN EXPRESSION

FOURTH EDITION

World
Regions
and
Cultures

Paul Thomas Welty
Miriam Greenblatt

GLENCOE

Macmillan/McGraw-Hill

New York, New York   Columbus, Ohio   Mission Hills, California   Peoria, Illinois

Dr. Paul Welty taught at Northeastern Illinois University for many years. He believed that world history texts should stress a cultural approach. In addition to writing *The Human Expression*, Dr. Welty also authored *The Asians: Their Evolving Heritage* and *Man's Cultural Heritage*. He edited *World Cultures Sourcebooks* (8 volumes), *Pageant of World Cultures*, and *Readings in World Cultures*.

Miriam Greenblatt is a writer, editor, and nationally recognized educational consultant. She is a graduate of Hunter College and the University of Chicago and is an adjunct teacher at New Trier High School. She has written for or contributed to more than twenty-five social studies programs. She is an officer of the American Historical Association's Committee on History in the Classroom. Greenblatt is listed in the *Who's Who of American Women* for 1988–1989.

Reviewers

Gerard San Gemino
Curriculum Coordinator
Social Studies, Grades 1–12
Nanuet Public Schools
Nanuet, New York

Gary Koeller
Administrative Assistant
Moline High School
Moline, Illinois

Gloria Sesso
Social Studies Supervisor
Half Hollow Hills School
   District
Dix Hills, New York

Dr. Crystal Sisler
Coordinator of Research and
   Evaluation
Duval County Public Schools
Jacksonville, Florida

Send all inquiries to:
Glencoe Division, Macmillan/McGraw-Hill
936 Eastwind Drive
Westerville, Ohio 43081-3374

ISBN 0-02-654000-2
   4 5 6 7 8 9   95 94 93

CONTENTS

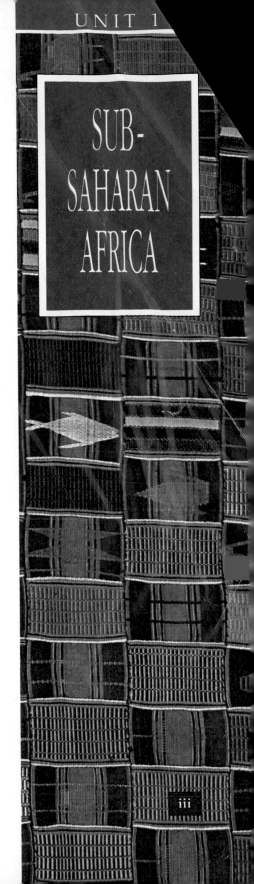

UNIT 1

SUB-SAHARAN AFRICA

iii

SOUTH
AND
SOUTHEAST
ASIA

UNIT 3

EAST ASIA

LATIN AMERICA

UNIT 5   394

UNIT 5

THE MIDDLE EAST

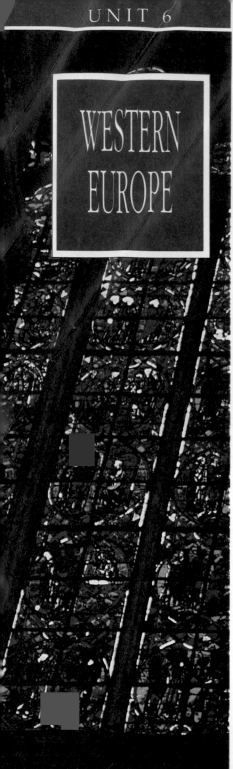

WESTERN
EUROPE

THE SOVIET UNION AND EASTERN EUROPE

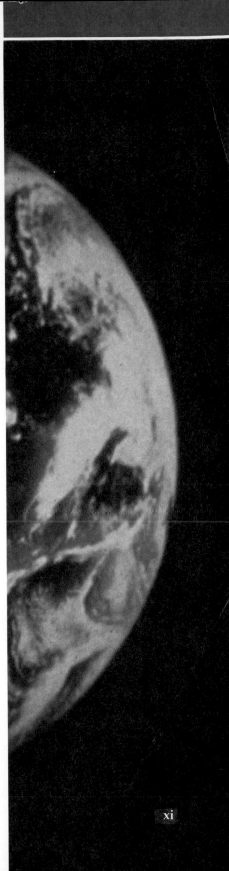

MAPS, TABLES, GRAPHS, AND CHARTS

THE SOVIET UNION AND EASTERN EUROPE

SOCIAL STUDIES SKILLS AND FEATURES

PROLOGUE: THE STUDY OF CULTURE

SUB-SAHARAN AFRICA

SOUTH AND SOUTHEAST ASIA

EAST ASIA

HOW TO USE THIS BOOK

The authors and editors of *The Human Expression: World Regions and Cultures* believe it would be helpful to you in using this book if you know how it is arranged. First, there is *Prologue: The Study of Culture* which introduces you to the terms and methods of the social sciences. It contains the basic vocabulary you will need to study each world region. Next, there are seven units arranged by regions. They are *Sub-Saharan Africa, South and Southeast Asia, East Asia, Latin America, The Middle East, Western Europe,* and *The Soviet Union and Eastern Europe.* Finally, there

is *Epilogue: The World Today* which presents to you the challenges facing the world in which we live. Because you take courses in United States history, geography, economics, society, and the arts, there is no need to provide a historical-cultural study of the United States.

Each unit is divided into chapters and sections. Below and on the following page, you will find sample pages from the textbook, pages 140, 153, and 157 of *South and Southeast Asia.* They are reproduced here to show you the features that will help you to use and enjoy this textbook.

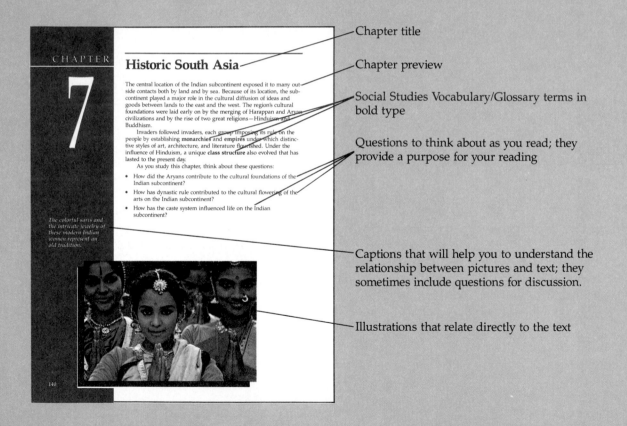

CHAPTER

7

The colorful saris and the intricate jewelry of these modern Indian women represent an old tradition.

Historic South Asia

The central location of the Indian subcontinent exposed it to many outside contacts both by land and by sea. Because of its location, the subcontinent played a major role in the cultural diffusion of ideas and goods between lands to the east and the west. The region's cultural foundations were laid early on by the merging of Harappan and Aryan civilizations and by the rise of two great religions—Hinduism and Buddhism.

Invaders followed invaders, each group imposing its rule on the people by establishing **monarchies** and **empires** under which distinctive styles of art, architecture, and literature flourished. Under the influence of Hinduism, a unique **class structure** also evolved that has lasted to the present day.

As you study this chapter, think about these questions:

- How did the Aryans contribute to the cultural foundations of the Indian subcontinent?
- How has dynastic rule contributed to the cultural flowering of the arts on the Indian subcontinent?
- How has the caste system influenced life on the Indian subcontinent?

140

Chapter title

Chapter preview

Social Studies Vocabulary/Glossary terms in bold type

Questions to think about as you read; they provide a purpose for your reading

Captions that will help you to understand the relationship between pictures and text; they sometimes include questions for discussion.

Illustrations that relate directly to the text

Section title

Section introduction and preview

Topic

Phonetic pronunciations

Easy-to-understand maps

Review questions at the end of each section

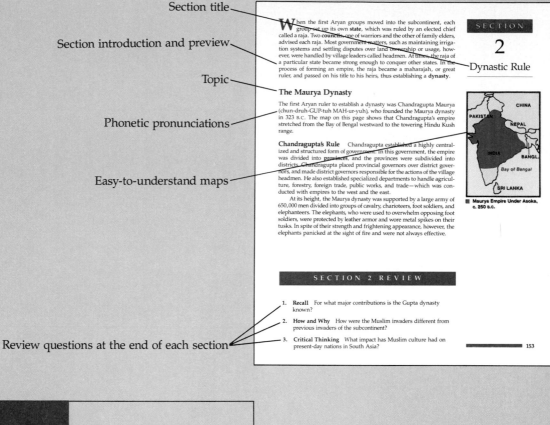

When the first Aryan groups moved into the subcontinent, each group set up its own **state**, which was ruled by an elected chief called a raja. Two **councils**, one of warriors and the other of family elders, advised each raja. Most government matters, such as maintaining irrigation systems and settling disputes over land ownership or usage, however, were handled by village leaders called headmen. At times, the raja of a particular state became strong enough to conquer other states. In the process of forming an empire, the raja became a maharajah, or great ruler, and passed on his title to his heirs, thus establishing a **dynasty**.

SECTION
2
Dynastic Rule

The Maurya Dynasty

The first Aryan ruler to establish a dynasty was Chandragupta Maurya (chun-druh-GUP-tuh MAH-ur-yuh), who founded the Maurya dynasty in 323 B.C. The map on this page shows that Chandragupta's empire stretched from the Bay of Bengal westward to the towering Hindu Kush range.

Chandragupta's Rule   Chandragupta established a highly centralized and structured form of government. In this government, the empire was divided into provinces, and the provinces were subdivided into districts. Chandragupta placed provincial governors over district governors, and made district governors responsible for the actions of the village headmen. He also established specialized departments to handle agriculture, forestry, foreign trade, public works, and trade—which were conducted with empires to the west and the east.

At its height, the Maurya dynasty was supported by a large army of 650,000 men divided into groups of cavalry, charioteers, foot soldiers, and elephanteers. The elephants, who were used to overwhelm opposing foot soldiers, were protected by leather armor and wore metal spikes on their tusks. In spite of their strength and frightening appearance, however, the elephants panicked at the sight of fire and were not always effective.

■ **Maurya Empire Under Asoka, c. 250 B.C.**

SECTION 2 REVIEW

1. **Recall**   For what major contributions is the Gupta dynasty known?

2. **How and Why**   How were the Muslim invaders different from previous invaders of the subcontinent?

3. **Critical Thinking**   What impact has Muslim culture had on present-day nations in South Asia?

153

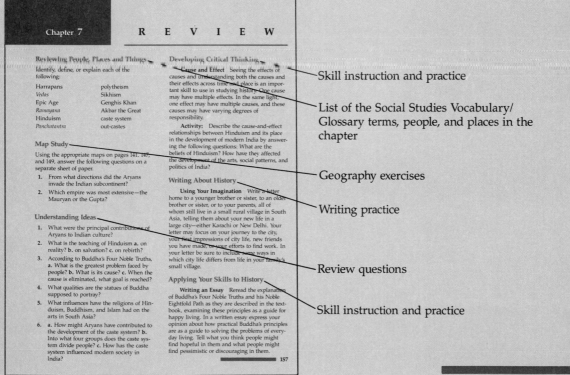

Chapter 7   R E V I E W

Skill instruction and practice

List of the Social Studies Vocabulary/ Glossary terms, people, and places in the chapter

Geography exercises

Writing practice

Review questions

Skill instruction and practice

Reviewing People, Places and Things

Identify, define, or explain each of the following:

Harrapans
Vedas
Epic Age
Ramayana
Hinduism
Panchatantra

polytheism
Sikhism
Genghis Khan
Akbar the Great
caste system
out-castes

Map Study

Using the appropriate maps on pages 141, 147, and 149, answer the following questions on a separate sheet of paper.

1. From what directions did the Aryans invade the Indian subcontinent?

2. Which empire was most extensive—the Mauryan or the Gupta?

Understanding Ideas

1. What were the principal contributions of Aryans to Indian culture?

2. What is the teaching of Hinduism **a.** on reality? **b.** on salvation? **c.** on rebirth?

3. According to Buddha's Four Noble Truths, **a.** What is the greatest problem faced by people? **b.** What is its cause? **c.** When the cause is eliminated, what goal is reached?

4. What qualities are the statues of Buddha supposed to portray?

5. What influences have the religions of Hinduism, Buddhism, and Islam had on the arts in South Asia?

6. **a.** How might Aryans have contributed to the development of the caste system? **b.** Into what four groups does the caste system divide people? **c.** How has the caste system influenced modern society in India?

Developing Critical Thinking

Cause and Effect   Seeing the effects of causes and understanding both the causes and their effects across time and place is an important skill to use in studying history. One cause may have multiple effects. In the same light, one effect may have multiple causes, and these causes may have varying degrees of responsibility.

Activity: Describe the cause-and-effect relationships between Hinduism and its place in the development of modern India by answering the following questions: What are the beliefs of Hinduism? How have they affected the development of the arts, social patterns, and politics of India?

Writing About History

Using Your Imagination   Write a letter home to a younger brother or sister, to an older brother or sister, or to your parents, all of whom still live in a small rural village in South Asia, telling them about your new life in a large city—either Karachi or New Delhi. Your letter may focus on your journey to the city, your first impressions of city life, new friends you have made, or your efforts to find work. In your letter be sure to include some ways in which city life differs from life in your family's small village.

Applying Your Skills to History

Writing an Essay   Reread the explanation of Buddha's Four Noble Truths and his Noble Eightfold Path as they are described in the textbook, examining these principles as a guide to happy living. In a written essay express your opinion about how practical Buddha's principles are as a guide to solving the problems of everyday living. Tell what you think people might find hopeful in them and what people might find pessimistic or discouraging in them.

157

1

PROLOGUE

Culture, as anthropologists use the term, means all the ways of life and knowledge—the learned behavior—of a people. This man is making sun-dried bricks the way his ancestors did for centuries. Culture, however, is not static. He is working to the music of a transistor radio.

The Study of Culture

The Human Expression: A History of the World will introduce you to the cultures—past and present—of the various peoples of the world. When scholars speak of **culture**, they mean all the ways of life and knowledge of a people. A culture includes the tools and other objects that people use, their language, their religious beliefs, customs, values, folklore, ways of eating and dressing, and their everyday activities. It includes a people's history and government as well as their achievements in art, literature, science, and technology.

Every group of people in the world has a culture. Scholars do not think in terms of one person or group being more cultured than another. All people are cultured in the sense that they grow up learning their own culture. This is so that as adults, they can function within their own group.

As you study the prologue, think about these questions:

- Why have different cultures fulfilled their basic needs in different ways?

- How have scientists found out about the early inhabitants of the world?

- How did the agricultural revolution influence the development of world cultures?

This cave painting of a horse was found in France. Does its appearance differ in any way from horses today?

4

H istorians who study human culture draw on research and analysis from other fields of study. Some of these fields include: anthropology, sociology, economics, and geography. These disciplines contribute to our understanding of what early human society was like and how and why cultures developed as they have.

Anthropology

The term *anthropology* comes from two Greek words: *anthropos*, which means "man," and *logos*, which means "word." Today, *anthropos* might be translated more acceptably as "people." Anthropologists in the past used the word *man* to mean both men and women. Anthropology is literally words about people. It is the study of people, their place in the natural world, their cultural development, and their differing ways of living and behaving. Two major divisions are physical anthropology and cultural anthropology.

Physical anthropologists study the physical development of humans since their appearance in **prehistory**, that is, in the time before writing developed roughly 5,000 years ago. Cultural anthropologists study the development of human culture and the ways that social groups behave. They may study dead cultures or living ones. Anthropologists use comparisons between peoples to study physical and cultural similarities and differences. From these studies they form general ideas, or generalizations, about human development. A generalization is a conclusion that is reached after gathering and analyzing information. It pulls together the common ideas behind a number of examples and specific facts.

How Scientists Study People

The field of anthropology is so large that it has been further divided into various branches. One of these is **archaeology**. *Archaeo* means "ancient." Archaeologists investigate the cultures of both prehistoric and historic peoples by studying the materials they left behind. These remains include anything people made or created such as tools, pottery, buildings, and writings.

Special Terms   Like all sciences, anthropology uses special terms. To anthropologists, the objects, such as pots and buildings that people make—whether by hand or machine—are called artifacts. Some ordinary words take on very exact meanings. For example, the word *dig* to an archaeologist means an excavation site.

Another special term that anthropologists use is *culture trait*. A **culture trait** is a characteristic that is held in common by members of the same culture. For example, bowing is a Japanese culture trait. Instead of shaking hands the way Americans usually do when they meet, Japanese people greet one another by bowing. Also, the person who is less important will bow low to one who is more important, while the more important person will simply nod his or her head.

Throughout history, there has been a flow of culture traits from one cultural group to another. Features of one culture are carried to others through such things as trade and conquest, and more recently through world telecommunications. An example of this process of **cultural diffusion** was the movement of the Buddhist religion from India south to what is now Sri Lanka and east to China, Korea, Japan, and the mainland nations of Southeast Asia.

Another term anthropologists use is *culture region*. By this they mean an area in which people of different cultural groups have adapted to their surroundings in similar ways. Thus many culture traits are held in common. Most farmers in central and southern China grow paddy rice for a living. So do most farmers in Korea. For over a thousand years, the two peoples have shared a common written language. Most people have lived in small villages, and most were and are Buddhists. Because they have so many common ways of life, the Koreans and the Chinese can be said to belong to the same culture region.

Culture regions may not have clear boundaries. For this reason, scholars may not always agree on the number of world culture regions and the countries included in these regions. This book divides the people of the world into seven culture regions: Sub-Saharan Africa, South and Southeast Asia, East Asia, Latin America, the Middle East, Western Europe, and the Soviet Union and Eastern Europe. North American culture—Canada and the United States—is not covered in this text.

Cultural Change   All cultures experience change. Sometimes this change is slow and may not be noticed for many years. In modern times this is true of groups that have not been greatly influenced by the revolutions in **technology**. However, the world of the late twentieth century is more than ever one of **interdependence**. Through technology and economics, all nations are connected. What happens in one part of the world may affect what happens in other parts.

In nations with a high level of **industrialization**, differences in way of life are noticeable within 10 to 20 years, or even less. In these nations, the ever-increasing pace of technology can bring about rapid changes in such things as the way people earn their living and the foods they eat.

Anthropologists use the term *acculturation* to describe a process of change that takes place when two cultural groups have contact with each other over a long period of time. In this process each may influence the cultural life of the other. The relationship between the United States and Great Britain since the industrial revolution is such an example. There are also times when one culture may strongly influence the other without being greatly affected itself. European colonial governments greatly changed traditional ways of African societies while being influenced very little in return.

Language Families

The scientific study of language is called linguistics. Language—either written or spoken—is a way of communicating that can be understood by all members of a group. It is an important part of a culture.

Not all people who speak the same language are necessarily of the same national origin. Many people in the United States have parents who came from Asia, Africa, Latin America, or Europe. All these people may speak English today, yet their parents came from different geographic areas of the world. In addition, even though people may live in the same geographic area, they may not speak the same language. For example, the Chinese and the Koreans are East Asians, but they speak different languages.

In the world of the late twentieth century, Western clothes, food, attitudes, and values have spread around the world. This is an example of cultural diffusion. For example, few young Japanese women wear traditional kimonos anymore. What specific Western culture trait has influenced Japan?

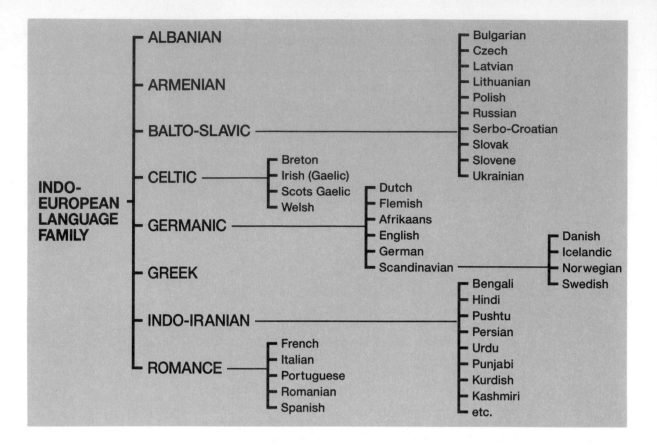

INDO-EUROPEAN LANGUAGE FAMILY

- ALBANIAN
- ARMENIAN
- BALTO-SLAVIC
  - Bulgarian
  - Czech
  - Latvian
  - Lithuanian
  - Polish
  - Russian
  - Serbo-Croatian
  - Slovak
  - Slovene
  - Ukrainian
- CELTIC
  - Breton
  - Irish (Gaelic)
  - Scots Gaelic
  - Welsh
- GERMANIC
  - Dutch
  - Flemish
  - Afrikaans
  - English
  - German
  - Scandinavian
    - Danish
    - Icelandic
    - Norwegian
    - Swedish
- GREEK
- INDO-IRANIAN
  - Bengali
  - Hindi
  - Pushtu
  - Persian
  - Urdu
  - Punjabi
  - Kurdish
  - Kashmiri
  - etc.
- ROMANCE
  - French
  - Italian
  - Portuguese
  - Romanian
  - Spanish

Many languages of the world belong to the same **language families**. They have words that come from the same source and that can be recognized in each of the languages of the same family. For example, the Latin word *mater* is *madre* in Spanish, *mutter* in German, and *mother* in English. All these languages belong to the Indo-European language family, which includes most of the languages of Western and Eastern Europe as well as Hindi of India and Farsi of Iran.

Through the study of ancient languages and languages that are related to one another, it is often possible to tell something about the movements or the origins of a people. By tracing the spread of Bantu languages back through South, Central, and East Africa, anthropologists have been able to discover the origins of the Bantu-speaking peoples in the Cameroon highlands in Central Africa.

Society and Social Groupings

People have always lived together in groups. Social scientists in describing these groupings use the term of *sociology*, the study of the development, organization, and functioning of human society.

The basic unit of human social contact is the family. It may be either nuclear or extended. A **nuclear family** is made up of a father, a mother, and their children. It is the usual type of family unit found in industrialized, urban areas. It may vary, however. For example, it may consist of brothers, sisters, and one parent. An **extended family** might include grandparents, aunts, uncles, and cousins. This type of family is quite common in Asia and Africa and in many rural areas of the world.

Everyone is related to someone. This relationship is called **kinship**. Kinship often determines how people behave within the group. For example, there are rules of relationship about who may or may not marry whom. In some cultures, uncles may marry their nieces. In other cultures, such a practice is forbidden. Other kinship rules determine how property is passed from generation to generation. In some cultures, custom dictates that only the oldest son may inherit. In other cultures, property is divided equally among all the children.

Some societies have traditionally large kinship systems that include all those who are descended from a common ancestor. Sometimes several families claiming an often remote, perhaps even mythical, common ancestor will form a **clan**. The clan system was once very important in China, and is still important to many Africans.

Families live in households. When larger numbers of people cluster together, they are said to live in villages. Not everyone lives a settled way of life. Some people are nomads, wandering from place to place in a seasonal pattern looking for grasslands for their herds. Such groups are called bands.

Many bands and villages may occupy the same territory. When they share a similar culture, they are known as tribes or **ethnic groups**. Some scholars prefer the term *people* to refer to this larger social grouping. Groups of peoples may organize themselves into a larger political, economic, and social unit defined by territorial boundaries. This is called a **nation** or country.

Another common term in sociology is *society*, meaning any group of people who have a shared culture and identity. Generally the group also occupies the same territory. The size of the group does not matter. An isolated village, a small band of nomads, or a nation of millions can be a society. When speaking of nations, however, one must be careful.

Some nations in the world are made up of people who share a common tradition, language, and origin—a common culture. Such countries are said to have a single society. An example is England. Other nations contain many societies within their geographic borders. For example, Nigeria has some 50 different societies while the Soviet Union has over 100.

The Meaning of Race

Race is a term that has been misused so frequently that its real meaning is lost to most people. Race is not an indicator of language, religion, or nationality. These characteristics are all part of an individual's cultural heritage. They are learned and may be changed.

Race is primarily a biological concept. All organisms of the same species, whether animals or plants, have the same basic form. For example, all members of the human species, *Homo sapiens sapiens* (HOH-moh SAP-ee-uhns SAP-ee-uhns), have two eyes, two ears, two hands, and two feet. But there are differences within species. Birds of the same species may differ in color, and each bird has a slightly different size or shape. There are also differences among people. Eye and skin color, shape of skull, hair texture, and nose shape may vary among individuals and among groups.

Anthropologists do not agree on the number of races because human beings do not fit into exact categories. All people are similar in some ways and different in others. But scientists do agree that every race belongs to the same species—*Homo sapiens sapiens*, "thinking human."

SECTION 1 REVIEW

1. **Recall**   What do cultural anthropologists study?
2. **How and Why**   How are features of one culture carried to another culture?
3. **Critical Thinking**   Why is race considered a biological concept and not a cultural or social idea?

SECTION 2

Early Inhabitants of Earth

There is still much mystery about the hominids—humanlike creatures—who lived in prehistoric times. Time and decay have destroyed most of the bones and artifacts that anthropologists need to reconstruct the beings and cultures of the past. They are forced to develop theories based on evidence that is often scanty. This is especially true of very ancient times. Anthropologists and historians are like detectives who arrive at conclusions from a few clues. They must keep an open mind. Later evidence may prove them right or wrong, or suggest that they modify their theories.

Accounts of prehistoric life are always subject to change or modification. What is said here is the generally accepted theory of anthropologists at present. Future discoveries may change these ideas.

Dating Prehistoric Remains   One of the greatest problems in archaeology is deciding the age of remains and the cultures they represent. About 1949, radiocarbon dating began to be used for this purpose. This method is used for objects up to 30,000 years old. For objects older than that, scientists use potassium-argon dating. They actually date the rocks in which the objects are found.

Tree-ring dating—called dendrochronology (DEN-droh-kruh-NAHL-uh-jee)—is used to date wooden objects such as house beams. Each year a tree grows a new ring. The size of that ring is affected by such things as rain or lack of it, fire, and changes in weather. By comparing the growth rings on the wooden object with a sample of the rings from an ancient tree still growing in the area, scientists can date the object fairly accurately.

Hominids   In 1974 Donald C. Johanson discovered the remains of a humanlike creature in the Afar Triangle region of Ethiopia. His find was a female hominid whom he named Lucy. Nearly half of her skeleton remained. By using scientific tests, Johanson estimated that Lucy had lived approximately 3.5 million years ago. She stood slightly over 3.5 feet (1.1 meters) tall and weighed about 60 pounds (27 kilograms). From examining her skeleton, Johanson decided that Lucy walked upright. Since the discovery of Lucy, other hominid fossils that may be as much as 4 million years old have been found in the same area.

As a result of these discoveries, anthropologists theorize that these hominid fossils belong to a species called *Australopithecus afarensis* (aw-STRAY-loh-PITH-uh-kuhs uh-fahr-EN-sis). Over thousands of years, *Australopithecus afarensis* grew larger and heavier, tripled its brain size, and eventually—about 2 million years ago—developed into the human genus, *Homo*.

Archaeologists are detectives of a kind. They fit together pieces of pottery like these ancient amphorae, or jars.

Homo Habilis   An important characteristic of *Homo* is the making of tools. The first toolmaker is known as *Homo habilis*, or "skillful one." *Homo habilis* was named by Louis S. B. Leakey and Mary Leakey, who first discovered its fossil remains in 1960 at Olduvai (OHL-duh-vey) Gorge in Tanzania. The Leakeys found some simple pebble tools with the remains. The tools were about the size of a human fist. Each tool had a rough cutting edge that was made by striking one pebble against another so as to knock off a few flakes. The edge was sharp enough for cutting meat. Using this method, the Leakeys were able to manufacture a pebble tool in less than 20 minutes.

Homo Erectus   *Homo habilis* was succeeded about 1.5 million years ago by *Homo erectus*, meaning "upright." Specimens of *Homo erectus* have been found in Africa, Europe, and Asia. Among the most widely known of these specimens are the Java remains found in Indonesia in Southeast Asia and the Beijing forms found in China.

The fossil record shows that *Homo erectus* was able to make fire, which enabled the people to cook food, warm themselves, and keep away animals. They made fire either by rubbing sticks together or by hitting flint against a rock to strike sparks. Two-thirds of the diet of *Homo erectus* was obtained by gathering fruits, nuts, berries, and insects. They also scavenged for meat, picking up whatever lions, tigers, and other animals left from a kill. Anthropologists believe that these early humans were able to communicate with one another through some kind of spoken language rather than just by gestures.

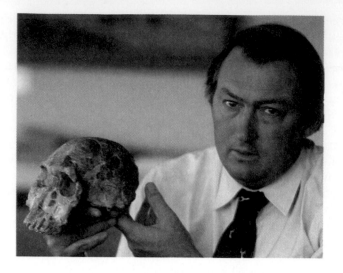

Homo Sapiens   *Homo sapiens*, which means "thinking," emerged rather recently, probably within the last 300,000 years. Between about 100,000 years ago and 12,000 years ago, *Homo sapiens* developed two major cultures. One was the Neanderthal (nee-AN-der-thahl) culture, named after the Neander Valley in Germany. The first skeleton of this type was discovered here in the 1850s. The second culture was Cro-Magnon (kroh-MAG-nuhn), named after the place in southern France where remains were first found. The Cro-Magnons, who looked very much like the people of today, are classified as *Homo sapiens sapiens*. All people now living are members of this sub-species.

Neanderthal Culture

By studying fossils, scientists have described the physical and cultural characteristics of the Neanderthal people. Their physical characteristics are often thought to be an adaptation to the extreme cold climate in Europe and Asia at the time they lived there.

Experts believe the Neanderthal people were about 5.5 feet (1.7 meters) tall. They had thick bones, heavy muscles, and an almost chinless lower jaw. They lived in small bands generally numbering between 40 and 60 people. They were nomadic food-gatherers and hunters. As the food supply in one territory gave out, the band moved on to a new territory. The average life expectancy of Neanderthals was about 20 years. Hardly anyone lived past 30.

In spite of such a comparatively short life span, the Neanderthals lived much more comfortably than earlier humans. The reason was technological. Neanderthal people steadily improved the design and effectiveness of their hand axes, scrapers, and stone knives. They used fire to dry and harden wood to make spearpoints, digging sticks, and other tools and weapons. This enabled Neanderthal bands to hunt for meat as well as to scavenge for it.

The Neanderthal people used animal skins to make clothing and shelters. In many places, they lived in caves. They obtained light by burning fatty bones in stone lamps and used storage pits for food shared by the entire band.

The Neanderthals buried their dead. Remains of food, weapons, and flowers have been found in their burial grounds. Because of this, many archaeologists think the Neanderthals believed in some form of life after death.

Between 40,000 and 35,000 years ago, the Neanderthal culture slowly disappeared. They may have been absorbed by the newer Cro-Magnon culture or wiped out by disease. No one knows for certain. In any event, by 35,000 B.C. only people of the Cro-Magnon culture remained.

Cro-Magnon Culture

The Cro-Magnon people stood about 6 feet (1.8 meters) tall. They had definite chins, graceful bodies, and were physically weaker than the Neanderthals.

The Cro-Magnons made many technological advances. They developed such devices as the spear thrower and the bow and arrow, which enabled them to hurl weapons with greater speed—and therefore greater killing power—than simple throwing had done. As a result, they were able to kill larger animals and obtain meat more easily. Other tools used to increase the food supply were fishhooks and harpoons made of bone, and rawhide snares for trapping waterfowl and small game. The increased food supply led to an increase in population. Scientists estimate that by 20,000 B.C. there were 3 million people living on the earth.

By the time the type Cro-Magnon had developed, about 40,000 years ago, artwork began to appear. Anthropologists theorize that the art may have been connected with a ritual or religious ceremony asking for good luck on the hunt. Above is a molded clay figure of a bison found in France. Below are cave paintings. The one on the left shows bison, and the one on the right is of oxen. The latter are part of the famous paintings at Lascaux, France.

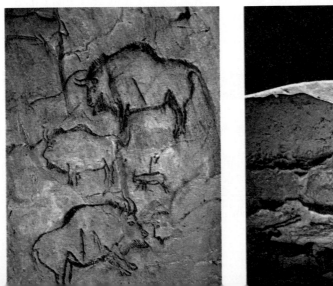

Cro-Magnon women invented needles made of bone. Instead of simply wrapping themselves in animal skins, they sewed close-fitting leather clothing. This enabled them to live in colder climates. Cro-Magnon men invented the stone axe. Now they could cut down trees, hollow out logs to make canoes, and voyage along rivers and seacoasts.

Pictures of animals painted by Cro-Magnon people have been found on the walls of caves in Spain and France. These paintings may have been part of a magic ritual used to bring good luck to hunters. Cro-Magnon people made clay figures and used heat to bake and harden them. The figures were of animals as well as people. Animal statues were also carved from bone and reindeer antlers. One of the oldest known musical instruments is a bone flute dating from Cro-Magnon times.

In addition to technological and artistic advances, the Cro-Magnons apparently also made certain political and social changes. The improvement in weapons led to a new hunting technique. Hunters would stampede a herd of animals into a dead-end ravine. Then they would kill and butcher the animals as needed. However, it took more than one band of hunters to run a large game drive. Probably five or six bands had to work together for weeks at a time. Until that time each band had followed its own customs. Cooperation now meant that all the bands had to observe the same hunting rules.

One result seems to have been the rise of distinct social groupings. Archaeologists have found the first **status burials** among the Cro-Magnons. Certain individuals were buried with amber beads, ivory daggers, and similar luxury goods. Archaeologists believe that individuals buried in this way were tribal religious and political leaders who planned and led the big game drives.

By about 10,000 B.C. the Cro-Magnons were living in nearly every climate on the earth. They had crossed from Asia to the Americas over a land bridge that had linked Siberia and Alaska in those years. They had **domesticated** the dog, which they probably used to help them hunt game. They made pots from clay, hardened the clay in the sun, and used the pots for cooking and storing food. They numbered about 10 million.

Then, begining about 9000 B.C. and continuing until about 4000 B.C., Cro-Magnons in several widely separated parts of the world made a cultural change that had such overwhelming results that it is called a **revolution**. They developed agriculture. It was the first economic revolution in human history.

SECTION 2 REVIEW

1. **Recall** When do anthropologists think *Homo sapiens* first lived on the earth?
2. **How and Why** Why must people keep open minds about anthropologists' theories about the origins of people?
3. **Critical Thinking** Why was the development of agriculture considered to be an economic revolution?

It is difficult to discuss stages of culture because not all groups of people arrived at the same cultural stage at the same time. For example, the Inuit did not use metal until it was introduced by Europeans. Therefore, the periods of cultural development described in the following pages are not exact historical or calendar periods for the world as a whole.

Development of Civilization

Calendar for Prehistory

Until recently, historians divided prehistoric times into stages named after the main material that people used to make tools. The earliest stage was the Paleolithic (PAY-lee-o-LITH-ik) Period, or Old Stone Age. It began when *Homo habilis* first appeared on the earth and lasted until about 8000 B.C. Then came the Neolithic (nee-uh-LITH-ik) Period, or New Stone Age. Although stone was still the main material people used for toolmaking, people now shaped stone by grinding instead of chipping.

Today historians divide prehistoric times on a different basis entirely. The earlier Paleolithic Period is when people were nomadic food gatherers and hunters. The Neolithic Period began when people learned how to produce their own food.

The Agricultural Revolution

Farming—the raising of crops and the domestication of animals—began independently in many parts of the world between 9000 and 4000 B.C. Among the places where people developed farming are the Middle East, China, Southeast Asia, and the Americas.

Different species of grain developed in each place, depending on the local climate, soil, and water supply. Neolithic farmers in the Middle East grew wheat and barley. Rice was first cultivated in Southeast Asia. Farmers there also cultivated bananas and root crops such as cassavas and yams. China was the source for a kind of grain called millet. Later, Chinese farmers added soybeans to their diet. Maize—an early ancestor of corn—was first grown in the Americas. Other plants domesticated there included squash, beans, and potatoes.

Neolithic farmers, probably women, cultivated the soil by loosening it with pointed sticks. Grain was harvested first by hand, later with knives or sickles made of a stone called flint. After a time, farmers learned that they could make their land more productive by fertilizing it with such materials as manure, fish, and ashes. They also learned how to bring water to their fields through ditches and canals. This technique is called irrigation.

With the growing of crops came the domestication of various animals. Sheep, goats, pigs, and horned cattle provided farming societies with steady supplies of meat and other products such as milk, leather, and wool. Farmers in Southeast Asia domesticated chickens, thus obtaining eggs as well as meat. Camels, donkeys, and llamas were used as pack animals.

As humans improved their tools, other changes in living took place as well. Farming first brought about improved stone and wooden tools and then metal ones such as the bronze sickles shown here (below). This painting from an Egyptian tomb (above) shows farmers breaking ground, sowing, and plowing.

As people slowly improved their methods of agriculture, revolutionary changes took place. Instead of wandering from place to place following animals herds, they were able to settle down in villages of about 200 inhabitants. A steady food supply meant that people lived longer. The average life expectancy rose to 30 years. Scholars estimate that by 4000 B.C. the world's population had soared to 85 million.

Agriculture as a way of life made it important to know the seasons, so people developed calendars to measure months and years. A settled life led to ideas about private property. People marked the boundaries of their fields and passed the land on to their children. Warfare came into being as village leaders competed for the most fertile territory.

Agrarian people made dozens of technological advances. They baked clay in a fire or a hot oven and produced pottery that was almost as hard as stone. They also produced bricks for building. They invented the loom and began wearing clothes of linen and wool instead of leather. They invented the wheel, using it first for transportation and later for turning out standardized pottery on a wide scale. They learned how to work metals and invented the plow.

At first Neolithic farmers produced just enough food to meet their own needs. This is known as **subsistence farming**. Then their technological efforts enabled them to produce food surpluses. This abundance allowed some people to spend their time in work other than farming.

Crafts and the arts developed. Some people were able to spend their time making pottery or weaving baskets or cloth. This is called specialization. People then traded their goods for food. The same was true of services such as those provided by the healer or priest.

Among the specialists in Neolithic villages were political leaders. They were usually a combination of wise village elders and the best warriors. Over the years these political leaders increased their power. They needed to make decisions about what crops to plant, when to plant them, which fields to use, how to share water, and how to defend the village's resources from attack. As the villages grew larger, the political leaders began to form a ruling class.

Neolithic political leaders were usually religious leaders as well. New Stone Age peoples were probably **animists** who believed that everything in nature contained a spirit. There were spirits in the earth, in the sky, in animals, and even in mountains and rivers. Depending on their moods, these spirits were either helpful or harmful to human beings. But whatever their behavior, the spirits were powerful—much more powerful than ordinary humans.

After a while, people began attributing humanlike characteristics to some of these spirits. They gave names to these spirits and developed ways to thank them for past favors or ask them for future favors. Neolithic peoples put up shrines, brought offerings of food and flowers, danced special dances, and recited special prayers. In short, they developed **polytheism**, the belief in many gods.

The most widely worshiped deity during the Neolithic Period was the Earth Mother, the goddess of fertility. Sometimes she had a husband, a son, or a daughter who died and then came back to life, just as the crops did. In addition, most Neolithic villagers worshiped a local god or goddess.

With farming and a settled way of life the making of pottery developed. Here an archaeologist fits together pottery shards or fragments. What can pottery tell archaeologists about a culture?

Civilization and Cities

Many historians do not use the terms *civilization* and *civilized* when speaking of cultures or peoples. If they do use the term *civilization*, they use it to describe a very complex level of development. Such a development would include the following: 1) a food-producing base that makes possible a large population; 2) increasing centralization of political and religious authority; 3) large buildings; and often, but not always, 4) the development of writing and written records.

The words *civilization* and *city* are closely related. Both words come from the same Latin word *civis* meaning "someone who lives in a city." The word *city* can be traced even further back in time to a Greek word meaning "to settle down in." People developed towns through divisions of labor, trade, and exchange of services. Some towns grew into cities, and civilization developed.

Urban life requires government. A way of regulating large groups of people is needed so they can live and work together peacefully. The administration of city governments in ancient times, as in modern times, required the keeping of records. This may have been the beginning of writing.

Civilization and Geography

About 3500 B.C. civilizations began to arise in several parts of the world. The earliest of these civilizations emerged in the Middle East. Later, civilizations developed in India and China.

In each instance, these early civilizations arose in river valleys. The first arose in Mesopotamia, the land between the Tigris and the Euphrates (yu-FRAYT-eez) rivers in what is now Iraq. Egyptian civilization was nourished by the Nile River. The Harappans (hah-RAP-anz) of ancient India depended on the Indus River, which is now in Pakistan. And the birth of Chinese civilization was made possible by the Huang He.

The rivers provided the people who lived along their banks with water, nutrients that increased the fertility of the soil, and fish as a source of food. The Nile, the Euphrates, and the Indus were also calm enough to serve as a cheap and easy means of transportation for people, goods, and ideas.

Although each civilization had a river, the rivers were different. This meant that the people had to adapt to them in different ways. Since the Huang He is violent and unpredictable in its flow, the Chinese people put their efforts into building dikes to protect themselves against floods. The Egyptians, who enjoyed a gentle and predictable river, concentrated on building an irrigation system that would bring water to their arid country. In both places, however—as well as in Mesopotamia and India—the people had to work together in order to make the best possible use of their river. Thus, geography played a major role in the development of early civilizations.

One example of economic interdependence is food. Many nations import food either because they do not grow enough to feed their people or because the people want variety in their diet. This photo shows a market in Oman. The boxes contain fruit from the Philippines.

The Role of Trade

These early civilizations, as well as more recent ones, carried on trade as a means of supplying some of their own needs or of adding to their wealth. Early trade items were usually natural materials such as gold or tin. As people recognized the importance of trade to an area, they formed trade networks. For example, by the 600s B.C., the Phoenicians (fi-NEE-shunz) of the Middle East were trading silver and tin from what is now Spain, cloth from Syria, and ivory from Central Africa.

Sometimes one area became dependent on another for such goods as grain or salt. In the 500s B.C., Rome depended on Egypt for grain. The empire of Ghana traded its gold for salt from the Sahara. Later, manufactured goods such as textiles and iron tools were added to the supply of trade goods. Some trade goods such as coffee, sugar, and cotton could be grown only in certain places. As a result, demand for these goods created interdependence among areas. Some areas began to specialize by growing or trading certain goods.

The growth of trade led to technological improvements in transportation. Better sailing ships were built, as well as more and improved roads. In modern times, railroads, trucks, and airplanes have speeded movement along the world's trade networks.

Economic Choices

Economics is the study of how people and nations make use of their resources. Economics as a science was not developed until the late 1700s. However, humans have been informally using principles of economics throughout their history.

Economists usually talk about three kinds of resources—land, labor, and capital. **Land** includes not just the ground but also such things as climate, minerals, rivers, fishing grounds, and the like. **Labor** in its simplest form is human muscle power. But it also includes people's mental skills and the effort they put into their work. **Capital** refers to goods that are used to produce other goods and services. These range from hand tools to power plants, from shovels to automatic assembly lines.

The basic fact of economics is scarcity. All resources are limited. A nation has only so much land, raw materials, labor, machines, and money. This means that at any given time, the amount of goods and services a nation can produce is limited. People's wants, on the other hand, tend to be unlimited. In the first place, people need such things as food, clothing, and shelter throughout their lives. Also, many things are consumed quickly and have to be replaced. In addition, no matter how much people have, it seems as if they always want more. As soon as one want is satisfied, another want takes its place. Even the richest nation in the world cannot produce enough goods and services to give everyone everything they want. Accordingly, every nation must decide how it will cope with the problem of scarcity.

In making economic choices, any time a nation decides to do one thing with its resources instead of another, it is making a **trade-off**. Suppose a nation wants to spend several billion dollars on a power plant. Then that money cannot be spent on something else, such as education or defense. What a nation is willing to give up or pay to reach its goals is called an **opportunity cost**. As you read about the economic growth of the peoples of the world, keep in mind the problem of scarcity and the trade-offs that they have faced and are facing as they make decisions.

SECTION 3 REVIEW

1. **Recall**   What revolutionary changes took place as a result of the improved methods of agriculture?

2. **How and Why**   Why did most cities and towns develop near water?

3. **Critical Thinking**   How do scarcity, trade-offs, and opportunity costs affect a nation's economic decisions?

Reviewing People, Places, and Things

Identify, define, or explain each of the following:

- culture
- anthropology
- prehistory
- archaeology
- interdependence
- industrialization
- extended family
- ethnic group
- Neanderthal
- Cro-Magnon
- Paleolithic
- Neolithic
- subsistence farming
- specialization
- civilization
- division of labor
- capital
- scarcity
- trade-off
- opportunity cost

Understanding Facts and Ideas

1. To an anthropologist, what does the term *culture* mean?

2. Why do you think cultural diffusion might take place more readily since the use of telecommunications?

3. Why is the world of the late twentieth century more than ever one of interdependence?

4. How are languages identified as being members of a language family?

5. What is the difference between a nuclear and an extended family?

6. How do kinship groups influence members?

7. Where have remains of *Homo sapiens* been found?

8. How do the technological advances of the Neanderthal people compare to those of the Cro-Magnon people?

9. How did the agricultural revolution affect the development of civilization?

10. How are a nation's economic decisions affected by scarcity, trade-offs, and opportunity costs?

Developing Critical Thinking

Comparing or Contrasting   When you compare ideas or facts, sometimes you look for the advantages or disadvantages that a certain factor might provide for a group of people. It is often helpful to prepare a matrix or chart listing the advantages and disadvantages so that they are easier to compare.

Activity: Extended families are most often found in rural rather than in urban areas. Prepare a matrix listing the advantages and the disadvantages that urban people and rural people have as a result of having or not having extended families. Then write a sentence or two summarizing these advantages and disadvantages.

Writing About History

Analyzing History   The physical characteristics of a region affect the ways in which the people make a living, but so do the skills and attitudes of the people themselves. Write a paragraph stating which of these factors you think is more important in the development of a region. Give reasons for your position.

Applying Your Skills to History

Using Maps   Using the population density map in the Reference Section of this text and a natural regions map for any culture region, draw a population density map for that culture region. Include the major geographical features that are on the natural regions map. Then write a conclusion about the relationship of population to the geographical features of that region.

1

SUB-SAHARAN AFRICA

Sub-Saharan Africa's history and prehistory are as varied and colorful as this weaving. Weavings such as this are now hung in museums around the world. This cloth from Ghana hangs in the Textile Museum in Washington, D. C.

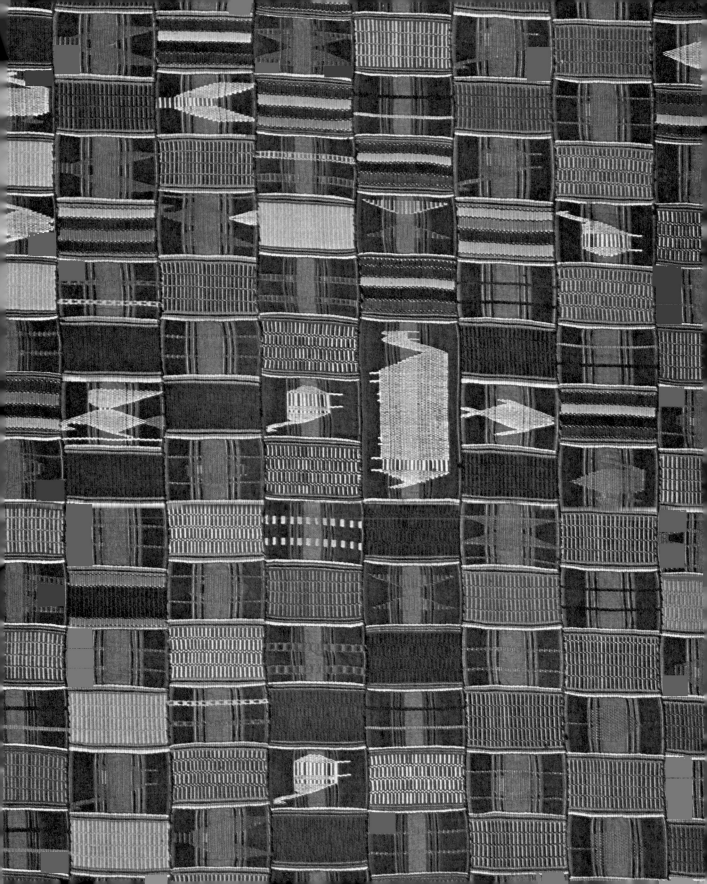

1

The Land and the People

Sub-Saharan Africa is one of the largest culture regions on earth. It is also one of the most varied. Its environment ranges from barren deserts to lush forests. Its inhabitants include a variety of ethnic groups who speak more than 1,000 different languages. Its cultures follow early traditions and reflect more recent colonial influences.

Sub-Saharan Africa is a difficult culture region in which to live. Much of it is infested by flies that spread destructive and often fatal diseases to livestock and humans alike. The Sahara has been creeping southward at a rate that will more than double the region's desert area within the next 50 years.

As you study this chapter, think about these questions:

- What are the geographic characteristics of Africa south of the Sahara?

- How did the development of agriculture and ironmaking affect the early peoples of Sub-Saharan Africa?

Art is an important cultural expression to the people of Sub-Saharan Africa. Rock paintings from as early as 400 B.C. have been discovered in Sub-Saharan Africa. Below is a painting by a modern Ghanaian artist, Poto Poto. What is the subject matter?

24

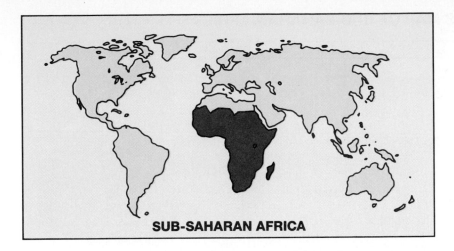

SUB-SAHARAN AFRICA

S ub-Saharan Africa includes about three-fourths of the African conti-nent, together with the large island of Madagascar and several smaller islands. From north to south, this culture region measures 3,500 miles (5 633 kilometers). At its widest, it is 4,700 miles (7 562 kilometers) across. This is roughly 1.5 times as wide as the continental United States. The region covers about 9 million square miles (23 million square kilometers), or about 15 percent of the earth's land surface.

Sub-Saharan Africa itself can be divided into four subregions: West Africa, Central Africa, East Africa, and Southern Africa. The map on page 26 shows these four subregions and the modern nations within each.

Like other peoples, the environment in which Africans lived has shaped their culture and history. Those who lived on the southern fringes of the Sahara or on the east coast were influenced by Islamic culture from the Arabian Peninsula. West Africans came more into contact with Western Europeans. The mass migrations of Bantu-speaking peoples over time across and down the continent brought new languages and ways of life to the peoples of Central and Southern Africa. Because of different climate and vegetation, agriculture and trade in the East African grass-lands were very different from that of the rainforests of Central Africa.

Plateau

Most of Sub-Saharan Africa is a giant plateau, slightly higher in the east than in the west. The plateau lies more than 2,000 feet (610 meters) above sea level. In most places, it does not slope gently to the ocean. It drops sharply into narrow coastal plains. As a result, a cliff-like barrier exists between the plateau and the coast. The broad rivers that flow from the interior to the sea are usually unnavigable when they reach this barrier. The barrier creates rapids and waterfalls like the tremendous Victoria Falls on the Zambezi (zam-BEE-zee) River, which plunges 335 feet (102.1 meters), or twice the height of Niagara Falls. For centuries, such obstacles kept outsiders from penetrating the interior.

(continued on page 28.)

A NATURAL REGIONS MAP OF SUB-SAHARAN AFRICA

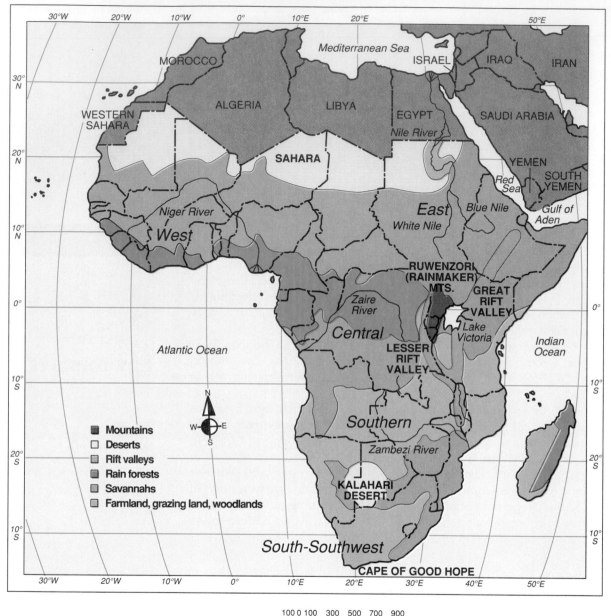

MOROCCO

Mediterranean Sea

ISRAEL

IRAQ

IRAN

WESTERN SAHARA

ALGERIA

LIBYA

EGYPT

Nile River

SAUDI ARABIA

SAHARA

YEMEN

SOUTH YEMEN

Red Sea

Niger River

West

East

Blue Nile

White Nile

Gulf of Aden

RUWENZORI (RAINMAKER) MTS.

Zaire River

GREAT RIFT VALLEY

Central

Lake Victoria

LESSER RIFT VALLEY

Atlantic Ocean

Indian Ocean

Southern

Zambezi River

KALAHARI DESERT

South-Southwest

CAPE OF GOOD HOPE

Legend:
- ■ Mountains
- □ Deserts
- ▨ Rift valleys
- ▨ Rain forests
- ▨ Savannahs
- ▨ Farmland, grazing land, woodlands

Statute Miles: 100 0 100 300 500 700 900

Kilometers: 100 0 100 500 900 1300

A POLITICAL MAP OF SUB-SAHARAN AFRICA

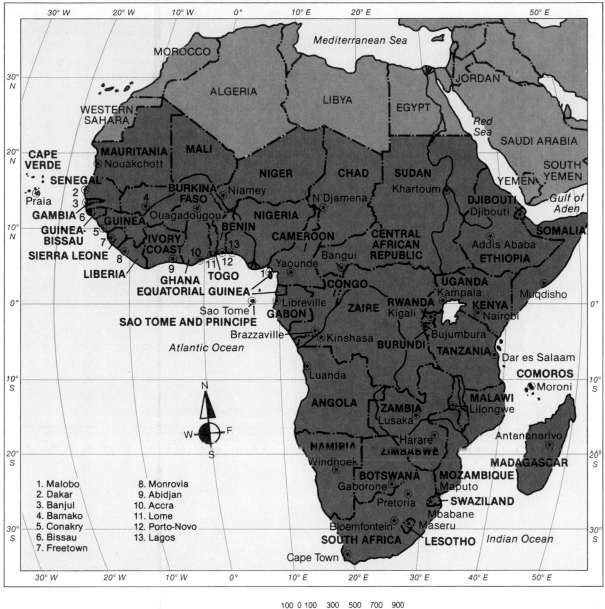

Mediterranean Sea

MOROCCO

ALGERIA

LIBYA

EGYPT

WESTERN SAHARA

Red Sea

JORDAN

SAUDI ARABIA

CAPE VERDE

MAURITANIA
⊙ Nouakchott

MALI

NIGER

CHAD

SUDAN
Khartoum ⊛

SOUTH YEMEN

YEMEN

Gulf of Aden

SENEGAL

2 ⊛
Praia
3 ⊛

BURKINA FASO
Niamey

DJIBOUTI
Djibouti ⊙

GAMBIA
6
4

Ouagadougou

N'Djamena ⊛

SOMALIA

GUINEA-BISSAU
GUINEA
5

NIGERIA

BENIN

CAMEROON

CENTRAL AFRICAN REPUBLIC

Addis Ababa ⊛

ETHIOPIA

SIERRA LEONE
7
IVORY COAST
8
10
11 12
13

Bangui ⊛

LIBERIA
9
GHANA
TOGO
Yaounde ⊛

UGANDA
Kampala ⊛

EQUATORIAL GUINEA

CONGO

Muqdisho ⊛

Sao Tome I
⊙ Libreville
GABON

SAO TOME AND PRINCIPE

ZAIRE

RWANDA
Kigali ⊛

Nairobi
KENYA

Brazzaville
⊛ Kinshasa

BURUNDI
Bujumbura ⊛

Atlantic Ocean

Luanda ⊛

TANZANIA

Dar es Salaam

COMOROS
Moroni ⊙

ANGOLA

ZAMBIA
Lusaka ⊛

MALAWI
Lilongwe ⊙

Harare ⊛

Antananarivo ⊙

NAMIBIA
Windhoek ⊙

ZIMBABWE

MADAGASCAR

BOTSWANA
Gaborone ⊙

MOZAMBIQUE
Maputo ⊙

Pretoria ⊛

SWAZILAND
Mbabane

Bloemfontein ⊛
Maseru

SOUTH AFRICA
LESOTHO

Indian Ocean

Cape Town ⊛

1. Malobo
2. Dakar
3. Banjul
4. Bamako
5. Conakry
6. Bissau
7. Freetown
8. Monrovia
9. Abidjan
10. Accra
11. Lome
12. Porto-Novo
13. Lagos

Statute Miles

100 0 100   300   500   700   900

Kilometers

100 0 100   500   900   1300

27

Several times in prehistory, volcanic activity raised parts of the plateau on its eastern side. This lifting of the earth caused deep fractures, mountains, and depressions. The fractures are called **rifts.** A chain of rifts runs for almost 4,000 miles (6 444 kilometers) from the Red Sea to Mozambique (MOH-zuhm-BEEK). The chain is called the Great Rift Valley, and it is so large that it can be seen from the moon. In some places the Great Rift Valley is as much as 1 mile (1.6 kilometers) deep. Its width varies from 20 to 60 miles (32 to 64 kilometers).

The highest mountain in Sub-Saharan Africa is Mount Kilimanjaro, which towers 19,340 feet (5 895 meters) and is always capped with snow. It is located in the rift system, in Tanzania. Other mountains in this culture region include the Drakensburg Mountains along the southeast coast, and the Ruwenzori or Rainmaker Mountains along the Uganda-Zaire (ZIYR) border. The peaks of the Ruwenzori are always shrouded in mist, giving them a ghostlike appearance. Because of this, the ancient Greeks referred to them as the Mountains of the Moon. Both swamps and glaciers are found in the Ruwenzori, and ordinary plant life reaches enormous size.

The depressions that were made by the earth's movement of the plateau are called **basins**. Water from surrounding mountains drains into these basins and forms rivers. However, about one-third of the region has no drainage to the sea.

Most of the region's coastline is inhospitable to ships. In some places the coastline is straight, so there are no natural harbors. In other places the coastline is gently shelving, which means that the sea along the coast is very shallow for some distance out. As a result, oceangoing ships cannot use the harbors directly but must anchor out to sea and send passengers and cargo ashore on small boats.

This is a section of the Great Rift Valley in Kenya. The area is used primarily for grazing.

Lakes

Most of the great lakes of Sub-Saharan Africa, such as Lake Tanganyika (TAN-guhn-YEE-kuh), lie on the floor of the rifts. Rift lakes are very long and deep. In contrast is Lake Victoria in Tanzania (TAN-zuh-NEE-uh). It is a shallow, circular lake that is not part of the rift system but simply marks a depression in the land. Lake Victoria is the world's second largest freshwater lake. Only Lake Superior in the United States is larger.

The lakes of Sub-Saharan Africa provide drinking water and fish. They are used for irrigation and hydroelectric power and are an important part of the region's inland transportation network.

Rivers

A more significant part of the region's inland transportation network consists of four large river systems that meander slowly through the interior before plunging to the coastal plains. They are the Nile, the Zaire, the Niger (NIY-juhr) and the Zambezi.

The best-known river is the Nile. The longest river in the world, it runs for over 4,100 miles (6 600 kilometers). It has two branches: White and Blue. The White Nile starts in the Lake Victoria area. The Blue Nile, which gets its name from the bluish-gray clay it carries down from the mountains, rises in Ethiopia. The rivers join in the Republic of the Sudan (soo-DAN). From there they flow northward into the Mediterranean.

The Zaire River is the fourth longest river in the world. The land drained by the river and its tributaries forms the Congo Basin, which is centered on the equator. The Niger River starts less than 200 miles (320 kilometers) inland from the Atlantic. But it curves northeast and then south, so that its journey to the ocean is almost 2,000 miles (3 200 kilometers) long. So important is this river that two nations are named after it: Niger and Nigeria. The Zambezi River flows eastward to empty into the Indian Ocean.

Climate Zones

The equator runs about midway between the northern and southern parts of the African continent. Similar climate and vegetation zones appear on either side of the equator. There are, however, some exceptions such as the East African highlands, where higher altitude modifies the climate and vegetation.

Along the equator lies the tropical-rainforest climate zone of West and Central Africa. This zone covers about 8 percent of the culture region. The direct rays of the sun keep temperatures moderately high, about 80°F (27°C) year round. But the air is often humid, so the heat soaks into the skin and feels uncomfortable. The warm, humid air holds enough moisture to produce rain almost every day. Yearly rainfall averages about 100 inches (250 centimeters).

The vegetation consists of a great variety of trees. Most are broad-leaved **evergreens** that keep their leaves year-round. Tropical-rainforest vegetation grows so thick that several layers are formed at different heights. The highest layer is formed by tall trees such as teak and mahogany, whose tops grow together to form a canopy. Under this layer are shorter trees and bushes. Vines and low, shade-loving plants grow on the floor of the rainforest where direct sunlight cannot reach. Where there are no tall trees to block the sun, especially along rivers, the vegetation consists of dense patches of bushes and vines. The soil in a tropical rainforest is usually too poor for farming. This is because the heavy rains wash away valuable minerals in a process called **leaching**.

North and south of the tropical-rainforest zone lies the tropical-savannah zone. **Savannahs** are grasslands with occasional clumps of trees. They cover about one-fourth of the region. The rainfall in these grassy areas averages between 30 and 60 inches (76 and 152 centimeters) a year. This is enough to turn vegetation a rich green and to support both farming and herding. But the rain is seasonal. High temperatures and the dry winter season cause rapid evaporation. The rainfall also varies from year to year, so farmers and herders may suffer from both floods and droughts.

North and south of the tropical-savannah zone is the desert zone. The Sahara covers most of the northern part of the region. The smaller Kalahari Desert lies in Southern Africa. Desert areas and the semiarid regions that border them average less than 10 inches (25 centimeters) of rain a year. Sometimes no rain falls. Then the desert sands bury the sparse shrubs. However, underground water may surface as a spring and support an **oasis**. Desert temperatures can be extremely hot during the daylight hours and then fall 50 or 60 degrees (10–16° C) to turn quite cold at night.

Although African nations are working to industrialize, most Africans still earn their living from the land. These women are picking tea in Tanzania.

At the southern tip of Sub-Saharan Africa is a slim zone of Mediterranean climate. Winters are mild and rainy. The sunny summers are hot and dry. Broad-leaved evergreens form the vegetation, and people can grow crops year after year.

Agriculture

Agriculture is the main economic activity in Sub-Saharan Africa. Almost 70 percent of all workers are farmers. Yet they are generally unable to produce enough food to feed all the people of the region adequately.

Much of Africa's soil is poor. It lacks **humus**, the organic material in soil that results from the decay of animal or vegetable matter. In addition, in rainy areas, heavy rains either erode the topsoil or leach the soil of its minerals.

With this type of soil, a farming method called **slash-and-burn agriculture** is used. Farmers clear a piece of forest or savannah land and plant crops. In a few seasons, the fertility of the soil is gone. The farmers move on and repeat the process. Farmers who use the slash-and-burn method grow enough to live on, but they have nothing extra to sell. They are **subsistence farmers**.

Slash-and-burn agriculture has other limitations as well. It usually takes several years for once-used plots to become productive again. In addition, this method requires a great deal of land. With population on the increase, slash-and-burn agriculture may not be possible in the future.

In areas of Sub-Saharan Africa where soil is more fertile and animal fertilizers are available, **sedentary agriculture** is practiced. River deltas and valleys, mountain slopes, and some highland regions support the permanent growing of **cash crops**, or crops that are sold in the market.

Some cash crops—such as grains—are sold locally. Others—including cotton, palm oil, cacao, bananas, rubber, peanuts, coffee, and citrus fruits—are exported. More than half of the region's export earnings come from the sale of such crops.

In dry areas where irrigation is not possible, Sub-Saharan Africans depend mainly on herding to earn their living. Cattle, goats, sheep, and camels can survive where crops cannot. The herders are generally nomads. Some wander in savannah and semiarid areas. Others migrate between lowlands and neighboring mountains. Diseases that attack livestock make herding in dry areas commercially unprofitable. In general, the livestock raised there produce less meat and milk than livestock raised in other parts of the world.

Some Africans combine farming and herding. The most extensive areas of mixed farming are in the grassy parts of South Africa and southern Zimbabwe (zim-BAHB-wee).

Meeting Food Needs

Only about 10 percent of the land in Sub-Saharan Africa is arable. But the culture region has the most rapidly growing population on earth. As a result, producing enough food is the region's most critical challenge.

Desertification   One factor limiting agricultural production has been **desertification**. The Sahara has been creeping steadily southward. Today about 20 percent of the culture region is desert. At the current rate of desertification, 45 percent will be desert within 50 years.

Desertification is caused partly by the lack of rainfall and partly by people cutting down trees to use as fuel. It is also caused by poor farming practices. When harvests are good, farmers usually let the soil lie fallow between plantings so it can store moisture for future crops. But most farmers lack a surplus to carry them over a bad year. So when a drought causes poor harvests, the farmers do not allow their land to lie fallow. As a result, the nutrients in the soil are quickly exhausted.

Another poor farming practice is overgrazing. Nomadic herders have purposely increased the size of their herds because they know that droughts kill many animals. The nomads hope that by raising more animals, they will have as many animals for milk and meat in a bad year as in a good year. The extra animals, however, eat more vegetation and kill more trees. As a result, the land becomes increasingly barren, and the desert continues to spread.

Overgrazing is made worse by a regional culture trait. Many Africans believe that animals are a sign of wealth. Herders try to own as many animals as possible, regardless of weather conditions.

Preventing Desertification   Some nations in Sub-Saharan Africa are trying to restore the forests that once formed a barrier to the expanding desert. However, it will be a long time before the trees become large enough to withstand recurring droughts. One possible way to

Using GEOGRAPHY Skills

Reading a Historical Map

Maps represent time as much as they represent space. Every map is drawn to depict an area (space) at a certain point in history (time). For example, a road map of your community drawn a century ago would be of limited value for a traveler today. Over time, roads have been built, destroyed, rerouted, and renamed. You would probably say that such a map is "out of date"—that the time of the map is not current.

Although these "out of date" maps are of little use to you as a traveler, they are of great importance to you as a student and a citizen. By comparing current maps to those drawn long ago (or those drawn recently that depict the world of long ago), you can gain important insights into the human experience.

The political map on this page depicts Africa in 1914. Compare it to the contemporary political map of Africa on page 27 to answer the questions.

1. Who controlled most of Africa in 1914?

2. Which country controlled a large area of central Africa in 1914? What country is that area today?

3. By comparing the two maps, what can you infer happened between 1914 and today?

4. Are the borders of contemporary Africa the same borders that existed in 1914? Why do you think this is so?

5. How would you feel if your region was controlled by a nation from another continent? Why?

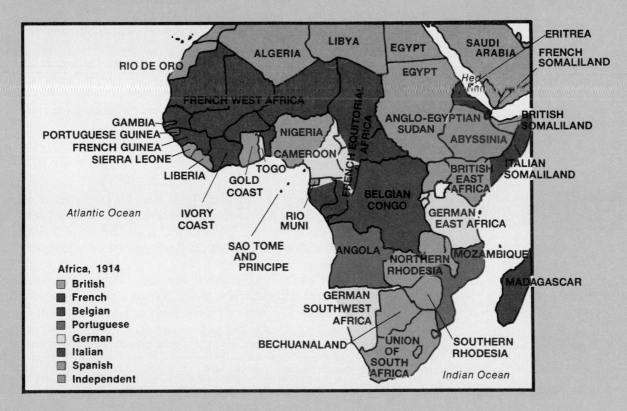

Africa, 1914
- British
- French
- Belgian
- Portuguese
- German
- Italian
- Spanish
- Independent

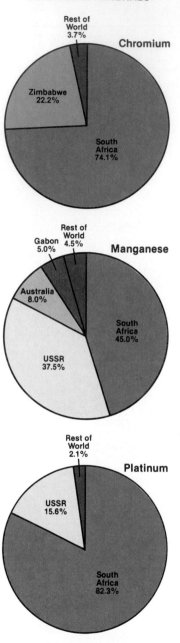

Chromium

Rest of
World
3.7%

Zimbabwe
22.2%

South
Africa
74.1%

Manganese

Rest of
World
4.5%

Gabon
5.0%

Australia
8.0%

USSR
37.5%

South
Africa
45.0%

Platinum

Rest of
World
2.1%

USSR
15.6%

South
Africa
82.3%

Source: *The World Almanac & Book of Facts*,
1984 edition, copyright © Newspaper Enterprise Association, 1983. New York, New York
10066

speed up tree growth would be to use fast-growing species of trees, such as the eucalyptus.

Another current effort involves the settling of nomads in new villages. These villages have been built in unpopulated areas of the region's river basins. Irrigation in these areas could increase the chances of successful farming. However, in order for the program to be successful, diseases—typhoid, malaria, sleeping sickness, and others—must be brought under control. Relocation of people to the river basins will also affect the traditional lifestyle of the nomads.

Tropical Diseases

People in much of Sub-Saharan Africa suffer from various tropical diseases. The three most widespread diseases are nagana, sleeping sickness, and river blindness.

Both nagana and sleeping sickness are carried by the tsetse (SEET-see) fly. When a tsetse fly bites a mammal to suck blood, it may inject parasites into the mammal's bloodstream. Nagana, carried by wild animals upon which the tsetse fly feeds, is fatal to cattle. This has severely limited the size of the region's cattle herds, as well as the quality of the animals that survive to reach the marketplace. In people, sleeping sickness eventually attacks the nervous sytem and the brain, causing death. However, early treatment of the disease can lead to a full recovery.

River blindness is carried by a blackfly that releases a tiny worm when it bites a person. The worms cluster in certain parts of the victim's body. Wrinkled spots and intense itching result, and eventually the person becomes blind.

Many solutions to the problem of the tsetse fly and the blackfly have been tried. Some of the most effective programs have been based on burning the woodlands and the grasslands where the flies breed. Unfortunately, this leads to soil erosion. Insecticides and radiation have also been used.

Resources

From early times, gold was an important trade item for West Africans. They exchanged it across the Sahara for salt and other goods they did not have. Ghana is still a major source of gold. Gold is also mined in South Africa, Zaire, and Zimbabwe. In fact, about 60 percent of the world's gold comes from this region.

Sub-Saharan Africa has many other mineral resources. It is the world's major source of diamonds, most of which come from the mines of South Africa and Zaire. The region produces about 60 percent of the world's cobalt. Guinea contains the world's second largest deposit of bauxite. Nigeria is a top producer of oil. Liberia boasts a rich iron ore deposit. The region has vast reserves of copper, tin, uranium, lead, nickel, and zinc. The mining and exporting of all these mineral resources offer great hope for the region's economic future.

Sub-Saharan Africa also has great potential for hydroelectric power. Using the region's many waterfalls and rapids promises cheap power for homes and industries. South Africa, Uganda, and Ghana have hydroelectric projects. However, most of this water power is as yet undeveloped. Most countries in the region lack the necessary capital and skilled workers.

Another resource of Sub-Saharan Africa is its population of wild animals, which inhabit the savannahs and the rainforests. This population has decreased greatly over the years because of hunting and overgrazing by domesticated animals. Some countries such as Botswana (baht-SWAHN-uh), Kenya (KEN-yuh), Tanzania, and Zimbabwe have set up wild-game preserves where protected animals roam freely. Tourist safaris to view these animals bring in much-needed income.

The Aksombo hydroelectric plant is one example of how Africans are using their rivers. The plant provides almost all of Ghana's electricity. The lake created by the dam supplies water for irrigation and fish.

Cities

Africans, like other people in the world, developed cities near the coast or near major rivers. These areas were the most accessible to the Africans and to the people who traded with them over the centuries. Many cities that are major trading centers in Africa today such as Lagos, Nigeria; Kinshasa, Zaire; Addis Ababa, Ethiopia; and Cape Town, South Africa; developed as early trade centers. Also, some cities such as Johannesburg, South Africa, developed around sites rich in resources. Other cities were political or cultural centers.

Today about 30 percent of the region's people live in cities. However, population patterns are changing. The urban population is increasing rapidly as people migrate to the cities in search of jobs, education, and what they hope will be a better life.

Capitals in particular are having a spectacular growth. This is because of the increasing need of African governments for workers. As government employees and their families come to the cities, more services and the people to provide them are needed. Stores, hospitals, schools, and government buildings must be constructed and staffed. Very often, trade and industry also cluster around capitals.

SECTION 1 REVIEW

1. **Recall** What is the main natural feature of Sub-Saharan Africa?
2. **How and Why** Why is the soil in a tropical rainforest too poor for farming?
3. **Critical Thinking** Why does South Africa have great potential for hydroelectric power?

SECTION

2

Early People

Most anthropologists believe the earliest ancestors of the human family lived in Sub-Saharan Africa around 3.5 million years ago. Only time and further investigations will tell if this theory is correct.

By about 10,000 B.C., much of Sub-Saharan Africa was inhabited by black-skinned individuals. Today their descendants make up about 90 percent of the region's population. Short people, sometimes called Pygmies, lived in the rainforests of the Congo Basin. Farther south lived the Khoisans (KOY-sahnz), a people with yellow-brown skin. Only some 100,000 Khoisans remain. White-skinned people, who today make up about 10 percent of the population, began moving into the region only within the last 2,600 years.

Language Divisions

Since prehistory, Sub-Saharan Africa has experienced sweeping movements of peoples from both inside and outside the continent. As a result, some 1,000 different languages developed. However, many of the languages share certain elements. Accordingly, linguists have grouped them in six major language families: Niger-Kordofanian, Afro-Asian, Nilo-Saharan, Khoisan, Indo-European, and Malayo-Polynesian.

The most widely spoken language family is Niger-Kordofanian. Within this group are the several hundred Bantu languages. They use tones to indicate differences in meaning. The most important Bantu language is Swahili (swah-HEE-lee). Over the centuries, many Arabic, Malay, and Persian words have become part of Swahili. Until about the 1800s, Swahili was written in Arabic script. Today it is written in Roman letters. Much of present-day African literature is written in Swahili.

Afro-Asian includes the languages of the Ethiopians, Somalians, and some North Africans. Ancient Egyptian is an Afro-Asian language. Nilo-Saharan—also known as Sudanic—includes the languages of people living in the Sahara, Sudan, and parts of East Africa. The Bushmen and the Hottentots speak Khoisan. Malayo-Polynesian is spoken in Madagascar. A leading Indo-European language is Afrikaans (af-ruh-KANZ) which was developed in South Africa by the Dutch who came in the 1600s. Many Africans also speak such Indo-European languages as French, English, or Portuguese, depending on the Western European nation that colonized their area during the 1800s.

The official language of most nations in Sub-Saharan Africa today is English or French. This enables government leaders and business people to communicate easily with other culture regions. However, in recent years a backlash has developed against colonial languages. Many Sub-Saharan Africans feel they should be speaking a local tongue rather than one that was originally imposed on them by European conquerors.

The Green Sahara

On a map of Africa, the dry and mostly barren Sahara is a prominent feature. It seems completely inhospitable to humans. Yet, that is where Sub-Saharan Africa's earliest cultures apparently began.

Between 10,000 to 8,000 years ago, the Sahara was an area of water and greenery. Giraffes, spotted oxen, elephants, rhinoceroses, wild sheep, and other animals grazed there. Trees grew. Rivers filled with fish cut through the land. Until about 2500 B.C., hunters and, later, herders and farmers, made the area their home.

Archaeologists can piece together the life of these Saharan people from what has been called "the world's greatest gallery of prehistoric art." About 15,000 paintings on cave walls have been discovered in the Sahara. The earliest paintings show a food-gathering and hunting people. Hunters used throwing spears, clubs, knives, and sticks to kill game. For fishing they used hooks made of bone.

Pictures dated between 4000 and 2000 B.C. show people herding cattle, sheep, and goats with the help of dogs. The prehistoric artists paid special attention to the cattle's horns—short and long, thick and thin, crescent and lyre-shaped. The abundance of cattle enabled the herders to settle in villages, where they built huts of wickerwork and dried grasses. They harvested wild grain, but there is no evidence that they cultivated cereal crops.

According to the rock paintings, a strict division of labor existed between men and women. Women cared for children, gathered and cooked food, tended cattle, and made baskets, pottery, necklaces, and bracelets. Men hunted with bows and arrows, and shaped stone and bone into tools and weapons.

The life of the herders seems to have been rich and peaceful. Many of the rock paintings show men and women dancing. The men wore flared leggings and masks; the women wore long, ribbonlike headdresses. They had flutes and stringed instruments. The dances may have had religious meaning.

The Tassili rock paintings were discovered in the Sahara by Henri Lhote. This particular picture shows cattle near huts. The huts are the white ovals. The figures are of women and children working.

37

About 2500 B.C. the climate changed and the Sahara began drying up. The rivers dwindled and disappeared, the forests died, and the grass was replaced by sand. By 1500 B.C. the drying-up process had ended. Some people remained on the few scattered oases. But most of the people, together with their animals, had migrated. Some probably settled in the Nile River valley. Others went to the highlands of Ethiopia. Still others moved to the savannahs and forests of West Africa.

Agriculture and Iron Making

Scientists disagree about when and where Africans south of the Sahara began to farm. What is certain is that by about 3000 B.C., farmers in the Nile Valley were growing wheat and barley, while farmers in West Africa were cultivating millet, sorghum, rice, and yams. Around 1500 B.C. new crops arrived by boat from Southeast Asia—bananas, sugar cane, and coconut trees. The cultivation of bananas in particular spread rapidly. They are easier to grow than cereal grains, and they are well suited to tropical forest conditions. By this time, too, people had domesticated pigs, donkeys, chickens, ducks, and geese.

The agricultural revolution brought about a gradual increase in population. Then another development helped expand the population still more. About 1000 B.C., the Phoenicians introduced the technique of smelting iron to northwestern Africa. About 666 B.C. the Assyrians introduced ironworking into the Nile Valley. From these two areas, the technique spread through Sub-Saharan Africa. Iron greatly improved the efficiency of tools and weapons. Iron tools and weapons are much stronger and last longer than those made of stone or wood. Iron axes made it easier to chop trees and clear land for farming. Iron hoes and other farm tools helped farmers cultivate land more easily. Iron-tipped spears meant more meat. The increased food production enabled more people to survive. In addition, iron objects became valuable items in African trade activities.

An Egyptian harvests grain. Sickles similar to his were used by the first farmers.

SECTION 2 REVIEW

1. **Recall**   About how many languages developed in Sub-Saharan Africa?

2. **How and Why**   Why are archaeologists able to piece together the way of life of Saharan people from thousands of years ago?

3. **Critical Thinking**   How did the introduction of ironworking in Sub-Saharan Africa improve the quality of life there?

Chapter 1

Reviewing People, Places, and Things

Identify, define, or explain each of the following:

Madagascar	leaching
Victoria Falls	humus
Zambezi River	cash crops
rifts	Khoisans
Mount Kilimanjaro	Swahili
basins	Afro-Asian
Lake Victoria	Afrikaans
Nile River	Sahara

Map Study

Using the maps on pages 26 and 27, determine the answers to the following questions:

1. What countries in Sub-Saharan Africa contain part of the Sahara?
2. What is the most prevalent natural region in Sub-Saharan Africa?
3. What countries in Sub-Saharan Africa contain rift valleys?

Understanding Facts and Ideas

1. Why are the rivers that flow from the interior of Sub-Saharan Africa to the sea usually unnavigable?
2. Why is most of the region's coastline inhospitable to ships?
3. What is the average rainfall in the savannahs?
4. What is the main economic activity in Sub-Saharan Africa?
5. Why are farmers in Sub-Saharan Africa generally unable to produce enough food to feed all the people of the region adequately?
6. In what countries in Sub-Saharan Africa is gold an important resource?
7. What are the major language families in Sub-Saharan Africa?
8. Why is the official language of most nations in Sub-Saharan Africa English or French?
9. Why has a backlash developed against colonial languages?
10. What have archaeologists discovered about the life of early Saharan people from paintings on cave walls?
11. Why had most people left the Sahara by 1500 B.C.?
12. Why did the cultivation of bananas in Sub-Saharan Africa spread rapidly?
13. How did the introduction of ironworking in Sub-Saharan Africa help expand the population?

Developing Critical Thinking

Analyzing Economics　Africa is rich in minerals and potential hydroelectric power. How can these resources best be developed? What problems must be solved for Africans to develop their resources? Consider such things as capital, technology, and labor.

Writing About History

Analyzing Geography　How Africans earn their living depends largely on the climate, plant life or vegetation, and type of soil of an area. How has climate affected the way of life of people in different parts of Africa?

Applying Your Skills to History

Making Special Maps　Study the population density map of the world in the Atlas in the back of the textbook and the natural regions map of Africa on page 26. Next, draw a new map combining the population density of Africa and the natural regions of Africa. Then write a generalization about the relationship of population density to natural regions.

2

Kingdoms, Empires, and States

Many kingdoms, empires, and states developed in Sub-Saharan Africa before the coming of the Western Europeans in the 1400s. Environment and location influenced the kinds of work the peoples did. Some areas were ideal for sedentary farming. Other areas were more suited to herding. Coastal peoples and those who lived at the edge of the Sahara became traders.

Natural resources affected the kind of materials people used. Forest peoples, for example, used wood for buildings and artwork. Where wood was scarce, people used mud bricks or stone.

Some of the kingdoms, empires, and states developed under the influence of cultural diffusion. Others developed with almost no outside influence.

As you study this chapter, think about these questions:

- How did geography affect the development of the kingdom or society?
- How did rulers use political power in Sub-Saharan Africa?
- What was the importance of trade in Sub-Saharan Africa?
- What was the role of religion in the cultures of Sub-Saharan Africa?

This soapstone sculpture of a head was carved in Sierra Leone sometime during the 1500s or 1600s.

These pyramids were built during the Meroitic period of the Kingdom of Kush. What other peoples built pyramids?

From around 3400 to 3100 B.C., fortified settlements began to appear along the Nile River in Egypt. A number of these towns and villages joined together to form two kingdoms—Lower Egypt and Upper Egypt. Lower Egypt was in the delta area that reached north from about Cairo to the Mediterranean Sea. Upper Egypt stretched south to the river's First Cataract, or rapids, at Aswan (as-WAHN). Around 3100 B.C. these two kingdoms were united under a single ruler called a pharaoh (FER-roh).

Nubia

During the Middle Kingdom period (c. 2050–1800 B.C.), one of the pharaohs extended the kingdom southward. He claimed all the area beyond Aswan to the land of the Nubians. The Egyptians had had contacts with the Nubians for many centuries. During the Empire period (c. 1580-1150 B.C.) pharaohs sent a series of invasion forces south. They wanted to control Nubian trade. Eventually Nubia became an Egyptian province.

Kingdom of Kush   Not much is known of Nubia again until the 700s B.C. During this time the Kingdom of Kush (KUHSH) arose among the Nubians. The Kushites built their capital at Napata (NAP-uh-tuh) on the Nile. Around 750 B.C. the Kushites were strong enough to conquer Egypt. Eventually the Kushite king Shabaka became the ruler of Kush and Egypt.

In the mid-600s B.C., Assyrians from the Middle East drove the Kushites back to their Nubian homeland. In the 500s B.C., the Kushites moved their capital from Napata farther south to Meroë (MER-uh-WEE). This later period of Kushite development became known as the Meroitic

SECTION

1

The Northeast

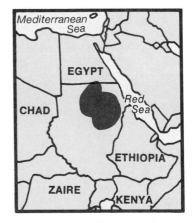

■ **Kingdom of Kush, c. 500 B.C.**

(mer-uh-WIT-ik) civilization. Around this time the Kushites began working in iron. Iron objects became part of their trade goods.

The Kushite trade network reached east to ports along the Red Sea and possibly as far southeast as Ethiopia. Kushite cultural influence may have spread as far west as Lake Chad or beyond. The Kushites continued their ties with the Egyptians. Later they developed friendly relations with Egypt's Greek and Roman rulers.

Over the centuries, the Kushites created a civilization which blended elements of these various peoples. Egyptian influence can be seen in temples, palaces, and the pyramid tombs built at Meroë for the royal family. It is also evident in the custom of wrapping the dead in cotton cloth and of placing glass and bronze objects in tombs. Some Kushite ruins also show Roman influence. One ruin is an imitation of a Roman bath. Evidence of contacts with the Arabian Peninsula and even India is apparent in Kushite cloth and **sculpture** designs.

However, Kushites did not lose their African culture traits. Royal women played important roles in society and **politics**. Succession to the throne may have come through the female side of the family. This was common in Africa. Kushites also believed that their rulers were divine. This belief too is part of Africa's long cultural tradition.

Beginning around A.D. 300, the Meroitic civilization began to decline. Desert nomads known as Red and Black Noba moved into the kingdom. Evidently some of the nomads passed south through Kush and into the Kingdom of Axum (AHK-soom) in Ethiopia. In 330, the king of Axum marched against the Noba. He chased them into Kushite territory and destroyed both Kushite and Noba towns. In the following centuries, other desert peoples settled among the Kushites. These peoples adapted many Kushite culture traits. From this blending arose three kingdoms in the 500s.

evidently:
clearly, obviously

Christian Kingdoms
Nobatia (noh-BAY-shee-uh) was located in the northern region of Nubia between the **First and Third Cataracts** of the Nile. Makuria (muh-KOOR-ee-uh) was the central kingdom. Alodia (ah-LOOD-ee-uh) was south not far from Meroë.

In the mid-500s these kingdoms were converted to Coptic Christianity. Coptic Christianity had arisen out of a disagreement about whether God as the Son had one nature or two. The Copts believed that Jesus had one nature. In the late A.D. 200s, Alexandria, Egypt, had become the leading center of Coptic teaching and writing. Religious leaders at Constantinople, however, held that Jesus had two natures— divine and human. The Roman Catholic Church called a meeting, the **Council** of Chalcedon (KAL-suh-dahn), in 451 to settle the question. It decided in favor of the teachings set forth by Constantinople. Those who continued to hold the Coptic belief were to be considered heretics. The Copts broke with the Church. However, they continued to make converts in the Nubian kingdoms and in Ethiopia.

From the 600s onward, the Christian Nubian kingdoms grew. Their prosperity was based on trade with Muslim Arabs—followers of Islam—

who occupied Egypt at the time. Around the 800s, non-Arab Muslims began to invade the kingdoms for their gold. The kingdoms held out for several centuries. But eventually they were conquered. In the latter part of the 1200s, Muslim rulers were able to take Nobatia. Makuria fell about a century later. Alodia remained independent until the 1400s.

Most Egyptians and people of the Republic of the Sudan are now Muslims. Coptic Christianity is very strong in Ethiopia, however. During their years of conquest, the Muslims permitted freedom of worship to Christians.

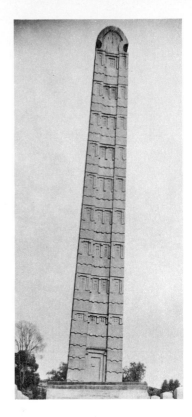

Ethiopia

Between 700 and 500 B.C., groups of people crossed the Red Sea from what is modern Yemen to the area known today as Ethiopia. They merged with people already living in the northern highlands. From this mixing of peoples and cultures there developed around 300 to 200 B.C. the Kingdom of Axum.

Axum became a great trading empire. Ivory, tortoise shell, spices, perfumes, and incense among other items passed through the kingdom. Its main port, Adulis (ah-DOO-lis), on the Red Sea, became the center of trade between the Mediterranean Sea and the Indian Ocean. Extensive trade grew with Egypt which was then ruled by Greeks. Greek merchants settled in Axum and began to dominate the kingdom's commerce. Greek became the language of trade and **diplomacy**.

The Ethiopians, however, developed their own language and **script** called Geez (GEE-ez). Among Axumite artistic achievements are **steles** — large carved stone blocks. Archaeologists believe that these were memorials to important people.

Around A.D. 300, the Axumites invaded Kush to the northwest. They also extended their power east across the Red Sea into the southern part of the Arabian Peninsula. During the 500s, the Persians from what is modern Iran drove them from most of inland Arabia. Ethiopian trade began to decrease. Axum declined. The capital was moved south to Nazaret. In the 600s, Muslim Arabs began moving into the northern and eastern portions of Ethiopia. They made large numbers of converts to Islam.

Around 1100 the Zagwe (ZAHG-wee) from southern Ethiopia seized power. In the 1200s they were driven out. The new rulers were supposedly descended from King Solomon and the Queen of Sheba. They were known as the Solomonian line.

In the 1300s the Ethiopians began a series of campaigns to subdue the Muslims. The fighting raged for over a hundred years. In 1527 the Muslims began an all-out war. Ethiopia appealed to Portugal for help. In 1541 the Portuguese joined the Ethiopians to defeat the Muslims. But by this time the empire had split into several kingdoms. It was not until Emperor Menelik (MEN-uh-lik) II came to power in 1889 that the country was once again reunited.

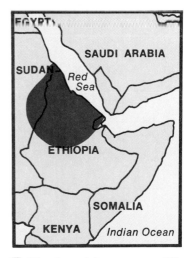

■ Kingdom of Axum, c. A.D. 400

1. **Recall**   What evidence shows that the Kushites had contact with the Arabian Peninsula?
2. **How and Why**   Why did Greek become the language of trade and diplomacy in the Kingdom of Axum?
3. **Critical Thinking**   Why had Ethiopia split into several kingdoms by 1541?

SECTION

2

Central and Southern Africa

The cultural development of the peoples of Central and Southern Africa is largely the history of the migrating Bantu-speaking peoples. The Bantu-speakers also contributed much to the history of peoples in East Africa.

Bantu Migrations

Most scholars believe that the original home of the Bantu peoples was the lightly wooded highlands region of present-day Nigeria. Around 500 B.C. the people were mostly herders, fishers, and farmers. They knew how to use iron.

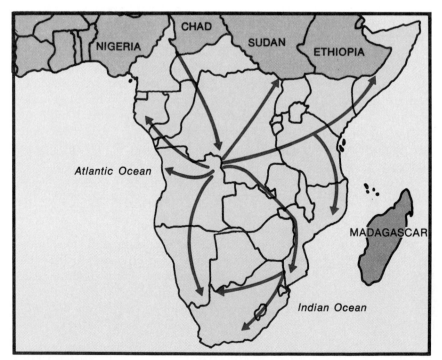

Bantu Migrations

About 2,000 years ago, the Bantu-speakers began moving out of their homeland. No one knows why. Their migrations were not a series of quick, sweeping invasions. Rather, they were gradual movements of small numbers of people. As the population increased in each new area, the groups divided. Some people remained, while others moved on. This pattern was repeated many times.

Gradually the Bantu-speakers made their way through the rainforest of the Congo Basin. When they reached the other side, they settled down for some time. Eventually, they resumed their migration, expanding in all directions. Some continued south and east along the interior river systems and eventually came to the Indian Ocean. Others turned west toward the Atlantic Ocean.

As generations developed, differences began to multiply among the Bantu-speakers. They adapted to the environments and peoples they met, and began to develop new customs and ways of doing things. Their original language split into hundreds of dialects. They began to call themselves by various names: Xosa (KO-suh), Sotho, Shona, Kikuyu, Zulu, and so on.

Yet, certain culture traits remained. For example, kinship ties are important among all Bantu-speaking peoples. Everyone in a community belongs to the same clan. This descent from a common ancestor is traced through the mother's side of the family. Property is also passed down through the mother's family. This kinship system binds clan members to each other. It also binds them to their ancestors. Bantu-speaking peoples share the belief that their dead ancestors live among them and watch over them.

At first the Bantu-speakers lived in small villages made up of family groups. In time the villages in an area would multiply. Gradually **chiefdoms**, or groups of villages, were formed and chiefs were appointed. Finally, some chiefdoms grew into kingdoms.

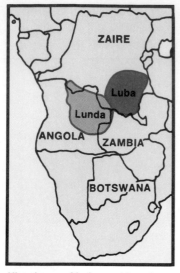

Kingdoms of Luba and Lunda
■ Luba
□ Lunda

Luba and Lunda

As early as A.D. 700 people living in the copper-rich area of modern-day Zaire were making pottery and working with metal. By the 1100s their copper trade reached to distant parts of Sub-Saharan Africa. The villages were ruled by family chiefs. They, in turn, were ruled by higher chiefs who were related to them.

Around the beginning of the 1500s, Kongolo, a warrior chief from the north, conquered parts of the region. He was succeeded by his son, Kalala Ilunga, who continued the process until he had formed a single kingdom—Luba. Kalala became the king.

To the idea of kingship, Kalala added the idea of divinity. He claimed that he was sacred. Only he and his family had the help of the spirits in protecting and guarding the well-being of the people. This claim, of course, kept power in Kalala's family.

According to oral tradition, around 1600, Kibinda Ilunga, one of Kalala's sons, conquered the neighboring state of Lunda and married its queen. He immediately cut himself off from Luba and ruled Lunda as an independent kingdom.

Like the political and social system of Luba, that of Lunda was based on kinship ties. Major positions of authority were held by relatives of the ruler. However, Lunda rulers also appointed some people who were not related to them—for example, chiefs of conquered lands. This insured the chiefs' support and that of their people, and enabled Lunda to expand and rule successfully. At its peak, more than a million people lived under Lunda rule. Lunda culture spread far beyond the kingdom's boundaries and influenced peoples all through Central Africa.

Malawi   Sometime around the 1500s, probably before Luba became a kingdom, people from Luba migrated southeast. They may have been the ancestors of people known as Malawi. In the beginning the political system of the Malawi developed differently than that of the Luba. By the mid-1500s, there were a number of Malawi chiefs. Their positions were strengthened when the people began long-distance trade with the east-coast city of Mozambique.

Malawi trade connected the interior with the east coast in the same way that the Luba-Lunda kingdoms connected the interior with the west coast. Gradually a network of trade routes grew which connected the southern east and west coasts from Angola to Mozambique. The routes of the southern savannahs also tied into these trade routes.

In the early 1600s Kalonga Mzura (kuh-LAHN-gah muh-ZOO-rah) became the most powerful of the Malawi rulers. He gained control of the territory from Lake Malawi south to where the Zambezi River empties into the sea. He considered himself no longer a king but an emperor. During his rule, his contacts included the Portuguese who began coming to Sub-Saharan Africa in the 1400s. After his death the empire of Malawi gradually declined. By 1800 it had disappeared.

Prior to the coming of the Europeans, most Africans used the barter system, but some used shells and beads as a medium of exchange. This is a money collar from the Congo.

The Congo   Around the 1100s, states began growing along the lower parts of the Zaire River. The greatest of these was the Kingdom of the Congo, or Kongo. Sometime before 1400, Wene (WAY-nay), the son of the chief of the small state of Bungu, conquered an area south of the Congo (Zaire). He and his followers made their rule legal by marrying into the major families they had conquered. Wene took the title manikongo (mah nee-KAHN-goh), or king. He ruled with absolute authority and was believed to have divine power.

During the 1400s the kingdom grew to include land north of the Congo River. It stretched across northern Angola from the Atlantic Ocean to the Kwango River, where it met the Lunda kingdom. Like other kingdoms in the area, trade was the basis of its economy. Pottery, cloth, and iron goods were traded. The Congolese also farmed. Their main crops were millet and bananas. In the 1600s maize, among other crops from the Americas, was introduced.

The arrival of the Portuguese in 1482 led to divisions within the kingdom. The royal family converted to Christianity. Those who did not convert opposed them. Throughout the 1500s, Portuguese greed for **slaves**, copper, and gold worsened the problems within the kingdom. These and other factors brought about the final division of the kingdom around 1664. Local kings and chiefs ruled small areas. The growing influence of merchants, however, undercut their power. By the beginning of the 1800s, little was left of the glory that once was the Kingdom of the Congo.

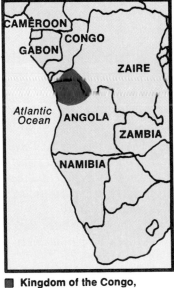

■ **Kingdom of the Congo, 1400s**

Zimbabwe   Between the Limpopo and Zambezi rivers in parts of modern Zimbabwe and Mozambique are many groups of stone ruins that Africans call Zimbabwe. Zimbabwe, from which the nation takes its name, means houses of stone. These ruins are among the earliest stone structures south of the Sahara. Elsewhere, wood and mud were the usual materials. Such buildings have long since disappeared.

Early in the Christian era, Bantu-speakers moved over this region in their migrations southeast. Perhaps as early as the A.D. 400s, some of them began mining gold in the area. These were probably ancestors of the modern Sotho people. These early people also made iron tools, herded, farmed, and made pottery.

Around the 700s, they began trading gold and locally made items with their neighbors. Their trade increased when news of their gold reached east coast traders. It may have been the experience of this trade which moved these people to begin building Zimbabwe sometime before the 1000s. Or they may have begun these buildings much earlier. Some archaeologists have dated the ruins to as early as the A.D. 500s.

Builders of the Zimbabwe did not use mortar. They carefully fitted together the stone blocks. The largest of the ruins is known as Great Zimbabwe. It is located near Fort Victoria in Zimbabwe. Archaeologists have named one group of buildings the Acropolis (uh-KRAHP-uh-luhs) because it was built on top of a hill like the Greek Acropolis. It may have been a fort. In the valley below are other stone structures.

Perhaps between 1000 and 1100, the Bantu-speaking ancestors of the Shona (SHOH-nuh) people began settling in the area. They gradually drove out the Sotho. The Sotho moved south to the Transvaal region of South Africa. The Shona took over the gold trade and began to create small states in the area. Then, in the first half of the 1400s, the Mono-motapa (muh-noh-muh-TAH-puh) Empire developed.

This is a part of the Temple Ruin at Zimbabwe. Some archaeologists believe it was the home of the ruling chief or king. Between it and the Acropolis is another group of walls and small buildings—the Valley Ruin. Ordinary people may have lived in these.

Monomotapa Empire Like most Bantu-speaking peoples, the Shona were divided into various clans. Clan unity came from sharing a common ancestor. Among the strongest of these groups were the Karanga (kuh-RAHN-guh). The dominant among the Karanga was the Rozwi (ROHZ-wee). They believed their kings had divine powers. The Rozwi took over the Great Zimbabwe. There and elsewhere, they continued to add to the stone structures that had been built earlier.

One of the Rozwi kings, Mutota (muh-TOH-tuh), began a conquest of the land between the Limpopo and Zambezi rivers around 1440. He gained control of the trade coming to and from the coastal cities. Taxing these goods made him rich. After his death, his son, Matope (mah-TOH-pee), continued the conquests. Matope took much of what is modern southern Mozambique, including Sofala (soh-FAHL-uh) and other harbors along the east coast. His empire came to be called Monomotapa.

Monomotapa was divided into provinces. The ruler lived in the north near the Zambezi Valley. This became the center of his government. The other provinces were ruled by relatives and trusted subjects called **vassals**. They paid annual dues to the ruler. Monomotapa was a **feudal** form of government. Like all feudal systems, however, some vassals grew strong enough to challenge their ruler. This happened with a Rozwi vassal named Changa.

Changa ruled a province in the southern part of the empire. After Matope died, around 1480, Changa brought the entire southern part of the empire under his rule. He changed his name to Changamira (CHAN-guh-mee-ruh) and named his empire after himself. Later, after killing the Monomotapa ruler, he gained control of the entire empire. After several years, he too was killed. But his son continued to hold and expand the southern part of Monomotapa. The Changamira Kingdom lasted from the late 1600s through the 1700s. Other Bantu speakers, the Ngoni, destroyed it.

Ultimately, Monomotapa fell not to other Africans but to the Portuguese. Around the beginning of the 1500s, the Portuguese took the coastal city of Sofala. The Portuguese then began to move up the Zambezi River. They were in search of the sources of the gold that flowed into Sofala. At first the Portuguese supported Monomotapa against its rebel vassals. But in return, the Portuguese began to ask more and more from the empire. When the king finally resisted in the 1620s, the Portuguese defeated him. They placed a puppet king on the throne. He ruled as he was directed by the Portuguese king.

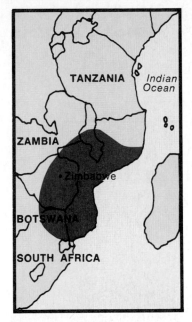

■ **Monomotapa Empire, 1400s**

SECTION 2 REVIEW

1. **Recall** Why did the original language of the Bantu-speakers split into hundreds of dialects?

2. **How and Why** Why are kinship ties very important among all Bantu-speaking peoples?

3. **Critical Thinking** In what way was the feudal form of government in Monomotapa weak?

People living along the east coast of Africa have a long history of contacts with non-Africans. The old Ethiopian port of Adulis on the Red Sea was a busy center of commerce. Greeks, Jews, Arabs, and Egyptians among others came there to trade. Farther south—in modern Somalia—was a trading region known in ancient Egyptian writings as the land of Punt.

Over the centuries trade gradually spread farther south. Gold, iron, ivory, and other goods in increasing amounts moved from the interior to the coast. Trading villages grew into cities and then into **city-states**. Muslim Iranians and Arabs played a large role in this expansion of trade. Many of them settled along the coast and on the offshore islands. They blended their culture and customs with the Africans already living there.

People living in the interior of East Africa were not exposed to these continuing outside influences. Traders generally stayed close to the coast. They were interested in the goods coming from the interior. They were not interested in the people who sent them. Thus the people of the interior developed their own ways of life without any great pressure from non-Africans.

East African Coastal Cities

Coastal Cities

Much of the earliest knowledge we have of the coastal centers of modern Somalia, Kenya, Tanzania, and Mozambique comes from Greek and Arab writings.

Around A.D. 110, an unknown Greek living in Alexandria wrote *The Periplus* (Guide) *of the Erythraean* (Red) *Sea*. The guide grouped the trading centers along the coast of Tanzania and Kenya under the name Azania (ah-ZAN-ee-uh). The people of Azania exported ivory, palm oil, rhinoceros horn, tortoise shell, and other goods to the southern Arabian Peninsula and India. They exchanged these goods for swords, hatchets, lances, glass, and other items. Not much is known about the social and political systems of east-coast people at this time. They apparently were governed by independent chiefs. Arabs handled most of the trade. By the 700s the trade route had grown to include China.

Monsoon winds played an important part in this trade. From November through April these winds blow from a northeast direction. They carried Arab ships from the west coast of India to the east coast of Africa. From May through October the winds blow in a southeast direction. Arabs and Asians used these winds to return to Asia.

In the 900s, an Arab historian, al-Masudi (ahl-mah-SOO-dee), wrote *Meadows of Gold and Mines of Gems*, after visiting the east coast. From al-Masudi's work, it is clear that the people had become skilled metalworkers and had increased the amount of their trade with Asia. Some of the east-coast settlements had developed into states. He wrote that the people were ruled by a king who had other kings under him.

In the 1100s, another Arab traveler, al-Idrisi (ahl-id-REE-see), wrote of his visit to the area that is modern Kenya. Trade goods from there went to such distant places as China, Indonesia, and Malaysia. Into the cities came, among other items, Chinese porcelain, Burmese pottery, and

This is an old ruin in the east coast trading center of Gedi or Malindi. What was the source of wealth of the east coast cities? How important was trade to the development of other areas of Africa? Do you think trade has always played a role in the development of cities?

Indian cloth and beads. Al-Idrisi was especially impressed by the iron trade. African iron was of excellent quality and easy to shape into blades and tools. Malindi was an important African center for iron.

Major coastal cities of this time included the island-port of Mozambique—for which the nation was later named—Zanzibar and Tumbatu in Tanzania, and Zeila and Berbera farther north in Somalia. Zeila was an outlet for the coffee trade of the Ethiopian highlands. It also traded in goatskins and slaves. Farther south along the Somalia coast were other centers. One of the most important was Mogadishu (mahg-uh-DISH-oo). Mogadishu merchants had trade contacts as far south as Sofala. By the 1200s, the island-city of Kilwa off the Tanzanian coast began to rise above these other cities in importance.

Sources of Information   Besides Greek and Arab writings, information about early east-coast Africa comes from chronicles written in the various cities. The oldest of these is the *Kilwa Chronicle*. It was written around the first half of the 1500s. Another source of information is oral history or tradition. There is also the information that comes from the work of anthropologists and archaeologists. These sources do not always agree. Often conflicts arise over the time something supposedly happened. For example, disagreement exists over Kilwa's early development.

According to the *Chronicle*, Iranians (Persians), known as Shirazi (shuh-RAHZ-ee), came to Kilwa in the 900s. Archaeologists, however, disagree. Their recent findings indicate that the Shirazi came two centuries later. Archaeologists have found coins in Kilwa which they date to this later period and link to the first Shirazi.

Still other scholars say that no one came directly from Iran to Kilwa. They claim that African descendants of the Iranians moved to Kilwa from earlier settlements in the north. Whatever the final theory will be, it is certain that Kilwa had become an important trading center by the 1100s.

Much of Kilwa's prosperity came when it took over the gold trade of Sofala in the 1200s. The Portuguese who captured Kilwa in 1505 described the city as having three- and four-story stone houses. Gold, pearls, silver, amber, and silk were abundant. The people ate a wide variety of food: lamb, goat, chicken, rice, millet, oranges, pineapples, limes, and many kinds of vegetables.

Muslim Influence As early as the A.D. 600s, Muslim Arabs had been bringing their religion as well as their goods over the trade routes to Africa's east coast. At first the religious element probably had little impact on the cultural development of the African peoples. It was not until the 800s that Islamic influence began to be felt. More Muslim Arabs came as trade increased.

The Arab traders began to settle permanently along the east coast and marry African women. This mixture of African and Arab peoples came to be known as Swahili. The Swahili were Muslims. They developed their own language, primarily of Bantu origin, with Arabic and some Persian words. Describing Kilwa in the 1300s, Ibn Battuta (IB-un bah-TOOT-tuh), a traveler from Morocco, reported that the Koran, the mosque, Islamic designs in architecture, and other Islamic influences had become part of the daily lives of the people.

It should be remembered that these east-coast cities were not Arab cities. They were African. The Africans living in them adopted Arab and other non-African influences. But the dominant political and social force was African.

Kingdoms of the Interior

Long ago, ancestors of the Hottentots and Bushmen hunted for food in East Africa's interior. Gradually they were pushed out by farming people moving south from Ethiopia. The newcomers spread through the area as far south as Tanzania. Over the centuries other peoples wandered into the Great Rift Valley from the north. Some settled in Kenya. Others moved south of Lake Victoria in eastern Tanzania. They were cattle herders.

Sometime after the A.D. 100s, Bantu-speaking peoples began migrating into East Africa from the west. The Bantu mixed with the earlier

This is an example of a Bushman cave painting. Bushmen were early inhabitants of East Africa.

peoples. Over the next thousand years or so, Bantu-speakers came to occupy all of southern and eastern Tanzania. They also took over the high region of Kenya east of the Great Rift Valley.

In Tanzania and Kenya, the various peoples lived mostly in clusters of villages ruled by a chief. They did not develop into kingdoms with a centralized government. Their economy was based mainly on farming. But they traded in such items as salt, iron, and pottery.

Kitwara   In some parts of the Lakes region kingdoms did develop. A non-Bantu-speaking people called Hima (HEE-ma) moved into Uganda around the 1300s. The Hima were herders. They began to dominate the Bantu-speakers already there. Strongest among the Hima clans were the Chwezi (KWEE-zee). The Chwezi became the rulers of a kingdom known as Kitwara (kit-WAH-ruh). This kingdom was divided into districts. Each district was ruled by a subchief. Rule was passed from father to son.

A social system developed based on occupations. Herders held the highest positions. Some people were farmers. Others made pottery or worked iron. All had to give part of their labor as well as other **tribute** to the rulers.

Bunyoro and Buganda   Meanwhile, other people had been moving into the area from the north. Sometime in the 1500s, a branch of these people—ancestors of the modern Luo—replaced the Chwezi as rulers. Their kingdom became known as Bunyoro (bun-YAH-roh).

Gradually smaller kingdoms elsewhere in Uganda came to be ruled by members of the Bunyoro family. One of these kingdoms was Buganda (boo-GAHN-duh). At first Buganda covered a small area centered around Kampala, which later became the capital of modern Uganda. Gradually Buganda's rulers expanded their territory and power. By the 1700s Buganda had become greater in power and status than Bunyoro. By the 1890s, Buganda was the greatest state in the interior. Its economy was based on long-distance trade. In Bunyoro and Buganda, the Luo rulers gradually adopted the customs and language of the Bantu whom they governed.

Rwanda and Burundi   South of Uganda, the kingdoms of Rwanda (roo-AHN-duh) and Burundi (bur-ROON-dee) developed. Rulers of both kingdoms came from the Hima people. Tradition states that the first kings were of the Chwezi clan. In the 1400s and 1500s the Tutsi (TOOT-see), also called Watusi (wah-TOO-see), migrated into the area. They took control of the Bantu-speaking Hutu (HOO-too), or Bahutu (bah-HOO-too).

The Hima people brought with them to Rwanda and Burundi their social system. At the top were the herding Hima people. Cattle meant wealth and status and belonged only to the king. However, he gave cattle to various lords to look after. Next were farmers, who were **serfs** for the Hima. At the bottom were the hunting and food-gathering Pygmies. As with the feudal system of Europe, farmers attached themselves to strong lords. In return for their labor, these lords gave them protection and security. Marriage between social classes was forbidden.

1. **Recall**   Why did the people living in the interior of East Africa develop their own ways of life without pressure from non-Africans?
2. **How and Why**   How did monsoon winds play an important part in the trade along the coast of East Africa?
3. **Critical Thinking**   Why had Islamic influences become part of the daily lives of the people of East Africa's coast by the 1300s?

SECTION

4

West Africa

By 5,000 years ago, West Africans were farming. Over 2,000 years ago, some—the Nok culture in what is modern Nigeria—had entered the Iron Age. The introduction of iron was important to the development of the West Africans. Superior tools and weapons gave them greater control of their environment. The stronger people began to dominate the weaker ones.

At various times between A.D. 500 and the 1700s, a number of states, kingdoms, and empires rose and declined in West Africa. They were based mostly on trans-Saharan trade. They traded gold, ivory, spices, and slaves in return for salt, cloth, metalware, and other items. As this trade grew, it helped to stimulate the growth of cities and states. One of the earliest of these West African states came to be known as the Empire of Ghana.

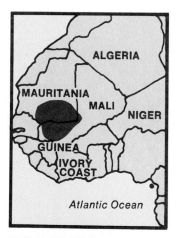

■ Empire of Ghana,
c. 300s-1076

Empire of Ghana

Ghana's beginnings may reach back to about A.D. 300. A people called Soninke may have developed and ruled it. The empire's exact boundaries are not known, but it extended into areas which are parts of the modern nations of Mauritania, Mali, Senegal, and Guinea. Ghana's location favored growth and prosperity. It was on a main north-south trade route.

Through Ghana passed the salt traders from the Sahara and North Africa and the gold traders from the south. The West Africans needed salt as much as the Arabs wanted gold. Ghana's king taxed both. Moreover, all gold found within Ghana itself belonged to him. He allowed only limited amounts on the market at any one time. By the 700s Ghana was known as the Land of Gold. Its ruler was described as among the wealthiest in the world.

Ghana's subjects considered their king divine. The position was also **hereditary**. When the king died, he was succeeded by the son of his sister. The various territories conquered by Ghana were generally ruled by local leaders. They paid tribute and provided soldiers to the king. In return, they received protection and were allowed to rule their own areas.

These figures are examples of gold work from Ghana. What was the source of Ghana's wealth? How important was trade to Ghana's growth?

The empire reached the height of its power in the mid-1000s. Then a slow decline began. Revolts from within and attacks from without occurred. The most serious invasion was that of the Almoravid (ahl-muh-RAH-vid) Berbers, an Islamic **sect** from North Africa. The Ghanaian ruler's refusal to become a Muslim angered the Almoravids. They conquered and looted Ghana's capital in 1076. Ghana fought and eventually regained its independence, but the war had seriously weakened it. Territories began to break away. In 1235, what remained of the empire was taken over by Susu, one of its former states.

Spread of Islam   During the 600s, Muslim Arabs swept out of the Middle East across North Africa. Many of the people in these areas became Muslims. North African traders carried Islam with them into West Africa. Sometimes—as in the Empire of Ghana—Islam was carried by invading armies.

By the late 1000s, the impact of Islam was very apparent in the savannah region just south of the Sahara. Ghana's kings had kept their traditional religion. But many of their advisors and **ministers** had become Muslims. Kumbi Saleh (KOOM-bee SAHL-uh), Ghana's last capital, was really two towns. Most of the Muslims lived in one. Non-Muslims lived in the other.

During the following centuries, Islam moved even farther into the savannah and forest regions of West Africa. Throughout these areas, the Koran began to be used as the basis for systems of justice and taxation. New buildings resembled those in other parts of the Islamic world. Since Islam stressed education, schools, universities, and scholars became important. Pilgrimages to Mecca (MEK-uh), the Muslim holy city in modern Saudi Arabia, brought West Africans into contact with peoples from all over the then-known world.

Islamic influence was stronger in cities and towns than it was in rural areas. There, many people held onto their traditional ways.

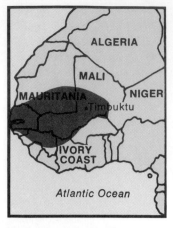

Empire of Mali, 1300s

Empire of Mali

The Empire of Mali achieved its greatness not only by trading in gold and salt as had Ghana, but also by actually controlling the sources of these two items. Mali's rulers gained control of both the gold fields and the salt region. Mali eventually covered an area from the Atlantic to the borders of modern Nigeria. Mali's rulers continued the tax practices of Ghana. All goods coming into and leaving the empire were taxed.

The empire was divided into states. The central region was governed directly by the ruler. He appointed governors—often members of the royal family—to administer parts of this region. Conquered states were generally left under their former rulers. They had to swear loyalty to Mali's ruler. To insure their loyalty, members of their families often had to live in the capital as hostages. The vassal states also had to provide soldiers for the empire's army. These soldiers kept peace and defended the empire. For a time this orderly system resulted in economic prosperity.

This burnt-brick mosque is in Mali. How important was Islam in West Africa? What areas of people's lives did Islam influence?

The greatest of Mali's rulers was Mansa Musa (MAN-suh MOO-sah, 1312–1337). In 1324, he made a pilgrimage to Mecca. On this journey, Mansa Musa met As-Saheli (ahs-sah-HAYL-ee), a Spanish writer and architect, who returned to Mali with him. As-Saheli built the first mosques and palaces of burnt-brick in the region. His materials and designs greatly influenced future building in West Africa.

During this time, the city of Timbuktu became famous. It endured for almost 1,000 years as part of various empires. At the peak of Mali's and later the Empire of Songhai's power, Timbuktu was known throughout the Islamic world. Early in the 1500s, a young Muslim traveler, Al Hassan ibn-Mohammed (ahl-hah-SAHN IB-un-moh HAM-uhd)—known to the Western world as Leo Africanus (af-ri-KAY-nus)—described the city. He wrote especially of the people's regard for learning. Scholars and students came from far and near to teach and study at Sankore, its university. Graduates of this university established schools of their own.

Like Ghana before, however, Mali became the object of invasions. In the early 1400s, Tuaregs (TWAH-regs), a group of Berbers from North Africa, attacked northern towns in the empire. Revolts occurred within the empire. The most serious of these resulted in the separation of the areas of Timbuktu and Gao (GAH-oh) from the empire. By the late 1400s Mali had lost much of its importance.

Empire of Songhai

The Songhai (sahn-GHEE) people of the area around Gao had carved out a kingdom along the Niger River perhaps as early as the A.D. 600s. In the 1000s their ruler converted to Islam. In the 1300s the kingdom became, for a time, a vassal state of the Mali. The Songhai people fought and regained their independence. They then began their own territorial expansion.

Sunni Ali (SOO-nee AH-lee), who came to power in 1464, drove out the Mossi people from the area around Timbuktu. He also drove out the Tuaregs. He made the area of the Niger bend and the central savannah the center of his empire. Generally local rulers were not allowed to remain as leaders after their territories were conquered. He appointed his own governors. He also introduced a **bureaucracy** of **civil servants** to run the central government.

Sunni Ali died in 1492. He was succeeded by his son who was deposed by Askia Mohammed (AHS-kee-uh moh-HAM-uhd, 1493–1528). Under Askia Mohammed the Songhai Empire reached the peak of its power and prosperity. He extended its borders in all directions and came to control the sources of gold and salt. Taxes on **imports** and **exports** brought much wealth into the royal treasury. Unlike Sunni Ali who was tolerant of traditional religious beliefs, Askia Mohammed wanted all his people to become Muslims. He supported the building of mosques and encouraged Islamic teachings throughout the empire.

Askia Mohammed continued the centralization of government. He divided the empire into four regions and appointed trusted officials to govern them. Each region included a number of provinces. No posts were hereditary. Askia Mohammed kept a well-trained army of both cavalry and foot soldiers. When he died, the empire began a slow decline. There were arguments over succession to the throne. Revolts resulted. But it was a Moroccan army that finally destroyed Songhai.

Hoping to gain control of the empire's gold, Sultan Al-Mansur (ahl-mahn-SOOR) sent an army south into the empire. The Songhai army was larger. But its swords, bows and arrows, and spears were no match for the firearms and cannons of the Moroccans. During 1591–1592, the Moroccans overran the main Songhai cities. Other peoples within the empire, including the Mossi and Hausa, took advantage of the situation to revolt. The Moroccans tried to hold onto their gains but could not. They retreated in 1618. By this time, however, the Songhai Empire was gone.

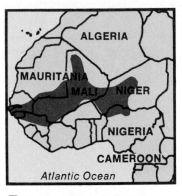

■ Empire of Songhai, 1500s

succession:
the order in which persons come to authority

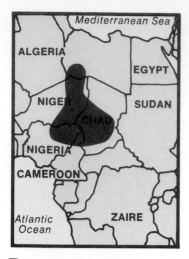

Empire of Kanem-Bornu, c. 1550

Empire of Kanem-Bornu

East of the Ghana, Mali, and Songhai empires was one known as Kanem-Bornu (KAH-nem-BOR-noo). Around A.D. 850, the Kanuri (kah-NOO-ree) people established the state of Kanem east of Lake Chad. Their leaders were members of the Sefuwa clan. Their location in the central savannah area put them at the crossroads of trade.

In 1086 the Kanuri king, Umme Jilma, was converted to Islam. Muslim laws, beliefs, and practices were introduced into the kingdom. This conversion tied Kanem into the cultural and economic community of Islam.

By the mid-1200s, the empire extended north to Fezzan in southwest Libya, east to the interior of modern Chad, and west to Kano in northern Nigeria. It also included Bornu, a territory southwest of Lake Chad. In the late 1300s, Kanem was conquered. The Sefuwa rulers moved their center of government to Bornu. Bornu also became the center of the empire's trade. In the early 1500s, the Sefuwa rulers brought Kanem again under their control.

In 1580, one of the greatest of their rulers came to power—Idris Alooma (EE-drees ah-LOOM-uh, 1580–1610). He introduced firearms and hired Turkish soldiers to train his army. With these new weapons and his armored cavalry, he further enlarged the empire. Idris Alooma built towns in the areas he conquered and placed troops in them to keep peace.

The wealth of Kanem-Bornu was built on trade. Its position of power was reinforced by a large army. This is one of the ruler's bodyguards. What advances in weaponry were introduced into the army in the late 1500s?

He made himself more powerful than the Council of Sefuwa Advisors who previously held as much power as the king. He continued the spread of Islam. At the end of his rule, Kanem-Bornu was a unified and strong state.

In the mid-1700s a series of internal revolts and outside attacks began to weaken the empire's power. In 1808 the Fulani (FOO-lahn-ee), conquerors of the Hausa States to the west, threatened to overrun the empire. An army from Kanem fought them off. In 1846 the last Sefuwa king died. With his death more than 1,000 years of Sefuwa rule ended.

This photo shows the old section of Kano. Why do you think that the Hausa states never combined into a single centralized government?

Hausa States

The area known as Hausaland is located in what is modern northern Nigeria and southern Niger. The Hausa (HOW-suh) people may have been descendants of several peoples. People from the Sahara and others from the Sudan may have come into the area and mixed with the original people. Possibly by around A.D. 500 this new mixture had become the Hausa.

Gradually the Hausa grouped themselves into walled villages. These villages grew into city-states ruled by kings. According to oral tradition, Daura was the first state. Kano (KAH-noh) is the best known historically because of the *Kano Chronicle*.

By 1300 each of the several city-states had well-marked boundaries. They did not form a single kingdom with a central government as did Ghana, Mali, Songhai, or Kanem-Bornu. Instead, they were clusters of settlements, each with a main city. These main cities became the centers of trade and manufacturing. In the 1400s, the cities also became centers of learning. By this time, Islam had reached Hausaland.

In the 1800s, the Hausa States were taken over by the larger Fulani Empire. The Fulani people may have originated in the area between the Niger and Senegal rivers. In the last days of the empire of Ghana, they began a series of conquests. Over the next several centuries their power grew. After they became Muslims in the early 1700s, most of their conquests were made in the name of Islam.

The Yoruba city-states became known for their artwork. The animal head is from Nok and the human figure is from Benin. Notice how the neck was built up by applying rows of bronze rings.

Yoruba City-States

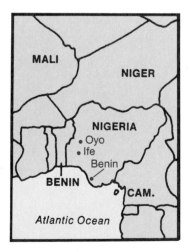

Yoruba City-States

The Yoruba (YOH-roo-buh) people speak a Kwa language of the Niger-Congo language family. According to their oral traditions, they trace their origins back to the first king of Ife (EE-fay), a city in western Nigeria. Archaeologists believe they may go back as far as the Nok culture—c. 500 B.C.–A.D. 200. Their language may be over 3,000 years old. Today the Yorubas live also in Benin and Togo.

According to one tradition, Ife was founded by a priest-king who had both religious and civil powers. As centuries passed, other Yoruba cities were founded. Oyo (OH-yoh) developed north of Ife around 1000. Benin grew to the southwest. Ife is world famous for its wood, terra-cotta, and bronze sculptures. Ife sculptors used a lost-wax technique that was used in ancient Egypt. In this process, a wax model is surrounded with clay. As molten metal is poured into the clay mold, the melting wax is replaced with the permanent metal.

Benin became the best known of the later Yoruba cities. The people of Benin learned about casting bronze from Ife. The Dutch who visited the city in the 1600s were impressed by the people's skill and the city's size and beauty. They described the great bronze plaques that graced the pillars of the palace. These plaques were scenes of life in Benin—hunting parties, court musicians, merchants, and acrobats.

During the 1700s, the Yoruba city-states began to decline. **Civil wars**, rivalries between states—especially over the slave trade—and the greediness of rulers caused the decline.

The Ashanti Union

The Ashanti (uh-SHAHN-tee) are one of the Akan-speaking peoples. The first states of Akan-speaking peoples developed along the coast of the Gulf of Guinea perhaps as early as the 1400s. These states were Adansi and Assin. Their prosperity rested on gold. Another early state was Bono-Manso. Later ones near the coast, such as Aguafo, Fante, and the Ga kingdom, were known as the Gold Coast States.

In 1695 the Ashanti leader combined these states into the Ashanti Union of Akan States. The capital was set up at Kumasi (koo-MAH-see). According to tradition, a golden stool came down from heaven to rest in front of the Ashanti leader. His advisor said this meant that the Ashanti chief was to unite the separate states into a **union**. Thus the states began to swear loyalty to the person who was elected to and sat on the Golden Stool of Kumasi.

Once united, the Ashanti started to expand. As they moved south, they met Europeans who were buying slaves. By the 1800s they controlled much of the modern nations of Ghana, the Ivory Coast, and Togo. The British were impressed by the union's power and prosperity. A messenger service operated to all parts of the union. A professional army trained by Germans kept peace. Only after a long and bloody war were the British able to crush the union. That was in 1901.

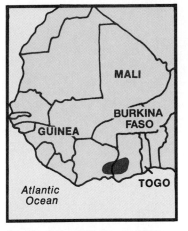

The Ashanti Union, c. 1700

This Ashanti gold work is a badge of honor. It was made by the lost-wax process. What can the types of object a culture makes and the materials it uses tell you about such things as its economy, politics, religion, and arts?

This is the Golden Stool of Kumasi. According to Ashanti tradition, the stool symbolizes power, bravery, and the welfare of the people.

Other States and Kingdoms

Sometime around the 1100s and 1200s, the Mossi people began developing kingdoms in what is now Burkina Faso. They had to fight Mali and Songhai to establish their states. The greatest of the Mossi states was Ougadougou (wahg-uh-DOO-goo). The city that bears that name is now the capital of Burkina Faso. In the late 1800s the French conquered the area and added it to French West Africa.

In what is modern Senegal, the Wolof (WOH-luhf) people built a kingdom. When Islam reached the area around 1000, the king converted. Most of the people continued to observe their traditional religion, however. The Portuguese came to Wolof in the 1500s and 1600s. For the next hundred years several European countries fought for control of the kingdom. The French won. In the 1800s, Senegal became the center of French West Africa.

The Kingdom of Dahomey began to develop in the 1600s with the expansion of the Fon people. By the mid-1700s Dahomey controlled the coast between the modern nations of Ghana and Nigeria. The kingdom's major source of income came from the slave trade. Dahomey sold prisoners from its wars with the Ashanti and Yoruba peoples. Many Africans who were brought to the U.S. as slaves came through Dahomey. In a series of wars between 1892 and 1904, the French conquered the kingdom. It too became part of French West Africa.

SECTION 4 REVIEW

1. **Recall** Why did the empires of Ghana, Mali, and Songhai grow and prosper?
2. **How and Why** How did the spread of Islam affect West Africa?
3. **Critical Thinking** Why did the West African empires decline?

Reviewing People, Places, and Things

Identify, define, or explain each of the following:

Kushites	Rwanda
Axum	Kumbi Saleh
Kibinda Ilunga	Mansa Musa
Great Zimbabwe	Timbuktu
Monomotapa Empire	Sunni Ali
Azania	Kanem-Bornu
Swahili	Hausaland
Ibn Battuta	Ife
tribute	Ashanti

Map Study

Using the maps on pages 54, 56, and 57, determine the answers to the following questions:

1. Which empire was smallest?
2. Which empire extended into a small part of modern Nigeria?
3. In what two modern-day countries were all three empires partly located?

Understanding Facts and Ideas

1. Why did the Egyptian pharaohs extend their power southward?
2. **a.** Where did Kushite cultural influences and trade contacts extend? **b.** How did Kushite civilization reflect these outside influences?
3. **a.** What do scholars not know about the early Bantu peoples? **b.** What do they know? **c.** What culture traits are shared by Bantu peoples?
4. **a.** How did Lunda rulers gain support of the chiefs? **b.** What was a result of this?
5. How important was trade to Malawi?
6. What caused the divisions within the Kingdom of the Congo in 1482?
7. What form of government did the Monomotapa Empire have?

8. What sources of information are there about early east-coast Africa?
9. **a.** What was the social system in Kitwara based on? **b.** Who held the highest positions?
10. What was the base of Buganda's economy?
11. How was the social system in Rwanda and Burundi like the feudal system of Europe?
12. Why was the introduction of iron important to the development of West Africa?
13. **a.** What was the consequence of the growth of trade in West Africa? **b.** What was the role of salt and gold in Ghana's trade?
14. What impact did Islam have on West African: **a.** justice and taxation? **b.** architecture? **c.** education? **d.** contact with non-Africans?
15. What method of power did Askia Mohammed use to strengthen the Songhai Empire?

Developing Critical Thinking

Examining Your Assumptions An assumption is an idea that a person takes for granted to be true. When examined, however, an assumption may prove to be false. Re-examine your ideas about early Africa. What have you learned from this unit that has changed any assumptions you had?

Writing About History

Analyzing Economics How did trade affect the growth of West African empires?

Applying Your Skills to History

Making a Table Make a table of African kingdoms, empires, states, and city-states. List dates, location, government, trade goods, and reasons for decline.

Colonialism

In the early 1400s Western Europeans began to look for a sea route to Asia. The Portuguese were among the first. As they moved south along the coast of Africa, they discovered the wealth it had to offer. They began to set up trading posts along the coast. The English, Dutch, and French soon followed.

In the 1700s Western Europeans began to explore the interior of Sub-Saharan Africa. Until then they had bought goods from African and Arab merchants. In the 1800s Western Europeans began to seize the sources of Africa's trade goods. Because of the **industrial revolution**, Western Europeans needed more **raw materials** and more **markets** for their manufactured goods. At this time Western European nations also began setting up **colonial** empires. Like Asia, Africa became caught in Western European power politics.

As you study this chapter, think about these questions:

- When Western Europeans first came to Africa, how did Africans use the rivalry among Western Europeans to their own advantage?
- How did the slave trade encourage an arms race among Africans?
- Why were Western Europeans eager to colonize Africa?
- How did Western Europeans deal with Africans in their colonies?

Portuguese forts, like the one pictured below, were the center of busy trade activity. They also showed Africans the force of Western European power.

It was a number of years before the Portuguese reached the southern tip of Africa. In 1486, while traveling along the west coast of Africa, Bartholomew Diaz's ship was blown out to sea in a storm. When he next saw land, it was to the west rather than to the east. He had rounded the southern end of Africa. The king of Portugal, John II, named this the Cape of Good Hope. He had every hope that the Portuguese would soon reach Asia and take over the spice trade.

Within ten years Vasco da Gama rounded the Cape and reached the east coast of Africa. He crossed the Indian Ocean to southern India. There he traded with Indian merchants for spices. He returned to Portugal in 1499 with two shiploads of spices.

Other Western Europeans began to follow the routes of the Portuguese. With the exception of Dutch farmers in South Africa, most Western Europeans stayed along Africa's narrow coastal strip in forts and trading stations. These early Western Europeans were interested in making money and then going home. They were also afraid of the tropical diseases of the interior such as malaria and sleeping sickness.

More importantly, however, the Africans limited these new people to the coast. The Africans wanted to keep as much of the profits as possible for themselves. By keeping the Western Europeans on the coast, they could control the flow of trade. Africans could also collect taxes on trade goods as they passed through their territories. Most African trade was in gold, ivory, skins, and food. In return, Western Europeans brought to them tobacco, cloth, alcohol, and later, guns and ammunition.

The Portuguese

Although other Western Europeans came to Africa, it was the Portuguese who dominated trade for several centuries. As they traveled down the west coast, the Portuguese came in contact with a number of the kingdoms and city-states described earlier.

The Portuguese established diplomatic and trade relations with several of these. Portugal and Benin dealt with each other on the basis of friendly equality for more than a hundred years. The possibility of force often kept the dealings friendly. The Portuguese were very polite when they discovered that rulers of kingdoms like Wolof and Dahomey could command armies of thousands. The Portuguese, and other Western Europeans also, came to respect African business sense.

Africans, for their part, learned that a great rivalry existed among Western Europeans. For a long time they used this knowledge to play one country against another. They tried to keep the Western Europeans from dominating them through trade or politics.

The Western Europeans, however, kept looking for weaknesses in the various kingdoms. Whenever an opportunity arose, they used trickery and force to get what they wanted. The Portuguese in East Africa are an example.

The Portuguese set up trading forts along the west coast of Sub-Saharan Africa. They were interested mostly in such African exports as gold, ivory, skins, pepper, and palm oil. In return the Portuguese brought the Africans cotton and linen cloth, glassware, kettles and pans of copper and iron, alcohol, and later, tobacco, guns, and ammunition.

The situation was different along the east coast of the culture region, with its numerous city-states. For a time the Portuguese used the coastal cities as stopovers on the way to Asia. But the wealth of the cities soon aroused their greed. Portuguese captains were told to try taking the cities by negotiating with the rulers. If that failed, they were to use force. In 1505 negotiations failed with the ruler of Kilwa. The Portuguese attacked, looted, and destroyed the city. The other cities soon fell.

The Portuguese rerouted trade from India through their island-port of Mozambique off the southern part of the coast. Cities north of Mozambique began to decline. Trade had been their only source of income. The merchants could no longer afford to send caravans to the interior to buy goods. Their income further decreased. As a result, these once strong and wealthy Swahili centers became weaker and poorer. A number of cities turned to smuggling. Sometimes a city would revolt. Such action brought swift punishment from the Portuguese.

During the 1600s Oman, a city-state on the Arabian Peninsula, began driving the Portuguese out. The Portuguese gradually retreated from the coasts of what are now Somalia, Kenya, and Tanzania. But they managed to cling to Mozambique. Around 1800 Oman was itself driven out by the Arab sultan of Zanzibar. By this time, several major changes had taken place in the Sub-Saharan culture region. They were related to the slave trade.

Rise of the Slave Trade

The Western Europeans did not introduce slavery to Africa. However, they introduced a new economic element to it.

Slavery had existed for many centuries in Africa. But it was different from the slavery later known among Western nations. Africans often took prisoners of war. Sometimes these prisoners were sold or traded back to their own people. Or, they were kept as laborers. They worked hard, but no harder than their masters. Their food, clothing, and lodging were almost the same as that of their masters. It was not uncommon for such captives to rise to positions of responsibility. Some even owned property and other slaves.

With the coming of the Western Europeans and the introduction of guns, the African pattern of slavery changed drastically in some areas. Slaves were traded or sold, not to other Africans, but to Western Europeans for guns and other goods. When one kingdom had guns, it became necessary for other kingdoms to have guns for their security. This was the case with Dahomey, Benin, and the Ashanti Union. An **arms race** developed and a vicious circle of war and slave trading began.

Western Europeans were eager to trade guns for people because they needed laborers. They were settling the Americas at the time. There, they opened gold and silver mines and started sugar cane and coffee planta-tions in Latin America. Later they grew tobacco and cotton in North

This is Regents, formerly a settlement of freed slaves in the British colony of Sierra Leone. What motives do you think prompted the British to abolish slavery in their own colonies and make Sierra Leone a haven for blacks?

America. In some areas, Western Europeans used Indian peoples as workers. But European diseases and abuse wiped out whole groups in a short time. In other areas, there were too few Indians to satisfy labor needs. As a substitute, Western Europeans began importing Africans to use as slaves.

As the demand for laborers increased in the Americas, slavery became big business. Africans were dragged from their homes or captured in battles. They were marched great distances from the interior to the coast. There they were branded and chained together in the hot, cramped holds of slave ships.

No one knows exactly how many Africans were brought to the Americas. The most commonly accepted estimate is 15 to 20 million. Additional millions were killed in the slave raids or died from disease or exhaustion on the march to the coast, or on the two-month, trans-Atlantic passage. The total number of victims may have run anywhere from 25 million to 50 million.

There was another slave trade, operated by the Arab traders who controlled the east coast of Sub-Saharan Africa. The Arabs sent their raiding parties deep into the interior. Some of the captured Africans were sent to the clove plantations on Zanzibar. Others were shipped to Arabia and the Ottoman Empire. Again, no one knows how many Africans the Arabs enslaved. But the total was in the millions.

End of the Slave Trade

A number of British and Americans opposed the slave trade on religious and humanitarian grounds. Beginning in the mid-1700s, churchmen in England preached that all human beings were equal in God's eyes and that slavery was immoral. Antislavery groups were organized. In the late 1700s the British colony of Sierra Leone in West Africa was made a refuge for freed slaves. Its capital was named Freetown. American Quakers freed their slaves before the American Revolution. After the Revolution, a number of states passed laws that forbade the importing of slaves. Some abolished slavery altogether.

Early in the 1800s both Britain and the United States passed laws making the slave trade illegal. In 1822 freed slaves from the United States landed in Liberia. The American Colonization Society had purchased land there for freed slaves. The settlement was named Monrovia after President James Monroe. The site is now the capital of Liberia. The colony was declared an independent republic in 1847.

However, many Western Europeans and Americans continued to operate as slavers. The profits and the difficulty of enforcing the laws against them caused many to risk capture. It was not until late in the 1800s that the slave trade decreased and finally ended.

Slavery itself was abolished by Great Britain in 1834 and by the United States in 1863. Brazil did not abolish it until 1888. Plantations in East Africa continued using slaves until 1898. And slavery persisted in the Arabian peninsula until at least World War II.

Consequences of the Slave Trade

The trans-Atlantic slave trade lasted for more than 350 years, from 1518 to the late 1800s. It had a number of serious consequences for Africans. The wealth produced by the trade influenced many West Africans to engage actively in the slave trade. They became slave hunters and captured increasing numbers of other Africans. This led to more and more wars and hostility among African peoples.

To escape the slavers, many Africans ran away from their homes. Traditions, families, kinship ties, and villages were torn apart. Because only healthy people would survive as slaves, the youngest and strongest were caught and sold. The old, sick, and weak were left to make out as best they could. Many areas were depopulated. This was especially true in Angola.

depopulated:
lost a great number of people from an area

Arts and **crafts** suffered. The energies of many Africans were used either to escape the slave hunters or to capture other Africans. Moreover, Africans could now get by trade what they had once had to make. A slowdown in African artistry and technology resulted.

Some African states prospered because of the slave trade. This was particularly true of Benin, Dahomey, and the Ashanti Union. All three kingdoms were originally located inland, between the Africans of the interior and the Western European slavers on the west coast. These kingdoms were thus in an excellent geographic position to control the flow of slaves to market. Gradually, they expanded their political control toward the Atlantic. As their power and importance grew, that of the savannah kingdoms—which depended on trans-Saharan trade routes—declined.

Overall, however, the effect of the slave trade was to weaken the economy, culture, and political strength of Sub-Saharan Africa's kingdoms. This made them increasingly vulnerable to outside control.

The slave trade had consequences for Western Europeans too. Western European slave merchants generally remained on the coast. They saw Africans either as slaves or slavers. They neither knew nor were interested in the culture of the various African peoples. There was no exchange of ideas, no attention given to African history or traditions. It was easier to sell people if they were thought of as property rather than humans.

Western European slave traders carried their ignorance and **prejudice** with them to Europe and the Americas. Seeing only this side, other Western Europeans and Americans developed a false picture of Africans. Greed and rationalizations—false reasons used to hide real motives—blocked from view the full range of African achievements.

SECTION 1 REVIEW

1. **Recall**   What methods did the Portuguese use to weaken east-coast cities?
2. **How and Why**   Why did most Western European traders stay along the coast of Africa?
3. **Critical Thinking**   How did the slavery of Western Europeans differ from the slavery that Africans practiced?

The only area in Sub-Saharan Africa where Western Europeans established a colony prior to the late 1700s was Southern Africa. Ever since 1497, the Portuguese and others had been rounding the Cape of Good Hope on their way to and from India. They stopped only to obtain fresh supplies of food and water. Then, in 1648, a Dutch ship went down in a storm off the Cape, and the shipwrecked sailors spent a year on shore before being rescued. When they returned to the Netherlands, they were so enthusiastic about the Cape's mild climate and fertile soil that the Dutch East India Company decided to set up a permanent colony there.

SECTION

2

Southern
Africa

The Boers

The Dutch settlers called themselves Boers (BO-uhrs), meaning farmers. At first they stayed at the tip of the Cape. There they grew vegetables and other food to supply ships traveling between Europe and Asia. The Hottentots and the Bushmen living in the area were pushed north.

After a while, the Dutch East India Company grew anxious about protecting its sea route to the Far East. So it started strengthening the Cape Colony. It granted homesteads of 6,000 acres apiece to its employees. It sent out Dutch orphan girls to marry the settlers. It imported Malay slaves to work on company-owned cattle ranches. It welcomed Protestant refugees from the religious conflicts in France.

The Boers gradually developed a new language called Afrikaans. Mostly Dutch, it contained a few French words and many African ones. The Boers were staunch members of the Dutch Reformed Church. They read little except the Bible. They believed it justified both slavery and the superiority of Europeans over peoples of non-European ancestry.

As its population grew, the Cape Colony kept expanding eastward. But at the same time that the Boers were moving east, another people were moving south. In the 1830s the two groups met in conflict.

The Zulus

The Zulus were Bantu-speaking cattle herders. During the 1700s they began migrating toward the Cape Colony in search of fresh pastures. They also wanted to avoid Arab slave raiders.

In the early 1800s, a Zulu chief named Chaka organized his people into a powerful military force. Between 1818 and 1828, Chaka's armies swept through much of Southern Africa. They established a great nation. After Chaka was killed by his two half brothers, one of the brothers, Dingane, became king. Dingane later led the Zulus in their battles against the Boers.

The Great Trek

In 1815, at the end of the Napoleonic Wars in Europe (about which you will learn in Unit 6), the Cape Colony was taken away from the Netherlands and given to Great Britain. The British allowed Afrikaans to remain the colony's official language and at first did not interfere with the Boer way of life.

Gradually, however, the values of the British and the Boers began to clash. The British did not believe in slavery; the Boers did. The British felt that individual Europeans should be limited in the amount of land they could claim. The Boers were used to taking as much land as they wanted. The British believed that Africans had the right to complain in court if their masters treated them badly. The Boers regarded that as nonsense.

In 1834 the British abolished slavery in the Cape Colony and made English the official language. That was too much for the Boers. In a journey known as the Great Trek of 1836, they moved northeast across the Orange River to find new homes. And there they met the Zulus.

The Zulus resisted the Boers valiantly. But the Zulus were armed only with spears, while the Boers carried muzzle-loading rifles. The decisive battle was fought in 1838 at Blood River. It received the name because the river ran red with the blood of 3,000 fallen Zulus. Three Boers were wounded.

The Boers set up two new colonies. One was called the Orange Free State. The other was called Transvaal, meaning across the Vaal River. For a number of years, the Boers lived undisturbed in their new homeland. Then British-Boer hostility erupted again.

The Union of South Africa

The renewed conflict between the British and the Boers was sparked by three things. These were diamonds, gold, and a man named Cecil Rhodes.

In 1867 diamonds were discovered along the Vaal River. Tens of thousands of British miners poured into the area, and in 1877 the Cape Colony annexed the mine fields. The action was taken at the urging of Rhodes, an English financier who had become prime minister of the Cape Colony. Rhodes envisioned a British empire in Africa that would stretch from "the Cape to Cairo"—that is, from Capetown in the Cape Colony to Cairo in Egypt.

In 1886 gold was discovered in Transvaal. Once again, tens of thousands of British miners poured in. The Boers, outnumbered two to one in their own country, thereupon denied the miners the right to vote. At this point the miners obtained guns and ammunition from Rhodes and planned an uprising. It failed, however, and Rhodes had to resign his post.

But friction between the British and the Boers continued, and eventually war broke out in 1899. The Boers waged **guerrilla warfare**, or hit-and-run tactics. The British burned Boer farmhouses and herded Boer women and children into concentration camps, where some 26,000 died from typhoid and hunger. After three years of bloody fighting, the Boers surrendered in 1902.

As a result of the Boer War, the Boer states became British colonies. In 1910 the Dutch states joined the English states to form the Union of South Africa. As it turned out, the majority of white settlers in the new nation were Boers, not British. While the British concentrated on mining and trade, the Boers gradually took over the government. They turned the Union of South Africa into a racist society. You will read more about this in the next chapter.

SECTION 2 REVIEW

1. **Recall**   Who were the Boers and Zulus?
2. **How and Why**   Why did the Boers believe Europeans were superior to Africans?
3. **Critical Thinking**   How were the Zulus and the Boers alike?

3

Scramble for Africa

In the late 1700s and 1800s, Western Europeans became interested in exploring the African interior. When the slave trade was banned, they began to look for other African goods to trade. The Industrial Revolution was underway. Greater and greater supplies of raw materials were needed to keep the machines working. Western Europeans also needed new markets in which to sell the output of their machines. Africa was seen as a possible source of both raw materials and markets.

At this time, too, Western European governments were beginning to think in terms of empire. A struggle for power among European nations was taking place. Having worldwide colonies, they believed, was one way of increasing a nation's power at home. To Western European missionaries, Africa presented the possibilities of millions of converts to Christianity. Western European scientists were curious about the various animals, plants, and resources they might find in Africa.

Western Europeans Move Inland

The first to enter the interior were explorers and missionaries. They were curious about two major rivers, the Nile and the Niger. At the time, Western Europeans knew so little about Sub-Saharan Africa that they believed the two rivers were part of one huge river system.

The first successful adventurer was Scottish explorer James Bruce. In the 1770s he found the source of the Blue Nile in the highlands of Ethiopia. In 1795 and again in 1805, Mungo Park, another Scotsman, explored part of the Niger.

There was a lull in exploration during the Napoleonic Wars. But no sooner had they ended than explorers once again pressed in upon the culture region. In 1823 two English brothers, John and Richard Lander, traced the Niger from its sources to its mouth. In 1827 Frenchman René Caillié (ruh-NAY ka-YAY) followed the Niger to Timbuktu. In 1848 missionary explorers Johann (YO-hahn) Rebmann and Johann Krapf of Germany were the first non-Africans to see the Ruwenzori Mountains. Other explorers included the husband-and-wife team of Sir Samuel Baker and Florence von Sass, Sir Richard Burton, and John Hanning Speke. It was Speke who located the source of the White Nile in 1862 when he took a detour by himself.

The most famous explorer of all, however, was medical missionary David Livingstone. Livingstone's goal was to stop the slave trade that Arab traders were carrying on. The way to do that, Livingstone felt, was to develop trade in other commodities, such as ivory, palm oil, coffee, and cotton. So Livingstone decided to map trade routes through Africa's interior.

From 1849 until his death in 1873, Livingstone crisscrossed the Sub-Saharan culture region. He learned several African languages. His journals were filled with detailed descriptions of the peoples, animals, plants, and natural wonders that he came across. His letters to London newspapers about the brutalities of Arab slaving raids helped arouse British public opinion against the slave trade.

This cartoon, from a British humor magazine, satirizes the European scramble for Africa. The character on the left symbolizes Germany, the one on the right, Italy. Why was Germany suddenly interested in Africa in the 1880s? Why did the rest of Western Europe fight for a piece of the pie?

In 1865 Livingstone set out on what was to be his last trip. By 1871 nothing had been heard from him. So Henry M. Stanley, an American journalist, was sent by a New York newspaper to look for him. Stanley found Livingstone at a village in what is now Tanzania and stayed to do some exploring himself. He spent three years tracing the course of the Congo or Zaire River.

Dividing the Continent

In the 1870's Stanley returned to the Congo Basin at the request of King Leopold II of Belgium. He succeeded in reaching Stanley Pool from the downstream end of the Congo River by finding a way around the falls. In doing so, he provided Leopold with claim to over 900,000 square miles (2 331 000 square kilometers) of territory in Central Africa. So Leopold's personal empire was larger than all of Western Europe. Moreover, it was rich in copper, ivory, and rubber.

As Africa was explored and mapped, Western Europeans began to move into the interior and take over. Many Western Europeans used the same argument they had used to build empires in Asia and elsewhere. First they ignored the cultures of the peoples they conquered. Then

Western Europeans claimed they had a mission to bring their way of life to the less-developed peoples of the world. Perhaps some actually believed this. Others used it to conceal their real motive—desire for power and wealth.

By now, Belgian, British, French, and Portuguese claims in Sub-Saharan Africa overlapped. In addition, other Western European nations also wanted to establish overseas empires. This was particularly true of Germany, which had recently been unified by Otto von Bismarck. As the rivalry over Africa increased, the threat of war between the Western European powers grew.

In November 1884 Bismarck called a conference in Berlin to settle the arguments. Fourteen European nations and the United States attended. Leopold's claim to the vast area of the Congo was recognized. Other nations, however, were allowed to trade in the Congo Basin and those areas washed by the Nile and Zambezi rivers. Other boundaries were also agreed upon. By February 1885 the Europeans had settled their differences—at the expense of the African peoples, none of whom were represented at the conference.

By 1914, when World War I broke out, all of Sub-Saharan Africa was under European control except for Liberia and Ethiopia. Many African peoples fought bravely for their freedom.

In West Africa, for example, the forces of Samori Touré (too-RAY) kept the French out of the area between the Niger River and the coast for almost 20 years. British settlements and trading posts in the Gold Coast were attacked repeatedly by the powerful Ashanti warriors beginning in 1824. In 1901 the British finally captured the Ashanti capital and took the king prisoner.

In the Sudan, followers of the Mahdi (MAH-dee), a Muslim religious prophet, destroyed British forces at Khartoum in 1885. The British—with the help of the newly invented machine gun—took their revenge at the battle of Omdurman in 1898. Eleven thousand Sudanese died. The number of Englishmen killed was 28.

The only nation that successfully resisted the European invaders was Ethiopia. This was due to the modernizing efforts of two kings, Tewodros and Menelik II (MEH-nuh-lik). Tewodros concentrated on building roads and on arming his soldiers with rifles and cannons. As he explained: "I know the tactics of European governments. First they send out missionaries, then [officials] to support the missionaries, then battalions to support the [officials]."

Menelik II likewise increased his army and equipped it with all the modern weapons he could buy. In 1895 Italy invaded Ethiopia. The following year, Italian troops were soundly defeated at the battle of Adowa (AH-duh-wah). The European nations then agreed to recognize Ethiopia's complete independence.

Liberia remained independent because of the influence of the United States. However, Liberia lost some boundary disputes to French and British colonies.

1. **Recall**   What are five reasons why Western Europeans began a scramble for control of Sub-Saharan Africa in the late 1700s and 1800s?

2. **How and Why**   How did Africans react to European plans to control Africa?

3. **Critical Thinking**   Why was Ethiopia able to resist Western European invaders?

Similar political and economic reasons drove the various Western European powers to seize African territory. However, each nation differed in its approach to colonizing and ruling the African peoples. At the same time, colonial rule had certain overall effects on Sub-Saharan Africa.

British Rule

For the most part, the British did not involve themselves directly in African affairs. They governed indirectly through African rulers. The British wanted law and order. They believed that fewer problems would be created if they did not change traditional ways.

The British allowed the local chief or king to continue ruling as long as he recognized and supported British authority. He had to enforce British laws. He also had to collect taxes and provide workers according to the demands of the top British official, called the resident. Some of the cooperating rulers and their followers were given British titles. A number of their children and other relatives were sent to schools in Great Britain. In this way the British hoped to strengthen the political and economic ties that bound African territories to Great Britain. However, the British government's official policy was that its colonies would eventually receive self-rule.

Uganda is an example of indirect British rule. The kingdom of Buganda developed around the northern part of Lake Victoria in what is modern Uganda. In 1900 the British made an agreement with the ruler of Buganda. He and his followers were allowed to rule as long as they recognized and supported British authority. As an additional reward, the British gave half of Buganda's land to these few thousand. The British later extended Buganda's rule to include other parts of Uganda.

SECTION

4

Colonial Rule

French Policy

In their colonies, the French practiced a policy of assimilation, or absorption, into French culture. Unlike the British, the French did not think that their African colonies might someday govern themselves. Rather, the French expected their colonies to become a part of France. In theory, colonial Africans would all become French citizens.

As a beginning, French citizenship was gradually given to all men who were born in certain towns in Senegal. These towns were settled mostly by French and mulattoes, descendants of both French and black Africans. A seat in the French Chamber of Deputies was given to a representative from Senegal.

The long-range aim of the French was to change the culture and traditions of their African colonists. They wanted them to speak, think, and act like the French. They had some success in training and assimilating an educated elite. After independence, many of these became the leaders and administrators of their former colonies. The vast majority of Africans, however, kept their traditional customs, attitudes, and language. Even the educated elite held to many of their traditional ways.

Because of their long-range goals, the French ruled in a more direct way than the British. A formal chain of command reached from the governor down to the local levels of government. Orders flowed down this chain to the various levels. Reports flowed back to the top through the same channels. At most levels above the local one, administrators sent from France held authority.

Belgian System

exploit:
take advantage of, especially for economic reasons

At first the Congo was ruled directly by Leopold II of Belgium, who exploited it for his personal benefit. The king developed large rubber plantations. In time he began to demand greater and greater outputs of rubber from his Belgian representatives. They, in turn, demanded more and more work from their African laborers. Workers were often whipped and tortured. Workers' families were held as hostages. It was not uncommon to kill laborers if they slowed down. These same methods were used on building projects and in mines.

In the early 1900s these brutalities came to world attention. In 1908 Leopold was forced to turn over his personal empire to the Belgian government. Some reforms were made. Forced labor was ended. The Belgians began to develop a more humane system of rule. They still exploited the colony, but they realized that satisfied workers produce more. Medical care, homes, clothing, and other benefits were provided.

The Belgians also set up primary and some secondary schools. Most of those who attended school never went beyond the lower grades. A few were sent to technical or vocational training schools. The Belgians wanted to provide enough education so that the Africans could contribute to the development of the colony. But they did not want to provide so much that Africans would become restless and demand change.

Other Governments

The Portuguese, the Germans, and the Spaniards were generally harsh in their colonial policies. They forced their colonists to work on plantations, rail and road construction, and other public works projects. Wages were low, and beatings were common. The Western European attitude was that the colonists were ignorant and uncivilized, and needed to be taught discipline and obedience.

Effects on the Africans

When the Western Europeans began taking over Sub-Saharan Africa, they knew little about the variety of peoples who lived there. To Europeans the peoples were Africans—not Zulus, or Masai, or Hottentots, or Yorubas. The cultural and ethnic qualities that made a group different from every other group were ignored. The Western Europeans were concerned only with exploiting the Africans to European advantage.

The political boundaries drawn at the Berlin Conference in 1884 cut across common grazing lands, farms, and even villages. This grouping of different peoples within the same borders often led to anger and violence among the Africans. When Western Europeans discovered this, they used it to make their rule more secure. They pitted one people against another. When independence came, colonial boundaries became the new national boundaries. The disunity and hostility encouraged by the Western Europeans were not easily forgotten. Disunity and hostility continue to hold back the nation-building efforts of modern African leaders.

Western Europeans also encouraged Indians to move into Sub-Saharan Africa. This was especially true in East Africa and in the Union of South Africa. Many of the Indians became merchants and shopkeepers, with one or two Indian families living in each town. Other Indians worked in railroad construction. The Indians added yet another

Exploitation of African mineral deposits, like this surface diamond mine, not only stripped Africa of its resources and put the profits in European pockets, but also changed African social and economic customs.

ethnic strain to the population, for they kept their own language, clothing styles, and customs. Their economic success bred resentment on the part of many.

New Crops   Western Europeans introduced new crops to Sub-Saharan Africa. The Portuguese imported the manioc from South America. Because manioc is resistant to locusts, it added considerably to the African food supply. The Portuguese also imported maize from South America. Because maize grows much more rapidly than other grains and requires little work, its cultivation became widespread. Unfortunately, maize lacks certain vitamins, and people who relied on it as a staple food developed "the disease of the mealies," otherwise known as pellagra. Cocoa beans for chocolate, also originally an American crop, eventually became one of Sub-Saharan Africa's major exports.

Economic Changes   Before colonization, most Africans used the barter system. A few kingdoms used shells as a medium of exchange. And among the east coast trading centers such as Kilwa, coins were used. But these were exceptions.

In some areas colonial administrators now placed a head or a hut tax on the Africans. This had to be paid in cash. In addition, Africans were being attracted to European goods that had to be paid for in cash. To obtain money, the Africans had to work for Europeans. They alone gave cash wages. For many Africans, this meant moving—either alone or with families—from the country to the new cities and industrial centers.

Social Changes   Christian missionaries from the United States and Western Europe established many schools and hospitals in Sub-Saharan Africa. The schools taught pupils how to read and write, and also trained them in technical skills. Some Africans studied to become ministers, teachers, and government clerks. Other Africans became professional soldiers. The hospitals treated such diseases as leprosy, malaria, and sleeping sickness. The death rate in Sub-Saharan Africa gradually decreased.

Western Europeans also brought to the culture region the Africans' first look at nationalism. This proved to be the undoing of European rule in Sub-Saharan Africa.

SECTION 4 REVIEW

1. **Recall**   Who ruled the Congo in the early 1900s?
2. **How and Why**   How did conditions change for Africans after King Leopold was forced to give up his African empire?
3. **Critical Thinking**   How did the British and the French differ in their approaches to governing their African colonies?

Chapter 3

Reviewing People, Places, and Things

Identify, define, or explain each of the following:

Industrial Revolution   Stanley
colonial   Leopold II
Caillié   assimilation
Burton and Speke   exploit
Chaka   barter
Livingstone   nationalism

Map Study

Using the map on page 33, answer the following questions.

1. What country controlled the southernmost part of Africa?
2. What color is used to indicate French colonies?
3. What country controlled the island in the Indian Ocean?

Understanding Facts and Ideas

1. Why did the Africans want to keep Western European traders along the coast?
2. How did the Portuguese and the Africans deal with one another?
3. Why did Western Europeans need laborers?
4. What were the consequences of slave trade for Sub-Saharan Africans?
5. Why did the Dutch East Indian Company found the Cape Colony?
6. What two kinds of Western Europeans were the first to enter Africa's interior?

7. How did the boundaries of today's African nations come about?
8. How do the political boundaries drawn at the Berlin Conference in 1884 hold back nation-building efforts today?

Developing Critical Thinking

Recognizing Stereotypes A stereotype is an oversimplified view of a person or group. It does not take into consideration individual differences, nor is it based entirely on facts. A stereotype may be complimentary but it is usually negative. Stereotypes often keep a person from understanding other people and from appreciating them and their way of life. This happened among the Europeans in Africa.

Activity: Western Europeans claimed they had a mission to bring their way of life to the less-developed peoples of Africa. But their real motive was usually a desire for power and wealth. Describe some of the stereotypes Western Europeans held about Africans. Explain how these stereotypes kept the Western Europeans from understanding the people of Africa.

Writing About History

Writing a Summary Write a paragraph to summarize the formal and informal methods used by Western Europeans to divide Africa.

Applying Your Skills to History

Using Special Maps Redraw and color the map from page 33. Using the political map on page 27, label with the current name the African holdings of Western European nations in 1914.

79

4

Independence and Growth

Colonial administrators set up European-run schools where students were taught about **self-government** and **nationalism**. Africans were also sent to study in Western Europe and the United States. After World War I, villagers began moving to mining and industrial centers to work. They too came in contact with Western European ideas. During World War II, Africa was a major supplier of materials and troops. They became increasingly aware of the benefits independence could bring.

At the end of the war, Africans increased their efforts for independence. In time most Western European governments were forced to give up their colonies. But the change from colonialism to independence was not smooth. Building a nation of many peoples has not been easy. A lack of skilled workers and capital adds to the problem.

As you study this chapter, think about these questions:

- What factors led to the end of colonial rule in Sub-Saharan Africa?
- What problems did new African governments face?
- How have African leaders tried to solve these problems?

This is a government building in Nairobi, the capital of Kenya. Kenya had a long and bloody struggle for independence.

Italian troops march into Axum in 1935. What significance does Axum have in the history of Sub-Saharan Africa?

In 1957 Ghana, a British colony, gained nationhood. From then on, independence in Sub-Saharan Africa came with a rush. Within a dozen years, most of the culture region was independent. By 1990 only South Africa remained under white rule.

Early Independence Movements

Two of the pioneers of African independence were Americans. One was Marcus Aurelius Garvey. The other was W. E. B. DuBois.

Garvey, who was born in Jamaica in 1887, came to the United States in 1916, where he published a newspaper called *Negro World*. Garvey called for a "back to Africa" movement on the part of American blacks. His efforts failed. His belief that "black is beautiful," however, stirred the imagination of many African leaders. It encouraged them to take pride in their cultural heritage. Along with the desire for acceptance of African cultural values by Africans and the outside world, came the desire for building political and economic unity—Pan-Africanism.

DuBois, who was born in 1868, was a university professor who helped found the National Association for the Advancement of Colored People (NAACP). In 1919 he attended the peace conference that ended World War I. DuBois tried to persuade the victorious Allies to grant African peoples the right of self-determination, or the right to decide for themselves what government they wanted. But all that happened was that German-owned territories in Sub-Saharan Africa were divided among Belgium, France, Great Britain, and South Africa.

DuBois then organized several Pan-African Congresses. The first was held in 1919 and was attended by black Americans and delegates from

governing minority and European settlers. The British, believing Kenyatta to be the head of the Mau Mau, imprisoned him. But the rebellion continued. It was finally suppressed in 1955, after four years of bloody fighting. Almost five times as many Africans—approximately 12,000—as European settlers were killed.

In 1960 Britain finally agreed to majority rule by black Kenyans. In 1961 the Kenya National Union Party won a majority in the legislature. Kenyatta, who had been released from jail, was its head. In 1963 Kenyatta became president of the new nation. He began easing out European landowners and Indian merchants and shopkeepers. Thousands in both groups left and were replaced by black Kenyans.

Kenyatta remained in office until his death in 1978. During that time, he increased the political powers of the presidency. Kenyatta, like most other leaders in Sub-Saharan Africa, wanted his nation to be ruled in the traditional African manner—by a king or a chief, but with the approval of the people's elders. Accordingly, Kenyatta rewarded his supporters but allowed freedom of the press.

Rhodesia to Zimbabwe

During the colonial period, Western Europeans poured into what was known as Northern Rhodesia, Southern Rhodesia, and Nyasaland. These areas have large mineral resources.

In 1953 the territories of Northern Rhodesia and Nyasaland and the self-governing colony of Southern Rhodesia joined in a **federation**. The European settlers of Southern Rhodesia dominated it. Black Africans—especially in Southern Rhodesia and Nyasaland—saw the federation as an attempt to interfere with their march toward independence. They pressured Britain into breaking up the federation in 1964. Northern Rhodesia became the independent nation of Zambia. Nyasaland became the independent nation of Malawi. Both came under control of their black African majorities.

Britain did not grant independence to Southern Rhodesia, however. Its European settlers refused to give black Africans adequate representation in the government. Black Africans make up about 95 percent of the population. With the end of the federation, Southern Rhodesia became known simply as Rhodesia.

In 1965 Rhodesia declared itself independent of Britain. Britain claimed the action was illegal. The UN agreed and ordered all trade with Rhodesia to stop. But some countries, such as South Africa and Portugal, continued to do business with Rhodesia. Leaders of Africa's black nations demanded that Rhodesia's black Africans be given majority rule. Zambia and Tanzania allowed their countries be used as bases for guerrilla operations against the government of Rhodesia.

In 1974 representatives of the white minority government and black leaders of the nationalist movement agreed on a program of reforms. Voting rights were to be given to greater numbers of blacks. By 1979 blacks

In 1980 Robert Mugabe became Zimbabwe's first black prime minister. Britain recognized the nation's independence soon after.

had gained control of the parliament. Independence was finally achieved in 1980. The nation took the name Zimbabwe for the stone ruins of the early African state. Robert Mugabe (moo-GAH-bee), a leader in the nationalist movement, became prime minister.

At first, unlike Kenyatta, Mugabe tried to persuade Western Europeans to remain. He valued the contributions they could make to commerce, industry, government, and military life. But Zimbabwe soon moved from a nonracial democracy to a black dictatorship. Almost no Western Europeans live there today.

The French Community

France's colonies gained their independence more rapidly than those of Britain did. After World War II France, like Britain, began to feel the economic burden of keeping a colonial empire. So it allowed its African possessions to determine their own futures. In 1958 French President Charles de Gaulle invited France's colonies in Africa to join France in what he called the French Community. In general, the colonies would control their domestic affairs. However, France would handle foreign affairs, finance, and defense. A constitution was drawn up and submitted to a vote of the people of the various territories.

De Gaulle made it clear that any nation voting "no" would receive immediate independence. But it would receive no future help from France. The people of Guinea, under the leadership of Sekou Touré (SEH-koo too-RAY), were the only ones to vote "no." De Gaulle kept his promise. Guinea was given immediate independence. But it was stripped of all French property that could be removed—even the desks in government offices. Economic assistance was cut off. Guinea was plunged into economic chaos for some years.

The other French colonies agreed to de Gaulle's proposal. But they were impressed by Sekou Touré's courage and demanded more freedom. By 1960 most of the French colonies were independent. Some nations have since dropped out of the French Community. Those that have remained guard their independence. France continues to give economic aid, but it has no power to force policy on its former territories.

In 1958 Sekou Touré of Guinea defied French President Charles de Gaulle and led his nation to complete independence.

SECTION 1 REVIEW

1. **Recall** What two Americans were pioneers of African independence?
2. **How and Why** How did Zambia and Tanzania help Rhodesia gain independence?
3. **Critical Thinking** Why did France's African colonies gain their independence more rapidly than those of Great Britain?

Since independence, African nations have followed many different paths. Some have had able leaders. Others have been plagued with many and violent changes in government. Some nations have a favorable location and valuable resources to exploit. Others have a poor environment and few natural resources. Most of the new nations have one thing in common, however. They are faced with dealing with the rivalries of the various peoples within their borders. This makes economic and social progress difficult.

Civil Wars

When independence came, most of the new nations kept their colonial boundaries. When outside enemies existed—the Western Europeans—the African peoples within these borders had been able to unite. But once independence had come and the Western Europeans were gone, unity sometimes broke down.

Nigeria The bloodiest attempt to change national boundaries occurred in Nigeria. The nation consisted of three regions, each with its own ethnic groups and economy. In the Northern Region lived the Hausa, Fulani, and Kanuri peoples. They were mostly farmers and Muslims. The Western Region was dominated by the Yoruba. It contained many bustling towns, and its peoples followed a variety of religions. The Eastern Region had vast coal and oil resources. Here the leading ethnic group was the Ibo, who were Christian and well educated.

The main problem was that although the Eastern Region was the richest of the three, political power rested with the Northern Region. Most government and army officials came from the north, which also received most of the revenue from the natural resources of the east. There was considerable inter-group prejudice as well. The Ibo looked down on the Hausa and Fulani because they were less educated. In turn, the Hausa and Fulani disliked the Ibo because they were arrogant.

In 1966 Ibo army officers in the Northern Region staged a coup. Many northern and western leaders were killed. Army officers from the Northern Region then staged a counter-coup. They also massacred civilian Ibo living in the area. More than 1.5 million Ibo refugees fled back to Eastern Nigeria. The following year, 1967, the Eastern Region seceded and declared itself an independent country—the Republic of Biafra.

The resulting civil war lasted for three years. The Nigerian government received military support from Great Britain, the Soviet Union, and Egypt. Biafra was aided only by France, although several African countries, notably Tanzania, gave it diplomatic recognition. The Nigerian government successfully blockaded Biafra, causing some 2 million Ibo to die through disease and famine. In 1970 Biafra surrendered to the Nigerian government.

Although Nigeria remained a united nation, the government realized that the political dominance of the Northern Region could not continue. So the country was divided into 12 ethnically based states, with a federal district for the capital of Lagos. Each state has considerable

Burundi and Rwanda have also experienced civil wars. Above, soldiers raise the flag of the newly independent kingdom of Burundi in 1962. The Tutsi people became dominant. Since then, the government has had to fight violent attempts by the Hutu people to take control.

powers of self-government. Nigeria was run by a military council from 1970 to 1979. Since then, it has been under civilian rule. The government has followed a policy of rebuilding the eastern part of the country after the destructiveness of the civil war.

Other Civil Wars The search for political stability and unity proved equally difficult in Ethiopia, Somalia, and Sudan, among other nations.

Ethiopia had regained its independence at the end of World War II. In 1952 it joined in a federation with the former Italian colony of Eritrea. Ten years later, in 1962, Ethiopia took over Eritrea and made it a province. The Eritreans rebelled. During 1990, the civil war was still in full swing.

In Somalia, conflict developed because of ethnic repression rather than politics. The one-party dictatorship of Major-General Mohammed Siyad Barrah represented the Sunni Muslim majority, which had made Islam the state religion. For twenty years, the government discriminated against the largest non-Muslim minority, the Isaak people. In 1988 a full-scale rebellion erupted. The government reacted savagely. Hundreds of civilians were slaughtered or swept into jails without a charge. The herding economy of the Isaaks was destroyed by the poisoning of wells and the killing of livestock. Cities in the northern area where the Isaaks lived were bombed so heavily that some 450,000 refugees fled into the Ethiopian desert, while another 600,000 were forced to move from one part of the country to another. By 1990, the civil war had not been settled.

A similar situation existed in Sudan, where non-Muslim blacks in the southern part of the country revolted against the Muslim Arabs in the northern part of the country. There were bitter charges that the Arabs had enslaved young boys from the Dinka people. In 1988 and 1989, hundreds of thousands of orphaned Dinka youngsters tried to make their way to safety in Ethiopia. About half survived the difficult trek.

African Identity

Some leaders have tried to build national unity by awakening their people's interest in their own heritage. Zaire's president, Mobutu Sese Seko, called for a program of national authenticity—a return to genuine Africanness—to do this. In 1971 he had the country's name changed from the Democratic Republic of the Congo to the Republic of Zaire. Zaire is the original name for the Congo River. The river was renamed Zaire. The people are now Zairese instead of Congolese. Lake Albert is now Lake Mobutu Sese Seko. The copper-rich province of Katanga became Shaba. This is the Swahili word for copper. Mobutu wanted his people to have African rather than European names. As an example, he changed his own name from Joseph Desire Mobutu to Mobutu Sese Seko.

In 1971 Major General Idi Amin Dada, former heavyweight boxing champion of Uganda, took over the government. The following year he gave 80,000 Indians and Pakistanis three months in which to sell their belongings and leave Uganda. The expulsion of the Asians was a serious blow to the nation's economy and government, for they controlled about 90 percent of its commerce and industry and held important jobs as

Once Joseph Mobutu (Mobutu Seso Seko) took power in the Congo and settled the civil war, he began an Africanization program.

teachers and clerks. But to Idi Amin, it was more important to have an all-black population. A few months later, he nationalized British-owned companies and tea plantations. However, Idi Amin's treatment of his own people was so abusive that in 1979 he was overthrown.

One-Party Systems and Military Takeovers

Leaders of the new nations discovered that the unity of political purpose their people had shown against the Europeans soon split apart. It seemed that the various postindependence political parties represented only local interests. National leaders felt that so many parties threatened national unity and economic development. After a time many leaders declared that only one party could exist within their countries.

Many Sub-Saharan governments have experienced military takeovers. You have already read about Uganda, Ghana, and Nigeria. Among other nations that have seen military groups seize power are Ethiopia and the Central African Republic. A number of reasons have moved these groups to overthrow their governments. Most seem to have been angered by worsening economic and political conditions within their countries. In some cases leaders had used their positions to reward their **kinfolk** and supporters. In other instances the leaders simply were not able to govern effectively.

South Africa: A Special Case

South Africa is still ruled by a white minority. For several decades, its black inhabitants and their supporters have been waging a struggle to gain control of the government.

Apartheid   At the time the Union of South Africa was formed in 1910, blacks in the Cape Colony had the right to vote. The British expected that the same would be true of the new nation. In 1948, however, the Afrikaner Nationalist Party defeated the British United Party, and Boer racist attitudes were enacted into law.

Under the segregationist system of apartheid, the population was divided into four groups: whites, Asians, black Africans, and Colored—people of mixed ancestry. The different groups were required to live in separate areas and to attend separate schools. They had to shop in separate stores, eat in separate restaurants, ride in separate buses, swim at separate beaches, and worship in separate churches. The areas set aside for whites were the most desirable areas in town. Blacks and other groups had to live in townships located on the outskirts of communities. That meant traveling long distances to work and shops.

Supervisory jobs in factories and mines were reserved for whites. Blacks who worked in the nation's mines had to live in fenced-in dormitories apart from their families for 6 to 18 months at a time. Strikes were illegal. Only whites could vote in parliamentary elections.

The government enforced apartheid in many ways. One was by means of pass laws. All nonwhite Africans had to carry a pass, or identity

This is an example of apartheid—separate entrances to the local post office.

card, in order to enter a white neighborhood. The government also restricted civil rights. Police could search homes without a warrant and arrest people and hold them without a trial. Organizations could be outlawed and newspapers, closed. People who persisted in opposing the government's policy were banned. This meant that they had to be in their homes every night, and could not go away on weekends or holidays. They were not allowed to see more than one person at a time. Nor could they speak out or be quoted publicly.

During the 1980s the government yielded to both internal and external pressure and repealed many of its apartheid laws. Pass laws were abolished. Most restaurants, hotels, and other kinds of public accommodations are no longer segregated. Neither is public transportation. Jobs are open to everyone, and workers may form unions and go out on strike. However, housing, elementary schools, high schools, and hospitals remain segregated. Also, whites receive more pay than blacks for the same job. In 1983 Asians and Coloreds received limited representation in government when the one-house parliament was replaced with three houses, one for each group. However, whites control the largest house and still hold most of the power.

Helen Suzman fought against apartheid as a member of the South African Parliament.

Bantustans   The government of South Africa also set up ten Bantustans, or ethnic homelands, for blacks. The Afrikaner theory was that each of the main groups of African peoples within South Africa would have its own homeland. Eventually all the blacks in South Africa would return to their own Bantustan, which would then become an independent nation. To date, four Bantustans have been declared independent. However, South Africa controls their laws, currency, immigration, and foreign policy. The Bantustans have not been recognized by any country except South Africa.

The idea of Bantustans cannot work economically. The amount of land set aside for the black 76 percent of South Africa's population represents only 13 percent of the total land area. Moreover, the soil is too dry and barren to feed the people. The only way blacks in the Bantustans have managed to survive is through remittances. Family members who work in white areas send them money.

Even for white South Africans, the idea of Bantustans is unrealistic. The nation's economy depends on black workers. Nevertheless, the government has so far forced 3.5 million blacks to move from white areas into a Bantustan.

The Struggle for Civil Rights   Opposition to South Africa's government has taken several forms. The first was passive resistance, similar to that practiced by Mahatma Gandhi in India; you will read about Gandhi in Unit II. The leading advocate of this approach was Zulu chief Albert John Luthuli. However, the situation in South Africa was unlike that in India. The Afrikaners, unlike the British, did not look on themselves as colonial rulers in a strange land. To the Afrikaners, South Africa was home, and they would fight for it the way their Boer ancestors had.

(Continued on page 92.)

Nelson Mandela

"I hate white domination. I hate black domination. I cherish the ideal of a democratic and free society in which all persons live together in harmony and with equal opportunities. It is an ideal for which I hope to live for and achieve. But if needs be, it is an ideal for which I am prepared to die."

These are the beliefs for which Nelson Mandella was sentenced in 1964 to life "plus five years" in prison by the white-ruled government of South Africa.

Branded a traitor, labeled a Communist, and sentenced as a saboteur and conspirator, Nelson Mandela is, above all else, a dreamer. His dream is one shared by many people: that of a world in which people of all races are respected as humans with equal rights.

Mandela lives in a difficult place to keep this dream alive. South Africa is a country whose government symbolizes injustice to people around the globe. The 26 million nonwhite (black, Indian, and mixed race) South Africans suffer under the oppressive rule of the nation's 5 million whites. In South Africa, nonwhites are routinely denied what we consider the most basic of human rights. Nonwhites cannot live where they choose. They cannot vote. They are brutalized by police. In South Africa, to be a nonwhite means to live in fear.

The horror of racism exists in most places, but what makes the racism of South Africa unique is that there it is institutionalized, legalized. The Population Registration Act, for example, classifies all citizens by race. The Group Areas Act requires segregation by race. These various policies, which are designed to insure white rule by oppressing nonwhites, are known collectively as *apartheid* ("apartness").

Nelson Mandela grew up under oppression. Born the son of a tribal chief in 1918, he rejected his hereditary right to become chief in order to study law, feeling that obtaining a legal education was the best way to help his people end the oppression. Mandela attended the black university at Fort Hare, but he was expelled in 1940 for his part in an anti-apartheid student strike. He continued to study law by correspondence, and eventually co-founded the first black law office in South Africa.

In 1944, Mandela joined the African National Congress, the oldest anti-apartheid group in South Africa. Committed to ending apartheid peacefully, Mandela played an important part in the ANC's Defiance Against Unjust Laws Campaign in 1952, the first nationwide organized protest against apartheid.

Mandela continued his campaign of nonviolence until the infamous Sharpeville Massacre in 1960, when white police fired into a peaceful crowd of black protestors, killing 69 and wounding 86 (many were shot in the back as they fled from the police). Believing that the government would continue the violence, Mandela renounced nonviolence and participated in a sabotage campaign. (The targets were carefully selected so as to not injure anyone.) "It would be unrealistic and wrong for African [black] leaders to continue preaching peace and nonviolence at a time when the government met our peaceful demands with force," Mandela claimed. With the police hot on his trail, he was forced to go underground. Eventually, however, he was discovered, tried, and sentenced to prison.

Mandela remained jailed for 27 years—more than a quarter of a century. Throughout this time, his status grew as a symbol of the cause of millions of oppressed nonwhites in South Africa and oppressed people everywhere. Mandela con-

Nelson Mandela speaking against apartheid at Wembley Stadium. After his release from prison in February 1990, he and his wife Winnie conducted a world speaking tour asking for donations to continue the protests against the South African government.

tinually refused government offers of release because they were based on the condition that he renounce violence or limit his activism. His defiance of the government and his heroic personal sacrifice are dramatic testament to his commitment to creating a just South Africa.

Growing demonstrations in South Africa and in other countries led to Mandela's release in February, 1990. He was heartily received and is continuing his fight—a man freed from prison but still imprisoned by apartheid in his native country.

As Nelson Mandela spoke to the tens of thousands of people who welcomed his freedom, he reminded them and insisted to the world that "Our march to freedom is irreversible. We must not allow fear to stand in our way."

1. Why do you think people discriminate against people of other races?

2. Do you think the United States should take action to end apartheid? Why or why not? If so, what should the United States do?

3. Why did Nelson Mandela refuse governmental offers of freedom? Do you agree with his position? Why or why not?

4. Write a letter to Nelson Mandela. Tell him what you think of his dream and the ways he has tried to achieve it.

5. Define "human rights," and give examples. What are some ways to insure people's rights are protected?

In 1960 there occurred the so-called Sharpeville massacre. In two separate instances, thousands of unarmed blacks, marching peacefully but without their required passes, were fired upon by the police. As a result, many blacks decided that the only way to bring about change was violence. Under the leadership of Nelson Mandela and Walter Sisulu, the African National Congress (ANC) committed more than 70 acts of sabotage against white-owned office buildings, business firms, and other institutions. Although property was destroyed, no one was killed. In 1964 the ANC leaders were tried and sentenced to life imprisonment. Mandela was offered his freedom several times if he would agree to live in a Bantustan, but he refused.

In the 1980s a public relations campaign developed in favor of **divestment**. Business corporations and universities in the United States and other Western countries were urged to sell their stock in South African companies. The economic losses would supposedly pressure the government to change its policy. Many firms and schools did as they were asked. However, some blacks—notably Mangosuthu Gatsha Buthelezi, chief of the Zulu—did not approve of divestment. He argued that blacks should seek not to destroy the nation's wealth but rather to obtain a share in it. On the other hand, such religious leaders as Bishop Desmond Tutu, who won the Nobel Peace Prize in 1984, supported divestment as a moral statement against apartheid.

Beginning in 1984, black unions launched several nationwide strikes to protest the behavior of police in black townships and to demand the adoption of ''one person, one vote.'' As many as 2 million workers at a time have taken part in such demonstrations. In addition, a guerrilla movement of about 10,000 blacks has been operating against South Africa from neighboring Mozambique.

South Africa's government has already made a considerable retreat from apartheid. The great majority of whites seem willing not only to live and work alongside blacks, but also to grant them a share of political power. In 1989 Sisulu was released from jail. In 1990 South Africa's President F. W. de Klerk released Nelson Mandela and legalized the ANC. De Klerk also lifted emergency restrictions on the press. It remains to be seen whether South Africa, unlike so many of its neighbors, can avoid a civil war.

Namibia   Namibia was formerly the German colony of South-West Africa. At the end of World War I, South Africa received control over it through a League of Nations mandate. However, in 1966 the United Nations ended the mandate, but South Africa refused to recognize Namibia's independence. South Africa also extended apartheid to Namibia and set up nine ethnic homelands in the country.

In 1971 a black guerrilla movement called South-West Africa People's Organization (SWAPO) began fighting to bring an end to South African rule. SWAPO established bases in Angola. South Africa responded by invading Angola to destroy the bases. South Africa also supported a rebellion against the Angolan government.

In 1989 a truce between the two sides was arranged by the United Nations. Elections for a constituent assembly to draw up a constitution for the new nation were held in November, 1989. This marked the end of colonialism in Sub-Saharan Africa. In March 1990, Namibia became an independent nation.

SECTION 2 REVIEW

1. **Recall**   What makes economic and social progress difficult in African nations today?
2. **How and Why**   Why was Nigeria divided into 12 ethnically based states?
3. **Critical Thinking**   How do you think the problems in South Africa can be solved?

During the colonial period, the countries that colonized Sub-Saharan Africa used the region's resources for their own benefit. Africa was a great supplier of raw materials. Some were agricultural and forest products that required little investment. These included cocoa, palm oil nuts, peanuts, cotton, and tea. Some were minerals that called for a large investment but yielded a high return. The most important minerals were gold, diamonds, and copper.

During this period, most technical, management, and business positions were held by non-Africans. As the Sub-Saharan nations gained independence, many of these trained people left. The new nations were faced with a lack of skilled labor. They also found that their economies were dependent on European markets. New markets had to be developed, new factories built, and skilled workers trained.

Capital

The major factor limiting the region's economic development has been a scarcity of capital. Without capital, a nation cannot put its resources to work to develop its economy. The capital needed to expand the economy comes from a nation's savings. But when an economy operates at a subsistence level, it cannot build up these savings.

One answer is for the nation to look to outside sources for capital. Foreign investment is one such source. Sub-Saharan nations can offer attractive incentives for foreign investors such as cheap labor, few regulations on business, and plentiful raw materials.

Another source of outside capital is foreign aid. African leaders recognize that they need this aid. The memories of colonialism, however, are still fresh. Many Africans fear a new colonialism. They are concerned that if they take aid from other nations, those nations will make demands on them. African nations do not want to find themselves in a position of being controlled once again by outsiders.

France aids the nations that are members of the French Community. Great Britain helps former British colonies. Canada, the United States, West Germany, and Israel also give aid in various forms. The Soviet Union and the People's Republic of China support some nations. Usually these nations have leaders with strong pro-Communist leanings.

Transportation

In addition to a scarcity of capital, most nations of Sub-Saharan Africa lack an adequate transportation system. As a result, they have not been able to exploit their natural resources. For example, large deposits of uranium were recently discovered in Niger. But there was no way to get it to market. Niger has no railroad and only unpaved dirt roads. Moreover, it lies several hundred miles inland, and the nations that border it likewise lack good transportation.

The lack of adequate transportation has had a political as well as an economic effect. Such landlocked nations as Botswana, Lesotho, Malawi, Zaire, and Zimbabwe carry on most of their foreign trade through the railway and harbor network of South Africa. As a result, although they oppose apartheid, they have been unwilling to do anything about it.

Industrialization

Industrial growth has been slow in most parts of Sub-Saharan Africa. There are many reasons for this lack of industrial development. The lack of capital is the main reason. Another important reason is the poor transportation system in this region. Waste and corruption in government has slowed development in many countries. Also, few countries have skilled workers to work in new industries. Furthermore, the great potential for hydroelectric power in Sub-Saharan Africa has not been tapped. Finally, the rapid population growth in the region has slowed economic progress throughout the region.

Even so, some of the Sub-Saharan countries have made strides in developing their economies. Kenya, for example, has focused on service-industry activities in order to develop its economy. Tourism is also an important industry in Kenya, particularly in the game parks and along the beaches. The Ivory Coast has begun to build its tourist industry. Liberia has a very large service industry related to the oil industry, and this nation registers and leases a large number of oil tankers and merchant-marine ships.

South Africa is the most industrialized country in the region. Automobiles, chemicals, clothing, processed foods, and iron and steel are among the goods produced in South Africa. Nigeria has experienced rapid industrial growth since the discovery of oil in the southern part of the country in the early 1900s. Since that time, Nigeria has been increasing its oil-refining capacity and developing its iron and steel industry.

Among the nations exploiting their resources is Botswana. The impurities of the ores that it mines are removed in smelters. This worker is pouring out a worthless material called slag.

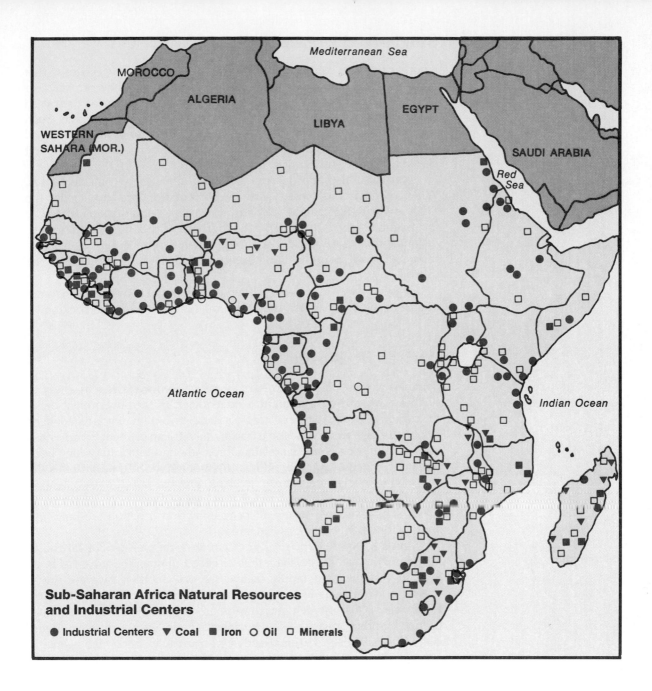

Sub-Saharan Africa Natural Resources and Industrial Centers

● Industrial Centers ▼ Coal ■ Iron ○ Oil □ Minerals

MOROCCO
ALGERIA
LIBYA
EGYPT
SAUDI ARABIA
WESTERN SAHARA (MOR.)
Mediterranean Sea
Red Sea
Atlantic Ocean
Indian Ocean

Single-Product Economies

Another problem confronting the nations of Sub-Saharan Africa is that many of them have only one or a few products that they can sell. For example, Niger and Senegal rely on peanuts and cotton for their cash crops. Zambia depends on copper for most of its export trade. Such dependence can turn out to be a disaster. In the case of an agricultural crop, the harvest might be bad. In the case of a mineral, the demand for it elsewhere in the world might fall.

Agricultural output in Africa is often affected by natural causes. When a drought hits, harvests are sharply reduced. This happened in the 1970s in Chad, Senegal, Mali, Mauritania, Niger, and Burkina Faso. The farmers and nomads living along the southern edge of the Sahara in these nations suffered the most. The drought was especially serious because the people had overgrazed and overcultivated the land and overcut the trees.

Nations have to diversify their economies. That way, if they are unable to sell one product, they have another product to fall back on.

African Socialism

Some leaders in Sub-Saharan Africa have chosen **socialism** as a way to further **economic development**. Under socialism the government owns the **means of production** and controls the distribution of goods. Modern Africans, however, have added a traditional African element to form their own kind of socialism. The relationships among kinfolk have long been basic to African peoples. Land has traditionally been thought of as the common property of a people, its clans, and the families. Cooperation was all-important. Africans added this idea of kinfolk to socialism. To them, socialism now means all peoples within a nation working and sharing. Such an example is Tanzania.

Julius K. Nyerere (ny-uh-REHR-ee), the first president of Tanzania, introduced a form of socialism that he called ujamaa (oo-jah-MAH). In Swahili this means a family feeling for one another. Nyerere wants everyone in Tanzania to work together for the common good. In rural areas this goal has taken such forms as **cooperatives** and communal farms. In other areas, banks, businesses, and even privately owned buildings have been **nationalized**. Unfortunately, Tanzania's economy has seen little growth because of a continuing **scarcity** of capital.

Famine Relief   In the 1980s a series of famines occurred in the northern part of Sub-Saharan Africa. The results were devastating. Famine caused malnutrition, disease, and death. Families left their homelands and wandered in search of food. Weakened by hunger and disease, many victims of famine did not live long enough to reach relief stations. More than 1 million people died in one year in Ethiopia alone.

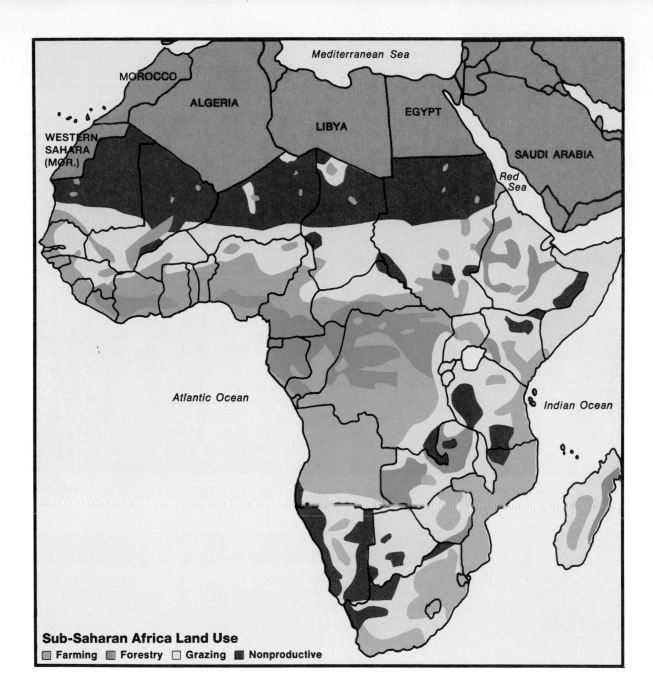

Sub-Saharan Africa Land Use

☐ Farming ☐ Forestry ☐ Grazing ■ Nonproductive

97

When Tanzania was created from Zanzibar and Tanganyika, Julius K. Nyerere began a series of reforms. One was the establishment of agricultural cooperatives and the introduction of modern farm equipment.

Food aid was sent to Africa from around the world, both by governments and by private relief groups. Yet much of the food did not reach the people quickly enough or even at all. Armed conflicts and a lack of roads made access to the people difficult. At times, corruption, mismanagement of relief money, and unfair distribution of food added to the problem. The government of Ethiopia, for example, has refused to deliver food to certain parts of the country unless the people there agree to be relocated to collective farms.

Increasing Food Production   Sub-Saharan nations need to make their land more productive. Sedentary agriculture will have to replace slash-and-burn agriculture. Farmers will need to plant a greater variety of crops. They will have to learn to use animal fertilizer to enrich the soil. In some instances, that means that farmers belonging to one group of people will have to cooperate with herders who belong to a different group of people. The nations' economic well-being will have to become more important than ethnic loyalties.

Large areas of land in Sub-Saharan river basins could be cultivated more intensely. But in order to bring this about, governments will have to invest their limited capital in agriculture instead of urban development or a huge army. This is difficult for governments that are run by the military or that are involved in a civil war.

Still another aid to greater food production would be for more technically advanced countries—the United States, Canada, Great Britain, France, and others—to share up-to-date agricultural ideas. New technology might be able to help control crop diseases, to deal with periods of unstable rainfall, and to increase crop yields.

SECTION 3 REVIEW

1. **Recall**   What factors are needed to speed economic growth in Sub-Saharan Africa?
2. **How and Why**   Why has food aid to Sub-Saharan Africa been unsuccessful?
3. **Critical Thinking**   How can Sub-Saharan African nations make their land more productive?

Chapter 4

R E V I E W

Reviewing People, Places, and Things

Identify, define, or explain each of the following:

self-government   Mugabe
Pan-Africanism   Touré
Haile Selassie   Amin
prime minister   Bantustan
Nkrumah   Mandela
Jomo Kenyatta   socialism
federation   cooperative

Map Study

Using the maps on pages 95 and 97, answer the following questions:

1. Where are the largest forests found in Sub-Saharan Africa?
2. What ocean do you think most of the industrial areas use for shipping?
3. How is the land on the island off the southeast coast of Africa used?

Understanding Facts and Ideas

1. What are three of the factors that led to the end of colonialism in Africa?
2. When did black Africans gain control of the Rhodesian parliament?
3. How has the French Community helped some African nations since they have become independent?
4. What factors have caused African nations to follow different paths since independence?
5. What caused the civil war in Nigeria in the 1960s?
6. What reasons are given by African leaders to justify one-party political systems?
7. How have black Africans in South Africa been affected by apartheid?
8. What is the purpose of the Bantustans?
9. Why have Sub-Saharan nations been faced with a lack of skilled labor since they gained their independence?
10. How has tradition been used to support socialism in Tanzania?

Developing Critical Thinking

Debating an Issue   A debate is a formal argument of two sides of a problem. One side is pro, for the issue, and the other side is con, against the issue. To prepare, each member of the debate team should read about the issue and take notes. The team decides together on the arguments. Each speaker is responsible for preparing and rehearsing a speech on his or her part of the debate.

Activity: Debate: The United States, Canada, Great Britain, France, and other technically advanced countries should share up-to-date agricultural ideas with Sub-Saharan Africa.

Writing About History

Relating Past to Present   Biafra's attempt to become an independent nation was put down in a costly war. Write a paragraph explaining how this war illustrated the problems of African nationalism.

Applying Your Skills to History

Using Economic Skills   Imagine you are a potential investor in an African nation. List the facilities and services you believe the government has to provide in order for you to build your factory. Consider labor force, transportation, public utilities, and postal service.

5

African nations, like many nations in the world, are a mixture of old and new, traditional and changing. This photo is a good example. What elements of modern and traditional ways are apparent? Is complete change necessary?

Tradition and Change

The move from colonialism to independence brought great changes to many people in Sub-Saharan Africa. Before the coming of Western Europeans, Africans felt a deep relationship with their land and their group. Life was known, certain, and secure. Then Europeans came and forced change on them. Independence, the world market economy, and the technology of the late twentieth century are forcing more change. Adapting to new ways is never easy. When conditions force people to change, more problems arise. But increasingly, Sub-Saharan Africans believe that change is necessary. They are trying to make those changes within an African framework. They are blending the old and the new into their own kind of future.

As you study this chapter, think about these questions:

* What are traditional Sub-Saharan African values toward the family, marriage, religion, and education?

* What are some themes of art, literature, and music of Sub-Saharan Africa?

S ub-Saharan Africans traditionally have thought of themselves not as individuals but as members of a group. From birth they are part of a community. Their joys and sorrows are all shared. What happens to one happens to the group. And what happens to the group happens to each member. Understanding this relationship is basic to understanding African society.

Ethnic Groupings

Today we speak of Africans as Ghanaians, Nigerians, Tanzanians, and so on. These are names that came with independence. But below the national level, Africans group themselves ethnically. Such groupings are usually identified by a number of common factors: language, culture, social and political ties, and geographical region. Underlying these common features is a shared religious experience.

Persons are born into an ethnic grouping. They cannot become part of it by moving from one region to another. Sometimes the group may consist of millions of members. The Hausa people of West Africa number 20 million. Or, the group may be very small. The El Molo people of Kenya are only a few dozen.

In Africa today there are between 800 and 1,200 different peoples. Sometimes groups cut across national boundaries. The Fulani people, for example, live in Nigeria, Senegal, and Cameroon. As we have seen, placing different peoples within national boundaries has led to tension and conflict.

To unify nations that contain many different peoples, leaders have to consider the interests of each group. The larger the group, the more consideration it is shown. Having the support of a large group can provide a person with a base for political office.

The Family

The family is the basic unit of the ethnic grouping. Within the family, children learn their rights and responsibilities. They learn that family members work together for the good of the whole group. Individuals may farm separate pieces of land, but they help each other. When harvests are poor, they share.

As children grow older, they are expected to help. Young girls care for old people or younger children. They may also learn a skill such as weaving that will enable them to earn money. They may learn to buy, sell, and trade goods in market towns. Young boys learn farming, fishing, and herding. Women, however, do much of the farm work. Fathers also teach their sons their particular trade—carpentry, blacksmithing, or winemaking, among others.

Some families are **matrilineal**. They center around the mother and the mother's brother. The son of a ruler does not inherit the ruling office. The son of the ruler's sister does. Sons do not inherit their father's property either. They inherit the property of their mother's brother, their

Africans are of many peoples or ethnic groupings. This woman is a member of the Kanuri people of northeastern Nigeria. Nigeria has at least 11 other large ethnic groupings and many smaller ones.

While the extended family is the general rule in the country, the nuclear family is the trend in the new African cities.

uncle. Children are sent at an early age to live in their uncle's home. It is the uncle's duty to care for them, teach them, and later see that they have suitable marriage partners. However, the **patrilineal** system, under which descent is traced through the father's side, is more widespread in Sub-Saharan Africa.

Families are grouped into clans. Clans in Sub-Saharan Africa often have hundreds and even thousands of members.

Initiation Ceremonies   In traditional Africa, as children reach the age of adolescence, they undergo initiation ceremonies. These ceremonies mark the end of childhood and the beginning of adulthood. They are usually for boys.

Initiation varies from place to place. In general, however, it prepares young people to assume adult roles in their clan. Initiation is not a single ceremony. The initiation period may last from several weeks to several months. In all instances, the individual is expected to show indifference to pain and hardship.

During the rituals, the full meaning of a group's kinship is explained to the candidate. In a way, a group is a secret society. It has beliefs and a history that are revealed only to full members, that is, adults. These secrets must be kept for life. To become full members, individuals have to prove themselves mature and responsible.

Age Sets   Among some peoples, initiation also prepares boys for entrance into an age set. The boys who are being initiated are not necessarily from the same clan, but are about the same age. Age sets are common among those peoples who need cooperation regardless of family or clan ties. For example, herders have age sets. They need to help one another look for water and grazing land. They also cooperate in protecting their cattle from wild animals and thieves.

During initiation, one person in an age set will emerge as the leader of the age set. This is a post he will hold for life. Members of an age set develop strong and lasting relationships with each other. Until they marry, age-set members often live together in a special area. They help each other when needed and, if necessary, fight side by side. In time they move as a unit to higher levels of authority in their community. Eventually they become elders and senior advisors. Under them, like a ladder, are other age sets. As each age set moves up, the next lower age set fills its place.

Age-set groupings cut across family and clan lines. But members often become related by marrying sisters or cousins of other age-set members. The age-set system helps unify a people. It lessens jealousies and divisions that sometimes arise between families and clans.

In Sub-Saharan Africa today, initiation rituals are that part of traditional life that has experienced the most drastic change. Pressure from missionaries and national governments has caused many rituals to be modified.

Marriage

Because family is so important in African society, marriage is a matter of concern not only to those being married, but to their families too. Some parents start looking for suitable mates for their children while their children are still young. A boy or girl may be engaged at an early age although the marriage takes place much later. This custom is common in traditional societies around the world. Many families, however, wait until the young reach mid- or late teens before arranging a marriage. In general, members of the same clan cannot marry.

The family generally considers their son's or daughter's feelings about a mate. If a person dislikes the one selected, the family will look for a more suitable choice. Sometimes a young person meets someone he or she likes and asks the family's approval to marry. If a person wishes to marry someone of whom the family disapproves, the individuals may

The traditional African family pattern is the extended family. Cooperation is a characteristic of this system. Here young women in Burkina Faso work in the family's fields.

Children are very important in African families. A mother braids her daughter's hair as mothers around the world have for centuries. Only the style varies.

103

In traditional societies the young learn about their past—their folklore—from village elders. Today in Tanzania this is still true, but with a difference. Formal education is considered necessary, but the Tanzanians are also trying to preserve their past. These students are on a field trip to learn about local history from a village elder.

choose to run away. Among traditional Africans this can cause serious problems. Among other things, the couple loses the security and protection of the group. Families and individuals all try to avoid pushing matters to so serious an end.

Once both families agree to the marriage, the family of the groom usually gives gifts to the father of the bride. These gifts are called bridewealth. The amount and kind depend on the customs, wealth, and status of the families. Most African women contribute greatly to their family's support by working in farming or trade. The gifts given at a marriage are to pay her parents for losing her.

Actual marriage rituals vary from one people to another. In some places, relatives of the bride and groom visit for several days in one or both of the families' communities. Sometimes the elders bless the marriage. All the elements of the ceremony stress the importance of the marriage to the community of relatives.

When the couple have a child, they are fulfilling the main purpose of their marriage. They are adding to the next generation of the clan.

Elders

As parents grow older, their authority and influence within the family and clan usually increase. Africans value older people. They believe that wisdom comes with age. In a matrilineal system, the mother's influence grows. In a patrilineal system, the father's influence increases. If he is of exceptional ability, the father may become a clan chief. Whether they reach high positions or not, elders are often consulted about community problems. Preserving the ways and customs of their ancestors is of primary importance to them. They want to keep alive and strong the kinship ties that give order and security to their community.

SECTION 1 REVIEW

1. **Recall**   What are some things that members of an ethnic group have in common?
2. **How and Why**   Why are marriages usually arranged, or at least approved, by families?
3. **Critical Thinking**   Why are older people important in African society?

Religion

Traditionally religion has been a vitally important part of African life. Religious ceremonies were community affairs in which all members took part. Local leaders often had religious as well as political roles.

Today millions of Africans still practice traditional religions. However, the degree to which they are observed depends on the particular group. Among many peoples, modern medicine, technology, and education challenge traditional beliefs. But among those peoples whose traditional ties are strong, especially in rural areas, traditional religions are still influential.

However, many young people are forced to move to urban or mining areas to find work. They no longer live as part of a clan or a people. They are suddenly individuals far from the rituals and customs that form their

These Coptic Christians are taking part in an Epiphany procession in Lalibela, Ethiopia. Epiphany commemorates the visit of the Three Kings to the Christ Child.

cultural and religious heritage. As a result, Christianity and Islam have made great numbers of converts among them. These two religions, however, have long histories in Sub-Saharan Africa.

Traditional Religions

The traditional religions of Africa are as varied as the hundreds of peoples who live there. However, there are some beliefs and rituals that are common to many peoples: belief in a Supreme Being, in a middle level of divinities, in ancestor spirits, and in life after death.

The Concept of God   Central to African religions is the idea of God as Creator. But after Creation, God withdrew. The affairs of earth and its people were left to lesser divinities and to ancestor spirits. Various peoples have different explanations for this. Basically, however, the reasons are the same. The attitudes and actions of humans were so unpleasant that they drove God away.

Lesser Divinities   Human beings are not left completely without protection, however. They have lesser divinities to help them. The divinities that are worshiped vary from people to people. The divinities may live in forests, rivers, or animals. Storms, thunder, lightning, the sun, and other forms of nature are controlled by the deities. Some are thought of as having human characteristics and of having once enjoyed human pleasures. Ogun, for example, is the Yoruba god of iron. The Yoruba people believe that when he was human, he was a hunter.

    At certain times of the year and during times of trouble, animals are sacrificed to the divinities, who usually live in sacred shrines. The people around Kano in Nigeria have a divinity that lives in a tree. The tree is encircled with a wall. Only the guardian of the shrine and other authorized persons may enter. Black goats, dogs, and fowl are sacrificed to this divinity. Among a number of peoples, black is regarded as a sacred color.

    If the sacrifices or offerings are not made, the community can expect trouble. According to an old legend, the empire of Ghana fell because one year the great snake Bida did not receive its annual sacrifice. Historically Africans have sacrificed the things they valued most: cattle, sheep, goats, chickens, and even humans. They also made offerings of grains and vegetables.

Ancestor Spirits   Ancestor spirits are closest to the everyday concerns of traditional Africans. Ancestors have died in a physical sense, but as spirits they are still present to their descendants. Ancestors generally stay near the community or even the house in which they lived. They will remain as long as they are remembered. Some Africans carve figurines into which the spirits can go. Sometimes a spirit enters an animal.

    For most traditional Africans, their present **values**, customs, duties, and responsibilities began with their ancestors. Thus traditional ways cannot be ignored or lightly discarded. Ancestors will protect and help their descendants if they are honored with rituals and ceremonies. If the

sacrificed:
offered to a deity

106

rituals are not observed, ancestors take their revenge. Among many people the young are not told the history of their clans and, therefore, their ancestors until their initiation. At that time they are warned that trouble awaits them if they stray from the ways of the ancestors.

Obedience to traditional ways has provided stability and security for the various African peoples. It has tended, however, to discourage change. Reliance on ancestors is found among other cultures besides African ones.

Masks and costumes are an important part of African traditional religions. These figures are part of a festival of the Dogon people of Mali.

Specialists   Traditional African religions have their special people as Christianity has its ministers and priests and Judaism, its rabbis. Among these special people are the guardians of the shrines of local divinities. The guardians may be either male or female. African community leaders and individuals consult the guardian for advice. The people believe that he or she has the power to communicate with the spirit. A guardian learns from the spirit the cause of someone's troubles and what must be done to end them.

Traditional Africans believe that mediums, diviners, and rainmakers also possess special powers. Mediums serve as contacts between the world of the living and the spirit world. Mediums are mostly women. The spirit speaks through the medium while the medium is in a trance. The medium gives advice and foretells the future. Diviners, who are usually men, also foretell the future. But they use omens and symbols. An omen is an occurrence or phenomenon such as an eclipse or the way sacred stones fall when the diviner throws them. A symbol represents or suggests something else. A lion, for example, may symbolize strength. Rainmakers supposedly have the power to bring rain or sometimes to stop it.

Another group of specialists are medicine men and women. They play a variety of roles in traditional African religions. They heal both physical and spiritual illness. Sometimes they are called herbalists. As apprentices they learn about the medicinal properties of a variety of herbs, roots, fruits, and minerals. Like modern medical doctors, they also understand that certain physical ills are brought on by the mind. They use rituals to cure these.

Christianity

Christianity came early to northeast Africa. Ethiopians were converted in the A.D. 300s. The majority of Ethiopians and a small number of Egyptians still practice Coptic Christianity. Elsewhere in the Sudan and northern Africa, Islam almost stamped out Christianity beginning in the 600s.

Christianity came late to the rest of Sub-Saharan Africa. In the 1400s and 1500s, Portuguese and Spanish traders brought missionaries with them. The missionaries established churches along the west coast. Not many Africans became Christians, however. Toward the end of the 1700s, a number of former slaves who had converted began moving to Liberia and Sierra Leone. From these areas Christianity began to spread along the west coast and into the interior.

During the early 1800s, Western European missionaries began going into the interior to set up missions and convert Africans. Some of them, including David Livingstone, became famous explorers. In the late 1800s European and American missionaries accompanied the new colonial rulers. As colonial power spread, the number of missionaries and their converts increased.

Many Africans saw Christianity as part of colonialism. The missionaries were mostly Western Europeans; so were the colonial rulers. Colonial officers generally gave aid and even military support to missionaries. In mission schools Western European—not African—languages, history, and culture were taught. Nevertheless, millions of Africans over the years converted to some form of Christianity. It is estimated that the total number of Christians in Sub-Saharan Africa today is between 120 and 130 million. This includes those who belong to the major Christian churches. It also includes members of the estimated 5,000 or so independent African Christian churches.

Both missionary churches and independent African churches are attempting to make Christianity more African in form and content. They want it to be more rooted in African social and religious traditions. Those attitudes and practices that come from European tradition and are not part of **doctrine** are being removed. Baptizing Roman Catholics with African names instead of saints' names is being encouraged.

Islam

substantial:
large; important

Islam swept across North Africa during the 600s and 700s. In the following centuries Muslims moved into West African communities along the southern fringe of the Sahara. Islam moved more slowly across the savannahs and into the forest areas of West and Central Africa. It spread up the Nile River to what is modern Sudan and Ethiopia. Today most Sudanese are Muslims. Ethiopia has a substantial minority of Muslims. At the same time Islam was spreading across North Africa, Arab and Persian traders were carrying it to the east coast of Africa. Somalia gradually became almost entirely Muslim. For centuries, however, Islam stayed in the trading centers and cities of the east coast. It began to reach the interior only in the 1800s. Today there are somewhere between 140 and 150 million Muslims in Africa south of the Sahara.

Islam came to Africa without a color barrier. Muhammad, the founder of Islam, is believed to have married an African woman to teach his followers that Islam was without prejudice. Wherever Islam spread, it merged with the traditional customs and practices of the people. Since Africans already believed in one God, they had little difficulty in accepting this key teaching of Islam. Many African converts initiate their young, but they include passages from the Koran—the sacred book of Islam—at the ceremony. Evil spirits are driven out with prayers from the Koran.

In a number of African nations Islam is also a political force. Some countries like Somalia and Mauritania have made Islam the state religion.

These Africans are praying at a mosque in Kano, Nigeria. Many Africans are Muslims. How did Islam come to Sub-Saharan Africa?

In other countries, such as Senegal and Mali, Islam was used as a rallying point in the fight for independence. Islam has also tied the Sub-Saharan Africans to a worldwide community of about 556 million Muslims. Large amounts of money and aid from Arab countries are coming to Africa through this tie.

Some Muslims are beginning to believe that they too must adapt their ways to the forces of change and modernization. Some Muslims are opposed to polygyny—the practice of having more than one wife—which Islam permits. Others say that Africa's Muslim leaders should do more to encourage education among the young.

Judaism and Hinduism

Followers of Judaism lived in northern Africa long before the first century A.D. Alexandria in Egypt was a famous center of Jewish learning. A number of Berbers converted to Judaism. Judaism also has a long history in Ethiopia. The first Jews came to the area in the A.D. 500s. Today about 15,000 Falasha still live there. There is also a large Jewish community in South Africa.

In various parts of Africa, there are communities of Hindus. Almost all are originally from India. There are very few African converts.

SECTION 2 REVIEW

1. **Recall**   What is the concept of God in traditional African religions?
2. **How and Why**   How have traditional religions been an important part of African life?
3. **Critical Thinking**   How is obedience to traditional ways, which is aided by ancestor worship, both good and bad?

The lives of many Africans have changed through their contacts with non-Africans. Some changes came through European-run schools. Other changes came through working for Europeans. In the cities and **towns** that grew around mining, manufacturing, and shipping centers, Africans from rural areas learned new **lifestyles**. During World Wars I and II, many Africans were recruited into Western armies and navies and sent to other areas of the world.

Since independence, outside influences are even more forceful. Through trade and foreign aid, African countries are becoming more closely tied to non-African nations. As Africans move toward industrialization and **urbanization**, more of their traditional patterns will change or be adapted to new ways. The question is how much and how useful will change and adaptation be.

Zambia is training workers to fill gaps in its industries. Trainees receive two-year courses in such skills as carpentry, electricity, or plumbing. This man is learning to be a welder. What industries would need welders?

Education

Traditionally the family and the clan were responsible for educating the young. It was within kinship groups and age sets that young people learned their history and roles in life. Some exceptions to this informal education existed. Along the east coast, Muslims set up schools where African students learned to read and write Arabic and/or Swahili. These schools, however, were usually limited to teaching Islam. Social roles or a people's heritage were not included.

Colonial Education   The real changes in African education began with Western European Christian missionaries. They opened schools across the continent. These schools were primarily for converting Africans to Christianity. But they also taught the culture and technology of the West. Some schools were supported by the colonial governments.

The results of this type of education on Africans were many. In some ways the educational system resulted in cultural conflicts. Africans learned more about Europe than about their own continent. They began to value Western European cultures and ideas more than those of their own peoples. The French tried to replace African cultures with French culture. Perhaps the British did not deliberately try to make African students into British copies. But their students learned to speak English with a British accent and adopted British attitudes and customs.

In other ways European-based schooling prepared Africans for independence and modernization. Africans learned about such political ideas as self-government and nationalism in these schools. They learned that by controlling their own economies, they would benefit more than if colonial powers controlled them.

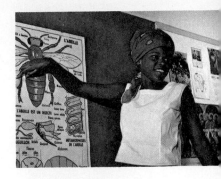

Higher education is becoming increasingly important in Sub-Saharan countries. The areas of law, science, medicine, and engineering are stressed.

Education Today   Since independence, many governments have been pouring money into their educational systems. Many African leaders consider modern education the key to the future. Most of the money has been spent to build primary schools. But students trained at high school, college, and university levels are also needed. Building and supporting such large educational systems place great economic burdens on nations. Resources are scarce, and needs are many. As a result nations must make **trade-offs**.

Because of economic factors, wide differences in the quantity and quality of education exist. Literacy rates in Sub-Saharan Africa vary considerably, from a low of 10 percent in Burkina Faso, Mali, Niger, and Senegal to a high of around 77 percent in South Africa and more than 60 percent in Zaire.

Two factors hinder a rapid increase in literacy. First, most of the languages of Sub-Saharan Africa have no written form. Therefore, in

Educational television is part of the school day in some Sub-Saharan nations. This classroom is in Niger. What do you think the benefits of educational television are?

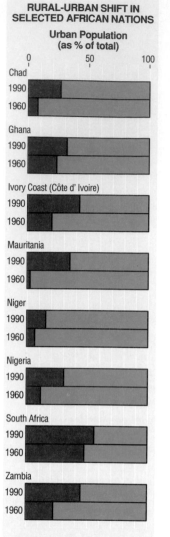

RURAL-URBAN SHIFT IN SELECTED AFRICAN NATIONS

Urban Population
(as % of total)

0   50   100

Chad
1990
1960

Ghana
1990
1960

Ivory Coast (Côte d' Ivoire)
1990
1960

Mauritania
1990
1960

Niger
1990
1960

Nigeria
1990
1960

South Africa
1990
1960

Zambia
1990
1960

Source: *World Development Report*, 1983.
1990 World Population Data Sheet.

order to read and write, most children must first learn a second language. Second, formal education is not highly valued by people who make their living from the land. Instead, parents believe that their children should learn survival skills, such as farming and hunting.

In most Sub-Saharan countries, education is more available in the cities than in the country. A lack of trained teachers adds to the problems. Some countries, such as the Ivory Coast and Nigeria, are using television to reach greater numbers of their citizens. Other countries are using radio and correspondence courses.

For African nations at this time, providing the right kind of education—not just providing education—is vital. Vocational training is essential. However, in countries where higher levels of education are available, many young are interested only in the kind of education that will get them government jobs. Government jobs have high status. While skilled workers are desperately needed, the bureaucracy in many countries is becoming overcrowded and inefficient. Graduates who have come from the country do not want to return even though few jobs exist in the city. To return home would seem an admission of failure. They are reluctant to return to the country even to teach.

Impact and Conflict   The ideas and practices that come from the new educational system are having a great impact on Africans. The young especially are greatly influenced. Their new attitudes often bring them into conflict with their families, clans, and peoples. In other instances, the young have been led to examine and rediscover the value of their own cultures. Still other people are trying to adapt the new ways to their old customs and beliefs.

Cultural conflicts take many forms. A young man might declare he no longer believes in the power of the clan's ancestor spirits. He would then be forbidden to take part in his clan's religious rituals. Such disbelief threatens the very foundation of the clan's traditional religious and social organization.

As we have seen, the traditional purpose of marriage was to produce as many children as possible. Marriage insured the continuation of family and clan. If a couple refuses to have more than two children, the family's future is threatened.

Conflict may also arise when a young man leaves his wife in the village and goes to the city to work or study. When they meet again, the ways of one may seem strange to the other. The man might be ashamed of his wife for being "old-fashioned." This affects the well-being of the marriage, which in turn affects the well-being of the clan.

Urbanization

In Africa, as in other parts of the world, cities are centers of change. Government and industry cluster in them. Residents are constantly exposed to a variety of customs and behaviors, opinions and attitudes. Most Sub-Saharan Africans, however, continue to live in rural areas. There the traditional ways of life are still strongly held. But as more and

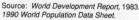

more people move to urban areas, they are caught up in a new experience.

They live and work with many different peoples who have different customs and beliefs. Their lives now are run by the clock and not by the seasons as they were in the country. City-dwellers often have to change from wearing traditional clothes to wearing Western ones. They may live with relatives, but they are not surrounded by family as they were in their villages. They are not under the constant watch of their elders. At the same time the city provides many opportunities to wander from traditional ways.

Many workers are required to join a labor union or other kind of organization associated with their job. This is not the kinship grouping they have known. These unions and other associations may comprise many unrelated people. Nor is it like the traditional age sets. People of all ages belong.

Urban living has not entirely displaced ethnic groupings, however. Associations of those who belong to the same people have been organized in some cities. These organizations teach newcomers the ways of the city and help them to find jobs. They also provide help for unemployed group members.

The first generation, especially, of city-dwellers go back to their old homes for marriages, deaths, births, and religious celebrations. Thousands of contract laborers, such as those who work in South Africa, return to their homes at the end of their contracts. But the ties are not all one way either. When relatives come to visit the city in search of a job or further education, they expect to stay with relatives. The obligations of kinship require city-dwellers to help members of their clan if possible.

Today second-, third-, and fourth-generation Africans are being

Cities in Sub-Saharan Africa are increasing in size and number. These are government buildings in Nairobi, the capital of Kenya. Why have cities grown up around the new capitals?

NATIONAL PROFILES/SUB-SAHARAN AFRICA

Nation/Capital	Population/ Area (in sq mi)	Urban Population (as % of total)	Per Capita GNP (in U.S. $)	Adult Literacy Rate (%)	Life Expectancy	Population Growth Rate* (%)
Angola/Luanda	8,534,000/481,351	25	**	20	45	2.7
Benin/Porto-Novo	4,741,000/43,483	39	340	20	47	3.2
Botswana/Gaborone	1,255,000/231,804	22	1,050	59	59	2.9
Burkina Faso/Ouagadougou	9,078,000/105,869	8	230	13	51	3.2
Burundi/Bujumbura	5,646,000/10,747	5	230	30	51	3.2
Cameroon/Yaoundé	11,092,000/183,568	42	1,010	65	50	2.6
Cape Verde/Praia	379,000/1,557	27	**	37	61	2.8
Central African Republic/ Bangui	2,877,000/240,534	35	390	33	46	2.5
Chad/N'djamena	5,017,000/495,753	27	160	17	46	2.5
Comoros Islands/Moroni	460,000/694	23	440	15	55	3.4
Congo Republic/Brazzaville	2,242,000/132,046	40	930	80	53	3.0
Ivory Coast (Côte D'Ivoire)/ Abidjan	12,596,000/322,460	43	740	35	53	3.7
Djibouti/Djibouti	406,000/8,494	78	**	20	47	3.0
Equatorial Guinea/Malabo	369,000/10,830	60	350	55	50	2.6
Ethiopia/Addis Ababa	51,667,000/471,776	11	120	35	41	2.0
Gabon/Libreville	1,171,000/103,346	41	2,970	65	51	2.2
Gambia/Banjul	858,000/4,361	21	220	12	43	2.6
Ghana/Accra	15,020,000/92,099	32	400	45	55	3.1
Guinea/Conakry	7,269,000/94,927	22	350	28	42	2.5
Guinea-Bissau/Bissau	987,000/13,948	27	160	9	45	2.1
Kenya/Nairobi	24,639,000/224,960	20	360	59	63	3.8
Lesotho/Maseru	1,774,000/11,720	17	410	65	56	2.8
Liberia/Monrovia	2,640,000/43,000	43	450	20	56	3.2
Madagascar/Antananarivo	11,980,000/226,657	22	180	53	54	3.2
Malawi/Lilongwe	9,158,000/45,747	14	160	25	49	3.4
Mali/Bamako	8,142,000/478,764	18	230	10	45	3.0
Mauritania/Nouakchott	2,024,000/397,954	35	480	17	46	2.7
Mauritius/Port Louis	1,070,000/790	41	1,810	83	68	1.3
Mozambique/Maputo	15,663,000/309,494	19	100	17	47	2.7
Namibia/Swakopmund, Windhoek	1,453,000/318,261	51	**	100 (whites) 28 (blacks)	56	3.2
Niger/Niamey	7,879,000/489,189	16	310	21	45	3.0
Nigeria/Abuja	118,819,000/356,667	31	290	30	48	2.9
Rwanda/Kigali	7,267,000/10,169	6	310	49	49	3.4
São Tomé and Principe/São Tomé	125,000/370	38	280	54	65	2.8
Senegal/Dakar	7,369,000/75,750	36	630	23	46	2.7

NATIONAL PROFILES/SUB-SAHARAN AFRICA, continued						
Nation/Capital	Population/ Area (in sq mi)	Urban Population (as % of total)	Per Capita GNP (in U.S. $)	Adult Literacy Rate (%)	Life Expectancy	Population Growth Rate* (%)
Seychelles/Victoria	68,000/175	52	3,800	65	70	1.7
Sierra Leone/Freetown	4,166,000/27,699	28	240	24	41	2.5
Somalia/Mogadishu	8,424,000/246,200	33	170	60	45	3.1
South Africa, Republic Of/ Bloemfontein, Cape Town, Pretoria	39,550,000/471,443	56	2,290	99 (whites) 65 (blacks)	63	2.7
Sudan/Khartoum	25,195,000/967,495	20	340	20	50	2.9
Swaziland/Mbabane	779,000/6,704	26	790	68	50	3.1
Tanzania/Dar es Salaam	25,971,000/364,898	19	160	85	53	3.7
Togo/Lomé	3,674,000/21,927	22	370	18	55	3.6
Uganda/Kampala	17,960,000/91,134	9	280	52	49	3.6
Zaire/Kinshasa	36,589,000/905,563	40	170	55 (male) 37 (female)	53	3.3
Zambia/Lusaka	8,113,000/290,584	45	290	56	53	3.8
Zimbabwe/Harare	9,721,000/150,803	25	660	77	58	3.2

Sources: *The 1990 Information Please Almanac* (Houghton Mifflin Company); *1990 World Population Data Sheet* (Population Reference Bureau, Inc., Washington D.C.)

*A nation with a population growth rate of 2% or more doubles its population within 35 years or less.

**Not available.

born and are growing up in the new cities. These later generations are not so closely tied to the traditional ways as earlier generations were, or rural Africans continue to be. Their education and experiences are very different from the traditional patterns. For example, these new Africans were probably brought up in a **nuclear** rather than an extended family. The authority of clan elders is unknown to them. They may have visited their ancestors' villages, but the way of life may have seemed strange. These new Africans are concerned with careers and with national and international events.

Women

Throughout history women have played important roles in a number of Sub-Saharan societies. Some scholars believe that the women of the old Nubian kingdoms held considerable power. Various empires were ruled by queens. In many cultures women acted as advisors to kings and chiefs. Among the Ashanti people, sisters and mothers of rulers often held the real power. Oral histories tell of women who served as generals and led warriors into battle. As we have seen, a number of peoples practiced, and still practice, the matrilineal system in which inheritance comes through the mother's side.

These computer technicians are civil servants in the Ivory Coast. What historical basis is there in Sub-Saharan Africa for women's involvement in politics, economics, and medicine?

In African religions, mediums are usually women. Some women also serve as rainmakers and diviners. Besides motherhood and household chores, African women are farmers and merchants. In West Africa, especially, they play—as they have for centuries—important roles in trade.

In modern Africa, women are also playing increasingly important roles in politics. Annie Jiagge was the first woman judge and Supreme Court Justice in Ghana. Angie Brooks of Liberia has held a number of government positions. Dr. Irene Ighodaro of Nigeria is known throughout the world for her work in medicine and education. Margaret Kenyatta, daughter of President Jomo Kenyatta of Kenya, worked with her father for the independence of that country. After independence she held a number of government positions, including mayor of Nairobi, Kenya's capital. In Chad, Fatime Kimto became that nation's first woman cabinet minister in 1982.

Modern African women are doctors, nurses, teachers, and engineers. Often they hold these jobs while also raising a family and managing a household. Some African women, especially Muslims, still lead lives that are centered on the home. Many spend their lives within the boundaries of their villages. But growing numbers of African women are taking on additional roles in society.

SECTION 3 REVIEW

1. **Recall** When did the real changes in African education begin?
2. **How and Why** How have kinship ties been affected by urbanization?
3. **Critical Thinking** Why is the right kind of education vital for African nations now?

Among many peoples of West Africa there exists a long tradition of visual arts such as weaving, sculpture, and metal casting. Along the east coast, creativity was more likely to be expressed in the spoken word and in music.

The arts of some peoples reflect non-African influences. Their many centuries of contact with Islam are evident in the works of the Hausa and Fulani, for example. Western Europe has had its greatest impact on modern African literature. Many writers use French or English rather than an African language. Non-African influences are also being felt in the contemporary visual arts. Some African artists are adapting Western styles and techniques to traditional subject matter.

Visual Arts

The Portuguese who came to West Africa in the late 1400s took back to Europe carved figurines and ceremonial masks. Objects such as these are still important in traditional African art. This art has been, and still is, deeply rooted in the religious life of the various peoples. These objects are not made for beauty alone or as a means of self-expression for the artist. They are made for religious or ceremonial purposes.

Some masks represent a divinity or force of nature. When worn during a funeral rite, they often serve as a bridge between the living and the dead. They are also worn among some peoples during initiation rituals. The Ibo people of Nigeria wear masks for many events including public holidays such as Nigeria's Independence Day. Some masks are

Much of African art is tied to traditional religions. Masks, such as the one shown below from the Luba culture of Zaire, are worn in ritual dances. These masks also influenced artists of other cultures, such as Picasso. The man on the right is carving a figurine. What materials is he using?

abstract:
in art, having little or no resemblance to an actual object

abstract representations of the human head. Others combine human and animal features. Still others may represent ideas such as beauty or ugliness.

Generally, carved figurines also have religious meaning. Some people carve these figurines to serve as places in which ancestor spirits can live. Some figurines carry the spirits of unborn babies. And some are symbols to bring fertility, strength, or other power to the bearer.

Traditional African artists use many materials for their carvings: wood, ivory, soapstone, and clay. Masks are often carved wood. But they may be made of animal skins, cotton or other fiber, or shells. In addition to carving masks and figurines, African artists carve boxes for cosmetics and jewelry, cups and other containers, headrests, chairs, stools, shutters, and doors.

Where natural materials—clay, raffia, and so on—are available, pottery, baskets, weavings, and leather goods are made. Leatherwork is found especially among herding peoples. The Ashanti and Baule people of West Africa have long worked with gold. Bronze, silver, brass, and copper are among the other materials used by African artists.

Early Art

Many early African art objects, especially those made of wood, have been lost. Dampness, termites, and wars have destroyed them. For the most part only works of metal, clay, or soapstone have survived.

We do have some knowledge of very early African creativity, however. Among the art which has survived are rock and cave paintings found from the Sahara to South Africa. The oldest of these are in the Tassili plateau in southern Algeria. As we have seen, ancient artists painted and carved scenes from their daily lives on cave walls and rocks.

In Sub-Saharan Africa, the oldest surviving art comes from the village of Nok in northern Nigeria. There, in the 1940s, terra-cotta—fired clay—heads of both humans and animals were discovered. Found with them were some iron tools. The earliest of these have been dated to between 400 and 300 B.C. As we have seen, scholars believe that this may have been the earliest date for making iron in West Africa. The influence of the Nok culture continued in the region after its decline around A.D. 200.

The Nok culture may have inspired artists of the later city-state of Ife. As we have seen, Ife artifacts include works in bronze, wood, terra-cotta, and ivory. The artists of Ife passed along their knowledge and techniques to other peoples in West Africa, especially those of Benin.

In the 1900s, traditional African masks and other sculpture became a major influence on Western art. French painters living in Paris came across African art objects in the city's shops and began to imitate them. At the time, European art was concerned mostly with showing the outward appearance of objects—color, mass, the play of light, and so on. The French painters admired the abstractness of the masks, the fact that they were more concerned with showing an idea than an actual person.

This terra-cotta head is from the Nok culture. How long did the influence of this culture last? Why do you think people imitate the art styles of others?

This picture shows Lagos, the capital of Nigeria. The architecture in modern cities in Sub-Saharan Africa is similar to the architecture of modern cities throughout the world.

Among the modern artists who were influenced by Sub-Saharan art were Pablo Picasso of Spain and Henri Matisse (ahn-REE ma-TEES) and Georges Braque (ZHORZH BRAHK) of France. Their paintings showed faces with long, square, simplified features that nevertheless conveyed the subject's personality.

Architecture

Mention has already been made of the great stone buildings made by the Nubians and the people of Zimbabwe. In most areas today—except in the large cities and towns—buildings are still made of the most easily available materials. In rural communities, stone buildings are rare. Clay or mud is used. Round houses of straw are common among some Sudanese and East African peoples. The Dogon people of Mali build multistory square houses of mud. The Ndebele people of South Africa decorate the outside walls with colorful geometric designs.

The buildings that are going up in the new cities belong to the school of design known as international. They look very much like glass skyscrapers in large cities elsewhere in the world.

Dance and Music

African dancing is highly symbolic and tied to traditional religions. There are dances for rain, a good harvest, a successful hunt. Dances are also performed to thank the spirits that guard the community. In many communities, there are dances of sorrow at a death. And at times people dance just for the joy of life.

Dancing is a community act, since the reason for the dance generally concerns all members. Among some peoples, however, such as the Watusi of Burundi, persons are trained as professional dancers. The participants in a dance usually move in a circle, in a single line, or in two parallel lines. Villagers who are not dancing form a circle around those who are, and clap their hands or cry out to the dancers.

Drums and gourd rattles often provide the rhythms for dancing. Rhythm is basic to all music. And complex rhythm is the trademark of African music. There may be three, four, or five rhythms going at the same time. Dancers move each part of their bodies—arms, legs, head, shoulders, and trunk—to a different rhythm. Dancing calls for great skill and practice.

The cultural diffusion of African music has been widespread. It has influenced blues and jazz in the United States, West Indian calypso, and Latin American dance music, among others.

Oral Literature

Over the centuries, most African literature has been oral. **Epics**, myths, poems, stories, and **proverbs** have been handed down from one generation to the next by word-of-mouth. Certain members of each community memorize the tales from their elders. They in turn pass them on to the next generation.

All over Sub-Saharan Africa, storytellers still recite their tales. They do not simply entertain; they also teach. They recite their peoples' legends about the creation of the world and humans. Epic tales of the exploits of ancestors and local heroes are also passed on.

Other African tales are about small animals who outsmart bigger and stronger enemies. Fables of the clever spider are found throughout West and Central Africa. There are also tales about the hare and the tortoise. Apparently Africans have long admired those whose intelligence enables them to overcome the greater physical strength of others. Through symbolism these tales teach listeners that cunning and cleverness can outwit injustice and evil.

In traditional Africa, storytelling is a community activity. The storyteller, usually an elder of the village, will act out all the parts of the story. Sometimes sound effects or music are used too. Very often the audience will sing any songs that are part of the tale. Often listeners will comment on the action of the story.

Sub-Saharan Africans also have an oral tradition of useful sayings. They also have a treasury of riddles, songs, and poetry whose origins have been lost in time.

Written Literature

The education and local circumstances of writers influence their choice of topics. Many of the writers were educated under the French, English, or

This drum is from Ghana. How has the drum been decorated? What part does music play in Sub-Saharan religious and social life?

Portuguese colonial systems. Many continue to write in the language of their former rulers.

Beginnings

Written literature in Sub-Saharan Africa began in the 1700s with such works as *The Early Travels of Olaudah Equiano*. It was written in English in 1789 by an Ibo who had been kidnapped when he was 11 years old and sold into slavery. It took ten years for Equiano to save enough money from a trading business to buy his freedom from his Quaker owner. In 1767 he went to England, where he became a leader in the antislavery movement. Equiano's autobiography helped inform people about the horrors of the slave trade.

The first great modern novelist of Sub-Saharan Africa was Thomas Mofolo of Lesotho, who wrote in the Sotho language in the 1920s and 1930s. *Pitseng* tells about the education and courtship of a contemporary African. *Chaka* is a fictional account of the Zulu chief.

Writers in French

As early as the 1930s, Africans writing in French began comparing the values of the West with those of Africa. They concluded that there was a naturalness and warmth in African culture that Western culture lacked. African culture was more in harmony with nature and with life. It seemed to them that Western culture was cold and exploitive. It had had a brutal impact on Africans and their cultures. These themes came to be grouped under the general heading of negritude (NEG-ruh-tood).

Among the best known writers of the school of negritude was the poet Léopold Sédar Senghor (lay-oh-POLD SAY-dahr SAHN-gohr). He later became the first president of Senegal. Most writers of the school of negritude are poets.

More recent African writers in French have been less concerned with negritude. Among them is Camara Laye, whose book *L'enfant noir (Dark Child)* is considered to be one of the culture region's best autobiographies.

Writers in English

Many Africans writing in English base their works on social, economic, or political themes. One of their great literary centers is in Nigeria. Among Nigerians, Ibo writers have been especially productive. Perhaps the best known is Chinua Achebe. In three of his novels, *Things Fall Apart*, *No Longer at Ease*, and *Arrow of Gold*, he deals with the clash of old and new values.

Among Nigeria's poets is Christopher Okigbo, who died in the Biafran civil war. Probably the most famous Sub-Saharan playwright is Nigerian Wole Soyinka. In his plays—*The Road, A Dance of the Forests, Kongi's Harvest, The Strong Breed, The Lion and the Jewel, The Trials of Brother Jero*, and *The Swamp Dwellers*—he pokes fun at strutting school teachers and so-called prophets. He also criticizes negritude and Sub-Saharan dictators.

Two of Ghana's playwrights are Efua Sutherland and Ama Ata Aidoo. Sutherland founded the Ghana Society of Writers and the Ghana Experimental Theater. She is known in the United States for *Playtime in Africa*, a children's book.

This is Léopold Sédar Senghor, poet and politician.

Weaving is one of the many arts that are practiced in Sub-Saharan Africa today. This tapestry is from Benin. The figure represents a king. For what other kinds of art objects have the cities of the Republic of Benin been famous?

During the 1960s several East African writers came into prominence. James Nguigi of Kenya wrote several works that explore the problems of harmonizing old and new ways. *Weep Not Child* and *The River Between* are two of these. In *Song of Lawino*, Okot p'Bitek of Uganda portrays the troubles an uneducated wife has in understanding the ways of her educated husband.

South African writers, both black and white, are caught up in the anger and anguish of living in an apartheid society. Ezekiel Mphahlele examines this theme in his autobiography *Down Second Avenue*. Peter Abrahams has also written on this subject. In *Kaffir Boy* and *Kaffir Boy in America*, Mark Mathabane describes his experiences first in South Africa and then in the United States, where he currently lives and works. Among the white authors who have written about apartheid are novelists Alan Paton and Doris Lessing and playwright Athol Fugard. Fugard's plays have been widely performed in American theaters and on television.

Writers in African Languages
Other Sub-Saharan Africans are also writing in their own languages. Poets B. W. Vilakazi and J. L. Dube wrote in Zulu. S. E. K. Mqhayi wrote poems in his Xhosa language. Both are Bantu languages.

The modern Yorubas of Nigeria and Benin have a strong literary tradition in their native language. In the 1940s Daniel O. Fagunwa began writing novels in Yoruba. Another writer in Yoruba is I. O. Delano. Herbert Ogunde writes plays in this language.

The earliest known Swahili writings date to the 1600s. Until the 1800s the only Swahili literature was poetry. Its themes were mostly religious. In the 1800s some poets began to write on other subjects. Two twentieth-century Swahili poets are Sheikh Amri Abedi and Mathias E. Mnyampala. James Mbotela and Muhammad Saleh Abdullah Farsi wrote novels in Swahili. Perhaps the best-known Swahili writer is novelist Shaaban Robert.

SECTION 4 REVIEW

1. **Recall**   What types of literature make up African oral tradition?
2. **How and Why**   How do the arts of some African peoples reflect non-African influences?
3. **Critical Thinking**   Why is dancing considered to be an important part of African life?

Chapter 5

R E V I E W

Reviewing People, Places, and Things

Identify, define, or explain each of the following:

matrilineal	Jiagge
patrilineal	Brooks
clan	Ighodaro
initiation ceremony	Margaret Kenyatta
doctrine	Nok culture
state religion	negritude
lifestyle	Senghor
urbanization	Laye
trade-off	Achebe
bureaucracy	Soyinka

Map Study

Using the maps on pages 26 and 27, answer the following questions:

1. What city is located near the White Nile and the Blue Nile?
2. What city is located nearest Lake Victoria?
3. In what kind of natural region are Luanda and Kinshasa located?

Understanding Facts and Ideas

1. How did persons in Africa become part of an ethnic grouping?
2. What is the matrilineal system of kinship?
3. What advantages do age sets have?
4. Why do traditional Africans honor ancestors with rituals and ceremonies?
5. Why did Christianity and colonialism appear to many Africans to go together?
6. Why have so many Africans accepted Islam?

7. In traditional Africa, who was responsible for educating the young?
8. What new experiences are Africans faced with when they move to urban areas?
9. How have art and literature played an important role in African life?

Developing Critical Thinking

Predicting Alternative Futures   When you predict an alternative, or choice, for the future, you do not choose the obvious solution. Instead you use the data from the present to imagine other possible solutions. To do this, you must be flexible and creative; both are valuable skills because that will help you to adjust to change and to the unexpected.

Activity: Imagine you are an African faced with rapid industrialization, urbanization, and modernization. Write a letter to a friend describing how you feel about your situation. Discuss what accepting Western ideas might cost you as a traditional African and suggest some alternative solutions besides complete rejection or acceptance.

Writing About History

Making Comparisons   Write a paragraph comparing the importance of family in Africa with the importance of family in the United States.

Applying Your Skills to History

Using Bar Graphs   Examine the bar graphs on page 112. Describe in a paragraph what they tell you about the change in Africa's population over a 20-year period. If the trend continues, explain the problems you foresee for Africa's future.

SUB-SAHARAN AFRICA

Reviewing Facts

1. What natural obstacles kept outsiders from penetrating the interior of Sub-Saharan Africa?

2. What causes desertification?

3. What is the economic significance of the location of Axum/Ethiopia?

4. From where do sources of information about early east-coast Africa come?

5. What was the result of the Boer War?

6. What was David Livingstone's goal as a medical missionary in Sub-Saharan Africa?

7. What is Pan-Africanism?

8. What is the main reason for the lack of industrial development in Sub-Saharan Africa?

9. What are some religious beliefs and rituals that are common to many Africans?

10. What two factors hinder a rapid increase in literacy in Sub-Saharan Africa?

Understanding Main Ideas

1. Why are rivers important in Sub-Saharan Africa?

2. How are kinship ties important among all Bantu-speaking peoples?

3. How did the slave trade in Africa change with the coming of the Western Europeans?

4. Why have one-party systems and military takeovers occurred in many countries in Sub-Saharan Africa?

5. Why is oral literature important to African culture?

Applying Chronology Skills

Chronology of African Independence
Study the time line below and answer the questions that follow.

1947	— Nkrumeh founded Convention People's Party
1951	— Mau Mau rebelled against Europeans
1953	— Northern Rhodesia, Nyasaland, and Southern Rhodesia joined in a federation
1957	— Ghana became independent
1958	— Guinea became independent
1960	— Nigeria became independent
1963	— Kenya became independent
1964	— Northern Rhodesia became independent nation of Zambia; Nyasaland became independent nation of Malawi
1980	— Southern Rhodesia became independent nation of Zimbabwe

1. How many years after Nkrumeh founded the Convention People's Party did Ghana become independent?

2. Did Kenya become independent before or after the Mau Mau rebelled against the Europeans?

Making Connections

Understanding Economics Study the table on pages 114 and 115 to make a bar graph

UNIT 1 REVIEW

showing the per capita GNP (In U.S. $) of countries in Sub-Saharan Africa and the per capita GNP of the United States ($19,780).

Understanding the Humanities

Analyzing Oral Literature   One African tale that has been passed on by word-of-mouth is about the tortoise and the hare. Make a list of tales that have been passed on to you.

Developing Critical Thinking

Determining Causes   Why were Western European nations interested in acquiring colonies in Sub-Saharan Africa?

Using Sources

In the following poem, David Diop, a famous poet from Senegal, expresses his bitterness toward the Western Europeans who colonized Africa and his hopes for Africa. Read the poem and then answer the questions below.

> **The Vultures**
> In those days
> When civilization kicked us in the face
> When holy water slapped our tamed
>   foreheads
> The vultures built in the shadow of their
>   talons
> The blood stained monument of tutelage.
> In those days
> There was painful laughter on the metallic
>   hell of the roads
> And the monotonous rhythm of the
>   paternoster
> Drowned the howling on the plantations,
> O the bitter memories of extorted kisses

> Of promises broken at the point of a gun
> Of foreigners who did not seem human,
> Who knew all the books but did not know
>   love.
> But we whose hands fertilize the womb of
>   the earth
> In spite of your songs of pride
> In spite of the desolate villages of torn
>   Africa
> Hope was preserved in us, as in a fortress,
> And from the mines of Swaziland to the
>   factories of Europe
> Spring will be reborn under our bright
>   steps.

*David Diop, "Vultures," trans. by Ulli Beier, in Langston Hughes, ed., POEMS FROM BLACK AFRICA (Bloomington, Indiana University Press, 1963), p. 145.

1.   Who do you think the vultures are?
2.   What kind of hope does Diop have for Africans?

Extension Activity

Making a Chart   Make a chart showing the exports and trade partners for selected Sub-Saharan nations.

Read More About History and Culture

Abrahams, Roger D. *African Folktales: Traditional Stories of the Black World (selected and retold).* New York: Pantheon Books, 1983. Collection from oral traditions of Sub-Saharan peoples.

Esedebe, P. Olisanwuche. *Pan-Africanism.* Washington, D.C.: Howard University Press, 1983. African nationalism.

2

SOUTH AND SOUTHEAST ASIA

South and Southeast
Asia has cultural
patterns that are
distinctive of the
region. Shadow
puppets, such as these
from Thailand, are
used in puppet plays
at wedding and birth
celebrations. The
puppets made of
leather or wood are
intricately carved and
painted.

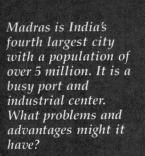

The Environment

Over the centuries the people of South and Southeast Asia have used the physical features of the culture region to create great civilizations with a high level of political, social, and cultural development. Some of these civilizations lasted thousands of years and produced an enduring **heritage** for the 17 independent nations and the more than 1.4 billion people that call South and Southeast Asia home. These nations include many ethnic groups, who speak hundreds of different languages.

The great religions of Hinduism and Buddhism originated in the culture region and helped shape the customs and traditions of the people, most of whom earn their living through agriculture. Most nations in the culture region, however, are making progress in modernizing agriculture and in industrializing their economies. As a result, the region is one that has seen great changes in recent decades.

As you study this chapter, think about these questions:

- How has the physical environment of South and Southeast Asia influenced its cultural development?

- How has the cultural environment of South and Southeast Asia influenced its political development?

Madras is India's fourth largest city with a population of over 5 million. It is a busy port and industrial center. What problems and advantages might it have?

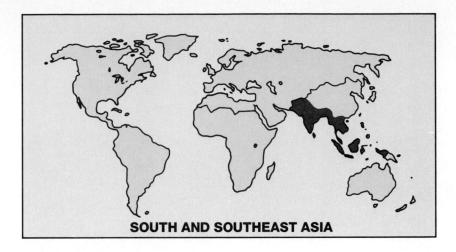

SOUTH AND SOUTHEAST ASIA

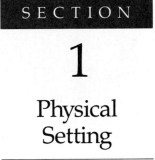

A glance at the map above and the maps on pages 130–131 shows that the nations of South and Southeast Asia are spread across the continental mainland and many offshore islands. The region of South Asia includes the nations of India, Pakistan, Bangladesh, Nepal, and Bhutan on the **peninsula** that is so huge it is called a **subcontinent**. South Asia also includes the island nations of Sri Lanka and the Maldives off the tip of the subcontinent.

The nations of Southeast Asia skirt the Bay of Bengal on the east. They then extend southeastward to include Myanmar (formerly Burma), Thailand, Malaysia on the Malay Peninsula and Singapore off its tip and continue across the Indochina Peninsula, which includes Laos, Cambodia (also known as Kampuchea), and Vietnam. Off the mainland are the island nations of Indonesia, Brunei, and the Philippines.

South Asia

The subcontinent of South Asia, usually known as the Indian subcontinent, extends into the Indian Ocean like a tapering jewel from the necklace of snowcapped mountains that separate the subcontinent from the rest of the Asian continent. The height and ruggedness of the mountain ranges reflect the force of the collision that joined the subcontinent to Asia as many as 50 million years ago.

The Landscape   The subcontinent has three distinct regions: the mountain wall, the Indo-Gangetic Plain, and the Deccan Plateau and coastal rim. The Himalayas, from an ancient word meaning "places of snow," are the highest of the three ranges that form the wall of mountains. The other two are the Karakoram and the Hindu Kush. Included in the Himalayas is Mount Everest, which soars more than 29,000 feet (8 839 meters) above sea level. Openings through the mountain wall, such as the Khyber Pass, provide a gateway to the subcontinent. It is through

(Continued on page 132.)

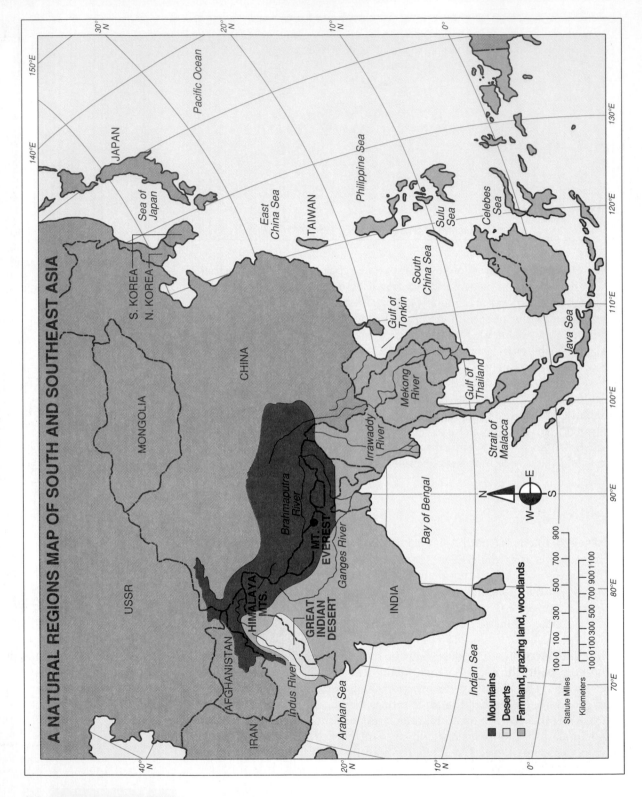

A NATURAL REGIONS MAP OF SOUTH AND SOUTHEAST ASIA

USSR

MONGOLIA

CHINA

JAPAN

S. KOREA
N. KOREA

Sea of
Japan

Pacific Ocean

East
China Sea

TAIWAN

Philippine Sea

South
China Sea

Sulu
Sea

Celebes
Sea

Java Sea

Gulf of
Tonkin

Mekong
River

Gulf of
Thailand

Strait of
Malacca

Irrawaddy
River

Brahmaputra
River

MT.
EVEREST

Ganges River

Bay of Bengal

HIMALAYA
MTS.

GREAT
INDIAN
DESERT

INDIA

Indus River

AFGHANISTAN

IRAN

Arabian Sea

Indian Sea

N
W—E
S

Mountains
Deserts
Farmland, grazing land, woodlands

900
700
500
300
100
100 0

Statute Miles

1001001003005007009001100

Kilometers

30° N
20° N
10° N
0°

150°E
140°E
130°E
120°E
110°E
100°E
90°E
80°E
70°E

40° N
20° N
10° N
0°

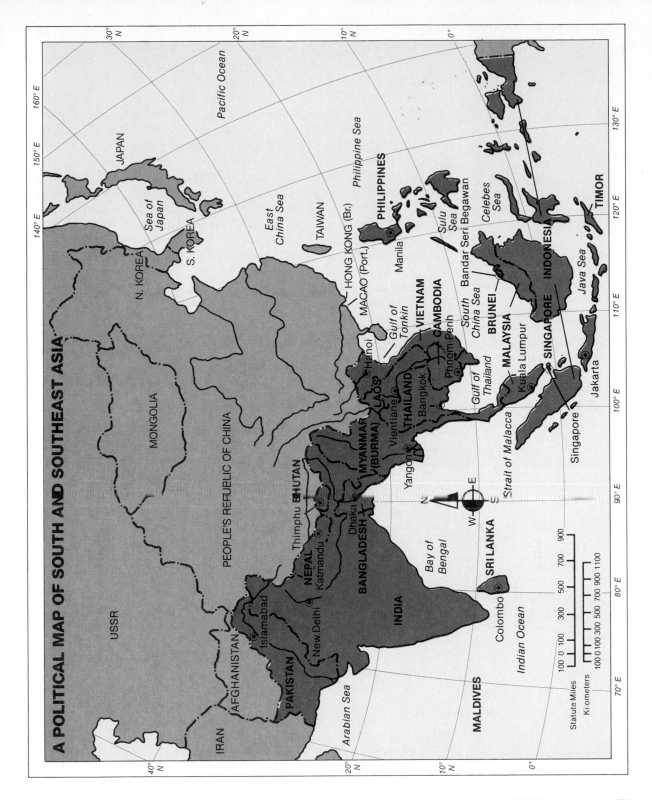

A POLITICAL MAP OF SOUTH AND SOUTHEAST ASIA

USSR

MONGOLIA

PEOPLE'S REPUBLIC OF CHINA

IRAN

AFGHANISTAN

PAKISTAN

Islamabad

New Delhi

INDIA

NEPAL
Katmandu

Thimphu BHUTAN

BANGLADESH
Dhaka

MALDIVES

SRI LANKA

Colombo

Arabian Sea

Bay of Bengal

Indian Ocean

MYANMAR (BURMA)

Yangon

LAOS

Vientiane

THAILAND

Bangkok

Gulf of Thailand

CAMBODIA

Phnom Penh

VIETNAM

Hanoi

Gulf of Tonkin

HONG KONG (Br.)

MACAO (Port.)

TAIWAN

East China Sea

N. KOREA

S. KOREA

Sea of Japan

JAPAN

Pacific Ocean

Philippine Sea

PHILIPPINES

Manila

Sulu Sea

Celebes Sea

BRUNEI

Bandar Seri Begawan

South China Sea

MALAYSIA

Kuala Lumpur

SINGAPORE

Singapore

Strait of Malacca

INDONESIA

Jakarta

Java Sea

TIMOR

30° N
20° N
10° N
0°

160° E
150° E
140° E
130° E
120° E
110° E
100° E
90° E
80° E
70° E

40° N
20° N
10° N
0°

Statute Miles
Kilometers

100 0 100   300   500   700   900 1100
100 0 100 300 500 700 900

N
W   E
S

131

Like many other nations, India is harnessing its rivers to provide electric power. The government rather than private power companies is building these hydroelectric plants. Why do you think this might be happening?

these passes that conquering invaders moved into the subcontinent, gradually contributing to the culture of South Asia and its people.

The Plain   South of the mountain wall lies the Indo–Gangetic (IN-doh-gan-JET-ik) Plain, a vast lowland that stretches in an arc from the Arabian Sea to the Bay of Bengal. Drained by the southwestward-flowing Indus River and the southeastward-flowing Ganges (GAN-jeez) River, the plain is home to many of the subcontinent's people. Like the Nile River in Egypt, the rivers flood seasonally. As the waters recede, they leave a rich deposit of silt that renews the land and makes the plain an important agricultural area for both Pakistan and India. A third great river, the Brahmaputra (BRAHM-uh-POO-trah) flows through Bangladesh. Where it joins with the Ganges and then continues southward on its journey into the Bay of Bengal, the Brahmaputra forms the largest delta in the world. All three river systems provide a potential source of hydroelectric power.

The Deccan Plateau and Coastal Rims   Most of the southern part of the subcontinent consists of a rocky plateau bordered on the east and the west by a narrow, but well-watered, coastal plain. A band of low-lying hills separates the Deccan from the Indo-Gangetic Plain on the north. Throughout history these hills have formed a barrier that prevented invaders and native rulers from extending their control over the southern portion of the subcontinent. As a result, the people in the southern part of the subcontinent developed a culture that differed sharply from that of the north.

The seaward edges of the Deccan are formed by two mountain ranges—the Western Ghats (GAWTS) and the Eastern Ghats. Extending from the Ghats are coastal plains of varying widths. The people of the coastal plain have traditionally been merchants and sailors who traded at first with people from the neighboring islands, and later with seafaring adventurers from other parts of the world—the Chinese, Romans, Arabs, Portuguese, French, and English.

Southeast Asia

Southeast Asia, which includes ten countries, is located partly on the Malay and Indochina peninsulas of the mainland and partly on the chain of islands called the Malay Archipelago. The largest island chain in the world, the archipelago consists of nearly 20,000 islands that are the tips of mountains rising from the seafloor.

The terrain of both mainland and island nations is mountainous and heavily forested. The mainland peninsulas are drained by the Irrawaddy, the Chao Phraya (CHOW PRAY-uh), and the Mekong (MAY-kong) rivers. Major farming areas are found along their banks and deltas.

The mountaintops that form the islands of the Malay Archipelago slope to fertile coastal lowlands containing rich volcanic soil. As part of the Pacific "Ring of Fire," the islands have some of the world's most active volcanoes and have been struck by major earthquakes.

archipelago: chain of islands

Using GEOGRAPHY Skills

Reading a Climatic Map

Monsoons are winds that reverse direction when the seasons change. Monsoons often bring heavy rainfall. Understanding the effects of monsoons is fundamental to understanding the cultures of the regions that monsoons affect. Monsoons largely determine the weather of these areas, and so influence such things as the types of agriculture, dwellings, and clothing.

Maps can be used to learn about monsoons. The two maps on this page depict the monsoons of India. One map shows the wind direction and precipitation levels in summer—the monsoon season—and the other map shows these conditions in winter. Study the maps to answer the questions below.

1. What general direction does the summer monsoon blow? The winter monsoon?

2. What body of water does the summer monsoon cross before it strikes India? After it crosses India?

3. Which parts of India receive the heaviest precipitation during the summer monsoon? Why do you think this is so?

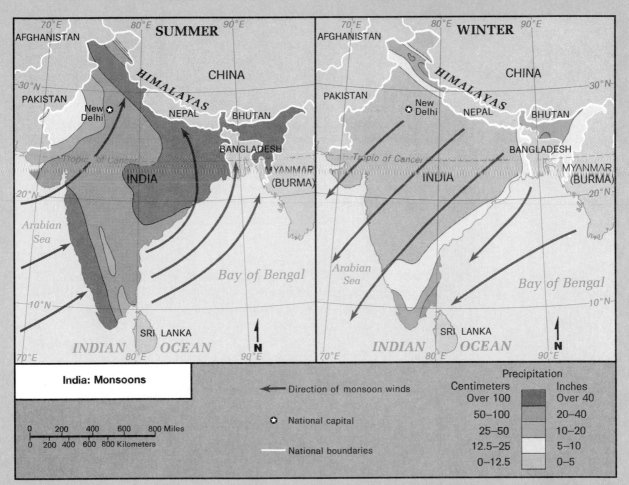

India: Monsoons

Monsoons and the Climate

Most of South and Southeast Asia lie in the low latitudes and have tropical climates. South Asian nations on the subcontinent lie north of the equator and have a subtropical climate that is characterized by wet and dry seasons. Many of the nations in Southeast Asia, especially its island nations, straddle the equator and have hot humid temperatures year round and rainfall patterns of wet and wetter. But the dominant climatic factor in this region is the monsoons.

South Asia   The monsoons give much of South Asia distinct wet and dry seasons. In winter, when the continental landmass is cooler than the ocean, the monsoon blows from the northeast out of Central Asia toward the ocean. This northeast monsoon, forming as it does over the cold land of the Asian continent, is a drought-producing wind for most South Asian nations.

In summer, when the oceans are cooler than the continental landmass, the monsoon blows from the southwest over the Indian Ocean toward South Asia. This southwest monsoon brings life-giving rains in varying amounts to different parts of the parched subcontinent. In general more rain falls on the coastal areas and the windward, or wind-facing, sides of mountains than in the Deccan. But the area surrounding the mouth of the Indus River is little affected by the southwest monsoon and remains a desert year round.

The time of year a particular monsoon arrives is crucial for farmers in South Asia. The early or late arrival of the wet monsoon can jeopardize the planting of crops, while the early arrival of the dry monsoon can shrivel crops before the harvest. Flooding is often severe during the wet monsoon season, especially in Bangladesh. City-dwellers often wade ankle-deep through flooded streets, and everyday life is completely dominated by the monsoon rains.

Southeast Asia   For much of Southeast Asia, the monsoons bring rain throughout the year because both winter and summer monsoons cross over stretches of ocean and pick up moisture that is dropped on the coastal plains and the windward mountain sides. Only the leeward sides of mountains—the sides facing away from the wind—experience a lessening of rainfall as the monsoon seasons change.

Because much of Southeast Asia lies across the equator, temperatures there are hot year round and the air is always humid. Only those areas away from the equator on the Malay and Indochina peninsulas of the mainland experience the variations in rainfall and humidity that the monsoons bring.

1. **Recall** What are the three distinct regions of the Indian subcontinent?
2. **How and Why** Why did the people in the southern part of the subcontinent of South Asia develop a culture that differed from that of the north?
3. **Critical Thinking** Why are the monsoons important to the region?

I n South and Southeast Asia the greatest contrast in living conditions is found between **rural** and **urban** areas. Both regions have large modern cities and ancient villages where time seems to have stood still for centuries.

Village Life

South and Southeast Asia probably have more than one million villages. In South Asia a village is frequently laid out in rows alongside a river or at the intersection of two roads. For centuries the people have lived in houses made of mud or mud bricks with thatched roofs tied down with bamboo strips. Rooms are small and few. Paper covers tiny windows. In many parts of Southeast Asia, houses shaded with fruit and palm trees sit on stilts above the ground, allowing the air to circulate. The houses also have roofed porches that give shade. In general, rural homes lack indoor plumbing and electricity.

Around most villages lie the fields that the villagers farm. About 80 percent of the labor force in the region is engaged in farming. The main crops are rice and wheat. Other food crops include barley, millet, sorghum, corn, soybeans, many kinds of vegetables, tea, peanuts, and sweet potatoes. Cotton and peanuts are often grown as cash crops because villagers today can no longer rely completely on barter and must buy some items.

The desire for **consumer goods** such as transistor radios and other small appliances, and the increase in a **cash economy** are changing village life in South and Southeast Asia. News about the world outside the village, through advances in radio, television, movies, and other **telecommunications**, has also raised villagers' expectations of what life can bring. The effort to improve the **standard of living** is one reason why many villagers have moved from the country to the city. The swelling of city populations by rural immigrants has also brought unrest to the nations of South and Southeast Asia.

SECTION

2

The Cultural Setting

thatched:
covered with straw or palm leaves

City Life

As long ago as 2700 B.C., people were living in cities on the South Asian subcontinent. Now as in the past these cities are centers of commerce and culture. Today more than 100 cities in South and Southeast Asia have populations greater than 500,000. Calcutta, Bombay, and New Delhi in India, and Karachi in Pakistan are among the largest cities in the world. In Southeast Asia the largest city in every country is its capital as well as its major port and industrial center.

Most of these large cities were first developed by colonial powers from Western Europe and have a Western appearance. They contain major international airports, universities, libraries, museums, parks, and other cultural centers. The streets are lined with high-rise office buildings and modern apartment complexes. Many of the inhabitants wear Western-style clothes, and, like their counterparts in Western cities, face traffic jams and air pollution.

In some parts of these large cities and elsewhere in the region, people still live in traditional houses built of brick or wood, and follow traditional ways of bargaining for food and clothing in open-air markets. Because of the rapid growth in population and the migration of rural people to urban areas, vast slums with no electricity and few sanitary facilities have risen in metropolitan areas. One of the most difficult tasks of nations in South and Southeast Asia is to improve the quality of life of their citizens.

Dams provide much of India's hydroelectric power. Because of the lack of heavy machinery in some areas, however, human power must be used to build dams.

NATIONAL PROFILES/SOUTH AND SOUTHEAST ASIA						
Nation/Capital	Population/ Area (in sq mi)	Urban Population (as % of total)	Per Capita GNP (in U.S. $)	Adult Literacy Rate (%)	Life Expectancy	Population Growth Rate* (%)
Bangladesh/Dhaka	114,700,000/55,598	14	170	33	51	2.8
Bhutan/Thimphu	1,500,000/18,000	5	150	15	48	2.1
Brunei/Bandar Seri Begawan	300,000/2,226	64	14,120	45	74	3.4
Cambodia/Phnom Penh	6,800,000/69,884	11	100	48	47	3.0
India/New Delhi	835,000,000/ 1,229,737	26	330	43	58	2.1
Indonesia/Jakarta	184,600,000/735,268	25	430	74	61	2.1
Laos/Vientiane	3,900,000/91,429	15	180	84	49	2.4
Malaysia/Kuala Lumpur	17,400,000/128,328	38	1,870	73	70	2.6
Maldives/Male	209,000/115	26	410	**	69	3.4
Myanmar/Yangon	40,800,000/261,220	24	210	78	60	2.2
Nepal/Katmandu	18,700,000/54,463	8	170	26	51	2.7
Pakistan/Islamabad	110,400,000/310,000	30	350	30	55	3.1
Philippines/Manila	64,900,000/115,830	41	630	86	64	2.4
Singapore/Singapore	2,700,000/220	100	9,100	86	73	1.1
Sri Lanka/Colombo	16,900,000/25,332	22	420	87	71	1.5
Thailand/Bangkok	55,600/000/198,445	20	1,000	91	65	1.9
Vietnam/Hanoi	66,800,000/127,246	19	200	78	66	2.6

Sources: *The 1990 Information Please Almanac* (Houghton Mifflin Company); *Universal Almanac, 1990* (Andrews-MacNeil)
*A nation with a population growth rate of 2% or more doubles its population within 35 years or less.
**Not available.

The Quality of Life

In measuring the quality of life of a nation—sometimes called the standard of living—economists look at many factors: life expectancy; per capita income; use of energy; the availability and cost of health care; the population growth rate; the literacy rate; the numbers of automobiles, telephones, radios, and televisions in use; newspaper circulation; and the **gross national product**.

By looking at these factors, economists have classified the nations of the world into two categories. Nations, such as the United States, Japan, Great Britain, and other Western European nations, are said to be fully industrialized, or **developed nations**. The rest of the world's nations, about 130, which are considered less developed, still depend mainly on agriculture, rather than on industry, for much of their gross national product. Many have high population growth rates and annual per capita incomes under $3,000.

The chart on this page provides a listing of the nations of South and Southeast Asia, all of which are characterized as **developing nations**.

In Simla, India, an oxcart, a traditional means of travel, is used alongside more modern means of travel. The contrast between old and new can be seen throughout India.

The list, however, shows that some developing nations are wealthier than others. Efforts to improve the quality of life depend on many factors, some of which are political, some economic, and some cultural. Lack of capital is an economic reason that frequently hampers government efforts. Without the money to spend on developing human and **natural resources**, a country cannot provide goods and services for its people. But other factors also limit economic growth. Among these are overpopulation, resistance to change, an unfavorable location or climate, political instability in government, and overreliance on military spending.

India, Pakistan, and Bangladesh, for example, suffer from overpopulation, lack of land suited to farming, and an unreliable water supply. Cambodia (Kampuchea) has been ravaged by political instability and a civil war, problems that have affected other nations in Southeast Asia. Still, progress is being made toward improving the quality of life for South and Southeast Asians, especially in those nations that have relatively stable governments.

SECTION 2 REVIEW

1. **Recall** What percent of the labor force in South and Southeast Asia is engaged in farming?
2. **How and Why** Why have vast slums risen in metropolitan areas of South and Southeast Asia?
3. **Critical Thinking** If you suddenly found yourself in a large city, what signs would you look for to decide if you were in a developing nation?

Chapter 6

R E V I E W

Reviewing People, Places, and Things

Identify, define, or explain each of the following:

subcontinent

Himalayas

Hindu Kush

Mount Everest

Indo-Gangetic Plain

Indus River

Deccan Plateau

Malay Archipelago

monsoons

rural areas

urban areas

cash crops

consumer goods

Calcutta

Karachi

standard of living

developed nations

developing nations

Map Study

Using the maps on pages 130 and 131, answer the following questions.

1. What are the natural regions into which South and Southeast Asia are divided?

2. Between what two nations is the Strait of Malacca located?

3. What direction is the Philippines from Vietnam?

Understanding Ideas

1. a. In what ways do the people of South and Southeast Asia depend on their rivers? b. What problems have rivers created for them?

2. Why do most large cities in the region have a Western look about them?

3. How has modernization affected village life in South and Southeast Asia?

4. How do developed nations differ from developing nations?

5. How do economists measure the quality of life of a nation?

Developing Critical Thinking

Negotiating Negotiation is the settlement of a disagreement by discussion and compromise. The negotiator's main job is to design a settlement acceptable to all parties. A skillful negotiator: 1. asks both parties to state their demands and reasons why they should be met; 2. helps all parties see the viewpoint of the other participants in order to make their demands realistic and reasonable; 3. plans a fair settlement that allows each party to compromise without weakening its position; and 4. redesigns the compromise as many times as needed to arrive at a solution that benefits each party.

A party to the disagreement also has certain responsibilities. A party: 1. does not ask for something that seriously weakens the other party's position; 2. compromises without seriously weakening its own position; 3. never allows emotions to interfere with the negotiating process.

Activity: Nation A pollutes the coastal waters of Nation B by dumping industrial wastes into the sea. Negotiate a solution by organizing volunteers to act as the negotiator, and other classmates to represent nations A and B.

Writing About History

Analyzing Geography Write a paragraph that gives a reasonable explanation about why almost all known civilizations of the world originally developed around rivers.

Applying Your Skills to History

Comparing and Contrasting Rivers, mountains, and monsoons are all important in South and Southeast Asia. Make a table showing how each has contributed to the development of the region and how each has been a disadvantage to the region.

Historic South Asia

The central location of the Indian subcontinent exposed it to many outside contacts both by land and by sea. Because of its location, the subcontinent played a major role in the cultural diffusion of ideas and goods between lands to the east and the west. The region's cultural foundations were laid early on by the merging of Harappan and Aryan civilizations and by the rise of two great religions—Hinduism and Buddhism.

Invaders followed invaders, each group imposing its rule on the people by establishing **monarchies** and **empires** under which distinctive styles of art, architecture, and literature flourished. Under the influence of Hinduism, a unique **class structure** also evolved that has lasted to the present day.

As you study this chapter, think about these questions:

- How did the Aryans contribute to the cultural foundations of the Indian subcontinent?

- How has dynastic rule contributed to the cultural flowering of the arts on the Indian subcontinent?

- How has the caste system influenced life on the Indian subcontinent?

The colorful saris and the intricate jewelry of these modern Indian women represent an old tradition.

The practice of agriculture, which began on the Indian subcontinent about 4000 B.C., gradually led to the development of villages and towns and the beginnings of civilization in South Asia. About 2500 B.C. the first known invaders made their way into the subcontinent through the Khyber Pass and other openings in the mountain wall. The bronze weapons of the invaders gave them a great advantage in conquering the local inhabitants who used only stone weapons. After conquest, the invaders settled in cities where they intermarried and adopted the language of the local inhabitants. By 2400 B.C. the subcontinent's first known civilization—the Harappan—was flourishing in the Indus River valley.

Cultural Foundations

The Harappans

South Asia's first known civilization, which was not discovered until the 1920s, centered around two cities—Harappa and Mohenjo-Daro (moh-HEN-joh-DAHR-oh). In these well-planned cities, north-south streets intersected with east-west streets in a grid fashion. One- and two-story houses, built with fire-hardened bricks of uniform size, lined the streets of the residential areas. Often the Harappan houses were built around an interior courtyard—a style still followed by the more well-to-do people of the valley. Many homes had private and public baths and toilets, conveniences that many other cultures did not have until recent times. The Harappans connected these conveniences to a network of sewers lined with baked brick and with shafts for inspection regularly placed.

In the center of each city stood a walled fortress containing a meeting hall and granaries where they stored grain for use in times of famine. The fortress also contained a large pool that scholars believe was used in a religious ceremony similar to the present-day Hindu practice of washing sins away in the sacred waters of the Ganges River.

The Harappans were mainly farmers and traders. The farmers raised chickens and grew wheat, which was used for barter as well as for food. The Harappans were the first known people to grow cotton, and cotton textiles were one of their main exports to Egypt and Sumer. Other exports included such luxuries as tea and jewelry. Imports were mostly copper and other metals. Harappan merchants used rulers made of shell to measure their cloth and metal weights to weigh their goods. The Harappan traders built docks far out into the sea, thus making it possible to load and unload cargoes during both high and low tides.

About 1700 B.C., the Harappan civilization entered a period of decline. Unearthed skeletons and remains of buildings suggest that war may have been one cause for the decline. A series of earthquakes may also have changed the course of the Indus River. Severe flooding caused by **erosion** may also have contributed to the decline because the nearby forests had been cut down to supply wood for the ovens used to make the Harappan bricks. About this time, however, a new group of invaders

■ Indus Valley Civilization, c. 2500–1500 B.C.

called the Aryans entered the subcontinent through the Khyber Pass. Some Harappans intermarried with the invaders, but others retreated to the southern part of the subcontinent.

The Aryans

About 2000 B.C., the Aryan invaders began migrating from the grasslands of their Central Asian homeland in search of fresh pastures for their cattle. The invaders reached the Indus River valley sometime between 1700 B.C. and 1500 B.C.

The Aryans made many contributions to the developing civilization of South Asia. One important contribution was their language, which was called Sanskrit and which belonged to the Indo-European family of languages. People in the northern part of the subcontinent adopted the Aryan language, and in time it formed the basis for the more than 300 languages that are spoken in present-day northern India. In the southern part of present-day India the people speak languages that belong to the Dravidian family of languages spoken by the Harappans. Other important contributions attributed to the Aryan way of life are the religious beliefs and customs that make up the foundations of Hinduism, many of which are traced through the literature of the Aryans.

The Vedic Age (1500–900 B.C.)
The term *Vedic* (VAYD-ik) *Age* comes from a group of sacred writings called *Vedas*, a collection of mostly hymns to the Aryan deities. Hindus today recite these hymns when celebrating births, marriages, and funerals. The *Vedas* were written originally in Sanskrit, which is now used only for religious and literary purposes.

As sources of information about the Aryans, the *Vedas* reveal that the Aryans fought from horse-drawn chariots; that they enjoyed music, dancing, and gambling with dice; that they measured their wealth by the number of cattle they owned; and that they were divided into three major social classes—priests, warriors, and commoners.

The Epic Age (900–500 B.C.)
In the Epic Age, the Aryans spread eastward across the Indo-Gangetic Plain. They cleared the dense forest growth along the Ganges with iron axes, cultivated the land with iron plows, and grew rice where water was plentiful. The Aryans began to use copper coins instead of cattle for money and established cities where trade flourished and a successful class of merchants arose.

This period is called the Epic Age because two religious epics, or heroic poems, began to take shape at this time. One epic is the *Mahabharata* (muh-hah-BAH-ruh-tuh). The other epic is the *Ramayana* (rah-MAH-yuh-nuh). The *Mahabharata*, the world's longest poem, describes a war between two Aryan families who fight over control of a kingdom. The war is a fierce one and many people are killed. Within the poem is the *Bhagavad-Gita* (buh-guh-vud GEE-tuh), a dialogue between the warrior Arjuna and the deity Krishna. The *Bhagavad-Gita's* basic thought—that duty should be done without emotion or desire—became

The Ganges River is sacred to Hindus. Each year thousands come to bathe in its waters. Some come to purify their souls. Others believe that the holy river will cure them of illness.

fundamental to Hinduism, a major religion of the subcontinent that traces its roots to the Aryans. Scenes from the *Mahabharata* are still repeated by storytellers, illustrated by artists, and dramatized on stage and screen.

The second epic, the *Ramayana*, is about Prince Rama and his devoted wife, who were exiled because of the jealousy of a stepmother. The *Ramayana* tells of their adventures, including the kidnapping of Rama's wife, Sita, by a demon king and her rescue by Prince Rama with the help of the monkey king, Hanuman. The story ends with the return of Sita and Rama to their homeland. Not only is the *Ramayana* an entertaining story with a happy ending, but its main characters have also become examples of what good Hindu men and women should be. Rama is brave, devoted to his wife, and always ready to fight against evil. Sita is always kind and loyal to her husband regardless of the circumstances.

Hinduism

By the end of the Epic Age, Hinduism was well established as a major religion of the subcontinent. Unlike many other religions, Hinduism has no fixed creed. It is more a way of looking at life than a set of established beliefs and rituals.

A Universal Spirit Hinduism teaches that reality is one. The many statues and pictures of deities displayed in temples, the countryside, and homes are merely symbols of a universal spirit. Hindus call this universal spirit Brahman. Every living thing in the universe is part of Brahman. Nothing stands apart from anything else. That is why most Hindus are vegetarians. They do not believe in eating a living thing to which they are related.

Many Deities in One   Hindus believe in as many as 330 million deities, each of which represents a different aspect of Brahman. The three most popular deities are Brahma, Vishnu, and Siva. Brahma creates the universe, Vishnu preserves it, and Siva destroys it so that it can be recreated. Other popular deities include Krishna, who appears in the *Bhagavad-Gita*, and Ganesha, the elephant-headed god of business. When Hindus pray to one or another of these deities, they are really praying to Brahman.

Rebirth   Hindus believe that every living thing contains a soul that is part of Brahman, and that when the body dies, the soul is reborn in a process called reincarnation, or rebirth. In reincarnation, the soul may assume a shape or form that is different from its previous existence. The form taken when a soul is reborn is determined by the law of karma. According to karma, the acts a person performs while alive determine the shape and form of the soul's rebirth. Good acts raise a person to a higher level in the next rebirth. Bad acts lower a person's status in the next reincarnation.

The purpose of reincarnation is spiritual progress. The final goal is reached when a person is freed from the cycle of rebirth and is united with Brahman for eternity. As a result of their belief in reincarnation, Hindus are cremated on a pyre, or pile of wood. If possible, the pyre is built near a river, preferably the holy Ganges.

Festivals   Two of Hinduism's major holidays are based on the *Ramayana*. Divali (duh-VAH-lee), also known as the Festival of Lights, celebrates the return of Rama and Sita to their home. City-dwellers string electric lights on rooftops and along roads.

People in rural areas light the wicks of oil-filled clay saucers. The lights are supposed to guide Rama and Sita. They are also supposed to remind Lakshmi, the goddess of prosperity, to bring good fortune to everyone in the coming year. Dussehra (DOO-suh-ruh), which lasts for nine days, recalls Rama's killing of the demon king. To celebrate Dussehra, the people act out scenes from the epic and explode wood and paper figures of the demon king that have been stuffed with firecrackers.

Buddhism

About 500 B.C. a second major religion arose in India. Its founder was Siddhartha Gautama (sid-DAHR-tuh GOW-tuh-muh), who is generally known as Buddha (BOOD-uh), the Enlightened One. Gautama was the son of a wealthy and powerful monarch who ruled a territory in the foothills of the Himalayas. At the age of 29, shocked by his first view of human suffering, Gautama decided to leave his wife, child, and his home to find the cause of human suffering and its solution. His search took six years. Then one day in a flash of enlightenment, or understanding, he received his answer. Buddha then gave up his life of meditation and began preaching his message to the people of India.

Diwali, *or Festival of Lights, celebrates the happy ending of the epic,* Ramayana. *The epic is no longer regarded merely as a story. The main characters have become examples of what good women and men should be.*

Buddha's Teachings   Seeing the young become old and die, the freshness of a flower at dawn disappear under the hot sun, and a cloudless sky fill with the rage of a storm, Buddha concluded that nothing is permanent except decay and change. With an understanding of the importance of change, Buddha preached the Four Noble Truths.

The First Noble Truth is that everyone suffers. Even pleasure is a cause of suffering because pleasure is not lasting, and this knowledge in itself is a sorrow. The Second Noble Truth is that desire is the cause of suffering. A person who fails to suppress all desires will continue to be reborn. According to the Third Noble Truth, the only way to end suffering is to suppress all desires and achieve nirvana, a condition or state in which a person is completely at peace. Once a person has achieved nirvana, the cycle of rebirth ends.

In the Fourth Noble Truth Buddha offered a series of ethical guidelines for achieving nirvana. Buddha called these guidelines the Noble Eightfold Path. They consist of: 1. right knowledge of the cause and end of suffering, 2. right intentions in actions and feelings toward others, 3. right speech about others, 4. right conduct in relations with others, 5. right living without hurting other living things, 6. right effort to train oneself, 7. right mindfulness about feelings, and 8. right meditation to improve an understanding of life.

meditation: deep concentration for religious or psychological awareness

Buddhism's Spread   Buddhism flourished on the subcontinent for about 800 years before it began to decline and almost disappear. One reason behind its decline on the subcontinent was the adoption of nonviolence and other Buddhist teachings by Hinduism. Another reason had to do with the importance people on the subcontinent attached to

Statues of Buddha are highly stylized. The knot on his forehead symbolizes wisdom. The foot pointing toward heaven shows that Buddha is meditating.

symbolize:
stand for another object or idea

rituals for birth, marriage, and death. They preferred Hinduism, which supplied these rituals, to Buddhism, which lacked them.

Outside the subcontinent, however, Buddhism spread to Southeast and East Asia where it became a thriving religion. It also split into two branches—Theravada Buddhism and Mahayana Buddhism. The Theravada branch, which follows the original teachings of Buddha, is popular today in Sri Lanka and throughout Southeast Asia. The Mahayana branch added new ideas to Buddhism by calling Buddha a god and by teaching that people could get help in attaining enlightenment from a bodhisattva (bo-dee-SAHT-wuh), a person who has achieved nirvana but who delays entering it in order to help others learn how to achieve it. Mahayana Buddhism is popular in China, North and South Korea, Mongolia, and Japan.

Buddhism and Art   Although Buddhism more or less died out as a religion on the subcontinent, it had a lasting influence on art. The Buddhist stupa, a domed structure of brick or stone that houses a sacred relic, is one of the oldest types of monuments found in present-day India. The stupa symbolizes Gautama's death and his attainment of nirvana. Buddhists gain merit by walking around a stupa while offering flowers, reciting prayers, or merely folding their hands.

Statues of Buddha are also found. These statues symbolize Buddha's characteristics and are not accurate portraits. For example, a bulge on top of the head symbolizes Buddha's wisdom; the long earlobes, once adorned with heavy jeweled earrings, are reminders that wealth is of little value; and a dot on the forehead represent Buddha's great spiritual powers.

SECTION 1 REVIEW

1. **Recall**   What evidence exists that the Harappans had achieved a high degree of civilization?

2. **How and Why**   How did the Aryans contribute to the developing civilization of South Asia?

3. **Critical Thinking**   Why did Buddhism decline on the subcontinent but thrive in areas outside the subcontinent?

When the first Aryan groups moved into the subcontinent, each group set up its own **state**, which was ruled by an elected chief called a raja. Two **councils**, one of warriors and the other of family elders, advised each raja. Most government matters, such as maintaining irrigation systems and settling disputes over land ownership or usage, however, were handled by village leaders called headmen. At times, the raja of a particular state became strong enough to conquer other states. In the process of forming an empire, the raja became a maharajah, or great ruler, and passed on his title to his heirs, thus establishing a **dynasty**.

The Maurya Dynasty

The first Aryan ruler to establish a dynasty was Chandragupta Maurya (chun-druh-GUP-tuh MAH-ur-yuh), who founded the Maurya dynasty in 323 B.C. The map on this page shows that Chandragupta's empire stretched from the Bay of Bengal westward to the towering Hindu Kush range.

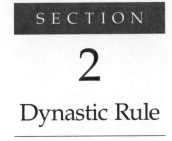

■ **Maurya Empire Under Asoka, c. 250 B.C.**

Chandragupta's Rule   Chandragupta established a highly centralized and structured form of government. In this government, the empire was divided into **provinces**, and the provinces were subdivided into districts. Chandragupta placed provincial governors over district governors, and made district governors responsible for the actions of the village headmen. He also established specialized departments to handle agriculture, forestry, foreign trade, public works, and trade—which was conducted with empires to the west and the east.

At its height, the Maurya dynasty was supported by a large army of 650,000 men divided into groups of cavalry, charioteers, foot soldiers, and elephanteers. The elephants, who were used to overwhelm opposing foot soldiers, were protected by leather armor and wore metal spikes on their tusks. In spite of their strength and frightening appearance, however, the elephants panicked at the sight of fire and were not always effective.

Asoka's Rule   One of the Maurya dynasty's most remarkable rulers was Chandragupta's grandson, Asoka (uh-SOH-kuh), who ruled from 273 to 232 B.C. Asoka's rule is remarkable because it consisted of two contrasting periods. In the first period, Asoka expanded the empire to its greatest extent. In the second period, realizing that his conquests had caused the death of millions of his subjects, Asoka turned from violence and war and became a Buddhist and a lover of peace. In his newly found fervor, Asoka forgave his former enemies, gave up hunting, and devoted the rest of his life to improving the lives of his people. As a result, Asoka improved medical services and irrigation systems and eased the life of travelers by having rest houses built throughout the subcontinent. At the same time, Asoka helped spread Buddhism by sending Buddhist missionaries to other lands. Among the missionaries was Asoka's own brother, who was sent to Sri Lanka where he converted the ruler.

Throughout the subcontinent, Asoka proclaimed his laws by having them carved on stones and pillars. Some of these pillars still stand, rising

The Buddhist ruler Asoka publicized his laws by carving them on stone pillars for all to see.

as much as 50 feet above the ground. The sculpture at the top of one of these pillars, which shows four stone lions back to back, is now the national emblem of present-day India.

The Maurya dynasty ended with the assassination of the last ruler in 185 B.C., which was followed by the breaking up of the empire into many small monarchies. Over the next 500 years, many groups from Central Asia invaded the subcontinent. Then in A.D. 320, another dynasty emerged that ruled for nearly 200 years. Buddhism, however, continued to advance abroad.

The Gupta Dynasty

The period of the Gupta dynasty, which extends from A.D. 320 to about 500, is known as the Golden Age of Indian culture. Religious tolerance was practiced, government was mild as rulers took a real interest in the people's welfare, taxes were low, and travelers moved about freely. Art, literature, and science flourished as did foreign trade.

Architecture and Art   Although tolerant of Buddhism, the Gupta rulers were Hindus and the art and architecture they sponsored reflected their religious beliefs. In the north, Hindu temples were cut from solid rock. In the south, cities were filled with tall temples that were completely covered with the humanlike figures of various Hindu deities.

Following detailed and strict rules, sculptors working in stone, bronze, and clay interpreted the humanlike forms of Brahma, Siva, Vishnu, and other Hindu deities. Some sculptors showed Brahma with four heads and four arms holding the *Vedas*. Siva was often sculpted in the pose of a dancer to show his powers of creation and destruction. Vishnu, who was sometimes portrayed riding a bird that was part human and part eagle, often was shown with four arms holding a shell, a staff of authority, a lotus flower, and a circular disk that represented the sun.

Literature   Writers during the Gupta dynasty developed the technique of teaching moral lessons through **fables**. In these fables, animals talk and behave like human beings. One such collection of fables is the *Panchatantra* (PAHN-chuh-tahn-truh). One of the fables, an account of a young girl named Sumandevi who becomes an Indian princess, was the inspiration for the story many children in the West know as Cinderella.

Gupta playwrights often wrote their plays in poetic form, using classic Sanskrit. The greatest of the poetic dramatists was Kalidasa, who wrote his masterpiece *Sakuntala* (say-kuhn-TAHL-uh) in the A.D. 400s. As the heroine of the story, Sakuntala represents an ideal vision of women. Besides being beautiful and strong of character, she is tender, merciful, generous, faithful, and as shy as the animals of the forest in which she lives. Like much of Indian literature, the play is based on a story from the *Mahabharata*. In addition, like all plays of the period, *Sakuntala* left the audience with a sense of peace and serenity.

Poets of the Gupta period, who also wrote in classic Sanskrit, loved playing games with words. For example, one poem was written without using any "s" sounds. Another poem was written so it had one meaning when it was read from left to right and a completely different meaning when it was read from right to left. Poetic competitions were often held at court with the Gupta monarch suggesting the theme just before the beginning of the contest.

Advances in Science   Indian scientists made remarkable advances in mathematics and astronomy during the Gupta period. Astronomers taught that the earth revolved around the sun and rotated on its axis centuries before Copernicus advanced the same idea in Europe. Astronomers also correctly calculated the moon's diameter, knew that the passage of either the Earth or the moon in front of the sun was the cause of an eclipse, and could predict the occurrence of an eclipse with great accuracy.

Mathematicians during the Gupta Age used the zero as a place holder and originated the decimal system. They developed algebra, worked with negative quantities, quadratic equations, and square root. They also created the system of numbering in use today, even though it is mistakenly called Arabic because Western Europeans learned of it through Arab traders.

Physicians during the Gupta Age studied anatomy and knew that certain physical characteristics are hereditary. They were familiar with the medicinal properties of many plants and herbs and used them in the treatment of leprosy and other diseases. Doctors during the Gupta Age

■ **Gupta Dynasty,** c. A.D. 400

Siva, the god of destruction, is one of the most important Hindu gods. This statue is more than 700 years old. It shows the god crushing a symbol of ignorance.

inoculated people to protect them against smallpox, a technique they probably learned from the Chinese. Surgeons sterilized wounds, performed gall bladder operations, and used plastic surgery to rebuild noses and ears and to remove scars.

Trade   During the Gupta Empire, trade was carried on with merchants in Southeast Asia and in the Roman Empire to the west. Much of the trade was handled by seafaring people called Tamils who lived along the southern coast of the subcontinent. Today the Tamils constitute about 25 percent of the population of Sri Lanka.

A major export was textiles. Manufacturing techniques developed on the subcontinent enabled Indians to produce such fabrics as calico, cashmere, chintz, and muslin. Other exports included brassware, monkeys, and parrots. All of these were traded in exchange for silk from China, Arabian horses and gold from the west, and spices from the Southeast Asia. Trade with Southeast Asia also led to the diffusion and adoption of Indian customs. People in Indonesia, Thailand, and Vietnam wore clothing styles, read literature, and enjoyed works of art imported from India.

A Shadowy Period   After the fall of the Gupta dynasty about the year 500, a period of chaos followed until another great king, Harsha (606–617), brought peace, unity, and security to the subcontinent. After Harsha's death, little is known about the history of India for more than 500 years. During the period, Hinduism survived in modified form while Buddhism almost completely disappeared from the subcontinent. Most of what is known about this period comes from stories about notable people whose **legends** survive in **folklore**.

The Coming of the Muslims

In the 1000s a people invaded the subcontinent who infused it with an enduring cultural and political character that is still visible. These new invaders, who entered from Afghanistan through the Khyber Pass, were mostly Turkish in origin. But they practiced the religion of Islam and were known as Muslims.

Culture Clash   Not since the coming of the Aryans had the invasion of a new people had such an impact on South Asia. Previous migrations and invasions of people from Central Asia had resulted in little change or challenge to the local inhabitants because of **assimilation**. But the influx of the Muslims was different.

Founded by Muhammad in the A.D. 700s, Islam had quickly spread throughout North Africa, the Arabian Peninsula, and Southwest Asia, lands collectively known as the Middle East. When the Muslims invaded the South Asian subcontinent, they showed little tolerance for people who did not practice **monotheism**. To the Muslims, the **polytheism** of Hinduism with its many deities, its elaborate rituals, and its fondness for imagery was contrary to all that they held sacred.

Social differences also existed. For example, while Hindus believed that some people have a higher status than others, Muslims believed that everyone is equal before God. While Hindus believed that a man should have only one wife, Muslims, believed that a man could have as many as four wives. While Hindu women moved about freely in public, Muslim women seldom left their households. While Hindus refrained from eating beef, Muslims refused to eat pork.

At first the Muslim conquerors destroyed Hindu temples and killed thousands of Hindus in an effort to impose Muslim customs on the people of the subcontinent. Gradually, however, the Muslim rulers found a way for the two groups to live side by side in relative peace by imposing a special tax on Hindus. As long as the Hindus paid the tax, the Muslims did not disturb the Hindu way of life.

Sikhism   The introduction of Islam also led to the creation of a new religion called Sikhism (SEEK-iz-uhm). Developed about 1500, Sikhism combined certain Hindu and Muslim ideas. Like the Hindus, the Sikhs practiced meditation and believed in reincarnation and karma. Like the Muslims, the Sikhs believed that fighting for their faith was a holy act. All Sikhs took the last name of Singh (SING), meaning "lion." Sikh men wore beards and hid their uncut hair under a turban.

Present-Day Impact   Eventually Islam became the religion of about 20 percent of the people in South Asia, mostly those who lived in the Indus River valley and the delta of the Ganges-Brahmaputra rivers. In the Indus River valley, most Muslims were descendants of the invading Muslims from Turkey. In the delta area, most Muslims were converts from Hinduism who wanted to improve their social status.

In 1947 when independence came to the subcontinent, two nations were established — the Muslim nation of Pakistan, which consisted of the Indus River valley and the delta of the Ganges-Brahmaputra rivers, and the Hindu nation of India on the remainder of the subcontinent. In 1971 the delta region seceded from Pakistan and became the independent nation of Bangladesh. But animosities between Hindus, Muslims, and Sikhs simmer under the surface and occasionally erupt into riots and other forms of violence in the region. For example, since independence India and Pakistan have clashed over the Indian states of Jammu and Kashmir. Muslims in the state are in the majority, but they are ruled by the Hindu minority. Twice India and Pakistan have gone to war over the right of the people to vote on whether they prefer to belong to India or Pakistan. During most of the 1980s the state was quiet, but disruptions in the area increased in the early 1990s, and pleas for holding a vote were renewed.

The Delhi Sultanate

After the Muslim invaders entered the subcontinent, they expanded their control during the 1100s. By 1206 a Muslim kingdom known as the Delhi Sultanate had taken control of most of the Hindu monarchies in the north. The southern part of the subcontinent was controlled by Hindu rulers. The subcontinent then experienced several waves of invasion by Mongols from Central Asia under the leadership of Genghis Khan (JIN-guhs KAHN) and later Tamerlane. It was the invasions under Tamerlane that weakened the Delhi Sultanate and brought about its destruction in 1398.

The Mogul Empire

In 1526 Turkish Muslims again entered the subcontinent. They were led by Babur the Tiger, a descendant of Tamerlane, who founded a new dynastic empire. It is known in Mongol as the Mogul Empire, after the Hindi pronunciation for Mongol.

Akbar the Great   The most outstanding Mogul ruler was Babur's grandson, Akbar the Great, who was only 13 when his father died in 1556. With the help of able and loyal followers, and later under his own

Akbar's son, Jahangir, ruled the Mogul Empire from 1603 to 1627. During this time, the art of Muslim painting reached its peak in India. This painting shows Jahangir on his throne receiving gifts from both Western Europeans and Indians.

leadership, Akbar brought the greater part of India under his rule. In doing so he displayed his talents as a magnificent organizer, astute diplomat, and a military leader who also cared about the welfare of his people.

Akbar set up land taxes that were fair and just, established a civil service under which government jobs went to qualified persons, and unified his people by encouraging religious toleration through his own example. Under his rule, the Muslim tax on nonbelievers was removed and Hindu temples were protected. Of his four wives, one was a Muslim, one a Christian, and two were Hindus.

A Flowering of the Arts Before Akbar, Persian had been the only language used at the Mogul court. Under Akbar, however, Persian was increasingly used by the common people. Eventually a mixture of Persian and Hindi languages resulted that became known as the Urdu language. Urdu is still spoken by many people in modern India and is the official language of present-day Pakistan. Other cultural elements also merged to produce a flowering of arts in the Mogul period.

Painting flourished as artists made realistic and detailed landscapes and portraits in miniature. Mogul printers often decorated the borders and bindings of their books with gold. People with beautiful handwriting became artists in their own right, and it was probably the Moguls who introduced the people of the subcontinent to paper. In building their places of worship—which were called mosques—their palaces, and the tombs of their rulers, the Moguls used arches and slender, graceful bulb-shaped towers to adorn their buildings. These buildings of marble and red sandstone were often surrounded by gardens with reflecting lakes and lagoons.

During the 1600s and 1700s, however, Mogul control of the empire was gradually weakened by divisions within the empire and by the growing power of Western European nations that were beginning to make their presence felt in South and Southeast Asia.

SECTION 2 REVIEW

1. **Recall** For what major contributions is the Gupta dynasty known?

2. **How and Why** How were the Muslim invaders different from previous invaders of the subcontinent?

3. **Critical Thinking** What impact has Muslim culture had on present-day nations in South Asia?

Beginning about 1000 B.C., people on the subcontinent developed a **social institution** known as the **caste** system. Although changes are occuring in the system, castes remain a central feature of life in present-day India.

The Structure of the System

Hindus are born into different groups within their society. The caste system groups most of them into four castes. This ranking according to caste has both an occupational and a religious significance.

Caste Divisions   The first caste is the Brahmin, or priestly caste. The Brahmins, the traditional teachers of Hinduism, were considered the highest in rank because of their spiritual and educational work. The second caste is the Kshatriya (kuh-SHA-tree-yuh), or warrior caste. Warriors were ranked next in importance because of their work of governing, protecting, and defending the land. The third caste is the Vaisya (VEESH-yuh), people such as merchants and farmers engaged in food production, commerce, and trade. The lowest caste is the Sudra (SHOO-druh), people whose lot in life was to serve the other three castes.

Out-castes   A fifth group of people belong to no caste. These people are called out-castes, untouchables, harijans, or scheduled castes. The untouchables performed those jobs that were regarded as the lowest—sweeping streets and floors, removing trash and other wastes, and working with leather. Hindus consider any item touched by an untouchable to be contaminated and unfit for use by any caste member. Contamination, which was not a matter of being physically dirty, meant being spiritually unclean. In order to prevent contamination, villages had two wells—one for untouchables and one for caste members. Untouchables had to live in a separate section of the village and walk along separate paths in the streets. Their children were not allowed to play or go to school with caste children.

contaminate
(kuhn-TAM-uh-nayt): make impure through contact

Hinduism and Caste   Hindus believe the castes were created by Brahman, the universal spirit. According to Hinduism, Brahmins were made from Brahman's head—making them wise and understanding and good teachers. Kshatriyas came from Brahman's heart and breastbone—making them strong, yet gentle and just right for governing and fighting. The Vaisyas were drawn from Brahman's thighs—making them hard workers as artisans, farmers, and merchants. The Sudras came from Brahman's feet—lacking wisdom and understanding they were unskilled laborers and servants. Untouchables, however, were made by Brahman from mud and so were fit only for the very lowest kind of work.

System Requirements   The caste system has three main requirements. First, members should marry within their caste. Second, caste members should eat and drink with members of the same caste and not with members of a lower caste. Finally, all members of a caste subdivision, or jati (JOH-tee), should practice the same occupation, which is usually hereditary. Some exceptions to these requirements exist, especially the last one. But the first two generally remain common. Various other rules of behavior for each caste and jati also exist. For example, drinking liquor is forbidden for a Brahmin, but is acceptable for a Vaisya. Rajputs are expected to seek revenge if someone questions their honor. Goalas are supposed to keep calm no matter what the provocation.

Origins and Development

Scholars disagree about the origins of the caste system. Some scholars believe that caste system began with the Aryan conquerors who entered the subcontinent between 1700 and 1500 B.C. These scholars speculate that the Aryans wanted to keep the highest status and most desirable kinds of work for themselves and their descendants. As a result the people of the subcontinent came to be separated by the kind of work they did, developing closely knit communities in the process.

The conquered Harappans, whose dark skin contrasted with the fair skin of the Aryans, were made to serve the higher classes of priests, officials, and warriors and thus became Sudras. People who handled waste products and the hides of dead animals were put outside the caste system as a way of protecting society because Aryans may have had a fear of catching diseases from them.

During the course of the subcontinent's history, a continuous flow of new physical types, occupations, and foreign elements found places within the caste system. Typical of this assimilation process is the story of the Rajputs (RAHJ-poots), a people who were powerful in the north and central parts of the subcontinent from about A.D. 650 to 1150 and who remained politically active as a separate group until the 1800s. The Rajputs were valiant warriors whom the Brahmins made into allies by making them a part of the caste system. Rajput priests became Brahmins, their warriors and chiefs became Kshatriyas, and the common people became Vaisyas.

Castes have died out and new castes have formed, but always the caste system has remained the basis of the social order with thousands of castes and subcastes coming into existence. Over the centuries even the out-castes have organized themselves on a graduated social scale into many groups.

Some changes in the caste system, however, have taken place in modern India. In 1950 the constitution of India abolished untouchability. In 1976 a constitutional amendment provided that untouchables were to be treated equally with members of the caste system. In practice, the amendment meant that untouchables could not be denied entrance to public places, and special provisions were made for their education at higher levels.

Legislation, however, has not changed the attitudes and emotions that are embedded in many Hindus' minds and hearts because of religion

Castes in India are mainly based upon occupation. To whom would this artisan rug maker teach his craft?

and other long-standing traditions. Clashes between untouchables and caste members have occurred in the past. They are likely to continue in the future as the government continues to support the equality of untouchables, as untouchables themselves continue to protest any discrimination or inferior treatment by caste members, and as members of the lower castes demand equal **civil rights** with the highest caste.

Advantages and Disadvantages

Supporters of the caste system say it has helped preserve Hindu culture and civilization and given Hindus a sense of identity and stability. By giving each Hindu a special duty in society, supporters say that the system has created cooperation instead of competition. They point out that invaders and rulers have succeeded one another with regularity, but the people have always kept their loyalty to the caste system. Overall, supporters believe that the caste system has freed people from anxiety about their lot in life. They believe that it has motivated Hindus to behave in an ethical manner to achieve rebirth at a higher level.

Some critics of the caste system believe it discouraged change and progress. Under the caste system, there was no incentive to become educated in order to obtain a better job, nor was there any incentive to try something new. In addition, untouchables were mistreated and humiliated, and led very difficult lives.

Some critics of the system have declared that present-day India cannot achieve real political unity until all Hindus are permitted to mingle freely. Other critics maintain that real social and economic progress is impossible while the rigid caste system governs people's activities and attitudes.

SECTION 3 REVIEW

1. **Recall** What is the religious and occupational basis of the caste system?

2. **How and Why** How has the caste system changed through the centuries?

3. **Critical Thinking** What are some of the advantages and some of the disadvantages of the caste system?

Reviewing People, Places and Things

Identify, define, or explain each of the following:

Harrapans	polytheism
Vedas	Sikhism
Epic Age	Genghis Khan
Ramayana	Akbar the Great
Hinduism	caste system
Panchatantra	out-castes

Map Study

Using the appropriate maps on pages 141, 147, and 149, answer the following questions on a separate sheet of paper.

1. From what directions did the Aryans invade the Indian subcontinent?
2. Which empire was most extensive—the Mauryan or the Gupta?

Understanding Ideas

1. What were the principal contributions of Aryans to Indian culture?
2. What is the teaching of Hinduism **a.** on reality? **b.** on salvation? **c.** on rebirth?
3. According to Buddha's Four Noble Truths, **a.** What is the greatest problem faced by people? **b.** What is its cause? **c.** When the cause is eliminated, what goal is reached?
4. What qualities are the statues of Buddha supposed to portray?
5. What influences have the religions of Hinduism, Buddhism, and Islam had on the arts in South Asia?
6. **a.** How might Aryans have contributed to the development of the caste system? **b.** Into what four groups does the caste system divide people? **c.** How has the caste system influenced modern society in India?

Developing Critical Thinking

Cause and Effect   Seeing the effects of causes and understanding both the causes and their effects across time and place is an important skill to use in studying history. One cause may have multiple effects. In the same light, one effect may have multiple causes, and these causes may have varying degrees of responsibility.

Activity: Describe the cause-and-effect relationships between Hinduism and its place in the development of modern India by answering the following questions: What are the beliefs of Hinduism? How have they affected the development of the arts, social patterns, and politics of India?

Writing About History

Using Your Imagination   Write a letter home to a younger brother or sister, to an older brother or sister, or to your parents, all of whom still live in a small rural village in South Asia, telling them about your new life in a large city—either Karachi or New Delhi. Your letter may focus on your journey to the city, your first impressions of city life, new friends you have made, or your efforts to find work. In your letter be sure to include some ways in which city life differs from life in your family's small village.

Applying Your Skills to History

Writing an Essay   Reread the explanation of Buddha's Four Noble Truths and his Noble Eightfold Path as they are described in the textbook, examining these principles as a guide for happy living. In a written essay express your opinion about how practical Buddha's principles are as a guide to solving the problems of everyday living. Tell what you think people might find hopeful in them and what people might find pessimistic or discouraging in them.

CHAPTER 8

India, Pakistan, and Bangladesh

Beginning in 1499, new invaders from Western Europe entered the Indian subcontinent, but unlike previous invasions, the newcomers came by sea and were mainly interested in trade. Gradually the traders from Western Europe moved inland from the seaports, gaining control of more and more territory and becoming colonial masters. As colonial rulers, the Western Europeans imposed Western ideas of government and culture upon the local people.

During the late 1800s, the people of South Asia began to look at ways to regain control of their lives through self-government, a movement that resulted in the splitting of the subcontinent into the independent nations of India and Pakistan in 1947 and the secession of Bangladesh from Pakistan in 1971.

As you study this chapter, think about these questions:

- How did the British come to dominate the subcontinent?

- How did nationalism develop in South Asia?

- What are the major political, economic, and social characteristics of modern India?

- What are the major political, economic, and social characteristics of modern Pakistan and Bangladesh?

The Taj Mahal was built as a tomb for Mumtaz Mahal. She was the favorite wife of Shah Jahan, who ruled the Mogul Empire from 1628 to 1658.

In 327 B.C., Alexander the Great opened up an overland trade route between India and the West. When the Islamic empire rose to power in the A.D. 600s, Arab traders carried goods from India across the Arabian Sea through the Arabian Peninsula and then to Western Europe.

The Rise of British India

Western Interest

In the 1400s, Western Europeans began searching for a way to bypass the Arab traders and reach India themselves. They came for spices, especially pepper, that could be obtained only from Eastern lands. In the days before refrigeration and canning, meat was often half spoiled by the time it was eaten. Spices improved the flavor and made the meat easier to eat. In the long journey from South Asia, however, the spices had to be loaded on ships that carried the goods to ports across the Arabian Sea where they were then transferred to land. Once on land, they were reloaded on pack animals for the journey by caravan to ports at the eastern end of the Mediterranean Sea. From here the spices were bought by other traders who then shipped them to ports in Western Europe. Each time someone handled the shipment, costs went up. By the time a cargo of spices reached Western Europe, the price was about 6,000 times the original cost.

The Spanish and the Portuguese were the first to look for an all-sea route to the Indies. The Spanish tried sailing west and reached the Americas instead. Vasco da Gama, a Portuguese captain, found a way to the Indies by sailing south around the tip of Africa and across the Indian Ocean. In 1499 his ship brought back to Portugal a cargo of precious spices.

The British in India

In the 1500s, the Portuguese were followed by the French and the Dutch. At first their ships would enter a harbor, exchange gold and silver for spices and cotton textiles, and leave. Later, the Westerners established trading posts and began to compete with one another for control of the profitable Indian trade. In 1611, a British company commonly known as the East India Trading Company established a trading post on the subcontinent's west coast. In 1640 the company established another post on the east coast. This second post became Madras, one of India's four largest cities. Two other British trading posts also developed into large cities—Bombay, on an island off the west coast, and Calcutta, near the mouth of the Ganges. From these trading posts, the East India Company slowly expanded its influence into the subcontinent. They ousted the French in 1757 after the Battle of Plessey, and the Dutch and the Portuguese were confined to small coastal enclaves and off-shore islands.

Imperialism in India, 1857

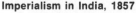

■ British possessions
■ Independent states

For the next 100 years the East India Company dominated the subcontinent by moving against the 500 or so monarchies into which the Mogul Empire had broken up in one of two ways. If the local raja was weak, the company took over the state and ruled it directly. If the raja was strong, the British signed an agreement under which they collected taxes and ran **foreign policy** in exchange for supporting the raja and training his troops in modern methods of warfare.

Economic and Social Change   Like the Muslims before them, the British brought about many changes in the subcontinent in a process called **westernization**. They did away with warfare between the monarchies and eliminated the robbers who had made it dangerous to travel on land. They built a railroad network that unified almost all parts of the subcontinent. They gave grants of land that formed the basis for a plantation tea industry.

On the other hand, the East India Company destroyed India's textile industry in order to further British manufacturing interests at home. Instead of using local factories to make cotton cloth, the company shipped raw cotton to England. There British manufacturers used newly invented machines to turn the cotton into cloth. The machine-made fabrics were then shipped back to South Asia for sale. The British also introduced the Western concept of landownership to the subcontinent. Previously, landowners had been able to collect rents from peasants but could not evict them. With British control, however, landowners could evict peasants and do whatever they wished with the land.

The British also tried to control the lives and customs of the people. They abolished slavery, made English the official language of government and the law courts, introduced secondary schools and universities, and reorganized the school system. Christian missionaries traveled everywhere, trying to make converts and talking about their dream of replacing both Hinduism and Islam with Christianity.

Many of the social and cultural changes the British introduced improved everyday life. Other westernization changes, however, were insensitive to local needs, **customs**, and **traditions**. For example, the mingling of people on railroad trains posed a threat to the caste system. Farmers did not understand how the new law courts operated. Millions of textile workers were no longer able to earn a living. In addition, many Britishers discriminated against Indians. They routinely treated their Indian servants and clerks with verbal abuse and would not allow Indians to hold positions of authority in either the army or the government.

The Great Mutiny   In 1857 discontent with British rule erupted into open rebellion. The uprising centered on the sepoy mutiny of Indian troops called sepoys. Hindu sepoys complained that the new rifle cartridges they had been issued were smeared with the fat of cows, while Muslim sepoys complained that the cartridges were smeared with the fat of pigs.

In all likelihood, the sepoy mutiny would have occurred without the cartridge incident. The changes under British rule came so quickly and

evict:
throw out

caused so much social and economic disruption that a reaction against them was only to be expected. In fact, the mutinous soldiers were soon joined by large groups of unhappy farmers. Unfortunately, there was no leader around whom the various groups could unite. After about a year of vicious fighting, with atrocities committed on both sides, the rebellion was crushed. Later in the 1800s, the British Parliament abolished the East India Company, made the subcontinent an official part of the British Empire, and established the British monarch as the subcontinent's official ruler.

SECTION 1 REVIEW

1. **Recall** What three British trading posts developed into large cities?
2. **How and Why** How did Western Europeans become interested in India?
3. **Critical Thinking** How did the Great Mutiny affect the subcontinent?

Nationalism on the Subcontinent

Over the next few decades after the ending of the Great Mutiny of the sepoys, Great Britain consolidated its control over the subcontinent. At the same time, it planted the seeds of **nationalism**.

The Rising Middle Class

The British presence in India consisted of only about 40,000 British soldiers and civil servants. Such a small number could not possibly govern a population of about 300 million local inhabitants without training Indians to assist them in the governing of a **territory** as large as the subcontinent. Thus the British trained Indians to teach in government schools and to serve as lawyers and court reporters in the westernized courts. Companies handling trade and manufacturing trained shipping clerks and accountants; engineers to build irrigation canals; stationmasters, ticket collectors, and mechanics to run the railroads; and foremen to supervise mills and other manufacturing plants.

Gradually India developed a middle class educated in the English language and familiar with Western ideas and history—especially the long struggle of the British people for self-government. Many members of this middle class could not understand why the British were **democratic** at home and in undemocratic India. More and more the educated class of India resented the British view that Indians were unfit and unready to govern themselves.

Mahatma Gandhi led the way of India's independence. His teachings influenced people around the world.

Finally in 1885, 73 members of this new middle class—mostly lawyers and mostly Hindu—met to organize the Indian National Congress. By 1890 the Congress was the primary voice of South Asian nationalism. At first the Congress called only for **reforms** in British rule, such as appointing more Indians to government positions. By 1906, however, the Congress was advocating complete independence for the subcontinent. Also in 1906, a separate **nationalist** organization called the Muslim League was formed by Muslims who feared political and economic domination by the Hindu **majority** on the subcontinent.

Mahatma Gandhi

In 1869 a man was born in the northwestern part of the subcontinent who was destined, more than any other single person, to unify the Indians and gain their freedom. This man was Mohandas K. Gandhi, a member of the Vaisya caste, who later was given the name of *Mahatma*, or "Great Soul."

Gandhi studied law in London, England, and returned to the subcontinent to practice. In 1893 he went to South Africa on a law case and stayed to fight against the discrimination that was practiced toward his people. It was in South Africa that Gandhi conceived and put into practice the idea of mass resistance through nonviolence. He called this approach *satyagraha*, or "soul-force." Gandhi believed in returning love for hate, good for evil, and unselfishness for selfishness. Tormented by his enemies, roughly handled by the police, and imprisoned, Gandhi never struck back. He suffered in silence and patience, hoping to make the government officials and people of South Africa ashamed of their behavior. In the end, the government agreed to change the discriminatory practices that Gandhi had fought against through satyagraha.

In 1915 Gandhi returned to the subcontinent to work for the freedom of his people. He gave up Western clothes and dressed in sandals and the traditional dhoti, a simple piece of white cloth. He practiced vegetarianism and owned little. If people rioted, he pleaded with them to practice nonviolence. When they did not listen, he fasted until his wishes were met.

The British found it difficult to cope with **civil disobedience**, or nonviolent protest, a term that Gandhi had borrowed from the American philosopher Henry David Thoreau. At Gandhi's urging, people began wearing clothing made of homespun fabric instead of British textiles. Women and children, who lay down on railroad tracks and in the streets as a form of nonviolent protest, accepted beatings from those who tried to remove them. After the British passed a tax on salt, people in the subcontinent made their own salt by evaporating it from ocean water. When the British passed a law that enabled them to imprison without a trial people suspected of anti-British activities, the people observed a nationwide day of prayer with workers staying away from their jobs and students absenting themselves from classes.

Gandhi was himself jailed for civil disobedience, and when the jails became filled with nonviolent protestors, the British stopped arresting them. As resistance stiffened, the British were left with no choice except to talk and negotiate with the leaders of the Indian National Congress. But progress was slow, and the talking went on until 1947 when the British announced that they would leave the subcontinent, granting independence to two nations—a Muslim-dominated Pakistan and a Hindu-dominated India.

With the British announcement, wild emotions and long-restrained hatreds erupted. Muslims fought Hindus, Hindus fought Sikhs, and Sikhs fought Muslims. At least one million people were killed. Partition created about 12 million refugees as Hindus in Pakistan and Muslims in India fled to the land of their choice.

Mahatma Gandhi pleaded and finally fasted almost to death in his efforts to halt the bloodshed and suffering dividing his native land. He succeeded in saving thousands of lives when he reluctantly agreed to partition and the creation of a separate Muslim state on the subcontinent, but he came to be hated by a few Hindu fanatics. One of these fanatics assassinated Gandhi in 1948, which left the subcontinent without the guiding force that had inspired it for so long.

fanatic:
person who acts with excessive enthusiasm and devotion to a cause

SECTION 2 REVIEW

1. **Recall**   Who assisted the British in the governing of India?
2. **How and Why**   How did a middle class develop on the subcontinent?
3. **Critical Thinking**   How was Mahatma Gandhi a guiding force in the drive for self-government?

From independence in 1947 until the end of 1989, with the exception of a short period, India has been led by three members of the same family—Jawaharlal Nehru (juh-WAH-hur-lahl NEHR-oo), his daughter Indira, and his grandson Rajiv (RAH-jeev).

Nehru

Jawaharlal Nehru was a long-time supporter of Mohandas Gandhi. A brilliant member of the Brahmin caste, Nehru studied law in England. But instead of practicing law on his return to the subcontinent, Nehru devoted himself to the struggle for independence and, like Gandhi, spent considerable time in prison for civil disobedience. In 1947 when India received its independence along with Pakistan, Nehru became the first prime minister of India's new parliamentary government. He remained in that position until his death in 1964.

Here Nehru is shown speaking at the UN. He supported a policy of neutrality in world politics. What are some advantages and disadvantages of neutrality?

Under Nehru's leadership, industrialization and modernization were pushed by the national government. Under Nehru, India adopted a **mixed economy** in which most industry remained in private hands, but the government nationalized such basic areas as energy, transportation, communications, banking, and life insurance. The government helped farmers by building dams and drilling wells. It also set up rural banks so farmers would no longer have to pay moneylenders the traditional high rate of 30 percent interest a year for loans. Education was made compulsory through the fourth grade and free to age 14. As a result, more than half the population is now literate.

Indira Gandhi

Nehru's daughter, Indira, who married a man by the name of Gandhi with no relation to the Mahatma, became prime minister in 1966. She continued her father's policies of modernization and industrialization. Like Nehru, she tried to steer clear of the worldwide contest for power between the United States and the Soviet Union that was then at its height. She accepted economic and military help from both **superpowers**, at the same time keeping India among the nonaligned nations of the world.

Indira Gandhi also faced internal political problems, especially with the Sikhs, who, by the 1980s, were demanding self-rule for the Punjab — the Indian state in which most Sikhs live. When militant Sikhs began carrying out acts of **terrorism**, Indira Gandhi ordered retaliation. Government troops then raided the Golden Temple in Amritsar, which Sikh militants had turned into a munitions storehouse. Hundreds of Sikhs were killed and the shrine was badly damaged in the raid. Four months later, on October 31, 1984, Indira Gandhi was assassinated by two Sikh members of her personal bodyguard.

Rajiv Gandhi

On Indira Gandhi's death, the Indian people turned to her son, Rajiv, for leadership. After succeeding his mother, Rajiv concentrated on improving India's **economy**. He removed hundreds of regulations that were restricting private businesses. He encouraged factory owners to import high-technology equipment. At the same time, he cracked down on businesses that were not paying taxes. He also put young, well-educated people rather than traditional politicians in many government jobs.

In 1989, however, charges of corruption and bribe-taking were leveled against officials in Rajiv's government. At about the same time, new parliamentary elections were held that brought an end to the Nehru-Gandhi dynasty that had ruled India since its independence. Since the elections left no party with a clear majority, the country is now governed by a **coalition** that is headed by Vishwanath Pratap Singh, a former member of Rajiv Gandhi's **cabinet**. The new prime minister must now tackle the major problems that beset the world's second most populous nation.

Major Problems

Most of India's problems are long-standing by-products of its history and culture. Building a true sense of **national identity** is one such problem. India is a mosaic of **nationalities** and is beset with traditional religious differences among Muslims, Hindus, and Sikhs. It has 16 official languages, only two of which—English and Hindi—are used nationwide. Because of language differences, many Indians are more loyal to the state in which they live than to the nation.

A second major problem is land reform. Many people work the land, mostly as day laborers, and only a small percentage of farmers own the land they work. Landowners are usually high-caste members who look down on the mostly low-caste laborers. In addition, the national government can do little about land reform because under India's constitution the states control agriculture. The members of state legislatures are frequently landowners who do not want their large estates to be broken up and redistributed to the landless. In recent years, landowners and day laborers have clashed in several northeastern states. State police have either not wanted to stop the violence or have been unable to do so.

A third major problem for India is the lack of balance between its population and its production of food. On the one hand, India's population has been increasing at such a rapid rate that the country is expected to overtake China as the world's most populous nation in the next 25 years. Under Indira Gandhi, the government started a vigorous campaign to reduce the birth rate. Many Indians, however, are opposed to birth control—especially people engaged in agriculture—because many children mean extra hands to help farm the land and earn money. Many Hindus to whom male heirs are important have as many children as possible to insure that they have at least one son survive to manhood.

On the other hand, India's food production has not kept pace with the population, even though farm production has increased through the use of new "miracle grains" that have a higher yield than native grains. India's farmers are also using fertilizers, pesticides, and other more advanced farming methods.

Indira Gandhi won by a wide margin when she was reelected prime minister in 1980. Despite her personal popularity with voters, she had to face many political problems. Besides India's economy, she also dealt with a separatist movement by Sikhs in northern India who sought independence.

The Arts Today

Indian music uses a tone system of 12 notes. Instruments native to India include flutes made of bamboo or metal and a set of small drums that are played with the hands. The **sitar** and the **vina** are plucked with the fingers like a guitar. For ceremonial occasions, Indians use a horn made from a conch shell. Indian musicians usually perform in groups of two to

The sitar was developed around the 1200s. It has 6 or 7 strings that are plucked and 12 to 20 strings that vibrate. Metal strips called frets are used to adjust string tension.

six. The traditional musical form of **raga** tries to capture religious moods or feelings, such as gratitude for the dawn of a new day.

Like Indian art and music, Indian dance is highly formal and uses symbolism. Every position of the body, every facial expression, every gesture of the arms and hands, and every tempo has a meaning attached to it. Several schools of classical dance have evolved from temple dancing. One type is dance drama. The great epics of Hinduism, especially the *Ramayana* and the *Mahabharata*, are often performed by dancers who mime the story while a chorus chants the verses.

One of India's greatest modern writers was Sir Rabindranath Tagore (rah-BIN-druh-naht tuh-GOR), who died in 1941. In 1913 he won the Nobel Prize for literature, the first South Asian to receive that honor. Writing first in the Bengali language, then translating it into English, he turned out some 50 plays, 40 novels, several books on philosophy, and thousands of poems—many of which he set to music himself. His hymn *Morning Song of India* is the country's national anthem. Tagore criticized nationalism and the caste system and urged people to renounce violence. He admired Western technology, but felt that people in Western nations were spiritually empty. Among the finest contemporary authors in India are R. K. Narayan (nah-RAH-yan) and Santha Rama Rau.

Indians are enthusiastic filmgoers, and India's film industry is the largest in the world. The government uses films to instruct the people on family planning, personal hygiene, and other planned reforms. The films are shown in the villages along with romances, adventure stories, and other popular movies. Director Satyajit Ray has won worldwide fame for films that portray modern Indian life with sensitivity and realism.

The Family Today

The traditional Indian family is typically an extended family. As the family head, the oldest male supervises family property and finances. Family members pool their resources and income, and the family head spends according to the needs of each. He is bound by tradition, custom, and public opinion to preserve and not to waste the family holdings. He consults with the elders of the family, and he seeks advice from his mother, if she is living.

Family members also possess personal property. For example, the jewelry that a bride receives from her family remains her personal property. Most women in India, except widows, wear gold or silver bracelets, earrings, nose rings, necklaces, and other jewelry. This is generally all they can call their own except for the clothes they wear. Widows are not supposed to wear jewelry, bright clothing, or cosmetics. It is assumed that all brightness left their lives when their husbands died. Society frowns upon their seeking another husband.

Traditionally the woman occupies a position subordinate to the male. As the Laws of Manu, which were codified about A.D. 100, put it: "Her father protects her in childhood, her husband protects her in youth, and her sons protect her in old age; a woman is never fit for independence." The ideal Indian wife is one who is submissive, obedient, modest,

Pinning money to a bride's or groom's clothes is the custom in a number of countries. Do you know any wedding customs?

retiring, and loyal. She serves her husband and her family quietly, efficiently, and without complaint. When she is the wife of the family head and mother of his children, she is respected. Her advice on household and other matters is asked for and often followed.

One of the most serious responsibilities of Indian parents is the marriage of their children. Traditionally, marriage in India is not a private romantic affair between two people. It is a family matter of grave importance. Two people are being brought together to preserve and continue the family, not merely to satisfy their own emotions. The Indians take the view that love should follow marriage, not precede it. As a consequence, the couple may not see each other before their engagement, and sometimes not before their marriage day. They may see only a picture of each other.

It is not always easy for parents to find suitable mates for their children. Many social concerns surround marriage in India. There is the question of caste, reputation, and the economic position of the families. The bride must have a trousseau and a dowry. These items are important to the family of the groom, for these are new resources she brings to the family.

dowry:
money or goods that a woman brings to a marriage

A successful marriage traditionally results in children. These children are primarily members of the extended family and are the responsibility of the extended family rather than of the parents alone. Children thus absorb a sense of responsibility toward the entire family.

Changes in Family Life Some change in Indian family life is apparent today. This is especially true in the cities and among those educated in Western ideas. The growth of industrialization has attracted many people to the cities from the villages. There is a wider range of jobs in urban areas than in rural ones. Sometimes only the nuclear family will

Although lack of teachers and money for education is a problem in India, educational opportunities are increasing there. These women work in an electronics plant in India.

go to the city to look for work. The rest of the family must stay in the village, for living conditions in the city are too crowded and rents too high for the relatives to go.

Some young people are seeking greater choice in the selection of a mate. Sometimes individuals personally select a candidate for their parents' consideration.

Women in India Since the 1960s, women's organizations in India have been campaigning for an end to the dowry system. The reason is the large number of so-called "dowry deaths" each year. Thousands of newly married women burn to death in kitchen fires, and shortly thereafter their husbands remarry, once again obtaining a dowry.

Women's organizations have campaigned for other goals as well. They would like the marriage age for girls raised from 15 to 18 years of age. They advocate establishment of day-care centers for the infants of poor women who work as laborers and must bring their babies to work with them. They also campaign for "equal pay for equal work." How fast women's roles will change and how these changes will affect society in India remain to be seen. As in the case of caste, the vast number of Indians still hold traditional values. As India passes through economic and political changes, social changes can also be expected. But no one can say how greatly these changes will modify Indian attitudes toward women.

SECTION 3 REVIEW

1. **Recall** What advances did India make under the leadership of Nehru? Indira Gandhi? Rajiv Gandhi?

2. **How and Why** Why is India's advancement as a developed nation hindered?

3. **Critical Thinking** How may modernization affect family life and attitudes toward women in India?

The Muslims, who entered the northern part of the subcontinent about A.D. 1000, gradually conquered most of the subcontinent where they established the Mogul Empire. Unlike previous conquerors, the Muslims refused to be assimilated into the Hindu population and kept their culture distinct and separate. The Muslims, however, were a **minority** surrounded by a Hindu majority. After the decline of the Mogul Empire, both Muslim and Hindu were governed by the British.

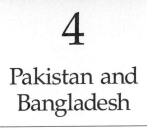

The Founding of Pakistan

Direction, purpose, and spirit were given to the Muslim minority by three men who led their fellow Muslims to dream of a country of their own and eventually to realize that dream with an independent nation that came to be called Pakistan.

Sir Sayyid Ahmad Khan (1817–1898) urged Muslims to learn from the West so that they might become strong once again as they had been under the Moguls. Ahmad Khan emphasized the need of Muslims to be strong because he predicted that Hindus would outnumber Muslims four to one in an independent India. Sir Mohammed Iqbal (1873–1938), who inspired Muslims to study science, was among the first to present Muslims with the dream of a separate homeland, which he called Pakistan. Sir Mohammed Ali Jinnah (1876–1948) was a supporter of the Hindu-dominated Congress Party. At first, he thought in terms of a united government for the subcontinent—a government in which Hindus would vote for Hindu representatives and Muslims would vote for Muslim representatives. When he realized in 1930 that the Congress Party would never grant Muslims equal representation with Hindus, however, he insisted on partition and became the leading voice for an independent Muslim nation of Pakistan. When the new nation was formed, it consisted of two parts—West Pakistan, which comprised most of the Indus River valley, and East Pakistan, which comprised most of the Ganges-Brahmaputra delta region.

Government   Just as Gandhi died soon after the founding of his nation, so Mohammed Ali Jinnah died soon after Pakistan received its independence. For the next ten years, from 1948 to 1958, Pakistan had a series of civilian governments as it tried to find a leader who inspired the kind of allegiance the people had given to Jinnah. Then in 1958, the military decided to take over the nation's leadership. General Mohammed Ayub Khan (ah-YOOB-kahn) seized power in a military **coup d'etat** and set up a **dictatorship**. At first Ayub Khan's government worked well. He seized supplies of rice and grain that people were hoarding and sold them to the needy at low prices. He resettled Muslim refugees from India on plots of land confiscated from wealthy landowners. He even had the streets of major cities thoroughly cleaned for the first time in years.

By 1965, however, a number of troubles weakened Ayub Khan's government. Corruption undermined the people's trust in his rule as

Mohammed Ali Jinnah is considered the founder of Pakistan.

many of Ayub Khan's friends made huge profits in the construction of Islamabad, Pakistan's new capital. At the same time the prices of goods rose faster than wages, and students clamored for democratic elections. Differences between East Pakistan and West Pakistan also became increasingly troublesome. When India intervened following the outbreak of civil war between East and West Pakistan, East Pakistan in 1971 became the independent nation of Bangladesh.

Recent Developments in Pakistan   After the separation of Bangladesh, Pakistan's military leader Yahya Khan, who had replaced Ayub Khan in 1969, was himself replaced by a civilian, Zulfikar Ali Bhutto (ZOOL-fih-kahr ah-LEE BOO-toh) in March 1977. Bhutto emphasized land reform, dividing large estates into small plots owned by peasants. He also nationalized Pakistan's banks and shipping industry. In July 1977 Bhutto was overthrown by General Mohammad Zia-ul-Haq (ZEE-ah-ahl-hak), imprisoned, and later hanged.

On taking over the government, Zia declared Pakistan an Islamic republic based on the traditional law of the Koran rather than on secular law. Pakistani women immediately began demonstrating against the government. After 11 years of protest, Zia announced that a democratic election would be held in November 1988. A month after making the announcement, Zia died in an unexplained midair airplane explosion. Nevertheless the election was held as scheduled, and as the leader of the party that won a majority of parliamentary seats in the election, Bhutto's daughter, Benazir (BEN-ah-zeer), was named prime minister. With her election Pakistan became the world's first Muslim nation to be led by a woman.

While Benazir Bhutto's election produced a severe reaction among conservative Muslims, the prime minister began moving ahead on her campaign promises. One of her promises was to improve Pakistan's standard of living. In 1987 the average income of a Pakistani was $350, and the literacy rate in the country was only 30 percent. Only 14 percent of its labor force was engaged in industry, while 49 percent depended on agriculture for a living. Like India, Pakistan must curb its population growth, which at its present rate of 3.1 percent gives promise of doubling its 110 million population in less than 35 years.

The Independence of Bangladesh

East Pakistan and West Pakistan were united by the common bond of Islam, but the two vastly separated sections of the country were divided in most other ways.

Divisions   West Pakistan was dry and mountainous, while East Pakistan was rainy and low-lying. People in West Pakistan spoke mostly Urdu, while people in East Pakistan spoke Bengali. West Pakistan contained several ethnic groups, but East Pakistan contained only

HISTORY AND PEOPLE

BENAZIR BHUTTO

"I must sacrifice everything for my country. This is a mission I shall live or die for."

Benazir Bhutto, former prime minister of Pakistan, did not speak lightly of life or death in service to her country. Her father, Zulfikar Ali Bhutto, president and later prime minister of Pakistan, was forced from office by the Pakistani military in 1977 and, despite appeals from world leaders, was hanged in 1979.

The coup was led by General Mohammad Zia ul-Haq, who ruled Pakistan with an iron hand until his death in an airplane crash in 1988. His death enabled Pakistan to return to a democratic system and provided an opportunity for the younger Bhutto to regain her prominence. At 35, she became the first woman and youngest person to be prime minister of Pakistan.

Although she was a powerful leader, Bhutto did not enjoy the influence her father had. She was forced to contend with a strong military voice in government and a more powerful president. The largest province of Pakistan, Punjab, is controlled by the opposing political party. Other Asian nations, after obtaining their independence from European control, developed systems of power sharing among their leaders. In Pakistan, however, power sharing was, before Benazir Bhutto became prime minister, unprecedented. A great deal of governmental energy was spent vying for control. These political battles checked her authority, making it especially difficult for her to improve conditions for her fellow Pakistanis.

Pakistan is faced with a host of serious problems. As a relatively poor country, Pakistan has a sizable foreign debt. The civil war in neighboring Afghanistan has forced approximately three million refugees to seek shelter in Pakistan. It is surrounded by powerful neighbors, and holds a long-standing enmity with neighboring India. The economy of Pakistan is weak, and many of the people suffer from inadequate education and medical care. Benazir Bhutto's job was to address these difficult issues—and others—while keeping Pakistan's fledgling democracy alive.

The challenges to Bhutto were redoubled by the fact she is a woman. Pakistan is a Muslim nation, and Bhutto is the first woman in modern times to rule a Muslim country. Muslim women are denied many of the civil rights of men, and rule by a woman is virtually unheard of. "I'm a Muslim woman in a Muslim society and there are certain topics Muslim women can't discuss," she had said. "I can't develop the kind of camaraderie that exists among men."

On August 6, 1990, President Ishaq Khan of Pakistan dismissed Bhutto as prime minister. Khan charged that Bhutto's government was ineffective and corrupt.

1. How did the fact that she is a woman make Bhutto's job more difficult?

2. What are some problems facing Pakistan today?

3. Do you think power should be shared among a nation's leaders, or should one person have great authority? Why?

Bengalis. West Pakistan's staple food was wheat, while East Pakistan's was rice. West Pakistan was moderately industrialized with factories that turned out cotton textiles, processed foods, tobacco, and natural gas. East Pakistan was mainly agricultural, producing only tea and jute, which is used in making burlap and rope. West Pakistan contained only 45 percent of the nation's population, yet it dominated the nation's political affairs with West Pakistanis holding most government and military offices. It also spent most of the nation's budget even though more than half of the national income came from East Pakistan.

Civil War   Troubles between East and West Pakistan came to a boiling point after the elections of 1970 in which East Pakistanis won a majority of seats in the national legislature. Sheikh Mujibur Rahman (shayk moo-JEE-bur RAH-mahn), the leader of the Awami League, then issued a series of demands that would have made East Pakistan virtually independent. Yahya Khan responded to the demands for a separate currency, army, and foreign affairs with a declaration of martial law.

In 1971 civil war erupted. Within a few months some 12 million East Pakistani refugees had streamed into India. Indira Gandhi, India's prime minister, did not want the refugees to remain on Indian soil. She also

This picture shows pro-Bhutto demonstrators in Karachi, Pakistan. How do most governments react to this kind of demonstration?

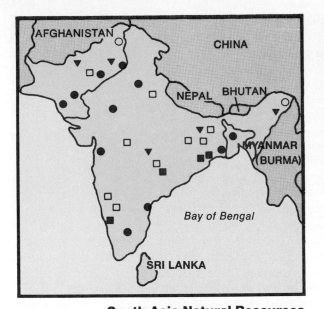

**South Asia Natural Resources
and Industrial Centers**

● Industrial Centers ▼ Coal ■ Iron ○ Oil □ Minerals

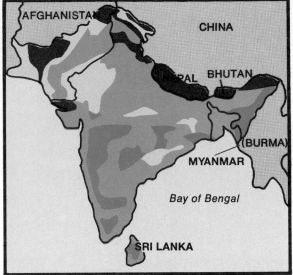

South Asia Land Use

▨ Farming ▨ Forestry □ Grazing ▧ Nonproductive

preferred having two weak Muslim nations on India's borders to one strong one. As a result she sent Indian armies into East Pakistan. In less than two weeks, the Indian army defeated the West Pakistani troops stationed there, and created Bangladesh. In February 1974 the leaders of Pakistan agreed to recognize the independence of Bangladesh, the land of the Bengalis.

Recent Developments   With independence Mujibur Rahman became Bangladesh's first chief of state. He was assassinated in 1975, and from then until 1982 the country went through several changes of leadership. In 1982 a military coup d'etat brought General H. M. Ershad (ur-SHAD) to power, and in 1983 he assumed the office of president.

Ershad has been faced with trying to alleviate the nation's economic problems. Because of its limited resources—jute makes up 75 percent of its exports—the country suffers from high unemployment, poverty, and a lack of capital. Bangladesh is also troubled by floods, made more devastating because the Himalayan forests that used to prevent flooding and erosion have been destroyed. The floods annually leave millions of people homeless and create conditions that lead to widespread malnutrition and starvation.

The population of about 115 million people has a growth rate of 2.8 percent. About 2,000 people, on the average, fill every square mile of the nation, giving Bangladesh one of the highest population densities in the world. Only about 33 percent of its people are literate. On the average, a Bangladeshi earns only about $170 a year.

Sri Lanka's economy is based on agriculture. Sri Lanka is the world's second leading exporter of tea. Workers called tea pluckers pick tea leaves in Sri Lanka.

SECTION 4 REVIEW

1. **Recall**   What leaders helped shape the drive for independence in Pakistan? In Bangladesh?

2. **How and Why**   How did East Pakistan and West Pakistan differ?

3. **Critical Thinking**   Why did India support an independent Bangladesh? Given traditional animosities on the subcontinent, why was this support unusual?

Reviewing People, Places, and Things

Identify, define, or explain each of the following:

Vasco da Gama

East India Trading Company

westernization

sepoys

Mahatma Gandhi

satyagraha

civil disobedience

Jawaharlal Nehru

mixed economy

Indira Gandhi

Rajiv Gandhi

nationalized

Hindi

sitar

R. K. Narayan

extended family

Sir Mohammed Ali Jinnah

dictatorship

Map Study

Using the maps on page 173, answer the following questions on a separate sheet of paper.

1. **a.** What natural resources are located in India? **b.** in Pakistan? **c.** in Bangladesh?

2. What is most of India's land used for?

3. In what country are most of the subcontinent's forests found?

4. In what country is about half the land suitable for grazing?

Understanding Ideas

1. How did the spice trade lead Western Europeans to take an interest in South Asia?

2. How did the East India Trading Company dominate the monarchies of the subcontinent?

3. What role did westernization play in the development of a middle class in India?

4. How did the British try to control the lives and customs of the people?

5. What political organizations were instrumental in fighting for partition of the subcontinent?

6. What effect did the practice of civil disobedience have on the struggle for independence?

7. Why was Indira Gandhi willing to support independence for Muslim-dominated East Pakistan?

Developing Critical Thinking

Debating an Issue A debate is a formal argument of two sides of a problem. One team—the pro side—takes a positive stand on the issue, while the con team takes a negative stand on the issue. To prepare for a debate, each member of the team reads about the issue and takes notes. The team decides together on the arguments to present and which team member is responsible for presenting each argument. The team also prepares responses called rebuttals to arguments presented by the other side, and decides who will do any rebuttals.

Activity: Self-government for Sikhs in the Punjab is an issue currently dividing opinion on the subcontinent. Prepare a debate on the topic: *Sikhs in the Punjab should receive self-government.*

Writing About History

Analyzing Leadership After reading short biographies about political leaders on the subcontinent, write a paragraph that describes the qualities of leadership that enabled these people to make contributions to their nations. Some people to write about include Mahatma Gandhi, Nehru, Ali Jinnah, Zulfikir Bhutto, Indira Gandhi, and Benazir Bhutto.

Applying Your Skills to History

Making a Time line Using the information presented in this chapter, make a card for each dated event, displaying the date and a short description of the event. Arrange the cards in chronological order.

CHAPTER

9

A Burmese artist created this religious portrait in lacquer. What religious symbols are shown in the picture?

Southeast Asia

Southeast Asia includes the nations of Myanmar (formerly Burma), Thailand, Cambodia (also known as Kampuchea), Laos, Vietnam, Malaysia, Singapore, Indonesia, and the Philippines. Almost two thirds of the region's 430 million inhabitants are Malays, with the Chinese ranking as the second largest ethnic group. A majority of the people today, as in the past, are rice farmers.

The cultures of Southeast Asia have been greatly influenced by the cultures of China, which will be studied in Unit 3, and India. Nations in the West have also played an important role in the region's history.

As you study this chapter, think about these questions:

- How has the mix of people in Southeast Asia influenced its development?

- What similarities and differences are found in the various ways the nations of Southeast Asia received their independence?

- What traits characterize the culture and social patterns of Southeast Asia?

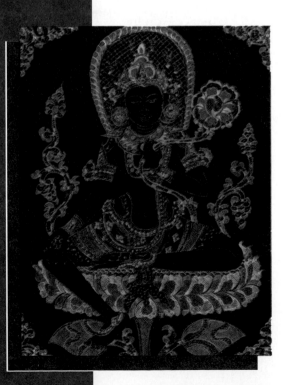

Buddhist shrines with golden domes rise above the countryside in Myanmar.

The archaeological evidence thus far uncovered in Southeast Asia indicates that early ancestors of Southeast Asians were living in the region as early as 500,000 years ago. About 15,000 B.C., a people known as the Hoabinhians (hwah-BIN-ee-uhns) apparently began the **domestication** of wild plants and animals. By 4000 B.C., they had invented a type of outrigger canoe, and by 3500 B.C., the people of the region were making copper tools.

About 2500 B.C., the ancestors of the present-day Malays began appearing in the area. They brought with them the practice of eating cultivated rice grown in irrigated fields. Sometime later they domesticated the water buffalo, using it as a beast of burden, raised chickens and pigs for meat, and built richly carved houses of wood. They also practiced **animism**, a form of religion in which people find spirits, some good and some evil, in natural objects such as trees, stones, mountains, and rivers. While most people today practice Hinduism, Buddhism, Islam, or Christianity, the influence of animism still lingers. For example, most people from Thailand and Laos still keep a "spirit house" in their garden or in their fields. Every day the people place an offering of fruit, rice, or flowers on the shrine to please the good spirits and to ward off the evil spirits.

The Chinese

In 111 B.C. the Chinese made present-day northern Vietnam part of their empire. Chinese teachings influenced the way the Vietnamese viewed the roles of individuals within family and society. The Vietnamese also accepted the Mahayana branch of Buddhism brought to them by the Chinese. So strong was the Chinese influence that the Vietnamese copied

cultivated:
crops that are seeded, cared for, and harvested (as opposed to plants that grow wild)

Vietnamese Migrations

Malay Migrations

Chinese dress, imitated the Chinese use of a family name as well as a personal name, adopted the Chinese writing system, added many Chinese words to their own language, and began using iron plows. Chinese officials supervised the construction of roads, bridges, and irrigation systems in Vietnam. At the same time, Chinese shopkeepers and bankers established themselves throughout most of the area.

Although the Vietnamese accepted many Chinese cultural contributions, they resisted Chinese rule. Among the major revolts was one led by the Trung sisters in the first century A.D. Finally, the Vietnamese drove out the Chinese in 939, and then sent a mission to pay **tribute** to the Chinese emperor. From the viewpoint of the Chinese, the payment of tribute allowed the Chinese to save face over the ouster and meant that China still ruled the area. Thus Chinese honor was saved, and the Vietnamese obtained self-government.

Chinese influence also spread to other parts of Southeast Asia. Between A.D. 700 and 1400 many Chinese went to the Philippines, where they settled mostly on the large island of Luzon, married the island people, and came to control a great portion of the trade and wealth of the Philippines. Today more than 10 percent of the Filipino population has some Chinese ancestry.

Some of the inhabitants of Malaysia and Myanmar and most of the inhabitants of Singapore are of Chinese descent. Beginning in the 1100s, many Chinese settled farther south in Indonesia, becoming so successful as traders and merchants that they eventually controlled much of the economy and resources of the Indonesia islands.

The Indians

Traders from India began coming to Southeast Asia about the year A.D. 1. Pushed by monsoon winds, their seagoing ships swept across the Bay of Bengal and through the Strait of Malacca. In addition to products, the South Asians introduced to the region three religions—Hinduism, Buddhism, and Islam.

Religious Influences   Hinduism lasted only on the Indonesian island of Bali, but Theravada Buddhism became a powerful force in present-day Thailand, Myanmar, and Cambodia where today it is the religion of the majority of the people. Each year thousands of young men leave their studies and their jobs to become Buddhist monks. Most enter the priesthood at the age of 20 for a three-to-six-month period. The monks wear a simple yellow robe, shave their heads, and beg for food. They serve as teachers in elementary schools, many of which are housed in temple buildings. They study Buddhist scriptures and use astrology to advise the people when to conclude a business deal or to make other important moves.

South Asians also introduced Islam to Southeast Asia after the 1200s, and it is now the dominant religion of modern Indonesians. In contrast to the more rigid observance of Islam by people in other parts of the world,

TRADE IN SOUTHEAST ASIA					
Nation	Major Exports	Total in millions of U.S. $	Imports	Total in millions of U.S. $	Major Trading Partners
Cambodia (Kampuchea)	agricultural products	3.2	foodstuffs, fuel, machinery	28.0	Vietnam, USSR, Japan, India
Indonesia	petroleum products, agricultural products, tin	17,136.0	grains, machinery, iron and steel	12,370.0	Japan, USA, Singapore, Hong Kong, W. Europe
Laos	forest products, electric power	58.5	foodstuffs, petroleum products, machinery	205.0	Thailand, Japan, Malaysia, Vietnam
Malaysia	forest products, petroleum products	20,771.0	machinery, transport equipment	16,585.0	Japan Singapore, USA, W. Europe
Myanmar (Burma)	agricultural products, ores	138.0	machinery, transport equipment	244.0	Singapore, Japan, W. Europe
Philippines	industrial machinery, textiles, forest and agricultural products	7,035.0	petroleum, industrial equipment, wheat	8,731.0	USA, Japan
Singapore	petroleum products, manufactured goods, electronics	39,305.0	machinery, manufactured goods, petroleum products	43,862.0	USA, Japan, Malaysia, Hong Kong, Thailand
Thailand	agricultural products, gemstones	11,546.0	machinery, fertilizer, petroleum products, chemicals	12,849.0	Japan, USA, Singapore, Malaysia, W. Europe, Hong Kong
Vietnam	agricultural products, coal, minerals	785.0	petroleum, steel products, raw cotton, fertilizer, grain	1,590.0	USSR, Singapore, Japan, E. Europe

Sources: *The 1990 Information Please Almanac* (Houghton Mifflin Company); *Universal Almanac, 1990* (Andrews and MacNeil).

the observance of Islam in Indonesia, where the people have absorbed elements of other faiths, tends to be more relaxed and more tolerant.

Political Influences   When an Indian ship captain came to a new locale, he often set up a trading post and married the daughter of a local chief. The chief's followers soon adopted South Asian customs and ideas, especially the idea of monarchy. Gradually a number of monarchies arose, a few inland, but mostly near coastal trade centers. One inland state was Funan, which was located in the southern part of present-day Cambodia. Another was Champa in the southern part of present-day Vietnam. But the greatest monarchy was the kingdom of Angkor in present-day Cambodia.

Khmers

Angkor was founded by a people called the Khmers (kuh-MERZ), who probably originated in India and southern China. The first written reference to them, which is found in the writings of a Chinese historian,

Khmer Migrations

This Khmer sculpture of a deva or divine warrior was made about 1100. This was just before the Khmer empire reached its peak in Cambodia.

places them north of Funan. The Khmers learned about Hindu culture from Indians and the skills of ironworking and rice cultivation from the Chinese. About A.D. 500, a Khmer ruler seized control of Funan. Over the next several centuries, the Khmers enlarged their territory. At the peak of Khmer development in the 1100s and 1200s, the Khmer Empire included present-day Thailand, Laos, and parts of Myanmar and Malaysia.

Khmer Society   Nobles and priests made up the ruling class. Next came the free middle and lower classes. At the bottom of the **social structure** were numerous slaves. The Khmers had a written language, built stone-surfaced roads, made tiles of lead, adorned their capital city of Angkor Thom with many sculptures, and built hospitals to care for the sick.

Their highly developed agricultural system was characterized by huge reservoirs that stored the excess waters of the wet monsoon period and by irrigation canals that distributed the stored waters for use during times of drought. In addition to rice, Khmer farmers grew a variety of fruits and vegetables.

The Khmer empire was noted for the high status that women achieved. Khmer women served as government officials and judges, were skilled doctors and astronomers, and handled most of the empire's trade. A Chinese visitor to Angkor Thom described how women merchants displayed their goods on straw mats from six in the morning until noon. The goods included textiles, silverwork, fish, and rice wine. The people used gold only for large transactions. For small transactions, payment was in grain.

Temple Architecture   The Khmers, who regarded their monarchs as divine, built royal temples in which the rulers' spirits could live after death. The largest and most remarkable of these temples is Angkor Wat, a Buddhist monastery built in the early 1100s. Every block of grey limestone in Angkor Wat is carved with battle scenes, royal portraits, men fishing, women dancing, Buddhas, or the Hindu god, Vishnu, to whom the temple was dedicated. Archaeologists believe that the Khmers transported the huge stones to the building site by ox-drawn carts.

But the Khmer empire faded and was gradually reduced to the size of modern Cambodia. Among probable reasons for the decline was a series of wars with the Thai and the Vietnamese, diseases, and weak leadership. In 1432 the capital was moved from Angkor Thom to the neighborhood of Phnom Penh (puh-NAHM PEN), the capital of Cambodia.

Westerners

During the 1500s Western Europeans came to Southeast Asia, attracted by the great profits to be made from the spice trade. They also introduced Christianity to the region. During the 1800s and early 1900s a second wave of Westerners arrived, driven mainly by **imperialism**, the desire for empire.

The Portuguese and the Spanish   The Portuguese came first in 1511. They captured and set up trading posts in the strategically located city-state of Malacca, a move that enabled the Portuguese to control trade through the Malacca Straits. In 1521, sailing under the Spanish flag, Ferdinand Magellan reached the Philippines. Once the conquest of the islands began 45 years later, Spanish rule lasted for more than 300 years. Under the Spanish, the Philippines became a Catholic country with numerous Catholic churches, monasteries, and convents. The Spanish also set up large estates that were owned by individuals or by religious groups. Filipino peasants worked the land, however, raising sugar cane and other crops.

The Dutch and the English   By the late 1500s Portuguese and Spanish power was on the decline in Western Europe and the power of the Netherlands and Great Britain was on the rise. The Dutch reached Java, a major island of present-day Indonesia, in 1596. The British arrived in Sumatra, also a part of present-day Indonesia, in 1602. For the next several decades, the two nations competed for Indonesia's riches, finally resolving their armed rivalry with a peace treaty that divided the Southeast Asian islands between them. The Dutch took over the Indonesian islands, which became known as the Dutch East Indies, and the British took over the Malay Peninsula and the island at its tip that became known as Singapore.

Today Singapore is one of the world's largest ports.

The Dutch traded in such local products as cloves and other spices. They also introduced the cultivation of sugar cane and coffee to the islands, reaping profits as high as 2,000 percent of their original investment. But the peasants who grew the crops remained poor. Moreover, the peasants were often forced into labor gangs and were so busy growing crops for export that they seldom had time to grow enough food for themselves. With such miserable labor conditions forced upon them, the islanders revolted against the Dutch several times. Each time, however, Dutch power prevailed.

The British controlled the Malay Peninsula and nearby islands in the same way that they controlled the South Asian subcontinent, ruling some monarchies directly and installing advisers in others. By the late 1800s, the Malay Peninsula was Great Britain's main source of tin and rubber. The British also turned the island of Singapore into a well-fortified naval base and made present-day Myanmar into a province of the British Empire.

The French   Although French missionaries reached Southeast Asia in the 1600s, the French made their main colonial inroads between 1862 and 1893 when they conquered Indochina, the peninsula that today includes the present-day nations of Laos, Cambodia, and Vietnam. Roman Catholicism became widespread, French became the language of instruction in public schools, and great rice and rubber plantations owned by French colonials and wealthy Southeast Asians were set up. Many peasants lost their lands and were forced to become low-paid day laborers farming the land or building railroads, highways, and port facilities. To

keep down opposition to their rule, the French organized a secret police and severely restricted freedom of speech and of the press.

The Americans   In 1898 the United States and Spain went to war over Spain's harsh treatment of its colonies. In the treaty following Spain's defeat in the Spanish-American war, the Philippines were awarded to the United States. During the war the Filipinos fought with the Americans against the Spanish. After the war, however, the Filipinos declared their independence under the leadership of Emilio Aguinaldo. Three years of bloody fighting between Filipino freedom fighters and the United States followed, ending with the capture of Aguinaldo in 1901. In 1916 the United States set up a Filipino legislature. By 1923 Filipinos held more than 90 percent of all government positions. In 1934 a Philippine government was established under the guidance of the United States, which promised and granted the nation full independence in 1946. During its caretaking period, however, the United States did nothing to change the system of land ownership and the power of wealthy landlords. As a result, the majority of Filipinos remained poor.

Rivers and canals are the roads in much of Asia. They are also where people live and do business. This is a market in Bangkok, the capital of Thailand.

The Independent Thai

The only nation of modern Southeast Asia that was never colonized by Westerners is Thailand. Formerly called Siam, Thailand takes its name from the Thai people who migrated to the region from southwestern China sometime about the A.D. 800s. The Thai intermingled with the Khmers, giving allegiance to the Khmers and even becoming soldiers in their armies. As the Thai became stronger and more numerous, however, they began to compete with the Khmers. About 1250, the Thai set up their own state, gradually expanding southward. As the Thai moved southward, they took their written language and some political ideas from the Khmers. The Thai also became Buddhists.

The Thai remained independent by playing the French and the British against each other. The Thai success in escaping the nets of Western **colonialism** was due largely to the efforts of King Mongkut (MAHNG-koot), who ruled the country from 1851 to 1868. A former Buddhist monk, Mongkut gave Thailand its first railroad, its first mint, and its first paved streets. Anna Leonowens, the British governess he hired to teach his children, was later the subject of a book that became a popular American musical and film, *The King and I*. Mongkut's son Chulalongkorn (1868–1910) continued the modernizing process by abolishing slavery, organizing an army and a civil service, and gearing the economy to producing rice for the world market.

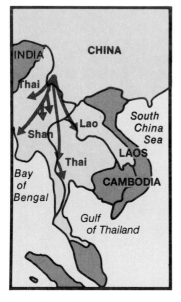

Thai Migrations

The Japanese

After World War II broke out in 1939, Southeast Asians came under the influence of the Japanese. After the Japanese attack on Pearl Harbor and the Philippines, the military leaders of Japan turned to Southeast Asia to make use of the region's rich resources of rubber, tin, and oil. Within six months, the Japanese had taken over all of Southeast Asia. At first

Japanese rule was welcomed by the peoples of Southeast Asia, who believed Japan's slogan, "Asia for the Asians," meant that changes would bring prosperity to many people in Southeast Asia. But when the Japanese turned out to be as greedy and exploitive as the Western colonizers had been under imperialism, Southeast Asian **guerrillas** began fighting the Japanese, especially in the Philippine Islands and in Indochina.

Most Southeast Asians were relieved when Japan surrendered in 1945, but their cheers did not mean they were willing to return to their prewar colonial status. Guerrilla fighters turned into independence fighters when Southeast Asians demanded self-government. Some peoples achieved independence with relatively little fighting, but others fought long and relentless battles before independence was granted.

SECTION 1 REVIEW

1. **Recall**   What evidence shows that the Khmers had a high degree of civilization?
2. **How and Why**   How did Western Europeans affect Southeast Asia?
3. **Critical Thinking**   Why was Thailand the only nation of Southeast Asia that was never colonized by a Western imperialist power?

Western imperialism helped create nationalism in Southeast Asia just as it had in the South Asian subcontinent. In both instances, an educated **elite** developed that was familiar with Western ideas about self-government and modernization. Even before the end of World War II, members of this educated elite became the leaders in the region's independence movements.

Indonesia

Sukarno, the leader of Indonesia's independence movement, started working for freedom as early as 1927 when he was a young engineering student. Because of his activities in support of nationalism, he spent about 13 years either in prison or in exile from his native land before the outbreak of World War II. During World War II he returned to the Indonesian islands and collaborated with the Japanese—all the while continuing to agitate for independence. After the war, the Dutch attempt to reassert control resulted in four years of fighting before the Dutch finally withdrew.

Sukarno became Indonesia's first president. Skeptical of **democracy**, he set up a government under which he appointed members of the legislature, provincial governors, and mayors. He also kept the press and

Jakarta, the capital of Indonesia, is an important port on the island of Java.

other media groups under tight control. At the same time, Sukarno promoted education and helped unify the country by making the Malay language of Bahasa Indonesia the nation's official language. He gave little thought to Indonesia's future, however, spending large sums of money on showy buildings and monuments. He preserved his political power by playing off the strong Communist Party against the military. Sukarno's rule came to an end in 1967, however, when the military led by General Suharto took over the country. Since 1969 Suharto has held the title of president and directed the country in a strong anti-Communist stance.

Suharto's rule has brought considerable stability to Indonesia, both in its politics and its economy. Suharto has encouraged foreign investments, especially in exploiting the nation's oil reserves, and has improved agricultural production. But the nation must still import food to feed its growing population. In addition, the economy has suffered because of Suharto's persecution of the nation's ethnic Chinese, who handle most of Indonesia's domestic trade.

The Philippines

Since the United States granted independence to the Philippines in 1946, the nation has passed through some troubling times. With the arrival of independence, the leading group of wartime guerrillas, which was Communist-led, became known as the People's Liberation Army, or Hukbalahap (HOOK-bah-lah-HAHP). The Huks, as the army was popularly called, organized the nation's tenant farmers and started a revolt in 1947. Ramon Magsaysay, who was president of the Philippines from 1953 until his death in a plane crash in 1957, and who had himself been a guerrilla during the Japanese occupation, finally put down the revolt. He then destroyed the Communists' main appeal to the nation's tenant farmers by breaking up many of the country's large sugar plantations and redistributing the land to the peasants.

In 1965 Ferdinand Marcos became president and ruled the Philippines until he was ousted by a revolt in 1986. Marcos's rule was marked by rampant corruption and by eight years of **martial law** (1972–1980) as a way of subduing opposition to his policies. In 1983 Marcos allowed his main political opponent, Benito Aquino (ak-KEE-noh) to return from exile. But as Aquino stepped off the plane that had brought him home, he was assassinated.

In 1986 Aquino's widow, Corazon (kor-ah-SOHN), ran against Marcos for the presidency. When it became obvious that the supporters of Marcos were stealing the election by force and by fraud, the nation's Catholic bishops called on the people to follow the "way of nonviolent struggle for justice." Carrying flowers and candles and led by priests and nuns, thousands of Filipinos took to the streets, urging the military to support them. When Marcos and his family fled the country, Corazon Aquino was sworn in as president. Since then, Aquino has renewed land reform programs. But her government has been hampered by Communist and Muslim opposition efforts to unseat her and by several failed military coup attempts.

Malaysia and Singapore

Following the end of World War II, Great Britain attempted to keep the Malay Peninsula and the northern part of the island of Borneo within the British Empire. The movement for independence, however, was too strong, and Malaysia was formed in 1963. Despite a strong economy that stemmed from rubber, tin, and iron ore resources and its geographic position as a leading trade center, Malaysia suffered from social disruptions among Malays, Indians, and the Chinese brought on by discrimination and **prejudice**.

When Malaysia became independent, the predominantly Malay government started discriminating against Chinese and Indians. The Malays resented the successful Chinese—who controlled the tin, rubber, and trucking industries—and considered them to be foreigners because they kept to themselves. The Malays, who were Muslims, disliked the Indians because they were Hindus. In addition, the Indians were the nation's moneylenders and merchants. The government decreed that the Chinese language could no longer be taught in schools, and it limited the number of Chinese and Indians in the civil service. It also stipulated that only Malays could own certain parcels of land. Finally in 1965, Malaysia insisted that Singapore, which was predominantly Chinese, become a separate nation.

Since separation, Malaysia has become a leader in the assembly of automobiles and exports cement, chemicals, textiles, and processed foods. The country has also experienced a number of riots led by Malay youths against the Indians and the Chinese.

Singapore, under the leadership of Lee Kuan Yew, has become a global economic center. Its duty-free port is the second busiest in the world. Its refineries process crude oil from Indonesia and other oil-rich nations, making Singapore the world's third biggest oil-refining center. In addition, Singapore's banking and insurance industry finances business ventures worldwide. The government emphasizes education and discourages industries that need large pools of unskilled labor. But the government is **authoritarian**, allowing little political opposition and controlling newspapers, radio, television, and the labor unions.

Vietnam

Ho Chi Minh, the leader of the Vietnamese independence movement, began working for his nation's freedom as a teen-ager in 1919. At that time he presented a petition calling for **self-determination** for colonial peoples to the peace conference that ended World War I. But instead of considering the petition, members of the peace conference had Ho Chi Minh thrown out of the room.

In 1930 Ho Chi Minh helped found the Indochina Communist Party. In 1941 he organized a group of nationalists called the Vietminh and carried on guerrilla warfare against the Japanese.

After Japan surrendered in 1945, Ho Chi Minh proclaimed the establishment of the Independent Democratic Republic of Vietnam. The French, who had reestablished themselves in southern Vietnam, promised to recognize North Vietnam as a free state within the French Union. But almost at once, they went back on their promise and attacked Ho Chi Minh's government. The French-Indochinese War lasted for seven and a half years. During that time, the United States—in an effort to contain the spread of communism—sent weapons and supplies to help the French. By 1954 when the French were finally defeated, the United States was paying more than 75 percent of France's military expenses in the war.

At the Geneva Conference in 1954, Vietnam was temporarily partitioned into the Democratic Republic of Vietnam, a Communist government under Ho Chi Minh, and the Republic of Vietnam, an anti-Communist government under Ngo Dinh Diem. But elections, which were scheduled for 1956 to reunite Vietnam under a single government, were never held because Diem refused to allow the elections to take place, fearing that Ho Chi Minh would win any nationwide election.

In 1957 the Communist-led Vietcong began guerrilla activity in South Vietnam. By the 1960s, the conflict had become a full-scale civil war as nationalists who wanted a united country, Buddhists who resented Catholic domination of government posts, and liberals who wanted land reform and freedom of the press sided with the guerrillas. The Soviet Union, the People's Republic of China, and other Communist countries supported the North Vietnamese and the Vietcong. The United States supported the South Vietnamese government, providing supplies and a fighting force that gradually built up to more than 500,000 soldiers. In the fighting, United States planes dropped more bombs on North

Vietnam than the Allies dropped on Germany during World War II. In an attempt to wipe out Vietcong hideouts, the military command also had the countryside sprayed with toxic chemicals that defoliated about 20 percent of South Vietnam's trees and crops. As a result, the nation changed from a rice exporter to a rice importer.

By 1973 an anti-war movement within the United States led to the withdrawal of American troops, but the fighting continued. In 1975, when the Saigon government surrendered to the Vietcong and the North Vietnamese, Vietnam was finally united. Saigon, the former capital of South Vietnam, became Ho Chi Minh City. The war cost the lives of at least 1.3 million people, including more than 56,000 Americans.

When the war ended, about one million Vietnamese fled the country. Some were South Vietnamese officials, but most were ethnic Chinese forced from the country for favoring free enterprise too much. They became known as "boat people" because many of them fled by sea to nearby nations. More than 600,000 refugees from South Vietnam have been resettled in the United States and another 100,000 in France. Many who fled are still living in refugee camps in Thailand and other Southeast Asian nations, hoping for permanent resettlement.

Since reunification, Vietnam has had to face many problems. The nation has suffered shortages of food, clothing, housing, and raw materials for its industries. The economy has continued to suffer despite some experiments in free enterprise that allowed some small private businesses to operate and villagers to grow crops for their own use and sale.

Ho Chi Minh led a successful Communist drive to oust the French from Indochina. What country became Ho's ally in 1949, supplying weapons and guerrilla training?

A man cleans a skull near a mass grave at the Chaung Ek camp in Cambodia. During the 1970s the Khmer Rouge leadership tortured and killed thousands of people to stay in power.

Cambodia and Laos

In 1953 Cambodia became independent of France. In 1955 Prince Narodom Sihanouk (SEE-hah-nook) became Cambodia's ruler, but the monarchy was overthrown in 1970. Fighting then broke out between the new pro-American government and Communist guerrillas known as the Khmer Rouge (ROOZH). In 1975 the Khmer Rouge took over Cambodia. The new government was headed by Pol Pot, a rigid Communist who considered trade to be evil. Accordingly he relocated all city-dwellers to rural areas to work as peasants. During the forced marches from city to countryside, one million Cambodians may have died, including many of Cambodia's educated people. The government discouraged the practice of religion and passed laws that required all people to dress alike.

In 1978 Vietnamese forces invaded Cambodia, defeating the Khmer Rouge and setting up a **puppet government** under Heng Samrin. By 1988, when the Vietnamese began withdrawing their troops, the United States, China, the Soviet Union, Prince Sihanouk, Heng Samrin, and the leaders of the Khmer Rouge entered into negotiations about Cambodia's new government. Political affairs in Cambodia in the 1990s, however, give little promise of peace and stability.

Laos, like Cambodia, became independent of France in 1953. For the next 20-odd years, the country was caught up in a civil war between government forces and the Communist Pathet Pao. In 1975 the Pathet Pao took control of the country. Since then, Laos has become self-sufficient in rice production. But its economic future is still uncertain.

Myanmar

The change of name from Burma to Myanmar in 1989 reflects one of the country's major problems—ethnic minorities. The name *Burma* reflected only the Burmese people even though major ethnic groups include the Chin, Kachin, Karen, and Shan peoples.

After World War II, like other Southeast Asian nations, Myanmar was briefly reoccupied by its colonial master, Great Britain. The British soon left, however, and in 1948 Myanmar became an independent republic. Since then minority and economic problems have led to several military takeovers, the most recent in 1988. The government nationalized industries, taking land and trade away from Chinese and Indian business people. The government also maintains a strict censorship of the press and frequently closes its borders to foreigners.

SECTION 2 REVIEW

1. **Recall**   Who was independent Indonesia's first ruler? Who succeeded him?
2. **How and Why**   How was Ferdinand Marcos overthrown in the Philippines?
3. **Critical Thinking**   Why have so many governments in Southeast Asia been prone to takeovers by the military or other authoritarian leaders?

Southeast Asian artistic development was largely influenced by the civilization of the Indian subcontinent. Local artists then adapted the Indian culture to suit their own needs. Southeast Asian artists have continued to be influenced by foreign styles but have kept a quality that is distinctive of Southeast Asia.

Arts and Crafts

The Vietnamese and the people of Myanmar are known for their fine lacquer ware—articles such as boxes, trays, dishes, and furniture that are covered with many layers of black varnish made from the resin of certain trees and then illustrated with pictures of many colors. The Indonesians and the Malaysians make beautiful patterns on cloth by a method called batik (buh-TEEK). Wax or rice paste is placed on cloth to keep dye from reaching certain parts. The cloth is then dyed and a pattern is formed by the dye's reaching only the uncovered parts of the cloth. Different shades of color can be obtained by repeating the process. The cloth is finally boiled to remove the wax.

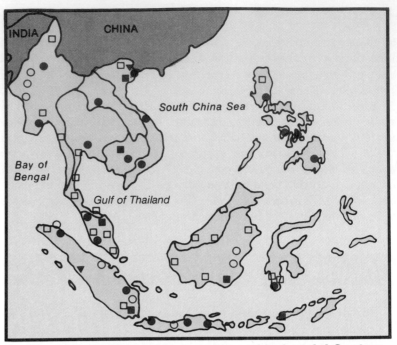

Southeast Asia Natural Resources and Industrial Centers

● Industrial Centers ▼ Coal ■ Iron ○ Oil □ Minerals

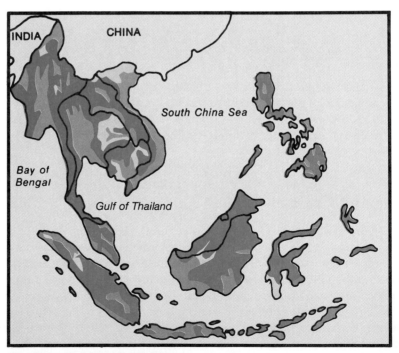

Southeast Asia Land Use

▨ Farming ▨ Forestry ▢ Grazing

In the Philippines, a delicate cloth is made from pineapple fibers. People throughout Southeast Asia weave palm leaves, bamboo, and other plants into baskets, mats, hats, and other goods for everyday use. The people of Myanmar create wall hangings known as kalaga. These wall hangings usually portray scenes from the life of Buddha or animals such as elephants and parrots. The artisans use thousands of multi-colored sequins, glass beads, and silk threads in their designs. The Thai are excellent woodcarvers. Their sculptures of cats and elephants, in either a reddish or a white-grained wood, are particularly attractive.

Music, Dance, and Drama

Traditional folk, religious, and court music remains strong throughout Southeast Asia. Music, dance, and drama are combined to portray legends or historical events. Many dances are based on stories from the *Ramayana*. Some dances have magical themes. For example, on Bali there is a dance that describes a battle between a witch and a dragon. The dances are formal, with every movement and gesture expressing a meaning. The musical instruments used are mostly gongs, drums, xylophones, and other percussion instruments.

Puppet plays are popular in many parts of Southeast Asia, especially Indonesia. These plays use local and religious characters to tell tales based on Hindu legends and, more recently, on political events. Puppet plays are often performed at birth and wedding celebrations that usually last all night long. The puppets made of leather or wood are intricately carved and painted. Light from an oil lamp throws their shadows on a screen. Traditionally men sit in front of the screen where they see all the vivid colors of the puppets, while women sit behind the screen where they see only the shadows.

Social Patterns

Southeast Asians live in extended families. Girls are raised to be wives and mothers. Young men usually accept the wishes of their parents regarding a marriage mate.

A spirit of helpfulness is a major characteristic of Southeast Asians. The spirit has stemmed from the environment, traditions, and religion. From earliest times, Southeast Asians have tried to resolve social conflicts through adjustment and **compromise**. They prefer working together to competition against one another. People also join in constructing community buildings, schools, and clinics and in building roads, dams, and irrigation canals. They help one another put up houses, cultivate fields, and find suitable mates for their children. When the dikes of a river burst because of flooding, people come from many villages to repair the damage. At funerals, births, and in the many religious and national festivals, people are ready to assist wherever they are needed.

irrigation canals:
deep cuts in the ground to carry water to crops

These students attend school in Laos. Many schools have been started since 1946. Educational opportunities, however, remain limited.

Like people elsewhere, Southeast Asians have found confusing the changes that modernization has brought to their customs and traditions. For example, at village meetings young representatives of the central government urge, and sometimes command, villagers to plant new crops and to make these crops part of their diets, thus changing their eating habits. Young people are encouraged to speak up before their elders, people are urged to limit the number of children they have, and families are told to send their girls to school along with the boys. But it is hard for older people to understand why many departures from custom and tradition are necessary. Without an understanding of the reason behind the changes, people resist modernization. As a result, modernization in less developed nations often takes place slowly.

SECTION 3 REVIEW

1. **Recall** What is batik?
2. **How and Why** Why is cooperation important to the people of Southeast Asia?
3. **Critical Thinking** Why is the ability to accept change a key element in the modernization of Southeast Asia?

Chapter 9

R E V I E W

Reviewing People, Places, and Things

Identify, define, or explain each of the following:

Myanmar

Hoabinhians

animism

Luzon

Angkor

Khmers

Phnom Penh

Ferdinand Magellan

Emilio Aguinaldo

Sukarno

Ferdinand Marcos

Corazon Aquino

Ho Chi Minh

Khmer Rouge

batik

puppet plays

Map Study

Using the map on page 190, answer the following questions on a separate sheet of paper.

1. What symbol is used to indicate industrial centers in Southeast Asia?

2. What generalization can you make about the location of oil resources in Southeast Asia?

3. a. What land use is the greatest in Southeast Asia? b. Which is the least?

Understanding Ideas

1. In what areas of Southeast Asia was the Chinese influence felt most strongly?

2. Who were the Trung sisters?

3. How did India influence the culture of Southeast Asia?

4. a. What group of people were noted for the high status women achieved? b. Why did these people build royal temples?

5. What makes Thailand different from other nations in the region?

6. Which country of Southeast Asia is presently ruled by a woman?

7. a. Why did the Vietnamese fight the French after 1945? b. What agreement was reached in 1954 concerning Vietnam?
   c. Why were elections never carried out?
   d. What was the result of the civil war between North and South Vietnam?

8. How is modernization affecting Southeast Asian village life?

Developing Critical Thinking

Forming a Generalization   A generalization is a conclusion reached after analyzing data. It pulls together common themes or ideas behind a series of facts or examples. For example, a generalization that can be derived from the chart on page 137 in this unit is as follows: The majority of people in Laos earn their living through agriculture because only 15 percent of the people live in urban areas.

Activity: Using the natural resources and land use maps on page 190 and the table of exports and imports on page 179, form a generalization about the relationship of raw materials to a country's economic growth.

Writing About History

Relating Past to Present   Choose a nation of Southeast Asia and trace the historical events behind current news stories about it. In your essay, show how the past influences the present in one or more areas of the country's life. If possible, illustrate your essay with excerpts and photographs from current news stories.

Applying Your Skills

Making a Chart   Look up in a world almanac, the population density (number of people living per square mile) for each nation in Southeast Asia. Use the data to make a chart, arranging the nations in order from the one with the fewest people per square mile to the one with the most people per square mile.

SOUTH AND SOUTHEAST ASIA

Reviewing Facts

1. What makes the Indo-Gangetic Plain an important agricultural area?
2. What is the dominant climatic factor in South and Southeast Asia?
3. What is Sikhism?
4. What are the caste divisions?
5. What economic and social changes did the British bring to South Asia?
6. What caused a rise in the middle class in South Asia?
7. What three major problems face India today?
8. What was the status of women in the Khmer empire?
9. Who was the leader of the Vietnamese independence movement?
10. What do much of the music, dance, and drama of Southeast Asia portray?

Understanding Main Ideas

1. Why do economists classify the countries of South and Southeast Asia as developing nations?
2. **a.** How do Hinduism and Buddhism differ? **b.** How do Hinduism and Islam differ?
3. Why is the period of the Gupta dynasty known as the Golden Age of Indian culture?
4. How did Mahatma Gandhi work for the freedom of his people from the British?
5. In general, how have Southeast Asians reacted to the changes that modernization has brought to their customs and traditions?

Applying Chronology Skills

Study the timeline below and answer the questions that follow.

Chronology of South and Southeast Asian History

1946	— Philippine independence
1947	— India independence Pakistan independence
1948	— Myanmar independence
1949	— Indonesia independence
1953	— Cambodia independence Laos independence
1963	— Malaysia independence
1965	— Singapore independence
1974	— Bangladesh independence

1. Which country in South and Southeast Asia was the first to gain independence?
2. How many years after Malaysia gained independence did Singapore gain independence?
3. How many years after Pakistan gained independence did Bangladesh gain independence?

Making Connections

Understanding Sociology Study the table on page 137 showing the population and area (in square miles) of countries in South and Southeast Asia. Calculate the population density of the countries using the following formula: population ÷ area (in square miles) =

people per square mile. Then write a generalization about the population density of the countries in South and Southeast Asia.

Understanding the Humanities

Comparing Drama Forms   Compare the following aspects of a puppet play in Indonesia to the aspects of a puppet play in the United States: themes, construction of puppets, lighting, and audience seating.

Developing Critical Thinking

1. Identifying Cause and Effect   Why were Western Europeans interested in colonizing South and Southeast Asia?

2. Supporting an Opinion   From what you have learned about South and Southeast Asia, which countries have the greatest possibility of becoming developed nations? Explain your answer.

Using Sources

Mahatma Gandhi was educated in an English university. In the following excerpt, Gandhi criticizes the basis of western civilization. Read the excerpt, and then answer the questions that follow:

...It has been stated that, as men progress, they shall be able to travel in airships and reach any part of the world in a few hours. Men will not need the use of their hands and feet. They will press a button, and they will have their clothing by their side. They will press another button, and they will have their newspaper. A third, and a motor-car will be in waiting for them. They will have a variety of delicately dished up food. Everything will be done by machinery.... This is civilization. Formerly, men worked in the open air only as much as

they liked. Now thousands of workmen meet together and...work in factories or mines. Their condition is worse than that of beasts. They are obliged to work, at the risk of their lives, at most dangerous occupations, for the sake of millionaires. Formerly men were made slaves under physical compulsion. Now they are enslaved by temptation of money and of the luxuries that money can buy....

1.   According to Gandhi, why won't men need the use of their hands and feet?

2.   How are men enslaved by civilization?

Extension Activities

1. Making a Map   Research information to make an industrial-products map of South and Southeast Asia. Include the cities that are major industrial centers and a map key.

2. Making a Diagram   Research batik as a method of hand-printing cloth. Make a diagram illustrating each step in the batik method.

Read More About History and Culture

Adams, John, and Igbal, Sabila. *Exports, Politics & Economic Development: Pakistan, 1970–1982.* Boulder, Colo.: Westview Press, 1983.

Basham, A. L. *The Wonder That Was India.* Lawrence, Mass.: Merrimack Book Service, 1983. Indian history and civilization. Illustrated.

Duft, Ashok K. *Southeast Asia: Realm of Contrasts.* Boulder, Colo.: Westview Press, 1983. Differences among Southeast Asian nations.

Franda, Marcus. *Bangladesh: The First Decade.* Columbia, Mo.: South Asia Books, 1982. One of the world's least developed nations.

Hahn, Emily. *The Islands.* New York: Coward, McCann & Geoghegan, 1981. American imperialism in the Philippines.

Karnow, Stanley. *Vietnam: A History.* New York: Viking Press, 1983. One thousand years of history.

EAST ASIA

Love of nature is often expressed in East Asian art. These trees were painted on a silk screen by a Japanese artist. His name was Nonomura Sotatsu, and he painted from about 1600 to 1630. Many Japanese and Chinese artists of this period painted on folding screens and sliding panels. Sliding panels are still used instead of doors in many homes in Japan.

The Environment

The culture region of East Asia includes the People's Republic of China, Mongolia, North Korea, South Korea, the Republic of China (Taiwan), and Japan. The region also includes the British crown colony of Hong Kong, which is scheduled to become part of the People's Republic of China in 1997. East Asia has about 8 percent of the world's total land area and a little more than 25 percent of the world's population. More than two-thirds of the people of East Asia live in rural areas. Nonetheless, with at least 18 cities having populations greater than 2 million, East Asia has the largest urban population in the world. As the most populated city in the world, Shanghai in the People's Republic of China has nearly 11 million inhabitants.

Physically, East Asia is separated from the rest of the Asian continent by high mountains and barren deserts. As a result, the civilizations of East Asia developed independently of civilizations in other culture regions.

As you study this chapter, think about these questions:

- What are the major landforms and natural resources of East Asia?

- What factors have affected where people in East Asia live?

- Why has the standard of living changed in East Asia in recent years?

Rice farming is a major source for food in many valleys of East Asia.

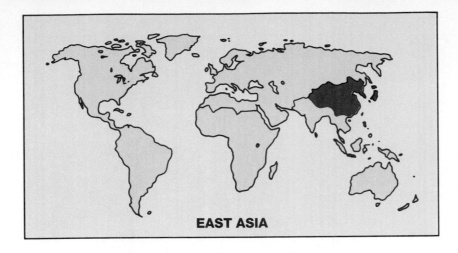

EAST ASIA

The culture region of East Asia covers about 4.5 million square miles (11.7 million square kilometers). Mainland East Asia includes that part of the Eurasian landmass that is south of the Soviet Union, and on which are located the People's Republic of China, Mongolia, North Korea, and South Korea. Off-shore East Asia includes two island nations— Japan, which is located on a series of volcanic islands that lie east of the Korean Peninsula, and the Republic of China on the island of Taiwan. Hereafter, to avoid confusion over the similarity of names, *China* will be used in referring to the People's Republic of China on the mainland, while *Taiwan* will be used in referring to the Republic of China.

The Mainland

Much of the East Asian mainland has a rugged landscape that is dominated by plateaus surrounded by mountain ranges, through which rivers have carved pathways to the sea. Lowlands, or plains, so important as farming areas, exist along river banks, on narrow bands along the coast, in northeastern China on the Manchurian Plain, and farther south in China on the North China Plain. The islands of East Asia, as the tips of mountains rising from the seafloor, also have a rugged landscape and few lowlands.

Mountains, Plateaus, and Deserts   The Himalayas form much of the southern border of East Asia. North of the Himalayas is the Plateau of Tibet, which averages in elevation between 10,000 and 16,000 feet (3 050–4 900 meters) above sea level. Northward from the Plateau of Tibet a series of mountain ranges rise, interspersed with plateau areas, basins, and deserts. One of these deserts is the Takla Makan. The name *Takla Makan* means "Go in and you won't come out" in the Turkic language, and the desert lives up to its name. Another desert east of the Plateau of Mongolia is the Gobi.

(Continued on page 202).

199

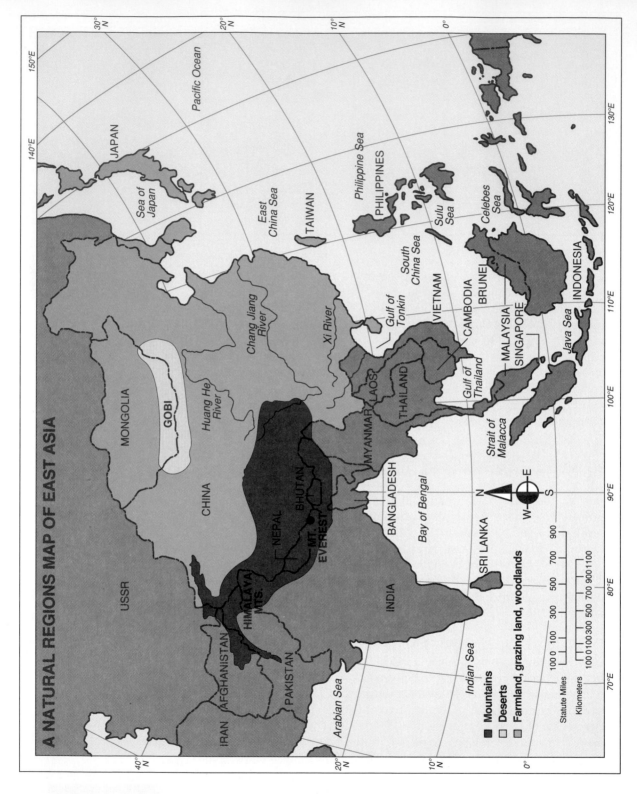

A NATURAL REGIONS MAP OF EAST ASIA

USSR

MONGOLIA

GOBI

CHINA

Huang He River

Chang Jiang River

Xi River

JAPAN

Sea of Japan

Pacific Ocean

East China Sea

TAIWAN

Philippine Sea

PHILIPPINES

Sulu Sea

Celebes Sea

South China Sea

Gulf of Tonkin

VIETNAM

LAOS

MYANMAR

THAILAND

CAMBODIA

Gulf of Thailand

BRUNEI

MALAYSIA

SINGAPORE

INDONESIA

Java Sea

Strait of Malacca

AFGHANISTAN

PAKISTAN

HIMALAYA MTS.

NEPAL

BHUTAN

MT. EVEREST

BANGLADESH

INDIA

IRAN

SRI LANKA

Bay of Bengal

Arabian Sea

Indian Sea

30° N

20° N

10° N

0°

40° N

20° N

10° N

0°

150°E

140°E

130°E

120°E

110°E

100°E

90°E

80°E

70°E

N

W   E

S

Mountains

Deserts

Farmland, grazing land, woodlands

Statute Miles

100 0 100   300   500   700   900

Kilometers

100 0 100 300 500 700 900 1100

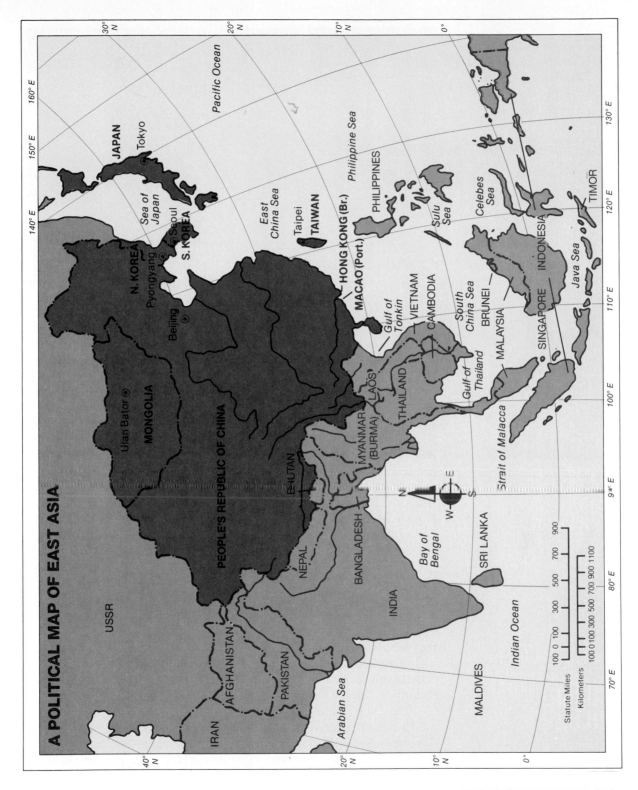

A POLITICAL MAP OF EAST ASIA

USSR

IRAN
AFGHANISTAN
PAKISTAN

MONGOLIA
Ulan Bator ⊛

PEOPLE'S REPUBLIC OF CHINA

Beijing ⊛

N. KOREA
Pyongyang ⊛
Seoul ⊛
S. KOREA

JAPAN
Tokyo ⊛

Sea of Japan

Pacific Ocean

East China Sea

Taipei
TAIWAN

HONG KONG (Br.)
MACAO (Port.)

Philippine Sea

PHILIPPINES

Sulu Sea

Celebes Sea

BHUTAN
NEPAL
BANGLADESH

INDIA

MYANMAR (BURMA)

LAOS
THAILAND

VIETNAM
CAMBODIA

Gulf of Tonkin

Gulf of Thailand

South China Sea

BRUNEI
MALAYSIA

SINGAPORE

INDONESIA

Java Sea

TIMOR

MALDIVES

SRI LANKA

Bay of Bengal

Arabian Sea

Indian Ocean

Strait of Malacca

N
W E
S

Statute Miles
100 0 100   300   500   700   900

Kilometers
100 0 100 300 500 700 900 1100

30° N
20° N
10° N
0°

40° N
20° N
10° N
0°

70° E
80° E
90° E
100° E
110° E
120° E
130° E
140° E
150° E
160° E

The Great Wall of China winds across northern China for about 1,500 miles (2 400 kilometers). It was built to keep out invaders from central Asia.

Some 2,000 years ago, a great trade route ran from one oasis city to another around the Takla Makan Desert. The route was called the Silk Road because the main product that moved over it from East Asia to the lands around the Mediterranean Sea in the west was silk. Tea, jewels, furs, and spices were other goods sent westward by East Asian traders. Goods from the West that reached China included glass, wool, linen, ivory, and especially horses and gold. Some cities along the Silk Road, such as the Chinese cities of Kashgar and Changan, now Xian (shee-AHN), are still flourishing. Other oasis cities disappeared, probably because the sources of water that supplied their wells dried up.

Major River Systems   Three great river systems dominate China. From north to south they are the Huang He (hoo-AHNG-huh), the Chang Jiang (CHANG JYAHNG), and the Xi (SHEE). All three rise in the western highlands and flow in a generally eastward direction.

The Huang He, which is generally not navigable, carries large amounts of yellowish soil, and historically in the West has been known as the Yellow River. The Chinese refer to it as China's Sorrow because of the difficulty it has caused for China's people over the centuries. As North China's soil washed into the river, the riverbed built up, raising the level of the river above the land. To contain the river, the Chinese built higher and higher dikes. But in heavy rains, the dikes weakened and broke, sending floods over the countryside that destroyed lives, homes, and crops and that often changed the river's course.

The Chang Jiang, also known as the Yangtze (YANG-SEE), forms the fourth longest river system in the world. Only the Nile in Africa, the Amazon River system in South America, and the Mississippi-Missouri system in North America are longer. About half of China's people live in the drainage basin of the Chang Jiang, which is commonly called the "land of rice and fish" because it contains most of China's farmland.

(Continued on page 204.)

Using GEOGRAPHY Skills

Understanding Latitude and Longitude

On this drawing of a globe, you can see lines drawn from the North Pole to the South Pole, and other lines drawn east to west. Look at the north-south lines. These are lines of **longitude**, or meridians, and they measure the distance east or west of the prime meridian. The east-west lines are drawn parallel to the equator. There are lines of **latitude**, or parallels, and they measure the distance north or south of the equator.

Lines of latitude and longitude are divided into degrees (°). These measures of degrees are shown on maps and globes.

Using the longitude and latitude on the map, answer the following questions:

1. What settlement is located at approximately 15°N and 121°E?

2. What is the location of Pondicherry?

3. What direction would a ship travel to go from 22°N 89°E to 8°S 98°E?

4. Using latitude and longitude, give directions to get from Batavia to Goa.

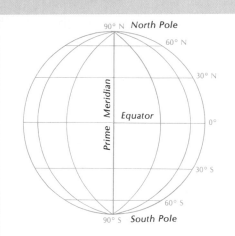

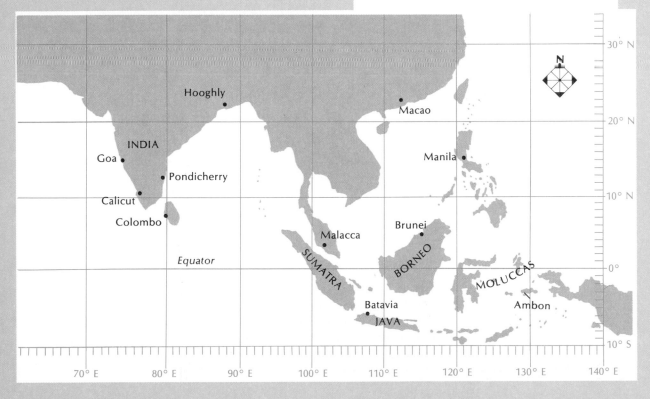

Navigable for almost 700 miles (1 100 kilometers) from Shanghai at its mouth, the Chang Jiang is a major transportation route.

The Xi River drains the southern part of China, flowing from its source through rugged terrain for nearly 1,700 miles (2 700 kilometers). The port of Guangzhou (GWANG-JOH), formerly Canton, is located near the river's mouth. Like the Chang Jiang, the lower stretch of the Xi is navigable, making it an important transportation route.

The Climate   The lands drained by the Chang Jiang and the Xi form a part of China known as South China. Here the climate is mostly subtropical, allowing at least two crops of rice to be grown the year round. The area drained by the Huang He and extending northward is called North China. The climate is colder, has four distinct seasons of the year, and the growing season is no longer than three to five months. West of North China, the climate is semiarid. Because rainfall is unpredictable and generally under 20 inches (51 centimeters) a year, grazing is the chief land use. The rest of the mainland is either desert or highland where climate depends on elevation.

Natural Resources   The mainland of East Asia contains a variety of natural resources. China, in particular, has large reserves of coal, oil, and iron ore. Other natural resources found on the mainland include tungsten, manganese, and other minerals. Except for the Korean Peninsula, however, the East Asian mainland contains only a small amount of forestland. Over the centuries, the people on the mainland cut down their forests for fuel. In recent years, China's government leaders have encouraged the planting of rows of poplar trees along the roads in an effort to block dust storms from the Gobi.

Fast-flowing rivers and waterfalls in the highland areas of the region are potential sources of hydroelectric power. Unfortunately, except in North Korea, most of these potential sources are too distant from centers of population to be developed.

Because level land is scarce, farmers cultivate every bit of soil they can. They plant crops up to the edge of the roads, and dig terraces up the hillsides and mountain slopes. The farming plots are usually small, and much of the work, especially in China, is done by hand.

The Islands

The main island nations of East Asia are Taiwan and Japan. Volcanic in origin, the islands are the tips of mountains that rise from the seafloor. With much of the East Asian mainland, they share a scarcity of level land for the location of cities and towns and for farming.

Oceanic Influences   Islands have climates that are influenced by winds blowing over ocean waters. Many of East Asia's islands, including Taiwan and Japan, are influenced by violent tropical storms called typhoons that are similar to hurricanes. Most typhoons occur between July and October and cause great damage to boats at sea and to coastal areas in their paths.

Japan is the leading fishing nation in the world. The coastline of Japan has many natural harbors that make safe ports for fishing vessels to unload their catch. Ocean currents around Japan, as well as the wide continental shelf off the East Asian mainland, create favorable fishing grounds. The Japanese also harvest seaweed—an excellent source of iodine and vitamins—and pearls. The western coast of Taiwan contains numerous ponds where farmers practice aquaculture, or fish farming. In addition, many Taiwanese make their living by fishing the ocean waters.

Seismic Influences   As part of the "Pacific Ring of Fire," the band of islands formed from volcanic action and earthquakes, the islands are also subject to **tsunamis**, waves caused by undersea earthquakes that travel long distances at high speeds until they strike land with great force. A tsunami may speed through the ocean at 400 miles per hour and strike the shoreline with waves that reach as high as 100 feet or more. The threat of earthquakes has other consequences as well. Buildings, especially high-rise buildings, must be constructed in such a way that a severe earthquake will cause little structural damage.

In Japan the volcanic nature of the islands has resulted in thousands of hot springs, around which health and pleasure resorts have been built. In some areas, the Japanese use steam from the springs to heat schools, police stations, village halls, and other public buildings.

This picture shows a bamboo forest near the city of Kyoto, Japan. Some kinds of bamboo grow to a height of 120 feet (36 meters). Others may grow only a few feet (meters).

SECTION 1 REVIEW

1. **Recall**   What are the major landforms of East Asia?
2. **How and Why**   Why is the Chang Jiang a major transportation route?
3. **Critical Thinking**   Why is Japan the leading fishing nation in the world?

E ast Asians have lived in villages for thousands of years. There are hundreds of thousands of villages in East Asia. However, for centuries East Asians have also known the conveniences of city life. Some East Asian cities are among the largest in the world.

Village Life

Over two-thirds of the people in East Asia live in rural areas. A village is frequently a network of tiny lanes and alleys that wind through closely packed houses. The narrow lanes permit only the passage of people and their animals. Some villages, particularly in Japan and southern China, are laid out in rows on one or both sides of a river, canal, or road. The roads are usually dirt.

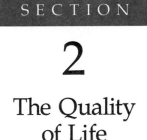

SECTION

2

The Quality of Life

The older houses in East Asia are made of mud bricks and have a tile or straw roof. Newer houses are made of clay bricks or stone and have a tile roof. Some villages have constructed apartment buildings. Rooms are small and few in all the housing. Most houses have electricity.

Just as in South and Southeast Asia, the desire for consumer goods and the increase in a cash economy are changing village life in East Asia. Most families have enough food and clothing, and own a sewing machine, a bicycle, and a radio. Some families even own television sets and other small appliances. News about the outside world has changed the villagers' expectations of what life can bring.

NATIONAL PROFILES/EAST ASIA						
Nation/Capital	Population/ Area (in sq mi)	Urban Population (as % of total)	Per Capita GNP (in U.S. $)	Adult Literacy Rate (%)	Life Expectancy	Population Growth Rate* (%)
China, People's Republic of/ Beijing	1,119,877,000/ 3,705,390	21	330	77	68	1.4
Japan/Tokyo	123,638,000/143,750	77	21,040	99	79	0.4
Mongolia/Ulan Bator	2,160,000/604,247	52	**	90	65	2.8
North Korea/Pyongyang	21,293,000/46,540	64	**	95	70	2.1
South Korea/Seoul	42,789,000/38,025	70	3,530	95	68	1.0
Taiwan/Taipei	20,219,000/13,885	97	**	92	76	1.2

Sources: *The 1990 Information Please Almanac* (Houghton Mifflin Company); *1990 World Population Data Sheet* (Population Reference Bureau, Inc., Washington D.C.)
 *A nation with a population growth rate of 2% or more doubles its population within 35 years or less.
**Not available.

The Largest Cities in East Asia

Even though East Asia is mostly rural, it has the largest urban population in the world. At least 18 cities in East Asia have populations greater than 2 million.

Housing shortages are common in much of urban East Asia. Most urban families live in apartments or houses of three rooms or less. In Japan, rapid industrial development has produced overcrowding and pollution problems. In Chinese cities two families must often share an apartment. Most homes in the cities have electricity, heat, and indoor plumbing. City people who can afford more space live in high-rise apartments or in single-family houses.

China's major cities are centers of industry. They are mostly located along the coast, along the Chang Jiang, or on the Manchurian Plain. These areas are near rail and sea transportation and raw materials. The port city of Shanghai has about 11 million people. The capital city of Beijing has almost 8 million people.

Japan's largest city is its capital city, Tokyo, which has over 8 million people. Three other Japanese cities—Yokohama, Osaka, and Nagoya— have more than 2 million people each. These cities are located in Japan's industrial area, and they form the Tokaido **megalopolis**—one of the world's most populous metropolitan areas. Nearly half of the Japanese population resides in this area.

The largest city in Korea is Seoul, the capital of South Korea. Seoul is an industrial and cultural center with a population of about 7 million. Other large cities in Korea include Pusan, in South Korea, and Pyongyang (pee-AWNG-YAHNG), the capital of North Korea. These cities have populations of about 2.5 million. Pusan is a major port city and a center of fishing and shipbuilding. Pyongyang, like Seoul, is a center of industry, culture, and government.

The largest city in Taiwan is its capital, Taipei. Taipei has many industries and a population of about 2 million. Mongolia's largest city is its capital, Ulan Bator, which has a population of about 400,000. This city has livestock-related industries and is the country's transportation center.

Hong Kong has a world famous harbor. The population of Hong Kong is over 4.5 million. Many of these people are refugees from mainland China. Overcrowding is a serious problem in Hong Kong, and has caused a great housing shortage.

Public transportation is another problem in Hong Kong.

Chinese artists often painted on scrolls. This painting, Plum Blossoms, *was painted on silk. Many families did not display their scrolls on their walls, but kept them rolled up in a safe place. From time to time the scrolls would be brought out for a leisurely viewing.*

A Rising Standard of Living

East Asia has become increasingly developed. This has caused the living standards throughout East Asia to rise. Japan is a developed nation. The Japanese have a high standard of living by world standards. Income is distributed fairly evenly. Nearly 90 percent of all Japanese consider themselves in the middle-income range. Workers at Japan's large companies have jobs guaranteed to them for their working life, and they enjoy many benefits.

The Taiwanese standard of living has been increased both by the country's rapid industralization and by a land-reform program. This program gave land to those who farmed it. South Korea has become increasingly prosperous. However, in South Korea, despite land reforms similar to Taiwan's, there still exists a group of landless peasants who farm for landlords.

The developing nations of China, Mongolia, and North Korea have also improved their people's standard of living. At present, however, these countries lack the capital to offer their people much more than enough to meet their basic needs.

SECTION 2 REVIEW

1. **Recall**   About how many people in East Asia live in rural areas?

2. **How and Why**   Why is village life changing in East Asia?

3. **Critical Thinking**   Why is the standard of living in China, Mongolia, and North Korea much lower than the standard of living in Japan and Taiwan?

Chapter 10

R E V I E W

Reviewing People, Places, and Things

Identify, define, or explain each of the following:

Himalayas	tsunamis
Takla Makan	Shanghai
Gobi	Beijing
Huang He	Tokyo
Xi	megalopolis
Guangzhou	Seoul
typhoons	Pyongyang
Pacific Ring of Fire	Taipei

Map Study

Using the map on pages 200 and 201, answer the following questions:

1. What countries contain the Gobi?
2. What countries border the Sea of Japan?
3. What countries border the USSR?
4. Which country in East Asia is the largest?
5. What is the main natural feature of East Asia?

Understanding Ideas

1. Why was the trade route that ran from one oasis city to another around the Takla Makan Desert called the Silk Road?
2. Why is the Huang He known as China's Sorrow?
3. Why are the Chang Jiang and the Xi River important transportation routes?
4. Why is it difficult to develop the potential sources of hydroelectric power in most of East Asia?
5. How has rapid industrialization affected Japan?

Developing Critical Thinking

1. **Comparing and Contrasting** Making comparisons among world regions or among countries within regions is an important part of studying world history. When you compare ideas, facts, causes, or effects, you are looking for similarities. When you contrast them, you are looking for differences. Sometimes comparisons or contrasts are directly stated. More often, however, you have to infer, or interpret, differences and similarities. Often putting information into a chart or a table can help.

   Activity: Study the chart on page 206. Then write six questions about the chart that compare and contrast the economic and social statistics of countries in East Asia. You might also make a bar graph using the statistics of countries in East Asia.

2. **Expressing an Opinion** The use of television and radio has brought news about the outside world to small villages in East Asia. This has changed the villagers' expectations of what life can bring. Do you think this change is good or bad? Explain your answer.

Applying Your Skills

1. **Using Statistics** Using an almanac, make a table comparing the populations of the ten largest United States cities and the ten largest East Asian cities.

2. **Writing a Report** Many East Asian countries are often hit by typhoons. Find information and write a report on the ways in which typhoons affect the people of Japan. Find out which areas of Japan typhoons affect.

The Chinese government and culture is centered in Beijing.

Traditional China

China covers almost 3.7 million square miles, (9.6 million square kilometers) and has a population greater than 1.2 billion, a figure that represents 25 percent of the world's total population. For the most part, Chinese culture developed independently from other cultures because of China's vast size and the mountains, deserts, forests, and ocean that formed protective barriers around it.

For centuries, the Chinese thought of their country as the center of the world and thought of themselves as culturally superior to all other peoples. They called their country Chung Kuo (JUHNG GWOH), or the Middle Kingdom. Among other things, the Chinese invented silk, paper, printing, paper money, the compass, and gunpowder. Knowledge of China spread to other peoples who borrowed the Chinese writing system, their form of government, styles of architecture, city layouts, and other elements of culture. But the Chinese thought that little from the outside world was worth borrowing.

Then in the 1800s with the coming of the Europeans to East Asia, the Chinese learned that centuries of isolation from the outside world had created a stagnant culture and that other peoples had surpassed them in many technological and cultural achievements.

As you study this chapter, think about these questions:

- How have Confucianism, Daoism, and Buddhism influenced China's development?

- How has Chinese culture influenced other parts of East Asia?

Chinese civilization developed in the highlands of the Huang He valley about 4500 B.C. The people grew wheat and millet, and raised pigs and cattle. They also fished and hunted wild game. Because wood was scarce, they built their houses of rammed earth. Kilns for making pottery were located to the east of the houses, while a cemetery was located to the north.

The Chinese say that their first dynasty started around 2000 B.C. and lasted until about 1766 B.C. It was called the Xia (shee-AH) dynasty. We know of the Xia dynasty chiefly through legends. No archaeological proof of it has been uncovered so far. However, ever since, the Chinese have divided their history into dynasties.

The dynasties followed a similar pattern. Each dynasty would set up a strong central government. It would help farmers by redistributing land and by building roads and canals. After several centuries, the dynasty would start to weaken. Government corruption would increase, taxes would go up, and the growth of population would outstrip the growth of the economy. After a while, the dynasty would be overthrown, either by rebels or by invaders. Then the pattern would be repeated.

Shang Dynasty (1766–1122 B.C.)

The first great historical dynasty, the Shang, arose in China around 1766 B.C. and lasted until 1122 B.C. Written records from this period reveal that the Chinese lived under a ruler who combined religious and political duties.

rammed:
pounded or compacted

Silk-making remained a Chinese secret for about 3,000 years. This scroll shows one stage of the process, pressing the silk. The scroll itself is silk.

The writing system the Shang developed contained about 3,000 pictographs; that is, each character represented an object. Over the centuries the Chinese added about 47,000 ideographic characters, each of which stood for an idea or a sound.

In Anyang (AHN-yahng), a major Shang city, archaeologists have dug up thousands of tortoise shells and ox bones carved with characters of Shang writing. The shells and bones are known as **oracle bones**. The Shang king would question the gods about such things as the weather, the next harvest, and the possible outcome of a military expedition. The priest would heat the oracle bone until cracks appeared on its surface. The priest would interpret the cracks as meaning "yes," "no," or "undecided." Then he would carve or write the question and the answer on the surface of the bone.

The Chinese writing system that developed from the Shang system helped unify the Chinese people. Although they spoke different dialects, they used the same script for writing. On the other hand, the large number of characters made it difficult to become literate. Nevertheless, other peoples, including the Japanese, later copied the Chinese script.

The Shang were apparently the first to raise silkworms and weave silk cloth from the fibers of the cocoons. Because so much skilled labor was needed to manufacture silk, it was very expensive. Only kings and nobles could afford to wear silk clothes and carry silk banners.

Zhou Dynasty (1122–221 B.C.)

The Shang dynasty was overthrown around 1122 B.C. by a group of soldier-farmers from the northwest called Zhou (JOE). The new dynasty ruled for nearly nine centuries, the longest dynastic reign in Chinese history. For the last 500 years of their rule, however, the Zhou kings were little more than figureheads as several states led by ambitious nobles rose to power and fell in succession.

The Zhou dynasty gave China the political concept of the **Mandate of Heaven**. This meant that the king had a right to rule as long as he did so justly and the people were contented. However, if the government became corrupt, or there was a famine, or bandits infested the roads, the people had the right to rebel and establish a new dynasty. Throughout Chinese history, this reasoning was used to explain the coming to power of each new dynasty. "An unsuccessful rebel is a bandit, a successful one a king."

During the last centuries of Zhou rule, many economic and cultural changes took place in China. Iron-working was introduced, and Chinese peasants were soon using iron plows and other tools to open and cultivate new land. The peasants also developed large-scale methods of irrigation. Dozens of walled towns grew up. Coined money came into use.

About this time, Chinese nobles began riding on horseback. They adopted the practice from nomadic groups to the northwest. One result was that communication within China improved. Another result was that nobles began wearing trousers instead of flowing robes. Gradually Chinese commoners—women as well as men—likewise began wearing trousers. Most Chinese still do.

In spite of the warfare between states that characterized the last four centuries of Zhou rule, the period is known as China's Classical Age. Among its greatest achievements were two philosophies that were to influence the Chinese for hundreds of years. You will learn about Confucianism and Daoism (DOW-iz-uhm) later in the chapter.

Qin Dynasty (221–206 B.C.)

In 221 B.C. the first Chinese empire was established by the Qin (CHIN) dynasty. China was united under one strong central government for the first time in its history. Although the dynasty lasted only 14 years, from 221 B.C. to 206 B.C., the empire continued for more than 2,100 years. In fact, the dynasty's founder and first emperor—Shi Huangdi (shi HWAHNG-dee)—accomplished so much that the entire country became known as China after Qin, the state in which he was born.

Shi Huangdi believed the empire could be more easily governed if political control was centralized. So he divided China into 40 provinces and appointed officials to oversee each province. To keep local nobles from rebelling, he had all metal weapons except those belonging to his own soldiers collected, melted down, and recast into bells and statues. He also had local nobles move with their families to the capital, where their activities could be watched.

Shi Huangdi standardized the system of weights and measures, which made it easier to collect taxes. He also standardized the currency and the writing system, which helped unify the nation. An extensive system of roads was completed. The system resulted in better communications within the empire and also enabled the army to be sent quickly anywhere in the realm.

To protect China against northern nomads, Shi Huangdi had the Great Wall completed by connecting existing walls. Soldiers could march quickly over a paved roadway along the wall's top. Caravans loaded with trade goods could enter and leave China through gateways in the wall.

The Great Wall was a remarkable engineering feat. But its construction made the Chinese people very unhappy. Farmers were forced to abandon their fields in order to dig trenches and bake bricks. The work was so hard that many of them died. And construction costs were so high that taxes on iron and salt, two necessities of life, skyrocketed. As a result, rebellions broke out as soon as Shi Huangdi died. In 206 B.C. the Mandate of Heaven passed to a peasant general who founded the Han (HAHN) dynasty.

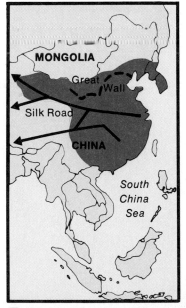

■ Han Dynasty, c. A.D. 100

Han Dynasty (206 B.C.–A.D. 220)

The Han dynasty lasted from 206 B.C. to A.D. 220. It strengthened China from without and within. Its achievements were so great, in fact, that even today many Chinese call themselves "Sons of Han."

Han rulers extended the empire's boundaries more than 2,000 miles (3 220 kilometers) westward into central Asia and moved some 700,000 Chinese settlers into the area. One result was that various nomadic groups also began moving westward to escape from the Chinese. Known as Huns, these nomads later became one of the reasons for the fall of the Roman Empire. You will read more about this in Unit 6. Chinese armies also moved east into Korea and south into Vietnam and Tibet. As a result, Chinese culture spread throughout Asia.

Another and more immediate result of Han conquests was the start of trade with Western Europe, especially with the Roman Empire. The trade moved primarily along the Silk Road. Long caravans of donkeys in the east and camels in the west wound their way through mountain passes and across arid plains. Each caravan covered one section of the route, moving back and forth from end to end. It took about one year for Chinese products to reach Rome, and vice versa.

Shi Huangdi had centralized China's government. Wu Di (WOO DEE), the leading Han emperor, carried this a step further. He developed a trained bureaucracy to administer the government. People who wanted to enter government service had to pass a series of examinations. These dealt with such topics as ethics, law, literature, and philosophy. The Chinese believed that scholars made the best administrators. If you were well-educated, they felt, you could always learn the details of a job while doing it. In 124 B.C. Wu Di set up a special school in the capital to help prepare candidates for the examinations.

This civil service system lasted for almost 2,000 years. Chinese government officials were generally able individuals. They shared a similar education and tended to administer laws in the same way. This made it easier to govern a large and heavily populated country. Also, because the examinations were open to everyone, it was sometimes possible for people to rise from the farming or merchant class to the ruling class.

Sui Dynasty (A.D. 590–618)

In A.D. 220 the last Han ruler was overthrown, and China was plunged into four centuries of chaos and disorder. **Warlords**, or rulers of small Chinese states, struggled to win control of the entire country. At the same time, nomads who occupied the vast arc of land stretching from Tibet to southern Manchuria began raiding northern China. At last, in 590, the ruler of northern China overwhelmed the states in the south and reunified the country. He established the Sui (SWEE) dynasty, which governed China for the next 28 years.

The Sui dynasty is noted for the construction of a canal system in the eastern part of China known as the Grand Canal. Another name for the 1,100-mile-long (1 770-kilometer-long) waterway was the "grain transport river." Freight boats loaded with rice from the rich fields of the Chang Jiang delta carried food north to the capital and to the armies defending China's northern frontier.

Tang and Song Dynasties (618–1279)

For most of the next 700 years, China was ruled by two dynasties. The Tang (TAHNG) dynasty held the Mandate of Heaven from 618 to 907. The Song (SOONG) dynasty was in power from 960 until 1279.

Both dynasties were noted for their cultural achievements. Sculpture flourished under the Tang, and painting, under the Song. Both dynasties also saw a flowering of poetry. You will learn about this later in the chapter.

Under the Tang dynasty, the Chinese sent their armies as far west as the Indus Valley. They also consolidated their control over Korea and Tibet. The Song emperors focused their attention on naval expeditions. Fleets of ships called junks—carrying both passengers and goods—sailed to Japan, India, and as far away as Africa, including Egypt.

The Tang capital was Changan. At the time, it was the largest city in the world, with a population of over 2 million. Surrounded by a wall, Changan was laid out in checkerboard fashion, with streets that were almost 500 feet (38 meters) wide and were crossed by canals. The emperor's palace stood on a hill called "Dragon Head Plain." People approached the palace over a blue stone-paved road that was shaped like a dragon's tail. Flower beds and weeping willows were reflected in the lakes of the imperial garden. In addition to the local population, there were numerous foreigners—Buddhist priests from India, Arab and Jewish merchants from the Middle East, Turks, and Japanese—who came to marvel, preach, and trade.

By the Sui dynasty, China's breadbasket had shifted from the dry, wheat-and-millet-producing lands in the north to the hot, moist, rice-growing lands in the south.

215

Genghis Khan became the leader of the Mongols in 1206 and united the various Mongol tribes.

The Mongols and the Yuan Dynasty

While the Song dynasty was reaching new levels of cultural development, a group of nomads from central Asia known as Mongols were coming to power. Although they numbered at most 1 million people, the Mongols eventually established the largest empire the world has ever seen. At its peak, the Mongol Empire stretched from the Pacific Ocean to the borders of Hungary and included much of what is modern China, Mongolia, the Soviet Union, India, and Pakistan.

Mongol Life   In their homeland, the Mongols had been primarily herders and hunters. They grazed either sheep or, in colder areas, yak, and used the wool from the animals to make felt for clothing. They also used felt as a covering for their yurts, or portable tents, which they carried on ox-drawn carts from one grazing area to another. Mongol boys began learning how to ride horseback and shoot steel-pointed arrows at the age of three. The Mongols hunted for food and practiced for war.

The Mongols used horses not only for transportation but also for food. Women made sausages out of horsemeat. Men churned mare's milk into a fermented drink called kumiss. The Mongols' taxes on conquered peoples took the form of horses.

Mongol women were considered to have the same rights as men. Women took part in making group decisions. They handled family property and traded with traveling merchants. They could ride and hunt as well as the men. And they helped in battle by cutting the throats of the enemy wounded.

The Mongols valued personal loyalty above all else. They also valued honesty, physical endurance, and, of course, courage in battle. On the other hand, murders among them were common, and families carried on blood feuds for generations.

Genghis Khan   The Mongols began their campaign of conquests under the leadership of Temujin (TEM-oo-jin), better known as Genghis Khan, or "Supreme Ruler." Genghis Khan was a military genius. He organized his troops into units of tens, hundreds, thousands, and ten thousands, ignoring clan and other kinship ties. He chose officers on the basis of merit. Using flags by day and torches by night, he developed a signaling system that enabled the different units to coordinate their movements on the battlefield. He set up a quartermaster corps to make certain that his soldiers had enough food. He also set up a medical corps of Chinese and Persian physicians to care for the wounded. Mongol soldiers wore silk shirts under their oxhide armor. That way, if a soldier was stabbed or shot, the silk kept the weapon from touching the wound directly. That reduced the chance of infection.

Genghis Khan was a ferocious conquerer who burned crops, leveled cities, and wiped out populations wholesale. On the other hand, he was a liberal ruler. He respected the property rights of conquered peoples. He chose local scholars and merchants to administer the government. And he issued numerous laws for complete religious freedom and for equal rights for women.

Kublai Khan Under Genghis Khan, the Mongols conquered Chinese territory north of the Huang He. By 1279 Genghis Khan's grandson Kublai (KOO-bih-ly) Khan had become the first non-Chinese to rule all of China. He founded a new dynasty called the Yuan (yoo-AHN) dynasty that lasted until 1368.

Gradually the Yuan dynasty became more Chinese than Mongol in nature. The Mongols adopted the Chinese system of government and followed the Chinese custom of building a temple in honor of one's ancestors. They extended the Grand Canal, built roads and reservoirs, and encouraged education. Kublai Khan's capital stood on the present site of Beijing. However, the Mongols kept certain culture traits. For example, they continued to drink fermented mare's milk and allow women to inherit property.

It was during the reign of Kublai Khan that a Venetian traveler named Marco Polo visited China. After returning to Europe, he published an account of his travels and observations. The Europeans of that day were so far behind the achievements of the Chinese that they could not believe what Marco Polo told them. They had never heard of paper money, for example. They were unfamiliar with "black stones that give heat when burned," otherwise known as coal. They could not even imagine a country with tens of millions of people and millions of farms.

Ming and Qing Dynasties (1368–1644)

The Mongol rulers who followed Kublai Khan were weak. By the mid-1300s a series of peasant "rice rebellions" broke out in southern and central China. In 1368 a military leader drove out the Mongols and restored to the country a new Chinese dynasty.

The Ming dynasty lasted from 1368 to 1644. Until about 1500, it was characterized by peace and prosperity. New land was brought under cultivation through the use of irrigation canals and reservoirs. Trading expeditions were sent to Southeast Asia, India, Arabia, and Africa. Cultural achievements, on the other hand, were few. Most of the art, architecture, literature, and philosophy imitated or interpreted the styles of the earlier Tang and Song dynasties.

After 1500, China turned in on itself and began to follow a policy of isolation. Chinese ships were not allowed to leave coastal waters. Chinese citizens were forbidden to have any dealings with foreigners. When Portuguese, British, Dutch, and French merchants reached China by sea, they were severely restricted. They could trade only during the four summer months, and only in the city of Guangzhou (gwahn-JOE, formerly known as Canton). They even had to live in special buildings outside the city walls.

The isolationist policies of the Ming severely limited trade. As the government's income declined, taxes were increased, and living conditions grew worse. Farmers turned bandit. Peasant rebellions broke out. At the same time, new invaders from the north—the Manchus—began attacking China. In 1644 the last Ming ruler hanged himself, and the Qing (CHING) dynasty of the Manchus took over. The Qing were to be the empire's last rulers.

■ **Manchu Dynasty, 1800s**
● **Treaty Ports**

217

SECTION 1 REVIEW

1. **Recall** According to historical evidence, what was the first great dynasty to rule China?
2. **How and Why** How did the Mandate of Heaven serve the wishes of the Chinese people?
3. **Critical Thinking** How did the isolationist policy of the Ming rulers contribute to the dynasty's downfall?

SECTION

2

Creativity

The Chinese have been sculpting, painting, working in metal, carving, and building from the earliest period of their history. Fortunately, some of their creations have survived the decay and destruction of the ages.

Since ancient times Chinese inventions have been passed along to people of other parts of the world. The Romans traded with China for silks; Chinese porcelains and lacquerware have been prized all over the world for centuries; and modern physicians have studied the Chinese technique of acupuncture as an aid in treating disease or relieving pain.

Sculpture

Among the oldest surviving pieces of Chinese art are works of bronze produced during the Shang dynasty. The Shang made bronzes for a variety of purposes. For drinking, they made tall slender cups. To hold their food, they made vessels with handles and three legs. To hold their wines, they fashioned containers in the shape of owls and other animals.

The Chinese continued making bronzes during the Zhou dynasty. On these bronzes the Chinese carved birds and animals, imaginative dragons, and abstract symbols. Some of the Zhou bronze bowls were used in rituals honoring ancestors and important state events.

The Tang dynasty was noted for its pottery. Graceful, dramatic figures of dancers, musicians, merchants, and animals such as horses and camels were modeled in clay and then glazed in rich colors of green, yellow, and brown. Thousands of these figures were placed in the tombs of Tang emperors and court officials.

From earliest times, the Chinese have worked in jade. Jade is a hard stone, harder even than steel, that is found in a number of colors. Green is the most common; cream is the rarest and most precious. Chinese artisans spent many long hours cutting and polishing jade by rubbing it with quartz. They carved such ornaments as rings, buckles, and hooks, as well as cups, bowls, vases, seals, and badges of authority. Articles of jade were also made for use in religious ceremonies. The Chinese believed that jade brought good fortune, good health, and long life.

Chinese archaeologists found this bronze horse in the tomb of a Han general. The horse is galloping, and one hoof brushes the back of a swallow in flight. The bird looks up in amazement at the flying horse.

Architecture

Many of the early Chinese buildings had curved roofs that overhung the walls. The roofs were supported by pillars, not by the walls, which served only to keep out harsh weather. The roofs were made of tiles of various colors, mostly blue and green. However, the tiles of the emperor's palace were yellow, the royal color. The pillars were carved and brightened with gold, lacquer, and a variety of inlays. These were the homes of the wealthy. The average Chinese could not afford the luxury of art.

The coming of Buddhism from India after the first century A.D. brought to China a type of tower known as a pagoda. A pagoda is generally a four- or eight-sided structure with an uneven number of stories. Early pagodas were mostly Buddhist temples. Later pagodas were built either as a memorial to honor the dead or to bring good fortune to a city or a site.

Chinese builders were famous for their graceful bridges. These were usually made of stone and had a high single arch that one reached by climbing a series of steps. The arches were high enough to allow ships with sails to pass under them.

Calligraphy and Painting

The Chinese greatly valued calligraphy, the art of beautiful writing. Painting and calligraphy were connected because the same type of brush was used for both. The force and skill that gave character and feeling to Chinese ideographs also gave meaning, strength, and beauty to Chinese paintings.

Little remains of the paintings of the Tang dynasty. But we know about them from copies and descriptions written by people who lived at

Jugglers, acrobats, and animal trainers were popular with the Chinese people. This bronze statue of a bear trainer was made during the Zhou dynasty.

the time. Then, and later in the Song dynasty, the Chinese painted mostly scenes from nature. Sometimes they portrayed horses, flowers, birds, and butterflies in fine detail. But they were especially talented in painting misty landscapes. Mountain peaks in their paintings were veiled with fog and clouds, and often a river, stream, or lake would be linked with the mountain or the cloud by mist. Tang artists were concerned with line and brushstroke, not with color. Sometimes people were introduced into the landscapes, but they were generally small and insignificant amid the grandeur of nature. The Chinese rarely painted portraits.

Literature

The Chinese have a vast literature, much of it nonfiction. At court, scribes were kept busy taking down in great detail everything that was said and done by the emperor. Scribes also kept histories of dynasties, provinces, localities, and special events. The past and its preservation have always been very important to the Chinese.

China's leading historian was Ssu-ma Ch'ien (soo-mah chee-YEN), who wrote during the Han dynasty. In addition to political events, Ssu-ma Ch'ien included information on economic conditions and biographies of important people. He also told about such aspects of daily life as music and fortune-telling, and he described the non-Chinese peoples the Han conquered. Ssu-ma Ch'ien's thorough and detailed work was imitated by later historians, which is why we have so much information about Chinese civilization.

The Chinese put together dictionaries and genealogies, or family histories. They wrote essays, romances, and poetry. Some of their finest poets lived and wrote during the Tang dynasty.

One was Li T'ai-po (LEE ty-BOO), who was fond of parties and congenial drinking companions. His unconventional ways eventually led to his exile from the court. His poetry shows a delicateness and sadness that do not seem to match his behavior.

Another poet of the period was Tu Fu. He sharply criticized the government for permitting the sufferings of the poor. But he also wrote about the beauty of the Chinese landscape.

"A boat on the Spring waters—
Like sitting on top of the sky."

Drama

Chinese drama started out as a way of remembering the deeds of one's ancestors. People would pantomime scenes from a famed ancestor's life to musical accompaniment. Instruments included cymbals, drums, flutes, and gongs.

Although regular plays were performed as early as the Han dynasty, the theater's greatest growth occurred during the Yuan dynasty. The

Potters were considered the most important of all Chinese artisans. This bowl was made during the Ming period for sale to Arabs. The arabic writing is a wish for good luck and power.

mostly illiterate Mongols encouraged the building of raised platforms over streets or in fields that could serve as stages for traveling bands of actors. There was no curtain and little scenery—perhaps a table and a few chairs, or a crude painting of a town wall with a gate. On the other hand, costumes were rich and elaborate. So, too, was makeup.

Both the makeup and the gestures of the actors were highly stylized. For example, a character carrying a wand with white horsetail hair was a supernatural being. Red makeup indicated an honest, upright person. Stooping showed that the actor was going through a door. Putting a hand on the heart meant the person was doomed to die. And so on. Actors spoke in high-pitched voices, and men usually took women's parts, at least until the 1900s.

Technology and Science

Throughout their history the Chinese have amassed a long list of technological and scientific achievements. Most of their discoveries were made long before the Europeans began their scientific and technological revolutions.

The earliest major Chinese invention was silk-making, which began under the Shang. The next major invention was paper, which dates from the Han dynasty. The Chinese made paper from the bark of the mulberry tree and from rags.

Some time before the 700s, the Chinese developed the art of printing with wood blocks. A written page was first pasted on a smooth block of wood. Then the wood was carved away, leaving the writing or characters raised. The raised characters were inked and then pressed on paper. One of the oldest printed books dates from this period. It is a Buddhist text printed in A.D. 868.

The Chinese also printed banknotes. Each note carried a serial number and two inscriptions. One inscription said: "Counterfeiters will

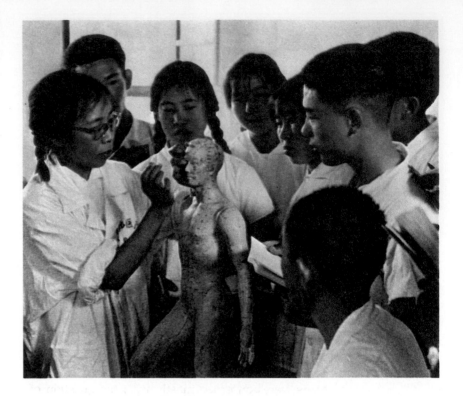

A physician teaches acupuncture to students in rural China. Skilled doctors are sent into the countryside to train others.

be beheaded." The other said: "The informer will be rewarded with three hundred strings of copper coins." In addition to printing with wooden blocks, the Chinese invented printing with movable type.

Other Chinese inventions include gunpowder, the crossbow, the compass, paddleboats, the wheelbarrow, the stirrup, mechanical clocks, and hand grenades. The Chinese invented a water-powered spinning machine and a calculating device called the abacus. They built suspension bridges and canals with locks. They used water mills and chain pumps, and made high-quality hard steel.

Among Chinese scientific achievements were the seismograph, which detects and measures earthquakes; a calendar; and an astronomical clock. Chinese astronomers knew about the existence of five planets. They observed and recorded such phenomena as sunspots, eclipses, and supernovae, or stellar explosions. In 210 B.C. they were the first to observe Halley's comet. They called it a "broom star" because its long tail looked like a broom sweeping across the sky.

The Chinese used a wide variety of herbs and drugs to treat diseases and to ease the pain of childbirth. Perhaps their best known medical accomplishment was acupuncture. In acupuncture, a doctor inserts steel needles in various parts of the body. Modern researchers have found that the spots used have a low electrical resistance and, as a result, may influence the nervous system. Chinese today use acupuncture rather than anesthesia for most operations. Many Americans have found it helpful in treating the pain of arthritis and cancer.

SECTION 2 REVIEW

1. **Recall**   Why was jade highly valued by the Chinese?
2. **How and Why**   How did the pagoda become part of Chinese architecture?
3. **Critical Thinking**   How did tradition and an emphasis on the past influence the creative arts in China?

A s you know, missionaries and travelers carried Buddhism to China about the first century A.D. However, the Chinese had already developed ideas that were quite different from the concepts of Buddhism. Unlike the Indians, the Chinese were optimistic about the possibilities of finding some happiness here and now. They wanted to improve society. They were not too much concerned with what might happen after death, although they did think about it.

The practical quality of the great Chinese philosophies— Confucianism, Daoism, and Legalism—may have been due to the troubled times in which they developed. You recall that warfare among the Chinese states was continuous during the last four centuries of Zhou rule. As a result, philosophers were concerned mostly with the question of how people could learn to live together in peace.

Confucianism

One answer to the question was given by Kong Qiu (KOHNG SHEE-oh), who is better known to Westerners as Confucius. He was born in 551 B.C. and died around 479 B.C. His basic writings are contained in a collection known as the Four Books. The most important is a book called the *Analects*, or "Conversations." Beginning with the Song dynasty, the *Analects* was the basic textbook used in Chinese schools. When Chinese children learned to read, the first sentence they read was Confucius's assertion that "Man is by nature good."

Sympathy   Confucius also said that people are by nature social creatures. To live apart from others is unnatural and harmful. To live with others is natural and will further the growth and development of humanity. The quality that makes people social creatures is called jen. It is often translated as human-heartedness, sympathy, or benevolence. It means all of these things, and more. Jen relates each human being to every other human being.

This relationship is so close that whatever affects one affects all others. Jen lies at the very root of society. Without it there could be no society, and jen can only exist when there is a society.

social creatures: beings who enjoy the company of others

223

Since all people have jen, they merely have to look within themselves to find the solutions to the problems of others. Thus, understanding oneself will give an understanding of others. The person who truly understands the importance and nature of jen will want to help others. In helping others, people are really helping themselves. Jen will always say, "Do not do unto others what you do not wish done to yourself." Confucius taught that jen must be expressed in action, and he defined some of these actions.

Right Action   Confucius insisted that individuals must play definite roles if they are to live in harmony with themselves and with others. He taught that there were five fundamental social relationships. These are between: ruler and subject; father and son; elder brother and younger brother; husband and wife; and friend and friend.

In these relationships there were duties and responsibilities that each person owed to the other. In each case, except between friends, one person had authority over the other. The subordinate should give loving obedience to the superior. The superior should be lovingly responsible for the subordinate. If there was any doubt about an action, one had merely to ask oneself: If I were a ruler, how would I wish my subject to serve me? If I were a friend, how would I want my friend to act toward me?

Confucius believed there had been a Golden Age in China's past when people lived together in peace and tranquility. He stressed the importance of learning from ancient texts. However, knowing what actions were right was not enough. People also had to have the courage to act on their knowledge. "To see the right and not do it is to be a coward."

Family and Government   To Confucius, the family was basic. Within the family, individuals learned to play their correct social roles. If people learned their roles well, they would naturally be good members of the community and good government officials, for the state was an extension of the family. The individual Chinese owed the same obedience and loyalty to political authorities as was owed to senior family members.

The emperor was considered the father of all the Chinese. He was responsible to Heaven for the welfare of all his children. He was responsible in much the same way that the father of a family was responsible to his ancestors.

If the emperor did not maintain a proper relationship with Heaven, he and his people would suffer. This proper relationship demanded that the ruler set a morally good example for his large family. "Lead people by doing right," Confucius said. "Then no one else will do otherwise." Leading a moral life was just as important as maintaining irrigation systems, the empire's defense, and other affairs of state—perhaps of greater importance.

Confucius urged that only the best and wisest men should govern. Those who wanted to govern should be educated in all subjects. Confucius wanted to establish a tradition in government of morally sound,

Confuscius taught the virtues of an ideal, orderly life.

educated men who worked solely in the people's interests. If such a tradition could be established, society would improve and the state would prosper. Then the people would be happy.

Influence on China　Starting with the Han dynasty, Confucianism came to be a powerful force in China. Family relationships were based on those spelled out by Confucius. A knowledge of the Four Books was essential in order to pass the civil service examinations. Confucius's teachings were even reinforced religiously. Schoolchildren offered a daily sacrifice to his memory, and temples in his honor were built throughout the empire during the 600s and 700s.

Confucianism gave unity but also a conversative slant to Chinese civilization. Confucian leaders were not inclined to accept different ideas of government and society. They were somewhat contemptuous of those outside the Middle Kingdom.

But during China's Classical Age, from 551 to 223 B.C., Confucianism was not yet the generally accepted philosophy of the Chinese. Some philosophers looked at life, society, and politics from other points of view. Much of what they taught also entered into the developing Chinese way of life. Among the most influential of these philosophies were Daoism and Legalism.

contemptuous:
feeling or expressing scorn

This symbol represents the basic Daoist philosophy of Yin/Yang. According to Daoism, two forces are at work in the world. Black represents Yin, the quiet or unifying principle. It is symbolized by the earth, the moon, and water. White is Yang, the active or transforming principle. It is symbolized by the sun, the sky, and fire. Daoists believe that the interaction of these two opposite forces influences everything that happens. Note that neither principle is absolute. There is some Yin within Yang, and vice versa.

Daoism

Daoism originated sometime during the 400s or 300s B.C. Its name comes from the Chinese word *dao*, meaning "the way." Laozi (LOW-dzuh) is traditionally believed to be the founder of Daoism and the author of the *Dao Te Ching*, the sourcebook of this philosophy.

Whereas Confucianism was concerned with family relationships and government, Daoism was concerned mostly with the individual. According to Daoism, at one time people had lived and moved about unhampered by artificial social restraints. In this natural state, people had been happy and in harmony with their nature and with the dao. Accordingly, to a Daoist, living a good life meant living as close to nature as possible.

Laozi's attitude toward government and laws was almost the opposite of Confucius's attitude. Confucius believed that the best-educated and most moral individuals should compete for public office. Laozi disagreed. He felt competition was arrogant, because each person was trying to be first. Only by refusing to compete could people truly develop their own distinctive talents. Moreover, Laozi questioned whether laws did any good. Locks and seals, he felt, only encouraged people to steal and to be dishonest. "If we do not prize things that are hard to get, there will be no more thieves. If we do not display things that arouse desire, the hearts of the people remain calm and undisturbed." Only by concentrating on inner matters rather than on wordly matters could people live a good life.

As time went on, Daoism took a religious turn. Chinese peasants began to associate Daoism with the world of spirits—the gods of rain, fire, agriculture, and the kitchen. Daoists were called upon to choose lucky days for weddings and funerals and to select good sites for houses and shops. Eventually, Daoism combined with Chinese Buddhism to form Zen Buddhism, which is popular in Japan.

Daoism influenced Chinese poetry, painting, and novels. It is mirrored in the great appeal that nature has for the Chinese. Daoism also influenced China's class structure. Because Daoism is pacifist, soldiers have traditionally held a low position in Chinese society.

Legalism

Legalism is another important philosophy of the Chinese. The main collections of Legalist writings are found in three works written between 350 and 100 B.C.

Confucius believed that people were naturally good, and that kindness and morality could keep order. Legalists believed that people were naturally selfish and cowardly. They were blind to the welfare of others, and would obey a ruler only in hope of reward or fear of punishment. Accordingly, the proper government was a strong, centralized state under the firm hand of one ruler. Laws were to be spelled out in detail and strictly enforced. Even the smallest offenses should be dealt with in a severe manner. For example, Legalists recommended that the hand that threw ashes into the street be cut off. They believed that if the ruler was harsh in small offenses, the people would not dare break the more important laws.

The Legalist philosophy was adopted by Shi Huangdi, the first emperor of China. Legalism lost its influence, however, with the overthrow of the Qin dynasty and the coming of the Han dynasty.

Buddhism in China

Buddhism appeared in China about the middle of the Han dynasty and was not welcomed. The Buddhist idea of rebirth seemed like nonsense. The practice of encouraging people to give up marriage and become monks or nuns was considered disgraceful. The Chinese felt strongly that every person should have descendants. It was the duty of children to look after their parents in old age and to honor them after death. Besides, Buddhism was a foreign religion. Its spread might undermine the authority of Chinese officials.

Despite its early rejection, Buddhism stayed in China and gradually became acceptable. By the A.D. 500s it had become a part of Chinese life and thought. A major reason was the political turmoil that engulfed China between the fall of the Han dynasty and the coming of the Sui dynasty. The Chinese grasped for hope and release from their troubles. Buddhism offered them this hope.

This glazed pottery figure is a larger-than-life portrait of a Buddhist monk. This figure was made in the style of Tang pottery in the A.D. 900s. It was discovered during this century in a cave near Beijing.

Buddhism had considerable influence on Chinese culture. As you know, the first book the Chinese printed was a Buddhist scripture. Pagodas were built everywhere. Sculptures of Buddha and various **bodhisattvas**—especially Kwan Yin, the goddess of mercy—were made in bronze, gold, and jade. Caves called grottoes were dug in sandstone and limestone cliffs, and their walls were covered with paintings of scenes from Buddha's life and with statues of Buddha. The Buddhist emphasis on charity became widespread, and many hospitals and free inns for travelers were built.

Toward the end of the Tang dynasty, a fanatical Daoist emperor came to the throne. In 845 he ordered thousands of Buddhist monasteries and shrines destroyed, and seized their gold and bronze statues for the royal treasury. Monks and nuns were told to return to secular life. Buddhism in China never recovered from the blow.

secular:
public, or nonreligious

SECTION 3 REVIEW

1. **Recall**   With what were Chinese philosophies mostly concerned?
2. **How and Why**   In what way can Confucianism be considered a conservative philosophy?
3. **Critical Thinking**   Why do you think Daoism appealed to the Chinese during the continuous warfare of the last centuries of Zhou rule?

SECTION

4

Society

The family and the clan were the most important units in Chinese society. The two main social classes were the peasants and the scholar-gentry.

Family

Traditionally, the family was so important in Chinese society that even the state was regarded as an extension of it. "Within the four seas [China] all men are brothers." Confucius stressed the importance of the family in his philosophy. Three of the five basic social relations he described had to do with the family. The Chinese write their family name first, ahead of their personal name.

To the Chinese, each individual was regarded as a member of a family. The individual's success or failure was the success or failure of the family. If individuals stole, the family had to pay back what was taken. If they offended another, the apology had to come from the family. If they revolted against the government, the family was punished. If they became honored officials, it was a family honor.

It was the duty of parents to teach children their proper roles. Boys

228

were taught field work or, if their families could afford it, were sent to school. Girls learned household duties and, if their families were farmers, helped in the fields as well.

Marriages were arranged by parents through a middleman. Marriages were designed to improve the family's fortunes. The bride and groom rarely even saw each other before the wedding. After the ceremony, the bride moved to the household of her husband's parents, where she was directly under the authority of her mother-in-law.

Women were considered far less important than men. Rarely were women taught to read and write. They had no need to learn because they were not eligible for civil service jobs. A woman who was very beautiful and talented might make a particularly good marriage. But in general, a woman's most desirable qualities were physical health and strength—so she could bear many babies, do the housework, and help in the fields. She also had to have a good reputation.

Children in traditional Chinese society were expected to give their parents loving obedience and support while they lived. The Chinese did not fear old age, for this was the best period of life. They were greatly respected. The burdens and work had shifted to others. They could now rest and prepare to become ancestors.

Clan

The Chinese traced the line of descent in clans from the father's side, not the mother's. Some clans had thousands of members and dozens of branches. Clan records were lengthy and elaborate. They often included biographies of individuals, a history of the locality, and many other details.

The clan maintained an ancestral center where family graves and an ancestral hall were located. Personal data about each clan member were kept in the hall. The individual's name, title, and birth and death dates were recorded on a rectangular piece of wood. Once or twice a year, clan members met to honor their ancestors with special rites. They also swept and tidied up the graves each spring. The Chinese believed that if they did not have sons to perform these rites, their spirits would roam about as hungry ghosts and bring misfortune to their descendants. As a result, a Chinese who had no son usually adopted one.

The clan also held property, generally in the form of land. The income from the property was used for the clan members. The clan had, in effect, its own welfare system. It supported orphans, widows, childless older members, and members unable to work. Often the clan paid for marriages and burials.

Peasants

Throughout China's history, peasants have made up the vast majority of the population. Their income came from the land they cultivated. It was supplemented by handicraft work, such as basketmaking or weaving.

For centuries calligraphy — fine handwriting—has been considered an important art in China.

Chinese peasants often lived on the edge of hunger and sometimes starvation. They had one main purpose—to get enough to eat. They greeted one another by saying, not "Hello" or "How are you?" but "Have you eaten?"

Chinese peasants were extremely hardworking and skillful. They saved human and animal manure to fertilize the soil, which is why streets and cart tracks were clean. They terraced hillsides so as to use every bit of available land. Since there were few draft animals, the peasants pulled plows and carried loads themselves.

Most Chinese peasants were illiterate. However, there was always the possibility that a peasant boy might rise to the scholar-gentry class. Sometimes the peasants of a village would pool their resources to pay for a tutor for one or more promising boys. If a boy passed the state examination and obtained a civil service position, the entire village would share in his good fortune.

About the only contact peasants had with the national government was paying taxes and being drafted to serve in the army. Disputes over boundary lines, thefts, and similar matters were settled on a local level by village elders, who followed custom rather than law. Usually these elders were members of the scholar-gentry class.

Scholar-Gentry

The members of the scholar-gentry were well-educated and well-to-do. They stressed etiquette and ritual. They were not expected to perform physical labor, and wore long fingernails to indicate this. Most government officials came from the scholar-gentry class. Members of this group also were teachers, patrons of the arts, writers, and professional people. They strongly supported Confucianism and the traditional system of thought and practice from which they benefited.

Some scholar-gentry lived in towns, others in villages. In addition to their government salaries, they usually earned their living either by renting land to landless peasants or by lending money, often at interest rates as high as 50 percent a month. Members of the scholar-gentry also owned local businesses, such as rice shops and pawnshops.

SECTION 4 REVIEW

1. **Recall** What were the most important units in Chinese society?
2. **How and Why** In traditional Chinese society, why was an education considered unnecessary for women?
3. **Critical Thinking** How did village elders benefit from Confucianism?

R E V I E W

Reviewing People, Places, and Things

Identify, define, or explain each of the following:

dynasty	Manchus
pictograph	calligraphy
ideograph	Ssu-ma Ch'ien
empire	seismograph
bureaucracy	jen
Changan	Legalism
Kublai Khan	bodhisattvas
Guangzhou	peasant

Map Study

Using the maps on pages 212 and 213, determine the answers to the following questions:

1. Which dynasty ruled the largest amount of territory?
2. Where was the Great Wall constructed?

Understanding Facts and Ideas

1. What were oracle bones?
2. What name was given to the last 400 years of Zhou rule?
3. Which emperor and dynasty established a civil service system in China?
4. What was the one great accomplishment of the Sui dynasty?
5. Where were the Mongols originally from?
6. What was the Yuan dynasty like under the leadership of Kublai Khan?
7. What are some of the oldest surviving pieces of Chinese art?
8. What are the five fundamental social relationships taught by Confucius?
9. What were the two main social classes in China?

10. How were local disputes handled in Chinese villages?

Developing Critical Thinking

Comparing and Contrasting Shi Huangdi and Wu Di are considered among China's greatest emperors. Compare the achievements of these rulers. In your opinion, which emperor had a more lasting or beneficial impact on the history and culture of China?

Writing About History

Relating Past to Present The Ming government's policy of isolation may have been an attempt to prevent other non-Chinese people, like the Mongols, from ruling China. In a brief essay, explain the effects that an isolation policy might have on a country. Discuss whether or not an isolation policy is an effective protective policy for a modern country to adopt.

Applying Your Skills to History

Writing a Paragraph The ability to write a clear, well-reasoned paragraph is a skill that you need whether you are writing an answer to an essay question, a one-page report, a ten-page research paper, or a book report. A good paragraph is made up of a topic sentence and its supporting details. Supporting details are sentences that develop and explain the main idea. Often the main idea, or topic sentence, is the first sentence of the paragraph. However, the topic sentence may be placed anywhere it makes sense and reads well.

Activity: Imagine that you are a member of a family in early China. Write a paragraph about your daily life that illustrates the Confucian ideas of social relationships and the importance of the family.

12

China and Its Neighbors

Between about 1800 and 1914, Europeans spread their rule, their civilization, and their culture throughout the world. In China, they competed for trading rights and divided the country into areas of influence. Eventually, political unrest within China brought an end to 2,000 years of imperial rule there.

In the 1930s, China was again invaded, this time by Japan. Following Japan's defeat in World War II, a civil war broke out in China that was won by the Communists. Since then, the country has continued struggling to solve its problems.

As you study this chapter, think about these questions:

- Why did the Chinese Empire collapse?
- What factors led to the establishment of China's present government?
- What changes have occurred in Chinese society since 1949?
- What are China's relations with its Far Eastern neighbors?

May Day—May 1—is an international holiday for workers. Shown below are Chinese workers celebrating May Day in Shanghai.

For centuries, the pattern of Chinese history had been that of dynastic cycles. The families of imperial rulers rose to power. Then, after a time, they fell into decline and finally were replaced by a new and more vigorous dynasty. The end of the Qing dynasty, however, was different. The reason was the introduction of a new element into Chinese life.

The Start of Trouble

As you learned in Chapter 11, the Manchus established the Qing dynasty in 1644. The Manchus came from Manchuria, a region to the northeast of China. Although not Chinese, the Qing emperors adopted Chinese culture and style of government. At the same time, however, they set themselves apart from the Chinese. For example, the Qing required all Chinese men to wear their hair in a single braid called a **queue** (KYOO). This braid symbolized Chinese acceptance of Manchu rule.

By 1800 the Qing dynasty, like its predecessors, was in serious trouble. Within China, it faced a tremendous population explosion—from 150,000,000 Chinese in 1650 to 350,000,000. Yet Qing rulers failed to increase public services to keep pace. There were no new irrigation projects to expand crop land to increase food supplies, and no additional soldiers to control bandits and protect China's borders against nomad attacks. At the same time, government officials became increasingly corrupt and taxes soared to 70 percent of a peasant's crop. As a result, peasant rebellions were common, and some areas of the country actually came under the control of warlords rather than the national government.

In foreign affairs too, the Qing dynasty was in serious trouble. For more than 250 years, it had restricted Western merchants to special foreign settlements in Guangzhou and regulated their activities and trade. And for 250 years, Western merchants had abided by these laws because they wanted Chinese porcelain, silks, brocades, and tea. These luxuries sold in Europe for many times the price that the merchants paid.

By 1880, however, world conditions had changed. The Industrial Revolution—about which you will learn in Unit VI—had developed in Western Europe, and European merchants and manufacturers were looking for additional markets for their goods. This was particularly true of Great Britain, which at that time was the world's leading industrial nation. However, when the British government attempted to gain further trading privileges in China, it was informed by the Qing emperor that "We lack no products within our borders. I have no use for your country's manufactures." The Qing rulers wanted to keep China free from foreign influence. To the Chinese, Westerners were "sea barbarians," and the less contact China had with them, the better.

Unfortunately for the Chinese, Western Europeans were not only aggressive traders, but they were also armed with cannon and steam-driven warships. The Chinese army and naval forces were no match for the better-armed and better-trained European forces. This overwhelming military imbalance proved decisive in the first Anglo-Chinese War, better known as the Opium War.

A Century of Turmoil

Opium had been used for medicinal purposes in China since the 600s, when it was introduced by Arab traders. During the 1600s, the Chinese started smoking opium. They adopted the habit from Dutch traders, who considered it a cure for malaria. The Chinese did not realize that opium was a habit-forming drug.

At first only a few Chinese smoked opium. Then, during the 1700s, the opium trade increased dramatically. British merchants set up a lucrative three-way exchange—English cotton textiles to India, Indian opium to China, and Chinese porcelain, tea, and silk to Great Britain. By the 1800s, about half a million pounds of opium were entering China each year. Thousands of Chinese were dying. Moreover, Chinese exports were not bringing in enough money to pay for the drug, and the consequent need to use silver to pay for it was creating a fiscal crisis.

In 1838 the Qing emperor ordered a stop to the opium trade. The next year, the Chinese destroyed 20,000 chests of opium found on British ships. The result was war.

The Opium War ended in 1842. China gave Great Britain the island of Hong Kong and opened four ports, known as **treaty ports**, to British trade without any restrictions. Foreigners living in these ports were granted the right of **extra-territoriality**. This meant that Chinese law did not apply. If disputes arose between Westerners and Chinese, they were tried in Western, not Chinese, courts of law. Within a few years, China was forced to grant similar rights to France, Germany, Russia, and the United States.

A Clash of Cultures   Basic cultural differences existed between the Chinese and Western Europeans. To Westerners, the individual was more important than the group. The Chinese took the opposite view. Westerners believed in the supremacy of law. The Chinese believed in an all-powerful emperor. Westerners placed a high value on technology and material wealth. The Chinese considered proper relationships far more important. According to Confucian thought, Chinese society at this time was divided into four classes. In order of importance, they were scholar-gentry, who governed in the name of the emperor; peasants, who provided food and taxes; artisans, who crafted useful objects; and merchants, who made profits by selling things that the peasants and artisans produced. Thus, while Westerners held merchants and business people in high regard, the Chinese tended to despise merchants, who "neither plow nor weed."

The Taiping Rebellion   One result of China's defeat and the overall ineffectiveness of the Qing dynasty was the Taiping Rebellion. The worst civil war in history, it lasted from 1851 to 1864 and cost between 20 million and 30 million lives.

The leader of the rebellion was a poor scholar named Hong Xiuchuan (HAWNG shee-oh-CHOO-ahn), who was influenced by Christian teachings. In 1837 he fell ill after failing the civil service examination and apparently had visions. According to his visions, Hong was supposed to

lucrative:
profitable

fiscal:
relating to taxation, public revenues

234

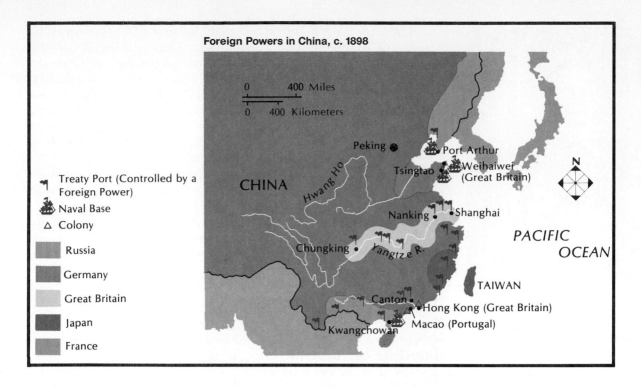

Foreign Powers in China, c. 1898

Treaty Port (Controlled by a Foreign Power)
Naval Base
△ Colony

Russia
Germany
Great Britain
Japan
France

CHINA
Hwang Ho
Peking
Port Arthur
Tsingtao
Weihaiwei (Great Britain)
Nanking
Shanghai
Chungking
Yangtze R.
PACIFIC OCEAN
TAIWAN
Canton
Hong Kong (Great Britain)
Macao (Portugal)
Kwangchowan

N

set up a new dynasty—the Taiping, which means "Great Peace." He then began gathering an army of followers. Their aim was to rid China of both Westerners and the foreign Qing dynasty.

By 1853 the Taipings controlled most of southern and central China. The Qing emperor continued to rule in northern China. But Hong was opposed by various groups in Chinese society, especially the scholar gentry, who were fearful of losing their land and their privileges. Also, Western countries supported the Qing emperor with arms and military training for his soldiers. The Westerners preferred dealing with a weak and corrupt government. In 1864, after a series of defeats, Hong committed suicide. The Taiping Rebellion was a failure, but it seriously weakened the Qing dynasty and the country.

The Boxer Rebellion   In 1861 Ci Xi (TSEE SHEE), or Empress Dowager, became the power behind the Qing throne. She remained in control of China until her death in 1908.

Ci Xi tried to strengthen the traditional Confucian values of honest government. At the same time, she adopted some Western technology, especially weapons manufacture. But she faced a series of revolts by ethnic groups in western China. Then came the Sino-Japanese War of 1894–1895. (*Sino* means "Chinese.") China lost and was forced to recognize the independence of Korea and to cede Taiwan and part of Manchuria to Japan. Western powers promptly renewed their interference in China, demanding the right to build railroads and set up factories wherever they wished. Foreign **spheres of influence** developed all along the coast.

One of the last Manchus to rule China was the Empress Ci Xi. She governed first in the name of her young son. After his death in 1875, she placed another child on the throne and continued to rule as regent. In later years, she was nicknamed the Old Buddha.

In 1899 the Boxer Rebellion broke out. A secret society known as the Society of Righteous and Harmonious Fists—called Boxers by Westerners—demanded the removal of all foreign and all Christian influence in China. The Boxers resented the fact that Western businessmen were making tremendous profits from their factories while Chinese workers labored 12 to 14 hours a day, seven days a week in those same factories. The Boxers disliked Christian missionaries because many of them made fun of Chinese customs and built churches and schools in locations the Chinese did not consider suitable.

In 1900 the Boxers succeeded in occupying Beijing. Many Westerners, fearing the Boxers, had fled to the protection of their embassies in Beijing. There a group of angry Boxers held the Westerners and Chinese Christians under siege for 55 days. An international army of American, British, French, German, and Japanese troops ended the siege and the Boxer uprising. China was forced to pay hundreds of millions of dollars in war damages.

Eleven years later, a third rebellion broke out. This one led to a major change in the government of China.

The 1911 Revolution

After the Boxer uprising, many Chinese began to question their government and philosophy, and their economic and social systems. They recognized that if their country was to protect itself against foreign domination, it would have to become a modern nation. Reform was needed. Finally, from among these Chinese there emerged one man, Sun Yatsen (YAH-SEN), who would later become known as the father of the Chinese Republic.

Of peasant stock, Sun was educated first in his village school and then in Hawaii, where an older brother was working. In Hawaii, Sun converted to Christianity. Later he studied medicine in British Hong Kong. He then began working for the establishment of a republican government in China.

Dr. Sun worked and traveled tirelessly to preach his doctrine of the Three Principles of the People. Through these he tried to adapt and blend the best of Chinese ideology and the best of Western thought. The first principle was nationalism. It called for the Chinese to think of themselves first as citizens of a nation and only secondly as members of a family or clan. Nationalism also meant that all foreigners, both Europeans and Manchus, should be driven out of China. The second principle was democracy. This meant a constitutional republic. All Chinese would have to be educated so that all could vote. The third principle was livelihood. All Chinese should be able to earn enough to feed their family and pay their taxes. Economic improvements were needed. Peasants would own the land they farmed, while the government would either own or regulate factories, transportation, and communication.

In 1911 Chinese students and soldiers revolted. Within a few months the rebels held most of southern China. They proclaimed the First

Chinese Republic and chose Sun Yatsen as president. But Dr. Sun soon realized that he was not strong enough to unite China and govern it. So he worked out an arrangement with Yuan Shikai (YOO-ahn SHI-ky), a powerful Qing general. If the emperor agreed to abdicate his throne, Dr. Sun would resign and allow General Yuan to become president in his place. The general agreed—and in February 1912 the 2,100-year-old Chinese Empire came to an end. Yuan, however, had little use for democracy. He ruled as a dictator until his death in 1916.

After Yuan's death, China was again divided among local warlords. They kept personal armies, taxed the people, and fought continually among themselves. So once again Dr. Sun attempted to unify the country and set up a republic. He appealed to Western countries for help but was ignored. He then turned to the Soviet Union. The Soviets supplied Sun and his followers—the Guomindang (gwoh-min-DAHNG), or National People's Party—with organizers, money, and guns. In return, Sun promised to cooperate with the Chinese Communist Party.

Sun Yatsen died in 1925, several years before his dream of a republic headed by the Guomindang was realized. His program was carried on by Chiang Kaishek (jee-AHNG jih-eh-SHEE).

Nationalist China

Chiang Kaishek had begun to support Sun Yatsen's program as a young military officer. He received much of his military training in Japan and also studied army organization in the Soviet Union. After Sun's death, he took command of the Nationalist army and led it north from Guangzhou. By 1928 all the major warlords had either surrendered to Chiang or joined him.

Chiang then broke with the Communists. In 1927 Shanghai's workers had gone out on strike and seized the police stations and government offices. When Nationalist soldiers reached Shanghai, the workers turned the city over to them. Three weeks later, Chiang's troops rounded up thousands of union leaders and Communists, and executed them. The surviving Communists then fled to a hilly area in Southern China.

Chiang set up his capital at Nanjing, which had been the capital during the Song dynasty. Over the next few years, the Guomindang worked hard to modernize the country. Railroads and airlines were built to connect the port cities. Business people were encouraged to set up banks, develop mines and factories, and expand trade. New houses and shopping centers went up in the major cities. The urban economy flourished.

But the price for these achievements was high. There were no elections. All government positions were filled by Guomindang members, who insisted on being bribed for every action they took. A secret police force and strict censorship of the press kept political opposition from developing. And little or nothing was done to help the peasants, who continued to groan under high taxes and high rents.

General Chiang Kaishek's Nationalist government ruled parts of mainland China from 1928 to 1949.

In 1912 Sun Yatsen became China's first president.

237

Mao Zedong and the Long March

The Communists who fled from Shanghai in 1927 were led by Mao Zedong (MAU dzuh-DOONG). The son of a peasant, he had fought in the 1911 revolution and worked as a librarian before becoming an organizer for the Communist Party. Mao's aim was to gain the support of the peasants by giving them their own land. Then he planned to organize them into a people's army that would take over the country.

Aware of the threat to his government, Chiang launched a series of "bandit extermination campaigns" against the Communist base in southern China. Outnumbered three to one, the Communists developed guerrilla tactics to defend themselves—retreating when the enemy advanced, attacking when the enemy tired, and obtaining weapons from the enemy itself. By 1934, however, Chiang's fifth campaign appeared to be on its way to success. So Mao and his companions decided to break through the Guomindang lines and head for north-central China, where another group of Communists had set up a base near the town of Yan'an.

The year-long, 6,000-mile (9 660-kilometer) journey of the Communists to Yan'an is known as the Long March. About 100,000 men—mostly in their late teens and early twenties—set out on the trek. There were also 35 women and about 100 children. The journey was an epic of courage and determination. There were running battles with Guomindang forces and with ethnic peoples who hated all Chinese. There were snow-capped mountains, raging rivers, deserts, and swamplands to cross. Fewer than 7,000 Communists managed to reach the journey's end.

The Long March was of tremendous significance. First, it enabled communism in China to survive. Second, it created a revolutionary spirit among the Communist leadership. No matter what sacrifices were needed to achieve victory, or how long the struggle would take, they were determined to reach their goal. It took them only thirteen years.

The Communist Triumph

In 1931 the Japanese, who already controlled part of China's province of Manchuria, took over the entire area. They set up a puppet state with the last Qing emperor as its head. In 1933 the Japanese took over all of northern China. Three years later, bowing to pressure from his own generals, Chiang agreed to suspend the civil war with the Communists and to form a united front with them to resist Japanese aggression. In 1937 Japan launched a full-scale war against China. By the end of 1938 the major coastal cities of China were under Japanese control. In 1941 Japan attacked the American naval base at Pearl Harbor, and the United States entered World War II.

As the struggle against Japan continued, the Communists became increasingly popular with the Chinese people, while support for the Nationalists grew ever smaller. There were several reasons for this.

The Communists followed a political strategy of winning over the peasants in the areas under their control. They paid peasants for food and

Under Mao Zedong's powerful and ruthless rule, China changed dramatically after 1949. Mao was a Marxian theorist and a champion of peasant revolution.

puppet state:
a government controlled by a power outside the country

238

supplies instead of simply taking what they needed. They redistributed land. They lowered rents by 25 percent or more. They helped peasants plant their fields and harvest their crops. They set up medical clinics, and schools where peasants could learn how to read and write. Above all, they treated peasants with respect. They also kept up a steady **propaganda** campaign against the Guomindang, accusing them of being the party of bankers and landlords, who had oppressed the peasants and collaborated with the Japanese.

For their part, the Nationalists suffered serious economic damage because of the loss of Manchuria and China's coastal cities. In addition, they were perceived as being weak, which lowered their prestige. Corruption among Guomindang officials and army officers was widespread. When a massive famine swept through the countryside in 1944, the Nationalists did not attempt to relieve the suffering by distributing food. On the contrary, they continued to insist that peasants pay the usual grain tax. Millions of peasants died.

At the end of World War II, the United States tried to persuade the Nationalists and the Communists to work together. But neither side trusted the other, and civil war between the two groups soon broke out. By 1949 the Communists had driven the Nationalists from power. Chiang, accompanied by about a million soldiers and civilians, moved the Nationalist government to the island of Taiwan and called it the Republic of China. The Communists took over mainland China, set up their capital at Beijing, and established the People's Republic of China.

collaborated:
cooperated with or willingly assisted the enemy of one's country

SECTION 1 REVIEW

1. **Recall**   What was the Chinese government forced to grant to Great Britain following the Opium War?

2. **How and Why**   Why did Western countries support the Qing emperor in putting down the Taiping Rebellion?

3. **Critical Thinking**   How did the actions of the Nationalists help Mao Zedong in his efforts to win the support of Chinese peasants?

SECTION

2

Communist China

Since 1949 Communist China—formally known as the People's Republic of China—has tried to reshape the country's economy, social structure, and government. It has been more successful in some areas than in others.

Changes in Agriculture

You will learn about the theory and history of communism in Units VI and VII. The important thing to remember about the Communists in China is that they focus their main attention on the peasants. In the Soviet Union, the main attention has been focused on city workers.

The Communists in China began by redistributing some 115 million acres (47 million hectares) of land. About 2 to 5 million landlords were killed in the process. Land reform weakened the power of the clan. The scholar-gentry class disappeared entirely.

Under land reform, however, each peasant family received only about half an acre of land. This was not large enough to produce as much food as was needed. So the Communists organized farm **cooperatives**. In a cooperative, all the peasants in a village shared tools, draft animals, labor, and harvest. As a result of the cooperatives, food production increased in China.

The next step was combining 300,000,000 individual farms into 750,000 collective farms. These resembled agricultural factories. The members of the collectives owned the means of production: land, animals, tools, seeds, and fertilizers. All the peasants were allowed to keep was a tiny garden for their own use. The managers of the collectives decided what crops to plant where. They also sold the crops and paid the peasants for their work. Food production again increased. However, the reason was not that collectives themselves were more efficient. Food production increased because hired peasants worked full-time at digging irrigation ditches and planting trees to prevent soil erosion.

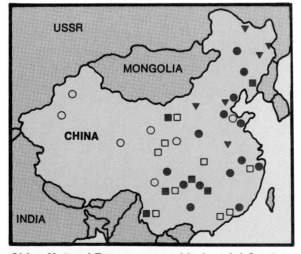

China Natural Resources and Industrial Centers
● Industrial Centers ▼ Coal ■ Iron ○ Oil □ Minerals

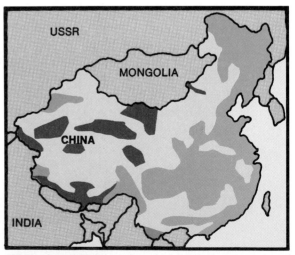

China Land Use
□ Farming ■ Forestry □ Grazing ■ Nonproductive

A busy farmer is havesting his crop in China.

The next step was combining the 750,000 collective farms into 24,000 even larger units called communes. The members of the communes not only owned the means of production, but they also ran their own schools, stores, and workshops. All the peasants in a commune had to eat at a central dining hall. And every peasant received the same amount of pay. This is an important part of Communist theory.

However, theory and practice were not the same. Food production on the communes fell drastically, and it has been estimated that as many as 20 million people died of starvation. The government then reluctantly reversed itself. It abolished communal dining halls, agreed to pay hard-working peasants more than lazy ones, and allowed peasants to sell the produce from their private gardens in nearby cities. In the 1980s, the government moved still closer to the kind of market economy that exists in the United States. Under the **household responsibility system**, each family on a collective farm was assigned its own plot of land to farm. The family had to turn over part of the crop to the government, but could do whatever it wanted to with the rest. The result has been that food production has increased.

Women

In traditional Chinese society, as you know, women were considered far less valuable than men. Women could not choose their husbands. And from the time of the Song dynasty, women's feet were bound by tight bandages to make them as small as possible. While Chinese society thought this made women more attractive, binding was painful and made walking extremely difficult.

Mao Zedong taught that women "hold up half the sky." The Communist government abolished foot-binding and allowed women to choose their own husbands. New laws also gave women the right to own property and to divorce. Women are entitled to an equal education and to equal pay for equal work. Child-care centers have been set up so that working mothers have a place to leave their children. However, less than one-half of all working mothers are able to take advantage of them. Others must use relatives, especially grandmothers, as babysitters.

In spite of laws guaranteeing equality, males are still valued more than women. In government, men hold most of the high positions. In factories, they have the more challenging jobs. Women are given the boring, routine jobs that pay less. Women lag behind in education, too. Only about one-fourth of all students entering college in China today are women. These female students are usually family members of high-ranking officials. Estimates are that 80 percent of Chinese women cannot read and write.

The Family

While Mao Zedong was alive, the government did not promote family planning. After his death in 1976, new government leaders felt that China could not support an ever-growing population and also make industrial and economic progress. So starting in 1979, the government encouraged families to have only one child. Radio broadcasts and bulletin boards at bus stops and other places where people gather are used to publicize the policy. Free information and material on family planning are provided by the government at special clinics. Men are not allowed to marry until they are 22, and women cannot marry until they are 20.

The one-child policy is reinforced economically. Families with only one child receive salary bonuses and preference in housing and job placement. Children of one-child families receive free medical care and

This "One-Child Family" poster reminds the Chinese to limit population growth.

These Chinese shoppers are buying clothes in a Beijing discount store. How does this clothing store differ from the clothing store where you shop?

education. The birth of a second child results in the loss of these benefits. Couples who have a third child are penalized 10 percent of their salary and must give up any pay raises.

However, not all families follow the one-child policy. The Chinese tradition of large families has been slow to change, particularly in rural areas. The mother who has a daughter may defy the government in order to have a son. She believes she has not done her duty as a wife until she has a male child. China's 56 ethnic minorities—who make up about 10 percent of the population—are mostly Muslim, and the government's policy is not even presented in the areas where they live. Also, China has no retirement pension system. Therefore, the Chinese people continue to depend upon their children to support them in their old age.

Nevertheless, the birthrate has been dropping. The Chinese government hopes to reach **zero population growth** by the year 2000. Zero population growth is a situation in which the death rate and the birthrate are equal. As a result, the population remains stable instead of increasing year after year.

The Cultural Revolution

In the mid-1960s, Mao saw himself growing old and his work of turning China into a successful Communist state unfinished. He was concerned that some leaders had lost their revolutionary spirit and were in favor of private enterprise. Mao was also concerned about China's future. New young leaders would come to power who did not know about the hardships of pre-Communist China.

In 1966 Mao began what came to be known as the Cultural Revolution. He wanted to wipe out any foreign influences and pre-Communist attitudes and customs that remained. He also wanted to remove from

The president of China, Deng Xiaoping.

power any officials who in his opinion were becoming like the old scholar-gentry and putting themselves ahead of the people.

To accomplish this, Mao relied on the Red Guards. These were some 10 million students and factory workers, most of them in their teens. For two years, the Red Guards held rallies, marched through city streets, and invaded homes, government offices, and factories. They denounced **bureaucrats** and "old-fashioned teachers." They burned books and destroyed religious relics and works of art. Many scientists and technicians not only lost their jobs but also had to stand for hours in public, wearing dunce caps and acknowledging their "crime" of being professionally trained. To Mao, being "red"—devoted to communism and the people—was more important than being an expert.

The Cultural Revolution resulted in chaos in China and personal tragedy for many. All schools except primary schools were closed. Industrial production fell dramatically. Some 17 million students were sent to western farming areas to learn firsthand about the difficulties of peasant life. In some areas, there were pitched battles between the Red Guards and their elders. Estimates of the number of people who died run to the hundreds of thousands. The suicide rate increased, and many people experienced a loss of hope and of ideals. When even relative turned against relative, it was hard to know whom to trust.

There were a few positive results of the Cultural Revolution. The government began spending less money in the cities and more in the countryside. It set up primary schools and free health clinics in every community. It trained so-called "barefoot doctors" for three months in hospitals and sent them to rural areas. There they held classes in hygiene and taught peasants how to get rid of disease-carrying flies and snails. As a result, such diseases as cholera, malaria, trachoma, and typhoid have been practically wiped out.

Recent Developments

When Mao died in 1976, two groups fought for power. They were the radical revolutionaries and those who wanted to take a more practical approach to China's problems. The radicals—including Mao's wife, Jiang Qing—considered Communist principles and politics more important than economic growth. The second group believed that China had to modernize in order to become one of the developed nations of the world. The second group succeeded in gaining power. The new leader was Deng Xiaoping (DUNG shee-ah-aw-PING), a Long March veteran. "It doesn't matter if a cat is white or black," Deng said. "If it catches mice, it's a good cat."

Beginning in 1978, China began a program called Four Modernizations. Its goals were to update China's industry, agriculture, science, and technology. Plans were made to build more iron and steel plants, to expand coal mining and railway lines, and to improve harbor facilities. Plans were also made to build hotels, office buildings, and apartment buildings in the large cities. China increasingly turned to Western countries and to Japan for technological and financial aid to reach these goals.

Deng introduced numerous reforms in the economic system. You read earlier about the household responsibility system in farming. Deng's industrial reforms included changing the wage system to encourage productivity. In the past, all factory workers had received the same pay. Under the new system, the more a worker produced, the more he or she earned. Also, the pay scale for professionals and technicians was increased so that it was higher than that for less-skilled workers.

There were changes in commerce as well as industry. Under Mao's rule, most small businesses and privately owned shops had disappeared. According to the reforms, city people were encouraged to open their own restaurants, retail establishments, and repair shops.

Economic conditions in China improved somewhat. But all was not well. And in the spring of 1989, popular dissatisfaction erupted in a remarkable student demonstration that was broadcast on television and witnessed by millions around the world. For seven weeks, nearly a million young people occupied Tienanmen Square in Beijing and peacefully called for still more—and somewhat different—reforms. The reforms they called for were primarily political rather than economic.

retail:
to sell in small quantities directly to the consumer

In the ballet called White-Haired Girl, *a young woman's hair turns white from poverty and hardship. In this scene, she meets enemies of her class while searching for food. Burning with hate, she attacks them. Why is class struggle an important idea in China?*

One cause of student dissatisfaction was due to a generation gap. Deng and most other senior Chinese leaders were in their 70s, 80s, and even 90s. To the students, these men were simply too old and too set in their ways to govern effectively. The students called on them to resign. They wanted rulers who would be more responsive to their needs.

The students also called for freedom of speech and freedom of the press. The students reasoned that even if China was not ready for multi-party elections, the people should not have to accept without question whatever the government decided.

Another complaint centered on the age-old problem of government corruption. Why should Communist Party leaders ride around in chauffeur-driven Mercedes-Benz automobiles when the average Chinese was lucky to own a bicycle? Why was the inflation rate 30 percent a year? The students resented the miserable conditions of the nation's colleges and universities. Buildings were filthy and crumbling, students were jammed eight to a cubicle in dormitories. And instead of being allowed to seek their own jobs after graduation, students were being assigned to low-paying work in the countryside.

The government would not talk with the students. At first, however, it did not move against them. In fact, the Communist Party hierarchy was split as to how best to respond. Moderate Zhao Ziyang (JOW dsih-YAHNG) favored meeting some student demands. Deng and Prime Minister Li Peng (PUNG) took a hard line.

Then hundreds of thousands of workers in some 40 cities, including Shanghai and Guangzhou, started demonstrating in support of the students. The parallels with 1911 and 1949 were obvious. Frightened at the possibility of a full-fledged revolt, Deng ordered a military crackdown. Although only a few thousand students remained in Tienanmen Square,

246 ▬▬▬▬

the Red Army stormed it, killing between 500 and 1,000 people. In the weeks that followed, dozens of student leaders and labor leaders were executed. Many more were arrested.

To some observers, it seemed as if the Communists were losing their moral authority to rule. In 1949 there had been an alternative to the government—the Communist Party. In 1989 no organized alternative existed within China. Only time will tell whether the Mandate of Heaven will remain with the Communists, or whether it will be withdrawn in favor of a new group of rulers.

The Arts Today

The modern Chinese have not lost pride in and appreciation for their past artistic achievements. They have carefully preserved their artistic treasures in museums. Many Buddhist temples and pagodas have been made into national monuments supported by the state. Under Deng, exhibits of **artifacts** from the Shang, Qin, Han, and other dynasties have been sent abroad.

For many years, Chinese musicians were permitted to play only Chinese music composed since the Cultural Revolution. Now, however, they may also play the works of Western composers. The Beijing Opera Company has been permitted to travel outside China. The government encourages ethnic and regional dance groups, as well as the more formal ballet.

In general, however, Chinese artists, musicians, and writers are expected to shape their work to fit the ideals of the Communist Party. The arts are used for propaganda purposes and are expected to glorify peasants and workers.

Tibet

Tibet is often called the "Roof of the World." It has always been a secluded land, with a population engaged mostly in grazing animals. The chief domestic animal is the yak, which can live on very sparse vegetation and whose thick coat enables it to withstand the intense winter cold of the Tibetan Plateau.

In the A.D. 600s the first historical kingdom was established in Tibet. The capital was Lhasa, the "City of Sun." The next 1300 years witnessed repeated wars of conquest by China. Sometimes Chinese control over Tibet was strong. At other times it was weak or nonexistent.

In 1912, when the Qing dynasty was overthrown, Tibet declared its independence. But in 1950, Chinese troops again invaded the country. The Communists effected a more even distribution of land to the peasants and established schools with instruction in both Chinese and Tibetan. They also encouraged small and medium-sized industries. At the same time, however, they tried to suppress the Tibetan form of Buddhism. In 1959 the Tibetans revolted, but the Chinese put down the rebellion with great ferocity, massacring about 20 percent of the population.

Since the death of Mao, Chinese control over the area has eased somewhat. Freedom of religion is allowed, and the Chinese government has restored some of the monasteries and shrines that were damaged during the Cultural Revolution. However, Tibetans are not permitted to demonstrate for their country's independence.

Tibet's form of Buddhism is known as Lamaism, from *lama*, or "superior one," the name for a Tibetan monk. The leader of Lamaism is called the *Dalai*, or "oceanwide," Lama. Tibetans believe that when a Dalai Lama dies, his spirit passes into the body of a newly born infant. It takes several years of searching and special tests to discover which boy is the proper reincarnation. Once he is found, he is carefully trained until he is old enough to assume his religious responsibilities. The present Dalai Lama fled from Tibet in 1959 when the Chinese invaded. He and thousands of his followers now live in exile in India. In 1989 the Dalai Lama was awarded the Nobel Peace Prize.

SECTION 2 REVIEW

1. **Recall**   What group of people is the main focus of attention for the Communists in China?
2. **How and Why**   Why did the Communists in China organize farm cooperatives, collective farms, and communes?
3. **Critical Thinking**   What steps do you think the Communists in China could take to decrease resistance to the one-child policy?

SECTION

3

China's Neighbors

China's immediate Far Eastern neighbors were all at one time under Chinese political control. Today, China's relations with Korea, Mongolia, Hong Kong, and Taiwan are varied.

Korea

Koreans often describe their land as a "shrimp caught between whales." Throughout history, the most influential "whale" has been China. Korea's cultural heritage is predominantly Chinese. The Koreans used the Chinese writing system, studied Chinese classics, and followed the Chinese practice of civil service examinations for government officials. They adopted Chinese styles of architecture and such technological accomplishments as movable type, gunpowder, and clocks. They became Buddhists, Daoists, and followers of Confucius. But the Koreans also modified much of what they borrowed. For example, they created their own porcelains and ceramics, and eventually developed their own writing system.

Politically, too, Korea—although officially independent—recognized China as its overlord. Then, in 1910, Japan took over Korea and maintained control until the end of World War II.

South Korea has reduced its imports of automobiles by building cars of its own. This worker is assembling a Hyundai car in Ulsan, South Korea. Automobiles are now an important export of South Korea.

Following Japan's defeat in 1945 and its withdrawal from Korea, the country was divided into two zones. The Soviet Union took control of Korea north of the 38th parallel, while the United States held the southern part of Korea. In 1948 both nations withdrew after setting up governments in the area each had occupied. The government of North Korea became Communist, while an autocratic regime under Syngman Rhee was established in South Korea. The South Korean government was supported by the United States. Both Korean governments were eager to rule the entire country, and each carried out repeated military raids against the other.

autocratic regime: government headed by one who holds absolute power

In 1950 North Korean armies invaded South Korea. The United Nations sent some 400,000 American and other, mostly Western, troops to help push the North Koreans back across the 38th parallel. However, instead of stopping at the dividing line, American General Douglas MacArthur led his soldiers northward. When they reached the Yalu River, the boundary between Korea and China, some 300,000 Chinese "volunteers" entered the war on the side of North Korea.

The Korean War became a bloody conflict. American casualties totaled 54,000 dead and twice that number wounded. China's losses were similar. But the Koreans suffered the most. In addition to military casualties, about 1 million civilians were killed and another 1 million were wounded. About 2.5 million civilians in South Korea were made homeless, and about 5 million of them were forced to seek government aid because of the destruction of farms and cities.

In 1953 a truce was finally arranged. The border between the two Koreas was fixed at the 38th parallel, exactly where it had been before the war.

Since that time, North Korean officials have emphasized industrialization and have organized collective farms. And as in most Communist nations, a single political party controls education and the media, as well as the government.

South Korea has likewise turned to industrialization. Among its major exports are clothing, automobiles, and electrical equipment. Politically, the nation had some difficulties. South Korea's recent presidents, even though elected, have ruled with an iron hand. Since 1987 the South Koreans have demonstrated for more political freedom. They have also demonstrated for reunification of the two Koreas.

Mongolia

As you have learned, in the thirteenth century the Mongols ruled China. By 1382 they were expelled. From 1691 to 1911, Mongolia was under Chinese control. After ten years of fighting among the Mongolians, the Chinese, and the Russians, an independent Mongolia was proclaimed in 1921. It became a Communist republic in 1924. Today, the Mongolian government cooperates with the Soviet Union on matters of economic concern.

Today there are more Mongols living in China than in the Mongolian People's Republic. The Chinese worry about attempts by Mongolian nationalists to combine the two groups of people under a single government.

Hong Kong

Hong Kong consists of one large island, some 215 tiny islands, and a small mainland area near the mouth of the Pearl River in China. For centuries, Hong Kong's islands and inlets served as a haven for coastal pirates. In 1842, following the Opium War, Great Britain made Hong Kong a British colony and developed it into a trading center. Hong Kong was captured by the Japanese in 1941 but was reoccupied by the British in 1945. When the Communists came to power in China, hundreds of thousands of Chinese began to flee their country. Many of these Chinese settled in Hong Kong.

Over the past 40 years, Hong Kong has become a major financial and light-manufacturing center. Hong Kong's banks and insurance companies provide service around the world. Hong Kong's skilled workers turn out textiles, clothing, motion pictures, and electronic equipment.

In 1984, China and Great Britain signed a Joint Declaration on the Question of Hong Kong. The British agreed to return Hong Kong to China on July 1, 1997. Deng Xiaoping promised that Hong Kong could retain its autonomy for at least 50 years. "One nation, two systems," said Deng. What that meant in theory was that Hong Kong would remain

autonomy:
the right of self-government

Mongolia's economy is based on raising livestock. The herders live in portable houses called yurts. The yurts are made of layers of felt covered with canvas or hides.

capitalist. However, since the Red Army massacres in Tienanmen Square, most Chinese in Hong Kong do not believe that the Chinese government will keep its promise.

Hong Kong's people have limited options. Great Britain will accept about 200,000 immigrants. Banks and other financial institutions are gradually relocating their senior staffs to such places as Singapore and Canada. The majority of the population will have to stay, because they cannot afford to leave or they are not wanted anywhere else. Some favor accommodation with Communist China. Others want Hong Kong to help free China from Communist rule. In the early 1900s, they point out, it was the **overseas Chinese**—those living and working outside China— who bankrolled Sun Yatsen's overthrow of the Qing dynasty. Today's overseas Chinese are being urged by people in China to support the students and others who want to bring democracy to China.

accommodation: settlement, adaptation

Taiwan

About 16 million of Taiwan's 19 million people are descended from Chinese who came to the island around 1600, when the Qing dynasty took over the Chinese throne and annexed Taiwan. In 1894–1895, as you have learned, China lost a war with Japan. As a result, it was forced to give up Taiwan. Fifty years later, at the end of World War II, the island was returned to China.

In 1949 some 2.5 million Nationalist troops and their families arrived in Taiwan from the mainland. They brought with them whatever money remained in the Chinese treasury. They also brought with them thousands of packing cases filled with paintings and other works of art. Since then, the island has been the seat of Nationalist China, formally known as the Republic of China. Nationalist leaders still claim to be China's true government. The Taiwanese army of 550,000 men is one of the largest in the world and always stands combat-ready.

COMPARATIVE STATISTICS FOR THE PEOPLE'S REPUBLIC OF CHINA AND TAIWAN IN A RECENT YEAR

	People's Republic of China	Taiwan
Area (square miles)	3,705,390	13,885
Population	1,119,877,000	20,219,000
Population per square mile	288	1,460
Arable land (%)	11	25
Annual growth rate of population (%)	1.4	1.2
Per capita income (U.S. $)	258	3,000
Televisions in use	92,000,000	6,000,000
Passenger cars in use	794,000	1,200,000
Telephones in use	7,000,000	6,000,000
Newspaper circulation per 1,000 people	50	179
Imports (U.S. $ billions)	55.2	34.8
Exports (U.S. $ billions)	47.5	53.8

Source: *The World Almanac and Book of Facts 1990*, published by the Newspaper Enterprise Association, Inc. © 1989; *1990 World Population Data Sheet*, Population Reference Bureau, Inc., Washington D.C.

In contrast to their behavior on the mainland, the Nationalists on Taiwan gradually instituted a land-reform program that gave land to those who farmed it. Taiwanese farmers use chemical fertilizers and small tractors and other machinery. The government helps with low-interest loans. As a result, the island is now able to grow 85 percent of its food.

Since 1949 Taiwan has become highly industrialized. Major exports include textiles and electronic equipment. The island has the advantages of good natural resources and a large supply of well-educated workers.

At first the "mainlanders" dominated the government and the army. After Chiang Kaishek's death in 1975, he was succeeded by his son Chiang Ching-kuo. Since that time, the government and the army have opened their ranks to the Taiwanese. Although the Nationalist government controls the media, and does not allow political criticism, individuals on Taiwan enjoy more personal freedom than the Chinese on the mainland.

SECTION 3 REVIEW

1. **Recall** What group of people has greatly influenced the culture of Korea?
2. **How and Why** Why did the United Nations send troops to Korea in 1950?
3. **Critical Thinking** Why do you think the Nationalists on Taiwan instituted a land-reform program?

Reviewing People, Places, and Things

Identify, define, or explain each of the following:

queue

treaty ports

Boxer Rebellion

Sun Yatsen

Nanjing

household responsibility system

Mao Zedong

Red Guards

Deng Xiaoping

Tienanmen Square

Dalai Lama

Korean War

overseas Chinese

Map Study

Using the map on page 235, determine the answers to the following questions:

1. Which European countries established naval bases in China?

2. What trading center did Portugal control?

3. Which country claimed the most territory in the interior of China?

Understanding Facts and Ideas

1. What development in China caused serious problems for the Qing dynasty in 1800?

2. What did the right of extraterritoriality mean to foreigners living in China?

3. What was the Guomindang?

4. How did Mao Zedong plan to gain the support of the Chinese peasants?

5. Why did Mao begin the Cultural Revolution?

6. In what way are the arts in China expected to fit the ideals of the Communist Party?

7. What has been China's policy toward Tibet since the death of Mao Zedong?

8. How did the Korean War end?

9. What kind of economy has Hong Kong developed in the last 40 years?

10. What are the major exports of Taiwan?

Developing Critical Thinking

Expressing Your Opinion   Millions of people expressed outrage and horror over the 1989 massacre of students and workers in Tienanman Square, and many countries condemned the leaders of Communist China. Why do you think the Chinese government reacted the way it did toward the demonstrators? What course of action do you think the government should have taken? What do you think the outcome might have been if the government had decided to meet with the demonstrators and discuss their demands?

Writing About History

In Someone Else's Shoes   Old age was the best time of life for people in China. The elderly were respected and cared for by their families. What would a society gain by giving such respect to the elderly? What would individual family members gain?

Applying Your Skills to History

Making a Map   Using reference materials, make a map of the 6,000-mile (9 660-kilometer) Long March made by Mao Zedong and the Red Army in 1934. Be sure that your map includes the following: major cities, the area controlled by the Guomindang, major rivers, the natural barriers encountered on the Long March (the Chang Jiang, the Dadu River, the Great Snow Mountain Range, the Great Grasslands), and a map key.

Japan

Japan is a land of contrasts. The people of Japan have alternated between maintaining close ties with their neighbors and isolating themselves from outside contacts. The Japanese have also shifted between borrowing cultural elements and developing their own patterns. The Japanese have borrowed heavily from China and, more recently, the West. For much of its history, Japan was a military dictatorship. Japanese society, however, placed great emphasis on manners and the arts.

During World War II, the cities of Hiroshima and Nagasaki were almost destroyed by humankind's first atomic bombs. Japan's rise to economic power has been especially dramatic since 1945.

As you study this chapter, think about these questions:

- How has the clan system influenced the social and political life of the Japanese?

- What has been the relationship between religion and politics in Japanese history? Between religion and the arts?

- How has the ability of the Japanese to adapt new ways to old values affected the nation's development?

- How and why has Japan changed since the end of World War II?

Japan has a modern, efficient transportation network of railroads, roads, and highways. The famed bullet-train shown below, with Mt. Fuji in the background, is a 130-mile-per-hour (209-kilometer-per-hour) electric train that connects the cities of Japan's main island of Honshu.

Most scholars believe that Japan was first settled about 25,000 years ago by people from mainland Asia and Indonesia. In 221 B.C. Shi Huangdi came to power in China. Many Chinese who opposed him fled to Japan, taking with them the knowledge of iron-making and rice cultivation. In A.D. 220 the fall of the Han dynasty set off a second wave of migration from China to Japan. Some entire villages moved. The people took with them such skills as silk manufacture, glass making, and shipbuilding.

About the same time, warriors from central Asia also arrived in Japan. Equipped with iron weapons and armor, they soon established themselves in positions of power. They were organized in some 120 clans. Each clan owned land and farmed it cooperatively. Each clan worshipped its own deity. The clans were ruled by chiefs who had both political and religious authority. This type of organization became the foundation of Japanese political, social, and economic life for many centuries.

The Yamato Clan

By the A.D. 300s, one of the competing Japanese clans, the Yamato (yah-MAH-toh), began to gain power in central and southern Japan. Over the next 200 years, it extended its rule to all Japan. The chief of the Yamato clan bore the title of emperor. The Japanese throne is still held today by a member of the Yamato clan. It is the oldest dynasty in the world.

The emperor claimed his power from Shinto, or "The Way of the Gods." Shinto is the native religion of Japan. Shinto taught that the emperor was of divine ancestry.

According to ancient Shinto legends, Ninigi, the grandson of the Sun Goddess, Amaterasu, came down from Heaven to rule Japan. He carried with him three treasures that had been given to him by his grandmother. These treasures—a bronze mirror, a cut jewel, and a sword—became the symbols of sovereignty. Ninigi went to the island of Kyushu. Later, one of his great-grandchildren, Jimmu Tenno, moved from Kyushu to Honshu, where he established the state of Yamato. Thus, in the year 600 B.C., the Japanese empire began. Jimmu Tenno—*Tenno* means "sovereign of heaven"—is traditionally considered Japan's first emperor.

Shinto

The story of the creation of Japan and the beginning of its long line of emperors is found in two Shinto texts. They were written between A.D. 700 and 800.

Shinto began as a form of **animism**. In Shinto, nature is divine. Deities called *kami* live within rocks, trees, mountains, and all the forces of nature. Shinto teaches that people should be thankful for the blessings of nature, for birth, growth, and life. Anything that interferes with these blessings, such as decay, sterility, and death, should be regarded as evil. The most joyous Japanese festivals are those related to the planting, growing, and harvesting of crops.

sterility:
in people, the inability to have children; in farming, the inability of land to produce crops

At first Shinto had no shrines except the soaring tree, the quiet stream, and the majestic mountaintop. Sometimes a small but striking natural object—a rock of unusual shape, for example—might be enclosed with sticks. It was only later, under the influence of Buddhism, that symbols for the divine were housed in shrines. Every 20 years these shrines are destroyed and erected again with unpainted wood. There is no place for a congregation. Generally, people approach the shrine, wash their hands, rinse their mouths, clap their hands, perhaps ring a bell, and make an offering. Then they bow and leave.

When Shinto worshipers wash their hands before a shrine, they are really cleansing themselves of dirt. Those who participate in the rituals of Shinto must be physically pure. Shinto is not concerned with moral guilt. It is actual physical uncleanliness that must be washed away. This emphasis on ritual purity helps explain why the end-of-the-day hot bath is so important in Japan. The Japanese also use the communal bathhouse as a social center, with more than a dozen persons soaking in a tub at the same time.

Learning From China

Beginning in the latter part of the A.D. 600s, the Japanese borrowed many cultural elements from the Chinese, who were experiencing a period of great creativity under the Tang dynasty. For some 200 years, the Japanese sent groups to China to learn and bring back all they could of Chinese ideas and inventions.

The Yamato rulers followed the Chinese style of establishing a central administration for their government. They divided the country into local units administered by officials appointed by the emperor. The new bureaucracy was financed by a land tax. The Yamato rulers also built a capital, called Nara, modeled after the Tang capital of Changan. Nara differed from Changan in that it was not protected by a wall.

Although the new system of government was Chinese in form, it was Japanese in spirit. China's administration, both central and local, was staffed by educated people who had passed a series of difficult examinations. In contrast, Japanese officials usually were chosen because of their rank and the strength of their family connections. The Chinese emperor's power was checked by the right of the people to revolt if the Mandate of Heaven was withdrawn. The Japanese believed that the emperor was divine. He could do no wrong; therefore, there could be no revolt.

In addition to a system of government and the idea of cities, the Japanese borrowed other cultural elements from China, including a writing system. But as with their government, whatever they borrowed was usually given a Japanese interpretation. This adaptation was especially true of Buddhism.

Buddhism

Buddhism clashed with Shinto, just as it had clashed with Chinese ideas when it first appeared in China. But in Japan it was not because people

This statue of Buddha was made in the 1200s in Kamakura, Japan. This was the capital city of the Kamakura shōgunate. By that time, Buddhism had existed in Japan for hundreds of years. Where did Buddhism originate?

objected to Buddhist beliefs. Buddhism did not threaten to destroy Shinto, for Shinto had few formal rules and teachings. The conflict between Buddhism and Shinto was part of a fight for power. Clans that were warring among themselves for control of Japan chose to attract followers either through Shinto or Buddhism. The supporters of Shinto lost, and Buddhism became the religion of the court and the wealthy.

But Shinto remained strong among the common people. Buddhism then began to adapt itself to Shinto, as it had done with the beliefs and attitudes of the Chinese some centuries before. Shinto deities became Buddhist holy ones. Some people proclaimed that the two religions were merely forms of the same religion. Buddhist monks took part in Shinto rituals. Gradually the Japanese became both Buddhists and followers of Shinto. This is still true today. For example, most Japanese are married by a Shinto priest but buried according to Buddhist ritual.

Buddhism in Japan split into several sects. Of these, the one that has had the most influence on Japanese culture is Zen.

To Zen Buddhists, the Buddha-nature is everywhere, and it is the purpose of each person to discover and understand this Buddha-nature. Each person must do it alone. There can be no assistance from others, no matter how devout and saintly they may be. Students cannot find much help in books, good works, or prayer, but only in meditation. This meditation may go on for years before enlightenment comes.

To meditate well, a person must live a quiet, serene, self-disciplined life. It is necessary to conquer oneself and to be simple in tastes and habits. Zen approves of gardening, the arts, and the tea ceremony.

What are the components of a quiet, serene Japanese garden?

Japanese gardens are usually made of rocks and sand rather than flowers, shrubs, and grass. These "dry gardens" are intended to symbolize nature rather than reproduce it. The proportions of a building are more important than its decoration. Japanese painters try to use as few strokes as possible when painting. The idea is to convey a mood rather than show every detail. The tea ceremony was designed to produce spiritual calm. Generally, a few people sat quietly together in a room while one person slowly made the tea. As they sipped their tea, they admired the beauty of nature in the garden that was located outside the room.

The cultural diffusion of Buddhism from China to Japan had practical as well as religious and artistic results. Buddhist monks were literate and often skilled in such areas as engineering and medicine. They set up schools near their monasteries and helped farmers improve their irrigation systems.

The Heian Period (795–1185)

In 794 the nation's capital was moved from Nara to the new city of Heian (HAY-ahn). Heian is now known as Kyoto (KYOH-toh). A major reason for the move was politics. The Fujiwara clan, which had risen to power, wanted to reduce the influence of the Buddhist monks of Nara, who were supported by other clans. Accordingly, even though Heian imitated Nara's design, it contained only a few Buddhist temples, all of which were placed as far away from the imperial palace as possible.

By this time the emperor was reigning but not ruling. His main duties were to attend ceremonies and conduct religious rituals. Although successive emperors continued to be members of the Yamato clan, their wives were always from the Fujiwara clan. After an emperor fathered sons, he was forced to abdicate and retire to a Buddhist monastery. The head of the Fujiwara clan then assumed the office of **regent** and ruled during the youth of the new emperor. This process was repeated when the young emperor became old enough to father sons. Members of the Fujiwara clan also filled all important government posts.

The elegant court life of the Heian period is well-described in the world's first novel, *The Tale of Genji*. This novel was written around the year 1000 by Murasaki Shikibu (moo-RAH-sah-kee SHKEE-boo), a lady of the court. Its central character is Prince Genji, the "Shining Prince." Besides being a well-told story of the life, loves, and thoughts of the prince, the novel paints a vivid picture of Japanese culture. Prince Genji personifies the qualities most admired by Japan's aristocrats. He is a calligrapher, a dancer, a musician, and a poet, as well as being handsome and a great lover. Another book of the period was a diary, *The Pillow-Book of Sei Shōnagon* (SAY show-OH-nah-gon), also a court lady. A gossipy work, it was known as a pillow-book because it was stored inside the wooden pillow on which the Japanese sleep.

The court ladies who produced most of the literature of the Heian period used a Japanese writing system called *kana*, rather than the Chinese writing system used by government officials. Kana was easier to learn. Its symbols stood for the 47 syllables of the Japanese language.

SECTION 1 REVIEW

1. **Recall**   What was the Yamato clan? Why was it important?
2. **How and Why**   Why was the Mandate of Heaven never used in Japan?
3. **Critical Thinking**   Why do you think Zen Buddhism approves of gardening, the arts, and the tea ceremony?

Beginning around the year 1039, control of the government slowly passed from the central administration at Kyoto into the hands of military lords outside the capital. These lords began to organize private armies. The members of these armies made up a warrior class called **samurai** (sah-MOO-rah-ee), or those who serve. The rise of the samurai led to the establishment of a military dictatorship called a **shōgunate** (show-OH-goo-nayt). Japan was a shōgunate for some 650 years, from 1185 until 1867.

Kamakura Shōgunate (1192–1333)

As the power of the Fujiwara clan declined, other clans fought among themselves for control of Japan. From this struggle the Minamoto clan, under the leadership of Yoritomo (yoh-REE-toh-moh), eventually emerged as the most influential. It was Yoritomo who assumed the title of **shōgun**, or barbarian-conquering general. The period that began with his rule is known as the Kamakura shōgunate (1192–1333). Kamakura

SECTION

2

Shōguns

The warrior Yoritomo founded Japan's first shōgunate, a feudal system of military government. The system lasted from the beginning of his rule in 1192 until 1867. This portrait of Yoritomo was painted on a silk scroll during his lifetime.

was the site of Yoritomo's capital. Yoritomo chose the small fishing village of Kamakura because he was afraid his samurai would become soft if they were headquartered in luxury-loving Kyoto. So while the emperor remained in Kyoto, the shōgun ruled from Kamakura.

Yoritomo set up a **feudal system** in Japan. Instead of giving his captains government positions, as the Fujiwara had done, he gave them tax-free estates in various parts of the country. The estates provided enough income so the captains could pay for their own horses, armor, and weapons and also those of their samurai.

The Way of the Warrior   A samurai's education started at the age of five and continued throughout his lifetime. He toughened his body by bathing in icy streams and fasting for days at a time. He learned to use a bow that was strong enough to pierce an iron shield. He learned to use a curved, two-handed sword that could cut an enemy in two with a single stroke. His armor consisted of small iron scales tied together with silk cord. It was not only strong but also light and flexible, enabling the wearer to move about with ease.

During the 1200s, the samurai formalized their code of behavior. It was called **bushido** (BOO-shee-doh). Its major virtues were courage and obedience. To lack courage was to lose respect in one's own eyes and in those of one's peers. Superiors had to be obeyed promptly and without doubt or question. Loyalty was valued above all else.

Bushido emphasized self-discipline and control over one's emotions. Everything was to be done in moderation. Bushido included a deep love for the wonders of nature and the land of Japan.

The values of the samurai were adopted by the Japanese people. Many of these values are still held today. For example, when Japanese workers join a company, they seldom leave. They consider it disloyal to change jobs. Similarly, large corporations usually guarantee their workers lifetime employment. Japanese people tend to hide their feelings. They avoid behavior that will bring shame to their family or their country. They strive to do their duty at all times. As part of their respect for nature, many Japanese sing songs to the full moon, picnic to celebrate the first cherry blossoms in spring, and attempt the climb to the top of Mt. Fuji.

The Mongol Invasions For almost 100 years, Japan flourished under the Kamakura shōgunate. Then, in 1274, the Mongol emperor of China, Kublai Khan, attacked the islands with a fleet of 450 ships and some 30,000 soldiers. As the Mongols neared the island of Kyushu, a great typhoon arose and wrecked their fleet.

In 1281 Kublai Khan again attacked, this time with 4,000 ships and 150,000 soldiers. Never before had the world seen such a large seaborne expeditionary force! For two months, the battle raged off the coast of Kyushu. Then history repeated itself. A great typhoon arose and wrecked the Mongol fleet.

Although Kublai Khan's attacks failed, Japan was politically weakened. The samurai were unhappy because they did not receive land

Stories have been written about the samurai for hundreds of years and have been expressed in other art forms, such as woodblock prints, plays, and films. This scene is from the film Rashomon, *directed by Akira Kurosawa. It shows a sword fight between a samurai (left) and a bandit.*

grants for their military services. Buddhist monks also felt that they should have received land grants because their prayers had led the gods to send the typhoons that had saved Japan. In 1331 a coalition of samurai and Buddhist monks rebelled against the Kamakura shōgun. Two years later, a new clan rose to power.

Ashikaga Shōgunate (1336–1573)

The Kamakura shōgunate was succeeded by the Ashikaga shōgunate (1336–1573). The nation's capital was moved back to Kyoto, where the Ashikaga shōguns built magnificent palaces filled with fine art. To help pay for these luxuries, the shōguns encouraged trade with China. Japan exported luxury items, such as swords and screens, and imported books, silk, and copper coins. Gradually the Japanese began using copper coins for money instead of rice and textiles.

Under the Ashikaga shōguns, the arts took on a new vigor. The Japanese developed their first form of drama, the Nō (NOH) play. Plays were dance dramas designed to teach the values of Zen Buddhism. Nō actors wore decorative masks and moved in stylized dance steps while a chorus chanted the story. There is little plot in Nō drama. The emphasis is on human relationships and feelings. Nō plays are still performed today.

But in spite of prosperity and cultural achievements, the Ashikaga shōgunate was politically unstable. The Ashikaga shōguns were weak rulers. Local lords began to ignore the shōgunate and to behave as if they were independent rulers. By the 1500s Japan was a country at war with itself.

By the 1600s, however, Japan was again united. Three men were primarily responsible. They were Odo Nobunaga, Toyotomi Hideyoshi, and Tokugawa Ieyasu (ee-AY-ah-soo). As Japanese children learn in school: "Nobunaga made a pie, Hideyoshi baked it, and Ieyasu ate it."

Nobunaga was called upon by the emperor to restore order and bring unity to Japan. By using the guns introduced in Japan by Portuguese traders in 1542, Nobunaga gained control over half the country. He put an end to the political power of the Buddhists by destroying their temple-fortresses. He standardized the currency, encouraged trade and industry, and turned the little fishing village of Nagasaki into a bustling commercial seaport.

In 1582, Nobunaga was assassinated. His best general, Hideyoshi, then took command of Nobunaga's armies and completed the unification of Japan. Hideyoshi made the great lords swear to obey him "down to the smallest particular." He also gained the support of the peasants through a fair tax system.

Hideyoshi then set out to establish a Japanese empire. Historians suggest two reasons for his action. First, Hideyoshi wanted to keep the samurai busy so they would not be tempted to revolt. Second, he had been born into a peasant family. Hideyoshi was very much aware that Japan's natural resources—especially arable land—were limited. Gaining an empire and increasing trade seemed an excellent way to solve this economic problem.

Hideyoshi's palace at his capital of Osaka had a strong influence on Japanese architecture and art. The palace's interior walls were covered with paintings on gold-leaf backgrounds. Gold-leaf screens are among Japan's most highly prized works of art. This gold-leaf painting shows a Portuguese ship stopping at a Japanese port. Japanese courtiers adopted the Portuguese clothing style of full trousers, long cloaks, and high-crowned hats.

Accordingly, Hideyoshi invaded Korea and took over most of the country. But when his troops reached the Yalu River, the Chinese entered the war on the side of the Koreans. Hideyoshi was forced to withdraw. Five years later, he tried again, and again he failed. He died in 1598.

Tokugawa Shōgunate (1603–1867)

Hideyoshi had wanted to leave his son in control of Japan. To achieve this, a council was formed to rule in his name and Ieyasu, another of Nobunaga's generals, was named chairman. But Ieyasu did not wish to turn the leadership over to Hideyoshi's son. Instead, he had himself appointed shōgun by the emperor in 1603. The Tokugawa shōgunate lasted until 1867.

Ieyasu established his capital at Edo (EH-DOH), the present site of Tokyo. To hold power over the great lords, he required them to spend every other year in the capital. When they left, some of their relatives had to remain in Edo as hostages. While in Edo the lords were required to work digging canals, filling in marshes, and building roads and bridges so they had no time to plan revolts.

The morning ceremony reinforces the traditional Japanese sense of identity with a group. Here are company workers at morning exercises.

A Regulated Society   Hideyoshi had believed that the best way to strengthen Japan was by establishing a colonial empire. Ieyasu felt the answer lay in stabilizing the country. After establishing control over the military lords, he turned his attention to the general public.

Ieyasu began by dividing the people into four classes. In descending order, these classes were the samurai, the farmers, the artisans, and the merchants. The samurai, most of whom were no longer soldiers, became the nation's bureaucrats. The artisans and merchants generally lived in the cities and towns. People within each class had to follow their hereditary occupation and marry within their class.

Ieyasu also issued codes regulating personal life. There were detailed rules about the kind of clothing to wear, the size of house to build, the sort of vehicle to ride in, and the amount of money to spend on a wedding or a funeral. The codes were reinforced by social controls. Families were organized into groups of five. Each group paid taxes as a unit and was expected to watch over the behavior of neighboring groups. There was also a government police force that observed individual behavior. Anyone who disobeyed the rules of his or her group was punished.

Although these rules no longer exist, Japanese society is still extremely group-oriented. Political and economic decisions are made by groups, not individuals, and only after extensive discussion has brought about a consensus, or general agreement. Generally, the Japanese feel more comfortable within a group. Even Japanese tourists tend to go sightseeing as a group, rather than as individuals.

An Isolated Society   In addition to regulating Japanese society, the Tokugawa shōgunate isolated the country in the early 1600s. The Western traders who began arriving in the 1500s had been followed by Christian missionaries. The missionaries came from several countries: Portugal,

Spain, England, and Holland. They tended to bring their national quarrels with them. At this time Western Europe was being torn apart by religious wars between Catholics and Protestants. (You will read about this in Unit 6.) By the early 1600s, a large number of Japanese had become Christians. Ieyasu and later Tokugawa shōguns became alarmed. They feared that the Japanese Christians might revolt against their rulers.

Finally the shōgun decided to act. He expelled all missionaries and ordered Japanese converts to either give up Christianity or be killed. To prevent further foreign influence in Japan, the shōgun then sealed off Japan. Only one Dutch ship a year and a few Chinese traders were permitted to enter. Japanese who were abroad at the time could not return. Similarly, no Japanese were allowed to leave the country. To make certain of this, the people were forbidden to build any ships, except for fishing boats and small coastal craft. This isolation was to last for about 250 years.

A Business Culture
Despite the efforts of the Tokugawa shōguns to stabilize Japanese society, a few internal changes *did* occur. One change was an increase in domestic trade. As commerce increased, the merchants grew richer. After a time, they were wealthier than the great lords. The cities and towns in which they lived grew larger. Edo, with 500,000 inhabitants, was the world's largest city in 1700. As Japan's urban areas expanded, there developed within them special sections where much of the art, recreation, and entertainment of the Tokugawa period centered.

Puppet shows known as bunraku (BUH-nrah-koo) became popular at this time. The puppets were about two-thirds life size and were

Below is a scene from a kabuki play. Kabuki drama combines singing, dancing, sword play, and gorgeous costumes. Since businessmen were required by law to dress simply, the rich fabrics and colors on a kabuki stage dazzled them.

operated by machinery that enabled them to open and close their mouths, roll their eyes, and even wave a fan. Some economists regard the bunraku puppets as Japan's earliest robots.

Kabuki, or popular drama, developed out of bunraku. At first the actors were women, but later only men played parts. Unlike Nō, kabuki plays emphasized exciting plots. One type of plot dealt with samurai loyalty to their lord. Another type dealt with young commoners outwitting samurai bullies. Elaborate sets were built on a vast revolving stage. When a crucial turning-point of the plot was reached, the actors would freeze for a minute to emphasize the drama. Kabuki performances still draw large audiences in Japan.

A popular form of recreation that developed during the Tokugawa period involved geisha (GAY-shah), or art people. These women were trained from youth to play musical instruments, sing, and carry on witty conversations. They wore special clothes and makeup. Merchants relaxed from their business problems by spending an evening in the company of one or more geisha. Businessmen today do the same.

During the 1600s, the Japanese began to write short poems called haiku (HY-koo), made up of three lines and 17 syllables. The poems were simple but they suggested more than was actually said. The reader was expected to supply the missing details, in a sense taking part in the creation of the poem. The leading master of haiku was Basho. Haiku were written in everyday Japanese rather than the more formal language used at the emperor's court. As a result, haiku were read by a great number of Japanese.

Painting was also popular during the Tokugawa period. Much of it took the form of woodblock prints. At first such prints were used only as advertisements for restaurants, plays, and other forms of recreation. Gradually, however, artists began painting landscapes. The leading woodblock artists of the 1700s and 1800s were Otamaro, Hokusai (hoh-KSY), and Hiroshige.

SECTION 2 REVIEW

1. **Recall** What three powerful shōgunates ruled Japan from 1185 to 1867?

2. **How and Why** How did shōguns rise to power in Japan?

3. **Critical Thinking** Why do you think the values of the samurai had such a lasting effect on the Japanese?

I t is impossible to prevent the development of social, economic, and
political changes within a country. It is also impossible to keep a nation
completely isolated from the outside world.

The Dutch traders at Nagasaki brought information into Japan along
with their goods. In 1720 a Tokugawa shōgun decided to allow Japanese
scholars to import books from Western Europe. The more the scholars
learned about Western science and democratic ideas, the more they
questioned their nation's policy of isolation.

During the same period, economic problems were developing within
Japan. Periodic famines caused farmers to flee to the cities. The farmers
who remained on the land then had to pay higher taxes. The result was
hundreds of peasant uprisings, especially after 1750. Then, too, many
feudal lords found themselves in debt to merchants and unable to pay
their own armies. Former soldiers roamed the countryside, leaderless and
penniless. A feeling of discontent and a desire for change swept through
the Japanese people.

The Opening of Japan

As part of their isolation policy, the Japanese government had refused to
give shelter to foreign ships during storms. They also treated shipwrecked sailors harshly. In 1853, an American fleet of four warships,
under the command of Commodore Matthew Perry, arrived in Edo Bay.
Perry informed the Japanese that they had to open up their ports to
American ships and had to guarantee the safety of American sailors.
American ships trading with China needed a place to refuel. American
whalers in the northern Pacific needed supplies of food and water.
American merchants and manufacturers were looking for additional
markets. And American missionaries were anxious to spread Protestant
Christianity.

Perry's display of power forced the Tokugawa government to sign a
treaty opening Japan to American trade. The treaty also granted extra-
territoriality to Americans. Although several feudal lords objected to the
government's decision to open Japan, the Japanese government realized
that it was useless to resist. Similar treaties were signed with France,
Great Britain, the Netherlands, and Russia.

The Japanese found themselves powerless against the Westerners.
So the feudal lords decided to learn from those who had humiliated
them. They did not want what had happened to China to happen to
Japan.

The Meiji Restoration (1868–1912)

In 1867 a group of lords, who wanted to reform Japan, removed the
Tokugawa shōgun from power and brought the emperor to Edo. The city
was renamed Tokyo, meaning "eastern capital." This marked the beginning of the Meiji (MAY-jee) Restoration, or the change from the Tokugawa

*Matthew Perry forced the
Tokugawa shōgunate to
open Japan to the West.*

shōgunate to imperial government. Each emperor gives his reign a name; Meiji means "enlightened government." During the Meiji Restoration, feudalism ended and Japan became a modern nation.

Under the slogan "Rich country, strong military," the reformers started a systematic study of Western technology and institutions. Within a few years, Japan had many Western features. Basic values, however, remained very Japanese.

Political Changes

The reformers emphasized the dignity and importance of the emperor. They asserted that the shōgun had stolen his position as head of the nation. To strengthen the national government, all feudal lords deeded their land to it. The country was then divided into large sections, with local governments appointed by the central government. Instead of paying taxes to a feudal lord, farmers now paid them to the central government.

The feudal lords also disbanded their private armies. Instead, a universal draft was put into effect. Promotion in the new national army was based on ability. This change wiped out the samurai as a separate class. "All Japanese are now equal in the empire and without distinction in their duty to serve the nation."

The Japanese adopted a constitution based on that of Germany and Great Britain. Legal courts were modeled on those of France. Japan had political parties, but the relationship between party leaders and their followers was like the relationship that had existed between feudal lords and their followers. Personal relations were more important than principles. Furthermore, only male property owners over the age of 25 were allowed to vote for members of the Diet, the national legislature. The electorate thus consisted of little more than one percent of the population. Cabinet members were of samurai background. Despite the many changes, political power in Japan still rested in the hands of a few.

Economic Changes

The Japanese established a banking system along Western lines. The British introduced the telegraph and helped to build Japan's first railroad. The Japanese set up factories to turn out iron and steel, textiles, and other products. However, since Japan has few natural resources, it had to import such raw materials as mineral fuels, metal ores, and textile fibers in exchange for its manufactured goods. Japan's economy began to depend heavily on foreign trade.

As Japan industrialized, a close relationship developed between the government and the zaibatsu. A **zaibatsu** was a large corporation controlled by a wealthy family of samurai background. Each corporation resembled a present-day American conglomerate. That is, it engaged in a wide range of economic activities and controlled numerous other companies. Among the more prominent zaibatsu established during the period were Mitsubishi and Mitsui, which are still in business today. The government treated the zaibatsu as partners, giving them tax benefits, tariff protection, and other kinds of assistance. The government also used tax money to build factories, which were then sold to private owners at a low price. Government and industry in present-day Japan still work very closely together.

conglomerate:
a widely diversified corporation

Social Changes   Slowly, Japanese society began to change. Universal education for both sexes was made compulsory for six years. Japan's literacy rate soared to 90 percent. The basic purpose of education was to train people to be of service to the nation. Pupils were taught the traditional Japanese virtues of obedience, loyalty, and submission to authority. Particular emphasis was placed on instilling devotion to the divine emperor.

There were many other social changes. Commoners were allowed to take a family name. They were also allowed to live wherever they wanted and to follow whatever occupation they chose. Those of samurai background no longer carried their traditional sword. Men stopped wearing the traditional kimono, at least in public, and put on European-style shirts, business suits, and hats. People also started eating beef as well as fish.

Japanese Imperialism

Japan's use of Western skills and technology had enabled Japan to rise from a feudal, farming nation to one of the world's leading industrial powers in less than 50 years. The Meiji leaders had achieved their goal of making Japan a modern nation. Japan had an efficient government, a vigorous economy, and a strong army and navy. But Japan needed more natural resources. And Japan felt threatened by the imperialist expansion

Japanese Empire: 1895–1942
■ Japan
— Extent of conquest by 1942

of Western nations in Asia. For these reasons, the Japanese began their own expansion program, competing with Western nations to establish colonial empires.

By the 1890s, the Japanese were beginning to make their power felt in Asia. As you have learned, the Japanese defeated the Chinese in the Sino-Japanese War of 1894–1895. In 1904–1905 they defeated the Russians. The Russo-Japanese War marked the first time that an Asian nation bested a European colonial power. The Japanese continued to expand and, by 1910, had incorporated Korea in their empire. By 1914 Japan was recognized as a world military power. The Japanese people developed strong feelings of patriotism and nationalism as a result of their nation's achievements. Japan's success inspired nationalist movements in other Asian nations.

The Japanese continued their drive toward empire during the 1920s. As Japan's industry continued to increase, so did the need for additional natural resources. Japanese expansion was also fueled by an economic depression that struck the industrial nations in 1929–1930. Everywhere, banks and factories closed, and millions of people lost their jobs. International trade slowed considerably. Hard-hit because of its dependence on trade, the Japanese renewed their desire to acquire colonies to supply raw materials and provide markets for manufactured goods.

The Japanese military leadership, which had risen to power in the government, supported expansion on the Asian continent. Their target was China. In 1931 Japan succeeded in seizing Manchuria and making it a colony. They renamed the colony Manchukuo. And in 1937, Japan invaded China. This resulted in full-scale, but undeclared, war. By 1940 Japan had entered an alliance with Germany and Italy and fought as a member of the Axis powers against the Allied nations in World War II.

Hiroshima after the first explosion of an atomic bomb on August 6, 1945. The blast was so powerful that it burned or suffocated persons 2.5 miles (4 kilometers) away. For years after the blast, hundreds of thousands of Japanese died from radiation sickness.

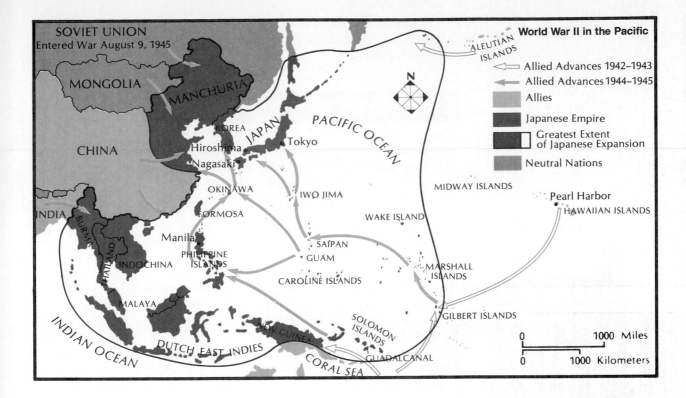

Map labels:
SOVIET UNION
Entered War August 9, 1945

MONGOLIA

MANCHURIA

CHINA

KOREA

JAPAN

Hiroshima

Tokyo

Nagasaki

PACIFIC OCEAN

N

World War II in the Pacific

Allied Advances 1942–1943
Allied Advances 1944–1945
Allies
Japanese Empire
Greatest Extent
of Japanese Expansion
Neutral Nations

OKINAWA

FORMOSA

IWO JIMA

WAKE ISLAND

MIDWAY ISLANDS

Pearl Harbor
HAWAIIAN ISLANDS

INDIA

BURMA

THAILAND

INDOCHINA

Manila
PHILIPPINE
ISLANDS

SAIPAN

GUAM

CAROLINE ISLANDS

MARSHALL
ISLANDS

MALAYA

SOLOMON
ISLANDS

GILBERT ISLANDS

INDIAN OCEAN

DUTCH EAST INDIES

NEW GUINEA

CORAL SEA

GUADALCANAL

0   1000 Miles
0   1000 Kilometers

World War II

On December 7, 1941, the Japanese formally launched a great expansionist move by bombing the United States naval base at Pearl Harbor in Hawaii. During the first year of the war, the Japanese were very successful. They conquered most of Southeast Asia.

But their control of these lands was brief. The United States, assisted by allies from Asia and the West, began to push the Japanese back. Resistance was stubborn. The Japanese had been well-trained in the values of bushido. Japanese soldiers fought to the last man. Japanese pilots crashed their bomb-laden planes on the decks of Allied ships to insure a direct hit. Nevertheless, the Japanese were pushed back island by island until Japan itself was threatened.

Then, in August of 1945, two things happened. The Soviet Union declared war on Japan and invaded Japanese-held Manchuria (Manchukuo). And on August 6, the United States dropped the world's first atomic bomb on the city of Hiroshima. Three days later, it dropped a second atomic bomb on Nagasaki. In a brief moment the A-bomb wiped out most of the life and structures in large areas of both cities.

Historians have long debated whether or not it was necessary to drop the atomic bomb. On the one hand, it is estimated that an invasion of Japan would have cost the lives of 1.5 million Allied soldiers. On the other hand, Japan had been sending out peace feelers for six months. There is considerable evidence to support the belief that the real reason the bombs were dropped was to deliver a warning to the Soviet Union.

In any event, the will of the Japanese to continue the war was shattered. They asked for peace and surrendered unconditionally on August 14, 1945.

SECTION 3 REVIEW

1. **Recall**   What was the Meiji Restoration?
2. **How and Why**   In what way did the military forces of Japan change during the Meiji rule?
3. **Critical Thinking**   In what way can the Meiji Restoration be considered a revolution?

SECTION

4

Modern Japan

In 1945 Japan was a devastated and demoralized country. Its cities lay in ruins. Military and civilian casualties ran in the millions. The Japanese people were fearful and bewildered. It was the first time in its history that Japan had suffered a defeat.

Japan rose from the depths of despair, however, and became a leading economic power whose influence has reached far beyond Asia. Today Japan is one of the two richest industrial nations in the world. It has gained far more from economic development than it could ever have hoped to gain from its Asian empire.

The American Occupation

United States military forces occupied Japan from 1945 to 1952. Under the command of General Douglas MacArthur, the Americans helped reorganize the political and economic life of the Japanese.

Political Changes   The first goal of the Americans was to eliminate militarism. Japan's government had been run by military men throughout the 1930s and 1940s. Accordingly, the new constitution the Americans wrote in 1947 stated that Japan "forever renounces war as a sovereign right of the nation." Japan's army, navy, and air force were abolished. The country was allowed to keep only a small self-defense force, mostly to maintain domestic order. One result of this has been that Japan spends about one percent of its **gross national product** for military purposes. This has enabled Japan to use most of its wealth for economic growth.

Emperor Hirohito told his subjects that he was not a god after all. He was only "the symbol of the State and of the people with whom resides sovereign power." The constitution guaranteed trial by jury, and freedom of religion, of assembly, and of the press. These rights cannot be done away with at the command of a ruler. Members of the two-house Diet are elected by universal suffrage. Japanese women were finally granted the vote in 1945.

Planting spring rice by hand is a centuries-old tradition.

Economic Changes The first economic change that MacArthur instituted was to give workers the right to form unions and to go out on strike. The second change was to reform the system of land ownership. Farms were limited to seven and one-half acres. Landlords with larger farms had to sell their excess acreage to tenants at low prices. Japan's individual farmers are now strong supporters of the democratic government that enabled them to own land.

These two changes lasted after the American occupation ended. A third economic change did not. The Americans broke up the gigantic zaibatsu into smaller, competing companies. But that was contrary to Japanese tradition. The Japanese believe in cooperation rather than competition. They regard the business firm for which they work as a family. They even start their workday with the company song. After 1952, Japanese business firms began merging with one another. However, instead of incorporating a wide range of industries the way the zaibatsu had done, the new firms usually concentrated in just one field, such as electronics or automobile manufacturing. Also, firms were no longer controlled by a family. Anyone can now buy shares of stock in a Japanese corporation.

An Economic Giant

Since the 1950s Japan has experienced dramatic economic growth. In the size of its economy, Japan is exceeded only by the United States, which has a population that is twice as large. Japan is the world's leading producer of cars, cameras, and ships. It is the second largest producer of computers, plastics, and television sets. Since 1986 Japan's per capita income has been higher than that of the United States. The value of Japanese stocks is almost equal to that of American and European stocks combined. The ten top Japanese banks control two-thirds of the world's financial capital. About one-third of the world's bank deposits are

per capita income: the amount of money per person that the people in a country or in a certain region earn

Japanese-owned savings accounts. About two-thirds of the world's industrial robots are employed in Japanese factories.

In trying to explain Japan's economic rise, analysts offer several explanations. One reason is Japan's limited resources. Because resources are scarce, people have had to turn to technology to find substitutes. This has caused Japanese technology to become highly developed. Also, the Japanese have a positive attitude toward technology. They do not fear robotization as something that will take away their jobs. They know that their company will provide them with other jobs.

Japanese workers are well-educated and highly skilled. They pay a great deal of attention to the quality of their products.

The Japanese economy has a very high rate of capital formation. The Japanese save more than 20 percent of their after-tax incomes. The banks holding these savings lend them to businesses and thus keep the economy growing. As you have learned, the Japanese spend very little of their national income for defense. Thus more capital is available to be used for economic development.

The government plays an important role in Japan's economic growth. For example, MITI—the Ministry of International Trade and Industry—guides Japanese production by encouraging the exportation of some goods while discouraging the exportation of others. The aim is to avoid competition among Japanese goods in foreign markets. The Ministry of Finance regulates banking. By allowing low-interest loans to corporations, the government decreases production costs, which in turn enables companies to charge lower prices.

Some sociologists believe it is Japan's cultural values that are largely responsible for the nation's economic rise. The Japanese grow up with a strong group feeling. They have a sense of obligation to others and generally put the demands of society ahead of their own wishes. In the workplace, they transfer these feelings to the firm. Because companies compete in the international marketplace, workers are motivated to do the best possible job to help their company succeed.

Some Pluses and Minuses

Japan's industrial growth has created a comfortable life for its people. Overall, income is evenly distributed. More than 90 percent of the Japanese consider themselves middle class. Health care is available to everyone regardless of their ability to pay. Public transportation is fast, efficient, and clean.

On the other hand, housing is extremely scarce, cramped, and costly. About 60 percent of Japan's 120 million people live in only four major urban areas. City housing is extremely expensive. Workers who are unwilling to live in tiny city apartments, and who move to a house in the suburbs, may have to spend four hours a day commuting to and from their jobs. Also, about two-thirds of Japan's cities lack adequate sewer systems.

(Continued on page 276.)

Japan Natural Resources and Industrial Centers

- ● Industrial Centers
- ▼ Coal
- ■ Iron
- ○ Oil
- □ Minerals

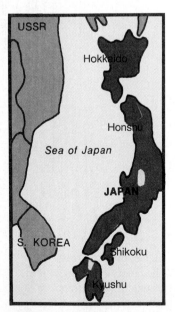

Japan Land Use
- ■ Farming
- □ Grazing
- ■ Nonproductive

HISTORY AND PEOPLE

SOICHIRO HONDA

As the Ford Model T chugged through the small town in Japan, a young boy ran after it. This was Soichiro Honda's first experience with what was to become his obsession and his life. Honda was born on December 17, 1906.

Honda worked his way up quickly from an apprentice mechanic to owning his own auto repair shop at the age of 22. His hobby was building racers, and one of his improved engines—in the body of a Ford—set a new Japan speed record of 75 miles per hour.

When World War II came to Japan, Honda's shop retooled to produce parts for fighter planes. The shop was eventually destroyed by bombings, but Soichiro Honda did not give up. He noticed the shortage of motor vehicles after the war and turned his attention and skills to building motorbikes. The small, awkward scooters sold quickly. By 1953 sales had reached $6.7 million.

Honda was not satisfied with being the best in Japan, however. He wanted the world. So he spent endless hours building and redesigning his motorcycle engines. Today, one-third of all motorcycles produced in the world are made by Honda Motor Company.

Motorcycles and the European market were but one step toward Honda's goal. He wanted to tackle the American market. With the help of a catchy slogan "You meet the nicest people on a Honda" and with a fresh, updated design and look for his product, Honda propelled motorcycles—and his name—into the mainstream of America.

Honda has never spared himself or his workers in the pursuit of efficiency and quality. "If you turn out a superior product, it will be patronized by the public," he said. He dressed like his workers, and many days worked beside them on the assembly line. Honda demanded as much attention to minute detail in production as in design.

In 1962, Soichiro Honda produced his very first automobile. In 1989, the Honda Motor Company celebrated its first American-produced Honda automobile. Through unflinching devotion to excellence and innovation in design and performance, Honda products have set the standard to which other automakers aspire.

Retired now, Soichiro Honda has been honored by the Automotive Hall of Fame with a long overdue ceremony ensuring him his place in history next to the Fords, Chryslers, and Dodges. And, in the Henry Ford Museum in Dearborn, Michigan, a Honda Accord now sits proudly on display—very close to a model of that same Ford that Soichiro Honda loved at first sight.

1. What qualities helped make Soichiro Honda a success in his chosen field?

2. Why do you think the Automotive Hall of Fame took so long to include Honda among its inductees?

3. What factors do you think contributed to Honda's rising share of the U.S. market?

Industrialization has resulted in pollution as well as a growing economy in Japan. The Japanese government has enacted some of the strongest anti-pollution laws in the world. Japan has reduced air pollution from factories and automobiles, but pollution of its lakes and streams is still serious.

Another negative result of industrialization has been the intense pressure placed on students. The best jobs go to graduates of Tokyo University. But only a small percentage of those who apply are admitted. As a result, youngsters start preparing for the admission exams in elementary school by taking extra classes every weekend. This leaves little time for sports, the arts, social development, or just plain fun.

The Family

The Japanese family is headed by the oldest male, who represents the family in all official matters. In the past, marriages were arranged. Today many still are, but the younger generation, especially in cities, demands more freedom of choice.

The Japanese love and want children, especially male children, because the family line is carried on by the male. If there are no sons, a younger son of the husband's brother, or the son of another relative, may be adopted. Sometimes if a couple have a daughter but no son, they may adopt a boy who then marries their daughter. He gives up his family name and takes the name of his adopted parents. Some of Japan's great business firms are headed by men who were adopted sons. Of course, the adopted son is chosen very carefully.

Women

During the early period of Japan's history, women had the same rights and privileges as men. They were companions rather than subordinates. In ancient Japan, women were chiefs of clans, and the Empress Jingu ruled Japan when it reportedly conquered Korea in A.D. 420.

During the Heian period, Japan's first literary masterpieces were written by women. Upper-class women had some property rights. But then Confucian ideas about the inferiority of women began to take hold. Japanese women were being taught that their only goals in life were to be good wives and mothers and that their primary virtues were obedience, patience, and self-sacrifice.

During the Kamakura period, samurai women were often trained in the use of daggers and other weapons. When their husbands were away at war, samurai women were expected to defend their castles. Nevertheless, the trend toward Confucian ideas grew stronger.

The Tokugawa period, when all of Japanese society was very regulated, marked the low point of women's status. They were considered stupid and "silly" and always in need of direction from men. It was thought that educating women would lead only to trouble. Marriages were not official until a son was born. Men could obtain divorces but women could not. A man could even send his wife away without any means of support.

The Meiji Restoration modernized Japan and industrialized the economy. Women became important to the labor force. By the mid-1930s Japanese women worked in many occupations. But they were kept in their traditional social role. For example, those who worked in factories were rarely permitted outside their walls. Managers took the place of parents. Factory women were expected to save their money for a dowry. Management offered them classes in traditional subjects, such as flower arranging, that would prepare them to be homemakers.

With the adoption of the postwar constitution, the status of Japanese women changed significantly. Legally they are equal to men. They have the right to vote, to own property, to hold political office, and to seek divorce. Today education is required for Japanese girls.

Increasing urbanization is affecting Japanese families. Especially in cities, husband and wife live as a nuclear family. The wife is no longer directly and immediately subject to her mother-in-law and the elders of the extended family.

Nevertheless, Japanese women still face many obstacles. Until 1985, companies had separate salary scales for men and women, with women being paid about 50 percent less than men. When the law was changed, companies simply downgraded the titles of women's jobs so that they would be paid less but still do the same work. Because women are responsible for housework, child care, and care of the elderly, they often have to take part-time work. This means they do not receive fringe benefits and are not eligible for pensions. Even full-time women workers are discouraged from taking paid vacations. And overtime work without extra pay is common.

However, some changes may soon take place. In 1989 the Liberal Democratic Party, which had controlled the upper house of the Diet since

Sports fans in Tokyo can choose from such events as a judo tournament (above left) or a home game of the Tokyo Giants (above).

its formation in 1955, lost its majority. The reason was the so-called "madonna factor." Japanese women voters, who outnumber men by 2.7 million, were outraged by a sales tax that cut into consumer buying power. They were also outraged by statements made by the agriculture minister. He said "women are useless in politics," and he called lawyer Takako Doi, head of the Socialist Party, unfit to be prime minister because she had never married or had children. A record number of women candidates ran in the election, and a record number were elected to office.

Literature and the Arts Today

The late Yasunari Kawabata is regarded as one of Japan's greatest modern novelists. His writing is lyrical but somewhat sad. In 1968 he became the first Japanese author to win the Nobel Prize for literature. Kawabata was the teacher of another great Japanese novelist, Yukio Mishima, who often wrote about violence and death. Mishima committed suicide in 1970 because he felt that Japan was moving too far away from its traditional samurai ideals.

Japanese musicians employ three traditional instruments. The samisen, with three strings, resembles a guitar. The koto, with 13 strings, is similar to a zither. The shakuhachi is a clarinet-like instrument made of bamboo.

Since the 1870s, Western music has been taught in Japanese schools, beginning in the elementary grades. The Suzuki method, introduced by Shinichi Suzuki, teaches very young children to play the violin. The Japanese have rock groups similar to those in the United States and Europe. Western musicals with all-Japanese casts are also popular.

The Japanese were introduced to motion pictures in 1896 when the film industry was also new in the West. Within a few years, Japan was producing its own films. Many of these films have won various international prizes. In 1951 *Rashomon* became the first Japanese film to win a Grand Prix Award at the Venice Film Festival. *Rashomon* portrayed an event as viewed by its three participants, each of whom saw it quite differently. Japanese films are known for their visual beauty. Their photographic technique is among the best in the world.

SECTION 4 REVIEW

1. **Recall** What rights does the Japanese constitution of 1947 guarantee?
2. **How and Why** In what way did Japan's lack of resources contribute to the country's dramatic economic growth?
3. **Critical Thinking** Despite Japan's dramatic advances, why do you think women still face obstacles and inequality?

Reviewing People, Places, and Things

Identify, define, or explain each of the following:

clan	kabuki
Heian	Diet
The Tale of the Genji	zaibatsu
kana	Manchukuo
shōgunate	Douglas MacArthur
Yoritomo	
Hideyoshi	Yasunari Kawabata
Edo	Suzuki method

Map Study

Using the map on page 274, determine the answers to the following questions:

1. Which of the four islands of Japan has no resources and is used exclusively for farming?
2. On what island are Japan's oil deposits located?
3. How is most of Japan's land used?

Understanding Facts and Ideas

1. What is the native religion of Japan?
2. What practical results did Buddhism have in Japan?
3. a. What was Japan's first form of drama? b. When did it develop? c. What was its purpose?
4. In his effort to stabilize Japanese society, into what four classes did Ieyasu divide society?
5. Why did the Tokugawa shōgunate isolate Japan?
6. What did the reformers of the Meiji decide to do in order to make Japan a modern country?
7. What results did the Meiji reforms in education have for the Japanese people?

8. Why did the Japanese begin a program of expansion under the Meiji?
9. a. Why did the Japanese resist the break-up of zaibatsu following World War II? b. How does the government's regulation of Japanese goods in foreign markets reflect this traditional attitude?
10. What have been some negative results of Japan's industrialization and urbanization?

Developing Critical Thinking

Analyzing a Society   In this chapter you have studied the changes that the Japanese have experienced throughout their history as Japan developed from a farming country to a feudal society to a military power, and ultimately, to a leading industrial nation. Despite these changes, tradition has had a lasting influence on the Japanese people. One example can be found in the work habits of the Japanese people, and in the business practices of large Japanese companies. What other examples can you cite? What effect has tradition had on the role or status of Japanese women?

Writing About History

Using Your Imagination   Imagine that you are one of the feudal lords who witnessed Commodore Matthew Perry's arrival in Japan. Write a letter to the Tokugawa shōgun stating your reasons why the government should or should not end the isolation of Japan and open the country to trade with Western nations.

Applying Your Skills to History

Making a Time Line   Using the information you have learned in this chapter, make a time line showing the Japanese shōgunates in chronological order. List the major events and artistic accomplishments of each period.

Reviewing Facts

1. Why has China's government recently encouraged the planting of rows of poplar trees along the roads?

2. What seismic influences cause problems in East Asia?

3. What are some inventions made by the Chinese?

4. Why did Confucius stress the importance of learning from ancient texts?

5. Who became known as the father of the Chinese Republic?

6. What rights did the Communist government in China grant to women?

7. What was meant by the Four Modernizations?

8. What economic changes did the Meiji rulers make in Japan?

9. How did the status of the Japanese emperor change following World War II?

10. What three economic changes did General MacArthur make in postwar Japan?

Understanding Main Ideas

1. How do the standards of living compare in the countries of East Asia?

2. How did the philosophy of Confucius influence the literature of China?

3. How did social roles within the family influence the development of government in early China?

4. In what way did Chiang Kaishek fail to carry out Sun Yatsen's plans for a republic in China?

5. How did Japan's rapid postwar economic growth affect the Japanese family?

Applying Chronology Skills

Study the time line below and answer the questions that follow.

Chronology of Chinese History

1911	— Sun Yatsen leads a revolution in China
1912	— Qing dynasty ends
1927	— Civil war between the Nationalists and Communists
1928	— Chiang Kaishek and Nationalists rise to power
1934–1935	— Long March of Red Army
1949	— Communists take power—establish the People's Republic of China; Nationalists flee to Taiwan—establish the Republic of China

1. How many years after Sun Yatsen's revolution was the People's Republic of China established?

2. Did the Long March take place before or after civil war broke out between Nationalists and Communists?

3. How many years elapsed between the time Chiang Kaishek came to power in China and when he set up the Republic of China?

Making Connections

Understanding Political Science Study the poster on page 242. Governments use various ways to publicize and promote their policies. How effective do you think this strategy is in gaining public cooperation?

UNIT 3 REVIEW

Understanding the Humanities

Analyzing a Poetic Form A major form of Japanese poetry is haiku—verse of three lines and seventeen syllables. The first and third lines have five syllables, the second line has seven syllables. Write a haiku of your own.

Developing Critical Thinking

1. Making Comparisons Reverence for the past and a strong sense of tradition have greatly influenced both China and Japan. How has tradition helped or hindered each country in adjusting to sweeping political, economic, and social changes?

2. Expressing Your Opinion For many years the United States did not recognize the People's Republic of China. Now the United States does. Do you think the United States change in policy was wise? Why or why not?

Using Sources

According to legend, Laozi was reluctant to record his wisdom, fearing that his beliefs would become an outer, formal faith rather than an inner, natural faith. Nevertheless, his 81 sayings, many in verse, were recorded in the *Dao Te Ching*. Read one of Laozi's sayings listed below and answer the questions that follow.

People starve
If taxes eat their grain,
And the faults of starving people
Are the faults of their rulers.
That is why people rebel.
Men who have to fight for their living
And are not afraid to die for it
Are higher men than those who, stationed
   high,
Are too fat to dare to die.

1. According to Laozi, what causes people to rebel against a ruler?

2. Who is responsible if people are starving?

3. Why does Laozi call those who rebel "higher men" than those stationed high?

Extension Activities

1. Writing a Paragraph Research and write a few short paragraphs on the work habits of the Japanese and the relationship between workers and employers in Japan.

2. Making a Report Research and compare the beginnings of the American civil service exam in the late 1800s to the beginnings of the civil service exam in China. Present your findings in an oral report.

Read More About History and Culture

Bloodworth, Dennis. *The Messiah and the Mandarins: Mao Tsetung and the Ironies of Power.* New York: Atheneum, 1982. China under Mao.

Christopher, Robert. *Japan Explained: The Mind of the New Goliath.* New York: Simon and Schuster, 1983. Modern Japanese civilization.

Gibney, Frank. *Miracle by Design: The Real Reason Behind Japan's Economic Success.* New York: Times Books, 1982. Economics.

Goulden, Joseph C. *Korea: The Untold Story of the War.* New York: Times Books, 1982. Korean War.

Kuo, Shirley W.Y. *The Taiwan Economy in Transition.* Boulder, Colo: Westview Press, 1983. Economic conditions in modern Taiwan.

Le, Ki-baik. *A New History of Korea.* (Harvard-Yenching Institute Series). Cambridge, Mass: Harvard University Press, 1983. Illustrated.

Maitland, Derek, ed. *China: The Land, the Cities, the People, the Culture, the Present.* New York: Exeter, 1981. Modern China.

Nien Chieng. *Life and Death in Shanghai.* Garden City, NY: Doubleday, 1989. One woman's recollections of the Cultural Revolution.

4

LATIN AMERICA

Gold objects, such as
this Chimu vest,
tempted Western
Europeans to come to
the New World in
search of treasure.
Some took the riches
and left. Others stayed
to settle the land they
seized from the
Indians. More Western
Europeans came and
brought with them
blacks from Africa. All
blended their ways to
make the Latin
American culture.

The Land and Ancient Peoples

Latin America includes Mexico, all the countries between it and the southern tip of South America, and the islands in the Caribbean Sea. The culture region is called Latin America because most of the people speak either Spanish or Portuguese, and both languages are derived from Latin. The culture region covers about 14 percent of the earth's land surface and stretches over 6,000 miles (9 654 kilometers) from north to south.

Latin America was settled by three waves of people. The first were prehistoric Asians, whose descendants came to be known as Indians. Then came Western Europeans, mostly the Spanish and the Portuguese. The third wave were Africans. The most noticeable cultural influences in Latin America today are those of the Spanish and the Portuguese. Their languages, society, arts, and religion dominate.

As you study this chapter, think about these questions:

- How has the geography of Latin America influenced its development?

- What effects did the development of farming have on the early peoples of Latin America?

There are many farms and villages on the shores of Lake Atitlán, Guatemala.

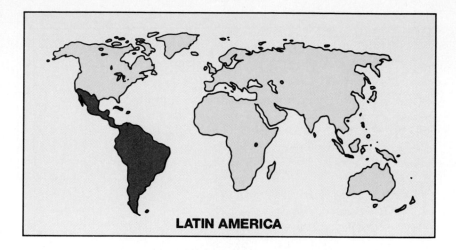

LATIN AMERICA

Latin America is marked by a great variety of physical features—soaring mountains, flat plains, vast river systems, tropical rainforests, and deserts. There are also great differences in the kinds and uses of the material resources found throughout the culture region.

Mexico

Mexico is the third largest country in Latin America. It is a federation of 31 states and a federal district. The district is Mexico City, the nation's capital.

Mexico is essentially a huge plateau bordered on the east and the west by mountain ranges and narrow coastal plains. The Sierra Madre Oriental runs along the country's east coast; the Sierra Madre Occidental runs along its west coast. Both ranges are part of the same chain as the Rocky Mountains in the United States. The elevation of the plateau averages 5,000 to 8,000 feet (1 500 to 2 400 meters) above sea level. The northern part of the plateau, as well as the peninsula of Baja (Lower) California, is desert. But the central and southern parts of the plateau produce much of Mexico's food. Because of the rich soil and temperate climate, most of the country's major cities are located there. The Valley of Mexico, where Mexico City is located, lies on the plateau.

Mexico's mountains, like those of all Latin America, are magnificent to see. They also contain rich deposits of silver and other minerals. At the same time, they have created problems. One problem is that they block transportation. As a result, the people of Mexico and other countries are sometimes more loyal to their region than to their nation. In addition, the mountains are geologically young, which makes volcanic eruptions and earthquakes common.

Traditionally, Mexico has had a strong agricultural economy, exporting cotton, sugar, and coffee. In recent years, however, it has become an industrialized nation. The basis of its industry is mining and oil. Mexico's

(Continued on page 288.)

A NATURAL REGIONS MAP OF LATIN AMERICA

75°W 60°W 45°W

30°N   30°N

UNITED STATES

Gulf of Mexico   Atlantic Ocean

YUCATÁN PENINSULA

Gulf of California   Caribbean Sea

Yucatán Channel

15°N   15°N

SIERRA MADRE ORIENTAL
VALLEY OF MEXICO
SIERRA MADRE OCCIDENTAL

Caribbean Sea

Lake Maracaibo

Panama Canal

Orinoco River

Lake Nicaragua

Magdalena River

0°   0°

Pacific Ocean

Amazon River

ATACAMA DESERT

15°S   Lake Titicaca   10°S

Paraguay River

Paraná River

N
W E
S

ANDES MTS.

Uruguay River

30°S   30°S

Rio de la Plata

- ■ Mountains
- □ Deserts
- ▨ Rain forests
- ▨ Pampas
- ▨ Farmland, grazing land, woodlands

45°S   45°S

Statute Miles 100 0 100 300 500 700 900

Kilometers 100 0100 300 500 700 9001100

CAPE HORN

120°W 105°W 90°W 75°W 60°W 45°W

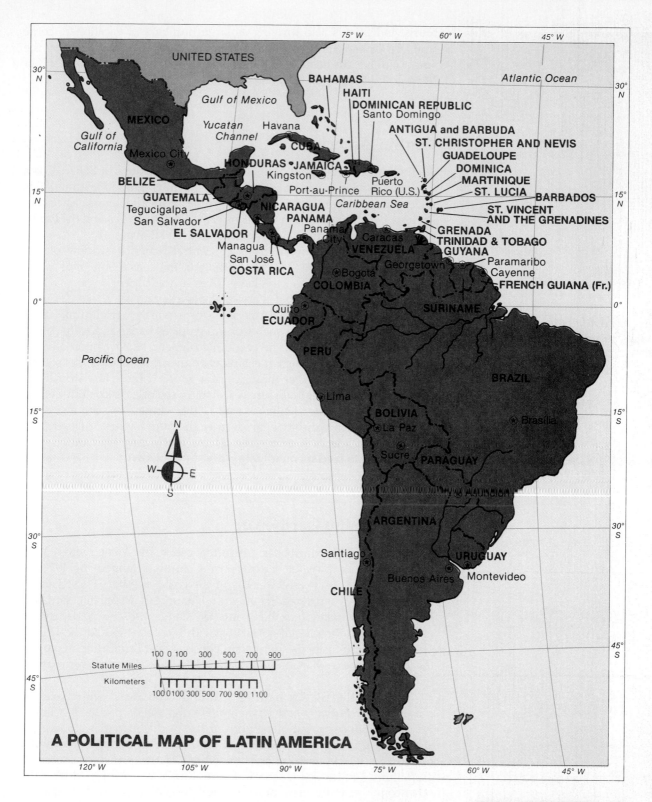

UNITED STATES

75° W   60° W   45° W

Atlantic Ocean

30° N

BAHAMAS

Gulf of Mexico

HAITI

DOMINICAN REPUBLIC
Santo Domingo

Yucatan
Channel   Havana

MEXICO

Gulf of
California

Mexico City

CUBA

ANTIGUA and BARBUDA

ST. CHRISTOPHER AND NEVIS

GUADELOUPE

HONDURAS **JAMAICA**

DOMINICA

MARTINIQUE

BELIZE

Kingston

Puerto
Rico (U.S.)

ST. LUCIA   **BARBADOS**

Port-au-Prince

15° N

GUATEMALA

Tegucigalpa

NICARAGUA

Caribbean Sea

**ST. VINCENT
AND THE GRENADINES**

San Salvador

PANAMA

GRENADA

EL SALVADOR

Panama
City

TRINIDAD & TOBAGO

Managua

Caracas

GUYANA

San José

VENEZUELA

Georgetown   Paramaribo

COSTA RICA

Cayenne

COLOMBIA

Bogotá

SURINAME

FRENCH GUIANA (Fr.)

0°

Quito

ECUADOR

PERU

BRAZIL

Pacific Ocean

Lima

15° S

BOLIVIA

Brasília

La Paz

Sucre

PARAGUAY

N

W   E

S

ARGENTINA

30° S

Santiago

URUGUAY

Buenos Aires   Montevideo

CHILE

45° S

100 0 100   300   500   700   900

Statute Miles

Kilometers

100 0100 300 500 700 900 1100

A POLITICAL MAP OF LATIN AMERICA

120° W   105° W   90° W   75° W   60° W   45° W

Costa Rica's economy has been improving steadily. Above, a young man picks coffee beans, one of the nation's major exports.

tourist industry is also thriving as large numbers of vacationers come from the United States and Western Europe during winter to enjoy the sunny climate, the beautiful beaches, and the warm waters of the Gulf of Mexico and the Pacific Ocean.

Central America

South of Mexico are the seven Central American nations of Belize, Costa Rica, El Salvador, Guatemala, Honduras, Nicaragua, and Panama. At its widest, Central America is about 600 miles (965 kilometers) across. In Panama, where the Panama Canal joins the Caribbean Sea and the Pacific Ocean, the land narrows to about 50 miles (80 kilometers).

On the east and west coasts of Central America are low plains. Between them lie highlands. The climate of the coastal lowlands is hot and humid. Most of the population lives in the higher regions where temperatures are milder but where there is less rainfall.

The nations of Central America are primarily agricultural. They produce lumber as well as such tropical crops as bananas, cacao, coffee, cotton, and sugar. Most of the economies depend heavily upon a single crop. This leads to problems. It is buyers on the world market, not sellers, who have traditionally set the price of a good. If there is a worldwide scarcity, the price is high. If there is a surplus, the price is low. But Central Americans can be the victims as well as the winners in such a system. Bad weather or crop diseases can destroy an entire harvest. Also, dependency on a single cash crop often means that a country cannot grow enough food to feed its rapidly increasing population.

Islands of the Caribbean

The islands of the Caribbean are often called the West Indies. They received this name when Christopher Columbus landed in 1492 and thought he had discovered islands off the coast of India. These islands include Cuba, Hispaniola (Haiti and Dominican Republic), Jamaica, Puerto Rico, Trinidad, and many smaller islands. Most are independent nations. Puerto Rico is self-governing with territorial ties to the United States. The Virgin Islands are ruled in part by Great Britain and in part by the United States. Martinique and Guadeloupe are considered part of France.

Most of the islands have agricultural economies, with bananas, cacao, coffee, lumber, and sugar among the major products. Central America produces about one-eighth of the world's bananas. Tourism is also extremely important. Jamaica is developing an industrial economy because of its deposits of bauxite, which is the principal source of aluminum. The textile industry in Puerto Rico is flourishing. Most of the other countries in the area, however, lack the capital to invest in factories and machinery. They also lack skilled workers and energy sources.

South America

South America accounts for 86 percent of Latin America's area and about 60 percent of its population of 400 million. South America contains 12 independent nations and one French colony.

Mountains   The largest area of mountains in South America is formed by the Andes, the longest mountain chain in the world. The Andes run along the western edge of the continent for more than 4,000 miles (6 436 kilometers). At their widest spot, in Peru and Bolivia, they are almost 500 miles (805 kilometers) wide. Most of their peaks are covered with snow year-round. The melted snow flows down the mountains and waters the dry coastal plains.

Plateaus   South America's landforms include large plateaus. One is the altiplano—from the Spanish word for "high plain"—located in Bolivia among the Andes. The altiplano, which has a cool climate, contains most of the country's population. Mining is the chief industry. A plateau called the Mato Grosso—from the Portuguese for "thick forest"—spreads over much of Brazil. Farther south, hills and low tablelands in southern Argentina and Chile form a flat, windswept area known as Patagonia that is well suited for the grazing of sheep. It is also rich in deposits of coal, iron ore, and petroleum.

Plains   Another important landform is plains areas. In addition to narrow coastal plains, there are several areas of broad inland plains. Two of these are the *pampas* of Argentina and the *llanos* (YAH-noz) of Colombia and Venezuela.

This mechanical reaper is being used to harvest grain on the pampas of Argentina. Most of the crops and animals raised in the nation are grown on the pampas.

The pampas make up about one-third of Argentina. Their flatness prevents erosion but allows for the buildup of rich soil deposits that wash down from the mountains. As a result, the pampas are South America's most productive farmland.

The llanos stretch from the delta of the Orinoco River in Venezuela westward into Colombia. The major economic activity here is cattle-raising. In the past, people suffered from alternating floods and droughts. Then a dam was built across the Guárico River. Now the llanos are protected against flooding, and ranchers and farmers have enough water for irrigation.

Deserts Argentina, Brazil, Chile, and Peru all have areas where rain seldom falls. The largest is the Atacama Desert, one of the driest places in the world. It extends 1,400 miles (2 240 kilometers) along the coast of northern Chile and southern Peru. In the Chilean section, miners dig tons of nitrates—used in the manufacture of fertilizers and dynamite—from the earth. However, the mineral reserves have been declining in recent years.

The geography of Latin America is one of many contrasts. On the left is a copper mine in the Atacama Desert. On the right is the green Amazon Basin. The Brazilian government is working to bring people and cities into the basin. How might that affect the area's environment?

Rainforests About 50 percent of Brazil is covered by a tropical rainforest. It is the largest such forest remaining on the earth.

In the rainforest, the trees grow into tangled masses that stay green year-round. The sun cannot penetrate this thick ceiling of leaves, but rain can. It falls almost daily, averaging 100 inches (254 centimeters) a year. The warm temperatures and heavy moisture create a hot, humid climate that is difficult for humans to tolerate. On the other hand, the rainforest contains over 50,000 species of plants—about 20 percent of all plant species on earth—and supports more species of animals than any other place on the planet.

(Continued on page 292.)

Using GEOGRAPHY Skills

Reading a Thematic Map

In recent years, significant weather changes have occurred in Latin America, the United States, and around the world. One of these is an unusual increase in the water temperature of the Pacific Ocean off the coast of Central and South America. This change has been seen several times since the 1950s, usually around the middle of December. The temperature increase is caused by a warm water current the Spanish named *El Niño*, or "The Child."

In 1982, El Niño arrived in the spring. Instead of lasting its usual six to eight weeks, El Niño lasted for more than a year. This large El Niño current near the equator covered 8,000 square miles (20 720 square kilometers) making it strong enough to influence weather conditions around the world. Along the usually dry coasts of Ecuador and Peru, El Niño's weather conditions brought torrential rains. The oceans near the coast warmed, almost destroying the rich fishing grounds. Many Latin American countries along the Pacific coast also experienced flooding and landslides.

In the United States, this strange current of water helped cause a severe drought in the plains, while at the same time resulted in tremendous storms on the west coast. High tides and heavy rains brought flooding and landslides to the coasts of California and Oregon. In fact, all countries with a Pacific coast were affected by El Niño.

Some scientists think that the major eruptions of the Mexican volcano El Chicón (EL-chee-KOHN) in 1982 might have caused the increase in the severity of El Niño. The eruptions sent large amounts of ash, dust, and sulfuric gases into the earth's atmosphere. The huge clouds formed by the ash, dust, and gases upset the heat balance of the earth and caused unusual weather patterns. The clouds prevented hot air from rising at the equator and changed

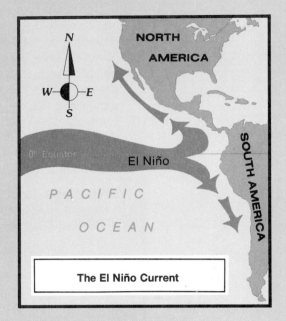

The El Niño Current

the pattern of the trade winds. The trade winds that normally blow over the Pacific Ocean died and then reversed direction. The sudden change in the trade winds was more severe than normal. Therefore, the effects spread farther and faster than expected.

Finally, water temperatures began to fall back to normal, and the unpredictable weather patterns caused by El Niño began to fade. Scientists and meteorologists now keep a much closer eye on the El Niño current.

1. What is El Niño?
2. Which continents would be most affected by El Niño?
3. What were some of the effects of the 1982 El Niño?
4. What do some scientists think caused the 1982 El Niño to be so unusual?

The soil in the rainforest is rich but is easily exhausted. Cultivation for even a few years, along with the heavy rains, robs the soil of the minerals that make it fertile. For this reason, the Indians who live in the rainforest practice slash-and-burn farming. They cut trees and burn them to clear the land. In a few years, when the soil wears out, the Indians move and begin again.

Over the years, people from other parts of Brazil have tried to move into the rainforest and develop it economically. However, raising cattle proved to be difficult and very expensive. Because many of the forest plants are poisonous to grazing cattle, the animals had to be fenced in or watched closely. Lumber companies have been more successful. But their success has left millions of acres of land stripped of all trees. The lumber companies did not practice **reforestation**—planting seeds of trees or young trees—where they had stripped the land. The thin layer of topsoil in these areas was exposed to heavy tropical rains that washed nutrients out of the soil. In some cases, the rains washed away the topsoil, leaving the land looking like a desert.

Rivers and Lakes Rivers are more important in South America than elsewhere in the culture region. The rivers are located east of the Andes and flow into the Atlantic Ocean or the Caribbean Sea.

The greatest river system is the Amazon, which drains some 2,700,000 square miles (7 020 000 square kilometers), or about 40 percent of the continent. The system is made up of more than 200 tributaries. From its source in the Andes to its mouth on the Atlantic Ocean, the Amazon measures about 4,000 miles (6 436 kilometers). Only the Nile River in Africa is longer—by a few miles. But the Amazon holds more water than the Nile. In all, the Amazon empties one-fifth of the total river water of the world into the Atlantic. Ocean steamers and riverboats can navigate the Amazon as far as Iquitos, Peru, more than 2,000 miles (3 200 kilometers) from the coast.

The continent's second greatest river system is the Plata system, which is formed mainly by the Paraná, the Paraguay, and the Uruguay rivers. The Paraná and Uruguay rivers join near the city of Buenos Aires in Argentina. The Orinoco River provides water for the plains of Venezuela. The Magdalena river system in Colombia empties into the Caribbean.

South Americans have been working to make their rivers more usable. To improve river travel, they have built deep-water channels. New dams generate electricity and provide flood control. Irrigation systems have increased the amount of arable land.

Latin America has relatively few large lakes. The largest is Lake Maracaibo in Venezuela. The highest is Lake Titicaca, in the Andes on the border of Bolivia and Peru. This lake lies 12,507 feet (3 812 meters) above sea level. On the other hand, there are many waterfalls in Latin America. Angel Falls in Venezuela, with a drop of 3,212 feet (979 meters), is the world's highest waterfall. Iguaçu (ee-gwuh-SOO) Falls, on the border of Argentina and Brazil, is composed of hundreds of waterfalls that are separated by rocky islands and are surrounded by national parks containing vivid orchids, millions of butterflies, and birds with brilliant hues.

1. **Recall**   What countries make up Latin America?

2. **How and Why**   How are two nations of the Caribbean islands developing new economies?

3. **Critical Thinking**   Why is the protection of South America's rainforests important to everyone?

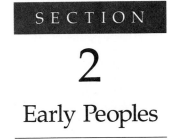

SECTION

2

Early Peoples

Latin America was one of the last culture regions to be settled. People did not walk the lands of the Western Hemisphere until hundreds of thousands of years after humans were living in Africa, Asia, and Europe.

As you know, most scientists believe that people arrived in the Americas from northeast Asia in two successive waves. The first wave came on foot between 35,000 and 25,000 years ago, across a land bridge that connected Siberia with Alaska. About 4,000 years ago, after the last Ice Age ended and the land bridge was submerged beneath the Bering Strait, a second wave of people came by boat.

The first migrants from Asia were hunters, who lived in bands of 25–50 persons. With spears and clubs they hunted mammoths, bison, llamas, and other large grass-grazing animals. They added to their diet by gathering fruits, nuts, and roots. They cooked their food, and wore furs and hides. They had not yet domesticated the dog.

From Alaska the migrants spread slowly southward, reaching the southern tip of South America by about 9,000 B.C. As they followed the animal herds, groups became separated from one another. According to where they finally settled, they developed different physical characteristics. The Indians of the Andes, for example, are shorter and have larger chests than the Indians of the lowlands. Larger chests make it easier to breath in high altitudes. The different groups of migrants also developed numerous languages—an estimated 1,800—as well as different religions and ways of life.

About 7,000 B.C. there was a dramatic change in the environment. The glaciers began to retreat, and the climate became hotter and drier. Most of the large grasslands disappeared, and with them, most of the large game. As a result, people began to rely more and more on plants for food. They found that some plants grew better than others. They learned that if seeds from these plants were gathered and planted, harvests would be larger. Gradually, these first Americans went from plant-gathering to farming.

So far, the earliest remains of domesticated plants in Latin America have been found in Mexico. By 6000 B.C., people there were growing squash, peppers, and beans. By 5000 B.C., they were growing maize, or corn. They were still semi-nomadic. They cleared the land and planted crops, but moved on when the soil was worn out.

Corn became part of the diets of the people of Mexico around 5000 B.C. The earliest corn was even smaller than the variety shown above. This was found with prehistoric remains in South America.

About 3000 B.C. the environment changed again, becoming somewhat cooler and rainier. Gradually, people began living in permanent villages. By then, farmers were producing hardier plants and had developed better ways of farming. They had also domesticated the dog and the turkey.

Less is known about early agriculture in South America. The earliest evidence of domesticated plants comes from the coast of Peru and dates to about 4500 B.C. Between 3000 B.C. and 2500 B.C., cotton, squash, and beans were being grown. Corn seems to have been introduced from Mexico by about 2000 B.C. The sweet potato was originally domesticated in the rainforests of the Amazon and Orinoco basins, while the white potato was developed by the highland Indians of Peru. Potato cultivation then spread throughout the culture region.

By about 2000 B.C., settled agriculture was a way of life in Latin America. In a few areas, farmers had devised irrigation systems that channeled water from the rivers and thus increased the farmers' ability to grow food. Farmers in the Andes extended their arable land by carving terraces into the steep slopes of the mountains.

By now, people were no longer living in pit houses with floors below ground level. Instead, their houses consisted of a framework of poles interwoven with cane and plastered with clay. The roofs were thatched with grass or palm leaves. This type of architecture is well suited to warm climates.

Also by this time, the peoples of the Latin American culture region were weaving textiles and making pottery containers in which to prepare and store food. Pottery apparently developed in Ecuador and spread northward into Mexico. Some archaeologists, however, believe that the craft of making pottery was brought to Ecuador by fishermen who drifted across the Pacific Ocean in canoes from Japan.

In addition to containers, the peoples of the culture region used clay to make figurines about four or five inches long. The earliest figurines were female, but after a while, male figures appeared. Anthropologists believe that the early Indians used the figurines as sacrifices to the gods for more children or increased crops.

SECTION 2 REVIEW

1. **Recall**   When do scientists think the first people arrived in the Americas?
2. **How and Why**   How did the early people of Latin American use pottery?
3. **Critical Thinking**   How did the development of different body types help early hunting groups to survive?

R E V I E W

Reviewing People, Places, and Things

Identify, define, or explain each of the following:

federation

Sierra Madre Oriental

Sierra Madre
    Occidental

Panama Canal

Andes

altiplano

Mato Grosso

Patagonia

pampas

llanos

Atacama Desert

rainforest

reforestation

Amazon

Plata river system

pottery

Map Study

Using the maps on pages 286 and 287, answer the following questions:

1. What are the two largest natural regions of Latin America?

2. What two bodies of water are joined by the Panama Canal?

3. What is the southernmost point in Latin America?

Understanding Facts and Ideas

1. **a.** Where are most of Mexico's major cities located? **b.** Why?

2. How has Mexico been able to move from an agricultural to an industrial nation?

3. Why do most of Central America's people live in its higher regions?

4. What problems can result from dependence on a one-crop economy?

5. What type of economy do most of the Caribbean islands have?

6. How are South Americans working to improve the use of their rivers?

7. Why did early Americans begin to depend more on plants for food?

8. By when was settled agriculture a way of life in Latin America?

Developing Critical Thinking

Classifying Classifying means to arrange data in a system by topic such as the advantages and disadvantages of some condition, event, or point of view. Often making a table listing advantages in one column and disadvantages in a second will help you in organizing your information. A table will make it easier for you to decide whether some piece of data is an advantage.

Activity: Latin America contains a great variety of geographic features. Make a table to help you list the advantages and disadvantages of these features to Latin Americans.

Writing About History

Analyzing Geography Write a paragraph explaining why certain geographical features provide an advantage or a disadvantage to the people of a region.

Applying Your Skills to History

Making a Chart Use encyclopedias and botany books to help make a chart of useful plants native to the Americas and unknown to Europeans before Columbus and of plants that were brought to the Americas from other parts of the world. Include the part of the world from which the plants were brought.

Pre-Columbian Civilizations

Permanent farming made possible the rise of complex Indian civilizations in Latin America. These emerged in two main geographic areas. One was centered in Mexico and Guatemala. The other was in the central part of the Andes Mountains, primarily Peru.

These Indian civilizations developed without the plow. No culture used the wheel—except on toys. Some of these peoples did not have a writing system. All were ignorant of iron and steel. Yet they built beautiful cities, ruled vast empires, and created dramatic works of art.

Archaeologists use the term Mesoamerica to refer to Mexico and Central America. They use the term pre-Columbian or pre-contact to indicate that the Indian civilizations arose before Christopher Columbus reached Latin America in 1492.

As you study this chapter, think about these questions:

- What was the basis of the economies of pre-Columbian civilizations?

- How did each civilization spread its power and influence?

- How have archaeologists learned about these civilizations?

Palenque (pah-LAYNG-kay) in northern Mexico was once the site of a large Mayan ceremonial center. To the right is the Temple of the Sun and to the left the Temple of Inscriptions. The latter pyramid is also a tomb for one of Palenque's rulers.

The first Indian civilization developed in Mesoamerica, in the steamy lowland forests of southern Mexico along the coast of the Gulf of Mexico. It began between 2000 B.C. and 1500 B.C. and lasted until about 100 B.C. This Olmec civilization is usually referred to as the "mother culture" of Mesoamerica. The Olmecs originated a religion, a form of government, a hieroglyphic writing system, a calendar, planned cities, and an art style, all of which carried over into later Indian civilizations.

Mesoamerica

Olmecs

The Olmecs were primarily farmers who raised corn, beans, and squash. The soil of their homeland was extremely fertile, so they needed to tend their fields for only four months of the year. They spent the rest of the time building ceremonial cities.

The cities stood on great artificial hills. They contained temples, houses for priests, huge stone heads, and steles—stone columns with hieroglyphs on them. They also contained large squares where the people celebrated religious festivals and met at regular intervals to trade food and other products. Around the cities were the villages where the people lived.

ceremonial:
belonging to a ceremony, which is a series of formal acts, such as a wedding

Building the cities required both engineering skill and great effort on the part of the Olmecs. They had no metal tools, draft animals, or the wheel to help them. The stone came from quarries at least 50 miles (80 kilometers) away, and a single block sometimes weighed as much as 50 tons (45 metric tons)! With great patience inspired by religious devotion, the Olmecs dragged the huge stones through the jungle and floated them on rafts along navigable rivers to the construction sites.

Olmec religion seems to have centered on worship of a half-human, half-jaguar god. Anthropologists believe the Olmecs chose the jaguar to symbolize physical strength and the forces of rain and fertility. Many finely carved jade figures of this god have been found. In addition, the Olmecs incorporated jaguar symbols in everyday objects. Their pottery was painted with spots and claws, their axes were carved with jaguar masks, and the beads of their necklaces were shaped like jaguar teeth.

The huge stone heads in the Olmec cities were as impressive as the cities. The heads stand up to 9 feet (2.7 meters) high and weigh as much as 20 tons (18 metric tons). They are characterized by feline eyes, flat noses, and thick lips that droop in a sort of open-mouthed snarl. The heads wear hats that resemble football helmets. Archaeologists believe that they may have been worn for protection. The Olmecs played a ball game in which they used hips, elbows, and shoulders to drive a hard rubber ball through a vertical stone hoop. Most archaeologists believe that only kings could play this game. The kings acted both as political leaders and as generals.

The Olmecs developed two calendars. One was a ritual calendar of 260 days. It showed the people the proper times to hold their religious ceremonies. The second calendar was a so-called "Long Count" that indicated how many years had gone by since the gods created the Olmec people. According to the "Long Count," the Olmec year 1 is the same as the year 3113 B.C.

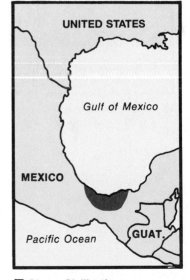

■ **Olmec Civilization, c. 2000s–100s B.C.**

Between 800 B.C. and 400 B.C., Olmec influence spread widely through Mesoamerica. It is not known whether the Olmecs conquered other peoples or spread their knowledge and art by trade and/or colonization. Some scholars believe that Olmec influence can be seen as far south as Peru. The jaguar god of Peru's Chavin culture may have been an adaptation of the Olmec god. Or, the situation may have been reversed, with the worship of the jaguar originating in Peru and then being carried northward by boat along the coast. As archaeologists continue to study Olmec sites, more of the mystery surrounding these early people may be solved.

About 100 B.C., the Olmecs disappeared. No one knows why. But even before they vanished, their civilization had been overshadowed by a more powerful culture to the south—that of the Mayas.

■ **Mayan Civilization,**
c. 1500 B.C.–A.D. 900

Mayas

Mayan civilization began around 1500 B.C. in the rainforests of Belize, Guatemala, Honduras, and the Yucatán Peninsula of Mexico. The greatest stage of Mayan development came during the Classic Period, which lasted from about A.D. 300 to 900.

Like the Olmecs, the Mayas lived in farming villages centered around ceremonial cities. They practiced slash-and-burn agriculture. Since they lacked plows, they planted seeds in holes that they poked in the ground with wooden digging sticks. In addition to the staple foods of corn, beans, and squash, they grew avocados, guavas, chili peppers, papaya, plums, pumpkins, sweet potatoes, and tomatoes. They also grew cacao trees and ground the bean to make chocolate. The farm land was owned by the villages rather than individual families.

Mayan ceremonial cities resembled those of the Olmecs. They were built of limestone blocks, with temples, market places, and houses for the priests. The cities also contained ball courts. While the Olmecs played only for sport, the Mayas attached a religious meaning to their games. They believed the games' outcome was a message from the gods that would help foretell the future.

The Mayas worshiped deities that were connected with the harvest. There were rain, soil, sun, and corn gods, and a moon goddess. An important part of Mayan worship was bloodletting. The Mayas would cut some part of their bodies—usually their tongues—and let the blood drip on the altars. The Mayas believed that unless the gods were fed with blood, they would not be strong enough to keep the sun moving across the sky. Then the crops would wither and the people would die.

The Mayas were fine astronomers, mathematicians, and inventors. Although they had no telescopes, they worked out the movements of the planet Venus and were able to predict eclipses of the sun and the moon. They developed the concept of zero hundreds of years before mathematicians in India did. They developed a numbering system with place value, similar to the decimal system except that it had a base of 20 rather than a base of 10. They invented paper independently of the Chinese.

The Mayas adopted the ritual calendar and the "Long Count" of the Olmecs. They also developed a solar calendar of 365 days. They used it to determine when to plant and harvest crops and what days were lucky or unlucky for getting married and going on trips. The Mayas also developed the belief that time moved in 52-year cycles, with dates and events repeating themselves every 52 years. The belief was based on the fact that every 52 years, the first day of the solar calendar was also the first day of the ritual calendar. This idea of 52-year cycles spread to other Mesoamerican civilizations. As you will read later, it was one reason why many Indians welcomed the Spaniards when they arrived in 1519.

In addition to being farmers, the Mayas were traders. Their oceangoing canoes brought luxury goods, especially jade and pearls, from Panama and Venezuela. Local trade moved along jungle paths or over cement-paved roads that were raised above ground level to keep from being flooded. The goods were carried, not by draft animals, of which there were none, but by slaves. Most of the slaves were Mayan criminals. The Mayas did not have jails.

About A.D. 900, the Mayan civilization collapsed. Their calendar stopped, their ceremonial cities were abandoned, and most of the people vanished. Only in the Yucatán did some Mayas and their culture survive.

The explanation seems to be poor soil management. As the Mayan population increased, slash-and-burn agriculture no longer provided enough food. The Mayas tried to increase the productivity of their farms by fertilizing the soil, building drainage and irrigation ditches, and similar techniques. But what rainforest soil needs is a rotation system that allows it to lie fallow for ten years after being cropped for five. The Mayas also expanded into highland areas, where they felled the trees and

The photo above shows the ruins of a Mayan ball court at Copán, Honduras. The Mayas played a game much like soccer. They batted a rubber ball back and forth by hitting it with their bodies. Archaeologists believe that the game had some religious meaning. A similar game has been found among the Hohokam of central and southern Arizona. This group may have moved into the area from Mexico.

299

terraced the land. But the removal of the forest cover increased the rainy season runoff, and the resulting floods eroded the soil or washed out its nutrients. Unable any longer to support themselves and their ceremonial cities, the Mayas moved away.

Teotihuacanos

About the time that the early Mayan culture was developing in southern Mexico, another civilization was developing north of modern Mexico City. It began in an area of the Valley of Mexico called Teotihuacán (TAY-oh-TEE-wah-KAHN).

People were living in the region by 300 B.C. or earlier. But some archaeologists believe that Teotihuacán and the civilization that bears its name developed about 2,000 years ago. Over the centuries the city of Teotihuacán came to rival any city of Europe in size, splendor, and planning. Estimates of the city's population, at the height of its influence, range from 60,000 to 200,000. Teotihuacán spread across nearly 8 square miles (21 square kilometers). Wide avenues, temple pyramids, palaces for priests and nobles, and houses for artisans and traders filled the city. Smaller communities grew out from it.

Of its architectural features, Teotihuacán is best known for the Pyramids of the Sun and of the Moon. They are located at either end of the Avenue of the Dead. The Pyramid of the Sun was built of adobe bricks and covered with stone. Possibly 10,000 workers labored 20 years to build it.

Some archaeologists believe that Teotihuacán may have been the largest city in Mesoamerica. Its prosperity was built on its trading network. This network spread Teotihuacán's influence from Guatemala in the south to the United States Southwest.

About A.D. 400 the Teotihuacanos began a series of wars of conquest. Sometime between the A.D. 600 and 900s, enemies—probably Toltecs from the north—burned the city. It never again regained its importance.

This stele was found at Piedras Negras, Guatemala. Archaeologists believe the figures to be that of a priest-ruler and his wife.

Toltecs

Other peoples—Zapótecs, Totonacs, and Mixtecs, to name a few—came to power in pre-Columbian America and then fell. The people they conquered regarded them as barbarians. The invaders usually had a less-developed culture. As has often happened, however, the invaders accepted many of the ways of the peoples they conquered. But they also left their own cultural mark on the conquered. As we have seen with the Olmecs, none of the cultures totally disappeared. Elements reappeared in one form or another in one culture or another. This fact is also illustrated by the merging of Mayan and Toltec cultures.

The Toltecs were originally seminomads who lived in northern Mexico. Around A.D. 750 a severe drought hit their homeland, and they began moving south into the central valley of Mexico. A warlike people,

the Toltecs gradually conquered the valley's ceremonial cities including Teotihuacán. By about A.D. 950 they ruled most of Mexico.

About that time, the first flesh-and-blood person in Mesoamerican history ascended the Toltec throne. He was fair-skinned and black-bearded, and his name was Topiltzin. Upon becoming king, he added the name Quetzalcóatl (ketz-uhl-KOH-ah-tuhl). This was the name of the god of Teotihuacán, who had given the people of central Mexico corn, art, and learning—in other words, civilization. Quetzalcóatl's symbol was a feathered serpent, which is why scholars often refer to pre-Columbian Mexico as The Land of the Feathered Serpent. It is also why the temples at Teotihuacán are decorated with carvings of massive snake heads.

Shortly after becoming king, Topiltzin-Quetzalcóatl moved his capital to Tula, 20 miles north of Teotihuacán. Tula was a showcase of the Toltecs' military spirit. Built on top of an easily defended hill, its buildings were covered with designs of skulls and crossbones and with pictures of grim-faced warriors. On the other hand, such facilities as public steam baths made life in Tula fairly comfortable.

Topiltzin-Quetzalcóatl ruled for about 20 years. Then a civil war broke out between his supporters and the worshipers of a god whom the Toltecs had brought with them from the north. Defeated in the war, Topiltzin-Quetzalcóatl and his followers left Tula and set sail for the Yucatán. They conquered the Mayas who were living there and reoccupied many of the cities the Mayas had abandoned, building pyramids in their own style over existing Mayan pyramids. The combined Toltec-Mayan civilization lasted until about 1400. Then it disappeared.

Topiltzin-Quetzalcóatl's memory, on the other hand, did not disappear. According to legend, when he left Tula he prophesized that he would return in the year Ce Acatl. (That is the name of a year in the 52-year cycle that other cultures adopted from the Mayas.) For more than 500 years, Indians throughout Mesoamerica looked forward to the time when the prophecy would be fulfilled. Then, in 1519—which was the year Ce Acatl—the fair-skinned, black-bearded Hernán Cortés led his Spanish troops into the Valley of Mexico. You will read about this in the next chapter.

Teotihuacán, located about 30 miles (48 kilometers) northeast of Mexico City, flourished between A.D. 300 and 700. The large grassy area in the foreground was once a giant market. Behind it are the city's most famous architectural features, the Pyramids of the Sun and of the Moon.

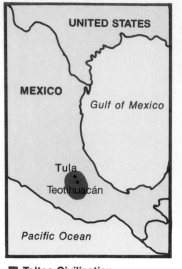

■ Toltec Civilization,
  c. A.D. 950

■ Aztec Civilization,
  c. 1200s–1521

segment:
portion or part

In the meantime, the Toltec Empire remained centered around Tula for some 200 years. Then, about 1160, another warlike people from the north conquered central Mexico. They destroyed Tula and established a group of city-states in the Valley. Around 1400 they were conquered in turn by still another warlike people from the north, the Aztecs.

Aztecs

We know more about the Aztecs than about any of the other Mesoamerican cultures. Many written accounts—both Aztec and Spanish—give details of Aztec civilization. Some of these records were written at the time of the Spanish conquest. Others were written shortly afterward.

The name *Aztec* comes from Aztlán, the area in northern Mexico where the Aztecs originated. In the late 1100s they began wandering south into the Valley of Mexico. In the early 1300s they came upon a large, shallow lake called Lake Texcoco. In the lake was a rocky island.

According to Aztec legend, their war god Huitzilopochtli (WEE-tsee-loh-POHTCH-tlee) had told them that they would someday be a great people. But they must follow his advice: Seek out good land. Plant corn and beans. War only when strong enough to conquer. Make sacrifices of war captives. The Aztecs would know that they had found the right place to settle when they came upon a small island where they would see an eagle perched on a cactus, with a serpent in its beak.

When the Aztecs arrived at Lake Texcoco, they supposedly found these signs. (Today the cactus, the eagle, and the snake form Mexico's national emblem.) Accordingly, they built a city on the island that they called Tenochtitlán (ten-och-tee-TLAHN)—meaning near the cactus. (Today the lake is gone but Mexico City stands on the dry lake bed.) Tenochtitlán soon became a great city-state. Gradually the Aztecs spread their military power throughout Mexico. By the late 1400s, their empire contained some eleven million people and was larger by far than any nation of Western Europe.

Politics and Society   The Aztec empire was headed by a semi-divine ruler. He was chosen by a council of nobles because of his bravery in battle and his devotion to public service. However, he had to be a member of the royal family.

The Aztecs had a rigid class system. At the top—just below the emperor—were the nobles, who served as administrators, generals, and priests. They were the only people in the empire who were permitted to drink cocoa. Below the nobles were the judges and the merchants. Then came the commoners, who formed the largest segment of the population. They included farmers and artisans. Intermarriage between the nobles and the other classes was rare. At the lowest social level were the slaves. People became slaves because they were prisoners of war, criminals, or debtors.

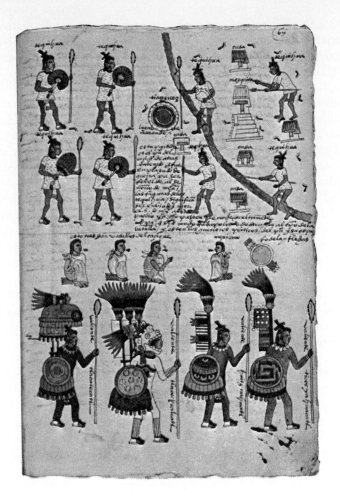

The commoners were organized into groups called *calpulli*, or group of houses. A calpulli might contain a few dozen families or a few hundred. Each calpulli was ruled by a group of three household heads. Each calpulli owned the land that its families farmed. Each calpulli also ran its own market, its own temple, and its own school. Only boys attended the schools, which taught religion, history, and military skills.

The Economy   The Aztec economy was based on agriculture. The Aztecs dug elaborate irrigation systems for their fields. In marshy areas, such as the land around Tenochtitlán, they built *chinampas*, or floating gardens. To make these gardens, they dug ditches through the marshland. Then they filled the enclosed areas with fertile mud dredged from the bottom of the ditches. The mud was kept in place with tree branches or cane. The Aztecs' main crop was corn, but they also grew fruit, vegetables, and flowers. Chinampa farming was extremely efficient and productive.

Aztec artisans produced a variety of goods in wood, feathers, and other materials. Because such luxury items as jaguar skins and jade were not available near Tenochtitlán, the Aztecs traded over long distances. Their traders did double duty as military spies.

War and Religion   Warfare was an extremely important part of Aztec life. The training of Aztec soldiers began at an early age. In the absence of metal, Aztec weapons were limited to wooden clubs, spears tipped with a volcanic rock called obsidian, bows and arrows, and slings. For protection, Aztec soldiers wore helmets and armor made of heavily padded cotton. Members of a calpulli fought as a unit.

The Aztecs fought wars mostly for religious reasons. Their main god, Huitzilopochtli, required human sacrifice. (There were no oxen, sheep, or other livestock in Mesoamerica that might have been sacrificed instead of people.) So prisoners of war were thrown face up on an altar, where a priest cut open their chest and tore out their still-beating heart. As many as 20,000 prisoners were sacrificed at a time.

Warfare also benefited the Aztecs economically. Defeated peoples sent vast quantities of tribute to Tenochtitlán. The roads to the city were always filled with thousands of porters carrying beans, corn, cotton cloth, firewood, rubber, and sisal.

A Great City   Tenochtitlán itself was one of the greatest cities in the world. By the late 1400s, its population of 300,000 was more than five times that of London, and it boasted many things unheard of in Europe—including clean streets, neat and well-regulated markets, an ample supply of pure water, a public police force, and public sanitation workers.

Two three-mile-long aqueducts carried fresh water to the city from springs on the mainland. Then municipal workers distributed the water to people's houses and took away human wastes, which were sold for fertilizer. The sanitation workers traveled by canoe, for Tenochtitlán's streets were a gridwork of canals. (The city as a whole was linked to the mainland by three causeways, or stone-paved roads.) People crossed the canals over wooden bridges that could be taken down if the city were attacked. In addition to the aqueducts, Aztec engineers built a large dike across Lake Texcoco to keep water from flooding the city during the rainy season.

Tenochtitlán's markets were not only trading centers but social centers as well. There, the women visited with their friends and the men discussed local events. Doing business in the markets took a long time, for the Aztecs did not use money and therefore had to resort to barter. Anyone caught selling stolen goods was put to death.

Tenochtitlán's inhabitants celebrated many religious festivals with feasting, music, singing, and dancing. The music was rhythmic rather than tuneful because most Aztec instruments—such as drums and rattles—could carry a beat but not a melody. Saunas and gardens were attached to most of the city's houses, while the palaces of the royal family and the nobles contained pools and zoos. Everyone who could afford it wore brightly colored clothes.

barter:
to trade goods or services without the exchange of money

1. **Recall** Where was the Olmec culture located?
2. **How and Why** How did the Aztecs spread their power and influence throughout Mexico?
3. **Critical Thinking** Why do we know more about the Aztecs than about any of the other Mesoamerican cultures?

Andean cultures developed along the mountains and coastal areas of western South America from southern Ecuador through Peru, Bolivia, and Colombia into northern Chile. Like those of Mesoamerica, Andean cultures were based on agriculture. The leading culture was that of the Incas. But it was preceded by other cultures that formed a basis for it.

SECTION

2

The Andes

Pre-Incan Cultures

All we know of pre-Incan peoples is what archaeologists have found. And there are various interpretations of what the artifacts mean. However, we know for certain that by about 3000 B.C., Andean peoples began farming. They cultivated such crops as lima beans, white potatoes, and peanuts that eventually spread to other culture regions. (Corn was introduced from Mesoamerica about 1500 B.C.) They also became skilled weavers, pottery makers, and stone carvers. They domesticated two relatives of the camel—the llama and the alpaca—which they used for wool, meat, and transport. So far, however, no traces of scientific accomplishments have been found. Neither calendars nor written material like Mayan steles have yet been discovered.

Very little archaeological work was done in the area before World War II. The expense of sending expeditions and the difficult working conditions kept archaeologists away. Also, because of a lack of records, it was difficult to know where to explore. The study of Spanish histories and new techniques such as surveys of sites from the air have helped solve this problem.

Chavin The oldest known Andean culture is the Chavin culture, which developed around 1000 B.C. The Chavin people built ceremonial centers similar to those of the Indians of Mesoamerica. These centers had great platformlike temples decorated with stone carvings of animals and humans. The most impressive ceremonial center is at Chavin de Huántar in northern Peru. It contains the so-called Castle, the oldest building in Peru. Like the structures of the later Incas, the Castle was built of stones that were fitted together without mortar. Apparently artisans and traders

■ **Chavin Civilization,**
   c. 1000s–400s B.C.

This bowl made in the shape of a jaguar was found at Chavin de Huántar. What other people used a catlike figure in their art?

cult:
a system or community of religious worship and ritual

Mochica-Chimú Civilizations
━**Mochica, c. 200s B.C.–A.D. 800s**
■ **Chimú, 1300s–1460**

from all parts of Peru would meet at the ceremonial centers and exchange products, techniques, and ideas. In this way, Chavin influence spread widely.

The Chavins worshiped a jaguar god similar to that of the Olmecs. Designs and figures with catlike features are prominent on Chavin pottery and textiles. The Chavins were also skilled in metalworking, for they made plaques, necklaces, and rings from copper and gold.

About 400 B.C. the jaguar cult apparently suffered a setback and the ceremonial centers declined. The overall Chavin culture was replaced by numerous local cultures as different groups competed for land and for power in the Andes.

Paracas and Nazca   Around 200 B.C., people on the Paracas peninsula of southern Peru began developing a culture. So far, its textiles are the most impressive aspect to be unearthed. Most that have been found are cloaks that were wrapped around mummies. The cloaks were embroidered with brilliantly colored birds, fish, animals, gods, and geometric designs. Various weaving techniques were used, and some pieces had more than a hundred different colors.

The Paracas culture gradually merged into the Nazca culture, which also developed along the desert coast of southern Peru but about 100 miles farther south. The Nazcas were famous for their polished pottery. They also created what seems to be Peru's most baffling archaeological mystery. On the dry plains north of Nazca are giant lines made in the shapes of animals and geometric forms. The Nazca lines were first spotted from an airplane; an entire pattern cannot be seen at one time from the ground. Archaeologists theorize that the straight lines served as astronomical calendars to determine when to plant crops and when to open irrigation ditches to catch the water from the seasonal rivers. Another theory is that the spirals and animal shapes were made as religious offerings to the gods who lived in the sky. Some writers have suggested that the lines are signals to visitors from another solar system.

Mochica-Chimú   About 200 B.C. the Mochica culture emerged along the northern coast of Peru. Mochica pottery indicates that warriors ranked high in the Mochica class system, that hunting was a favorite sport, that doctors practiced bone surgery, that musical instruments included flutes and a sort of bagpipe, and that men always dressed more luxuriously than women. The Mochicas also developed a unique pottery design—the portrait jar, which represented specific individuals from all walks of life. The Mochicas, like the later Incas, sent messages from one area to another by means of knotted strings. They built their ceremonial pyramids of adobe bricks that lasted for centuries because of the absence of rainfall in their homeland.

The Mochica culture declined sometime between A.D. 600 and 800. But the Chimú culture rose on its base. The Chimú were richer than the Mochicas. They lived mostly in well-planned cities. At one time, their capital contained 200,000 inhabitants in ten separate districts, each of which was protected by an adobe wall. There were numerous parks and

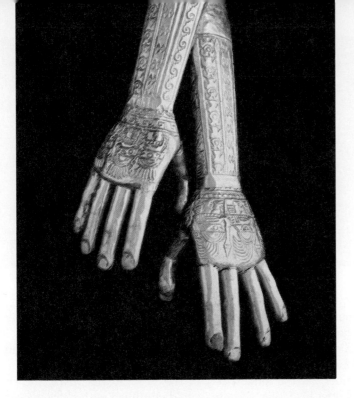

The peoples of the Mesoamerican and Andean cultures had been working in metals for centuries before the Western Europeans came. This is an example of Chimú goldwork. Human and animal figures as well as abstract designs were beaten into the gold.

lagoons scattered throughout. Chimú farmers terraced the mountainsides and built an extensive irrigation system. They fertilized their fields with guano (the droppings of sea birds) which they carried from the coast up the valleys.

In the 1300s the people of Chimú began to expand. They waged a series of highly successful wars and conquered several neighboring peoples. They resettled the conquered peoples near the capital, and moved loyal settlers into the new distant territories. Then, around 1460, the Chimú were themselves conquered by the greatest of the Peruvian civilizations, that of the Incas.

Incas

Little is known about the Incas before the 1200s. By the time the Spaniards arrived in the 1500s, however, the Incas ruled an empire of almost 400,000 square miles (1 million square kilometers) that included all or part of five nations. Its population numbered about ten million people. At one time, the word *Inca* was applied only to the ruler. The Spaniards, however, used it to describe the entire culture.

Religion   Among the legends the Incas told about their origins is the story of Manco Capac and his sister-wife Mama Ocla. They were created by Inti, the sun god, who told them to search for a place where they could push a gold stick all the way into the ground. When they found such a fertile place, they were to "Stay there, build a city, start a family, make a

At right is a highly decorated jar from the Nazca culture. To the far right is a Mochica jar in the shape of a llama. Both cultures used their pottery to describe objects and scenes from daily life. Why would people take such care and use so much talent to make an ordinary item such as a jar?

nation." Manco Capac and Mama Ocla founded the city of Cuzco, which became the capital of the Inca empire. The Incas believed that their rulers were descended from these two gods.

The Inca religion centered around Inti, and the most important religious celebration was the Festival of the Sun. It was held around December 22, the longest day of the year. At daybreak, the emperor would offer his father, the sun, a gold cup filled with chica, a beer made from corn. In exchange, Inti promised the Incas light, warmth, and good crops for the coming year. The emperor also offered the god gifts of gold and silver, and sacrifices of black alpacas and llamas.

Organization

Archaeologists believe that the Incas were originally a small group of farmers and shepherds who lived in the Cuzco basin. In the early 1400s, as their population increased, they began spreading beyond the basin. At first they fought bloody wars with neighboring cultures, including the Chimú. After a while, however, their reputation as fighters became so great that other peoples simply surrendered when asked, without any resistance at all.

The main architect of the Inca empire was Pachacuti, who ruled from 1438 to 1471. Pachacuti was an excellent administrator as well as a good general. He adopted the Chimú practice of resettling conquered peoples among loyal subjects. He built a gold-plated Temple of the Sun in Cuzco and ordered his subjects to worship Inti in addition to their own gods. This helped to unify the empire. Another unifying technique was the use of Quechua (KECH-uh-wuh), the Inca language, as the language of government.

Pachacuti also expanded the system of roads that had been built by earlier people. The Inca highway network eventually extended more than 10,000 miles (16 000 kilometers) from the coast of the Pacific to the rainforests of the Amazon. Two main roads ran parallel for the length of the empire, with small roads connecting them. The roads were paved with stone. In coastal areas, they were lined with shade trees. In mountain areas, they were lined with low walls that provided protection against the wind. Wherever the route crossed mountain chasms or rivers, the Incas built suspension bridges of wood and fiber. A special staff kept the roads clean and in repair.

The Incas used their roads only for government business. Messengers carried news from one part of the empire to another. Inspectors toured the countryside, making certain that people paid their taxes, that crimes were properly punished, and that local officials were honest and hard-working. Soldiers tramped from one roadside station to another. The stations were situated a day's journey apart and were stocked with food, weapons, and sandals. Ordinary persons were not permitted to use the roads. As a result, it was almost impossible for subject peoples to revolt against the Incas.

A Welfare State
Inca society was one of the most highly organized in the world. At the same time, the government tried to see to it that everyone had food, clothing, and shelter.

The emperor made all political and religious laws for his subjects. For administrative purposes, the empire was divided into four districts. The governor of each was a member of the royal family and was directly responsible to the emperor. Each district was divided into smaller districts, each with a governor. Under him were local officials who conducted the census, recorded wealth, and set tax rates. Each local official was responsible for the welfare of a group of ten families. If a farmer stole food because he was hungry, the official responsible for him was also punished for having failed in his duty.

All land was owned by the emperor but worked by the people. Its products were divided into three parts. One part was kept by the people. Products of the second part were used in religious ceremonies and to support the temples and priests. The third part was for the use of the emperor, the army, public officials, and such government employees as teachers, architects, and engineers. A portion of the emperor's third, however, was stored in warehouses. In times of drought or crop failure, the emperor would send some of this emergency supply to the needy areas.

■ Inca Empire, c. 1200s-1533

The Incas had no writing system but used quipus instead. Quipus were made of one long rope with shorter ropes knotted to it and shorter ropes tied to these. The knots were used to show units, tens, and hundreds. The cords were dyed. Each color represented a different item such as land or tribute.

Machu Picchu is one of the largest examples of the Inca culture to be found. It is set high in the Andes, not far from Cuzco. Its ruins include a temple, a fort, and walled terraces. The Incas raised crops on these terraces.

Technology   The Incas inherited much of their technology from earlier peoples. But they adapted and expanded these ideas to their own needs. They were especially skilled at engineering. They did not surround their cities with walls. Instead, they built citadels on mountaintops where people could seek shelter in case of attack. An Inca fortress outside Cuzco contains three rows of masonry walls. The walls were angled so that attackers would be caught in a crossfire of stone balls and spears.

A Basic Weakness   In spite of its wealth, military strength, and administrative organization, the Inca empire had a basic weakness. Like the ancient Roman Empire, it lacked a law of succession. The throne could be claimed by any royal son, not just the oldest. To avoid trouble, it was customary for an emperor to name his heir. But in 1525 the emperor died without having done so. The resulting civil war between two half-brothers devastated the empire and made it difficult for the Incas to resist the invading Spaniards. You will read about this in the next chapter.

SECTION 2 REVIEW

1. **Recall**   What is the most impressive aspect of the Paracas culture to be unearthed?
2. **How and Why**   Why is the Chavin culture considered to be the oldest Andean culture?
3. **Critical Thinking**   How did communication affect the Inca empire?

Chapter 15

Reviewing People, Places, and Things

Identify, define, or explain each of the following:

Mesoamerica

pre-Columbian

Olmecs

hieroglyphic

ceremonial

Mayas

Toltecs

Teotihuacán

Tula

Aztecs

Tenochtitlán

calpulli

chinampa

artisans

barter

Incas

Chavins

cult

Cuzco

Pachacuti

Map Study

Using the maps on pages 298 and 308, answer the following questions:

1. What body of water bordered both the Maya and the Inca lands?
2. In what direction from the United States did the Mayas live?
3. Along what coast of South America was the Inca Empire located?

Understanding Facts and Ideas

1. What special skills did the Olmec people have?
2. What have archaeologists been able to determine about the Mayas?
3. The Mayan deities were connected with what activity?
4. What evidence is there of a sudden decline of Mayan culture?
5. Why did the Toltecs move into the central Valley of Mexico?

6. What was the class system of the Aztecs?
7. What methods did the Chimú use to control their empire?
8. What did the Incas learn from others, especially the Chimú?

Developing Critical Thinking

Comparing and Contrasting   To compare things means to look for similarities. To contrast them means to look for differences. Organizing information about ideas, movements, and cultures will make it easier to think critically.

Activity: Make a table listing Mesoamerican and Andean cultures. Use headings such as: Name, Dates, Political Organization, Class System, Economy, War, Technology, Religion, and Other. Write four or more summary statements comparing and contrasting these cultures.

Writing About History

Expressing Your Opinion   Write a paragraph defending the explanation of why the Mayan culture ended that seems most reasonable to you.

Applying Your Skills to History

Making a Historical Map   Using the maps in this chapter as reference, make a combined map of Mesoamerican and Andean cultures. Be sure to use a different color or marking for each culture and to include a legend.

Like other conquistadores, Vasco Nuñez de Balboa claimed land and people in the name of God and his monarch. This statue of Balboa stands in Panama City.

Coming of the Western Europeans

The European discovery of the Americas was an accident. It was the result of efforts during the 1400s to find a sea route to the riches of Asia. The conquerors, regardless of nationality, treated the Indians as objects to rob. They set up colonies for the benefit of their Western European homelands.

Between 1500 and 1800 the British, French, and Dutch fought with the Spanish and Portuguese for control of parts of Latin America. Except for several small territories and some islands in the Caribbean, the Spanish and Portuguese were able to hold onto their claims.

As you study this chapter, think about these questions:

• What was the attitude of Western Europeans toward the Indians?

• How did the colonization of Spanish and Portuguese areas differ?

• Why were blacks from Africa brought to Latin America?

Christopher Columbus's first voyage to the Americas took place in 1492. He landed on an island in the Bahamas and also on Hispaniola. Believing that he had reached India he called the people he met Indians. In all, Columbus made four voyages to Latin America in search of the Asian mainland.

Although he never brought back great riches, Columbus's discoveries aroused considerable interest in Spain. That country had just defeated the last of the Moors and become a unified nation. The victory created a great sense of pride in being Spanish and Christian. It also left thousands of soldiers unemployed. So the soldiers—later known as conquistadores, or conquerors—began coming to the Americas. For the possibility of gold, they fought mountains, rivers, jungles, cold, heat, and Indian resistance. One-fifth of what they found went to the Spanish monarch. They were permitted to keep the rest.

In time the Spaniards began claiming the land as well as its mineral resources. They also claimed the people living on the land, whom they looked down on because of their dark skins and their religious beliefs. The level of civilization of the Indians did not matter. Within less than twenty years, the Spanish conquistadores destroyed both the Aztec and the Inca empires and established a vast colonial empire of their own. It was to last for about three centuries.

The Conquest of Mexico

By 1515 the Spaniards controlled Hispaniola, Puerto Rico, Cuba, and other Caribbean islands. Rumors of the Aztec wealth prompted Hernán Cortés, the mayor of the Spanish settlement of Santiago, Cuba, to lead an expedition to Mexico in 1519. The expedition included about 400 conquistadores and 16 horses.

After landing on the Yucatán peninsula, Cortés received a gift from a local chief: a beautiful slave named Malinche. The Spaniards called her Doña Marina. She was an Aztec who had been sold to the Mayas, and she spoke both the Aztec and the Mayan languages. Doña Marina acted as an interpreter for Cortés. With her help, he learned that the Aztecs were hated by their subjects because of their custom of sacrificing war prisoners to the god Huitzilopochtli. Cortés promised to help overthrow the Aztecs, and thousands of non-Aztec Indians allied themselves with him. Knowing that he was outnumbered even with Indian allies, Cortés burned his ships so that his men would have to fight if they wanted to survive. Then he and his army began moving inland.

Word of Cortés's arrival reached the Aztec ruler, Montezuma II, long before the Spaniards entered Tenochtitlán. Montezuma believed that Cortés fulfilled the ancient prophecy of the fair-skinned, black-bearded god Topiltzin-Quetzalcóatl, who had promised to return out of the east in the year Ce Acatl. Accordingly, Montezuma sent rich gifts to the Spaniards, as well as requests that they leave Mexico. But the gifts merely excited the greed of the Spaniards, who continued on their way.

When Cortés reached Tenochtitlán, he was welcomed by Montezuma as a god. Soon after, he took Montezuma hostage. He correctly

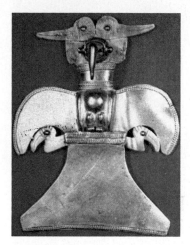

Gold works, such as this, tempted the Spaniards into exploring the Americas. When they found the peoples who made these objects, the Western Europeans seized their land and valuables and killed them or made them slaves on their estates.

313

This picture shows Hernán Cortés in Mexico in 1519. On the far right is Malinche. How did she help Cortés defeat the Aztecs?

assumed that the Aztecs would not risk harming their emperor even if they harbored doubts about Cortés's divinity. Therefore the conquistadores were relatively safe from attack as long as Montezuma was their prisoner.

A few months later, Cortés left Tenochtitlán for a short time. In his absence, the greedy Spaniards murdered 600 unarmed Aztec nobles during a religious feast and removed all the gold jewelry from the dead bodies. The Aztecs, who no longer respected Montezuma's authority because of his refusal to act against the conquistadores, besieged the Spanish quarters. They also stoned Montezuma to death when he tried to calm them. When Cortés returned, he realized the danger of his position and left quickly.

In 1521 Cortés re-entered the Valley of Mexico with a new army of Spaniards and Indians. The Aztecs fought valiantly for more than four months. But the conquistadores had two overwhelming advantages. One was technological. They were armed with guns and steel swords. The second—and more significant—advantage was medical. The Spaniards had carried smallpox germs with them on their first invasion, and the Aztecs—who lacked a natural immunity against the new disease—had died in great numbers. When Cortés entered Tenochtitlán for the second time, he found more than half the people dead from smallpox. Historians estimate that by 1600, the disease killed from 80 to 95 percent of Mexico's population.

By August 1521, the conquistadores had conquered and almost completely destroyed what Cortés called "the most beautiful city in the world." The era of Spanish rule in Mexico had begun.

The Conquest of Peru

Shortly after Cortés's successful conquest of the Aztecs, a group of about 180 Spanish adventurers set sail from Panama in search of the wealth of the Incas. In 1530, these conquistadores, led by Francisco Pizarro, landed in what is now Ecuador. From there, they made their way south toward the center of the Inca empire.

As it happens, the empire was extremely unstable at that time. Although a civil war between two half-brothers for the throne had ended, the country was in ruins, partly because of the fighting and partly because not enough men had been left behind to cultivate the fields and maintain the irrigation systems. To make matters worse, the dread disease of smallpox had entered the empire from Panama and was slowly but steadily wiping out the population.

In 1532, Pizarro's force entered the undefended Inca city of Cajamarca (CAH-huh-MAHR-kuh), high in the Andes. At that time, the Inca Atahuallpa (AHT-uh-WAHL-puh) was camped near the city. Pizarro sent **emissaries** to invite Atahuallpa for a visit. Surprisingly, the Inca agreed and entered the city with 5,000 unarmed nobles. Pizarro, copying Cortés's tactics in Mexico, ambushed the Inca. He massacred about half of them and took Atahuallpa prisoner.

In captivity, Atahuallpa continued to issue orders, and he was treated very well. Meanwhile, Inca nobles were reluctant to attack the Spaniards for fear that such a move would bring harm to the sacred emperor.

Atahuallpa soon realized how much the Spaniards wanted gold. So he offered to fill a huge room with the precious metal in return for his release. Pizarro hastily accepted the offer. And well he might. His share of the ransom came to $425,000—a small fortune in those days. His soldiers likewise received tidy sums: $50,000 for each cavalryman and $20,000 for each foot soldier.

Nevertheless, when the ransom was complete, Pizarro had Atahuallpa executed. The grounds were that the Inca had killed his half-brother and had plotted against the Spaniards. Without an emperor to guide them, the Incas were unable to organize any effective resistance. By 1535, Spanish control of the Inca empire was complete. The only poetic justice was that in 1541, Pizarro was assassinated by the friends of a former partner whom he had killed in 1538 in a struggle for power.

Atahuallpa (above) was the last Inca. His death came as a result of the efforts of Spaniards under Francisco Pizarro (below) to obtain Inca gold.

The Spanish Empire

Spain's empire in Latin America was the largest colonial empire in the world at the time. Its establishment had profound effects on the culture region. Many of these effects have lasted until the present, although the empire itself disappeared in the early 1800s.

Government The original Spanish explorations and conquests were the result of individual action. Columbus, Cortés, and Pizarro were all soldiers of fortune. Gradually the government in Spain realized that their conquests had placed a huge territory under its authority.

Accordingly, in 1535 the Spanish king divided the vast empire into two administrative units called **viceroyalties**. In the north was New Spain, composed of Mexico and Central America. (In those years, Mexico included present-day southern United States.) Farther south was the Viceroyalty of Peru, which included most of Spanish South America. A viceroy, or royal governor, appointed by the Spanish king governed each area. Both viceroyalties, in turn, were divided into smaller units. In the 1700s, the Viceroyalty of Peru was divided twice again. The new territories were the Viceroyalty of New Granada and the Viceroyalty of La Plata. The viceroys ruled in an authoritarian manner. The only appeal to their decisions was to the king in Madrid, a costly and time-consuming process.

Like the ancient Romans, the Spaniards established cities that became strongholds of power and centers of culture. For example, even before setting out of Tenochtitlán, Cortés founded Veracruz in the Yucatán. Pizarro shifted the capital of Peru from Cuzco in the Andes to a new city called Lima, about eight miles (12 kilometers) from the coast.

The Spaniards laid out their colonial cities in Spanish style. On one side of the central square stood the church. Opposite it were government buildings. Flanking the square was a rectangular grid of streets on which stood the homes and businesses of the Spaniards. Indian dwellings were located on the city's outskirts.

These are the front and back of a Spanish coin called a piece of eight. Gold and silver from Latin America were sent to Spain and minted into millions of such coins.

The Economy   Eager for riches and land, Spaniards flocked to Latin America. The Spanish monarch, who was considered the owner of all Spanish lands, granted these adventurers large estates, where they farmed or began mining for gold and silver. In addition, through a policy known as *encomienda*, the Indians who lived on these vast estates were entrusted to the new owners' care.

Laws governing the encomienda described the rights and responsibilities of both the Spaniards and the Indians. Spanish landholders would develop the land for their own profit. In return they were to care for and protect the Indians and convert them to Christianity. The landowners could use Indian labor as a tax for taking care of them. Legally the Indians were free. In reality, however, they were bound to the land and were slaves in all but name.

At first the Spaniards searched mainly for gold. But in 1545 prospectors discovered Mount Potosí in Bolivia. The 2,000-foot (610-meter) mountain proved to be almost solid silver, and mining and shipping the precious metal turned into an international trade. Each year, Spanish galleons carried silver from the Mexican port of Acapulco across the Pacific to the Philippines, where it was exchanged for silks and spices from China and the East Indies. Back in Mexico, the silks and spices were loaded on mules and taken crosscountry to Veracruz. There, another fleet of Spanish galleons carried the goods, together with bars of silver and gold, across the Atlantic to Spain.

It was in the area of agriculture that major cultural exchanges between Latin America and Spain took place. The Spaniards introduced the wheel, which made possible the cart. They introduced draft animals, especially horses and mules, as well as animals for food—cattle, chickens,

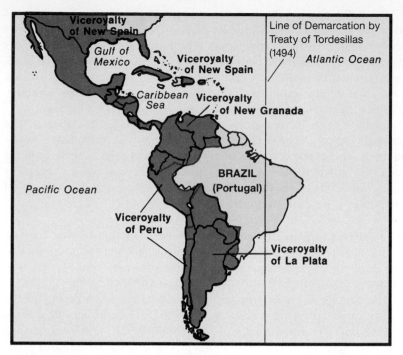

Spanish Colonial Administration, 1790

Map labels: Viceroyalty of New Spain, Gulf of Mexico, Viceroyalty of New Spain, Caribbean Sea, Viceroyalty of New Granada, Line of Demarcation by Treaty of Tordesillas (1494), Atlantic Ocean, BRAZIL (Portugal), Pacific Ocean, Viceroyalty of Peru, Viceroyalty of La Plata

pigs, and sheep. They also introduced sugar, wheat, barley, onions, grapes, bananas, oranges, and coffee. For their part, the Indians gave the Spaniards beans, corn, peanuts, potatoes, sweet potatoes, tomatoes, and turkeys. As you know, the Indians were the first people to drink chocolate and to smoke tobacco. And they contributed such medicinal plants as cinchona (quinine), used in the treatment of malaria.

The main agricultural exports of the Spanish empire were sugar cane and beef. The sugar cane was grown mainly in the West Indies. As disease and overwork killed off most of the Indian population there, black slaves from West Africa were imported to insure an adequate labor supply. The beef was raised mostly on the pampas of Argentina. The cowboys there were known as gauchos. They were part Spanish and part Indian, and during the 1800s they became the subject of much Argentinian literature. For example, the epic poem *Martín Fierro* by José Hernandez tells the first-person story of a gaucho who relies on himself, his horse, and his knife to gain control over a cattle herd so that he can continue his free and self-sufficient life away from the city.

Society   The Spaniards brought their strict class system to Latin America. They also added two factors: birthplace and race.

The leading posts of viceroys, judges, and bishops were held by peninsulares, or men of the peninsula, meaning those who had been born in Spain. Below them in rank were the creoles. They were the descendants of the original Spanish colonists. They owned plantations or profitable trading businesses but had only a limited say in the government.

The third, and largest, social class consisted of mestizos, or persons with a Spanish father and an Indian mother. Mestizos worked mostly as artisans, tenant farmers, and small shopkeepers. Below the mestizos came the Indians, followed by the mulattoes (of mixed Spanish and black parentage) and the zambos (of mixed Indian and black parentage). Black slaves were at the bottom of the social system. Mestizos, Indians, mulattoes, zambos, and slaves had no say at all in the government.

In addition to bringing their class system to Latin America, the Spaniards brought over definite ideas about the role of women. Upper-class peninsulare and creole women spent most of their time secluded at home. If unmarried, they could not go anywhere without a chaperone. Lower-class women, on the other hand, were expected to work. Most were domestic servants and farm laborers.

The Church   Since the desire to spread Christianity was a major motive for Spanish colonization, the conquistadores were accompanied to Latin America by missionaries. Religious leadership in Mexico was provided by the Franciscans, in Peru by the Dominicans.

The Roman Catholic Church became a major part of life in the Spanish empire. It ran the schools, including the University of Mexico and San Marcos University at Lima—the first two universities established in the Americas. It operated numerous businesses, including flour mills, shipyards, ranches, mines, and all the printing presses. It owned vast amounts of land—almost half of Mexico, for example. And since it did not pay taxes, it soon became extremely wealthy. Nuns—most of whom came from the upper classes—ran the empire's orphanages, hospitals, women's prisons, and retirement homes for widows.

In addition to the Franciscans and the Dominicans, many Jesuits came to Spanish America. They specialized in establishing mission villages where Indians were protected against slave hunters and where they were trained in crafts and farming. By 1750 about one out of three Indians was living in a mission village. Then, in 1767, the Spanish monarch—jealous of their influence—expelled the Jesuits from the empire, and most of the mission villages disappeared.

SECTION 1 REVIEW

1. **Recall**   Why did Montezuma welcome Cortés?

2. **How and Why**   Why were the Spaniards able to conquer Mexico with such ease?

3. **Critical Thinking**   How were the Indians affected by the encomienda system?

In 1500 a Portuguese captain named Pedro Alvarez Cabral reached the coast of northeast Brazil and claimed it for Portugal. According to Cabral, he had been blown off course while on the way to India. Many historians suspect, however, that Cabral set out to claim new land for Portugal under the Treaty of Tordesillas. In this treaty the pope divided the uncharted world between Spain and Portugal.

Early Colonists

At first the Portuguese neglected Brazil, which apparently did not contain either spices, silver, or gold. Then, three factors led Portugal to take an interest in its new possession. The first factor was the growth of Western Europe's textile industry. Brazil contained a tree similar to Asian brazilwood, used to make red dye. The second factor was a sharp decline in Portugal's spice trade with India. And the third factor was an attempt by France to take over Portugal's claims to Brazil and exploit the area's resources.

In 1530 Martim Affonso de Souza sailed for Brazil with a fleet of five ships and instructions from the Portuguese king to stop French interference. De Souza seized several French vessels, captured a fort the French had established in Brazil, and founded the country's first permanent European settlement.

In 1532 the king moved to colonize Brazil. He divided the country into a number of districts called captaincies and gave these grants of land to wealthy Portuguese called *donatarios*. The donatarios agreed to find settlers and to promote farming and trade. They also were to fight off invaders and guard the spiritual well-being of the Indians. In exchange, they had the right to rule the captaincies more or less as they wished.

It took some time before Brazil began flourishing. For one thing, it was hard to obtain settlers. Portugal's population totaled only about one million, and the country was more concerned with maintaining its foothold in India than in settling Brazil. As a result, many settlers were either Jewish converts frightened by the recently established Portuguese Inquisition, or individuals who were considered trouble-makers and were exiled to Brazil.

In 1549 the king appointed Tomé de Souza as captain-general of Brazil with orders to make the colony profitable. De Souza set up his headquarters at Bahia in the northeast. The introduction of sugar cane in the 1530s had made this area the center of Brazil's economy. In the 1700s, when prosperity shifted from sugar to minerals, the government moved to Rio de Janeiro, which was closer to the mines.

The Jesuits

De Souza brought with him Jesuit missionaries. The Jesuits were the first Western Europeans to brave Brazil's wilderness. They set up mission villages in remote areas along the Amazon River. Thousands of Indians

promote:
bring about; encourage

■ Portuguese Colonial
Administration, 1790

were baptized, gathered into fortified settlements, and taught farming. These missions provided a place of safety for the Indians against slave raiders. They also became outposts of Portuguese political and economic influence. At the same time, they disrupted the hunting and gathering life of the Indians.

The Jesuits vigorously opposed enslavement of the Indians. Land-owners who were expanding their sugar plantations resented the Jesuits' attitude. Moreover, some of the mission settlements were themselves becoming wealthy sugar plantations and were competing with the dona-tarios for profits. The donatarios finally united against the Jesuits and had them driven from the colony in 1759.

The Blacks

Many times between 1530 and the mid-1600s, Brazil's colonists had to drive out French, Dutch, and British forces. The Portuguese gave them no aid. In 1565 this fleet of Brazilians sailed to Rio de Janeiro to fight the French.

By the early 1600s, many of the forests of northeastern Brazil had been cleared for giant sugar plantations. Brazil soon became the world's leading producer of sugar. As more and more people were needed to work the cane fields, a labor shortage developed. The Indians in Brazil, as in Spanish America, were unable to withstand European diseases and overwork. Scholars estimate that about 1.8 million, or 90 percent of them, died. The Portuguese had to look elsewhere for workers. Black slaves from Africa seemed the solution. The first slaves were imported in the

For many years Brazil's prosperity was based on sugar. This picture shows slaves operating a sugar mill.

1530s. By 1700 there were so many slaves in Brazil that in some places they outnumbered the Europeans 20 to 1. The importing of slaves ended in 1850. But slavery itself was not abolished until 1888.

The Portuguese were more racially tolerant than other nationalities such as the Spanish and the English. Portuguese men not only had children by black women but also recognized these children as their own. Mulattoes became clerks, supervisors, and priests.

The Africans made numerous contributions to Brazil's culture. They added many words to the Portuguese language. They brought their religions, especially macumba, which includes ancestor worship and a belief in magic. It is still widely practiced. They brought the samba, which is now the national dance of Brazil. They brought the drum and other percussion instruments. Brazilian composer Heitor Villa-Lobos (AY-tohr VIL-uh-LOH-buhs)—perhaps the most famous of Latin America's composers—has based many of his works on African themes. And African artisans filled Brazil's churches with statues, candlesticks, and other religious objects fashioned from wood, clay, and metal.

The Bandeirantes

The last group that helped establish Portuguese rule in Brazil were the *bandeirantes*, or fortune-hunters. Part Portuguese and part Indian, they traveled in bands of from fifty to several thousand men, moving along the rivers deep into the jungle. At first they pursued runaway black slaves and also captured and sold Indians. When gold was discovered in the 1690s, they became leaders in the gold rushes, especially the one in Minas Gerais (MEE-nuh zhuh-RYS). It attracted tens of thousands of people, not only

This polychrome—many colors—and gilt wooden statue is of St. Peter as Pope. It stands in a church in São Paulo. The statue is done in the ornate and colorful baroque style.

from the coastal cities and southern Brazil but also from all over Europe. Mining camps and boom towns became common in the interior, and many turned into permanent settlements.

The discovery of gold was most fortunate because it occurred just when Brazil's sugar industry was declining. The country's economy expanded still further with the introduction of coffee growing and the discovery of diamonds in the early 1700s.

SECTION 2 REVIEW

1. **Recall** What did Africans contribute to Brazil's culture?

2. **How and Why** Why did Bahia become important to the Brazilian economy?

3. **Critical Thinking** Why were more slaves brought to Brazil than to any other area in the Americas?

R E V I E W

Reviewing People, Places, and Things

Identify, define, or explain each of the following:

conquistador	penisulare
Cortés	creole
Doña Marina	mestizo
Montezuma	mulatto
Pizarro	zambo
Atahuallpa	Cabral
viceroyalty	donatario
encomienda	bandeirante

Map Study

Using the maps on pages 317 and 319, answer the following questions:

1. Which Spanish viceroyalty included part of present-day United States?
2. What European country claimed the vice-royalty of Brazil?
3. Which Spanish viceroyalty extended the furthest south?

Understanding Facts and Ideas

1. Why did the conquistadores look down on the Indians?
2. Why were the Aztecs hated by their subjects?
3. What conflict within the Inca Empire helped Pizarro's forces?
4. Why did the Spanish set up viceroyalties?
5. How did the Spanish administrators regard the missions?
6. Why did Jesuits set up missions in the Brazilian wilderness?

7. How did the Portuguese solve their labor shortage?

Developing Critical Thinking

Recognizing Stereotypes A stereotype is an oversimplified view of a person or group. It does not consider individual differences, nor is it based entirely on facts. Stereotypes often keep a person from understanding other people and from appreciating them and their way of life. This happened among Western Europeans in Latin America. The following activity will help you recognize some of the stereotypes that Western Europeans held about Indians.

Activity: Spanish conquistadores and missionaries were the first Europeans to have contact with the Indians. Write a paragraph to explain the following: 1. What stereotypes did they hold about the Indians? 2. Why did they develop these stereotypes? 3. How did they use these stereotypes to their advantage?

Writing About History

Expressing Your Opinion Write a paragraph explaining why you think Montezuma and Atahuallpa were unable to win against the Spanish even though they led powerful empires.

Applying Your Skills to History

Using a Flow Chart A flow chart shows the steps in a process or the way something is organized. It uses arrows to show directions and may be read from left to right, top to bottom, bottom to top, or in a circle. Using your text as your source, make a flow chart showing the class structure in Spanish America.

Wars of Independence

The American and French revolutions of the late 1700s spread new ideas about government throughout Europe and the Americas. These ideas, in turn, helped touch off a series of wars against the colonial rulers of Latin America. Haiti led the way with a successful revolt against France between 1791 and 1804. Between 1808 and 1825, all of Spain's mainland possessions gained their independence. However, Spain was able to keep the islands of Cuba and Puerto Rico until 1898. Other Latin American nations—notably Brazil in 1822—obtained independence fairly peacefully. Today, only French Guiana and a few islands in the Caribbean remain under Western European control.

   As you study this chapter, think about these questions:

- What were the successes and failures of the leaders of independence in the former Spanish colonies?

- Why did the development of Brazilian independence differ from that of the Spanish colonies?

This statue of Benito Juárez honors one of Mexico's greatest heroes.

L atin America's wars of independence were preceded by several generations of unrest. One of the earliest revolts against Spanish rule occurred in Peru. It was led by Tupac Amarú II, a descendant of the Inca kings. In 1780 he protested against the forced labor of Indians in Spanish mines and on Spanish farms. When his protests were ignored, he organized an army of Indians, hoping that a show of strength would make the Spaniards reform their colonial system.

After six months of fighting, the Spaniards captured Tupac Amarú II. First they cut out his tongue because he had spoken against their rule. Then they tied a horse to each of his arms and legs and had him torn apart. The Indians were shocked. Although they had few weapons, they tried to drive the Spaniards from Peru. But after two years of fighting and 80,000 casualties, the rebellion was put down.

Nature of the Revolutions

The Indians were not the only ones dissatisfied with Spanish rule. Black slaves longed for freedom. And through the years, the mestizos and creoles had likewise become increasingly unhappy.

The mestizos, although part Indian and part European, were denied by both. Yet their numbers grew rapidly, and they collected into separate settlements. Often a mestizo village sprang up between a European town and a nearby Indian settlement. Mestizos were an important link between the two cultures. They also became wholeheartedly Latin American. No European monarch could claim their loyalty. When the wars of independence came, the mestizos were ready.

The leaders of the revolts, however, were usually creoles. Like the middle class in France before the French Revolution, the creoles—although educated and well-to-do—had little say in the government. Their taxes were high, and they were not allowed to trade with other countries.

It should be noted, however, that the creoles were primarily interested in gaining power for themselves. They were not particularly concerned with improving the conditions of the lower classes. The protection of creole interests was a dominant factor in the revolutions. It was also a factor in determining the course the new nations would take, and it continues to be a factor in Latin America today.

Between 1799 and 1815 much of Europe was fighting Napoleon Bonaparte and the French. In 1808 Napoleon's troops took over Spain. The Spanish king was overthrown, and Napoleon's brother Joseph was placed on the throne. The viceroys in Latin America tried to continue their rule as before. But to no avail. The events in Europe were the signal for rebellion in Spain's colonies.

Francisco de Miranda

One of the early leaders of the independence movement was Francisco de Miranda. He was a creole, born in Caracas, the capital of modern Venezuela. At the age of 22, he became a captain in the Spanish army. Charged with misusing army funds, he fled to the newly founded United States. There he met several leaders of the young republic, and Miranda formulated a plan to free his homeland from Spain.

For years Miranda traveled throughout Europe seeking help for his plan. In 1792 he fought in the French Revolution, rising to the rank of general. He obtained funds from England and Russia. Finally, in 1806, with soldiers recruited in the United States, Miranda landed on the coast of Venezuela to begin the revolution. The attempt failed, and he escaped to London. Four years later, however, Venezuela declared itself independent, and Miranda returned home. He was named commander-in-chief of the revolutionary army and dictator of Venezuela. But the Spaniards had not given up. In 1812 they counterattacked, inflicting a heavy defeat on Miranda's troops. To make matters worse, a disastrous earthquake struck the region where the rebels were strongest, killing many. Dismayed by the twin blows, Miranda surrendered and prepared to flee once again to England. Instead, his disillusioned followers turned him over to the Spaniards in exchange for their own safety. He died in a Spanish prison in 1816.

Simón Bolívar

Simón Bolívar—known as the Liberator—was also a wealthy creole who was born in Caracas. In 1798, at the age of fifteen, he went to Europe to further his education. He cheered the spread of France's revolutionary ideals and was captivated by the drama of Napoleon's crowning himself emperor. In Italy he visited the place where the plebeians of ancient Rome had first demanded their rights from the city's patricians. After swearing an oath never to rest until all Spanish South America was free, Bolívar returned to Venezuela. He participated in the nation's first declaration of independence in 1810 and joined Miranda's forces. After Miranda's capture (which he helped arrange), Bolívar left the country. He returned to retake Caracas in 1813 but was forced to flee again the following year.

Between 1814 and 1817, Bolívar spent his time gathering support and writing down his thoughts and hopes for the future. He criticized the creoles' lack of political experience. Spain "has kept us in a sort of permanent infancy with regard to public affairs." He hoped that all of Spanish America might become a single nation, "greatest not so much by virtue of her area and wealth as by her freedom and glory." But because he did not think that was possible, he proposed the establishment of several small republics.

In 1817 Bolívar landed in Venezuela once again. This time, instead of attacking Caracas, he concentrated on training an army in the Venezuelan lowlands along the Orinoco River. Some of his recruits were *llaneros,* or cowboys; others were blacks. Additional volunteers included English,

This is a painting of Simón Bolívar. He hoped that the new Latin American countries would become republics after achieving their independence.

Irish, Scottish, and German adventurers. In 1819, with about 3,000 troops, Bolívar began a march to Bogotá, the capital of the Viceroyalty of New Granada. (Today Bogotá is the capital of Colombia.) He felt that if he could capture the Spanish capital, he would seriously hurt Spanish morale.

morale:
good feelings

Bolívar's army had to march 600 miles (970 kilometers) across the rugged, snow-capped Andes. More than one-quarter of the soldiers and almost all the horses died. At Boyacá, 60 miles (97 kilometers) from Bogotá, the rebels fought a large Spanish army and were victorious. A few days later, Bolívar rode into Bogotá and declared it free. He then proclaimed the existence of a new independent nation called Gran Colombia, to consist of Colombia, Venezuela, and Ecuador.

In 1821 Bolívar advanced from Colombia into Venezuela and drove most of the Spanish forces from the area. In 1822 a comrade of Bolívar defeated another Spanish force and occupied Ecuador. By 1824 rebel troops had driven the Spaniards from Peru. The fight at Ayacucho was the final battle for independence in South America. In addition to Peru, a separate nation named Bolivia in honor of the Liberator was formed. Bolívar had indeed kept his oath: all Spanish South America was free.

However, by the time of Bolívar's death from tuberculosis in 1830, the Gran Colombia that he had created was no more. Jealousy and a scramble for power among leaders had driven the nation's three areas apart. Shortly before he died, Bolívar wrote bitterly: "America is ungovernable. Those who have served the revolution have plowed the sea."

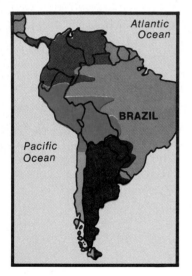

**Independent
South America, 1825**

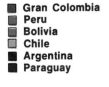
- **Gran Colombia**
- **Peru**
- **Bolivia**
- **Chile**
- **Argentina**
- **Paraguay**

José de San Martín

Just as Bolívar was the liberator of northern South America, José de San Martín was the liberator of the south. He was born in a Jesuit village in Argentina and studied in Madrid for a military career. He served in the Spanish army for 22 years but resigned his commission when Joseph Bonaparte took over the throne of Spain. In 1812 San Martín returned home and offered his services to a *junta* (HOON-tuh), or political council, in Buenos Aires that had proclaimed its independence. Unlike Venezuela, the territory of Buenos Aires had not been recaptured by the Spaniards. However, as long as Spanish troops remained in Chile and Peru, Buenos Aires was not safe.

So San Martín organized a trans-Andean expedition against the Spaniards. Between 1814 and 1817, he recruited troops and collected weapons. Funds came mostly from the creole ladies of Buenos Aires, who contributed their jewels to the cause of independence. Most of the guns, bullets, swords, and bayonets came from factories set up by a priest named Luis Beltrán. Beltrán even melted down church bells to obtain the necessary raw material for the weapons.

In 1816 all of Argentina declared its independence of Spain and in January 1817, San Martín scaled the Andes with his army. In February he met and defeated the main Spanish army not far from Santiago, the

328

present capital of Chile. By 1818 Chile was independent. The people elected San Martín as their first president. But unlike Bolívar, San Martín had no ambition to be a ruler. So he stepped aside in favor of Bernardo O'Higgins, a Chilean who had been fighting for his country's freedom since 1810.

After freeing Chile, San Martín moved on to Peru. Realizing that their army could not march across the Atacama Desert, the rebels began assembling ships with the help of Lord Cochrane, a former admiral in the British navy. Some of the ships were stolen from the Spaniards; others were bought from foreigners. In 1820 San Martín sailed north and blockaded Peru's ports. The Spanish viceroy left Lima and took his army to the mountains. San Martín then entered the capital and declared Peru independent.

At this point, Lord Cochrane—who had not yet been paid for his services—seized the government treasury and made off with the ships. San Martín, realizing that he could not defeat the Spaniards by himself, wrote to Bolívar. In July 1822 the two liberators met at Guayaquil (gwy-uh-KEEL), Ecuador. Their conference did not bring agreement as to how one could help the other. Among other differences, Bolívar wanted Peru to be a republic, while San Martín favored a constitutional monarchy. Also, both men wanted to add Ecuador to their territories. Finally, San Martín withdrew rather than risk endangering the independence movement. He went into exile in Europe and died there in 1850. As you read, Bolívar ultimately freed Peru.

In the meantime, Paraguay declared its independence of both Spain and Buenos Aires in 1813. Uruguay became independent in 1828 after several years of fighting against both Brazil and Argentina.

Mexico's Struggle

What has been said about the dissatisfaction of creoles and mestizos in South America can also be said of these classes who lived in Mexico. The creoles in particular felt that they should control their own affairs. When Napoleon occupied Spain in 1808, many began to work for independence. However, the first open rebellion against Spanish rule was an Indian revolt in 1810.

Hidalgo   Father Miguel Hidalgo y Costilla, a creole priest, was among the first to fight for the poor. His parishioners in Dolores, a small town about 100 miles (161 kilometers) northwest of Mexico City, were mostly Indians and mestizos. Hidalgo believed that along with their spiritual welfare, their material life needed to be improved. He taught them better ways to cultivate their vineyards. He introduced silk manufacturing. He established a brickyard, a pottery works, and a tannery. He even organized an orchestra. Hildalgo was strongly influenced by the philosophes, especially Rousseau.

Father Miguel Hidalgo led the first revolt against the Spanish in Mexico.

philosophes: any of the leading philosophical, political, and social writers of the French Enlightenment

When Napoleon deposed the king of Spain in 1808, secret societies were organized in Mexico to oust the Spaniards. Hidalgo belonged to one such group. In 1810 the authorities uncovered the society's plot to overthrow them. Instead of escaping, Hidalgo rang the church bells in Dolores and called on his assembled parishioners to revolt against Spanish rule and take back the land their forefathers had owned 300 years before. His final words were: *"Viva Nuestra Señora de Guadelupe, muera el mal gobierno, mueran los gachupines!*—Long live our Lady of Guadelupe (the Virgin Mary), down with bad government, death to the Spaniards!" His words became known as the Grito de Dolores—the cry of Dolores.

Hidalgo was neither a military leader nor a good organizer. But he became the center of an army of 60,000 rebels, mostly barefoot Indians. Women accompanied their men on the campaign, cooking meals and scouring the countryside for supplies. Hidalgo's followers fought with clubs, knives, and their hands against the guns of the Spaniards. For a time they were successful. They captured several large cities and provinces, and came near Mexico City. Hidalgo set up a government for the freed territories. Slavery was abolished, and Indians were given back their land.

By 1811 the creoles had become frightened by Hidalgo's policies, which threatened their economic position. So they called on the peninsulares to help end the revolution. Spanish troops defeated Hidalgo's followers, and Hidalgo was shot. Although the Grito de Dolores movement did not free Mexico, September 16—the day Hidalgo issued his call to arms—is celebrated as Mexican Independence Day.

Morelos   Another Mexican priest, a mestizo named José María Morelos, continued the struggle. He had joined the revolt in 1810. When Hidalgo was defeated, Morelos took his place as leader. He was a far better soldier and administrator. By 1813 he had conquered enough of southern Mexico that he declared the nation independent.

Morelos urged his followers to adopt a constitution that would abolish slavery. Neither the army nor the Roman Catholic Church were to enjoy any special privileges. Everyone, regardless of class or race, was to have equal rights. Large estates were to be broken up and given to the poor peasants who worked the land.

Again, the program of the rebels frightened the creoles. They supported the peninsulares, and in 1815 Morelos was captured and shot.

Iturbide   In 1821 Spain experienced a revolt of its own. Liberals forced the king to accept a constitution. They also called for land reform and the abolition of forced labor in colonial Mexico. The creoles realized that they could no longer depend on Spain to help them maintain their privileged position. The only solution was for Mexico to become independent.

Agustín de Iturbide (ee-tur-BEE-day), a creole who had fought for the Spanish cause against Hidalgo and Morelos, became the creoles' agent. In February 1821, he deserted the Spaniards and signed an agreement with Vicente Guerrero, who had replaced Morelos. Backed by both wealthy creoles and poor Indians and mestizos, Iturbide led forces to defeat the Spanish and Mexico became independent.

At this point, the coalition fell apart. Iturbide had no intention of considering the rights of Indians and mestizos. What he wanted was for creoles to have the same political power as peninsulares. He also favored continuing the Roman Catholic Church's official and privileged position. In 1822 Iturbide declared himself Emperor Agustín I. However, poor administration and the lack of money to pay the army and the bureaucrats forced him to abdicate the following year. Mexico was then proclaimed a republic.

Mexico and United Provinces of Central America, 1825

■ Mexico
■ United Provinces of Central America

Central America

Five of the six modern nations of Central America—Costa Rica, El Salvador, Guatemala, Honduras, and Nicaragua—were part of the Captaincy-General of Guatemala. In 1821 they peacefully declared their independence from Spain. The following year they united with Mexico under Iturbide.

abdicate:
to give up high office

After Mexico became a republic, the five nations set up their own federal system, called the United Provinces of Central America. Although a capital was established in Guatemala City, each state had its own president. Slavery was abolished. But the federation was plagued by conflicts between liberals and conservatives and by Indian revolts. In 1838 it collapsed, and the five nations went their separate ways.

abolished:
done away with

Toward the end of the 1800s, Guatemala tried several times to reunite the nations by force, but it was never successful. Proposals for reunion are still being discussed today.

SECTION 1 REVIEW

1. **Recall** Where did the independence movement in Spanish America begin?

2. **How and Why** Why did Bolívar's Gran Colombia fail to remain united?

3. **Critical Thinking** Why do you think the Central American nations were unable to remain united?

The desire for independence spread to other parts of Latin America during the eighteenth and early nineteenth centuries. In one instance, it was achieved more or less peacefully. In other instances, it came only after a series of wars.

Brazil

Brazil never experienced any revolts that affected the entire colony. From time to time, however, there were local rebellions. One of the earliest was an uprising by black slaves, who escaped into the interior in 1633 and set up the Republic of Palmares, named after its forest of palm trees. An estimated 20,000 runaways lived in the republic, which remained a refuge for slaves until it was finally destroyed in 1697 by a Portuguese military expedition.

A desire for economic improvement prompted another Brazilian uprising. In 1788 workers in the gold and diamond mines of Minas Gerais rebelled because the Portuguese king had lowered their wages and raised their taxes. The leader of the workers was Joaquim José de Silva Xavier. Because he was a dentist, he was nicknamed Tiradentes, the tooth-puller. Besides voicing the workers' complaints, Tiradentes called for the abolition of slavery. He also urged independence for Brazil and asked that a university be established in Minas Gerais. The rebels were quickly subdued, however. Tiradentes was taken prisoner and hanged.

Brazil's steps toward independence, like those in Spanish America, were sparked by Napoleon Bonaparte. In 1807 he invaded Portugal. The British government promptly put the Portuguese royal family—together with thousands of followers and court officials, the national treasury, art, jewels, and a huge library—aboard a fleet of 37 ships and sent them to Brazil. The Brazilians welcomed the government-in-exile enthusiastically. They hoped it meant that Brazil's importance to the Portuguese empire would be recognized.

The Brazilians were not disappointed. In 1815 João VI (ZHWOWN) declared Brazil an equal partner with Portugal in the empire and made Rio de Janeiro its capital. He also made numerous changes in Brazil. He opened trade to all nations, with special privileges for English merchants. He granted Protestants freedom of worship. He set up a printing press, a national library, a university and an art museum. He also set up medical and law schools. However, João VI removed Brazilian-born officials and replaced them with Portuguese. This angered the Brazilians.

After Napoleon fell from power in 1815, liberal forces began to emerge in Portugal. By 1820 they were demanding many reforms. João VI had to return to Portugal if he wanted to keep his throne. He did so, taking with him all the gold in the treasury but leaving behind his son Pedro to rule in his name.

In the meantime, the Portuguese parliament began limiting the rights of Brazilians. They wanted to return Brazil to the status of a colony. In 1822 the parliament ordered Pedro back to Portugal "to complete his education." They were afraid he might lead a Brazilian revolt. Sure enough, instead of returning, Pedro ripped the Portuguese colors from his uniform and declared "Independence or death!" Then, with British help, he drove out the Portuguese, practically without bloodshed. In December 1822, he was crowned emperor of an independent Brazil. Brazil was the only nation in Latin America to choose constitutional monarchy as its form of government.

Liberation of Haiti

The first area in Latin America to win its independence was neither a Spanish nor a Portuguese colony but a French one—Saint-Domingue (san-duh-MANG), or modern Haiti. It occupied the western third of the island of Hispaniola. The French had seized the area from Spain in the early 1600s.

Saint-Domingue was one of France's most profitable colonies. Its exports of sugar, coffee, cotton, indigo, and spices accounted for about one-half of France's colonial trade. Almost 500,000 black and mulatto slaves worked its plantations. About 32,000 French creoles ruled the colony and formed the upper class. In addition, there were about 24,000 free blacks and mulattoes.

When the French Revolution broke out in 1789, the creoles tried to take control of Saint-Domingue's government from French officials. The creoles used arguments drawn from the French Revolution. But terms like liberty, equality, and fraternity also appealed to blacks and mulattoes—free and slave. While the creoles and free mulattoes attempted to bargain for self-rule, the slaves rebelled. Perhaps as many as 100,000 took part in the revolt.

Leadership of the revolt soon passed into the hands of Pierre Dominique Toussaint L'Ouverture. The reputed grandson of an African king, Toussaint was born a slave in 1743. His owner taught him to read and write and set him free when he was in his mid-30s.

By 1799 Toussaint was head of Saint-Domingue's government. Surprisingly, he ruled in the name of France, which appointed him governor-general in 1801. That same year, Toussaint conquered the Spanish-held eastern part of Hispaniola (the modern Dominican Republic) and abolished slavery there.

A year later, Napoleon Bonaparte decided to return his Caribbean possession to its former colonial status. He sent over an army headed by General Charles Leclerc, one of his many brothers-in-law. Although Toussaint's troops fought bravely and inflicted heavy casualties, the French superiority in munitions and manpower told. Direct French rule over Saint-Domingue was reestablished in 1802. The next year, Toussaint was captured by Leclerc and shipped in chains to France, where he died.

In the meantime, the revolt resumed under the leadership of Jean-Jacques Dessalines (days-uh-LEEN), formerly a general under Toussaint. Dessalines was aided by an epidemic of yellow fever that killed thousands of French soldiers. By 1804 Dessalines and his troops were victorious, and Saint-Domingue proclaimed its independence. The nation was renamed Haiti, meaning mountainous, the original Indian name for the island.

Toussaint L'Ouverture led the first successful revolt against colonialism in Latin America. What was different about the leadership of this revolt as opposed to the revolts on the mainland?

Throughout the 1800s there were various attempts by Cubans to free their land from Spanish rule. The last one was led by Jose Martí (right) and Antonio Maceo. Martí was a creole, and Maceo, a mulatto. Why do you think the social class of the leaders made a diffeence in the direction that movements and their later governments took?

Cuba

After Cuba was discovered by Columbus, it became the base of operations for Spanish conquistadores on the mainland. Control of Cuba meant control of the gateway to Mexico and South America. By the end of the 1700s, however, the island was attracting settlers for its own sake. Its plantations were flourishing. Tobacco, cattle, coffee, and especially sugar were being produced in great quantities. Slavery was widespread.

When the colonies on the mainland rebelled, Cuba remained quiet. Many of its plantation owners and merchants were creoles. And like the creoles in Mexico, they feared the influence of liberal ideas. Instead of seeking change, wealthy Cubans tried to keep the island as it was.

Around the mid-1800s, however, some creoles began suggesting annexation by the United States. Many Americans favored the idea, especially southerners, since Cuba would be another slave state. In 1853 the United States offered to buy Cuba for $130 million, but Spain was not interested in selling.

Meanwhile, a group of young Cubans began talking of independence. Talk soon turned to action. First came a series of short-lived uprisings. Then, in 1868, the Ten Years' War broke out between Spanish troops and Cuban guerrillas. In 1878, after the loss of 200,000 lives and the destruction of $700 million worth of property, Spain promised to abolish slavery and to institute land reform and other economic changes.

Spain kept the first promise but not the second. In fact, its behavior soon brought economic disaster to Cuba. The island's economy depended on the sale of sugar and tobacco to the United States. Yet Spain kept imposing new taxes and restrictions on Cuban sugar and tobacco growers. The final straw came in 1894. Spain canceled Cuba's trade agreement with the United States, plunging the island into a depression. At this point, Cuban businessmen decided that the time had come for *Cuba libra*—a free Cuba.

In 1895 revolts broke out in eastern Cuba. They were supported by the business community and by a government-in-exile that had been maintained in New York City ever since the end of the Ten Years' War. The leaders of this government-in-exile were José Martí, a creole poet and journalist; Antonio Maceo (may-SAY-oh), a mulatto ex-slave; and Máximo Gomez, a Dominican. Martí in particular had worked for years collecting money for guns and powder and trying to convince Americans to support Cuban independence. In May 1895, Martí, Maceo, and Gomez landed in Cuba with an army of volunteers. Martí was killed in battle, but additional volunteer groups kept arriving.

At first it seemed as if the rebels might be successful. Then Spain appointed General Valeriano Weyler commander in chief. The general soon became known as "Butcher" Weyler. He herded hundreds of thousands of Cubans—men, women, and children—into concentration camps to prevent them from helping the rebels. Unfortunately, the lack of food and sanitation in the camps resulted in some 200,000 deaths. Weyler also destroyed cattle and crops in an attempt to starve out the guerrillas. In return, the guerrillas burned Spanish-owned sugar plantations.

In the meantime, the interest of the United States in the revolt kept rising. Many Americans were worried about their investments in Cuba. Then, too, the United States had decided to build a canal through Central America to join the Atlantic and Pacific oceans. Having Spain in control of Cuba might interfere with this plan. In addition, many Americans were shocked by the stories of Weyler's brutality.

The cartoon with its caption, "The Duty of the Hour—To Save Her Not Only from Spain, but from a Worse Fate," was designed to build public support for American intervention in Cuba.

Buildings such as this fortress in San Juan remind Puerto Ricans of their Spanish heritage. What other ethnic groups have contributed to the heritage of Puerto Ricans?

In 1898 President William McKinley sent the USS *Maine* to Havana to protect American citizens in case of emergency. On February 15, the battleship exploded in the city's harbor. Two hundred and sixty-six American lives were lost. To this day, no one is certain why the explosion occurred. But newspaper headlines across the land called on Americans to "Remember the *Maine*!" And on April 11—despite Spain's offer to give Cuba home rule—the United States declared war.

The Spanish-American War ended three months later with Spain's defeat. As part of the peace treaty, the victorious United States took over Cuba. After four years of military rule, the island was declared independent in 1902. But as you will read later in this unit, its relations with the United States remained close.

Puerto Rico

For much of its history, Puerto Rico was a military outpost of Spain. Its economy was limited to subsistence farming, and it was supported mostly by taxes raised elsewhere in Spanish America. By 1800, however, such Puerto Rican products as coffee and sugar had become important on the world trade market.

When rebellions broke out in Mexico, Venezuela, and other colonies, Spain grew fearful of losing Puerto Rico, too. Accordingly, it extended full Spanish citizenship to the islanders in 1812. Slavery was abolished in 1873 after a brief uprising and Puerto Rico was given representation in the Spanish parliament in 1876. The Puerto Ricans, however, wanted to govern themselves. In 1895 the revolt against Spanish rule in Cuba caused widespread unrest in Puerto Rico. So in 1898 Spain decided to give the Puerto Ricans what they wanted.

One of the great national leaders to emerge from Puerto Rico's campaign for independence was Luis Muños Rivera (moon-YOHS rih-VAY-ruh). Unfortunately, the reforms that he had worked for were short-lived. Two months after Puerto Rican self-rule went into effect, the United States and Spain were at war. In July 1898, the United States invaded and occupied Puerto Rico. By October the island was a United States possession and had a military government.

In 1900 the United States Congress passed the Foraker Act giving Puerto Rico a civilian government. However, the people could elect members of only the lower house of the legislature. The senate, as well as the governor, were appointed by the president of the United States. And most appointees were Americans, not Puerto Ricans. In 1917 the Jones Act granted United States citizenship to Puerto Ricans and allowed them to elect their own senate. However, the governor could still veto all legislation.

Over the years, Puerto Ricans continued their struggle for more self-rule. The 1930s especially were a time of violent protest, largely because of economic conditions. Puerto Rico now had a one-crop sugar economy. But since most of the land was used for sugar, farmers were unable to grow enough food. Moreover, the United States had introduced sanitary improvements, which in turn had contributed to a population explosion. These problems gave rise to a strong nationalist movement for independence.

In 1940 Luis Muños Marin (muh-REEN) became the leader of the Popular Democratic party and made great strides toward home rule. (His father had led the campaign for self-rule in the 1890s.) In 1946 the first Puerto Rican governor was appointed. Two years later, Muñoz Marin became the first popularly elected governor.

This oil refinery is just one example of the industry that Operation Bootstrap helped bring to Puerto Rico. How have the investments made in Puerto Rico by United States firms since the 1950s been different from the investments of the 1930s?

In 1952 Puerto Rico became a self-governing United States territory, the Commonwealth of Puerto Rico. Puerto Ricans do not pay federal income tax, and they cannot vote for an American president. They do not have voting representation in the United States Senate or House of Representatives. The United States administers Puerto Rico's foreign relations, defense, postal, and customs services. Until the end of the draft in 1973, Puerto Rican men were subject to military service.

The island's voters have been asked several times to choose among commonwealth status, independence, or statehood. Each time they have voted for the status quo, although by increasingly narrow margins. Another election on the issue will probably be held in 1992.

Only about 5 percent of the population of Puerto Rico seems to prefer independence. The main objections to statehood are economic and cultural.

Under Muñoz Marin's leadership, Puerto Rico launched Operation Bootstrap, designed to pull the island up "by its bootstraps" from poverty to prosperity. Muñoz Marin realized that the island had to move from one-crop agriculture toward industrialization. He offered ten-year tax exemptions to encourage United States business people to build factories there. The program accomplished what it set out to do. But if Puerto Rico becomes a state, it will not be able to continue its program of tax incentives, and its economy will decline. Even under commonwealth status, tens of thousands of Puerto Ricans flock to the mainland each year in search of work.

Culturally, Puerto Rico's language is Spanish. About 60 percent of the people do not speak English at all. Statehood would mean that the United States would officially become a bilingual nation.

SECTION 2 REVIEW

1. **Recall**   Who drove the Portuguese out of Brazil?

2. **How and Why**   Why were the 1930s a time of especially violent protest in Puerto Rico?

3. **Critical Thinking**   Why do the people of Puerto Rico object to statehood?

R E V I E W

Reviewing People, Places, and Things

Identify, define, or explain each of the following:

revolution	Hidalgo
Tupac Amarú II	Grito de Dolores
Miranda	Iturbide
Bolívar	Tiradentes
Gran Colombia	Pedro
San Martín	Toussaint L'
junta	Ouverture

Map Study

Using the maps on pages 328 and 331, answer the following questions:

1. At what time do these maps show the status of Latin America?
2. How many modern countries were part of Gran Colombia?
3. In what direction from Mexico is Cuba located?

Understanding Facts and Ideas

1. Why were mestizos and creoles dissatisfied with Spanish rule?
2. What events in Europe signaled rebellion in the Spanish colonies?
3. What was Simon Bolívar's dream?
4. Where and when was the final South American battle for independence?
5. How were Bolívar and San Martín different?
6. Who led Mexico to defeat Spanish forces and become independent?
7. Why did the United Provinces of Central America collapse?
8. What was the first area in Latin America to win its independence?
9. During mainland rebellion, why did Cuba oppose change?
10. How did Spain try to keep from losing Puerto Rico in 1812?

Developing Critical Thinking

Continuity and Change Continuity is an unbroken series of events. In history a continuous or connected series of events may gradually lead to change. The change may appear abrupt, but if you study the change carefully you may find a long series of causes behind it. This pattern of continuity leading to change makes up the history of many nations and peoples.

Activity: Consider what you have read in Chapter 17 and write a paragraph stating the continuity of purpose behind the wars of independence in Spanish America and describing the resulting changes.

Writing About History

Writing a Paragraph Write a paragraph explaining why you think Spain was able to retain possession of Cuba while the mainland nations won their independence.

Applying Your Skills to History

Making a Time Line Construct a time line of the wars of independence in Latin America. Indicate which were successful.

CHAPTER 18

The Evolving Political Scene

For most of their history, Latin Americans tended to support a single, strong leader. Since independence, this leader, known as a caudillo (kaw-THEE-yoh)—a Spanish word for chieftain—has usually been a member of the military.

During the 1900s, groups demanding economic and social changes began to play a more active role in government. These groups included peasants and labor unions. Today, democratic government is the goal of many Latin American nations. But the military remains strong.

Adding to Latin America's political instability has been foreign intervention, especially by the United States. Sometimes such intervention has been direct: the sending of troops to overthrow a particular government. Sometimes it has been indirect, with business companies exercising control through investments.

As you study this chapter, think about these questions:

- What were the causes and results of the Mexican Revolution?
- What factors have led to political changes since the 1930s?
- What has been the relationship between Latin American nations and the United States in this century?

This photo shows the changing of the guard at the government palace in Lima, Peru. Like many Latin American countries, the nation was hard hit by economic problems in the later 1970s and 1980s.

As you know, Mexico became a republic in 1823 after the forced resignation of Agustín de Iturbide as emperor. For the next 100 or so years, the Mexican people struggled to build a stable government. The struggle centered in the nation's cities.

On one side were the liberals, mostly mestizo merchants and professionals. The liberals called for the breakup of large estates, separation of church and state, and civilian control of the military. They also favored a weak central government, with provincial control over local matters. On the other side were the conservatives, mostly creole landowners, church officials, and army officers. The conservatives supported the status quo and a strong central government. In between were the peasants, who simply worked and fought. They could not vote because they did not own property and were illiterate.

For most of this 100-year period, Mexico was ruled by caudillos. For that matter, caudillos have ruled every nation in Latin America at one time or another, and often for very long periods. Why has there been such a widespread dependence on authoritarian leadership in Latin American society? There are several reasons.

The Basis for Caudillos

When independence came, ordinary citizens were not prepared to govern themselves. They had no experience. Indian kings and chiefs had exercised absolute authority. The Spanish and Portuguese who replaced the native rulers governed in the same way. They taught their subjects that the laws and the government that controlled them were not their concern. When the Latin Americans broke free of Western European control, the leaders of the revolts—who were usually creole men—simply replaced the foreign rulers and continued to govern from above. Considering the lack of political experience on the part of the ordinary people, the rulers could always say that the people were not ready for a republican form of government.

The European pattern of settlement also encouraged the power of the privileged. In Argentina and Brazil especially, the small number of European descendants were scattered over wide areas. A few families acquired vast landholdings. They were able to dominate not only the laborers on their estates but also the small towns that sprang up around them. After independence, these people used their wealth and local authority as a base from which to widen their power.

Religion also reinforced belief in the need for central authority. The Roman Catholic Church preached strict obedience and acceptance of authority. The Spanish and the Portuguese did not want newly converted Indians and blacks to be exposed to heresy. So they were isolated from ideas that might cause them to question religious authority. Moreover, religious and civil authority were closely connected. If religious authority were questioned, civil authority might be challenged as well. After independence, religion continued to be used to reinforce the authoritarian tradition.

Mexican troops in the Mexican-American War were mostly Indian peasants who were sent to fight by their landlords. In addition to being poorly trained, they were badly armed because the businessmen who supplied the army's weapons cheated on quality. This is a scene of the Battle of Molina el Rey.

Another factor that encouraged the rise of caudillos was a demand for law and order after the bloodshed and chaos of the wars of independence. Cities and farmlands had been destroyed, ports had been blockaded and business interrupted. Transportation and communication systems had to be restored or built. Outlaws and groups of unemployed soldiers roamed the countryside. The need for law and order seemed more important than insuring freedoms that few people had heard about.

Santa Anna

From 1824 to 1855, Mexico's politics were dominated by a caudillo named Antonio López de Santa Anna. He was a rich creole who greatly admired Napoleon Bonaparte and tried to walk, talk, and dress like the late French emperor. Unfortunately for Mexico, Santa Anna was a poor general and a worse administrator. It was during his on-again, off-again rule that Mexico lost more than half of its territory to the United States.

When Santa Anna first came to power, Mexico included Texas, California, and the desert between. During the 1820s and early 1830s, more and more Americans settled in Texas. At first they were welcomed by the Mexican government, which gave the newcomers large grants of land. But a culture clash soon developed. The Americans spoke English rather than Spanish, even though they were now citizens of Mexico. Also, the Americans were Protestants rather than Catholics, and—most important of all—they owned slaves. Mexico had outlawed slavery elsewhere in the nation in 1829.

In 1830 Mexico decided to ban further American immigration into Texas. But it lacked the soldiers and guns to enforce its decision. In 1833 the Texas Anglos, as they were known, petitioned for independent statehood within the Mexican republic. Their petition was denied, and their leader—Stephen Austin—was imprisoned for 18 months. By 1836 the growing hostility between the two groups erupted into war. Texas rebelled.

Santa Anna, anxious to build up his dwindling popularity by a show of military strength, led a large army against the rebels. On March 6 he attacked a group of 150 Americans in the Franciscan mission of the Alamo in San Antonio. After a ten-day siege, the Mexican troops surged over the mission walls and killed the surviving defenders. Two weeks later, Santa Anna ordered the massacre of more than 300 American prisoners at Goliad.

Santa Anna's behavior infuriated the Anglos. Cries of "Remember the Alamo! Remember Goliad!" swept Texas. On April 21, under Sam Houston, the Anglos defeated the Mexican army and captured Santa Anna. In exchange for his freedom, Santa Anna signed a treaty recognizing Texan independence. He reneged on his promise as soon as he returned home, but it was too late. The former Mexican province was now the Lone Star Republic.

reneged: went back

In 1845 the United States annexed Texas. It also offered to buy California and other land for $40 million. When Mexico rejected the offer, American troops moved into a disputed area along the Mexican-American border. The Mexicans, who saw the American move as an invasion of their territory, attacked—and the United States declared war.

The Mexican-American War—or, as the Mexicans call it, the War of the North American Invasion—lasted three years. During its course, American troops captured Mexico City and also defeated Mexican forces in California. In February 1848, the two nations signed the Treaty of Guadelupe Hidalgo. In exchange for $15 million, Mexico gave up all claim to Texas and also ceded what is now California, Nevada, New Mexico, Utah, and most of Arizona and Colorado.

As a result of Mexico's humiliating defeat, Santa Anna was forced to step down. The reform-minded liberals who succeeded him then adopted a new constitution. It reduced the influence of the army and established a secular system of public schools. It also called on the Roman Catholic Church to sell whatever land it was not using for religious purposes. The liberals hoped the land would be bought by the peasants who farmed it. But the peasants had no money. So most of the Church's landholdings were bought either by the creole middle class or by foreign investors. The great mass of the people were no better off than before.

Benito Juárez

From 1855 to 1876, Mexico's politics were dominated by a different kind of caudillo, one who cared about the needs of the people. A Zapotec Indian, he was named Benito Juárez (HWAHR-ehz), and he is held by Mexicans to be their finest liberal reformer. In fact, the period is known as *La Reforma*, or the reform.

Emiliano Zapata was one of many who fought for power in Mexico. He was supported mostly by landless peasants.

Although orphaned at the age of three, Juárez managed to obtain an education and become a lawyer. His practice consisted mostly of protecting the land and water rights of poor Indians against creole landowners. He served as a state governor for a time and then became head of the nation's supreme court.

In 1858 a civil war broke out in Mexico. The Church, the regular army, and wealthy citizens overthrew the liberals. The liberals, on their part, set up a rival government in Veracruz under Juárez. After three years of fighting, the liberals won, and Juárez returned to Mexico City.

Juárez wanted to reconcile his opponents. So instead of seeking revenge, he pardoned them. He also allowed complete freedom of speech and press. Then, because Mexico was almost bankrupt, he stopped all repayments of loans to European creditors for two years.

This made bankers in France, Spain, and England very unhappy. They were so unhappy, in fact, that France determined to take control of Mexico. In 1862 French troops landed in Mexico and drove Juárez out of the capital north to the Texas border. Two years later, in 1864, Napoleon III sent his cousin, the young Austrian archduke Maximilian, to Mexico as emperor.

Maximilian was a well-meaning man with little ability and no political sense. Within a few months, he tripled the nation's debts. He not only agreed to pay foreign bankers immediately, he also took out an additional loan to cover the palatial remodeling plans of his ambitious wife, Carlota. At the same time, he antagonized his conservative supporters by calling for freedom of speech and press. He sharply criticized the ruling groups for their mistreatment of the Indians and for their general behavior. The creoles, he wrote, "are [not] familiar with their duties, and they live for money alone. The judges are corrupt, the officers have no sense of honor, and the clergy are lacking in Christian charity and morality."

In 1865 the Civil War in the United States ended, and President Abraham Lincoln recognized the Juárez government. The United States also demanded the withdrawal of French troops and began selling arms to the republican forces. In 1866 Napoleon III announced that he was calling his soldiers home. He wanted them in Europe to face the growing military might of Prussia. In 1867 Juárez defeated Maximilian in battle and executed him.

The liberals were now supreme, and Juárez was free to carry out the constitution's reform program. He established a national public school system, reduced the size of the army by two-thirds, and began construction of several railroad lines. But there was very little money, and considerable resistance by the conservatives. In 1872 Juárez died. La Reforma was over.

Porfirio Díaz

Mexico enjoyed republican government for four years. Then another caudillo came to power. Porfirio Díaz, a mestizo, dominated Mexico's politics from 1876 to 1910.

Orphaned at three, Benito Juárez managed to receive an education and become a lawyer. From 1847 to 1852, he was governor of the state of Oaxaca. His term in office was a model for later officials. Why do you think the wealthy objected to Juárez's reforms?

Díaz believed that Mexico's future lay in encouraging foreign investors. Accordingly, he offered them tax benefits, land concessions, and favorable treatment in the nation's courts. By 1900 Mexico's oil wells and its gold, silver, and copper mines were owned mostly by the Americans and the British. The textile industry was in the hands of the French. Hardware and drugs were under German control, the tobacco fields and the grocery stores were run by the Spaniards, and everybody except the Mexicans owned and operated the public utilities.

The results of Díaz's policy were mixed. On the one hand, the nation experienced a tremendous increase in foreign trade. It built up a national railroad system, maintained a balance in the treasury, and set up some public schools. On the other hand, any attempts at land reform or improvements in the standard of living of the mestizos and Indians died. Instead, peasants were forced off whatever land they owned, and the acreage was either given to a few hundred creole families or sold to Americans. By 1910, 99 percent of the peasants—or about 84 percent of the population—were peons. Under the system of **peonage**, workers were bound to the land by debt. They were forced to buy everything from the landowners. Prices were high and wages were low. The peons remained constantly in debt. Sometimes the debts of the fathers were passed on to the sons.

In 1910 Díaz was reelected president for the eighth time. Less than a year later, he was fleeing to Europe, where he died in 1915. What happened?

The Mexican Revolution

In 1910, a century after Father Hidalgo issued the Grito de Dolores, another revolution broke out in Mexico. It was organized by three discontented groups: intellectuals, factory workers, and peasants. The intellectuals called for the usual reforms of the Church, the army, and the schools. The workers wanted a minimum wage, an eight-hour day, a six-day work week, and some health and old-age benefits. Their strikes for these improvements had been repeatedly crushed by the army. The peasants wanted land of their own. Their leader was a tenant farmer named Emiliano Zapata. The story is told that Zapata became a revolutionary when he saw the tiled stables in which his landlord's race horses were kept. The stables were much larger, cleaner, and more comfortable than the miserable dirt huts of the peasants.

The three groups rallied around liberal Francisco Madero. In 1911 Madero was elected president after rebel troops forced Díaz to resign. Two years later, however, a general named Victoriano Huerta seized power and had Madero shot. He then tried to put down Zapata's followers, who had been taking land for themselves in the southwest. At the same time, a former cattle rustler named Francisco "Pancho" Villa (VEE-ah) organized an army in the nation's north, while Madero's supporters united behind Venustiana Carranza.

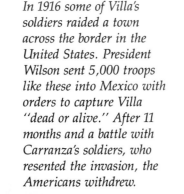

In 1916 some of Villa's soldiers raided a town across the border in the United States. President Wilson sent 5,000 troops like these into Mexico with orders to capture Villa "dead or alive." After 11 months and a battle with Carranza's soldiers, who resented the invasion, the Americans withdrew.

The leaders of the Revolution of 1914 sit for their portrait. Mexico was to endure several more stormy years, but by the 1940s the nation was politically and economically stable. Industrialization was making rapid progress.

Soon a coalition made up of Carranza, Villa, and Zapata was fighting the Huerta government. The coalition received support from United States President Woodrow Wilson, who disapproved of Huerta. Wilson blockaded Mexico's ports to prevent foreign aid from reaching Huerta and, at the same time, allowed the rebels to purchase arms and ammunition in the United States.

In 1914 Huerta resigned and Carranza assumed the presidency. But the political coalition that had backed him did not last. Zapata's followers wanted more land reform, while Villa was interested in personal power. And neither Zapata nor Villa was willing to cooperate with urban workers, who in turn despised the mostly Indian peons.

It took three years of fighting among the various factions before Carranza was victorious and order returned to Mexico. In 1917 a constitutional convention met to write a new constitution. Carranza, himself a wealthy landowner, did not want much reform. But the convention delegates had other ideas. They realized that the peasants and the workers had to be satisfied if the nation was to be politically stable.

Accordingly, the Constitution of 1917 gave the Mexican government the power to break up large estates and divide them among the peasants. It gave workers the right to form unions and go out on strike. It also provided for equal pay for equal work for women. It took control of education away from the Church. And it said that subsoil minerals, such as oil, belonged to the nation as a whole and not to the landowner.

Unlike other Latin American countries, mestizos, not creoles, came to dominate Mexican politics. The government acted to restore and preserve Indian monuments. The Indians' pride in themselves and in their ancestors was encouraged.

The revolution destroyed the tradition of the caudillo in Mexico. All men and women have the right to vote, and freedom of speech and press is guaranteed. Mexican presidents now take their power from the office they hold instead of from the army.

Carlos Salinas de Gortari is the new president of Mexico. What changes do you anticipate from this new administration?

Aftermath

In the late 1920s, various political factions in Mexico united in a single party. Over the years, the party has been known by different names, the most recent being the PRI, or Partido Revolucionario Institucional. Although other parties have been free to nominate presidential candidates, the PRI candidate has always won, sometimes by an overwhelming margin.

In 1988, for the first time, there was serious opposition to the PRI. A leftist faction under Cuauhtemoc Cárdenas, the son of a former president, split from the party and demanded that more attention be given to the needs of peasants and workers. Since half the present population of Mexico is under the age of fifteen, the nation faces enormous demands for food and jobs. The PRI candidate—an American-trained economist named Carlos Salinas de Gortari—narrowly won the presidency with a 50.3 percent majority. But it was evident that the opposition would have a much greater say in the future.

SECTION 1 REVIEW

1. **Recall** What was the excuse of every Latin American caudillo and junta that has seized power?
2. **How and Why** Why were ordinary citizens not prepared to govern themselves in Latin America?
3. **Critical Thinking** Why was the period of Benito Juárez's influence known as *La Reforma*?

Two world wars and the Great Depression of the 1930s had their impact on the economies and social awareness of Latin Americans. Most nations tried to industrialize in order to end their dependence on a single product. As they did so, their middle class and urban working class expanded and became educated. The two classes also grew dissatisfied with the status quo.

As a result, the nations of Latin America experienced one political upheaval after another. The new governments ranged from the authoritarian right to the Communist left. By 1990, however, most Latin American nations had adopted some form of electoral democracy—although the army was always waiting in the wings. Three examples of the varying political changes that have swept the culture region are Argentina, Brazil, and Cuba.

Responses to Change

Argentina

Unlike Mexico, Argentina had almost no peasants. The pampas contained mostly cattle ranches. Technological improvements such as the steam vessel and a technique for chilling meat made it practical to ship Argentine beef thousands of miles to overseas markets. British and other foreign firms gladly provided the capital to build Argentina's packing houses, railroads, and docks and to establish companies to handle the nation's shipping, banking, and insurance. Italian and Spanish laborers flocked to Buenos Aires and other cities. Western Europeans soon made up about one-third of the population.

As a result, land reform was not an issue in Argentina. What *did* arouse the people were populism and nationalism—that is, the demands of urban workers and a desire to do away with foreign ownership of businesses.

The individual who personified these interests was Colonel Juan D. Perón. He was elected president of Argentina in 1946. Unlike some previous presidents, Perón did not outlaw labor unions. Instead, he used them as a base for political power. Describing Argentina as "a country of fat bulls and undernourished peons," he moved to give the urban workers more. He encouraged strikes, which the government then settled in favor of labor. He increased wages and fringe benefits. In less than four years, labor's share of the national income jumped by 25 percent.

Perón satisfied nationalist feelings by taking over the British-owned railroads, the American-controlled telephone system, and the French-owned dock facilities. He also instituted high tariffs to protect local industry.

Perón also moved to increase his own power. He outlawed freedom of the press and freedom of speech. And he abolished the constitutional clause that prevented him from succeeding himself as president.

Perón's wife, Maria Eva Duarte, helped him to win the support of organized labor. A former radio actress who had been snubbed by the society matrons of Buenos Aires, "Evita" set up a personal foundation that distributed money to the poor, the sick, widows, and orphans. She was especially interested in women's rights. She organized women workers and helped women gain the vote. She was highly effective. When she died of cancer in 1952, the Argentine working class went into mourning for one month.

With his wife's death, Perón's popularity began to decline. He lost favor with the Roman Catholic Church when he pushed through legislation legalizing divorce and placing parochial schools under government control. In 1955 Peronist crowds demonstrated against the Church and even set fire to cathedrals in Buenos Aires. In response, the Vatican excommunicated Perón and his cabinet. At which point the army told Perón that if he did not resign, the country would be plunged into civil war. Perón resigned and went into exile. His supporters, however, remained active.

Perón's resignation did little to bring stability to Argentina. The next 18 years saw worsening economic conditions and a series of military and civilian governments. Then the Peronists won the presidency, the successful candidate stepped down, and Perón returned to power in 1973. He died the next year and was succeeded by his vice president and widow, Isabel. She ruled until 1976, when she was ousted by a military junta.

The junta put down all opposition, much of it through torture and kidnappings. It abolished labor unions and denationalized many state-owned businesses. But the military was unable to solve the country's problems of inflation, unemployment, and a large foreign debt.

In 1982 Argentina invaded the Falkland Islands (Las Malvinas), a British possession off its southeastern coast that it had claimed for some time. The government hoped to draw the nation's attention away from its troubled economy. At first the Argentine people reacted with an outpouring of patriotic fervor. But when the British regained control of the Falklands after only two months, the Argentinians turned against the junta.

Peronists, supporters of Juan Perón's policies, celebrate in 1982. The picture of Perón is flanked on the left by a picture of Evita; on the right by one of Isabel.

In the presidential election of 1983, the Peronists lost to a moderate, Raul Alfonsín. Alfonsín promised to end Argentina's human rights violations and ease the nation's economic problems. He succeeded in the first goal but failed in the second. In 1989 Carlos Saúl Menem became president. Although elected with Peronist support, Menem took certain actions that angered the working-class electorate. Peronists believe it is the role of the state to guarantee jobs to workers, and markets and profits to business. Menem felt that the solution of Argentina's economic difficulties lay in reducing the size of the government and its role in the economy. In March 1990, mass strikes erupted to protest the inflation rate of 100 percent a month. There were widespread rumors that unhappy army officers would soon join with the Peronists to overthrow the government.

Brazil

The transition from colony to independent nation was more orderly in Brazil than in any of the former Spanish-ruled nations of Latin America. But freedom from Portuguese rule did not bring social reform.

The rule of Emperor Pedro I was not a happy one. Among other things, he ignored the constitution and governed as a dictator instead of consulting the elected legislature. In 1831 regents took control of the government and ruled for Pedro's five-year-old son.

Pedro II was crowned emperor in 1840. He followed a program of encouraging Brazil's economic development. Roads, railroads, and port facilities were built. Rubber plantations were started. Coffee replaced sugar as the leading crop. And the government paid for the trans-Atlantic passage of millions of European workers, especially Italians and Germans. Many Japanese workers immigrated to Brazil as well.

As Pedro II's long reign continued, groups of Brazilians grew restless. Plantation owners were becoming very influential in the nation's politics. Many feared for their interests if Pedro's daughter Isabel should succeed him. As it was, while Pedro II was in Europe for his health, Isabel had freed the slaves. Army officers were also unhappy. They wanted more money spent on modernizing the army, and they wanted the right to express their political views in public.

In 1889 a combination of plantation owners, army officers, and liberals who favored a republic toppled Pedro II and sent him into exile. The new constitution established a federation of 20 states, with a nationally elected president. Between 1889 and 1945, either the military acted as a watchdog over the president, or else the president was himself a military man.

The caudillo who ruled the longest in Brazil was Getulio Vargas. He moved into the presidential palace in 1930 following a military coup, and remained in power until another military coup in 1945. Like Perón in Argentina, Vargas gained working-class support by increasing wages, shortening working hours, and giving unions the right to organize.

Dom Pedro II ruled Brazil from 1840 to 1889. His overthrow by the military was an example of the importance the military has played and continues to play in Latin America.

In time, however, the United States began to use the Monroe Doctrine as a cloak for its own expansion. In the 1830s and 1840s, American settlers in the Mexican territories of Texas, California, and the Southwest wanted the United States to annex those territories. President James K. Polk agreed that the Monroe Doctrine prevented transfer of American land to a European state. However, it did not forbid changes in ownership among the nations of the Western Hemisphere. And as you know, the United States acquired all these territories as a result of the Mexican-American War. In 1898, the United States acquired Puerto Rico and Cuba (the latter as a protectorate) as a result of the Spanish-American War.

Theodore Roosevelt

An American hero of the Spanish-American War was Theodore Roosevelt, who resigned as assistant secretary of the navy in order to fight against the Spaniards in Cuba. Later as president, Roosevelt was responsible for several major American interventions in the Latin American culture region.

The Panama Canal   Victory in the Spanish-American War gave the United States possessions off the coast of Asia as well as in the Caribbean. As a result, the United States had to be able to move its fleet quickly between the Atlantic and Pacific oceans. It needed a canal across Central America.

In March 1903, the Senate approved a treaty with Colombia to finish a canal that the French had started in the Colombian province of Panama. The new Colombian government, however, rejected the treaty. It was afraid it would lose sovereignty over Panama.

sovereignty: supremacy of authority or rule

On November 2 an American warship entered the harbor of Colón in Panama. The ship's commander had instructions from President Roosevelt to take over the Panama Railroad in case a rebellion against Colombia broke out and to prevent Colombian troops from landing in the area. Sure enough, the next day a rebellion against Colombia broke out and government troops were unable to reach Colón to suppress it. On November 4 ten more American warships appeared off the coast of Panama. On November 6 the United States recognized Panama as an independent nation. And on November 17 the new Panamanian government signed a treaty with the United States for construction of the canal. Panama received $10 million at once and an annual rental fee after nine years. In return, the United States received complete control of a canal zone 10 miles (15 kilometers) wide "in perpetuity," that is, forever. Panama also agreed to the principles of the Platt Amendment, which permitted American intervention in its domestic affairs.

The Roosevelt Corollary   Construction of the Panama Canal aroused tremendous resentment against the United States on the part of many Latin Americans. They felt the United States was following a policy of political and economic imperialism. They became even more unhappy when President Roosevelt extended the Monroe Doctrine in 1904.

By the mid-1800s Europe was becoming industrialized. Merchants and manufacturers were on the lookout for sources of raw materials and for areas in which to invest money. Latin America fit the bill in both respects. Naturally, Europeans expected the repayment of loans and regular returns on their investments. In a number of cases, however, Latin American governments borrowed money that they either could not or would not repay. When that occurred, the European governments threatened the offending nations with blockades. This alarmed American officials. They feared a repetition of France's takeover of Mexico under Maximilian. They also saw the extension of European influence in the hemisphere as a threat to the position of the United States.

Accordingly, in 1904 Roosevelt proclaimed what is known as the Roosevelt Corollary to the Monroe Doctrine. Whenever a nation in the Western Hemisphere failed to repay its debts to foreign investors, Roosevelt said, the United States would exercise "an international police power." It would assume supervision of that country and see to it that the debts were paid. In other words, preventing European intervention justified American intervention.

During the next three decades, the United States applied the Roosevelt Corollary a number of times. For example, in 1905 American bankers took over administration of the customs revenue of the Dominican

Colonel Theodore Roosevelt poses with his Rough Riders atop San Juan Hill, Cuba, during the Spanish-American War. What events led to this war?

Republic. In 1916 the United States established a military government there that lasted for eight years. American marines landed in Haiti in 1914 and remained until 1934. They also landed in Nicaragua in 1912 and stayed until 1933.

In addition to military intervention, the United States exercised considerable economic influence in Latin America. An example was the United Fruit Company (UFCO), which controlled the banana trade of Costa Rica, Guatemala, Honduras, and Panama. On the one hand, UFCO paid its workers up to three times the going rate and provided them with housing. It built schools, hospitals, docks, and roads. On the other hand, it kept vast amounts of land in reserve against hurricanes and plant disease. This made it difficult for peasants to acquire land of their own or to grow enough food. Because profits flowed from the so-called "banana republics" to the United States, they were unable to accumulate enough capital to industrialize. Furthermore, UFCO undervalued its land for tax purposes.

Good Neighbor Policy

In the 1920s, the United States changed its policy. It tried to assure Latin Americans that it had no imperialistic designs. President Herbert Hoover went on a goodwill tour of the culture region. He repudiated the Roosevelt Corollary and withdrew American marines from Nicaragua. After his election in 1933, President Franklin Roosevelt continued the Good Neighbor policy. He convinced Congress to abolish the Platt Amendment, and the United States pulled out of Haiti as promised.

The years between 1933 and 1945 were relatively free of tension. The Good Neighbor policy was especially important during World War II. After Asian sources of war materials were cut off, the United States was able to buy copper, tin, and rubber from Latin America. Many people began to see the possibility for a new spirit of cooperation.

The Good Neighbor policy continued after World War II. In 1948 the Organization of American States (OAS) was established on the foundations of an existing organization. The OAS provides means for the peaceful settlement of disagreements. It promotes regional cooperation and also aims to improve the social and material welfare of the citizens of its member nations.

In 1961 President John Kennedy proposed a program of economic aid known as the Alliance for Progress. Funds from the United States were to be matched by funds from those Latin American countries participating in the program. The money was to be used to bring about a peaceful social revolution. Schools and houses were to be built, large estates were to be broken up, tax laws that benefited the rich were to be changed, and health and sanitation facilities were to be installed.

Ten years of the Alliance for Progress accomplished little. Some of its inspiration was lost when Kennedy was assassinated in 1963. But it failed, too, because the landowning class in Latin America resisted change. In addition, the United States compromised its aims even as they were

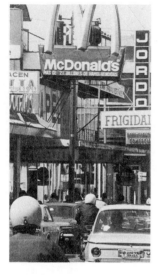

Although some **multinational companies**—*companies that do business in more than one country—are American-owned, like McDonald's, many are European- or Japanese-owned. What effects might multinationals have on the economy of the nations in which they invest?*

Since the late 1970s, El Salvador has been a battleground between government forces and guerrillas. A major issue is land reform. How might land reform help peasant farmers like this one?

announced. Because of the cold war and the fear of Communist influence in Latin America, two thirds of the Alliance's funds went for weapons instead of social reform.

Support of the Status Quo

Between 1950 and 1990, the United States pursued a hard anti-Communist line in Latin America. Often this meant supporting right-wing dictatorships. Sometimes it meant attaching the label of communism to any change in the status quo.

In 1953 Jacobo Arbenz Guzmán was elected president of Guatemala. Although Arbenz had accepted Communist support in the election, he was actually a moderate who tried to strengthen private industries. He also instituted a program of land reform under which he himself lost 1,700 acres (688 hectares) of land. The United States, however, considered Arbenz "soft" on communism and a potential threat to the Panama Canal. So in 1953 it organized an exile invasion that overthrew Arbenz. The new government reversed the land reform.

In 1963 President Lyndon B. Johnson sent marines into the Dominican Republic to put down a supposedly Communist revolt. In 1973 the United States financed strikes against the elected socialist government of Salvador Allende in Chile. Throughout the 1980s, the United States sent weapons to the government of El Salvador, which was fighting left-wing guerrillas—and also slaughtering about 70,000 labor union organizers, teachers, peasant leaders, and priests and nuns who opposed its policies. The most extensive American intervention, however, took place in Nicaragua.

In 1970 Salvador Allende (ah-YEN-day) Gossens of Chile became the first freely elected Marxist president in Latin America. His policies angered landowners and the middle class, and in 1973 he was overthrown by a violent military coup.

You recall that United States marines left Nicaragua in 1933 after 21 years of military occupation. During that time, the Americans trained a police force known as the National Guard, which more or less ran the country for the benefit of its large landowners. Between 1933 and 1979, most of Nicaragua's rulers were members of the Somoza family. In 1979 the Somoza dictatorship was overthrown by a combination of three rebel groups known as the Sandinista National Liberation Front.

The Sandinistas set up a mixed government. They took over the land holdings of the Somozas but left the rest of Nicaragua's land in private hands. They censored or shut down opposition newspapers but allowed opposition political parties to function. They controlled the army and the police. They also mounted a massive attack on illiteracy and tried to improve public health facilities.

At first the United States provided some financial help to the Sandinistas. In 1981, however, President Ronald Reagan cut off all assistance on the ground that the Sandinistas were Communists. The United States then launched a trade embargo against Nicaragua that severely damaged the country's economy. The United States also funded an exile army known as the contras, led in part by former Somoza army officers. Despite hundreds of millions of dollars in American aid, the contras were unable to overthrow the Sandinistas. But they forced the government to spend half of its budget on defense rather than on social needs. The country was devastated, casualties reached the 50,000 figure, and an additional 500,000 Nicaraguans fled for safety to Honduras.

In 1987 the five major Central American nations signed a peace plan known as the Arias plan after the man who drew it up, Costa Rican President Oscar Arias Sanchez. Under the Arias plan, the Sandinistas and the contras were to negotiate a peace. Nicaragua would then hold a free election to determine its new government. The plan also called for a

360

(Continued on page 362.)

HISTORY AND PEOPLE

ARCHBISHOP OSCAR ARNULFO ROMERO

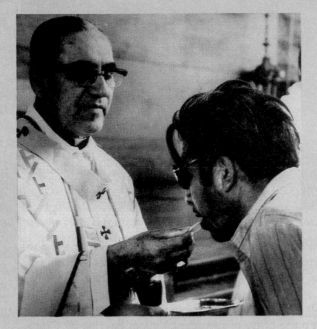

Archbishop Oscar Romero from San Salvador was an outspoken champion of human rights

I n 1979, an outspoken defender of human rights was nominated for the Nobel Peace Prize by 23 members of the United States Congress. They described him as follows:

> An individual of unsurpassed courage and integrity, Archbishop Romero has not allowed government persecutors to frighten him into silence or submission. He has remained a forthright and compelling advocate of human rights, nonviolence and social progress—setting a standard in defense of human liberty which can be applied not only in Latin America, but throughout the world.

Any country where an elite 2% of the people own 60% of the land, where crops are sold for cash rather than fed to a malnourished population, and where dissent is outlawed needs a champion. The small, overpopulated Latin America country of El Salvador found one in Archbishop Oscar Romero.

Romero served as bishop in the village of Santiago de Maria from 1974 to 1977 and was considered part of the conservative clergy at that time. He began to change, however, as he witnessed the poverty of the peasants and their continued repression by the government. In addition, he was greatly moved by the Vatican's increasingly active support of human rights worldwide.

When he was appointed Archbishop of San Salvador in 1977, the government was unhappily surprised to find an influential activist for social change in their midst. The archbishop rapidly garnered enemies within the regime. The country's newspapers denounced him regularly, while printing none of his sermons in which he spoke outright against the tyrannical rule of the government. He was also opposed by upper levels of the clergy as well, many of whom thought him aligned with the communist rebels fighting the government.

On March 23, 1980, as Archbishop Romero stood in his church praying and pleading for the end of the violence and persecution, he was assassinated by a lone gunman. The people of El Salvador lost a prominent spokesman in their struggle for peace and justice. The influence of the martyred archbishop will continue to be felt, but the struggle for peace and justice continues.

1. In what ways is it not surprising that the archbishop was murdered?

2. How is the situation in El Salvador similar to the situation in much of Latin America today?

3. What do you think causes division and fighting in a country like El Salvador?

A ship passes through the Panama Canal. How did the United States gain control of the Canal Zone? What is the present status of Panamanian-American relations?

SECTION 3 REVIEW

1. **Recall**   What was the Roosevelt Corollary to the Monroe Doctrine?

2. **How and Why**   How did the United Fruit Company affect the so-called "banana republics"?

3. **Critical Thinking**   Do you think political unrest will continue in Latin America for a long time?

Reviewing People, Places, and Things

Identify, define, or explain each of the following:

caudillo

Santa Anna

Texas Anglos

Treaty of
   Guadelupe Hidalgo

Juárez

Díaz

peonage

Zapata

Madero

Huerta

Villa

status quo

Perón

Bay of Pigs

Monroe Doctrine

Panama Canal Zone

Good Neighbor
   Policy

Noriega

Map Study

Using the map on page 363, answer the following questions:

1. Between what two cities does the railroad in the Canal Zone run?

2. What two bodies of water are connected by the Panama Canal?

3. In what direction from Colón is Panama City located?

Understanding Facts and Ideas

1. What issues caused dissent between Americans and Mexicans in Texas?

2. Why were the results of Díaz's policy considered to be mixed?

3. What changes did the Mexican Revolution bring about?

4. What were Juan Perón's policies?

5. How does Collor hope to solve the economic problems of Brazil?

6. What reforms did Castro begin?

7. How did the United States apply the Monroe Doctrine differently in the 1830s and 1840s than it did in the 1820s?

8. Why did the Alliance of Progress accomplish little?

9. What was the Arias plan?

Developing Critical Thinking

Predicting Alternative Futures   Prepare a diagram to show the possible outcomes of the United States using a different policy in its relations with Castro. Then discuss whether the United States' opposition to Castro was justifiable according to United States and Cuban interests.

Writing About History

Analyzing Economics   Consider the military takeovers discussed in this chapter and write a paragraph discussing how military takeovers affect the economy of a nation.

Applying Your Skills to History

Debating an Issue   With your classmates, debate whether Grenada should or should not have been invaded in 1983.

Society in Transition

Today, industrialization and urbanization are bringing changes to Latin America. The changes, however, are uneven. They are more noticeable in some countries and in some areas of social and economic development than in others. Two groups—a rapidly growing middle class and a large urban working class—are beginning to exercise power.

As you study this chapter, think about these questions:

- How are power and wealth divided in Latin America?
- How is industrialization affecting Latin America's social and economic development?
- What factors have shaped the arts in Latin America?

The Indian man and child below are dressed the way their ancestors dressed for hundreds of years, but they are playing with a Frisbee.

With independence, the distinction between American-born and European-born Spanish and Portuguese disappeared. The new upper class of Latin America included anyone with money and all-European ancestry. The two usually went together. Independence did little for Indians, blacks, mestizos, mulattoes, and zambos. They remained at the bottom of the social system.

Modern Social Structures

In most Latin American nations today, the same small upper class still holds the wealth. Their families have owned the large landholdings since colonial days. Now these few also hold key positions in industry and government. The successful children of later immigrants from Europe, Asia, and the Middle East also rank high in Latin American society today.

In some nations, such as Argentina and Uruguay, the growing middle class is becoming important. It is made up of doctors, lawyers, government clerks, and other white-collar workers. Education and industry have made the middle class possible.

Most Latin Americans, however, belong to the lower class. They are subsistence farmers, wage hands on large commercial farms, construction workers, part-time carriers of firewood or water, and artisans. Their wages are low and their future often seems hopeless. They usually have little or no education.

For upward social mobility—movement from one social class to another, higher social class—it is a person's dress, speech, education, and wealth that are important. Immigrants perhaps have had the best chance of moving up the Latin American social ladder.

SECTION

1

Social Patterns

white-collar workers: people who are paid weekly or monthly salaries instead of working for an hourly wage

It is estimated that more than 12 million immigrants entered Latin America from about 1885 to the mid-1900s. More than 4 million came from Italy alone. Others included English and Germans as well as Spanish and Portuguese. They settled mostly in Mexico and in countries with temperate climates—Argentina, southern Brazil, Chile, and Uruguay.

Of all the Latin American countries, Brazil offers the greatest opportunity for upward mobility. The experience of the Japanese is an example. They began arriving in large numbers about 1908 to work on coffee plantations. But they soon abandoned the harsh working conditions there and turned to other ways of making a living. They began growing cotton, jute, and pepper. They started a poultry industry and modernized commercial fishing.

After World War II, the Japanese began moving into urban areas. The move signaled a cultural change. On the farms, they had kept much of their Japanese culture, including their language. In the cities they were exposed to Brazilian culture. They exchanged the Japanese language for Portuguese. Many young Japanese took jobs outside agriculture. They became engineers, economists, and doctors—members of the middle class.

Education

Until independence, most Latin Americans were illiterate. Since then, all the governments have established free public schools. Today, literacy rates range from 25 percent in Haiti to 95 percent in Argentina and Uruguay. Overall, about three-fourths of the population can read and write.

However, there are numerous problems. Only a fraction of young people are enrolled in secondary schools. Most children have to work from an early age to help support their families. Providing education for children who live in remote areas is difficult. More than half the teachers lack teaching degrees. They are generally poorly paid and have little prestige. Also, Latin America's population is growing so quickly that each year additional hundreds of thousands of children reach school age. As a result, governments must give education a larger share of their budgets just to maintain existing standards.

Higher education has expanded more rapidly. Argentina, Brazil, Colombia, Mexico, and Peru combined have more than a hundred universities. Since Latin American countries need people who can develop the economy, the universities concentrate on such subjects as engineering and medicine.

In addition, Latin America contains other institutions with an educational purpose. For example, Argentina, Brazil, and Mexico have almost 1,000 museums and 5,000 public libraries. One of the most impressive museums in the culture region—if not the world—is Mexico City's National Museum of Anthropology, with its displays of Olmec, Mayan, Aztec, and other Indian artifacts.

NATIONAL PROFILES/LATIN AMERICA

Nation/Capital	Population/ Area (in sq mi)	Urban Population (as % of total)	Per Capita GNP (in U.S. $)	Adult Literacy Rate (%)	Life Expectancy	Population Growth Rate* (%)
Antigua and Barbuda/St. John's	64,000/171	58	2,800	90	71	1.0
Argentina/Buenos Aires	32,291,000/ 1,068,297	85	2,640	94	71	1.3
Bahamas/Nassau	246,000/5,380	58	10,570	95	71	1.5
Barbados/Bridgetown	257,000/166	32	5,990	99	75	0.7
Belize/Belmopan	220,000/8,867	50	1,460	93	69	3.1
Bolivia/La Paz, Sucre	7,277,000/424,162	49	570	63	53	2.6
Brazil/Brasília	150,368,000/ 3,286,472	74	2,280	74	65	1.9
Chile/Santiago	13,173,000/292,257	84	1,510	96	71	1.7
Colombia/Bogotá	31,819,000/439,735	68	1,240	88	66	2.0
Costa Rica/San José	3,033,000/19,575	45	1,760	93	76	2.5
Cuba/Havana	10,620,000/42,803	72	**	96	75	1.2
Dominica/Roseau	85,000/290	**	1,650	80	75	2.1
Dominican Republic/ Santo Domingo	7,170,000/18,816	52	680	74	66	2.5
Ecuador/Quito	10,737,000/109,483	54	1,080	85	65	2.5
El Salvador/San Salvador	5,310,000/8,124	43	950	69	62	2.7
Grenada/St. George's	84,000/133	**	1,370	85	71	3.0
Guatemala/Guatemala City	9,197,000/42,042	40	880	51	63	3.1
Guyana/Georgetown	765,000/83,000	33	410	86	67	1.9
Haiti/Port-au-Prince	6,504,000/10,714	26	360	23	53	2.2
Honduras/Tegucigalpa	5,138,000/43,277	42	850	56	63	3.1
Jamaica/Kingston	2,441,000/4,243	49	1,080	76	76	1.7
Mexico/Mexico City	88,598,000/761,601	66	1,820	88	68	2.4
Nicaragua/Managua	3,856,000/50,193	57	830	87	62	3.6
Panama/Panama City	2,418,000/29,761	52	2,240	90	72	2.2
Paraguay/Asunción	4,277,000/157,047	43	1,180	84	67	2.8
Peru/Lima	21,906,000/496,222	69	1,440	80	65	2.4
St. Kitts and Nevis/ Basseterre	40,000/100	45	2,770	**	68	1.3
Saint Lucia/Castries	153,000/238	46	1,540	78	71	2.2
St. Vincent and the Grenadines/Kingstown	113,000/150	21	1,100	85	72	1.9
Suriname/Paramaribo	397,000/63,037	66	2,450	65	68	2.0
Trinidad and Tobago/ Port-of-Spain	1,345,000/1,981	64	3,350	95	70	2.0
Uruguay/Montevideo	3,037,000/68,037	87	2,470	96	71	0.8
Venezuela/Caracas	19,636,000/352,143	83	3,170	88	70	2.3

Sources: *The 1990 Information Please Almanac* (Houghton Mifflin Company); *1990 World Population Data Sheet* (Population Reference Bureau, Inc., Washington D.C.)

*A nation with a population growth rate of 2% or more doubles its population within 35 years or less.

**Not available.

Religion

Most of the people of Latin America are Roman Catholics. Roman Catholicism is the state religion of seven countries in the culture region, although all countries allow freedom of worship. Many people of Indian or African descent identify themselves as Roman Catholics even though they perform dances and practice rituals related to the religions of their ancestors. Voodoo drums still beat in Haiti, for example. And in spring, Guatemalan farmers still bury a statue of the Mayan corn god in the ground along with the seeds for a new crop.

A few Latin Americans have accepted Protestant Christianity. Some Protestant denominations—notably Methodists and Seventh Day Adventists—have been active as missionaries, especially among Indians and blacks. In remote regions such as the Amazon Basin and the mountains of Bolivia, the missionaries often combine their religious message with clinics and schools. There are also Jewish communities in Argentina, Chile, Mexico, and Uruguay.

The wars of independence brought about changes in the position of the Roman Catholic Church. In countries where church and state were separated, the government took over the Church's educational, health, and welfare services. Religious instruction was no longer allowed in the public schools, and marriages had to be performed by civil as well as religious authorities. In some countries, as you know, the Church lost much of its land and business holdings. The resulting shortage of funds, combined with a shortage of priests, helped lessen the Church's influence.

On the right is a photo of a traditional Good Friday religious procession. On the left a priest celebrates an outdoor mass. How has the Roman Catholic Church's policy toward the activities of its priests changed in recent years?

For many years, the Church took a direct part in political activities, urging parishioners to support certain candidates. However, in 1990, when Pope John Paul II visited Latin America, he said that the Church should seek social justice only by using Christian principles, not through politics. The pope stated that priests should neither seek nor hold government offices.

In line with this approach, many Catholic clergy have concerned themselves with problems of land reform, labor, and the strengthening of political democracy. They have organized credit unions and food cooperatives, and have helped workers form labor unions. They have helped city dwellers set up organizations to obtain running water, regular waste disposal, paved streets, and other services from local governments. They have led protests against government violations of human rights.

From the beginning of the conquest, the church was often the largest and most impressive building in a settlement. This church in Columbia is an example of Spanish colonial architecture.

The Family

Traditionally, the family has been an important institution in Latin America. Today, Latin Americans still retain a strong family sense. Everyone may not live under the same roof, but important questions are discussed among family members. Businesses are often family enterprises. Everyone gathers to celebrate birthdays, weddings, and other events. Political leaders often depend on family members to help them

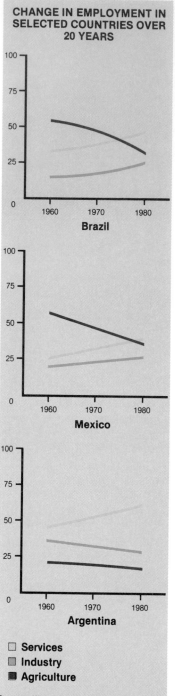

CHANGE IN EMPLOYMENT IN SELECTED COUNTRIES OVER 20 YEARS

Brazil

Mexico

Argentina

☐ Services
☐ Industry
■ Agriculture

Source: *World Development Report 1983*, copyright © 1983 by the International Bank for Reconstruction and Development/The World Bank. Reproduced by permission of Oxford University Press.

run the government. And when problems arise that might reflect upon family pride, the members present a united front to the public.

The extended family is strongest among the upper and lower classes. Family ties are somewhat weaker among the growing urban middle class. This is partly because many young people leave home for better jobs. Also, in cities, family ties are often less important than education and ability as a basis for hiring.

Among many lower-class families, marriages are common-law unions. That is, the husband and wife live together without a legal or religious ceremony. There are several reasons for this. Having a formal wedding with a celebration afterwards is very expensive. Often the family of a bride just cannot afford to go into debt for several years. Then, too, if a common-law marriage does not work, it is easier for the couple to break up if they do not have to worry about religious or legal difficulties.

Women

To understand the present status of women in Latin America, it is necessary to understand one of the values of Latin American society—*machismo* (mah-CHEEZ-moh). The term comes from the Spanish word *macho*, meaning manliness. It is an attitude that always implies the superiority of men over women. Men are required to act bravely, to have a large family that relies on them for financial support, and to dominate women. Women are to be treated as personal property and are useful mostly for bearing children and keeping house. Violence toward women is considered acceptable male behavior.

Traditionally, the Spanish and Portuguese kept upper-class women shielded from the public. Their bedrooms were in the inner part of the house, and the windows were barred. The women went out only to attend church or for social reasons. Marriages were arranged. Women were supposed to be quiet, obedient, and understanding about their husbands' illegitimate children. Wives never interfered in their husbands' business or political affairs.

Poor people, of course, did not follow this ideal. And even among the wealthy, the ideal was not achieved completely. There were always a few upper-class women who took an active part in society. For example, Sor (Sister) Juana Inés de la Cruz (1650–1695) was among the first Latin American poets. She learned to read at the age of three. She constantly criticized the attitude toward women and the lack of education for them. She reportedly became a nun so that she might devote her life to study.

In the 1800s, during the struggle for independence, there were many heroines, some of whom were executed for their activities. Maria Josefa Ortíz de Dominquez warned Father Hidalgo of his coming arrest, resulting in his issuing the Grito de Dolores. Teresa Heredia, a Venezuelan teacher, was tarred and feathered by Spanish authorities and exiled to the United States to keep her from helping the independence movement. During the Ten Years' War, Mariana Grajales organized a field hospital for rebel soldiers deep in the Cuban jungle. And there were many others.

Not all Latin American women are as fortunate as this one. The nation a woman lives in and whether she is from a city or village will in large part determine her opportunities.

In 1928 the Inter-American Commission of Women was formed. Its purpose was to promote the civil, political, and economic rights of women. The Commission's first task was gaining suffrage for women in Latin America. Ecuador led the way in 1929. Paraguay brought up the rear in 1961. Today women's suffrage is universal throughout the culture region.

Since 1966 the Commission has been working on a long-range program to improve women's economic status through education. It is trying to outlaw discrimination against women. It is popularizing the work of women folk artists. It has established agencies to look after the legal and social welfare of working women.

In recent years, women in some Latin American countries have been in leadership positions. Eva Perón and Isabel Perón of Argentina are two examples. Lidia Gueilar Tejada served as president of Bolivia, and in 1990 Violeta Barrios de Chamorro was elected president of Nicaragua, while Ertha Pascal-Trouillot (AIR-tah pahs-KAHL TROO-yō) became provisional president of Haiti. In general, however, political, economic, and social freedoms remain only dreams for most Latin American women.

SECTION 1 REVIEW

1. **Recall** What factors are considered important for upward social mobility?
2. **How and Why** How has the Inter-American Commission of Women worked to improve the status of women?
3. **Critical Thinking** How have the activities of the Catholic Church changed since 1980?

Most of the nations in Latin America are considered to be developing nations, that is, they are not yet highly industrialized. Yet they are rich in mineral and other natural resources. Among the main reasons for the culture region's economic difficulties are the need for land reform, overpopulation, and a shortage of capital.

Land Reform

In no other area of the world is so much land owned by so few people as in Latin America. In Brazil, for example, the top two percent of landowners control 60 percent of the arable land. In Paraguay, the top one percent of landowners control 80 percent of the arable land. And similar situations exist in other countries. This pattern of land ownership had its origin in the colonial practice of rewarding loyalty with large land grants.

Big landholdings are of two kinds: haciendas and commercial farms. **Haciendas** are usually owned by absentee landlords and farmed by peasant sharecroppers, who keep one-third to one-half of what they grow and give the rest to the landlord as rent. Productivity on haciendas is low. Absentee landlords often do not want to spend the money needed to improve farm equipment. They find it more economical to use cheap labor. Tenant farmers often grow only enough food to meet their own needs. Because they do not own the land, they lack the desire to produce more. In addition, they do not earn enough to buy manufactured goods, which keeps industry from growing.

Latin American Indians still live according to the traditions of their ancestors even though the social, economic, and political base of their way of life was destroyed long ago. They are unsure about adopting Western European ways because their experience with those in power has seldom been good. Do you think their fear of change is reasonable?

Almost half of all Latin Americans earn their living from agriculture. Many of them rent land from or work as laborers for large landowners. Why would land reform appeal to them?

Commercial farms produce such crops as bananas, cereals, coffee, meat, sugar, and wool for sale on the world market. Productivity is high because the farms use large quantities of machinery, fertilizers, and insecticides. Many nations depend on commercial farms for more than half their export earnings. At the same time, the emphasis on growing crops for export means that these nations are plagued by food shortages and are unable to feed their own people.

Some Latin American farmers—especially Indians living in the Andes—own small plots of land. For the most part, they practice subsistence farming. They use simple tools, such as hoes and digging sticks, and employ horses, burros, and llamas for transportation. Unfortunately, their farms are usually too small and the soil too poor to provide them with a decent living. Some try to supplement their income by making handicrafts for sale, running small stores or produce markets, or working for large landowners. But even so, their lives are hard and often short.

The movement for land reform in Latin America has a long history. It has succeeded politically in four countries: Mexico, Cuba, Peru, and Nicaragua. In all four, revolutionary governments forced the large landowners to give up their estates. But in none of the four has agricultural productivity improved enough to keep up with the growth in population.

The most successful land reform took place in Mexico beginning in the 1920s. It was part of the social revolution that continued beyond the fighting. Mexico redistributed land in two ways. It divided large estates into workable units and gave them to individuals. It also delivered land grants to entire communities. This communal arrangement, known as the *ejido* system, was based on the Aztec system of land organization. But the government soon found that it was not enough just to give land to the people. People needed instruction, seeds, equipment, and credit. Unfortunately, the government did not invest enough money in this. Also,

credit:
a loan against which a person can borrow, or charge goods and services

(Continued on page 378.)

375

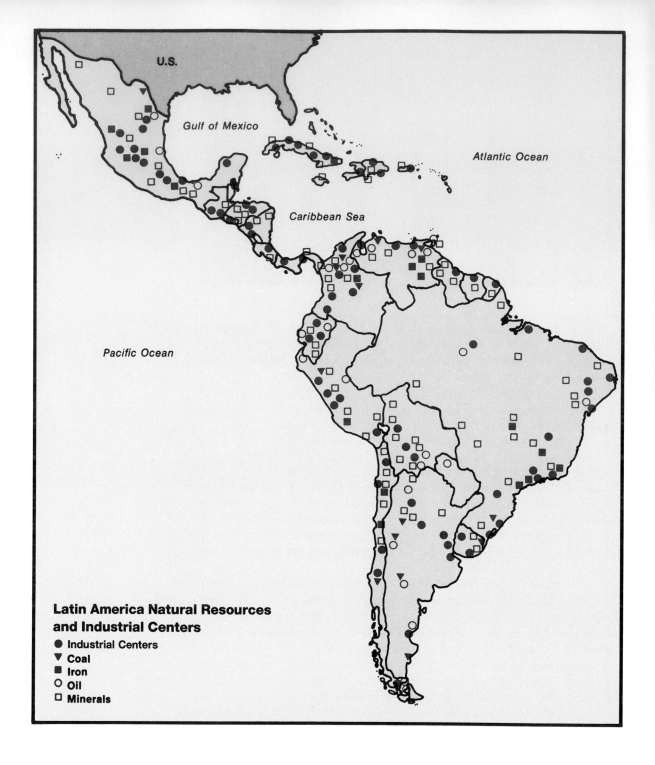

Latin America Natural Resources and Industrial Centers

- ● Industrial Centers
- ▼ Coal
- ■ Iron
- ○ Oil
- □ Minerals

U.S.

Gulf of Mexico

Atlantic Ocean

Caribbean Sea

Pacific Ocean

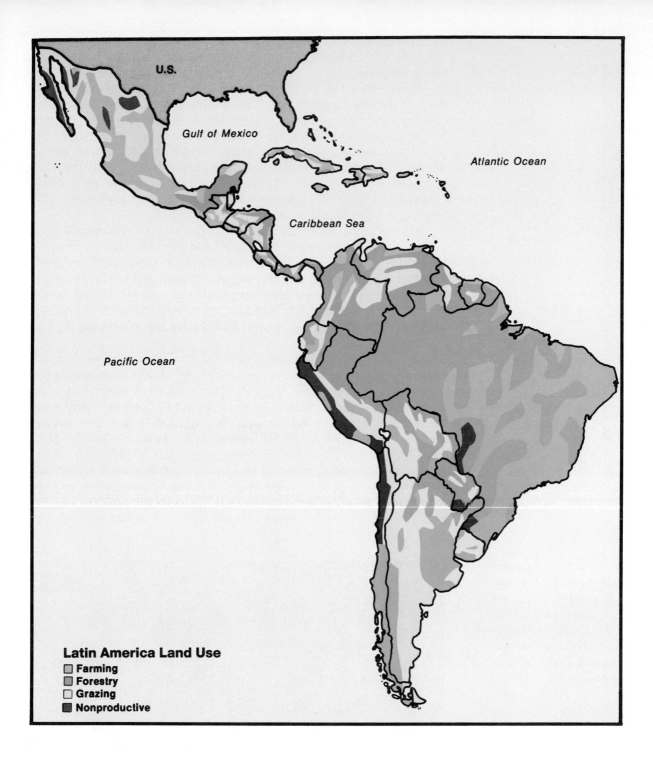

U.S.

Gulf of Mexico

Atlantic Ocean

Caribbean Sea

Pacific Ocean

Latin America Land Use
☐ Farming
☐ Forestry
☐ Grazing
■ Nonproductive

Mexico's population has been growing at a very high rate, more than twice that of the United States. As a result, Mexico has to import grain to feed its city-dwellers.

Brazil has tried a different approach. Instead of attempting to destroy the old landholdings, the government has been setting up colonies within the country's interior. Ideally, the colonization program will accomplish four goals. First, unsettled lands will be brought into production. Second, the rubber, lumber, and mineral resources of the interior will be tapped. Third, poor rural Brazilians, especially from the impoverished northeast, will have a chance to improve their living conditions. And fourth, colonies will receive some of the peasants who might otherwise migrate to already crowded cities.

However, the colonization program has run into numerous difficulties. It requires vast sums of money. Land must be cleared and roads built. The colonists must be taken to the new areas and then given financial assistance until they become self-supporting. Most of the colonization schemes guarantee government-financed educational and health services. Moreover, the new land may not be productive. Brazil discovered this. Once the vegetation was cleared from the rainforests, the soil quickly wore out.

Brazil's efforts at colonization have run into yet another problem: the Indians who still live in the interior. Brazil's 1988 constitution calls for the setting aside of about 9 percent of the country's land as reservations. The reservations would be off limits to development by outsiders. Within the reservations, Brazil's remaining Indians could decide their own future. However, Brazil's newly elected president, Fernando Collor de Mello, finds himself torn between conflicting interests. On the one hand, in order to attract more foreign investment, he wants to show international public opinion that he is trying to preserve the Amazon Basin and not mistreat the Indians. On the other hand, he was elected with the support of miners, loggers, and ranchers who are anxious to exploit Indian lands.

Soccer is the most popular sport in Latin America. Soccer stars, such as the Brazilian known as Pelé, are rich and world famous. Becoming a professional soccer player is one way out of poverty.

Squatter settlements such as this one have sprung up in many Latin American cities in recent years. Why? How do squatter settlements begin? What are governments trying to do about them?

Urbanization

Some experts suggest that Latin America's landownership problems will disappear as more peasants migrate from rural areas to the cities. But the region's cities are likewise facing difficulties.

Overall, Latin America is about two-thirds urban. In Argentina, Chile, and Uruguay, more than 80 percent of the people live in urban areas. Brazil, Mexico, and Venezuela are only slightly behind. Since World War II, cities in Latin America have grown faster than those in any other part of the world. Mexico City, for example, jumped from about 3 million people in 1950 to 16 million in 1980 and an estimated 20 million in 1990. It is now the second largest city in the world; only Tokyo is larger. Other large cities in Latin America include Buenos Aires, Rio de Janeiro, and São Paulo, Brazil.

Urban growth has come from two major sources: population growth and migration. Latin America's very high birthrate has been the greater cause.

Latin Americans have large families for several reasons. One is the opposition of the Roman Catholic Church to birth control. Another reason is machismo. Latin American men believe that one way to show their masculinity is to father a lot of children. A third reason is the lack of information about family planning.

Some of the migrants to the city are from outside the nation. But most are from rural areas within the same country. Most are young. They are usually illiterate, inexperienced, and unskilled. Some are lucky and find work, although the wages are very low. Many do not. About one-half of all workers in Mexico City, for example, are unemployed. Even those who find jobs live in poverty. But they remain because whatever faint hope the city offers is better than the certain poverty of the countryside.

The constant arrival of newcomers has made existing problems in the city worse. At first, newcomers usually stayed with relatives. But over

Latin America has an abundance of natural resources. Various nations are beginning to exploit them. The welder is working in a plant in São Paulo, Brazil's new industrial center. The oil rig is in Ecuador.

one-half of all urban families already sleep in single rooms. So most migrants have moved to squatter settlements located on the hillsides and lowlands around the cities.

Squatter settlements generally consist of patched-together shacks of wood scraps and discarded trash. The settlements have no running water, sewers, or electricity. They are known by various names depending on the country. In Brazil, for example, they are called *favelas*. In Venezuela, they are known as *barrios*; in Mexico, as *barriadas*.

Squatter settlements usually begin as an invasion of unoccupied land. They represent a demand for the right to own and improve property when existing housing is not available. They also provide the poor with free or inexpensive living quarters. On the average, 40 percent of the people in Latin American capitals live in such settlements.

Many governments are trying to improve urban living conditions. But they cannot build low-cost housing as rapidly as the people need it. Nor have governments been able to build enough schools or provide adequate health services. Disease and malnutrition are widespread in Latin American cities.

Industrialization

Until the worldwide depression of the 1930s, most Latin American nations depended on the exports of a few agricultural products or minerals. Tin from Bolivia, oil from Venezuela, and coffee from Brazil and Colombia were all sent to foreign processing plants. Latin Americans then had to import the finished products at high prices. When the depression hit, foreign nations stopped buying raw materials. Latin American nations found themselves without markets for their goods and without the money to buy what they themselves needed.

After World War II, Latin Americans were determined to avoid such economic disaster again. One nation after another adopted policies favoring industrial growth. Governments offered tax incentives and direct money grants to industry. They established tariffs to protect new local industries against the products of foreign competitors. They also allowed foreigners to invest heavily in industry.

By the 1980s, Argentina, Brazil, and Mexico were fairly well industrialized. Together, they accounted for 70 percent of Latin America's industrial output. Brazil's manufactured goods range from trucks to computers. Mexico's major industries include steel, chemicals, electrical goods, textiles, and rubber. Argentina produces chemicals, textiles, and machinery. All three nations are leaders in food processing.

Industrialization has helped diversify the economies of various Latin American countries. An industrial nation no longer depends on the size of a single harvest. Nor does it depend on the world market price for a single product. Local consumers have a wide range of manufactured goods from which to choose. More Latin Americans can be better dressed and fed than in the past.

At the same time, Latin American nations that industrialized had to borrow money from foreign countries to build factories and to purchase new equipment. There was not enough capital available from within the culture region. Between 1973 and 1983, international bank lending to Latin America grew tenfold, from $35 billion to $350 billion.

Unfortunately, some of the borrowed money was squandered. Military governments used it to help keep themselves in power. Local elites used it to keep up the value of their currency, thus enabling them to

In the San Telmo flea market In Buenos Aires the prices are negotiable. How do store owners cope with changing inflation?

continue to import luxury goods. And some of the money was simply exchanged for domestic savings that wealthy Latin Americans sent to banks in Miami, New York, and Switzerland, where it would be safe and would earn high interest rates.

By the mid-1980s, Argentina, Brazil, Mexico, and other Latin American nations were in serious trouble. A global recession lowered the demand for the region's exports. At the same time, the interest rates the nations were required to pay on their foreign debt shot up.

Since the late 1980s, creditors have been lengthening the terms of their loans to Latin American nations from 7 years to as much as 20 years. They have also been making new loans to enable the debtor nations to pay at least the interest on their original loans. In some instances, foreign banks have swapped loans for a share of local business companies. For their part, Latin American nations have begun selling off government-owned enterprises and cracking down on tax cheats. They are also trying to curb runaway inflation rates of as much as 100 percent a month.

It remains to be seen whether these and other measures will succeed. If not, political discontent and violence may sweep the culture region.

SECTION 2 REVIEW

1. **Recall** What factors have held back Latin America's agricultural growth?
2. **How and Why** How have Latin American economies changed since the 1930s?
3. **Critical Thinking** Why has industrialization created problems for Latin American countries?

SECTION

3

Creativity

The creative arts of Latin America reflect the influence of the three major ethnic groups that settled its nations. The Indian influence is most strongly felt along the west coast of South America and in Mexico and Central America. Africans have provided the dominant cultural expression in the Bahia region of Brazil and several islands of the Caribbean. Elsewhere, Spanish and Portuguese influences are most evident.

Weaving and Metalwork

As you know, weaving reached a high development in the Andes long before pottery appeared. The peoples of Paracas and Nazca spun llama fleece and cotton fibers for their garments. The art of weaving is still carried on today in such nations as Bolivia, Guatemala, Mexico, and Peru. Patterns vary from one area to another. By studying the design, it is possible to tell where a weaving was done.

This Guatemalan woman is using a backstrap loom just as her ancestors did 5,000 years ago. The loom is attached to a tree and then tied around the weaver's back. By pulling against the weaving, the tension is kept tight and an even weave is achieved.

Metalwork likewise originated among the Andean cultures of South America. Early metalworkers used many techniques, including wire coiling, casting, and inlaying. So highly perfected was the metalwork of the Incas that in the 1600s a Spanish priest wrote a book on their technology that became a reference for people elsewhere in the world.

Metalwork remains an important way of expressing creativity in Latin America today. In Mexico, Taxco has been known since colonial times as the City of Silver. Originally it was so named because of the silver mines found nearby. Today the city still has the title because of the many silversmiths there.

Music

Nowhere in Latin American creativity is culture diffusion stronger than it is in music. Into the creation of Latin American music have gone the folk songs of the Indians, the drum rhythms and chants of the Africans, and the melodic moods of the Spaniards and the Portuguese.

The Indians who lived in pre-Columbian Latin America had a definite musical style. Aztec instruments included drums, rattles, flutes, and horns made of conch shells. The Andean peoples used long-tubed pipes, flutes, and other wind instruments. They made these instruments from cane or the bones of llamas.

The Spaniards introduced stringed instruments such as the guitar, harp, and violin. The Indians combined these instruments with their own to create exciting new sounds.

Although black musicians have not made as much use of the harp and the violin as the Indians, they do use the guitar and a wide assortment of drums. Trinidad is the home of calypso music. The lyrics of

A band of steel pans plays the music of Trinidad. How is the steel pan a consequence of modernization?

calypso songs are witty and often satirical. They may contain political or social comment. Reggae music, which comes from Jamaica, is connected with the Ras Tafari, a religious sect.

Trinidad is also the home of a relatively new instrument—the steel pan. The pan is made from an empty steel oil drum. Four types corresponding to the human voice can be made: soprano, alto, tenor, and bass. When the pans are played together, they make a pleasing sound that has become very popular.

Latin America has produced many instrumental performers and singers of exceptional talent. Among them are pianist Claudio Arrau of Chile, singer Bidu Sayao of Brazil, and violinist Jaime Laredo of Bolivia. The Pablo Casals festival in Puerto Rico, held each summer, attracts musicians from all over the world.

Dance

Many dances have originated in Latin America. The conga, like the samba, is of African origin. The beguine began among the blacks on Martinique and St. Lucia. Cuban blacks gave the world the rhumba. The limbo comes from Trinidad. In the limbo, the dancer passes under a bar— sometimes flaming—that is gradually lowered.

In recent years, several fine dance companies have been formed in Latin America. The Ballet Folklórico of Mexico performs traditional Indian and Spanish dances. The New World Ballet of Caracas, Venezuela, performs ballet and modern dance.

This Andean boy makes the miles to market pass more quickly by playing his pipe.

Quechua Indians celebrate a festival in Concepción, Peru. How have traditional Indian and Christian themes been blended in festivals?

The people of Rio de Janeiro take to the streets during Carnival. Across the country, people celebrate. What is the reason for this festival? How is Brazil's past a part of the celebration?

Festivals

Festivals with music and dancing are a part of Latin American life. Some aspects of the festivals have their roots in pre-Columbian times. Dancing was always important in ancient Indian rituals. Many dances, such as the pole dance of the Aztecs, were unique to a particular people. After the Indians were converted to Christianity, some adapted their earlier rituals to the new religion. Native costumes and music were kept, but the themes took on Christian elements. What may have been an Aztec war dance, for example, became a dance that showed saints fighting devils.

Not all festivals have Christian significance, however. The festival of Alacitas in Bolivia, for example, is purely Indian. It is a week-long celebration held in late January. Its theme is good luck. People buy a small figure called an ekeko and load it with tiny items. Usually the ekeko is hardly visible beneath miniature pots and pans, trucks, sacks of food, baskets, and brooms. The idea of Alacitas is that everything bought in miniature during the festival week will become a reality during the year. To insure good luck, the ekeko must be given away.

Some of the most exciting festivals are those that precede Ash Wednesday, the beginning of Lent in Christian churches. The most famous is the Carnival of Rio de Janeiro. During Carnival, business stops and government comes to a standstill. For four days, the streets belong to everyone—rich and poor. Rio's Carnival reflects the cultural influences of all the Brazilian peoples. Even the brief period of Dutch rule in the northeast is recalled in some of the costumes.

Literature

The Aztecs, Mayas, and Incas had their own literary traditions long before Western Europeans arrived. Theirs was largely an oral literature. When the Spaniards came, they used the Roman alphabet to represent the sounds of Indian words. For example, a Dominican priest named Francisco Ximinez (hih-MAY-nays) recorded a version of the *Popul Vuh* in both Spanish and Quiché. This is the story of the creation of the universe and the beginning of humankind as believed by the Quiché-speaking Mayas of Guatemala.

Early colonial literature consisted largely of diaries kept by conquistadores and missionaries. Hernán Cortés described his conquest of the Aztecs in a series of reports called the *Five Letters*. Another view of the campaign was presented by Bernal Díaz del Castillo in his chronicle *The True History of the Conquest of New Spain*, notable for its magnificent description of Tenochtitlán. Garcilaso de la Vega, who was half Inca, dramatized the history of the Incas in *Royal Commentaries*. And Fray (Father) Bartolomé de Las Casas passionately condemned Spanish treatment of the Indians in two works, *History of the Indies* and *Brief Account of the Destruction of the Indies*.

Romanticism   Between the conquest and independence, comparatively little Latin American literature was produced. Then a literary style called romanticism swept Western Europe. A particularly popular romantic theme was the "noble savage"—a non-European who had not been corrupted by Western civilization. The theme appealed to Latin American writers, who made Indians the heroes of their novels.

Probably the finest of the Latin American romantic writers was José Martiniano de Alencar (a-LAYNG-kar). He is known for his deep feelings toward the Indians and the landscape of his native Brazil. His novel *O Guaraní*, written in 1857, concerns the love of an Indian and a Brazilian of European descent.

Realism   In the late 1800s, romanticism gave way to realism, which described the actual conditions of life and showed the relationship between people and their social environment. The most important realist was probably Joaquim Maria Machado de Assis (ma-SHAH-doo day a-SEES). Born in poverty in Brazil, his talent took him to the heights of success. He founded the Brazilian Academy of Letters and wrote numerous poems and books. Some of his works, such as *Dom Casmurro* and *Epitaph of a Small Winner*, are noted for their character development and narrative technique. Both books have been translated into almost every modern language.

Modernismo   Realism was, in turn, followed by modernismo, which flourished between 1888 and 1910. The two leading writers of this period were Rubén Darío of Nicaragua and José Enrique Rodó of Uruguay.

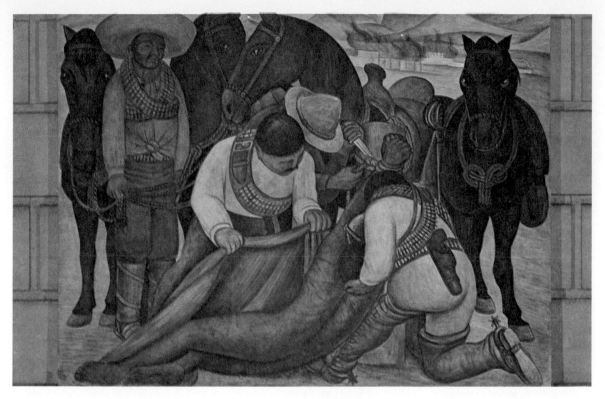

Darío, who spent much of his life in Paris, was both a poet and a diplomat. His experiments with themes, verse forms, and language revolutionized Latin American literature. He did not believe that poetry should carry a political or social meaning. The important thing was the beauty of the language. Nevertheless, Darío's poems helped to awaken an awareness among Spanish Americans of the cultural ties that bind them together.

Rodó, in his essay "Ariel," published in 1900, called upon the young people of Latin America to be aware of the differences between the United States and their own civilization. The United States was a technical genius, Rodó wrote. But it was interested only in material things. Latin Americans should not accept its cultural values uncritically. Instead, they should emphasize idealism and high spiritual goals.

Diego Rivera painted Liberation of the Peon *as an attack on Mexico's old social and economic system. Revolutionary soldiers are cutting the rope from the wrists of a peon. His body shows the scars of the landlord's whip. The master's house is in flames. Rivera's message is that the revolutionaries will right the wrongs done by the landowners. Do you think that art should be used for propaganda?*

The "Boom"   During the twentieth century, two main groups of Latin American writers attracted widespread international attention. One group consisted of poets, the other of novelists.

The leading poet was Gabriela Mistral of Chile, who won the 1945 Nobel Prize for literature. She was the first Latin American to receive that award. Many of her poems deal with the feelings of women in a male-dominated society. Pablo Neruda, also of Chile, experimented with form and technique. He received the Nobel Prize for literature in 1971. His

Rufino Tamayo's style and subject matter are very different from that of fellow Mexican, Rivera. This painting is called Watermelon.

social commitment: sense of social responsibility to improve the conditions of society

poetry ranges from lyrics to pleas for social commitment. Octavio Paz of Mexico wrote about his country's history and national identity.

The most famous novelist of the "boom" period is Gabriel García Márquez of Colombia, who received the Nobel Prize for literature in 1982. His *One Hundred Years of Solitude* combines historical facts with dreams and fantasy. Both time and space are shifted around. *Love in the Time of Cholera* is a lyrical work that likewise mixes extraordinary characters and magical happenings with historical events and scenes from everyday life.

Painting

As we have seen, pre-Columbian peoples painted pottery based on the world around them. During colonial times, painters were often trained in Europe. Their themes are usually religious—Jesus, the saints, and scenes from the Bible.

Toward the end of the 1700s and in the 1800s, Latin American artists began to show a sense of nationalism in their choice of subjects. They depicted battle scenes and the leading figures of the independence movement.

In the 1900s, a group of artists emerged who sought to teach reform through their works. Many had fought in the Mexican Revolution.

Perhaps the most important of these artists were Diego Rivera, José Clemente Orozco, and Davíd Alfaro Sequeiros (si-KAY-rohs), who covered the walls of Mexico's public buildings with their vivid murals. More than a thousand years earlier, Mayan artists had likewise painted murals on temple walls.

Rivera's murals tell of Mexico's legends, traditions, and history. He wanted ordinary people, many of whom were illiterate, to know and appreciate their past, both Indian and Spanish. He hoped to give to all Mexicans a sense of the ideals of the revolution and the progress that it would bring.

Where Rivera expressed hope in his work, Orozco was more pessimistic. He hated the brutality that people inflict on each other. He was particularly moved by the sufferings of Mexico's Indians. Orozco wanted his paintings to shock. And they do.

Siqueiros also painted pictures with social messages. In some of his works, he curved the wall to create a feeling that the viewer is actually part of the scene.

More recent Latin American artists use a wide variety of styles similar to those of European artists. The work of Mexican Rufino Tamayo is bright and colorful.

Architecture

Many modern Latin American architects have welcomed the challenge of rapid urbanization. They view it as an opportunity to influence the total environment.

Perhaps the best example of this is Brasília, the new capital of Brazil. In 1960 Brazil moved its capital from Rio de Janeiro inland to what had

This is Brasília's Chamber of Deputies, designed by Oscar Niemeyer. Brasília in the 1960s was as much a frontier as the Americas had been to Europeans in the 1500s.

A building in Brasília designed by Oscar Niemeyer.

once been a barren, isolated plain. An inland capital was seen as a way to unify the nation. It was also designed to be a stimulus to the development of the interior.

Oscar Niemeyer, Brazil's most famous architect, was given the contract to design Brasília's government buildings. Niemeyer also had final authority over the design of all other structures in the city. Under his direction, architects have created impressive buildings of concrete, glass, steel, and bronze. Niemeyer himself made considerable use of curved sculptures and of Indian designs in his mosaics.

SECTION 3 REVIEW

1. **Recall** What was the status of music in pre-Columbian Latin America?
2. **How and Why** Why was the twentieth century considered to be the "boom" period of Latin American writing?
3. **Critical Thinking** How do you think Rodó's essay "Ariel" might have affected the values of Latin American people?

R E V I E W

Reviewing People, Places, and Things

Identify, define, or explain each of the following:

social mobility	squatter settlement
machismo	ethnic group
Grajales	Alencar
developing nation	Mistral
hacienda	Niemeyer

Map Study

Using the maps on pages 376 and 377, answer the following questions:

1. Where are most of the industries located in South American countries?
2. What natural resources are found in the Caribbean islands?
3. For what is most land in Brazil used?

Understanding Facts and Ideas

1. Which people make up the middle class and the lower class?
2. What are two problems governments face in providing education?
3. Who were some women who tried to improve the status of women in Latin America?
4. Where has the most successful land reform in Latin America taken place?
5. What two sources have contributed to Latin America's urban growth?
6. What three ethnic groups have influenced the creative arts in Latin America?
7. What European influences are evident in Latin American literature?

8. How have the styles in painting and architecture developed in Latin America?

Developing Your Critical Thinking

Relating Past to Present to Future   Relating the past to the present can often help you predict what might happen in the future in regard to historical events. Looking at social changes in a culture region and seeing the rate of change from past to present can help you decide what you might expect to happen in the future.

Activity: Make a chart to show the changes in status of women in Latin America since the 1800s. Then use the chart to predict how you think the status of women might change during the next 50 years.

Writing About History

Writing a Letter   Pretend you are living in a Latin American country. Write a letter to a friend in the United States describing what your family life is like.

Applying Your Skills to History

Making a Collage   Make a collage to depict the society of Latin America today. Cut pictures from old magazines, photocopy pictures, or make drawings to show various aspects of Latin American culture such as schools, architecture, cities, art, music, and literature.

LATIN AMERICA

Reviewing Facts

1. What countries are included in Latin America?
2. Where and when did the Mayan civilization begin?
3. What is the oldest known Andean culture?
4. Why did conquistadores come to the Americas?
5. What was the attitude of the Spaniards toward the Indians?
6. What role did Bolívar and San Martín play in Latin America?
7. What factors encouraged the rise of caudillos in Latin America?
8. What was the Alliance for Progress?
9. Which Latin American social class is largest?
10. Where has Indian influence been strongly felt in the creative arts?

Understanding Main Ideas

1. How was the development of farming important to the early people of Latin America?
2. How were the Mayan and Aztec civilizations alike and how were they different?
3. How were the attitudes of all Western European conquerors toward the Indians and their lands alike?
4. Why did Brazil gain its independence more peacefully than the Spanish colonies did?
5. How has the relationship between Latin America and the United States changed since the 1800s?

6. Why have the Latin American countries had economic difficulties?

Applying Chronology Skills

Study the timeline below and then answer the questions that follow.

1500	— Cabral reached Brazil
1519	— Cortés arrived in Mexico
1530	— De Souza sailed for Brazil
1532	— Pizarro entered Cajamarca
1541	— Pizarro was killed

1. Who was the first European conqueror to arrive in the Americas?
2. Did Cortés arrive in Mexico before or after Pizarro entered Cajamarca?
3. How long before Pizarro was killed did De Souza sail for Brazil?

Making Connections

Analyzing a Political System   Laws governing the encomienda described the rights and responsibilities of both the Spanish and the Indians. Why were abuses of the system frequent? What was wrong with the system?

Understanding the Humanities

Analyzing Literary Trends   Using the information in the text, write a brief description of the literary development of the Latin American countries. Use specific examples to illustrate your description.

UNIT 4 REVIEW

Developing Critical Thinking

1. Comparing and Contrasting How does Brazil, as a result of its colonial experience, differ from the Spanish nations of Latin America?

2. Analyzing a Society The Teotihuacanos built great temple pyramids. To do this, what kinds of wealth, power, and organization must have been necessary?

Using Sources

The following selection describes how San Martín led his army across the Andes to win independence for Chile and Peru. Read the selection and answer the questions.

At last, in January of 1817, the Army of the Andes was ready to march.... The army numbered around 5,000 men including 800 cavalry, 1,200 volunteer helpers and 120 engineers. There were 1,600 horses, 7,200 pack mules and 261 pieces of artillery....

For 18 days men and beasts struggled onward through Andean valleys which narrowed to rock-walled gorges, picking their way over ribbon-like trails and clinging precariously to rocky ledges. On the barren Andean plateau, they were lashed by frigid winds and pelted with hail when it stormed. In the rarefied air at 12,000 feet (3 658 meters) above sea level, both men and animals gasped for breath. The army lost 6,000 mules and 1,200 horses, but the soldiers survived the ordeal remarkably well, thanks to San Martín's foresight in providing warm and durable footwear and clothing. When weary and numbed with cold, San Martín, O'Higgins, and Beltran cheered them on, marching at their side and setting examples of indefatigable courage. Onward, upward and over the towering Andes they pushed; then through the two passes and down toward Chile's verdant, sundrenched Central Valley.

The impossible had been accomplished. The Army of the Andes had crossed the world's highest mountains, excepting the Himalayas, in one of the greatest feats in military history—before or since.

(From *Jose de San Martin*, Washington, D.C.: Pan American Union, 1954. Reprinted courtesy of the General Secretariat, Organization of American States.)

1. How did San Martín's foresight help the army survive the ordeal?

2. Why is the crossing of the Andes by San Martín's army considered to be one of the greatest feats in military history?

Extension Activity

Making a Map Using references, make a map showing where the various missions were located in Latin America.

Read More About History and Culture

Altimar, Oscar. *The Extent of Poverty in Latin America.* Washington, D.C.: The World Bank, 1982. Social and economic issues.

Betancourt, Juan, ed. *From the Palm Tree: The Cuban Revolution in Retrospect.* Secaucus, N.J.: Lyle Stuart, 1983. Communism in Cuba.

Cheney, Glenn Alan. *El Salvador: Country in Crisis.* New York: Franklin Watts, 1982. Political upheaval.

Fincher, E. B. *Mexico and the United States.* New York: Thomas Y. Crowell, 1983. Historical and contemporary issues.

Hemming, John. *Monuments of the Incas.* Boston: Little, Brown, 1982. Incan stonework.

Lernoux, Penny. *Cry of the People.* New York: Penguin Books, 1982. Struggle for human rights in Latin America.

393

5

THE MIDDLE EAST

Archaeologists learn about peoples from many different sources. One of the most important sources for students of ancient Egypt is its tombs. This tomb painting shows Nakt, a priest to the pharaoh Thutmose IV in the 1400s B.C., and his family.

The Land and Early Peoples

The Middle East is sometimes called the Near East or the Mideast. Geographically, it includes the northern part of Africa, the Arabian Peninsula, the peninsula of Asia Minor, and the southwestern part of Asia. To the north are the Black, Caspian, and Mediterranean seas; to the south, the Arabian Sea; and to the west, the Atlantic Ocean. The region covers about 5.5 million square miles (14.2 million square kilometers) of land, or about 10 percent of the earth's land surface. However, it contains only about 5 percent of the world's population.

In general this culture region has a rugged terrain and a desert climate. However, it also contains fertile river valleys that fostered the development of some of the world's earliest civilizations. Farmers of the region were the first to raise many of the cereals, vegetables, and animals still used as staple foods in much of the world. Three of the world's major religions originated in the Middle East.

As you study this chapter, think about these questions:

- What are the region's major natural resources? How have these resources influenced the development of the Middle East?

- What do we know about humankind's earliest villages?

Most of Libya is part of the Sahara Desert. How much of the Middle East is desert? What physical features explain this fact?

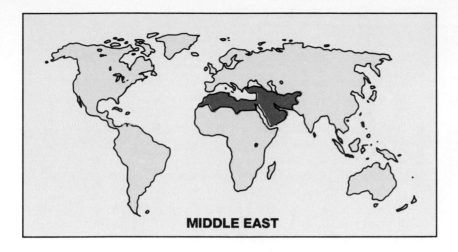

MIDDLE EAST

The largest single land feature of the Middle East is the Arabian Peninsula. Millions of years ago the area was attached to the African continent. But a weakness in the earth's crust caused a part to split from Africa. This section became a peninsula. The resulting rift filled with water, thus creating what we now call the Red Sea and the Gulf of Aden.

Other peninsulas in the region include the Sinai (SY-ny) Peninsula and the Anatolian Peninsula. The Sinai Peninsula is a very small triangle of land that extends south into the Red Sea between the Arabian Peninsula and northern Africa. The Sinai Peninsula divides the Red Sea into the Gulf of Aqaba (AH-kuh-buh) on the southeast and the Gulf of Suez on the southwest. The Anatolian Peninsula, also known as Asia Minor, is in the northernmost part of the region. This peninsula is bordered on the north by the Black Sea and on the west and the south by the Aegean (i-JEE-uhn) and Mediterranean seas.

The large bodies of water surrounding the Middle East enabled the region to become an important trading center. Merchants traded to the north with Europe, to the south with Sub-Saharan Africa, and to the southeast with India, China, and the islands of Southeast Asia.

Steppes and Deserts

Parts of Turkey, Iran, and some coastal areas, especially in Syria, Lebanon, and Israel, receive large amounts of rain. Little rain falls over much of the Arabian Peninsula, Iraq, and the North African nations. Mountain ranges along the coast stop the rain-bearing winds that blow in from the sea.

Because of the dryness, there are vast stretches of steppe and desert. In the steppe area enough rain falls for some grasses and trees to grow. Nomads roam the steppes with their herds. The best steppe lands are in the eastern part of the culture region—Turkey, Iran, Iraq, and Afghanistan.

(Continued on page 400.)

397

A NATURAL REGIONS MAP OF THE MIDDLE EAST

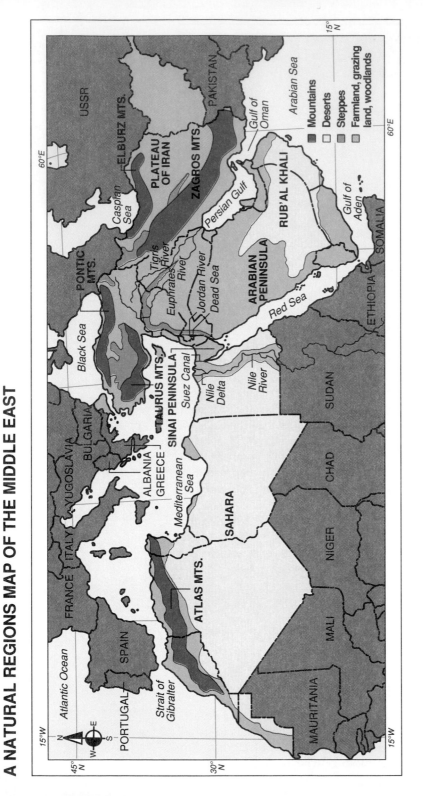

Legend:
- ■ Mountains
- □ Deserts
- ▨ Steppes
- ▤ Farmland, grazing land, woodlands

Atlantic Ocean

45° N
30° N
15° N
15°W
60°E

PORTUGAL
SPAIN
FRANCE
ITALY
YUGOSLAVIA
BULGARIA
ALBANIA
GREECE
Strait of Gibraltar
Mediterranean Sea
ATLAS MTS.
SAHARA
MAURITANIA
MALI
NIGER
CHAD
SUDAN
ETHIOPIA
SOMALIA

Black Sea
PONTIC MTS.
TAURUS MTS.
SINAI PENINSULA
Suez Canal
Nile Delta
Nile River
Red Sea
Caspian Sea
ELBURZ MTS.
PLATEAU OF IRAN
ZAGROS MTS.
Tigris River
Euphrates River
Jordan River
Dead Sea
Persian Gulf
Gulf of Oman
ARABIAN PENINSULA
RUB' AL KHALI
Gulf of Aden
Arabian Sea
USSR
PAKISTAN

Statute Miles
100 0 100   300   500   700

Kilometers
100 0100   300   500 700

N
W E
S

398

A POLITICAL MAP OF THE MIDDLE EAST

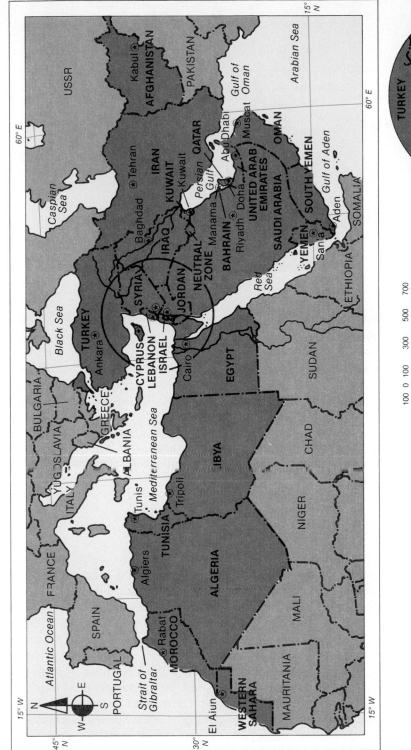

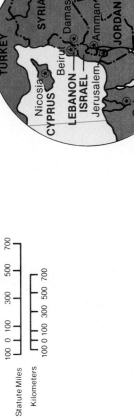

Statute Miles

100 0 100   300   500   700

Kilometers

100 0 100 300 500 700

Turkey's borders are mostly mountainous. This area is near the western border.

Much of the Middle East consists of barren deserts. One such desert is the Rub'al Khali (RUB-al KAHL-ee), or "empty quarter," in southern Saudi Arabia. Its sandy dunes contain almost no vegetation. The Sahara, which takes its name from the Arabic word for "tan," stretches across the North African countries. About two-thirds of the Sahara consists of sand dunes. The remainder is mostly a rocky gravel. Despite the lack of rain, however, there are occasional oases where people grow crops of dates and figs.

The majority of the people of the Middle East live either along the rainy coasts of the region or in its river valleys. About two-thirds of the culture region is uninhabited.

Mountains and Plateaus

The dominant landforms of the Middle East are hills and low tablelands. Much of the Arabian Peninsula, for example, is a rocky plateau with mountains along the west coast. Most of the Anatolian Peninsula is likewise a rocky plateau, as are both Iran and Afghanistan.

The Elburz and Pontic mountains run along the northern borders of Iran and Turkey. East of the Anatolian Peninsula, the Zagros Mountains extend southeast through Iran to the eastern shore of the Persian Gulf. In ancient times, passes in Iran's mountains provided invasion routes into the Middle East from the north and east. At the easternmost part of the region, mountains that are part of the Hindu Kush range reach altitudes of 25,000 feet (7 620 meters). As you know, Turkic invaders from central Asia entered India through passes in the Hindu Kush. The mountains of northern Africa include the isolated Ahaggar Mountains in southern Algeria and the Atlas Mountains, which extend from northern Algeria to central Morocco.

Many of the mountain areas of the Middle East are centers of earthquake activity. For example, the Zagros Mountains and the Taurus Mountains are along an earthquake belt, and quakes in that area are often severe.

Rivers

The major rivers of the Middle East are the Tigris, the Euphrates, and the Nile. For many centuries Middle Easterners have used these rivers to irrigate their fields and to ship their goods.

The Tigris and Euphrates rivers begin in the mountains of Turkey. They flow southeast through Syria and Iraq. Before they empty into the Persian Gulf, the two rivers join to form one waterway, known as the Shatt-al-Arab. The ancient Greeks called this area Mesopotamia, or land between the rivers.

The land between the rivers and the green land bordering the Mediterranean are sometimes called the Fertile Crescent. When shown on a map, the area looks like the curved shape of a new moon. This area was the home of the earliest civilization for which we have written records.

The Nile River, which flows north from mountains in Africa to the Mediterranean, is the longest river in the world—4,145 miles (6 670 kilometers) from its source to its mouth. Although the largest portion of the river flows through Sub-Saharan Africa, the Nile is vital to the Egyptians. In the past it regularly overflowed its banks each year. This seasonal flooding left silt, or particles of soil, on the land bordering the river. Where the river enters the sea, the soil deposits formed a triangle of land called the Nile Delta. The ancient Egyptians called the annual deposit of silt the "black land" in contrast to the sterile "red land" of the desert. The silt was extremely fertile and enabled the people in the Nile valley to develop a flourishing civilization based on agriculture.

The Jordan is another important Middle Eastern river. It flows southward between Jordan and Israel and empties into the Dead Sea.

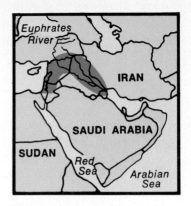

■ **Fertile Crescent**

In ancient times the Fertile Crescent and the Nile River Delta were the two most fertile areas in the Middle East. Over the centuries much of the Crescent has been made unproductive by the invasion of salt water. How might changes in the ecology of a region affect its development?

There are very few permanent streams in the Middle East. Instead, water from rainstorms creates **wadis**. Wadis are streambeds that are dry except during periods of heavy rain. At such times the wadis become rapidly flowing rivers. But because the region's soil is very porous, the water is quickly absorbed. Once again the land is dry.

Agriculture

About four out of every ten Middle Easterners earn their living by some form of agriculture. However, as much as 90 percent of the land cannot be farmed. The people struggle to grow crops on the 10 percent that is arable.

Wheat and other cereal crops are widely grown. Many of the coastal areas are well suited for the growing of citrus fruits. Olives and grapes are important crops in Syria. Iraq grows almost two-thirds of the world's dates. Non-food crops include cotton and silk. Cotton grows well in the lands near the Nile River and along the coast of Turkey. Silk is produced in the northern part of Iran, along the coast of the Caspian Sea.

Middle Easterners also raise animals. Camels—the "ships of the desert"—are still needed for transportation in some areas. When they outlive their usefulness as beasts of burden, they are killed for food. Sheep and goats, however, are the main sources of meat for Middle Easterners. Their fleece is spun into yarn and woven into cloth. Their skins are made into coats and other articles of leather.

Mineral Resources

The Middle East has the largest known oil, or petroleum, reserves in the world. The major oil-producing countries are Saudi Arabia, the United Arab Emirates, Iran, Kuwait, Iraq, and Qatar. They are grouped around the Persian Gulf and on the Arabian Peninsula. Algeria and Libya in North Africa also are among the world's leading producers of oil.

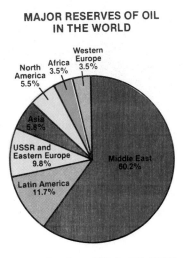

MAJOR RESERVES OF OIL IN THE WORLD

Western Europe 3.5%
Africa 3.5%
North America 5.5%
Asia 5.8%
USSR and Eastern Europe 9.8%
Latin America 11.7%
Middle East 60.2%

Source: Based on 1982 *Annual Energy Review*, Information Administration. U.S. Department of Energy.

Although the nomadic way of life has almost disappeared, some Middle Easterners are still herders. Here a goatherd watches over his flock.

Egypt, Turkey, and Iran have some coal deposits. In general, however, the nations of the Middle East lack large amounts of minerals other than oil. The area did have large deposits of copper and tin. But these deposits have been exploited for thousands of years and are almost gone.

SECTION 1 REVIEW

1. **Recall** Name four major natural resources of the Middle East.
2. **How and Why** How have settlers used the natural resources of the Middle East?
3. **Critical Thinking** Why is about two-thirds of the culture region uninhabited?

The peoples of the Middle East are a product of the blending of peoples from Europe, Asia, and Africa. From very early times migrants and conquerors crisscrossed the region. Peoples from Europe passed back and forth across the Mediterranean. Peoples from Asia and Africa used the Middle East as a land bridge.

Early Peoples

Archaeologists have not found any remains of *Homo erectus* in the Middle East. However, archaeologists have uncovered artifacts that *Homo erectus* used in other parts of the world. These early gatherers and hunters left behind scrapers, hand axes, arrowheads, and other stone tools. As a

Over 11,000 years of history can be seen in this photo. In the background is the Dead Sea. Next are the remains of an "old" town, then mounds that reveal ancient settlements. In the foreground is a group of contemporary dwellings.

result, archaeologists believe that *Homo erectus* at least traveled through the region, possibly coming north from Sub-Saharan Africa. With more digging, *Homo erectus* skeletons may be found.

Neanderthal remains have been found in Israel and Iraq. Cro-Magnon sites have been found around the Mediterranean from Egypt to Turkey.

Jericho   Some of the world's oldest towns have been found in the Middle East. The oldest settlement so far discovered has been named *Jericho*. It is near the modern village of Jericho, in the Jordan River valley north of the Dead Sea.

Archaeologists have found layer upon layer of settlement there. The site was used at least ten times. A fresh-water spring made it an ideal choice. At each level different types of buildings, tools, and pottery have been found.

The lowest level of Jericho dates from about 8000 B.C. By 7400 B.C. Jericho had about 2,000 inhabitants and was surrounded by a stone wall for defense. The wall reached more than 11 feet (3.4 meters) high and was nearly 5 feet (1.5 meters) thick. The town was a trade center. The people exported mostly salt that they evaporated from the waters of the Dead Sea. They also exported sulfur and bitumen, a natural asphalt used to waterproof materials. Among the goods Jericho received in return was obsidian, a shiny black glass made by volcanic action. Obsidian is hard enough to be used for knife blades and other cutting tools. People also used it for jewelry and mirrors.

Çatal Hüyük   In south-central Turkey archaeologists have found the ruins of a larger town dating from about 6500 B.C. The site is called Çatal Hüyük (CHAH-tuhl hoo-YUK) and covers approximately 32 acres (13 hectares). It probably housed some 6,000 people.

The people of Çatal Hüyük lived in houses made of sun-dried mud-brick, with flat roofs made of reeds that had been plastered over with

404 ■■■■■■■■■■■■■

(Continued on page 406.)

Using GEOGRAPHY Skills

Reading a Physical/Cultural Map

Although geographic factors do not strictly determine how people live, they do have a fundamental influence on where people live, what foods they grow, and so on. This influence of geography is universal. We know, for example, that most early farming societies developed in similar geographic situations. They also developed similar land use and settlement patterns.

Maps are an important way to see how geography has influenced the human experience. The map on this page combines features of a physical map with those of a cultural map to depict the relationship between geography and the patterns of settlement common to many early farming societies. It shows a hypothetical region in the ancient Middle East. Study the map carefully. Then answer the following questions:

1. Within what geographic environment did the earliest farming villages develop?

2. What factor may have caused early farming societies to move between about 8000 and 3000 B.C.?

3. What do the earliest and latest farming villages depicted by this map have in common? Why do you think this is so?

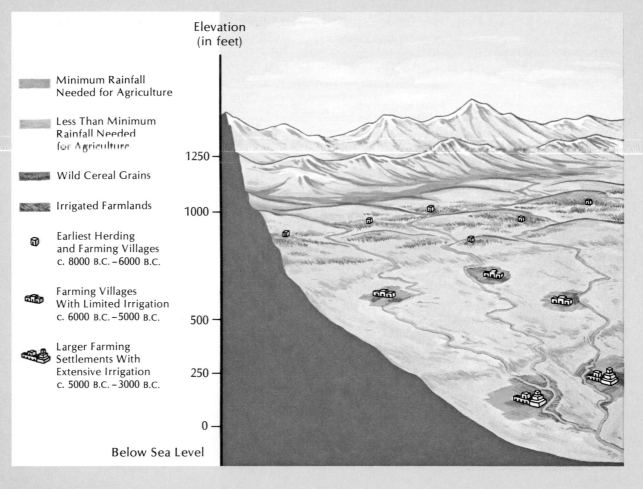

Elevation (in feet)

Minimum Rainfall Needed for Agriculture

Less Than Minimum Rainfall Needed for Agriculture

Wild Cereal Grains

Irrigated Farmlands

Earliest Herding and Farming Villages c. 8000 B.C.–6000 B.C.

Farming Villages With Limited Irrigation c. 6000 B.C.–5000 B.C.

Larger Farming Settlements With Extensive Irrigation c. 5000 B.C.–3000 B.C.

1250

1000

500

250

0

Below Sea Level

Ancient Cities

mud. There were no doors. People entered their houses through a hole in the roof, which they reached by a ladder. The outer houses of Çatal Hüyük stood against each other, thus forming a solid wall as a protection against attack.

The protective walls of both Jericho and Çatal Hüyük indicate to archaeologists that townspeople who farmed and traded were much richer than nomadic herders. The walls also indicate that the towns had a large labor force and a strong government. The walls are too large to have been built without central planning.

The houses in Çatal Hüyük also indicate the people's wealth. They painted walls with colorful pictures of flowers and animals, hunting scenes, and geometric designs. They tossed mats on their sleeping platforms, and covered the floors with carpets made of swamp plants called rushes. They decorated benches and pillars with bull horns. Bull horns were used by the later Minoan civilization (c. 5000–1100 B.C.), and archaeologists believe that traders from Çatal Hüyük and surrounding areas carried the symbol with them. It was probably associated with the people's religion. The bull represented strength and power. Many of the buildings in Çatal Hüyük appear to have been shrines, and the town itself may have been a religious center.

Several other town sites—including Jermo and Hassuna—have been unearthed in the Middle East. In April 1985 archaeologists discovered a remarkable collection of artifacts near the Dead Sea in Israel. These included fragments of the earliest textiles yet found. Some pieces of cloth had been woven with as many as 11 different designs. Also among the artifacts were necklaces and other jewelry and the world's oldest painted mask. As more discoveries are made, we will learn more about the early peoples of the Middle East.

SECTION 2 REVIEW

1. **Recall**   Archaeologists have found the remains in the Middle East of which two early peoples?

2. **How and Why**   What are two reasons why Jericho is an important archaeological discovery?

3. **Critical Thinking**   How do early wanderers differ from early settlers?

R E V I E W

Reviewing People, Places, and Things

Identify, define, or explain each of the following:

Arabian Peninsula

Red Sea

Anatolian Peninsula

Rub'al Khali

Sahara

Atlas Mountains

Euphrates River

Fertile Crescent

Nile Delta

wadi

Jericho

Dead Sea

Çatal Hüyük

Jarmo

Map Study

Using the map on page 399, determine the answers to the following questions:

1. Which Middle Eastern countries are in North Africa?

2. Which Middle Eastern country is the farthest north?

3. About how many miles (kilometers) is it from Baghdad to Tehran?

Understanding Facts and Ideas

1. How did the Arabian Peninsula form?

2. **a.** Why are there vast stretches of steppe and desert in the Middle East? **b.** In which two areas of the Middle East do most of the people live?

3. **a.** Why are the Zagros Mountains important in Middle Eastern history? **b.** What areas of the Middle East are centers of earthquake activity?

4. **a.** What are two uses that Middle Easterners have made of their rivers? **b.** Why was the Nile River vital to Egyptians?

5. **a.** What portion of Middle Easterners earn their living by some form of agriculture? **b.** What percent of the land cannot be farmed?

6. What is the major mineral resource in the Middle East?

7. **a.** Middle Easterners are a product of the blending of peoples from which areas? **b.** Why did this occur?

8. Why do archaeologists believe that *Homo erectus* traveled through the Middle East?

9. **a.** What geographical feature made Jericho an ideal place to settle? **b.** What did the protective walls of both Jericho and Çatal Hüyük indicate to archaeologists?

10. What made the collection of artifacts discovered by archaeologists near the Dead Sea in April 1985 remarkable?

Developing Critical Thinking

Analyzing Geography From very early times, migrants and conquerors have crisscrossed the Middle East. How did the location and geography of the Middle East encourage migration and conquest?

Writing About History

Relating Past to Present to Future
Archaeologists study the arts and crafts of peoples from the past to learn about their life. In a brief essay explain what the arts and crafts of a people from the past tell us about their life. Discuss also the forms of art that we have today that might be of interest to archaeologists a thousand years in the future.

Applying Your Skills to History

Writing a Paragraph: Examine several paragraphs in this chapter to find the topic sentence. Then see how the supporting details develop that main idea. Read "Developing Critical Thinking" above and write a paragraph answering it.

Ancient Kingdoms and Empires

Like people in other cultures, the ancient peoples of the Middle East built their civilizations where there was water and fertile land. These civilizations grew slowly over thousands of years. The work of hundreds of generations contributed to their development. These early Middle Easterners were skilled artisans, builders, and writers. They also made many technological and scientific achievements that were passed on to other culture regions.

As you study this chapter, think about these questions:

- What kinds of culture traits spread from group to group among the ancient peoples of the Middle East?

- How did government develop in each society?

- What effect did the various conquerors and the peoples they conquered have on one another?

Darius the Great receives an official on this bas relief or carving found on a wall at Persepolis. Persepolis was the capital of Persia under Darius and later kings. Alexander the Great destroyed much of it in 331 B.C.

The earliest known civilization in the Middle East arose in Mesopotamia, where the Tigris and the Euphrates rivers join. This was the civilization of Sumer (SOO-muhr).

The Sumerians were a combination of peoples. Some were farmers from the foothills of the Zagros Mountains who migrated into the river valley about 4000 B.C. in search of fertile farmland. Others were nomadic herders from the deserts of Saudi Arabia. By 3500 B.C. the two peoples had blended their cultures into what is now known as Sumerian culture.

Sumer

Agriculture and herding were the foundations of Sumerian wealth. The Sumerians grew barley, wheat, dates, and other crops. They built dikes to contain the floodwaters of the Tigris and Euphrates. This water was used to irrigate their fields. The Sumerians raised cattle, sheep, goats, and oxen. The oxen were used to pull plows. Oxen as well as donkeys pulled carts and chariots. The first known use of the wheel was in this area. These early wheels were made of wood and had leather or copper tires.

Around 3000 B.C. the Sumerians began to build walled cities. These cities became the political, economic, religious, and cultural centers of Sumerian life. The center of each city was the temple. The temple was a business center, a storehouse for grains, and a bank. From the temple the priest-king administered the city and surrounding land. Much of the farmland around the cities was thought to be owned by the deities, and was managed for them by the priest-king. Ordinary citizens owned the rest of the land. Each city and the land around it was known as a **city-state.**

Sumerian temples were called **ziggurats** (ZIG-uh-rats). They were multi-layered structures that stood on stone platforms. The platforms kept the temples from being washed away by spring floods. The ziggurats were covered with glazed or enameled bricks, a different color for each layer. Stairs led to the shrine on top, where the Sumerians kept a statue of their local god. The Sumerians probably built ziggurats because in their original homeland, they had worshiped their deities on hills. Since there were no hills in Mesopotamia, the ziggurat was substituted.

As cities grew, trade developed. Sumerians exported textiles, wool, and grain. They imported gold, silver, copper, lead, woods of various kinds, ivory, and jewels. Sumerian land routes reached east into Iran. Sumerian traders sailed down the Persian Gulf into the Arabian Sea. They went as far east as the Indus Valley of India. They went west to Africa.

Among the great city-states of Sumer were Ur (UHR), Erech (EE-rek), Nippur (nip-UHR), and Lagash (LAY-gash). These cities often warred among themselves. Weapons included spears, swords, and bows and arrows. The Sumerians fought mostly over canals and irrigated land. But they also fought to prove that their city-state was stronger than another.

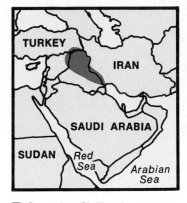

■ Sumerian Civilization, c. 2800 B.C.

Above left is the ziggurat at Ur. The photo was taken by a University of Pennsylvania expedition in the 1920s. The men are workers for the expedition. The tablet was found in Nippur in the 1890s. It is from a medical text and gives prescriptions for various diseases.

We know so much about the life of the Sumerians for two reasons. First, some of their architectural inventions were copied by later peoples. The arch, the vault, and the dome were Sumerian inventions that are still used in modern buildings.

We also know about the Sumerians because they developed the oldest known form of writing. Sumerians used a sharpened stick or the tip of a reed to scratch wedge-shaped marks on soft clay tablets. This type of writing is called *cuneiform* (kyoo-NEE-uh-form). The word means "having the shape of a wedge." The tablets were baked in large ovens until they hardened.

Libraries of these clay tablets have been found in the remains of Mesopotamian temples and palaces. Some tablets are account records. Others tell of Sumerian work in mathematics, astronomy, and medicine. The Sumerians used a mathematical system based on the number 6. This system was the basis for our 60-minute hour and 360-degree circle.

Akkad

For hundreds of years, the Sumerians farmed, traded, and fought with each other. Then around 2400 B.C. they were conquered by the Semitic-speaking Akkadians (uh-KAYD-ee-uhns) from the north. The Akkadian leader King Sargon I united the Mesopotamian city-states into one empire. At its peak the new empire extended from the Persian Gulf to the Mediterranean Sea. With this conquest the decline and disappearance of the Sumerians as a people began. However, elements of their civilization survived in the civilization of their conquerors.

The Akkadians had not developed a form of writing. They adapted the Sumerian writing system to their own language. Akkadian became the official language for diplomacy and commerce. But the Sumerian tongue continued to be used for religious purposes.

Sargon I's empire lasted for about 160 years before being overthrown by new invaders. Various city-states assumed leadership for a while. Then about 1800 B.C. a third major civilization arose in Mesopotamia. It was established by the Amorites (AM-uh-ryts) and is known as Babylonia (bab-uh-LOH-nee-uh) after the capital of Babylon.

■ Akkadian Empire, c. 2300s B.C.

Babylonia

The Amorites were originally from an area northwest of Mesopotamia. They spoke a Semitic language similar to that of the Akkadians. And like Sargon's, their form of government was a centralized monarchy.

The most famous Babylonian king was Hammurabi (ham-uh-RAHB-ee), who lived in the 1700s B.C. He is remembered as one of the first great lawmakers. Codes, or systems of laws, had been used before Hammurabi. But the earlier laws had been those of individual cities. Hammurabi researched past and present laws and customs. He selected those that seemed to be important. To these he added new laws he felt were needed. They were then arranged into a code and proclaimed as law for his entire empire.

■ Babylonian Empire, c. 1760 B.C.

Hammurabi's Code covered the daily lives of his subjects. It dealt with military service, business, marriage, divorce, alimony, child welfare, and the rights of women. Although women were not considered equal with men, they had the right to own property and to borrow and lend money. Slaves likewise had the right to own property, and they could also sue a free person in court. Since there were no prisons in Babylonia, punishments consisted of fines, mutilation, or death. The punishment usually depended on the social status of the victim. For example, if someone knocked out the eye of an aristocrat, his or her own eye was knocked out in return. This is how the expression "an eye for an eye and a tooth for a tooth" originated. However, if someone knocked out the eye of a slave, he or she was simply fined half the slave's value.

Hammurabi's Code helped unify his widely spread empire. He also brought his subjects together by setting up a common religion. In addition to worshiping their own local god, people were expected to worship Marduk, the god of Babylon. Each spring a great religious festival was held in the capital during which the gold statue of Marduk was wheeled through the streets. Thousands of pilgrims from all over the empire would crowd into Babylon for the occasion.

Hammurabi's empire lasted for about 200 years. Then new invaders, probably from central Asia, entered the valley. The most important of these invaders were a people known as Hittites (HIH-tyts), who spoke an Indo-European language. The Hittites introduced a new weapon: the horse-drawn chariot. Archers standing in the chariots were able to direct showers of arrows against the Babylonian foot soldiers. The Hittites were also the first people to make weapons of iron. These were much stronger than the copper and bronze weapons used by other Middle Easterners. Moreover, since iron ore was more abundant than copper and tin, iron weapons cost less to manufacture.

The Hittites were followed by the Kassites, who ruled Babylonia for about 400 years. Then about 1100 B.C. a new empire began to rise along the upper Tigris where the river runs out of the mountains. This empire was known as Assyria.

Assyria

The Assyrians were a warlike people. This characteristic can be explained by the fact that their original homeland lacked natural defenses and was continually being invaded. As a result, the Assyrians became used to fighting.

Beginning around 1200 B.C. the Assyrians started their own conquests. From the Hittites they had learned to make weapons of iron and to use the horse and chariot in battle. The Assyrians also invented weapons—such as battering rams, armored towers on wheels, and other siege equipment—that enabled them to break down city walls. In addition, the Assyrians organized their armies, not by village, but according to the type of weapon used or job performed. They had separate units of infantry, archers, and engineers. As their conquests grew, they made soldiering a year-round profession. Until then Middle Easterners had fought only during the months between planting crops and harvesting them.

The warlike nature of the Assyrian people is reflected in their art. Bravery, struggle, and death are frequent themes. The best-known examples of Assyrian art are wall carvings of hunting scenes and battles. The

The Assyrians conquered much of the Middle East because of the superiority of their weaponry. However, they did not invent all their weapons. They borrowed some ideas, such as the horse and chariot. From whom did they take this idea? This bas relief was found at Nineveh.

Assyrians admired bigness. They judged beauty and usefulness by this standard. Their capital at Nineveh (NIN-uh-vuh) was surrounded by huge brick walls that ran for several miles along the Tigris River. The city itself was filled with palaces and temples. In building these, the Assyrians borrowed the idea of arches and domes from the Sumerians.

The Assyrians also borrowed the cuneiform style of writing from the Sumerians. But they greatly simplified it by reducing the number of signs and symbols. They also preserved much of the culture of the Sumerians and the Babylonians. In the 700s B.C. King Sargon II started a library of Sumerian and Babylonian clay tablets. The following century, King Ashurbanipal (ahsh-uhr-BAHN-uh-pahl) built a library to house some 25,000 cuneiform tablets. He also had a Sumerian dictionary compiled.

The Assyrians taxed their subjects heavily. However, they were efficient administrators. One of their major achievements was the construction of a system of "royal roads" to connect the different parts of their empire. The roads were paved only near major cities. But they were level enough for carts and chariots to use. Every 20 or 30 miles (32–48 kilometers) stood a military post manned by government soldiers. The soldiers protected traveling merchants from bandits. The posts also provided government messengers with fresh horses for their journey.

The Assyrians reached the peak of their empire under Sargon II. However, their authority was constantly challenged by revolts in the provinces. Thus the Assyrians were forced to keep large armies. Over the centuries this constant warfare drained Assyrian strength. Finally, in 612 B.C., Nineveh was destroyed. A coalition of Medes from northern Iraq and Chaldeans (kal-DEE-uhns) from the south marched against the Assyrians.

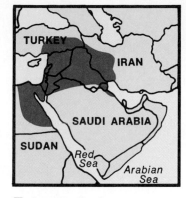

■ Assyrian Empire, c. 671 B.C.

New Babylonian Empire

Around 1000 B.C. the Chaldeans, a Semitic-speaking people, established the base of their empire in southern Babylonia near the Persian Gulf. For centuries they warred against the Assyrians. With the fall of Nineveh, the New Babylonian Empire of the Chaldeans became dominant in the Middle East.

The empire reached the height of its glory under Nebuchadnezzar (NEHB-uh-kuhd-NEZ-uhr) II, who ruled from 605 to 562 B.C. To show the empire's strength and wealth, Nebuchadnezzar had Babylon rebuilt along both sides of the Euphrates River. The city's walls were so wide that chariots could be driven on the road that ran along their top. Beside the road were covered walks. One hundred bronze-plated gates opened through the huge walls. About 200,000 people lived in Babylon.

Within the city, Nebuchadnezzar built his palace. Its sides were covered with brilliantly decorated glazed tiles. Around the palace were terraces, one above the other. On the terraces many varieties of trees, plants, and shrubs were planted. They grew in such numbers and to such length that they hung down like tapestries from terrace to terrace. These were known as the Hanging Gardens of Babylon.

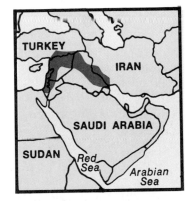

■ New Babylonian Empire, c. 570 B.C.

phenomena:
facts or events that can be
observed

Besides their architecture, the Chaldeans are also remembered for their knowledge of astronomy. They accurately recorded eclipses and other heavenly phenomena. They used a seven-day week in which the days were divided into 12 hours of 120 minutes each. They knew the length of the year to within less than one-half hour.

The New Babylonian Empire did not last long after Nebuchadnezzar. In 539 B.C. it fell to the armies of Cyrus the Persian.

Persian Empire

The Persians, who spoke an Indo-European language, came from the grasslands of southern Russia. Between 1000 and 900 B.C. they settled in what is now Iran, or "land of the Aryans." They were divided into two classes: fighting nobles who were skilled at shooting arrows from horseback, and farmers who supported the military aristocracy by raising wheat, barley, and sheep.

Around 550 B.C. Cyrus became king. Under his leadership the Persians conquered a great part of the Middle East. Cyrus's son added Egypt to the empire. He was succeeded by the greatest Persian conqueror of all, Darius the Great (521–486 B.C.), who extended the empire's boundaries from Greece to India.

The Persians were tolerant rulers. Persian subjects could use their own languages and follow their own religions, laws, and customs so long as they accepted Persian authority and paid taxes. This mild policy won Persian leaders the loyalty of their subjects.

The Persians set up a bureaucracy to administer their empire. The land was divided into 20 provinces, with three main officials in charge of each province. One official was responsible for carrying out the laws the

This is a reconstruction of the main gate of Babylon. Besides their architecture, what else are the Chaldeans noted for?

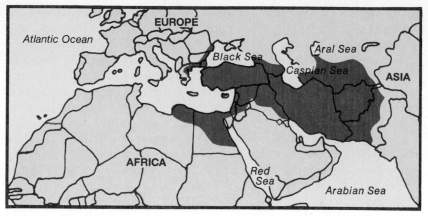

■ Persian Empire, c. 500s B.C.

king ordered, a second collected taxes, and a third was in charge of the local army. Since the three officials reported separately to the king, it was difficult for any one to be dishonest. The king also maintained a group of inspectors known as "The Eyes and Ears of the King." They traveled throughout the empire seeing to it that officials were performing their work properly and that the people were not overtaxed.

As warriors and farmers, the Persians looked down on merchants, whom they considered to be naturally dishonest. Nevertheless, the Persians were responsible for two great aids to trade. They improved and extended the road system the Assyrians had begun. As a result, trade with the Far East boomed. Silk was imported from China, and chickens from India. The Persians also adopted a uniform system of coinage. They borrowed the idea of coinage from the Lydians, one of the peoples they conquered. Until then people had relied upon a system of **barter**, trading one type of goods for another. By 500 B.C. the most widely used coin in the Middle East was the gold daric, named for Darius.

Under later rulers the Persian Empire declined. The armies of Alexander the Great finally conquered it around 330 B.C.

Greek Rule

Alexander the Great was a Macedonian (mas-uh-DOH-nyuhn) from the northern part of the Greek peninsula. His father Philip had conquered Greece, and Alexander continued his father's conquests. He not only defeated Persia, but also pushed deep into India.

As a youth, Alexander had been taught by the Greek philosopher Aristotle. As a conqueror, he wanted to spread Greek knowledge and culture throughout his empire.

Alexander and the Macedonian generals who followed him founded cities that became centers of Greek thought and science in the Middle East: Alexandria in Egypt, Antioch (ANT-ee-ahk) in Syria, and Seleucia

■ **Seleucid Dynasty,
c. 200s B.C.**

(suh-LOO-shee-uh) along the Tigris. Greek became the language of the educated and the ruling class. Greek philosophy, education, art, and science became known throughout the Middle East. Buildings were constructed in the Greek style, merchants used Greek banking methods, and people attended Greek plays for entertainment. The period during which Greek culture spread around the Mediterranean and through the Middle East is known as the Hellenistic period. You will learn more about it in Unit 6.

After Alexander died in 323 B.C., his generals fought over control of his empire. No one was able to gain complete control. Eventually the empire was broken into three parts. Egypt came under the control of Ptolemy (TAHL-uh-mee) who founded the Ptolemaic dynasty. The Ptolemaic dynasty lasted until the death of Cleopatra in 30 B.C. Egypt then became a Roman province.

Syria and portions of Asia Minor came under the rule of Seleucus (suh-LOO-kuhs) who began the Seleucid dynasty. Macedonia came under the rule of Antigonus (an-TIG-uh-nuhs). These two parts also later came under Roman rule.

Roman Rule

Between 146 and 30 B.C. the Romans extended their rule into the Middle East. The Romans respected the arts, science, and learning of the people they conquered. They generally allowed the peoples to live as they wished so long as they accepted Roman authority.

Although Roman rule lasted in some places in the Middle East for 600 years, little evidence of their rule remains. There are some aqueducts for carrying water and some buildings and monuments. In North Africa scattered ruins of temples, villas, and coliseums, or stadiums, still stand. In some places Roman laws are the basis of the present legal systems.

SECTION 1 REVIEW

1. **Recall**   List one major culture trait for each of the following cultures: Assyria, Persian Empire, and Roman Empire.

2. **How and Why**   How did each culture group build upon the achievements of earlier groups?

3. **Critical Thinking**   Why are laws important to a society?

This monument is called a sphinx and represents the ruler as having the strength of a lion. In the background is a pyramid, or royal tomb.

The civilization that developed in the Nile River valley is one of humankind's longest-lasting civilizations. It began formally in 3100 B.C. and continued almost without change for 2000 years. One reason for this continuity is geographical. The inhabitants of the Nile valley were protected against invaders by vast expanses of desert to the east and west. To the south, cataracts, or rock-filled rapids, made it difficult for enemies to come down the Nile. Danger from the north was limited by the difficulty of crossing the Mediterranean. And the river itself brought fertile silt to the land, enabling Egyptian farmers to grow large quantities of wheat, barley, grapes, and vegetables.

Old Kingdom

Perhaps as early as 5000 B.C. an ancient people known today as Egyptians settled along the Nile River. They spoke a language related to Semitic. From evidence found at various sites it is known that these people built canals and irrigation ditches and farmed. They wove linen and cotton cloth. Gold and silver ornaments and pottery were also made. These early Egyptians also developed a form of writing. Sometime before the 3100s B.C. two separate government units began to emerge. In the Nile Delta area the Kingdom of Lower Egypt arose. Farther south along the Nile, the Kingdom of Upper Egypt was formed.

Around 3100 B.C. a prince from Upper Egypt named Narmer, whom the Greeks later called Menes (MEE-nees), united the two kingdoms.

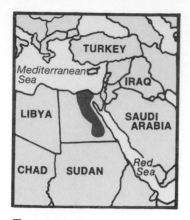

Old Kingdom, c. 3000 B.C.

Narmer is the earliest individual in recorded history. To help unify his nation, Narmer built a new capital at Memphis, at the border between the two former kingdoms.

Narmer and the kings who succeeded him were believed to be the direct descendants of the sun-god Re (RAY). During the 1500s B.C. they received the title of **pharaoh**, or "great house." Historians apply the title to all of Egypt's rulers. Pharaohs usually married members of their own family because they believed that if deities married humans, their children would be human rather than divine.

The Old Kingdom lasted from 3100 to 2200 B.C. It was a period of peace, prosperity, and political stability. Around 2200 B.C., however, a power struggle erupted between the pharaoh and the nobles who acted as governors of the country's provinces. The civil war continued for 200 years. Then, once again, a prince from Upper Egypt conquered Lower Egypt and reestablished national unity. The new dynasty of pharaohs marked the beginning of the Middle Kingdom.

Middle Kingdom

During the 250 years of the Middle Kingdom, nobles grew more powerful and wealthy. In return for favors and services that the nobles provided, the pharaohs had to grant them land. Gradually, under a series of weak rulers, the office of pharaoh lost much of its power.

Economically, however, the Middle Kingdom benefited from widespread international trade. Egyptian merchant ships sailed to such places as Somalia, Syria, Palestine, and Crete. The Egyptians exported mostly linen, gold, and **papyrus**, a type of paper made from reeds that grew in the Nile. They imported mostly cedar wood, which they used for furniture and coffins.

In the 1200s B.C. the pharaoh, believed to be Ramses II, used the labor of enslaved Hebrews on public works projects, such as this building at Luxor.

The Middle Kingdom ended about 1800 B.C. when a new power struggle took place between the pharaoh and the nobles. Until around 1570 B.C. various groups of invaders known as Hyksos (HIK-sohs)—Princes of the desert—seized power. Egyptian weaponry was no match for their war chariots. However, just as the Assyrians learned from their conquerors, the Egyptians learned from theirs. The Egyptians added horses and chariots to their stock of weapons.

The invasions of the Hyksos taught the Egyptians another lesson. They learned that in order to overcome an invader they had to put aside disagreements among themselves. They found, as others have, that disunity results in weakness. Toward the end of the 1600s B.C., the Egyptians were able to unite. Gradually the conquerors were driven out. By around 1570 B.C. Egypt was free of the Hyksos. A new pharaoh took the throne and began the New Kingdom, or the Empire Period.

■ Empire Period, c. 1450 B.C.

Empire Period

From around 1570 to 1165 B.C. Egypt played the dominant role in the Middle East. Determined to avenge the disgrace of foreign rule and to protect their country against future invasions, the Egyptians set up a professional army and then marched into neighboring lands. By the 1400s B.C. the Egyptian empire included Palestine and Syria to the northeast and Nubia, or Kush, to the south. The wealth of the conquered lands poured into the Egyptian treasury and, for the first time, slavery—in the form of prisoners of war—became widespread.

The Egyptians made many enemies by their conquests. Their wealth attracted more enemies. A major conflict with the Hittites, whose iron weapons were stronger than the bronze weapons of the Egyptians, greatly weakened Egyptian power during the 1200s B.C. The death of Ramses (ram-SEES) III, the last of the great pharaohs, marks the end of the Empire Period. From then on, a series of foreign conquerors ruled Egypt until 1952.

Science and Art

The Egyptians were a practical people. This quality is reflected in their science and technology. The Egyptians were able to compute the area of squares, triangles, rectangles, and circles. This knowledge enabled them to measure fields and construct pyramids and other buildings. They were also able to figure accurately the amount of supplies needed by their armies and workers.

As astronomers, the Egyptians made careful observations of the heavens. These observations too were turned to practical use. Because they were farmers, they depended on the yearly flooding of the Nile. They observed that the Nile overflowed its banks soon after the star Sirius (SIR-ee-uhs) appeared on the horizon before dawn. They made the rising

horizon:
the visual meeting point of earth and sky

The Book of the Dead contained magical verses and was supposed to guarantee a happy life in the next world.

of Sirius the beginning of their year. The Egyptian year was divided into 12 months of 30 days each. The five extra days were saved at the end of the year for feasts.

Egyptian doctors were likewise practical. They knew which injuries could be repaired and which could not. They were skillful at dressing wounds, setting broken bones, and diagnosing certain diseases. They fastened loose teeth together with gold wire, and used various drugs and minerals—such as sodium bicarbonate—that doctors still use today. At the same time, however, they often prescribed what today would be considered improbable remedies, such as a mixture of dates, a dog's toes, and a donkey's hoof as a cure for baldness.

Pyramids   During the Old Kingdom the Egyptians built pyramids as tombs for pharaohs. The most massive of these, the pyramid of the Pharaoh Khufu, contains over 2 million blocks of limestone, each weighing almost two tons (two metric tons). An estimated 100,000 workers labored 20 years to complete it. Egyptian farmers carried on this and similar public works projects during the three months that the Nile flooded their fields each year.

When a pyramid was finished and the dead pharaoh was placed in the tomb, the entrance was sealed and hidden. Nothing was supposed to disturb the peace of the pharaoh. The Egyptians believed that as long as their pharaoh enjoyed peace, the kingdom would too.

The Egyptians stopped building pyramids after the Old Kingdom. However, they continued to create huge stone temples. The temples at Karnak and Luxor are the most famous examples. Egyptian architects were the first to use stone columns and pillars to support roofs.

Writing   The earliest form of Egyptian writing was **hieroglyphic** (hy-ruh-GLIF-ik), or based on pictures. In time a kind of writing developed in which part of each picture represented a syllable. Still later, in order to make writing easier, the Egyptians developed two types of shorthand in which the picture symbols were rounded off and connected. The Egyptians wrote with sharpened reeds and ink on papyrus.

Only a few people in ancient Egypt knew how to write. Boys trained to be scribes from age 5 to age 17, and the right to become a scribe was hereditary. Scribes worked as bureaucrats in the government, keeping records of the pharaohs' decrees, compiling tax returns of grain and labor, and supervising public construction projects. They were known as the "white kilt class" because they were exempt from manual labor and their white linen kilts were always clean.

During the Old Kingdom, Egyptian scribes also began writing books. Among these are the oldest known books on medicine and surgery. During the Middle Kingdom, fine literature was written. Much of it was religious. It included hymns to the sun god Re, and poetry that told of eternal life and the ways to gain it. Ancient Egyptian literature also included love poems, tales of adventure, and fables.

Egyptian hieroglyphs were first decoded in the early 1800s. French soldiers on an expedition to Egypt with Napoleon discovered a stone with three inscriptions. One was in Greek, one in hieroglyphs, and one in a later form of Egyptian. A French scholar reasoned that all three inscriptions said the same thing, and since he knew Greek he was able to decode the hieroglyphs. The stone is known as the Rosetta Stone because it was discovered near the Rosetta, a branch of the Nile.

Society

Ancient Egypt had a rigid social system. Pharaohs, priests, nobles, and government officials held the highest positions. Below them in descending rank were scribes, merchants, and artisans. Still further down were the farm workers. Lowest of all were the slaves.

Egyptian nobles lived comfortably in large, cool villas along the river. For privacy, the houses were surrounded by high walls. Within the walls trees shaded the house, walks, and gardens. A typical villa had two stories and was built of brick and wood. The floors were tiled. Tapestries decorated the walls. Soft leather cushioned the chairs and couches. The wooden frames were inlaid with ivory and ebony. On the roof of the house was a garden. A linen awning shaded it.

A man of noble rank wore a linen kilt. A noblewoman wore a long, sleeveless dress of linen. It was starched and pleated. She also wore necklaces and bracelets. She used a black powder to darken her eyebrows and eyelashes. She also used green eye shadow. The juice of the henna plant was used to color her nails. She kept her own hair short, but wore wigs of various styles and colors.

In ancient Egypt women generally enjoyed a good position in society. Women were consulted in family and business matters. No man could have more than one legal wife. Descent was matrilineal. Women of the royal family often exercised great influence in affairs of state.

Beginning in 1503 B.C. a royal woman ruled as pharaoh. Her name was Hatshepsut (haht-SHEHP-soot), and she reigned for 22 years. To insure the people's obedience, she always appeared in male clothing and

The statue is of a scribe. Could everyone in Egyptian society read and write? What advantage do people who can read and write have over those who can't?

These sandstone figures were made during the Hyksos or Empire periods. The statues are of an official and his wife. What was the role of women in upper-class Egyptian society?

wore the false beard that male pharaohs traditionally wore. She was the only pharaoh of the New Kingdom who emphasized trade rather than war. She also carried on an extensive construction program.

Farmers worked hard to survive. Their lives were a weary routine of planting, irrigating, and harvesting. Some farmers had oxen for their plows. A few had donkeys for carrying their produce. They used river water to irrigate their fields.

The farmers paid high rents to nobles or priest landowners. Their possessions were few: some cooking pots, a wooden bed, and an outdoor brick oven for baking. Their diet was barley or wheat bread and beer. They also planted flax for linen thread. Farmers ate little meat, except when they were lucky enough to catch a wild duck in the marshes. Fish, however, were plentiful.

This Egyptian wall painting shows workers winnowing grain with wooden scoops. They are throwing it up in the air so that the waste matter—dirt and chaff—will be separated from the usable grain.

SECTION 2 REVIEW

1. **Recall**   What steps did the Egyptians take to change their kingdom into an empire?
2. **How and Why**   How did the Egyptians make practical use of mathematics and astronomy?
3. **Critical Thinking**   What factors other than geographical might account for the duration of Egyptian civilization?

SECTION

3

Smaller Mediterranean States

While the empires of Mesopotamia and Egypt were rising and declining, other Middle Easterners were founding small kingdoms along the eastern and southern coasts of the Mediterranean. Two of these peoples were the Phoenicians and the Hebrews (HEE-broos). Both made important cultural contributions to other civilizations.

Phoenicians

The Phoenicians lived in several independent city-states along the eastern Mediterranean. The name *Phoenician* means "purple people." Outsiders called them Phoenicians because of the purple dye they manufactured from shellfish. The dye was expensive as well as beautiful, so only kings and wealthy individuals could afford it.

Much of the area where the Phoenicians lived is part of the modern nations of Lebanon, Syria, and Israel. The section of their land between the Jordan River and the coast was known to the ancients as Canaan (KAY-nuhn). The ancestors of the Phoenicians probably migrated to this area around 2000 B.C. Their original homeland is not known. But they spoke a Semitic language. Over the centuries they were influenced by the

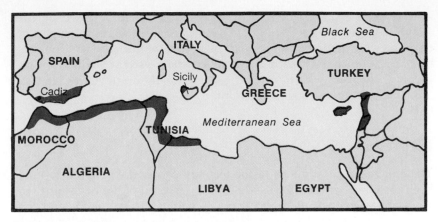

■ **Phoenician Sphere of Influence, c. 500s B.C.**

cultures of the Egyptians, the Mesopotamians, and the Hittites among others. Often the Phoenicians were targets for invasion by these peoples. Then, between 1200 and 1100 B.C., the Phoenicians began their own period of expansion.

The Phoenicians expanded their holdings through trade, not war. They were excellent sailors. Once they discovered that the North Star maintains a fixed position in the sky, they no longer had to sail their ships within sight of land. They traveled the Mediterranean coast of Africa as far west as the Strait of Gibraltar (juh-BROL-tuhr). They built settlements all along the coast. Carthage (KAHR-thij) was their most famous North African site. The Phoenicians also sailed through the Strait and down the coast of West Africa. They went north to the British Isles and perhaps beyond.

From their trading trips Phoenicians brought back tin, copper, ivory, and silver. Artisans fashioned the raw materials into decorative or useful objects. These items then became Phoenician trade goods and were exchanged for more raw materials. The Phoenicians also traded glass objects, wool cloth, the purple dye they were known for, and lumber from cedars that grew along the coast. The Phoenicians also used cedar for their own ships.

The most important cargo the Phoenicians carried, however, was neither raw materials nor manufactured goods. It was an alphabet. In their writing, other peoples had used symbols to represent syllables, objects, or ideas. But the Phoenicians were the first people to use a symbol—a letter—to represent a sound. The Phoenician alphabet, which developed out of a simplified form of Egyptian hieroglyphs, contained 22 letters, written from right to left. All 22 letters were consonants. This alphabet was later adapted by the Greeks, who added symbols for vowels, and then by the Romans. The Roman alphabet is the one used today for English and other languages of the Indo-European language family. The word *Bible* comes from a Greek word meaning "book." This word was taken from the name of the Phoenician city-state of Byblos, a major manufacturing and trading center for papyrus.

Between 800 and 700 B.C. the Phoenicians were harassed by the Assyrians. Later, in the 500s B.C., Phoenician city-states became part of the New Babylonian Empire and then part of the Persian Empire. Carthage, which at one time controlled the western Mediterranean, fought three wars with Rome and was eventually destroyed in 146 B.C. You will learn more about this in Unit 6.

Hebrews

The first historical writings of the Hebrew people are believed to have been recorded between 1000 and 800 B.C. They tell of the beginnings of the Hebrew people, the great flood, Abraham, Isaac, Jacob, and the journey out of Egypt. Modern archaeologists have found evidence that supports much of these writings. For example, an inscription on a monument of the Pharaoh Merneptah (MER-nep-tah), who ruled in the 1200s B.C., confirms that the Hebrews were in Egypt as mentioned in the Old Testament of the Bible.

■ **Kingdom of David and Solomon, c. 1000–900 B.C.**

The Promised Land   The early Hebrews were nomadic herders who worshiped many gods. Between 2000 and 1600 B.C. they left their home in the land of Ur (modern Iraq) in Mesopotamia. Under the leadership of Abraham—who told them there was only one God—they went into the land of Canaan. This is approximately the modern nation of Israel. According to Jewish tradition, this land was promised to them by their God.

In time Abraham's grandson, Jacob, became leader. Jacob was renamed *Israel*. It is from this name that the Jewish people took the name *Israelites* (IZ-ree-uh-lyts)—children of Israel. Jacob, or Israel, had 12 sons. Their descendants later became known as the Twelve Tribes of Israel.

From the land of Canaan, a number of Israelites traveled to Egypt. The Old Testament tells of Joseph, a son of Jacob, who was sold into slavery in Egypt by his brothers. He became a favorite of the pharaoh and was set free. He brought his father and brothers to Egypt. But later pharaohs made the Israelites slaves. They were forced to work on building projects for the pharaohs in the 1300s and 1200s B.C.

During the 1200s B.C. a man named Moses was born among the Israelites in Egypt. According to the Old Testament, Moses was a prophet—a messenger of God. He told the Israelites that God would deliver them from slavery. After threatening the pharaoh with God's anger if he did not free the Israelites, Moses was allowed to lead the Israelites out of Egypt and back toward Canaan. This journey is known as the Exodus (EK-suh-duhs). It is remembered today in the Jewish feast of Passover.

The Israelites wandered in the wilderness for 40 years. During this time God gave Moses the Ten Commandments, which have provided a basis for ethical conduct for both Jews and Christians. *Ethical* means "right" or "good." After Moses died, Joshua led the Israelites into Canaan and divided the land among the 12 tribes.

![Masada ruins photograph]

After the fall of Jerusalem and the destruction of the Temple by the Romans in A.D. 70, Masada was the last Jewish stronghold in Palestine. Today it is in ruins, but originally it was a mountaintop fortress. Fifteen thousand Roman soldiers spent almost two years fighting a thousand men, women, and children. In the end the Jews killed themselves rather than surrender.

Once in Canaan the Israelites had to fight to survive. Under military leaders called Judges, they fought such enemies as the Philistines (FIL-uh-steens), the Canaanites (Phoenicians), and the Aramaeans (ahr-uh-MEE-uhns). It was from the name Philistine that the land of Canaan later became known as Palestine.

The years between 1000 and 900 B.C. were a great period in Israel's history. During this time David and then Solomon ruled. Israel dominated a large part of the surrounding area. David, a powerful warrior, was also a poet. His Book of Psalms (SAHMS) contains some of the most beautiful poetry in the Bible. David's son Solomon built the first Temple in Jerusalem. It was made of gold, cedar, and stone, and gradually became the center of Jewish religious life. Several times a year, thousands of pilgrims, laden with offerings of grain and fruits, came to the Temple to celebrate Passover and other important holidays.

The Jews Around 925 B.C., after Solomon died, a division occurred among the Israelites over taxation. As a result, two kingdoms were formed. The two southern tribes became the Kingdom of Judah (JOOD-ah). Its capital was Jerusalem (juh-ROO-suh-luhm). It is from the name Judah that the word Jew comes. The ten tribes in the north made up the Kingdom of Israel.

Around 721 B.C. the Assyrians overran the Kingdom of Israel. The ten tribes were scattered across the Middle East. Their identity as a people was lost. They are known as the Ten Lost Tribes of Israel. Many legends have sprung up about them. In the 1700s religious writers in New England even identified them with the Indians of North America.

In 586 B.C. the Chaldean king, Nebuchadnezzar destroyed Jerusalem and the Temple. He deported most of the people to Babylon. This

Hebrews, c. 933–912 B.C.
■ Kingdom of Israel
■ Kingdom of Judah

period in Jewish history is known as the Babylonian Captivity. After Cyrus of Persia conquered Babylon, he allowed the Jews to return to their homeland. Around 539 B.C. they rebuilt Jerusalem and the Temple.

Unfortunately their troubles were not over. Around 332 B.C. they came under the rule of Alexander the Great. In 168 B.C. the Jews revolted against the Seleucid dynasty that had taken control of part of Alexander's empire. The Jews were fighting for their religious freedom, for the Seleucid king had ordered the Jews to abandon their religion and to set up their own dynasty of the Maccabees. Hanukkah (HAHN-uh-kuh)—the Feast of Lights—commemorates the victory of the Jews over the Seleucids.

Around 63 B.C. the Romans took control of Palestine and its people. During Roman rule there were many revolts. One, which lasted from A.D. 66 to 70, ended in the second destruction of the Temple. The Jews revolted again in A.D. 135. This time the Romans scattered the Jews throughout the empire. This is known as the Diaspora (dy-AS-puh-ruh). From then until 1948, when the independent state of Israel was established, many Jews were without a country. Some Jews, however, remained in the area that is now the state of Israel.

SECTION 3 REVIEW

1. **Recall**   What role did trade play in the expansion of the Phoenicians?

2. **How and Why**   Why did the Kingdom of David and Solomon split?

3. **Critical Thinking**   The Romans generally allowed the peoples they conquered to live as they wished so long as they accepted Roman authority. Why do you think there were many revolts among the Jews during the period they were under Roman rule?

R E V I E W

Reviewing People, Places, and Things

Identify, define, or explain each of the following:

Mesopotamia	hieroglyphic
ziggurat	Rosetta Stone
cuneiform	Hatshepsut
Nebuchadnezzar	Abraham
Darius the Great	Moses
Alexander the Great	David
pharaoh	Ten Lost Tribes of
papyrus	Israel

Map Study

Using the map on page 423, determine the answers to the following questions:

1. Which North African countries were under Phoenician influence about 500 B.C.?

2. Which body of water did the Phoenicians probably use for trading purposes?

Understanding Facts and Ideas

1. How did elements of Sumerian civilization survive?

2. **a.** Why are laws important to a society? **b.** How did Hammurabi develop his code of laws?

3. **a.** Who were the earliest users of iron weapons in the Middle East? **b.** What was the advantage of iron over copper and bronze?

4. What did the Assyrians learn from: **a.** the Hittites? **b.** the Sumerians?

5. Describe Chaldean achievements in: **a.** architecture. **b.** astronomy.

6. How did the Romans treat the peoples they conquered?

7. How did the rule of the pharaohs begin in Egypt?

8. What two lessons did the Egyptians learn from the Hyksos invaders?

9. How did the Phoenician city-states extend their influence?

10. **a.** How did the Jews come to be called Israelites? **b.** What happened to the Kingdom of Israel?

11. What events are commemorated: **a.** in Passover? **b.** in Hanukkah?

12. What caused the Diaspora?

Developing Critical Thinking

Working with Hypotheses   A hypothesis is a prediction, an educated guess, or a suggested reasonable possibility. It is used as the basis for considering the different possibilities for a solution. It is not fact. Facts are what are used to test whether a hypothesis works. Forming questions to find out the kind of data needed to test a hypothesis is a way to begin testing it.

Activity: Write three questions that would test this hypothesis: Religious organization was the major factor in bringing about a civilization at Sumer. For example: What is a civilization?

Writing About History

Expressing an Opinion   In a brief paragraph explain how you think social scientists use hypotheses in their work.

Applying Your Skills to History

Using a Map for Comparisons   Make one map showing the major empires and kingdoms described in this chapter. Use the map as the basis for a discussion on geography's influence on trade, invasions, and conquests in the Middle East.

A Cradle of Religions

Early Middle Easterners, like people in other parts of the world, looked beyond themselves for answers to their problems. At first they worshiped nature. Gradually some groups came to believe that there was only one God, supreme above nature and humans.

Nearly 4,000 years ago the Hebrews began to teach belief in one God. Christianity came from the same base 2,000 years later. Islam in the A.D. 600s built on both earlier religions. Many of the practices, traditions, and moral laws of each religion are different. But Judaism, Christianity, and Islam have certain basic beliefs in common. Besides religious influence, each religion has had great social and political influence on its followers.

As you study this chapter, think about these questions:

- What religious beliefs did ancient Middle Easterners hold?
- What are the major beliefs of Judaism, Christianity, and Islam?
- How have the teachings of these three major world religions influenced their believers?

Within the city of Jerusalem are the Jewish Western Wall, the Christian Church of the Holy Sepulchre, and the Muslim Dome of the Rock.

The Sumerians, most of the Semitic-speaking peoples of the Middle East, and the Egyptians believed in many gods and goddesses. Some deities were thought to be more powerful than others. Deities were represented in many forms and worshiped in many different ways. Often the ruler was looked on as a representative of the chief deity. Sometimes rulers themselves were considered divine. This was true in Egypt.

Gods and Goddesses

Early Deities

Because Sumerians and Semitic-speaking peoples depended on farming for their living, nature was very important to them. Nature and agriculture became the bases of the religions. Among the greatest of their deities were Entil, the storm god; Enten, the god of farming; and Ishtar, the goddess of love and fertility. During the 1800s B.C. and later, the Babylonian god Marduk and the Assyrian god Ashur became important.

The Sumerians and Semitic-speaking peoples were afraid of their deities. The people thought their gods and goddesses were able to feel the same violent emotions that humans felt. To protect themselves, the people made sacrifices and gave gifts to their deities. When one deity became angry, the people asked other gods and goddesses for help.

Evidently deities often became angry. One example is found in the *Gilgamesh* (GIL-guh-mesh) *Epic* of Babylonia. The deities became so angry that they threatened to destroy humanity with a flood. A man who was liked by one of the gods was warned. He was told to build a boat to save himself and a few others. This story is similar to the Old Testament account of Noah and the ark.

Interest in life after death was not an important part of the religions of these early Middle Easterners. They were more concerned with their lives on earth. They did not build elaborate tombs or monuments for their dead. But they did show concern for them. They buried them in cemeteries or under the floors of their houses.

Egyptian Deities

With the beginning of the Old Kingdom, the sun god Re became the most important Egyptian deity. This was because the sun was essential to life and to the agricultural wealth of the country. The worship of Re became the **state religion**. The pharaoh was supposedly his representative on earth. Re was not concerned with the welfare of individuals. He preserved the state and the people as a whole. Most Egyptians felt closer to the special deities of their cities and regions than to Re. These local gods were usually portrayed as animals—apes, bulls, cats, crocodiles, hunting falcons, and hippopotamuses.

Gradually Osiris (oh-SY-ris), the god of agriculture, became important. It was Osiris who had supposedly taught the Egyptians how to farm. Osiris had a jealous brother named Seth. Seth chopped Osiris to pieces and scattered his body across the earth. Isis (EYE-sis), who was both Osiris's sister and wife, roamed the earth collecting the pieces. Then she brought Osiris back to life.

This alabaster figurine of a Sumerian worshiper was made between 2800 and 2550 B.C. Why was sacrifice an important part of Sumerian religion?

Queen Nefertiti was Ikhnaton's wife. She greatly influenced his religious ideas. Why did she and Ikhnaton try to change the religious practices of their subjects? Do you think this is wise policy for leaders to follow?

Osiris eventually became the god of the underworld, who judged the goodness or badness of the dead. Books were written containing instructions about how to pass Osiris's judgment. At first the Egyptians believed that only the pharaoh and his family were immortal. But by the Middle Kingdom, they believed that everyone was immortal.

The Middle Kingdom saw another change in Egypt's religious beliefs. The ruling dynasty came from Thebes (THEEBZ), so that city's local deity, Amon, became known as Amon-Re. The New Kingdom was founded by yet another Theban dynasty. Accordingly, Amon-Re became the nation's supreme deity and was soon known simply as Amon. Gradually the priesthood of Amon became extremely rich. The Egyptians believed that the growth of their empire was due to Amon's good will. So they gave the priests vast quantities of land, cattle, and gold. As the priesthood grew richer, it assumed more political power.

In the 1300s B.C. the priesthood and the pharaoh came into political conflict. As a result, Amenhotep IV turned away from Amon and announced a new god, Aton (AH-tuhn), a single and loving god. Amenhotep changed his name to Ikhnaton (ik-NAHT-uhn), or "serviceable to the Aton," and moved his capital away from Thebes. He announced that the royal family would worship Aton, while the Egyptian people would worship Aton's son, the pharaoh.

Ikhnaton's rule had considerable effect on Egyptian art. Before, pharaohs had been portrayed as massive figures with no individuality. Portraits of Ikhnaton, on the other hand, were realistic and personal. They showed him with a large head and a pot belly.

Unfortunately, Ikhnaton neglected the Egyptian empire, especially its holdings in Syria. Hittite invaders overran the land. This caused political trouble within Egypt. Also, the people were afraid that the worship of Aton would cause them to lose immortality. After Ikhnaton's death they quickly returned to the worship of the old deities.

Zoroastrianism

For many centuries the Persians practiced a religion called Zoroastrianism (ZOHR-uh-WAS-tree-uh-NIZ-uhm). They believed a man named Zoroaster (ZOHR-uh-was-tuhr) had received the truths of this religion from the creator of goodness and light—Ahuramazda (uh-HUR-uh-MAZ-duh). This was sometime between 1000 and 600 B.C. The sacred book of Zoroastrianism is the *Zend-Avesta* (zen-duh-VES-tuh).

Zoroastrianism emphasizes certain ethical concepts. It teaches that good and evil are waging a constant battle for control of the universe and humanity. The force of good is Ahuramazda, who created all living things. The force of evil is Ahriman (AHR-ih-man). The battle will end in a final judgment day, when the dead will rise and be judged. Those who led good lives will be rewarded with eternal happiness, while the evildoers will receive eternal punishment. A good life includes being honest, giving to charity, obeying the king, and not doing to others what one does not wish done to oneself. An evil person is one who is lazy, arrogant, greedy, or deceitful.

This wall painting shows Osiris and the gods of burial. Why did the Egyptians see the story of Osiris as a triumph of life over death?

Zoroastrianism was largely replaced by Islam. This occurred when the Muslims conquered Persia in the 600s. A few thousand Iranians still practice Zoroastrianism. A larger group of people who practice Zoroastrianism lives in India. They are descendants of Zoroastrians who fled Persia to escape the Muslims. They are known today as Parsis (PAHR-sees), from the Persian word for Persians.

SECTION 1 REVIEW

1. **Recall** On what did Sumerians and Semitic-speaking peoples base their religion?

2. **How and Why** How did Sumerians and Semitic-speaking peoples think about the traits of their gods and goddesses?

3. **Critical Thinking** What political advantage might the pharaohs have gained by linking politics and religion in Egypt?

A man blows the shofar or ram's horn to mark the beginning of Rosh Hashanah, the Jewish New Year. The shofar is also used at the end of Yom Kippur, the Day of Atonement. Ancient Hebrews used it as a battle signal.

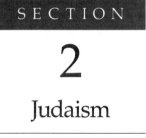

SECTION

2

Judaism

The first of the three great world religions to begin in the Middle East is Judaism (JOOD-uh-IZ-uhm). The ancient Hebrews gave to the world a knowledge of the one God whom they called Yahweh (YAH-way). For almost 4,000 years Hebrews and their descendants—the Jewish people of today—have preserved knowledge of this one God. Their writings make up the Jewish Bible. It is part of the sacred writings of both Christianity and Islam.

The Jewish Bible consists of three parts: The Torah (TOHR-uh), or The Law, also known as The Five Books of Moses; The Prophets; and The Writings. The Torah begins with the creation of the world and ends with the death of Moses at the edge of the Promised Land. It describes the Jewish concept of God, and sets out the moral and ritual laws that God gave to the Jewish people. Among these laws are the Ten Commandments, which form the basis for the civil and criminal codes of Western civilization. The Prophets is an account of the activities and sermons of the **prophets**, a group of religious teachers who preached from 900 to 500 B.C. The Writings are a collection of psalms, poems, proverbs, and history.

In the Christian Bible these three parts are called the Old Testament. The New Testament—the second half of the Christian Bible—has accounts of the life and teachings of Jesus of Nazareth and his followers, especially Paul of Tarsus.

Beliefs and Institutions

Other Middle Easterners were polytheists. The Jews, in contrast, became **monotheists**, or believers in a single God. Moreover, their concept of God was different from that of other Middle Eastern peoples.

Yahweh is spiritual, which means that he cannot be represented by a statue or a painting. Nor is he tied to a specific place on earth. He exists everywhere. Yahweh is also just. Both people and society should reflect this justice. Jews are supposed to worship God, not by offering sacrifices, but by following a moral way of life. Jews are expected to work for social justice through charity, education, and laws. According to the Jewish Bible, the Jews made a covenant, or agreement, with Yahweh to carry out his wishes, in exchange for which he promised them a homeland in Palestine.

In ancient times the Temple in Jerusalem was the center of Jewish religious life. After the first destruction of the Temple in 586 B.C., a number of Jews went to Babylon. There they developed a new way of worship. Small groups met to pray and to hear someone read from the Torah. Out of these meetings there developed the synagogue (SIN-uh-gahg), the present-day Jewish house of worship.

Every synagogue contains a copy of the Torah handwritten in Hebrew on parchment scrolls. An excerpt is read aloud each week, so that by year's end, all five books have been read. Accompanying the reading from the Torah is a reading from The Prophets.

After the Jews were scattered in the Diaspora, the synagogue became a school and a seat of local government as well as a place of worship. There, Jewish boys learned to read and write Hebrew. Also, people brought their quarrels before the rabbi (RAB-iy), or teacher, who settled them according to Jewish law.

Many of these laws were contained in a collection of 63 books known as the Talmud (TAHL-mud). Originally, these laws were oral laws that had been handed down among the Jews by word of mouth. During the Babylonian Captivity, however, scholars in Babylon gathered the oral laws together. Besides laws, the Talmud contains biographies, stories, debates and discussions with unbelievers, practical wisdom, and a code of ethics.

For centuries after its completion, the Babylonian Talmud was the main textbook in Jewish schools. Jews from different communities used Talmudic Hebrew, which differs somewhat from Biblical Hebrew, for their international correspondence.

Orthodox, Conservative, Reform

Over the centuries, divisions have taken place among Jews over the interpretation of Jewish laws. Modern Judaism is made up of three major groups: Orthodox, Conservative, and Reform.

Orthodox Judaism emphasizes tradition and observance of ritual. Extremely Orthodox Jews believe in the actual coming of the Messiah (muh-SY-uh)—the promised leader. They believe the Messiah will usher in the Kingdom of God on earth. To most Jews, however, the coming of the Messiah is not the coming of one person. It means a time when all humanity will begin to work together for peace and justice.

Orthodox Jews strictly observe Saturday as the Sabbath—the day of

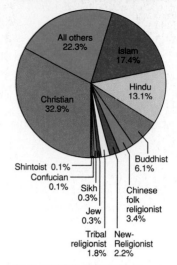

MAJOR WORLD RELIGIONS

All others 22.3%
Islam 17.4%
Hindu 13.1%
Christian 32.9%
Buddhist 6.1%
Shintoist 0.1%
Confucian 0.1%
Sikh 0.3%
Chinese folk religionist 3.4%
Jew 0.3%
Tribal religionist 1.8%
New-Religionist 2.2%

Source: *1989 Brittanica Book of the Year,* copyright © 1989 by Encyclopedia Brittanica, Inc. Reproduced by permission.

rest and worship. No business, work, or travel is allowed. The Hebrew language is used for prayers and ceremonies. Women sit in separate places in the synagogue. Dietary laws, which were given in a book of the Torah, are carefully followed. These laws are called kosher (KOH-shuhr)—that is, correct according to ritual. Animals for food must be killed as painlessly as possible and be free of disease. Jewish laws also forbid eating the meat of animals that eat other animals. Killing animals for sport is forbidden.

Conservative Jews follow many of the practices of Orthodox Jews. But they are less strict about it. Conservative Jews observe the Sabbath, holy days, and traditional festivals. However, they believe that it is sometimes necessary to change traditions. They are more flexible in their hours of religious service and in the use of Hebrew for prayers. Women may sit with men at services.

Reform Jews depart more from tradition than do Conservative Jews. They allow women equality in the synagogue. Prayers are said mostly in the **vernacular** (ver-NAK-yuh-luhr)—the language of the region. Reform Jews are less strict about dietary laws and have simplified such rituals as the wedding ceremony.

Although Orthodox, Conservative, and Reform Jews differ on various points of law, they all agree basically on the ethical and moral teachings of Judaism. They also agree on the need for prayer, worship, and belief in the one God to whom the Hebrews are the chosen people. They call themselves that because they believe Yahweh chose them to set an example of moral behavior to other peoples.

Teachers and Students

Judaism does not have a religious **hierarchy**, or group of officials of different ranks. Each congregation is independent. It is led by a rabbi or, if it is very large, by two rabbis. Rabbis are trained at schools called yeshivas (yuh-SHEE-vuhs). Rabbis preach, conduct religious services, and offer guidance to members of their congregation when needed. They also perform religious ceremonies concerned with birth, confirmation, marriage, and death.

Cantors are also important in Jewish worship. Jewish prayers are not spoken; they are chanted. As the cantor begins each prayer, the congregation takes up the chant. The cantor also helps with the religious education of the congregation, especially in preparing a young man for his Bar Mitzvah (bahr MITS-vuh). This is a Hebrew term meaning "son of the Law."

When a Jewish boy reaches the age of 13, he is ready to take on the responsibilities of adulthood. During the ceremony that marks this event, the boy promises to live up to the highest ideals of his religion. He also promises to dedicate himself to the Torah. It is a time of joy and celebration. Among some Reform and Conservative congregations, a similar service—a Bas (or Bat) Mitzvah—is held for girls.

A boy becomes a man when he has his Bar Mitzvah. What other religions mark the change from child to adult with religious ceremonies?

Jewish Philosophers

During the Diaspora, Jews were scattered over many lands. They settled in Europe and elsewhere. Among them were many scholars. Philo (FY-loh) of Alexandria worked to blend Greek and Jewish thought. He lived sometime between 20 B.C. and A.D. 80. During the A.D. 900s Saadia Gaon (SAH-dyuh GAH-ohn) translated the Hebrew Bible into Arabic. He also wrote poetry as well as religious works.

By the end of the 700s, Spain had become a center of Jewish learning and culture. Some Jews had been living there since the Diaspora. In the early 700s Islam reached Spain. The Muslims practiced religious tolerance. This attracted Jewish scholars to Spain. There they helped to preserve the culture of ancient Greece. Some made translations from Greek to Arabic. Later, other scholars made translations from Arabic to Latin and passed the works along to European Christians.

The greatest Jewish philosopher of this period was Moses Maimonides (my-MAHN-uh-deez). He was born in Spain in 1135 but went to Egypt after a strict Islamic **sect**, or group, known as the Almohavids, invaded Spain from Morocco and insisted that the Jews convert to Islam. In Egypt, Maimonides became a doctor and was soon appointed chief physician at the royal court. In addition to his medical works, he wrote

435

books explaining Jewish laws and arguing that the study of science would not harm religion, because both recognize the existence of one creator.

SECTION 2 REVIEW

1. **Recall** Describe the three parts of the Jewish Bible.
2. **How and Why** How was the Talmud used by Jews for centuries after its completion?
3. **Critical Thinking** Name the three major groups within modern Judaism. Describe their basic similarities. Describe their basic differences.

SECTION

3

Christianity

Christianity developed from the teachings of Jesus almost 2,000 years ago. Jesus was a Jew who was born in Palestine. What we know of his life and teachings is found mainly in the first four of the 27 books of the New Testament. They are the Gospels of Matthew, Mark, Luke, and John. Gospel means good news.

According to the Gospels, Jesus grew to adulthood in Nazareth. When he was about 30 years old, he began what can be called his public life. For the next several years he preached about the way God wanted people to act toward one another. Those who heard and saw him believed that he had extraordinary powers. In the third year of preaching, Jesus went to Jerusalem to celebrate Passover. His arrival caused great excitement.

The Gospels tell that Jesus was arrested and asked if he claimed to be the Messiah. He was brought to trial and put to death at the command of Pontius Pilate, the Roman procurator, or governor. Much of the Middle East was part of the Roman Empire at that time. Roman records show that Pilate was later removed from office for cruelty.

Jesus was crucified and died on a cross. Crucifixion was a common form of Roman punishment then. Most of his followers scattered. The few who remained buried him. The Gospels record that when his followers went to his tomb two days later, they found it empty. An angel told them that Jesus had risen from the dead. His followers began to teach that Jesus was the Messiah promised by the Old Testament.

Teachings of Jesus

According to Christian belief, everything Jesus said and did centered on God's love for humans and the love people should have for one another. He used parables—stories—to make his point. He told his followers to love everyone. Christians had to show this love by their actions. The Gospels tell that Jesus once told his followers to sell their possessions and

Jesus is shown blessing the faithful in this enamel picture. During the 1000s, the Christian Church became divided into the Roman Catholic and Greek, or Eastern, Orthodox branches. This artwork is from an Orthodox church.

share the money with the poor. The real treasures, he said, were in Heaven. Because of such teachings, early Christianity had great appeal for the poor.

Not all Christians today agree on how the teachings of Jesus should be interpreted. There is, however, agreement on a number of beliefs. Most Christians believe in the Trinity: three separate persons in God—Father, Son, and Holy Spirit—all with one nature. Each is fully God. Christians consider Jesus to be the Messiah who came to earth to make up for humanity's sins. Most Christians accept the word of God as revealed through the Bible. Christians believe that the coming of Jesus marked a new covenant with God. For that reason, they place special emphasis on the New Testament.

Spread of Christianity

Many people were drawn to the warmth, sincerity, and goodness of Jesus. He chose 12 of his followers to spread his teachings. These special

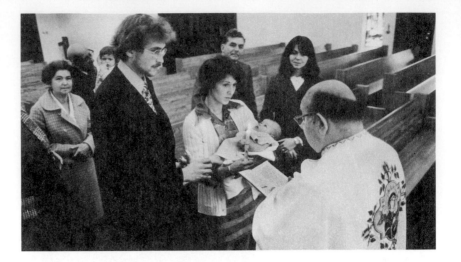

Baptism brings a person into Christianity. Some denominations have infant baptism, and others believe a person should not be baptized until he or she is older. This a baptism in the Roman Catholic Church.

messengers were called Apostles (uh-PAHS-uhls). Chief among them was Peter. Small groups of Jews began to accept Jesus as the Messiah and follow his teachings.

Within a few years after his death, Christianity began to reach gentiles (JEN-tyls) or non-Jews. One of those responsible for this was Saul of Tarsus. He had once fought against the Christians. But after seeing a vision from God, he became a Christian. He changed his name to Paul and spent the rest of his life preaching. Through his efforts Christian communities were set up in Syria, Asia Minor, Greece, Egypt, and even Rome itself. Paul kept in touch with the various groups of Christians by epistles (ih-PIS-uhls). This is another word for letters. In these he interpreted Christian teachings. These messages and those of the Apostles make up the Epistles—21 of the books of the New Testament. The other two books are Acts and Revelation. Revelation, also known as Apocalypse (uh-PAHK-uh-lips), is the last book of the New Testament. It is a book of prophecy.

Early Christian Church   In the beginning Christians saw little need for organization. Some expected the kingdom of God to come within their lifetimes. They achieved a sense of unity by observing common rituals called sacraments. These sacraments were signs of God's love for them. Originally, the most important sacraments were baptism and the eucharist, or communion. Through baptism one became a Christian. Through the eucharist (YOO-kuh-ruhst)—taking bread and wine—early Christians commemorated the death and resurrection of Jesus.

Gradually Christianity spread throughout the Roman Empire. Its spread was helped by the excellent system of roads and by the fact that the empire was at peace. In addition, most of the people spoke either Latin or Greek, so the missionaries who were preaching Christianity could address them directly.

Roman authorities, however, saw Christianity as a threat to their rule. Christians refused to serve in the army, hold public office, or honor the emperor as a god. As a result, the authorities often blamed Christians for such disasters as famines, fires, and plagues. Many Christians were persecuted or killed. Finally the Emperor Constantine ended the persecution. He said that he had received a vision from God that had helped him in battle. In A.D. 313 he issued an order, the Edict of Milan, which granted freedom of worship to Christians. By 392 Christianity was the official religion of the Roman Empire.

As the number of Christians increased, the need for organization became clear. The Church adopted the organizational structure of the Roman Empire. At the bottom was a parish headed by a priest, who led services and performed such rituals as baptism and marriage. Several parishes made up a diocese (DY-uh-sis) headed by a bishop, who managed Church property and looked after people's welfare. Several dioceses made up a province headed by an archbishop. Each archbishop was headquartered in one of the major cities of the Roman Empire: Rome, Alexandria, Antioch, Constantinople, and Jerusalem. The archbishop of Rome came to be looked upon by many Christians as holding a special position. By A.D. 600 he was known as the pope, from a Latin word meaning "father."

Differences Arise   During the first centuries of the Christian Church, a number of differences arose over the interpretation of Church teachings. In A.D. 325 the first church council was held to settle the argument over the nature of the three persons in the Trinity. Once a Church council defined a teaching, Christians were obliged to accept it. If people doubted or denied the definition, they were considered **heretics** (HER-uh-tiks). Heretics were excommunicated. All rights of Church membership were taken from them.

Central to Christian worship is communion. Here a young woman drinks the wine and a man gives the host, a wafer of unleavened bread. What are the different beliefs about the nature of communion held by the various denominations?

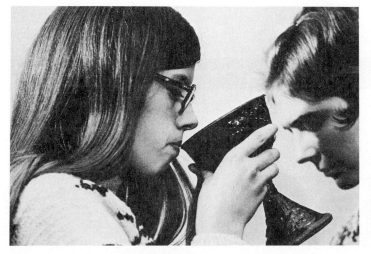

Between A.D. 100 and 500 certain clergy—who became known as Church Fathers—wrote works that had a major impact on Christian thought. St. Jerome translated the Bible into Latin, the Church language of that time. Known as the *Vulgate*, it became the only approved version of the Bible. St. Augustine wrote *City of God*, in which he presented a Christian view of history.

Divisions Within Christianity

While Emperor Constantine made Christianity legal, he set the stage for a split within the Christian Church. He divided the Roman Empire into two parts: east and west. He built a new capital in the east on the site of the ancient city of Byzantium. It was later named Constantinople in his honor. The western half of the empire declined and finally fell apart in the 400s. The eastern section remained until the 1400s.

Ordinary Christians of the two parts of the former empire began to drift apart. In culture and language the two regions were very different. People in the west spoke Latin. Those in the east spoke Greek. The eastern region also contained a greater mixture of peoples and cultures. In time the Christians in the east began to call their church the Eastern Orthodox or the Greek Orthodox Church. This was to distinguish it from the Roman church which later became known as the Roman Catholic Church. Catholic means universal.

Over the centuries the two churches adopted different rituals and even followed a different calendar. They disagreed strongly over how much influence the pope should have. Finally, in 1054, the split between them became official.

Christianity—both eastern and western—continued to grow. In Western Europe corrupt practices began to creep into the Church. A reform movement developed in the 1500s. This led to formation of the Protestant branches of the Christian Church. You will read more about this in Unit 6.

SECTION 3 REVIEW

1. **Recall**   What are the chief teachings of Jesus?

2. **How and Why**   Describe the conditions that contributed to the spread of Christianity.

3. **Critical Thinking**   Do you think the Christian Church would have remained united if Emperor Constantine had not divided the Roman Empire into two parts? Explain your answer.

Muslim places of worship are called mosques. This one is in Damascus. Muslims also believe the world is a mosque and they, therefore, may pray wherever they are when the call to prayer is sounded five times each day.

The third great world religion to begin in the Middle East is Islam (is-LAHM). It started on the Arabian Peninsula. Much of this region is controlled today by the Kingdom of Saudi Arabia.

By the A.D. 500s the peninsula was dominated by Arabian nomads known as Bedouins (BED-uh-wuhns). They lived mostly by herding. A few towns and cities dotted the trade routes between Asia and Europe. One of the largest was Mecca (MEK-uh), on the Red Sea.

Mecca was also a religious center. It was the site of the Kaaba (KAHB-uh) and a holy well. The Kaaba housed an ancient black stone said to have come from Heaven. The shrine also contained several hundred statues of deities that were worshiped by the peoples of the region. Each year hundreds of Arabs visited the Kaaba. The holy well, which stands nearby, dates to the time of Abraham.

Abraham fathered a son—Ishmael (ISH-mee-uhl)—by his wife's maid Hagar. But Abraham's wife, Sara, later had a son, Isaac. To protect Isaac's legal rights, Ishmael and Hagar were sent away. While wandering in the desert, they were saved by the angel Gabriel (GAY-bree-uhl) who showed them the well. Gabriel also promised that Ishmael's descendants would create a great nation. Arabs trace their ancestry to Ishmael.

Muhammad

The story of Islam begins with Muhammad (moh-HAM-uhd). He was born in Mecca around A.D. 570. Muhammad was orphaned at an early age and raised by relatives. During his youth he worked as a herder. He married Khadijah, a rich widow. For many years he managed her cloth business and was a successful merchant.

441

One of the Five Pillars of
Islam is a pilgrimage to
Mecca. These Muslims are
fulfilling this part of their
law. What is the purpose of
the pilgrimage? Do other
religions encourage
pilgrimages? Are they
voluntary?

Muhammad was also a religious man. He often went to a cave near
Mecca to meditate. According to Islamic teaching, it was there one night
in 610 that God began speaking to him. The revelations—or messages—
came through the voice of the angel Gabriel.

At first Muhammad told only his family and close friends what he
heard. Later he began preaching publicly in Mecca. He gained followers
among the poor because he taught that the rich should share their wealth.
But when he preached against the deities in the Kaaba, he made enemies.
He threatened the economic security of those who profited from the
pilgrimages. They turned against him. Muhammad decided to leave
Mecca in 622. He went to Medina (muh-DEE-nuh), a city farther north.
This journey is known as the Hegira (hih-JY-ruh). The event marks the
beginning of the Islamic calendar.

Muhammad wanted all Arab people to know the one God of the
Jews and the Christians. The revealed teachings he preached came to be
known collectively as the religion of Islam. The word Islam means
submission—that is, to Allah (AL-uh) or God. Followers of Islam took the
name Muslim. Muslim means one who submits.

In Mecca Muhammad had preached a religious message of social
justice and equality. In Medina he found himself in a new role—political
leader. He was called on to settle arguments and make laws.

Later Muhammad took on a third role. In 624 fighting broke out
between Mecca and Medina. Muhammad led a group of Muslims in
battle against Mecca. They were victorious. Muhammad proved himself
to be a military as well as a religious and political leader. By 630 he had an
army strong enough to seize Mecca. He marched on the city and ordered
all the statues removed from the Kaaba. Only the black stone was to
remain.

After that many people converted to Islam. Muhammad sent missionaries all over Arabia to preach. Muhammad returned to Medina where he died in 632.

Teachings of Muhammad

Muhammad taught that there is only one God—Allah. Allah is the creator of all things. Muslims believe that Allah is the same God who spoke through the prophets Abraham, Moses, and Jesus. Muslims believe that Muhammad was chosen to complete this series of revelations.

Muhammad's revelations are recorded in a sacred book called the Koran (kuh-RAN), which is written in Arabic. It also contains dietary laws and rules about marriage, inheritance, and business. Although people in different nations speak different forms of Arabic, they all write the language the way it appears in the Koran. The more chapters a person can recite by heart, the better educated he or she is considered to be.

Five Basic Pillars

Islamic devotion is based on five articles of faith. They are known as the Five Pillars of Islam.

The first pillar is recital of the words: *There is no God but Allah; and Muhammad is His Prophet*. Muslims say this many times a day. They believe that the oneness of God must be engraved in their minds and hearts. A sincere public recital of this creed is all that is necessary to become a Muslim. In repeating these words, Muslims will be reminded that Muhammad was only a prophet. He was a human and must not be worshiped.

The second pillar of Islam is prayer. Muslims are required to pray five times a day: at dawn, noon, midafternoon, sunset, and nightfall. Services are held at noon on Fridays in mosques. Any Muslim may lead the prayers. When Muslims pray, they face in the direction of Mecca. This is to remind them of the unity within Islam.

The third pillar is charity. Muslims are required to share what they have with others. This is to show appreciation for God's generosity. Muslims are asked to pay a tax each year on all their possessions. The tax is used for charitable purposes. Islam also tries to give its followers a social conscience—a sense of obligation to help ease the suffering of others.

The fourth pillar is fasting during Ramadan (RAM-uh-dahn). This is the ninth month of the Muslim calendar. It was during Ramadan that Muhammad first received God's revelations. It was also in this month, several years later, that Muhammad went to Medina. During Ramadan Muslims fast each day from sunrise to sunset. They avoid eating,

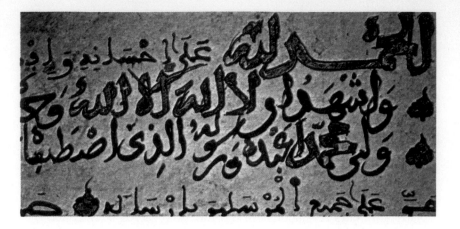

The Koran is the holy book of Islam. The copy from which this page comes dates from the 1400s. What are the major teachings of Islam?

pilgrimage:
a journey, especially to a shrine or sacred place

drinking, or other earthly pleasures. Fasting is supposed to remind Muslims that they are weak and need the constant help of God. It is also supposed to remind them to be sympathetic and helpful to the less fortunate.

The fifth pillar is a pilgrimage to the Kaaba, the shrine in the Great Mosque of Mecca. Islam teaches that Muslims should visit this shrine at least once, if possible. The pilgrimage will strengthen their faith. In the mosque at Mecca, no distinctions are made because of a person's wealth or status. All are equal before Allah. All pilgrims dress alike in plain white cloth. This coming together of Muslims from all over the world symbolizes the international community of Islam. The pilgrimage is known in Arabic as the Hajj, and, draws hundreds of thousands of believers each year. A man who has made the Hajj is entitled to wear a green turban.

All Muslims are expected to practice the five pillars of Islam. Some try to reach the highest form of Islam—Sufism (SOO-fiz-uhm). Its followers, called Sufis, strive for a personal experience of God. They seek a personal union with their creator. In the early days of Islam, they founded monasteries where they lived lives of prayer, meditation, and self-sacrifice. Sufis have also been the great missionaries of Islam. Many of the great Persian poets of the 1000s and 1100s were Sufis. Among them was Omar Khayyam. His work, called the *Rubaiyat* (ROO-by-aht), contains numerous love songs and is widely quoted today.

SECTION 4 REVIEW

1. **Recall**   List and describe the Five Pillars of Islam.
2. **How and Why**   Why are Muslims encouraged to make a pilgrimage to Mecca?
3. **Critical Thinking**   How are Muhammad's teachings an extension of Jewish and Christian beliefs?

R E V I E W

Reviewing People, Places, and Things

Identify, define, or explain each of the following:

Re	Moses Maimonides
state religion	sect
Ikhnaton	Constantine
Zoroaster	heretic
prophet	St. Jerome
monotheist	mosque
vernacular	Ishmael
hierarchy	Koran

Map Study

Using the map on page 398, determine the answers to the following questions:

1. What natural region is indicated on the map by the color brown?

2. What natural region is found along the Nile River?

3. What natural region makes up most of the land in the southern half of the Arabian Peninsula?

Understanding Facts and Ideas

1. **a.** What were the bases of the religions of Sumerian and Semitic-speaking peoples? **b.** Why? **c.** Why did these peoples fear their deities?

2. How did Ikhnaton's worship of Aton weaken the Egyptian empire?

3. What religion did the Persians practice for many centuries?

4. **a.** Name the three parts of the Jewish Bible. **b.** What are they called in the Christian Bible?

5. What things are found in the Talmud besides laws?

6. **a.** Where did the Jews serve as a cultural bridge between the ancient Middle East and medieval Europe? **b.** What attracted them to that area? **c.** What caused them to leave?

7. **a.** How do we know about the life and teachings of Jesus? **b.** What did the teachings of Jesus center on?

8. **a.** Why did early Christians see little need for organization? **b.** Why did organization become necessary?

9. **a.** Where did Islam originate? **b.** Why was Mecca important at that time?

10. **a.** Why did Muhammad decide to leave Mecca? **b.** What was Muhammad's religious message?

Developing Critical Thinking

Comparing and Contrasting   In reading history you may find that you need to **infer**, or interpret, a comparison or contrast from the information you are given. Often making a table listing in one column the similarities and in a second, the differences, will help. Make a table to help you answer the following question: Judaism, Christianity, and Islam began in the Middle East. What do these religions have in common? How do they differ?

Writing About History

Expressing an Opinion   Judaism, Christianity, and Islam have certain basic beliefs in common. These beliefs may be similar because they fulfill universal human needs. In a brief essay discuss the human needs that you think are met by Judaism, Christianity, and Islam.

Applying Your Skills to History

Using Pie Graphs   Using the pie graph on page 433 and library references, make a similar pie graph for religions in the United States. Compare the two graphs and write a statement about what you have inferred from the data.

CHAPTER

23

In this fresco, or wall painting, a Persian ruler receives a foreign delegation. In the 1500s Persian Muslims fought Turkish Muslims for power. Each side tried to gain allies. What attracts allies to one side or the other?

The Rulers and the Ruled

The teachings of Muhammad inspired his followers with a missionary spirit. They became determined to spread the will of Allah and their own power as widely as possible. Within a century most Middle Easterners were Muslims. As Islam spread, peoples of many different backgrounds were tied together by a shared religion and culture. A vast civilization was created that at one time reached from Southeast Asia to Spain.

In the 1000s the Muslims were overrun by non-Arabic invaders from the east—Turkish nomads. The Turks quickly accepted Islam and continued to spread its teachings and their own power. Their expansion was finally checked in the late 1600s. After that, Turkish power slowly declined. By the end of the 1800s, European nations dominated the Middle East.

As you study this chapter, think about these questions:

- How did the teachings of Muhammad influence his followers?

- How did the series of invasions of the Middle East between 900 and 1300 affect the spread of Middle Eastern culture?

- Why did European nations fight for control of the Middle East?

From the beginning Islam was more than a religious force. Its impact was felt in social, political, and economic areas as well.

SECTION

1

The Islamic Empire

Successors to Muhammad

When Muhammad died in 632, most of the Arabian Peninsula was under his control. However, he had not chosen a successor. His followers elected as his successor Abu Bekr, his closest friend and also his father-in-law. After Abu Bekr's death, three other leaders were elected one after the other. They bore the title of caliph, from the Arabic phrase *Khalifat Rasul Allah*, or "Successor of the Messenger of Allah." These first four caliphs were called the upright caliphs because they had known Muhammad personally and tried to imitate him in daily life. They were also called the barefoot caliphs because they lived simply.

These first four caliphs were also military conquerors. Under the leadership of Abu Bekr, the Arabs invaded the Persian Empire and also took Syria and Palestine away from the Byzantines. Under the second caliph, Umar the Great, the Arabs not only conquered the entire Persian Empire but also took Egypt from the Byzantines. By the time the fourth caliph, Muhammad's son-in-law Ali, came to power, the Islamic Empire stretched from North Africa to India.

The Arabs were mild rulers. People who submitted to Arab control could keep their land and follow their own religion in exchange for paying taxes. People who resisted, however, had to turn their land over to the Arabs but continue farming it in order to feed the Arab armies. They also had to pay taxes.

In the 660s problems arose in the Islamic Empire. The third caliph had favored members of his own Umayyad (uh-MY-ad) clan when giving out government positions. The fourth caliph, Ali, a member of the Hashemite clan, had followed Muhammad's instructions that all Muslims should be treated equally. As a result, the governor of Syria, an Umayyad named Mu'awaiya (moo-AH-wih-yah), challenged Ali for the caliphate. For the next several years there was bitter fighting between the two clans. In 661 Ali was assassinated. Mu'awaiya declared himself caliph and moved the capital of the Islamic Empire from Medina to Damascus, Syria. This was closer to the empire's geographical center.

Ali's death created a religious split within Islam. Two major groups emerged: Sunni and Shia. The Sunnis consider the caliph's position to be elective. They follow the Koran closely and also follow the teachings of those whom they believe to be the rightful successors of Muhammad. About 85 percent of Muslims today are Sunni.

The Shia sect began in Persia as a political group. The word *shia* means "partisan of Ali," and the Shi'ites (SHEE-ytes) believe that Muhammad intended his successors to be descendants of Ali. Today Iran is a Shi'ite nation, and more than half of Iraqi Muslims are Shi'ites. Large groups of Shi'ites are also found in Afghanistan, Pakistan, India, and Yemen.

Sunni Muslims and Shi'ite Muslims have organizational as well as political differences. Sunni Muslims do not have a religious hierarchy.

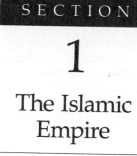

■ Islamic Empire Under Muhammad, c. A.D. 632

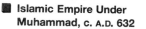

447

Shi'ite Muslims do. Their most important leaders are known as ayatollahs (iy-uh-TOHL-uhs). Also, Shi'ite Muslims observe not just one pilgrimage but two. In addition to the Hajj to Mecca, Shi'ite Muslims journey to Kerbela, near the Euphrates River. There they fast and pray for ten days. Often men will strip to the waist and beat themselves until blood flows down their backs. They are commemorating the "Tragedy of Kerbela"—the murder in 680 of Ali's son, Husein (hu-SAYN), by the son of Mu'awaiya.

Umayyad Dynasty

The Umayyad dynasty that Mu'awaiya founded lasted for about 100 years. During this time the position of caliph became hereditary rather than elective. And there were other political changes as well. Instead of relying only on Arabs as government workers, Mu'awaiya set up a bureaucracy made up mostly of Syrian Christians. However, he adopted Arabic instead of Greek or Persian as the official language of government. He also replaced Byzantine and Persian coins with coins that had a quotation from the Koran engraved on them.

During the Umayyad dynasty a class system emerged. At the top were the ruling nobles. They were descended from the leading families of Mecca and Medina and were usually soldiers. Much of their wealth came from land given to them by the caliph. Directly below the nobles were Muslim non-Arabs. They formed an urban middle class of artisans, merchants, and storekeepers. The third group were non-Muslims who believed in one God. These included Christians and Jews. The lowest

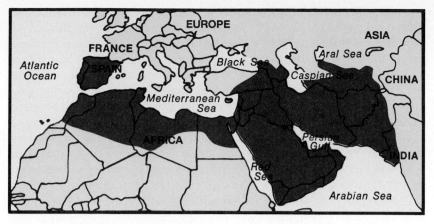

Umayyad Dynasty, c. A.D. 632–750

group were slaves. Muslims did not enslave fellow Muslims. Instead, they imported slaves from East Africa, Scandinavia, and Russia. Slaves were generally treated fairly, and talented slaves were able to rise in the military.

The most important military achievement of the Umayyads was the conquest of Spain. It was carried out in the early 700s by the Moors, a people of mixed Arab and Berber background. The Berbers were a North African people who had themselves been previously conquered by the Arabs and had converted to Islam. In Spain the Moors created a brilliant civilization that lasted until 1492. It was under the Moors that Jewish philosophy and scholarship flourished in Spain.

Another important military achievement was the conquest of Samarkand, a city in central Asia. In Samarkand the Muslims learned about the Chinese art of making paper. In 794 they set up a paper factory of their own in Baghdad (BAG-dad). One result was the establishment of public libraries throughout the Islamic Empire. By the 1400s the use of paper had spread through Christian Europe.

Eventually a group of Shi'ite Muslims in Persia and Iraq revolted against the Umayyad dynasty. They brought about its downfall in 750. The new caliph was Abdul Abbas, of the Hashemite clan. He was the founder of the Abbasid (AB-uh-suhd) dynasty.

Abbasid Dynasty

Under Abbasid rule (750–1258) the Islamic Empire reached its peak. Al-Mansur, the second Abbasid caliph, established a new capital at Baghdad. The city's splendor was known throughout east and west. The caliph, his family and advisers, and the nobles lived in luxury. They dined off gold and silver plates decorated with jewels. Such luxury was possible because of the empire's profits from trade. Baghdad had an excellent geographical position. It was located on the trade routes between Asia and Europe.

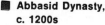
Abbasid Dynasty, c. 1200s

The Abbasid dynasty marked a turning point in the government and culture of the Islamic Empire. The Persians especially began to exercise considerable influence. Most government bureaucrats were now Persians rather than Syrian Christians. A new post of prime minister was set up and was usually filled by a Persian. The Arabs adopted Persian clothing styles, household goods, foods, and pastimes. Instead of wearing long robes, Arabs took to wearing trousers. They ate off tables instead of eating cross-legged on the ground. Arab diets included such Persian foods as chickens, bananas, oranges, peaches, and sugar cane. Arab houses now contained cushions, mattresses, and ovens. Arab nobles engaged in such games as archery, chess, and polo. The Persians themselves had obtained some of the foods and games through cultural diffusion from India.

Eventually the wealth and luxury of Baghdad corrupted the caliphate. The caliph's political power fell into the hands of Persian prime ministers and their paid Turkish soldiers. Parts of the empire—such as Spain, Egypt, and Tunisia—broke away and set up their own caliphates. Then a series of invasions occurred, and by 1258 the Abbasid dynasty was no more.

SECTION 1 REVIEW

1. **Recall** What are the differences between Sunni and Shi'ite Muslims?
2. **How and Why** Why did the Muslim Empire grow rapidly?
3. **Critical Thinking** How were some of Muhammad's teachings corrupted under Umayyad and Abbasid rule?

SECTION

2

Invaders

During the disunity of Abbasid rule, people from the steppes of central Asia began moving into the Middle East. They were a nomadic people who spoke a Turkic language and came to be called Seljuk Turks. They took their name from an early leader, Seljuk.

Seljuk Turks

Under Togrul Beg, Seljuk's grandson, the Seljuk Turks began a conquest of the Middle East. In 1055 they captured Baghdad. The Abbasid caliph was allowed to keep his religious authority. But the Seljuk Turks took political control. Their leader took the title of sultan, meaning "he who has authority." The Seljuk Turks eventually became Muslims.

The Seljuk Turks were very devout in their religious observances. To promote the study of Islamic law, they established a series of schools called madrasas. The largest of these was Al-Azhar in Cairo, Egypt. Until the 1900s Al-Azhar and other madrasas were the only source of higher education in most Islamic countries.

This fresco shows two crusaders in camp. Thousands of men, women, and children joined the crusades. What were the consequences of the crusades in the Middle East?

Another result of the religious strictness of the Seljuk Turks was their intolerance of other religions. Under the Arabs, Christian pilgrims from Europe had been able to journey to Jerusalem without interference. The Seljuk Turks, in contrast, levied heavy taxes on the pilgrims and often subjected them to physical assault and even slavery.

Europeans also felt threatened by Turkish military expansion. In their continued campaign for territory, the Turks overran Armenia and Georgia (now part of the Soviet Union). In 1071 they crushed the Byzantine army stationed in Asia Minor. The next step would probably be an attack against the Byzantine capital of Constantinople and an invasion of the Balkan lands to the north.

As you know, the Eastern Orthodox Church and the Roman Catholic Church had split in 1054. Nevertheless, the Byzantine emperor—having nowhere else to turn—appealed to Rome for help. His first plea went unanswered. But his second appeal led to action.

■ States of the Crusaders

Crusaders

In 1096 Urban II, the Roman Catholic pope, answered the emperor's appeal. He called for rich and poor, knights and peasants, and men, women, and children to drive the Turks out of the Holy Land—Jerusalem and the area surrounding it. It is so called because most of the events mentioned in the Bible took place there. The pope's call resulted in a series of crusades, or holy wars. In all, nine major crusades were launched. The fighting continued on and off for 200 years.

In 1099 the crusaders took Jerusalem with savage fury. They kept control for 88 years, during which time they established four states in the area. Then, in 1187, Jerusalem was recaptured by the Turks under Saladin, who also recaptured several other cities.

Before the end of the 1100s, the crusaders had been driven from most of the Holy Land. They had failed as much because of their own greed as because of the bravery and skill of Muslim warriors. Many crusaders were more interested in easy wealth than in religion. They used the crusades as an excuse to pillage, or forcibly rob, Jewish and other communities on their way to the Holy Land, especially in the Rhine Valley. In 1204 crusaders looted Constantinople, stealing or destroying thousands of manuscripts and art treasures. This attack seriously weakened the Byzantine Empire.

Many Middle Eastern cities were destroyed and people killed during the crusades. However, the crusaders left little physical evidence of their presence in the Middle East. They did leave behind a distrust of Westerners. They also left a contempt on the part of Muslims for what they considered the inferior culture of Western Europe, especially in medicine and science. You will learn more about Islamic achievements in these fields later in the unit.

The greatest material impact of the crusades was the cultural diffusion that occurred as the crusaders returned home. They had learned much about the arts, literature, and way of life of the Middle Easterners. They had learned about ancient Greek philosophies and sciences that had been preserved and added to by Arab and Jewish scholars. The crusaders also carried home a taste for new luxuries, such as spices, sugar, fine fabrics, and exotic foods. To fill the demand for these goods, European trade with the Middle East became important. Middle Easterners were a link in the chain between Western European and Asian merchants. Eventually Western Europeans began searching for their own sea routes to the Far East, routes that would not be under Muslim control.

exotic:
unusual, foreign

Mongols

Control of the Middle East by the Seljuk Turks finally collapsed in the 1200s. Their place was taken by another people from central Asia, the Mongols. Under Genghis Khan, the Mongols swept through Iran and Afghanistan. Mongol conquest of the Middle East was extended by Genghis Khan's grandson Hulegu (hoo-LEH-goo). In 1258 Hulegu captured and destroyed Baghdad, thus ending the Abbasid dynasty. He then moved westward into the Holy Land. But his expansion was checked by an army of Mamluks from Egypt. The Mamluks were Turkish soldiers who had been slaves. They had been purchased by the Egyptian sultan when they were very young, and trained as warriors and palace guards. Within a few years, the Mamluks had murdered the sultan and installed their own leader. They not only stopped Mongol expansion, but they also drove the crusaders from the last of their holdings in Syria.

Hulegu's successors then settled in Iran. There they accepted Islamic beliefs and culture. Mongol influence gradually faded. By 1355 a number of small dynasties had risen in what had once been Hulegu's Mongol Empire.

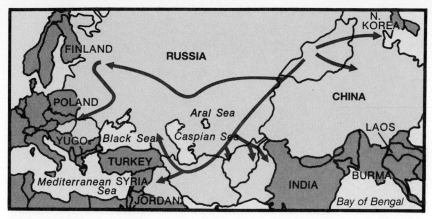

Mongol Invasions, c. 1200s

The last of the major Mongol conquerors to invade the Middle East was Tamerlane, or Timur the Lame. Between 1370 and 1402 Tamerlane's armies swept from India to Russia and then to Syria. He was a brutal conqueror who gloried in having his enemies beheaded and pyramids made out of their skulls. At the same time he was a scholar who turned his capital of Samarkand into a center of Muslim learning. In 1405, on his way to conquer China, Tamerlane died. His empire quickly fell apart.

Ottoman Turks

In the 1300s, while Mongol influence was fading, another group of people—the Ottomans—began their rise to power. They were nomadic Turks from central Asia, who began migrating westward as early as the 1100s. When they reached the Anatolian Plateau, they were hired by the Seljuk Turks to protect the border. In exchange for this service, the Ottomans were given a small piece of land.

Ottoman Expansion   In 1299 Osman I began to expand this territory. Within 20 years his soldiers had conquered almost all of the Byzantine Empire except for Constantinople. His successors continued the conquests, moving into the Balkans as far as modern Yugoslavia. In 1453, under Mehmet the Conqueror, they captured Constantinople after breaching the city's walls with cannons. This was the end of the Byzantine Empire. Constantinople became popularly known as *Istanbul*, meaning "the city," although its name was not officially changed until 1930. It became the capital of the Ottoman Empire.

The military strength of the Ottomans was based upon a professional army made up of janissaries (JAN-uh-ser-eez), or new troops. These were mostly Christians who had been taken from their families as young boys and forcibly converted to Islam. The brightest among them were specially trained for high government positions. The others joined

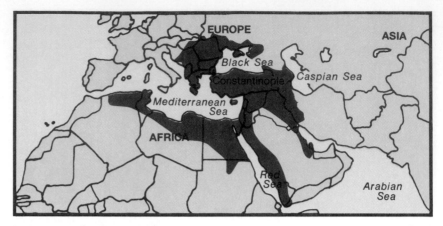

■ Ottoman Empire, c. 1683

the army. They were not allowed to marry or even to grow beards. However, they lived very comfortably and were well taken care of when they became sick or old. The janissaries were infantrymen. They were the first military unit in the world to be armed with guns. The Mongols had brought gunpowder to the Middle East from China.

By 1520, when Suleiman (SOO-lay-MAHN) the Magnificent came to the throne, the Ottoman Empire was the strongest in the world. By this time the Ottomans had conquered Syria, Egypt, and Arabia, including the Muslim centers of Mecca and Medina. That made the Turkish sultan caliph of all Muslims. Ottoman warships ranged throughout the Mediterranean. They raided Algeria, Libya, and Tunisia and added these lands to the empire. In Europe Suleiman's armies defeated the Hungarians and then laid siege to Vienna. They failed to capture the city. But they instilled a deep fear of the Ottoman Turks among the Europeans.

Suleiman's government was highly centralized. All the land in the empire was considered his personal property. Although he granted land to members of his cavalry to provide them with an income, the land reverted to him when they died. That way, it was not possible for a landed aristocracy to challenge the sultan's authority. Government bureaucrats were directly responsible to the sultan. They kept detailed census and tax records of the people. The tax burden fell on farmers and merchants. Soldiers, government officials, and religious leaders did not have to pay taxes.

The Ottoman Empire contained many ethnic and religious groups. Each group—known as a millet—had certain rights of self-government. Although Islam was the official religion, millets could follow their own religion in return for paying a special tax.

A Slow Decline   Suleiman's rule marked the peak of Ottoman conquests. With his death in 1566, a period of slow decline set in. Corruption within the bureaucracy increased. Also, as guns improved, the janissaries became much more effective soldiers than the cavalry. To support more janissaries, the sultans began taking land away from the cavalry. The dispossessed cavalry rebelled repeatedly.

Another problem was caused by the shah, or ruler, of Persia. In the early 1500s the shah had declared his nation to be officially Shi'ite. He had also encouraged Shi'ite Muslims within the Ottoman Empire to revolt. After putting down the revolt, the Ottomans reacted by becoming extremely conservative, not only in their Sunni religion, but also in their schools. If something was not mentioned in the Koran, it was ignored. Thus, Ottoman bureaucrats continued copying documents by hand instead of using the printing press that had been developed in Europe. The Ottoman army also failed to adopt new techniques of warfare from the West.

From time to time, sultans would try to reform the empire, but without success. Either the janissaries would mutiny, or religious leaders would insist that the solution to problems was to pay more attention to Islamic law.

In 1683 the Turks suffered a major military setback outside Vienna at the hands of John Sobieski (soh-BYES-kee), the Polish king. By 1699 the Turks had been driven from Hungary back to the Danube. In the 1700s the Ottomans fought a series of wars with Russia. They were defeated and forced to give up their lands along the Black Sea.

Several more Turkish-Russian wars erupted in the 1800s. The most important was the Crimean (kry-MEE-uhn) War. Named for the Crimean Peninsula on the Black Sea where the fighting occurred, the war lasted from 1853 to 1856. The Turks were aided by Great Britain and France, who wanted to keep Russia out of the Mediterranean.

The war was extremely bloody. Generals on both sides had received their commissions because they were aristocrats, not because they were competent. Most weapons and other equipment were obsolete, and no preparations had been made for winter fighting. Hospital care was so poor that almost half a million soldiers died from cholera, dysentery, and neglect.

A compromise agreement ending the war was reached at the Congress of Paris in 1856. This agreement returned the Ottoman Empire to its prewar boundaries. But Russia continued to support revolts in the Balkans by various non-Turkish groups that wanted to become independent. In 1877 another Turkish-Russian War broke out. This time, the Ottoman Empire lost most of its Balkan territory.

In 1908 a group of young army officers known as Young Turks seized control of the Ottoman government. Well-educated and idealistic, they tried to institute reforms. But their efforts were generally ineffective. Economically, the empire was on the edge of collapse. Islamic leaders refused to accept anything that they thought was non-Muslim, and thus opposed most of the reform measures. And once again, rebellions erupted in the Balkans.

In 1914 World War I broke out. Under Enver Pasha, a Young Turk general, the Ottomans allied themselves with Germany and Austria-Hungary. This was partly because they feared the Russians, who were on the opposite side. As a result, the Ottoman Empire was on the losing side in World War I. It lost all its territory except for modern Turkey. You will learn about World War I in Unit 6.

Under Suleiman the Magnificent, the Ottoman Empire reached its peak. How did his successors go about delegating authority? How did their policies weaken the central government?

1. **Recall** What actions of the Seljuk Turks caused the Crusades?
2. **How and Why** Why did the crusaders fail in their attempts to gain control of the Holy Land?
3. **Critical Thinking** Which factor do you think was most responsible for the collapse of the Ottoman Empire? Explain your answer.

SECTION

3

European Domination

Almost every Middle Eastern nation has been dominated to some extent by Western Europeans. Eventually, however, economic problems at home and nationalist movements within the Middle East forced Western Europeans to give up their holdings.

Egypt

In 1798 the French tried to conquer Egypt. They were defeated by the combined forces of the Ottoman Turks and the British. In 1805 Muhammad Ali, a Turkish general who had been appointed governor by the Ottomans, seized control. He killed the Mamluk ruler, drove out the remaining British, and began a dynasty that ruled Egypt until 1952.

Ali wanted to modernize Egypt. He brought in French technicians to reorganize the army. He brought in European engineers to build canals and an irrigation system that employed steam-driven pumps. One result was that the English textile industry became dependent on high-quality Egyptian cotton.

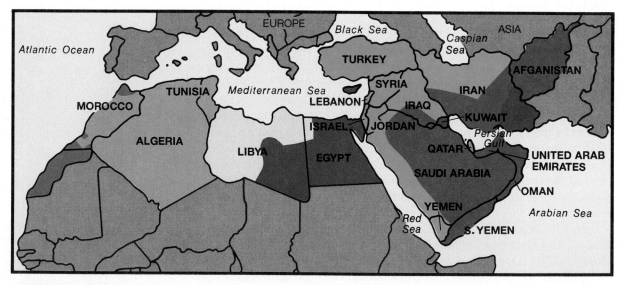

Middle East, 1914

■ British ■ French ☐ Italian ■ Spanish ■ Russian ■ Ottoman Empire ■ Independent

Under Ali's grandson Ismail Pasha, French engineers built the Suez Canal. It connected the Mediterranean and Red seas through the Gulf of Suez. The canal immediately became Britain's "life line" to India, which was then the most important part of the British Empire. The opening of the canal was marked by the first performance of Verdi's opera *Aida* (iy-EE-duh), which is set in ancient Egypt and was specially commissioned for the occasion.

Modernizing Egypt, however, cost a great deal of money. By 1876 the country could no longer keep up interest payments on its foreign debt. Egypt was forced to sell its share of Suez Canal stock to Great Britain. English bankers took over control of Egypt's finances. A few years later British troops put down an anti-European nationalist revolt and made Egypt a protectorate. A **protectorate** is a country whose foreign affairs are controlled by another country.

Increased nationalist sentiment among Egyptians, as well as Britain's weakened condition after World War I, led Britain to give Egypt its independence in 1922. The British agreed to withdraw all troops except those in the Suez Canal Zone. British troops remained in the Suez Canal Zone until the mid-1950s.

The Suez Canal was originally a joint project between a French company and the Egyptian government. Later the Egyptians had to sell their stock to the British. Egypt came increasingly under British domination.

The Barbary States

Apart from Egypt, North Africa consisted of the four Barbary States of Morocco, Algeria, Tripoli (modern Libya), and Tunisia. They were called Barbary States because of their Berber inhabitants. Morocco was an independent kingdom. The three other states in North Africa were semi-independent provinces of the Ottoman Empire.

During the 1600s and the 1700s the area was a stronghold for pirates. They demanded money from European and American merchant ships in return for safe passage through the Mediterranean. Sometimes the pirates would seize a ship's passengers and crew and hold them for ransom. This practice eventually led to the Tripolitan Wars. The new navy of the United States broke the power of the Barbary pirates in the early 1800s. That is why the official song of the U.S. Marine Corps opens with the words: "From the halls of Montezuma to the shores of Tripoli."

In the 1820s a dispute between France and Algeria led to war. The Algerians resisted for seventeen years but were finally defeated. French

Mandates
- ■ British
- ■ French
- ■ Independent

settlers then moved in. They took the best farmland and made the dispossessed Algerians work for them in the fields. In 1871 Algeria became a province of France. However, only people of French or other European descent could vote. Algerians could not.

The remaining Barbary States also came under European control. In 1881 France invaded Tunisia and set up a protectorate. Together with Spain, it did the same in Morocco in 1912. The previous year, 1911, Italy conquered Tripoli and set up the colony of Libya.

Iran and Afghanistan

During the 1800s and early 1900s, both Russia and Britain became interested in Iran—still known at that time as Persia. The British were interested because it was near India. The Russians were interested because they wanted an outlet on the Persian Gulf.

In the early 1900s oil was discovered in Iran. The British began to develop the country's rich oil fields. Together with the Iranian government, they formed the Anglo-Iranian Oil Company. The Iranian people, however, objected to foreigners having economic privileges. In 1907 Russia and Britain signed an agreement dividing Iran into spheres of influence. The Russians took the northern part of the country. The British took the south. The Iranians reacted bitterly. But World War I intervened. Iran was neutral during the war but was occupied by Russian and British troops. After the war Britain and Russia canceled their agreement. A new dynasty took over the Iranian government in the 1920s.

The British and the Russians were also rivals in neighboring Afghanistan. Both saw it as a possible threat to their empires. The British invaded Afghanistan in 1839. For many years the Russians and the British fought the Afghans and each other in a series of Afghan Wars. Finally, in 1879, the British gained the dominant role. In 1919, after another war, the British granted Afghanistan its independence.

The Mandates

When the Ottoman Empire collapsed after World War I, the breakup of its territory led to the creation of several mandates along the eastern Mediterranean. A **mandate** is a territory administered by another country. Syria and Lebanon became French mandates, while Iraq and Palestine became British mandates. In 1922 the Palestine mandate was divided by Britain into Jordan and Palestine.

SECTION 3 REVIEW

1. **Recall**   What practice led to the Tripolitan Wars?
2. **How and Why**   How did Muhammad Ali try to modernize Egypt?
3. **Critical Thinking**   Why did Europeans seek to dominate Middle East nations?

R E V I E W

Reviewing People, Places, and Things

Identify, define, or explain each of the following:

Abu Bekr
Mu'awaiya
ayatollah
Moors
Seljuk Turks
madrasas
Urban II
Holy Land
Mongols
Genghis Khan

Tamerlane
Ottoman Turks
janissaries
Suleiman the Magnificent
Crimean War
Young Turks
Suez Canal
protectorate
Barbary States
mandate

Map Study

Using the map on page 454, determine the answers to the following questions:

1. On which three continents were Ottoman holdings found?
2. How far west did the Ottoman Empire extend?
3. To which five bodies of water did the Ottomans have direct access?

Understanding Facts and Ideas

1. **a.** What problems did Ali's death cause? **b.** How do the Sunnis and Shi'ites regard the position of the caliph?
2. What was the new direction Mu'awaiyah gave the empire?
3. **a.** Why did Urban II begin the crusades? **b.** When? **c.** How long did they last?
4. **a.** Why did crusaders fail in their attempts to free the Holy Land? **b.** What was the greatest material impact of the crusades?
5. What ended the Byzantine Empire?

6. What caused Ottoman power to weaken?
7. Why were the Young Turks ineffective?
8. **a.** How did Britain obtain part ownership of the Suez Canal? **b.** How long did British troops remain in the Suez Canal Zone?
9. What parts of North Africa came under control of: **a.** France? **b.** Italy? **c.** Spain?
10. How did Russia and Britain gain increasing control of Iran's internal affairs?

Developing Critical Thinking

Cause and Effect Middle Easterners have developed a distrust of Westerners. Based on what you have read, what historical reasons (causes) can you give for this distrust (effect)?

Writing About History

Relating Past to Present Sunni and Shi'ite Muslims have clashed in modern times in the Middle East. In a brief essay give the historical causes for their hostility. Discuss also the political and organizational differences between them.

Applying Your Skills to History

Testing a Hypothesis The text states that Islam was more than a religious force—its impact was felt in social, political, and economic areas as well. Reread Chapter 23 and take notes for a table listing each caliphate and dynasty named and the ways in which Islam's impact was felt in social, political, and economic areas. Analyze the table to test the text's explanation. Do you think the text's statement is reasonable? Answer in a paragraph, giving the evidence for your conclusion.

Kuwait's oil fields have made it one of the world's richest nations. However, a wide gulf separates the very few rich from the majority of citizens. The nation supports a large welfare system for these people. At the same time, the rich enjoy such holdovers from British days as soccer.

Recent Years

The Ottoman Empire collapsed after World War I. With its end came the beginning of the new nation of Turkey. This event also began the movement for independence among other peoples in the Middle East. Western nations, however, tried to increase their control over the region. But after World War II, they pulled out.

Beginning with the 1920s, the Middle East has been the scene of much fighting. Since 1948 much of the conflict has been between Israel and its Arab neighbors over Israel's very existence. Other conflicts have arisen between Iraq and Iran, and between different groups within Lebanon.

As you study this chapter, think about these questions:

- How did Islam affect the efforts of governments to build nation-states in the Middle East?

- What is the historical basis for the Arab-Israeli conflict?

- What problems must Middle Eastern nations overcome to achieve economic growth?

The movement toward nationalism started late in the Middle East. Most Middle Easterners had been part of the Ottoman Empire for centuries. During that time they identified themselves not with a nation but with Islam. Before they could form a national identity, a sense of oneness, Middle Easterners had to adapt Islam to the modern world. Many national leaders have found the process of blending the old and the new a long, slow one.

Modernization of Turkey

Turkey was the first Middle Eastern nation to move toward modernization. The changes were brought about by Mustafa Kemal Ataturk (moos-tah-FAH kuh-MAHL ah-tah-TOORK). Ataturk was a war hero. During World War I he directed the successful defense of the Dardanelles against British attack. It was the only major Turkish victory of the war. In 1919, when a Greek army invaded Turkey, Ataturk again led the fight against his country's enemies. His forces took Constantinople and deposed the sultan. In 1921 they defeated the Greeks. In 1923, under the Treaty of Lausanne, Turkey was allowed to keep all of Asia Minor, Constantinople, and the Dardanelles. It did lose its Arab territories, however. That same year Ataturk became the first president of the Turkish republic. He moved the capital from Constantinople to Ankara, in Turkey's heartland.

Ataturk was guided by several principles. They included nationalism, secularism, statism, and revolutionism.

By nationalism, Ataturk meant that all people within the borders of Turkey were Turks. Their origins, physical appearance, and beliefs did not matter. All would be treated alike. This policy led to conflict with two ethnic minorities, the Armenians and the Kurds. Their demands for independence were crushed.

Secularism meant separating the government from religion. When Ataturk became president, Turkey was a religious state. The legal system was based on Islamic law. All parts of daily living—dress, education, and so on—were tied to Islam. Ataturk's first step was to abolish the caliphate. He then changed the legal system. Laws were no longer to be interpreted according to the Koran or other Islamic sources. Instead, they would be based on European legal codes. Religious shrines were closed. Sunday replaced Friday as the day of rest. Schools were placed under government operation. They no longer taught Islam. Instead, they taught such subjects as mathematics, science, and social studies. By the time Ataturk died in 1938, Turkey had become a secular state.

Statism was concerned mostly with improving the Turkish economy. State aid was granted to private industry. Railroads, shipping, banks, and other businesses were taken over by the government. The government also built additional railroads and entered into the manufacturing of such items as sugar, tobacco, and textiles.

Revolutionism meant making changes in daily life. For example, Ataturk felt that the Arabic script used by the Turks was not suited to modern business. In 1929 he ordered that it be replaced with the Roman alphabet used by Western nations. Typewriters then came into wide-spread use. Furthermore, since Arabic has only three vowels while the Turkish language has eight vowels, using the more phonetic Roman alphabet made it easier to spread literacy among the Turkish people.

There were social changes as well. Men were no longer allowed to wear the round, red, brimless hat known as a fez. It was considered old-fashioned. Government employees had to wear Western-style business suits. In 1935 Ataturk introduced the Western culture trait of last names. Until then, Turks had had only one name, to which they added descriptive words and phrases. For example, a man might be Selim the Proud, or Selim the son of Ismet, or Selim the shoemaker. Now Turks took as their last names the name of a river or a city, or a fanciful name such as *Arslan*, meaning "lion." Ataturk himself had been named only *Mustafa* at birth. He had acquired the nickname *Kemal*, meaning "excellent," in school. He was given the last name of *Ataturk*, meaning "Father of the Turks," by the national assembly.

Ataturk did much to improve the status of women. Polygyny—having more than one wife—was discouraged. Women were given the right to vote and encouraged to seek political office. They were also encouraged to pursue careers in science and the arts.

Iran's Nationalism

Ataturk's reforms influenced Riza Khan of Iran, a military man who seized control of his country in 1921. In 1925 he proclaimed himself shah and founded the Pahlevi (PAHL-uh-vee) dynasty. It was Riza Shah who changed his country's name from Persia to Iran.

acknowledge:
recognize, accept

Riza Shah forced the various peoples in Iran to acknowledge the authority of the central government. He broke the power of Muslim religious leaders who opposed reforms. European codes of law replaced Islamic laws. An educational system was set up patterned after that of France. Riza Shah encouraged industry and built factories and railroads. Banks and currency controls were created to put the nation's finances in order.

Religious and social customs that Riza Shah considered too extreme were abolished. Women in particular benefited from such reforms. Polygyny was discouraged. A man was not allowed to take a second wife unless the first and the prospective wives agreed. Nor could girls marry before the age of 15.

Despite his efforts, Riza Shah was far less successful in his attempts at modernization than Ataturk. Many of Turkey's businessmen and other members of the middle class had been educated in Western Europe. This was not true of Iran. So Riza Shah's reforms did not receive widespread support. Islamic leaders resented his changes. Riza Shah himself became cruel and greedy, murdering political enemies and stealing money. Finally he supported Nazi Germany during World War II. Great Britain and the Soviet Union wanted to prevent Germany from taking over Iran's oil fields. So in 1941 the Soviets invaded from the north, and the British invaded from the south. Riza Shah was forced to step down. He was succeeded by his son, Mohammed Riza Pahlavi.

After several years of internal turmoil and a brief period of exile, by 1959 Shah Mohammed Pahlavi seemed secure on his throne. He started a land reform program, and gave women the right to vote. He encouraged a literacy campaign in the villages. But discontent within Iran kept growing. Inflation was high. Also, in carrying out his reforms, the shah often violated the political and civil rights of Iranians. His opponents were arrested, and many were tortured or murdered. The cultural changes the shah encouraged angered many mullahs, or Muslim leaders. In 1978 the shah faced a revolt by Muslims who wanted the return of their exiled leader, an ayatollah named Ruhollah Khomeini (koh-MAY-nee).

In January 1979 the shah left Iran for medical treatment abroad. Two weeks later Khomeini returned. Within days his revolutionary followers had gained control of the government. In March Iran became an Islamic republic. Mullahs were placed in charge of all government offices. Even the police now operated out of the local mosque instead of the town or village hall. Khomeini called for a return to Islamic traditions. He forbade Western dress for women. Alcohol was banned, as was Western music. The new government nationalized local and foreign industry, banks, and other businesses. Many educated Iranians fled the country.

As Khomeini consolidated his power, anti-American feelings in Iran were rising. The United States had long supported the shah. So in November 1979, Iranian militants invaded the U.S. Embassy in Tehran and seized the staff. This began an international crisis that lasted for 444 days. Khomeini refused to free the hostages until the United States met several demands. Among them was the return of the shah's fortune. Khomeini also wanted the shah returned to Iran to stand trial for ''crimes against the Iranian people.'' After long negotiations, the 52 Americans were released in January 1981. The shah died abroad of cancer.

In the meantime Iran's neighbor, Iraq, became frightened by the actions of the Khomeini government. Khomeini wanted to export his Islamic revolution. He urged Iraq's Shi'ite majority to revolt against the country's Sunni and secular leadership, and to set up an Islamic republic like that of Iran.

In 1980 Iraq launched a surprise attack against Iran. Iraq was confident that its well-equipped armies would win a quick and easy victory. Instead, Iranians responded enthusiastically to Khomeini's call for a jihad (ji-HAHD), a holy war. Boys as young as thirteen volunteered to fight against Iraq. They believed that if they died in battle, they would go at once to Paradise.

The war between Iraq and Iran dragged on for more than eight years, claiming the lives of more than 300,000 soldiers. At one point Iran threatened to block the Strait of Hormuz at the entrance to the Persian Gulf. That would have prevented the flow of oil from Iraq and Kuwait to the rest of the world. The threat caused the United States, Great Britain, and France to send warships to the Persian Gulf. But in spite of several incidents, the situation eventually calmed down. In 1989 Iraq and Iran agreed to a truce.

This news photo shows Iranian demonstrators at the gates of the American embassy that they seized, taking 60 hostages. Why did the Iranians capture the embassy?

Gamal Abdel Nasser was a controversial leader. What tactics did he use to gain and keep power? What reforms did he bring about?

extremist:
one who uses extreme measures

Also in 1989, Khomeini died. He was promptly succeeded by another ayatollah. It seemed clear that, in Iran, the process of developing a national identity meant the rejection of many Western values and an emphasis on traditional Shi'ite beliefs and institutions.

Egyptian Nationalism

After World War II feelings of discontent in Egypt erupted into violence. Egyptian nationalists resented the continuing presence of British troops in the Suez Canal Zone. They were also angered by the corruption within their government and by Egypt's defeat in the 1948 Arab-Israeli war. In 1952 a group of army officers led a revolution. They expelled the king and set up a republic. In 1952 Colonel Gamel (juh-MAHL) Abdel Nasser became prime minister. He was elected president in 1956 and led the country until his death in 1970.

Nasser's first goal was to remove foreign influence from Egypt. In 1954 he signed an agreement with the British to remove their troops from the Suez Canal Zone by June 1956. The following month he nationalized the canal. He also nationalized the business holdings of most foreigners.

Nasser's second goal was to improve the standard of living of Egyptian farmers. He pushed hard for land reform. He broke up large estates and reduced rents. The government lent money at low interest rates to farmers to buy land. Nasser sought to increase agricultural production. Irrigation projects were improved, expanded, and paid for by the government. Cooperatives were set up to distribute farm supplies and machinery. Perhaps Nasser's greatest project was construction of the Aswan High Dam, on the Nile River, built with the aid of the Soviet Union.

Nasser was also dedicated to **pan-Arabism**, or the political unity of all Arab nations. He did not wish to force this unity, however. He wanted to encourage a spirit of cooperation. In 1958 he joined Egypt and Syria into the United Arab Republic. But the union only lasted for three years, until Syria's new military rulers withdrew.

Nasser's efforts were not the first to unite Arab nations. In 1945 Egypt was one of the founding nations of the Arab League. Members cooperate on military, cultural, and economic matters. Agencies within the League coordinate Arab scientific efforts, tourism, telecommunications, postal rules, and the exchange of agricultural information. The League also provides a common front in publicizing Arab concerns in the Arab-Israeli conflict.

Nasser was a charismatic leader with great popular appeal. After his death in 1970, pan-Arabism lost momentum. Nasser's successor, Anwar Sadat, preferred to concentrate on Egypt's internal problems. He lowered government restrictions on business, and called for a new constitution to guarantee individual rights. He also moved away dramatically from other Arab nations by signing a peace treaty with Israel. In 1981 Sadat was murdered by extremist Muslim soldiers. He was succeeded by Hosni Mubarak (moo-BAHR-ahk), who promised to continue Sadat's policies.

Saudi Arabia's Religious Nationalism

By the 1500s the Ottoman Turks had conquered parts of the western Arabian Peninsula. The rest of the peninsula was occupied by various people who were bound together by kinship ties. In the 1700s Abd-al-Wahhab (ahb-dool-wah-HAHB) began a reform movement within some of these groups. He felt that Islam had been corrupted. He wanted to enforce Muhammad's teachings that gambling, drinking wine, smoking, wearing luxurious dress, and using tombstones were wrong. He also wanted Muslims to follow strictly the teachings of the Koran with regard to prayers, fasting, and the pilgrimage to Mecca.

Eventually Abd-al-Wahhab made an alliance with the Saud (sah-OOD) family of central Arabia. By 1926 the Saud family under King ibn Saud had expanded its control to the present boundaries of Saudi Arabia. In 1932 Saudi Arabia became the official name of the country. Mecca became the religious capital. Riyadh (ree-YAHD) became the political capital.

Ibn Saud died in 1953. He was succeeded by his son Saud, who was replaced by his brother Faisal (FY-zal) in 1964. Faisal began a program of gradual social and economic reform. One of his first acts was to abolish slavery. Some of the profits from the sale of the country's vast oil resources were spent for free medical services and free schools. Faisal ruled until his assassination in 1975. A family council selected his brother Khalid as successor. When Khalid died in 1982, he was succeeded by his half-brother Fahd.

Religion is the heart of Saudi Arabian life. The law of Islam is the only law. The first pillar of Islam appears on the nation's flag. Most national holidays are religious holidays. The people want better health care, transportation and communication systems, and education. But always these improvements must be kept within the framework of Islamic tradition.

Saudi Arabian nationalism is built on Islamic traditions. How does this differ from Egyptian nationalism? King Faisal (above) used profits from oil to move the technology and industry of his country into the twentieth century while keeping Islam strong.

Other Nations

Nasser's triumph in Egypt influenced the nationalist movement in Algeria. Both Morocco and Tunisia obtained independence from France peacefully in 1956. But the situation in Algeria was different. About one out of nine inhabitants was descended from French colonists. To them, Algeria was home. When Algerian Muslims demanded independence, the European population vowed to resist to the death.

As a result, Algeria's war for independence was a long, bloody struggle that lasted seven years and cost the lives of 1 million people. The conflict even tore apart France's government and brought former French President Charles de Gaulle (duh-GAWL) back to power. He negotiated Algeria's independence, and a majority of the French people agreed. Algeria's European population then fled the country.

Libya, which became independent in 1951, came under the control of Colonel Muammar Qaddafi (kuh-DAHF-ee) in 1969. After taking power Qaddafi used Libya's oil wealth to improve his people's standard of living.

He built irrigation systems, freeways, and harbors. Most Libyans are on the government payroll. Most work is carried on by immigrants from other countries.

Qaddafi also used Libya's vast oil resources as a tool to gain prominence for his country in Middle Eastern and world politics. He strongly opposed Egypt's peace treaty with Israel. In 1980 Libyan troops entered Chad to help Muslims in the northern part of that country who were fighting Christians and **animists** in the south. Libyan terrorists in other countries have carried out attacks against Americans, British, Jews, and others. Hundreds of people have been killed as a result. In 1986 American planes bombed terrorist installations in Libya.

Military leaders have also taken over in Syria, Turkey, and Iraq. In Afghanistan a military coup in 1973 was followed by a leftist coup in 1978. The new government signed a treaty with the Soviet Union. In 1979, when it appeared that the new government was about to fall, the Soviet Union sent thousands of its troops into Afghanistan. This action created strong anti-Soviet feelings among the Afghans. Afghan guerrillas began a war against the Soviets. To escape the guerrilla fighting, over 2.5 million Afghans fled to Pakistan. In 1989 the Soviet Union withdrew its troops. But the fighting within Afghanistan continued as various Muslim groups—some in favor of an Islamic republic and others, not—struggled for power among themselves and also against the country's leftist leaders.

Perhaps the country that has had the most difficulty in forging a national identity in recent years is Lebanon. It changed from a mandate to an independent nation in 1942. Since then, it has known mostly war. At one time Christians were the majority. However, since the 1970s Muslims have been in the majority, and they seek a greater role in running the country.

In 1975 a civil war broke out between the two groups. Syrian troops intervened. A cease-fire lasted until 1981, when Lebanese Christians and Syrians began fighting. In 1982 Israel invaded Lebanon to break up Palestinian guerrilla strongholds there. An international peacekeeping force of French, Italian, British, and American troops tried to keep order. But their efforts were hampered by terrorists. The Lebanese president was assassinated. Several hundred of the peacekeeping troops, including more than 250 Americans—mostly Marines—were killed. To complicate matters further, a pro-Iranian Muslim group began fighting against a more moderate Muslim group.

Part of the Saudi Arabian armed forces lines up for inspection. Why do Middle Eastern nations use so much of their budgets for the military?

Why the Military?

Ataturk, Riza Shah, Nasser, and Qaddafi, among others, have all been military men. One reason why military takeovers have been common in the Middle East is that army officers are often better educated then most people in the region and have the organizational abilities to govern. Also, next to religion, the army is the most effective power base in most countries. The middle class is small, and the peasants are not organized.

Then, too, the historical tradition of the region favors military rule. Muhammad, the founder of Islam, was a military leader as well as a political ruler and a religious prophet. The Abbasid dynasty came to power through force. The centuries of centralized Ottoman rule were followed by a colonial period during which the people had no experience in self-government. Under these circumstances, it is not surprising that many Middle Easterners have turned to strong military leaders in times of change.

SECTION 1 REVIEW

1. **Recall**   List ways Ataturk modernized Turkey.
2. **How and Why**   Why do the Saudi Arabians promote religious nationalism?
3. **Critical Thinking**   Compare and contrast the policies of the shahs with the policies of the ayatollahs.

The longest-lasting conflict in the Middle East, and the one that is probably the most difficult to resolve, centers around the Arab-Israeli struggle over possession of the land once known as Palestine.

The Diaspora in A.D. 135 caused many of the Jewish people living in Palestine to be scattered throughout the world. Some Jews did remain, however. Of those who left and their descendants, many believed they could never return until the coming of the Messiah. But some Jews did not want to wait for that indefinite day.

In the 1800s Jews were being persecuted in Russia and its territories in Eastern Europe. Many fled, especially to the United States. Some of the younger ones, however, chose to go to Palestine.

Zionism

During the late 1800s a movement to reestablish Palestine as the Jewish homeland was founded. The movement came to be known as Zionism. Publication of a pamphlet called *The Jewish State* by Theodor Herzl (HERT-suhl) helped the cause of Zionism. An Austrian journalist, Herzl was disturbed by European prejudice against Jews. He was especially influenced by the Dreyfus case.

SECTION

2

Arab-Israeli Conflict

In 1894 Alfred Dreyfus, a Jew and an officer in the French army, was found guilty of treason. He was sentenced to life imprisonment in the penal colony of Devil's Island in the Caribbean. When it was shown that the evidence against him had been forged, he was retried. But **anti-Semitism**, or prejudice and discrimination against Jews, ran so high that he was again found guilty. It took the election several years later of a liberal French government to overturn the verdict.

Herzl believed the solution to such prejudice was a mass exodus of Jews from Europe to a nation of their own. At the time many ethnic groups in Europe and the Middle East were clamoring for independence, whether from the Ottoman Turks, or Austria-Hungary, or Russia. In 1897 Herzl and others held the first Zionist Congress in Basel, Switzerland. There they organized the World Zionist Organization. Its goal was the establishment of a Jewish state.

Further attacks against Jews in Eastern Europe and Russia started the second migration to Palestine in the early 1900s. Among the migrants was David Ben-Gurion (ben-goor-YON). He was a Polish Jew who later became Israel's first prime minister.

During World War I Chaim Weizmann (HIYM VYTS-mahn) won British recognition for Zionism. In 1917, in a paper by Arthur J. Balfour, the British foreign secretary, Britain formally stated that it "viewed with favor the establishment in Palestine of a national home for the Jewish people." This statement is known as the Balfour Declaration.

At the same time the British made vague promises about independence to Arab leaders in what is now Lebanon, Syria, Israel, and Jordan. The Arabs then revolted against the Ottomans and began a guerrilla war against the Turks on the Arabian Peninsula. Leading the Arabs was a British scholar and adventurer named T. E. Lawrence. Later he became known as Lawrence of Arabia.

When World War I ended, both the Jews and the Arabs were disappointed. No independent nations were formed in the area. Instead, as you read earlier, Great Britain and France created mandates over the states that were carved out of the former Ottoman Empire. Britain was given the authority to govern Palestine.

From the 1920s on, many Jews migrated to Palestine. Their numbers increased in the 1930s as Jews from Germany and German-occupied countries in Europe fled to Palestine to escape persecution and murder. The Arabs living in Palestine protested that the land could not hold so many people. The Jewish newcomers would have to be put out—with violence if necessary. On the other hand, the Jews regarded Palestine as their ancient homeland. Their ancestors had been removed from there by force. Both groups were determined to push their claims.

The British offered a proposal to limit Jewish migration. But World War II began before a decision could be made. During the war Jewish organizations smuggled refugees out of war-torn Europe into Palestine.

After the war Britain continued to rule Palestine. To satisfy the Arabs, the British limited the number of Jews who could enter Palestine legally each year. This decision angered the Jews. Many Jews had been left homeless in Europe. Violence increased. Arabs attacked Jews. In spite of

British patrols, Jews continued to be smuggled into Palestine. Finally, in 1947 the issue was submitted to the United Nations. The United Nations is an international organization established after World War II to help maintain peace and security in the world.

Partition

Both Arab and Jewish leaders presented arguments to the United Nations. To the Arabs, Palestine was a land that had been inhabited mostly by Arabs for centuries. They did not want what they regarded as an outpost of Western Europe in their midst. The Jews argued that Palestine had been a Jewish nation until Roman times, and the Arabs already had a dozen nations of their own. The Germans had murdered more than 6 million Jews during World War II, and the Jews needed the protection of a Jewish state. Moreover, Jewish settlers in Palestine had "made the desert bloom" through modern agricultural techniques. They had built cities, set up hospitals that cared for Jew and Arab alike, and greatly improved the standard of living.

The United Nations General Assembly decided that both sides were right. Under the circumstances, "the most realistic and practicable settlement" was the partition of Palestine into three parts: a Jewish state, an Arab state, and the city of Jerusalem. Jerusalem would be administered by an international body. The British were to withdraw in eight months.

In May 1948 the new state of Israel came into being. Chaim Weizmann was the first president. David Ben-Gurion was prime minister.

Israel, 1948

Fighting

Although the Palestinian Jews had agreed to the UN partition plan, the Palestinian Arabs had not. They refused to recognize the new state of Israel. Fighting broke out as soon as the British troops left. Jewish settlements were attacked by Palestinian Arabs supported by troops from six Arab nations. Although the Israelis were outnumbered, they defeated the invading Arabs. In 1949 UN diplomats arranged a cease-fire.

The war settled nothing, however. The Arab countries still refused to recognize Israel's right to exist. They talked about the day when Arab armies would drive the Israelis into the sea. In the meantime an Arab state in Palestine was not established. The territory assigned to it by the UN was occupied partly by Israel and partly by Jordan. Egypt moved into the Gaza Strip along the coast.

The war also left an enormous refugee problem. Some 900,000 Palestinian Arabs either fled or were expelled from old Palestine. These people lived in other Arab countries in squalid camps amid great hardships. Arab leaders felt the refugees had a right to return to Israel. Jewish leaders wanted the refugees to be resettled in Arab countries. Because Arab countries provided little assistance to the refugees, they were supported largely by the UN.

The Suez Canal Crisis

In July 1956, as you know, Nasser nationalized the Suez Canal. He then closed it to Israeli ships. He also accepted arms from the Soviet Union. Fearing an Egyptian move, Israeli armies attacked Egypt in October 1956 and occupied most of the Sinai Peninsula. Great Britain and France, who resented the nationalization of the canal and also wanted to keep the Soviet Union from gaining influence in the Middle East, entered the war on the side of Israel. They bombed Egyptian bases and landed soldiers in the Suez Canal Zone.

This is a Palestinian refugee camp. The settlement of Arab refugees became a major issue in the Arab-Israeli conflict. Explain both sides of the question.

Again the UN intervened. Another truce was arranged. British, French, and Israeli forces withdrew from Egyptian territory. A UN peacekeeping force was then set up to patrol the border.

The Six-Day War

For the next ten years there was an uneasy peace between Egypt and Israel. Then, in 1967, Nasser took a series of aggressive actions. First he moved Egyptian troops into the Sinai Peninsula and ordered the UN peacekeeping forces stationed there to withdraw. The UN removed its troops. Egypt then signed a defense pact with Jordan, and Jordan's King Hussein placed his army under the command of an Egyptian general. Finally Egypt blockaded the Gulf of Aqaba, thus preventing Israeli ships from entering the Red Sea.

Israel found itself in a dangerous position. The Israeli cabinet voted to go to war. The fighting began in June 1967. Within six days the Israelis had overrun the Sinai Peninsula and occupied the east bank of the Suez Canal. They took Old Jerusalem and the West Bank of the Jordan River. They also occupied the neighboring Golan Heights of Syria. The extent of Soviet aid to the Arabs was revealed when the Israelis captured or destroyed huge quantities of Soviet military equipment. During the Six-Day War the United States supported Israel. Arab nations retaliated by cutting diplomatic relations.

■ Israel, 1967

The Yom Kippur War

The results of the Six-Day War were as inconclusive as the results of earlier conflicts. Israel was not willing to return the territory it had occupied until Arab nations recognized its right to exist. Arab leaders wanted all Palestinian refugees resettled in Israel before entering into peace talks. In the meantime the Soviet Union kept supplying Egypt and Syria with military aid and the United States kept supplying Israel with military aid.

In October 1973, on Yom Kippur—the Day of Atonement and the holiest day in the Jewish calendar—Egypt and Syria launched surprise attacks against Israel. At first the two Arab nations were successful. Then the tide turned, and Israeli troops pushed back Egyptian and Syrian forces. Once again the UN arranged a truce.

The Camp David Accords

In 1977 a major break in the Arab-Israel conflict took place. Israeli Prime Minister Menachem Begin (BAY-gihn) invited Egypt's new leader, President Sadat, to visit Jerusalem and address Israel's parliament. The visit was watched on television by millions of people around the world.

The following year the two leaders met again, this time in the United States, at the presidential retreat of Camp David, Maryland. With the

In 1977 Anwar Sadat risked the anger of Arab leaders by going to Jerusalem and meeting with Menachim Begin. This meeting led the way for the Camp David Peace Accords in 1978.

encouragement of President Jimmy Carter, Begin and Sadat reached an agreement for which they were jointly awarded the Nobel Peace Prize. In 1979 they signed a formal peace treaty. Israel returned the Sinai Peninsula to Egypt. Egypt recognized Israel's legal existence and promised to demilitarize, or not station troops in, the Sinai.

The Camp David Accords held advantages for both countries. The largest Arab state was removed as a military threat to Israel. Egypt got back the Sinai oil fields, and the government was able to devote more resources to raising the people's standard of living instead of supporting the army. But although Israel's relations with Egypt improved, relations with other Arab states remained hostile. Much of the Arab opposition to Israel came from the Palestine Liberation Organization (PLO).

The PLO

The PLO is a coalition of several groups of Palestinian guerrillas. Their current leader is Yasir Arafat (YAH-sir AHR-uh-faht). Between 1964 and 1971 the PLO was based in Jordan. From there it staged a number of raids into Israel. The PLO also engaged in terrorist activities such as hijacking airplanes. The Israelis responded by attacking Palestinian bases and camps in Jordan.

As the guerrillas grew stronger, they began to pose a threat to King Hussein's power. The Palestinian refugees in Jordan outnumbered the Jordanians. In 1971, after the PLO murdered two of the king's closest associates, Hussein drove them from Jordan.

Many PLO members then went to Lebanon and set up bases in the southern part of the country. They continued raiding Israel. Israel responded by raiding Lebanon. In 1972 PLO members attacked and killed Israeli athletes who were competing at the Olympic Games in Munich. In the late 1970s the PLO began receiving large numbers of Soviet tanks and heavy artillery. They also received help from Syria in the form of troops.

In 1982 Israel moved into southern Lebanon. After bitter fighting PLO members were surrounded in Beirut. With the help of American diplomats, an agreement was reached that called for the evacuation of the PLO to other Arab countries. But the assassination of Lebanon's new president and the massacre of Palestinian refugees by Lebanese militia during the Israeli occupation heightened tension. And although the PLO withdrew from Lebanon, it was not destroyed.

The Intifada

Attention then shifted from Lebanon to the West Bank of the Jordan River. The West Bank, you recall, had been occupied by Israel during the Six-Day War. Thousands of Jewish settlers had moved into the area. Following the Camp David Accords, its Palestinian inhabitants looked forward to the establishment of a Palestinian state. But the Israeli occupation continued without any signs that that might happen.

472

(Continued on page 474.)

HISTORY AND PEOPLE
WOMEN OF PEACE IN ISRAEL

In a region of the world marked with violence and tension between Jews and Palestinians, many Arab and Jewish women of Israel are diligently working for peace. These women have organized more than fifty groups to work for human rights for everyone—an end to discrimination in the workplace, civil rights and liberty for all people, and a peaceful coexistence for Arabs and Jews.

One Arab woman, Dr. Mariam Mar'i, an instructor at the University of Haifa, is co-president of Shutafut ("Partnership"). This is an organization that seeks cooperation between Jews and Palestinians in community work. She also is active in HaGesher ("The Bridge")—the Organization of Jewish and Arab women for Coexistence and Peace.

A Jewish woman, Hanna Knaz, is the chief nurse at Gen Shemu'el kibbutz, a communal settlement, near Tel Aviv. She is an organizer for the Women in Black movement—an activist group striving for an end to hostility in the West Bank and the Gaza Strip. This organization began after several Jewish women visited refugee camps and were appalled by the treatment of Palestinians. The women dress totally in black and stand in nonviolent vigil to make people aware of the hatred that is destroying Israeli society.

The Palestinian women are torn between their allegiance to the Jewish state and their identity as Arabs. The Israeli women are accused of eroding Israeli security by their actions for peace. However, Arab and Israeli women are united in their efforts to gain peace, freedom, and full citizenship for all people regardless of race or sex.

1. Why might you be surprised to learn that Israeli women are leading a peace movement in their nation?

2. Why have the women of Israel organized more than fifty groups?

3. Who is Dr. Mariam Mar'i? What are the goals of the organizations that she works with?

4. Who is Hanna Knaz? Why was the Women in Black Movement organized?

5. What personal conflicts do Arab and Israeli women face in their search for peace?

Israel, 1973

Israel, 1990

In 1987 a traffic collision in the Gaza Strip led to the death of several Palestinians. Immediately rumors spread through the Gaza refugee camps that the collision had not been an accident. According to one rumor, the collision had been engineered by the Israeli security police in revenge for the stabbing of an Israeli the previous week. As is often the case, the incident released long-standing feelings of resentment. Teenagers armed with slingshots and stones began attacking Israeli vehicles. From there the violence escalated. It spread from the Gaza strip to the university towns in the West Bank, and then to the rest of the West Bank. Almost every day, there were clashes between Israeli troops and demonstrating Palestinian youngsters. In addition, Palestinian policemen and tax collectors resigned their jobs and Palestinian businesses stayed open only in the morning as a protest against the Israeli occupation. The movement was called the *intifada*, which means "throwing off."

In 1988 Yasir Arafat more or less acknowledged that Israel had a "right to exist." However, he did not specify what that meant as far as boundaries were concerned. Nor did he renounce military action against Israel. In 1989 Israeli Prime Minister Yitzhak Shamir (shah-MEER) called for local elections in the West Bank. However, the Israeli government said that while it would negotiate with local Palestinians and with Jordan, it would not negotiate with the PLO. As of 1991, the Arab-Israeli conflict remained a major problem in the Middle East.

SECTION 2 REVIEW

1. **Recall**   What are the origins of Zionism?
2. **How and Why**   How did the state of Israel come to be?
3. **Critical Thinking**   Why were the Camp David Accords a major break in the Arab-Israeli conflict?

SECTION

3

Economic Development

Over the centuries the Middle East has been the victim of destructive invasions, careless handling of the environment, changing trade routes, and interfering foreign powers. Today the scarcity of capital keeps many nations from using their resources fully. The exceptions are Israel and the nations with large oil reserves.

Land and Water Management

By overgrazing animals, using poor drainage systems, and overcutting trees, among other actions, Middle Easterners have drastically changed the region's **ecology**—the relationship between living things and the environment. One result has been a decrease in the amount of arable land. Although farmers have been able to increase harvests by using new strains of seeds, most countries must still import food.

The most urgent problem facing Middle Eastern farmers is a scarcity of water. In recent years several governments have undertaken major irrigation projects. For example, Turkey has built a dozen dams, including one on the Euphrates. In addition to water for irrigation, these dams provide flood control, hydroelectric power, and fishing areas.

In making changes that affect the environment, people may solve one problem only to cause another. For example, the Aswan High Dam created farmland in the Nile River Valley. It had the opposite effect on the Delta. The trade-off is that by cutting the flow of the Nile, the dam has caused salt water from the Mediterranean to back up into the Delta. Also, the fertile deposits of silt that once formed and fertilized the Delta no longer accumulate. As a consequence, Egyptian farmers have to invest scarce capital in chemical fertilizers to maintain the fertility of their fields. In addition, much of Egypt's coastal fishing industry has been ruined.

The scarcity of water has political implications, too. For example, four-fifths of Iraq's water originates outside its borders. In 1975 and again in 1984, Iraq accused Syria of using its dams on the Euphrates to hold back water from Iraq. Jordan has accused Israel of pumping so much fresh water out of Lake Tiberias that the Jordan River has become too salty to use for irrigation. Syria supports an independence movement by Turkey's Kurdish minority because it does not want Turkey to reduce the flow of the Tigris and Euphrates rivers. West Bank Palestinians complain that Jewish settlers are allowed to dig deeper wells than Arabs. It is likely that competition for scarce water resources may become a growing source of tension in the Middle East.

Industrialization

Economic development in much of the Middle East is slow for several reasons. Many nations lack the skilled and semiskilled workers needed to run construction equipment or complicated machines. In order to gain such workers, these countries need technical and vocational schools to train them. In the meantime they use foreign workers, whose pay leaves the culture region instead of being spent locally.

Another problem is a scarcity of raw materials. If a nation imports needed materials, it has to pay for them. This money cannot be used to develop other parts of the economy. The money that is used to import food, for example, cannot be used to build automobile plants.

The factor that most limits economic development is a scarcity of capital. For a country to get the capital needed to expand, it must build up its savings rate. But this is almost impossible to do if the nation is at a subsistence level. The oil-rich nations are luckier because they have been able to sell their oil to build capital.

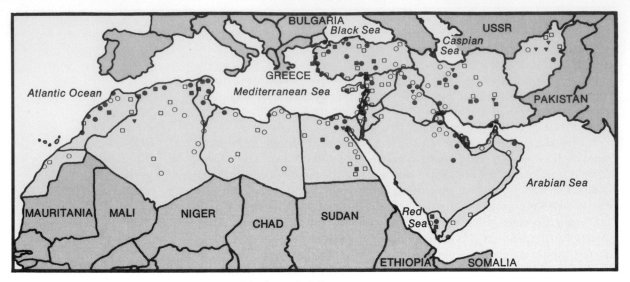

Middle East Natural Resources and Industrial Centers

● Industrial Centers ▼ Coal ■ Iron ○ Oil □ Minerals

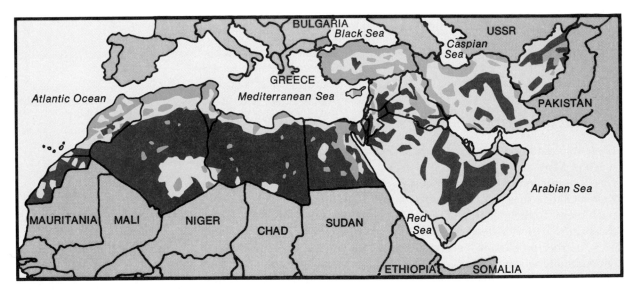

Middle East Land Use

▨ Farming ▢ Grazing ▮ Nonproductive

Impact of Oil

Oil is the one major industry of the Middle East. Saudi Arabia offers an example of the industry's development. Oil was first discovered there in the late 1930s by Standard Oil of California. Until that time Saudi Arabia's economy was based on the export of a few items such as horses, dates, and animal hides. Eventually Standard Oil joined with several other American oil companies to form the Arabian American Oil Company (Aramco). Aramco developed and marketed the oil. Saudi Arabia received a percentage on each barrel sold. Gradually Saudi Arabia began to take control of Aramco. First it was 25 percent. Then, in the early 1970s, it was 60 percent. Finally plans were made for Saudi Arabia to own 100 percent. Aramco then took on a new role. It became a partner with Saudi Arabia in developing and building industries to make use of oil by-products.

In the early 1960s Saudi Arabia, Kuwait, Iraq, and the non-Arab nations of Venezuela and Iran joined to form the Organization of Petroleum Exporting Countries (OPEC). Their goal was to gain a greater financial return for their oil. Later other oil-producing nations joined OPEC. In 1973 OPEC decided to raise prices. The cost of a barrel of oil zoomed from $3 to over $11.

After the Arab-Israeli war of 1973, the Arab members of OPEC imposed an oil embargo. Oil shipments to the United States and the Netherlands were halted for a time because of the pro-Israeli position of these nations.

OPEC continued to raise prices and limit production. In 1981 oil was selling for $36 a barrel. The increase in oil prices worsened the already-existing problem of world inflation. High oil prices caused consumers to turn to smaller cars, energy-efficient appliances, and other sources of

embargo: government order forbidding ships from entering or leaving a port

energy. As a result of lower demand, an oil glut developed. Oil prices fell. By 1983 a barrel of OPEC oil cost $29. In August 1990, Iraq, led by President Saddam Hussein, invaded Kuwait for its oil resources. An international embargo of Iraq's ports caused oil prices to continue to rise.

Israel's Economy

As you read earlier, Israel is now home to immigrants from all over the world. Immigrant Jews are automatically granted citizenship. By the 1990s, over 85 percent of Israel's population was Jewish. The rest was made up of Muslims, Christians, and other minorities. Many of the newcomers have technical skills needed for advancing the nation's economy. Those who arrive illiterate and unskilled are provided with job training and educational programs. New citizens are immediately given courses in Hebrew, the language of Israel.

Israel lacks most raw materials and energy reserves and must import these. Inflation is also a serious problem. In spite of these limitations, Israel has one of the most advanced economies in the Middle East. Diamond cutting, food processing, chemicals, textiles, and fertilizers are important to its trade. In recent years tourism has also become important to the economy.

Grants and loans from other countries and foreign investments are encouraged. Jews living elsewhere in the world have poured large sums of money into Israel. This capital has brought a rapid expansion of Israel's economy. Immigrants have also boosted the nation's economy. They have enlarged the home market for goods and added to the labor force. But

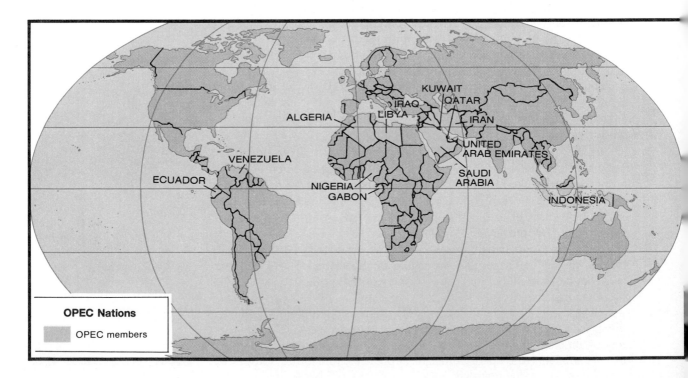

This kibbutz was founded in 1922. Today its income comes from light industry as well as agriculture. What is the difference between light and heavy industry? Why do you think kibbutzim have turned to light industry?

they have also strained the economy. Government expenses for their resettlement have increased as their numbers have grown.

Israel has economic problems too because of its large defense and military needs. A major portion of Israel's budget is devoted to defense. Each time war breaks out, the whole country is mobilized—that is, called into military service. Industry suffers. Israel does not have enough people or money to keep both sectors working at a peak level at the same time. Israel has made its largest gains in agriculture. The Israelis have almost reached their goal of complete food self-sufficiency. Their most serious farming problem is lack of water. Israel has tried to expand its arable land through large irrigation projects. Water resources are strictly controlled and new methods of irrigation are constantly being researched. Israel has introduced some crops new to the region, such as cotton. Its citrus fruits, especially Jaffa oranges and grapefruits, are famous throughout the world.

An unusual element of Israel's agriculture is the **kibbutz**, or collective settlement. Although only about 4 percent of the population live on kibbutzim, these village collectives have played an important role in Israel's development. They began with the early Zionist settlers.

Property is collectively owned on a kibbutz. Decisions are made collectively, and men and women work side by side. No one is paid a wage. Instead, members give their labor and talent in return for food, housing, clothing, and social services. A nursery cares for the children. And people eat together in a common dining room.

Although the kibbutzim were originally agricultural, they have since branched out into light industry, such as assembling television sets and electronic equipment.

Nation/Capital	Population/Area (in sq mi)	Urban Population (as % of total)	Per Capita GNP (in U.S. $)	Adult Literacy Rate (%)	Life Expectancy	Population Growth Rate* (%)
Afghanistan/Kabul	15,862,000/249,999	18	**	12	41	2.6
Algeria/Algiers	25,567,000/919,591	41	2,450	80	59	3.1
Bahrain/Manama	520,000/240	81	6,610	40	67	2.3
Cyprus/Nicosia	702,000/3,572	62	6,260	89	76	1.0
Egypt/Cairo	54,706,000/386,660	45	650	43	60	2.9
Iran/Tehran	55,647,000/636,293	54	**	48	63	3.6
Iraq/Baghdad	18,782,000/167,924	68	**	55	67	3.9
Israel/Tel Aviv	4,586,000/8,019	89	8,650	92	75	1.6
Jordan/Amman	4,123,000/37,737	64	1,500	75	69	3.5
Kuwait/Kuwait	2,143,000/6,880	94	13,680	71	73	2.5
Lebanon/Beirut	3,339,000/4,015	80	**	75	68	2.1
Libya/Tripoli	4,221,000/679,359	76	5,410	50	66	3.1
Morocco/Rabat	25,630,000/172,413	43	750	28	61	2.6
Oman/Muscat	1,468,000/82,030	9	5,070	20	55	3.3
Qatar/Doha	491,000/4,247	88	11,610	70	69	2.3
Saudi Arabia/Riyadh	15,081,000/829,996	73	6,170	52	63	3.4
Syria/Damascus	12,558,000/71,498	50	1,670	55	65	3.8
Tunisia/Tunis	8,124,000/63,170	53	1,230	64	65	2.0
Turkey/Ankara	56,704,000/301,381	53	1,280	80	64	2.1
United Arab Emirates/Abu Dhabi	1,588,000/32,278	81	15,720	68	71	1.9
Yemen Arab Republic/San'a	7,161,000/75,290	20	650	15	49	3.5
Yemen, People's Democratic Republic of/Aden	2,585,000/128,559	40	430	25	52	3.4

Sources: *The 1990 Information Please Almanac* (Houghton Mifflin Company); *1990 World Population Data Sheet* (Population Reference Bureau, Inc., Washington D.C.)
 *A nation with a population growth rate of 2% or more doubles its population within 35 years or less.
**Not available.

Transportation

Roads and highways in the Middle East serve mostly to connect the region's major cities with oil fields and seaports. Elsewhere in the region, the rough terrain makes it difficult and costly to build roads. Privately owned automobiles are common in the large cities. For poorer people, buses are the major means of transport. Bicycles, donkeys, and horses are commonly used in rural areas. Camels are often used for transportation through desert lands.

Because of the difficulty and cost of building across deserts and mountains, railroads are likewise scarce in the Middle East. Those rail lines that have been built usually carry natural resources from the interior to the coastal cities for export.

On the other hand, there are numerous airlines in the region. Most are government owned and operated. Air flights connect the region's major cities with cities in other culture regions. Beirut, Cairo, Istanbul, and Tel Aviv have major airports that provide international connections. The airport at Jidda, Saudi Arabia, is the largest in the world in terms of area. This giant facility spreads across 26,240 acres (10 619 hectares). Each year hundreds of thousands of pilgrims use the Jidda airport as they make their way to Mecca on the Hajj.

Because of the oil industry, the Middle East also contains numerous pipelines. These run from the oil fields to seaports. Oil-producing countries without Mediterranean seaports have built pipelines through nearby countries in order to increase their export capacity to Europe and the United States.

The major international waterway in the Middle East is the Suez Canal. It has no locks because there is little difference between the levels of the Mediterranean and Red seas. In the past the canal was used extensively by oil tankers. Newer tankers, however, are too large to pass through the canal. They go the long way around Africa.

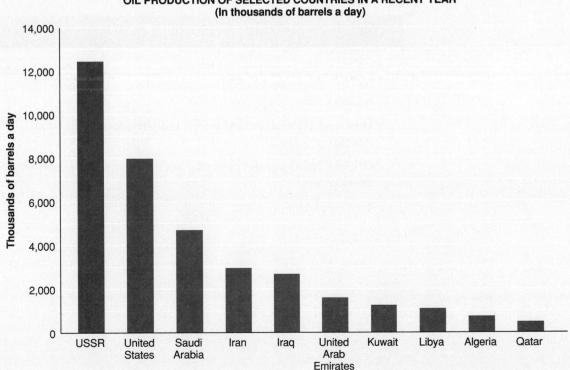

OIL PRODUCTION OF SELECTED COUNTRIES IN A RECENT YEAR
(In thousands of barrels a day)

Source: *The 1990 Information Please Almanac,* copyright © Houghton Mifflin Company, 1989, New York, New York 10003.

Education and Economic Growth

Although the number of students attending elementary and secondary schools and colleges in the Middle East has increased considerably since the 1960s, education still remains one of the region's most critical problems. There are not enough qualified teachers. In addition, Islam has traditionally stressed learning by memorizing—especially memorizing the Koran. Muslims are taught the Koran by hearing it read. Thus it has not been necessary to learn to read. In addition, many young people still must quit school to work. Some students do not want to take certain subjects, such as the sciences. But these subjects are needed to create a modern society.

The absence of skilled and educated people continues to hold back economic growth. It also tends to create rule by a few. The few are not the wealthy so much as the educated. Except for those countries with monarchies, where family and wealth are important, education is the key to social mobility.

The Israelis are very aware of the importance of education to economic growth. Also, the Jews have an ancient tradition of education. School in Israel is free and compulsory for all children between the ages of 5 and 16. Israel has several universities. Emphasis is placed on scientific research. A major research center is the Weizmann Institute.

SECTION 3 REVIEW

1. **Recall** Give two examples of Middle Easterners' water management.

2. **How and Why** How did the oil industry develop in Saudi Arabia?

3. **Critical Thinking** Why is education important to economic development?

Reviewing People, Places, and Things

Identify, define, or explain each of the following:

Mohammed Riza Pahlevi

Ruhollah Khomeini

Gamal Abdel Nasser

pan-Arabism

Arab League

Anwar Sadat

Saud family

Zionism

Theodor Herzl

anti-Semitism

David Ben-Gurion

Menachem Begin

PLO

Yasir Arafat

ecology

OPEC

kibbutz

Map Study

Using the maps on page 476, determine the answers to the following questions:

1. Where are most of the industrial resources of North Africa found?

2. How is most of the land on the Arabian Peninsula used?

3. In what part of the Middle East is most of the nonproductive land found?

Understanding Facts and Ideas

1. Why did Middle Easterners' identification with Islam cause their movements toward nationalism to be delayed?

2. **a.** Describe in a paragraph Ataturk's four principles. **b.** How did Ataturk influence Riza Shah's steps toward nationalism?

3. What is Islam's strength in Saudi Arabia?

4. Why was the nationalist movement slower in North Africa than elsewhere in the Middle East?

5. **a.** List two reasons why most Middle Easterners lack the political knowledge to deal with independence. **b.** Why have they turned to strong military leaders in times of change?

6. **a.** What is the basis for the Arab-Israeli conflict? **b.** How did the British attempt to satisfy Arab demands that Palestine was Arab?

7. **a.** Why was the question of Palestine put to the UN? **b.** What was the reaction of the Arabs to partition?

8. What were the Camp David Accords?

9. Why is capital important to the economic development of a nation? List three ways Middle Easterners are working to solve their water crisis.

10. **a.** Where is most of the Middle East's oil located? **b.** How has oil been used as a weapon? **c.** How have high oil prices affected consumers?

Developing Critical Thinking

Debating an Issue   Debate: OPEC does have/does not have the right to charge as high a price as possible for its oil.

Writing About History

Doing Research   Saudi Arabian nationalism is based almost entirely on religion. Research and write a paper on how its nationalism brought modernization without disturbing Islamic traditions.

Applying Your Skills to History

Using a Statistical Table   A table can be used to compare statistics. Use library references to make a table showing the per capita GNP, life expectancy, infant mortality rate, urban population, adult literacy rate, and birth rate for Middle Eastern nations. Study the table to determine if there is a relationship between a nation's GNP and the other categories. Write a paragraph explaining why or why not.

25

In 1947 two shepherd boys found these scrolls—known as the Dead Sea Scrolls—in a cave on the western shore of the Dead Sea in an area of Khirver Qumran. These scrolls, written in Hebrew, are parts of Bible text dated between the second century B.C. and the first century A.D.

Society and Creativity

The late twentieth century has brought many changes to the Middle East. More land is being made available for farming. Industry is creating new kinds of jobs. The nomadic way of life has almost disappeared. Cities are taking on a new look. But the most dramatic changes have been in the status of women.

In the areas of arts and sciences, the Middle East has given much to the world. Muslims and non-Muslims working in Arab-held countries have acted as preservers, adaptors, and creators. They have preserved and transmitted the accomplishments of earlier peoples. They have also made great contributions of their own, especially in the areas of science and medicine.

As you study this chapter, think about these questions:

- What factors are bringing about change in the Middle East?
- Why is women's status in the Middle East slow to change?
- How do the arts of Middle Easterners reflect their values?
- What have Middle Easterners contributed to other culture regions?

A bout one-half of Middle Easterners live in cities. The shift in population from rural to urban areas is only one of the many changes taking place in this region. People are living longer, the roles of women are changing, and family patterns are changing, too.

Nomads

Nomads represent less than 5 percent of the Arab people of the Middle East. Nomads own little except their animals, tents, and a few personal items. They exchange wool, milk, meat, or their services as herders to villages for such items as grain, fruits and vegetables, coffee, utensils, and tools.

Nomadic herding in the Middle East is concentrated in the drier areas of Saudi Arabia and the Sahara. It is also practiced in the mountain and plateau lands of Afghanistan, Iran, Iraq, and Turkey. In these nations nomads practice a form of herding called **transhumance**. They graze their animals in mountain lands during the summer months. In the winter they move their flocks down to the valleys, where some grass and water is available.

Although nomads no longer make up a majority of the population, some of their culture traits are still found among Arabs. One such culture trait is hospitality to guests. Nomads spend most of their time getting food for themselves and their animals. They never know when they might find themselves needing shelter in someone else's tent. Accordingly, they offer it willingly to others.

Village Life

Most of the Middle Easterners who live in rural areas are farmers. They live in villages, surrounded by their fields. A few nonfarming villagers, such as shopkeepers, provide services for the rest of the people.

Villagers do not have an easy life. There are few modern conveniences. Most people live in small one- or two-room houses made of mud or sun-dried bricks. The houses often have dirt floors and usually are windowless. The people have little furniture. The family may sleep on mats. Women cook outside in a community oven. Since most villages have no electricity, villagers use oil lamps for light. Usually there is no running water or indoor plumbing. Water must be carried from wells.

The diet of villagers consists mainly of grains. Millet is usually eaten as a cooked cereal. Wheat and barley are baked into bread. Rice is boiled. Locally grown fruits and vegetables are also important to the diet. Goats and sheep may be slaughtered for special occasions. Muslims are forbidden to eat pork. In general, Middle Eastern villagers seldom eat meat. Coffee and tea are popular drinks.

City Life

The Middle East has a long history of urban life. Some of the great cities dating from ancient times are located there: Alexandria, Baghdad, Damascus, Cairo, Istanbul, and Jerusalem. Traditionally the city has served as the center of political and economic activity. The rich and the powerful have always lived in cities.

The general pattern of many Middle Eastern cities today is an old Arab city next to a modern one. The old cities were built around a fortress and the major mosque. These were surrounded by covered bazaars or marketplaces such as the Casbah in Algiers, the Grand Bazaar in Istanbul, or Mushi in Cairo. Sellers on the narrow, crowded streets of the bazaars are usually grouped by occupation—leather workers are on one street, goldsmiths on another, and so on. The Middle Eastern custom of bargaining for goods is still practiced in these places. Surrounding the bazaars are food markets, public baths, and private homes. The old cities are usually enclosed by high walls with several gates.

The new cities look like cities of the Western world. The architecture is international in style. There is a central business and shopping district. Residential areas surround it. On the outskirts of the city are slums.

In recent years Middle Eastern cities have experienced an extremely rapid growth. People seeking better jobs or educational opportunities come to urban areas in large numbers. This often creates problems: housing shortages, overcrowding in the schools, strains on the transportation systems, and lowered health standards. The new arrivals expect the cities to provide jobs, education, water, housing, and health services. Most often the cities do not have the funds for these services.

In some instances people have not left their villages, yet find themselves living in an urban setting. In a short time oil prosperity has

Rush hour in some Middle Eastern cities might remind you of the United States. But outside the cities, such as Riyadh, shown here, there are few cars and few roads.

changed some villages of the Persian Gulf region into urban areas complete with high-rises and paved highways. The newly created oil cities are not faced with the problems of other Middle Eastern urban areas. They have the money to cope with rapid urbanization. Services such as schools, housing, and health care are available because of the wealth brought by the oil boom.

Family Ties

The extended family in the Middle East today is more the ideal than the reality. Poverty is widespread, and managing a large household is impossible for most Middle Easterners. The trend is toward the nuclear family. Beyond the nuclear family, people feel loyalty to a few generations of their family—grandparents and grandchildren.

City-dwellers, especially those who are educated, are more independent of family ties than are villagers or nomads. By moving to the city, members of a kinship group have less contact with one another. In an urban, industrialized environment, more emphasis is placed on a person's achievements than on family background. People are more likely to make their own way without depending on their kinfolk. This independent attitude is beginning to extend to the choice of a mate, a decision traditionally made by the families.

Marriage

Traditionally marriages among Middle Easterners have been arranged by male members of families. The bride leaves her family to live with her husband and his family. Marriages frequently take place between relatives. Often the bride marries the son of her father's brother.

At the time of the marriage, the husband or his family has to provide a sum of money—a bride-price—for the bride. The bride uses it to buy clothing, articles for her home, or items that will insure her future financial security, such as jewelry or livestock.

If a husband divorces his wife, she is allowed to keep the bride-price. However, if she divorces him and he objects to the divorce, he can demand that the amount of the bride-price be returned.

The Koran permits a man to have four wives at one time. But a man who takes more than one wife must be able to support, love, and treat all equally. Because of Islam's strict rules, the majority of Muslim men rarely have more than one wife.

Under Islamic law, divorce is easy for men to obtain. A husband divorces his wife simply by stating three times, ''I divorce you,'' before two witnesses. In recent years many Arab countries have instituted divorce laws. More and more, as women seek social equality, divorces are becoming matters for the courts.

This young woman is a nomad in Iran. She has little chance to obtain an education or to be paid for her work. Why?

Women

The prophet Muhammad did much to improve the lives of women. A woman could not be left without support by her father or her husband. Islamic law requires that she share with male heirs in her father's property. As mentioned earlier, at the time of her marriage, a woman is provided with a bride-price to guarantee her financial independence.

Veiling One of the distinctive culture traits of the Middle East is the veiling of women. Scholars disagree as to how veiling came about. Some believe it is a pre-Islamic custom that was adopted through cultural diffusion. In ancient Assyria veils were worn only by respectable married women. Single women and women who ran taverns were not supposed to cover their faces. The Persians adopted the practice, and when the Arabs conquered the Persians, they adopted it, too. Other scholars feel that veiling is part of the Muslim religion. The Koran suggests that veiling helps preserve the "modesty" of women. Conservative Muslims like the followers of Ab-dal-Wahhab in Saudi Arabia believe that a woman who shows her face dishonors both her family and her religion.

Veiling customs have varied. Muslim women in cities and towns were more likely to cover their faces than were Bedouin or Berber women. Some veils were light and transparent; others were thick.

Veiling was often combined with segregation by sex. Men and women occupied separate living quarters within a home. If the family had only a one-room hut or a tent, the men would go to a village meeting place at night while the women stayed at home. Women seldom went to a mosque to pray. The mosque was considered a meeting place for men rather than a holy place of worship.

As with veiling, segregation by sex varied. Within a nomadic kinship group, for example, men and women were generally not segregated at all. Everyone in the kinship was considered to be part of the same tightly knit family, without any distinctions.

Changing Patterns   During the 1800s and early 1900s the British, French, and other Western Europeans came to dominate much of the Middle East. They criticized the way Arab women were treated. These Westerners claimed the women were given little respect and no social equality. Muslims who visited Western Europe began to speak out about the treatment of Arab women too. By the 1920s a few women were appearing in city streets without their veils.

The issue of veiling has often had political overtones. Both Kemal Ataturk and Riza Shah issued laws requiring women to be unveiled as part of their program of modernization. In 1923 an Egyptian woman named Huda Sharawi made history in that country by throwing her veil into the Mediterranean, thus becoming the first woman to be unveiled. Her husband promptly divorced her. The next year she became the leader of the Egyptian Feminist Union, which worked for nationalism, education for women, and the outlawing of the veil. In the 1950s the French in Algeria used the issue to discredit nationalists who were trying to drive them out. The French claimed the nationalists would compel women to veil themselves again. The Ayatollah Khomeini ordered women to wear the veil when he established an Islamic republic in Iran.

Some Middle Eastern women see veiling as an advantage. It symbolizes the fact that they are protected. They can go out without worrying about dressing in a particular manner. They can walk city streets without being subjected to whistles and comments. Other women feel the veil is not only old-fashioned, but it also prevents them from achieving equality.

Women's Suffrage   The first Middle Eastern nation to give women the right to vote was Turkey, which did so in 1934. Israel has had women's suffrage since it was established in 1948. As of the early 1990s, women are able to vote in Iran and in all major Arab countries except Jordan, Kuwait, and Saudi Arabia.

These women are students at the University of Algiers. Why are their opportunities greater than those of a nomad woman? What cultural differences explain this?

Israel   The status of women in Israel is very different from that of women in most Muslim nations. Israeli women work alongside men in fields and factories. Their equality is guaranteed by law. Generally, however, women receive less pay than men.

Women serve with men in the armed forces, although no longer in combat. As in most Western countries, fewer women than men become doctors and lawyers. And few women hold government positions. One notable exception is the former prime minister of Israel, Golda Meir (me-IHR). She held that office from 1969 until her defeat in the elections of 1974.

SECTION 1 REVIEW

1. **Recall**   What social changes are taking place in the Middle East today?

2. **How and Why**   Why are city-dwellers more independent of family ties than are villagers?

3. **Critical Thinking**   Why do you think the position of women in most Middle Eastern nations has been slow to change?

SECTION

2

Creativity

Through conquest, the Muslims extended their influence from Spain to India. In these diverse areas the Muslims took what interested them from the arts and sciences of the various cultures. They blended these with their own ideas and developed a composite style that we call Islamic.

Early Islamic Arts

The Islamic style developed over several centuries. We can see how the blending of styles occurred by examining Muslim architecture.

Architecture   Muslim buildings throughout the empire were usually built by the conquered people. Thus the materials, size of the structures, degree of ornamentation, and features such as domes vary from place to place. These characteristics depend on the skill of the peoples who built them and the materials available.

The major Muslim buildings are mosques, tombs, fortresses, and palaces. The most common is the mosque. On the wall that faces Mecca is

490

the mihrab, or prayer niche. It is a central point of worship much like an altar in a Christian church. Outside the mosque is a tower called a minaret. Some mosques have several such towers. The minaret may be part of the mosque or a separate structure. Five times a day a man climbs the steps of the minaret to call faithful Muslims to prayer. In the past, muezzins were often blind. This provided employment for blind men. It also protected people's privacy, because a blind muezzin could not see into a private courtyard.

Early mosques were simply wooden structures without the mihrab or minaret. They were designed to resemble Muhammad's house in Medina, with a walled courtyard and a hall for prayer. But as Muslim power and wealth grew and spread, the buildings became more elaborate. First the mihrab was added. Later the minaret, which originated in Egypt, was included. Eventually domes became a part of the design. Domes were copied from the Byzantines. Stone, brick, or marble replaced wood. Ornately carved stone columns replaced wooden pillars. Often these columns had been taken from Roman or Byzantine buildings or ruins.

Among the most famous mosques are those at Cordova, Spain, and Damascus, Syria. Today the Cordova mosque is a Christian church. In Istanbul, however, this process was reversed. The Byzantine church of Hagia Sophia (HAH-yah suh-FEE-uh) became a mosque in the 1400s. It is presently a museum.

Orthodox Islam does not allow the pictures of any creatures—human or animal—to be used in architecture or art. Early Muslim leaders feared the people would return to the practice of worshiping statues. Instead, artists were encouraged to decorate buildings and art objects with geometric and floral patterns. Often Arabic script was used. The writing usually was a passage from the Koran. The ban on living figures in art was not strictly followed, however. For example, carved marble lions were used as part of a fountain in the courtyard of the Alhambra, a Moorish fortress in Spain.

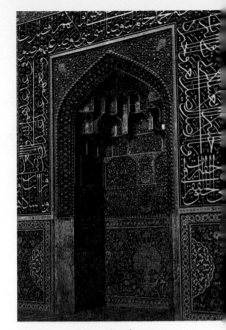

This is an example of a mihrab or prayer niche in a mosque.

Other Visual Arts   Islamic creativity was not limited to buildings. Muslims made colorful silks and tapestries. Their painted pottery, leather goods, and objects of brass, copper, ivory, gold, and silver were in demand as trade goods. Steel swords made in Damascus, Syria, and Toledo, Spain, were also valuable trade items. Linens woven in Damascus were of such fine quality that they took the name of that city—damask.

The Persians were not as strict as other Muslims about not using creatures in their art. They painted miniatures of people and landscapes that included animals. The peak of Persian miniature art was reached in the 1400s. This form had great impact on the art of India.

Literature   Early Islamic literature was mostly poetry. Poets writing in the Arabic language composed verses on many subjects and for every occasion. They also enjoyed compiling folk tales and hearing them read aloud.

An early work that is well known to Western readers is the *Thousand and One Nights*, sometimes called *Arabian Nights Entertainments*. These 200 tales were taken from many peoples—Persians, Indians, Arabs, and others. The collection was first put together in Arabic translations, probably during the 900s. Among the more popular stories are "Ali Baba and the Forty Thieves," "The Magic Carpet," "Sinbad the Sailor," and "Aladdin and the Magic Lamp."

Although considered fiction, the stories give us a picture of life in Baghdad during Abbasid rule. One of the important characters is Harun al-Raschid (hah-ROON al-RASH-id), a real caliph of the Abbasid dynasty, who ruled in the late 700s. The stories about Sinbad the Sailor are likewise apparently based on real life. They have been interpreted as being exaggerated accounts of Arab trading voyages in the Indian Ocean. For example, one story has Sinbad landing on what appears to be an island but is really a whale. When Sinbad builds a fire, the whale dives below the surface of the ocean—just the way a volcanic island sinks into the sea. In another story a bird called a roc carries Sinbad across a mountain range and drops him in a valley covered with diamonds. Arab traders had secret business arrangements with Indian princes that enabled them to obtain diamonds and other precious gems.

Early Islamic literature was in Arabic. But by the 900s, Persians began using their own language to express their ideas. They used Arabic script and many Arabic words, however. Omar Khayyam, author of the *Rubaiyat*, is one of the most famous Persian writers. His descriptions of love and nature were translated into English in the nineteenth century and became popular throughout the Western world. Also famous is the Persian poet Firdausi (fir-DOO-see). He is the author of *Shah Namah (Chronicle of the Kings)*, the national epic of Iran. In the poem's 40,000 lines, mythological heroes and historical figures show the rise of the Persians and their triumph against evil. Portions of the epic are still memorized by Iranians today and recited in private homes and coffee-houses. Still another well-known Persian poet is Saadi, who wrote the *Bustan (Fruit Garden)* and the *Gulistan (Rose Garden)*. His works have great humor and wisdom.

History   The most important historian of the Islamic Empire was Ibn Khaldun (IB-in kahl-DOON). In addition to writing an exciting account of the empire, he developed a theory of history to explain why empires rise and fall.

In Ibn Khaldun's opinion, an empire's rulers became soft and selfish after several generations. Instead of taking a personal interest in government, they relied on laws and bureaucrats. Instead of maintaining their military skills, they surrounded their cities with walls for protection and devoted themselves to luxurious living. The result was that another, stronger group of people would come along and conquer them.

Music   Islamic prayer services do not contain music because Muhammad objected to it. In everyday life, however, Muslims enjoyed singing. They developed a high-pitched, nasal style that is still popular today.

Beginning in the seventh century, singers accompanied themselves on musical instruments. The earliest was the tambourine. Later singers added drums, flutes, harps, lutes, cymbals, guitars, and castanets. Some musical styles spread through cultural diffusion from Spain to Latin America and from there to North America.

Early Science and Technology

During the rule of the Abbasids, the capital of Baghdad was a dazzling city. Many artists, poets, and musicians went there. It was a time of great creative expression. It was also a time of intellectual development.

Muslim and Jewish astronomers understood that the earth rotates on its axis and revolves around the sun. Omar Khayyam was commissioned by the sultan to revise the solar calendar. He devised one that was more accurate than the Gregorian calendar used today in the Western world. Navigators made improvements on the astrolabe, an earlier Greek invention used for observing the position of stars. By the 1100s the geographer al-Idrisi had mapped the lands from Spain to Indonesia with great detail and accuracy.

Of all the sciences, medicine was the one in which the greatest contributions were made. Most Islamic doctors were Arabic-speaking Persians. They were able to diagnose stomach cancer. They knew antidotes for poison as well as ways to stop bleeding and infection. They established hospitals, clinics, pharmacies, and medical libraries throughout the Islamic Empire. Medical students learned through study and practical experience. When they had completed their training to the

The astrolabe is a navigational instrument that originally came from the ancient Greeks. Middle Easterners improved it, and it was their instrument that Western Europeans used on their voyages around the world in the 1500s.

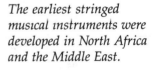

The earliest stringed musical instruments were developed in North Africa and the Middle East.

satisfaction of their teachers, they took special tests. If they passed, they received a license to practice on their own.

Razi (RAY-zee), known in Western Europe by his Latin name of *Rhazes* (RAY-zeez), was the first to diagnose smallpox and distinguish it from measles. He wrote over 100 books on medicine. One of his works was an encyclopedia containing medical information from Greek, Persian, and Hindu sources as well as his own experience. The encyclopedia was later translated into Latin and helped shape medicine in Western Europe.

Ibn Sina, called Avicenna (av-ih-SEN-uh) in Latin, knew that diseases could be spread by dirt or contaminated water. Around the year 1000 he wrote the *Canon of Medicine* on the treatment of diseases. From the 1100s to the 1600s, the *Canon* was the most widely used medical textbook in Western Europe. Even today this book is still used in some parts of Asia. Avicenna also wrote some 170 works on physics, mathematics, astronomy, and religion.

Baghdad and other Islamic cities attracted scholars from as far away as China. Such Chinese inventions as paper, printing, and the compass were first known in the West through Arabs. The system of numbers known as Arabic was likewise passed along to the Western world by way of the Middle East. The system began among the Hindus during the Gupta dynasty. Khwarizmi (KWAH-riz-mee), a Persian mathematician who lived in the 800s, made use of the numbers when he compiled a textbook on algebra. The book was translated into Latin in the 1100s and introduced algebra into Western Europe. Khwarizmi and other Persian mathematicians also transmitted the decimal system and the concept of zero, which originated in India, to the Western world.

Islamic Arts Today

Modern Islamic creativity is a mixture of religious tradition and folk art. Over the centuries people have expressed themselves most often through literature and handcrafts. These forms are encouraged today because they are so much a part of the people's cultural heritages.

One of the most beautiful examples of Middle Eastern art is the Persian rug. Not all rugs of this type are made in Persia (Iran) today, but the name remains. Compare this to the use of the word china *for porcelain. This rug was woven in Turkey in the 1500s.*

Literature   In recent times the Middle East has produced some excellent poets. The one probably best known to Western readers is Kahlil Gibran of Lebanon. He wrote *The Prophet*, a collection of mystical prose poems dealing with freedom, love, and death. An accomplished painter, Gibran also illustrated his writings.

Today writers in many parts of the culture region deal with the problems of change in a traditional society. Much of the modern literature also has nationalistic themes. The outstanding contemporary novelist is Egyptian Naguib Mahfouz, who won the Nobel Prize for literature in 1988.

Visual Arts Handcrafted objects remain an important part of Middle Eastern creativity. Iranians, especially, are famous for their beautifully designed carpets. These are made mostly of wool, with the addition of some cotton or silk. They are either woven or, more commonly, knotted. The Persians began making carpets when they were nomadic cattle herders. Carpets were practical, for they could be rolled up and slung over a donkey's back whenever the Persians moved from one pasture to another. When the Persians settled on the brown plateau of Iran, they made carpets that resembled gardens, as a contrast to their surroundings. Persian carpets are of such fine quality that they are often hung on walls.

The artistry of Middle Eastern craftworkers is also evident in articles of gold, silver, and brass, particularly jewelry. The region is also well known for colorful pottery, glassware, and ceramics. Other crafts include embroidery and, particularly in North Africa, leather work.

Music Singing, dancing, and instrumental music are very much a part of Middle Eastern Muslim life. As with other peoples, music expresses emotion and is a form of entertainment. Traditional ballads and hudas—songs of camel drivers—are still very popular. In Egypt folk singers and musicians travel throughout the countryside singing old melodies and playing such stringed instruments as the lute, zither, and kanoun. Folk dances are very popular.

Middle Eastern music may sound strange to Western ears because the musical scale is different. Arabic music uses many more notes within the range of a Western octave. Recently some efforts have been made to develop a musical style more like that of Europe.

Traditional music is still an important part of Middle Eastern Arab culture. Musicians, such as those above, travel through the countryside singing, dancing, and playing the old music.

Israeli Arts

In literature Israel has produced a Nobel Prize winner: novelist Shmuel Yosef Agnon. Aharon Appelfeld's novels deal with the murder of 6 million Jews by Nazi Germany during World War II. The novels of Amos Oz are more concerned with modern life and its problems. Among the leading poets is Yehuda Amichai.

A number of Israeli artists have turned to their Jewish past for inspiration. Marc Chagall, a Russian Jew and member of the Paris school of Jewish painters, has been very influential in depicting Jewish folklore. Younger Israeli artists often utilize abstract forms. For example, Joseph Zaritsky's abstract paintings make powerful use of color. Yitzhak Danziger's sculptures are large-scale abstract works of great originality and vigor. Another form of contemporary art is kinetic painting, which changes in appearance as the viewer moves. Among the leading kinetic painters is Agam.

Music and dance are important in Israel. The country supports several symphony orchestras, including the Israel Philharmonic. Dance companies include the Batsheva and the Inbal group, which specializes in the athletic folk dances of Yemenite Jewry.

This is a model for a stained-glass window that Marc Chagall designed for the Hadassah-Hebrew University Medical Center in Jerusalem. In all he designed 12 windows for the center. Each honors one of the Twelve Tribes of Israel.

The National Theater of Israel is the *Habimah*, meaning "the stage." It was founded in 1917 in Moscow by Nahum David Zemach (TSEH-mahk), who believed that Zionism as a political movement should be reflected in the arts. Actors had to learn Hebrew in order to perform.

As the Israelis seek to trace their past, archaeology has become a major national pastime. Ancient sites that have been reconstructed include Caesarea, where mosaics from a synagogue dating back to the 500s B.C. were discovered by a farmer plowing his fields. Construction of a post office at Akko led to the uncovering of a Greek shrine from the second century B.C. The most impressive feat of archaeological research has been the excavation of the fortress of Masada. By following information in the Bible, archaeologist Nelson Glueck found the ruins of King Solomon's copper mines. He also obtained evidence that the desert of the Negev was densely populated between 200 B.C. and A.D. 200. As a result, many of Israel's newer kibbutzim were established there.

SECTION 2 REVIEW

1. **Recall** What contributions did Middle Easterners make to medicine?
2. **How and Why** How did the Islamic style of art develop?
3. **Critical Thinking** How does modern Islamic creativity reflect traditional values?

R E V I E W

Reviewing People, Places, and Things

Identify, define, or explain each of the following:

transhumance   Firdausi

Golda Meir   Saadi

mihrab   al-Idrisi

minaret   Ibn Sina

damask   Khwarizmi

Omar Khayyam   Kahlil Gibran

Map Study

Using the map on page 399, determine the answers to the following questions:

1. What body of water separates Africa from the Arabian Peninsula?
2. What direction is Kabul, Afghanistan, from Riyadh, Saudi Arabia?

Understanding Facts and Ideas

How has the population in the Middle East shifted in recent years?

Describe in a paragraph each the life of: **a.** nomadic people; **b.** village people.

a. What is the general pattern of many Middle Eastern cities? **b.** What problems are the cities facing today? **c.** Why?

a. How did Muhammad improve the lives of women? **b.** What effect did Europeans have on the way Arab women were treated? **c.** How did Khomeini's policies affect Iranian women?

How is the status of women different in Israel than in Muslim nations?

a. Why were human and animal forms not used in most Islamic architecture? **b.** What forms were used instead?

What collection of folk tales of many Middle Eastern peoples is well known throughout the world?

8. Why was Baghdad a center of creativity?
9. What Chinese inventions were introduced to the West through the Arabs?
10. Where did Arabic numbers begin?
11. Why does Middle Eastern music sound strange to Western ears?
12. Why has archaeology become a major national pastime in Israel?

Developing Your Critical Thinking

Analyzing Geography The geographical location of Iran made it an ideal place for the blending of Eastern and Western knowledge. With modern transportation and telecommunications, does the geographical location of a country still play a major part in its development?

Writing About History

Using Primary Sources Read some of the stories in *Thousand and One Nights*. In a brief essay explain whether the stories confirm what you have learned about the Middle East.

Applying Your Skills to History

Using Primary Sources A primary source is any firsthand or eyewitness account of an event. It may be a letter, diary, speech, autobiography, document, song, poem, legend, myth, or folk tale. It may be a painting, cartoon, photograph, or poster. A primary source may also be an artifact such as a coin, building, pottery, or weaving. Almost all the illustrations in this book are primary sources. They were created at the time they are describing, not in a later period.

Activity: Collect illustrations of Middle Eastern art and architecture, including Israeli examples. Add a note to each explaining it.

THE MIDDLE EAST

Reviewing Facts

1. What are the main geographical features of the Middle East?
2. Describe humankind's earliest settlements.
3. What kinds of culture traits spread from group to group among the ancient peoples of Mesopotamia?
4. Describe the religious beliefs of ancient Middle Easterners.
5. What is the importance of Mecca?
6. What words best describe the style of rule by the caliphs?
7. Describe Nasser's three goals.
8. List three problems that Middle Eastern nations must overcome to achieve economic growth.
9. Describe Israel's agricultural kibbutzim.
10. What are some of the problems affecting Middle Eastern cities today?

Understanding Main Ideas

1. How have people used the resources of the Middle East to develop the region?
2. How did government develop in ancient Egypt?
3. Why did divisions occur in the Christian community?
4. How did the Ottoman Turks rise in power?
5. Why did the movement toward nationalism start late in the Middle East?
6. How have Middle Easterners contributed to other culture regions?

Applying Chronology Skills

Study the time line below and answer the questions that follow.

Chronology of Recent Middle Eastern History

1967	Six-Day War breaks out between Israel and Arab nations
1973	Arab members of OPEC impose oil embargo on the United States and the Netherlands
1975	Civil war breaks out between Muslims and Christians in Lebanon
1978	Israel and Egypt sign Camp David Accords
1979	Ayatollah Khomeini establishes Islamic republic in Iran
1980	Iraq launches surprise attack on Iran
1982	Israel invades Lebanon to break up Palestinian guerrilla strongholds
1986	American planes bomb terrorist installations in Libya
1989	Soviet Union withdraws its troops from Afghanistan
1990	Iraq invades Kuwait

1. When did the Soviet Union withdraw its troops from Afghanistan?
2. Did Iraq launch a surprise attack on Iran before or after Ayatollah Khomeini established an Islamic republic in Iran?
3. How many years after the Six-Day War did Israel and Egypt sign the Camp David Accords?

498

UNIT 5 REVIEW

Making Connections

Understanding Geography Using an atlas or encyclopedia map of the average rainfall in the Middle East, compare where the rain falls with the natural regions shown on the map on page 398. Explain in a paragraph the relationship between the amount of rainfall and the types of natural regions—desert, steppe, mountains—in the Middle East.

Understanding the Humanities

Analyzing Islamic Architecture Study the photographs on pages 441 and 491 and write a brief paragraph describing the characteristics of Islamic architecture.

Developing Critical Thinking

Making Predictions What effect do you think modern telecommunications might have on Middle Eastern music in the future?

Using Sources

The excerpts below are taken from the Koran. Read the excerpts carefully, and then answer the questions that follow.

The Creator
Men, bear in mind Allah's goodness towards you. Is there any other creator who provides for you from heaven and earth? There is no god but Him. How then can you turn away from Him?

Alms
Have you thought of him that denies the Last Judgment? It is he who turns away the orphan and does not urge others to feed the poor.

Woe to those who pray but are heedless in their prayer; who make a show of piety and give no alms to the destitute [poor].

1. What is the subject of the first excerpt?
2. According to the second excerpt, what will happen to those who try to appear pious but do not help the poor?

Extension Activity

Making a Time Line Construct a time line showing the different groups of peoples that invaded the Middle East between 900 and 1500. Include the important events that took place during the period of each group's influence.

Read More About History and Culture

Edwards, Holly. *Patterns and Precision: The Arts and Sciences of Islam.* Washington, D.C.: Smithsonian Institution Press, 1982. Islamic civilization.

Fairservis, Walter A., Jr. *Ancient Kingdoms of the Nile.* New York: New American Library. Covers all the ancient kingdoms bordering the Nile.

Gilsenan, Michael. *Recognizing Islam: Religion and Society in the Modern Arab World.* New York: Pantheon Books, 1983. Islamic response to Western influences.

Herzog, Chaim. *The Arab-Israeli Wars.* New York: Random House, 1982. War and peace.

Holden, David, and Richard Johns. *The House of Saud: The Rise and Rule of the Most Powerful Dynasty in the Arab World.* New York: Holt, Rinehart & Winston, 1981. Saudi Arabia's ruling dynasty.

Leone, Bruno, ed. *The Middle East: Opposing Viewpoints.* St. Paul, Minn.: Greenhaven Press, 1982. Readings on the issues facing the modern Middle East.

Potok, Chaim. *Wanderings.* New York: Fawcett Crest, 1978. History of the Jewish people.

6

WESTERN EUROPE

The making of
stained-glass windows
began in Western
Europe in the Middle
Ages. These windows
are in the Cathedral of
Saint Gatien in Tours,
France. The church
was built in the 1200s
and is an example of
Gothic architecture.

CHAPTER

26

This bronze horse and chariot and gold disk were made in Denmark around 1000 B.C. Like early Greeks and Romans, Danes believed the sun was driven around the earth.

The Environment

Western Europe lies in the far western section of Eurasia—the land-mass formed by Europe and Asia. Western Europe covers about one-third of Europe. The rest is made up of the nations of Eastern Europe and the Soviet Union, which also extends into Asia. Eastern Europe and the Soviet Union will be presented as a separate region because their development was far different from that of Western Europe.

Although Western Europe is the smallest of the seven culture regions you are studying in this book, it has had the greatest influence on other parts of the world. Western European ideas, technology, and political institutions have made a great difference in the way many people in the world live.

As you study this chapter, think about these questions:

- How has the environment influenced Western Europe's development?

- How is Western Europe divided into natural regions?

- What have archaeologists learned about early cultures in Western Europe?

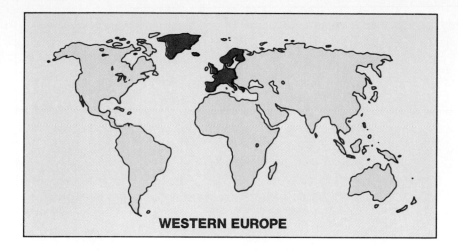

WESTERN EUROPE

The culture region of Western Europe covers about 4 million square miles (10.4 million square kilometers) of land including some large islands to the north and west. The region extends from the Arctic Ocean southward to the Mediterranean Sea. Many peninsulas jut out from Western Europe, and numerous islands fringe its coasts. Therefore, the region has a long coastline despite its relatively small size. Seas and oceans separate a number of areas of Western Europe. Western Europe's geographic position and its many excellent harbors helped it to become a major trade and commercial center.

Peninsulas, Islands, and Seas

The large Scandinavian Peninsula is located in the northernmost part of Western Europe. Norway and Sweden occupy this peninsula. The Scandinavian Peninsula is fringed by the Atlantic Ocean, the Arctic Ocean, the North Sea, and the Baltic Sea. Opposite the Scandinavian Peninsula is the small Jutland Peninsula, which is occupied by Denmark.

Three large peninsulas lie in the southern part of Western Europe. The largest is the Iberian Peninsula, on which Spain and Portugal are located. The Iberian Peninsula extends into the Mediterranean Sea and the Atlantic Ocean. A narrow strait—the Strait of Gibraltar—separates the Iberian Peninsula from the northern part of Africa. Italy is located on the boot-shaped Italian Peninsula, which extends into the Mediterranean Sea. The Balkan Peninsula, which is occupied by Greece, also juts out into the Mediterranean Sea.

Iceland and Greenland are large islands in the northern part of the Western European culture region. Greenland, which mostly lies above the Arctic Circle, is geographically part of North America. However, it is usually treated as part of the Western European culture region because it is governed by Denmark and has historical and cultural ties to Western

(Continued on page 506.)

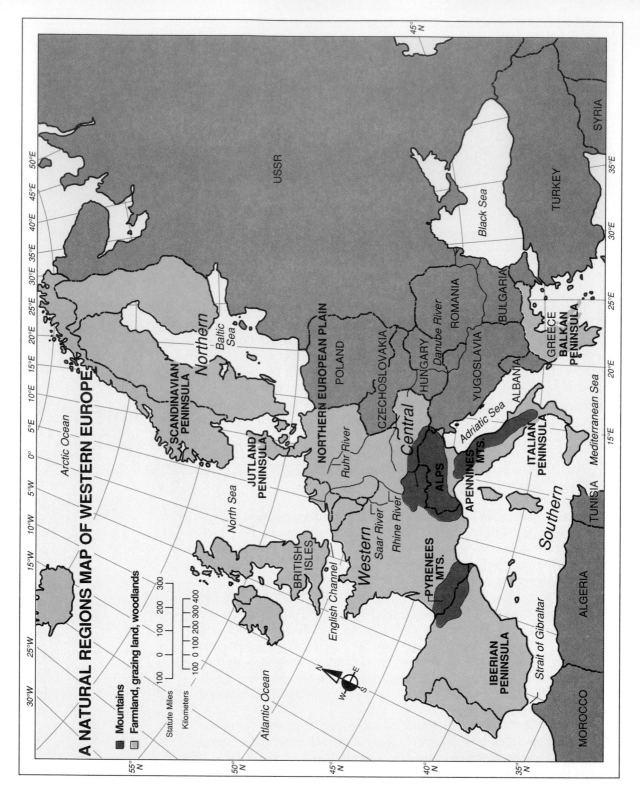

A NATURAL REGIONS MAP OF WESTERN EUROPE

Mountains

Farmland, grazing land, woodlands

Statute Miles
100 0 100 200 300

Kilometers
100 0 100 200 300 400

N
W · E
S

Arctic Ocean

SCANDINAVIAN PENINSULA

Northern

Baltic Sea

USSR

NORTHERN EUROPEAN PLAIN

POLAND

CZECHOSLOVAKIA

Ruhr River

JUTLAND PENINSULA

North Sea

BRITISH ISLES

English Channel

Atlantic Ocean

Western

Saar River

Rhine River

Central

ALPS

PYRENEES MTS.

IBERIAN PENINSULA

Strait of Gibraltar

MOROCCO

ALGERIA

TUNISIA

Southern

APENNINES MTS.

ITALIAN PENINSULA

Adriatic Sea

Mediterranean Sea

HUNGARY

Danube River

ROMANIA

YUGOSLAVIA

BULGARIA

ALBANIA

GREECE

BALKAN PENINSULA

Black Sea

TURKEY

SYRIA

30°W 25°W 20°W 15°W 10°W 5°W 0° 5°E 10°E 15°E 20°E 25°E 30°E 35°E 40°E 45°E 50°E 55°E

35°N 40°N 45°N 50°N 55°N

45°N

35°E 30°E 25°E

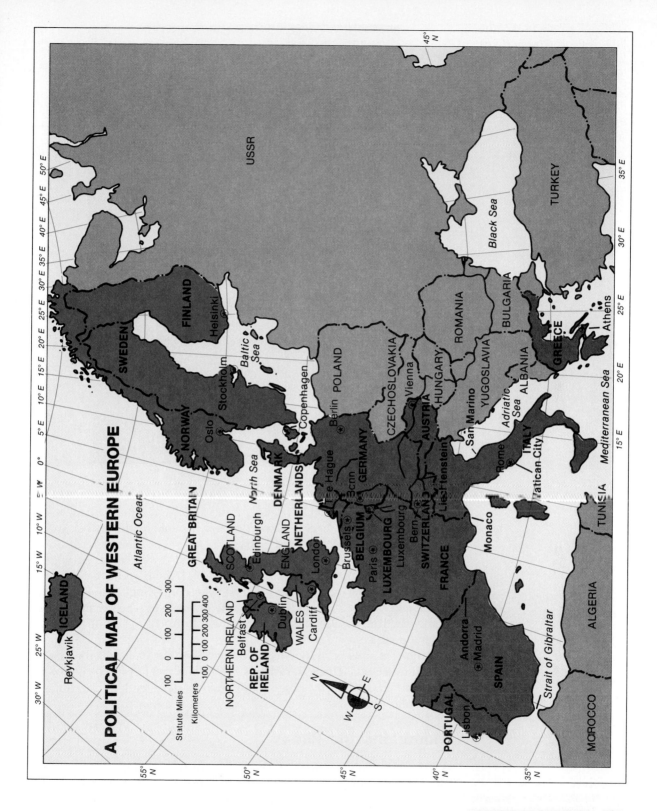

A POLITICAL MAP OF WESTERN EUROPE

ICELAND
Reykjavik

Atlantic Ocean

NORTHERN IRELAND
Belfast

REP. OF IRELAND
Dublin

WALES
Cardiff

GREAT BRITAIN

SCOTLAND
Edinburgh

ENGLAND
London

NORWAY
Oslo

SWEDEN
Stockholm

FINLAND
Helsinki

North Sea

Baltic Sea

DENMARK
Copenhagen

NETHERLANDS
The Hague

Berlin
GERMANY
Bonn

POLAND

CZECHOSLOVAKIA

BELGIUM
Brussels

LUXEMBOURG
Luxembourg

Paris

SWITZERLAND
Bern

Liechtenstein

AUSTRIA
Vienna

HUNGARY

ROMANIA

FRANCE

Monaco

San Marino

ITALY
Rome

Vatican City

YUGOSLAVIA

Adriatic Sea

ALBANIA

BULGARIA

Black Sea

GREECE
Athens

TURKEY

USSR

PORTUGAL
Lisbon

SPAIN
Madrid

Andorra

Strait of Gibraltar

MOROCCO

ALGERIA

TUNISIA

Mediterranean Sea

Statute Miles
100   0   100   200   300
Kilometers
100 0 100 200 300 400

N
W   E
S

30° W   25° W   20° W   15° W   10° W   5° W   0°   5° E   10° E   15° E   20° E   25° E   30° E   35° E   40° E   45° E   50° E

55° N

50° N

45° N

40° N

35° N

45° N

35° E   30° E   25° E   20° E   15° E

Through passes in the Alps like this one, Roman armies came to conquer Switzerland. Today the Alps provide the Swiss with income in winter from tourists who come to ski and in summer from those who come to mountain climb.

Europe. Greenland's 840,000 square miles (2 175 600 square kilometers) make it the world's largest island. Iceland lies just south of the Arctic Circle between Greenland and Norway.

The British Isles lie in the Atlantic Ocean northwest of the European continent. The largest islands in the group are Ireland and Great Britain. Two nations, Ireland and the United Kingdom—England, Scotland, Wales, and Northern Ireland—occupy the British Isles. The North Sea lies east of the British Isles and separates them from the Scandinavian and Jutland peninsulas.

Many islands lie in the Mediterranean Sea. The Balkan Peninsula is skirted by islands. The larger islands of Sardinia and Corsica lie between Italy and France. Sicily lies off the southwestern end of the Italian Peninsula.

Mountains and Plains

A large mountain system stretches across much of Western Europe. This mountain system consists of the Alps and several smaller ranges including the Pyrenees (PIR-uh-NEEZ) and the Apennines (AP-uh-niynz). The

Alps stretch westward through Austria, southern West Germany, northern Italy, Switzerland, and southeastern France. Most of the highest mountains in the Alps are located in Switzerland. The Pyrenees lie on the border between Spain and France, creating a natural barrier between the two nations. The Apennines run lengthwise through the center of the Italian Peninsula.

North of the mountains is the huge Northern European Plain. Within this plain lies most of France, Belgium, the Netherlands, and Denmark, and parts of the United Kingdom, Sweden, Finland, West Germany, and East Germany. The plain borders the seas in most places. It has very fertile soil and contains some of the most productive farmland in the world. It also contains some of Western Europe's major cities, as well as most of its industry.

The absence of natural barriers on the Northern European Plain has had a great effect on Western Europe's history. Invading armies from the Romans to the Nazis have found it easy to march across the plain, and national borders within the culture region have changed with every war.

Rivers, Lakes, and Fjords

The rivers of Western Europe form a vital transportation network. Many of the culture region's cities—such as Rome, Paris, and London—were built on rivers.

The most important river of Western Europe is the Rhine, which flows through the region's industrial heartland. The Rhine connects West Germany's Ruhr industrial basin with the Dutch port of Rotterdam, and has been crucial to West Germany's development. Through a series of canals, the Rhine is connected with the main rivers of France and Belgium. The Rhine carries a greater volume of freight than any other river system in the world. It can be navigated as far as Basel, Switzerland, thus providing that landlocked country with a water access to the Atlantic Ocean. Many industrial centers of Western Europe are situated on tributaries of the Rhine River.

The Danube River, which begins in West Germany's Black Forest, is the longest river on the European continent. A canal in West Germany connects the Danube with the Rhine River. This link makes it possible to ship goods to ports on the North Sea. Other major rivers in Western Europe include the Loire and the Seine in France, the Thames (TEMZ) in Great Britain, and the Po in Italy.

The rivers in the southern European countries are generally unsuitable for navigation and tend to have irregular courses. They also have low water levels during the summer but are flooded during the winter.

The only large lake that lies within Western Europe is Lake Vänern in Sweden, which is 91 miles (146 kilometers) long. There are, however, a large number of lakes in various parts of the region. Finland and Sweden are covered by thousands of lakes. Scotland's highland region has many deep lakes, known as **lochs**. The lochs were created by glaciers. Lake Constance and Lake Geneva are located in Switzerland on a high plateau. Lake Como in northern Italy is known for its natural beauty.

A spectacular natural feature of Western Europe is the coastal scenery of Norway. Its long, narrow bays fringed by steep-walled cliffs called fjords (fee-AWRDZ) have become great tourist attractions. Most of Scandinavia's rivers have so many waterfalls they are difficult to navigate, but they are major sources of hydroelectric power.

Minerals and Other Resources

Western Europe has some important mineral deposits. West Germany, the United Kingdom, France, and Sweden have large deposits of iron ore. Greece is rich in magnesium ore and France in sulfur. West Germany and France have large amounts of potash. Uranium is found in Spain, France, and Sweden. Copper is mined in East Germany. The region also has some deposits of lead, zinc, and bauxite. Other metals, however, are scarce.

West Germany ranks highest in the region and fifth in the world in coal reserves. Major coalfields are also found in the British Isles, the Netherlands, and Belgium. Other energy sources found in the region include oil and natural gas. Western Europe's major oil and natural gas deposits lie beneath the North Sea.

The fast-flowing rivers of Norway, Sweden, and Switzerland are good sources of hydroelectric power. Iceland and Italy generate some of their energy by tapping heat sources produced in the ground by the volcanic activity present in these two nations. Another energy source, used primarily in Ireland, is **peat**—a kind of decayed vegetable matter— which is burned for heat.

The Rhine River flows through several countries. In 1981 France, Switzerland, West Germany, Luxembourg, and the Netherlands agreed to work together to clean up the river. In 1986, however, pollution from a fire in a chemical warehouse caused damage to the Rhine River.

1. **Recall**   What features make up the physical setting of Western Europe?
2. **How and Why**   Why does Western Europe have such a long coastline despite its relatively small size?
3. **Critical Thinking**   How have the natural features of Western Europe affected the region's history?

Western Europe's mountain ranges and other natural features have created four natural regions. These four areas are the western, northern, central, and southern regions.

Western Region   France, Belgium, Luxembourg, the Netherlands, the United Kingdom, and Ireland are included in the western natural region of Western Europe. This region has a temperate, humid climate because of the North Atlantic Drift. The drift is an ocean current that brings warm water from the Caribbean Sea and the Gulf of Mexico across the North Atlantic Ocean. The westerly winds pick up this warm water and carry it overland where it falls as rain. Therefore, the climate of the western region is milder than its northerly location would suggest. It is also rainy and damp.

France has many good seaports and rivers for trade, rich soil for farming, and natural resources for industry. Although most of its borders are protected by mountains or seas, France's northeast corner is part of the Northern European Plain. This section has been a weak spot in France's defense. Invading armies have found the plain very inviting.

Wedged in the northwest corner of Western Europe between West Germany, France, and the North Sea are the Low Countries: Belgium, the Netherlands, and Luxembourg. Their location has been both a blessing and a problem. The harbors and rivers of Belgium and the Netherlands have helped make them cultural and commercial centers. These same harbors and rivers have also made them targets for invaders. The Netherlands has also had to fight the sea. The Dutch have built dikes, canals, and windmills to keep back the water and reclaim land for agriculture. More than half the Netherlands consists of reclaimed land.

The United Kingdom and Ireland generally consist of rugged highlands and rolling hills in the northern areas, and lowlands in the south and east. Much of the Fens, a marshy lowland in central Great Britain, has been drained and turned into productive farmland. The English Channel separates the British Isles from the rest of Europe. The relative isolation of the isles has greatly influenced their history and development.

Northern Region

Northern Region   The northern region of Western Europe includes Norway, Sweden, Denmark, Iceland, Greenland, and Finland. It is generally known as Scandinavia. However, only Norway and Sweden actually occupy the Scandinavian peninsula.

Most of Scandinavia has long cold winters and short cool summers. Large sections of Norway, Sweden, and Finland are part of the subarctic. The land there is covered by vast evergreen forests and has a short growing season. Farther north lies tundra where few crops can be grown because the soil is frozen most of the year.

Most of Norway and Sweden is covered by mountains, although southern Sweden lies on the Northern European Plain. Since the climate and soil are not suited to most types of farming, Norwegians and Swedes generally depend on wood products, mining, fishing, and shipping for their livelihood.

Denmark is located on the Jutland Peninsula and on about 500 nearby islands. While Denmark's land is flatter than the rest of Scandinavia, the soil is not particularly fertile. The Danish economy depends partly on fish, livestock, and dairy products, and partly on manufactured goods, such as machinery, electronics, and furniture.

Most of Iceland is covered by volcanic mountains and ice fields. Its climate, however, is moderated by the North Atlantic Drift. About 84 percent of Greenland, a territory of Denmark, is ice-capped. Iceland and Greenland are mostly uninhabited, except for a few coastal areas. The few hundred thousand people who live on these islands generally make their living by fishing, grazing animals, or mining.

Southern Finland is flat with thousands of lakes. The northern section of the country is mountainous. The Finns earn their living from the forest and the sea.

grazing:
way of raising cattle, sheep, goats by letting them feed on grass

Central Region

Central Region   The countries of central Western Europe are West Germany, East Germany, Switzerland, Austria, and Liechtenstein (LIK-tuhn-stiyn). In the central region, winters are colder and summers are hotter than in the coastal areas.

After World War II Germany was divided into two parts—West Germany and East Germany. West Germany's development has been influenced by the United States and other Western European nations. East Germany's development has been dominated by the Soviet Union.

The rich coal and iron mines of the Ruhr and Saar river valleys have been the foundation of West Germany's industrialization. A network of rivers cheaply transports goods across the European continent or north to the Baltic Sea. The northern part of West Germany lies on the flat Northern European Plain. Forested highlands cover the central area. The Bavarian Alps are located in the southern part of the country.

Nearly all of East Germany lies on the Northern European Plain. The largest industrial centers are found in the southeastern part of the country near coal and other mineral deposits in the Elbe River valley.

Although the Alps mountain range covers about 75 percent of the country, Austria's farms are very productive and supply almost all the

(Continued on page 512.)

Using GEOGRAPHY Skills

Reading a Special Purpose Map

The industrial revolution began in Great Britain during the latter half of the eighteenth century. Industrialization spread to Belgium, France, and Germany during the first decades of the nineteenth century. The factors necessary for the shift to an industrial economy—an abundance of raw materials and sources of power, a large and efficient transportation network, and a growing population—helped these countries to be at the forefront of the Industrial Revolution. Germany in particular possessed the elements necessary for rapid industrial growth.

The map on this page will help you understand how geographic factors contributed to industrialization in Germany. Study the map. Then answer the following questions:

1. What relationship do you see between the location of industrial centers and population density? Between the industrial centers and the railroads? Between the industrial centers and the location of resources?

2. Hamburg and Bremen are not located in areas of especially dense population. They are not located near large resource deposits. What factors do you think contributed to their rise as industrial centers?

3. Control over the Alsace-Lorraine area was disputed for decades by Germany and France. Why do you think this is so?

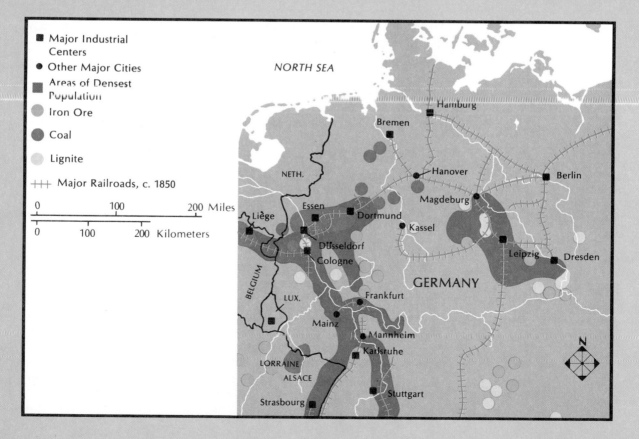

food needed by that nation's people. Switzerland lies in the midst of the Alps. Within its borders are the sources of most of Europe's important rivers. The Swiss have harnessed these rivers to produce hydroelectric power. Switzerland possesses few minerals, and the soil is generally poor. Therefore, the Swiss have had to depend on the manufacture of high-quality precision instruments, such as watches and electronics, and on service industries, such as banking and tourism, to make a living. The people of the tiny alpine nation of Liechtenstein have done the same.

Southern Region　　The southern part of Western Europe is occupied by Spain, Portugal, Greece, Italy, and the small states of Andorra, Monaco, San Marino, and Vatican City. Except for the mountain regions, the southern region's climate is similar to that of southern California. The summers are long, hot, and dry, while the winters are mild and somewhat rainy.

Spain and Portugal, located on the Iberian Peninsula, are isolated from the rest of Western Europe by the Pyrenees mountains. In some ways, these two countries have been more influenced by the culture of nearby northern Africa than by that of Europe.

Although agriculture is important to the economies of both Spain and Portugal, farming is often hindered by poor rocky soil and lack of rain. Most farming takes place on the coastal plains and in fertile river valleys. Some of the crops grown include grapes, olives, and citrus fruits. Portugal has an important fishing industry, and Spain has some rich mineral deposits. Both countries, however, are industrially and technologically behind the rest of Western Europe.

In the northern part of Italy between the Alps and the Apennine mountains lies the fertile Po Valley. This region is the site of Italy's richest farmland and its major industries. The center of Italy, between the Arno River and Rome, has some agriculture but is best known as the nation's intellectual, political, and cultural heartland. Southern Italy, including the islands of Sicily and Sardinia, is primarily agricultural and is the poorest region of the country.

Greece is a mountainous country. Because of the rugged terrain and the fact that the soil has been greatly eroded over the centuries, crops are limited. Many Greeks depend on raising livestock or on fishing to earn a living.

The tiny nation of San Marino, located in the Italian Apennines, is primarily agricultural. The tourist trade is also a major source of income there. Andorra, which is situated on the French-Spanish border in the Pyrenees, is also agricultural, but tourism is the mainstay of the economy. Monaco is in the southeast corner of France on the Mediterranean Sea. Its mild climate and beautiful scenery, as well as its famous gambling casino at Monte Carlo, make it a tourist resort. Vatican City, an independent nation, is located within the Italian city of Rome. It occupies less than one quarter of a square mile of land. The pope, the head of the Roman Catholic Church, lives there and governs.

1. **Recall**   What are the four natural regions of Western Europe? Name the countries in each of these regions.
2. **How and Why**   How have the Swiss taken advantage of the mountains that cover most of their country?
3. **Critical Thinking**   Why is the climate of Western Europe milder than its northerly location would suggest?

SECTION

3

Early Cultures

For over fifty years, the British government has worked with scientists and other people to make needed repairs on Stonehenge. Why do you think some people want to preserve Stonehenge?

Archaeologists have pieced together the story of the **prehistoric**— before written history—cultures that existed in Western Europe. Although much is still unknown, evidence has been found to indicate that prehistoric cultures existed in nearly every Western European nation.

Excavations of sites in northern Europe reveal the presence of a reindeer-hunting people as early as 10,000 B.C. Their tools and other **artifacts**—objects made by people—have been found by archaeologists. Some of these early people also gathered plants for food. Eventually people learned to grow crops and keep animals for food. By around 4000 B.C. farming villages had been established in most of Western Europe.

513

Megalith Builders

By about 3500 B.C. groups of people in Western Europe were building with **megaliths**—massive stones. Megalithic structures have been found from Scandinavia to the Mediterranean Sea. They are important to the study of the development of Western Europe's early people because they show how **architectural**—building—skills developed. Some megalithic structures were used as tombs. Others may have been used for religious purposes.

The most famous megalithic structure is Stonehenge on the island of Great Britain. Many archaeologists believe that Stonehenge was built as an **astronomical observatory**—a place to study the movements of the stars and planets. The groups of stones seem to align with various events in the skies. Astronomers have shown that the changes of the seasons could have been predicted using the arrangements of the megaliths at Stonehenge. This was important knowledge for the farming people who built Stonehenge. By predicting seasonal changes they could determine when to plant and harvest their crops.

Building monuments like Stonehenge required some knowledge of mathematics. It also required the cooperation of large numbers of people. One scientist calculated that it would take 80 people using ropes to move a 5-ton (4.5-metric-ton) stone. Some of the stones at Stonehenge weigh ten times that much. Experts believe that some of the huge stones were brought to Stonehenge from Wales—several hundred miles away.

Metalworkers

Sometime after 5000 B.C. people in Western Europe began to use metals. The first metal objects were made of copper. About 2000 B.C. people in various parts of the region began making objects of bronze. Iron objects began to appear in Western Europe about 1000 B.C. Some of the earliest ironworking cultures have been identified in northern Italy and in Austria.

The development of metalworking encouraged trade in Western Europe. For example, Britain had large deposits of the tin needed for making bronze. Britons traded tin for other goods, such as **amber**—a highly valued stone—and furs from Denmark. Trade brought wealth and exchanges of ideas to Western Europeans.

SECTION 3 REVIEW

1. **Recall** Why might Stonehenge have been built?
2. **How and Why** In what ways were the people of Western Europe affected by the development of metalworking?
3. **Critical Thinking** Why was it important for those who built Stonehenge to be able to determine the changes of the seasons?

Chapter 26

Reviewing People, Places, and Things

Identify, define, or explain each of the following:

Eurasia
Mediterranean Sea
Scandinavian
  Peninsula
Iberian Peninsula
Italian Peninsula
Balkan Peninsula
Iceland
Greenland
British Isles
Alps
Pyrenees
Apennines
Northern European
  Plain

Rhine River
Danube River
fjords
peat
Low Countries
United Kingdom
Fens
English Channel
Scandinavia
East Germany
West Germany
megaliths
astronomical
  observatory

Map Study

Using the maps on pages 504 and 505, determine the answers to the following questions:

1. Which bodies of water skirt the countries in the northern region of Western Europe?
2. Which peninsulas lie fully or partially in the Mediterranean Sea?
3. Which Western European nations have no coastline?

Understanding Facts and Ideas

1. Why does Western Europe have a long coastline despite its relatively small size?
2. What body of water separates the Iberian Peninsula from Africa?
3. Why is Greenland usually treated as part of the Western European culture region even though it is geographically part of North America?
4. What natural feature of Western Europe has proven to be inviting to invading armies from the Romans to the Nazis?
5. Why is the Rhine the most important river in Western Europe?
6. Why is the climate of the western region of Western Europe milder than its northerly location would suggest?
7. What resources have been the foundations of West Germany's industrialization?
8. How have the Swiss thrived economically despite the fact that Switzerland has few mineral resources?
9. a. What two small nations are located within Italy? b. What small nation is located in the Pyrenees on the French-Spanish border?
10. Why do many archaeologists believe Stonehenge was built?

Developing Critical Thinking

Expressing Problems Various megalithic structures, such as Stonehenge, have been found in a number of places in Western Europe as well as in other places throughout the world. Why is it difficult for archaeologists to determine the purposes of these structures?

Writing About History

Analyzing Geography Write a paragraph explaining why many important Western European cities such as Paris, London, Rome, and Vienna developed on rivers.

Applying Your Skills to History

Comparing and Contrasting Create a chart comparing and contrasting the geographic features of the four natural regions of Western Europe. Compare and contrast such things as mountain ranges, rivers, plains, peninsulas, islands, coastlines, and resources.

515

Classical Greece

Western civilization is said to rest upon three legs: Judeo-Christian morals, Greek thought, and Roman law. The ancient Greeks had a high regard for the individual, and one of the most important legacies of the classical Greeks is the institution of democracy, although Greek democracy was limited.

The classical Greeks believed that it was possible to understand the world through the use of reason. The Greeks are considered to be the developers of many fields of learning, including political science, philosophy, geometry, the natural and physical sciences, and medicine. They wrote epic poems, plays, and other literary works that are still popular. The ancient Greeks were also talented sculptors and builders. The architecture of many public buildings in Washington, D.C., and other cities resembles that of ancient Greece.

As you study this chapter, think about these questions:

- What was the Greek concept of political power?
- What was the role of trade in the development of Greek civilization?
- What were the ideas of the major Greek philosophers?
- What elements from Greek civilization are still in use today?

The ruins of Old Corinth guard the Isthmus of Corinth. Founded in the 700s B.C. by the Dorians, Corinth was once the largest city in ancient Greece.

The origins of Greek civilization can be traced to several sources. The first major influence was the Minoan (muh-NOH-uhn) civilization of the island of Crete. The second was the Mycenaean (MY-suh-NEE-uhn) civilization established on the Balkan Peninsula by Indo-Europeans from the grasslands of southern Russia. Trade between these peoples and the Middle East brought new ideas and lifestyles. By about 800 B.C. classical Greek civilization had begun to develop.

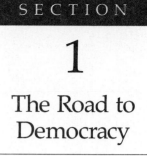

The Road to Democracy

Minoans

The island of Crete lies across the entrance of the Aegean Sea. By the time the Mycenaeans came into contact with the Minoans around 1700 B.C., they had developed a highly sophisticated civilization based on international sea trade.

sophisticated: highly developed and complex (as opposed to simple and natural)

The Minoans lived well. They had hot and cold running water, bathrooms, and elaborate furniture. They protected their valuables with metal locks and keys. The plastered interiors of their homes were colorfully decorated with paintings called **frescoes**. This technique of painting on wet plaster is still used today.

We have learned much about Minoan culture from their art. They were fond of dancing, as well as boxing, racing, and other sports. There was one sport, however, in which the Minoans seem to be unique. That was bull-leaping. Minoan paintings show men and women leaping over a bull's horns, turning handsprings on its back, and landing upright behind the bull. Bull-leaping apparently began as a religious ritual and developed into a sport over time.

From their paintings, it appears the Minoans were slender, short, and had dark, curly hair. The women wore hats, tight jackets and long, bell-shaped skirts. Women apparently held a high position in Minoan society. Their chief deity was a goddess who was often represented in gold or ivory statues holding a snake. Minoan art also reveals that the people had a feeling for nature and peace. They did not portray scenes of war but pictured landscapes, sports, and festivals.

Minoan civilization centered around cities, the most important of which was Knossos (NAHS-uhs). Unlike the cities of Sumer and other early Middle Eastern civilizations, Minoan cities were unwalled. Crete's forests provided the raw material for the Minoan shipbuilding industry. Among the trade goods the Minoans carried between Egypt, Phoenicia, and the lands bordering the Aegean were vases, enameled bronze daggers, rings, and other items made of gold, silver, and bronze.

Minoan civilization flourished until about 1450 B.C. Then it collapsed. Some historians believe a volcanic eruption on the nearby island of Thera caused huge tidal waves that smashed against Crete, destroying the cities and drowning most of the inhabitants. Other historians argue that Crete was simply overrun by the Mycenaeans.

Mycenaeans

The Mycenaeans began filtering into the Balkan Peninsula around 2000 B.C. Several waves of Mycenaeans moved in over the next four centuries. By 1600 B.C. these warlike people had conquered the inhabitants of Greece (who were called Hellenes) and set up a group of kingdoms.

Each kingdom centered around a hilltop fortress that contained the king's palace, workshops for royal artisans, and offices for the royal scribes who kept tax records. The fortress also sheltered the kingdom's inhabitants in case of attack. Land was divided into estates that were owned by warrior nobles and cultivated by slaves and tenant farmers. When needed, the nobles turned out in horse-drawn chariots to fight for their king.

Whether or not the Mycenaeans invaded Crete, they adopted many elements of Minoan culture. These included a writing system, clothing styles, and especially the skills of shipbuilding and navigation. By about 1400 B.C. the Mycenaeans had replaced the Minoans as the major sea-trading power in the Aegean Sea. Two great epic poems testify to this.

The poems tell the story of the Mycenaean expedition against the rival city of Troy. Because Troy overlooked the waterway between the Mediterranean and Black seas, it controlled the trade route between Russia and Greek lands. One epic poem, the *Iliad*, tells of the ten-year-long siege of Troy, which took place around 1200 B.C. The other epic, the *Odyssey*, relates the fantastic adventures of the warrior-hero Odysseus on his way home to Greece after Troy's fall. It is believed that the two epics were composed by a blind Greek poet named Homer.

siege:
surrounding a place in an effort to capture it

The *Iliad* and the *Odyssey* later became the basic textbooks about classical Greece. They present the values important to Greek civilization: a pride in being Greek, a desire for honor, a love of life, an emphasis on the individual, and courage in the face of whatever fate the gods have decreed.

Although the Mycenaeans won the Trojan War, their power came to an end within a century. They were greatly weakened by conflict among themselves. Then invaders from the north, known as Dorians, entered Greece and conquered the Mycenaeans. The bronze weapons of the Mycenaeans were no match against the iron weapons possessed by the Dorians.

The period from about 1100 to 800 B.C. is known as the Dark Age in Greek history. This was a period during which overseas trade ceased, and the fine arts and crafts disappeared. Thousands of refugees abandoned mainland Greece for the Aegean islands on the Turkish coast. Then, around 800 B.C., Greek civilization began to revive. However, it took a very different form.

The Polis

politics:
the art or science of government

The English words *politics* and *politician* come from the Greek word *polis*, meaning "city-state." The polis was the center of the new civilization that developed in the area around the Aegean Sea. Each city-state contained a

Besides the subject of a poem by Homer, the siege of Troy became the theme for other artwork. This large pottery container is decorated with a relief of the Trojan horse.

hill called an **acropolis**, on top of which stood public monuments and temples to the local gods and goddesses. At the foot of the acropolis was a public square called the **agora**. The city-states were usually walled.

The typical city-state was about 100 square miles (259 square kilometers). This was a large enough area for people to earn a living. It was also small enough so that citizens could carry on the public business.

The main purpose of the city-state was politics. "We do not say that a man who takes no interest in politics is a man who minds his own business. We say he has no business here at all." The citizens of a city-state could vote, run for office, and own property. They enjoyed freedom of speech and of assembly. Their civic responsibilities included participating in government and supporting their city-state in battle. Citizenship, however, was limited. Women, children, foreign-born workers, or slaves were not considered citizens. Prior to about 500 B.C., people who did not own land were also excluded. Nevertheless, the city-state was the first step on the road to democracy. Democracy comes from the Greek word *demos* meaning "rule by the people."

Although the various Greek city-states shared a common language and common deities, they seldom cooperated with one another. The Greeks were so devoted to their own city-state that they never developed a group or national loyalty. Another reason for the lack of unity among the Greeks was geography. The rugged, mountainous countryside and the sea isolated the city-states from one another.

There was, however, one occasion when city-states cooperated—the Olympic Games. The Olympic Games were held in honor of Zeus, the

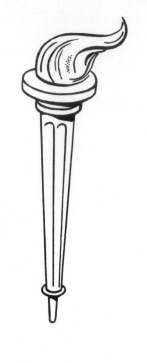

The modern Olympic Games begin with the lighting of the Olympic flame from a torch that is carried from Olympia Valley in Greece. The five interlocking rings appear on the official Olympic flag.

father of the Greek family of gods and goddesses. Every four years Greeks gathered in a valley called Olympia for five days of athletic contests. These were individual rather than team contests, since Greek civilization generally emphasized the individual. The games consisted of foot races, chariot races, discus and javelin hurling, the broad jump, and other displays of individual physical ability. Wreaths of olive or laurel leaves were placed on the heads of winners, and more honors—parades, public banquets, and sometimes cash gifts—awaited them when they returned to their city-state. Only citizens could take part in the games. Foreigners and single women could watch, but married women could not. The earliest recorded date of the games is 776 B.C.

Two Societies

Different city-states had different values and lifestyles. Sparta and Athens are good examples of the wide differences that existed among the Greeks.

Sparta   Sparta was located in the southern part of Greece called the Peloponnesus (PEL-uh-puh-NEE-suhs). The Dorians, ancestors of the Spartans, had migrated there from the north. By about 500 B.C. the Spartans ruled the entire area. They ruled because their bodies and minds had been toughened and shaped for war since childhood.

Spartan babies were examined for physical fitness. If they did not meet the required standards, they were abandoned on a hillside to die. At the age of seven, a Spartan boy left home and began the severe training designed to make him into a soldier

He was given too little food so that he would be forced to steal. This taught him how to live off the land in wartime. A boy who was caught stealing was whipped to teach him to be more careful. If he whimpered, he disgraced himself. A Spartan boy learned endurance by walking barefoot and wearing only a single piece of cloth in both summer and winter. He marched, wrestled, fought with weapons, and hardened his muscles with gymnastics. He spoke little; his deeds in war would speak for him. Because of this rigid training, Sparta had the best army in Greece.

At the age of 30, a Spartan man married. His wife had also been taught to keep her body healthy for child-bearing. Spartan women, unlike those in other Greek city-states, had a voice in public affairs. They ran the city-state when men were away at war. After a battle, Spartan women asked first whether Sparta had won or lost the battle. Only afterward did they inquire about their husbands or sons.

Fighting was the primary job of Spartan men. Everything else, including making money or engaging in the arts, was secondary. Slaves worked the fields, which were equally divided among Spartan citizens. In a sense, however, the Spartans too were slaves. Although their city-state was governed by men whom they elected, the Spartans lived to fight, breed, and die for the glory and preservation of Sparta.

Athens   The city-state of Athens developed much differently than Sparta. The early Athenians were ruled by kings and later by landowning nobles. Over time, opposition to the hereditary rule of the nobles developed. Most Athenians did not own land. The fields they worked as tenants produced scarcely enough to pay their rent. When crops failed, they had to borrow money. Sometimes they were forced to sell themselves into slavery in order to pay their debts. Merchants, laborers, independent farmers, and sailors were no better off.

Beginning around the 600s B.C., a series of military leaders supported by the people seized power in Athens. These men were called **tyrants**. Although most were aristocrats, they were concerned about the common people's welfare.

The tyrant Draco gave the Athenians their first written code of law around 621 B.C. Although Draco's code was extremely severe, the fact that it was set down in writing meant that everyone knew what the laws were.

code:
a systematic body of law

Solon, who assumed power in 594 B.C., instituted both economic and political reforms. He canceled all land debts, freed those already enslaved because of debt, and placed a limit on the amount of land any one person could own. He also opened the Assembly, one of the two governing bodies of Athens, to all citizens rather than just landowners. Solon's reforms became a permanent part of Athenian government.

Solon's reforms, however, did not completely satisfy all Athenians. Social unrest within the city-state continued. Then, in 508 B.C., Cleisthenes (KLIYS-thuh-neez), another tyrant, came to power. It was Cleisthenes who established Athenian democracy.

Every male citizen over the age of 20 became a member of the Athenian Assembly. The Assembly had the sole power to make laws, decide on matters of war and peace, and approve treaties and the city's budget. The Assembly also served as a supreme court. Any citizen could express his opinions freely in the Assembly. About 45,000 men were considered citizens of Athens. Decisions could be made if there were at least 6,000 at the open-air meetings of the Assembly.

The Assembly was much too large to administer the everyday business of government. This was handled by the Council of Five Hundred. Council members were chosen each year by lot. The Athenians did not elect members to the Council because they felt that people who were rich or who spoke well in public held an unfair advantage in such elections. The Athenians also believed that as a result of their educational system, every citizen was qualified to hold public office. No Athenian citizen could serve on the Council of Five Hundred more than twice.

by lot:
to decide something by chance; for example, to choose straws to see who does something

The only position that called for special expertise was that of general. Each year the Athenians chose ten generals to oversee the armed forces. If a general was found to be a successful and effective leader, he might be elected over and over again.

The Athenians trusted justice from the many but not from the few. The Athenians reasoned that if the number of jurors hearing a case were large enough, there was less chance that they might be moved by bribery, threat, or prejudice. Each year 6,000 citizens over 30 years of age were chosen as jurors. For each trial a jury of 201 or more was drawn by a complicated system of lots. The jurors determined guilt or innocence by majority vote. The jurors also fixed the penalty.

As has been stated, the Athenian democracy had flaws. Women had no political rights. Slaves were not considered citizens, and, although usually treated well, had no share in Athenian freedoms. Foreigners were permitted to live in the city-state, but they were not allowed to own land. Only rarely were foreign men permitted to become citizens.

Athenian men who lived in the city found it easier to attend Assembly meetings than the farmers who lived in the countryside. Thus, the Assembly came to be dominated more and more by city-dwellers. For its time, however, the Athenian experiment in rule by ordinary citizens—even a limited number—was daring. Its success provided an example for future states.

SECTION 1 REVIEW

1. **Recall**   Which two groups of people laid the foundation for classical Greek civilization? What happened to these peoples?
2. **How and Why**   Why did the Greek city-states seldom cooperate with one another?
3. **Critical Thinking**   How does the development of Sparta compare with the development of Athens?

Rise and Decline

colonies:
a body of people living in a new territory but retaining ties with the parent state

Between 750 and 500 B.C., the people of Athens, Corinth, and other city-states set up some 250 colonies along the shores of the Mediterranean Sea and beyond. Greek colonies dotted the edges of the Black Sea and included the city of Byzantium (modern Istanbul). You will read about the Byzantine Empire in the next chapter. The Greeks also moved westward to Sicily, where they built Syracuse, and then to the mainland of Italy, where they set up so many cities that the area became known as Greater Greece. The Greeks also colonized southern France.

It was not difficult to recruit Greeks to settle in these colonies. Greece's soil was generally poor and the amount of land available for farming was limited. Greece's growing population was always in danger of exceeding the food supply.

Colonization changed Greece's economy. Many colonies were set up in places with fertile soil, where colonists could raise surplus grain to send home to their parent city-state. Farmers in the city-states shifted from growing grain to growing such cash crops as grapes and olives for sale overseas. Growing grapes and olives required fewer workers than growing grain. The displaced farm workers became artisans, turning out pottery, textiles, weapons, and other goods for sale overseas. By 600 B.C., the Greek economy depended on international sea trade rather than on farming.

The Persian Wars

During the sixth century B.C., the mighty Persian Empire arose to the east of Greece. The once-great empires of Egypt, Assyria, and Babylonia all came under Persian control. In addition, the Persians conquered the Greek colonies in Ionia—the area along the Turkish coast.

The Persians generally left their subjects in peace if they acknowledged Persian rule and paid **tribute**—a tax. The Greeks, however, considered the Persians to be barbarians. The Greeks disliked the fancy clothes the Persians wore, the fact that Persian men curled their beards and used perfume, and especially the Persian belief that the king ruled by divine right. The Greeks believed that citizens had the right to choose their government.

In 499 B.C. the Greek colonies of Ionia, with the support of Athens, rebelled against Persian rule. The rebellion was ruthlessly put down by the Persian king Darius I. Seeking revenge for Athens's role in the uprising, Darius invaded the Greek mainland in 490 B.C. Although outnumbered two to one, the Athenians soundly defeated the Persians on the plain of Marathon. Ten years later Darius' successor, Xerxes (ZUHRK-seez), led the Persian army and navy against the Greeks. In the battle at Thermopylae, the Persians crushed a small force of Spartans and others defending a mountain pass. Xerxes then led his army on to Athens and burned the city. Several days later the Persian navy attacked the Greek fleet at Salamis. The Persian fleet was destroyed, and the Persians retreated. The following year, the Persians again invaded Greece. They were defeated at the battle of Plataea (pluh-TEE-uh).

The above shows two sides of a coin minted about 413 B.C. in the Corinthian colony of Syracuse on the island of Sicily. The area is now part of Italy.

The Athenian Empire

Despite the fact that the Greeks had been able to defeat Persia, they still feared invasion by this powerful empire. Therefore, the Greek city-states decided to form a defensive alliance called the Delian League. Since the

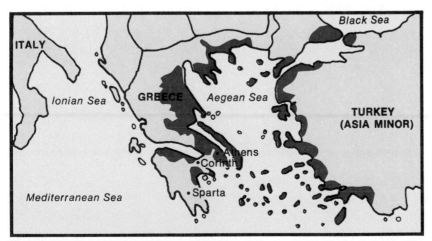

■ Athens in the Age of Pericles, c. 450 B.C.

Persians had been defeated in large part by the Athenian navy, Athens became the league's head. Sparta did not join.

The Athenians began a large fleet-building program financed by the other city-states. Soon Athens was the leading naval power in the eastern Mediterranean. As Athenian naval power grew, its commerce, industry, and political control also grew. Other city-states began using Athenian coins and the Athenian system of weights and measures. Criminals were no longer tried in their own city-state but were sent to Athens for judgment. Funds from the treasury of the Delian League were used to beautify Athens. Eventually, the Delian League became the Athenian empire.

The Peloponnesian War

The growing power of Athens alarmed many Greek city-states, including Athens' chief rival, Sparta. In 431 B.C. Sparta, supported by several allies, went to war against Athens. This struggle, known as the Peloponnesian War, lasted for 28 years. In 404 B.C. the Spartans finally defeated the Athenians. As a symbol of their victory, the Spartans tore down the wall surrounding Athens. Athens was forced to give up its navy and its overseas colonies.

The long years of conflict damaged the city-state as a political institution. In almost every city-state, people no longer considered the common good. Instead, they concentrated on making money and enjoying themselves. Bitterness between aristocrats and commoners grew more intense, and social unrest and rebellions were widespread.

This helmet is called Corinthian. It was developed in the city-state of Corinth during the 500s B.C. Later, Corinth joined with other city-stages to fight Athens' growing power.

Alexander the Great fought and defeated Darius III and his Persian armies three times between 333 and 330 B.C. The final defeat opened Alexander's way into India.

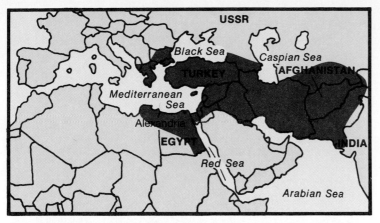

Empire of Alexander the Great

The victory of Sparta over Athens did not bring peace to Greece. Sparta had been weakened by the long years of war against Athens. Attempts to unify the city-states under Spartan rule failed. No city-state was strong enough to rule Greece. Lack of unity greatly weakened the Greeks. Philip II, the ruler of Macedonia, soon took advantage of this weakness.

Philip and Alexander

The Macedonians were a mixture of Greek and other cultural groups. From the time Philip became king in 359 B.C., he schemed to unite Macedonia and Greece. In 338 B.C. Philip overthrew the combined forces of Athens and Thebes and became overlord of Greece. In 336 B.C. he was murdered by an assassin allegedly hired by his wife.

Philip was succeeded by his son Alexander, whose military exploits earned him the title Alexander the Great. Alexander dreamed of uniting the world into one empire. For a brief time, until his death in 323 B.C., he united almost all the territory from Macedonia in the north to Egypt in the south and from Greece eastward to India.

Alexander attempted to blend the customs and institutions of the Greeks with those of the peoples he conquered, especially the Persians. He began by taking a Persian wife and encouraging his officers and troops to do the same. He brought Persian soldiers into his army and put Persian officers in charge of Greeks. He even followed the Persian custom of claiming that he was a divine ruler.

Alexander founded about 70 cities, many of which he named Alexandria. The most famous Alexandria was the one in the Nile delta of Egypt. Alexander encouraged Greeks and Macedonians to settle in these cities. In this way, as well as through trade, Greek culture spread throughout the ancient world. The mingling of the cultures in Alexander's empire evolved into a new culture—the Hellenistic culture.

institution:
a significant practice, relationship, or organization in a society or culture

525

The Hellenistic Age

Soon after Alexander's death his empire was divided into three parts, each ruled by one of his leading generals. For the next 250 years, Alexander's successors ruled the lands he had conquered. Greeks and Macedonians formed the ruling class.

During the Hellenistic Age, trade between the Mediterranean world and Asia increased. Sea traders from India traveled through the Persian Gulf and up the Tigris River. Overland caravans then transported trade goods farther west. Around 120 B.C., sailors learned how to use the monsoon winds to enable them to sail directly across the Indian Ocean instead of hugging the coastline. Soon ships were carrying spices, jewels, and other luxury goods from India around Arabia to Egypt. The main items of trade, however, were grain and slaves. Farmers in Egypt and southern Russia produced grain for the cities around the Aegean Sea. In exchange, these cities exported wine, olive oil, fish, and wood. The slaves were mostly prisoners of war, although some were people kidnaped by pirates. Slaves worked in mines, fields, and private homes. Their labor formed the backbone of the Hellenistic economy.

Despite their prosperity and cultural achievements, which you will read about later in this chapter, the empires of the Hellenistic world were torn by conflict. It was difficult to hold together empires with so many different peoples and cultures. Revolts erupted, smaller kingdoms broke away, and the empires established by Alexander's generals fell apart. During the 200s and 100s B.C., they gradually fell under the rule of the Italian city-state of Rome. You will learn about the Roman Empire in Chapter 28.

SECTION 2 REVIEW

1. **Recall** How far did the empire of Alexander the Great extend?
2. **How and Why** Why was the Delian League formed?
3. **Critical Thinking** Why was there really no winner in the Peloponnesian War?

Despite political turmoil, the centuries between 500 and 200 B.C. were a time of great cultural and scientific achievements by the Greeks. Many of the most important achievements took place during the Age of Pericles—461 to 429 B.C. Pericles was elected as a general 30 times by the people of Athens. Pericles dominated Athens and other parts of Greece as well. His leadership and words expressed the spirit of the time. Other important Greek achievements, primarily in science, occurred during the Hellenistic Age.

Gods and Goddesses

The Greeks believed in a family of gods and goddesses that could protect and aid them in their daily lives. It is believed that many of the Greek deities originally represented the forces of nature, such as rain, wind, and the sea. Their chief deities were believed to live on Mount Olympus in northern Greece. Zeus, the lord of the sky, was chief among the Greek gods. Hera, his wife, was the guardian goddess of women and marriage. Poseidon, a brother of Zeus, was god of the sea. Aphrodite, the daughter of Zeus, was the goddess of love and beauty. The Greeks believed that the gods and goddesses were immortal and had powers far superior to those of humans, but also had human characteristics. Gods and goddesses fell in love, quarreled, and often became jealous. Although all Greeks worshiped the same deities, every city-state had its own special god or goddess who was honored as its protector. For example, Athena was the patron of Athens.

immortal:
free from death

The religious beliefs of the Greeks had a strong influence upon their literature, art, and architecture. Some of the greatest Greek sculptures were portrayals of their deities. Among the finest Greek public buildings were temples. Many Greek poems were hymns in praise of the gods and goddesses. Greek drama had its beginnings in religious festivals honoring Dionysus, god of the springtime and giver of wine.

527

Thinkers

The Greeks came to believe there was a rational explanation for the existence of the universe and of humans. They were determined to reason out that explanation.

The first known Greek philosopher is Thales (THAY-leez) of Miletus, in Ionia, who lived just after 600 B.C. He believed there was a single substance that was basic to all matter. Thales' ideas were developed by Democritus, who declared that all matter was composed of invisible small particles called atoms.

By the 400s B.C. Greeks were becoming more interested in human existence than in the basic stuff of matter. They wanted to know more about themselves so they could live happier and more useful lives. A group called Sophists, or wise teachers, believed that truth is relative. What is beautiful, true, just, and good for one may not be considered as such by someone else in another place at another time. Sophists saw the world as a jungle. For them, might made right.

Sophists taught pupils how to speak and debate in a way that would help them succeed whether or not they spoke the truth. Other Greeks, however, challenged the ideas of the Sophists. Among them were Socrates, Plato, and Aristotle.

Socrates

The philosopher Socrates, who lived in Athens from 469 to 399 B.C., was perhaps the greatest teacher of classical Greece. He used a technique that came to be known as the Socratic method. He would ask his listeners a series of questions, and would continue the questioning until the listeners either contradicted themselves or could no longer answer. In this way, Socrates hoped to lead people to think correctly and to discover the truth.

Socrates believed that people should know and understand themselves. "An unexamined life is not worth living," he said. Striving for money or fame was much less important than improving the soul. Socrates was opposed to the Sophists, for they used words to deceive, and they failed to admit ignorance of what they did not know. Socrates held that there was an ultimate truth and a correct course of action for each individual. Further, each person had the ability to discover it.

Socrates' method of seeking the truth led many Athenians to accuse him of threatening established laws and values. He was brought to trial on the ground of misleading the young, found guilty, and condemned to death. Although he was given an opportunity to save his life by fleeing Athens, Socrates refused to do so. He believed that a citizen should obey the laws of his city-state even if those laws were unjust. At the age of 70, Socrates ended his life by drinking a cup of **hemlock**—a deadly poison.

Plato

Plato was a student of Socrates and founder of the Academy—a school—that lasted until A.D. 529 Plato's writings, called dialogues, were discussions among fictional people about such topics as government, religion, law, and justice.

Plato believed that nothing in the material world ever remains the same. An object described today may have changed by tomorrow. Thus, the way to gain knowledge is not by observing the material world but by thinking about universal truths. Plato called these truths *Ideas*.

In *The Republic*, the first book ever written on political science, Plato described an ideal government. Most people would be farmers and merchants. Above them would be the soldiers. And at the top would be the rulers, the philosopher-kings. They would be specially educated by the state in such subjects as philosophy, music, art, and poetry. This special training would make them brave, wise, good, and devoted to the welfare of the community. In Plato's republic there were no slaves, and all things were held in common. Women as well as men could become rulers if they were intellectually qualified.

Aristotle   When Aristotle was 17, he became a student in Plato's Academy. Later Aristotle served for seven years as tutor to Alexander the Great. When Aristotle returned to Athens, he founded a school called the Lyceum. In addition to teaching, he wrote or edited some 200 books, thus gaining for himself the title of "master of them that know."

Aristotle described things according to their similarities and differences. As a biologist, he collected facts about plants and animals, which he organized and classified according to genus and species. With only a few changes, this classification system is still used today. Before Aristotle wrote a book called *Politics*, he analyzed the constitutions of 50 city-states. He believed the best government lay somewhere between an

Aristotle was a student of Plato. Compare and contrast Aristotle's ideas on government with those of Plato.

oligarchy—government by a few—and a democracy. He favored rule by the middle class, because he believed the rich seldom obeyed, while the poor lacked experience in directing others.

Other Philosophies

Later Greek philosophers were not always interested in discovering truth. Zeno, who founded Stoicism, was an Athenian who taught around 300 B.C. Zeno and his followers wanted peace of mind. They found it in resignation, duty, and self-discipline. They believed that everything that happened to people, bad or good, was for the good of the universe. It was useless for people to rebel against the evils that came to them. The Stoics also taught that all peoples should live together in tolerance and equality. They spoke out against slavery and war, and they urged everyone to take an active part in public affairs.

The Epicureans believed there was neither reward nor punishment after death, only nothingness. They urged people to seek what pleasure they could find here and now. They were especially interested in the pleasure that comes from a tranquil mind. They cautioned people to seek this pleasure in moderation. Excess would bring pain.

The Cynics, contemporaries of the Epicureans, believed that living a virtuous life was all-important. Everything else was useless.

The Skeptics did not believe that a person could have definite knowledge about anything. There was no use in seeking absolute truth or knowledge because it could never be obtained. They said a person should abandon the search and suspend judgment. Then peace of mind would follow.

1. **Recall**   What did Plato describe in *The Republic*? Explain his views.
2. **How and Why**   In what ways did the religious beliefs of the Greeks influence their literature, art, and architecture?
3. **Critical Thinking**   How did the beliefs of the Epicureans compare with the beliefs of the Skeptics?

The Greeks believed that one of the essentials of excellence was to do nothing in excess. They tried to achieve this goal of balance and proportion in their architecture and their sculpture. Their interest in moderation also affected their day-to-day living. At the same time, the Greeks delighted in words. Their epics, lyric poems, and plays have greatly enriched Western literature. Their histories have served as models for present-day scholars.

SECTION

4

The Arts, Science, and Society

Architecture and Sculpture

After the destruction of Athens by the Persians in 480 B.C., the Athenians rebuilt their city. They followed the words of Pericles, who said: "We are lovers of the beautiful.... What I desire is...that you should fix your eyes every day on [Athens]...and that you should fall in love with her."

From 447 to 431 B.C., Athenian artists decorated their acropolis with beautiful temples and statues. Probably the best known example of Greek architecture—the Parthenon—was built at this time. Constructed as a temple to the goddess Athena, its floor plan resembled the main hall of a Mycenaean palace. It was rectangular shaped with an entrance porch along one of the short sides. There were two doors—one facing east and the other, west—but no windows. Rows of columns supported the roof of the building on the outside. Between the top of the columns and the pitched roof were sculptures of gods, goddesses, and people. The entire building was constructed of marble. Within the Parthenon stood a massive gold and ivory statue of Athena. It was carved by one of the greatest of Greek sculptors—Phidias (FID-ee-uhs).

Most classical Greek sculpture, however, showed individual human beings rather than gods and goddesses. But the statues did not portray specific people. Rather, they were ideal representations of the human body. Hellenistic sculpture, on the other hand, was realistic. It replaced the order and balance of classical Greek sculpture with emotion and energy. Among the well-known sculptors of the Hellenistic Age were Praxiteles (prak-SIT-uh-leez) and Myron.

The Theater

Greek theaters were open-air constructions called amphitheaters. Their stone seats and benches were set in the natural bowl of a hillside and curved around three sides of the stage. The theaters were very large. For example, the one at Athens seated 14,000 people.

To enable audiences to hear better, the actors walked on raised shoes and spoke through canvas-and-plaster masks, the mouths of which were shaped like a megaphone. The masks also showed the characters' sex, age, and personality type. Only males performed on the Greek stage, so some were trained to play the parts of females. There was no scenery. At times a chorus—a group of singers and speakers—described events that were happening offstage. They explained the background of the play or told a part of the story.

Greek tragedies explored the struggles of people to free themselves from the flaws in their characters. It was these flaws that caused individuals to perform acts that led to their destruction. Among the Greek dramatists of the 500s and 400s B.C. whose works are still performed are Aeschylus (ES-kuh-luhs), Sophocles, and Euripedes (you-RIP-uh-deez). Aeschylus wrote about the way people misuse power. Sophocles stressed the importance of meeting fate with dignity. Euripides bitterly criticized war and the suffering it brings. Several of his plays, including *Electra* and *The Trojan Women*, are about women.

According to Greek mythology, Athena was the goddess of war, wisdom, arts, and crafts. She was the special patron of Athens. This bronze statue of Athena was made in the 300s B.C. and stood in Piraeus, the port city of Athens.

The Greeks balanced their tragedies with comedies that poked fun at the important and the disliked. The most famous of the comedy playwrights—also called satirists—was Aristophanes (ar-uh-STAHF-uh-neez). In *The Clouds* Aristophanes ridiculed Socrates. The philosopher is shown talking from a basket suspended in midair. Aristophanes implies that Socrates' words were impractical and full of hot air. Only those whose feet are firmly planted on the ground have wisdom and common sense.

History

The two greatest Greek historians were Herodotus (hi-RAHD-uh-tuhs) and Thucydides (thoo-SID-uh-DEEZ), both of whom lived during the Golden Age. Herodotus wrote a popular history of the Persian Wars many years after the wars had ended. He relied in large part upon the memories of those who had survived the conflict. Although he tended to

exaggerate numbers, his work contained a great deal of information about the events and everyday life of the period. Thucydides wrote a scholarly history of the Peloponnesian War, in which he himself had participated. Using many factual details, he hoped to lead his readers to a clearer understanding of past events.

Although in ruins, the Parthenon, above left, is still a good example of Greek architecture. Above right, modern Greeks still attend performances of ancient Greek plays. Today, however, women play the female roles as in this production of Euripides' play Hippolytus.

Science

During the Classical Age, science was generally studied by philosophers who were searching for a way to explain the forces of nature. Great strides were made by these early Greeks. By careful reasoning, they came to realize that nature was ruled by fixed laws, not by gods and goddesses. They also came to realize that these laws could be discovered and systematically studied.

Many of the leading Hellenistic scientists worked and studied in Alexandria, Egypt. The city contained a government-supported library with as many as 700,000 rolls of papyrus and parchment manuscripts. Next to it stood an institution for advanced studies called the Museum, where scholars could carry out experiments.

Medicine   In the fifth century B.C. Hippocrates, the "father of medicine," taught that doctors should observe their patients carefully, draw

This picture of a young man writing on a clay tablet is on the inside of a kylix, a two-handled drinking cup. The Greeks decorated their cups, vases, pitchers, and various jars and containers. Much of what we know of the early Greeks comes from such objects. Why would people decorate everyday items like these?

conclusions from their observations, and compare notes with one another. He often recommended rest and an improved diet to his patients. Hippocrates founded a medical school for which he drew up a list of rules known as the Hippocratic oath. The rules included never betraying anything about a patient's private life and never administering a deadly drug. Many medical school graduates still take the Hippocratic oath today.

Early Greek physicians included many women. Physicians had a knowledge of simple surgical methods and of the functions of the heart and the importance of the pulse. They also knew that the brain was the center of human thought.

Astronomy Great strides were made in astronomy during the Hellenistic Age. The solar year was calculated to within about 6 minutes of modern calculations. The lunar month was computed to within 2 seconds of the figure accepted today. Aristarchus, who lived during the 200s B.C., speculated that the earth and the other planets revolve around the sun—an idea known as the **heliocentric theory**. However, he was unable to prove his ideas. As a result, Aristotle's **geocentric**, or earth-centered, theory remained generally accepted for about 1800 years.

Eratosthenes, a contemporary of Aristarchus, knew the earth was spherical, not flat. He also argued that all the world's oceans are connected. Seventeen centuries before Columbus, he claimed that if one sailed west from Spain one would eventually reach the coasts of India. Eratosthenes made a fairly close estimate of the earth's circumference.

Hipparchus, who lived in the 100s B.C., is generally considered to be the greatest astronomer of ancient Greece. He catalogued nearly 900 stars and knew the approximate distance of the earth from the moon as well as the moon's diameter. He did all this without the aid of a telescope!

Greek science did not begin with the Hellenistic period. Anaximander, for example, who lived from 611 to 547 B.C. is credited with designing a sundial and introducing mapping. Above is his description of the universe.

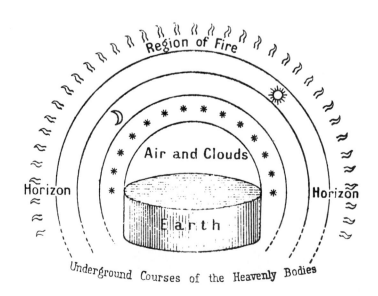

Mathematics   Perhaps the most important scientific developments during the Hellenistic Age took place in mathematics. Around 300 B.C. Euclid gathered together much of the Greeks' mathematical knowledge and developed the basic principles of geometry. His approach is still found in geometry textbooks today.

Archimedes (AHR-kuh-MEED-eez) was one of Euclid's students. He continued the mathematical work of his teacher and uncovered various laws of physics. Archimedes developed the pulley and the lever. He once used them to pull a loaded ship out of the sea by himself. He also laid the foundations of calculus. Although Archimedes and other Hellenistic scientists developed many mechanical devices, they usually regarded the devices as practical demonstrations of mathematical or scientific ideas.

At Home, School, and Work

The Greeks were not obsessed with material comforts. Their daily life was simple and focused toward the practical. City-dwelling Greeks lived in houses that were tightly packed along narrow lanes. The lanes often smelled of garbage because there were no drains or sewer systems. Water had to be carried from wells.

Most houses consisted of two main rooms and several smaller ones. One main room was a dining room with couches on which the men reclined during meals. The other was a wool room where the women spent their time spinning wool and weaving it into cloth. The Greeks hung their pottery, writing tablets, and weapons on pegs on the wall. The houses were lighted with olive-oil lamps.

The Greeks ate simply—fish, onions, lentils, barley cakes, and grapes. They washed down their food with a mixture of wine and water. Only the Spartans ate meat on a regular basis.

The Greeks dressed as simply as they ate. The men draped themselves in rectangular cloths called tunics, which they pinned at the shoulders and belted at the waist. When they went out, they merely threw another piece of cloth over their shoulders. Women dressed in a similar fashion, but their tunics were longer. Both men and women wore sandals.

The family unit consisted of husband and wife, all unmarried children, and married sons and their wives and children. A married woman lived with the family of her husband.

The father was the absolute head of the household. He arranged the marriages of his daughters, although he usually consulted with his wife. A girl was usually only 14 or 15 years old when she married, and she rarely saw her husband before the marriage. The father gave each daughter a dowry, which had been agreed upon with her future husband's family. Women in Greek society stayed mostly in the home. They did not shop in the market. They did not go to banquets with their husbands. Even when a man entertained at home, a wife was expected to keep out of sight.

dowry:
the money, goods, or estate that a woman brings to her husband in marriage

The rather limited life of Greek women did not represent a scorn for them. The Greek deity of wisdom was a female, Athena. Women characters played central roles in Greek drama. Sappho, who wrote in the 600s B.C., is considered one of Greece's greatest poets. However, woman's place was generally considered to be in the home rather than in public.

At the age of six or seven, Greek children whose parents could afford it were sent to private schools. Schooling consisted of reading, writing, public speaking, literature, mathematics, and music. A well-balanced Greek needed a healthy body as well as a healthy mind, so boys also learned to hurl the discus, throw the javelin, jump, race, and wrestle. Girls learned gymnastics.

If the family could afford it, a boy at 14 went on to advanced studies in government and astronomy, among other fields. If his family was poor, a boy was apprenticed to his father. At 18 young men entered the armed forces for a year. At 19 they were admitted to full citizenship. Upon the death of the father, all sons shared equally in the inheritance.

Most Greek city-dwellers owned small businesses. They were potters, weavers, blacksmiths, or metalworkers. In general, Greeks worked only for what was necessary to support themselves and their families. Business was not their whole life. They took an active role in public affairs, and they spent much of their time exchanging ideas.

SECTION 4 REVIEW

1. **Recall** In what field did the most important scientific developments take place during the Hellenistic Age? What were some of these developments?

2. **How and Why** How did Greeks feel about work?

3. **Critical Thinking** How did classical Greek sculpture compare with sculpture from the Hellenistic period?

R E V I E W

Reviewing People, Places, and Things

Identify, define, or explain each of the following:

Troy

acropolis

agora

democracy

Olympic Games

Sparta

Athens

tyrants

Persians

tribute

Delian League

Peloponnesian War-

Philip II

Alexander the Great

Hellenistic Age

Zeus

Socrates

Plato

Aristotle

Stoics

Cynics

Skeptics

Parthenon

Euripides

Hippocrates

Archimedes

Map Study

Using the map on page 525, determine the answers to the following questions:

1. How far east did Alexander the Great's empire extend?
2. How far west did Alexander's empire extend?
3. How would it be possible to travel by sea from India to Egypt?

Understanding Facts and Ideas

1. **a.** What is the major source of information about Minoan culture? **b.** What are two things we have learned?
2. What do the *Iliad* and the *Odyssey* tell us about the early Greeks?
3. What effect did geography have on the development of the city-states?
4. What were four of Solon's reforms?
5. Why was the Delian League formed by the Greek city-states?
6. What was the result of the Peloponnesian War?
7. Who were the Macedonians?
8. How did Alexander the Great attempt to blend the customs and institutions of the Greeks with those of the peoples he conquered?
9. What were some ideas Plato wrote about in *The Republic*?
10. What did Greek tragedies explore?
11. **a.** Who was Hippocrates? **b.** What is the Hippocratic oath?
12. What was life like for Greek women?

Developing Critical Thinking

Recognizing Values   The Spartans and the Athenians had far different values. What were some values that were important to the Spartans, and what were some values that were important to the Athenians?

Writing About History

Relating Past to Present   The Stoics believed that all peoples should live together in tolerance and equality. They spoke out against slavery and war. They urged everyone to take an active part in public affairs. In a brief essay, discuss whether this philosophy was accepted by the majority of Greeks. Also discuss whether people today would accept the Stoics' philosophy.

Applying Your Skills to History

Summarizing   To summarize material means to restate what you have read in general terms. A summary should be short, complete, and accurate.

Activity: Read and summarize a Greek myth or poem.

The Roman Era

During the days of its greatness, Rome ruled an empire that stretched from Persia and Africa to the Danube and Rhine rivers and to southern Scotland. At their best, the Romans showed a sense of duty and sacrifice. They displayed tolerance and common sense in governing the peoples of their empire. In time the empire declined, and Roman rule passed to others. In the West the empire was divided and ruled by Germanic peoples. In the East the Byzantine emperors ruled. The center of the Christian Church in the West, however, remained in Rome.

As you study this chapter, think about these questions:

- How did the Romans govern the peoples they conquered?
- How did other cultures influence the development of the Romans?
- What caused the fall of the Western Roman Empire?
- What factors influenced the development of the Byzantine Empire after the fall of Rome?

Remains of Roman rule can be seen throughout Western Europe and the Middle East. This Roman aqueduct—a structure for carrying water—is in France.

Sometime after 2000 B.C. groups of migrating peoples discovered the passes through the Alps that separate Italy from the rest of western Europe. For more than a thousand years, members of these groups straggled through the passes to settle the Italian peninsula. Some lingered in the rich green valley of the Po River. Others continued down the western plains that lay between the Apennine Mountains and the Tyrrhenian (tuh-REE-nee-uhn) Sea.

Among the groups that moved south were a people called Latins. They settled on one of seven hills overlooking a ford of the Tiber River. The Latins were the ancestors of the Romans. Their development was greatly influenced by the Etruscans.

Roman Beginnings

Many scholars believe that the Etruscans came from Lydia, in western Turkey. By the 600s B.C. they had established a series of city-states in central Italy.

Etruscan cities were walled and stood on hilltops for protection against attack. The Etruscans paved their streets with pebbles and lined them with raised sidewalks. They designed arches for their gates and laid underground sewers. They built their houses and temples of wood and sun-dried mud bricks. They used stone only for their underground tombs. Tomb walls were decorated with colorful paintings of the Etruscans feasting, dancing, and playing such musical instruments as the flute, the trumpet, and the lyre. The Etruscans earned their living by mining iron, copper, and tin and exporting these minerals to Greece and the North African city of Carthage in exchange for silver and gold.

About 616 B.C. the Etruscans conquered the Latins and ruled them until 509 B.C. During this period, the Latins absorbed many culture traits from their conquerors. First, they learned to use the arch in construction. Second, they adopted the alphabet the Etruscans had borrowed from the Greeks. The later Romans modified this alphabet, which is the one we use today. Third, the Latins adopted the practice of consulting soothsayers in an attempt to foretell the future. The soothsayers would examine animal livers or observe the direction in which a flock of birds was flying. Then they would interpret these signs from the gods. A fourth Etruscan custom adopted by the Latins was that of having two slaves fight to the death when a noble died. The spirit of the dead slave was supposed to accompany his master's spirit to the underworld. In later years, similar fights were carried on with hundreds and even thousands of men and animals. Known as gladiatorial games, they became Rome's main form of entertainment. Finally, the Latins adopted the Etruscan custom of the triumph—a parade to honor a victorious general returning from battle.

The Latins also retained certain values of their own. These values later became part of Roman culture. One value was a strong sense of duty. It was unthinkable for a Roman sentry to desert his post. Roman soldiers never surrendered. They either retreated to prepare for another attack or else committed suicide. A soldier who proved cowardly in battle was stoned to death.

Ancient Italy
- Etruscans
- Latins
- Greeks

Etruscans decorated the
walls of their homes as well
as their tombs.

Another basic characteristic of the Latins was an emphasis on the
clan. Clan members gave one another financial support. They also helped
one another win elections. For many years, members of the top 20 or so
clans held most of Rome's public offices.

In 509 B.C. the Latins revolted against the Etruscans and drove them
from Rome. They replaced the Etruscan monarchy with a republican form
of government that lasted until 31 B.C. The Latins eventually became
known as Romans, taking their name from the city of Rome. The word
republic comes from the Latin words *res publica* meaning "the public
business." A republic is governed by elected representatives.

The Republic

The Romans wanted to prevent the return of a monarchy. Therefore, they
divided the powers of government among several branches. In that way,
no one person could obtain total control.

Structure of Government   At the head of the republic were two
officials known as **consuls**. They were chosen each year by the Senate.
They administered the laws and also served as military leaders. If either

consul disagreed with the other consul's orders, he said "Veto—I forbid," and the orders did not have to be obeyed. Sometimes, during a war or civil emergency, the consuls, with the consent of the Senate, would appoint a **dictator**, or absolute ruler, to govern for a maximum of six months.

The Roman Senate was composed of 300 members who were appointed for life. The Senate determined foreign policy, approved building contracts for roads and temples, and advised the consuls on taxation and finance. Most senators were former consuls.

There was also an assembly, but it had few powers. Additional government officials included **praetors**, or judges, and **censors**, who took the census. Censors also passed judgment on the morals of Roman citizens and drew up the lists of citizens from which senators were selected.

census:
the official counting and collecting of information about a people by its government

Patricians and Plebeians

At the time the Romans overthrew the Etruscans, they were divided into two classes: **patricians** and **plebeians** (pli-BEE-uhns). Patricians, who made up about 10 percent of the population, were wealthy landowners. Plebeians—common citizens—included small farmers, artisans, merchants, and laborers. Women had no legal status.

At first only patricians had the right to participate in government. Laws were not written down, so a patrician judge could say that something was against the law and a plebeian had no way to prove the judge wrong. Plebeians were not allowed to declare bankruptcy. If they fell into debt, they were sold as slaves. In addition, marriages between patricians and plebeians were prohibited.

In 494 B.C. the plebeians decided to band together to gain more rights. All Roman men were required to serve in the army. But that year, when a call to arms was issued, the plebeians refused to respond. They threatened to leave Rome and set up a rival city if the patricians did not make some changes. A political compromise quickly followed.

A special Assembly of Tribes was created to represent the plebeians. The Assembly could participate in making laws. Each year, it also elected

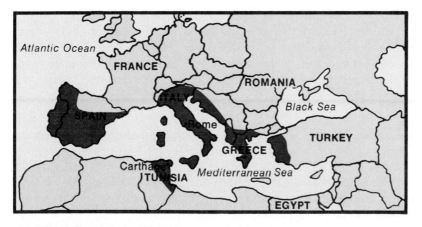

■ Roman Republic, c. 133 B.C.

ten tribunes, who had the power to veto any act of the Senate, the consuls, or the judges that was unjust or that violated the rights of the plebeians.

Gradually, plebeian power and social conditions improved. Around 450 B.C. the laws of Rome were set down on 12 bronze tablets. The Twelve Tables, as they were called, defined property and family rights and duties. They also guaranteed all citizens the right to appeal severe court sentences. In 445 B.C. plebeians gained the right to marry into the patrician class. In 367 B.C. they won the right to be elected as consuls. By 300 B.C. plebeians were eligible for all public and religious offices of the republic. In addition, enslavement for debt was abolished.

Despite these improvements the government remained largely in the hands of patricians. Public offices did not pay a salary, and the cost of running a political campaign was high.

War and Conquests

Soon after the Romans expelled the Etruscans from Rome, they started conquering Etruscan cities. Thus began an expansion that continued until the name of Rome was known and feared in Europe, Africa, the Middle East, and other parts of Asia.

Reasons for Success   One reason the Romans were so successful in expanding their boundaries was the manner in which they organized, trained, and provisioned their armies. Every Roman male was expected to be a soldier, and no one could run for office unless he had served in the army for ten years. Wealthy Romans provided their own helmet, shield, sword, and javelin. They also served without pay. Poorer citizens were equipped and paid by the government.

Roman soldiers were organized into legions of about 5,000 men. The legions were subdivided into groups of 60 to 120 soldiers who could split off from the main force to encircle the enemy. The soldiers were tough and skillful. Every day, they practiced fighting with their double-edged iron swords. They also made a forced march of 20 miles.

Another reason the Romans were successful conquerors was because they made allies of the friendlier peoples in Italy and enlisted their help in conquering the more hostile ones. Often they offered the conquered peoples special privileges and even citizenship in return for their help. By 264 B.C. the Romans held all of Italy south of the Po River.

The Punic Wars   As the Romans extended their power farther and farther south, they came into conflict with the powerful trading empire of Carthage. From its founding in 800 B.C., Carthage had expanded its lands, and held colonies in northern Africa and on the islands of Sicily, Corsica, and Sardinia. It also controlled the trade routes of the eastern Mediterranean.

Between 264 and 146 B.C. the Romans and the Carthaginians tested each other in a series of three wars known as the Punic (PYOO-nik) Wars. Rome began the First Punic War in 264 B.C. by building a fleet to match Carthage's naval strength. For nearly 23 years, Rome battled Carthage on the seas. Losses on both sides were staggering. Neither side was able to invade the other's home territory. Finally, in 241 B.C., Carthage was forced to ask for peace. As a result, Rome obtained Sicily, Corsica, and Sardinia.

The Second Punic War was started by Carthage. The Carthaginians had established themselves in Spain. In 218 B.C. a brilliant Carthaginian general named Hannibal led 40,000 soldiers, 37 war elephants, and 8,000 cavalry from Spain across the snow-covered Alps into Italy. For nearly 15 years, Hannibal ravaged the peninsula. Although he defeated the Roman armies many times, he was unable to capture the walled cities or totally defeat Rome. Finally, the Roman general Scipio cut Hannibal's supply lines in the Mediterranean and attacked Carthage itself. Hannibal returned to northern Africa to defend his native city. In 202 B.C. Hannibal was defeated at the battle of Zama, and Rome gained control over the entire western Mediterranean. The battle of Zama ensured that Roman and not Carthaginian culture would form a basis for Western civilization.

Despite their victory, however, many Romans still felt threatened by Carthage. They also wanted revenge for the damage that Hannibal had inflicted on Italy. In 149 B.C. Rome launched an attack against Carthage. Three years later, the Third Punic War came to an end. The Romans burned Carthage to the ground and plowed its site with salt so no crops could grow. The captured Carthaginians were sold into slavery, and Carthage became a Roman province in Africa.

By the end of the 100s B.C. Rome had also conquered Greece, Macedonia, and parts of Western Asia, and had made Egypt a protectorate. The Romans had become the rulers of much of the all-Hellenistic world. They could truly call the Mediterranean *mare nostrum*—"our sea."

SECTION 1 REVIEW

1. **Recall**   What was the structure of the government of Rome?

2. **How and Why**   Why were the Romans so successful in expanding their boundaries?

3. **Critical Thinking**   Why do you think Hannibal chose to cross the Alps to invade Rome rather than launching a sea attack from Carthage?

From Republic to Empire

The Punic Wars launched Rome on the road to empire. They also brought about economic and social changes that eventually undermined the republic and led to the reestablishment of one-person rule.

A Time of Troubles

Rome's economic difficulties began in the countryside. Many of Italy's farms had been devastated during Hannibal's invasion, and the returning farmer-soldiers did not have enough capital to bring their land back into cultivation. Therefore, they were forced to sell their land to patricians and rich businessmen, who combined the small farms into large estates.

Instead of hiring the displaced farmers to work the land, the estate owners employed slaves. Originally, Rome had not taken slaves from conquered peoples. Then Rome's power spread into the Hellenistic world, whose economy rested on slave labor. The luxurious lifestyle of the Hellenistic kingdoms greatly impressed the Romans, and soon they were bringing in tens of thousands of war prisoners as slaves to grow their food, clean their houses, and work in their businesses.

The unemployed and landless farmers sought refuge in Rome, but finding work in the city was extremely difficult. There were almost no industrial jobs except in construction. Commercial enterprises were usually run by Greek slaves, who were better educated and more

By the end of the Roman Republic, fights between gladiators were a favorite form of entertainment. This mosaic shows a wounded gladiator dropping his dagger. Why might this type of game appeal to the masses of poor Romans?

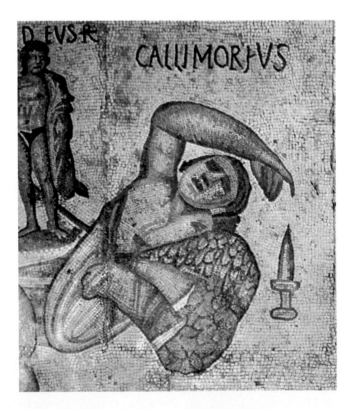

knowledgeable about business than Roman farmers. Finding a place to live was also a problem. Most displaced farmers ended up in crowded wooden tenements that lacked sanitation, were subject to frequent fires, and sometimes collapsed because of their cheap construction. The farmers could not even reenlist in the army, because the Romans believed that only property owners had a stake in fighting for Rome.

The only thing of value that the displaced farmers possessed was the right to vote. Accordingly, they sold their votes to whichever office-seeker paid the most. Payment consisted of *panem et circenses*—"bread and circuses." Candidates for public office distributed wheat at low prices, and put on free such spectacles as chariot races, fights to the death between animals, and gladiatorial games—fights between armed men. The gladiators—usually criminals, slaves, or prisoners of war—were trained in special schools and then hired out.

Public corruption was not limited to buying votes. When Rome expanded beyond Italy, it began collecting taxes as well as slaves. To collect taxes the Roman government used private individuals called **publicans**. A publican would pay Rome a certain amount of money for the right to collect taxes in a city or a province. Then he would try to collect enough to make a profit. With such opportunities for **graft**, most publicans became very rich very quickly.

As social unrest within Rome increased during the century after the end of the Punic Wars, a series of popular leaders tried to keep the republican system of government from dying. Some of these leaders were politicians. Others were soldiers.

Attempts at Reform

The first reformers were the Gracchi (GRAK-eye) brothers—Tiberius and Gaius. Tiberius was elected as a tribune in 133 B.C. He proposed a limit of 600 acres on the amount of land that any one family could own, and urged that the surplus land be distributed to unemployed citizens. His proposal frightened and angered wealthy landowners in the Senate, who stirred up a mob that clubbed Tiberius to death.

Gaius was elected as a tribune in 123 B.C. He suggested that the government take over the distribution of cheap wheat to the poor. His proposal was eventually adopted. By 100 B.C. free wheat was being distributed to the poor, and one out of three Romans was on welfare. Gaius also did away with the publicans and substituted a direct income tax. He also wanted to extend Roman citizenship to all Italians, but once again, an alarmed Senate resisted reform. A mob killed 3,000 of Gaius's followers, and Gaius himself committed suicide to avoid being captured.

The next group of reformers was all military men. First came Gaius Marius. Marius abolished the citizen-soldier army and replaced it with a professional army whose soldiers served for a fixed period of time and were paid by their general. This helped reduce unemployment, because the professional soldiers did not have to be landowners. But it transferred the loyalty of the legions from Rome to their general.

Another military reformer was Sulla, who declared himself dictator after several years of civil war between himself and Marius. Sulla tried to make the patrician Senate the most powerful branch of government, as it had been in the early years of the republic. He doubled the number of senators and did away with the power of the tribunes to veto legislation. He extended Roman citizenship to all Italians, and he placed the legions under the command of provincial governors rather than the consuls. This last reform led to the rise of perhaps the most famous Roman of all—Julius Caesar.

Julius Caesar

Julius Caesar was a well-educated, athletic man with great personal charm and speaking ability. In 61 B.C. he joined forces with an ambitious general named Pompey and a wealthy noble named Crassus. By combining their power, the three men were able to dominate the Roman government.

Crassus was soon killed in war, leaving Pompey and Caesar. Each wished to rule alone. Pompey had gained great popularity by conquering Syria and Jerusalem. He had also put down a year-long rebellion of some 70,000 slaves. Caesar, too, knew that the way of the soldier was now the way to permanent power.

While consul in 59 B.C., Caesar had himself appointed governor of the province of Gaul. In 58 B.C. he started a military campaign that in nine years brought what is now Belgium, Holland, France, part of Germany, and part of Great Britain under Roman rule. Caesar sent back to Rome progress reports on his victories. These reports were collected and published as *Commentaries on the Gallic Wars*. In addition to helping spread Caesar's fame, the book provided a wealth of information about the Gauls, the Germans, and other peoples.

In 49 B.C. the Senate, fearful of Caesar's growing power and popularity, demanded that he resign as governor and return to Rome without his army. Caesar responded by marching on Rome. When he reached the Rubicon River, which separated Gaul from Italy, he was met by a messenger from the Senate. The messenger stated that if Caesar entered Italy with his troops, the Senate would consider him a rebel. Caesar replied, "The die is cast!" and crossed the river. He quickly captured Rome.

Pompey, who had been elected consul and who now opposed Caesar, fled first to Greece and then to Egypt, where he was killed. Most senators fled as well. In 46 B.C. Julius Caesar had himself appointed dictator for ten years. In 44 B.C. he became dictator for life.

Caesar used his dictatorial powers to tackle many of the republic's problems. He resettled 80,000 landless army veterans and their families in the provinces. He started a public works program of building roads and draining marshes. Owners of large estates were required to fill at least one-third of their labor needs with unemployed citizens. Caesar chose his officials carefully and tried to make the tax collection system more honest and efficient. He extended Roman citizenship to Greeks, Spaniards, Gauls, and others who lived outside Italy, thus knitting the empire closer together. He also appointed non-Romans and business people to the Senate, making it more representative.

Leaders like Caesar often arouse fear and envy. Especially if, like Caesar, they wear royal purple robes in public and put their portrait on coins—something that only Hellenistic kings had done in the past. Convinced that Caesar meant to abolish the republic and declare himself a divine monarch, a group of 60 senators—led by Caesar's trusted friend Brutus—formed a conspiracy. On the Ides of March (March 15), 44 B.C., they stabbed Caesar to death and left his bloodied corpse lying at the foot of a statue of Pompey.

The End of the Republic

Caesar's death did not restore the republic. Instead, Octavian—Caesar's adopted son and chosen heir—and a leading general and consul, Mark Antony, combined their power to rule Rome for nearly 11 years.

In 32 B.C. civil war broke out between the forces of Octavian and those of Antony. The following year at Actium, off the coast of Greece, Octavian defeated Antony and became supreme in Rome. He ruled for 45 years, until A.D. 14. Throughout the period, the structure of the republic was kept, but the actual power was in the hands of one man. Although the only title Octavian accepted was that of Augustus, or great one, he is considered the first Roman emperor.

Julius Caesar used his role as a soldier to rise to power. What other leaders have used their military positions to gain control of government?

SECTION 2 REVIEW

1. **Recall**   Who were the Gracchi brothers? What were their goals?

2. **How and Why**   Why were many farmers displaced after the Second Punic War?

3. **Critical Thinking**   Why do you think Caesar's friends turned against him and even participated in his assassination?

The Roman Republic lasted for almost five centuries. So, too, did the Roman Empire. Its first 200 years were a period of stability and prosperity known as the *Pax Romana*, or Roman peace. Its last 300 years were a gradual decline.

The Age of Augustus

Under Caesar Augustus (Octavian) the expansion of the Roman Empire was halted, and frontiers became well-defined by such natural features as the Atlantic Ocean in the west, the Rhine and Danube rivers in the north, and the Sahara in the south. Augustus stationed Rome's legions permanently along the borders. The only troops remaining in Rome were 3,000 members of an imperial bodyguard called the Praetorian Guard. Under later emperors, border security was reinforced by stone walls built across southern Scotland and along the Rhine and Danube rivers.

Augustus reformed public administration of the empire in several ways. He set up a bureaucracy of slaves and freedmen that reported directly to him. He eliminated graft by paying provincial governors large salaries, and also by punishing them severely if they stole public funds. He ordered a periodic census so that the tax rates on land and property would be fair.

Augustus also improved life in Rome. He distributed wine and olive oil as well as grain. He set up a public police force and a public fire department. He ordered the construction of more aqueducts and sewers, and he had numerous public baths built.

This inscription in Latin and Neo-Punic (bottom) is the dedication for a Roman theater built in A.D. 1–2 in what is modern Libya.

The Pax Romana

Succeeding emperors continued Augustus's administrative techniques. In general, the Romans interfered little in the local affairs of their subjects. The Romans asked them only to pay taxes, fill their quotas of soldiers, acknowledge the emperor, and keep the peace. Having done this, the Romans left their subjects to follow their accustomed ways of life.

Nevertheless, Roman rule had a substantial influence upon conquered peoples. For the first time cities sprang up throughout Western Europe. Many—including London, Vienna, Bonn, and Cologne—were originally Roman army camps.

The Latin language spread throughout the empire and gradually developed into the Romance languages of the Indo-European language family: French, Italian, Portuguese, Rumanian, and Spanish. Also, many Latin words have been incorporated into English.

During the Pax Romana, trade between the empire's provinces and cities greatly expanded. The Mediterranean Sea was cleared of pirates, and new trade routes were opened. The government built docks and lighthouses to improve the movement of goods. Tariff barriers between provinces were eliminated. A uniform currency and improved banking practices further encouraged commerce. In addition, luxury goods—

■ **Roman Empire at Its Peak, c. A.D. 117**

such as amber and furs from northern Europe, spices and jewels from India, and especially silk from China—flowed into the empire.

Inner Weaknesses

Despite the stability and prosperity of the *Pax Romana*, the Roman Empire faced several problems that gradually led to its decline and fall. The first problem was political. Because Rome was officially still a republic, there was no rule about succession. Sometimes the son of an emperor took over, or an emperor designated a hard-working, popular man as his successor. At other times, an ambitious general would march into Rome at the head of his troops and declare himself emperor. Occasionally, the Praetorian Guard simply auctioned off the throne to the highest bidder.

Until A.D. 180 the transfer of power was usually peaceful. After that date, it was not. Between A.D. 180 and 284, Rome had 35 emperors, most of whom were assassinated by their own troops. The average reign lasted less than three years. Needless to say, under such circumstances the emperors paid little or no attention to government.

This political problem led to an economic one. An emperor who wanted to stay in office had to pay his troops, and pay them well. Since the empire had stopped expanding, there were no new sources of wealth. Therefore, the tax burden on civilians skyrocketed.

In addition, Rome began to suffer from inflation. Although no more gold was coming into the empire, a great deal was going out to pay for luxury goods. Accordingly, the government issued new coins that mixed gold with copper or lead. Because such coins were worth less than the old coins, prices went up. During the A.D. 200s they soared 20,000 percent! In some areas, people stopped using money altogether. They used grain, clothing, or labor for exchange instead. The Roman economy was reduced to a barter system.

Quarreling between military factions also weakened the empire. At the same time Rome became subject to invasions by groups of Germanic peoples from across the Rhine and Danube rivers. The Germans were seminomadic herders who kept pigs and cattle and practiced slash-and-burn agriculture. They also were excellent fighters, who trained for war in much the same way the Spartans had. In A.D. 258 a Germanic people called Goths invaded Greece and sacked Athens. Another Germanic people called Franks swept across northern Gaul. The Alemanni invaded southern Gaul, and the Saxons threatened England. Even Rome was forced to put up a brick wall for protection.

Attempts at Reform

The collapse of Rome was delayed for some years by the able rule of two emperors. Diocletian ruled from A.D. 284 to 305. Constantine I ruled from A.D. 312 to 337.

Diocletian   Diocletian focused his attention first on Rome's external problems. He strengthened the forts along the empire's borders. He also organized a special army that he shifted from place to place as needed to repel Germanic invasions.

Diocletian next turned his attention to internal problems. He increased his prestige by asserting that the emperor ruled by divine right. He dressed in purple robes and wore a crown of gold set with pearls. He insisted that people kiss the hem of his robe before addressing him.

Diocletian realized that the Roman Empire was too large to be administered by one person. So he divided it into two parts—eastern and western. Diocletian chose a co-emperor to govern the western division, while he spent most of his time in the eastern portion.

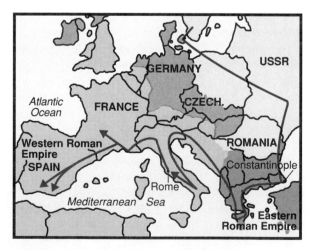

Invasions of the Visigoths, c. A.D. 300s-500s

Diocletian then tackled Rome's economic problems. Because the government needed certain goods, workers producing those goods were not allowed to quit their jobs. Diocletian also fixed maximum prices for goods and wages in an attempt to control **inflation**—rising prices. Diocletian's economic reforms were not successful. They led only to an increase in the number of government officials.

Constantine I   Constantine continued Diocletian's reforms, making the Roman Empire even more regimented than before. Not only were workers forbidden to change jobs, but sons also inherited their fathers' occupations. City officials were made personally responsible for community taxes. If for some reason—such as poor harvests or a plague—a community could not pay its taxes, the official had to make up the difference himself.

Constantine's economic policies were no more successful than Diocletian's had been. The only result was that wealthy landowners, in order to avoid the government's heavy hand, left the cities and set themselves up in self-sufficient country estates called villas. Gradually, farmers living near the villas gave up their lands to the estate owners in return for protection against government officials, Germanic invaders, and wandering outlaws. At first these farmers paid for the use of land with the crops they raised, but soon they became **serfs**, who were bound to the land they tilled.

Constantine's religious and political reforms, however, were lasting. In A.D. 313 he legalized Christianity by the Edict of Milan. He also built a capital for the eastern part of the Roman Empire on the site of the ancient Greek colony of Byzantium. He named it Constantinople.

The Final Stand

Despite the efforts of Diocletian and Constantine I, the Roman Empire continued to decay. Plagues depopulated large areas of Italy. The number of poor continued to increase. The government, near bankruptcy from trying to meet the costs of the military and feeding the poor, was forced to raise taxes again and again. Although Roman leaders talked about the old virtues of responsibility and simplicity, their personal lives were often selfish and corrupt.

As you have read, the Germans began moving into the western regions of the empire after the second century. In A.D. 376 one of these Germanic groups—the Visigoths, or West Goths—sought peaceful entry into the empire. They were being threatened by the Huns, fierce warriors from central Asia. However, the Romans did not live up to a promise of land and food for the Germans. As a result, they rose up under their leader Alaric and decisively defeated the Romans at Adrianople in A.D. 378. The main reason for the German victory was a technological development the Germans had learned from the Huns, who in turn had learned it from the Chinese. This was the iron stirrup. Stirrups enabled a

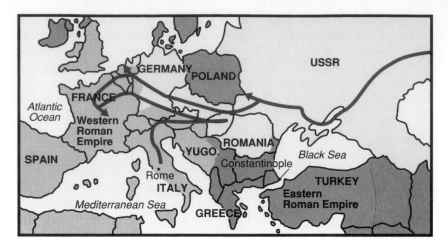

Invasions of the Huns, c. A.D. 300s-500s

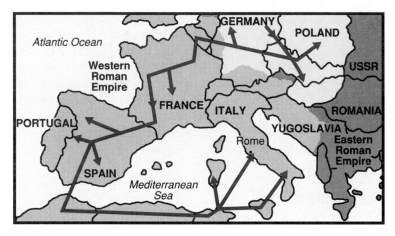

Invasions of the Vandals, c. A.D. 400s

horseman to change direction easily and also to add the thrust of a charging horse to the thrust of a spear. Not even a Roman legion could stand up to the force of a cavalry charge.

By A.D. 410 the Visigoths had reached Rome. The marauders shocked the empire by plundering the city. The victory of the Visigoths opened a floodgate through which poured other Germanic peoples. In A.D. 455 Rome was again plundered and sacked, this time by the Vandals. In A.D. 476 a Germanic general named Odoacer (OHD-uh-WAY-suhr) seized control of Italy and proclaimed himself king. Other Germanic kingdoms were carved out of the remaining lands in the west. The once-great Roman Empire had come to an end.

1. **Recall**   What was the period in Roman history known as the *Pax Romana*?
2. **How and Why**   In what way did the problem of succession weaken the Roman Empire?
3. **Critical Thinking**   Do you think it was wise of Diocletian to divide the Roman Empire into eastern and western regions? Why or why not?

The Romans took the thoughts and works of the Greeks and others of the Mediterranean area and blended them with their own ideas. For example, much of the knowledge we have of Greek sculpture is from Roman copies.

However, the Romans were creators as well as adaptors and preservers. They invented instruments for surgery and passed on to later Europeans a tradition of public hospitals and public hygiene. They built a legal system that people continue to follow. Roman domes, arches, and amphitheaters are still copied, and the foundations and routes of Roman roads are still in use. Roman writings are still read for their style and view of life.

SECTION

4

Beliefs and Accomplishments

Spirits and Deities

Roman religion was both private and public. The male head of a family was responsible for carrying on household sacrifices and other religious ceremonies. Elected priests conducted public observances.

The spirits that protected the household and its fortune were called *lares* (LAR-eez). Other spirits called *penates* (puh-NAYT-eez) guarded the storeroom. The Romans set bronze statues of the lares on the table while they were eating. They burned incense or candles before statues of the penates. The Romans also worshiped spirits that watched over the grain from its sowing to its storing.

The most important Roman spirit was Vesta, guardian of the hearth. As the hearth was central to the Roman household, so Vesta was the center of Roman worship. Within the temple of Vesta in Rome—the only round building in the city—a sacred fire always burned, attended by six vestal virgins. They came from leading Roman families and served for 30 years, from about the age of ten. The Romans believed that if the vestal fire died out, Rome too would perish.

The Romans also accepted deities from other peoples. For example, the Greek god Zeus became the Roman god Jupiter, and Hera became the Roman goddess Juno. Aphrodite was known to the Romans as Venus.

553

The Greek messenger of the gods, Hermes, was changed to Mercury. The cult of Mithra, which emphasized fighting for good causes, came from the Persians. It was very popular among the Roman legions. Many Roman women followed the cult of Isis, the Egyptian fertility goddess. Judaism made numerous converts, and after the first century A.D., some Romans accepted the God of the Christians. By the end of the fourth century, Christianity was Rome's official religion.

During the time of the empire, the Romans also practiced emperor worship. However, this was political rather than religious. Worshiping the emperor was considered a means of expressing publicly one's loyalty to Rome.

The Stoic Appeal

The Romans adopted the philosophies as well as the deities of the Greeks, particularly Stoicism. The Stoic insistence on the obligations of citizens appealed to the Romans, who had their own ideas of duty and public spirit. The Stoic idea of the unity of people agreed with the Roman idea of empire.

Emperor Marcus Aurelius was both a soldier and a follower of Stoicism. Does this statue portray both sides of his character? If so, how?

Among the leading believers in Stoicism was the emperor Marcus Aurelius (A.D. 161–180). He spent considerable time fighting on the frontiers of the empire, and knew the hardships that doing one's duty often requires. He related in his book *The Meditations of Marcus Aurelius* that he was often tempted to remain under his blankets in the cold early morning. Then he would remember his obligations, throw off his warm coverings, and begin his day.

Law

Rome's most important legacy to Western civilization was Roman law. It was based upon reason, tolerance, and justice. When Cicero (SIS-er-oh), one of Rome's greatest lawyers and orators, was asked to define the legal ideal, he replied, "It is of a sort that cannot be bent by influence or broken by power or spoiled by money." To Cicero, obeying the law was central to civilization. "We are servants of the law in order that we may be free."

As you know, the first Roman code of law, the Twelve Tables, was written down about 450 B.C. It was designed for the simple farm life of the early republic. However, life did not remain simple for long. As the Romans expanded their empire, they expanded their law. They adapted it to meet the customs of their new subjects. As a result, they were able to govern millions of people of varying cultural backgrounds.

Roman judges were flexible in interpreting the law for each case that came before them. Their interpretations became what is known as "case law," or precedents for other judges to follow and upon which to base further interpretations. Roman law grew in much the same fashion that later English common law grew — daily, gradually, and practically.

Roman law emphasized certain principles that have since become part of the legal systems of much of the Western world. Among these principles are:

1. The law applies equally to everyone.
2. Laws are just, not because they are enforced by the power of the state, but because they are reasonable.
3. A person is considered innocent until proven guilty.
4. No one suffers a penalty for what he or she thinks, only for what he or she does.
5. In inflicting a penalty, one should consider the age and inexperience of the guilty person.

Architects and Engineers

Although Roman sculpture in bronze and marble is still admired, the Romans are best remembered as builders. At first they copied Greek styles of architecture, using rectangular forms and graceful columns. Later, they developed their own style. It involved the use of the arch,

The Appian Way, which ran south 366 miles (589 kilometers) from Rome to Brindisi, was the first of Rome's great roads. It was begun in 312 B.C. by Appius Claudius Caecus, who also built the first of Rome's great aqueducts.

which the Romans had originally learned from the Etruscans, and also the vaulted dome. The Romans used the arch not only in their buildings but also in their bridges and aqueducts. The Romans also built arches as monuments to commemorate military victories. They decorated these arches with elaborate sculptures of Roman soldiers and prisoners of war. The largest dome in Rome capped the Pantheon—a temple dedicated to all the gods—and measured 142 feet (43.3 meters) in diameter and 142 feet (43.3 meters) from floor to ceiling. The Romans covered the dome on the outside with bronze so that all over the city, people could see its gleam.

The Romans made their buildings massive and strong to demonstrate their might. Perhaps their most imposing structure was the Colosseum (kahl-uh-SEE-um). It was built during the A.D. 70s, mostly by Jewish prisoners of war. It seated more than 50,000 spectators, who watched gladiatorial games and other spectacles under awnings that protected them from the sun. Vendors in the aisles sold bread, sausage, and wine. Gladiators and animals were kept in cells underneath the arena's floor until it came time for them to fight and die.

The Romans were also noted for the network of roads that linked the empire together. They tried to route the roads in as straight a line as possible, going over a hill rather than around it. They also built roads on an embankment that was higher than the surrounding land. In that way, the roads could be kept clear of mud in summer and snow in winter. The Romans built their roads as solidly as possible so they would need little or no maintenance. Roman roads had four layers of foundation topped with a watertight paving, and most of them lasted 80 to 100 years without needing repairs. Only Roman military forces and government postal messengers were allowed to use the roads. Ordinary people, their trading carts, and their animals moved along the roads' unpaved shoulders. Many modern roads are laid over old Roman ones.

Literature

The Age of Augustus not only marked the start of the *Pax Romana*, it also was Rome's greatest literary period. The emperor wanted the Roman people to be proud of themselves and of Rome. Accordingly, he encouraged such writers as Virgil, Horace, and Livy.

Virgil was influenced by a sense of the destiny and greatness of Rome. His finest creation is the epic poem, the *Aeneid* (ih-NEE-uhd). The *Aeneid* tells the legendary story of Aeneas, who escaped the destruction of Troy by the Greeks. After much wandering and many adventures, he settled in Italy, where his descendant Romulus founded the city of Rome.

Horace wrote hundreds of poems. Some dealt with love or nature, others praised Augustus and called on the people to observe the old Roman values of living simply and doing one's duty. Many of Horace's poems were intensely patriotic. *"Dulce et decorum est pro patria mori*— 'Tis sweet and glorious to die for one's country."

Livy was Rome's leading historian. Although he tended to exaggerate Roman accomplishments, his writing was vivid and full of detail.

Writers after the Age of Augustus were generally not so talented. There were exceptions, among them Petronius, Juvenal, and Tacitus. Both Petronius and Juvenal satirized the vices of Rome under the empire. Tacitus wrote a classic description of the early Germans. In his history, *Germania*, he compared the hardiness and simplicity of the Germans to the softness of many Romans.

satirized: criticized or poked fun at people's ideas or actions

Below left is an outside view of the Colosseum in Rome. At right is the interior. The Colosseum was built for fights between gladiators and humans and animals. By the 1400s Romans had begun using it as a source of building materials. Today the Colosseum is a major tourist attraction.

How did the life of Roman women differ from that of Greek women?

Family Life

The Roman family was an extended one. In addition to the husband and wife, the household included unmarried children and married sons and their families. Property was held in the father's name. When he died, it passed to his sons in equal shares. By the time of the empire, however, women as well as men could inherit property.

Legally, a father's authority over his family was absolute. He could sell his children into slavery and even kill a family member in order to protect the family's honor. In practice, however, Roman families were very affectionate. A father usually consulted all the men in the household before making any major decision.

It was up to the father to arrange his children's marriages. Girls were usually engaged by the age of ten and married in their mid-teens. Boys were older. Under the empire, divorce became common among the upper class, and many people married as often as five or six times.

Originally the primary duty of Roman women was the bearing and raising of children and the care of the home. Because they had no legal status, they could not vote or run for office. Unlike Greek women, however, Roman women had social freedom. They did the marketing, helped entertain at home, and frequently went out with their husbands on business and social engagements. Poor women worked at such occupations as spinning, weaving, making clothing, nursing, hairdressing, and selling fish and other foods. Under the empire, upper-class women sometimes became lawyers and doctors.

The Romans did not provide free schooling, but private schools were open to both boys and girls. In addition, wealthy Romans were sometimes taught at home by an educated slave or by a private tutor. After graduation, a young man might attend one of the famed schools of philosophy or medicine in Athens or Alexandria.

SECTION 4 REVIEW

1. **Recall**   What philosophy of the Greeks especially appealed to the Romans? Why?

2. **How and Why**   How did Roman law help the Romans to govern millions of people of varying backgrounds?

3. **Critical Thinking**   Why do you think only Roman military forces and governmental postal messengers were allowed to use the roads built by Rome?

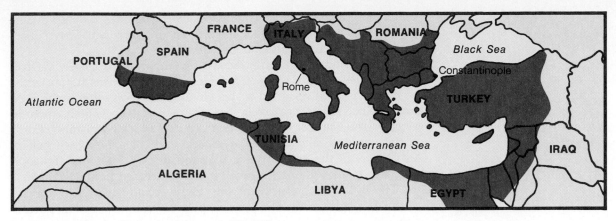

■ Byzantine Empire Under Justinian, A.D. 527–565

W hen Constantine I chose the site for the eastern capital of the Roman Empire, he chose well. Constantinople, formerly Byzantium, boasted a strategic location. It lay along the waterway between the Black Sea and the Mediterranean Sea. The city was at the crossroads of trade routes between Asia and Europe. Its landlocked harbor provided a calm and safe anchorage for ships. Three sides of the city were surrounded by water. The fourth side was protected by strong walls.

Within a short time Constantinople surpassed Rome in importance. Although the empire in the west fell, the eastern provinces survived for another thousand years. The people of the eastern Roman Empire considered themselves Romans. Because they differed culturally from the western Romans, they are referred to as Byzantines (BIZ-uhn-teens).

The Second Rome

Constantinople resembled Rome in many ways. The Byzantines copied Roman architectural styles in their public buildings, roads, bridges, aqueducts, and sewer systems. The emperor employed a Roman-style bureaucracy. Byzantine courts followed Roman principles of law. The government provided bread and circuses to the poor. Even Constantinople's slums were as jammed and unhealthy as those in Rome, and much of the economy rested on slave labor.

Constantinople also differed from Rome in several ways. From the day Constantinople was founded, it was a Christian city dedicated to the Holy Trinity and the Virgin Mary, the mother of Jesus. Public buildings were decorated and topped with crosses. Everywhere stood magnificent churches and shrines containing the bodies of saints. Each year thousands of pilgrims journeyed to these shrines in search of cures for their illnesses. Because of the Christian emphasis on charity, Constantinople was also filled with orphanages and old-age homes. Churches served free meals daily to the poor. Furthermore, the Byzantines did not put on gladiatorial games, which they considered un-Christian. They substituted chariot races and other amusements.

Church and state in the Byzantine Empire were closely related. Although the emperor was not considered divine, he was supported by the divine. He was regarded by his subjects as God's representative on earth. He had more voice in religious affairs than the patriarch whom he selected. The emperor also had the right to choose and dismiss church officials, to settle all church disputes, and to decide all religious beliefs. All citizens of the empire were required to be Christians. If people preferred to keep other religions, they were excluded from citizenship.

The Byzantine government was highly centralized. The emperor controlled all government finances, appointed and dismissed all government officers, made all laws, served as supreme judge, and directed the army and navy. The official language of government was Latin, although in daily life the Byzantines generally spoke Greek.

Justinian and Theodora

codify:
arrange items in a system

The most outstanding of the Byzantine emperors was Justinian, who ruled from 527 to 565. One of his greatest contributions was in the field of law. He ordered a group of legal experts to gather all the laws of the empire—including the legal opinions of judges—and codify them. Through Justinian's Code the main ideas of Roman law became part of the legal system of most Western European nations. The code also incorporated certain Christian principles. Judges were urged to put human rights above property rights. The emperor was reminded, when making new laws, to take into account the welfare of the people. At the same time, the penalties set forth in Byzantine law would probably seem very cruel to us. The Byzantines considered the death penalty un-Christian. Instead, they blinded criminals, tore out their tongues, or cut off their noses or hands.

Justinian succeeded in reuniting parts of the Western Roman Empire. A major reason for this success was his appointment of an extremely talented officer named Belisarius as his general. Belisarius not only reorganized the Byzantine army, but he also developed new battle techniques. In later years the Byzantines became famous for their textbooks on military strategy and for training their generals.

Justinian's wife Theodora greatly influenced the emperor. When a revolt broke out and the emperor's advisors urged him to flee, Theodora urged him to stand firm.

"In a crisis like the present we have not time to argue whether a woman's place is in the home, and whether she ought to be meek and modest in the presence of the lords of creation. We have got to get a move on quick. My opinion is that this is not the time for flight—not even if it is the easiest course. Everyone who has been born has to die; but it does not follow that everyone who has been made an emperor has to get off his throne."

These mosaics of the Emperor Justinian and Empress Theodora were made in the 500s. What reasons can you give to explain why Byzantine rulers wanted to enlarge the empire?

Justinian took his wife's advice and succeeded in putting down the revolt.

Theodora also worked to improve the place of women in Byzantine society. As a result of her efforts, Byzantine women gained the right to own a certain amount of land. Widows could raise their children the way they wished and manage their late husbands' property.

The Byzantine Economy

Constantinople ranked among the most prosperous trading centers of the world. Goods poured in from everywhere. Furs, hides, ivory, gold, silver, spices, jewels, slaves, wine, and foods of all varieties came into the city daily from far and near. The government benefited greatly from this trade because taxes were charged on all imports and exports. The government also controlled the profitable silk industry, which began during Justinian's reign. It eventually became a major source of Byzantine wealth. According to legend two Christian monks smuggled silkworm cocoons out of China in their hollow bamboo walking sticks.

Each worker within the empire had to belong to a **guild**—a group of workers who followed the same trade or craft. The government set wages and hours and told certain guilds where they could carry on their work. Byzantine artisans were known throughout Western Europe and the

Middle East for the high quality of their luxury goods. Brightly colored silks, heavy gold brocade, richly colored glassware, sparkling enamel and jewelry, and delicate ivory carvings were some of the products made in Byzantine workshops.

The fall of the western Roman Empire was preceded by the substitution of barter for money. The Byzantine Empire, on the other hand, continued to use currency. Its gold coins were so highly regarded that places as far away as India and Axum accepted them without question. The coins were engraved with a portrait of Christ and the words "Jesus Christ, King of Rulers."

The Byzantine Empire was built on trade. This gold bracelet from the A.D. 600s is an example of the type of goods Byzantine merchants would have traded.

Education and the Arts

The Byzantines placed a high value on education. Most young men between the ages of five and twenty attended school. After learning how to read and write, they studied grammar, which included memorizing the epic poems of Homer. They also studied public speaking, astronomy, mathematics, music, and philosophy. Although Byzantine women were often well-educated, they were taught only at home.

A significant aspect of Byzantine education was the fact that Byzantine scholars preserved the writings of the ancient Greeks. Thus, Greek ideas, learning, and literature were kept alive for people in other lands and other times.

Byzantine literature consisted mostly of religious works, such as the biographies of saints. There were, however, two notable Byzantine historians. Procopius wrote a vivid *History of the Wars of Justinian*. Anna Comnena described the reign of her father, Alexius I, in her history, *Alexiad*.

One of the finest expressions of Byzantine art was in the architecture of the churches. Byzantine architects developed a way to support domes on four columns rather than by circular walls. This enabled them to set domes over rectangular, square, or cross-shaped spaces as well as round ones. The outstanding example of a Byzantine church is Hagia Sophia, the "Church of Holy Wisdom," which was built by Justinian. Hagia Sophia was rectangular, and its dome was so huge that it seemed to float on air. Dozens of windows circled its base. The ceiling was overlaid with gold, the walls and floor were of marble decorated with mosaics, and the altar was solid gold. The story is told that when Justinian first saw the completed interior, he exclaimed, "I have outstripped you, O Solomon!" Hagia Sophia was the model for domed churches in Western Europe, Russia, and Turkey.

The Religious Atmosphere

Christianity was an important part of the lives of the Byzantines. From the emperor down to the most ordinary citizen, religious matters were discussed and debated as fiercely as politics. Often, issues were both religious and political in nature.

At first it was only natural for Christians to think of the pope in Rome as holding a central position in the organization of the Church. Rome had long been the center of government power. The authority of the pope was strengthened by the **doctrine** of Petrine supremacy. This doctrine states that the pope is the divinely appointed head of the Church. He is the successor to Rome's first bishop, Peter, to whom Jesus had given leadership of the Church.

Some early popes vigorously asserted their authority, at least in the western part of Europe. Eastern Christians, however, did not accept the supreme authority of the pope. They gradually began to look on both the patriarch and the emperor living in Constantinople as their religious leaders.

In the 800s Byzantine missionaries went out to convert the Slavs and other peoples of Eastern Europe and Russia. The Byzantine missionary brothers, Sts. Cyril and Methodius, invented an alphabet still used by the Soviets, the Serbs of Yugoslavia, and the Bulgarians. It is called the Cyrillic alphabet in honor of Cyril.

Friction between the patriarchs and the popes, however, continued. Eastern Christians conducted church rituals in Greek instead of Latin. There were also disagreements over the use of **icons**, or images, in worship. In addition, there were disputes over the nature of God. Finally, as you know, in 1054 a **schism**, or formal division, split the Church. The eastern Christians referred to their church as the Eastern Orthodox or Greek Orthodox Church to distinguish it from the Roman Catholic Church.

Fall of the Empire

In the late 1000s, the Byzantine Empire began to decline. Many of the later emperors spent so much money that taxes on small farmers skyrocketed. The farmers were forced to sell their land to large landowners and become tenants because they were unable to pay their taxes. The loss of the farmers' independence caused them to lose their willingness to serve in the army.

As a result, when the Byzantines were attacked in 1080 by a European soldier of fortune named Robert Guiscard, they had to call on the city-state of Venice for military assistance. In exchange, the Byzantines gave the merchants of Venice the right to trade in Byzantine cities without paying the usual tax. Within a few years, most of Byzantium's trade was in the hands of the Venetians, and the empire itself—having lost most of its tax revenues—was almost bankrupt.

In 1204 the Fourth Crusade went to Constantinople instead of the Holy Land. The crusaders plundered the city as though it were the stronghold of a hated enemy. The Byzantines regained Constantinople in 1261, but their power was considerably reduced. In 1347 the city was devastated by a form of bubonic plague that killed almost two-thirds of its population. In 1453 Constantinople's walls were demolished by a new weapon—cannon—and the Byzantine Empire fell to the Ottoman Turks. Constantinople is known today as Istanbul and is still part of Turkey.

SECTION 5 REVIEW

1. **Recall**   Where was Constantinople located? Why was this location important?

2. **How and Why**   In what way was Justinian's Code important to Western Europe?

3. **Critical Thinking**   Why did the Byzantine Empire decline beginning in the late 1000s?

R E V I E W

Reviewing People, Places, and Things

Identify, define, or explain each of the following:

Etruscans	Brutus
republic	Marc Antony
consuls	Caesar Augustus
Senate	(Octavian)
censors	Pax Romana
patricians	Constantine I
plebeians	Edict of Milan
Assembly of Tribes	Visigoths
Twelve Tables	lares
Carthage	Penates
Punic Wars	Virgil
Scipio	Horace
Julius Caesar	Constantinople
Crassus	Theodora
Pompey	guild

Map Study

Using the map on page 549, determine the answers to the following questions:

1. How far west did the Roman Empire extend at its peak?
2. How far south did the Roman Empire extend?
3. Between which two bodies of water was Constantinople located?

Understanding Facts and Ideas

1. **a.** Who were the Latins? **b.** What group of people greatly influenced their development?
2. **a.** What were the Punic Wars? **b.** What was the final result of these wars?
3. What change made by Gaius Marius brought about military rule in the Roman Empire?

4. How did Julius Caesar strengthen his control of the Roman Empire?
5. What administrative techniques were used during the Pax Romana to keep the Roman Empire together?
6. **a.** Which Greek deities were comparable to Roman ones? **b.** What Stoic ideas appealed to the Romans?
7. How did Roman buildings differ from Greek buildings?
8. How did Theodora work to improve the place of women in Byzantine society?
9. How did the loss of land by small farmers greatly weaken the Byzantine Empire?

Developing Critical Thinking

Analyzing Cause and Effect   Write a brief essay explaining what you believe was the primary cause in the fall of the Western Roman Empire. Explain why.

Writing About History

Analyzing Geography   Write a short paragraph explaining why Rome's location helped it build a vast empire in Western Europe.

Applying Your Skills to History

Analyzing Political Power   Strong leaders who bring about political reform or who lead a nation to greatness are often feared and envied. Julius Caesar was such a leader. While many Romans believed it was good to have a strong leader, many others thought it was not.

Activity: Use encyclopedias and other reference books to research a strong leader of the twentieth century. Write a brief essay discussing whether or not you think this strong leadership was good for the country involved. Explain why or why not.

Some crusaders were more interested in what they could take for themselves than in fighting Muslims. Why were castles like this one necessary?

The Medieval Scene

From the late 400s through the 1000s—the early part of the period known as the Middle Ages—Europeans struggled to survive as monarchs, knights, and raiders divided Western Europe. There were few towns, little trade, almost no education, and almost constant warfare. The people found hope and stability in Catholicism. They also developed a new form of government called feudalism and a new kind of economy known as manorialism. After the 1000s, conditions in Western Europe changed. The period from around 1100 to 1450—the later Middle Ages—may be viewed as the introduction to a new age. In some countries, an economically powerful middle class began to experiment with national legislatures. In other countries, monarchs used force to centralize the power of the new nations in their own hands.

As you study this chapter, think about these questions:

- What were the major forces shaping Western Europe in the Middle Ages?

- What effects did the ending of feudalism and manorialism have on the economic, social, and political development of Western Europe?

- How did religion and philosophy influence the arts of the Middle Ages?

For several centuries after the fall of the Western Roman Empire, Western Europe was divided into many different kingdoms ruled by Germanic kings. By the 800s, however, most of the culture region was part of a great empire ruled by the Franks.

Franks

In the late 400s the various Frankish tribes began to unite. Under their king, Clovis, they established themselves as rulers of much of what is now France and western Germany. Clovis became a Christian in 496 and encouraged the conversion of his people. From then on, the Franks and the Roman Catholic Church cooperated closely. The clergy supported Clovis's wars and helped him administer his conquests. Clovis adopted certain practices of the Roman Empire. He dressed in purple robes and insisted that government officials and courtiers use Latin instead of German.

The Franks ruled for several centuries, but their practice of dividing land among the sons of the ruler led to constant civil war. Gradually the real power of the crown was taken over by a royal officer called the mayor of the palace. One of the greatest of these mayors was Charles Martel, or Charles the Hammer. In 732 he defeated an army of Muslim Arabs and Moors at the battle of Tours. This victory preserved Christianity in Western Europe. Martel's son Pepin III officially assumed the title of king in 751.

At this time, another Germanic tribe called the Lombards were threatening to overrun much of Italy. The pope called on Pepin for help. Pepin marched into northern Italy and defeated the Lombards, who were forced to return some of the lands they had seized. These lands became known as the Papal States. They remained under the political control of the pope until 1860. In exchange for his support, the pope anointed Pepin as king and blessed him. This action not only established the concept of divine kingship, but it also drew the Church into greater political involvement in Western Europe.

Charlemagne   Pepin's son Charlemagne (SHAHR-luh-mayn), or Charles the Great, ruled from 768 to 814. He received his nickname because he stood six feet three inches at a time when most men were about a foot shorter. Historians consider him to be great because of his accomplishments.

Charlemagne doubled the size of his empire until it reached from the Danube River to the Atlantic Ocean and from Rome to the Baltic Sea. On Christmas Day of the year 800, Pope Leo III crowned Charlemagne as the emperor of the Romans. Once again an emperor ruled most of the West, but he was a Frank, not a Roman. The coronation showed that the Roman idea of a universal empire still existed in Western Europe.

Charlemagne ruled his vast empire by dividing it into hundreds of districts run by local officers called counts. Each year he sent out royal investigators to check on the counts and to listen to complaints. The

■ Charlemagne's Empire

567

investigators worked in pairs—one noble and one clergyman. This demonstrated the close relationship between church and state. Charlemagne regarded himself the way the Byzantine emperor did, as the Christian head of a Christian state. He appointed bishops as well as counts. If someone disobeyed the Church, it was considered treason against the emperor.

Charlemagne also worked to promote learning in the empire. He was very proud of his ability to read Latin and a little Greek, even though he was never able to master the skill of writing. He urged priests to study Latin and mathematics and to improve their education. "Although it is better to *do* the right than *know* it, nevertheless knowledge should precede action." He had a palace school set up and ordered bishops to set up similar schools. Irish monks were brought to the empire to correct and to rewrite old manuscripts, including those of Julius Caesar and Virgil. The Romans had used only capital letters in their writing. The monks developed a new script that contained lower-case letters as well. The new script was much easier to read than the old script and also took up less room.

Division of the Empire   Charlemagne's rule brought law and order to Western Europe. His personality and ability enabled him to hold his empire together. But his successors were neither strong enough, energetic enough, nor talented enough to follow his example.

In 843 the empire was divided among Charlemagne's three grandsons. One received what is now Germany. Another received most of what

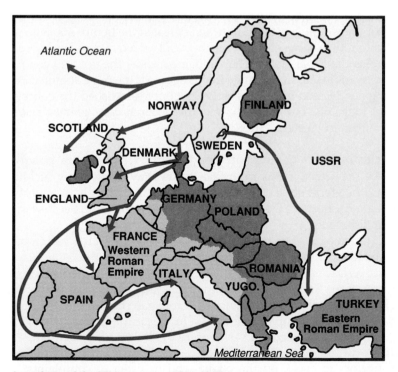

Invasions of the Vikings, c. A.D. 700s-1000s

is now France. The third received the title of emperor and a strip of territory between the other two kingdoms.

This division brought constant war to Europe. The middle kingdom was eventually absorbed into the eastern part. The central government was weakened as local lords asserted their independence. The breakdown of authority was hastened by continued invasions from various directions. The most terrifying raiders were the Vikings.

Vikings

The Vikings were a group of Scandinavian people. Beginning around 800, they raided settlements along the coasts and up the rivers of Western Europe. The Vikings would make surprise attacks and then withdraw quickly before a defending army could be gathered to attack them. Wherever the Vikings struck, they plundered villages, destroyed churches, and spread terror among the people. The people of Western Europe prayed: "From the fury of the Northmen, O God, deliver us!"

The Vikings were fierce warriors. They were also excellent sailors. Their wooden ships carried square sails and were long and narrow in shape. The Vikings decorated the bows of their ships with dragons' heads to frighten both enemies and ocean spirits.

After a time, the Vikings began to settle in the areas they raided and in lands beyond Western Europe. By 900 the Norwegian branch of the Vikings had settled in Iceland. In 930 the Icelanders drew up a constitution and established a governing body. The Norwegians also traveled to Greenland, where they founded a colony under the leadership of Eric the Red. It is believed that Eric's son, Leif, sailed farther west to the North American coast around 1000. It was in England, Ireland, and other parts of Western Europe, however, that the Vikings had their most important effect.

The Danes, another group of Vikings, conquered large portions of England during the 800s and 900s. The Anglo-Saxons, led by Alfred the Great, resisted, and the Danes were able to hold only the eastern third of the country. In 1017 a Dane named Canute succeeded in conquering all of England. His line did not last, however, and in 1042 England again came under Anglo-Saxon rule.

In 911 another group of Danes led by a warrior named Rollo attacked the city of Paris, France. After a ten-month-long siege, the king offered Rollo gold and a province of his own if Rollo would help defend France against other Vikings. Rollo agreed and thus became the first Duke of Normandy. The former Vikings—now known as Normans—adopted Christianity, the French language, and other elements of French culture.

In 1066, led by William, Duke of Normandy—later called William the Conqueror—the Normans crossed the English Channel and attacked England. They defeated the forces of King Harold at the battle of Hastings and began their long rule of England. Over the centuries, the traditions, languages, and customs of the Anglo-Saxons and the Norman French mixed and evolved into a new culture.

HIC EXEVNT:CABALLI DE NAVIBVS:· ET HIC:MILITES: FESTINA VERVNT:HES

On September 26–27, 1066, William the Conqueror and a fleet of 3,000 ships crossed the English Channel from Normandy to England. Within three months, William was king. Above is a section of the Bayeux Tapestry. According to legend, Matilda, William's wife, embroidered it.

The Vikings also attacked Ireland. The Irish had originally inhabited Britain but had been forced to leave by the Anglo-Saxons. In Ireland they set up a simple fishing and farming society. Because Ireland lay west of Britain, it remained free of Germanic attacks. Scholars, artists, and monks from the European continent were attracted by its peace and safety. After the Irish were converted to Christianity, the island became a center of education and the arts. Irish monks created beautiful **illuminated**—illustrated—manuscripts.

From around 800 to 1000, the Vikings fought over Ireland. They were able to conquer the principal cities largely because they wore armor, while the Irish did not. Then an Irish leader named Brian Boru overthrew Viking rule, and the Vikings were eventually absorbed by the Irish. In the late 1100s the Norman English invaded Ireland. This began a long conflict between the English and the Irish.

The Norwegian and Danish Vikings had crossed the stormy North Sea to raid and later to conquer. The Swedish branch of the Vikings, however, sailed across the Baltic Sea and became rulers of the first Russian state.

By 1000 the beginnings of modern Western European states could be seen in faint outline. There were independent units called England, Scotland, Ireland, Wales, Denmark, Norway, and Sweden. The German Otto I had been crowned Holy Roman Emperor and extended his rule to include northern Italy. France had a king, although he governed only a very small portion of France. There were Christian kingdoms in northern Spain, but the Muslims controlled most of the country.

SECTION 1 REVIEW

1. **Recall**   What practice led to constant civil war among the Franks?
2. **How and Why**   In what ways did Charlemagne promote learning in his empire?
3. **Critical Thinking**   How were the Vikings able to travel from their homeland in the northern region of Western Europe to other parts of the area and beyond?

A mid the puzzle of scrambled political authorities and the uncertainties of existence, there stood an unshakable institution in Western Europe—the Roman Catholic Church. It gave stability to the lives of medieval people and hope to their future. By the 1000s the non-Christian was an oddity in Western Europe, and the rare person who denied Christian truths was considered a heretic.

Stability Amid Instability

The Roman Catholic Church

The Church conditioned people to look at life very differently from the way the earlier Greeks and Romans had. The welfare of the soul became all-important. Life on earth was a period of testing and waiting, a preparation for a better life after death. Because of this attitude, the Middle Ages was a time of acceptance rather than doubt. People endured rather than rebelled. Most did not question their short life span, their poor living conditions, the feudal system, and secular or clerical authorities.

Church and State   Through the doctrine of Petrine supremacy, the pope possessed the authority of God on earth. During the Middle Ages strong and able popes molded the Roman Catholic Church. Gregory the

This medieval woodblock print shows a church procession. Printing pictures from woodblocks was an important art form during the Middle Ages. The method was first developed by the Chinese in the A.D. 700s.

Great (590–604) expanded the membership of the Church. His missionaries converted the inhabitants of northern Italy, England, and Spain. Leo III (795–816) asserted the political power of the pope by crowning Charlemagne emperor.

As in the eastern empire, politics began to play a large part in religious matters. In the 1000s Gregory VII forced the emperor of Germany, Henry IV, to do penance for opposing the pope's authority. Henry had to travel to Italy and stand outside the papal residence, barefoot and robed in burlap, for three wintry days. Innocent III (1198–1216) regarded kings and emperors as his subordinates.

The pope had weapons to enforce his power. Chief of these were **excommunication** and **interdict**. Excommunication was the cutting off of an individual from the sacraments of the Church. Fellow Catholics were told to avoid this person. Interdict was excommunication applied to an entire country or region rather than to an individual.

If punishment, or the threat of punishment, is to be effective, it must be fitted to time and circumstance. The Western Europeans of this period were very religious people. They feared that their souls would burn in hell forever if they died while excommunicated. Western Europeans—whether nobles, merchants, or peasants—wanted no part of a life without the comfort of the Church. Consequently, the mere threat of these punishments was usually sufficient to bring the disobedient into line.

Cardinals, archbishops, and bishops generally came from the nobility while parish priests were usually peasants. An intelligent man from a peasant family could sometimes rise to a high position in the Church. The Church offered one of the few ways for sons of the lowly to become educated and gain power.

The Church was the most powerful political and economic institution in Western Europe. It was the largest landowner, and its income exceeded that of all the region's kingdoms combined.

The Monastic Life   The idea of withdrawing from the world to follow a monastic life—a life of religious contemplation and prayer with other people—started among Christians during the third century. In the early sixth century, a monk named Benedict wrote a set of rules that became the basis of monastic life during the Middle Ages. The rules were based on poverty, chastity, and obedience. Those who followed Benedictine rules promised to own no worldly goods, to remain unmarried, and to obey the head of the monastery or the convent. Their lives were given to prayer and to manual labor.

Monks and also **nuns**—women who joined organizations that followed the same type of rules established for monks—cultivated orchards, reclaimed swampland, and devised and used the best farming practices then known. They made clothes, tools, and leather goods. Some monasteries became famed for their wine and beer. Monasteries and convents were often used as inns by travelers. They were the charitable centers of Western Europe, distributing clothes and food to the poor. They also served as hospitals, where sick people from the surrounding countryside could obtain medicines and nursing care.

In the silence of monasteries, monks studied, wrote, and copied what they thought to be the best of the ancient classics. Many of these works had been saved by Jewish scholars working in Arab-ruled countries. By copying these works, the monks preserved them and also increased the number available for study. The monks were concerned mainly with spiritual matters. As a result, they destroyed manuscripts they felt were opposed to Christian teachings.

Monasteries began to collect documents and manuscripts. These collections eventually became libraries. The monasteries also began schools. During the Middle Ages the libraries and schools established by the monasteries were often the only ones in Western Europe.

The Benedictine monks were also a missionary order. They traveled throughout Western Europe trying to convert people to Christianity. In the 1200s two other religious orders were founded, known as the Franciscans and the Dominicans after their founders, St. Francis of Assisi and St. Dominic. The members of these groups, generally called friars, went into the world to minister to spiritual and physical needs and to make converts.

The Inquisition

During the 1100s and 1200s, several **heresies** arose in Western Europe that posed serious problems. The most widespread of these was the Albigensian heresy that spread throughout southern France. The Albigensians believed that in order to lead a good life, people should avoid material things. They criticized the luxurious living of the clergy in Rome and went so far as to reject the Church hierarchy. The Albigensian heresy became mixed up in politics when a heretical noble murdered a representative of the pope and rebelled against the French king. The pope supported the king, and a crusade was launched against the Albigensians. The heresy was suppressed with considerable bloodshed.

The room where monks copied manuscripts was called a scriptorium from the Latin word scribo, to write. Why was the work of copying important?

Monks decorated the manuscripts they copied. The first letter of a new section would have a picture painted through it. At left is such a letter from a copy, made in the 1400s, of the work Natural History *by Roman naturalist, Pliny (A.D. 23–79).*

As you have read, the Church had weapons of interdict and excommunication to enforce its authority. But unlike a government, it had no power to punish with fines, prison, or other such penalties. Pope Gregory IX decided that stronger weapons were needed. In 1229 he created a court known as the Inquisition. It was to seek out and punish heretics and prevent new heresies from gaining followers. It was staffed mostly by Dominican friars.

At first the Inquisition took the form of an **interrogation**, or questioning, of a suspected person. If the person was found guilty, punishment ranged from fines to the taking away of a person's private property. In later years the Inquisition used torture to gain a confession. If a person refused to deny the heresy, he or she was sentenced to death. The Inquisition was especially active in Spain during the 1400s and 1500. As you will read later, Jews as well as suspected heretics were persecuted.

Problems of Power   As the Middle Ages wore on, some people began to question the Church. They usually did not doubt its teachings, but they often doubted the actions of some clergy. Sometimes a bishop or cardinal seemed more interested in advancing his own power or wealth than in spiritual matters. Some popes seemed to work only to gain land for themselves or to help a particular monarch. The welfare of the Christian community seemed second in importance.

Feudalism

Besides the Roman Catholic Church, **feudalism** helped people adjust to the decentralized life of Western Europe in medieval times. Although feudalism varied from place to place and developed later in some areas than in others, it had certain basic characteristics.

Feudal Structure   The feudal system was based on a set of obligations between a landholding noble and a person to whom the noble gave certain land rights. The noble was called a lord, and the person to whom the noble granted the use of the land was known as a **vassal**. The name vassal was an honorable title. In theory every noble was a vassal to someone above him or her. The ruler was the exception. He or she sat at the top of the feudal pyramid. The land itself was called a **fief** (FEEF). Both men and women could be lords and vassals, for daughters and widows could and did inherit property. Many lords and vassals were members of the secular clergy.

The grant of a fief was a contract that placed responsibilities on both lord and vassal. The lord promised to protect the vassal and to administer justice. The vassal promised to remain loyal to the lord and to give aid when needed. This aid was usually military. Vassals provided and equipped soldiers for battle and paid their expenses while at war. Should the lord be captured in battle, the vassal had to contribute to the **ransom**.

These obligations reflect the chief activity of the period—war. Little wars were constantly being waged to gain glory, to kidnap the rich for ransom, or to extend borders.

Knights

War was the pastime of men called knights. A man did not inherit knighthood. He earned it. At an early age he became a page in his lord's or lady's household. When he reached his teens, he became a squire and learned the use of arms. He was then assigned as a servant to a knight whom he accompanied into battle. When the squire had proven himself in battle, he was knighted in a formal ceremony.

The medieval ideal of chivalry held that a knight was supposed to be fair, honorable, brave, honest, respectful to women, eager to protect the weak and helpless, and ready to die defending the Church. In practice, of course, a man did not suddenly become loyal to the death or unable to live without honor just because he had been knighted. The knight was a man of his times—times when strength of arms was more important than education and when peasants and women were generally degraded.

When there were no real wars, knights kept in shape by staging tournaments. These were warlike games in which two groups of knights battled. One of the favorite tests of strength was the joust. Two riders fought to unseat each other with lances. Knights also took pleasure in hunting.

chivalry: behavior of knights; they were supposedly always fair, honorable, brave, honest, respectful, and generous

Living Conditions

At first lords lived in one-room wooden houses set on the top of a hill for protection. By the 1100s they were living in stone castles, with a central tower surrounded by high, thick walls and a deep moat. A drawbridge that was drawn up at night or during an attack was the only way across the moat. The drawbridge led into the castle yard. Around the yard stood stables, rooms for knights and servants, and storehouses. The storehouses held enough wheat, salt beef, and ale to enable the castle's inhabitants to withstand a six-month-long siege. However, since vassals were usually required to give only 40 days of military service a year, such long sieges were rare.

The castle itself contained not only a main hall but also private bedrooms on the second floor. Nobles slept on wool mattresses, and beds were surrounded by hangings that could be closed around the beds whenever the weather turned cold.

Manorialism

The economic system of medieval Western Europe was based on agriculture. Thousands of farming units known as **manors** were scattered throughout the region. The manors were held by feudal lords. Some manors contained thousands of acres, others only a hundred or so. Some lords held many manors; others owned only one. Over time, peasants became bound to manor lands. The peasants worked the land for the lords. This relationship between the peasants and the lords is called **manorialism**.

A typical manor included a manor house—the home of the lord and his family. It also usually included a mill to grind grain, a central oven, a blacksmith shop, pasture land, fields, and a peasant village. Surrounding this settlement was often a forest, which separated the manor from the outside world. The forests sometimes harbored outlaws. By the 1100s manors were usually self-sufficient. They bought little from the outside world except salt, iron, and stones for the mill. Sometimes the lord might purchase luxury items such as fine cloth. However, these goods cost money, and even nobles had little ready cash.

Serfs and Freemen   Two kinds of peasants lived on a manor—**freemen** and serfs. Freemen paid rent to the lord for the land they farmed. They were usually free to move from one manor to another. Most peasants, however, were serfs. Serfs were not slaves, but neither were they free. They were bound to the land and could not even marry without the lord's permission. Serfs had to give the lord of the manor a certain amount of animals or crops as a tax. They had to work on the lord's land for a certain amount of days each week—usually two or three. Even more time was required during planting and harvesting seasons. In addition, the serfs performed other services for the lord, such as repairing roads and

harbored:
gave a place to hide

This Spanish woodblock print of an armored knight on horseback dates from the 1500s. The introduction of gunpowder in the 1300s in Western Europe made armored knights on horseback impractical. Eventually they were replaced by foot soldiers with rifles.

bridges, digging ditches, carrying things to and from the manor house, and cutting wood. Serfs also had some rights that were protected. They did not have to serve in the army. They could not be bought or sold, nor could they be driven off the land.

Farming Methods   The farmlands on the manor were generally divided into three fields. One field was used for spring planting, another was set aside for fall planting, and a third field was left fallow so that it might regain its fertility. The fields were divided into long strips averaging one acre (0.4 hectares). The best strips were used to grow the lord's crops. Some of the strips were given to the Church. The rest of the strips—usually the poorest land—were used by the peasants to grow food for their families. Everyone shared the farming equipment and work animals.

The manor also had common land. Everyone could use the meadows for grazing animals, such as oxen, sheep, and pigs. They could also gather wood from the forest for fuel and for building purposes.

Living Conditions   The homes of the peasants were one-room huts with thatched roofs. The walls were sometimes wood, sometimes stone. If there was no fireplace, the fire was built on the dirt floor. Smoke filtered out through small openings in the roof. Peasants owned a few pots, perhaps a spindle and a loom, a bag of straw for a bed, a wooden plank or two for a table, and a few rough utensils. At night or during bad weather, peasants shared their small huts with their animals.

Ordinary people usually ate black bread, cheese, cereals, soup, cabbage and a few other vegetables. They also ate eggs and salt pork when they were available. In northern Europe peasants drank beer, and in the south they drank sour wine. Nobles had basically the same diet as the peasants but also ate meat. Despite the harsh lives of the peasants, they did have occasional times of enjoyment. Sometimes wandering players, acrobats, and storytellers entertained in the district of the manor. There were also holidays—usually religious ones—when everyone might rest. In general, however, the life of a peasant was one of back-breaking toil.

SECTION 2 REVIEW

1. **Recall**   What was the Inquisition? What was its purpose?

2. **How and Why**   In what ways could the pope enforce his powers?

3. **Critical Thinking**   How was the granting of a fief a contract between lord and vassal?

During the later Middle Ages, political, economic, and social changes took place in Western Europe. The growth of long-distance trade and the rise of towns gradually led to the decline of the manorial and feudal systems. An epidemic of bubonic plague called the Black Death also helped bring about an end to serfdom.

Growth of Commerce

Trade did not cease entirely after the fall of the Roman Empire. Some merchants and peddlers risked the dangers of robbers to travel from manor to manor to sell goods the manors could not produce. Frequently a market town served several manors.

Trade fairs were held in many parts of Western Europe during the Middle Ages. The fairs lasted for a certain number of days or weeks. They sometimes became yearly events. Merchants came from far and near to display their goods. People from the manors and the surrounding area came to look, to bargain, and to buy.

Beginning in the 1100s the pace of trade steadily increased. As sea and land routes expanded and became safer, more traders dared to travel them. One of the reasons for this expansion of trade was the crusades.

The Crusades   The crusades began as military campaigns to capture the Holy Land (Palestine) from the Seljuk Turks. During the 600s Arab Muslims had taken the Holy Land from the Byzantine Empire. Because Islam preached tolerance toward Christians and Jews, the ruling Muslims allowed them to visit and live in Palestine.

In 1070 the Seljuk Turks—a more warlike group of Muslims from Central Asia—conquered the part of the Middle East that included the Holy Land. They made it difficult for Christians to visit the shrines in the Holy Land. When the Turks threatened Constantinople, the Byzantine emperor asked the pope for help. In 1095 Pope Urban II called upon Western European Christians to unite and go to war against the Turks.

Many people answered the pope's call. They became crusaders for a number of reasons. First, many believed that if they died in battle in this holy war, their sins would be forgiven, and they would go directly to heaven. Second, many crusaders sought adventure and glory. Third, by joining the crusades, criminals were pardoned, and debtors had their debts cancelled. Finally, some crusaders sought to find land and wealth for themselves.

There were four major crusades and a number of smaller ones between 1096 and 1270. One of the lesser crusades was even undertaken by children. The crusades ended without achieving their final purpose. By the late 1200s the crusaders had been driven from all the areas of the Holy Land that they had gained earlier.

The Crusades, however, had certain lasting effects that the crusaders had not foreseen when they first set out with the cry "God wills it!" A significant outcome of the crusades was an increase in trade between

This broadsword once belonged to a crusader. Broadswords were double-edged and longer than the old Roman swords.

Western Europe and the Middle East. New foods and fabrics, such as cotton and satin, were brought to the West. New trade routes were opened. The crusaders' contact with the Byzantines and the Muslims led them to learn about advances in science, mathematics, medicine, and the arts. This knowledge led to a renewed interest in learning in Western Europe. The crusades gave Western Europeans a better knowledge of geography and stimulated their spirit of adventure and their interest in other lands.

In addition, the crusades had an effect on the growth of towns in Western Europe. Nobles needed money to equip themselves and their followers for the journey to Palestine. Therefore, they sold special privileges to towns under their control.

Finally, the crusades led to the decline of feudalism. Many nobles had lost their fortunes because of the costs of joining the crusades. Many of the most powerful nobles were away from their lands for many years or even lost their lives in the crusades. The increase in trade after the crusades brought about the wide use of money. This meant that kings could hire knights and pay them with money rather than reward them with fiefs.

The crusades also marked the beginning of persecution for many Western European Jews. Crusaders traveling to the Holy Land often attacked Jewish villages or the parts of cities inhabited by Jews. These areas were known as ghettos. Many Jews were murdered, their possessions were stolen, and their homes were destroyed.

New Patterns of Trade   Spurred by the need to furnish supplies for the crusaders, the cities of Italy—especially Venice—became leading commercial centers. The Venetian government did everything it could to encourage business. It built ships and leased them to merchants. It examined business contracts. It insisted that manufacturers maintain certain standards and even destroyed substandard products.

On the shores of the North and Baltic seas, cities such as Hamburg, Lubeck, and Bremen grew prosperous and powerful through trade. In the latter part of the 1200s, the merchants of these cities established an organization known as the Hanseatic League. The league provided protection for its merchants and supplied them with maps of harbors and other navigational aids. The league continued into the 1700s.

Trade routes tied all parts of Western Europe together. For example, fleets of ships took salt from the coast of France to Scandinavia where it was used to preserve fish for export. Wine was carried in great quantities from southern to northern Europe.

The most important industry that developed was the textile industry. At first it centered in Flanders, in what is now northern France and western Belgium. Flemish manufacturers imported raw wool from England and exported cloth. Then, around 1200, England encouraged the immigration of Flemish textile workers and set up its own factories. England remained Western Europe's leading manufacturer of textiles until about 1900.

Rise of Banking   Increased trade also led to the growth of banking. Business became increasingly complex, and traders began traveling great distances. Letters of credit and bills of exchange—similar in idea to credit cards—became necessary so that traders could conduct their business more easily.

Merchants lent money to kings, nobles, and Church officials as well as to businessmen. They also began to charge interest on the money they lent. During the early Middle Ages, the charging of interest—known as usury—was forbidden by the Roman Catholic Church. Moneylending therefore became one of the few occupations open to Jews. However, the growth of business and the need for capital later changed the Church's attitude, and by the 1400s moneylending was almost entirely in Christian hands.

Many bankers were Italian, and perhaps the most famous banking city was Florence. The bankers of Florence laid the foundations for modern banking systems. From Italy the banking business spread to other areas of Europe.

Growth of Towns

The expansion of trade, wealth, and capital as well as population hastened the growth of towns during the later Middle Ages. Fourteenth-century towns and cities were usually small by modern standards. Populations ranged from 5,000 to 10,000 people. But even this relatively small number of persons found themselves packed tightly within the protecting walls of the city.

This picture of Marco Polo leaving Venice is from an English manuscript of the 1400s. Polo set out for China about 1271. He did not see Venice again for 24 years. His book, Description of the World, *became an important guide in the 1400s. But during his own life, Europeans did not believe his tales. What attitude on the part of Europeans does this show?*

Townspeople solved the problem of space by building upward. They built their houses with four, five, and six stories. To gain additional space, each story was extended a little farther out so that the top floors of facing buildings almost met over the narrow streets. This gave the townspeople more space but it also made life hazardous for passersby since everyone emptied their garbage out the windows.

The towns lacked sewers and drainage systems. Rotting garbage and waste from horses and oxen were a breeding ground for disease. Drinking water was often polluted, so city-dwellers drank beer, ale, and wine. Once a fire started among the crowded houses, it quickly spread from one dwelling to another. There was also danger at night from robbers, so most towns had a curfew at sunset.

This Portrait of a Banker *was painted about 1530 by the Flemish portrait painter Jan Mabuse. How did the crusades promote the rise of banking?*

Guilds

As towns grew in size, more services were required to meet the needs of townspeople and those in the surrounding area. Increasingly, workers specialized. Shoemakers, weavers, bakers, tailors, embroiderers, masons, carpenters, goldsmiths, and other craftspeople responded to the growing needs. As their numbers increased, they began to organize into guilds. At first the membership of a guild included all the merchants and artisans within a town. Later, as business grew even more, a guild was formed for each particular craft. A widow was sometimes admitted to a guild when she carried on her husband's trade. In general, however, women were rarely allowed to join craft guilds.

Guilds fixed wages, hours, working conditions, and even the price that could be charged for products. They disciplined members who violated rules. Guilds also acted as welfare agencies. In time guild members developed high standards of excellence, and full membership was reserved to experts known as masters. Those who wanted to be master workers had to undergo a long period of training.

New Privileges

During the early Middle Ages, towns were usually governed by the lord on whose land the town stood. Like the serfs on a manor, the inhabitants of a town had to give their lord a certain amount of labor and follow the lord's rules.

With the growth of trade, it became obvious that a relationship that worked between lords and serfs did not work between lords and urban business people. Gradually, the people of the growing towns obtained greater liberties and privileges from their lords. Often they bought these privileges with their new wealth. At times they took them by force.

Townspeople were gradually released from a number of obligations, including the payment of feudal dues. A town was generally given a **charter**—a document stating the rights of the townspeople. Charters usually gave towns the right to buy and sell goods as they chose, to elect their own officials, to organize their own courts of law to enforce contracts and property rights, and to levy and collect taxes.

A Political Alliance

As time went on, a political alliance developed between townspeople and monarchs. With the rise of a money economy, kings and queens who wanted to expand their power no longer needed

After medieval merchants and townspeople bought their freedom from a feudal lord, they received a town charter. The charter guaranteed certain rights to the townspeople and freed them from most feudal obligations.

land to give vassals. What they needed was cash to pay soldiers and bureaucrats. Townspeople owned property that was subject to royal taxes.

For their part, townspeople realized that doing business would be much easier under a strong central government than under dozens of feudal lords. A strong central government could provide a uniform currency, a uniform system of weights and measures, a uniform system of courts, and protection of a large territory.

Accordingly, the monarchs of Western Europe, with the help of townspeople, began to assert their power and authority over the nobles and the Church. Feudalism was ending in Western Europe, and the formation of the modern nation-state was beginning.

The Black Death   In the mid-1300s towns grew and gained still more rights. The reason was that a dreadful epidemic of bubonic plague—known as the Black Death—struck Europe. The germ causing the disease was spread by flea-infested rats carried to Europe in the holds of merchant ships from Asia. People infected with the disease developed dark patches over their entire bodies. Their tongues also turned black. Victims generally ran a high fever and died within three days. Historians estimate that one-third to one-half of Europe's population was wiped out by the plague.

As a result of Western Europe's loss of population, the number of workers fell sharply. Serfs demanded and often received freedom and wages for their work. Many former serfs moved to the towns where opportunities for advancement were greater. The towns demanded and received still more rights from lords.

SECTION 3 REVIEW

1. **Recall** What was the Black Death? What effect did this disease have upon the population of Western Europe?

2. **How and Why** In what way did increased trade lead to the growth of banking in Western Europe?

3. **Critical Thinking** How did the crusades affect trade and learning in Western Europe?

The works and thoughts of medieval people reflected the world in which they lived. Religion was often the source of their inspiration. This is reflected in the great medieval cathedrals and in plays based on the Bible. There was, however, a lighter side to the lives of medieval people. This side is reflected in the poetry, romances, and music of the time.

Languages and Literature

Throughout the Middle Ages, Latin remained a spoken language in Western Europe. It was used in the rituals of the Roman Catholic Church, as well as by the clergy, who served as government officials and school-teachers. Much of the literature of the time was written in Latin.

Latin, however, was the language only of the educated. During the Middle Ages national or vernacular languages were developing. French, Spanish, and Italian came into being. German, the Scandinavian languages, and English also developed.

Gradually, literature composed in the vernacular began to appear. For example, *Beowulf*, an Anglo-Saxon epic poem, was composed in the 700s. The French *Song of Roland* was written in the 1100s. The Spanish *Poem of the Cid* was written in the 1200s. Both the *Song of Roland* and the *Poem of the Cid* were national epics glorifying heroes who had fought against national enemies.

SECTION

4

Artists,
Artisans, and
Philosophers

Some of the most popular romances written in the vernacular were the English tales about King Arthur and the Knights of the Round Table. Literature dealing with chivalry was especially pleasing to lords and ladies. The townspeople, however, preferred works that poked fun at chivalry, such as the tales of Reynard the Fox.

The main dramatic forms of the medieval period were religious in nature and designed to teach a moral lesson. These were the mystery, miracle, and morality plays. Mystery plays were based on stories from the Bible and were usually about Jesus. Miracle plays dealt with the life of the Virgin Mary or with the lives of saints. Morality plays taught a lesson or were concerned with the struggle between good and evil. The characters in these plays were abstractions—Vice, Riches, Faith, Charity, or Death. For example, in *Everyman*, the most famous morality play, Death comes for Everyman. Everyman seeks help from those whom he considers his friends, including Riches. But they all refuse to go with him. At last he calls upon Good Deeds, who is weak through long neglect. Good Deeds agrees to go with Everyman and be his guide, ''in thy great need, to go by thy side.''

Music

Early medieval music consisted of plainsong, or Gregorian chant. Choirs would chant the words of church services to a single melody. By the 1200s, church choirs were combining several melodies. Musicians developed a system of notes to enable singers to follow the different melodies. We still use this notational system today.

Beginning in about 1100, a group of poet-singers started providing almost the only medieval music that was not religious in nature. They wrote and sang of love, war, and politics with a freedom of speech surprising for the period. These poet-singers performed for the nobles who were their patrons. In southern France, northern Italy, and northern Spain, they were called **troubadours**. In Germany they were known as **minnesingers**.

Gothic Architecture

Prior to 1100, Western Europeans imitated the Roman style of architecture. They built churches, palaces, town halls, and houses with thick walls, narrow windows, heavy pillars, and rounded arches. The windows were small and few because builders feared that too many windows would weaken the walls, the walls would not be able to withstand the weight of the roof, and the building would collapse. This architecture—known as Norman in England and Romanesque on the continent—gives a general impression of heaviness.

Between the mid-1100s and 1500, northern Europeans developed a style of architecture—later known as Gothic—that had an air of lightness,

This stone monster called a gargoyle overlooks the city of Paris from atop Notre Dame Cathedral. Gargoyles were used as spouts to carry rainwater from the roof.

This stained-glass window called Holofernes Crossing the Euphrates *dates from 1246. According to the Book of Judith in the Bible, Judith killed Holofernes, a Babylonian general, in order to save her people, the Hebrews.*

Playing cards like this one first came into use in Europe in the 1300s. This one dates to about 1540. Lancelot was a knight in King Arthur's court. Can you explain how interest in a subject such as knights might become the basis of works in many art forms?

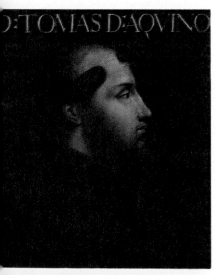

Thomas Aquinas believed that the teachings of Catholicism could be proven by reason.

a feeling of spaciousness, and a sense of soaring upward toward the sky. Gothic buildings had steeply slanted roofs and tall spires. The walls were supported by armlike supports called **flying buttresses** that leaned against the outside walls of a building. They enabled the walls to withstand the outward thrust from the weight of the roof. As a result, most Gothic cathedrals had many windows. The windows were usually made of stained glass. Small pieces of colored glass were fitted together with metal strips to show Biblical stories and the lives of the saints. The brilliant colors in the windows and the sunlight shining through them formed a vivid contrast to the gray stone of a cathedral.

Schools and Universities

At first, medieval schools were generally associated with religious institutions—monasteries, convents, and cathedrals. Students followed a liberal arts curriculum consisting of grammar, logic, rhetoric, arithmetic, astronomy, geometry, and music. Teachers would read aloud from a text in Latin and then explain the material. Since books were scarce and expensive, most students did not own any. Instead, they would listen to the same lecture several times and memorize the most important points.

By the 1100s **universities** had developed. They began as organizations of students and teachers similar to guilds. Classes met regularly and covered a fixed amount of material. Students had to pass oral examinations in order to graduate.

The leading university in Western Europe was the University of Paris, which specialized in theology and philosophy. Oxford University in England also specialized in these two fields. Later, students who were unhappy at Oxford founded a new university—Cambridge. The Italian University of Salerno prepared doctors, and the University of Bologna turned out lawyers. Many university graduates looked forward to careers in the service of the ruler or the Church.

Thinkers

During the Middle Ages, philosophy and theology were closely related. The combined study of the two led to a system of philosophy called **scholasticism**. Among those prominent in founding this philosophy was the Dominican friar Thomas Aquinas (1225–1274).

In his major work *Summa Theologica (A Summary of Religious Thought)*, Aquinas argued that both reason and faith belong in Christian thinking. Reason helps people understand the world around them. Faith reveals truths that are beyond reason and leads people to an everlasting life after death. Therefore, there are no conflicts between Christian teachings and reason.

Roger Bacon, an English friar, disagreed with any reasoning that began by accepting something as true on the basis of authority or faith. He believed that experience was important. First one must prove by experimentation that an idea is factually correct. Then one can reason to a conclusion. This is the method that is used by scientists today. Through his own personal experimentation, Bacon made some startling predictions about the future. He predicted the invention of the submarine, the mechanized ship, the automobile, and the airplane. They are not exactly as Bacon imagined them, but he sketched the general outline of what was to come.

SECTION 4 REVIEW

1. **Recall**   What was scholasticism?

2. **How and Why**   In what way were the main dramatic forms of the medieval period the same? How did they differ?

3. **Critical Thinking**   Why were the builders of Gothic cathedrals able to use so many windows?

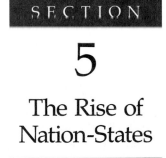

During the late Middle Ages, powerful monarchies began to replace feudalism as the dominant political system in many parts of Western Europe. The strong central governments of these nation-states did not develop at the same time or in the same way throughout the region. However, by 1500 four clearly defined nations—England, France, Portugal, and Spain—existed in Western Europe. It was these four nations that would take the lead in extending Western Europe's political control around the world.

SECTION

5

The Rise of Nation-States

England

The first nation-state to develop in Western Europe was England. The story begins with the conquest of Anglo-Saxon England by William the Conqueror, Duke of Normandy, in 1066.

William imposed his own type of feudal system on England. He took away much of the land that had belonged to Anglo-Saxon nobles and gave it to his personal followers. However, he did not completely trust these nobles so the manors he gave them were widely scattered. William also required that the nobles take an oath of allegiance to him. Decentralization of authority was basic to the feudal system, but the new Norman ruler wanted as much power as possible in his own hands.

William's successors continued to try to lessen the power of the nobles. Henry I (1100–1135) began to pay his officials salaries, making them more dependent upon him. He also established a royal court and a treasury that audited the accounts of the kingdom. Henry established one system of law for all his subjects. It incorporated much from both Anglo-Saxon and feudal customs and practices.

Judges and Juries   Henry II (1154-1189) continued to improve the processes of the law in England. He sent judges into the countryside to try cases. These judges were assigned to hold court along regular routes at regular times. They were called circuit judges.

To assist the judges in uncovering cases, the king appointed juries in each district. These juries consisted of respected persons who gave the judges the names of individuals they thought had committed crimes.

The king also gave authority to a jury of 12 men to function as sworn witnesses to the facts in cases concerning land. This is the origin of the jury system. In time, juries came to be used to decide criminal cases. The jury is now a fixed institution in British and American courts. The replacement of private feudal law by the king's law assisted in the breakdown of English feudalism.

Magna Carta   Henry II was succeeded by his son, Richard the Lion-Heart (1189–1199). During most of Richard's reign he was out of the country fighting against the French and later against the Turks in the Middle East. Richard's brother John followed him on the throne (1199–1216).

When John inherited the throne of England, he owned more land in France than the French king and his nobles did. However, John was so incompetent militarily that he soon lost most of his French possessions, including the province of Normandy. Determined to win back his lands, John asked his vassals to lend him money to hire foreign troops. Most of

This is a section of the Magna Carta. *What rights did this charter give the English? Why was it unusual?*

his vassals refused. He then raised the nobles' feudal dues and threatened to take back the freedoms of towns if they did not give him money. He also angered the Roman Catholic Church by disagreeing with the pope's choice for archbishop of Canterbury, England's highest church official.

Furious with the king's behavior, the nobles—supported by the archbishop and the leaders of London—organized against him. On June 15, 1215, at a meadow along the Thames River called Runnymede, they forced him to sign a document known as the Magna Carta, or Great Charter.

In the document's main provisions, John promised that he would not impose unusual taxes without the consent of his council; that the city of London could keep its old privileges; that no free person could be imprisoned, banished, or deprived of property except by the lawful judgment of a jury of peers—equals—or by the law of the land; and that he, the king, must give justice to all.

The Magna Carta also guaranteed various personal rights of English men and women, mostly nobles. However, its importance for the future lay in its definition of the king's power. The king was not above the law. He had to obey it.

Development of Parliament   The king's council came to be called Parliament sometime in the 1240s. At first it consisted only of nobles, but in 1265 it expanded to include two knights from each county and two **burgesses** from each town. The knights, later known as gentry, were well-to-do landholders who formed the rural ruling class. The inclusion of the burgesses showed the growing influence of towns in national affairs.

Under Edward I (1272–1307), Parliament became a tax granting body. Edward needed money to pay for his wars with Wales and Scotland. During the 1300s and 1400s, later kings were forced to call more and more upon Parliament for money. The members of Parliament learned to use this need as a bargaining weapon. They refused to approve new taxes until the king gave them a voice in how the money would be spent. They also demanded that certain laws be passed. Parliament eventually became England's lawmaking body.

As they found their interests moving closer together, the knights and the burgesses began to work together. They started meeting away from the nobles and high clergy. This happened as early as 1332. Thus the Parliament of England slowly came to be divided into the House of Commons, where the knights and burgesses met, and the House of Lords, where the nobles and high clergy met.

France

England has been united since 1066. In contrast, France at that time was made up of more or less independent provinces, each with its own ruler, courts, army, currency, and even dialect. The French king controlled only

Paris and its surrounding area, about 2 percent of what is now France. French kings thus had an especially hard task expanding their rule.

Rise of the Monarchy   The king who did the most to make France a strong kingdom was Philip II, known as Philip Augustus, who ruled from 1180 to 1223. It was Philip Augustus who defeated King John of England and conquered most of his lands in France. Philip gained still more territory as a result of the Albigensian Crusade. Philip Augustus divided the conquered land into districts. But instead of giving these districts to feudal nobles, he appointed middle-class lawyers to run them. These officials were paid by the king and were responsible only to him. By the time of his death, Philip Augustus was stronger than almost all the nobles of his kingdom put together.

Philip IV (Philip the Fair), who ruled from 1285 to 1314, was responsible for calling the first Estates General, a body representing each of the three estates, or groups, of French society—the clergy, the nobility, and the common townspeople. The king called the meeting to gain support in a dispute with the pope. However, the Estates General— unlike the English Parliament—had no power over taxation. Instead, the king obtained needed revenue from the lands he himself owned, from the Church, from the towns to which he gave rights, and from the Jews, whom he would expel from a region and then charge a fee for permission to return. As a result, the Estates General never became a powerful governing body as did Parliament. Instead, the French ruler grew increasingly absolute. Another result was that without a uniform, efficient system of taxation, the French government was always running short of cash. This eventually helped bring about the French Revolution.

The Hundred Years' War   From 1337 to 1453 the French and the English fought a series of wars which together are known as the Hundred Years' War. The fighting stemmed chiefly from English claims to the French throne and French territory. During the early part of the war, English armies made great gains. At the battle of Crécy (kray-SEE) in 1346, gunpowder and English foot soldiers armed with Welsh longbows completely defeated the armored knights of the French. Military power no longer rested with the noble soldier on horseback. The English won another major victory in 1415 at the battle of Agincourt (ah-zhan-KOOR). As a result of this battle, Henry V of England was granted the French crown.

Then, in 1428, the French gained courage and national pride behind a young woman named Jeanne d'Arc, or Joan of Arc. She had been led, she said, by visions and voices belonging to the archangel Michael and other saints. The voices told her to drive the English out of France. Under her leadership, the French won victories at Orléans and elsewhere. In 1431 Joan was captured. She was put on trial, convicted of heresy, and burned at the stake. However, the French victories continued. By 1453 the city of Calais was the only English possession on the continent, and France had become a unified kingdom under Charles VII.

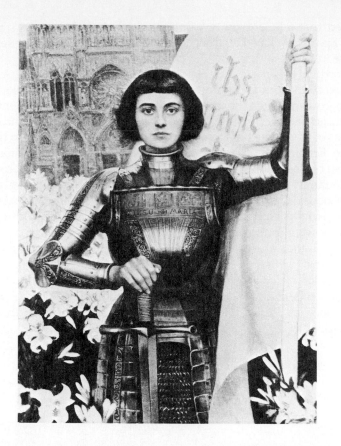

The end of the Hundred Years' War had important results. The French victory ended England's attempts to conquer France. In addition, the feudal system—with its emphasis on loyalty to the lord—declined. Perhaps most important, a sense of *patriotism*—loyalty to one's country—began to develop in France and in England. Consequently, the power of the nobles declined and stronger monarchies developed.

Other Kingdoms

The Moors conquered most of the Iberian Peninsula in the eighth century. They developed a high level of culture and transmitted much of the learning of the Islamic Empire to Western Europe. But the Christians who still lived in the northern parts of Spain fought to drive the Moors out. The Spanish kingdoms that led the 600-year-long struggle were Aragon and Castile. In 1469 Ferdinand of Aragon married Isabella of Castile. In 1492 their joint armies defeated the last Moorish kingdom of Granada, and the *Reconquista*—the Reconquest—was over. The establishment of Spain as a nation had strong religious overtones. The Spaniards were fighting not only for Spain but also for Christianity. The rulers

Holy Roman Empire, c. 1000

Map labels: Atlantic Ocean, North Sea, ENGLAND, GERMANY, FRANCE, ITALY, Mediterranean Sea

believed that religious unity would strengthen their country's political unity. Spain developed a strong self-image that later helped it set up an empire in the Americas.

Portugal became an independent nation in 1139 when King Alfonso I defeated the Moors. Germany and Italy, however, did not develop strong central governments. The area remained a league of independent states. Known as the Holy Roman Empire, it was roughly the central and eastern sections of Charlemagne's former empire. The main difficulty in the Holy Roman Empire was that imperial succession was not hereditary. The German nobles retained the right to elect the Holy Roman emperor. Thus, a noble family seldom ruled long enough to develop the power and the loyalty necessary to unify the country. To keep their own power, the nobles usually elected a relatively weak emperor. In addition, the emperors were continually trying to consolidate their power over northern Italy. In the process, they paid little attention to unifying the German duchies and towns.

This interference of the Holy Roman emperors also helped prevent the emergence of a strong central government in Italy. Instead, small city-states, such as Venice, Florence, and Milan, developed on the Italian Peninsula.

SECTION 5 REVIEW

1. **Recall**   What four clearly defined nations existed in Western Europe by 1500?

2. **How and Why**   In what way did the Magna Carta define the power of the English king?

3. **Critical Thinking**   Why did Germany remain disunified as many other parts of Western Europe formed nation-states?

Chapter 29

Reviewing People, Places, and Things

Identify, define, or explain each of the following:

Franks
Vikings
William the
  Conqueror
excommunication
Inquisition
feudalism
knight
manorialism
Venice
Hanseatic League
Flanders

Florence
guilds
charter
Black Death
troubadours
flying buttresses
Thomas Aquinas
Roger Bacon
Henry II
Magna Carta
Parliament
Reconquista

Map Study

Using the map on page 568, determine the answers to the following questions.

1. What areas of Western Europe did the Norwegian Vikings invade?
2. What areas did the Swedish branch of the Vikings invade?
3. What area did the Danes invade?

Understanding Facts and Ideas

1. How did Charlemagne rule his vast empire?
2. What weapons did Roman Catholic popes have to enforce their power?
3. What Benedictine rules formed the basis for the monastic way of life?
4. How was the granting of a fief a contract?
5. a. How was the farmland on a manor generally divided? b. How was common land used?
6. Why did many European Christians join the crusades?

7. How did the crusades lead to the decline of feudalism in Western Europe?
8. How did the guilds help their members?
9. How did universities begin in Western Europe?
10. How did Henry II improve the process of law in England?
11. What was the main cause of the Hundred Years' War between England and France?

Developing Critical Thinking

Recognizing Values   How did the Roman Catholic Church condition people during the Middle Ages to look at life? How did these values affect their lives?

Writing About History

Analyzing a Trend   A trend is a general direction in which something is moving over a period of time. A trend may refer to a particular path a movement is taking or the line of development of some action or theory. Write a paragraph describing how the Roman Catholic Church became centralized under the leadership of a strong pope while political power in Europe was being divided by many groups. Discuss how these two trends were related.

Applying Your Skills to History

Using a Flow Chart   A flow chart illustrates the steps in a process or the way something is organized. It uses arrows to show direction and it may be read from left to right, top to bottom, bottom to top, or in a circle.

Activity: Make a flow chart showing the relationships between people in the feudal system. Be sure to title your flow chart and label each part.

Creation of the **Stars and Planets** *is one of 21 scenes from the Bible that* **Michelangelo** *painted on the ceiling of the Sistine Chapel in the Vatican.*

The Renaissance and the Reformation

The period in Western history from around 1350 to about 1600 is usually labeled the Renaissance (REN-uh-SAHNS), which means rebirth. It refers to the political ideas, art, and literature of the ancient Greeks and Romans that were rediscovered. The Renaissance was also an attitude of mind. People began to show an interest in earthly life as well as life after death. They began to think of themselves as individuals as well as members of a group. They began to make up their own minds instead of accepting the voice of authority. This period also marked the end of the thousand-year era of religious unity in Western Europe.

As you study this chapter, think about these questions.

- In what areas did the differences between the medieval and the Renaissance way of thinking show themselves?

- Why was the printing press such a significant invention?

- What factors led to the Reformation?

- How did the Reformation influence the development of Western Europe?

For centuries Western Europeans had quietly accepted the hardships of their lives as a preparation for life after death. By the 1300s, however, they were beginning to question this attitude. This was partly because of the rediscovery of the works of Greek and Roman philosophers. The early Greeks and Romans found beauty in humanity and believed that humans might find happiness on earth. The Greeks in particular believed strongly in individual excellence. Western Europeans did not lose their religious spirit. However, they started to believe that life on earth was important and good in itself. They also started to believe that people have a tremendous potential for accomplishment. These beliefs are called **humanism**.

Italy

The first humanists were Italian. The Italians had long been acquainted with the Byzantines and Muslims, who had preserved much of the Greek and Roman heritage. In addition, the Italian city-states of Venice, Genoa, Pisa, Florence, and Milan had become centers of trade and commerce. Trade and commerce always speed the growth of worldly values and ideas. They also encourage personal achievement and a willingness to accept change. Because the Italian nobility looked down on merchants socially, the Italian merchants turned to the arts as a means of gaining prestige.

Soon the city-states of Italy were trying to outdo one another in obtaining Greek and Roman writings, in supporting humanist scholars, and in subsidizing the creation of paintings and sculpture. From Italy the Renaissance spread northward to other parts of Western Europe.

Renaissance Art

While medieval artists had often produced their works as offerings to God, the artists of the Renaissance were often hungry for fame and material rewards. They wanted all to know that the works were theirs and they wanted to be paid for them. Unlike medieval artists who worked anonymously, Renaissance artists signed their work. Moreover, the new wealth of the period worked in favor of artists. Popes, kings, and wealthy merchants all competed for their services. Artists were often richly supported and showered with official positions, money, and favors. The showing of a new painting or sculpture was an important social event attended by all the leading families.

Some Renaissance artists continued to paint religious themes but with a new approach. Saints were not only symbols of miracle-working, but they were also human beings with human emotions. Even the most spiritual ideas came to be expressed in terms of physical and worldly beauty. Other Renaissance artists responded to the emphasis upon individuals and their worldly activities by painting portraits. They pictured church officials, kings, queens, nobles, and wealthy merchants and

This Madonna and Child *is by Giotto. One of the earliest Renaissance painters, he is considered the most important artist of the 1300s.*

their families. The paintings were more than likenesses; they attempted to express the personalities of their subjects.

Many Renaissance artists found their inspiration in Greek and Roman art, which was very realistic. They studied anatomy and learned to depict the human body in idealized beauty. Some painted the gods and goddesses of Greek and Roman mythology. Scenes of important contemporary events also interested Renaissance painters.

Around the 1400s, oil paints came into wide use. Until this time, paintings had been done chiefly with tempera—colored powder mixed with egg whites, milk, or other liquid. Tempera paints were applied to a surface that had been prepared with a coat of glue. The paints were almost transparent, and very beautiful effects could be achieved. But it was necessary to work quickly before the paints dried. Once the paints were applied, it was very difficult to make changes.

Oil paints, on the other hand, were very slow-drying. This made it possible for artists to work more slowly and carefully. Because oil paints were not transparent, mistakes could be painted over. Also, oil paints provided a much wider choice of colors than tempera paints.

Renaissance artists experimented with new techniques. They wanted to give a three-dimensional quality to the flat surface of their paintings. They did this by the skillful use of colors and detail and by contrast between light and shade. Renaissance artists also developed perspective. They made objects at the front of a painting larger than those at the rear to create the impression that the objects at the rear were farther away.

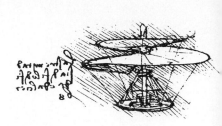

Renaissance Artists

In an age of artistic greatness, none were greater than Leonardo da Vinci (dah-VIN-chee) and Michelangelo (my-kuh-LAN-juh-loh).

This is a sketch of a flying machine from one of Leonardo da Vinci's many notebooks. He was a scientist and inventor as well as an artist of unusual talent.

Da Vinci   Da Vinci was a true "Renaissance man," one who has many talents. In addition to being a painter, he was a natural scientist, an inventor, an architect, a mapmaker, and a musician. He was also an excellent swordsman and horseman, as well as a delightful conversationalist.

Da Vinci's most famous paintings are the *Mona Lisa*, which shows a smiling woman, and *The Last Supper*, which depicts Christ and his disciples at the Passover **seder** the night before Christ's crucifixion. Da Vinci's notebooks contain more than 5,000 pages on which he sketched plants, animals, the human body, and inventions that ranged from two-level highways to a repeating rifle. He built a model of the human heart, as well as a model airplane that he was reported to have tested—unsuccessfully—in 1505.

Botticelli painted Birth of Venus *over a hundred years after Giotto worked. Do you see any difference in style between the two men? Is the use of light different? Is one figure more lifelike than the other? Since both men were Renaissance painters, how can you explain any differences?*

Michelangelo Michelangelo Buonarroti worked on a gigantic scale. Lying on his back, he painted the Biblical story of the creation of the world on the ceiling of the Sistine Chapel in the Vatican. It took him four years to complete the painting. Michelangelo was also a sculptor. Among his works is a statue of the Biblical hero David which the Florentines found so full of vigor that they adopted it as a symbol of their city-state. Another of Michelangelo's sculptures is the Pietà, which shows the Virgin Mary holding the dead Christ in her arms.

Other Artists More than Italian artists, artists from Flanders, Belgium, and the Netherlands began to picture ordinary people and scenes from everyday life in their paintings. This is known as genre (ZHAHN-ruh) painting. Pieter Brueghel (BROI-guhl) the Elder is a good example of a genre painter.

Albrecht Durer (DYUR-er), Lucas Cranach, and Hans Holbein (HOHL-byn) the Younger are among the best known of the German painters of this era. Durer was noted for his engravings and woodcuts. Cranach's work combined classical and religious elements. Holbein concentrated on portrait painting.

Return of the Hunters *by Pieter Brueghel the Elder portrays ordinary people and everyday life. Such painting is known as genre painting.*

St. Peter's Basilica in Rome dates from the 1500s and 1600s. What features of Greek and Roman architecture can you find in this building? What brought about the Renaissance interest in ancient architecture?

Renaissance Architecture

The architecture of the Renaissance followed classical lines. Architects were commissioned to design palaces and churches that reflected ancient Greek and Roman forms. As a result, the buildings of this period show many Greek columns and Roman arches and domes.

The best-known example of this style is St. Peter's Basilica in Rome. It is the largest church in the world. Although Michelangelo designed the dome, Bramante (bruh-MAHNT-ee) and Palladio (puh-LAHD-ee-oh) designed the rest of the building. Palladio was the most influential architect of the Renaissance. Publication of his work *Four Books on Architecture* kept his influence alive for the next two centuries.

Renaissance Music

Since very little ancient Greek or Roman music existed to revive, Renaissance music continued to develop medieval forms. The most noteworthy contributions were in musical instruments and in composition. The violin and the harpsichord were developed, and instrumental music became as important as vocal music. The oratorio—a religious drama set to music—appeared around this time. It combined vocal and instrumental music and foreshadowed modern opera.

1. **Recall** What was the architecture of the Renaissance like?
2. **How and Why** What made Leonardo da Vinci a "Renaissance man"?
3. **Critical Thinking** Why did the Renaissance have its beginnings in Italy?

Renaissance authors no longer confined themselves to religious and spiritual subjects. Instead, they began to write about social and political ideas, about human behavior, and about earthly matters. They also began writing in the vernacular instead of in Latin.

Renaissance scientists began to question ideas about the world of nature and the physical laws that they believed governed the universe. They looked at the world with new awareness and asked new questions. The old answers were no longer satisfactory.

Renaissance Literature

One of the earliest vernacular writers was Dante Alighieri (DAN-tay al-uhg-YEAR-ee) of Florence, who lived from 1265 to 1321. His book *The Divine Comedy* tells of an imaginary trip through hell, purgatory, and paradise. Many famous people are seen on the journey. Dante tells their stories as a way of pointing out the vices of the time. Dante wrote in his native language, the dialect of Tuscany, a region in Italy. Gradually, Italian writers began using the Tuscan language and it became the language of all Italians.

Another early writer in the vernacular was Geoffrey Chaucer (CHAW-suhr) of England, who lived from c.1340 to 1400. He wrote *The Canterbury Tales* in Middle English, the form of English spoken at the time. The book is a collection of 25 tales told by pilgrims on their way to Canterbury. Although the book belongs to the period considered the late Middle Ages, it is Renaissance in tone. Through descriptions of the pilgrims and their stories, Chaucer satirizes the clergy, the wealthy, and the code of chivalry.

Petrarch (PEE-trark), who lived from 1304 to 1374, is sometimes called the father of humanism. He was a traveler, a student of archaeology, a lyric poet whose work has been widely imitated, and a coin collector. He was also a collector of old manuscripts, which he found dusty and unused in monasteries and cathedral libraries throughout Italy, France, and Germany. Petrarch had these manuscripts copied for his private library. Other people followed his example, and by 1444 the first library open to the public was set up in Florence.

Petrarch wrote in both Latin and Italian. Writing in Italian made his works popular with many people, but his Latin writings were also influential. Lay people as well as monks began to study Latin. Soon humanists were working as lawyers, accountants, bookkeepers, and teachers. Monks no longer held a monopoly on such jobs.

Desiderius Erasmus (deh-zi-DAY-ree-us ih-RAZ-muhs), a Dutch scholar who lived from c.1466 to 1536, was one of the greatest humanists. He believed that evil came only from ignorance and the human tendency to make mistakes. He showed his strong support for education for everyone, including women, in his satire *The Abbot and the Learned Lady*, in which he poked fun at ignorant monks. Another example of his sharp humor was his *In Praise of Folly*. Erasmus was ever aware and respectful of the potential in humanity. He cited Jesus, Socrates, and Cicero among others as examples of the best in human nature. He traveled throughout Europe and taught at some of its finest universities. Erasmus also published a translation of the New Testament in Greek. It differed in some ways from the official Roman Catholic version in Latin called the Vulgate. These differences raised doubts in the minds of some about the accuracy of the official version.

Probably the most powerful critic of chivalry was the Spanish author and soldier Miguel de Cervantes (suhr-VAN-teez), who lived from 1547 to 1616. His most famous work, *Don Quixote de la Mancha*, was the earliest European example of the literary form that later became the novel.

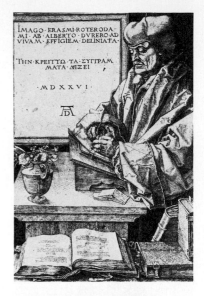

This woodblock print of the humanist Erasmus was done by Albrecht Durer. The top inscription gives the name of the subject, the artist, and the information that the painting was done during Erasmus' life. The date is 1526. The second inscription says, "His writings depict him even better."

Political Philosophy

Niccolò Machiavelli (MAK-ee-uh-VEL-ee) was a political philosopher who lived from 1469 to 1527. After serving as an ambassador and secretary of defense for the city-state of Florence, he wrote *The Prince*, which deals with the relationship between government and the people. Machiavelli actually preferred a government like that of the ancient Roman Republic. When he looked at Renaissance Italy—where the city-states were constantly fighting either one another or France, and where everyone carried a knife and was afraid to go out alone at night—he decided that the only practical government was rule by a strong prince.

Medieval scholars believed that the power of the king came from God. A king should therefore be just. Machiavelli believed that the state was a secular institution. A ruler should therefore be "a lion and a fox," both strong and clever. A ruler should also use whatever means were needed to remain in power and to build a strong, peaceful state. These included lying and pretending to be charitable in order to impress people. Even though many of Machiavelli's ideas seem immoral or, at best, unethical, they influenced later political philosophers. Not surprisingly, they influenced many rulers and politicians as well.

Another political philosopher was the Englishman Sir Thomas More, who lived from 1478 to 1535. He was a close friend of Erasmus and corresponded frequently with him. More criticized many Western Europeans for their greed and their ruthless search for power. In his book

Utopia, More described an ideal society. Everyone obeyed the laws because everyone participated in making them. People worked and shared their goods in common, so there was no poverty. Medieval scholars had argued that war and corruption existed because people were weak and evil. More argued that the real explanation was the failure of social institutions to work properly. It was not enough to improve the behavior of individuals, More said. It was also necessary to improve society.

Renaissance Drama

Renaissance drama centered in England. Its masterpieces were written during a period in English history known as the Elizabethan Age, after Queen Elizabeth I, who ruled from 1558 to 1603.

Christopher Marlowe made a major contribution by adapting **blank verse**—unrhymed poetry—to drama. He is best known for his plays *Doctor Faustus* and *Tamburlaine*. Ben Jonson is remembered for his comedies and court masques. Masques are fanciful productions with music, dance, and elaborate costumes and scenery.

However, one playwright stands above all other English dramatists: William Shakespeare. No dramatist before or since has approached his scope, dramatic ability, inventiveness, or graceful use of the English language. His plays have probably been performed more often than those of any playwright in history. Among his many works are tragedies, such as *Hamlet, Othello, Macbeth, Romeo and Juliet,* and *King Lear*; comedies, such as *Twelfth Night* and *Midsummer Night's Dream*; and histories, such as *Richard III* and *Henry V.* Eight of Shakespeare's ten historical plays deal with England between 1397 and 1485. The plays chronicle the rise of the house of Tudor, the royal family to which Elizabeth I belonged.

Elizabethan drama differed from medieval drama not only because of its subject matter but also because after 1576, it was performed in specially designed theater buildings instead of cathedral courtyards. Shakespeare himself was manager of the Globe Theater, in which many of his plays were performed. In the theater's pit stood "groundlings," who paid the lowest admission price. In the balconies that ran along the sides of the theater sat higher-paying spectators. Nobles sat on the stage, which had neither a curtain nor scenery. Female roles were played by young boys whose voices had not yet changed. Their roles were almost always shorter than male roles and less important to the action of the play.

Importance of Printing

Humanism spread so widely during the Renaissance because Western Europeans had perfected the art of printing. The Chinese had first developed printing under the T'ang emperors in the A.D. 800s. They carved their writings on blocks of wood, which were then inked and pressed against silk or, later, paper. Western Europeans learned about

Shakespeare's plays were performed in the Globe Theater (above model) and others like it. The theaters were adapted from the design of inn courtyards. These were, in fact, the first theaters.

block printing and used it to make playing cards and to reproduce drawings. In the 1000s the Chinese invented movable type. However, because the Chinese language contains thousands of characters, movable type was impractical for them.

Western Europeans still copied manuscripts by hand. This meant that very few books were produced. Also, errors crept into works as they were copied again and again. In the 1440s, however, a German named Johann Gutenberg developed a method of molding individual letters from metal. The letters were arranged in a frame, then inked. A sheet of paper was pressed on them. These molded letters could be used over and over. The first book that Gutenberg printed was an illuminated Bible written in Latin.

Gutenberg's metal type revolutionized bookmaking. Printing presses were much faster and more accurate than hand copyists. At first, printed books were very expensive and only the rich could afford them. After a while, however, printing made it possible to produce inexpensive books that appealed to a wide reading public. Historians estimate that in 1450, there were about 100,000 handwritten manuscripts in Western Europe. By 1500 at least 9 million books had rolled off the presses. By 1600 roughly 200 million machine-printed books were in circulation throughout the culture region. Their contents included many new ideas in science.

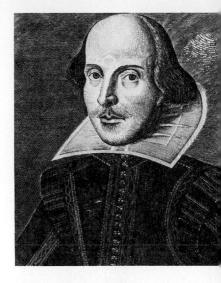

William Shakespeare is considered the greatest playwright in the English language, because of the variety and quality of his works.

Astronomy

During the Middle Ages most Western Europeans relied on the teachings of the Catholic Church to explain how and why the universe worked. These teachings followed the ideas of Aristotle, and were considered part of Church dogma. The Aristotelian universe was geocentric. The sun, planets, and stars moved around the earth on a series of transparent spheres. This theory was accepted not only because it seemed to accord with the evidence of the senses, but also because it fitted well with the view of humans as the crowning achievement of creation.

The first significant challenge to the Aristotelian universe was raised by Nicolaus Copernicus, a Polish astronomer who studied in Italy. Because astronomical instruments were limited, astronomers used mathematics to help them form theories about the universe. Copernicus could not make his mathematics agree with the popular theory that the earth was stationary and the planets and stars revolved around it. Copernicus believed that the earth and other heavenly bodies moved around the sun. His publication of *On the Revolution of the Heavenly Spheres* in 1543 marks the beginning of the Scientific Revolution. After Copernicus, more and more scientists began to use the scientific method. Instead of simply thinking about a problem, they would first collect data, either by observation or by experimentation. Then they would suggest a hypothesis, or possible explanation, for the data. Thirdly, they would test the hypothesis to see if it was correct. What that meant, of course, was that science was no longer part of religion.

popular:
accepted widely by the public

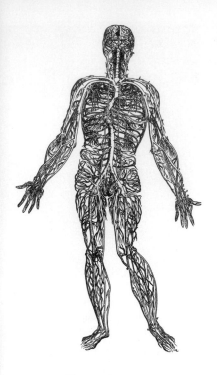

A Chart of Veins *illustrates Andreas Vesalius' view of the human circulatory system. This woodblock print was made in the workshop of the Renaissance artist Titian and is reproduced from a book published in 1543. This was the same year that Copernicus published his theory of the universe. The works of Copernicus mark the beginning of modern astronomy; those of Vesalius, the beginning of modern anatomy.*

Tycho Brahe (TEE-koh BRAH), a Danish astronomer, tried to combine Aristotle and Copernicus. He theorized that although the sun moved around the earth, the planets moved around the sun. His assistant, a German named Johannes Kepler, tested Brahe's theory and found that the data did not fit the way the planets moved. Copernicus was right: the universe was heliocentric. Kepler then added his own theories, known as Kepler's Laws: the planets move in elliptical, or oval, paths, not in circular ones; they move faster when they are closer to the sun and slower when they are farther away; and the length of a planet's year depends on its distance from the sun. Kepler developed a set of tables of planetary movements. These tables later proved a great help to navigators at sea.

In the 1600s, Galileo Galilei (gal-uh-LEE-oh gal-uh-LAY-ee), an Italian, constructed a telescope and saw moons revolving around the planet Jupiter. His observations supported the theory of Copernicus. For publishing these radical findings he was brought before the Inquisition. Threatened by punishment, Galileo promised to remain silent about his observations. But his book *Dialogue Concerning the Great World Systems* circulated throughout Western Europe, and the ideas of the new astronomy spread.

Because of expanding knowledge in the field of astronomy, the Julian calendar, which had been used since Roman days, was found to be inaccurate. In 1582 Pope Gregory XIII ordered that the calendar be set back ten days. Thus the new Gregorian calendar would correspond exactly with the solar year.

Medicine

Another area in which the Scientific Revolution began to take hold was medicine. During the Middle Ages, physicians relied on the theories and writings of Galen, a Greek physician who lived in the A.D. 100s. Galen was considered the authority in medicine just as Aristotle was considered the authority in astronomy. Among other ideas, Galen believed that blood flowed through the body in one direction and then reversed itself to flow in the opposite direction.

Andreas Vesalius, a Flemish physician, was one of the first to challenge Galen's theories on anatomy. Galen had never dissected a human body. He based his descriptions on the bodies of pigs. Vesalius, however, obtained the corpses of executed criminals and based his anatomical descriptions on what he actually saw. He published his findings in *The Fabric of the Human Body* and demanded that the study of anatomy be part of medical training.

William Harvey, an English physician, also challenged Galen's teachings. Using direct observations, Harvey traced the system of blood circulation in the human body. He was the first to recognize that the heart acted like a pump, moving the blood continually in one direction.

These are instruments of Nicolaus Copernicus' time. On the wall is an astrolabe. To the right is an astronomical globe and to the left, a triquetrum, used for measuring altitudes in astronomy.

SECTION 2 REVIEW

1. **Recall** Why were the writings of the Italian Dante Alighieri and the Englishman Geoffrey Chaucer important?

2. **How and Why** How did Sir Thomas More describe the ideal society?

3. **Critical Thinking** How did the invention of printing affect Western Europeans?

3

The Reformation

Others before Martin Luther had asked for reforms within the Roman Catholic Church. But historians consider Luther's actions the beginning of the Reformation.

The atmosphere of the Renaissance had its effects on the Roman Catholic Church as well as on art, literature, and science. As monarchs gained power, they began to view the popes as threats to their political strength. They envied the tax-free status of Church lands, which made up between one-fifth and one-third of all the land in Western Europe. They were annoyed that clergy accused of crimes should be tried in Church courts rather than in national courts.

In addition, many Western Europeans criticized such Church abuses as **simony**—the buying and selling of high Church offices. They did not understand why they had to make gifts to the Church whenever anyone was baptized, married, or buried. They felt that many Church leaders were more concerned about worldly power than about the spiritual needs of Christians. They resented the lavish lifestyle of some popes. It was not long before questions arose about the very doctrines that the Church preached.

A Divided Papacy

Papal prestige and authority had been shaken when, from 1309 to 1377, the popes lived in Avignon (a-veen-YOHN), France, rather than in Rome. This period, sometimes called the Babylonian Captivity, began when a Frenchman was elected pope and decided to move to Avignon. He and his successors were strongly influenced by the French rulers, a situation greatly resented by other Western European countries.

When the papacy was returned to Rome, a quarrel arose between French and Italian factions. The French cardinals elected a rival pope who again moved to Avignon. There were now two popes. Each excommunicated the other and called him false. This split, called the Great Schism, lasted for about 40 years. Catholics throughout Western Europe were worried about the salvation of their souls because they did not know which pope to believe. The Great Schism was finally ended by a Church council in 1417, but little was done about reforming the Church.

Lutheranism

A hundred years later, the Protestant Reformation began. On October 31, 1517, a German monk and professor of theology named Martin Luther (1483–1546) nailed a list of 95 theses, or propositions, to the door of All Saints' Church in the town of Wittenberg. The work sharply criticized the practice of selling indulgences. An indulgence was a papal pardon for sins that, when combined with true repentance, freed a sinner from punishment after death. Indulgences had originally been granted during the crusades. Crusaders were promised forgiveness from God if they died fighting for the cross.

In the 1500s, Church leaders needed money to rebuild Saint Peter's Basilica in Rome. Therefore, they offered indulgences in return for donations. Unfortunately, some monks and priests failed to explain that indulgences were valid only when accompanied by true repentance.

This woodcut cartoon was made about 1520. It satirizes the practice of selling indulgences. What is an indulgence? Was Luther excommunicated because of his stand against this practice? Or were there other reasons?

To Luther's amazement, his theses soon spread far beyond the bounds of Wittenberg. They were translated from Latin into German and reproduced on the printing press. Before long, demands for Church reform were being heard all over Germany. Luther's criticisms had obviously touched a raw nerve on the part of many people.

In 1520 Luther published three books in which he challenged other teachings and practices of the Church. He argued that instead of accepting papal authority, people should read and interpret the Bible for themselves. Luther's insistence on reading the Bible helped the spread of literacy in Germany. His translation of the New Testament helped to establish the modern German language.

Luther also taught that the only way to gain forgiveness for sins was through faith. Clergy, although helpful, were not essential to salvation.

The pope condemned Luther's teachings and declared him a heretic. Luther burned the pope's order of excommunication. In 1521 the Holy Roman Emperor called a **diet**, or meeting, of nobles and religious leaders in the city of Worms. Luther was ordered to appear before the diet to defend his views. Luther refused to deny any of his teachings. "I cannot . . . go against my conscience. Here I stand. I cannot do otherwise. God help me."

The diet declared Luther a heretic and an outlaw and forced him to flee. However, he was helped by a number of German princes. Some believed in Luther's religious ideas. Others realized that rejecting the authority of the pope meant that they could stop paying taxes to Rome and could seize Church property within their states. Accordingly, these princes became Lutherans and set up Lutheran churches.

From the 1520s to the 1550s, the Holy Roman Emperor, who remained a Catholic, fought against the Lutheran princes. As the conflict dragged on, both sides realized that neither would destroy the other. In 1555 the Peace of Augsburg ended the fighting and gave German princes the power to decide whether their subjects would follow Catholic or Lutheran teachings. In general, Lutheranism was established in northern Germany, while Catholicism remained the religion of southern Germany.

Lutheranism quickly spread beyond the borders of the German states. In slightly more than ten years it became the official religion of Denmark and Norway. A short time later it also became the state religion of Sweden.

Calvinism

Another major figure in the Protestant movement of the mid-1500s was John Calvin (1509–1564). Born in France, he became a Protestant in 1533. The following year, a wave of religious persecution caused him to flee to Geneva, Switzerland. In 1536 he published his beliefs in a book entitled *Institutes of the Christian Religion.*

Many of Calvin's ideas resembled those of Luther. For example, he believed that each Christian should study and interpret the Bible independently. He also believed that all Christians should have a voice in the operation of their church.

Once the Reformation began, many different religions sprang up in Europe. One was founded by John Calvin. What did Calvin preach? Why do you think people were attracted to Calvinism?

Calvin, however, added a belief called **predestination**. He felt that Christians were born already judged by God. Nevertheless, they should obey God's laws and strive always to live moral lives. That included working hard at whatever job for which they were best suited. Calvin believed that wealth and personal success were outward signs of goodness. His emphasis on the work ethic, on thrift, and on investing money for profit encouraged his followers to play an active role in business. Calvinism provided a moral justification for the material goals of the middle class.

Calvin became all-powerful in Geneva, where he tried to develop a godly society. He forbade dancing, card-playing, fancy clothing, and worldliness. The city was clean and orderly, and old and poor people were well cared for. Anyone who disobeyed Calvin's rules was exiled. People came to Geneva from all over Western Europe to hear Calvin. Then they returned home to spread his words.

John Knox came to Geneva from Scotland. When he returned home, he founded the Presbyterian Church, which gradually replaced Catholicism. From Scotland, Calvinist ideas also flowed into England.

The Reformation in England

In England, as in Germany, politics and religion were mixed. In fact, the Protestant Reformation came to England largely because King Henry VIII needed a son to inherit the throne.

Henry's father had come to power after a civil war, known as the War of the Roses, that had raged for some 35 years. Henry's only child by his wife, Catherine of Aragon, was a daughter, Mary. He desperately wanted a male heir to the throne. This was because it was not certain that the English people could accept a female ruler. A woman heir to the throne might mean revolution. By 1527, however, Catherine was too old to have any more children. To Henry, the only solution was for the pope to **annul**—set aside—his marriage to Catherine so that he might remarry. Henry had already set his eyes on Anne Boleyn (BUL-in), a lady-in-waiting at the court, but the pope refused to annul Henry's marriage. For one thing, the Roman Catholic Church did not grant many annulments. Also, Catherine had powerful political connections. She was the aunt of the Holy Roman Emperor, whose troops at the time were in control of Rome. Henry therefore decided to proceed on his own.

With the help of the new archbishop of Canterbury, Henry had his marriage to Catherine annulled. He then wed Anne Boleyn. She gave him another daughter who later became Elizabeth I. Next, Henry obtained from Parliament the Act of Supremacy. This made the English monarch head of the Church of England—the Anglican Church—and cut all ties with the pope. From then on, it was the English monarch who would appoint church officials and collect church revenues.

Henry used the Act of Supremacy to further his other political interests. He closed some 500 monasteries and convents and seized their lands and properties. Some he kept for himself. Some he sold or gave to nobles, merchants, and wealthy farmers, thus gaining their support for

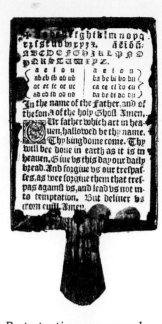

Protestantism encouraged its followers to read the Bible. Because of the need to be able to read, education grew during the 1500s. Above is a hornbook. It is the typical way Elizabethans were taught reading. The alphabet is at the top, followed by the vowels, various combinations of vowels and consonants, and then prayers.

annulment:
cancellation; a doing away with an agreement as if it never existed

For a time Henry VIII was a champion of Catholicism. He was given the title "Defender of the Faith" for a pamphlet he wrote attacking Luther. English monarchs still carry that title. This painting is by Hans Holbein the Younger.

his dynasty. Henry authorized the use of an English Bible rather than a Latin one. He also allowed priests to marry. He did not, however, change religious rituals and practices.

Henry was succeeded by Edward VI, the ten-year-old son of his third wife. (He had six wives in all.) Edward's advisors, heavily influenced by Calvinism and Lutheranism, carried England even farther along the Protestant way. During Edward's reign, a new worship service called the *Book of Common Prayer* was published in English. After six years, the sickly Edward died and was succeeded by Henry's daughter Mary, who was a Catholic. Mary tried to restore England to Roman Catholicism. She married the Catholic king of Spain and had some 300 Protestants burned at the stake for heresy, earning her the nickname of "Bloody Mary." She ruled for only five years and was succeeded by her Protestant half-sister, Elizabeth I.

During her 45-year reign (1558–1603), Elizabeth I brought England some of its greatest prestige. She presided over the Elizabethan Age of literature. During her reign, England decisively defeated Spain, at that time the most powerful country in Western Europe.

Elizabeth I also firmly established England as a Protestant nation. Under the Thirty-Nine Articles, the Anglican Church became the official English Church, supported by state taxes. Some of the beliefs and ceremonies of Catholicism were kept but its head was the ruler of England, not the pope. At the same time, Elizabeth followed a policy of religious toleration. She wanted to keep her realm free of religious wars.

SECTION 3 REVIEW

1. **Recall**   What caused the Great Schism in the Catholic Church?
2. **How and Why**   How did the Protestant Reformation begin?
3. **Critical Thinking**   How were politics and religion mixed during the Protestant Reformation in England?

The Reformation left permanent marks on Western Europe. It strengthened the position of the middle class, which became the base of future democracies in the culture region. It also strengthened the growing feeling of nationalism. The religion of a people became closely identified with the politics of their state. Rulers were often suspicious of subjects who followed a religion different from their own or from that of the majority. After the mid-1500s, Western Europeans began to refer to their nations as either Catholic or Protestant. The Reformation also led to various changes on the part of the Catholic Church.

Catholic Responses

The Protestant Reformation did not leave the Roman Catholic Church unchanged. In addition to Martin Luther, there were many other Catholics who called for reform. The movement by Catholics to reform the Church was known as the Counter-Reformation.

One reformer was a Spanish noble named Ignatius Loyola (1491–1556). After being badly wounded by a cannonball, Loyola decided to devote his life to religious service. In 1540 he received permission from the pope to set up the Society of Jesus. This was a new order of priests organized along military lines. Its head was called a general, and its members were expected to give absolute obedience to their superiors. They looked on themselves as engaged in a war on behalf of Catholicism.

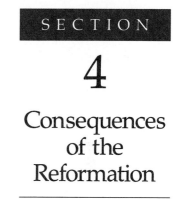

SECTION

4

Consequences
of the
Reformation

The Jesuits, as Society members were called, became excellent teachers. The schools they established set high standards that attracted the children of nobles and wealthy merchants. Jesuit missionaries sought converts in places as far away as Brazil, India, and Japan.

Additional reforms were carried out by the Council of Trent, which met a number of times between 1545 and 1563. First, the Council restated the important doctrines of Roman Catholicism. Second, it affirmed the supremacy of the pope. Third, church services were to continue being held in Latin, although sermons might be preached in the vernacular. Fourth, good works as well as faith were considered necessary for salvation. Fifth, priests and nuns were not allowed to marry. Sixth, both simony and the sale of indulgences were prohibited. In addition, seminaries were set up to improve the education of priests, and the pope was authorized to issue an Index of Forbidden Books that Catholics were not supposed to read. The Council of Trent helped to give the Roman Catholic Church much of its modern shape.

French Religious Wars

Just as the Reformation led to warfare between Germany's Catholic princes and Lutheran princes, so it led to civil war between Catholics and Huguenots within France. Huguenots followed Calvin's teachings. As in Germany, there were political as well as religious factors. Two families were competing for the French throne. The Guise family headed the Catholic party; the Bourbons headed the Huguenot party. At the time, about one-sixth of the French people were Huguenots.

The civil wars began in 1562 and lasted until 1598. Both sides committed atrocities. The most famous was the St. Bartholomew's Day Massacre of 1572. Henry of Navarre, leader of the Huguenot party, was marrying Margaret, daughter of the Catholic regent, Catherine de Medici (MED-uh-chee). Catherine had hoped the marriage would reconcile the two sides. For some reason she changed her mind. Catherine hired assassins to kill the Huguenot nobles who had come to Paris to witness the marriage and encouraged a Catholic mob to murder all the Huguenots in the city. From Paris, the massacres spread into other parts of France.

In 1588 both the duke of Guise and the Catholic king were assassinated, leaving only Henry of Navarre as a possible heir to the throne. Henry realized that he could not hold the throne if he belonged to a minority religion. Saying that "Paris is worth a Mass," he converted to Catholicism and became King Henry IV.

Henry wanted to strengthen the monarchy and play down differences among his people. So in 1598 he issued the Edict of Nantes (NAHNT). It granted Huguenots the freedom to worship as they pleased, both privately and in public. It also gave them many of the civil and legal

An old engraving shows the burning of witches by the Inquisition in a German market place.

rights enjoyed by Catholics, including the right to hold public office. France thus became the first nation in Western Europe to allow two Christian religions to exist within its borders.

The Witchcraft Panic

Periods of great social upheaval often cause people to look for scapegoats to blame for their troubles. During the decline of the Roman Empire, the Christians were blamed for the barbarian invasions. When the Black Death struck Western Europe, the Jews were blamed for the spread of the disease. Now, the split in the unity of the Roman Catholic Church led to a mass hysteria about witchcraft.

Witches were people who had supposedly rejected Christianity in favor of worshiping the devil. They were believed to fly around on broomsticks and to have the power to make cattle sicken and die. Both Martin Luther and John Knox condemned witchcraft as heresy. Henry VIII and Elizabeth I supported the passage of anti-witchcraft laws in England.

Historians estimate that between the mid-1500s and the mid-1600s, at least 500,000 people—mostly old women—were tortured and condemned to death for being witches. Executions of witches were considered great public entertainment. They were widely advertised and drew large crowds. Ballads such as the following became popular.

"So listen Christians to my Song
The Hangman's swung his rope,
And on these Gallows hath been done
An end to Satan's Hope;
Give the News from Chelmsford Town
To all the world be spread,
A crew of Evil Witches have gone Down
Hang'd by the neck, all three are Dead."

SECTION 4 REVIEW

1. **Recall**   What was the Counter-Reformation?

2. **How and Why**   Why did the Huguenot Henry of Navarre decide to convert to Catholicism when he became the only possible heir to the French throne?

3. **Critical Thinking**   In what way did the split in the unity of the Roman Catholic Church brought about by the Reformation lead to mass hysteria about witchcraft?

R E V I E W

Reviewing People, Places, and Things

Identify, define, or explain each of the following:

Renaissance

humanism

Leonardo da Vinci

Michelangelo

genre painting

Hans Holbein

Dante Alighieri

Geoffrey Chaucer

Petrarch

Desiderius Erasmus

Miguel de Cervantes

Niccolo Machiavelli

Sir Thomas More

Christopher Marlowe

William Shakespeare

Johann Gutenberg

Nicolaus Copernicus

Galileo Galilei

Gregorian calendar

Protestant Reformation

Martin Luther

John Calvin

John Knox

Henry VIII

Elizabeth I

Counter-Reformation

Council of Trent

Huguenots

Understanding Facts and Ideas

1. Who were the first humanists? What did they believe?

2. Why did wealthy Italian merchants turn to the arts?

3. How was the attitude of Renaissance artists different from that of medieval artists?

4. What new materials and techniques did Renaissance artists use?

5. What lines did Renaissance architecture follow?

6. What was the most noteworthy contribution of made in music during the Renaissance?

7. How did printing revolutionize bookmaking?

8. What did Copernicus believe about the relationship between the earth and the sun?

9. Why did Western European monarchs see the popes as threats to their political strength?

10. Why was Martin Luther excommunicated from the Roman Catholic Church?

11. How did the spread of Lutheranism affect the Holy Roman Empire?

12. What did the Act of Supremacy accomplish in England?

13. Why did Henry's daughter Mary earn the nickname "Bloody Mary" during her short reign?

14. How did the Reformation leave permanent marks on Western Europe?

15. What did the Edict of Nantes accomplish in France?

Developing Your Critical Thinking

Analyzing Continuity and Change
Some scholars believe that the Renaissance was a time of transition—movement from one thing to another. Elements of the dying medieval era existed along with the first breaths of the modern age. Which characteristics of the Middle Ages continued into the Renaissance? Which characteristics were new?

Writing About History

Relating Past to Present   Erasmus believed that evil comes from ignorance and human mistakes. In a brief essay, explain how this philosophy reflects the attitude of the Renaissance.

Applying Your Skills to History

Using Primary Sources   Find books about Renaissance life written by people who lived at the time. Locate an interesting passage and share it with the class.

CHAPTER

31

The Spanish galleons of the Armada were designed as troop transports to aid Philip II of Spain's planned invasion of England.

Exploration and Governments

In the 1400s many Western Europeans still believed that the world was flat and the seas were filled with monsters. Others viewed the seas as a path to trade and wealth, to the conversion of souls to Christianity, and to exciting adventure. Gold, God, and glory led these Western Europeans on voyage after voyage of discovery all over the world. These explorations brought changes to Western Europe as well as to the lands the Western Europeans visited and colonized.

At the same time, the nations of Western Europe were developing two patterns of government that were to continue into the twentieth century: one was absolute monarchy; the other was the constitutional state.

As you study this chapter, think about these questions:

• What changes in everyday life in Western Europe resulted from the voyages of exploration?

• How did French government change during the 1600s? How did English government change?

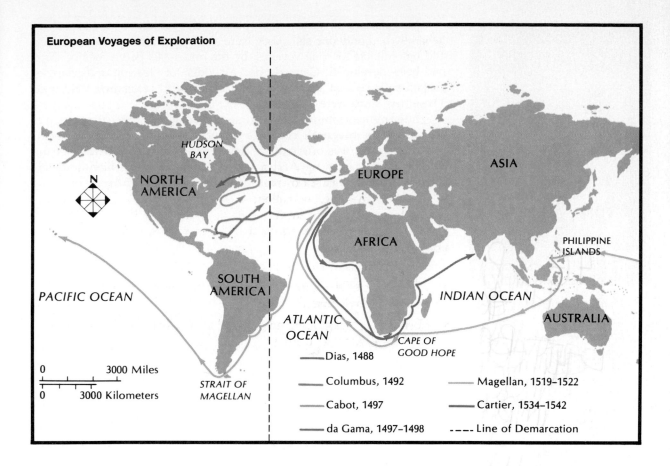

European Voyages of Exploration

HUDSON BAY

NORTH AMERICA

EUROPE

ASIA

N

PACIFIC OCEAN

SOUTH AMERICA

AFRICA

PHILIPPINE ISLANDS

ATLANTIC OCEAN

INDIAN OCEAN

AUSTRALIA

CAPE OF GOOD HOPE

STRAIT OF MAGELLAN

0   3000 Miles

0   3000 Kilometers

——— Dias, 1488

——— Columbus, 1492   ——— Magellan, 1519–1522

——— Cabot, 1497   ——— Cartier, 1534–1542

——— da Gama, 1497–1498   - - - - Line of Demarcation

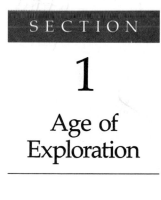

Portugal, Spain, the Netherlands, France, and England led the age of exploration. Their ships sailed in all directions. Their explorers charted unfamiliar seas and claimed great parts of the lands they reached. Often these claims resulted in disagreements and conflict.

Conquering the Seas

The Western European voyages of exploration would not have been possible without certain technological advances. These included more accurate maps, safer and faster ships, and new navigational instruments.

During the Middle Ages, mapmakers in Western Europe had based their work on religion. Following Christian tradition, they put Jerusalem at the center of the world. This meant that Western Europe, Asia, and northern Africa were completely out of proportion. During the 1300s, **cartographers** began drawing maps based on the reports of sailors and merchants engaged in trade with the East. Renaissance geographers also rediscovered the works of ancient Greek geographers. Soon they were producing more or less accurate maps of Western Europe and parts of Asia and Africa.

Age of Exploration

Prince Henry of Portugal never made a voyage himself, but he encouraged others to explore. As a result, he is remembered in history as Henry the Navigator.

New developments also took place in shipbuilding. Medieval ships generally had only one sail. They were also large, difficult to maneuver, and not suitable for long voyages. By the mid-1400s new types of ships had been developed. **Caravels** had a rudder for steering and triangle-shaped sails so that ships could sail either with or against the wind. These new ships were also fast.

Improvements in sailing instruments also helped make navigation at sea easier. The **magnetic compass** showed which direction was north. This instrument was originally an invention of the Chinese. Europeans learned about it from the Arabs. The **astrolabe** enabled sailors to determine their location at sea by measuring the positions of the stars.

The Portuguese

Prince Henry of Portugal was a religious man who wanted to spread Roman Catholicism. He was also a practical man who wanted to break the **monopoly** the Italian city-states had over trade with Asia and gain some profits for Portugal. Around 1420 Henry established a shipbuilding and maritime training center at Sagres on the southwestern end of Portugal. For 40 years he sent sea expeditions down the west coast of Africa. As Portuguese explorers went along, they set up a series of trading posts and developed a rich trade in ivory, gold, and slaves with the West Africans. Although Henry died in 1460, Portuguese rulers continued to encourage the search for a sea route to India.

In 1488 Bartolomeu Días, a Portuguese sea captain, rounded the southern tip of Africa—the Cape of Good Hope. In July 1497 Vasco da Gama set sail for India. He sailed around Africa, crossed the stormy Indian Ocean, and finally reached Calicut, India, in May 1498. This voyage gave Portugal an all-water route to the East. When da Gama returned to Portugal with a cargo of luxury goods, he received a hero's welcome.

Within a few years, the Portuguese had established a fairly large empire in the East. From India they fanned out to the islands of the East Indies—the islands near Asia, the Chinese coast, and even Japan. Although the Portuguese sent some priests to convert the local peoples to Catholicism, they were not particularly interested in large-scale conquest or colonization.

The Portuguese continued exploring, trading, and setting up trading posts. In 1500 Pedro Cabral sailed west and reached the coast of Brazil, where Portugal established some settlements.

During the 1600s, most of the Portuguese trading posts were taken over by the Dutch, English, and others. They followed the sea routes the Portuguese had first explored. Ultimately, Portugal's overseas empire consisted primarily of Brazil.

The Spanish

Like the Portuguese, the Spanish wanted to spread Roman Catholicism. They also wanted a share in the wealth of the East. In Spain's first venture,

Christopher Columbus reached the American continent, and the Spanish were on their way to building a vast empire.

Columbus   Columbus was born in the Italian seaport of Genoa, Italy. Like most educated people of his time, Columbus knew that the world was round. Therefore, he reasoned that by sailing west across the Atlantic Ocean, he would reach Asia. Columbus spent eight years trying to obtain financial backing from the monarchs of Europe's emerging nation-states for a voyage to prove his theory. He finally convinced Ferdinand and Isabella of Spain to give him a chance. In August 1492 Columbus set sail westward from Palos, Spain with three ships. In the early hours of October 12, 1492, land was sighted.

Columbus believed he had reached the East Indies. Therefore, he called the gentle people he found on the islands "Indians." Columbus actually landed on an island in the Bahamas. He sailed on to explore the northern coasts of Cuba and Hispaniola—present-day countries of Haiti and the Dominican Republic. Columbus made three other voyages across the Atlantic, but he was never able to find the riches Spain demanded. When Columbus died in 1506, he was still unaware that he had reached an unknown continent. Although Columbus believed he had failed, his discoveries set off a period of exploration that eventually made Spain the richest nation on earth.

Although Christopher Columbus' voyages made others wealthy, he received little for his efforts. At one time he was imprisoned for supposed mismanagement of his governorship in the Americas.

Spain and Portugal Divide the Earth   The Spanish and Portuguese voyages of exploration led to conflict between the two nations, especially when Spain asked the pope to grant it control of all non-Christian lands discovered in the Indies. The conflict was settled in 1494 by the Treaty of Tordesillas. The pope drew a north-south line, called the Line of Demarcation, on a map through the Atlantic Ocean. The Portuguese received all non-Christian lands east of the line, including Brazil, Africa, and most of Asia. The Spanish received all non-Christian lands west of this line including North America, South America (except for Brazil), and the Philippines. The Dutch, French, and English did not accept the division and made any claims they could either east or west of the line.

New Spanish Discoveries   In 1513 a Spaniard named Balboa crossed the **isthmus** of Panama and saw the ocean that was later called the Pacific. His discovery confirmed that Columbus had discovered a new land.

In 1519 Ferdinand Magellan, a Portuguese in the service of Spain, set out with a fleet of five ships to **circumnavigate**—sail around—the earth. He sailed along the coast of South America through the dangerous passage at the southern tip of South America—later named the Strait of Magellan—and entered the Pacific Ocean. Magellan sailed as far as what are today the Philippines, where he was killed. At last, in 1522, one of Magellan's ships with 18 tattered and half-starved men returned to Spain. Magellan's expedition was successful, however, for two important reasons. First, it showed that the landmass Columbus had discovered was not one but two continents. It also helped people understand the true size of the earth.

Unlike Portugal, Spain had a large enough population to send thousands of people to claim, conquer, and colonize large areas of the Americas. Its new lands soon yielded vast amounts of gold and silver for the Spanish treasury. Spain shortly controlled much of the world's production of precious metals.

The Decline of Spanish Power   Despite the great amount of wealth that flowed into Spain from its colonies, by the 1600s, Spanish power began to decline. There were several reasons for this decline. First, the flood of precious metals into Spain led to a high inflation rate. Second, most of the wealth from the colonies was concentrated among the Spanish monarch and the nobility, who used the money for military buildups or for luxury goods. Third, since the Spanish upper classes considered manufacturing and trade vulgar, they did not develop industry or commercial enterprises in Spain. They bought what they needed from England and the Netherlands. Therefore, the gold and silver flowed out of Spain nearly as fast as it flowed in. When the sources of precious metals wore out, Spain did not have an economic base strong enough to maintain its prosperity.

The Dutch

The Dutch were industrious, thrifty people. By offering cheaper shipping rates, more cargo space, and faster service than their competitors, they soon dominated the international trade of Western Europe. Dutch ships were familiar sights in all Western European ports, and their cities, especially Amsterdam, were centers of commerce and banking. The Dutch also benefited from the fact that their country was tolerant of various religious groups. For example Jews who had been expelled from Spain and Huguenots who had fled from France contributed to the prosperity of the Netherlands.

From the late 1500s until the late 1700s the Dutch roamed the seas in their privateer and merchant ships. They attacked Spanish and Portuguese shipping and trading posts. Their greatest triumph was taking over the spice trade of the East Indies from the Portuguese. The Dutch seized most of what is modern Indonesia. The area became a rich island empire for the Dutch. They introduced coffee plantations and developed production of rubber, palm oil, and sugar among other items. Dutch merchants formed the Dutch East India Company and used it to direct their overseas business.

The Dutch were the first Europeans to reach Australia and New Zealand. They also sailed to the Americas. They whaled in the Arctic Ocean and searched for a northwest passage to Asia through North America. On such a trip Henry Hudson sailed up the river that now bears his name as far as present-day Albany, New York. The Dutch settled the present site of New York and called it New Amsterdam. They also found their way into the Caribbean Sea. They fought with the Portuguese for a part of Brazil and lost. In Africa the Dutch planted a

colony on the Cape of Good Hope. Descendants of the Dutch still make up the majority of the white population of the Republic of South Africa.

Dutch ships roamed the world. By 1600 the Dutch had about 10,000 ships in their merchant marine. They were building them at the rate of one a day.

The English

English exploration began in 1497 with the voyages of John Cabot. It is believed that Cabot, financed by Henry VII, landed somewhere on the eastern coast of Canada. He may also have sailed as far south as Cape Hatteras off what is now North Carolina. Although Cabot believed he had reached mainland Asia, his voyages laid the foundation for later English territorial claims in North America.

By the late 1500s the only interest the British had in the Americas was in capturing treasure ships en route to Spain from the American colonies. In this way a good deal of gold and silver was diverted to England. England was also busy colonizing Ireland. It was not until the 1600s that the British turned their attention to colonization and trade in more distant parts of the world. The reasons for this interest were partly due to the English defeat of the Spanish **Armada**—a huge fleet of ships—in 1588. This victory made England a strong naval power. Also, the round-the-world voyages of Sir Francis Drake encouraged interest in new lands.

In 1600 Queen Elizabeth I chartered the East India Company and gave it a monopoly of all eastern trade. By the late 1600s the company was well established in the Indian cities of Madras, Bombay, and Calcutta. Eventually, the British pushed out the Dutch, Portuguese, and French, and India came almost entirely under British rule.

In 1607 the first permanent English settlement was started at Jamestown, Virginia. Three years later, Henry Hudson sailed into Hudson Bay, reinforcing England's claims to Canada. In 1620 a shipload of Pilgrims seeking religious freedom established the colony of Plymouth in Massachusetts. Gradually, a line of British colonies developed along the eastern coast of the present-day United States from Georgia to Maine. The British also explored and claimed land in northeastern South America and on several Caribbean islands.

The French

By the late 1600s the French claimed vast stretches of territory in various parts of the world. Their claims in North America were primarily based upon the explorations of Jacques Cartier, Father Jacques Marquette and Louis Joliet, and Robert de LaSalle. Cartier sailed up the St. Lawrence River deep into Canada. Marquette and Joliet explored parts of the Mississippi River, and LaSalle followed the river to its mouth near present-day New Orleans. The explorers claimed the land drained by these rivers for France, which gave them a huge empire in North America. France also made claims in the Caribbean. On the other side of the world, France extended its empire into parts of Africa and Asia, including India.

Rivalry Between Britain and France   In both North America and India, the British and French were fierce rivals. Between 1689 and 1763, the two nations clashed in a series of wars. Britain emerged victorious and gained possession of French claims on the North American continent. Britain also gained control of French interests in India.

Economic Effects

The explorations of Western Europeans brought about many economic changes. For the first time a truly worldwide trading network existed. This in turn called for new methods of raising capital, because few merchants could finance an expensive overseas venture by themselves.

As a result, the idea of the **joint-stock company** developed. Joint-stock companies were groups of investors who pooled their resources in the hope of making profits from international trade. To gain the money needed, the company sold **stock**, or shares in the company. Shareholders did not have to be directly involved in the company's operation. Most companies, in fact, were run by professional managers. Profits were distributed among the stockholders, and losses were shared by all. The most successful of joint-stock companies were the East India companies that were chartered by the English, the Dutch, and the French. All three played a major role in financing the establishment of colonies and trading posts around the world.

The growth of international trade also helped end the guild system of manufacturing goods, which was not at all suited to a rapidly expanding economy. The guild system restricted output and limited profits. Middle-class merchants wanted to increase both.

As a result, merchants developed what is known as the putting-out system, or the cottage system. No longer did the same person produce and sell a product. Instead, each step was handled by a different individual. For example, merchants who wanted to sell textiles would buy raw wool. Then they would put out, or assign, the work of spinning and weaving to workers who worked in their own cottages. After the work was finished, the merchants would pay the workers for each piece of cloth they produced, and sell the finished textiles themselves.

The putting-out system enabled merchants to try out new products, to increase or decrease production depending on the market, and to keep labor costs down. Workers, however, were no longer independent artisans. They were insecure day laborers instead. However, the advantages of the putting-out system outweighed its disadvantages. From the 1500s until the 1800s, it was the dominant form of industrial organization in Western Europe.

Social Effects

Revenues from the trading empires helped raise the standard of living for members of Western Europe's growing middle class. This middle class began buying enclosed stoves, which warmed a room much more effectively than an open fireplace. They began sitting on chairs instead of stools. They furnished their houses with carpets and wallpaper and began using linen tableclothes and napkins.

Many new products from around the world became popular in Western Europe. Tea, which came from China, was first considered medicinal. It was claimed that tea would cure a number of ills from headaches to paralysis. New foods that came from the Americas included bananas, corn, peanuts, beans, squash, pineapples, potatoes, tomatoes, and turkeys. Potatoes, which grew well in the cool, damp climate of northern Europe, soon became a staple in a number of these nations. The new foods were partly responsible for a huge increase in the European population during the 1700s. The Americas also furnished Western Europeans with tobacco and a drink called chocolate.

The Age of Exploration also caused a number of problems. Conflicts over colonies and trade led to wars among European nations. Also, the native peoples in the colonies were often treated badly and ended up on the bottom rung of the social ladder. For example, in the Americas, Indians were forced to work to the death in mines and on plantations. The Indians who survived overwork often died from a lack of immunity to

European diseases, such as smallpox, measles, and tuberculosis. Between 1520 and 1750 the American Indian population fell from nearly 78 million to less than 7 million. The Indians were soon replaced by African slaves. Sea captains and merchants prospered greatly by this trade in human misery.

SECTION 1 REVIEW

1. **Recall**   What was accomplished by the Treaty of Tordesillas?
2. **How and Why**   Why did the power of Spain begin to decline by the 1600s?
3. **Critical Thinking**   Why was a joint-stock company a good way to invest in overseas ventures?

SECTION

2

Absolute Monarchies

During the late Middle Ages centralized governments with powerful monarchs began to replace the feudal system as the dominant political structure in many parts of Western Europe. This process was often interrupted. Rulers found it difficult to limit the powers of the feudal lords, who resisted the loss of their personal power. Rulers were also faced with religious conflicts and wars that prevented the growth of stable governments.

By the early 1700s, however, strong governments whose rulers held varying amounts of power had been established in several Western European nations. In two of these nations—Spain and France—absolute monarchies developed.

Philip II of Spain

Following the Peace of Augsburg, which was supposed to end the religious warfare between the Catholic and the Lutheran states of Germany, the Holy Roman Emperor, Charles V, retired to a monastery. The lands Charles V willed to his son Philip included Spain, the Spanish Americas, the Netherlands, and parts of Italy.

Philip II, who ruled Spain from 1556 to 1598, set up his capital at Madrid. He established a civil service to administer his widely spread empire and demanded that no decisions be made without his approval. The huge bureaucracy Philip created made decision-making a very slow process. One saying of the time was "If Death came from Spain, we should live forever."

Philip had two main goals. First, he wanted to make Spain the strongest and most important nation in Europe. Second, he wanted to stamp out Protestantism and restore the Roman Catholic Church in Protestant nations. In 1554 he married Mary Tudor, the English queen.

Queen Elizabeth I—the Armada Portrait *is by the Flemish painter Gheeraerts. The Protestant Gheeraerts fled to England from Catholic Flanders. Flanders is now part of Belgium and France.*

Together they tried unsuccessfully to restore Roman Catholicism to England. After Mary's death, Philip proposed marriage to her successor, Elizabeth, but was rejected. His attempt to restore the Catholic faith in the Netherlands led to a rebellion. The Dutch defeated the Spanish forces, and set up an independent nation in 1581. Philip took the Portuguese throne when it became vacant in 1580, and Portugal remained under Spanish control until 1640.

Gradually rivalry between Spain and England grew. Philip still dreamed of restoring Catholicism to England, and he also sought a way to halt England's growing power. He was greatly angered by the attacks of English sea captains on Spanish treasure ships. In 1588 Philip sent an Invincible Armada of 130 ships and 30,000 sailors and soldiers across the English Channel to battle the English navy and conquer England. The armada, however, was doomed for several reasons. First, the Spanish lacked both ammunition and adequate supplies of food and water. Second, although greatly outnumbered, the smaller English ships were faster and more maneuverable than the bulky Spanish galleons. Third, a number of the English captains, such as Sir Francis Drake, were expert and daring sailors. The English, however, were able to sink only a few Spanish ships. The rest, including some that were badly damaged, were forced to scatter. The final reason for ultimate Spanish defeat was due more to nature than to the English navy. High winds and strong currents forced the armada into the stormy North Sea, where many ships ran aground or sank. It is estimated that the Invincible Armada sailed back to Spain with only about 75 ships. Around 20,000 lives had been lost. After this crushing blow, the power of Spain declined.

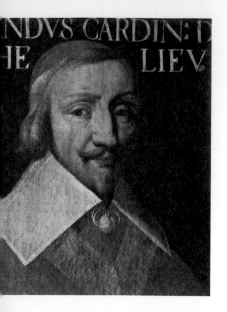

Cardinal Richelieu was more interested in furthering France's power than in meeting the spiritual needs of the country's Catholics. What facts can you find to support this statement?

Growth of the French Monarchy

Henry IV, who became a Catholic in order to keep his throne, was a capable ruler. In addition to issuing the Edict of Nantes, he carried out economic policies that strengthened his alliance with the middle class. He reduced government corruption and inefficiency, built roads and bridges, and encouraged industry and commerce. He also used gold and titles to bribe the most prominent nobles to obey the king's rule.

Henry's successor, Louis XIII, was a weak ruler. During the early years of his reign, the nobles tried to regain some of their powers. Then, in 1624, Louis chose Cardinal Richelieu (RISH-uhl-oo) as his chief minister. Richelieu worked to make the crown the sole political authority in France. To this end, he ordered the destruction of fortified castles, which had provided refuge for rebellious nobles in the past. Having destroyed the nobles' military power, Richelieu attacked their political power. He expanded the system of **intendants**—commissioners of justice and finance. Intendants were mostly from the middle class and were directly responsible to the king. They were sent into the provinces, where they exercised strong financial, judicial, and police powers. As the authority of the intendants increased, the power of the nobles over local government decreased.

Richelieu also worked to establish France as the major power in Europe. In 1618 a religious war, known as the Thirty Years' War, broke out between Protestant factions and the Roman Catholic rulers of the Holy Roman Empire—the Hapsburgs. France eventually entered the war on the Protestant side, despite the fact that the Hapsburgs and Louis XIII were both Catholic rulers. Richelieu's main concern was to destroy Hapsburg power. He knew that a disunited Hapsburg Empire in Germany would cause no threat to French power in Europe.

The Thirty Years' War finally ended in 1648 with the Treaty of Westphalia. The treaty greatly weakened the Hapsburg monarchy and reinforced the powers of the independent German princes. Thus, it ensured that Germany would not become a unified nation for some 250 years.

Louis XIV

Louis XIV was the model of an absolute monarch. He ruled France from 1643 to 1715—longer than any other monarch in the history of Western Europe. Louis believed that he ruled by divine right: God had planned his birth and position in life. He was God's agent on earth, and his subjects had a duty to obey his commands without question. *"L'état, c'est moi!*—I am the state!" asserted Louis. Because Louis believed that he was the center of France just like the sun was the center of the solar system, he became known as the Sun King.

Louis XIV further reduced the power of the French nobles. He removed them from all high government positions and appointed members of the middle class in their place. He also set up a secret police force and opened people's private letters to make certain that they were not plotting against him.

It had always been customary for French kings to travel from one part of the country to another. Louis XIV, however, established himself permanently at the town of Versailles (vehr-SY), about ten miles outside Paris. There he built a spectacular palace as a symbol of his power. Leading nobles, as well as the king's ministers, were required to live at Versailles. Deprived of governmental offices and local power, the nobles became completely dependent upon the king for their livelihood.

Louis's minister of finance, Jean Baptiste Colbert (kohl-BEHR), helped strengthen the monarchy by increasing government control over the economy. France previously had imported such products as textiles, steel, and weapons. Under Colbert the government subsidized French manufacturers who agreed to produce such items themselves. The government also regulated the quality and prices of goods.

Louis XIV set up the first modern army in Western Europe. Medieval armies had disbanded after each campaign. Louis's army was a permanent military force. Also, instead of being employed by individual nobles, it was employed by the state. The government provided the soldiers with weapons and uniforms, trained them in battle maneuvers, and instituted a regular system of pay and promotions. In 1643, when Louis became king, the royal army had consisted of fewer than 20,000 soldiers. By 1688 the French national army was 290,000 strong. For the next hundred years, its numbers never dropped below 200,000. Although most of the soldiers were **mercenaries** hired from Switzerland, Germany, and Ireland, all the officers were French.

In an effort to make France the leading power in Europe, Louis XIV began a series of wars. Other European powers, fearing a strong France,

Under Louis XIV, French architecture, clothing, cooking, and manners became part of the culture of other European countries. French became the second language of educated Europeans and the language of diplomacy.

united to oppose Louis's territorial ambitions. As a result, between 1667 and 1713, France was defeated in four separate wars. These wars seriously weakened the French economy. They drained the royal treasury and led to higher taxes. The economy was further weakened in 1685 when Louis revoked the Edict of Nantes. France lost about 300,000 of its best and most industrious artisans and merchants, most of whom fled to England and the Netherlands. France also lost the taxes the Huguenots had paid.

By the time Louis XIV died in 1715, the absolutism of the French king was firmly established. However, Louis's expensive lifestyle and his unsuccessful wars left the government with financial problems that were to plague his successors.

SECTION 2 REVIEW

1. **Recall**   What were Cardinal Richelieu's goals for France?
2. **How and Why**   Why did rivalry between Spain and England grow during the late 1500s?
3. **Critical Thinking**   How was the Invincible Armada defeated?

SECTION

3

The Constitutional State

In England, as in France, a strong monarchy slowly replaced feudalism during the late Middle Ages. Although France evolved into an absolute monarchy in which the Estates-General did not play a role, England moved in a different direction. Between 1603 and 1690, the English Parliament developed into an active legislative body that effectively limited royal power.

Stuarts Versus Parliament

Because Elizabeth I had died without a direct heir, her cousin, James VI of Scotland, became James I of England in 1603. He was the founder of the Stuart dynasty and the first monarch to rule both Scotland and England.

James encouraged scholars to make the King James translation of the Bible. The beautiful writing style in this translation greatly influenced English literature. Although James was learned, he was an unattractive person. He dressed shabbily, seldom washed, and was always lecturing members of Parliament about English law. Worse, James's concept of law was that he could do as he wished. Like Louis XIV of France, James I believed that he ruled by divine right. This belief angered the members of Parliament. They maintained that they possessed certain rights, including control over finances and a voice in foreign policy.

James I also angered Parliament by discriminating against Puritans and Separatists and insisting that they conform to the Anglican Church. Puritans wanted to "purify" the Anglican Church of Roman Catholic

King Charles I of England believed in rule by divine right. What does this mean? Can you name other rulers throughout history who believed in divine right monarchy?

practices, such as elaborate rituals, the use of incense, and ornate church decorations. Separatists wanted to break away from the Anglican Church and worship God in their own way. Among the Separatists were the Pilgrims who founded the Plymouth colony in North America in 1620.

James was always in need of money, and Parliament controlled the purse strings. Its members were often unwilling to grant James money because they disagreed with his policies. Therefore, James dismissed Parliament and ruled without it for some years.

The struggle for power between Parliament and the king continued during the reign of Charles I, James's son, who ruled from 1625 to 1649. Charles was even more convinced of rule by divine right than James had been. He dissolved Parliament and tried to rule as an absolute monarch. In 1628, however, Charles found it necessary to call Parliament into session to ask for new taxes. In return, Parliament insisted that the king accept the Petition of Right.

The Petition of Right, like the Magna Carta, became a foundation stone in the rights of the English people. The petition placed important limits on royal power. For example, no taxes could be collected without Parliament's consent, and no one could be forced to make loans to the king. Also, no one could be imprisoned without showing just cause. In addition, martial law could not be imposed during peacetime, and the king's practice of forcing his subjects to house soldiers in their homes was forbidden.

Charles agreed to the Petition of Right, but he was furious. After he was granted the taxes, he dismissed Parliament and refused to call it back into session for the next 11 years. To obtain money, he imposed heavy taxes on towns and levied heavy fines. He also pawned the crown jewels.

Charles, like his father, hated the Puritans. He persecuted them so severely that thousands migrated to North America. He especially angered the Scots, who were Presbyterians, by ordering them to use the Anglican prayer book. In 1639 the Scots revolted and invaded England. Charles was forced to call Parliament together once again to raise funds.

The Parliament that convened in 1640 was in a rebellious mood. During its first two years, it passed legislation stating that it could not be dismissed without its consent. It also stated that the king could not impose taxes without its consent, and that no one could be imprisoned without a fair and public trial. Charles had followed the practice of having people who opposed him brought before the Star Chamber, a special court that tried people without a jury. Charles agreed to these laws but later tried to arrest some of the leaders of Parliament. They escaped, and civil war broke out. Charles fled London in 1642.

Oliver Cromwell

Charles was ultimately defeated by the Roundheads—those who supported Parliament. They were called Roundheads because they cut their hair short to distinguish themselves from the long-haired Cavaliers who supported Charles I. The Roundheads were under the leadership of Oliver Cromwell. In 1648 Cromwell and his army captured King Charles. He was tried and beheaded for treason in 1649.

The idea that a monarch could be executed for treason was entirely new. Until this time only a person who conspired against the monarch was considered a traitor. No one had ever acted on the idea that a monarch might be a traitor to the people.

Oliver Cromwell changed England into a commonwealth ruled by a council. Later he became a dictator under the title of Lord Protector. He and the Puritans had been helped in their overthrow of the king by more moderate Protestants. They wanted a constitutional monarchy, but Cromwell controlled the army, and his will was carried out. He could have been king, but he refused the title.

constitutional monarchy: rule by a king or queen whose powers are limited by a constitution

Cromwell tried to maintain and increase English power on land and sea. He fought against Spain and seized Jamaica in the Caribbean. He defeated the army of the Scots, and savagely put down a rebellion in Ireland.

Cromwell encouraged the growth of the English economy. He ordered that only English ships carry English goods, which helped the merchant marine. He also brought about peace between the various Protestant sects by allowing all of them to believe and worship as they chose. He welcomed Jewish merchants and artisans. The Jews had been expelled from England in 1292.

In other ways, however, Cromwell's government was restrictive. Like most Puritans, Cromwell believed that people should spend their free time praying and reading the Bible. Therefore, sports, dancing, and the theater were made illegal. In addition, the press was censored, and judges who opposed the Puritans were fired.

When Cromwell died, he was succeeded by his son Richard. He lacked his father's strength, and it was clear that the English wanted an end to strict Puritan rule. In 1660 Parliament, supported by the army, recalled Charles I's son, Charles II, from exile.

The Restoration

The period between 1660 and 1688, marking the reestablishment of the monarchy in England, is known as the Restoration. Two Stuarts, Charles II and then his brother, James II, ruled during this time.

Charles II did not argue with Parliament. He had had enough of exile. Under Charles II, life in England again became gayer. Theaters, dancing, card playing, and other pleasures were once again permitted. The English, however, were suspicious of Charles's friendship toward France and of his leaning toward Roman Catholicism.

James II ascended the throne in 1685. He was publicly a Catholic who wanted to restore Catholicism in England. He chose Catholics as advisors and reopened Catholic churches in London. He also claimed the right to issue laws without the consent of Parliament. The idea of a Catholic

Oliver Cromwell, a member of Parliament in 1628 and 1640, became the leader of the Puritans. Below is the warrant issued for Charles I's death. Cromwell's signature is in column one.

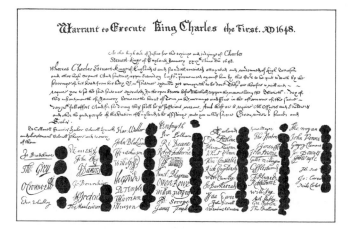

restoration greatly alarmed Parliament, and it decided to change rulers. So began what is known as the Glorious Revolution. During this revolution there was no bloodshed.

The Glorious Revolution

Parliament secretly asked Mary, the Protestant daughter of James II, and her husband, the Dutch prince, William of Orange, to come to England and occupy the throne. They accepted the offer, and in 1688 "Dutch Billy" landed with 14,000 troops. James had no support and fled to France. Before formally accepting the reign of William and Mary, Parliament had them agree to a Bill of Rights.

The Bill of Rights is one of the most important documents in English history. It put an end to divine-right monarchy in England and set up a constitutional state. Only Parliament could make laws, and laws could not be suspended without Parliament's consent. Only Parliament could levy taxes. Only Parliament had the right to maintain an army in peacetime. Individual liberties—such as freedom of speech, freedom of petition, and the right to a fair and speedy trial by a jury of one's peers—were guaranteed. The use of excessive bail and fines, as well as cruel and unusual punishments, were outlawed. Judges were considered independent of the crown and could not be fired except for immoral behavior. The Bill of Rights had a deep effect upon the writers of the Constitution of the United States. A number of the rights in this bill were incorporated into the first ten amendments to the U.S. Constitution.

In 1689 Parliament also passed the Act of Toleration. It granted freedom of worship to all Protestants. However, only Anglicans had the right to vote and hold public office.

Over the next several decades, parliamentary government continued to evolve. Political parties arose. The monarch began to choose cabinet ministers from the majority party to head executive departments. Thus the leaders of the majority party gradually came to control the executive as well as the legislative branch of the English government.

Parliament also gained other powers, such as those of declaring war and removing bad judges from the bench. Custom turned into an unwritten law that no act of Parliament could be vetoed by a monarch. By the mid-1700s the English had erected the government structure that continues to the present.

SECTION 3 REVIEW

1. **Recall** What factors led to disputes between James I and Parliament?
2. **How and Why** How did civil war break out in England? How did the war end?
3. **Critical Thinking** How did the English Bill of Rights later affect the United States?

Reviewing People, Places, and Things

Identify, define, or explain each of the following:

Cape of Good Hope

East Indies

Ferdinand and
  Isabella

Treaty of Tordesillas

Jacques Cartier

Robert de LaSalle

joint-stock company

Elizabeth I

Henry IV

Louis XIII

intendants

Versailles

mercenaries

Petition of Right

Cavaliers

James II

Bill of Rights

Understanding Facts and Ideas

1. What advances took place in Western Europe that led to exploration?

2. What two reasons did Prince Henry of Portugal have for encouraging exploration?

3. What did the voyage of Vasco da Gama accomplish?

4. **a.** How did Christopher Columbus hope to reach Asia? **b.** Where did he land on October 12, 1492? **c.** Where did he believe he was?

5. Why was Magellan's circumnavigation of the earth important?

6. Why did Portuguese power decline during the 1600s?

7. What food from the Americas became a staple in a number of nations in northern Europe? Why?

8. What were the two main goals of Philip II of Spain?

9. How was the Invincible Armada ultimately defeated?

10. Why did France enter the Thirty Years' War on the Protestant side?

11. Why did Louis XIV become known as the Sun King?

12. How did Puritans differ from Separatists?

13. How was Oliver Cromwell's government restrictive?

14. What did William and Mary have to agree to before they were accepted by Parliament as the monarchs of England?

15. Why did Parliament pass the Act of Toleration in 1689?

Developing Critical Thinking

Cause and Effect   The Age of Exploration affected both Western Europeans and the peoples in the lands they colonized. Describe the effects increased trade and colonization had on both these groups.

Writing About History

Analyzing Geography   The wars among European powers during the 1600s and 1700s were not limited to Europe. They extended to the colonies. In a brief essay describe how the location of Britain was an advantage in the wars that were fought both on the European continent and in other parts of the world.

Applying Your Skills to History

Making a Time Line   A time line shows historical events in chronological order. Studying events in this way helps you better understand them. A time line is divided into equal segments representing equal periods of time—years, decades, or centuries. Important events are then put on the time line to show when they occurred. Time lines often cover certain periods, such as the Age of Exploration. Time lines sometimes have themes, such as the monarchs of France.

Activity: Construct a time line showing the important events that occurred during the Age of Exploration.

Exploding Ideas and Revolution

The spirit of the Renaissance influenced the thinking of many Western Europeans. The scientific and philosophical gains made during the Renaissance brought about profound changes in many aspects of life. Gradually, these changes led to a change in people's attitudes toward government and to a rejection of traditional authority.

Western Europeans also began to emphasize the value of reason. This emphasis reached its peak during the **Enlightenment**—the Age of Reason. The Enlightenment lasted from about 1650 to about 1790. The ideas of the Enlightenment sometimes led to violent revolutions, as they did in France in the late 1700's.

As you read this chapter, think about these questions:

- What effects did the Enlightenment have on science, education, and government?

- What factors influenced the development of the arts in Western Europe during the 1600s and 1700s?

- How did the French Revolution change France's political and social organization?

- Why did Napoleon appeal to the French and to many other Western Europeans?

The pace of political and scientific change was rapid in the 1600s and 1700s. The detail of an eighteenth-century painting below shows a cabinet of scientific inventions.

The Enlightenment was more a state of mind than an actual movement. In general, it emphasized naturalism, rationalism, progress, and humanitarianism. Naturalism was a belief in science and natural law. Rationalism held that human reason could determine the principles of natural law, which governed not only the universe but society as well. Progress and humanitarianism expressed a belief in the rights of the individual and the possibility for the perfection of society. From these principles came serious efforts to reform government, society, and education.

Isaac Newton

The leading scientist of the Enlightenment was the Englishman Sir Isaac Newton, who was born in 1642. Newton's outstanding work was *Principia*, which was published in 1687. The work explained the laws of **gravity**—why objects fall and why the planets move in the pattern they do. By providing mathematical proofs for his explanations, Newton showed that the universe was a well-ordered system operating according to certain fixed laws.

Newton's work on gravitation marked the beginning of calculus. Calculus was a major scientific development with many practical applications. For example, it enabled engineers to determine stresses in construction. Calculus also helped to explain the properties of matter and the behavior of gases.

Gallileo had been forced by the Inquisition to recant his scientific opinions. In contrast, Newton was made a knight and received a lucrative government position. After Newton's death in 1727, British poet Alexander Pope wrote:

"Nature and Nature's laws lay hid in night:
God said, 'Let Newton be!' and all was light."

This microscope was made in the 1600s for a wealthy patron of the sciences.

Other Scientists

The founders of modern chemistry are Robert Boyle of Britain and Antoine Lavoisier (lay-vwah-ZYAY) of France. Boyle formulated a law about the relationship between the volume and the pressure of gas that later contributed to the development of the steam engine. Boyle also distinguished a number of elements and compounds and worked on chemical reactions. Lavoisier explained combustion as the union of a burning substance with oxygen.

Geology began to develop as a separate science because of the work of Englishman James Hutton. In general, Hutton believed that the earth's surface was constantly **eroded**—worn down—by the forces of water and wind. These same forces, Hutton argued, were constantly adding new layers to other areas of the earth's surface. These changes occurred over vast stretches of time. In other words, the earth was very old, much older than most people thought. Hutton believed that by studying the different layers of the earth, scientists could determine the earth's age.

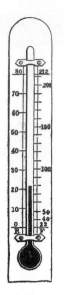

This is a reproduction of Gabriel Fahrenheit's thermometer. His differed from earlier ones because he used mercury instead of alcohol. Mercury is more accurate.

Descartes believed people could use reason to find truth. Compare this to Aristotle's philosophy.

Advances were also made in biology. Anton van Leeuwenhoek (LAY-ven-HOOK), a Dutch merchant whose hobby was grinding lenses, built almost 200 microscopes before discovering bacteria, or tiny cells of living matter. His discoveries started a field of research called microbiology. In Sweden, Carl Linnaeus (luh-NEE-uhs) established the present system of classifying plants and animals.

In medicine, probably the most important development of the Enlightenment was the practice of **inoculation**—infecting a person with a mild form of a disease to cause the person to become immune to a more serious form of the disease. Inoculation apparently originated in China and spread by cultural diffusion to Istanbul. There, Lady Mary Wortley Montagu, wife of the British ambassador to Turkey, learned about the practice. An epidemic of smallpox was raging at the time. Smallpox was a dreaded disease. It was often fatal, while those who recovered were permanently disfigured by deep pits on their faces. Lady Montagu had herself and her children inoculated against smallpox. All three escaped the disease. When she returned to England, she began urging everyone to follow her example. But people considered her a "notorious eccentric" and ignored her idea. It was not until 1796 that Dr. Edward Jenner proved that vaccination prevents smallpox.

Rationalism and Religion

The scientific triumphs of the 1600s and 1700s deeply influenced religious and philosophical thought. Some educated people saw no conflict between science and religion. For example, Newton believed that the Biblical prophets possessed scientific knowledge. They had merely simplified it for their followers. Others felt that science and logic left little room for religious belief. Many thinkers in Western Europe tried to solve this dilemma.

René Descartes (day-KAHRT) of France believed that humans are made of two substances—mind and matter. He said that matter is governed by reason and by the laws of nature. Faith and belief, however, are part of the mind and are impossible for science to understand. This idea became known as dualism.

By the 1700s thinkers developed a philosophy called **deism**. This philosophy held that God created the universe and also the natural laws that govern its operation. After creation, however, God withdrew and left the universe to run according to its natural laws. It was as if God was a master watchmaker who had made a watch, wound it, and left it alone to run on its own. Deism was not an organized religion with rituals and ceremonies; it was a personal philosophy of life based on reason.

John Locke

The anti-authority ideas of the Enlightenment affected the way in which people viewed their relationship with government. One of the leading political philosophers of the period was John Locke of England.

Locke believed that government should be based on the consent of the governed rather than on divine right. According to Locke, people are born with certain natural rights—life, liberty, and property. They enter into a social contract with their government. The government must rule wisely and protect people's natural rights. In return, the people are to obey the government. However, if the government abuses or takes away the people's rights, the people then have the right to overthrow the government. Locke expressed his views in a work entitled *Two Treatises of Government*, published in 1690.

The Philosophes

A number of Enlightenment philosophers were French. They were known as the *philosophes* (FEE-luh-ZAWFS). They were not true philosophers in that none of them created a system of philosophy as had Aristotle or Aquinas. Rather, the philosophes were intellectuals who shared a belief in the ability of reason to solve problems and to correct abuses. They also shared a hatred of intolerance, ignorance, superstition, and persecution. Some philosophes, however, could be very intolerant of anyone who disagreed with them.

Voltaire   One of the best known of the philosophes was Voltaire, who lived from 1694–1778. His novels, histories, plays, and other works fill more than 100 volumes. Much of Voltaire's work questioned and criticized accepted beliefs and practices. Voltaire was especially critical of the French monarchy and nobility. He compared France unfavorably with Britain. Voltaire wrote that the British king, instead of being absolute, "had enough power to do good but not enough to do harm." Voltaire also strongly championed free speech. He stated: "I do not agree with a word you say but I will defend to the death your right to say it."

Voltaire was a deist. He pointed out the hypocrisy and the intolerance of the Roman Catholic and Protestant churches and called for an end to religious wars and persecutions. He declared: "Tolerance is the natural attribute of humanity. We are all formed of weakness and error; let us pardon reciprocally each other's folly. That is the first law of nature. It is clear that the individual who persecutes a man, his brother, because he is not of the same opinion, is a monster."

Montesquieu   The function of government was carefully studied by another philosophe, Baron de Montesquieu (MOHN-tuhs-KYOO). Montesquieu had a strong influence on the writers of the United States Constitution.

In his popular work *The Spirit of Laws*, published in 1748, Montesquieu analyzed many laws and constitutions of the world. He argued that the only way to preserve political liberty was to prevent any one person or group from becoming too powerful. Accordingly, Montesquieu recommended that government powers be separated into legislative, executive, and judicial branches, so that one could check the actions of the others.

This portrait bust of Voltaire was sculpted by Jean-Antoine Houdon. What characteristics of Voltaire does Houdon appear to have captured?

Rousseau believed that arts and sciences had corrupted people. Why was this an unusual view for the Age of Enlightenment?

Rousseau   Jean Jacques Rousseau (roo-SOH) observed that people are by nature good, not evil. He believed in living a simple life and felt that the development of civilization had corrupted people. In *The Social Contract*, published in 1762, Rousseau argued that people would obey the laws of a government only if they made the laws for themselves. He wrote that the people are sovereign, and everyone is equal before the law. He viewed a just society as one in which each individual acts out of concern for the good of all, not out of self-interest.

Rousseau also wrote about education. He advocated learning by experience. For example, he argued that before studying maps, pupils should climb hills and swim rivers.

Diderot   In the 1740s, Denis Diderot (dee-DROH) was commissioned to work on a French translation of an English encyclopedia. Diderot saw the project as an opportunity to collect all the knowledge of his age and to bring about "a revolution in the minds of men to free them from prejudice." He convinced his publisher to start on an entirely new encyclopedia instead of a translation. Many well-known persons in the arts and sciences contributed articles. Many volumes contained detailed drawings of machinery and manufacturing processes. Diderot believed that people who applied scientific principles to practical problems were just as deserving of respect as the scientists who discovered the principles. The *Encyclopédie* helped spread the ideas of the Enlightenment throughout Europe.

SECTION 1 REVIEW

1. **Recall**   What did Isaac Newton explain?
2. **How and Why**   In what way did the scientific advancements of the Enlightenment affect religious thought in Western Europe?
3. **Critical Thinking**   How did the work of Montesquieu influence the writers of the U.S. Constitution?

SECTION

2

The Arts and Literature

The Enlightenment was a period of great artistic and literary development. Some artists and writers of the Enlightenment developed new styles. Others looked back to the ancient Greeks and Romans for inspiration.

Music

Music flourished during the Enlightenment. New instruments were developed, and new forms of musical expression were created.

Instruments   An exciting new instrument, developed in the early 1700s, was the piano. Unlike earlier keyboard instruments, such as the harpsichord, the piano produced both soft and loud tones. Therefore, it could produce very expressive sounds. The piano's popularity spread quickly throughout Western Europe.

Another instrumental change that occurred during the Enlightenment was the composition of the orchestra. In the past, all four sections of an orchestra—string, woodwind, brass, and percussion—had been the same size. Then, the string section was tripled so that it would be more prominent than before.

Opera
A new musical form that developed during the Enlightenment was the **opera**—a drama set to music. Its chief creator was Claudio Monteverdi. At first operas were highly structured. Plots dealt only with subjects from Greek and Roman mythology. Composers followed strict rules as to the length and sequence of sung and spoken words. Gradually, however, opera became more natural and varied. Composers began presenting such human emotions as love and grief.

Composers
In 1710 German-born George Frederick Handel arrived in London. He later became a British citizen. Handel had been thoroughly trained in all forms of musical composition. He composed a great number of works: operas, concertos, overtures, and **oratorios**—operas without scenery or action. Most oratorios have a religious theme. Handel's most famous oratorio is the *Messiah*.

Many composers of the Enlightenment concentrated upon the use of instruments rather than voices in their compositions. One of these instrumental composers was Johann Sebastian Bach, who was born in Germany in 1658. Bach wrote largely for the organ and is probably best known for his religious compositions including *The Passion According to St. Matthew* and *Mass in B Minor*. He also wrote secular music. *The Well-Tempered Clavier* explores all the possible keys in which keyboard music can be played. Bach composed many kinds of **polyphonic** music—music that blends several melodies into a harmony.

Also important during the 1700s was Franz Joseph Haydn (HIYD-uhn) of Austria. He developed the musical forms of the **sonata**, the string quartet, and the **symphony**. A sonata is usually played either on a piano or on a solo instrument—such as a violin—accompanied by a piano. A symphony is performed by a full orchestra. Haydn wrote more than 100 symphonies and dozens of string quartets. At first he wrote to order for two Hungarian princes. In the 1790s he visited London and learned that English composers wrote for the public. Delighted by the idea of writing

The line of music is from Fugue in A-flat *for organ by Johann Sebastian Bach. Although Bach lived most of his life in the 1700s (1685–1750), his work was baroque in character. Overlapping of trends and time periods is a drawback in grouping people into schools of thought. As a student can you see any advantages to grouping artists or thinkers by common characteristics? The lute is a Middle Eastern instrument that became popular in Europe.*

for ordinary people instead of the nobility, Haydn composed two oratorios that are generally considered his greatest works—*The Creation* and *The Seasons*.

Haydn sponsored a young musical genius named Wolfgang Amadeus Mozart. Mozart further developed the symphonic form. In addition, he wrote hundreds of other works, including several magnificent operas that combine a deep understanding of human nature with a rare gift for melody. These operas include *Don Giovanni*, *The Magic Flute*, and *The Marriage of Figaro*. Mozart also composed **chamber music**. Chamber music was written to be performed by a small group of musicians in private homes or in small concert halls.

Architecture and Art

The 1600s and the 1700s were also times of great artistic development. This period is generally known as the **baroque** era. Baroque architecture was elaborate, extravagant, and highly decorative. Baroque art was grand and emotional. Baroque art and architecture expressed the growing power of individuals.

By the early 1700s another style of art, called rococo, developed. Rococo made use of S- and C-curves, and many of its designs were based on natural forms—flowers, shells, and animals.

Sir Christopher Wren designed St. Paul's Cathedral in 1675. Compare it with the picture of St. Peter's Basilica, page 599, built along classical lines during the Renaissance.

The Palace of Versailles, southwest of Paris, was begun by Louis XIV in 1661. Later monarchs added to it. The best architects, artists, and landscapers were used in its design and decoration. In 1789 the Estates-General met there to consider Louis XVI's money request.

Later in the 1700s, some architects and artists reacted against the elaborate styles of baroque and rococo art. They returned to the classical forms of Greek and Roman art. This type of art became known as **neoclassical**.

Architecture Baroque architecture began in Italy with the work of architect and sculptor Gianlorenzo Bernini (1598–1680). It was Bernini who created the curving arms of the colonnade in St. Peter's Square that give the impression of drawing worshipers into the church.

One of the greatest examples of baroque architecture is the palace of Versailles, begun by Louis XIV. Its sheer size was overwhelming. The building covered 17 acres, with a façade that measured a quarter of a mile. Its formal gardens contained some 1,400 fountains. The dazzling Hall of Mirrors was 240 feet long. It was a palace truly worthy of the Sun King! Although Versailles's appearance and public rooms were awe-inspiring, its private rooms were not. They were tiny, dark, unventilated, and jammed with the 2,000 courtiers and 18,000 servants who lived at Versailles. The palace was also poorly designed for comfort. The kitchens were so far away from the dining rooms that food usually arrived at the royal table cold. The only plumbing was outdoors.

In England the greatest architecture was neoclassical rather than baroque in style. The leading architect was Sir Christopher Wren. In 1666 much of London was destroyed by a fire that blazed for four days. Wren was commissioned to rebuild St. Paul's Cathedral, which had been the

From left to right are Portrait of an Officer *by Franz Hals;* Prince Baltasar de Carlos *by Velasquez; and* Head of One of the Three Kings *by Peter Paul Rubens.*

largest medieval cathedral in Western Europe. The building that Wren designed is a huge yet perfectly proportioned example of the neoclassic style. Wren also designed many smaller churches.

Painting   The baroque style in painting is characterized by bold, sweeping curves and sharp color contrasts. Painters tried to capture a feeling of movement and space.

The Flemish painter Peter Paul Rubens was among the first and greatest of the baroque artists. His works were rich with color and full of action and life. He employed many assistants to turn out such details as hands, animals, or backgrounds under his supervision. He created portraits, hunting scenes, and enormous murals of religious events, village feasts, and scenes from mythology.

Other Dutch artists of the 1600s were Franz Hals, Jan Vermeer, and especially Rembrandt van Rijn (RYN). Hals's works are alive with cheerfulness. His interest in good living is reflected in the subject matter of many of his paintings. In contrast to Hals, Vermeer painted scenes of quiet home life. Rembrandt painted with both sympathy and understanding. He did not favor bright colors but relied more on contrasting lights and shadows to bring out the inner character of his subjects.

One of Spain's greatest seventeenth-century painters was Diego Velasquez (vuh-LAHS-kez). At first he painted chiefly religious or domestic subjects. Later his paintings became less detailed and more naturalistic. He often contrasted silver tones with more brilliant colors. His subjects—whether kings or dwarfs—were always portrayed with dignity and a sense of individual worth.

Rococo painting—with its delicate lines and carefree style—was especially popular in France. Jean-Antoine Watteau (wah-TOH), who was born in 1684, created paintings that captured the very spirit of rococo. Misty outdoor settings are filled with young nobles dressed as shepherds and shepherdesses. They appear to be living in a world devoted to pleasure. Watteau used shimmering pastel colors in his work, which strongly influenced fashion and garden design. Francois Boucher's (boo-SHAY) paintings also portray a gaiety and luxury typical of eighteenth-century court life.

Literature

The spirit of the Enlightenment was reflected in its literature. In the 1600s the center of Western Europe's literary world was the court of Louis XIV of France. Three dramatists—Corneille (kor-NAY), Molière (mohl-YAIR), and Racine (rah-SEEN)—were at work. In tragedies like *Le Cid*, Corneille glorified the concept of duty. Racine also wrote tragedies. His characters were usually drawn from Greek and Roman legends. Molière wrote comedies satirizing human weaknesses. In *Le Bourgeois Gentilhomme*, he poked fun at social climbers and snobs. In *Tartuffe*, he mocked religious hypocrites.

In seventeenth-century England the most notable literary works were those of John Milton. Among his best known poems is the epic *Paradise Lost*, in which he described Satan's rebellion and tried to explain why evil exists in a world made by God.

During the 1700s literature began reaching out to a wider public, especially the growing middle class. Novels began to replace classic tragedies and elegant comedies. Heroes and heroines were no longer ancient Greeks and Romans but ordinary people in everyday situations.

In France, the leading novelists included such philosophes as Voltaire and Rousseau. Voltaire's *Candide* satirized the idea that "this is the best of

Below is The Mill *by Rembrandt. To the left is* The Artist in His Studio *by Jan Vermeer. From the description in the text, what characteristics of baroque art can you find in these two paintings?*

all possible worlds." His hero, an innocent young man named Candide, experiences one disaster after another. At last, he and his companions end up living and working on a small farm, trying to ignore the supidities of life.

A famous British novelist of the 1700s was Samuel Richardson. In *Pamela* he told about a beautiful servant girl who so impressed her employer that he married her. Another British novelist, Jonathan Swift, amused readers with *Gulliver's Travels*, written in 1726. Swift pointed out the foolishness of war and the humorous behavior of people.

Another important British literary figure of the 1700s was Samuel Johnson. His *Dictionary of the English Language* became the model for all succeeding dictionaries. His work had a tremendous impact on the development of the English language.

In an illustration from Jonathan Swift's Gulliver's Travels, *Gulliver inspects the Lilliputian army. Although considered by many to be a children's story, Swift's work is an attack on English society and government of the early 1700s. Why do you think art is used as propaganda? Is satire propaganda?*

SECTION 2 REVIEW

1. **Recall**   What advances in music took place during the 1600s and 1700s?
2. **How and Why**   In what ways did baroque painters try to capture the feeling of movement and space?
3. **Critical Thinking**   How did art and architecture develop during the 1600s and 1700s?

SECTION

3

The French Revolution

In France the worship of reason reached its high point during the French Revolution. However, men such as Montesquieu, Voltaire, and Rousseau did not intend to overthrow the French monarchy. They wished only to reform abuses. The philosophes hoped to change the French monarchy to one like that of England. Some people, however, felt it necessary to destroy the system.

The Road to Revolution

By the mid-1700s France found itself in an economic crisis. The government was staggering under a huge royal debt, caused mostly by the many wars France had fought and by the support France had given to the American colonies in their struggle for independence from Britain. More than half of the national budget went to pay the interest on the debt. Since another quarter of the budget went to support the army and navy, and about a tenth to support the court, that left very little money for running the government.

In addition, the burden of contributing to the government lay on the shoulders of those least able to pay. As you know, French society was divided into three estates. The First Estate was the Roman Catholic clergy. It made up less than one-half of 1 percent of France's total population, but owned about 10 percent of the land. The Second Estate was the nobility. It comprised about 2.5 percent of the population and owned about 20 percent of the land. Neither the First nor the Second Estate paid taxes. The Third Estate consisted of the peasants, urban workers, and the **bourgeoisie**—middle class. It was the peasants who bore the heaviest tax burden. In fact, they not only supported the government, but the clergy and the nobility as well. French nobles still received feudal dues from peasant farmers, and the clergy received a tithe—about one-tenth of a peasant's yearly income. Some historians estimate that many peasants paid as much as one-half their income in taxes.

The people looked bitterly upon the extravagant lifestyles of the king, the nobility, and the upper ranks of the clergy. The bourgeoisie, in particular, grew angrier and angrier. They paid taxes and contributed to the nation's prosperity through their work as doctors, lawyers, chemists, engineers, bankers, manufacturers, and so on, but they were generally barred from holding high rank in the military, the Church, and the government. These posts were usually reserved for nobles.

Many of the literate French had read Voltaire's satiric attacks on the privileges of the upper class. They knew about Montesquieu's idea of the separation of powers. Many of them believed with Rousseau that humans were basically good. Society had corrupted them. The French also found in the newly formed United States a model of government by, for, and of the people.

The final spark was a series of poor wheat harvests in 1786, 1787, 1788, and 1789. The price of a loaf of bread rose above a laborer's daily wages, and famine resulted in many parts of France. Also, the high cost of food meant that people could not afford to buy other goods. Thousands of artisans and small merchants lost their jobs. In Paris the unemployment rate stood at 25 percent, and idle, ragged crowds milled restlessly on the city's streets.

Phase One: A New Government

Historians often divide the French Revolution into two phases. During the first phase, revolutionary leaders—drawn largely from the bourgeoisie—ended feudalism in France and transformed the absolute monarchy into a limited one. During the second phase, more radical leaders took control and set up a republic. Their use of terror as a political weapon, however, turned many people against them. A conservative reaction against the Revolution occurred, and after several years France ended up under a military dictatorship.

The Estates General   By 1789 the French were ready for change. In that year Louis XVI—desperate for money—called a meeting of the Estates General—the French assembly—which had not met for 175 years.

At once a dispute arose over the way in which voting would take place. Traditionally, the estates had voted as separate units, each with one vote. Thus the conservative clergy and nobility could outvote the commoners two to one. Representatives of the Third Estate wanted the estates to meet together in a national assembly where the ballots of individual representatives would be counted. In this way the commoners hoped that, with some support from liberal nobles and clergy, they might gain control of the assembly.

Louis refused to allow this, but the commoners were not to be denied. They declared themselves to be the National Assembly and took an oath that they would not disband until they had written a new constitution. Louis gave in and ordered representatives of all three estates to meet as the new National Assembly.

The National Assembly   Although Louis XVI had agreed to the demands of the Third Estate, he still believed in the divine right of kings, and began making arrangements to reassert his power. He secretly brought 30,000 Swiss and German mercenaries into Paris. When the people learned of this, tensions grew, and many Parisians armed themselves. On July 14, 1789, an angry, violent mob stormed and captured the Bastille (ba-STEEL), a fortress-prison that had become a symbol of the wrongs done to commoners by the ruling class. This event marks the beginning of French independence.

The Revolutionary tricolor—a flag of blue, white, and red—soon flew over the city of Paris, and revolution spread throughout France. The estates of the nobility were plundered and destroyed. Government officials were killed. Records of debts were burned. The slogan of the Revolution became liberty, equality, and fraternity.

Meeting in an atmosphere of change and violence, the National Assembly swept away the ancient feudal structure of government. Serfdom and special obligations to royalty and church were abolished. The privileges of the old governing class were removed. Anyone could now hold public office. Everyone would pay taxes.

These sweeping changes were capped with a statement known as the Declaration of the Rights of Man. This document proclaimed the principles of the Revolution. It followed in the tradition of the English Bill of Rights and the American Declaration of Independence. It made all people equal before the law and defended the rights of liberty, ownership of property, security, and resistance to oppression. Women, however, were excluded from politics.

Nevertheless, it was women who were responsible for the next development in the Revolution. During the fall of 1789, food shortages, especially in Paris, had become more and more critical. Therefore, a crowd of about 7,000 Parisian women marched 20 miles through mud and pouring rain from Paris to Versailles to demand bread. The crowd began shouting, "We want the baker, Mrs. Baker, and the baker's boy." They were referring to Louis XVI, his wife, Marie Antoinette, and their son. As a result of this demonstration, both the royal family and the National Assembly moved from Versailles to Paris. Once there, the fiery Parisian crowds began to play more of a role in the Assembly's actions.

In 1791 the National Assembly wrote a constitution for France, which transformed the absolute monarchy into a limited one. A government of three separate branches was established. The old court system was reorganized and the people gained the right to trial by jury. However, the tax requirements for voting and for holding office were very high. As a result, only the bourgeoisie and the wealthier peasants were able to participate in the new government. Poorer peasants and city workers were left out.

The National Assembly also instituted other changes. It confiscated lands belonging to the Roman Catholic Church. These lands were sold to the bourgeoisie and to wealthier peasants. As a result, independent farmers eventually became an important stabilizing force in France. The Assembly also took over the handling of education from the Church, and established freedom of religion. For the first time, Jews were allowed to become citizens. The assembly went even further and made the Church subject to government control. Church officials were to be elected and were to be paid by the government. The pope's authority was no longer recognized in France. More than half of the country's priests and nearly all of its bishops rejected these measures. The reforms also angered many peasants, whose enthusiasm for the Revolution disappeared.

The Bastille dates to the 1300s when it was used as a fortress. Later it was turned into a jail for political prisoners. The storming of the Bastille marked the beginning of the French Revolution.

Phase Two: The Radical Turn

In October 1791 a Legislative Assembly was elected according to the rules set down in the new constitution. As before, its membership was drawn mostly from the bourgeoisie, but it included many more radicals. The Assembly members took their seats according to their political views, with the radicals on the left side of the hall and the moderates on the right.

The Legislative Assembly   The Legislative Assembly faced several challenges. Émigrés—nobles and clergy who had fled France and were living in foreign capitals—were working against the Revolution. Also, war with Austria, Prussia, and many smaller German states appeared imminent. The rulers of these kingdoms feared that the Revolution might inspire their own people to revolt. So they organized an army to restore absolute monarchy in France.

The Assembly decided to strike first. In April 1792 France declared a war of "people against kings" on Austria and Prussia. However, the French army soon suffered several defeats at the hands of the well-trained Austrians and Prussians. By summer's end, the invaders were only 200 miles (320 kilometers) from Paris.

Emotions flared in the capital. Fearing the violent Paris mob that backed the radicals, the Legislative Assembly voted to suspend the monarchy. A new assembly, called the National Convention, was elected to change the constitution and create a democratic republic. In September 1792, the monarchy was abolished and the First French Republic was proclaimed. Nearly all adult males became eligible to vote.

Louis XVI was tried, convicted, and executed for treason. The republic immediately found itself confronting increased dangers at home and abroad. Great Britain, the Netherlands, Spain, Portugal, Sweden, and several Italian states joined Austria and Prussia in the war against France. Also, a counterrevolutionary insurrection broke out in the Vendeé, a poor but very religious farming section of France.

The Jacobins   Because the moderate faction in the Assembly faced too many problems they were unable to resolve, radicals seized control of the government. Led by a brilliant but fanatical young lawyer named Maximilien Robespierre (robes-PYAIR), the radicals—known as Jacobins (ZHAK-uh-buhns)—established a revolutionary dictatorship. They set up a Committee of Public Safety with extraordinary powers. It was the Committee that conducted the Reign of Terror from September 1793 to July 1794. Moderates were purged from the National Convention. People suspected of opposing the Revolution or hoarding food were exiled from France or were killed. Among those whom the guillotine beheaded was the former queen, Marie Antoinette. Historians estimate that 2,700 persons were executed in Paris and another 20,000 or more were killed throughout the rest of the country. Tens of thousands of people were arrested and jailed. No evidence was needed for conviction. It was enough to be denounced as an enemy of the people. Fear spread across France.

At the same time, however, the Jacobins moved to improve economic conditions for their political supporters, especially the working poor of Paris. The price of bread was fixed at a low level, and food was rationed. A social security system was set up to help the aged, the disabled, war widows, and couples with large families. Women gained the right to control their property, and divorce was allowed. The government promised free primary education to all.

The Jacobins also moved on the foreign front. They adopted an idea that had been suggested by the Paris workers: a universal draft. All unmarried, able-bodied men between 18 and 25 were called up for service. The French army soon numbered more than one million, making it the largest army in Western Europe. Inspired by love of France and by the revolutionary principles of liberty, equality, and fraternity, French soldiers adopted a new battle technique: mass charges with fixed bayonets. Victory quickly followed victory, and by 1795 Prussia and Spain had made peace. By this time France once again had a new government.

The End of the Revolution

The Committee of Public Safety had maintained and defended the Revolution against enemies from without and within. However, the ruthlessness and bloodshed of the Reign of Terror disgusted and exhausted the people. In July 1794 a reaction set in. Robespierre and his chief followers were themselves guillotined, and a moderate government called the Directory was formed.

The Directory was led by a committee of five and lasted from 1795 to 1799, but it was neither honest nor efficient. Prices rose, anti-draft riots swept the countryside, and all was in confusion. There was even talk of restoring the monarchy. In 1799 the Directory's most powerful general, Napoleon Bonaparte, took over control of the government in a military coup. It was Napoleon and his conquering soldiers who were to spread the ideas of the French Revolution across Europe.

Marie Antoinette, once queen of France, is bound and on her way to the guillotine. Is this how you expect to see a queen? Does this drawing reflect the French Revolution's idea of equality? How?

SECTION 3 REVIEW

1. **Recall** What groups were represented by each of the estates in the Estates General?

2. **How and Why** In what way do historians often divide the French Revolution?

3. **Critical Thinking** How did the Declaration of the Rights of Man follow the tradition of the English Bill of Rights and the American Declaration of Independence?

Napoleon Bonaparte is still regarded as one of France's greatest heroes. He centralized the government, improved communication, and unified French law in the Napoleonic Code. He continued the process that the Revolution had started of unifying the French people. He also sought to make France an international power. Under Napoleon, the French people were constantly reminded that they were being asked to fight for the glory and honor of their nation. Thus French citizens became conscious of the oneness of their culture and their land and developed a spirit of patriotism and nationalism.

Rise to Power

Napoleon was born on the French island of Corsica and studied at military schools in France before joining the revolutionary army. He rose quickly in the ranks and proved to be brilliant in military tactics. Under the monarchy, he would never have risen above the rank of captain. However, the Revolution opened the door for talented commoners in all fields. Napoleon became a brigadier general at the age of 24. His marriage to Josephine de Beauharnais (boh-ahr-NAY), who had influence with the Directory, also helped his career.

In 1795 Napoleon was given command of the French forces fighting the Austrians in Italy. Within a few months he defeated Austria and gained much of northern Italy for France. This left only one nearby military opponent—Great Britain. Napoleon decided to strike at Britain by cutting its trade routes with India. In that way, Napoleon hoped that France could regain the overseas empire it had lost in 1763, but the Middle Eastern campaign went badly. Although the French invaded and easily conquered Egypt, British naval hero Admiral Horatio Nelson destroyed the French fleet. This cut French communication and supply lines and left the French army stranded in a strange land. The long hot months and the stiff opposition that the French encountered from the Ottoman rulers of the Middle East soon wilted the French soldiers' desire for the campaign. Plague and a virulent form of eye disease that caused widespread blindness made matters worse. The only positive result of the campaign was the discovery of the Rosetta Stone, which enabled scholars to read the hieroglyphic writing of the ancient Egyptians.

The debacle in Egypt gave Napoleon an opportunity to return to France in 1799. There he and his followers overthrew the weak and corrupt Directory and seized power for themselves. They set up a new government called the Consulate, with Napoleon as First Consul. From this powerful position Napoleon ruled France.

The French people generally approved. In fact, more than 3 million voted in favor of the new constitution, as compared to only 1,500 against. The French were willing to accept a military dictatorship because Napoleon represented law and order in place of revolutionary strife. At the same time—unlike the royalists who wanted to restore the monarchy—Napoleon promised to keep the changes the Revolution had brought about.

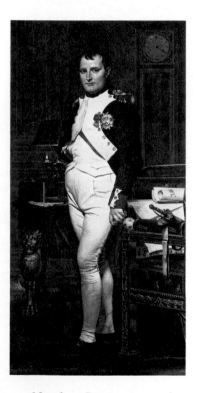

Napoleon Bonaparte posed in 1810 for this portrait by the neoclassical painter Jacques Louis David, who also drew the sketch of Marie Antoinette on page 649.

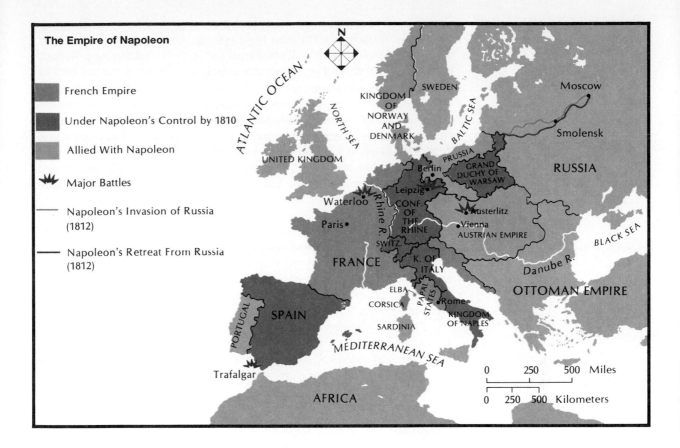

The Empire of Napoleon

French Empire

Under Napoleon's Control by 1810

Allied With Napoleon

Major Battles

Napoleon's Invasion of Russia (1812)

Napoleon's Retreat From Russia (1812)

In 1802 Napoleon was chosen First Consul for life. Two years later he asked the French people for their approval to become emperor. Again they agreed. The pope came to Paris to crown Napoleon in the Cathedral of Notre Dame. When the pope was about to place the crown on Napoleon's head, Napoleon took it and crowned himself. The power expressed by this gesture was not lost on Europeans. From 1804 to 1815, Emperor Napoleon I was the dominant force in Western Europe.

Napoleonic Reforms

One of Napoleon's first efforts at coping with domestic problems was making peace with the Roman Catholic Church. The French government and the Church had been at odds since the Revolution began. Although Napoleon was not a religious man, he realized that an agreement with the pope was needed for political stability, especially since the majority of the French people were staunch Roman Catholics.

Accordingly, Napoleon and the pope signed the Concordat of 1801. This document reestablished the Church in France. However, other religious groups retained freedom of worship. Church buildings were returned, but land confiscated from the Church was not. In addition, the state was to continue the practice of paying the salaries of the clergy and of nominating bishops to their office.

One of Napoleon's most important accomplishments was the codification of French law. The new legal system, known as the Napoleonic Code, was finished in 1804. It combined old French common law, Roman law, royal decrees, and revolutionary legislation. Most of the reforms of the Revolution were kept. Thus, all persons were equal before the law. They could work in whatever occupation they wished. Torture was outlawed. People were guaranteed a public trial by jury. However, married women lost the right to control their property, and marriage was described as follows: "A husband owes protection to his wife, a wife owes obedience to her husband." The Napoleonic Code eventually influenced the legal codes of Germany, Italy, Holland, and many nations in Latin America.

Napoleon also made other lasting changes. He established public education under the supervision of a government body. He centralized the government to bring the country more firmly under his control. He improved the economy by making tax collection more efficient, building roads and bridges, and establishing the Bank of France to handle the finances of government. He also set up the Legion of Honor to reward merit in various fields.

Despite Napoleon's accomplishments, he did away with liberty. There was no more freedom of speech in France. Newspapers were censored, and a vast spy system was established to keep an eye on people suspected of holding subversive ideas. Political opponents were often arrested without charge.

Empire

Through diplomacy and war, Napoleon was able to defeat his enemies. The Austrians, who had again gone to war against France, asked for peace in 1801. In 1802 Great Britain did likewise.

Napoleon then turned his attention toward America. He dreamed of a vast colonial empire built around Haiti in the Caribbean and the Louisiana Territory. He had forced Spain to give the latter to France in 1801. However, Napoleon's costly wars in Europe, the continued resistance of the Haitians, and yellow fever among his troops changed his plans. In 1803 Napoleon sold the Louisiana Territory to the United States for $15 million. In 1804 Haiti won its independence, and Napoleon reluctantly abandoned his dream of an overseas empire.

Instead, Napoleon focused his attention on Western Europe. In 1805 war broke out again between France and Britain. Napoleon prepared to cross the English Channel and conquer Britain with the help of his ally, Spain. Britain, however, had more experienced sailors and better ships. At the battle of Trafalgar, Admiral Horatio Nelson destroyed almost the entire combined French and Spanish fleet without the loss of a single British vessel. Although Nelson died on the deck of his ship, his victory gave the British navy control of the seas, and Napoleon was unable to cross the English Channel.

Napoleon was far more successful on the European continent. Between 1805 and 1807 he defeated the Austrians, the Prussians, and the

Russians, and reached the summit of his glory. As you can see from the map on page 651 he was—either directly or indirectly—the master of almost all of Europe.

As Napoleon's power spread, so did many ideas of the French Revolution. Serfdom disappeared in many places. Everyone was considered equal before the law. Religious freedom for all was guaranteed, and the Catholic Church lost much of its political power. Jews were admitted to citizenship and allowed to live outside ghettos. The Napoleonic Code and the French system of administration were widely used.

The Road to Defeat

Because Napoleon could not defeat Britain militarily, he began an economic blockade. He hoped to destroy British trade with Western Europe. The blockade, however, was never completely successful because it could not be strictly enforced. British goods kept being smuggled into the continent, mainly through ports in Portugal and Spain.

Napoleon then made a major blunder. Although Spain was an ally, Napoleon arrested the Spanish royal family, installed one of his brothers as king, and invaded Portugal. Furious at the insult to their national pride, Spanish civilian fighters promptly began a guerrilla war against the French. In 1808 the British sent troops under the command of the Duke of Wellington to help the Spanish. The Peninsular War drew 300,000 French soldiers into Spain, but even this large army was not enough for a French victory. Napoleon was forced to pull back behind the Pyrenees.

In 1812 Napoleon made another major blunder that would end in disaster. He assembled an army of nearly 600,000 soldiers and set out to

Napoleon flees Moscow as tens of thousands of his troops die in the snow. This scene was painted by Jan Chelminski, a Polish painter of the early 1900s.

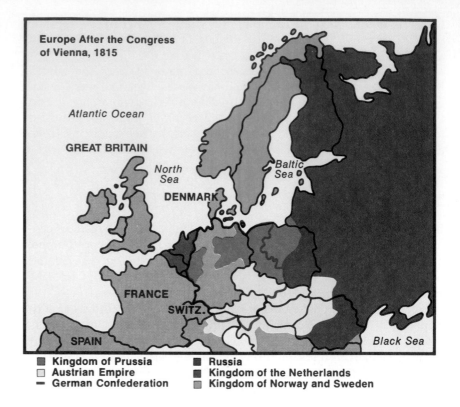

Europe After the Congress of Vienna, 1815

Atlantic Ocean

GREAT BRITAIN

North Sea

Baltic Sea

DENMARK

FRANCE

SWITZ.

SPAIN

Black Sea

- ■ Kingdom of Prussia
- □ Austrian Empire
- — German Confederation
- ■ Russia
- ■ Kingdom of the Netherlands
- ■ Kingdom of Norway and Sweden

the east to conquer Russia. The Russians' strategy consisted of retreating into the Russian interior. The Russians burned their fields to prevent the French from living off the land.

In mid-September, Napoleon entered Moscow with only about 100,000 troops, but the Russians had withdrawn beyond the city. Napoleon waited for a month. Then he began a retreat. The Russian winter had begun, and the French army was not equipped for it. Fewer than 30,000 soldiers made it back to France.

Most of Europe entered into a coalition against Napoleon. In October 1813 he was defeated at the battle of Leipzig. The following April, coalition armies occupied Paris. Napoleon abdicated and was exiled to the tiny island of Elba.

In March 1815 Napoleon returned to France. Once again the coalition formed against him. In June 1815 Napoleon was defeated in the battle of Waterloo. He was exiled, and he died in 1821.

SECTION 4 REVIEW

1. **Recall**   What was the Napoleonic Code?

2. **How and Why**   In what ways did Napoleon do away with liberty in France?

3. **Critical Thinking**   How was Napoleon defeated in Russia, even though the Russians never won a decisive battle?

Reviewing People, Places, and Things

Identify, define, or explain each of the following:

Enlightenment
Isaac Newton
gravity
Robert Boyle
deism
John Locke
philosophes
Voltaire
Jean Jacques
  Rousseau
Johann Sebastian
  Bach
Sir Christopher Wren
Peter Paul Rubens

Corneille
Moliere
Jonathan Swift
bourgeoisie
Estates General
Louis XVI
Bastille
Jacobins
Directory
Napoleon Bonaparte
Rosetta Stone
Napoleonic Code
Elba
St. Helena

Map Study

Using the map on page 651, determine the answers to the following questions:

1. How far east did Napoleon's empire extend?

2. How far north did Napoleon's empire extend?

3. What do you think prevented Great Britain from becoming a part of Napoleon's empire?

Understanding Facts and Ideas

1. Why was Newton's development of calculus important?

2. What did deists believe about the relationship between God and the universe?

3. What did John Locke believe people have a right to do when a government abuses or takes away their rights?

4. What was Voltaire's attitude toward free speech?

5. What changes took place in Western European literature during the 1700s?

6. Why did the members of the Third Estate want to meet in a National Assembly?

7. a. Why did thousands of women march on Versailles in the fall of 1789? b. What was the result of this march?

8. Why were radicals able to seize control of the revolutionary government?

9. a. What was the Napoleonic Code? b. How did it affect other nations?

10. What were Napoleon's two major blunders that eventually led to his fall?

Developing Critical Thinking

Expressing Problems Clearly   There were many reasons behind the outbreak of the French Revolution. List and explain three major problems in French society that caused the Revolution.

Writing About History

Analyzing Leadership   Within a few years, France was ruled by an absolute monarch, an Assembly led by radicals, and a military dictator. Write a short essay comparing the leadership of Louis XVI, the Jacobins, and Napoleon.

Applying Your Skills to History

Forming a Generalization   Some people believe that the arts influence social and political changes. Others believe that the arts only reflect the changes that are already taking place in society. Both beliefs are generalizations.

Activity: Reread Section 2 and decide whether you think the arts reflected changes that were taking place in society or the arts influenced society to change. Write a paragraph stating and explaining your conclusion.

The Industrial Revolution

The industrialization of Western society began during the industrial revolution. This revolution started in England in the middle of the 1700s and spread to Western Europe and the United States. Although the term *revolution* is used, the changes actually were gradual. The rise of industry took place over several centuries and its growth continues today.

The basic change caused by the industrial revolution was the introduction of machines into all areas of economic life. As a result, society changed from one based on farming to one based on an ever-increasing production of goods. In turn, the economic, philosophical, artistic, and social organization of Western society also changed.

As you study this chapter, think about these questions:

- What factors made the industrial revolution possible?

- What were the basic economic, social, and political changes that resulted from the industrial revolution?

- How were science and philosophy affected by industrial developments?

- What factors influenced the arts of the 1800s?

This 1876 engraving shows four inventions of the industrial revolution: a steam-driven printing press, telegraph, locomotive, and steamboat.

P rior to the industrial revolution, most people in Western Europe earned their living by farming, handcrafts, or both. Farmers still used the methods of their ancestors. Most manufacturing was done at home by hand and sold in surrounding communities. Transportation was slow and inadequate.

England as the Hub

The industrial revolution began in England because certain conditions there were particularly favorable. The British lived on an island defended by the finest navy in the world. They were, therefore, protected from the destructive European wars of the eighteenth century. Moreover, during that time Britain became a leading colonial power. Britain's colonies provided merchants and manufacturers with raw materials and expanded markets for goods. Also, Britain had many wealthy people who were interested in investing in growing industries.

The atmosphere in Britain was pro-business. The middle class was highly regarded, and many Protestant groups looked favorably upon the idea of earning a profit. Also, the Bank of England offered long-term credit at low interest rates. After 1762 insurance companies provided protection against shipping losses and other risks of doing business. A patent system—which did not exist in most other countries of Western Europe—allowed inventors to benefit personally from the use of their machines.

Britain had an abundant supply of such basic raw materials as coal, iron ore, and wool. In addition, transportation within Britain was excellent. The island nation was small, and was crisscrossed by roads and canals over which bulk cargoes could move cheaply and conveniently.

A Revolution in Agriculture

One of the first areas to feel the impact of new ideas and new machinery was agriculture. The resulting changes increased food production, freed farmers for industrial jobs, and brought about a growth in population.

In the late 1700s England changed from an open-field system of farming to an enclosed system. Since medieval times, farmers had cultivated small plots of land and shared a common pasture. With enclosure these small plots were grouped into large farms. Agricultural output and efficiency were increased. But many farmers lost their land and were forced to find work in the cities. Enclosure also led to the concentration of land in the hands of a few. By the 1870s fewer than 7,000 landowners held about 80 percent of the land in Great Britain.

Many inventions and discoveries contributed to making farming practices more efficient. In 1701 Jethro Tull invented a horse-drawn cultivator for loosening the soil and a drill for planting seeds. The cultivator enabled the soil to absorb moisture more efficiently and kept down weeds. The drill helped farmers plant seeds in straight rows, which

Eli Whitney's cotton gin (left) is an example of a machine created to fill a need. The earlier invention of the spinning jenny (right) by James Hargreaves made it possible for large amounts of cotton to be spun quickly into thread. But until the cotton gin, cotton could not be cleaned fast enough to keep the jennies running efficiently.

speeded up harvesting. Charles Townshend found that wheat, turnips, clover, and barley could be planted in alternate years to improve the fertility of the soil. The discovery that crops could be rotated made it unnecessary to allow land to lie fallow every third year.

During this time more scientific approaches to the breeding of animals were also discovered. Among the pioneers in scientific animal breeding was Robert Bakewell, who developed new breeds of sheep and cattle. Through his experiments it became possible to produce larger animals, thereby increasing the supply of meat. For the first time, meat became an important part of the diet of average people.

A Revolution in the Textile Industry

Britain had dominated the wool textile industry ever since the Middle Ages. In the 1700s it became the leader in the cotton textile industry as well. Cotton goods became extremely popular because they could be washed more easily than wool and were more comfortable to wear. Also, cotton fibers were adaptable to machines.

Machines   The first textile machine was an instrument for weaving called the **flying shuttle**, which was invented in 1733. The flying shuttle enabled weavers to double the amount of cotton cloth they wove each day. A shortage of cotton yarn quickly developed, however, because spinners could not keep up with the demand. In 1767 James Hargreaves invented the **spinning jenny** which spun eight threads at once. As the machine was improved, the jenny produced as many as 120 threads at a time. Richard Arkwright harnessed water power for spinning, and Samuel Crompton combined the jenny and Arkwright's water frame into a single machine called the **spinning mule**.

Weavers could no longer keep pace with spinners. In 1785, however, Edmund Cartwright found a method of using water to power looms, and the production of cotton textiles soared.

Increased production methods created a shortage of raw cotton fiber. The seeds of the cotton plant had to be removed by hand in a slow, painstaking process. Then in 1793 Eli Whitney, an American, developed a machine to remove the seeds. This invention—the **cotton gin**—eventually became a thousand times more productive than the average worker.

Factories   The development of textile machines not only increased production, but it also brought an end to the putting-out system. The new machines were too large, expensive, and complicated for a domestic worker to maintain. As a result, they were soon housed in a single building known as a **factory**. Instead of the merchant bringing raw materials to the workers' cottages, workers came to the factory.

After a time, factories became highly organized. Workers were supervised by foremen, and shop rules were established. Work became more and more specialized, with each worker performing a smaller part of the overall operation. Productivity lowered prices, and goods became available to more people. Work, however, became less skilled and more monotonous.

Steam Power   At first textile machines were driven by water power, and textile factories were located near swift-running streams. In 1769,

This is James Watt's first steam engine. How did the use of water power and then of coal quicken the pace of the industrial revolution?

This is a model of Thomas Edison's first successful light bulb.

however, a Scot named James Watt invented an engine that could provide power without using running water. His steam engine ran on coal. Manufacturers were then able to build factories near towns that supplied both markets for their goods and workers to operate their machines.

Steam power was soon applied to transportation as well as manufacturing. An American, John Fitch, built a steam-driven ship in 1787. Soon steam was propelling ships on rivers, lakes, and canals. In the 1880s, a fuel-efficient engine was developed that enabled steamships to cross the ocean as well.

The steam locomotive was invented in 1804 by Englishman Richard Trevithick. In 1829 George Stephenson's steam-powered locomotive won a race against a horse-drawn vehicle, and the cotton merchants of Manchester, England, decided to build a railroad connecting Manchester with the port of Liverpool. By 1850 Britain had the world's first railroad network.

Coal, Iron, and Steel

Great Britain has large deposits of coal, and the British quickly developed efficient mining techniques. Once a suitable fuel for powering factories was found, a strong, durable metal for building machines was needed. Machines contain many movable parts that have to withstand continuous strain.

At first iron was used to make machines but by the mid-1800s they were generally made of steel. Steel had been known since ancient times, but it was very expensive. People used it only for small items such as swords and razors. In the 1850s, however, Henry Bessemer of England and William Kelly, an American, both developed a technique for making steel by blasting air through molten iron to remove impurities. In 1866 German-born Sir William Siemens developed the open-hearth method of making steel, which was even cheaper and more effective than the Bessemer-Kelly technique. Steel could then be produced cheaply and in large quantities. Coal, iron, and steel became the cornerstones of industrialization.

The Electrical Revolution

In the late 1700s, about half a century after Benjamin Franklin's experiments with electricity, Italian Alessandro Volta generated an electric current in a device that resembled a modern battery. In 1831 Englishman Michael Faraday invented the dynamo, which changes mechanical energy into electricity. That same year American Joseph Henry combined the two devices and built an electrical telegraph. Samuel F. B. Morse, an American, improved the telegraph and convinced people of its commercial possibilities. Newspapers used the telegraph to send accounts of events, and railroads used it to send information between train depots.

Later, telecommunications were greatly improved by two inventions. One was the telephone, invented in 1876 by American Alexander Graham Bell. The other was Italian Guglielmo Marconi's wireless, which eventually evolved into the radio. Electrical current was also applied for many other purposes. By the 1860s dynamos were producing electricity to drive factory machines.

The Spread of Industrialization

Until about 1825 the industrial revolution in Western Europe was more or less limited to Great Britain. The British forbade skilled mechanics from leaving the country and refused to allow the export of textile and other machines. In addition, Napoleon's wars reduced Western Europe's working population and led to severe inflation that made it hard to accumulate money for investment in industry.

Eventually, industrial growth spread to the European continent. It came most quickly to Belgium, which had adopted British technology. Industrialization came much more slowly to France and Germany. During the first half of the nineteenth century, the French began to industrialize slowly. Political disunity in Germany greatly hindered German industrialization. Germany, however, had abundant natural resources needed for industrial development. Once the trade barriers between the German states were removed, German industry began to grow. By 1900 Germany was one of the world's industrial leaders.

SECTION 1 REVIEW

1. **Recall** What advances took place in Britain's textile industry in the 1700s?

2. **How and Why** In what way was the making of steel revolutionized?

3. **Critical Thinking** How did the industrial revolution spread throughout Western Europe?

2

The Machine and Change

Once machines were housed in factories, the face of Western Europe really began to change. In order to make a living, workers had to spend most of the day in factories. People began to build their homes or rent rooms near their jobs. Tradespeople were needed to serve these workers, and government was needed to preserve law and order. Gradually these communities became cities. Where cities already existed, factories turned them into overcrowded slums.

City Life

Urban industrial centers, especially in Great Britain, grew rapidly during the first half of the 1800s. For example, Liverpool's population soared from 77,000 in 1801 to 400,000 in 1851. As a result, cities could not keep pace with the demand for housing. Buildings became dangerously overcrowded. Pollution became a major problem. Sewage flowed through open trenches. Factories dumped their wastes into the rivers. Garbage was allowed to rot in alleys and basements until it could be sold as fertilizer. The air was filled with thick black smoke from factory chimneys. One result of the pollution and overcrowding was a sharp increase in urban death rates. In the 1830s epidemics of cholera, typhoid, and tuberculosis swept through British cities.

Gradually, national and local governments began taking steps to improve city life. For example, in 1848 Great Britain passed the first national public health law. Soon cities were installing iron pipes to bring in water, and underground sewers to carry off wastes. Building codes were drafted to fix minimum housing standards.

Working Conditions

Working conditions in the industrial towns were often miserable. People generally worked 12 to 16 hours a day, six days a week. There were no vacations or sick leaves. Many factories were dingy, poorly lit, improperly ventilated, and unsafe. Workers often lost fingers in machinery or contracted lung disease from inhaling fibers.

The great need for cheap labor led to the exploitation of children in factories and mines. Children generally received little pay. Ruthless factory owners sometimes employed children as young as five and six.

In the 1830s the efforts of British reformers led to investigations of working conditions in factories by committees of Parliament. As a result, Parliament passed the Factory Act of 1833, which prohibited child labor below the age of nine. A nine-hour workday was established for children between the ages of nine and 13, and a 12-hour workday was set for workers between the ages of 13 and 18. Government inspectors enforced the new law. In 1842 Parliament outlawed the labor of woman and children in British mines. In 1847 the Ten Hours Act established a standard workday for women and children. By the 1870s most British industrial workers were adults.

This is the city of Leeds, England, in 1885. Note the closely packed houses. The city is still an industrial center, manufacturing farm tools, glass, leather goods, and woolens.

Other industrial nations moved more slowly to reform working conditions in factories. For example, the 10-hour workday did not become standard in France until 1900. Child labor was not abolished until 1914 in both France and Germany.

New Political Forces

Two major political forces—the middle class and labor unions—grew out of the changes caused by the industrial revolution. In England, merchants, bankers, and manufacturers began demanding voting reforms in the early 1800s. At the time, suffrage was restricted to males who were rich landowners—about 6 percent of the male population. Also, the boundaries of election districts had not changed since 1664. This meant that sparsely populated districts were represented in the House of Commons while growing industrial cities such as Birmingham and Manchester had no representation at all.

Beginning in 1832 the British middle class was able to win greater voting privileges and representation in the House of Commons. Property qualifications for voting were lowered and eventually abolished. By 1918 all Englishmen over the age of 21 had gained the right to vote. Other industrial nations in Western Europe followed Britain's example.

Women's Suffrage   In Britain the struggle for women's suffrage, which began in 1867, started out mildly. Women—mostly from the middle class—passed out leaflets and held marches. Later, these women adopted more militant tactics. They chained themselves to seats in the House of Commons, went on hunger strikes, and threw stones at government officials. Many women were imprisoned as a result. Public opinion eventually swung in their favor, however, when they went on hunger strikes and were forcibly fed. In 1918 English women over 30 gained the right to vote.

The industrial revolution brought lower-class women out of the home and into the factory. At right is Emmeline Pankhurst, a major force in gaining the right to vote for English women. Suffrage was fought for and won largely by the middle class. Why do you think the fight might not have seemed important to women such as these mill workers?

Labor Unions   As workers became increasingly angry and frustrated with the insecurity of their jobs and their miserable working and living conditions, they banded together and formed **labor unions** to negotiate for them with business owners. At first, unions were opposed by the governments of industrial nations. For example, Great Britain declared them illegal in 1800. Even when the law was repealed in 1824, workers were not allowed to go out on strike. Over time, however, the British government modified its position. In 1859 it allowed peaceful picketing, and in 1871 it granted unions the right to strike.

Elsewhere in Western Europe, labor unions developed more slowly. Belgium did not allow them until 1866. France legalized them in 1884, and Germany in 1890.

As unions grew they gained political power. Their votes began to be heard by governments, which passed laws to improve working conditions, wages, and benefits, and to reduce the number of working hours. In some countries of Western Europe, unions helped form labor parties to advance their interests.

SECTION 2 REVIEW

1. **Recall**   What were working conditions like in industrial towns?
2. **How and Why**   In what ways did pollution and overcrowding become problems in industrial cities?
3. **Critical Thinking**   Why did conditions in British factories improve in the 1830s and 1840s?

The industrial revolution influenced the way people viewed the relationship between government and the **socioeconomic** system. Economists developed several new theories to explain how the industrial revolution worked and to propose solutions to the problems it had created. In general, these theories can be divided into three main groups: laissez-faire capitalism, socialism, and communism.

Laissez-Faire Capitalism

Laissez faire is French for "let it be." **Laissez-faire capitalism** is an economic theory that supports little or no government regulation with regard to business and international trade. The economist who best explained its principles was a Scottish professor named Adam Smith. His book *The Wealth of Nations*, published in 1776, had tremendous influence.

During the sixteenth and seventeenth centuries, Western European nations believed that the basis of their wealth lay in gold and silver. Smith disagreed. He believed that the only true source of wealth was manufacturing, because it created value where none had existed before. It did this by the **division of labor**. When each worker performed just one step in an operation rather than the entire operation, production soared.

Smith believed in certain principles of the Enlightenment. Just as there was a natural order in the physical world, so there was a natural order in the economic world. For example, it was natural for people to look out for their own interests. Accordingly, the government should not interfere in the economy but should allow the "invisible hand" of free competition to regulate the market. Free competition, according to Smith, rewards efficiency and hard work, and penalizes laziness and poor judgment. Under free competition, people would naturally produce more and more goods; the country would become richer; and individuals, including workers, would also become richer.

Smith believed that government should maintain a sound currency and should break up monopolies, which give some firms an unfair economic advantage. Other than that, however, Smith believed government should leave business alone. Smith also supported free trade among nations. He disapproved of protective tariffs and other restrictions. Smith argued that if there were free trade, each nation would produce the goods it could most cheaply produce, and everyone would benefit.

Some economists supported laissez-faire capitalism but believed that government legislation was needed to correct the problems that industrialization had caused. One such scholar was Englishman John Stuart Mill. In 1848 he published *Principles of Political Economy*, in which he distinguished between the production of goods and their distribution. Mill said that the natural law of free competition was the best way to determine how goods should be produced. Distribution, however, was another matter. Mill argued that distribution depended, not on natural law, but "on the laws and customs of society." Consequently, Mill favored government legislation to fix minimum wages and maximum hours, to protect working children, to tax inheritances, and to break up monopolies. Mill believed that government should advance the well-being of all its citizens by passing social legislation.

Socialism

Some economists believed that laws were not enough to correct the miserable working and living conditions of industrial workers. The only solution, they felt, was to have the government intervene directly in the economy. Instead of private property, they favored government ownership of the means of production—factories, farms, and mines—and the means of distribution—railroads, trucking lines, ships, and other transportation systems. Instead of the profit motive, they believed in social justice. Instead of competition, they favored central planning. Instead of a great gap between the rich and the poor, they wanted everyone to share in the profits of an industrial society.

Economists with this point of view were known as socialists. Although socialists generally believed in the same goals, they disagreed about how their ideas should be put into action.

Utopian Socialists   One group of socialists were known as utopian socialists, after Sir Thomas More's book *Utopia*. Utopian socialists called for the establishment of model industrial communities. They hoped these communities would set an example as to how society should be organized.

Probably the most famous utopian socialist was Robert Owen, who lived from 1771 until 1858. As the owner-manager of a large textile mill in New Lanark, Scotland, he was able to put his ideas into practice. He raised his workers' wages and shortened their working hours. He built good homes for them, set up a store where they could buy food at cost, and even established a school where their children could learn how to read and write. Opponents of his ideas had predicted that he would become bankrupt. Instead, his mill was tremendously profitable, in large part because worker productivity was high.

This drawing recreates a meeting of several members of the Fabian Society, which laid the basis for the British Labour party: from left, playwright George Bernard Shaw; the society's founders, Beatrice and Sydney Webb; and political scientist Graham Wallas.

Democratic Socialists   Another group of socialists were known as democratic socialists. They believed that the way to achieve a socialist society was through political parties and legislatures. Once people were convinced that socialism was preferable to capitalism, they would elect socialist representatives, who would gradually change the economy. Most democratic socialists did not support government ownership of all means of production and distribution. Mostly, they favored government owner- ship only of large industries, such as steel mills and railroads. Democratic socialists also believed in a multi-party system and in individual rights.

During the twentieth century, many Western European nations have been governed for varying periods of time by democratic socialist parties, either alone or in a coalition with other parties. These nations include Austria, France, Great Britain, Italy, Norway, Portugal, Spain, Sweden, and West Germany.

Communism

Communism was a more radical and revolutionary kind of socialism. It was developed by Germans Karl Marx and Friedrich Engels. In 1848 the two men published a pamphlet entitled *The Communist Manifesto*, which presented the foundations of communism. Later, Marx expanded his ideas in *Das Kapital*.

Theory   Marx believed that what shaped a society was its economic system. According to Marx, history was a continuous struggle between classes. It was a conflict between the haves and the have-nots, between "those who hold economic power and those whose labor is exploited."

Marx agreed that capitalism had helped people by turning out goods on a gigantic scale. Instead of creating abundance for all, however, capitalism was exploiting the workers. Factory workers throughout West- ern Europe were working long hours under bad conditions for very low wages, while factory owners were growing rich.

Marx argued that capitalism carried the seeds of its own destruction. Because workers were so poorly paid, they could not buy the products they manufactured. Falling sales would lead to unemployment and depression. Eventually the depression would run its course, factories would reopen, and workers would be rehired. Marx said that the cycle would repeat itself and each succeeding depression would be worse than the previous one. Eventually the frustrated workers would revolt, over- throw the capitalists and their governments, and seize the means of production and distribution. Although Marx believed that revolution was inevitable, he called for an immediate uprising. "Let the ruling classes tremble at a communist revolution," he wrote. "The proletarians [workers] have nothing to lose but their chains. They have a world to win. WORKING MEN OF ALL COUNTRIES, UNITE!"

Marx called his post-capitalist system "the dictatorship of the prole- tariat." There would be no economic classes, because everyone would own everything in common. The state would be unnecessary. It would wither away and die. All workers would produce according to their abilities and be rewarded according to their needs.

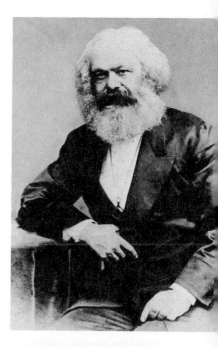

Karl Marx was a member of the middle class. How might this have shaped his view that communism needed a middle class?

Evaluation   As an economist, Marx's theories have not proved correct, and his predictions have not come true. He predicted that under capitalism, the rich would get richer and the poor would get poorer. Generally, in capitalist countries, both groups have gotten richer, although the gap between them remains. Since the early years of the industrial revolution, when Marx was writing, workers have achieved tremendous improvements in wages, hours, and working conditions. Marx predicted that depressions would grow increasingly severe. Instead, most governments have taken an increasingly active role in providing an economic safety net for workers through such means as unemployment compensation and spending for public works. Marx believed that "the working men have no country," but most industrial workers have been intensely patriotic. Marx predicted the withering away of the state. Instead, in countries in which communism has been established, governments have grown tremendously.

On the other hand, Marx's writings made people aware of the influence of economic forces. Governments in Western Europe, frightened at the thought of Communist revolution, probably adopted social legislation earlier than they would otherwise have done.

SECTION 3 REVIEW

1. **Recall**   What were some of the theories of Karl Marx?
2. **How and Why**   In what way did Adam Smith explain the wealth of nations?
3. **Critical Thinking**   Robert Owen provided high wages and excellent working conditions for the workers in his textile mill. Although opponents of Mill's ideas predicted that he would be bankrupt, his mill was tremendously profitable. Why do you think other mill and factory owners did not follow his practices?

SECTION

4

Science and Philosophy

The industrial revolution brought about many changes in science. New theories developed about the origin and evolution of living things. Discoveries were made about the nature of matter and of the universe. Medical care was greatly improved, and new theories were developed to explain human behavior.

The Theory of Evolution

In 1831 Charles Darwin, an English biologist, accepted the post of naturalist aboard H.M.S. *Beagle*. From 1831 to 1836, the *Beagle* sailed along the coast of South America and to the Galápagos (guh-LAP-uh-gohs) Islands in the Pacific. Darwin explored the area, carefully collected hundreds of specimens of plant and animal life, and filled his notebooks with an immense amount of information. After he returned to England, he spent years analyzing his data. Darwin published his theories in 1859 in his book *On the Origin of the Species*.

Darwin's Theory   Darwin believed that all forms of life evolved — gradually changed — from an earlier, simpler form. Simply stated, Darwin's theory held that all forms of life produced more offspring than could survive to adulthood. Darwin believed that this resulted in a constant battle to stay alive. He called this battle the "struggle for existence." Darwin also held that organisms vary within each species. Because of this variance, an organism might carry a special trait that could enable it to adapt more easily to a certain environment and to survive where organisms that lacked that trait would die out. This theory became known as "survival of the fittest." Darwin also believed in the concept of "natural selection." This meant that an organism that possessed a trait helpful to survival would pass that trait on to the next generation. The trait would then be passed on to succeeding generations. Darwin believed that in this way all forms of life gradually changed over time.

Many scientists have continued to probe the mysteries of evolution and heredity. In the 1860s botanist Gregor Mendel, an Austrian monk, experimented with garden peas. He found that certain laws govern the way characteristics are passed from one generation to the next. Mendel's work formed the basis of the science of heredity.

The man responsible for new theories in physics, biology, and medicine was Charles Darwin.

Social Darwinism   Darwin applied his ideas only to biological science. Some Western Europeans, however, adapted them to the study of society. Englishman Herbert Spencer argued that competition existed, not only in nature, but in society as well. Spencer believed that civilization's progress depended on the "survival of the fittest." He opposed programs to help the poor and the sick because he felt they would weaken society. Money was the reward for society's fittest members. Such ideas are known as **Social Darwinism**. Many laissez-faire capitalists quoted Spencer to justify their opposition to labor unions, to social legislation, and to the income tax.

Another Social Darwinist was German philosopher Friedrich Nietzsche (NEE-cheh). In his book *Thus Spake Zarathustra*, which was published in 1884, Neitzsche argued that the true goal of people and nations is power. He attacked Judeo-Christian values because he felt they encouraged compassion, which in turn encouraged a slave mentality. Neitzsche called for a new breed of "supermen," who would be free of old ideas and social restrictions and who would have control over their emotions. Only such "supermen," he said, were "capable of leading the dumb herd of inferior men and women." Nietzsche's philosophy had a strong influence on twentieth-century Nazi Germany.

Some Social Darwinists extended their ideas still further. Arthur de Gobineau of France argued that people with dark skins were naturally inferior to people with white skins. The proof supposedly lay in the fact that the industrial revolution had originated in Western Europe, not in Asia or Africa. Gobineau's ideas became known as **racism** and were often used to justify Western European imperialism in other culture regions.

A New View of the Universe

New scientific ideas were not limited to the biological sciences. They flourished in the physical sciences as well. As the nineteenth century drew to a close, the way in which scientists interpreted the universe changed dramatically.

The atomic theory—which holds that matter consists of invisible and indestructible particles called atoms—was first proposed in the 400s B.C. by the Greek Democritus. Democritus, however, had no way to prove his theory, and for almost 2,000 years no one paid much attention to it. Instead, Western Europeans believed that matter consisted of varying combinations of earth, air, fire, and water.

By the early 1800s, however, scientists had come round to a belief in the atomic theory. The change in attitude grew out of the experiments of Robert Boyle, Antoine Lavoisier, and especially Englishman John Dalton. A practical result of their theoretical work was the development of dozens of new products. There were beautiful synthetic dyes for clothing, and explosives for use in mining and construction. Medical patients benefited from anesthetics, disinfectants, and aspirin.

During the late 1800s and the early 1900s, however, experiments in electricity and magnetism showed that the atom itself was made up of even tinier, electrically charged particles. One of the first important discoveries in this field was made in 1895 by German physics professor Wilhelm Roentgen (RENT-guhn). He discovered that certain invisible energy rays pass through human skin and body tissues. By photographing the shadow cast by these rays, a person's bone structure becomes visible. Because Roentgen did not know where the rays came from, he called them "X-rays." X-rays are now widely used for medical diagnosis.

Other developments soon followed Roentgen's experiments. By the late 1890s, French scientist Antoine Becquerel observed that the element radium gave off energy as it disintegrated. Polish-born chemist and physicist Marie Sklodowska Curie, working in France, used the term *radioactive* to describe this behavior. She and her husband, Pierre Curie, discovered three more radioactive elements: thorium, polonium, and radium. Experiments by other physicists demonstrated the existence of three subatomic particles.

Even more revolutionary discoveries were made by German mathematician Albert Einstein. In a series of three papers published between 1905 and 1916, Einstein presented several new laws of physics. He expressed some of his ideas by the formula $E = mc^2$, that is, "energy equals mass times the speed of light multiplied by itself." In other words, a small amount of mass can be transformed into an incredible amount of energy.

Since the Renaissance, science has become very practical. For example, Albert Einstein's work on the quantum theory contributed to the invention of talking movies.

Marie Sklodowski Curie, a Polish chemist and physicist, discovered the elements polonium and radium. She became Professor of Physics at the Sorbonne in Paris and won two Nobel Prizes.

Einstein also overturned Newton's view of the universe. Newton believed that time, space, and motion are absolute and can be measured. Einstein's **theory of relativity** maintains that only the speed of light is fixed. Everything else is relative, or changeable, depending on the observer. Einstein's ideas led to an expanded understanding of how the universe works. They also showed that even scientific laws are subject to change.

Medical Advances

During the 1800s many advances occurred in medical science. In the 1860s French chemist Louis Pasteur found that many diseases are caused by bacteria. This is known as the **germ theory of disease**. Pasteur developed a process of killing bacteria by heat. As a result, milk could be pasteurized, or heated, so it would not turn sour. Pasteurization also saved France's silk industry by killing the bacteria that were destroying silkworms. Pasteur developed a vaccine against rabies, a generally fatal disease usually transmitted by the bite of a rabid animal. His vaccine against anthrax helped wipe out that disease among France's cattle and sheep.

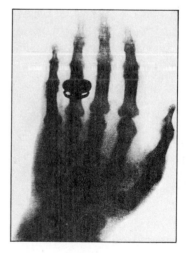

This is one of the first X-rays ever made. It was taken by Wilhelm von Roentgen, the discoverer of the X-ray.

German country doctor Robert Koch built on Pasteur's work. He developed a water-filtration system to prevent disease. He discovered the bacteria that cause tuberculosis and Asiatic cholera, among other diseases. He also investigated outbreaks of malaria, sleeping sickness, and bubonic plague in such places as India and southern Africa.

English surgeon Joseph Lister used many of Pasteur's ideas to show how important it is for surgeons to wash their hands and sterilize their instruments before operating. He also began to disinfect open wounds. By the 1890s the number of patients who survived surgery had increased dramatically. Also, the death rate in hospital maternity wards in Western Europe had fallen from 18 percent to less than 1 percent.

The Social Sciences

During the late 1800s and early 1900s a number of developments took place in the social sciences. Scholars began to apply the scientific method to the study of human behavior. Social scientists tried to combine and apply the knowledge of several different areas in their work. Field investigations and sociological studies were conducted. Statistics were employed as a tool of measurement.

John Stuart Mill published several books on political science. Many of them were written in collaboration with Harriet Taylor, who eventually became his wife. In *On Liberty*, which appeared in 1859, Mill argued that the only purpose of government was to prevent harm to others and that individual freedom was essential for progress. Mill asserted that society would not improve unless people were allowed to develop, and people could only develop if they were allowed freedom of thought and freedom of speech.

Mill strongly supported women's suffrage in his work *The Subjection of Women*. Putting his ideas into practice, he helped organize England's first women's suffrage society in 1867.

Psychology, like economics and political science, had originally been considered part of philosophy. But in the mid-1800s, it became experimental as people began trying to find out what factors influenced human behavior.

One interpretation of human behavior was offered by the Austrian physician Sigmund Freud (FROYD), who lived from 1856 to 1939. Freud concluded that people often behaved according to desires and feelings of which they were not aware. He developed a technique for investigating the unconscious called psychoanalysis. The psychoanalyst listens to patients talk about their dreams, their present, and their past—whatever enters their minds. By analyzing this data, Freud claimed, it is possible to uncover the unconscious desires and feelings that affect behavior. Once that happens, Freud believed, people can change their behavior and handle life's problems more successfully. Freud's major work was *A General Introduction to Psychoanalysis*, published in 1920. Freud's work had a great influence on the treatment of mental illness.

Sigmund Freud was the founder of a branch of psychiatry called psychoanalysis.

1. **Recall** What were the major parts of Darwin's theory of evolution?

2. **How and Why** Why were many laissez-faire capitalists eager to accept the theories of Social Darwinism?

3. **Critical Thinking** How did Sigmund Freud interpret human behavior?

During the 1800s new trends in literature, art, and music developed. The first half of the century was dominated by a movement known as romanticism. By midcentury this glorification of nature, the supernatural, and the emotional was being replaced by realism. The industrial revolution and the resulting changes were felt in the arts. By the century's close, painters began to emphasize color and design rather than real scenes and people.

Romanticism

The arts in the 1700s had been dominated by reason and by strict rules and standards. Near the end of the century, some artists, writers, and

Goya's work The Third of May *was inspired by Napoleon's occupation of Spain. Goya influenced various schools of art far into the 1900s.*

673

composers began to revolt against classical forms and subjects. The revolt climaxed in the 1800s, and the romantic movement began. Nature and the simple things of life were the inspiration for the arts and literature. Interest developed in the Middle Ages, folklore, and national heritage. Emotion and imagination were emphasized.

Literature   **Romanticism** had a great impact on the literature of England, France, and Germany. Poetry became the most important literary form, although novels and science fiction also flourished.

William Wordsworth was a romantic poet of the early 1800s, who often wrote about nature. Wordsworth and other romantic poets such as Samuel Taylor Coleridge, author of *The Rime of the Ancient Mariner*, preferred the natural life of the country to city life, and chose to live in the Lake Country of northern England. They have since become known as the Lake poets.

Other romantic English poets included Lord Byron, Percy Bysshe (BISH) Shelley, and John Keats. Generally they rebelled against politics and all forms of authority. They admired youth and despised life "after thirty." As Byron wrote in his poem *Don Juan*:

" 'Whom the gods love die young' was said of yore,
    And many deaths do they escape by this:
The death of friends, and that which slays even more—
    The death of friendship, love, youth, all that is,
Except mere breath."

Appropriately, perhaps, all three poets died at a young age—Byron at 36, Shelley at 30, and Keats at 25.

Several romantic prose writers were also active in England in the early 1800s. Sir Walter Scott wrote historical accounts of romantic adventure and chivalry in such works as *Ivanhoe, Kenilworth*, and *Waverly*. Mary Wollstonecraft Shelley wrote *Frankenstein* in 1818.

An outstanding romantic novelist was the German Johann Wolfgang von Goethe (GURH-tuh). His sorrow over an unhappy love produced the sensitive and gloomy novel *The Sorrows of Young Werther*. In the English-speaking world, Goethe is best known for his dramatic poem *Faust*—the story of a scholar who sells his soul to the devil in exchange for knowledge and eternal youth.

Other romantic writers of the 1800s included the French dramatist and novelist Victor Hugo. His most famous works are the novels *Les Miserables* and *The Hunchback of Notre Dame*. French novelist Alexandre Dumas wrote exciting adventure stories—such as *The Three Musketeers* and *The Count of Monte Cristo*—set in the days of Cardinal Richelieu. German scholars Jacob and Wilhelm Grimm gathered and published a collection of German folk stories under the title *Grimm's Fairy Tales*.

Music   Romanticism had a major impact on music as well as on literature. Composers began to express emotions and to emphasize beautiful melodies. They wrote music for everyone, not just for the Church or for the privileged upper classes, as they had done in the past.

Ludwig van Beethoven used what he had learned from his teachers—among them, Mozart and Haydn—and added his own talents for arrangement and development of form. His music was powerful and passionate, and celebrated human heroism.

674

The orchestra grew larger and richer-sounding. The piano in particular became an important solo instrument.

Romantic music was dominated by German and Austrian composers. Foremost was Ludwig van Beethoven, many of whose compositions were written after he began going deaf in 1801. Other outstanding romantic composers included Frédérick Chopin, Felix Mendelssohn, Franz Schubert, and Robert Schumann.

The climax of the romantic movement in music, however, came in opera. German Richard Wagner (VAHG-nuhr) was strongly nationalistic, and many of his works—such as *Tannhauser, Lohengrin, The Flying Dutchman*—are based on medieval German legends. Wagner revolutionized opera by treating it as a musical drama. Italian Giuseppi Verdi composed three popular operas in the 1800s—*Aïda, La Traviata,* and *Rigoletto.*

Art and Architecture Romantic painters, like romantic writers and composers, broke away from traditional themes and forms to rely on color, emotion, and imagination. Landscapes, legends, and struggles for freedom were common subjects. Francisco Goya, a Spaniard, painted both royal portraits and ordinary people. After Napoleon invaded Spain, Goya attacked war's brutality in such works as *The Disasters of War* and *The Third of May*, which depicts an execution.

Romantic ideals revived medieval Gothic architecture in Western Europe between 1830 and 1870. Buildings with spires, towers, and arches were constructed. The best example is the Houses of Parliament in London.

Realism

In the second half of the 1800s, a new movement began to affect literature, art, and music—**realism**. Realists rejected romanticism and portrayed everyday life as they believed it really was. They examined ordinary people and their problems.

Above is Honoré de Balzac *by the sculptor Auguste Rodin.*

George Bernard Shaw's life (1856–1950) spanned a number of schools of writing. But his style and subjects changed little.

This is L'Estaque *by Paul Cézanne. Can you see any differences in style between this and the impressionist work of Claude Monet on page 677? Are there any differences in light? color? shapes?*

Literature

The leading English realistic writer was Charles Dickens. He was a prolific writer, who wrote his books in monthly installments, sometimes turning out more than one at a time. Dickens created some of the most memorable characters in literature. At the same time, he portrayed the social ills caused by the industrial revolution. For example, *Oliver Twist* exposed the horrors of **workhouses**. *David Copperfield* portrayed the difficulty of getting out of debt. *Hard Times* showed the bleakness and misery of factory towns. Even the light-hearted *Pickwick Papers* described the grimness of debtors' prisons. Dickens's works did much to change existing social conditions in Britain.

A favorite dramatist of the period was Irishman George Bernard Shaw. His many plays emphasized witty intellectual arguments. Shaw mocked the military in *Arms and the Man*, condemned slum landlords in *Widowers' Houses*, and attacked poverty in *Major Barbara*. *Pygmalion* was a satire on the English class system.

In France the leading realistic writer was Honoré de Balzac. Although he wrote some 100 novels about people at all levels of French society, he was especially devastating in his descriptions of the middle class, as in *Père Goriot* and *Cousine Bette*. Balzac criticized the bourgeoisie for being interested only in money and power. Gustave Flaubert, another French realist, portrayed an ordinary woman crushed by the dullness and hypocrisy of bourgeois life in his novel *Madame Bovary*. Some of the novels of Emile Zola dealt with the effects of poverty on the working class.

Norwegian playwright Henrik Ibsen, like Shaw, attacked mostly middle-class morals and attitudes. *An Enemy of the People* presented the conflict between honesty and financial success. *A Doll's House* suggested

Claude Monet was especially interested in the effects of light in creating mood. This is his painting of Old St. Lazare Station in Paris.

that marriage should be an equal partnership between husband and wife. Ibsen's plays greatly shocked his Scandinavian audiences, who were not accustomed to having social problems presented on stage.

Art   The leading realist painters were two Frenchmen, Gustave Courbet and Honoré Daumier. Courbet painted detailed pictures of peasants and nature. Daumier produced thousands of lithographs of ordinary people, especially workers. He also developed the technique of leaving parts of his paintings "unfinished," that is, with only a few details so that the viewer's eyes focus on one or two main objects. This technique had a great deal of influence on the next major movement in art—impressionism.

Impressionism

Impressionism began in the 1870s. Technical advances in photography had made many artists feel there was no longer any need to recreate reality. If people wanted realism, they could take a picture. Instead, the impressionists chose to convey their personal impression of a scene, before the mind had a chance to analyze its details. The impressionists were particularly interested in showing the effect of light—especially sunlight—on an object. Instead of working in studios, they often painted out-of-doors or in cafés.

Most impressionist painters were French. They included Claude Monet, who specialized in landscapes; Edgar Degas, who became well-known for his paintings of ballet dancers and racetracks; Pierre August

Paul Gauguin painted this self-portrait in 1889. What differences do you see between this painting and the postimpressionist work of Cézanne on page 676?

Renoir, who painted the French entertainment world as well as women with their children; and Georges Seurat, who developed the technique of applying tiny dots of paint rather than broad brush strokes to his canvasses. As a result, Seurat's paintings must be viewed from a distance.

Impressionism influenced music as well as painting. Impressionist music tried to create a mood by breaking away from the usual melody and chord patterns. Foremost among the impressionist composers was Claude Debussy of France. His symphonic poems *Afternoon of a Faun* and *Le Mer* are dreamy in sound and very expressive.

Postimpressionism

Postimpressionism, which developed in the late 1880s, was even more individualistic than impressionism. Some postimpressionist artists were interested in form and mass. Others concentrated on expressing their feelings about nature and life.

French painter Paul Cézanne (say-ZAHN) displayed little emotion in his work. What interested him was the relationship between light and form. He often painted part of a scene from one eye level, and another part of the same scene from a different eye level. This created the impression of seeing the scene from a distance and up close at the same time.

Paul Gauguin (goh-GAN), a well-to-do French stockbroker, was a weekend painter at first. Later he deserted his family and fled to the South Pacific island of Tahiti to paint. His work was noted for its simple, flat designs; its bold lines; and its remarkable colors.

Dutch painter Vincent van Gogh (van GOH) was also interested in color. He used different colors to express his feelings. For example, yellow showed God's love for humankind. Blue, green, or pale violet indicated peacefulness or sleep.

Sculpture also reflected the developments in science, literature, and painting. The foremost sculptor of the late 1800s was Auguste Rodin (roh-DAN) of France. Rodin cannot be put into a particular school. At various times and in different works, he has been considered a realist, a romantic, and an impressionist. In general, though, he tried to express an idea in sculpture and varied his technique accordingly. Some of his statues are smooth and polished, while others are rough and gouged. Rodin is considered to be the first modern sculptor.

SECTION 5 REVIEW

1. **Recall**   What was the result of the revolt of some writers, artists, and composers of the 1700s against classical forms and subjects?
2. **How and Why**   In what way did Charles Dickens expose social ills of the 1800s?
3. **Critical Thinking**   Why did impressionism develop in the 1870s?

R E V I E W

Reviewing People, Places, and Things

Identify, define, or explain each of the
following:

James Watt

Henry Bessemer

Michael Faraday

Factory Act of 1833

labor unions

laissez-faire
   capitalism

Adam Smith

Stuart Mill

socialism

communism

evolution

radioactive

Albert Einstein

theory of relativity

Sigmund Freud

Sir Walter Scott

Ludwig van
   Beethoven

realism

Charles Dickens

Claude Monet

Understanding Facts and Ideas

1. What conditions existed in England that
    caused the industrial revolution to begin
    there?

2. How did increased agricultural production
    help make the industrial revolution
    possible?

3. What machines revolutionized the textile
    industry?

4. Why was the development of steam power
    important?

5. What happened to cities as a result of the
    industrial revolution?

6. What political forces grew out of the
    changes caused by the industrial
    revolution?

7. How did mill owner Robert Owen put
    utopian socialism into practice?

8. How did Karl Marx explain history?

9. What did Darwin believe about the evolu-
    tion of life?

10. How did each of the following contribute
    to scientific developments: a. Wilhelm
    Roentgen? b. the Curies? c. Louis
    Pasteur?

11. Why did the romantic movement begin in
    literature and the arts?

12. What did realist artists and writers try to
    portray?

13. Why did impressionism begin in art?

Developing Critical Thinking

Comparing Points of View   Adam Smith
and John Stuart Mill both believed in laissez-
faire capitalism. They disagreed about the role
of the government in business. Compare their
points of view.

Writing About History

Analyzing Economics   Karl Marx had
many ideas about where the industrial revolution would lead in regard to the power of the
workers. Write a paragraph comparing Karl
Marx's ideas with the actual effects of the
industrial revolution in regard to the power of
the workers.

Applying Your Skills to History

Interpreting Cartoons   Cartoons can
express opinions about events and issues. They
often use symbols to show their meaning. A
symbol is a sign or an object that stands for
something else. For example, the figure of
Uncle Sam stands for the United States. Historical cartoons are sometimes difficult to understand because you may not be familiar with the
symbolism. To interpret a cartoon you should
first identify the subject of the cartoon. Second,
you should identify any symbols and determine
who or what they represent. Third, you should
identify the artist's point of view.

Activity: Choose some person, event, or
situation of the industrial revolution and draw a
cartoon about it. You need not use symbolism,
but you will have to decide what you think
about the subject in order to determine your
point of view.

In some eras artists glorified war and war heroes. In other periods they painted the cruelty and destruction of war. This is Pablo Picasso's Guernica (1937, May–early June). It symbolizes the terror and death caused in the bombing of the town of Guernica during the Spanish Civil War (1936–1939).

Europe Warred and the World Followed

Like many peoples throughout history, Western Europeans have often wasted their energies and resources in war. For centuries they fought among themselves and with one another on the European continent. In the 1600s they extended their quarrels to their colonies overseas. In 1914 and again in 1939, European conflicts exploded into global warfare.

As you study this chapter, think about these questions:

- What factors in the nineteenth century led to unrest and wars?

- How did the problems of the nineteenth century spill over into war in the early twentieth century?

- Why did dictators appeal to some Europeans after World War I?

- What effects of World War I became the causes of World War II?

- What role did racism play in Nazi Germany?

The word *nationalism* means a sense of the unity, exclusiveness, and common interests of a people. At its best, nationalism preserves the independence and culture of each nation-state. However, nationalism can also be an excuse for hatred, violence, and the extension of one nation's power over another. In the 1800s, nationalism played an ever-increasing role in Western Europe.

Nationalism and France

After Napoleon's defeat, the monarchy was restored in France. The throne was held first by Louis XVIII. A weak ruler, he was succeeded by Charles X, who tried to wipe out the liberal reforms brought about by the French Revolution. Charles X announced that he ruled by divine right. He restored control of education to the Catholic Church, censored the press, and limited suffrage to those people who agreed with him.

In 1830 a revolt broke out and Charles X was forced from the throne. He was replaced by Louis Philippe. Although in theory Louis Philippe was a constitutional rather than an absolute monarch, only wealthy property owners were allowed to vote. Other members of the bourgeoisie, as well as the steadily growing working class, were denied suffrage. Furthermore, Louis Philippe declared labor unions illegal, had the police break up strikes, and denied freedom of the press.

In 1848 the French rebelled again. This time, even government troops refused to support the king unless reforms were made. Finally, Louis Philippe abdicated and the Second French Republic was proclaimed, with every male citizen having the right to vote.

The Second French Republic lasted only four years. The middle class, frightened by bloody riots on the part of unemployed Paris workers, looked around for a strong president. They found him in Louis Napoleon Bonaparte, nephew and heir of the former emperor. In addition to supporting law and order, Louis Napoleon had the advantage of a glamorous last name that appealed to French nationalism. Many of the French hoped to recapture the magic of the Napoleonic period, when France was the most powerful nation in Western Europe.

Louis Napoleon believed that he alone should rule France. In 1851 he seized control of the government. The following year, by popular vote, he proclaimed himself Emperor Napoleon III. The Second French Empire was born.

Napoleon III hoped to glorify both France and himself through his foreign policy. In 1853 he joined with Great Britain and the Ottoman Empire in the Crimean War against Russia. In 1856 the war was ended by the Treaty of Paris. Napoleon III played host to the peace delegates, a situation that brought him great satisfaction. His next attempt to extend French prestige took place in Mexico. In 1864 Napoleon III installed Hapsburg Archduke Maximilian there as emperor. The Mexicans, however, fought for their independence, and Maximilian was eventually executed.

In 1870 Napoleon III undertook yet another foreign adventure, which was to be his undoing. Outmaneuvered by the Prussian chancellor

Napoleon III ruled France from 1848 to 1871. Compare and contrast his policies and methods of controlling the people with those used by Napoleon Bonaparte.

Italy in 1852 Before Unification

■ **Kingdom of Sardinia**
■ **Kingdom of the Two Sicilies**
■ **Papal States**

Otto von Bismarck, Napoleon III declared war on Prussia and other German states. Within a few months, the well-trained and well-equipped Prussians had captured Paris and forced France to surrender.

Under the treaty ending the Franco-Prussian War, France had to give up the province of Alsace-Lorraine and pay $1 billion in damages. German troops remained in France until the sum was paid. The French were humiliated and wanted revenge. Moreover, the Franco-Prussian War proved that the newly unified Germany had replaced France as the leading nation in Western Europe. The bitter rivalry between France and Germany was to be a major force in bringing about World War I.

Nationalism and Italy

At the end of the Napoleonic Wars, Italy consisted of numerous states. Many were controlled by members of Austria's ruling house of Hapsburg. The Italian regions of Lombardy and Venetia were part of the Austrian Empire. The only Italian states ruled by Italians were Sardinia and the Papal States.

Italian unification was brought about through the efforts of three people: Giuseppi Mazzini (maht-TSEE-nee), idealist and poet; Giuseppe Garibaldi (gar-uh-BAWL-dee), sailor and activist; and Camillo di Cavour (kuh-VUR), aristocrat and diplomat. Although they differed in their methods and the type of government they wanted—Mazzini and Garibaldi wanted a republic and Cavour a limited monarchy—all three were nationalists.

Mazzini spent much of his life in exile or prison. While in exile in Switzerland, he organized a secret society known as Young Italy. In 1848 his followers seized Rome and Venice and founded republics. However, the cities were recaptured by the Austrians with French help. Mazzini fled to Switzerland again, but his dedication continued to inspire others.

"Two seas and the Alps shall our Italy bound,
The Oppressor no more in our land shall be found."

Garibaldi was a member of Young Italy. When discovered by the police, he escaped to Latin America. He returned to Italy in 1848 to help found a republic in Rome. When the republic fell, he went into exile but returned in 1854. Over the next several years, he took part in various attempts to drive Austrian armies out of Italy.

The main agent of Italy's unification, however, was Cavour, who became prime minister of the Kingdom of Sardinia in 1852. Besides the island of Sardinia, the kingdom included the Piedmont region of northeastern Italy. Cavour wanted to make Sardinia strong enough to drive the Austrians from Italy and put his king Victor Emmanuel II on the throne of a united Italy.

Cavour turned to Napoleon III of France. In a secret treaty, France promised to support Sardinia if it went to war against Austria. As a reward, France would receive the provinces of Nice and Savoy. Cavour then provoked Austria into declaring war. The combined Italian and French troops drove the Austrians from northern Italy.

At this point, Napoleon III double-crossed Cavour and signed a peace treaty with Austria. He probably began to realize that a united Italy might pose a threat to France along its southern border. However, the feelings of nationalism in Italy were too strong to be thwarted. Revolts against Hapsburg rule broke out all over northern Italy. In the south, Garibaldi raised a small army and invaded Sicily. The people rallied around him, and he soon controlled all of southern Italy. In the meantime, Cavour invaded central Italy and occupied the Papal States, with the exception of Rome.

In 1861 King Victor Emmanuel of Sardinia was declared the first king of a united Italy "by grace of God and the will of the nation." In 1866 Austria gave up the last of its Italian territory, and in 1870 Italian troops occupied Rome and made it their capital. Italy began to assume an important role in Western Europe.

Nationalism and Germany

The unification of Germany, like the unification of Italy, came about through the leadership of a single state. The architect of German unification was Otto von Bismarck, who became chancellor of Prussia in 1862. He was known as the Iron Chancellor because of his belief that the only basis for government was force and fear. According to Bismarck, "the great questions of our time will not be decided by speeches and majority resolutions...but by blood and iron."

Giuseppe Garibaldi is wearing a red shirt, his famous uniform, in this 1860 photograph.

Prussia had begun its rise to power during the Thirty Years' War. After Napoleon's armies invaded the German states, the spirit of nationalism began to grow. When Bismarck became chancellor, Prussia was one of thirty-eight Germany states in a confederation dominated by Austria. Bismarck believed that Prussia had been chosen by God to create a German nation. So he set about to carry out "God's will."

First, Bismarck militarized Prussia. He created an efficient general staff that drew up detailed war plans. He replaced a small army of professional soldiers with a large army of draftees. He equipped his troops with the latest weapons, especially steel cannon and a rapid-fire rifle. In addition, Bismarck built an excellent railway system that enabled large numbers of soldiers to be moved quickly to where they were needed.

In 1866, when his army was ready, Bismarck provoked Austria into declaring war on Prussia. In seven weeks of fighting, the Prussians defeated the Austrians. All but four of the German states united with Prussia in a North German confederation.

In 1870 Bismarck repeated his tactics. As you read earlier, he provoked Napoleon III into declaring war. The four remaining independent German states promptly joined the confederation, and a united Germany swept to victory against France.

Wilhelm I of Prussia became **kaiser**—emperor—of the German empire in 1871. His coronation was held in the palace of Versailles built by Louis XIV. The ceremony added to French humiliation and made France even more determined to revenge itself against Germany.

■ **Prussia, 1866**

Otto von Bismarck created the German Empire from a confederation of states. What methods did he use? How did the theory of nationalism influence him?

■ **German Empire, 1871**

Nationalism and the Austrian Empire

In the Austrian Empire nationalism proved to be a force for destruction. The Austrian Empire was a multinational empire, made up of many peoples speaking many languages. About one-quarter of the population was German. The second largest national group were the Magyars, in Hungary. There were also Italians in Lombardy and Venetia, as well as various groups of Slavs, notably Poles, Czechs, Slovaks, and Serbs. The empire did not allow the different nationalities under its rule to use their own language or even to celebrate their own holidays. The official language of government and education was German, the official religion was Roman Catholicism, and the power of the emperor was absolute.

As nationalist feelings spread through Western Europe, the subject peoples of the Austrian Empire grew restless. In 1848 a series of revolutions occurred in which the Hungarians, the Italians, and the Czechs all declared themselves independent. However, the revolutions were soon suppressed.

In 1866, when Austria was defeated by Prussia, the Magyars took advantage of the situation to demand independence again. Emperor Franz Joseph I agreed to a compromise. Henceforth, the empire was to be known as Austria-Hungary. It would have a single ruler—the emperor—

who would control foreign policy. It would also have a unified army, postal system, and customs union. However, Austria and Hungary would each have separate capitals, separate parliaments, and separate civil services, and each country would use its own language.

The compromise satisfied the Magyars, but it did not satisfy the other national groups within the empire. They continued to agitate for independence or, at the least, self-government. Also, many Slavs within Austria-Hungary began to turn to other Slavic nations such as Russia for help. This increased the traditional hostility between the Germans and the Slavs and was to be another major force in bringing about World War I.

SECTION 1 REVIEW

1. **Recall**   Which German state was responsible for the unification of Germany?
2. **How and Why**   In what ways did the Austrian Empire resolve its problems with the Magyars?
3. **Critical Thinking**   How did nationalism lead to the unification of Italy?

A delicate balance of political, economic, and social forces existed in Europe between 1871 and 1914. During these years, industrialism spread, and great colonial empires were founded by Western European nations. Relations among the European powers were soon strained, however, as arms races and misunderstandings became commonplace. Gradually, alliances divided the continent into two opposing sides. In 1914 the two sides went to war.

Imperialism

In the late 1800s, another great era of imperialism by Western Europeans began. The leaders of Belgium, France, Germany, Great Britain, Italy, and the Netherlands looked beyond their culture region to other parts of the world. Western Europeans saw lands that were tempting in their military weaknesses and potential wealth, and moved to acquire them.

One reason for this **new imperialism** was the industrial revolution. Colonies provided markets for the manufactured goods of the imperialist powers. In addition, colonies were an important source of raw materials—such as cotton, jute, oil, rubber, silk, and tin.

Another reason for the scramble for colonies was nationalism. The acquisition of colonies added to a nation's prestige. The newly unified nations of Germany and Italy were especially eager to exhibit their national strength. France sought to compensate for its defeat in the Franco-Prussian War by overseas adventures.

The imperialistic drive of the late 1800s included a military factor as well. Colonies were considered important because they could serve as military and naval bases to protect a nation's trade routes. Colonies were also thought of as huge troop reservoirs from which armies could be recruited.

Many Western Europeans also felt that they had a mission to bring Western civilization to the so-called "backward" peoples of the world. It did not matter that many of these peoples had cultures far older than that of Western Europe. This "civilizing" viewpoint was held sincerely by some Western Europeans. A number of political leaders believed that the rule of their governments could bring law and order to areas suffering from internal warfare. Religious leaders believed it was their duty to spread Christianity, and doctors wanted to introduce Western medical techniques. Other Western Europeans sought only to exploit the colonies. Many military and colonial officials viewed colonies strictly as a means for rapid advancement. Western European settlers often saw them as a source of free land and cheap labor.

Still another motive for the new imperialism was racism. Many Western Europeans, influenced by Social Darwinism, began to believe that the white race was superior because it had developed the industrial revolution. It was therefore essential for Western Europe to dominate the non-Western world in self-defense against the more numerous "inferior races."

Western Europeans were so successful at gaining overseas territory that by the beginning of the 1900s they dominated almost all of Africa and much of Asia. However, they paid a heavy price in jealousy and rivalry with one another. In no area was the price higher than in their mounting military budgets.

The Arms Race

The military successes of Prussia impressed Europeans with the advantages of a general staff and a reserve army. As a result, most nations established a system under which all able-bodied men were drafted for duty, trained, and then returned to civilian life. They could be **mobilized**, or called up, whenever they were needed.

By 1890 Germany had the strongest army in Western Europe, but Britain had the strongest navy. However, the new German kaiser, Wilhelm II, began to build up the German navy in an attempt to overtake Britain. The British, who not only depended on international commerce but also imported most of their food, were determined to protect their supply lines by maintaining their control of the seas. So the British built more and more ships, especially big-gun battleships. The French and the Italians, unwilling to be left behind, also began enlarging their fleets.

Industries arose to produce more and better arms. National budgets were increased to meet increased defense needs. For example, by 1914 Germany was spending ten times as much for weapons as it had spent in

1870. Austria-Hungary's military budget quadrupled over the same period, and Great Britain's military expenditures tripled. The arms race, far from bringing a sense of security to the nations of Western Europe, only added to their tenseness. Ultimately, arms were not enough.

Kaiser Wilhelm II of Germany was photographed reviewing his troops. By 1914, the German army was the most powerful army in the world.

Alliances

In order to increase their power, the nations of Europe began to form alliances. First Germany proposed a defensive alliance with Austria-Hungary. According to the alliance, either country would come to the aid of the other if attacked by a third nation. Austria-Hungary agreed and the pact became known as the Dual Alliance. Germany then turned to Italy and proposed the same conditions. Italy agreed, and the Dual Alliance became the Triple Alliance.

France was now alone in Europe. It frantically sought allies to counterbalance those of Germany. As long as Bismarck had controlled the diplomacy of Germany, he had managed to keep France without allies. The policies of Wilhelm II, however, unwittingly helped bring Russia and France together. Britain, fearful of Germany's growing strength, also sought an alliance with France. The alliance of France, Russia, and Britain became known as the Triple Entente. By 1907 two great power blocs faced each other in Europe. Other, less powerful, nations allied themselves with each group.

World War I was the first war in which airplanes were used. This is a photograph of an aerial dogfight.

spoils:
property or land taken from the losing side in a war

Perhaps none of the nations of Europe wanted war. Yet they all wanted things they could not have without war—more territory, more wealth, and more power. The forming of alliances and the military buildups set the stage for armed conflict.

The Great War

World War I mushroomed from the assassination of Archduke Franz Ferdinand, heir to the throne of Austria-Hungary. He was killed by a young member of a secret Serbian nationalist organization called the Black Hand. Its goal was to unite the Serbs of Austria-Hungary with the independent nation of Serbia.

After several weeks of diplomatic maneuvering, Austria-Hungary declared war on Serbia on July 28, 1914. The government of Austria-Hungary was confident it would be a "bright, brisk little war." Russia, which had a defensive alliance with Serbia, quickly mobilized its forces. On August 1, 1914, Germany declared war on Russia. On August 2, when the French refused to state whether or not they would remain **neutral**, Germany declared war on France. The Belgians remained neutral. However, the easiest land passage to France was through Belgium. On August 3 Germany invaded Belgium. As a result, Britain declared war on Germany and Austria-Hungary. World War I had begun.

Italy had been secretly promised some spoils from the war if it would join France, Britain, and Russia. Therefore, Italy deserted the Triple Alliance. France, Italy, Britain, and Russia came to be known as the Allies. Japan saw an opportunity to profit and joined them. Romania and Greece also joined the Allies. The Ottoman Empire and Bulgaria joined Germany and Austria-Hungary. Germany and the nations associated with it became known as the Central Powers. The war spread overseas to the British dominions and drew in Canada, Australia, and New Zealand among others. China likewise joined the Allies. In 1917 the United States entered the conflict. Thus the war extended around the globe.

About 93 percent of the world's population took part in the struggle. Some 65 million troops were mobilized. The military casualties numbered more than 13 million killed and over 20 million wounded. At least 17 million civilians also perished from starvation, disease, and military actions. Another 10 million civilians became refugees.

A New Kind of Warfare   During the initial battles of World War I, almost everyone remained dedicated to traditional military maneuvers and strategies. Massed cavalry still made heroic, saber-swinging charges, and infantry still advanced in regular formations with fixed bayonets. This soon changed.

Much of the fighting in World War I took place on the Western Front, a section of muddy, barren land along the Franco-German frontier. Soldiers lay in trenches protected by barbed wire. Each side would bombard the other, often for days at a time. Then the soldiers would attempt to cross over into the enemy's trenches. This exposed them to machine-gun fire, which resulted in enormous casualty figures. The battle of Verdun, for example, resulted in 900,000 casualties. Despite the slaughter, little ground changed hands.

Both sides attempted to break the stalemate by using new weapons. In 1914 the Germans introduced a heavy gun known as "Big Bertha," named after the wife of a German munitions manufacturer. "Big Bertha" had a range of 70 miles (113 kilometers) and could knock out steel and concrete fortifications. In 1915 the Germans also introduced poison gases. People who were gassed with chlorine gas suffocated. Mustard gas blinded and burned the skin of its victims. In response, gas masks were made standard equipment for both sides, and antigas defensive techniques became normal battlefield training.

In 1916 the British introduced the tank, which was able to cut a path through barbed wire and to advance against machine guns. Both sides built airplanes and began to learn the possibilities of air power. However, planes were used mostly for scouting rather than for combat or bombing.

Sea power also played an important role in the war. The Germans used submarines—U-boats—to sink millions of tons of Allied shipping. The British, however, ruled the surface of the sea and were able to bottle up the German navy and to cut Germany's overseas supply lines. One result was that Germany could no longer import chemical fertilizers for its farms, and by 1917 it was suffering from widespread famine.

Economic and Social Changes   The production of all the new weapons that were used during World War I required a massive industrial effort on the home front. Governments on both sides took over control of their economies. They assigned supplies of coal, steel, and other materials to factories producing war goods. They also assigned workers to jobs and set their wages. Food was rationed, and the production of consumer goods was cut.

World War I was the first war fought with heavy guns and tanks. This is a field in Flanders (now part of France and Belgium) after the French and British attacked the Germans in the area in 1917.

With so many men in their armies, the warring nations faced constant labor shortages. As a result, women joined the work force in unprecedented numbers. They also filled many jobs that had traditionally been held by men. Women's contributions to the war effort helped bring about the postwar adoption of women's suffrage in Austria, Germany, Great Britain, and the United States.

Another result of the war's demands was that Western Europe's place in the world economy changed. Before World War I, Western European nations had been the world's leading producers of manufactured goods. They had also been the world's chief lenders of money. As the war went on, however, Western Europe fell to second place in manufacturing, behind the United States. The Allies also became debtors instead of creditors. They borrowed billions of dollars from the United States, both to wage the war and later to repair the war damage.

The Nightmare Ends   The tide of war in Europe turned in 1917 when the United States threw its power behind the Allies. Gradually the nations on Germany's side began to ask for peace. Then German sailors mutinied, German workers rebelled, and Kaiser Wilhelm II was forced to abdicate. On November 11, 1918, the chancellor of the new German socialist government signed an armistice, or truce.

The war's costs were staggering. In addition to the millions of people killed and wounded, the direct cost of the war was placed at about $180 billion. The indirect cost—property damage and lost farm and factory

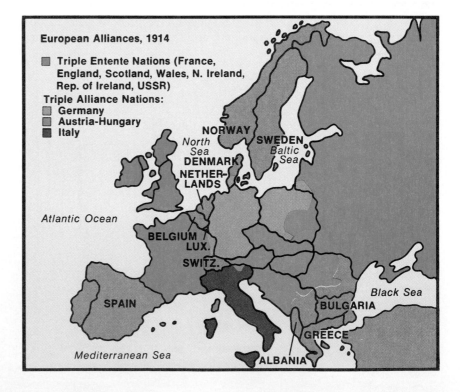

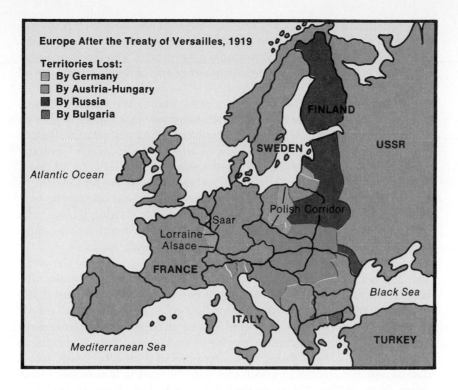

production—was about $150 billion. Economies were shattered, political life was disrupted, and the society of Western Europe lay in disorder.

Seeds of a New War

United States President Woodrow Wilson called World War I "a war to end wars." He pleaded for a peace that would make "a world safe for democracy." As a guideline for peace negotiations, Wilson formulated a program known as the Fourteen Points. Among other things, he called for freedom of the seas, freedom to trade, a reduction of armaments, open diplomatic agreements, and self-determination for nationalities. This means that the boundaries of European nations would be redrawn so that most national groups would govern themselves. Wilson also called for the creation of a League of Nations—an international organization to maintain peace.

From the beginning of the peace conferences, it was clear that— except for the League of Nations—Wilson's Fourteen Points would not be followed. Many of the allied leaders believed that the only way to prevent future conflict in Europe was to create a new balance of power in favor of the Allies. They wanted to weaken the Central Powers so that they would be unable to take part in another war.

The peace conference began in the Palace of Versailles, outside Paris, on January 18, 1919. Although 70 delegates from 27 nations attended the conference, all the major decisions were made by the Big Four—the leaders of Britain, France, Italy, and the United States. Russian representatives were not allowed to attend the conference because the Allied powers did not recognize the new Communist government. The Big Four wrote the Versailles Treaty without even consulting any of the defeated Central Powers.

In spring of 1919 the Treaty was presented to the Central Powers. They found the terms to be very harsh. Germany lost a great deal of its prewar territory and all its colonial empire in Africa and the Pacific. France received the provinces of Alsace and Lorraine, which Germany had taken as a result of the Franco-Prussian War in 1871. In addition, France was to administer Germany's coal-rich Saar Valley for 15 years, in order to replace coal production from mines destroyed during the war. Germany was forced to take full responsibility for starting the war and make huge **reparations**—payments—to the Allied Powers for war damages. The German military was also severely limited.

Separate treaties with similiar terms were made with the other defeated countries. The terms were equally harsh. These treaties disbanded the empire of Austria-Hungary and the Ottoman Empire. Independent nations were formed according to nationalistic and ethnic divisions. In many areas, however, ethnic groups were intermingled. Therefore, it was impossible to draw new boundaries strictly according to ethnic divisions. This meant that a number of minority groups found themselves in countries in which they did not want to live. In particular, about three million German-speaking people found themselves in a region of Czechoslovakia, known as the Sudetenland, rather than in Austria. In 1938 this gave Germany an excuse to invade Czechoslovakia. The invasion was a major step on the road to World War II.

The Versailles Treaty was a disastrous blow to the pride of the Central Powers, especially to Germany. The German people felt that their army had surrendered with the understanding that the peace settlement would be just. The Germans felt betrayed, bitter, and resentful. These feelings proved to be major factors in the events that took place in Germany in upcoming decades.

SECTION 2 REVIEW

1. **Recall**   What new kinds of warfare were introduced during World War I?
2. **How and Why**   In what way did the industrial revolution bring about a new imperialism?
3. **Critical Thinking**   How were the seeds of a new war sown as a result of the Treaty of Versailles?

Political, economic, and social conditions in Western Europe—especially in Italy and Germany—worsened after World War I. These conditions, in addition to the problems created by the Treaty of Versailles, eventually led to the rise of **totalitarian regimes**, in which the government held limitless power over the lives of the people. These factors would also lead to World War II.

Mussolini and Fascism

The Italians were discontented and frustrated after World War I. Although they were among the victors, they had not received all the territory they had been promised. In addition, Italy suffered from severe inflation and unemployment. There were sit-down strikes in factories, and calls for land reform by peasants. The nation's industrialists and large landowners became afraid that Italy might follow Russia's example and turn Communist. Italians looked to their government for help, but the government changed hands rapidly as one group after another failed to solve the nation's problems. The king was only a figurehead.

In the midst of this turmoil a new political leader emerged—Benito Mussolini. He told the Italians that he had the answers to their problems. He promised them that if they would follow him, he would make them proud members of a powerful nation.

Il Duce (DOO-chay), the leader—as Mussolini was commonly called—organized the **Fascist** party in 1919. It was composed mainly of army veterans and frustrated nationalists. The name *Fascist* came from a symbol of authority in ancient Rome—the *fasces* (FAS-EEZ)—a bundle of rods with the blade of an ax projecting from them. The Fascists—who wore a uniform of black shirts, breeches, and boots—started out by

figurehead:
a person who has the title of a ruler but not the power

breaking up strikes and beating workers. From there, they moved to breaking up meetings of socialists and Communists. In 1922 Mussolini and his Fascists marched on Rome. Instead of resisting, the king appointed Mussolini prime minister and gave him wide powers to restore order. By 1930, Mussolini had destroyed democracy in Italy and had made himself master of the country.

Mussolini abolished all political parties in Italy except the Fascist party. A special court was set up to punish anyone who did not conform to Fascist beliefs. Mussolini closed down opposition newspapers and censored those that remained. Teachers who failed to instill Fascist ideas in their students were fired. Labor strikes were prohibited, political prisoners were often tortured by the secret police, and posters that read "Mussolini is always right" were everywhere.

Mussolini dreamed of building a new Roman Empire. To achieve this goal, he built up Italy's armed forces. Mussolini asserted that only war "puts the stamp of nobility upon the peoples who have the courage to meet it." In 1935 Italy invaded and occupied Ethiopia in East Africa.

In 1929 Mussolini settled a long-standing dispute with the Roman Catholic Church over the relationship between the Church and the Italian government. Under an agreement called the Lateran Accord, Vatican City in Rome was recognized as an independent nation ruled by the pope. In addition, the Roman Catholic Church was recognized as Italy's official religion.

German military leaders and high party officials accompany Hitler at a Nazi party rally in Nuremberg.

Under Fascist rule, the material well-being of many Italians improved, but the price was high. Like other peoples throughout history, the Italians gave up freedom for security.

Hitler and Nazism

A new political leader arose in Germany amid the economic turmoil of the early 1930's. This leader was Adolf Hitler. Hitler was born in 1889 in a small Austrian town near the German border. When World War I broke out, Hitler joined the German army and served on the western front. He won an Iron Cross for bravery and rose to the rank of corporal.

Germany's defeat in the war was a bitter disappointment to Hitler. In 1919 he returned to Munich, Germany, where he joined a radical political group known as the National Socialist German Workers' party—the Nazi party. The Nazis wore uniforms and armbands and carried flags bearing a **swastika**—a hooked cross. Like most radical groups of the period, the Nazis were extremely nationalistic. They were also opposed to democracy and were anti-Semitic.

In 1923 Germany suffered a severe inflation. Money became cheaper than the paper it was printed on. Germans collected their salaries in large bags. People found that their savings were worthless. Money that had been worth hundreds of thousands of dollars, was worth only a few cents.

Under these circumstances, Hitler decided the time was ripe to launch a *putsch* (PUCH)—revolt—against the local government in Munich. But the revolt failed and Hitler was sent to prison. There he wrote a book called *Mein Kampf (My Struggle)*. In *Mein Kampf* Hitler expressed some of his major ideas. First, Hitler wrote that the German people were too crowded within their postwar borders and needed more land. Second, he described his passionate hatred of the Jews. According to Hitler, Germany did not lose World War I because the Allies were stronger. The Jews—about 1 percent of the German population—had caused the loss. Third, Hitler declared that only he could save Germany from economic ruin or a Communist takeover and only he could lead the German people to a glorious future.

The Road to Power   After serving eight months of a five-year sentence, Hitler was released from prison. He immediately started working to strengthen the Nazi party. Hitler was a remarkably effective speaker. He would begin quietly, almost hesistantly, and then build to a fiery conclusion. He put everything in simple terms, which he repeated over and over. Party rallies were spectacular, with thousands of uniformed Nazis marching under the glare of powerful lights, their right arms upraised, roaring as if with a single voice: "Seig Heil! Seig Heil!— Hail victory! Hail victory!"

Hitler appealed to many groups. Military leaders were attracted because Hitler promised to rearm Germany. Industrialists favored the party because the Nazis opposed communism. Young people favored the movement because it promised rapid change.

The factor that gave Hitler the final successful push occurred in 1930. Germany, like other nations in Western Europe, was hit by a great depression. Unemployment rose to more than 40 percent, and there were frequent clashes between unemployed workers and police. Fear and insecurity gripped the country. That year the Nazis polled 6.5 million votes. Two years later, in 1932, they polled 14.5 million. In January 1933 Hitler was appointed chancellor, and in March, the national legislature gave Hitler the dictatorial power to rule by decree.

The Nazi Dictatorship   Hitler moved quickly to control Germany's political, social, and economic life. All political parties except the Nazi party were banned. Judges and local officials were replaced by Nazis. Hitler's chief lieutenant, Hermann Göring (GUR-ing), set up a secret police, the Gestapo, with the power of life and death. Anyone could be beaten, tortured, sent to a **concentration camp**—a large prison camp—or even killed.

Teachers were trained in Nazi ideas, and textbooks were rewritten to reflect the Nazi party's views. Books the Nazis disapproved of were tossed onto huge bonfires and burned. The Nazis tore the paintings of such artists as Gauguin, Matisse, and van Gogh from museum walls and replaced them with paintings of mothers with several children or young men in Nazi uniform. Nazi party leader and propaganda specialist Dr. Joseph Goebbels was put in charge of all publications, films, and radio broadcasts.

The Nazis attacked religion and religious leaders. They closed Catholic schools and sent thousands of priests and nuns to concentration camps. Catholic and other youth groups were dissolved. Instead, German young people were organized into the Hitler Youth (for boys) and the Union of German Girls. In addition to military training, members were taught to worship Hitler, to obey orders without question, and to hate the Jews.

Nazism and Race   The Nazi racial policies were based on the idea of a superior **Aryan** race. According to Nazi thinking, the Germans were the finest example of the great and pure Aryan race. People who were not Aryans, such as Slavs and Jews, were considered inferior and were fit only to be enslaved or exterminated. Nazis believed that all human culture, art, science, and technology were almost exclusively created by the Aryans.

The Nazis also believed that the Jews were the cause of all Germany's problems. According to the Nazis, the Jews sought to dominate the world. The Nazis, therefore, instituted strict racial policies that would keep the Jews from reaching the imaginary goal of world domination.

After the Nazis came to power in Germany, they instituted a campaign of **anti-Semitism**—measures against the Jews. Jews were not allowed to hold government offices or practice medicine or law. Jewish musicians and actors could not perform in public. In 1935 the citizenship of German Jews was taken away. Soon after, Jewish children were expelled from schools. Jews were forbidden to use hospitals, eat in restaurants, stay out after 8:00 P.M., or even have radios or telephones in their homes.

The Nazis did not limit themselves to passing laws. In 1938 they carried out a series of bloody riots against the Jews known as "Kristallnacht" or "The Night of the Broken Glass." Synagogues were burned, windows in Jewish homes and stores were smashed, and almost the entire male Jewish population between the ages of 18 and 65 was sent to concentration camps.

The History of Anti-Semitism   Anti-Semitism in Germany, as in most of Europe, has deep roots. For centuries, Jews were called "Christ-killers" and were accused of using the blood of Christian children for religious purposes and of causing such disasters as the Black Death. During the Middle Ages, Jews were forced to wear a yellow identification badge and to live in ghettos. They were not allowed to farm land or to join guilds, but were restricted to such occupations as peddling and moneylending. As moneylenders, they were often employed by monarchs and nobles to collect taxes and perform other financial tasks. This increased popular feelings against the Jews. It also gave rise to the false idea that "the Jews control all the money." Jews were repeatedly attacked and their homes and property destroyed. At various times they were expelled from England, France, Germany, Italy, Portugal, and Spain.

In the late 1800s, racist ideas spread through Europe, and Jews began to be looked on, not as members of a religion, but as a race. In 1881 an "Anti-Semites Petition" was presented to Bismarck urging that Jews be removed from government. Soon dozens of anti-Semitic publications appeared in Germany, including *The Protocols of the Elders of Zion*. This book, which was later proved a complete forgery, was supposedly the secret plans of the "international Jewish conspiracy" to take over the world. It greatly impressed Hitler.

The Nazi Economy   The Nazis controlled the German economy as rigidly as they controlled politics. For example, manufacturers were told what to make, where to sell, and what prices to charge for goods. Despite government controls, however, giant businesses made huge profits. In part these profits were made because of Hitler's rearmament program.

Rearmament and public works were two of the main activities the Nazis used to end unemployment. A network of superhighways was built to connect German cities. At the same time, factories poured out tanks, guns, airplanes, and warships to equip the growing German military machine. By 1938, 75 percent of Germany's budget was being spent on the military. Even though there were plenty of jobs, German workers had no

During Francisco Franco's 36 years in power, he supported the wealthy. He was against social change and economic reforms aimed at the poor. Censorship was imposed. Those who opposed him were jailed.

rights. For example, strikes were banned, workers could not change jobs without permission, and farmers were not allowed to leave their land.

To further reduce unemployment, the Nazis fired all women from government jobs, including teaching. The wages of other women workers were cut to 40 percent of men's wages. The Nazis believed that women belonged in the home and that their main role in life was to bear soldiers for the German army.

By 1938 there was no more unemployment in Germany. But the Germans, like the Italians, had traded freedom for security. Adolph Hitler had begun his march toward World War II.

Civil War and Franco

The third major country of Western Europe to set up a totalitarian regime was Spain. In 1931 a republican-socialist government came to power. The new leaders separated church and state, and divided large estates among the peasants. But the army, the clergy, the wealthy, and many big businesses opposed the government, and in 1936 a civil war broke out.

General Francisco Franco was chosen to lead the rebels. He received large amounts of equipment and about 85,000 troops from Fascist Italy and Nazi Germany. The Soviet Union sold some tanks and planes to the republicans, who were known as Loyalists. The Loyalists were also helped by some 40,000 volunteers from Western nations. In 1939, after about a million Spanish casualties, the civil war ended with Franco's victory. The equipment and troops from Germany and Italy had helped him defeat the Loyalists. Franco set up an absolute dictatorship in Spain, with a single political party.

In a sense, the Spanish Civil War was a rehearsal for World War II. Germany in particular took the opportunity to test the new weapons it was producing. It also tested new military techniques, such as the terror bombing of Guernica. The town had no military significance. The purpose of the bombing was strictly to break the people's will to resist. It was a technique that Hitler would soon unleash against almost every nation in Europe.

1. **Recall**   What did Italians have to give up to improve their material well-being?
2. **How and Why**   In what ways did the Nazis institute a campaign of anti-Semitism?
3. **Critical Thinking**   How did Hitler and the Nazis come to power?

W orld War II, which lasted from 1939 to 1945, was even more widespread and devastating than World War I. In addition to fighting in Europe, there were land campaigns in northern Africa and Asia, and naval battles in the Pacific. Trench warfare was replaced by the sweeping movement of battle lines. Airplanes also played a major role in the war. In 1945 the atomic age began with the dropping of the first atom bombs.

Civilians were affected by the war as never before. They suffered nightly bombings and sieges that lasted as long as three years. Millions were forced into slave labor. **Partisans** carried on guerrilla warfare behind enemy lines, and millions of people were systematically murdered in the Holocaust. In the end some 56 million human beings perished in World War II. The financial cost cannot even be estimated.

Hitler's Diplomatic Victories

Hitler began to pursue his dream of world conquest by violating the Versailles Treaty. In 1935 he ordered compulsory military training for German youths. The following year, he sent German soldiers into the Rhineland, a demilitarized area between France and Germany. In both instances, Britain and France protested weakly but did not back their protests with action. The two nations had suffered heavy casualties and destruction in World War I and great economic problems during the worldwide depression of the 1930s. They did not want to spend money on arms. They also believed that a strong Germany would act as a buffer against Russian communism. Therefore, Britain and France decided to "do business" with Hitler.

In the spring of 1938, Hitler marched into Austria and annexed it to the Third Reich—the new Germany. His justification was that the German-speaking Austrians were naturally part of the German nation. Again, Britain and France protested the German move but failed to act.

Hitler then cast his eyes on Czechoslovakia. He told Britain and France that if the Sudetenland, with its 4 million German-speaking inhabitants, were not annexed to Germany the result would be war. However, Hitler promised that the Sudetenland would be "the last territorial claim I have to make in Europe." So British Prime Minister Neville Chamberlain flew to Munich, Germany, where he, Hitler, Mussolini, and the French premier signed the Munich Pact giving Hitler what he wanted. Unfortunately, Chamberlain was tragically mistaken in his policy of **appeasement**, or making concessions for the sake of maintaining peace. In March 1939 Hitler ordered German soldiers to take over the rest of Czechoslovakia.

Later the same year, Western Europe was stunned when Hitler signed a nonaggression pact with Germany's enemy—the Soviet Union. Under a secret section of this treaty, Germany and the Soviet Union agreed to divide Eastern Europe into German and Soviet spheres of influence. This agreement allowed Hitler to turn to his next target—

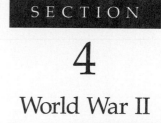

On September 1, 1939, Adolf Hitler (arrow) announces the beginning of what was to become World War II. Claiming that the Polish had fired first, Hitler said he had decided to send the German army into Poland.

Poland—without fear of Soviet opposition. The German-Soviet treaty also meant that Hitler would not have to face enemies on two fronts—eastern and western.

On the morning of September 1, 1939, German armed forces smashed across the Polish border. On September 3, Britain and France declared war on Germany. World War II had begun.

A New Kind of War

Hitler's attack on Poland marked the start of a new type of warfare: **blitzkrieg**, or lightning war. Waves of German dive bombers destroyed the Polish air force on the ground and then blasted troop positions, supply depots, and transportation lines. While the air strikes were going on, masses of German tanks, followed by *panzer*—armored—divisions in motorized transport, raced across the Polish countryside. It was impossible to resist the speed, force, and precision of the German attack. Within two weeks, the Germans were at the gates of the Polish capital of Warsaw, and the Soviet Union had invaded Poland from the east. Caught between two powerful armies, the Poles surrendered in late September 1939.

France and Britain were not as well prepared for war as Germany. After World War I French power declined and its economy weakened. A great fortification of steel, stone, and guns, called the Maginot (mazh-uh-NOH) Line was supposed to guard the French borders against the Germans. The French, however were unprepared for blitzkrieg warfare. The British had also had economic problems during the postwar years. Because so much capital was needed to update British industry, and British colonies were increasingly demanding more freedom, little attention was paid to improving the efficiency of the military.

After their declaration of war, French and British troops moved into the area around the Maginot line. Hitler moved quickly elsewhere. In April 1940 he conquered Denmark and Norway. This victory so startled the British that they asked for Neville Chamberlain's resignation, and Winston Churchill became the new British prime minister. Then Hitler unleashed a new blitzkrieg and quickly took the Netherlands, Belgium, and Luxembourg. German forces then ripped into northern France and trapped British and French forces at the port of Dunkirk, hoping to surround and destroy them. Through a daring naval operation, the British soldiers and some of the French troops were rescued. As the Germans raced through France, Italy declared war on the Allies and attacked France from the south. The French surrendered in June 1940. In September 1940, Japan joined the Germans and Italians.

Next, Hitler turned on Great Britain. For three months, German planes bombed the country day and night. Winston Churchill addressed the British people on radio. He had nothing to offer them, he said, but "blood, toil, tears, and sweat." Nevertheless, he promised that "We shall defend our islands, whatever the cost may be. We shall fight on the beaches, we shall fight on the landing-grounds, we shall fight in the fields

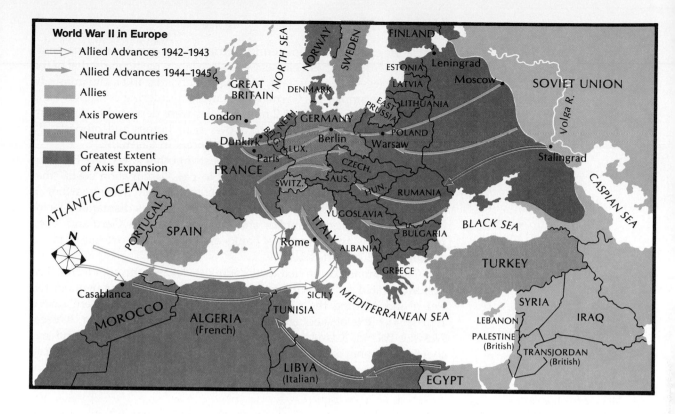

World War II in Europe

- Allied Advances 1942–1943
- Allied Advances 1944–1945
- Allies
- Axis Powers
- Neutral Countries
- Greatest Extent of Axis Expansion

and in the streets, we shall fight in the hills. We shall never surrender."
The courageous defense of Britain by the British Royal Air Force—
combined with the use of a new weapon, radar, that enabled the
defenders to spot incoming planes at a distance even at night—forced the
Germans to give up their raids. Great Britain's situation, however,
remained desperate. Many of the ships that brought supplies to the
embattled British Isles were sunk by German submarines. Only massive
American aid enabled Great Britain to remain in the war.

In June 1941 Hitler shifted his attention from the west to the east and
launched a surprise attack on the Soviet Union. At first the now familiar
blitzkrieg invasion went well. Within a few months the German army
surrounded the city of Leningrad and had reached the outer defenses of
Moscow. The Soviets were able to turn the tide with their scorched-earth
policy. As the Soviet army retreated, everything that could not be moved
eastward beyond Moscow was destroyed—farms, crops, cities, bridges,
railroad yards, and power stations. This strategy gave the Soviets the time
they needed to prepare for a counteroffensive. Also, the Soviet retreat
drew the invading forces deeper into Soviet land. In 1941 winter came
early. Rain turned the roads into thick mud, the temperatures dropped,
and the snows came. The German offensive was halted. In December
1941 the Soviets counterattacked, and the Germans were pushed back.
The bitter battle of Stalingrad forced the German army to surrender in
early 1943.

Hitler's "New Order"

Hitler's program for administering Germany's conquests was known as the "New Order." A basic element was slave labor, particularly that of the Slavic peoples—Poles, Russians, Estonians, Latvians, and Lithuanians. In Poland, for example, the Germans began by murdering or imprisoning the country's leaders. Then 1.2 million Poles were deported to Germany, while 500,000 German settlers took over their homes and property. By 1944 there were some 7.5 million slave laborers in Germany.

The Germans exploited their conquests in other ways, too. Belgium and the Netherlands, for example, had to pay "occupation costs" that came to two-thirds of their national income. About three-quarters of France's food production went to Germany. The Nazis dismantled factories in the occupied countries and shipped them to Germany. They removed all the gold in nations' banks and even looted art museums of paintings and sculptures.

The Germans controlled their conquests largely through terror. The police operated without restriction, seizing suspected opponents of the Reich and sending them to concentration camps. There were severe reprisals for acts of sabotage. Entire villages in Czechoslovakia, Greece, Norway, Poland, Russia, and Yugoslavia were burned to the ground and their inhabitants killed. In France 100 civilians were shot for every German soldier who lost his life. Despite such reprisals, small bands of partisans continued to resist the Germans in every way they could.

The Holocaust

The term *Holocaust* is used to describe the time between 1933 and 1945 when European Jews and some other minorities were singled out for

General Eisenhower seen talking to American paratroopers on D-Day, June 9, 1944. These battalions had many casualties during the invasion of France.

persecution by the Nazis. When the war ended in 1945, over 6 million Jews had been killed in Nazi concentration camps and in massacres such as the bombing of Poland's Warsaw ghetto. This number represents about two-thirds of all Jews living in Europe at the time.

After German armies overran most of Europe in 1941, the planned extermination of the Jews in Nazi-occupied lands was carried out by Hitler's generals in death camps run by the SS (storm troopers). Crowded railroad freight cars brought the Jews to the camps. The able-bodied were used as slave laborers, but most—men, women, and children—were killed with poison gas upon their arrival at the camps.

In late 1944, as the Nazis saw they were losing the war, they tried to hide the horror of the death camps. Allied troops, however, found some of the camps before the Nazis could destroy the evidence.

The Fall of the Third Reich

As you know, on December 7, 1941, the Japanese attacked the American naval base of Pearl Harbor, and the United States entered World War II on the side of the Allies. The Big Three leaders—British Prime Minister Winston Churchill, Soviet dictator Joseph Stalin, and United States President Franklin Roosevelt—worked out a global strategy for victory. They decided that the Allies should concentrate on defeating Germany first. After the Third Reich was destroyed, they would turn their efforts toward defeating Japan. Accordingly, in the months that followed, the Allies mounted their major efforts in Africa and Europe, while they carried on the war in the Pacific on a somewhat limited basis.

Between 1941 and 1943 the Americans and British concentrated on pushing the Germans and Italians out of North Africa. The Allies then invaded Sicily and moved into Italy. Mussolini resigned as prime minister and fled to German protection. The new Italian government surrendered to the Allies, but the Germans moved down the Italian peninsula and made it difficult for the Allies to take Italy north of Rome. In the meantime, Soviet armies were pushing the Germans out of the Soviet Union. By early 1944 the Soviets had forced the Germans back to the Polish border.

As early as 1942 Stalin had asked the British and the Americans to relieve the German pressure on the Soviet Union by invading Western Europe and establishing a second front. This finally became possible in the spring of 1944. Operation Overlord, as the invasion was called, was headed by American General Dwight D. "Ike" Eisenhower. It was the largest amphibious operation in history. On June 6, 1944, the Allies landed on the beaches of Normandy, France. Within three months after D-day, some 2 million soldiers and half a million vehicles had been transported across the English Channel to the continent of Europe.

Germany was now caught between powerful armies attacking from both the west and the east. As German troops slowly but steadily retreated, a group of German generals attempted to assassinate Hitler and negotiate a peace. Although Hitler's conference room was damaged

Through her diary, Anne Frank has come to symbolize the millions of Jews who died under Nazi persecution. She and her family were hidden by a Dutch couple when the Germans overran the Netherlands. Discovered in 1944, she died in a concentration camp at the age of fifteen.

Smoke rises over Nagasaki, Japan, after being hit by an atomic bomb on August 9, 1945. The use of the bomb there and at Hiroshima ended the war. How do you feel about the use of the bomb?

by a time bomb, Hitler himself was barely scratched. Some 5,000 conspirators and their families were arrested, tortured, and killed.

Nevertheless, the end was near. By late April 1945 Germany and its military machine lay in ruins, and American and Soviet troops had linked up at the Elbe River. Faced with certain defeat, Hitler decided to "go out in fire, like some warrior of legend." After dictating a will in which he blamed the Jews for Germany's defeat, he shot himself. His followers then doused his body with gasoline and burned it.

Following Hitler's death, German resistance collapsed, and Germany surrendered unconditionally. The Allied leaders proclaimed victory in Europe on May 8, 1945—V-E Day.

The Allies then turned their attention to defeating Japan. The Japanese had advanced through the Pacific until the spring of 1942. Then the naval battles of the Coral Sea and Midway Island stopped the Japanese advance. Beginning in 1943, the Allies gradually island-hopped toward Japan itself. In August 1945 the Soviet Union declared war on Japan, and the United States dropped two atomic bombs. On September 2, 1945, the Japanese signed an unconditional surrender aboard the USS *Missouri* in Tokyo Bay. World War II had officially come to an end.

SECTION 4 REVIEW

1. **Recall**   What event led Great Britain and France to declare war on Germany?
2. **How and Why**   In what way did the British prevent the Germans from invading Britain?
3. **Critical Thinking**   How did the military strategy of the Germans eventually lead to their defeat?

R E V I E W

Reviewing People, Places, and Things

Identify, define, or explain each of the following:

Napoleon III
Franco-Prussian War
Giuseppe Garibaldi
Sardinia
Otto von Bismarck
Magyars
Triple Alliance
Triple Entente
neutral
Fourteen Points
Versailles Treaty
totalitarian regimes
Benito Mussolini

Fascist
Nazi
concentration camp
Aryan
Francisco Franco
Sudetenland
appeasement
blitzkrieg
Maginot Line
Holocaust
Big Three
Operation Overlord
Normandy

Map Study

Using the maps on pages 690 and 691, determine the answers to the following questions:

1. What territories were lost by Germany after the Versailles Treaty?
2. Which nation lost more land, Germany or Austria-Hungary?
3. Which nation lost Finland?

Understanding Facts and Ideas

1. What are some positive and some negative points about nationalism?
2. How did Bismarck militarize Prussia?
3. What incident was responsible for the beginning of World War I?
4. How did World War I change Western Europe's place in the world economy?
5. What problem occurred as a result of the formation of new nations along nationalistic and ethnic divisions after World War I?
6. Why were the Italians discontented after World War I?
7. Why did Hitler appeal to military leaders, industrialists, and young people?
8. What anti-Semitic events took place on *Kristallnacht*?
9. How did some British and French troops avoid capture when they were trapped at Dunkirk by the Germans?
10. Which battle forced the German army to surrender in Russia?

Developing Critical Thinking

Making Comparisons   The Germans and the Italians had been on opposite sides during World War I. However, they faced many similar problems after the war that enabled dictators to take over their governments. Describe some of the postwar problems faced by both Italy and Germany.

Writing About History

Analyzing Leadership   The unification of Italy was achieved by the leadership of several people. Write an essay describing how the efforts of Mazzini, Garibaldi, and Cavour contributed to Italian unification.

Applying Your Skills to History

Recognizing Propaganda   Propaganda is the deliberate spreading of information, beliefs, and ideas to influence people for or against someone or something. It usually tries to arouse strong emotions such as loyalty, fear, or hatred. Propaganda may contain some truth, but more often it is biased, or one-sided, and built on half-truths.

Activity: Consider how the German people were so deceived by Hitler that the Holocaust was allowed to happen. Write a paragraph explaining the role propaganda played in the Holocaust.

CHAPTER

35

This indoor shopping mall is in Hamburg, West Germany. West Germany is one of the most prosperous of Western European nations.

A Changing Western Europe

Since the end of World War II, change has been an important fact of Western European life. The war left the region in economic ruin. With help from the United States, much of the region was rebuilt by the mid-1950s. Since 1945 technological and scientific advances have changed the way Western Europeans live and work. Their arts have reflected these changes. Today, Western Europeans enjoy some of the highest standards of living in the world.

Since the end of the war, the importance of regional cooperation has been stressed, particularly economic cooperation. By 1992 Western Europe will function as a single economic unit. Political changes are also taking place within the region.

As you study this chapter, think about these questions:

- What postwar developments have helped shape Western Europe?
- What factors have influenced philosophy, the arts, and the sciences of Western Europe?
- How has Western European cooperation helped shape the region's present, and how will it shape the region's future?

With the return of peace in 1945, the war-weary peoples of Western Europe struggled to rebuild their devastated countries. However, political differences between the Western democracies and the Communist world soon led to new fears, tensions, and divisions. One point all the victors agreed upon was that the Nazis had to be punished for their horrible crimes.

War-Crime Trials

In August 1945, the United States, Great Britain, France, and the Soviet Union set up an international military **tribunal**—court—to try 22 Nazi leaders for crimes against world peace, war crimes, and crimes against humanity. The trials were held in Nuremberg, Germany, and became known as the Nuremberg Trials. During the more than 12 months the trials continued, 12 Nazi defendants were sentenced to be hanged, seven were imprisoned for life, and three were acquitted.

Over the next five years, an additional 10,000 Germans were tried in military courts. The defendants included leaders of the Nazi party, high-ranking military officers, death-camp guards, and industrialists who had employed slave laborers. About one in five defendants was convicted.

Administering Germany

While the Allied powers were dealing with war criminals, they also faced the problem of setting up a government in devastated postwar Germany. During an Allied conference at Yalta in February 1945, Roosevelt, Churchill, and Stalin agreed to divide Germany into four separate zones of occupation—American, British, French, and Soviet. The city of Berlin, 110 miles (177 kilometers) within the Soviet zone, was also to be divided and occupied by the four powers.

At a conference in Potsdam, Germany, in July, 1945, the Allies decided to fix Germany's eastern border so that part of prewar Germany became part of Poland. The transfer was made to compensate Poland for the loss of some of its eastern territory to the Soviet Union.

The change in Germany's eastern border, however, created economic difficulties. First, the area annexed by Poland had formerly produced about one-quarter of Germany's food supply. Second, the Poles expelled the Germans living in this region in order to avoid having a German minority within their country. The refugees flooded into Germany, which now had to house, feed, and provide jobs for 13 million additional people.

The Division of Germany

By 1948 a major dispute had arisen among the occupying Allied powers over Germany's future. The Soviet Union—which had been invaded by Germany twice within a single generation and had suffered 26 million casualties in World War II—wanted to keep Germany divided, neutral, and primarily agricultural. The Western Allies, however, felt that rebuilding Germany was essential to rebuilding Western Europe. They pointed out that unless Germany were allowed to industrialize fully, it would be unable to support its population.

In 1948 France, Great Britain, and the United States decided to merge their zones of occupation in Germany, including their zones in Berlin. In response, the Soviets blockaded Berlin, cutting off all railroad, highway, and water access to the city. They hoped this action would force the Western nations to either reconsider their decision or leave Berlin. Instead, the three Allies began to supply their zones in Berlin by air. For nearly a year, a huge airlift of food, fuel, and other supplies poured into the city. When the Soviets realized that the other Allies would not leave Berlin, the blockade was lifted in May 1949.

Two German States   The Federal Republic of Germany—West Germany—was created on May 23, 1949, out of the American, British, and French zones of occupation. Konrad Adenauer (AD-uhn-OWR) became chancellor, and Bonn became the nation's capital. The three Western-occupied zones of Berlin, known as West Berlin, were also considered part of West Germany. In October 1949 the communist-controlled German Democratic Republic—East Germany—was proclaimed in the Soviet sector of Germany. Its capital was East Berlin. Although East Germany supposedly became independent of Soviet control in 1954, Soviet troops remained in the country.

The Berlin Wall   The people of West Germany enjoyed both political freedom and a high standard of living. Between 1949 and 1969 over 2.5 million East Germans seeking freedom and better living conditions fled to West Germany through West Berlin. Many of these refugees were educated professionals and skilled workers, whose flight severely damaged East Germany's economy.

On the morning of August 13, 1961, the citizens of Berlin awoke to find that during the night, government workers and troops from East Germany had begun construction of a wall through the heart of the city. At first the wall was simply a 29-mile (47-kilometer) expanse of cinder blocks topped with barbed wire. Eventually the wall became a 103-mile (166-kilometer) stretch of concrete and steel, standing 15 feet (4.6 meters) high. Armed soldiers constantly guarded the wall. The Berlin Wall was built to prevent East Germans from traveling to West Berlin. Over the next 28 years, however, some 10,000 East Germans attempted to escape to the West by going over, under, or through the Berlin Wall. About half succeeded, but nearly 200 people were killed, and about 5,000 were captured.

From 1961 to 1989, the Berlin Wall served as the world's most dramatic symbol of the **cold war**—a condition of hostility without actual fighting that existed between the Western democracies and the Communist bloc. It was not until late 1989 that cold-war tensions had eased enough for the East German government to open the Berlin Wall to unrestricted traffic.

(Continued on page 710.)

HISTORY AND PEOPLE

ROBERT SCHUMAN

Born near France's border with Germany in 1886, Robert Schuman grew up with a deep appreciation of the conflicts that can arise where countries meet. A devout Christian, he decided early to devote his life to public service, convinced that religion and civic responsibility go hand in hand. He rose to prominence as a lawyer and later as a statesman, serving as France's Finance Minister in 1946 and 1947, and as Premier in 1948 and 1949. In these positions, he worked diligently to reconstruct the French economy and political system amid the devastation left by World War II.

But Schuman, while working for France, always remembered that narrow and selfish nationalistic policies often led to war in Europe. He carefully sought, therefore, to develop policies that would help all of Europe, as well as France. Schuman believed that economic integration of the continent was the key to peace, that countries that relied on each other for trade would be far less likely to go to war.

Schuman's search for a means to achieve this economic cooperation culminated in 1950 when he proposed what came to be known as the Schuman Plan (officially, the European Coal and Steel Community). Dean Acheson, United States Secretary of State at the time, spoke for many world leaders when he called the Schuman Plan "a step towards unification of Western Europe which takes one's breath away."

The Schuman Plan called for six European nations to pool their coal and steel resources and to drop trading barriers among themselves. The Plan was an enormous success, both economically and, more important, as a decisive step toward a peaceful, unified Europe. The governing body of the Schuman Plan eventually evolved into the European Parliament in 1962. For nearly 30 years the European Parliament has worked to expand Robert Schuman's dream of an economically integrated—and thereby peaceful—Europe.

On December 31, 1992, twelve European nations, under the auspices of the European Parliament, will remove many of the remaining trade and regulation barriers that fragment the continent. Europe will virtually share the same economy, promoting harmony on the continent and creating a formidable economic competitor to Japan and the United States. Robert Schuman died in 1963, but the process of achieving peace through cooperative economic ties continues to grow toward fruition.

1. What did Robert Schuman believe was the best way to keep peace in Europe?

2. What do you think is the best way to maintain peace?

3. What might be some disadvantages to countries sharing the same economy?

North Atlantic Treaty Organization

Alarmed by the political disagreements between the Soviet Union and the West, the nations of Western Europe sought to form an organization to unify the military security of the region. In 1949 ten European nations joined the United States and Canada to form the North Atlantic Treaty Organization (NATO). The ten original European members were Belgium, Denmark, France, the United Kingdom, Iceland, Italy, Luxembourg, the Netherlands, Norway, and Portugal. They were later joined by Spain, Turkey, Greece, and West Germany. The heart of the NATO treaty states that "An armed attack against one...shall be considered an attack against all." The treaty provided that United States soldiers and weapons would be placed in Western Europe to discourage a Soviet attack and that all NATO members would take military action to repel attacks.

Beginning in the mid-1960s, however, differences over policy arose between some European members of NATO and the United States. For example, in 1966 France requested that the United States give up its NATO bases in that country and withdraw its troops. France wanted to be responsible for its own military defense. In the 1980s, when the United States installed a new system of nuclear missiles in Western Europe, huge protests erupted in Great Britain and West Germany. Also, a number of Western European members of NATO, unlike the United States, wanted to relax restrictions on trade in technology with the Soviet Union and Eastern Europe.

By the late 1980s it was clear that changes in NATO were inevitable as the cold war began winding down. NATO may play less of a military role and develop more of a political and economic role during the 1990s.

The Marshall Plan

The battles and bombs of World War II had devastated much of Western Europe. Fields, forests, villages, and cities had been destroyed. Factories were gutted, mines were ruined, and railroads and bridges were damaged. National currencies were nearly worthless. Millions of people were homeless. Countless numbers suffered from illness, lack of food, injuries, and despair. The war had drained the region of its wealth and energy. The tremendous task of rebuilding was beyond the ability of Western Europe alone. The United States provided the region with a great deal of help.

After World War II the official United States policy regarding communism was to keep it contained within its current borders. The United States believed that communism could be better contained if the countries of Europe could rebuild their economies. To accomplish this goal the United States instituted the Marshall Plan in 1947. This plan was named for Secretary of State George C. Marshall, who urged its passage. Massive aid was offered to all the nations of Europe. However, the Soviet Union and the Communist-dominated governments in Eastern Europe feared American influence and rejected American help. Between 1948

World War II was the most destructive war in the world's history. Many Western European cities such as Coutances, France (left), were left in ruins after shelling and bombing.

and 1952 about $13 billion in economic aid was given to Western Europe. As a result, the countries of this region were able to resist the Communist threat and reestablish their economies. By 1952 agricultural and industrial production in 16 Western European nations had surpassed prewar levels, and the region was headed toward an economic boom.

Economic Cooperation

In addition to the Marshall Plan, a major reason for Western Europe's economic recovery was increasing regional cooperation. In 1951 the European Coal and Steel Community (ECSC) was formed. It consisted of six nations: France, Italy, West Germany, and the Benelux countries— Belgium, the Netherlands, and Luxembourg. The six nations agreed to remove all barriers, such as tariffs, quotas, and import restrictions, to coal, iron, and steel trade among themselves. They also agreed to allow coal- and steelworkers from one member nation to take jobs in any other member nation. The standard of living in ECSC countries soon rose.

In 1957 the six ECSC nations decided to cooperate still further. They established the European Economic Community, sometimes known as the Common Market. Members agreed to end import quotas and tariffs on all raw materials and finished products. In effect, they set up a free-trade market about the size of the United States. They also decided to levy a common tariff on all goods imported from nonmember countries.

As a result of the establishment of the Common Market, trade among the member countries increased by more than 700 percent between 1958 and 1972. Nations began to specialize in what they did best. They also became increasingly interdependent. For example, coal-poor Italy relies mostly on coal supplied by other Western European nations to power its industries. On the other hand, Italy's citrus fruits, olives, and grapes are in great demand in the northern nations of the region.

Soon many U.S. companies set up subsidiaries in Western Europe to take advantage of the Common Market's huge protected market. Also, millions of people from rural areas in Western Europe and former European colonies in North Africa migrated to Common Market industrial centers to take jobs. In 1973 Denmark, the United Kingdom, and Ireland became Common Market members. Greece joined the Common Market in 1981, and Spain and Portugal became members in 1986.

Several Western European countries that did not belong to the Common Market have formed their own economic association, known as the European Free Trade Association (EFTA) in 1959. The current members of EFTA are Austria, Finland, Iceland, Norway, Sweden, and Switzerland. Like the Common Market, EFTA has almost no restrictions on trade between member countries. However, unlike the Common Market, EFTA does not regulate its members' trade with nations outside the group. The standard of living in EFTA countries has greatly increased.

United Nations

In April 1945, representatives of 50 nations—many of them European—met to draw up a charter for the United Nations (UN). According to the charter, the UN was to maintain world peace and security, promote friendship among nations, settle disputes among nations peacefully, and foster international cooperation in solving global economic, social, and cultural problems. Today, 159 nations are members of the UN.

The UN Charter set up a number of major bodies within the UN to help the organization carry out its work. These major bodies include the **General Assembly**, Secretariat, Economic and Social Council, Trusteeship Council, International Court of Justice, and **Security Council**. The General Assembly is composed of representatives from all member nations. Each nation has one vote. The General Assembly discusses important questions and recommends action to other UN bodies. The Secretariat is the administrative body of the UN. The Economic and Social Council oversees the improvement of worldwide social and economic conditions. The Trusteeship Council watches over people and territories that are not yet independent. The International Court of Justice decides on disputes brought before it by members and gives advisory opinions on matters of international law. The Security Council tries to settle international disputes. The Council is composed of five permanent members—the United States, the United Kingdom, the Soviet Union, China, and France—and ten other members elected by the General Assembly for two-year terms. Each of the five permanent members possesses veto power. If any one of the five votes against a proposal, the Security Council cannot act.

The UN is also made up of many specialized agencies. A number of these agencies are headquartered in Western Europe. For example, the International Atomic Energy, which aims to promote safe and peaceful

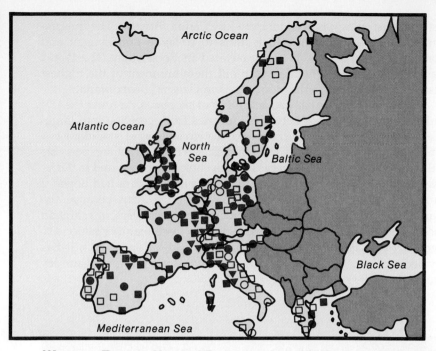

Western Europe Natural Resources and Industrial Centers
● Industrial Centers ▼ Coal ■ Iron ○ Oil □ Minerals

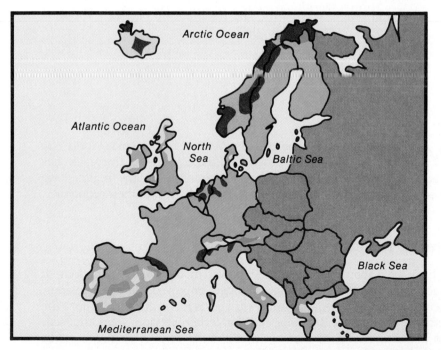

Western Europe Land Use
□ Farming ■ Forestry □ Grazing ■ Nonproductive

uses of atomic energy, is headquartered in Vienna, Austria. The International Labor Organization, which aims to promote employment and improve labor conditions, is headquartered in Rome, Italy. The World Health Organization, which aims to aid the attainment of the highest possible level of health, is headquartered in Geneva, Switzerland.

The United Nations has had a number of successes. At times the UN has helped keep disputes between countries from growing into large-scale wars. It has also helped improve education and living conditions in a number of parts of the world. The UN has also been largely responsible for the near eradication of diseases such as cholera, leprosy, and malaria. However, the UN has not been as effective as its founders had hoped it would be. Its peacekeeping powers have been limited because the organization depends on the cooperation of its members to maintain peace. In addition, the UN has little power to force member nations to accept UN decisions. Although the UN has had its drawbacks, it has provided a place where member nations can air their grievances and try to solve their differences.

SECTION 1 REVIEW

1. **Recall**   What alliance was formed to protect Western Europeans from attack?
2. **How and Why**   In what way did the Marshall Plan help the war-torn nations of Western Europe?
3. **Critical Thinking**   Why did the Soviet Union want to keep Germany divided?

Many changes have taken place in Western Europe since World War II. Democracy has flourished, and the economy of the region has steadily improved. In addition, several countries in the region have chosen to incorporate a number of socialist policies into their economies.

United Kingdom

In 1945 the Labour party came to power in the United Kingdom. It established a **welfare state** that provided improved old-age pensions, unemployment income, and health-care costs for all citizens. At first the medical care was free, but later, fees for certain services were imposed. The Labour government also nationalized the Bank of England, public utilities, and industries such as railways, trucking firms, coal mines, and iron and steel plants.

The Commonwealth of Nations   The British Empire came to an end in the years after World War II. Australia, Canada, New Zealand, and South Africa had been granted independence in the early 1930s. After the war the peoples living in British colonies in Africa and Asia began to increase their demand for independence. In the late 1940s, India, Pakistan, Ceylon (now Sri Lanka), and Burma (now Myanmar) achieved independence. Since 1950, all remaining British colonies have become independent nations.

Many former British colonies have chosen to continue their ties with their former rulers through the Commonwealth of Nations. Members are not tied to the Commonwealth by formal treaties. Each nation makes its own foreign policy. However, the members of the Commonwealth negotiate favorable trade agreements with each other, and developing nations within the association receive aid from wealthier members. Australia, New Zealand, and Canada were among the original members of the Commonwealth of Nations. Today, 47 independent nations plus a number of British dependencies are members of the Commonwealth.

Conservative Rule

Although control of the British government alternated between the Labour and Conservative parties between 1951 and 1979, national policy hardly changed. Then, in 1979, Conservative Margaret Thatcher became the new prime minister, the first woman in British history to hold that office. Thatcher's policy was to reduce the government's role in the British economy. She sold most nationalized businesses to private owners, cut government expenditures by ending a number of expensive social programs, and refused to subsidize, or support with money, manufacturing industries that were in financial trouble. She also tried to reduce the power of British labor unions. Thatcher succeeded in lowering government spending and in raising the standard of living for the middle class. Also, the inflation rate dropped significantly. However, working class unemployment tripled, and the northern part of the United Kingdom became a depressed area.

Although many of Britain's colonies demanded and gained their independence after World War II, one trouble spot remained: Northern Ireland. The difficulties can be traced to the English conquest of Ireland in the 1500s. Moreover, deep religious differences divided the Catholics and Protestants in Northern Ireland.

Many Catholics in Ireland disliked the division of their island into two areas. The southern part of the island, where most Catholics lived, had been an independent country—the Republic of Ireland—since 1937. The smaller area—Northern Ireland—was a self-governing part of Britain. The Catholics in Northern Ireland were a minority who believed that the Protestant majority discriminated against them in jobs and housing. They wanted to unite with the Republic of Ireland.

In the late 1960s, bloody clashes between Catholics and Protestants broke out in Northern Ireland. The British government sent soldiers to stop the fighting. When this proved unsuccessful the British government took over control of Northern Ireland in 1972. However, this step, as well as calls by religious leaders for peace, failed to end the violence and bitterness. By the 1990s a solution still seemed far away.

France

After World War II the French, like the British, nationalized some important industries. Wages were generally improved, and people were protected by such government social programs as health care and unemployment insurance.

The Fourth French Republic was created in October 1945. War hero Charles de Gaulle was elected president of the republic. Because the new French constitution did not provide strong executive powers, de Gaulle opposed it and resigned from the presidency in 1946.

After the war, French colonies, like the British colonies, began to demand their independence. Revolts began in Southeast Asia in 1946. French Indochina was eventually divided into Cambodia, Laos, and Vietnam. The French withdrew from Indochina in 1954 after heavy losses. Later in 1954, a revolt broke out in the French colony of Algeria in North Africa.

After four years of fighting, most French people felt that Algeria should be independent. However, French settlers in Algeria and some military leaders were opposed. This led to a revolt that threatened to overthrow the French government.

France Under de Gaulle   In the midst of this chaos, de Gaulle was asked to become France's prime minister and was given emergency powers to rule. De Gaulle had a new constitution written that gave the president more powers and established the Fifth French Republic. It was approved by the voters in 1958, and de Gaulle was elected president. De Gaulle ended the fighting in Algeria by agreeing to give the Algerians their independence. In 1962 Algeria became an independent country.

De Gaulle sought to make France a dominant power in Western Europe. He ordered scientists to develop nuclear weapons and took French soldiers out of NATO. After the Common Market was established in the late 1950s, de Gaulle hoped to use the organization to promote French influence. De Gaulle successfully blocked a British move to join the Common Market in the 1960s. He believed that Britain would be a rival of France. Amid growing criticism, de Gaulle resigned from the French presidency in April 1969.

France After de Gaulle   Georges Pompidou (PAHM-pi-DOO) was elected president of France after de Gaulle resigned. Pompidou's foreign policies were designed to improve relations with the United States and the United Kingdom. In 1971 he agreed on the United Kingdom's entering the Common Market. He also worked to improve French industry. Pompidou died in office in 1974.

Valery Giscard d'Estaing (zhis-KAHR des-TENG) was elected the new president of France. He worked to lower the voting age to 18 and to raise retirement pensions. He also worked to raise minimum wages and to increase benefits for workers.

In 1981 Francois Mitterand (MEE-ter-ahn), a socialist, was elected president of France. He and his party promised to increase government's role in business. The French government quickly nationalized five industries and most private banks. In addition, the minimum wage was raised again, and French workers received more benefits, such as longer vacation times and fewer working hours. Mitterand was reelected to a second seven-year term in 1988.

The Germanys

After World War II Germany was divided into two nations commonly known as West Germany and East Germany. Both nations developed very differently in the years after the war. West Germany's government was democratic, and it was influenced by the United States and Western Europe. East Germany's government was Communist, and it was dominated by the Soviet Union. By the 1990s, however, the two Germanys stood at the brink of reunification.

West Germany   West Germany rebuilt its industries after the war using the newest technological equipment. Its economy soon boomed. Its gross national product grew from $23 billion in 1950 to over $103 billion in

1964. West Germany is sometimes called an economic miracle. It has become one of the world's economic giants and has developed one of the highest standards of living.

Under the leadership of Chancellor Konrad Adenauer during the 1950s, West Germany again became an important part of the international community. In 1969 Willy Brandt, the former mayor of West Berlin, became chancellor. He was an outspoken peacemaker who worked to reduce tensions between Communist and non-Communist countries in Europe. Brandt especially worked to ease tensions between West Germany and East Germany. In 1974 Helmut Schmidt became West Germany's chancellor. He worked for greater economic cooperation in Western Europe and continued the trend toward cooperation with East Germany. Helmut Kohl was elected chancellor in 1982. He has worked to improve West Germany's economy and has strongly supported reunification of West and East Germany.

East Germany   East Germany was formed from the Soviet sector of Germany after World War II, and was ruled by a single party—the Communist party. East Germany suffered severe economic problems until the mid-1960s, when further industrialization of the nation was made a priority. By the early 1970s the East German economy was highly industrialized, and East Germany's standard of living was raised. However, growth began to slow in the late 1970s because of shortages of natural resources and skilled labor.

In 1981 Chairman of the Council of State Erich Honecker declared that German reunification might eventually be possible. He eased border restrictions on exchanges with West Germany. In 1987 Honecker made a landmark visit to West Germany.

In late 1989, as a result of the lifting of restrictions by the Soviets in its satellite nations, East Germany made preparations for the nation's first free elections. The elections were held in March 1990, and the Christian Democrats won a solid majority in the East German Parliament. A month later the Parliament elected Lothar de Maizière (may-ZHAHR) the Christian Democratic leader as prime minister. One of the Parliament's first acts was to endorse the rapid unification of the two Germanys. De Maizière and his Christian Democrats face the task of transforming the East German economy into a free market.

The Wall Came Tumbling Down   The events that led to free elections in East Germany began in late 1989. In 1961 the Berlin Wall had been built to prevent East Germans from emigrating to a better life in the freedom of the West. In 1989, however, Soviet President Mikhail Gorbachev decided that major reforms were needed in both the Soviet Union and the Communist-controlled nations of Eastern Europe. Many East Germans had long disapproved of their government. In 1982 the pastors of St. Nicholas Church in the city of Leipzig (LYP-sig) began holding Monday evening vigils to protest the installation of short-range nuclear missiles in Europe. Over the years people attending the vigils started to express grievances over Communist misrule of their country. They

criticized such things as the loss of 70,000 old apartments to decay. They complained about industrial pollution. They objected to low wages, the shortages of consumer goods, and the false economic statistics that the government put out.

On October 9, 1989, some 70,000 people in Leipzig paraded for multi-party elections. The next week 100,000 people turned out and the week after, 300,000. The huge marches continued for seven weeks. By this time the Soviet government had indicated that it would not send in troops to support the Communist East German government. Other events in Eastern Europe also added to the government's problems. In May Communist Hungary removed the fortifications along its border with Austria. East Germans had always been allowed to travel to Hungary. Now tens of thousands fled from Hungary through Austria to West Germany. Soon after, additional thousands escaped by way of Czechoslovakia, which had also opened its borders.

By the end of October 1989, the East German government was in full retreat. First, the old-line Communist party chief was replaced by a more moderate individual. Then the government promised free elections. Finally, it opened the Berlin Wall. People throughout the world watched on television as exuberant East Germans danced through the checkpoints. Soon people started tearing down the wall, a symbol of division and oppression.

Economic Problems   The East German government hoped that opening the Berlin Wall would stem the flow of refugees to the West. The government thought that people would visit West Berlin and then return home. Instead, a steady stream of people—almost 2,000 a day—kept crossing the border and not coming back. The mass migration posed serious economic problems for both Germanys.

For East Germany, the continuing exodus of the most able members of its work force meant that the country's already low level of productivity dropped still further. For West Germany, the arrival of so many new-comers meant much higher spending for such social services as unemployment benefits, pensions, and health care. Moreover, the newcomers were competing with West Germans for low-cost housing and jobs, both of which have been in short supply in recent years.

In February 1990 the two Germanys began talks on adopting a common currency. The most crucial decision was what exchange rate to set. In April the exchange rate was set at one to one. This exchange rate of one virtually worthless East German mark for one strong West German mark was set to protect East German wages, pensions, and savings. It was also set to protect workers from higher costs of living in the West and from the loss of the subsidies that existed in the socialist system. The union of East and West German currencies took place in mid-1990.

Unification   By early 1990 many people in both East and West Germany began calling for political unification as well as economic unification of the two nations. A few months later unification seemed inevitable. Unification of East and West Germany will bring a number of changes to West Germany.

West Germany is already the leading economic power in Western Europe. It will be even stronger after unification. A unified Germany will have the second largest land area in Europe. Its population will grow to 78 million, the highest in Europe. The city of Berlin will have a population of nearly 4 million, making it the third largest city in Europe behind Moscow and London. On October 3, 1990, Germany reunited.

Scandinavia

Sweden was neutral during World War II. Therefore, it did not suffer devastation. After the war, Sweden's economy grew tremendously and it is one of the world's most prosperous nations. The Swedish welfare system insures that everyone in the nation has a high standard of living. The government provides free education, largely free health care, pensions for the elderly, and financial aid for housing.

After World War II, U.S. aid helped Norway rebuild its industries and its merchant fleet. Soon, the nation's economy was thriving. Norway has one of the largest merchant marines in the world. The discovery of oil in the North Sea during the 1970s has added to Norway's economic prosperity. Although Norway is a member of NATO, it has refused to allow NATO bases or nuclear weapons on its soil. In 1959 Norway, with five other nations, founded the European Free Trade Associations. Like Sweden, Norway has many social welfare programs including pensions for the elderly, job retraining, and aid for handicapped persons.

During World War II, Finland held an uneasy truce with the Soviets. After the War, the Finns adopted a strict policy of neutrality. They did not join NATO. Finland is the least industrialized of the Scandinavian countries. Its economy is based on its timber resources. Agriculture is another major source of income. Industries such as metal working, machinery manufacturing, and shipbuilding have become important to Finland's economy. Finland is bound to the Soviet Union by strong economic ties.

The people of Denmark have a prosperous economy and they have achieved one of the highest standards of living in the world. After the war, United States aid helped the Danes rebuild their industries. The nation's economy soon became strong again.

Italy

Italy made a good economic recovery after World War II, partly due to its membership in the Common Market. Italy's people, however, remain divided economically along geographic lines. Northern Italy is far more industrialized than the southern part of the country, which is chiefly agricultural. Therefore, the standard of living is much higher in the north than in the south.

Greece

Shortly after the war, Communist-led rebels revolted against the government of Greece. The rebels were defeated in late 1949 after a bitter civil war. The United States provided the Greek government with a massive amount of military aid.

In 1963 George Papandreou became prime minister of Greece. He soon clashed with King Constantine II over the king's political powers and control of the Greek armed forces. The king dismissed Papandreou and confusion and government instability followed. In 1967 a military coup seized control of the country. When Constantine II tried to overthrow the ruling junta and failed, he and his family were forced to flee. Free elections were not held again until 1974. Since that time the Greek government has proven to be unstable. Some governments are in power for only a few months. Government instability has hindered Greek economic advancement.

Spain and Portugal

After military dictator Francisco Franco died in 1975, Spain became a constitutional monarchy under King Juan Carlos. In 1977 the government held free elections, and in 1978 it approved a new constitution based on democratic principles. Minority groups within the country, such as the Basques, have pushed for self-rule. Although Spain's economy expanded throughout the 1970s and 1980s, inflation and a lack of technology made progress slow.

The dictatorship of Oliveira Salazar in Portugal lasted from 1932 until 1968. In 1974 a military group seized control of the nation. They restored rights to the people and established a provisional government to administer the country. Political parties were permitted in Portugal for

Denmark is known for its high-quality ceramics. This skilled artist is hand-painting porcelain dishes and plates.

This well-stocked open-air produce market is on the island of Madiera in Portugal. This photo helps illustrate the growing economy in that country.

the first time in over 40 years. In 1976 Portugal held free general elections. Since then, Portugal's government has changed hands a number of times. In 1986 Portugal joined the Economic Community and the nation looks forward to a growing economy.

Belgium and the Netherlands

Belgium recovered its economic prosperity quickly after World War II. It played a leading role in international affairs during the postwar years. Belgium was a founding member of the United Nations, the Common Market, and NATO. In the 1960s Belgium granted independence to its African colonies. Belgium has lacked unity because it is divided into two ethnic and language groups. The Flemish people, who live in the north, speak Flemish, which is close to Dutch. The Walloons live in the South and speak French. The rivalry between the Flemish and Walloons has increased in recent years. This division had led to a lack of cooperation in solving problems that affects the entire country of Belgium.

World War II left much of the Netherlands in ruins. Nearly half the nation's factories, shipping, and railroads were destroyed. Much of the land was flooded because of damage to the dikes during the war. When the war was over, the Netherlands began to rebuild. By 1955 the industrial production of the Netherlands had increased to about 60 percent over prewar levels. The Netherlands enjoys a high standard of living.

Switzerland and Austria

Switzerland maintained its neutrality during World War II, as it had since 1815. It has prospered from its neutrality. Switzerland has become a world banking center with one of the world's most stable currencies.

The Republic of Austria was established in 1945, under the occupation of the Allies. Full independence was granted in 1955. Austria has declared itself to be permanently neutral.

SECTION 2 REVIEW

1. **Recall** What Western European nation remains divided economically along geographic lines?
2. **How and Why** In what ways did de Gaulle seek to make France a dominant power in Western Europe after the war?
3. **Critical Thinking** How were West Germany and East Germany formed?

Thought, Art, and Science

The philosophy and arts of the twentieth century reflected the period's political, economic, and psychological turmoil. Philosophers, psychologists, writers, painters, sculptors, architects, and composers broke away from traditional standards to interpret the modern world in a new way. Although there was no central theme or dominant school, there was a tremendous amount of creativity.

Science and technology experienced an even more spectacular development. In addition to the atomic bomb—which was developed largely by scientists who fled from Nazi Germany and Fascist Italy—the twentieth century witnessed the invention of everything from microchips to space ships, from television to an explanation of how heredity works. A major reason for these successes was the growth of "big science." Individual scientists no longer worked alone in laboratories. Instead, teams of scientists worked together on projects financed by governments and industry.

Philosophy

Most twentieth-century philosophers in Western Europe followed one of two movements: logical **empiricism** in Britain, and **existentialism** on the European continent.

Logical empiricism originated with Ludwig Wittgenstein, an Austrian who later settled in England. Wittgenstein argued that it is foolish to discuss such topics as God, freedom, and morality because there is no scientific or mathematical way you can prove your statements. It is all a matter of opinion. Wittgenstein said that the only thing worth studying is language. Language is what connects the mind to the real world.

Existentialism was a non-God-centered attempt to deal with a world of uncertainty and terror. Many existentialists were **atheists**; they believed that human beings simply existed. Once they "appeared on the scene," however, they defined themselves by their actions. In other words, human beings were personally responsible for their own lives. They could not shift that responsibility either to God or to society. The leading existentialists were Jean-Paul Sartre and Albert Camus of France. Both argued that in Western Europe in the twentieth century, people defined themselves by how they responded to Hitler. Either they went along with his tyranny and viciousness, or they fought against it in every way they could, no matter what the cost to themselves.

Psychology

You recall that Sigmund Freud had interpreted human behavior as being caused by people's basic inner drives—especially for power and pleasure. During the twentieth century, some people disagreed with aspects of Freud's theories.

One such person was Alfred Adler, a Viennese colleague of Freud. Adler insisted that all personality disorders stem from inferiority complexes and people's attempts to make up for them. Another psychiatrist who broke with Freud was Carl Jung (YUN) of Switzerland. Jung argued that self-preservation was the strongest drive in humans. Others like Eric Fromm and Karen Horney believed that mental health depended on cultural rather than personal factors. They were especially concerned about the influence of a society's economic structure. Fromm, for example, argued that people are bound to become alienated from themselves in an industrial society because they feel isolated and insignificant, with no control over what happens to them.

Whatever their beliefs, however, most psychologists agreed that human beings are motivated primarily by emotion. This view stood in sharp contrast with the Enlightenment thinkers' confidence in reason and progress.

In recent years, some psychologists have focused their attention on biological causes of behavior. They believe that conditions such as aggression, forgetfulness, and sleeplessness may be caused by the presence or absence of key chemicals in the brain.

Literature

Twentieth-century literature in Western Europe reflected the confusion of modern life. Writers emphasized the individual rather than society. They developed a new literary style, and sometimes wrote plotless novels and plays that dealt with characters' thoughts and feelings rather than their actions.

In the late 1800s, Marcel Proust of France had experimented with a literary style that was later known as stream-of-consciousness. In his 16-volume novel *Remembrances of Things Past*, Proust examined the smallest details of his childhood and youthful love in an effort to understand their meaning.

Jean Piaget of Switzerland spent over 40 years studying how children learn. He showed that children reason differently from adults and often do not understand logic.

James Joyce, an Irish writer, who lived from 1882 until 1941, refined the stream-of-consciousness technique in order to explore his characters' inner life. Joyce's novels—especially *Ulysses* and *Finnegans Wake*—are difficult to read and understand. His sentences ran for pages without paragraphs or even periods. He used puns, foreign words, references to classical literature—whatever came to mind. He mixed a description of a street, for example, with accounts of everything the street reminded him of. Joyce wrote the way people actually think—on various levels at the same time.

Since World War II, writers in Western Europe have dealt mostly with political and social problems. West German novelist Günter Grass, for example, criticized his countrymen for paying too much attention to possessions and for refusing to deal with their Nazi past. His best known work is *The Tin Drum*. Simone de Beauvoir of France analyzed women's rights in *The Second Sex*. English novelist George Orwell defended personal freedom and opposed dictatorship in his satires *Animal Farm* and *Nineteen Eighty-Four*.

In the field of drama, probably the most influential playwright was Irish-born Samuel Beckett. He spent most of his life in Paris and even wrote in French, later translating his work into English. Beckett's most important play is *Waiting for Godot*. It features two tramps who are waiting for a salvation that never comes. While they are waiting, they do vaudeville routines, discuss the universe, and present Beckett's belief that all of life involves waiting for something. It is up to individuals to make the waiting period worthwhile. Beckett was a pessimist who always searched for hope. As one of his characters says: "You must go on, I can't go on, I'll go on." And as another character puts it: "Try again. Fail again. Fail better."

In the late 1950s and early 1960s, a new school of drama developed in England. It was begun by John Osborne. In his play, *Look Back In Anger*, Osborne wrote about lower-middle-class people who were frustrated, restless, and above all bitter over what they regarded as the mismanagement of postwar Britain. A critic labeled Osborne an "angry young man," and the label was soon applied to other English playwrights such as Harold Pinter, author of *The Birthday Party* and *Homecoming*. Pinter often used pauses and silences in his plays in order to create a menacing atmosphere.

Painting

You recall that by the 1890s, such postimpressionist painters as Cézanne, Gauguin, and van Gogh were striking out in new directions. Twentieth-century art in Western Europe has been even more diverse and individual. Many painters have been fascinated only with form. Other painters have used art to portray mood or to make statements about the world rather than to show real objects.

Pablo Picasso drew this charcoal sketch of a violin about 1912. This was during his cubist period. He changed his style several times during his career.

Fauvism   The first important art movement of the 1900s was **fauvism**. The *fauves*—which means "wild beasts" in French—did not wish to convey a message but simply to paint happy pictures that showed the vividness and excitement of nature. They used bold colors but often did not paint objects in their natural color. Thus, a sky could be red or green. The originator of fauvism was French painter Henri Matisse.

Cubism   Both George Braque of France and Pablo Picasso of Spain had originally worked with the fauves. In 1907, however, they broke away and developed **cubism**. Instead of copying "reality," Braque and Picasso painted the underlying geometric forms of their subjects. Often they rearranged the forms to show an object from several angles at the same time.

Undoubtedly the most influential and innovative artist of this century has been Picasso. As a young man, he left his native Spain to study in Paris. His works move through many stages. His early work, known as his Blue Period because he used mostly shades of blue paint, is conventional in form, although it deals with such themes as loneliness. His first cubist painting, *Les Demoiselles d'Avignon*, was strongly influenced by the forms and features of African masks.

By 1912 Picasso was doing **collages** incorporating newspaper clippings, bits of cloth, and similar items in his paintings. During the early 1920s, Picasso's style changed again, this time to neoclassical. His figures became huge and dignified.

During the late 1920s and the 1930s, Picasso's paintings had a feeling of life about them even though they were not representational. After World War II, his paintings became more relaxed and gentle. It was Picasso who painted the dove that has become the symbol for peace movements throughout the world.

Because of the Spanish Civil War, Picasso vowed never to return to Spain while Franco was in power. Therefore, he worked in France until his death in 1973.

Dadaism   **Dadaism** developed under French painter Jean Arp. Dadaists believed that life made no sense. Therefore, many dadaist paintings made no sense. They were designed mostly to shock viewers into realizing that Western civilization was destroying itself. A major dadaist was Marcel Duchamp who also practiced "found art." That is, he would pick up ordinary objects, give them a fanciful title, and present them as art. He wanted to show that traditional standards of art had no meaning.

This picture by Edvard Munch is called The Scream. *Can you explain the feeling that this picture seems to express to you? How do the various elements—colors, shape, use of light—bring about this feeling?*

Expressionism

In contrast to fauvism and cubism, a movement known as **expressionism** emerged. The expressionists believed a painting should convey emotion. The Norwegian Edvard Munch (MOONGK) portrayed people's unhappiness and the world's social problems. Munch used thick paint in pure colors, and often enclosed his masses of color in heavy outlines.

A more lighthearted expressionist was Paul Klee (KLAY) of Germany. His pictures were filled with whimsical images of imaginary birds and machines. He was remarkably productive, turning out more than 9,000 works. After the Nazis came to power, Klee fled to Switzerland.

Surrealism

Surrealism was influenced by Freud's theory of dreams. Surrealists claimed there was a reality more real than what we can see: the world of our unconscious mind where dreams originate. The surrealists wanted to probe the unconscious and capture this world of dreams in painting.

Two groups emerged from surrealistic thought. In one group were painters like Salvador Dali, who portrayed melting watches in strange landscapes, and combined fantasy creatures with ordinary objects. The other group of surrealists, including artists such as Max Ernst, developed automatism. They no longer wanted to create art consciously. Instead, they let their brushes wander over the canvas. The results were considered the efforts of the subconscious mind of the artist.

Sculpture

Influenced by the movements in modern painting, sculptors also rebelled against tradition. Many worked with new materials such as aluminum, rubber, stainless steel, and junked auto parts. While still using the human figure as subject, they also experimented with form and shape. For example, Albert Giacometti (JAH-kuh-MET-ee) of Switzerland created elongated, somewhat distorted figures in bronze. British sculptor Henry Moore used holes or openings in his sculptures to emphasize their three-dimensionalism. He also simplified his figures into abstract shapes. Moore's most characteristic pieces are huge, reclining figures.

Among the most impressive Scandinavian sculptures are the figures of Gustav Vigeland (VEE-ge-lahn) in Frogner Park, Oslo, Norway. Swedish sculptor Carl Milles, a disciple of Rodin, is well known for his fountains and human figures, most of which are on display in Millesgarden in Stockholm, Sweden.

Architecture

The underlying principle of modern architecture is functionalism. In other words, the appearance of a building should correspond to its purpose. Many modern architects have discarded elaborate decoration. Instead, they emphasize simple lines and high-quality materials. Steel and glass are commonly used.

Albert Giacometti only attempted to suggest the subject of his sculptures. This is his Walking Man. *Besides a figure in motion, does it express any other feeling to you? What? What people and schools influenced modern sculptors?*

This is a model of an apartment building designed in the Bauhaus style by Walter Gropius. Note the use of glass. This is a characteristic of the Bauhaus school, which was the basis for the international—also called modern—style of architecture.

Among the leading modern architects of Western Europe were Le Corbusier (luh-KAWR-BOO-zee-AY) and Walter Gropius. Le Corbusier, who was born in Switzerland, designed houses of white reinforced concrete, topped with flat roofs. He was also interested in city planning and designed the new city of Chandigarh, India, in the 1950s. Gropius helped found the Bauhaus school of architecture in Dessau, Germany. The Bauhaus group believed that architects and engineers should work as a team. After the Nazis came to power, Gropius moved to the United States, where he helped popularize European ideas of architecture.

Functionalism influenced furniture design as well as architecture. Designers used new materials—foam rubber, molded plywood, synthetics, and plastics—that were easy to care for. They developed modular and multiple-use furniture that fit into small apartments and could be combined in various ways. The term Danish Modern refers to sleek, clean-lined styles of furniture and home furnishings. Much of the furniture is made from light-colored woods such as teak.

Music

Classical and romantic music in Western Europe had been based on melodies. Modern composers, on the other hand, often ignored harmonies in favor of strong rhythmic patterns.

A leading composer of expressionist music was the Austrian Arnold Schoenberg. Schoenberg replaced the familiar eight-note scale with a twelve-note scale. Instead of being organized by a key—like C major, for example—the notes were related to one another by a mathematical pattern. The resulting music often sounded dissonant, or noise-like. Not until after World War II did audiences come to accept it.

Another interesting trend in recent years has been the growth of electronic music, pioneered by French-born Edgard Varèse (vah-REHZ). The tape recorder and electronic instruments such as the Moog Synthesizer have opened a new world of possibilities for the modern composer.

Medical Science

Western Europeans made tremendous achievements in science during the twentieth century. Those in the area of medicine were particularly significant.

The era of wonder drugs began with the discovery and development of penicillin, which stops the growth of disease-carrying bacteria. The work of the Scottish biologist Sir Alexander Fleming, the German Ernst B. Chain, and the Englishman Howard W. Florey was followed by a stream of discoveries such as sulfa drugs and cortisone, and diphtheria and tetanus vaccines. Many formerly fatal illnesses can now be cured, and infections from surgery have been greatly reduced.

Knowledge about the origin of life and the secrets of heredity increased when three French scientists discovered how the activities of body cells are regulated. Another breakthrough in genetics came with the discovery of the structure and function of DNA (deoxyribonucleic acid). DNA is the basic ingredient in genes, the small units that transmit physical characteristics from parent to child. British scientists Francis Crick and Maurice Wilkins, along with the American James Watson, solved this mystery in the 1950s. Their research led to the field of genetic engineering, which offers the hope of someday eliminating such hereditary conditions as hemophilia, a blood disease.

SECTION 3 REVIEW

1. **Recall** What did twentieth-century literature reflect and emphasize?

2. **How and Why** Why did Schoenberg's music often sound dissonant?

3. **Critical Thinking** Why has twentieth-century art in Western Europe been so diverse?

The spirit of cooperation that began in Western Europe after World War II has strengthened over the years. European nations have cooperated in such fields as the aerospace industry and transportation. Soon much of the region will function as one economic unit. The region is hoping to use the same spirit of cooperation to take a united stand on saving the environment.

Europe 1992

Members of the European Community (EC—formerly the European Economic Community) have traded without tariffs since 1968. Physical barriers to trade, however, have remained. Trucks carrying goods endure delays at customs posts. Taxes are inconsistent from one country to another. Air travel is costly. In addition, some European Community nations have instituted national product standards that are anticompetitive. For example, all beer sold in West Germany has to be brewed according to purity specifications established in the sixteenth century.

In 1987 the European Community adopted the Single Europe Act. This act sets 1992 as the target year for the free movement of goods, people, services, and capital. Under the new act members of the European Community would be able to travel across national borders as easily as Americans can travel across state borders. The act includes 279 directives, or Economic Community orders, to individual nations. The directives involve specific economic areas, such as farming, banking, communication, transportation, and taxation. Some of the EC directives have already been put into place, such as standards for a Europe-wide cellular-phone system and the loosening of some customs formalities.

The purpose of the Single Europe Act is to create a single economic superpower that will be able to compete on the world market with such nations as Japan and the United States. It would control about 20 percent of the world's trade. The EC is also moving toward the creation of a central bank and a common currency for the organization.

Leaders of the Economic Community have also begun talking about full membership in the organization for EFTA countries and the countries of Eastern Europe. Several EC leaders even suggested that the nations of Europe take steps toward political unification as well as economic union. Their proposals ran along the lines of a confederation of nations that would closely cooperate in such areas as education, the environment, and research and development.

Whatever the result, it is clear that Europe is changing rapidly—both politically and economically. The 1990s will be an exciting decade in the development of the region.

The European Parliament

In June 1979 the first members of the European Parliament were elected by the people of the European Community. The Parliament met in

Strasbourg, France, in July of 1979. The Council of Ministers representing 12 member nations of the economic community discussed mutually important issues.

In June 1989 the third European Parliament was elected. It is believed that the establishment of the Europe-wide market in 1992 will give the Parliament opportunities to set forth important initiatives, particularly in social, economic, and environmental areas. The Parliament's main role today is that of a forum. The Single Europe Act, however, may move the Parliament toward playing the role of a decision-making body.

The Chunnel

In the past European nations have cooperated to develop the Concorde—a supersonic transport—communications satellites, and a space program. Today Britain and France are cooperating to build the chunnel—a 23-mile-long (37-kilometer-long) tunnel for transportation beneath the English Channel. The massive project involves the construction of three parallel tunnels. Two "running" tunnels will carry passenger trains and car-shuttle trains. The third tunnel will act as a service tunnel for maintenance and emergency rescue.

Eurotunnel, the British-French joint venture sponsoring the building of the $12 billion chunnel, hopes to have it in operation by June 1993. By then rail passengers should be able to travel from London to Paris without ever stopping to get off. Motorists will be able to drive directly onto double-deck rail cars that will take them under the English channel at speeds of nearly 75 miles per hour (120 kilometers per hour).

Saving Western Europe's Environment

For many years Europeans have shared a variety of pollution problems. It is only in recent years that there has been a united effort to clean up the environment.

Acid rain has been a major problem in a number of areas of Western Europe. It does not stop at national borders. Acid rain occurs when the burning of gas, oil, and coal sends pollutants into the air. When the pollution mixes with water vapor, acid rain forms and falls to the earth in the form of rain or snow. Some scientists believe that acid rain has played a major role in the widespread decline of forests in Europe. In West Germany this plague is called *waldsterben*—forest death. In 1982 about 8 percent of all forests in West Germany seemed to be in poor health. In 1985 about 52 percent of West Germany's forests showed visible decline. Forest damage has also been reported in at least 12 other European nations.

The Black Forest and Bavarian Forest areas of West Germany have been especially hard hit by *waldsterben*. Trees have been stunted, growth has been abnormal, and some trees have lost more than half their leaves. The weakened trees are also more vulnerable to damage by wind, insects, and fungi. Some scientists believe that the pollution carried into West Germany comes from Eastern Europe, where high-sulfur brown coal is burned.

NATIONAL PROFILES/WESTERN EUROPE						
Nation/Capital	Population/ Area (in sq mi)	Urban Population (as % of total)	Per Capita GNP (in U.S. $)	Adult Literacy Rate (%)	Life Expectancy	Population Growth Rate* (%)
Andorra/Andorra la Vella	52,000/175	64	**	100	77	0.8
Austria/Vienna	7,623,000/32,374	55	15,560	98	75	0.1
Belgium/Brussels	9,893,000/11,749	95	14,550	98	74	0.2
Denmark/Copenhagen	5,135,000/16,629	84	18,470	100	75	0.0
East Germany/Berlin	16,307,000/41,826	77	**	100	73	0.0
Finland/Helsinki	4,984,000/130,119	62	18,610	100	75	0.3
France/Paris	56,367,000/211,207	73	16,080	99	77	0.4
Greece/Athens	10,050,000/50,944	58	4,790	95	77	0.2
Iceland/Reykjavik	260,000/39,768	89	20,160	100	78	1.1
Ireland/Dublin	3,538,000/27,136	56	7,480	99	74	0.6
Italy/Rome	57,664,000/116,303	72	13,320	93	75	0.1
Liechtenstein/Vaduz	28,000/61	81	**	100	74	0.6
Luxembourg/Luxembourg	371,000/998	78	22,600	100	75	0.2
Malta/Valetta	352,000/122	85	5,050	83	75	0.8
Monaco/Monaco-Ville	29,000/0.73	100	**	99	76	0.0
Netherlands/Amsterdam, The Hague	14,886,000/14,405	89	14,530	99	77	0.4
Norway/Oslo	4,247,000/125,181	71	20,020	100	76	0.3
Portugal/Lisbon	10,354,000/35,553	30	3,670	80	74	0.2
San Marino/San Marino	23,000/23.6	90	**	98	76	0.3
Spain/Madrid	39,405,000/194,896	91	7,740	97	77	0.3
Sweden/Stockholm	8,527,000/173,731	83	19,150	100	77	0.2
Switzerland/Bern	6,700,000/15,941	61	27,260	100	77	0.3
United Kingdom/London, England	57,410,000/94,525	90	12,800	100	75	0.2
West Germany/Bonn	63,237,000/95,976	94	18,530	99	76	0.0

Sources: *The 1990 Information Please Almanac* (Houghton Mifflin Company); *1990 World Population Data Sheet* (Population Reference Bureau, Inc., Washington D.C.)
*A nation with a population growth rate of 2% or more doubles its population within 35 years or less.
**Not available.

Italy and Greece have also suffered the effects of acid rain. Their famous buildings and many outdoor artworks are being damaged by acid rain. Their surfaces are gradually being eaten away.

Another pollution problem that faces European nations bordering the Mediterranean Sea is water pollution. This pollution has been caused by oil from the large number of ships and pleasure boats that travel in the Mediterranean. Industrial wastes and garbage have also polluted the sea.

Western Europe has a lot of cleaning up to do. Weak environmental laws and lack of enforcement in many countries allowed industries to pump wastes into the air and water without reprisal. Led by the European Community, the cleanup has begun. The EC has passed legislation that imposes strict limits on emissions from new power plants and requires existing ones to meet the standards by 2003. Meanwhile, governments in the region are rushing to meet or surpass EC regulations.

Many consumers have started to blame European industries for such disasters as a recent chemical spill that devastated the Rhine River, the poisoning of North Sea seals, and black snowfall over Sweden's mountain resorts. Companies throughout the region are scurrying to meet consumer demands. Scandinavian paper manufacturers have been prodded into using bleach-free products that do not pollute lakes. Italy's chemical industry is embarking on a $10 billion program to reduce toxic wastes by 2000. Throughout the European Community, sales of unleaded gasoline, recycled paper, "ozone-friendly aerosols," and biodegradable diapers are skyrocketing. Many Western Europeans are willing to pay more for products that will not harm the environment. The so-called "green movement" in Western Europe has proven to be formidable and well organized, and businesses in the region are listening.

SECTION 4 REVIEW

1. **Recall** What will be the result of the Single Europe Act?

2. **How and Why** In what way does the chunnel show international cooperation in Western Europe?

3. **Critical Thinking** Why does Western Europe have a lot of cleaning up to do in regard to the environment?

R E V I E W

Reviewing People, Places, and Things

Identify, define, or explain each of the following:

tribunal	Charles de Gaulle
Potsdam	François Mitterand
NATO	Willy Brandt
Marshall Plan	Lothar de Maizière
Common Market	Oliveira Salazar
EFTA	existentialism
General Assembly	Carl Jung
Security Council	Salvador Dali
welfare state	Single Europe Act
Margaret Thatcher	chunnel

Map Study

Using the map on page 713, determine the answers to the following questions:

1. What is most of the land in France used for?
2. What is the land in Spain used for?
3. Which nation has the most unproductive land?

Understanding Facts and Ideas

1. Why were war-crime trials held after World War II?
2. **a.** How did the Soviet Union hope to get the Western Allies to leave Berlin? **b.** How did the Western Allies respond?
3. What is the function of the World Health Organization?
4. What is an advantage of belonging to the Commonwealth of Nations?
5. How did Georges Pompidou try to improve relations with the United Kingdom?
6. What changes will occur in West Germany after unification?

7. How do the beliefs of twentieth-century psychologists differ from those of Enlightenment thinkers?
8. Why did Picasso work in France until his death in 1973, even though his homeland was Spain?
9. What do modern Western European architects emphasize?
10. What will the Single Europe Act ensure?
11. What is the main role of the European Parliament today?
12. What are two effects of acid rain in Western Europe?

Developing Your Critical Thinking

Cause and Effect   Determine the causes of each of the following effects:

a. the Berlin Wall
b. the Marshall Plan
c. NATO

Writing About History

Analyzing Geography   Study the natural resources and land use maps on page 713. Choose one nation and write a paragraph describing how its natural resources have helped shape its history.

Applying Your Skills to History

Negotiating   Nation A has proposed to the European Community that Nation B reduce its steel exports to Nation A. This will help Nation A's steel industry, which has been badly hurt by a worldwide recession and by cheaper imports. Nation B objects. Imagine that you are a negotiator appointed by the European Community to work out a solution. List the steps you would take and the evidence you would need from each side to negotiate a settlement.

WESTERN EUROPE

Reviewing Facts

1. What is the most important river in Western Europe?

2. What monument in Britain was probably an astronomical observatory built by ancient people?

3. What Macedonian leader created an empire that stretched from Greece to India?

4. What was the Pax Romana?

5. Which Frankish leader founded the Holy Roman Empire?

6. In which Western European country did the Renaissance begin?

7. What did Ferdinand Magellan's attempt to circumnavigate the earth prove?

8. What document were William and Mary asked to sign before becoming the monarchs of England?

9. In which Western European nation did the industrial revolution begin?

10. Who was responsible for the unification of Germany?

Understanding Main Ideas

1. Why does Western Europe have such a long coastline despite its small size?

2. How did Julius Caesar become the sole ruler of the Roman Empire?

3. How did the feudal system work?

4. What factors led to the defeat of Spain's Invincible Armada?

5. How did the Versailles Treaty lay the groundwork for a new war?

Applying Chronology Skills

Chronology of English Rights
Study the time line below and answer the questions that follow.

1620	— Petition of Right
1642	— English Civil War begins
1648	— Charles I beheaded
1658	— Death of Oliver Cromwell
1660	— Restoration of monarchy
1688	— Glorious Revolution
1689	— English Bill of Rights

1. In what year was the Bill of Rights signed?

2. What event occurred in 1660?

3. How many years passed between the Petition of Right and the Bill of Rights?

Making Connections

Understanding Geography   Study the map on page 566 showing the Allied and the Axis powers. Note that this map includes major associated powers of the Allies and conquests made by the Axis powers. Study the map carefully. Then write a paragraph discussing the role geography played in the defeat of the Axis powers.

Understanding the Humanities

Analyzing Schools of Architecture   Study the examples of baroque and neoclassical architecture on pages 640 and 641.

UNIT 6 REVIEW

Write a paragraph describing the differences between them.

Developing Critical Thinking

1. Predicting Alternative Futures Imagine that the Treaty of Versailles had brought about a just peace after World War I based on Woodrow Wilson's Fourteen Points. How might this have changed the events that occurred in Europe during the 1920s and 1930s?

2. Making Comparisons Compare the development of government in England and France during the 1600s and 1700s.

Using Sources

Some Roman emperors tried to ignore the early Christians rather than go out of their way to persecute them. Belief in Christianity was still regarded as a crime in the early days of the religion. During the reign of the Roman emperor Trajan — A.D. 90–117 — the emperor wrote to a governor of an eastern province in the empire:

> They [Christians] are not to be searched out. If they should be brought before you, and the crime [of being a Christian] is proved, they must be punished; with the restriction, however, that where the party denies himself to be a Christian, and shall make it evident that he is not, by invoking [appealing to] our Gods, let him...be pardoned upon his repentance. Information without the accuser's name...ought not to be received...as it is introducing a very dangerous precedent, and by no means agreeable to the equity [justice] of my government.

1. According to the emperor's directive, is the governor to hunt down Christians?

2. What restriction was given to punishing a suspected Christian?

3. How did Trajan feel about using anonymous information against a suspected Christian?

Extension Activities

1. Writing a Research Paper Research and write a short report on the development of the atomic bomb.

2. Developing Historical Empathy Imagine that you are either an inventor, a factory owner, or a factory worker during the industrial revolution in Britain. Write about events in your daily life.

Read More About History and Culture

Ashley, Maurice. *The People of England: A Short Social and Economic History.* Baton Rouge: Louisiana State University Press, 1983. Illustrated.

Chartok, Roselle, ed. *The Holocaust Years: Society on Trial.* New York: Bantam Books, 1978. Commentary on the nature of prejudice and scapegoating.

Craig, Gordon A. *The Germans.* New York: G. P. Putnam's Sons, 1982. Social history of Germany since World War II.

Degrand, Alexander. *Italian Fascism: Its Origins and Development.* Lincoln: University of Nebraska Press, 1982.

Dickens, Charles. *A Tale of Two Cities.* New York: Bantam Books, 1981. The French Revolution. (fiction)

Kersaudy, Francois. *Churchill and DeGaulle.* New York: Atheneum, 1983. Two of the 20th century's greatest leaders.

More, Thomas. *Utopia.* New York: W. W. Norton, 1976. Ideal community.

Morris, Jan. *The Spectacle of Empire.* New York: Doubleday, 1982. The British Empire at its height.

Steadman, Ralph. *I, Leonardo.* New York: Summit Books, 1983. Life and work.

Woodford, Susan. *The Art of Greece and Rome.* New York: Cambridge University Press, 1982. From Homer to Alexander the Great.

THE
SOVIET UNION AND EASTERN EUROPE

These distaffs are examples of Russian folk art. Distaffs are used in spinning raw wool into yarn and flax into linen fiber. These are part of the collection in Moscow's Folk Art Museum. Why do you think people would spend so much time and talent in decorating tools?

36

This Scythian gold plaque of a stag was probably a shield decoration. The Scythians based much of their metalwork on Greek models. Ideas as well as goods flowed along the trade routes between the two peoples.

The Land and Early Peoples

Geography has played an important part in shaping the culture of the Russians and the Eastern Europeans—the people of the Soviet Union and of Albania, Bulgaria, Czechoslovakia, Hungary, Poland, Romania, and Yugoslavia. The East European Plain, the steppe of Central Asia, and the region's rivers have often served as roadways for invaders. As a result, the modern nations of the region contain a mixture of many ethnic groups with different religions, languages, and customs. Suspicion and conflict between ethnic groups has been common in the past. Today it is nowhere more evident than in the Soviet Union itself.

As you study this chapter, think about these questions:

- How has the geography of the Soviet Union and of Eastern Europe influenced the region's development?

- What effects have the many migrations of peoples had on the development of the region?

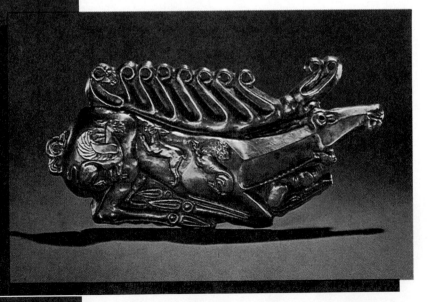

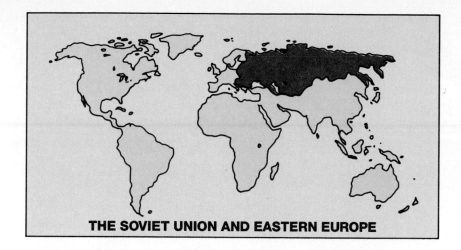

THE SOVIET UNION AND EASTERN EUROPE

The culture region of the Soviet Union and Eastern Europe has an area of more than 9 million square miles (23 million square kilometers). The Soviet Union makes up about 95 percent of this. The region's population numbers about 400,000,000. There are some 100 ethnic groups speaking about 90 different languages and writing in four different alphabets.

The World's Largest Nation

The Union of Soviet Socialist Republics (USSR) is a federation of 15 states called republics. The largest of these is Russia, which was the name of the entire country before the Communists came to power. The term *Soviet Union* will be used when describing the country's physical regions and for its history since the Revolution of 1917. The term *Russia* will refer to an earlier period of history.

The Soviet Union is the world's largest nation in terms of land area. It covers one-sixth of the earth's landmass. Its area of approximately 8.6 million square miles (22.3 million square kilometers) is about two and one-half times that of the United States. The Soviet Union spans two continents—Europe and Asia—and 11 time zones.

The Soviet Union borders two oceans—the Arctic and the Pacific—and two seas with access to the Atlantic—the Baltic and Black seas. The Caspian and Aral seas are landlocked. The Pacific Ocean forms the Soviet Union's eastern coast, far from the country's population and industrial centers. The Arctic Ocean forms its northern border. For about nine months of the year, most of the Arctic coastline is frozen.

The country's northern location has influenced its development. Winter is the longest season. Some of the coldest temperatures on earth outside the North and South poles occur there. The long severe winters limit the amount of food that can be grown. But winter has also been one of Russia's strongest weapons against invaders.

(Continued on page 744.)

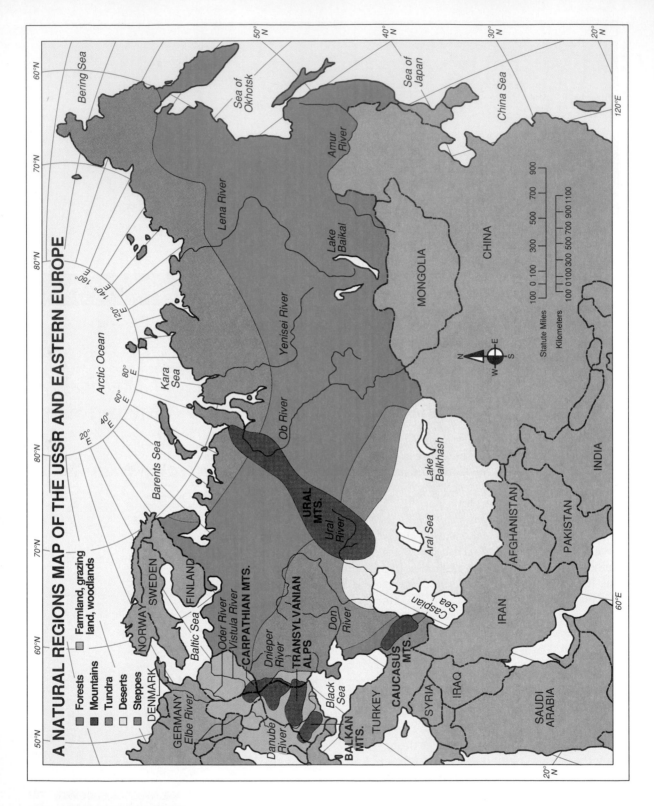

A NATURAL REGIONS MAP OF THE USSR AND EASTERN EUROPE

Legend:
- Forests
- Mountains
- Tundra
- Deserts
- Steppes
- Farmland, grazing land, woodlands

Statute Miles
100 0 100 300 500 700 900

Kilometers
100 0 100 300 500 700 900 1100

Labels on map:

Bering Sea
Sea of Okhotsk
Sea of Japan
China Sea
Arctic Ocean
Lena River
Amur River
Lake Baikal
Yenisei River
MONGOLIA
CHINA
Ob River
Lake Balkhash
Aral Sea
Kara Sea
Barents Sea
URAL MTS.
Ural River
Caspian Sea
AFGHANISTAN
PAKISTAN
INDIA
IRAN
IRAQ
SYRIA
SAUDI ARABIA
TURKEY
CAUCASUS MTS.
Black Sea
BALKAN MTS.
TRANSYLVANIAN ALPS
Don River
Dnieper River
CARPATHIAN MTS.
Danube River
Oder River
Vistula River
Elbe River
GERMANY
DENMARK
Baltic Sea
NORWAY
SWEDEN
FINLAND

120°E
60°E
20°N
20°N
30°N
40°N
50°N
50°N
60°N
70°N
80°N
80°N
70°N
60°N
50°N

20° E
40° E
60° E
80° E
120° E
140° E
160° E

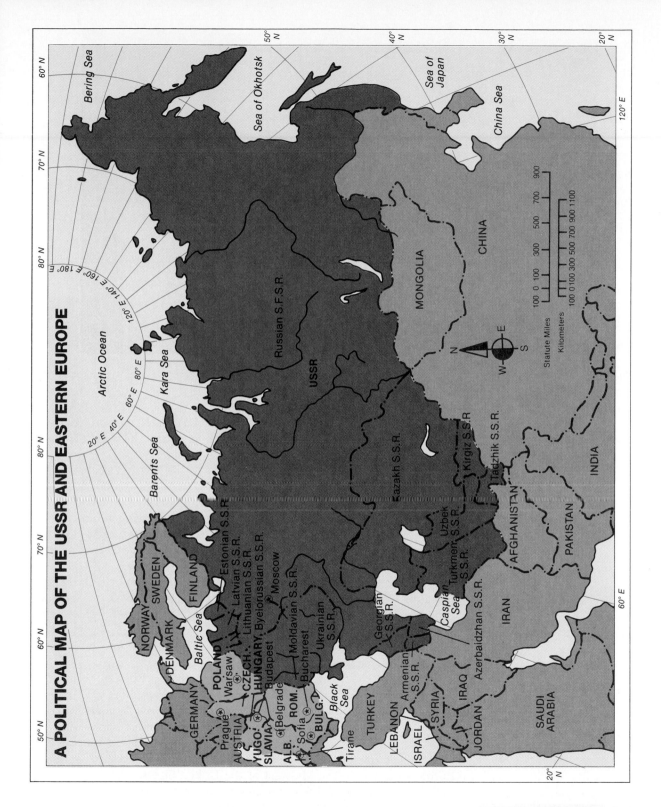

A POLITICAL MAP OF THE USSR AND EASTERN EUROPE

Arctic Ocean

Bering Sea

Sea of Okhotsk

Sea of Japan

China Sea

Barents Sea

Kara Sea

Russian S.F.S.R.

USSR

MONGOLIA

CHINA

Statute Miles

100 0 100   300   500   700   900

100 0 100 300 500 700 900 1100

Kilometers

Kazakh S.S.R.

Kirgiz S.S.R.

Tadzhik S.S.R.

Uzbek S.S.R.

Turkmen S.S.R.

Caspian Sea

Azerbaidzhan S.S.R.

Georgian S.S.R.

Armenian S.S.R.

AFGHANISTAN

PAKISTAN

INDIA

IRAN

IRAQ

SYRIA

LEBANON

ISRAEL

JORDAN

SAUDI ARABIA

TURKEY

Black Sea

Baltic Sea

NORWAY

SWEDEN

FINLAND

DENMARK

GERMANY

POLAND
Warsaw

AUSTRIA

CZECH.
Prague

HUNGARY
Budapest

YUGO-
SLAVIA
Belgrade

ALB.
Tirane

ROM.
Bucharest

BULG.
Sofia

Estonian S.S.R.

Latvian S.S.R.

Lithuanian S.S.R.

Byelorussian S.S.R.

Moscow

Moldavian S.S.R.

Ukrainian S.S.R.

743

The steppes are the richest farmland in the Soviet Union. This photo shows tea harvesting in the steppe area of Georgia. What other part of the world has a steppe area?

Vegetation Zones   The Soviet Union can be divided into four vegetation belts that span the country from north to south. These are tundra, forest, steppe, and desert.

The northernmost of these belts, next to the Arctic Ocean, is the **tundra**. This is a huge, nearly flat land with no trees, only shrubs and low grasses. Tundra winters are long and dark, summers short and cool. The soil, called **permafrost**, is frozen most of the year. During summer, the soil turns marshy. This makes growing crops difficult and causes buildings to shift on their foundations. The few people who live on the tundra make their living by hunting, fishing, or herding reindeer.

The treeless tundra merges with the next vegetation belt, the **taiga** (TY-guh), from the Russian word for forest. The taiga is the largest continuous evergreen forest area in the world. Its trees—fir, pine, and spruce—make up about one-fourth of the world's timber supply. The taiga covers almost half the Soviet Union. The people who live there make their living mostly from timber and furs.

South of the forest lies the **steppe**, from the Russian word for lowland. The steppe is a vast, treeless plain that extends about 4,000 miles (6 400 kilometers) from the European part of Russia into Asia. Before the steppe was cultivated, it was covered with grasses that grew taller than a rider on horseback. The European part of the steppe is the Soviet breadbasket. Its rich black soil, almost 5 feet (1.5 meters) deep, is similar to the fertile soil of the Midwest of the United States. Most of the 290 million inhabitants of the Soviet Union live on the steppe. Most of the invaders of Russia have come by way of the steppe.

The southernmost zone is a desert that stretches from the Caspian Sea to Mongolia. The people who lived there in the past were nomads who wandered from place to place in search of pasture for their herds. Today, modern methods of irrigation have made some farming possible. The area has become the major cotton producer of the Soviet Union.

Geographical Regions   In addition to vegetation zones, the Soviet Union can be divided into four geographical regions. These are European Russia, Siberia, Soviet Central Asia, and the Transcaucasus.

The most striking feature about the geography of the Soviet Union is that the country is flat. All the highest mountain ranges are located on the fringes of the country and do not break the monotony of the vast plain. The Ural Mountains serve as the dividing line between European Russia and the rest of the Soviet Union. They also mark the natural boundary between Europe and Asia. Yet the Urals do not form a serious barrier because they are low and easily crossed.

Siberia occupies the northern third of Asia. Temperatures are extreme and can range from 90° F below zero (-68°C) in the winter to 90° F above zero (32° C) in the summer. Building roads is extremely difficult, water mains and sewers require extra insulation, and steam-heat pipelines are built above the ground.

Siberian development is sometimes compared to that of the early American West with its rugged frontier society. Peasants fleeing their brutal landlords sought refuge in Siberia. Under both the tsars and the Communists, Siberia was a prison and slave-labor camp for criminals and political prisoners.

Siberia did not open up for voluntary settlement until the Trans-Siberian Railroad was begun in 1891. It took 26 years to complete the railroad. Today it stretches 5,777 miles (9 295 kilometers) from the capital of Moscow to the port city of Vladivostok on the Pacific, an eight-day ride.

Only about one-tenth of the Soviet people live in Siberia. Most have settled in towns along the railroad in the south and in the rich farmland of the west. However, the main value of Siberia lies in its tremendous supplies of iron ore, coal, gold, and other natural resources. The government is trying to develop these resources and bring more people and industry to Siberia.

South of Siberia lies Soviet Central Asia. This is fertile steppe with some desert. Its western, southern, and eastern borders are mountainous. The area is known for cotton and grain. Minerals such as coal and copper are also produced in the area.

The Caucasus Mountains run west to east between the Black and Caspian seas. The area south of the mountains is called the Transcaucasus. It contains most of the country's oil reserves.

Rivers   The rivers of the Soviet Union are a physical feature of great importance. Despite its 30,000 miles (48 000 kilometers) of coastline, the country is largely landlocked because most of the coastline is frozen for most of the year. As a result, the Russians have come to depend on their long, slow-flowing rivers for communication and trade. Rivers have been

Russia's highways for hundreds of years. Although railroads, trucks, and airplanes are now used for transportation, the rivers remain the most vital communication links in Soviet life. The nation's leading cities are all located on the banks of rivers.

The most important Soviet river is the Volga. The longest river in Europe, the Volga rises in the Valdai Hills near Novgorod and winds south to the Caspian Sea. A series of canals connects it with many other rivers, as well as with the Baltic and White seas in the north. The Volga handles almost half of the river-freight traffic of the Soviet Union. To the Russians, the Volga is more than a river; it is their Main Street. Many stories and songs—including the famous "Song of the Volga Boatmen"—have been written about it.

Several other major rivers of European Russia begin in the Valdai Hills. Among these are the Dnieper (NEE-puhr), on which the city of Kiev is located, and the Neva, which flows through Leningrad to the Baltic.

Four of the longest rivers in the world flow through Siberia. The Ob, Yenisei, and Lena rivers cross its vastness northward to the Arctic Ocean. The Amur River wanders east along part of the border with China and empties into the Sea of Okhotsk. The Ob, Yenisei, and Amur rivers are frozen for most of the year; so they are not vital communication links like the rivers of European Russia. The Lena, however, is a major waterway. Oceangoing ships are able to travel nearly 2,000 miles (3 218 kilometers) inland from its mouth.

Natural Resources and Energy   The Soviet Union is rich in natural resources. As a result, the country is self-sufficient in many of the raw materials needed for industry. It leads the world in the production of iron, nickel, and platinum, and is second in the production of copper and gold.

The Soviet Union is the world's leading producer of oil. It also has huge coal reserves. They account for 20 percent of the world's coal production. Natural gas is even more abundant. The Soviet Union has 40 percent of the world's known gas reserves and leads the world in its production. In the early 1980s, the Soviets built a natural gas pipeline that carries natural gas from Siberia to Eastern Europe and several Western European nations.

The Soviet Union opened the world's first nuclear power plant in 1954. Many more have been built since then. However, the 1986 disaster at the Chernobyl (cher-NOH-buhl) power plant in the Ukraine alarmed both supporters and opponents of nuclear energy. The accident released radioactive material that spread into Western Europe, and it caused a severe setback to Soviet nuclear policy.

Water power is also an important source of electricity. Some of the largest dams in the world are on Soviet rivers. The Soviets get about one-fifth of their electricity from such hydroelectric projects. However, many of the projects are located far from industrialized areas, which limits the usefulness of this energy source.

Moscow, the USSR's capital, is built on the Moscow River. Factories and high rises dot its skyline. The city manufactures vehicles, machinery, and textiles.

Eastern Europe

The seven nations of Eastern Europe make up about five percent of the culture region's landmass. However, the population numbers approximately one-fourth of the total.

Eastern Europe consists of alternating bands of mountains and plains. To the north, in Poland, lies the Baltic Plain. It is a continuation of the Northern European Plain of Western Europe. South of the Baltic Plain are the Carpathian Mountains. They form a great arc extending from Czechoslovakia eastward into the Soviet Union, then southward and westward through Romania. Farther south is the Danube River Basin, which includes most of Hungary and parts of Austria, Yugoslavia, and Romania. The Danube River Basin is the most fertile part of Eastern Europe. South of the basin are two mountain ranges. The Dinaric Alps run parallel to the Adriatic coast of Yugoslavia and into Albania. The Balkan Range extends through Bulgaria from the Yugoslav border to the Black Sea.

There are several important rivers in Eastern Europe. The Danube, which rises in West Germany and flows through Austria, is a vital traffic artery that touches almost every nation of Eastern Europe. After forming the border between Czechoslovakia and Hungary, it flows through Hungary and Yugoslavia, along the Bulgarian-Romanian border, and through Romania into the Black Sea. Like the Volga, the Danube has had many stories and songs written about it, including the enormously popular "Blue Danube" waltz.

Other rivers in Eastern Europe include the Elbe, which rises in the mountains of Czechoslovakia and flows northwestward through Germany into the North Sea. The Oder and Vistula rivers of Poland empty into the Baltic Sea.

Like the Soviet Union, much of Eastern Europe is rich in mineral resources. Poland and Czechoslovakia rank high among the countries of the world in coal reserves. Bulgaria and Romania contain large supplies of petroleum and natural gas. And there are rich deposits of iron ore in the Dinaric Alps and in the Balkan Range.

SECTION 1 REVIEW

1. **Recall**   What are the Soviet Union's vegetation regions? Its geographic regions?
2. **How and Why**   How did oceans and rivers affect the Soviet Union's development?
3. **Critical Thinking**   The development of the Soviet Union has been compared to that of the United States. How were they similar? How were they different?

SECTION

2

Early Peoples

The inhabitants of the Soviet Union and Eastern Europe have evolved from a long mixing of peoples. Most came out of Central Asia and pushed westward across the steppe.

Slavs   The vast majority of the people in the culture region are of Slavic origin. They are known by various names, including Russians, Ukrainians, Poles, and Czechs. The exact place of origin of the Slavs is still unclear. But historians agree that they were Indo-Europeans. Thus they are related to the Aryans who invaded India, the Hittites who moved into Turkey, and the Persians who entered what is now Iran.

The Slavs emerged as a distinct group about 600 B.C. in what is now eastern Poland and the western part of the Soviet Union. They were primarily hunters and fishers, although they raised some crops. They lived in villages of about 25 families that were related by blood or marriage. The families lived in their own houses but owned the land in common and shared all food and supplies. They were ruled by the oldest male of the village, who supervised the farming and served as a military leader in case the village was attacked.

About A.D. 300 the Slavs began to move into other areas. The West Slavs moved toward the Vistula River Basin. They were the ancestors of the Poles, Czechs, and Slovaks. The South Slavs traveled beyond the Carpathian Mountains into the Balkan Peninsula. Their descendants are the Croats, Serbs, and Slovenes of Yugoslavia. The East Slavs moved

748

(Continued on page 750.)

Using GEOGRAPHY Skills

Exploring Language and Culture

Nation	Cultural Region	Major Languages Spoken
Nigeria	Africa	Native Bantu languages, French, English, and Portuguese
India	South and Southeast Asia	Hindi, English, and 14 other languages
Japan	East Asia	Japanese, Chinese, English
Argentina	Latin America	Spanish, English, Italian, German, and French
Jordan	Middle East	Arabic, Hebrew, English, and Indo-European languages
Switzerland	Western Europe	German, French, Italian, and Romansch
Czechoslo-vakia	USSR and Eastern Europe	Czechoslovakian, German, Russian, and other Balto-Slavic languages
Soviet Union	USSR and Eastern Europe	Russian, Georgian, Slavic languages, Turkish, Persian, German, and English

Cultural diffusion, as you know, is the process of spreading cultural traits, beliefs, and customs from one group of people to another. One example of this process was the movement of Buddhism from India to Sri Lanka and Southeast Asia. This religion then moved from India across Central Asia to China, Korea, Japan, and Vietnam. Another example is the spread of languages to other specific regions. The table above will reveal cultural influences that European languages (such as English, French, Spanish, and Portuguese) have had on people throughout the world. Use the table to answer the following questions:

1. For which nations is German listed as a language? List the cultural areas where these nations are located.

2. What kinds of foods could a person order in restaurants in Switzerland?

3. How many different languages are spoken in the Soviet Union? How many of those come from European nations? What influences in the Soviet Union are missing as influences in Japan?

4. Name two European nations that influenced life in Argentina.

5. Would people in Switzerland be able to communicate with people in Argentina? What languages would they have in common?

north and northeast into the forests of modern Russia, settling along the upper reaches of the Dnieper and Volga rivers. The East Slavs are the ancestors of the Great Russians who today form the major ethnic group in the Soviet Union. The East Slavs are also the ancestors of the two next largest ethnic groups in the Soviet Union, the Belorussians (White Russians) and the Ukrainians. This movement of Slavs took place over four centuries.

These silver objects of dancing men and a lion were made by Slavs in the Ukraine in the A.D. 500s or 600s.

nomadic people: people who wander from place to place to find grazing land and water for their herds

Nomads   While the Slavs were establishing themselves in their new homelands, various nomadic groups kept moving westward across the steppe. They moved because of overpopulation, droughts, and the pressure of other and stronger groups.

The first nomadic people were the Scythians. Excellent horsemen and superb archers, they established an empire on the Black Sea about 700 B.C. There they came in contact with the ancient Greeks, who were founding colonies along the sea's northern shore. The Scythians admired and imitated Greek art and metalwork. They became known for their beautiful cups, bowls, and ornaments of gold.

The Scythians were able to preserve their empire until about 200 B.C. Then they were overthrown by the Sarmatians, a people from what is modern Iran. The Sarmatians controlled the area for the next 400 years, until they were conquered by the Germanic Goths.

Goth rule, however, did not last long. About A.D. 370, the fierce Huns, under their great leader Attila, swept in from the steppe of Asia. You recall that the Visigoths, or West Goths, moved into the crumbling Roman Empire in order to escape. The Huns conquered the Ostrogoths, or East Goths. Then, instead of stopping at the western border of the steppe, the Huns kept going and almost succeeded in conquering Europe. But Attila died in A.D. 453, a plague killed many in his army, and the remaining Huns rode back to their homeland in the eastern steppe.

The Huns were followed by several other groups, including the Khazars and the Mongols. You will learn about these groups in the next chapter, which describes the rise of the Russian state.

SECTION 2 REVIEW

1. **Recall**   What were the three groups of Slavs? Name some modern ethnic groups that stem from each.
2. **How and Why**   Why did nomadic groups migrate westward across the steppe?
3. **Critical Thinking**   How was it possible for so many early peoples to be migrating continually in the region of the Soviet Union and Eastern Europe?

R E V I E W

Reviewing People, Places, and Things

Identify, define, or explain each of the following:

Union of Soviet
  Socialist Republics
Caspian Sea
Aral Sea
Arctic Ocean
tundra
permafrost

Ural Mountains
Vladivostok
Caucasus Mountains
Danube River
West Slavs
South Slavs
East Slavs

Map Study

Using the maps on pages 742 and 743, determine the answers to the following questions:

1. What natural region is the most extensive in the USSR and Eastern Europe?
2. What countries of Eastern Europe have farmland, grazing land, and woodlands?
3. What natural region is located in much of the northern part of the USSR?

Understanding Facts and Ideas

1. Which countries make up Eastern Europe?
2. What was the early importance of the Trans-Siberian Railroad?
3. What is Siberia's chief value to the Soviet Union?
4. Why are the Soviet Union's rivers more useful than its coastline for communication and trade?
5. What is the most important river in the Soviet Union?
6. a. What are the major rivers of Siberia?
   b. What major rivers of the western Soviet Union originate in the Valdai Hills?
7. How does the main geographic feature of Eastern Europe differ from that of the Soviet Union?

8. In which Eastern European countries are there important mineral resources?
9. What is known about the origin of the Slavs?
10. In what ways did the Greeks influence the Scythians?

Developing Critical Thinking

Analyzing Geography   The Ural Mountains are low and easily crossed. If the Urals were higher and few passes existed through them, how different might the history of Russia have been?

Writing About History

In Someone Else's Shoes   Imagine that you are one of the volunteer settlers who moved to Siberia in the late 1890s. In a letter to your relatives in Moscow, explain what your new life is like and mention your reasons for settling in Siberia.

Applying Your Skills to History

Writing a Paragraph   The ability to write a clear, well-reasoned paragraph is a skill that you need whether you are writing an answer to an essay question, a research paper, a book report, or a letter. A good paragraph is made up of a topic sentence, or main idea, and its supporting details. There are sentences that develop and explain the topic sentence. Often the topic sentence is the first sentence of the paragraph. However, it may be placed anywhere in the paragraph where it makes sense and reads well.

Activity: Imagine you are a passenger on the Trans-Siberian Railroad. In a letter home describe in several paragraphs your eight-day journey from Moscow to Vladivostok. Refer to the maps in the textbook.

CHAPTER 37

The Rise of the Russian State

Although Russia was settled by Slavs in the northern forest and a succession of nomads from Asia in the steppe, its first rulers were Vikings from Scandinavia. Kievan Russia depended for its livelihood on trade with the Byzantine Empire. The Byzantines gave the Russians a religion, an alphabet, a legal system, and many other aspects of their culture.

After the decline of Kievan Russia, the Mongols ruled the land during the 1200s and 1300s. They were succeeded by the princes of Moscow, who expanded their power over more and more territory. Finally, a unified Russian nation was established under the rule of several strong tsars and tsarinas.

As you study this chapter, think about these questions:

- How did the Byzantine Empire influence Russian civilization?

- What effect did the Mongols have on Russia?

- How did the Romanovs change Russia from a disorganized feudal state into a world power?

Russian royalty had a vast treasure of gold and jewels, such as this orb, crown, and scepter.

By A.D. 700 the East Slavs were well established in the forests along the Volga and Dnieper rivers. They built towns on the riverbanks and developed a prosperous trade in such forest products as honey, beeswax for candles, furs, and timber. The merchants collected their products in winter. In late spring, after the ice on the frozen rivers melted, the merchants sailed south with their goods to the Black Sea. In Constantinople they exchanged their products for wheat, wine, jewelry, and textiles, returning home before the winter snows began to fall. The most important trading towns along the vital river roads were Novgorod in the north and Kiev in the south.

The Slavic merchants had no trouble crossing the western steppe to Constantinople. Instead of fierce warriors like the Huns, the western steppe was now inhabited by a peaceful group of former nomads called the Khazars. The Khazars were a Turkic people who traded with both the Byzantine and Arab empires. Since the Byzantines were Christians and the Arabs were Muslims, the Khazars converted to Judaism so as not to offend either of their trading partners. In exchange for a peaceful passage through their territory, the Khazars levied a 10 percent tax on the Slavic merchants. The Khazars also allowed Slavic farmers to move onto the steppes and cultivate grain.

The Kievan State

According to tradition, the official history of Russia began in 862. In that year, the inhabitants of Novgorod issued an invitation to a Scandinavian prince named Rurik. "Our land is vast and fertile, but there is no order in it. Come govern and rule over us." Rurik and his fellow Varangians were warrior-traders related to the Vikings who invaded the British Isles and France and later came to North America. Rurik accepted the invitation to rule Novgorod. After his death in 879, his successor Oleg took over Kiev as well, thus forming the first Russian state. The word *Russian* comes from *Rus*, another name for the Varangians. Rurik's descendants ruled Russia for about 700 years.

The Rus set up their capital at Kiev. The choice was a good one. The city was strategically located on a high bluff near the place where the forest met the steppe. Thus its soldiers could stand guard against invading nomads from central Asia. The city also overlooked the anchorage where the trading ships from upstream combined into a single fleet before sailing to Constantinople. Whoever controlled Kiev controlled all Russian trade with the Byzantine Empire.

The Kievan state did not form one country unified under a single ruler. Instead, there was a loose alliance of a dozen or so city-states under the leadership of the Grand Prince of Kiev. Each city-state was ruled by a prince who paid tribute to Kiev in exchange for military protection. The more powerful the Grand Prince, the more loyal the local princes, and the more tribute Kiev collected.

Kievan Russia, 1054

The boyars often had a great deal of influence over the rulers of early Russia. By the late 1500s, however, their power had diminished.

Russian society was divided into several classes. At the top were the princes. Then came the **boyars**, or wealthy merchants, and the landowning nobles. The majority of the Russian people were free peasants. They had few rights, were subject to military service, and had a difficult time simply earning a living. Below them were the slaves, with no rights. They included prisoners of war and Slavs who had sold themselves to pay their debts.

Vladimir I and the Eastern Orthodox Church

One of the most important rulers of Kievan Russia was Vladimir I, a great-grandson of Rurik. He ruled from 980 to 1015. The fact that he bore a Slavic name rather than a Scandinavian one indicates that, by this time, the Russians had absorbed the Varangian culture.

Vladimir I was an excellent military leader. He defeated the Lithuanians to the northwest and extended Russia's boundaries to the Baltic Sea. In the west he defeated the Poles, and in the south he pushed back a new group of nomads called Pechenegs. However, his significance does not lie in his conquests. Vladimir I is important because he was responsible for making Eastern Orthodox Christianity the official religion of Russia. The story is told that Vladimir invited missionaries from different faiths to explain their beliefs to his boyar council. He rejected Islam because Muslims are not supposed to drink wine. Vladimir considered drinking "the chief pleasure of the Russians." He rejected Judaism because the Romans had expelled most of the Jews from Palestine in A.D. 135. To Vladimir, this meant that the God of the Jews had no political power.

The prince then sent envoys to observe Christian services in Germany and Constantinople. The envoys reported that the most magnificent ceremonies were those held at the Eastern Orthodox Cathedral of Hagia Sophia. "We knew not whether we were in heaven or on earth. For on earth there is no such splendor or such beauty, and we are at a loss how to describe it. We only know that God dwells there among men." After Vladimir I was baptized, he had his subjects baptized also.

The Eastern Orthodox Church greatly changed Russian life. The priests who came from Constantinople brought many elements of Byzantine culture with them. They brought the Cyrillic (suh-RIL-lik) alphabet that had been created by two Byzantine missionaries, St. Cyril and St. Methodius. The priests opened schools for the sons of boyars and priests (Orthodox priests are allowed to marry) and taught reading and writing as well as religion. It was in these schools that the earliest Russian literature was produced. The priests imported the architectural style of stone churches with domed roofs, although the Russians changed the round dome into an onion-shaped one. The priests also brought the arts of making mosaics and painting icons.

Moreover, the Eastern Orthodox religion strengthened the power of the ruler. It taught that all power comes from God. Therefore, to disobey the ruler—God's representative—was to sin. The Orthodox Church further gave the Kievan Russians the beginnings of a sense of national identity. People now shared certain beliefs and practices. In the centuries to come, when political strife shook the country, the Eastern Orthodox Church would provide stability for the Russian people.

Iaroslav the Wise and the Golden Age of Kiev

The second great ruler of Kievan Russia was Iaroslav (yuh-ruh-SLUHF) the Wise. One of Vladimir I's 12 sons, Iaroslav ruled from 1036 to 1054.

Iaroslav's main contributions to Russia were cultural. He applied himself to books and read them continually day and night. He set up a large library in Kiev and invited Byzantine scholars to come there and translate the writings of the ancient Greeks into Russian. He set up trade schools where Russian artisans could study masonry, painting, pottery making, and shipbuilding. He also saw to it that his daughters learned how to read and write. Thus his daughter Anna, who married King Henry I of France, was able to sign her marriage contract, while her illiterate bridegroom had to mark it with an "X."

Iaroslav became known as "the Wise" because he was responsible for Russia's first legal code. It combined Slavic customs with Roman law, which had reached Russia through cultural diffusion from Constantinople. The code was rather mild. Neither torture nor the death penalty was allowed, and most crimes were punishable by fines rather than imprisonment. However, because Kievan Russia was a commercial state, the fines for crimes against property were much higher than those for crimes against people.

The Decline of Kievan Russia

Before he died, Iaroslav divided Kievan Russia into five principalities, giving one to each of his sons. He hoped that the sons would take turns

The Russians adopted the Byzantine style in making icons, portraits of religious figures. This is a portrait of St. Barbara, a patron saint of builders.

being Grand Prince of Kiev. Instead, there were almost constant civil wars, and the country became seriously weakened.

To make matters worse, steppe nomads, especially the fierce Polovtsy, increased their attacks against the Russian merchant fleets. Then, as you recall, Constantinople was captured and sacked by crusaders during the Fourth Crusade. Trade between Russia and the Byzantine Empire fell away to a trickle.

Gradually, people abandoned Kiev and fled northward to the safety of the forests along the upper Volga River. When the Mongols swept out of central Asia during the 1200s, there was no one strong enough to withstand them.

Mongol Invasion and Rule

You recall that in the early 1200s the Mongols began expanding under the greatest of their leaders, Temujin, or Genghis Khan. In 1223, one of Genghis Khan's armies reached the Ukraine. But after inflicting considerable damage, the Mongols withdrew. Fifteen years later, however—under the leadership of Batu Khan, Genghis Khan's grandson—they returned in force and stayed.

The Mongol invasion of Russia was terrifying and brutal. In some towns, it was said that "no eye was left open to weep for the dead." In other towns, children reportedly drowned in the blood that ran through the streets. When the Mongols captured Kiev—whose population of 80,000 made it the equal of Paris, then the largest city in Western Europe—they massacred its inhabitants and burned the city. Barely 200 houses were left standing. As a result of this destruction, Russia became even more rural, and learning and craftsmanship declined.

The dead and the poor, however, could not provide soldiers or pay tribute. Mongol rule over Russia—which lasted for almost 250 years, from 1240 to about 1480—was fairly mild. The Russians were allowed to keep their language and customs. Local princes who gave obedience and money to their Mongol masters were allowed to keep their titles and their land. The Mongols themselves established a capital at Sarai, on the lower Volga. From there they continued their nomadic ways, camping in winter and moving their herds from pasture to pasture during the summer.

Perhaps the most significant effect of the Mongol conquest on Russia was that the country became isolated from both the Byzantine Empire and Western Europe. As a result, the Eastern Orthodox Church, although strengthening Russian nationalist feelings, turned inward and became increasingly conservative. It emphasized ritual and ceremony rather than behavior. It frowned on education, calling it "a spiritual sin . . . to study astronomy and the books of Greece." The Russian people grew more and more suspicious of foreign ideas. And in fact, very few ideas even reached Russia. During the 1300s, as you know, the Renaissance began in Western Europe, laying the foundation for modern Western civilization. But Mongol rule kept the Russians isolated from the influence of these exciting changes.

1. **Recall**   How did the princes of Moscow rise to prominence?
2. **How and Why**   How did the Kievan Rus come to adopt the Eastern Orthodox religion? What significance did the Orthodox Church have in Kievan Rus?
3. **Critical Thinking**   How did Iaroslav's division of Kievan Russia lead to its downfall?

Just as Kiev was the center of the first Russian state, Moscow was the center of the second Russian state. It is still the capital of the Soviet Union.

The Rise of Moscow

In the early days of Russian history, Moscow was a small, unimportant trading town deep in the northern forest along the Moscow River. During Mongol rule, however, it began to grow in importance.

There were several reasons for this. The first was Moscow's geographic location. Many of the refugees who fled northward from Kiev settled there. Their numbers and their skills helped Moscow become stronger and richer. Second, Moscow's princes were shrewd men. Instead of rebelling against the Mongols, they cooperated with their new rulers and soon were administering the other city-states, collecting taxes and drafting soldiers for the Mongols. Moscow's princes also adopted the principle of primogeniture—passing the throne from father to oldest son—instead of dividing the land among all the sons. In this way, the princes preserved what they acquired. They also enlarged Moscow's territory by marrying well, by buying land from boyars impoverished by war, and by accepting tribute in the form of forests and villages rather than money or furs. By the 1300s, Moscow was Russia's chief principality.

In 1378 Prince Dimitri of Moscow refused to pay the Mongols their usual tribute. Instead, he raised an army of 150,000 men and attacked the Mongols on the banks of the Don River. Although half his soldiers were killed, he won a tremendous victory, and Mongol influence in Russia dwindled to almost nothing. It was Dimitri Donskoy—Dimitri of the Don—who tore down the wooden and earthen walls surrounding Moscow and replaced them with a **kremlin**, or fortress, made of stone.

Ivan III the Great

The man who actually founded the second Russian state was Ivan III the Great (1462–1505). He was determined to "gather the Russian land" and rule over all Orthodox Russians. He began by conquering or buying Novgorod and the other city-states. He also recaptured much of the land west of the Dnieper River that had been conquered in the 1300s by the Lithuanians and the Poles.

In 1472 Ivan III married Zoe, the niece of the last Byzantine emperor. Ivan III used the marriage to claim for himself the personal power of a Byzantine emperor. Like the emperor, he said that he received his right to rule directly from God. He assumed the Byzantine title of autocrat—a ruler with complete power over his subjects—and became Autocrat of All the Russias. He also called himself tsar—a monarch who owes allegiance to no one.

Zoe—who changed her name to Sofia—brought several elements of Byzantine culture to Moscow. Under her influence, palaces, cathedrals, and mansions of stone began to replace those made of wood. Courtiers began wearing garments of silk, and manners became important in obtaining government office.

The marriage between Ivan III and Sofia greatly strengthened the ties between the tsar and the Eastern Orthodox Church. The Church now regarded Moscow as the "Third Rome." The first Rome had fallen to corruption and foreign invasion. The second Rome—Constantinople—had been conquered by the infidel Turks. Moscow now inherited their position as the center of the true faith.

In 1480 Ivan III the Great warned the weakened Mongols not to bother his country or its people any more. Russia was now an independent nation, with a monarch who held absolute power over both church and state.

Ivan IV the Dread

Ivan IV, whose long reign lasted from 1533 to 1584, was known as Ivan Grozny or Ivan the Dread (sometimes mistakenly translated as Ivan the Terrible). The first 27 years of his reign were filled with actions that won him the love of the Russian people. But during the last 24 years of his reign—after the death of his wife, a member of the Romanov family—it was said that "his mind...turned to the nature of the wild beast and he became a traitor to his own country."

Ivan IV began his reign by revising Russia's laws and encouraging local self-government. He appointed a special minister to hear his subjects' grievances. He welcomed English merchants to his court and set up direct trade relations with England. He invited foreign artisans, physicians, and scholars to Russia. He broke the power of the old noble class and encouraged the rise of a new class of military-service landholders known as the **gentry**. The gentry received land from the tsar in return for military service in time of need.

After learning the use of gunpowder from Western Europeans, Ivan IV sent his armies eastward. He drove the Mongols from along the middle Volga and established Russian rule over the steppe as far south as the Caspian Sea. However, his attempt to expand Russia's borders westward to the Baltic Sea failed. He was stopped by the Poles and the Swedes.

From boyhood, Ivan IV had been surrounded by intrigue and attempts at assassination. He had always been somewhat unpredictable in his behavior. His wife's death in 1560 apparently removed a major restraining influence on him. Gradually, Ivan IV began to trust no one. People whom he suspected of disloyalty were tortured by being roasted over slow fires or impaled on sharp stakes. Their families and even their animals were killed. Under orders from the tsar, security police roamed the countryside with full powers to punish suspected traitors. Wearing black uniforms and riding black horses, the police struck fear into the populace. In 1581, in a fit of rage, Ivan IV hit his elder son and heir so hard with his steel-pointed staff that the young prince died. The tsar himself died three years later.

Boris Godunov is the subject of an opera by the nineteenth-century composer Moussorgsky.

The Time of Troubles

Ivan IV was succeeded by his second son, the feeble-minded Fedor, whose chief joy was ringing church bells. However, the real ruler of Russia was Fedor's brother-in-law, Boris Godunov.

For 14 years, all went well. Ambassadors came to Moscow from all the nations of Western Europe, seeking trade agreements and military alliances against the expanding Ottoman Empire. Silks, spices, and other goods from China and Southeast Asia were sold in the city's great bazaar. Hundreds of churches dotted the skyline, and dozens of suburbs, complete with orchards and meadows, stretched into the surrounding countryside.

Far to the east, groups of Russians were moving farther and farther into Asia. The process had started some 200 years earlier, when monks from the Holy Trinity-St. Sergius Monastery north of Moscow set up new monasteries in the forest. The monks were followed by hunters, fur trappers, peasants tired of paying taxes, and especially by Cossacks. The Cossacks were bands of frontiersmen who lived along the Don, Dnieper, and Volga rivers. A mixture of Slavs, Mongols, and Turks, they were tough, disciplined fighters. By 1572 they had crossed the Ural Mountains and were making their way eastward across Siberia toward the Pacific Ocean.

In 1598 Fedor died without an heir, and the dynasty Rurik had established in 862 came to an end. Boris Godunov was elected tsar by a hand-picked assembly. But Tsar Boris, like Ivan IV before him, saw opposition everywhere and he began to rule harshly, confiscating property and executing his opponents.

Then, beginning in 1601, one trouble after another hit Russia. First the grain harvest failed for three successive years. Famine was followed by a plague in which thousands of Russians perished. After Boris died in 1605, a series of false pretenders laid claim to the throne. The boyars struggled with the landholders for power, there was a mass uprising of peasants and Cossacks, and an army of Poles and Lithuanians took advantage of the chaos to invade Russia and capture Moscow. The country appeared doomed.

SECTION 2 REVIEW

1. **Recall** What city became the center of the second Russian state? Who founded the second Russian state?

2. **How and Why** How was Ivan III able to gain complete control over his subjects?

3. **Critical Thinking** How do you think the Moscow princes' attitude of cooperation toward the Mongols aided them in eventually freeing Moscow from Mongol rule?

Russia was saved by the Russian people. Alarmed at the prospect of another foreign conquest, the Russians rallied against the Poles. Everyone—boyars, other merchants, Cossacks, priests, and peasants—joined in. In 1612, the Poles in Moscow surrendered to a Russian army. And in 1613, an assembly of nobles chose Mikhail Romanov—a relative of Ivan the Dread's wife—as the country's new tsar. The Romanov dynasty lasted for a little more than 300 years, until the Revolution of 1917.

A Feudal Society

Mikhail ruled from 1613 to 1645. He was succeeded by his son Alexis I, who ruled until 1676. The two tsars restored law and order to Russia. At the same time, they created a society that stood in sharp contrast to that of Western Europe.

You recall that after the Black Death, serfdom in Western Europe disappeared. Trade and industry grew, and with it the economic and political power of the middle class. By the late 1600s, the middle class in England had carried out the Glorious Revolution.

In Russia the situation was almost the opposite. To maintain themselves in power, the Romanovs needed the support of the nobility. Ivan the Dread had weakened the old boyar class by taking away their political power and often their lands. Many he had killed. Accordingly, the Romanovs turned to the new gentry class for help in running the government, as well as for military service. They paid the gentry by giving them land to use during their lifetime. In order to make money from this land, the gentry increased taxes on their peasant tenants. Faced with the prospect of paying double taxes—to both the tsar who owned the land and the gentry who used the land—the peasants ran away,

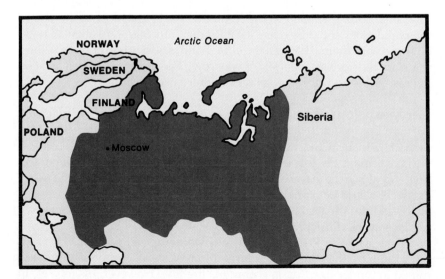

■ Russia, 1613

mostly to Siberia and the Ukraine. Without peasants, the gentry could neither fulfill their military obligations nor avoid economic ruin. So the landlords asked the government to prevent the peasants from leaving the land. In 1646 most formerly free peasants became bound to the soil as serfs. They had no legal rights and could be sold or traded at will.

Government control was extended over the middle and working classes as well. If a manufacturer built up a business, for example, the tsar simply took it over as a royal monopoly. Then he ordered the gentry to send entire villages of serfs to work in the government-owned factories and mines.

Peter the Great

Under Vladimir I and Iaroslav the Wise, Russia had been part of the European community of nations. Under the Mongols, it had been cut off from Western Europe. Now, under Alexis's son Peter, Russia once again turned its face to the West.

Peter I the Great became tsar in 1689 at the age of 17 and ruled until 1725. He was very tall—six feet eight inches—with dark hair and eyes. He loved eating, drinking, dancing, and setting off fireworks. He also loved to work with his hands. He learned 15 trades, including carpentry, cobbling, dentistry, and stonemasonry. Strong and energetic, he had a violent temper and could be as cruel as Ivan the Dread. Peter reportedly tortured his eldest son to death because he suspected him of treason. Peter I considered himself a servant of the state. He gave the greater part of his income to the government and never spent public funds on pleasure. He died as a result of rescuing some soldiers from drowning in the icy Neva River. This was the tsar who was determined to make Russia a modern nation.

Before Peter's reign, Russian rulers and ordinary people alike had been fearful and suspicious of foreigners, whom they knew chiefly from invasions. Foreigners had to live in quarters segregated from the rest of the population, and only a few loyal Russian officials were allowed to do business with them. Peter, on the other hand, spent many of his boyhood years in the foreign quarter of Moscow. There he developed a keen interest in Western technology and military organization.

European Journey Eight years after becoming tsar, Peter visited Western Europe for 18 months. He did not travel in the grand manner of a monarch. Instead, he went under an assumed name, disguised as an ordinary sailor. He worked for a time in the shipyards of Holland and England, where he learned about map making, navigation, and the use of guns. He studied canal building and munitions manufacture. He observed how Western Europeans dressed. He even noted that they used napkins at the dinner table.

Peter and the Russians with him were amazed at what they saw. They realized that Russia was far behind Western Europe. Peter determined to modernize Russia within his lifetime. However, his interest in

the West did not extend to democratic systems of government. He was interested only in technological advances. He had no intention of endangering his personal power.

Modernization Efforts   Peter began his campaign "to sever his subjects from their Asiatic customs" by ordering his nobles to cut off their beards, stop wearing long coats, and learn to speak either French or German. He forbade the seclusion of noblewomen and the wearing of veils in public. He also forbade the sons of nobles to marry until they were able to read, write, and do arithmetic.

These changes affected only the nobility. Most of Peter's other changes, however, had a much wider impact.

Determined to build up Russia's army and navy, Peter saw the need for a strong economy to support the military. Accordingly, he set up iron foundries to produce weapons, textile factories to produce cloth for uniforms, and so on. He promoted prospecting for coal, iron, and other mineral resources. He hired chemists and engineers from Western Europe to come to Russia to help manufacture goods. He also established a standing army of 200,000 soldiers who were drafted for life. Officers were promoted on the basis of merit rather than birth.

The tsar copied Western European forms of administration. He divided the bureaucracy into departments, each of which was run by an official loyal to the tsar. Here, as in the army, commoners were admitted and promotion was by merit. Nobles who were not in the army or navy were required to serve in the civil service in return for their titles and lands.

Men were able to keep their beards if they paid a tax and carried a beard license.

Among the new government departments was one called the Holy Governing Synod. It was designed to run the affairs of the Eastern Orthodox Church in place of the patriarch. This change in the Eastern Church's operation aroused great opposition. Opponents known as Old Believers even referred to the tsar as the Antichrist. But Peter wanted his control over the Church to be absolute.

To further Westernization, Peter substituted Arabic numbers for the less workable Slavic ones. He ordered the old alphabet simplified. He encouraged the printing of books and also instituted the use of the Julian calendar. Until then, Russians had used an ancient calendar which at that time placed them in the year 7208. The Julian calendar was already incorrect by 11 days in 1700, but at least the year was the same as the Gregorian calendar used throughout Western Europe.

Foreign Policy   Although Russia was already three times as large as the rest of Europe, Peter the Great spent most of his reign fighting for still more land. His goal was to obtain warm-water ports—ports that were open year-round.

The tsar's main thrust was to the northwest. There, Poland and Sweden blocked Russian access to the Baltic Sea. Assuming Sweden's 18-year-old king Charles XII to be the easier opponent, Peter signed a secret treaty with Poland and attacked Sweden.

The Great Northern War lasted from 1700 to 1721. At first the Swedes defeated the Russians. Then Peter's modernization of the army and the navy paid off. By 1709 Russia had replaced Sweden as the major power in northern Europe. By the end of the war, Russia had gained considerable territory along the Baltic coast, including Estonia and Latvia.

St. Petersburg   Louis XIV of France had built a new palace, Versailles. In 1703 Peter the Great—convinced of his eventual victory over Sweden—decided to build a new city on land captured from the enemy. It would be his "window to Europe" and a fitting capital for the great European power that Russia was in the process of becoming.

Accordingly, Peter chose a site at the place where the Neva River empties into the Baltic Sea. Although the land was marshy, the climate damp, and the site itself hundreds of miles (kilometers) from anywhere, ships could sail directly from St. Petersburg to the ports of Western Europe. (The city was renamed Petrograd during World War I and Leningrad after the Russian Revolution.)

The construction of St. Petersburg demonstrated the tsar's approach to many of Russia's problems. Nobles were ordered to live there year round instead of staying on their estates. In that way, the tsar could keep his eye on them. Merchants and artisans were assigned to special quarters and required to pay for the city's streets, canals, bridges, and parks. And, of course, peasants were drafted without pay to do the construction work. Many peasants died from accidents, disease, and the lack of food. But in the end the tsar got what he wanted—a city where Western culture, thought, and achievements merged with those of Russia.

Catherine the Great

For 75 years after Peter the Great died in 1725, powerful nobles and regiments of soldiers stationed in St. Petersburg seated and unseated the Romanov rulers. Only two lasted long on the throne. Both were women.

The first was Peter's younger daughter Elizabeth, who ruled from 1741 to 1762. Elizabeth's reign is noted chiefly for Russia's increasing participation in the affairs of Western Europe, especially the struggles between Austria and Prussia to determine which would be the dominant German state. Elizabeth also built the first theater in Russia and established the French language, clothing styles, and other aspects of culture firmly at court and among the aristocracy.

Elizabeth chose as her successor her nephew Peter, a grandson of Peter the Great. As Peter's wife, the empress selected Sophia, a princess from a minor German state. Sophia—who was extremely intelligent and ambitious—learned Russian, converted to the Eastern Orthodox religion (unlike her Lutheran husband), and took the name Catherine. Peter was crude, incompetent, and mentally unstable. A few months after he became Tsar Peter III in 1762, several regiments of soldiers led by one of Catherine's lovers placed her on the throne. Peter III died mysteriously a few days later.

Catherine II reigned from 1762 to 1796. She hoped to make her adopted country a major European power. During her long rule, she accomplished many of her goals and earned the name Catherine the Great.

Expansionism

Catherine greatly admired Peter the Great and his expansionist policies. She set out to imitate him. To the south, her armies warred against the Ottoman Turks and took from them the northern

During Catherine's rule Russia continued to expand abroad, while many new towns were built at home.

Built for Peter, the Great Palace near Leningrad was enlarged during Catherine's reign by Bartolomeo Rastrelli. World War II left the palace and gardens in ruin. The Soviet government rebuilt and restored them.

coast of the Black Sea. Russia also gained the long-sought right of free passage for its ships through the Black Sea and into the Mediterranean Sea.

To the west, Russia joined Austria and Prussia in the three partitions of Poland that took place in 1772, 1793, and 1795 and removed Poland from the map of Europe until after World War I. Russia received the lion's share of Poland's territory and population, including half of Lithuania. Catherine's soldiers also took the Crimean Peninsula from the remnants of the Mongols and added the entire Ukraine to Russia.

These conquests brought many new peoples into Russia. Catherine wanted them to become part of Russian society. To accomplish this, she set up a program called **Russification**. This meant that the people had to speak Russian and adopt Russian ways. The conquered peoples fought back in an effort to keep their ethnic identities and customs. Nevertheless, Russification remained an official government policy.

Domestic Policy   Catherine read and wrote Russian, German, and French and was a patron of the arts. Like Elizabeth, she admired the French and took them as her model. She hoped to make the Russian court as elegant and splendid as that of France. She corresponded with some of the greatest thinkers of the Enlightenment, including the philosophe Voltaire. For a time she saw herself as an enlightened despot, a ruler who would use her absolute power for the benefit of her subjects. She tinkered with reform of the government and even considered the possibility of emancipation, or freedom, for the serfs. Then a major rebellion broke out—and Catherine's reform ideas were not realized.

The rebellion lasted from 1773 to 1775. It included fugitive serfs, forced laborers from the mines, dissatisfied clergy, and Cossacks. The rebel leader, Yemelyan Pugachev, even posed as Catherine's dead husband, Peter III. Promising to free the serfs and hang the landlords, Pugachev had some initial success. Then Catherine recalled her best generals from the war against the Turks, and the rebellion was crushed. Pugachev was brought to Moscow in an iron cage and executed. It was the greatest uprising in Russia before the 1917 Revolution.

Pugachev's rebellion frightened Catherine, who realized that it might have overturned her rule. No longer did she believe it wise to loosen the bonds of the serfs. She needed the support of the nobility, who would never tolerate emancipation. So she distributed royal and Church lands to important nobles and gifted them with hundreds of thousands of serfs. She extended serfdom into Russia's conquered territory in the Ukraine and the Crimea. She also released all the nobles from the service requirements that Peter the Great had imposed.

The French Revolution of 1789—with its ideas of liberty, equality, and fraternity—gave Catherine II further reason to give up reform. By overthrowing the monarchy and beheading their king, the French revolutionaries threatened the idea of monarchy everywhere. Many nations went to war against France, but Catherine kept Russia out of the conflict in order not to endanger her absolute power.

fraternity:
a feeling of closeness because of shared interests and goals

Catherine the Great died in 1796, leaving behind a large and powerful Russian nation that spanned both Europe and Asia. It was also a nation in which most people lived in misery under nobles who cared nothing for their welfare.

Catherine the Great had intended for her grandson Alexander to succeed her, but she died before signing the decree. Paul, the neurotic son she despised, became tsar. In 1801, however, palace guards staged the last palace revolution under the Romanovs and strangled Paul. Alexander I assumed the throne.

Alexander I

Catherine had raised Alexander to be an enlightened despot, and he was well-educated in Western thought by his Swiss tutor. At the same time, his father reared him in the military life and gave him a love of power. As one of his friends said of the new tsar, "He would gladly give freedom to everyone, if everyone would freely do exactly what he wanted them to do."

Alexander I began his reign with several reforms. He freed many political prisoners, abolished torture, allowed foreign books to be sold, founded several universities, and even formed a committee to draw up a constitution. The tsar pushed reforms aside, however, when Napoleon threatened the peace of Europe.

As you know, Russia played a major role in defeating Napoleon and also in the peace conference, the Congress of Vienna, that followed. Alexander I returned home from Vienna with the cheers of Europe ringing in his ears. But his country was in serious trouble. The war had destroyed dozens of towns and villages and cost hundreds of thousands of lives. In addition, many young army officers had seen firsthand the industrial and political progress of Western Europe. They wanted Alexander to return to the reforms he had dropped in 1805: a constitution, the emancipation of the serfs, and independence for Poland. When Alexander ignored them, they formed secret societies to work for reform.

SECTION

4

Unrest at Home

Constant war had turned Alexander I's interest from the philosophy of the Enlightenment to Christianity. What were some ideas of the Enlightenment?

The Iron Tsar

In 1825 Alexander I died and was succeeded by his younger brother Nicholas I. Nicholas was not popular, especially among the reformers. On December 26, when the Russian troops were to take the oath of loyalty to the new tsar, they revolted. This revolt became known as the Decembrist uprising. The revolt, however, was quickly put down. Five leaders were hanged, and the rest were exiled for life to Siberia, many at hard labor in the coal mines.

Nicholas I reacted to the Decembrist uprising by clamping down on all personal freedom and individual thought in Russia. He expanded the power of the secret police and imposed strict censorship throughout the empire. There was even a separate government department to watch the censors! Only one religion—the Eastern Orthodox religion—was recognized. All other religions were persecuted. Anyone who criticized either the government or the Church was sent at once to Siberia.

Yet despite the tsar's efforts to tighten control and stifle change, unrest in Russia continued. The **intelligentsia**, or intellectuals, smuggled in books from Western Europe and held meetings to discuss reform. And about every other week of every year of Nicholas's reign, from 1825 to 1855, another group of serfs rose in revolt—burning their owner's barns, murdering a brutal overseer, or banding together to resist the payment of taxes.

The Tsar-Liberator

In 1853 the Crimean War broke out between Russia and the Ottoman Empire. The British, French, and Austrians helped the Turks defeat the Russians. Nicholas I died during the war. His son Alexander II, who reigned from 1855 to 1881, quickly made terms with the victors. Alexander was stunned by his country's defeat. Not only did Russia lose land in the Balkans and a great deal of prestige in Europe, it also lost 250,000 soldiers because there was not enough food, supplies, and equipment for the army. It seemed obvious that Russia must increase its agricultural and industrial production and improve its transportation system. In addition, as you have learned, during this period liberal revolts were breaking out in many nations of Western Europe. Alexander felt that, if Russia were to avoid revolution, it would have to reform. The most obvious reform was to free the 50 million serfs who supported the 1 million nobles, gentry, and clergy of Russia.

Accordingly, in 1861, after long preparation, Alexander II signed the Emancipation Edict abolishing serfdom in Russia. Peasants were no longer bound to the soil. Nobles could no longer flog a peasant to death or tell a peasant whom to marry. But freedom did not necessarily improve the former serfs' economic condition. For one thing, the land they had farmed was not given to them outright. Instead, they had to pay the government for it over a 49-year period. Many peasants were unable to do so; they either fell into debt or became tenant farmers. Also, peasants often did not receive enough land to provide a decent living. Furthermore, about half the land was not assigned to individuals as private property but to the community as a whole, the *mir*. And the elected councils of the mir reassigned the land to families. Thus, there was no individual incentive to adopt better farming methods. In addition, house serfs did not receive any land at all and had to find work or starve.

Alexander's reign brought many other reforms to Russia. He abolished the censorship of books, newspapers, and magazines. He reformed the courts by introducing trial by jury and by publicizing court proceedings. He reduced the period of military service from 25 years to 6 years, and insisted that members of the armed forces be taught how to read and write. He also extended the draft to everyone, not just the peasants.

Alexander established town councils with elected representatives. The councils were responsible for such new projects as building local roads, establishing hospitals and elementary schools, and providing relief for the poor. Alexander also built railroads, encouraged new industries, and organized a banking system and joint-stock companies.

On the foreign scene, Russia turned its attention eastward. In 1864 Russian troops captured the cities of Tashkent and Samarkand in central Asia. (This area now contains five of the 15 republics of the Soviet Union.) Soon after, the troops reached the frontiers of Afghanistan and Persia. They seized territory from China all the way to the Pacific coast. And they obtained the Pacific island of Sakhalin from Japan in 1875. The only area where the Russian Empire retreated was in the Western Hemisphere. In 1867 Russia sold Alaska to the United States for $7 million. Yet despite all these accomplishments, unrest in Russia continued. Seven attempts were made on Alexander's life before a terrorist's bomb killed him in 1881.

Repression

Alexander II's son, Alexander III, had none of his father's liberal leanings. Harsh, narrow-minded, and reactionary, he believed Russia would be destroyed unless the ideas of Western Europe were shut out. To the new tsar, the only way to save Russia from anarchy was to clamp down on the people. "Autocracy, Orthodoxy, and Nationality" became the watchwords of his government.

Alexander III restored press censorship and increased the powers of the secret police. Once again, anyone who spoke or wrote against the government was arrested and sent to Siberia without a trial. Everyone was expected to follow the Eastern Orthodox religion, and those who did not were regarded as traitors. Nationalities that had hitherto enjoyed local freedom—such as the Poles, Ukrainians, Finns, and Mongols—were required to speak Russian, be ruled by Great Russians, and become as Russian as possible.

Alexander III persecuted the Jews in particular. Many Jews from Western Europe had settled in Poland during the 1500s and in the Ukraine during the 1600s. Since the Jews were often the tax collectors and administrators for the absentee landlords, they were hated by the peasants. During the 1700s the Cossacks killed thousands of Jews because they represented the enemy. When these areas became part of Russia, the ill-feeling against the Jews continued.

Nicholas I tightened control over Russia. His son, Alexander II, tried to enact reforms. Neither was successful. What do you think might account for this?

Alexander III encouraged this. The Jews made useful scapegoats for the country's social unrest. They were blamed for everything from high taxes to cholera epidemics. Government troops organized dozens of **pogroms**—a Russian word meaning devastation—in which Jews were murdered and their houses burned. Some 2 million Jews fled from Russia between 1881 and World War I. Some went to Palestine. The majority settled in the United States. Among those who remained were several who were to become leaders of the Russian Revolution.

Economic Developments

When Alexander III died in 1894, his successor, Nicholas II, continued the government's repressive policies. But certain economic developments were taking place that eventually made it impossible to stem the tide of reform.

First, Russia's peasants were growing poorer. Population had increased, which meant there were more mouths to feed. It also meant that peasants were forced to subdivide their farms so that each son would have some land. That usually made the farms too small to be economically productive. The government set up banks to lend the peasants money to buy or rent more land. Soon the top 20 percent of the peasants owned more than half the land. This increased agricultural output. But it infuriated those peasants who lost their land.

Second, Russia was industrializing. There were textile factories in Moscow and iron and steel plants in St. Petersburg. The production of coal and other mineral resources was booming. The Trans-Siberian Railroad was only one of the many railroads that were beginning to cross the countryside.

As it had in Western Europe, however, industrialization brought problems. Wages were low, and the typical work day was 12 to 14 hours long. Many families lived in a single room. Many workers did not even have a room in which to live, but slept on the factory floor. Unions were illegal, and worker protests were forcibly suppressed by the police.

Yet the factories were hotbeds of unrest. One reason was their size. About half the Russian proletariat worked in super-factories of more than one thousand workers. The Russians set up such large factories to compensate for their late start in industrializing. As a result, political reformers found a concentrated audience for their ideas. You will learn about this in the next chapter.

SECTION 4 REVIEW

1. **Recall**   What caused the Decembrist uprising?
2. **How and Why**   How did Russia's defeat in the Crimean War affect Tsar Alexander II's policies?
3. **Critical Thinking**   Why did the liberal movement in Russia make little progress during the 1800s?

Reviewing People, Places, and Things

Identify, define, or explain each of the following:

Khazars	Boris Godunov
Novgorod	Cossacks
Rurik	Michael Romanov
boyar	St. Petersburg
Vladimir I	Yemelyan Pugachev
Iaroslav the Wise	Crimean War
tsar	Emancipation Edict
Third Rome	mir

Map Study

Using the maps on pages 753 and 761, determine the answers to the following questions:

1. What do the appearance of Kiev on the map of 1064, and Moscow on the map of 1613 signify?
2. What coastline had the Russian state acquired by 1613?

Understanding Facts and Ideas

1. Of what importance were the Varangians?
2. What advantage did the city of Kiev have for becoming a trade center?
3. Describe the social organization of the Kievan city-state.
4. What effect did Mongol rule have on Russia and its people?
5. What steps did Ivan III take to create a Russian state?
6. **a.** What was the gentry class? **b.** How did it come to exist in Russia?
7. **a.** How did Ivan the Dread extend Russian rule? **b.** How did this increase his own power?
8. **a.** How did Peter the Great develop an interest in the West? **b.** What elements of Western culture interested him?
9. **a.** How did the Enlightenment influence Catherine the Great? **b.** What caused Catherine to give up reforms?
10. What economic reforms did Alexander II make in Russia?

Developing Critical Thinking

Expressing Your Opinion Peter the Great wanted to advance Russia's power and greatness. Which of his changes helped Russia most? Which might have harmed Russia? Do you think he deserves to be called "Peter the Great"? Explain your answer.

Writing About History

Role Playing The year is 1812. You are Napoleon. You must teach Tsar Alexander I a lesson. He looks down on you for being an upstart monarch. He does not support your Continental System and allows Russians to trade with your enemy, the hated British. Using your knowledge about the geography of Eastern Europe and Russia, Tsar Alexander I, and Western European history, determine what is the best course of action to force Alexander to act as you wish. Would you use war or diplomacy? Study maps in atlases and read the histories of the Napoleonic Wars. Develop your plan and write a report.

Applying Your Skills to History

Writing an Essay Write an essay on the reign of Catherine the Great. Point out the difficulties she had to overcome in becoming empress. How did her background and means of coming to power affect her domestic policies? Was she really the enlightened despot that the philosophes envisioned? What were her accomplishments? How do they resemble those of Peter the Great? Does Catherine deserve being called "the Great"?

Communism in the Soviet Union

The Russians had borrowed technology and minor practices in government from the West since the time of the early Romanovs. Russians serving with the armies that defeated Napoleon also learned about Western ideas. During the 1800s and early 1900s, more ideas spread to Russia. These included basic human rights: the right to decent living conditions, the right to participate in government, and the right to live without fear. The new ideas inflamed peasants and workers who were already angry and desperate. Revolutionaries determined to change the government worked to gain widespread support among the people.

As you study this chapter, think about these questions:

* What were the causes of the Russian Revolution?

* How does communism in theory differ from communism as practiced in the Soviet Union?

* How successful have the Communists been in solving the problems of the Soviet people?

* What forces have shaped Soviet foreign policy?

The theory of **communism** was originally developed by two German revolutionaries, Karl Marx and Friedrich Engels. The *Communist Manifesto* of 1848 and *Das Kapital*, finished by Engels after Marx's death in 1883, contain their revolutionary philosophy. In *What Is To Be Done?*, published in 1902, the Russian revolutionary, V. I. Lenin, formulated a plan of action for the working class to take over the government and establish Marx's communism. Together, their philosophies and strategies have served as the basis for revolutionary movements throughout the world during the 1900s.

Communist Theory

Marx and Engels formulated a philosophy of history based on economics and the **class struggle.** Different economic systems developed during each period of history. The first was based on slavery, the next on serfdom, and the last on capitalism. In each period, one class—the slaveowner, the feudal lord, and the capitalist—was the exploiter. At the same time, the exploited classes—slaves, serfs, and laborers—were struggling to gain a greater share of wealth and power. Marx saw history as a continuous class struggle between the "haves" and the "have nots."

But Marx believed that a final struggle was coming. It would take place between the capitalists and the **proletariat** (proh-luh-TAYR-ee-uht), or workers. Under capitalism, the means of production—factories, railroads, machines, and land—are privately owned. Under communism, the means of production would be owned by the workers.

Marx predicted that the workers would win the struggle against the capitalists and seize the means of production. The new working-class rulers would set up a **dictatorship of the proletariat**. State and class distinctions would wither and die. The perfect system—communism—would then exist.

Marx argued that communism would come first only to highly industrialized countries like Great Britain or Germany. It was necessary to have a revolutionary middle class, the bourgeoisie, end privileges based on tradition and birth. The bourgeoisie were the class of the factory owners. By the early 1900s, Russia was just beginning to become industrialized. Its middle class was small but growing. Yet communism was first put into practice in Russia—an agricultural society.

The Road to Revolution in Russia

The last tsar of Russia was Nicholas II, who reigned from 1894 to 1917. Nicholas was charming and intelligent, a good family man, and a conservative like his father, Alexander III. Nicholas II, however, lacked his father's strength of character. He was not a good judge of people and was easily influenced. It was said that his decisions were those of whomever he last spoke with. His wife Alexandra had a strong influence over him. Like Catherine the Great, she was a German princess who converted to

The last of the Romanovs sat for this family portrait in 1913, 300 years after the first Romanov took the throne. The family was executed in 1918.

the Eastern Orthodox faith. Unlike Catherine, Alexandra showed little wisdom and her actions helped bring about the downfall of the Romanovs. Neither Nicholas nor Alexandra understood the great social and economic problems facing Russia.

Industrial Expansion   During the first ten years of Nicholas II's reign, industrial expansion increased 100 percent. The total value of industrial output exceeded that of agriculture. Yet industry employed only ten percent of the work force while eight times as many people worked on the land. The fastest growing industry was textile manufacturing, followed by such heavy industries as mining and metallurgy.

Foreign capital was important in developing Russian industries. Some 90 percent of the mining and 42 percent of metallurgical investments were foreign. Most of these investors came from France, Great Britain, and Germany. The French held about 80 percent and the British about 14 percent of the Russian government's debt. However, Russian investors still provided the largest share of the capital needed for Russian industrialization.

Russia still had to import such important goods as machine tools, electrical equipment, and precision instruments. The lack of these goods affected Russia's trade balance and severely handicapped the nation's war effort during World War I.

The economic growth brought discontent and unrest among the growing class of industrial workers. Strikes were common in the 1890s. Discontent continued among the peasants as well. No longer serfs, they remained unhappy with their inability to obtain clear title to the land. It was natural that the economic dislocations and discontent should bring about the creation of political parties.

New Political Parties

The first and largest party was the Socialist Revolutionary party, formed in 1901. It was formed in response to dissatisfaction in the countryside. The aim of the Socialist Revolutionaries was to seize all land from the large landholders and redistribute it to the peasants. Unfortunately, many members of this party were terrorists. They carried out assassinations of important people in the government and even members of the imperial family. This obscured the real value of the Socialist Revolutionary party's essentially humanitarian political platform.

A second party formed of middle-class liberals was called the Union of Liberation. It grew out of its members' association in district and provincial assemblies called *zemstvos* (ZEMPST-vohs). Founded in the 1860s during the reign of Alexander II, the *zemstvos* had provided for public roads, public health, and education. Through their association in the *zemstvos*, the members of the Union of Liberation represented many points of view. They came from many professions and were either Slavophiles (lovers of things Slavic) or Westernizers. The Union of Liberation wanted Russia to have democracy and a constitution. All supported human rights and individualism.

The third party was the Russian Social Democratic Workers' Party. It was formed in London by exiled supporters of Karl Marx's theories. In 1903 the Social Democrats split into two **factions**. The Mensheviks (MEN-chuh-viks) favored gradual change. The Bolsheviks (BOHL-shuh-viks) wanted immediate revolution and the establishment of a dictatorship of the proletariat.

The Bolshevik leader was Vladimir Ilyich Lenin (LEN-uhn). Lenin's political pamphlet, *What Is To Be Done?*, described how the party should achieve power. He did not favor a mass party like the Social Revolutionaries. Instead Lenin said that only a strong, disciplined revolutionary party—the **vanguard** of the proletariat—could educate and lead the working class toward the revolution.

Russo-Japanese War

Industrial growth slowed somewhat during the early 1900s. Economic conditions throughout Russia grew worse. Yet Nicholas II insisted on expanding Russian territory eastward. He wanted a warm-water port on the Pacific. There Russia ran into opposition with Japan over spheres of influence in Manchuria and Korea. Efforts to settle the matter peacefully failed, so in 1904 the two countries went to war.

The Russo-Japanese War went badly for the Russians. The Japanese defeated the Russian armies in Manchuria and established control of the seas. The Russians next sent their Baltic Sea fleet all the way to the Pacific. At the Battle of Tsushima in 1905, the Japanese decisively defeated it. The Treaty of Portsmouth (New Hampshire) ended Russian expansion in Asia. The Russians were defeated by a nation they considered a third-rate power. The defeat brought opposition to the tsar out into the open.

Bloody Sunday

On a Sunday morning in January 1905, the workers of St. Petersburg, with their wives and children, marched in a peaceful procession to the tsar's palace. They wanted to ask the tsar for better working conditions and better government. Nicholas gave the order to fire on the marchers and then left. Hundreds were wounded.

Russians across the country were shocked. Thousands of workers went on strike, and sailors on the battleship *Potemkin* mutinied. In St. Petersburg and Moscow, workers formed **soviets**—the Russian word for "councils"—to organize and direct the strikes. Mensheviks and Bolsheviks were prominent among the organizers. A **general strike** brought the nation to a standstill. No mail was delivered, shops were closed, and trains stopped running. The spontaneous strikes had become the Revolution of 1905.

The strikes frightened Nicholas II. His prime minister, Count Witte (VYEET-tyay), told the tsar that he would either have to establish a military dictatorship or create a national assembly. Against his will, the tsar promised to grant universal manhood suffrage and establish an assembly called the Duma (DOO-muh). It was expected that the Duma would make laws and write a constitution for Russia. The Duma met for four sessions from 1906 to 1916, but it had no power and proved to be little more than a platform from which to criticize the tsar and his government. The tsar and his officials undermined the Duma's attempts at reform.

Stolypin's Reforms   In 1906 Peter Stolypin (stuh-LIP-yin) succeeded Witte as prime minister. Stolypin saw that the Revolution of 1905 threatened the stability of the state. He believed that stability could be achieved if the peasants could be made supporters of the tsar. They must be drawn away from revolutionary action. The best way to do this was to give them land.

Russians flee as soldiers fire on their march to the Winter Palace. This was Bloody Sunday, the beginning of the first nationwide Russian revolt.

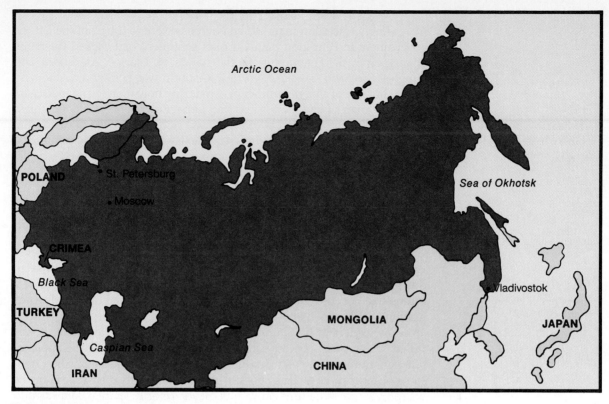

■ **Russia, 1914**

Since the emancipation of the serfs in 1861, most peasants still did not own land. The land was still owned by the mir. Stolypin had laws passed that freed the peasants from the constraints imposed by the mir. The peasants were to be given their land in a single piece, not in scattered plots that would be difficult to farm.

Of the 12 million peasants in European Russia, some 6 million petitioned to get land. Unfortunately, the laws were complicated and by 1915 only about 2 million claims had been settled. Lenin said that, had Stolypin's land reforms succeeded, the Bolsheviks might have had to give up on their land reform. The peasants would have become bourgeoisie and strong supporters of the monarchy! Luckily for Lenin, World War I intervened. Not enough peasants had achieved possession of their land outright. They remained dissatisfied. As for Stolypin, he was assassinated in 1911.

The Turning Point   World War I changed the course of Russian history. In the late 1800s, the Russian government had joined an alliance with Great Britain and France. When war against Germany and Austria-Hungary came in 1914, Russia was unprepared. Many soldiers at the battlefront had no weapons. Millions were killed, wounded, or taken prisoner. At home, the war drained the country of its scarce resources. Shortages of food, fuel, and labor hindered Russia's war effort.

The people still looked to the tsar for hope, but they saw an increasingly uncertain man. When Nicholas went to the front, he left the government in Petrograd (anti-German sentiment had caused the name change from St. Petersburg) in the hands of Tsarina Alexandra and Gregory Rasputin (ras-PYOO-tuhn). Rasputin was neither a monk nor a priest, but one of a large number of wandering holy men found in Russia. He was a man of low morals and bad behavior, but he was nonetheless introduced to the tsar and tsarina because of his supposed faith-healing powers. Nicholas and Alexandra's son Alexis suffered from hemophilia, a rare hereditary blood disease. Whatever methods Rasputin used—drugs or hypnosis—seemed to help Alexis. Alexandra became convinced that Rasputin had been sent by God and from then on, she followed his advice. Rasputin's influence on governmental policy and appointments was disastrous for Russia. In 1916 a group of noble conspirators murdered him, but the damage had already been done.

faith-healing powers: the ability to cure illness through prayer

On March 8, 1917, a food riot broke out in Petrograd. This quickly turned into a general strike and marked the beginning of the Russian Revolution. Conditions rapidly grew desperate. Railroad workers made it impossible for the tsar to return to Petrograd. Nicholas abdicated. Romanov rule ended and the family was placed under arrest.

The leaders of the Duma set up a Provisional Government. It was called "provisional" because its decisions would later need the approval of a constitutional convention. Elections would be held later. The Provisional Government faced impossible tasks. It tried to keep Russia in the war and at the same time provide domestic reform. Unrest continued to grow. As the Provisional Government wavered, the soviets became more powerful. They opposed the war and spread feelings of defeatism in the country. Then Lenin stepped to the forefront.

Lenin and the Bolshevik Revolution

Lenin was first acquainted with the revolutionary movement at age 16. Lenin's older brother, Alexander, belonged to a terrorist organization that plotted to kill Tsar Alexander III. He was arrested, proudly admitted his role in the plot, and was hanged in May 1887. After his brother's death, Lenin himself became a revolutionary. In 1896 he was arrested and sent to Siberia for three years. Police photographs of Lenin show a bearded and balding young man.

From Siberia he went into exile in Switzerland where he became the leader of the Bolsheviks. In 1917 the Germans allowed Lenin to return to Russia. They hoped he would foment revolution and take Russia out of the war.

Lenin's View of Marxism   Lenin wrote a great deal on the revolutionary aspects of Marxism. He emphasized that the workers would never be free until the capitalists and their governments had been overthrown by violent revolution. However, the workers needed to be organized and led by trained professional revolutionaries—the Bolsheviks. The Communists have used this argument as a justification for

their power ever since. Unlike Marx, Lenin believed that revolutions could occur in industrially undeveloped countries such as Russia. Lenin fit theory to reality.

Lenin as Revolutionary

The Provisional Government proved unable to improve conditions. Food and fuel shortages continued. Large numbers of soldiers deserted at the front and people continued rioting at home. The Bolsheviks promised "Peace, Bread, and Land," and helped the soviets gain strength. The Provisional Government arrested many Bolsheviks, and Lenin was forced to go into hiding for a time. When he returned, he promised that a Bolshevik government would give land to the peasants. In fact the peasants had already seized most of the land. The Bolsheviks got the soviets to pass a law guaranteeing worker control of the factories. About 80 percent had already done so. And the Bolsheviks wanted to negotiate peace with Germany on the basis of no annexations and no indemnities. The Bolsheviks kept none of these promises, but they were organized as no other group was.

In the meantime, the Provisional Government had scheduled national elections for November 25. Lenin knew that the Bolsheviks would not win a majority. So he devised a daring plan to bring the Bolsheviks to power. On November 6, 1917, the Bolsheviks called a strike.

devised:
made up

This photo of Leon Trotsky at about age 25 is from Russian police files. Trotsky had been arrested by the tsarist government for his activities.

Soldiers, sailors, and armed workers known as the Red Guard marched on government buildings. They arrested Provisional Government officials and took control of the government. They met with little resistance.

Two days later the All-Russian Congress of Soviets met in Petrograd. Those who opposed the Bolsheviks walked out. This left control of the soviets in the hands of the Bolsheviks. When the elections were held later in the month, the Bolsheviks received only one-fourth of the vote. The new assembly duly convened, but Lenin had the Red Guard disperse it. That was Russia's last relatively free election for 73 years. In this manner, the Bolsheviks gained control of Russia. Once in power, they changed their name to Communists.

Peace and Civil War   The Bolsheviks still faced a powerful German army in the west. Lenin had promised peace and his new government now obtained it. However, the Treaty of Brest-Litovsk of March 1918 stripped Russia of the Ukraine, its Polish lands, and its Baltic provinces. But the Bolsheviks were free to fight their enemies at home.

The Communists had to fight to keep and enlarge the power they had seized. Russians fought a bitter civil war for three years. On one side was the Red Army. On the other were the Whites—often several competing armed groups of former army officers, supporters of the tsar, landowners, and political parties opposed to the Communists. Great Britain, France, Japan, and the United States intervened in the civil war on behalf of the Whites. All sent troops and supplies. Nevertheless, the Red Army finally defeated the Whites. The Communists had the advantage of controlling the center of the country from Moscow to Petrograd. By the end of 1920, the Communists ruled all of Russia.

The New Soviet State   Marx's theory maintained that the Communist government would be a dictatorship of the proletariat. However, it soon became clear that the government was a dictatorship of Lenin and the Communist party. To strengthen their power, Lenin and the Communists began eliminating anyone who opposed them. The Communists organized a secret police that was more thorough than that of the tsars. They had Tsar Nicholas II and his family executed to prevent their rescue. Nobles, landlords, and members of the bourgeoisie were murdered.

In 1918 the Soviet constitution was established and the capital was moved to Moscow. The soviets were the basis of local government, and they in turn elected a national congress. The national congress appointed a Council of People's Commissars under the leadership of Lenin. The Communist party was the only political party allowed, so everyone in the government had to be a Communist. The Communist party had a parallel organization. Its Central Committee had a small group, the Political Bureau—**Politburo**—headed by Lenin. Thus, Lenin was the leader of both the government and the Communist party.

The new government took over all the factories, banks, mines, and land. In Communist theory, the workers owned the factories and the land, but in practice the government controlled everything. Under the

Communists, workers received low wages and were little better off than they had been under the tsars. In 1921 Lenin realized that his system of communism was not working. He took a step backward to capitalism with his New Economic Policy (NEP). Under the NEP, the peasants were allowed to keep some of their produce and sell it themselves. Factory workers received higher wages and some shops were even returned to private ownership.

In January 1923 Lenin changed the name of the country from Russia to the Union of Soviet Socialist Republics (USSR). It is commonly called the Soviet Union. At that time, the new union had only four republics. The Russian Soviet Federative Socialist Republic (RSFSR) was and is the dominant member of the Soviet Union. Each republic has a Communist party and a government of its own, but it is responsible to and closely watched by the Communist party of the entire nation.

Two of Lenin's associates played major parts in the Russian Revolution and the Soviet state that grew from it. One was Leon Trotsky (TRAHT-skee). The other was Joseph Stalin (STAHL-uhn). After Lenin's death in 1924, a three-year struggle for power developed between the two men. They had fundamental disagreements over the course communism should take.

Trotsky and Stalin

Trotsky was born Lev Davidovich Bronstein in 1879. His Jewish parents were well-off farmers in the southern Ukraine. Lev was a handsome youth who became a radical journalist at the University of Odessa. The police arrested him and he spent time in Siberian exile and Moscow jails. He adopted the name of one of his jailers—Trotsky—and escaped with his new name on his false passport. In 1902 he went to London as a reporter for *Iskra ("The Spark")*, a radical journal. There he met Lenin and became one of his most trusted friends.

When the revolution began, Trotsky returned to Petrograd, where he organized the Red Guard. He later commanded the Red Army and led it to victory during the civil war. He also negotiated the peace Treaty of Brest-Litovsk with Germany that ended Russia's role in World War I.

Trotsky became commissar, or minister, for foreign affairs. He believed in a world revolution of workers. He did not believe the revolution would succeed in underdeveloped Communist Russia until a worldwide revolution of workers had occurred.

Trotsky's ideas can be traced in a direct line back to Marx. Karl Marx started the International Workingmen's Association, or First International, in 1864. Its purpose was to promote the unification and revolution of workers throughout the world. However, its members disagreed and the First International soon fell apart. The Second International, founded in 1889, collapsed because of World War I. When the Bolsheviks came to power, they organized the Third Communist International, or Comintern, to help other countries overthrow capitalist governments. The Soviet Union dominated the Comintern until it was officially disbanded in 1943.

Here is Joseph Stalin taking a stroll in 1925. Can you find any similarities between his government and that of the Romanovs?

The same year Trotsky was born, 1879, Joseph Vissarionovich Djugashvili was born in Georgia, the son of a former serf. His mother, a washerwoman, was widowed in 1890. She sent the boy to a church school, hoping he would become a priest. Joseph was a good student and learned Russian. While at the seminary in Tbilisi (tuh-BIL-uh-see), however, he joined a secret Marxist debating society. The monks expelled him. Until 1917 he lived underground, planning strikes and riots, and stealing money to finance the revolutionary cause. Later he adopted the name of Stalin. Historians disagree over Stalin's role in the revolution. All that is certain is that after the revolution, Lenin appointed him commissar for national minorities. By 1922 Stalin had become general secretary of the Communist party. As secretary he made many friends and appointed them to high places. In this way he developed a following within the party.

Unlike Trotsky, Stalin was convinced that world revolution would come only after communism had been made strong in Russia. He believed Russia could accomplish this by itself.

When Lenin died, the choice for new party leader was between Trotsky and Stalin and their opposing points of view. Stalin's shrewdness in building up a major following and playing one side against the other enabled him to take command of the Communist party and become dictator of the Soviet Union.

Stalin expelled Trotsky from the party and sent him into exile. Between 1927 and 1940, Trotsky wrote a series of books and articles opposing Stalin's dictatorship. In 1940 Trotsky was murdered in Mexico City by agents of Stalin.

SECTION 1 REVIEW

1. **Recall**   According to Karl Marx, which two groups would the final class struggle be between?

2. **How and Why**   How did Trotsky's idea of revolution differ from Stalin's?

3. **Critical Thinking**   Do you think parliamentary democracy had a better chance of succeeding in Russia under the tsars or under the Provisional Government? Why?

With the defeat of Trotsky, Stalin became the undisputed dictator of the Soviet Union. Like Peter the Great, Stalin saw that Russia was far behind the nations of Western Europe. He was determined to change the Soviet Union into a major industrial state within his lifetime. In doing so, he created a totalitarian society characterized by the removal of his political opponents, the establishment of a secret police whose effectiveness far outstripped that of the tsars, and forced labor camps.

Stalin's Dictatorship

To accomplish his goal of making the Soviet Union an industrialized state, Stalin discarded Lenin's New Economic Policy and began the first of his Five-Year plans. These Five-Year plans provided for a planned economy. All the means of production and the items and quantity to be produced were controlled by the government. This system is called **central planning**.

Stalin moved even further away from basic Communist theory. He started a capitalistic system of reward and punishment. If factory managers did not meet government quotas, they were punished. If workers produced more than their quota, they were rewarded with higher wages and paid vacations.

Stalin concentrated his efforts in the area of **heavy industry**: steel, machines, and equipment for making machines. Since he paid little attention to **consumer goods**, the life of the average Russian did not improve.

Stalin's Five-Year plans faced serious problems. The Soviet Union had a very poor transportation system and few skilled workers. Vast portions of the country remained undeveloped.

The success of Stalin's industrialization program, however, hinged on agriculture. Most people in the Soviet Union still made their living by farming. Stalin needed workers for his factories, but he also needed high agriculture production to feed these workers and have a surplus. Stalin needed a large surplus of farm products to export in exchange for modern machinery.

To increase farm production, Stalin ordered the peasants to merge their small farms into huge **collective farms** run by the government. Large farm machinery could be used on these collective farms. The peasants would work together on the farms and share the profits.

Most Russian peasants had always hoped to own their own farms. Many had fought for the Communists because the Communists had promised them land. Many who had received land now refused to give it up. Stalin responded with a brutal policy of forced collectivization by which the government confiscated the peasants' land. In the next section, you will learn more about agriculture and the economy in the Soviet Union.

Purges   By 1934 Stalin had accomplished collectivization of agriculture and the end of the first Five-Year plan. He had defeated the opposition to his rule within the Communist party. Trotsky was in exile. At the Seventeenth Party Congress of 1934, former party opponents showered Stalin with praise. Nevertheless, Stalin became especially fearful of opposition. He created special military courts to try people and carry out immediate death sentences. No appeals were allowed. He sent his secret police, the NKVD (People's Commissariat of Internal Affairs), to spy on and arrest anyone who disagreed with him. This activity reached a peak in the **purges** of 1935–1936. Half a million party members were expelled. Hundreds of thousands were either executed or sent to Siberian labor camps. Execution or exile became convenient tools for officials who wished to get rid of personal enemies. Children were urged to spy on their parents. Women were urged to divorce husbands who were arrested. The victims ranged from the lowliest peasants to high-ranking party members. A number of former top Bolsheviks such as Bukharin, Rykov, Kamenev, and Zinoviev were sentenced to death. In "show trials" they confessed to any number of crimes. These included plotting to murder Stalin, restoring capitalism, and plotting with the British, German, or Japanese secret services to have those countries attack and divide up the Soviet Union. The people placed on trial showed no evidence of guilt except their fabricated and signed confessions. At the final trial in 1938, the prosecuter Andrey Vyshinsky concluded:

> Over the road cleared of the last scum and filth of the past, we, our people, with our beloved teacher and leader, the great Stalin, at our head, will march ever onwards, towards communism.

Stalin replaced party officials with his own people. In this way he was able to build a police state in which no one dared oppose him.

The Police State

One wonders why top Communists confessed to nonexistent crimes. The answer seems to be that investigators broke the prisoners by endless interrogations, beatings, and threats against their families. The prisoners duly signed confessions and admitted guilt in court. But the promises that their lives and those of their families would be saved were rarely kept. In any case, most people brought to Stalin's courts never had public trials. Some learned of their sentences in their prison cells.

Communist party members were not alone as victims of Stalin's terror. Everyone was suspect. The purges greatly weakened the military leadership of the Soviet Union. Stalin purged three of the army's five marshals, all three of the top army commanders, all of the 12 second-rank military commanders, and 60 of 67 corps commanders. Even the secret police were not safe. Two heads of the NKVD were executed. Members of the secret police working in countries outside the Soviet Union were simply murdered on the spot. The Mexican government jailed Trotsky's murderer, but Stalin gave him a decoration.

By 1939 the purges ended. Lavrenty Beria, the head of the NKVD, did not want to end up like his predecessors. Furthermore, the entire

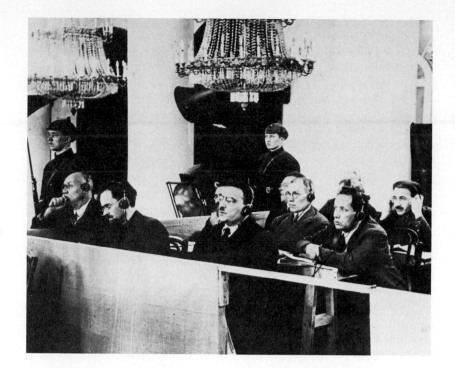

Communist party leaders, purged from the party by Stalin for so-called crimes against the state, listen intently to the court proceedings during their trial. All of these defendants pleaded guilty and were sentenced to prison terms ranging from five to ten years.

Soviet economic, scientific, and military communities were feeling the effects of the purges. Instead of killing people, Stalin's police state now found a more economically effective means of dealing with the opposition: the labor camp.

Labor Camps

Lenin established the first concentration camps in 1918. Most of their occupants were political prisoners and they did no forced labor. By the late 1920s, however, a severe labor shortage gave Soviet officials the idea that prisoners might be employed. To put prisoners into the service of the planned economy would save money and help solve the labor shortage.

The first big project built by forced labor was the White Sea-Baltic Canal (1931–1933). It was designed as an escape route for the Baltic Sea fleet in case of war. As it turned out, the canal was too shallow to be of any use. The forced laborers, promised **amnesty** if they completed the canal in time, were simply transferred to other forced labor projects. These included logging, gold mining, coal mining, and all kinds of construction. Most of the camps were built in areas that were not attractive to free labor. Some of the worst camps were in the Soviet Far East, hundreds of miles from any town in the frozen wastes of Siberia. During the 1930s, some construction sites near cities employed forced labor. These camps were surrounded by barbed-wire fencing and guard towers. No matter where forced labor existed in the Soviet Union, Soviet writer Aleksandr

Solzhenitsyn called it an **archipelago**, a region cut off from the rest of the world but linked by its own communications network.

Slaves have no incentive in achieving high productivity, but Soviet central planners did not accept that economic fact. They set high production targets which they achieved by using food rations. A normal ration was set. Forced laborers who did not achieve their production quotas were punished with lower rations of food, usually a small amount of bread and a thin soup in the morning and evening. On top of that, Soviet planners encouraged the collective spirit. No one would receive a normal ration unless the entire team to which he or she belonged met the production quota. Needless to say, the standard ration alone was not enough for a slave laborer to work at hard manual labor for 10 to 15 hours a day in below-freezing temperatures.

The slave laborer in a Soviet camp faced a slow death from exhaustion, malnutrition, overwork, and disease. The only escape was to get an administrative job in the camp. In many camps, however, criminal prisoners held these positions. Operating like the Mafia, criminal prisoners terrorized and subdued the political prisoners within the camps.

Nearly everyone in the Soviet Union had a friend or a relative in a labor camp. Statistics are uncertain, but about 12 million people died in Stalin's camps from 1936 to 1950. This figure does not include criminals or the earlier peasant victims of Stalin's forced collectivization of agriculture.

World War II

On June 22, 1941, Hitler launched Operation Barbarossa against the Soviet Union. It was a surprise blitzkrieg attack along the entire border between the Soviet Union and German-occupied Poland and Czechoslovakia. Within five days, the Germans captured Minsk, the capital of Belorussia. By the end of August, German forces reached Kiev and were approaching Leningrad. By late September, the autumn rains created muddy roads that slowed down the motorized German units. Nonetheless, the Germans were on the outskirts of Moscow.

Nazi-Soviet Pact   In 1933 Adolf Hitler came to power in Germany and began his policy of expansion. Stalin urged Great Britain and France to form a **popular front** to oppose him. Instead, Stalin saw Great Britain and France do nothing when Hitler seized the Rhineland, Austria, and Czechoslovakia. Stalin suspected that they might even be encouraging Hitler to turn against the Soviet Union. In 1939 it was clear that Hitler's next target was Poland. Stalin realized that he needed to reach an understanding with Hitler. In late August, one week before the German invasion of Poland, Stalin signed a **nonaggression** pact with Hitler. The Nazi-Soviet Pact gave Hitler the green light to attack Poland and to wage war against Great Britain and France without Soviet interference.

When Hitler's conquest of Poland was nearly complete, Stalin seized the eastern half of the country. This partition of Poland was made according to secret agreements in the Nazi-Soviet Pact. Stalin next took the Baltic republics of Estonia, Latvia, and Lithuania. He later took

Moldavia and part of Finland. He hoped the additional land would act as a **buffer zone** between the Soviet Union and Germany. His desire to increase Soviet territory also prompted these moves.

Now, in June 1941, two years after the pact had been signed, Hitler's armies overran the buffer zone and invaded the Soviet Union. Most of the Soviet air force was destroyed on the ground, as were thousands of tanks. The Nazis captured hundreds of thousands of Red Army troops. In the invaded regions, party officials burned their papers and NKVD agents shot their prisoners before fleeing east.

The population often welcomed the Germans. They hoped the Germans would let them farm private lands and attend church again. Nationalists in Belorussia and the Ukraine hoped that Germany would help them set up independent states. Germany's failure to accommodate these wishes helped Stalin win the war.

Great Patriotic War   Stalin quickly showed his courage and iron will. In October 1941, while German guns could be heard outside Moscow, he appeared on Lenin's tomb to celebrate the October Revolution. He proved to be a good administrator. Unlike Russia during World War I, the Soviet Union was able to coordinate military and civilian activities quite well. Stalin was of course head of both the civilian State Defense Committee and the military's Supreme Command.

The Soviet people rallied behind Stalin. The German invaders had not only invaded the Soviet people's homeland, but also regarded Slavic peoples as subhuman. The Germans shipped many Soviet soldiers and civilians to Germany to work in concentration camps as slave laborers.

German forces fighting in the Soviet Union had to contend not only with fierce resistance but also with severe winter conditions. Soviet soldiers were accustomed to the harsh weather. The Germans, however, were unprepared for the bitter cold and heavy snowfall that they encountered.

The Germans also executed Jews and Communist party officials on the spot in areas they conquered. Stalin—for all his terrors, purges, and forced collectivizations—managed to form an alliance between the government and the people to drive out the invaders. He made concessions to them in wartime that he would never have made in peacetime. For example, Stalin restored the patriarchate of the Russian Orthodox Church. To Stalin and the Soviet people alike, World War II became the Great Patriotic War.

Stalin mobilized people and resources. Many industries were moved east of the Urals—out of the path of invasion—and put into full production. Food supplies were in short supply. The Germans captured nearly 40 percent of the Soviet Union's grain-producing regions. In addition, many farm workers became soldiers. Women, young people, and old men replaced them. The government imposed **rationing** because items such as dairy products, sugar, and vegetables were either scarce or unobtainable.

From the German invasion of Poland in 1939 to the German attack on Russia in 1941, the Soviet Union had sat on the sidelines. After the German attack, the Soviet Union formed alliances with Great Britain. The United States became an ally of the Soviet Union after the Japanese attack on Pearl Harbor brought the United States into the war. The Americans began sending supplies to the Soviet Union. The Soviets used the same methods that their ancestors had used against Napoleon. This was the scorched-earth policy in which they destroyed everything in front of the invading army. The terrible Russian winter caught the Germans without the proper clothing and vastly extended supply lines.

The winter—with temperatures 40° below zero (Fahrenheit and Celsius)—also was harsh for the Russians. From August 1941 to January 1944, the Germans besieged Leningrad. During the winter the Russians could supply the city only by trucking goods across 30 miles (48 kilometers) of frozen Lake Ladoga. People burned furniture or books to keep warm. Nearly one million people died of cold or starvation in Leningrad.

Stalingrad   In the spring of 1942, the Germans resumed their advance across the Soviet Union. By September they reached the city of Stalingrad (now called Volgograd) on the Volga River. Then the Soviets began their counterattack and surrounded Leningrad. Hitler ordered the German forces in the city to fight to the death. The turning point of the war came in February 1943 when the Soviets recaptured Stalingrad.

The Red Army, under brilliant battle-seasoned commanders such as Georgy Zhukov (ZHOO-kuhf), then began pushing the Germans back through Eastern Europe. After a long, difficult campaign, the Soviets entered the German capital of Berlin in May 1945. At the same time the Allies invaded Europe, fought their way across France, and into Germany. The war in Europe was over. The Soviet Union lost 26 million people, or about 70 times the losses of the United States in World War II. The scale of suffering by a single nation in that war is unparalleled.

Wartime Conferences During the war, Stalin had met several times with Winston Churchill, the British prime minister, and President Franklin D. Roosevelt of the United States. In these Big Three conferences, Stalin promised to help the Allies against Japan once the war with Germany was over. The Big Three decided that control of Germany should be divided among the Soviet Union, the United States, Great Britain, and France. Stalin agreed to participate in the founding of the United Nations. He insisted, as did the United States, that the major nations have **veto power** in the Security Council and that the Soviet Union be a permanent member of the council. The Soviet Union also got three votes in the General Assembly. The Soviet republics of Belorussia and the Ukraine got one vote each, as did the Soviet Union.

The decisions reached by Churchill, Roosevelt, and Stalin at the Yalta Conference profoundly affected postwar Europe.

The Cold War

The Soviet Union emerged from World War II as a **superpower**. It was the strongest nation in Europe and second only to the United States in the world. Stalin chose this time to begin his own policy of expansion. He wanted to spread communism and to protect Soviet borders from future invasions. He began a policy that was to place large sections of Europe under Communist domination.

After the war, Stalin refused to withdraw his armies from the Eastern European countries through which they had fought. In each country Communist parties took over the government. These nations became called Soviet **satellites**, meaning they were lesser states subservient to the Soviet Union. Stalin signed special treaties and economic agreements with them. Europe thus became divided into two **blocs**—free nations and Communist nations. The Soviet Union and its satellites shut themselves off from the rest of the world. Winston Churchill described their action as the lowering of an iron curtain between East and West.

American leaders were especially displeased with Stalin's policies. They had requested free elections in Eastern Europe, but the Soviets ignored them. A period of mutual distrust and antagonism known as the cold war developed from these conflicts. The United States decided on a policy of containment. Under the containment policy, the United States would provide economic, political, and sometimes military aid to countries to prevent their becoming Communist.

antagonism: hostile feelings

The United States sponsored programs to carry out the aims of containment. The Truman Doctrine stopped communism in Greece and Turkey. The Marshall Plan provided economic aid to Western Europe. The North Atlantic Treaty Organization (NATO) was formed in 1949 for the mutual defense of the United States, Canada, and ten Western European nations.

The Soviets responded with programs such as the Communist Information Bureau (Cominform), founded in 1947. The Cominform coordinated the political activities of Communist parties in the Soviet bloc and Western nations, such as France and Italy, which had large Communist parties. The Council for Mutual Economic Assistance (CMEA) was founded in 1949 to coordinate the economic activities of Communist nations, particularly in their efforts to industrialize. Finally, the Soviet Union formed the Warsaw Pact with the nations of Eastern Europe as a defense against NATO.

At home Stalin moved decisively, too. World War II had left the Soviet Union almost in ruins. The population was imbalanced. There were only 59 men for every 100 women in the Soviet Union. Stalin introduced his fourth Five-Year Plan. He seized machinery and entire factories from East Germany and Austria, and shipped them back to Russia. He drove the Soviet people relentlessly to rebuild the country.

The Communist party reasserted its power in the country. Andrei Zhdanov (ZHDAH-nuhf) emerged as its leading figure after Stalin. He directed party ideology and denounced Western influences that had crept in during the war. The party continued the encouragement of Russian nationalism begun during the war. The film director Sergey Eisenstein was criticized for not making Ivan the Dread and his police look more humane in his film.

When Zhdanov died suddenly under mysterious circumstances in 1948, Stalin began new purges. The secret police sent thousands to slave labor camps. The Communist party met in the Nineteenth Party Congress in 1952. The congress abolished the old Politburo and replaced it with the Presidium. The new leaders feared that Stalin might be getting ready to purge them, too. But on March 5, 1953, Stalin died suddenly. Party leaders executed NKVD head Beria before he could seize power. Stalin's death left a great void in the Soviet Union's leadership. For more than a quarter of a century, Stalin had governed. He had eliminated all his rivals and industrialized the Soviet Union. He had fought a war that left the Soviet Union in ruins. But he rebuilt the country. Finally, Stalin made the Soviet Union a superpower. All this was accomplished at a terrible price.

SECTION 2 REVIEW

1. **Recall** What did the Nazi-Soviet Pact of 1939 accomplish?

2. **How and Why** How did Stalin's purges during the 1930s affect the Soviet Union's preparedness for war?

3. **Critical Thinking** How did the Soviet Union at the end of World War II differ from Russia at the end of World War I?

Since 1953 the Soviet Union and the United States have been the world's two superpowers. Soviet expansion had subsided, but the United States and its allies continued to regard the Soviet Union as a threat. The fear of nuclear war was ever present, although its use in accomplishing political aims was less dangerous than the possibility that someone might begin such a conflict accidentally. At home Soviet leaders coped with endless problems with the economy. Consumer needs were never satisfied. Production on the agricultural collectives remained static, and heavy industry seemed stymied by bureaucratic management and a lack of incentive. In the late 1980s, the last of the old generation of Kremlin leaders died in office. A new, energetic leader, Mikhail Gorbachev, emerged. He faced the perennial challenges of the Soviet economy with new ideas, and he reconsidered the Soviet Union's role as a superpower and as the leader of world communism.

From Coexistence to Détente

Since Stalin had liquidated all rivals, his death in 1953 left a gap in the Soviet leadership. At first a collective leadership was formed in which several men shared power. After two years of struggling for power, Nikita S. Khrushchev (kroosh-CHOF), emerged as the sole leader—both premier and first secretary of the Communist party—of the Soviet Union.

Khrushchev   Nikita Khrushchev had been a coal miner before he became a member of the Communist party in 1918. During the revolution he was active in the Ukraine. He rose to power by using many of the same methods Stalin had used in his rise to power. He made many friends and placed them in high positions. He was trusted by Stalin and worked faithfully for him.

But once Khrushchev was in power, he changed many of Stalin's policies of terror. He realized that times had changed and so should the face of communism. He began a policy of revisionism or change known as de-Stalinization. His rivals were forced to resign, but they were not executed. At the Twentieth Communist Party Congress in 1956, Khrushchev denounced Stalin as a dictator and murderer.

During his rule, Stalin had history books rewritten to glorify himself, placed statues and pictures of himself throughout the country, and had cities and streets renamed for him. Khrushchev attacked Stalin for these actions, what he called "the cult of personality." Khrushchev had the pictures removed, the history books rewritten, and the names changed again. Stalingrad, for example, became Volgograd. Stalin's body, which had been placed beside that of Lenin in a tomb on Red Square, was moved to a simple grave site.

Khrushchev tried to improve the life of the average Soviet citizen by producing more consumer goods. However, the Soviet economy was unable to increase production of both consumer goods and heavy industry.

In 1960 Khrushchev came to the UN. During an angry debate, he pounded the desk with his shoe. When order was restored, he left the shoe for all to see. Why?

Khrushchev also faced the problem of lagging farm production. The collective farms still did not produce enough foodstuffs to increase the Soviet Union's badly needed foreign capital. In case of a poor harvest, the Soviets did not even have extra food for themselves. Khrushchev's biggest effort to increase production was the virgin lands program. He selected sections of southern Siberia and Central Asia to be turned into major food-producing areas. Thousands of student volunteers and farm workers were shipped to collective farms in these regions. However, the program did not work immediately, and Soviet agricultural problems remained unsolved.

In international affairs, Khrushchev wanted to promote communication and trade between Communist and free nations. In 1956 he declared a policy of **peaceful coexistence** in which total war was to be avoided. He was the chief salesman of this policy, and he traveled throughout the world, including the United States. Khrushchev had not given up on communism, however. He believed that the struggle with capitalist nations would be carried on by economic or political means and, if necessary, by war among third-party nations. He began to use foreign aid to undeveloped nations—the **Third World**—as a weapon against the United States.

Confrontations still occurred in Soviet relations with the United States. In Germany, Khrushchev built the Berlin Wall in 1961. The next year President John F. Kennedy forced him to remove Russian missiles from Cuba.

During Khrushchev's period in office, bitter disputes developed within the Communist bloc. Because the Soviet Union had been the first Communist state, Soviet leaders considered themselves the leaders of world communism. Leaders of other Communist countries began to dispute the Soviet Union's claim to leadership. Yugoslavia broke with the Communist bloc as early as 1948. Later the Chinese Communists became the most vocal opponents of the Soviets. They argued that war was inevitable if capitalism was to be overthrown. They also actively supported Communist activities in Third World nations. Relations between the Soviet Union and the People's Republic of China have been stormy since the early 1960s. At times fighting broke out along their common border.

The Brezhnev Era   Despite improved relations with the West—such as a treaty ban on nuclear weapons tests—many of Khrushchev's policies were unpopular with other Soviet leaders. The break with the Chinese, the Cuban missile crisis, and problems in his agricultural and industrial programs forced Khrushchev to retire in 1964. The Politburo once again turned to collective leadership, but by the early 1970s Leonid Brezhnev (BREZH-nef) emerged as the sole leader.

Brezhnev continued many of Khrushchev's policies but emphasized efficiency and achievement. He tried to achieve a better balance between the production of consumer goods and heavy industry. As a result, the standard of living in the Soviet Union rose slowly.

Brezhnev's Soviet Union showed no weakening of its hold on the satellites. This was demonstrated in 1968 when Soviet troops moved into

Czechoslovakia to stop the movement toward greater personal freedom. The struggle between China and the Soviet Union continued as each country tried to exercise control over the Communist world and win over the Third World nations.

By the early 1970s, Brezhnev went beyond peaceful coexistence by showing a willingness to maintain world peace through **détente**. This is a policy of relaxing international tensions through negotiations. Détente means that major crises between the United States and the Soviet Union were avoided. Sometimes both sides used their influence to achieve peaceful settlement. This happened in the Middle East. Over the years, the United States had sent supplies to Israel, while the Soviet Union helped arm the Arab nations. Then both superpowers promoted the cease-fire of 1973 between Israel and the Arab nations.

The policy of détente was strengthened by several summit conferences between Brezhnev and American presidents, and the signing of trade agreements and the Strategic Arms Limitations Treaty (SALT) to limit nuclear weapons.

However, détente was threatened when the Soviet Union sent troops into Afghanistan in December 1979. Soviet-American relations cooled. President Jimmy Carter ordered an embargo on grain sales to the Soviet Union and called for a worldwide boycott of the Summer Olympic Games held in Moscow in 1980.

Brezhnev died in 1982. His two elderly successors were Yuri Andropov (an-DROH-pov) and Konstantin Chernenko (CHERN-yen-koh). Both died in office after serving as general secretary for very short periods of time. Their replacement, first as general secretary and then as president, was Mikhail Gorbachev (GOHR-buh-chof). He was to shake the static Communist world and the Soviet Union to their foundations.

After Khrushchev's fall from power, Leonid Brezhnev (above) and Aleksei Kosygin shared power for a time. Both men came from the Soviet middle class. How would Marx have viewed this fact? Did he believe that a middle class could exist in a Communist society?

The New Face of Communism

In 1989 Mikhail Gorbachev added the duties of president of the Soviet Union to that of general secretary of the Communist party. He defeated conservative opponents in getting constitutional changes made that strengthened the powers of the presidency. His powers as president are vastly different from those of Andrei Gromyko (gro-MEE-koh), his predecessor. The president of the Soviet Union had been a ceremonial position as head of state, much like that of the Queen of England. It is too early to tell if Gorbachev will be successful in using his new powers.

Constitutional Changes   Even before the Communists won the civil war, Lenin created a new government and a constitution for the Soviet Union. Stalin wrote a new constitution in 1936. On paper, power rested with the local Soviets. They, in turn, sent representatives to a Supreme Soviet, the supreme legislative body of the Soviet Union.

The constitution appeared democratic. Everyone 18 years old or older could vote by secret ballot for representatives to the parliamentary body. However, there was only one legal political party, the Communist party. The real power lay with the Politburo. Stalin controlled the Politburo and had eliminated his opponents, so he was in fact the dictator of the Soviet Union. His successors also remained in power by virtue of controlling the party apparatus.

This constitution remained intact for more than 50 years. The real power continued to lie with the Communist party leadership. Then Gorbachev initiated changes in December 1988. For the first time, candidates for the upper house, the 2,250-seat Congress of People's Deputies, could run against each other in elections. In the elections held in early 1990, several old-line Communist party members lost their seats. The Supreme Soviet selects the president, who can serve for a maximum of two five-year terms. Gorbachev was elected president, but he still retained his post as general secretary of the Communist party. There he got rid of many political opponents from the Central Committee. Gorbachev solidified his power base in the party and in the government. He was then ready to make the changes he believed were necessary for the Soviet Union.

Glasnost and Perestroika   In April 1986, a little more than a year after Gorbachev became general secretary of the Communist party, people in the Soviet Union first heard about the nuclear disaster at Chernobyl. They learned about it from foreign broadcasts. The Soviet government at first denied the reports. However, something so vital to the welfare of the people could not be denied. The decision to tell the truth about Chernobyl facilitated Gorbachev's determination to develop glasnost.

In January 1987, before the Central Committee of the Communist party, Gorbachev attacked a wide range of political, economic, and social ills: stagnation in the economy, political conservatism and inertia, the spread of apathy and cynicism among the people, and the failure of officials to take responsibility for their actions. Gorbachev said that the Soviet Union needed perestroika. He said that perestroika must encompass the political system, the ideology and operation of the Communist party, society at large, and particularly the economy.

The Economy

The general weakening of the Soviet economy caused Gorbachev to begin his policy of perestroika. A weak economy meant unrest and instability within the Soviet Union. It also meant a weakening of the Soviet Union as a world power.

This was the economic picture Gorbachev faced. The growth rate was stagnant—only 1.5 percent for both 1987 and 1988. Inflation was rising. Experts predicted that the Soviet Union's budget deficit would reach $160 billion in 1990. Because of low wages and poor working conditions, coal miners throughout the Soviet Union walked out. Soviet farms were losing money while as much as one-third of their produce rotted before it could be distributed to consumers.

(Continued on page 796.)

HISTORY AND PEOPLE

MIKHAIL GORBACHEV

As the leader of the Union of Soviet Socialist Republics, Mikhail Gorbachev is at the center of the most dramatic and far-reaching series of events the world has experienced since World War II. Gorbachev's mission is to preserve the Communist party's domination at home by changing the socialist system. He is essentially borrowing from capitalism to revitalize socialism. He has made a commitment to the elusive goal of *perestroika*, an effort to "restructure" the economy so that it produces what the people want to consume. He is further committed to *glasnost*, "open discussion" among the people and the end to official lying within the government.

Born in 1931 into a family of peasants, Gorbachev lived a typical working-class life. He was an average student in law school. In 1952, he joined the Communist party and began his active involvement in politics. Rising rapidly in the Communist hierarchy, Gorbachev joined the powerful Central Committee in 1971.

Gorbachev's election as general secretary of the Communist party in 1985 brought out two divergent viewpoints among Communist leaders: "reformers" who longed for the renewal of the party, and "conservatives" who feared the loss of powers and privileges of the elite. During his first years, Gorbachev began the pursuit of economic development for his country by consolidating his own power, removing corrupt officials, and building an effective party organization.

Gorbachev has wrought tremendous change within his own political system. Much more far reaching, however, has been this man's influence on shaping current and future world history. In 1989, *Time* magazine proclaimed Gorbachev "Man of the Decade." The cold war between the East and West that existed since World War II virtually ended because of his efforts toward

reconciliation. Unprecedented changes throughout the Communist bloc have inspired people to embrace rapid transformation of their entire lives. As the world watched, economic policies moved toward capitalism, the hated Berlin Wall came crashing down, governments changed and with them, outdated seclusionist ideas.

What these changes mean to Gorbachev is that he must struggle to keep his hold on his power in the Soviet Union. Countries long part of the bloc are demanding freedom and trying to become independent of all Soviet political ties.

What this means to the rest of the world is that a new global focus must emerge. Without the perennial threat of "the Red Menace," American and European views of the future must necessarily change.

1. Do you agree or disagree with *Time* magazine's naming of Gorbachev as "Man of the Decade"? Give reasons for your opinion.

2. Define "the Red Menace." How did that phrase fit into the concept of the cold war?

3. What are the problems that the United States government now faces in its relationship with the Soviet Union?

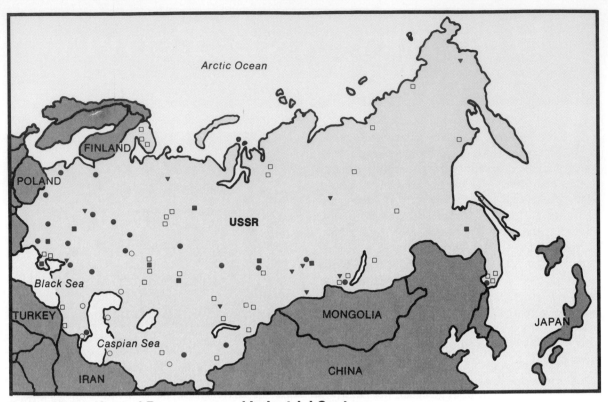

Soviet Union Natural Resources and Industrial Centers
● Industrial Centers ▼ Coal ■ Iron ○ Oil □ Minerals

As you have read, under the Soviet system, the economy is centrally planned. The state owns and controls all the nation's resources—mines, factories, the transportation system, domestic and foreign commerce, and most of the land. People may own automobiles and home furnishings, but not the land on which their houses are built.

All the central planning, however, has not produced a strong economy. Production goals are not met and consumer goods are in short supply.

Agriculture   Agriculture is the weakest part of the Soviet economy. Even though one-third of the total labor force are farm workers, the country cannot produce enough food to feed its expanding population.

Part of the problem is the geographical location of the Soviet Union. Where the land is arable, the rainfall is uncertain. One year may bring an abundance of rain, and the next year a drought. In addition, much of the land lies above 50° north latitude where crops can be grown only during the short summer months. Soviet scientists are working to develop fast-growing crops and improve land use and irrigation. The process remains slow and frustrating.

Despite these geographical limitations, Russia was an exporter of farm products before World War I. But both Lenin and Stalin considered

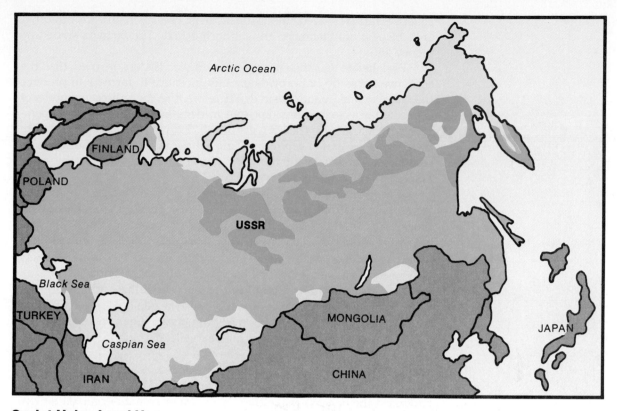

Soviet Union Land Use
◼ Farming ◼ Forestry ◻ Grazing

the peasants to be capitalists, and Stalin forced them onto collective farms. The peasants resisted collectivization. They destroyed their crops and livestock, burned their farm buildings, and smashed their tools. Stalin answered with brutal force. He knew he had to wipe out the rich peasants, the **kulaks**, as a class if collectivization was to succeed. So he seized their property and shipped the kulaks to work as slave laborers in the mines or building roads in Siberia. Stalin won, but at a great cost. After forced collectivization, the Soviet Union has had to import food.

The Soviet Union has two kinds of farms: the collective farm and the state farm. On collective farms, a number of families work together on government-owned land. The farmers own the buildings and machinery. Each farm is run by an elected chairperson who makes sure the collective farm delivers its quota as determined by the central planners in the government. A farmer cannot move from a collective without permission from the chairperson. This is much like the mir in the days of the tsars.

The products grown on the collective farm are sold to the state at a price fixed by the state. The state then sells the produce to consumers through state-operated stores. A small amount of collective farm produce may be sold on the **open market**, that part of the economy not controlled by the state. The money earned from the sale of all produce from the collective farm is shared among the farmers. Fees for insurance, building, and the cost of machinery are subtracted first. The farmers share any money left.

Well before Gorbachev's reforms, Soviet leaders learned that the collective farms do not provide enough incentive to farmers to produce the quantity and quality desired. Therefore, they permitted members of collective farms to have small private gardens. Farmers may grow vegetables, or whatever else they can eat or sell. Farmers are also permitted to own a cow, several sheep, a pig, and all the poultry they can raise. A significant percentage of the agricultural produce sold on the open market is grown on these private plots.

A second type of farm is the **state farm**. The average size of state farms is around 75,000 acres (30,000 hectares). They are from four to five times larger than collective farms, and the state owns not only the land but also the buildings and machinery. State farm workers are paid like factory workers, according to the kind and amount of work done. Workers also receive paid vacations, sick pay, and a retirement pension.

Soviet leaders have been forced to give agriculture a high priority. Khrushchev's downfall came in part because he could not solve the farm problem. Continued large imports of grain, meat, sugar, and cooking oils show the failure of central planning and collectivization.

Industry The industrialization of the Soviet Union began in the late 1800s. Foreign capital played an important role in this. The Communists continued the drive to make the Soviet Union an industrialized nation, but without foreign investment. The move to industrialize was helped by the enormous natural resources of the Soviet Union.

Central planning has dominated economic life. The top planning commission is located in Moscow. Below it, regional councils coordinate the plans of all industries in the region. Local factories are at the bottom of the planning ladder. They make plans that are sent for consideration and approval to the planning agencies above them. Because the state owns all the factories, the government in Moscow is the ultimate authority for each factory. It sets the yearly quotas and production plans.

Soviet leaders have concentrated on **heavy industry**. This means building industries to serve other industries rather than people. Until recently they were not concerned with producing consumer goods. The emphasis was on power plants and dams, trucks, machine tools, and military equipment. People were expected to sacrifice for the future.

Economic Reform Central planning has left the Soviet economy in a shambles. The people who do the planning have enormous power and privileges. They have access to goods that the ordinary Soviet citizen cannot obtain easily, if at all. Until recently, the planners kept prices of food, housing, and transportation low. But cheap goods are not plentiful and shortages are common. **Rationing** is in effect on basic items such as salt, soap, tea, and sugar. Ordinary people spend a part of each day standing in long lines for the few goods available. They often do this during working hours. Their philosophy is "They pretend to pay us, and we pretend to work." The Soviet people hoard many basic items. Even medicine is scarce. Doctors sometimes cannot perform surgery because they have no antibiotics.

Gorbachev inherited this abysmal state of affairs when he took office. At first he tried to instill discipline and put life into the existing system. Then he began perestroika in a limited way. In agriculture, he encouraged collective farm chairpersons to give long-term land leases to families. In March 1989, Gorbachev said that this did not mean abandonment of collective farms and a return to private ownership of the land.

Soviet farmers have not been eager to lease land. They fear that the government could change its policy again. This fear is based on Stalin's forced collectivization. The farmer needs assurances that the government is permanently committed to private farming. Some economists even argue that after 60 years of collective farming, the Soviet farmer no longer has the skills to operate a single-family farm. In the meantime, farmers leave the land for the cities, and agricultural production continues to lag. Perestroika has not been a success.

The scarcity of many things in the Soviet economy has resulted in a rebirth of private enterprise, or what is called the "cooperative" sector. As many as 3 million Soviet citizens work in the cooperative sector. This form of free enterprise—restaurants, fruit and vegetable stands, repair shops, small manufacturers, doctors and lawyers—exists primarily in cities where it competes with state enterprises. The cooperatives provide higher quality goods and services, but they charge from four to ten times the price one would pay in a state enterprise. People resent the private economy with its high prices. In 1989 the government began to regulate what cooperatives can do or sell and what prices they can charge. Because the cooperatives have no protection under existing Soviet law, their existence is insecure.

End of the Cold War

Since the beginning of Communist rule in 1918, the Soviet leadership has been suspicious of the rest of the world. This suspicion is grounded in the Allied intervention on the side of the Whites, the Bolsheviks' opponents, in the civil war. On the other hand, the Communists did nothing to help matters with their ideological warfare against the "bourgeois" West. Through the Comintern and Communist parties in other countries, they worked to undermine and overthrow governments everywhere.

During World War II, Stalin joined the United States and Great Britain to fight against Nazi Germany. But he did so only after the Soviet Union itself was invaded by Germany in 1941. He did not declare war against Japan until the last days of the war in the Pacific—after the United States had dropped the first of two atomic bombs on Japan.

The wartime cooperation—never really warm—turned into a cold war. Two blocks—East and West—developed. Both were armed and prepared to fight one another. The arms race intensified. Both sides knew that no one wins a nuclear war, so they agreed to some arms limitations

President George Bush and
Mikhail Gorbachev meet the
press at the Malta Summit.

before Gorbachev came to power. Still, it looked in 1985 as if the 40-year-old cold war would move into old age and the world would continue to be divided into two irreconcilable blocs.

Gorbachev had other ideas. As you have read, he took stock of the Soviet Union's economic situation. Clearly the country could not afford to keep up the arms race. He also examined the Soviet Union's role as one of the world's two superpowers. He concluded that the defense needs of the Soviet Union could still be satisfied without the continual sparring with the West.

This decision led to the agreement with the United States in late 1987 to eliminate intermediate range missiles and to reduce strategic arms, and to the Soviet Union's withdrawal from Afghanistan in 1988. In December 1988, the **unilateral** decision to reduce conventional forces along the Chinese border and in Eastern Europe took effect.

Gorbachev has held **summit meetings** with the United States president every year since 1985. In the Communist countries of Eastern Europe, Gorbachev gave the go-ahead for other political parties to develop. He still did not allow this at home, but the Soviet Union released most political prisoners and established a human rights commission. Within a remarkably short time, tensions between the Eastern and Western blocs have been reduced tremendously. Gorbachev has achieved understandable popularity throughout the world for his actions in easing this tension. Whether he can achieve as much in the Soviet Union remains questionable.

SECTION 3 REVIEW

1. **Recall**   What did Khrushchev do to ease international tensions?
2. **How and Why**   Why has agriculture continued to be a problem that Soviet leaders seem unable to solve?
3. **Critical Thinking**   Define *glasnost* and *perestroika*.

Chapter 38 — R E V I E W

Reviewing People, Places, and Things

Identify, define, or explain each of the following:

communism
means of production
Socialist Revolutionaries
Bolsheviks
soviets
Peter Stolypin
Gregory Rasputin
Treaty of Brest-Litovsk
Politburo
New Economic Policy
Leon Trotsky
central planning
Nazi-Soviet Pact
Stalingrad
satellites
cold war
containment
Warsaw Pact
peaceful coexistence
détente
SALT
kulaks
open market
state farm

Map Study

Using the maps on pages 796 and 797, determine the answers to the following questions:

1. In what area of the Soviet Union are the least amounts of natural resources located?
2. How is most of the land in the Soviet Union used?
3. Where are grazing lands found in the Soviet Union?

Understanding Facts and Ideas

1. What effect did the Revolution of 1905 have upon reform in Russia?
2. How did Stolypin plan to stabilize Russia?
3. a. What were three effects of World War I on the Russian homefront? b. How did the Russian Revolution begin?
4. How did Lenin's government differ in practice from Marxist theory?
5. What methods did Stalin use to achieve complete power in the Soviet Union?
6. a. What was Stalin's goal for the Soviet Union? b. How did it affect the lives of the Soviet people?
7. Why did Stalin create labor camps?
8. a. How did Khrushchev try to improve the life of the average Soviet citizen? b. How successful was his plan?
9. Why did Mikhail Gorbachev initiate sweeping reforms in the Soviet Union after 1986?
10. a. What areas of the Soviet economy are controlled or owned by the government? b. By individuals?

Developing Critical Thinking

Analyzing Effects When Lenin returned from exile in 1917, he made several promises to the Russian people. What were these? Did Lenin accomplish the things he promised?

Writing About History

Relating Past to Present Karl Marx claimed that workers would no longer be exploited once communism replaced capitalism. In a brief essay, explain whether or not communism has supported Marx's theory.

Applying Your Skills to History

Predicting Alternative Futures Most of the tsars tried to suppress ideas of reform and freedom. Would it have been possible for them to bring about democratic reforms in Russia and still keep their power? Could they have prevented the Communist takeover in Russia? Explain your ideas in a brief essay.

CHAPTER

39

This photo shows a collective farm in the southern Ural Mountains. Why did the Communists turn farms into collectives when they came to power? How successful have the collectives been?

Life in the Soviet Union

The Russian Revolution brought more than a change in rulers. The new Communist leaders created a federation based on nationalities. They also wanted to shape a new kind of society. This society would follow the teachings of communism and would produce a new kind of person: the ideal Soviet citizen. To create this ideal, all non-Communist influences such as nationality and religion had to be stamped out. Despite these efforts, Communist leaders found that such strong forces could not be as easily directed as they wished. Differences between Communist theory and practice have developed.

As you study this chapter, think about these questions:

- How did Soviet leaders hope to use nationalism for the benefit of the new federation of Soviet republics?

- What has the Soviet Union done to improve the quality of life of its citizens?

- How has religion survived in a state founded by leaders hostile to its existence?

- What forces have influenced the development of the arts in Russia?

The Soviet Union is a federation of republics and autonomous regions based on nationality. Not every nationality has its own republic, but since Stalin's time most Soviet citizens have had their nationality stamped on their passports.

More than 72 percent of the Soviet population are Russians, Belorussians, or Ukrainians. These three groups are descendants of the East Slavs. As Russia expanded its borders, many non-Slavic peoples became part of the country. The history of a number of these peoples goes back farther than that of the Slavs. They have their own language, culture, and customs.

The hundreds of languages spoken in the country serve as a barrier to **cultural integration**. The tsars tried to surmount this barrier through Russification. They had some success among ethnic elites, but ultimately Russification failed to achieve cultural integration. Over the centuries, the non-Slavs became resentful and bitter about domination and persecution by the Russians. The Communists took another route, but they did not achieve cultural integration either.

Communism and Nationalism

From Lenin's time, the Communists believed that social classes were far more important than nations. They used national **self-determination**, or independence, as a means to get support from national groups during the Revolution. By doing so, they encouraged nationalism. During the civil war, the Communists lost large amounts of territory that had belonged to the Russian Empire of the tsars. Poland and Finland were lost. They did not recover the Baltic provinces, eastern Moldavia, and parts of Belorussia and the Ukraine until World War II.

Lenin was faced with the challenge of building a Communist state. He had driven out or killed the old ruling class. Many who were left were illiterate. Such people were incapable of running the day-to-day business of government. It was important to educate people. During the 1920s and 1930s, the Soviet government brought primary education to people throughout the Soviet Union. This education was taught in the vernacular, or native languages of the people. This indirectly encouraged the rise of nationalism in some areas.

The Communist education system allowed cultural but not political independence. The nationalities could keep their styles of dress, arts, and customs as long as they did not interfere with communism. However, the content of education and writing and the economic way of life had to be Communist.

The government and Communist party of each republic bound the nationalities closely to the national state of the Soviet Union. In addition, the Communist regime believed that indoctrination in the party line, teaching the same material in all the schools, and the migration of Slavic peoples through the Soviet Union would help loosen ethnic ties and lead to the creation of a special Soviet citizen. The advent of glasnost and perestroika in the late 1980s showed how wrong the government was in holding this belief.

Nationalities

Ukrainian girls in native dress reflect their ethnic origins.

Russians, Ukrainians, and Belorussians

The Soviet Union has been called the last of the great European empires. It resembles the Hapsburg and Ottoman empires in that it is a large territory held together by the domination of a single nationality.

Russians   The Russians are the dominant group—52 percent of the population—in the Soviet Union. They live in the largest republic, the Russian Soviet Federative Socialist Republic, or simply Russia. This republic comprises 76 percent of the territory of the Soviet Union. It stretches across the northern part of the Soviet Union from the Ukraine to the Bering Sea, and includes Siberia. Russia's largest city, Moscow, with 9 million people, is located within this republic. From Moscow, the Communist party rules the entire union.

Stalin said that the Russians are the "elder brother" in the Soviet Union. They clearly dominate the territory, the government, and the Communist party. However, the Russians have not always received the treatment one might expect from a dominant people. Other minorities, particularly in the Baltic region, are more prosperous. The Russians' peasant heritage was ruthlessly changed by Stalin. The Communist government has persecuted the Russians for their faith. It has also forced many of the greatest Russian artists and writers into hiding or exile.

Ukraine   The Ukraine, or Little Russia, is the section of the Soviet Union just north of the Black Sea. Its capital, Kiev, was the center for early Russian culture. The Ukrainians, while similar to the Russians and

Belorussians in language, religion, and custom, are very independent. Since the 1300s, they have fought various countries for their freedom. The Ukraine achieved a short-lived independence during the Russian civil war, from 1917 to 1921. Today, the people continue to be restless under Soviet rule.

Aside from the Russian republic itself, the Ukraine is the most important of the republics. With a population of 42 million—16 percent of the total—it lies in the heart of the Soviet Union. The Ukraine's **chernozem**, or rich, dark soil, provides 25 percent of the Soviet Union's food supply and one-third of its industry. The Communist government, no less than that of the tsars, would find it unthinkable to lose the Ukraine.

Ukrainians developed a strong national consciousness as a result of the famine of the 1930s, the Stalinist purges, and the Nazi occupation and guerrilla warfare against the Soviets during World War II. During the 1950s and 1960s, Ukrainian nationalism arose again, inspired by poets. The Soviet regime used force to suppress it. On the other hand, the Ukrainian language has declined in the schools. Parents send their children to Russian-language schools, because this education provides opportunities in higher education and employment elsewhere in the Soviet Union.

Belorussia Belorussia, or White Russia, is located on the steppe between Russia and Poland. It has a population of 9 million, which represents 4 percent of the total population of the Soviet Union.

Like the Ukrainians, the Belorussians have close ethnic ties to the Russians. They also have historic ties with the nearby Lithuanians. Stalin extended his terror to the Belorussians. The discovery of mass graves of his victims near Minsk, the capital, helped reawaken nationalism among the people. In 1988 a **popular front**—a political coalition—grew up in opposition to the Belorussian Communist party.

Baltic Republics

No peoples have been more unhappy belonging to the Soviet Union than the Lithuanians, Latvians, and Estonians. These tiny countries on the Baltic Sea were dominated for centuries by Poles and Swedes before becoming provinces of tsarist Russia. Their countries bear a similarity to the Scandinavian nations, but the people are distinct ethnically, neither Scandinavian nor Russian. Each country has its own language. They have the highest standard of living in the Soviet Union.

Estonia The smallest republic is Estonia. The Estonians are ethnically related to the Finns. Most belong to the Lutheran Church. Of Estonia's 1.6 million people, about 65 percent are Estonians. A large number of Russians have moved into the country. They now account for 28 percent of the population. Although about 20 percent of the land is marshland, agriculture is the principal occupation.

The Soviet Union has allowed Estonia to develop its own economy as a free zone where some forms of capitalism may exist. This may not be

Lithuanian demonstrators ask for freedom from the Soviet government. When did they become part of the USSR?

enough to satisfy the aspirations of Estonians, however. Many Estonians are calling for independence. A Citizens' Committee has invited Estonians who left the country at the time of Soviet annexation to return home.

Latvia   Latvia is the middle Baltic republic, lying between Estonia to the north and Lithuania to the south. Of its 2.7 million people, about 54 percent are Latvians. Russian immigrants comprise a large minority of 33 percent. Agriculture dominates the Latvian economy, but it has growing industrial potential.

Latvia's Popular Front was the first group in the Baltic republics to call for independence. In local elections held in 1989, 75 percent of the seats went to candidates who supported independence.

Lithuania   The largest Baltic republic is Lithuania. It has a population of 3.7 million, of whom 80 percent are Lithuanians. Only about 9 percent are Russians and another 8 percent are Poles. Like its neighbors, Lithuania is chiefly agricultural, but it is the most industrial of the Baltic republics. The Roman Catholic Church plays an important role in the life of Lithuanian people, and its language is the oldest language still spoken in Europe. During the 1100s, Lithuania had an extensive empire, but more powerful neighbors such as Poland and Russia extinguished it.

Lithuania declared its independence in March 1990. This resulted in increased tension between Lithuania and the Soviet Union. However, the Lithuanians seem willing to negotiate the matter rather than precipitate a violent reaction from the Soviet government.

The Baltic countries were independent democracies during the period between the world wars. Then the Nazi-Soviet Pact between Hitler and Stalin handed them over to the Soviet Union in 1940. Stalin's **annexation** was so brutal that even many local Communists refused to support rule by the Soviets. The United States government never recognized Estonia, Latvia, or Lithuania as part of the Soviet Union.

The Baltic republics were receptive to perestroika. The Soviet government has allowed Estonia and Lithuana to develop a free-market economy. But this was not enough. The Baltic republics said that Stalin's annexation was outside the bounds of international law. Moreover, it was carried out by force and without the approval of the people involved. Therefore, Soviet annexation had no validity. Gorbachev has said that the mistreatment of the nationalities explains the current dissatisfaction in the republics. The independence movements have attracted worldwide attention. The Soviet government is alarmed at the strength of these movements because they could destroy the Soviet Union.

Transcaucasian and Moldavian Republics

Most nationalities throughout the Soviet Union have clung to their individual languages and have used them as a means of keeping and reinforcing their cultural identity. One republic that obtained official status for its language is Moldavia.

Between the Black Sea and the Caspian Sea are three small republics: Georgia, Armenia, and Azerbaijan. They were originally a single republic called the Transcaucasian Federation when the Soviet Union first formed in 1922. They became separate republics in 1936. All have rich, ancient heritages. Two of them are Christian and one is Muslim.

Moldavia   In the southwestern corner of the Soviet Union is the small republic of Moldavia. About two-thirds of its 4.3 million people are Moldavians. Ukrainians represent 14 percent and Russians 13 percent of the total. Moldavia is the most densely populated republic in the Soviet Union. Until 1940 part of it belonged to Romania. It was then known as Bessarabia. A smaller section belonged to the Ukraine. The nationalist movement in Moldavia is expected to favor reunification with Romania.

Georgia   Bordering the Black Sea and Turkey is the Georgian Soviet Federated Republic. Georgia has a population of 5.4 million, about 69 percent of whom are Georgians. The rest are a mix—less than 10 percent each—of Armenians, Russians, and Azerbaijanis. The Georgians are a European and Christian people. They had a powerful kingdom during the Middle Ages, but by the time the Russians took over Georgia in the 1800s it had broken down into many small principalities. While strongly nationalistic, Georgians are also proud that Stalin was a native son. Georgia is a prosperous land whose livestock business provides meat for the Soviet Union. It also has important raw materials.

The Communist party in Georgia has no popular support. Georgian nationalism has revived, but the movement is divided. Nevertheless, it aims to preserve the Georgian language and prevent further Russification and Russian immigration. Some of its leaders have seized upon human rights and environmental issues such as oil pollution in order to press for Georgia's right to secede from the Soviet Union. Anti-government riots, in which several people were killed, took place in March 1989.

Armenia   To the east of Georgia is Armenia. It is the smallest republic of the Soviet Union in area—12,000 square miles (31 080 square kilometers). After Moldavia, it is the most densely populated republic. About 90 percent of the population of 3.3 million are Armenians. Only 2 percent are Russians.

The Armenians adopted Christianity in A.D. 301. They have a long and varied history. Like the Jews, the Armenians have been forced to move from their homes time and again by more powerful enemies. The Armenian patriarch asked the tsars for protection against the Muslims in the 1600s. Part of the land inhabited by Armenians was incorporated into the Russian Empire in 1828. During World War I, the Ottoman Turks believed that the Armenians collaborated with the advancing Russians. They deported and massacred hundreds of thousands of Armenians. The Armenians hate the Turks and their Muslim neighbors, the Azerbaijanis.

Azerbaijan   The largest of the three Transcaucasian republics is Azerbaijan. Its population is 7 million, of which 78 percent are Azerbaijanis. Oil is the most important industry. It is centered at Baku, the capital of Azerbaijan.

This republic was part of the Persian Empire, but its people are not Persians. The Azerbaijanis are descendants of the Mongols of the Golden Horde and speak a Turkic language. Azerbaijanis converted to Islam in the 1300s. They belong to the same Shiite branch of Islam as the Iranians. As such, they worry the leaders of the Soviet Union. Azerbaijani nationalists tore down the border fencing between the Soviet Union and Iran, and they would like to form a larger state that would include other Shiites. More alarming, however, is the struggle between Azerbaijanis and Armenians.

Right in the middle of Azerbaijan is Nagorno-Karabakh (nuh-GAWR-noh kar-uh-BAHK), an autonomous region inhabited by Armenians. The Armenians were unhappy when the Soviets decided in 1921 to include Nagorno-Karabakh within the Azerbaijani republic. Azerbaijanis discriminate against Armenians in employment and housing. Worse, after four years of primary schooling, Armenian parents must decide if they want their children to continue schooling in the Russian or Azerbaijani language. The Armenian language is not taught. This helps explain why Armenians want Nagorno-Karabakh to be part of the Armenian republic.

Not until 1987, when glasnost gave them encouragement, did Armenians plead their case to the Soviet government. They got no response. Since then, the Armenian nationalist movement has gathered steam. Karabakh has been the scene of considerable violence and bloodshed. An earthquake in December 1988 provided an excuse for Moscow to begin **direct rule** in Nagorno-Karabahk. The government also sent large numbers of troops into the Armenian republic to restore order.

Central Asia

Five republics occupy a huge area in Central Asia on the Soviet Union's southeastern border. The region used to be known as Turkestan. For centuries Russia, China, Persia, and Afghanistan fought over it. The Russian tsars extended their control into Turkestan in the 1800s. The people, who are chiefly descendants of Turkish nomads, did not form separate regions until the Communists created the republics during the 1920s and 1930s. The five republics are Kazakhstan (kuh-ZAK-stan), Uzbekistan (uz-BEK-i-STAN), Turkmenistan (turk-MEN-i-STAN), Tadzhikistan (tah-JIK-i-STAN), and Kirgizia (kir-GEE-zhee-uh). All are Turkic-speaking except for the Tadzhiks. They speak a form of Persian.

The Soviet government has encouraged each republic to develop its own distinct written language. Schoolchildren learn that language first, and Russian as a second language. The result has been increased literacy and the development of a native literature. The people are predominantly Muslim, and their culture is closely tied to their religion.

Kazakhstan The second largest republic in the Soviet Union, after the Russian Soviet Federative Socialist Republic, is Kazakhstan. It is flat, semidesert country and covers an area about one-third the size of the continental United States. It stretches from the Caspian Sea to China. Until recently, the building of irrigation canals allowed agriculture to prosper in the region. Kazakhstan also has rich mineral deposits, notably coal and oil.

Since World War II, many people from European Russia have moved to Kazakhstan. The result has been that a larger number of Russians than Kazakhs now live there (41 percent to the Kazakhs' 36 percent). With the simultaneous weakening of the Soviet economy and Gorbachev's perestroika, unemployed Kazakhs were the first ethnic group in the Soviet Union to riot. They took out their resentment on the more prosperous ethnic Russians and Ukrainians (6 percent) living there.

Uzbekistan In the middle of Soviet Central Asia is the republic of Uzbekistan. It was once part of the land of the Golden Horde and a center for Muslim learning. Uzbekistan contains the famous trade-route cities of Khiva and Bukhara. The 2,500-year-old ruins of the ancient city of Samarkand are near the modern city of that name. Timur (Tamerlane) is buried there. Tashkent, the capital, was destroyed by an earthquake in 1966. The city was completely rebuilt and serves as a model of Soviet city planning. Uzbekistan was one of the last areas to be conquered by the tsars. The Soviets established the republic in 1924.

Like Kazakhstan, the region is flat. Irrigation has made it possible to grow one-third of the Soviet Union's cotton.

The Uzbeks represent 69 percent of the population of 19.9 million. Russians comprise 11 percent. Small minorities of peoples from neighboring republics make up the rest. Most of the people are Muslim, so religious freedom is an important element in the nationalist movement. Anti-Russian sentiment is not new. Back in 1969, when a Russian soccer team defeated an Uzbek team in Tashkent, Uzbek sports fans harassed Russian university students.

However, conflict is directed not only against Russians but also against other Muslim peoples. In 1989 Uzbeks attacked the dwellings of Meskhetian Muslims and killed 100 of them. Stalin had deported these unfortunate people from the Caucasus in 1944. They were never allowed to return home. The violence erupted from a marketplace dispute over the price of strawberries. This example shows how economic and ethnic problems merge. It is common throughout the Soviet Union. In this case, Uzbeks were outraged at having "foreigners" placed among them. The Soviet government had to send in troops to stop the killings.

Turkmenistan To the west of Uzbekistan is the Turkmen Soviet Socialist Republic, or Turkmenistan. On its southern borders are Iran and Afghanistan. To the west is the Caspian Sea. Turkmenistan was mostly a barren desert, but modern irrigation methods made the land bloom. However, the republic is poorer than either Uzbekistan or Kazakhstan. Its population is also smaller, only 3.5 million. The people are 68 percent

An old man of Turkmenistan wears a traditional wool cap.

Turkmen, 13 percent Russians, 9 percent Uzbeks, and 3 percent Kazakhs. The republic is largely unaffected by Gorbachev's reforms, and has no active nationalist movement.

Tadzhikistan   The smallest of the Central Asian republics can claim the highest mountain peak in the Soviet Union. This is Mount Communism in the Pamirs, at 24,584 feet (7 500 meters). This republic borders on troubled Afghanistan to the south and China on the east. Unlike the peoples in the neighboring Soviet republics in Central Asia, the Tadzhiks are of Persian rather than Turkic background. Cotton and livestock are important occupations in this basically agricultural republic.

The Tadzhiks make up 59 percent of the population of 5.1 million. They are not immune to ethnic unrest. They direct their resentment against the Russians who are 10 percent of the population.

Kirgizia   East of Turkmenistan on the Chinese border is Kirgizia. It is a rugged, mountainous region inhabited by nomadic peoples who make a living from livestock herding. At 48 percent, the Kirgiz make up less than half the population of 4.3 million. Russians comprise 26 percent and Uzbeks 12 percent of the total. Kirgizia has many of the same economic problems that face the rest of the Soviet Union. They have led to riots and demands for economic autonomy but so far, not for independence.

Citizens Without Republics

In addition to the 15 republics, the Soviet Union also has 19 autonomous soviet socialist republics (ASSRs) and nine autonomous regions, or *oblasts*. The **autonomous republics** were designed to provide a territorial homeland for ethnic groups that were not large enough to be given a republic. They have their own constitutions but are not considered sovereign states in the Soviet constitution like the republics are. They are administered by the union republic in which they are located. **Autonomous regions** are even smaller and do not qualify for republic status.

Most Soviet citizens have their nationality stamped on their passports. Curiously, the government denies this to a few peoples: the Germans, Tartars, and Jews.

Germans   The Soviet Union contains nearly 2 million Germans. Most of them are descendants of Germans invited by Catherine II to settle in Russia. From 1924 to 1941 they had their own autonomous republic along the Volga River in southern Russia.

Fearing their disloyalty during World War II, Stalin deported them. A large number of them—about 46 percent—live in Kazakhstan or in the border areas of the Russian republic. Khrushchev rehabilitated the Volga Germans as a people but did not return them to their homeland.

Tartars   The 6 million Tartars are descendants of the Mongols of the Golden Horde. Like the Germans, they had their own autonomous republic in the Crimea until World War II. Stalin believed they collaborated with the Nazis, so he deported all of them to Central Asia and Siberia. Their homeland was given to the Ukraine.

Soviet leaders have not allowed the Tartars to return to the Crimea. They are concerned that the Tartars might be Muslim nationalists.

Jews   Members of the third group are labeled Jews on their passports, but the government denies that they are a nationality. However, Jews do have their own autonomous region. In the 1920s, the Soviet government created the Jewish Autonomous Region of Birobidzhan (bir-OH-bi-ZHAHN). It is located along the Trans-Siberian Railroad in the Far East next to Manchuria. However, most Jews are unwilling to live there. The population of Birobidzhan is no more than 10 percent Jewish.

The political structure of the Soviet Union clearly reveals that it is a multinational state. Even so, about 60 million people do not live within their ethnic homelands. Whether they have a union republic, an autonomous republic, an autonomous region, or none at all, the aspirations and grievances of all the nationalities have not been satisfied. The tsars tried Russification without success. The Communists created a union based on nationalities, but the leaders in Moscow continued to give the orders. They clamped a firm lid on any real independence for the nationalities.

Glasnost allowed national aspirations and grievances to come into the open during the late 1980s. Violence took place and many people have become refugees in order to avoid it. The strife could very well lead to the breakup of the Soviet Union.

1. **Recall** How did the Communists organize the Soviet Union as a political unit?
2. **How and Why** Which of the divisions of the Soviet Union has taken the lead in the independence movement and why?
3. **Critical Thinking** How does the Soviet Union's nationalities policy work against forming one Soviet people?

SECTION

2

Religion

Kievan Rus gained wealth through its trade with the Byzantine Empire. At the same time, the Kievan Rus adopted many aspects of Byzantine civilization, most notably its religion.

The official religion of the Byzantine Empire was Eastern Orthodox Christianity. Emperor Constantine made Christianity the official religion of the Roman Empire in A.D. 313, but eastern and western Europeans gradually drifted apart. They disagreed over politics, culture, and the interpretation of their religion. In 1054 eastern and western Christians made a permanent break. Eastern Christians followed the patriarch in Constantinople. Western Christians obeyed the pope in Rome.

The Kievan Rus had chosen to follow the rituals and beliefs of the Orthodox Christians of the Byzantine Empire many years before the official split. Afterward they remained loyal to the Orthodox Church.

The Russian Orthodox Church

The Kievan Rus were nature worshipers until Vladimir I of Kiev became a Christian in the 980s. Vladimir wanted his people to follow some religion but he was unable to choose among the Muslim, Jewish, and Christian faiths. He sent out agents to find the best religion for his people.

These men went to religious services all over the known world. They reported to Vladimir that the most magnificent ceremonies were held at the Orthodox cathedral of St. Sophia (Hagia Sophia) in Constantinople. The ritual, sincerity of worship, and beautiful churches of the Eastern Orthodox faith overwhelmed Vladimir's agents. After Vladimir was baptized a Christian, he had his subjects baptized. Eastern Orthodox Christianity became the official religion of Kievan Rus and the Russian state that followed.

The Orthodox Church vastly changed Russian life. The church shaped and colored morals, family and national values, laws, language, literature, and art. The Russians had no written language of their own, so they used the Slavic or Cyrillic (suh-RIL-lik) alphabet created by saints Cyril and Methodius, the missionaries credited with converting the Slavs to Christianity. Byzantine priests opened schools and taught religion, reading, and writing. The first Russian literature was produced from these church schools. First came religious books; then came historical works such as the *Primary Chronicle*, which dates from the 1100s. The Russians also began to use the ancient Roman laws that the Byzantines had preserved. The earliest Russian commercial code was called the *Russkaya Pravda*. It contained regulations on loans, interest rates, wages, and working conditions.

The Church and the Tsars The Orthodox Church grew stronger with the development of the Russian state and the power of the tsars. Close ties grew up between church and state. During the Time of Troubles, the Orthodox Church provided unity and kept learning and culture alive.

However, with the beginning of the Romanov dynasty, changes occurred within the Orthodox Church that would eventually tear it apart. In 1652 Tsar Alexis appointed Patriarch Nikon as head of the Church. The Church emphasized ritual and ceremony. Nikon standardized the ritual of the Church and introduced a new prayer book that corrected errors in the language. Many of the words in old Cyrillic had lost their meaning. Nikon brought in Ukrainian scholars to help make these changes. Nikon's reforms, however, alienated the suspicious, uneducated masses. They did not understand the language of the Church, but they were accustomed to hearing the language of the old prayers and observing the practices of the rituals. To change them was heresy. Some members of the upper clergy feared that the Ukrainians might introduce Western, Catholic influences into the Orthodox Church.

Because he had moved too rapidly in his reforms and alienated the tsar, Patriarch Nikon was forced to resign. Nevertheless, his reforms stayed in place. Thousands of Russians left the Church. These dissenters were called Old Believers. They believed it was their mission to preserve the old and traditional forms of the Church. However, because the Old Believers were against the Church and its changes, the tsars said they also were against the state. Persecutions began and thousands were tortured and killed.

The persecutions continued almost to the end of the Russian Empire. But the Old Believers starved themselves to death, buried themselves alive, and burned whole congregations in their churches rather than accept the changes. In 1905 they were officially tolerated. Today the Old Believers persist and number perhaps 5 million.

You recall that when Peter the Great became tsar, he abolished the position of patriarch. Instead he established a **synod**, a group of men loyal to him, to govern the church. From the reign of Alexander I, the Church taught that the tsar was chosen by God to rule Russia. The people were to consider the tsar their Little Father. Church and state were probably linked more closely in Russia than in any other European country.

Because of these links, the clergy grew into a powerful class. Monasteries became centers of culture and education. Monks became owners of large tracts of land and thousands of serfs. Their increasing wealth had a corrupting influence on the Russian Orthodox Church.

tracts of land: areas of land

813

The life of the parish priests, however, was very different. They lived close to the peasants and usually were themselves peasants. To support themselves and their families, the priests worked in the fields alongside their parishioners. They were often uneducated and did not always provide the religious training that the people needed. Occasionally priests led or joined the people in revolts. On the whole, however, the Church was a strong support for the tsars and their policies.

Communist Persecution   The Communists believe the basic assumptions of religion to be false. They consider religion to be, as Karl Marx described it, "the opium of the people." They disliked the clergy and hated the Orthodox Church because of its close ties to the tsars. When the Communists came to power, they nationalized church property, seized church valuables, forbade priests to teach, sent many into exile, and imprisoned and executed others. Churches were made into museums or taxed so heavily that they closed.

The persecution of the 1930s under Stalin was the worst the Church ever experienced. When Stalin collectivized agriculture, many village churches were closed or destroyed. The priests were killed or exiled along with the kulaks. For a time the children of priests could not obtain a university education. Children under 18 could be taught religion only at home and in groups of three or less. Only people who cared little for their careers and their lives dared to practice religion openly.

When World War II broke out, relations between church and state improved. Stalin needed support from all the people if the enemy was to be defeated. Persecution eased for a time but was renewed under Khrushchev.

The Cathedral of the Annunciation was built by Ivan the Great. It stands within the walls of the Kremlin in Moscow. The Kremlin—which means fort—was once the home of the royal family and later of the Soviet government.

The Church Today   Today the Orthodox Church and all denominations in the Soviet Union operate under very strict regulations and government control. Religious congregations that hold public worship services must register all their members. The state must approve appointments of all clergy. This ensures that bishops and priests will be people who will work with the Communist party.

The membership of the Russian Orthodox Church is estimated to number from 40 million to 60 million. For many years, most worshipers seemed to be older women. Today religious activity appears to be on the rise, especially among young people and intellectuals. Some writers, including the exiled Aleksander Solzhenitsyn, see the Orthodox Church, with its simple peasant faith, as the holder of Russia's purest cultural and moral values. However, other educated and urban Soviet citizens have looked elsewhere for a more intellectual, literate faith that can compete with Marxism. Furthermore, some observers think that church attendance, the wearing of religious emblems, and making the sign of the cross are less signs of religious fervor than ways of striking back at the government.

In 1988 the Orthodox Church celebrated its 1,000th birthday. Many churches were restored for the occasion and opened to worship. This renewed activity coincided with the government's realization that it alone could not solve the country's social problems: poor work habits, alcoholism, corruption, and weakening of family life. The government and the Communist party are looking to the Church for help in this quarter.

The question seems to be whether the Orthodox Church is able to help solve these problems. After more than 70 years of persecution, the Church was put to its greatest test by simply surviving. And it has survived largely because it did what the state told it to do. Nevertheless, the revival of faith among the Soviet people—unable to get spiritual sustenance from communist ideology—will benefit the Church.

Russia's policies of expansion brought many new peoples and new religions into the Soviet government. Since the time of Catherine the Great, rulers have tried to force these people to accept the Orthodox Church. Many, however, continued to practice their own religion. Later the Communists made it as difficult for them as for members of the Orthodox Church.

Judaism

Before 1939 some 7.5 million Jews lived in the Soviet Union and Eastern Europe. The Nazis killed 5.5 million. After the war, thousands of those remaining emigrated to the new state of Israel. This nation was created after World War II as a national homeland for the Jews.

Most Soviet Jews live in the western part of the country, especially in lands taken from Poland during the reign of Catherine the Great. Tsarist Russia had some 4.5 million Jews. Today the figure is somewhat less than 2 million.

Before the rise of Kievan Rus, the ruling class of the Khazars converted to Judaism. Later, Polish kings allowed Jews from Western

Europe to settle in their lands. Others settled in the Ukraine. The Jews have been especially persecuted. In the 1600s and 1700s, the Cossacks killed thousands of Jews because they served as tax collectors and administrators for absentee Polish landlords. The persecutions continued when these areas became part of Russia.

Jews were allowed to live only in certain places in Russia. They were not permitted to join some professions. Usually they could not own land and only a few were allowed to go to school. Jews could not observe their Sabbath, which falls on Saturday, because they were supposed to work. At times their synagogues and schools for training rabbis were closed.

Even though many early Bolsheviks were Jews, Communist propaganda has continued to single out the Jews for attack. It has accused them of being agents of international imperialism. Stalin killed many of his Jewish party comrades during the purges. Since that time Jews have rarely held high government office. When the Nazis invaded the Soviet Union in World War II, they massacred many more Jews.

The Jews remaining in the Soviet Union represent the largest number outside Israel and the United States. Anti-Semitism is still strong and glasnost has brought it much more into the open. Anti-Semitic organizations not sanctioned by the government, particularly among the Russians, accuse the Jews of being behind all the ills affecting the Soviet Union.

Jews naturally have been unhappy with their status in the Soviet Union. Many wanted to emigrate to Israel, but the Soviet government alternated between refusing and allowing them to go. Part of the explanation in the past has been Soviet support of the Arabs in the Middle East conflict. However, an even larger number of Jews wishing to emigrate preferred to go to the United States. During the 1970s, as many as 4,000 Jews emigrated each month. Then the Soviets tightened up their policy of granting visas. The "Refusniks"—Jews who did not receive permission to leave—often lost their jobs or were intimidated by the police. Nevertheless, thousands of Soviet Jews did manage to emigrate.

Islam

The Soviet Union is the fifth or sixth largest Muslim country in the world, after Indonesia, Pakistan, Bangladesh, India, and possibly Turkey. Muslims are the second largest religious group after the Orthodox Church. They number about 55 million, most of whom live in the Central Asian republics. This is only 19.2 percent of the total population, but Muslims have double the population growth rate of other peoples in the Soviet Union.

When the tsars conquered Central Asia in the 1800s, millions of Muslims became citizens of Russia. At that time they were severely persecuted. Many fled. The Communists promised religious freedom for all when they came to power. Islam is a flexible religion that shared with the Communists the common struggle against Western imperialism and a belief in equality.

The early alliance between Muslims and Communists soon broke up. Communist atheism did not mesh with Islam. Muslim roots were closer to Asia than to European Russia. In any case, the Communists began persecuting Muslims as ruthlessly as the tsars had. Stalin closed almost all of the 26,000 mosques that existed in 1917. The mullahs were killed or sent to forced labor camps. Stalin forced Muslims to give up the Arabic script in their Turkic languages and use the Cyrillic script.

During the long period of Soviet rule, the Muslims lived quietly in the villages or the countryside. They did not migrate to the Soviet cities and have stayed in their homelands. They kept up their traditions as much as possible.

Unlike Christianity, Islam has been able to mix secular and religious customs. For example, Muslims are expected to fast from sunrise to sundown during the holy month of Ramadan. The Communists claimed this interfered with work schedules. To accommodate the Soviets, a Muslim laborer might fast only a few days instead of a whole month in order to be strong enough to work. Muslims are also expected to go to their mosques to pray five times a day. Muslim workers will stay at the workplace and say their prayers fewer times. These issues were of much less concern to Muslims than family and community customs relating to marriage and death.

When he came to power, Gorbachev said that Islam was the "enemy of progress and socialism." Now glasnost has made Muslims more assertive. Muslims in Tadzhikistan want their religion to be the official religion. Television and radio programs regularly feature Muslim programs. Many long-closed mosques are open again and new ones have been built. Some strict Muslims insist that women wear the veil, as they are required to do in fundamentalist Iran. Long repressed, Islam is attracting young members in the Central Asian republics. Arabic-language schools are operating again. Saudi Arabia has shipped thousands of copies of the Koran to the Soviet Union.

Many Muslims are less interested in political independence than in complete religious freedom, the right to use their script, and equal treatment with non-Muslim peoples. Given the revival of fundamentalist Islam in the Muslim Middle East, however, Soviet leaders fear a similar explosion in their land. Soviet soldiers encountered fundamentalist Muslims firsthand in Afghanistan. There, rebels, fighting with primitive weapons and a few rocket launchers supplied by the United States, fought the Soviet forces to a standstill. Gorbachev was forced to evacuate Soviet forces from Afghanistan in 1989.

Soviet authorities have continued to forbid the existence of the Sufi brotherhoods. These secret religious orders spearheaded the resistance to Russian settlement in the 1800s. They remain uncompromising in their dedication to their Islam. Not much is known about the activities of the Sufis today. But they have fertile ground on which to work, because Muslims in general distrust Europeans. While Muslim opposition usually takes the form of passive resistance, violence has become more common. Some of it has been aimed at Muslims who belong to different ethnic groups.

An old mosque near the town of Buna in the Bosnia region of Yugoslavia. About 10 percent of the people who live in Bosnia are Muslims.

Roman Catholicism

Catholics in the Soviet Union are a minority. Most of the approximately 4 million Roman Catholics are Lithuanians, Latvians, or Poles. The most important group is the Lithuanian church with more than 2.5 million members.

After Lithuania became part of the Russian Empire as a result of the Third Partition of Poland in 1795, the Roman Catholic Church became the focus of Lithuanian nationalism. The Church suffered under the tsarist Russification program and its lands were confiscated. Lithuanian Catholics had only a short period of freedom, from 1917 to 1940. Stalin's regime imprisoned or killed the bishops and many priests, and Khrushchev cracked down again with his antireligion campaign.

In the 1970s, Lithuanians began to press for religious freedom. The new Polish pope, John Paul II, took an active interest in Lithuania. He has managed to get the Soviet government to make some concessions concerning the appointment of bishops and the arrangement of diocesan boundaries.

The number of Catholics in Latvia is only about 10 percent of that of Lithuania. Roman Catholics—mostly of Polish background—also live in Belorussia. Even fewer Roman Catholics live in the Ukraine.

A special situation exists in the Ukraine. It has the Ukrainian Catholic Church, often called the Uniate Church. The Uniates recognize the pope but follow Orthodox rites. Stalin suspected the Uniates of collaborating with the Nazis. In 1946 he forced the church to merge with the Russian Orthodox Church. Many Uniates refused to attend the Orthodox Church and formed an underground church. Even though the Communists imprisoned or exiled its leaders, this underground church has thrived. Pope John Paul II has openly supported the Ukrainian Catholic Church. It not only provides Ukrainians with a church that uses their language, but it also has become associated closely with Ukrainian nationalism. In April 1987, on the anniversary of the Chernobyl disaster, a 12-year-old peasant girl claimed to have seen the Virgin Mary. This created a sensation. Some Uniates went on pilgrimages. Others claimed that they too had seen the Virgin Mary, who urged the Ukrainians to separate from the Soviet Union. The Soviet government has made no concessions concerning the Uniates.

On December 1, 1989, Mikhail Gorbachev paid a historic visit to Pope John Paul II in Rome—the first such visit ever by a Soviet head of state. The visit clearly indicates a shift in the position of the Soviet Union away from confrontation and toward better church-state relations, at least with the Roman Catholic Church.

Pope John Paul II was greeted by thousands of Poles on his visit to his native land in 1983. The Roman Catholic Church is a popular force in Polish society.

Protestantism

Protestant churches are not as rigidly organized as the Roman Catholic Church. Because of their differences, Soviet authorities have treated them in varying ways. Nevertheless, Protestants in the Soviet Union have been persecuted as severely as any other religious group.

Baptists   The Baptists form the largest Protestant group in the Soviet Union. They may well be the largest Christian group after the Orthodox Church itself. There could be as many as 1.5 million baptized adults and an additional 3 to 4 million family members. Total membership is difficult to determine, however, because of government refusal to register all Baptist communities, and a schism within the Baptist Church that dates from 1961. After World War II, the All Union Council of Evangelical Christians and Baptists was formed. Its members accept state regulation. During Khrushchev's persecution, dissident members refused to accept Soviet rules on paying taxes on church income, the holding of Sunday schools, and **proselytization**, or seeking to convert new members. The dissidents broke away and their leaders have been imprisoned.

The Baptists were first organized in Russia in the 1880s. Tsarist persecution was at first severe and then relaxed after the Revolution of 1905. The new Communist regime took no action against the Baptists, because they had opposed the tsars and held attitudes similar to those of the Communists toward drinking, sexual freedom, and hard work. Baptists even formed their own collective farms and youth movement. But Stalin's persecution began in 1928 when the Baptists refused to join the state collective farms. In addition, Soviet religious policy has always called for strict regulation of all churches. This put the Baptists squarely in the opposition with their advocacy of the separation of church and state and the complete autonomy of each congregation.

Nevertheless, the Baptists have attracted large numbers, particularly among the working class. Their emphasis on study of the Bible has been aided by the increasing literacy of Soviet citizens. At the same time, scripture reading has proved difficult because the government does not allow many Bibles to be printed.

Lutherans   The Lutherans are prominent in the Baltic republics. An estimated 350,000 Lutherans live in Estonia and 500,000 live in Latvia. The Soviet government has not interfered with the Lutherans to the extent it has with the Roman Catholics or the Baptists. This may be because the Lutheran Church is an established church with a long tradition of state regulation. At the same time, it does not have an influential international leader like the pope, nor has it thrust itself into conflict with the state as have the evangelists of the Protestant Church.

Pentecostalists   The only religion that came to the Soviet Union after the Russian Revolution was Pentecostalism. It was brought from the United States by a returned immigrant. The Soviet government persecuted the Pentecostalists as harshly as the Jews and Uniates. Soviet persecution may be explained by Pentecostalist insistence on proselytizing, setting up religious schools, and refusing to serve in the military. Stalin killed many of them and deported many others to Siberia. They have been allowed to work at only the poorest jobs and some were put in psychiatric hospitals. Young Pentecostalist men were forced to serve in the army because **conscientious objectors** are not recognized under Soviet law. They may number one half million, but this figure is approximate because many are not registered with the government.

1. **Recall**   How have organized religions been treated by the Soviet government?
2. **How and Why**   How does Soviet policy toward religion compare with that of the tsars?
3. **Critical Thinking**   Why do the Soviets fear Islam?

SECTION

3

Society

Under communism the Soviet Union has produced its own unique society. Most Soviet citizens have a similar standard of living and are entitled to equal social welfare benefits. The Communists provided freedom of opportunity. A person's birth or economic status no longer were important; ability was. But ability requires a certain amount of education. The Communist regime made education free to everyone. Soviet women participate fully in all areas of Soviet society. At the same time, the Communist leaders have become a new ruling class. They have replaced the tsars and the old aristocracy. The party has become the means for one to advance in society. The reformist mood present in the Soviet Union today, however, may well bring about changes in the Communist system. We have examined Soviet nationalities and religions. Let us turn now to other elements in the Soviet social fabric.

Social Organization

According to communism, history is an unfolding drama of conflict between different classes in society. The triumph of communism would mean the abolition of classes and the disappearance of conflict. But people do not always evolve according to a formula. The classless society has created its own classes. Private ownership of the means of production may not exist in the Soviet Union, but someone controls that production. It is the Soviet upper class.

At the top of Soviet society are the members of the Politburo and the Presidium, the members of the Council of Ministers, and ranking Communist leaders and officials. At this level also are generals and the most outstanding artists, writers, and scientists. They are few in number—less than one percent of the population. They live in luxurious houses or apartments, are driven in chauffeured automobiles, and have villas in the country or at the seaside. They shop in special stores not open to other Soviet citizens. When they die, they are even buried in special cemeteries. Their children behave much like the children of rich families in capitalist countries. Many have come to take the good life for granted.

The next group consists of the second level of Communist leaders. These are the managers of industry, the planners, high officials, engineers, university professors, artists, and scientists. They too get housing, food, and medical attention not available to most Soviet citizens. Their status roughly parallels that of the middle class elsewhere.

Lower down the social ladder are the men and women who are technicians, factory supervisors, better-paid clerks, and others of similar rank. They make up the lower middle class. Often they live with their families in an apartment in the city or in a small house in a village. In the city, two or more families may share an apartment. Each family has one room and shares the kitchen and the bathroom. Sometimes older buildings lack modern conveniences. Many high-rise apartment buildings have no elevators. A telephone is a real luxury.

The average Soviet citizen finds basic items such as meat, eggs, and vegetables expensive. Both husbands and wives must work in order to meet expenses. After paying for food and rent, little money is left for entertainment. However, many kinds of entertainment like movies and the theater are free or very cheap. The Soviet people spend much of their time reading. Many books are available, although all have been censored. The lower middle class makes up between 30 and 40 percent of the population.

At the bottom of the social scale are the industrial and agricultural workers. These people do not starve, but their life is hard. They must budget very carefully, and the daily routine of making a living occupies much of their time.

Economic differences have led to social differences. These differences result in growing gaps between the classes. Members of a group tend to follow similar ways of life and to associate only with others of that group. Through education or membership in the Communist party, it is possible to climb to a higher level. In the past, young, ambitious, loyal, intelligent Communists have raised themselves and their families to the upper levels of Soviet society.

In the 1990s, however, the Soviet economy is badly in need of reform. Opportunities for advancement are limited not only by the failing economy but also by older people staying in their jobs longer. These problems are now being publicly addressed in the spirit of glasnost and perestroika by the reform-minded government of Mikhail Gorbachev.

The GUM department store in Moscow is the largest in the Soviet Union. Once a collection of shops, it is now a state-owned store that offers consumer goods from foreign nations.

Education

If the nationalities and religious groups tend to point up the differences among Soviet people, the educational system does not. Soviet education has tended to eliminate these differences. It has achieved what would have been unthinkable less than a century ago: almost total literacy.

History   Under the tsars, only male Russian aristocrats could read. The great mass of the population, including most women and the ethnic minorities, were illiterate and ignorant. The Orthodox Church ran the primary schools and the government established a few universities. The tsars considered these universities hotbeds of radicalism and sometimes closed them. The reform-minded Tsar Alexander II introduced some educational reforms, but his successors abandoned them.

After the Russian Revolution, education became of major importance. The Communists wanted the Soviet Union to become an industrialized country. This required an educated public. The Soviet leaders began at once to educate the people. They were determined to create the New Soviet Citizen. Every person who had some education was required to teach others. Classes were held on farms, in city apartment houses, in factories, and in army camps. By 1930 the Soviets said that the Soviet people were 81 percent literate.

The Soviet Union has never tried to hide the fact that political indoctrination of its citizens is part of its educational program. To produce the New Soviet Citizen, they taught students Communist values. These values include honesty, obedience, hard work, truthfulness, and consideration and sharing. Through all ages, the Soviet educational system emphasizes the collective or group interest over that of the individual. Teachers encourage students to help others who do not learn as fast. Students are encouraged to compete, but individual success is shown as benefiting the class or school rather than the individual.

Primary and Secondary Schools   More than 50 percent of Soviet children begin their education in state-operated nurseries and kindergartens. The 1984 school reform legislation requires children to begin primary school at age six instead of age seven as formerly required. Many Soviet parents protested sending children to the regimented school system at such an early age.

Soviet children must attend primary and secondary school for a minimum of eight years. Most attend for ten years. The lower grades of the Soviet secondary school are similar to American elementary schools. However, students in the Soviet Union attend school for six days a week instead of five. The Ministry of Education in Moscow prepares the course of study for everyone. The same textbooks are used throughout the Soviet Union. Teachers maintain strict discipline in the classroom. Students spend from four to five hours each day on homework.

Mathematics and science are the most important subjects at the primary and secondary level. Students take a heavy load of two mathematics courses every year, about five years each of biology, physics, and geography, four years of chemistry, and one year of astronomy. Everyone must learn Russian. Students in the non-Russian republics also learn their national language. In the sixth grade, students begin the study of foreign languages such as English and German.

The Soviet educational system requires that students study Marxism-Leninism and materialism, and the history of Russia, the Soviet Union, and the Communist party. The humanities and social sciences are of much less importance. Because Soviet students lack these studies, it has been said that they "usually do not exhibit much intellectual spontaneity. Soviet education tends to produce technicians rather than intellectuals."

Students may go to work after completing the minimum number of years in secondary school. Others may choose to go to vocational school for an additional two years and then take a job. A third option is to enter a *technicum*. This is an advanced vocational school where students can specialize in courses on medical technology, nursing, or machine tools. Special schools also exist for the handicapped, for preparation for military careers, and for advanced levels of mathematics, foreign languages, and the arts. The latter are the most prestigious secondary schools. Its graduates are most likely to enter the post-secondary schools which are the equivalent of American colleges and universities. By 1986, 70 percent of the population of the Soviet Union had secondary educations.

Post-Secondary Schools   It is difficult to gain admission into the Soviet Union's post-secondary schools. Admission is based on a student's school records, a rigorous entrance examination, and political reliability. The limited number of openings are determined by the Five-Year plans. Only students who continue their schooling beyond the secondary level can hope to rise to very high positions in the Soviet Union. For this reason, politically influential parents have succeeded in entering children with average records. Bribery of examination scorers is not unknown.

At the post-secondary level, the Communists are chiefly interested in producing engineers and scientists. The Soviet Union produces more scientists and three times as many engineers as does the United States.

In 1959 only about 2 percent of the population of the Soviet Union had attended post-secondary schools. By 1986 nearly 9 percent had done so. One might expect that the future looks brightest for the Soviet student who graduates from the university. In the past this was true. Even the least talented graduate found exciting employment. Today they are now over educated for jobs that require few talents. One reason is demographic. The system of Communist party appointments has kept officials in their jobs for life. Consequently, fewer young graduates are hired for important jobs. The jobs they do get do not match their qualifications. This has led to disillusionment with the bureaucracy on the part of young people.

Although graduates may be disturbed by the employment outlook, they have countered disappointment by becoming active in other ways. Glasnost has permitted the formation of clubs and voluntary associations. These have to be registered but some have not done so. By 1990 an estimated 60,000 of these organizations existed in the Soviet Union. Members pursue a wide variety of interests: international peace, environment, historic preservation, sports, yoga, rock music, and building a memorial to Stalin's victims. Many young Soviets have joined them.

Technology and Science   The Soviet Union's emphasis on the sciences has deep roots. In 1724 Peter the Great founded what later became the Imperial Academy of Sciences. Its task was to promote scientific achievement. This is one of the oldest scientific groups in the world. During the 1800s, Russian reformers such as Alexander Herzen (HERT-suhn) came to believe that progress for Russia would only come through an understanding and mastery of the natural and social sciences. The Crimean War pointed out the continued backwardness of the country.

Under the tsars, Russia produced such great scientists as Mendeleyev, Metchnikoff, and Pavlov. In 1869 Dmitri Mendeleyev created a

After devising the Periodic Chart, Dmitri Mendeleev continued his research. This drawing shows him making a balloon flight in 1887 to study the atmosphere.

system for classifying chemical elements according to their atomic weight and properties. Ilya Metchnikoff received the Nobel Prize for medicine in 1908. His research showed how white blood corpuscles fight and kill bacteria within the body.

Probably the best-known Russian scientist is Ivan Pavlov. He won the Nobel Prize in 1904 for physiology. Pavlov studied conditioned reflexes and used dogs in his experiments to show how habits are learned unconsciously. His work made a major contribution to psychology and the theory of learning.

When the Communists took control of the government, many scientists and technicians left Russia. Nevertheless, the new Soviet leaders went ahead with the encouragement of scientific work. They asserted that communism itself was based on scientific principles.

The Imperial Academy was transformed into the Academy of Sciences of the USSR. This academy controls research in fields as varied as science, engineering, literature, and history. The Soviet government funds most research and has built and equipped great scientific laboratories. After 1928 scientific research became part of the Five-Year plans. This action stopped people from duplicating one another's work, but it also hampered experimentation.

Soviet science is directed toward the practical. Under the Five-Year plans, science took second place to heavy industry. Today scientists and technicians continue to be put to work solving specific problems in industry, weaponry, and agriculture. For example, a great deal of work is done on transportation, pollution, and fuel and energy. The Soviets are experimenting with water heaters, refrigerators, portable wells, heaters, and air-conditioners operated by solar energy. Sometimes, however, scientists can be held back by too much central planning.

To help this situation and yet continue to solve practical problems, the Siberian branch of the Academy of Sciences set up a science center near Novosibirsk (noh-voh-suh-BIRSK). The center contains separate institutes for each of the sciences. Each institute is free to experiment in the study and development of Siberia.

Siberia holds great natural resources that the Soviet Union needs. It is believed that their discovery and development for industrial use is possible only through science. Novosibirsk has proved so successful that the government has made plans for other science cities.

The Soviets have demonstrated the greatest scientific skill in the fields of military weaponry and space technology. After World War II, Stalin used all available Soviet resources to develop nuclear weapons. Captured German scientists were put to work developing the Soviet Union's atomic arsenal. In 1949 the first Soviet atomic bomb was exploded. This was followed in 1951 by the explosion of a hydrogen bomb. Since then the Soviets have built a vast stockpile of nuclear weapons. The Soviet Union and the United States are the world's leading nuclear powers. During the cold war, the two nations competed in an arms race to build more and better weapons.

By the late 1960s, many Soviet scientists had become aware of the dangers of the arms race. They became supporters of the human rights movement as a way of making Soviet leaders responsible for their acts.

Andrei Sakharov was a human rights advocate and a successful scientist. How was he punished for his beliefs?

The inventor of the Soviet Union's hydrogen bomb, Andrei Sakharov (1921–1989), became a champion of human rights. The state punished Sakharov and other scientists rather lightly. The government regarded their scientific research as too important to do otherwise. In 1980 Sakharov was sent into exile at Gorky, a large city 250 miles (402 kilometers) east of Moscow, and was not dismissed from the Academy of Sciences. Gorbachev allowed him to return from exile before his death in 1989. By then Gorbachev's changes in arms policy had helped to abate the arms race.

The Soviets were also pioneers in space research and exploration. They were the first to launch a spacecraft. In 1957 they put *Sputnik I* aloft. They followed this in 1961 with Yuri Gagarin's orbit of the earth. In 1963 the Soviets sent the first woman, Valentina Tereshkova, into space. The Soviets have landed spacecraft on the moon, obtained lunar dust and rock samples, and returned them to earth. In 1975 they launched a joint space program with the United States. The Soviets have also launched the Salyut space stations and telecommunications satellites.

The Soviet Union is not as advanced as the United States and other Western nations in some areas of technology. For example, the Soviets lag in the field of microelectronics, which deals with miniature components such as the silicon chip used in computers and other electronic equipment. Because the West does not want the Soviets to have this technology, it has banned sales of such items as silicon chips to the Soviet Union.

The picture above shows workers on a construction site in Novosibirsk in the western part of Siberia in the Soviet Union.

Soviet Women

Equality for women in the Soviet Union is a reality. They make up more than half of the total labor force. There are few fields of endeavor—skilled or unskilled, professional or nonprofessional—in which women do not work. More than 70 percent of the doctors and teachers of the Soviet Union are women. Women are a sizeable minority in engineering, agricultural technology, and economics.

Many women were revolutionaries during the tsarist period and in the Bolshevik movement. Large numbers of women served on active duty during World War II. Today they comprise only one-fourth of the Communist party's membership and about half the total representation in the local soviets. However, only one woman, Yekatarina Furtseva, was ever appointed to the Politburo.

Male chauvinism—an attitude of superiority toward women—is strong in the Soviet Union. Women get equal pay but they are generally found in lower-paying jobs. They tend to stay in these jobs longer than men. While women have achieved important jobs in the Communist party and the Soviet government, they also sweep streets, shovel snow, drive tractors, and dig ditches.

Women monopolize the medical profession. However, women doctors are found more often in the less desirable rural areas than men doctors, who prefer to work in the cities. In recent years, Soviet health care has improved significantly. Epidemic diseases such as cholera have been virtually wiped out. Infant and maternity care have improved greatly. Venereal disease has been controlled, but AIDS has surfaced. The

epidemic diseases:
diseases that quickly spread among a group

Soviets compete in many sports. Here a speed skater and a cross country ski racer show their determination. Do you think governments should support athletes?

life expectancy in the Soviet Union is now 64 years for men and 73 years for women, and a national average of 68.5 years. Medical care, including hospitalization, is provided free by the state. Medicine can be purchased at a minimal cost. Doctors are employed by the state but some practice privately in the cooperative sector. However, they are taxed heavily for this extra income.

The Soviet government has encouraged women to work for several reasons. During World War II, the Soviet Union lost an estimated 26 million people. Immediately after the war, Soviet figures showed only 59 men for every 100 women. This disparity now exists chiefly in an aging segment of the population, although alarming figures show that the mortality rate of young men has again become very high, some say owing to alcoholism. The low number of men created an acute labor shortage. Women were needed to fill the vacancies. Today many women work to help support their families. But most important, the Soviet government considers women a valuable national resource that should be used.

The Soviet family underwent great disruption in the years of revolution and civil war, forced collectivization, industrialization, and world war. The Communists wanted to sever all connections between the family and marriage on the one hand, and the Church and tradition on the other. They made provision for simple civil marriages and easy divorces.

But large numbers of homeless orphans and fatherless families resulted from the purges and deportations. Stalin tightened up the rules for divorce and abortion in order to increase the birthrate and stabilize the family. Doctors who performed abortions went to prison. Married couples seeking a divorce found they had to go through expensive and complicated court proceedings.

After Stalin's death, however, more liberal laws reappeared. Divorce is granted automatically if both partners agree and there are no children. Property is divided equally between husband and wife. If children are involved, the matter must go to a people's court for a ruling. Couples must allow a month for a reconciliation. If they cannot reach an agreement, the court will grant the divorce, decide who should have custody of the children, and determine how the property should be divided.

Like many other modern working mothers and wives, Soviet women have problems taking care of their families. The state has tried to ease their burden. It runs a network of nurseries and kindergartens where working mothers may take their small children for the working day. Parents pay part of the cost of these schools, but the state pays most of it.

The Soviet government gives financial assistance and prestige to mothers. Pregnant women receive paid maternity leaves and cannot be fired from their jobs. The state gives special awards to women with large families. A child allowance is paid to mothers after their third child. Women who have given birth to and brought up 10 children receive the title of Heroine Mother. Unmarried mothers receive low monthly child allowances as do low-income families. Abortion was legalized again in 1955.

Women can retire at age 55, five years earlier than men. Usually they receive lighter sentences when they have broken the law.

This is the opening ceremony for the 1980 Summer Olympic Games in Moscow. Why did the United States and other nations boycott these games? Do you think sports should be used for political purposes?

Sports

The Soviet people in general are athletic. Sports are emphasized in schools, youth groups, at work, and on vacation. The government believes that physical fitness and good health produce better workers and soldiers. It sponsors physical fitness programs under the slogan "Ready for Labor and Defense." Soviet workers do exercises on their work breaks.

The Soviet climate encourages winter sports. The Soviet people are great fans of skiing, ice hockey, and skating. They also enjoy hunting, fishing, and swimming. They mob the beaches in summer, and in winter many swim in outdoor pools. Soccer is the national sport, and many Soviets are devoted fans of some soccer team.

Through its youth organizations, the government supervises all athletics. Officials are able to select and train the best youths. These then compete in such world competitions as the Olympic Games. The Soviets, especially women athletes, have been very successful in these events. All athletes in the Soviet Union are considered amateurs, but those groomed for competition are supported by the government.

SECTION 3 REVIEW

1. **Recall**   What important roles have women played in the Soviet Union?
2. **How and Why**   What are the social divisions within the Soviet Union, who belongs to them, and why have they developed?
3. **Critical Thinking**   What is the chief purpose of Soviet education and how is it accomplished?

Prior to the reign of Peter the Great, the Russian arts were closely tied to the Orthodox Church and the Byzantine Empire. Russia also had a strong folk culture. When Peter became tsar, he ended Russia's isolation from Western Europe. Western culture, however, reached only the educated classes. Catherine the Great continued to bring Western influences into Russia. But Russian rulers were quick to censor any foreign ideas that might interfere with their power. They also executed or sent into exile artists who opposed them.

Russian cultural achievements reached their peak in the 1800s. Much of this work, especially in literature, spoke out against the tsars and demanded government reform.

After the Russian Revolution, artists were told that their works should reflect Communist ideals. In the 1930s, through the Ministry of Culture, Stalin took control of the arts. He and ministry officials decided what would and would not be published or shown. The Writers Union was established in 1932. All Soviet writers who wanted to publish had to belong to the union. Soviet writing had to go through editors, censors, and party critics. As a result, it was bland.

Stalin and the Communist party imposed socialist realism on all art forms. According to this doctrine, the only purpose of art was to glorify communism and to inspire Communist ideals. In literature, for example, this meant showing the Communist heroes in a positive light and reaching a positive conclusion. Art has to be understandable and available to everyone. It should reflect the reality of the socialist state. Socialist realism underwent some modification following Stalin's death, but its stifling effects continued until recently.

Writers as Social Critics

During the 1840s, small revolutionary groups met to discuss politics and philosophy. They published their ideas in literary journals that covered a

Dostoevski was one of Russia's greatest writers. Beside him is part of the handwritten manuscript for his novel, The Brothers Karamazov.

wide range of subjects. Russian literature of the 1800s contains some of the masterpieces of world literature. Some of the country's greatest writers exposed in their works the political and social corruption of tsarist Russia.

Masters of Literature   One of these writers was Nikolai Gogol, who is considered the father of the Russian novel. In *Dead Souls* (1842), Gogol dealt with serfdom. Gogol's hero plans to buy all the serfs who have died since the last census. The government makes landlords pay taxes on these serfs until a new census is taken. The hero offers to pay a small sum for the serfs and pay the taxes on them. Then he will mortgage his newly acquired "dead souls" and use them to buy property elsewhere. Soviet critics have accepted Gogol's novel as faithful to life in tsarist Russia.

One of the greatest Russian writers was Feodor Dostoevski (dahs-tuh-YEF-skee), who lived from 1821 to 1881. In his youth Dostoevski belonged to a secret society that studied the forbidden works of the French utopian socialists. They were arrested and sentenced to death for supposedly setting up a secret printing press. As he stood before the firing squad, an order came reducing his sentence to four years at hard labor in Siberia followed by an additional four years of military service. He wrote about this close brush with death in *The Idiot* (1868). The hardships Dostoevski experienced gave him a great sympathy toward the underprivileged. In prison he had been allowed to read only the New Testament. Religious themes became prominent in his novels. He was convinced that the most miserable creature could be saved. His novels *Crime and Punishment* (1866), *The Possessed* (1871), and *The Brothers Karamazov* (1879–1880) deal with guilt, crime, and redemption. Dostoevski was a master of the realistic novel. His reputation is perhaps greater outside the Soviet Union. The Soviet authorities were long critical of Dostoevski's dislike for socialism and the importance he gave to religion and psychology.

Count Leo Tolstoy was a Russian noble whose masterpiece, *War and Peace* (1864–1869), covers Napoleon's invasion of Russia. This immense novel grew out of Tolstoy's own experiences in the Crimean War. The author attempts to demonstrate the futility of war. Tolstoy's second great novel was *Anna Karenina* (1873–1876). While working on this, Tolstoy began to develop his views on life. He accepted the moral and ethical teachings of Christianity, but his rejection of Christ's divinity and his criticism of the Orthodox Church led to his excommunication. Tolstoy also began crusading for social justice. He developed the doctrine of passive resistance that influenced Gandhi of India. Tolstoy grew to hate capitalism and all private property. Family relations worsened when he proposed to divide his property among the poor. His wife stopped him, knowing full well that the money Tolstoy earned from the sale of his books supported their large family. He spent his final years working in the fields, mending shoes, and writing. Tolstoy died in 1910 on his way to a monastery.

Censorship and Dissidence   The Communist repression of the artistic spirit has gone far beyond that of the tsars. In 1921 the Tenth Party Congress forbade criticism of the Communist party line. Many writers fled the country. Those who remained had to accept the increasing censorship imposed by Stalin or risk exile or death. Therefore, Soviet writers stayed close to the party line and the triumphs of socialism.

After Stalin died in 1953, Soviet writers began to grow more daring, especially those critical of Stalin. This period became known as the "thaw," after a novel of that name published in 1955 by the Soviet writer Ilya Erenburg. However, Soviet writers were still under the control of the Writers Union.

Restrictions tightened again in the late 1960s, especially after the 1968 uprising in Czechoslovakia. Still, people found out what was happening. They listened to foreign broadcasts and kept abreast of the world around them. They began to form small circles like those of the revolutionaries of the 1800s. The circles took a strong interest in human rights. Their members were called **dissidents**.

From the circles developed the *samizdat*, or "self-publishing." Individuals typed several copies of material that interested them, passed them on to other people, who in turn would type additional copies. Through the samizdat, people got around government censorship. Entire novels and journals got a widespread reading through the samizdat. Others were smuggled out to the West and published there.

Despite the "thaw," Khrushchev made the spread of the samizdat a crime. In 1966 Yuli Daniel and Andrey Sinyavsky were tried and sentenced to labor camps for smuggling their works out of the country. Worldwide protests over this incident were ignored by the Soviets. Still, the dissident movement spread. When the Helsinki Accords of 1975 included a clause on human rights, it struck a responsive chord among the dissidents. A Human Rights Commission formed, of which Andrei Sakharov was a member. The government could not return to the terrors of Stalin's regime, but it did strike back. By 1980 most of the dissident leaders had been exiled, put in labor camps, or locked away in psychiatric hospitals.

One of these dissident exiles was perhaps the Soviet Union's best-known writer, Aleksandr Solzhenitsyn (sohl-zhuh-NEET-shun). After serving as an officer in World War II, Solzhenitsyn was sentenced to eight years of hard labor in Siberia for having referred to Stalin as "the boss." This was followed by exile to Kazakhstan where he taught school. From his experiences he wrote the short story, *One Day in the Life of Ivan Denisovich* (1962). Khrushchev was engaged in his de-Stalinization campaign so he approved its publication. The story describes the horrors of a single day for a political prisoner in one of Stalin's labor camps. Two other works, *The First Circle* (1968) and *The Cancer Ward* (1968), deal with Solzhenitsyn's experiences as a prisoner and an exile. Solzhenitsyn's first nonfiction work was *The Gulag Archipelago* (1973). It describes and condemns the Communist system of police terror. These later works had to be published outside the Soviet Union. Solzhenitsyn fled the Soviet Union in 1974 and settled in Vermont. From exile he has advocated an end

Solzhenitsyn talks to the press in Switzerland after his deportation. Why do you think Soviet leaders deported him rather than exiling him to Siberia? What does this say about Soviet politics?

to Communist rule and the right of non-Russians to secede from the Soviet Union. He continues to write. *August 1914*, a novel in the tradition of Tolstoy, describes the first 11 days of World War I. Solzhenitsyn belongs to the Slavophile tradition. He sees communism as the latest Western influence that is undermining Russia's unique heritage. He received the Nobel Prize for Literature in 1970.

The dissident movement remained repressed by the government until 1986. The Chernobyl disaster helped to unlock the government's policy on the dissemination of information. In the spirit of glasnost, the government began to take a second look at socialist realism. Works by the Nobel Prize winner and author of *Doctor Zhivago* (1957), Boris Pasternak, and the poet Anna Akhmatova were reconsidered. Solzhenitsyn's works can now be published in the Soviet Union. While Stalin had long been under attack by the dissidents, now even Lenin is no longer safe from criticism as Soviet writers examine the past.

The Fine Arts

Russian art of the 1800s has never received the attention that literature of that period did. Yet it produced the realist painter Ilya Repin (1844–1930). Repin faithfully reconstructed on canvas the same harsh realities of daily life in Russia that Dostoevski recorded in his novels.

When the Communists seized power, they insisted on conformity in painting and sculpture as well as in literature. Artists were reluctant to experiment for fear that their works would not be accepted and that persecution and exile would follow. Two of the most famous Russian artists, the abstract painter Vassily Kandinsky (1866–1944) and Marc Chagall (1887–1985), left Russia to work elsewhere. Despite his long absence from his homeland, Chagall often painted scenes of Russian village life and Jewish persecutions based on his childhood memories.

Socialist realism became the official style in art. This art adapted well to the **propaganda** purposes of the Communist state. It consists mainly of realistic murals depicting the Soviet worker. Nevertheless, the state sees itself as the preserver of the past. The Communists have taken

The Bolshoi Theater Ballet dates to the late 1700s. Here the company performs Nutcracker *by the nineteenth-century composer Peter Tchaikovsky.*

classics:
works of art that are considered of lasting importance

care of the artistic treasures they inherited. The Soviet Union has superb impressionist paintings collected by capitalists before the Russian Revolution, as well as the huge art collections amassed by the tsars. Orthodox churches with their beautiful icons and the palaces of the tsars have been turned into museums.

The Performing Arts

Theater and filmmaking too have been held back by socialist realism. Since the government owns and controls all forms of communication—theaters and film studios as well as newspapers and television and radio stations—it insists that the party line be followed. This usually means that the media are used for propaganda purposes, not for artistic works. Nevertheless, one of the world's great film directors, Sergey Eisenstein (1898–1948), set precedents in film technique. Two of his classics are *Potemkin* (1926) and the uncompleted trilogy, *Ivan the Terrible* (1941–1944). On the Soviet stage either the classics or works about the glories of communism are performed. While Soviet actors are very skillful, Soviet drama lacks interest.

For generations the world has paid tribute to Russian achievements in music. The works of such renowned composers as Tchaikovsky, Rimsky-Korsakov, and Moussorgsky are heard everywhere. More recently, the composers Prokofiev, Shostakovich, and Khachaturian have received critical praise. One of the century's greatest composers, Igor Stravinsky, left Russia before the revolution.

The Russians are considered supreme in ballet. Both the tsars and the Communists have supported this art form. The Russian Imperial School of Ballet produced such great dancers as Anna Pavlova and Vaslav Nijinsky. Many Soviet cities have their own ballet companies, but the finest of all performs in the Bolshoi Theater in Moscow. Among Soviet dancers, competition to become a member of this group is keen.

Like the writers, a number of Soviet artists and musicians felt the lack of freedom. The ballet dancers Rudolf Nureyev, Mikhail Baryshnikov, and Natalia Makarova, and the cellist Mstislav Rostropovich fled to the West. Such individuals were among the elite of the Soviet Union. They were not leaving for economic or ideological reasons, but for artistic freedom. They disliked the party's determination of what they had to perform and their inability to experiment with new art forms.

SECTION 4 REVIEW

1. **Recall**   How have dissidents circulated their ideas?
2. **How and Why**   How has the Communist party controlled the arts in the Soviet Union?
3. **Critical Thinking**   How do modern Soviet writers resemble the great writers of the past?

R E V I E W

Reviewing People, Places, and Things

Identify, define, or explain each of the following:

self-determination

Baltic Republics

Nagorno-Karabakh

autonomous republics

Old Believers

Uniates

Academy of Sciences

Andrei Sakharov

Nikolai Gogol

Feodor Dostoevski

Leo Tolstoy

dissidents

samizdat

socialist realism

Aleksandr
  Solzhenitsyn

Map Study

Using an outline map of the USSR, label the republics, autonomous republics, and autonomous regions that make up the USSR. Then complete the map as one of the following: a resource map, a products map, or a land-use map. Include a map key and symbols where needed.

Understanding Facts and Ideas

1. How has the federation of Soviet republics worked against developing the New Soviet Citizen?

2. Which republic dominates the others? Why?

3. Which republic is the most important? Why?

4. How did the Russian Orthodox Church contribute to the power of the tsars?

5. Why did Stalin's policy toward religion change during World War II?

6. How did glasnost affect Russian attitudes toward the Jews?

7. What is the position of women in the Soviet Union?

8. What is the role of sports in Soviet life?

9. **a.** What was the major influence on the arts under the tsars? **b.** Under the Communists?

10. **a.** How have artists and writers been affected by socialist realism? **b.** Glasnost?

Developing Critical Thinking

Comparing and Contrasting How did gaps develop between the classes in the Soviet Union? How do the economic and social classes of the Soviet Union compare with those classes in the United States?

Writing About History

Relating Past to Present to Future Based on what you have learned about the republics and regions in the USSR, the sweeping changes in the Communist world during the late 1980s and early 1990s, and the unrest in certain areas during the early 1990s, write a newspaper story on the fate of one of the Soviet republics. Set your story in the mid- or late 1990s.

Applying Your Skills to History

Holding a Panel Discussion A panel discussion is led by a moderator. Unlike a debate in which only two sides are given, panel members represent a number of viewpoints. Each panel member researches the topic and prepares and rehearses a presentation. Panel members need to work together so that no two people represent the same point of view. The moderator keeps the discussion moving and makes sure each member of the panel has equal time to speak.

Activity: Hold a panel discussion on the nationalities in the Soviet Union. Consider the following questions: Has the federation form of government allowed sufficient expression of national sentiments in the Soviet Union? How has nationalism been at odds with Communist theory? Should nationalities within the Soviet Union be allowed to secede?

CHAPTER

40

Eastern European nations are becoming more industrialized, but agriculture is still important. Below are farmers at a collective in Hungary.

Eastern Europe

Geography has played a paramount role in the history of Eastern Europe. Perhaps no culture region in the world has been more affected by its location. For centuries the countries of this culture region have been caught in power struggles between the countries to the west and east. They achieved political independence between the two world wars, only to see the Soviet Union seize control and install Communist governments. Throughout these changes, Eastern European peoples kept a strong sense of nationalism. Beginning in 1989, great changes in Soviet policy allowed the Eastern Europeans once again to make decisions concerning their own futures.

As you study this chapter, keep these questions in mind.

- What forces slowed down the development of nation-states in Eastern Europe?

- What changes have occurred in the social and economic patterns of Eastern Europe since World War II?

- How did the countries of Eastern Europe respond to the changes made by the Soviet Union under Gorbachev?

Geographically, Eastern Europe is divided into the Baltic Plain, the Danube River Basin, and the Balkan Peninsula. The Baltic Plain runs 300 miles (483 kilometers) from the Baltic Sea in the north to the Carpathian Mountains in the south. This is open land with no natural eastern or western boundaries; it is a natural invasion route.

South of the Baltic Plain lies the Danube River. It winds through great portions of Eastern Europe and has served as a major route for both traders and armies. The Danube River Basin is the land on either side of the river. It is the most fertile region in Eastern Europe.

For 45 years, the German Democratic Republic, or East Germany, belonged to the Soviet bloc. It was one of the most loyal of the satellites, but its citizens were not happy. Thousands fled across the boundary to West Germany. The loss of productive workers led the Communist regime to construct the Berlin Wall and to fortify the entire frontier heavily. Then the Communist regime was forced to give up its power after Gorbachev allowed the states of Eastern Europe to reform their own economic and political institutions. In March 1990 freely held elections brought to power a non-Communist government pledged to the reunification of Germany. The two remaining states in this part of Eastern Europe are Poland and Czechoslovakia.

States of the West Slavs

Poland

Poland lies between the Baltic Sea and the Carpathian Mountains. It is part of the Baltic Plain, and until recently was primarily an agricultural region. The Oder and Vistula rivers are its major waterways. Poland's capital, Warsaw, lies on the Vistula. In the west, the former German province of Silesia (sy-LEE-zhee-uh) provides Poland with its industrial strength through its large deposits of coal and iron ore.

The 39 million Poles are West Slavs. They were first united in the 900s under the Piast (PYAHST) dynasty. The first Piasts were baptized and established the Roman Catholic faith throughout Poland. Perhaps no people in Eastern Europe are as devout as the Poles. Ninety-four percent of the Poles are Roman Catholics. Their religion has been a great force of strength and unity for them.

When the Piast dynasty died out in 1370, the Polish throne passed to King Louis of Hungary. He had no male heir, so Polish nobles arranged for his granddaughter, Jadwiga (yahd-VEE-gah), to be crowned queen. Jadwiga married the grand duke of Lithuania. This marriage united Poland and Lithuania under the Jagellon (yah-GEL-uhn) dynasty from 1386 to 1572.

The Poles reached their military height during the 1600s. They defeated the Russians, and in 1683, under King John III Sobieski, saved the Hapsburg capital at Vienna from capture by the Ottoman Turks. At the same time, however, Poland's monarchy lost power to the nobles. Nobles elected the kings, and each member of the Polish parliament, the Diet, had veto power. This effectively weakened the government and allowed Poland's neighbors to intervene in the country's affairs.

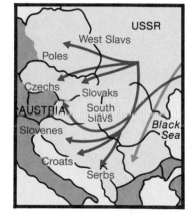

Migrations, A.D. 500–1000

- ■ Bulgars
- ■ Magyars
- ■ Slavs

Thaddeus Kosciusko led a peasant army against the Prussians, Russians, and Austrians in 1794 in a fight to prevent the third partition of Poland. The revolt was defeated.

In 1772 these neighbors—Prussia, Austria, and Russia—divided Poland among themselves. Twenty years later, Russia and Prussia partitioned Poland a second time. During this time, Thaddeus Kosciusko (kahs-ee-UHS-koh) returned from America where he had fought in the American Revolution. Kosciusko formed a peasant army to fight the invaders. At first it was victorious, but eventually Kosciusko was captured and the movement collapsed.

A third partition, in which Austria participated, took place in 1795. Poland no longer existed as a separate political unit. But it remained a nation to Polish patriots. For the next 125 years, many Poles fought and died in an effort to reestablish a united Poland. After Napoleon's defeat, the diplomats at the Congress of Vienna put most of Poland under Russian control but allowed Poland to have its own constitution. When the Poles rebelled in 1830 and again in 1863, the Russians crushed the rebellions and abolished the constitution. They subjected the Poles to intense Russification.

Not until 1918 did Poland again receive land and independence. The new republic began as a parliamentary democracy, but by 1935 Poland was a military dictatorship. Danzig, Poland's seaport on the Baltic, was made an independent city under the supervision of the League of Nations. Poland was given access to Danzig through a strip of land that ran through Germany. This became known as the Polish Corridor. It became the source of conflict between Germany and Poland.

In the secret pact signed a week before World War II began, Germany and the Soviet Union agreed to partition Poland. When the Poles rejected Hitler's demand that Danzig be turned over to Germany, German troops invaded Poland on September 1, 1939. A few weeks later the Soviet Union invaded Poland and seized its share of land agreed upon in the secret pact.

Poland saw fighting again as the Red Army pushed the Nazi forces back into Germany. Eastern Europe and Poland were principal topics at the wartime conferences held at Tehran, Yalta, and Potsdam by the leaders of Great Britain, the United States, and the Soviet Union. The Allies agreed that the Soviet Union should have 70,000 square miles (181 300 square kilometers) of Polish territory in the east. About 11 million Poles lived there, but so did many Ukrainians and Belorussians. In return, Poland was given about 39,000 square miles (101 000 square kilometers) of former German territory, including Silesia, in the west.

The Red Army occupied Poland and placed Polish Communists in power. Communist-controlled police spread terror throughout the country and prevented free elections from being held. By 1947 Poland was completely under Communist domination and bound to the Soviet Union politically and economically. Poland became a member of the Warsaw Pact.

The Poles have never been easily suppressed, however. On several occasions Polish workers organized demonstrations to protest economic and political conditions. In 1956 workers in Poznan marched through the streets demanding food. The problems continued. In 1980 a strike began in the shipyards of Gdansk (guh-DANSK), as the Poles call Danzig. It spread quickly to other industries. This led to the formation of a united labor front called Solidarity. Its founder was Lech Walesa (LEK wah-LEN-sah), a Polish worker.

The Communist leaders saw Solidarity as a threat to their power. Another strike in 1981 brought General Wojciech Jaruzelski (voy-CHEK yahr-uh-ZAHL-skee) to power. Jaruzelski declared martial law. Solidarity was banned. Walesa was arrested but later released.

Martial law did not end the unrest, however. Riots and street clashes in Gdansk and elsewhere continued. Several thousand Poles were arrested. Poland's economy suffered. The government alternated between concessions and stern measures. The Poles, however, did not submit to Communist control. Faced with no solution to mounting problems, Jaruzelski eventually allowed free elections to take place in 1989. Not surprisingly, Solidarity won the elections. Prime Minister Tadeusz Mazowiecki (MAH-zuh-vee-YET-skee) heads the new non-Communist government. He has had some success in restoring Poland's economy.

The leader of the Polish Solidarity party is Lech Walesa. How is he serving his country now?

Czechoslovakia

Czechoslovakia is not a large country. It covers an area about the size of New York State and has a population of 15.6 million. Economically its industry and coal and iron ore deposits make it an important country. Completely landlocked, Czechoslovakia shares its borders with several other nations and lies in the middle of Europe within the Danube River Basin.

West Slavs moved into this area before A.D. 700. In the 800s, the Moravian kingdom was formed in the regions of Bohemia, Moravia, and Slovakia. The West Slavs were first converted to Christianity by saints Cyril and Methodius. They might thus have become Orthodox Christians like the Russians. However, the West Slavs later became Roman Catholics because of powerful German influences.

German influences also became stronger when Bohemia became part of the Holy Roman Empire and was ruled by German-speaking emperors. The Holy Roman Empire occupied large and varying portions of Europe between 962 and 1806. Through a series of marriages and wars, Bohemia, Moravia, and Slovakia became possessions of the Hapsburg family in the 1600s. During the Reformation, many Bohemians became Protestant, but the Hapsburgs defeated the Protestants and their king. The Counter-Reformation brought most Czechs back to Roman Catholicism. Austria continued to rule the three areas until its defeat in World War I.

As part of the peace settlement, Czechoslovakia became an independent country in 1918. Thomas G. Masaryk (MAHS-uh-rik) and Eduard Benes (BEN-esh) founded the new republic. Masaryk became its first president. As an independent and democratic country, Czechoslovakia had a history of about 20 years.

Thomas G. Masaryk fought for Slavic rights against the Austro-Hungarians. His son, Jan, fought the Communist takeover of Czechoslovakia. In 1948 Jan died mysteriously.

837

The new president of Czechoslovakia is Vaclav Havel.

Many ethnic Germans lived in the region known as the Sudetenland (soo-DAYT-uhn-land) bordering Germany. Hitler agitated for the inclusion of these Germans in his Reich. At a meeting in Munich in 1938, Great Britain, Italy, and France agreed to the division of Czechoslovakia in order to appease Hitler and avoid war. The Munich Pact allowed Hitler to take the Sudetenland. Czechoslovakia lost about 30 percent of its territory, including its fortified border regions. In 1939 Hitler easily took over the rest of Bohemia and Moravia. Slovakia became a puppet state of the Germans.

At the close of World War II, the Red Army occupied Czechoslovakia. The original borders of Czechoslovakia were restored and the Sudeten Germans exiled. The Communists joined a coalition government, but by 1948 they dominated it. Czechoslovakia became a satellite nation with its government and constitution modeled after that of the Soviet Union.

Many Czechs fled west. In 1968 a power struggle within the Communist party brought Alexander Dubček (DOOB-chek) to power. He introduced reforms and expanded civil rights. Dubček's reform movement was called the Prague Spring.

These measures disturbed Soviet leaders. In August 1968 troops from the Soviet Union and other satellite states occupied Czechoslovakia. Dubček was removed and his reforms were stopped by the new Communist leader, Gustav Husak. Husak purged party members who had supported Dubček. He reimposed censorship and reorganized Czechoslovakia's political and economic structure. All this was meant to be a lesson to other Soviet satellites.

Despite efforts by several hundred Czech writers, artists, and intellectuals to speak out against the communist dictatorship, hard-line Communists remained in power until 1989. Then Gorbachev's new policy opened the way for the satellites to determine their own course in politics. The Communists faded away without bloodshed. One of the dissident intellectuals, the playwright Vaclav Havel (VAHK-lahv HAHV-uhl), became president of Czechoslovakia. The Soviet Union began pulling out its troops. Always the most Western of the Eastern European countries, Czechoslovakia seemed well on the road to becoming a democracy again.

Free Czechoslovakia is not without problems, however. The Slovaks, who represent one-third of the country's people, would like to change the name of the Czechoslovak Socialist Republic to the Federation of Czecho-Slovakia. The Czechs want simply the Czechoslovak Republic.

SECTION 1 REVIEW

1. **Recall** What nations participated in the partitions of Poland? How were they able to do this?

2. **How and Why** What territory did Hitler demand from Czechoslovakia in 1938 and why?

3. **Critical Thinking** How did Poland and Czechoslovakia differ in removing Communists from power?

L iving south of the lands of the West Slavs in Eastern Europe are a mixture of peoples that reflect the paths of invasions over many centuries. Until recently, all they had in common was a tie either to communism or membership in the Soviet bloc.

The Danube River Basin is particularly fertile where it passes through the Hungarian Plain. It has been home to the Magyars, or Hungarians, for centuries. South of the Danube River Basin is the Balkan Peninsula. It is a rugged region of mountains and valleys ringed on three sides by the Adriatic, Aegean, and Black seas. The Balkans—shared with Greeks and Turks—is home to the many southern Slavic peoples and to the Romanians. The number of countries has led to the term **balkanization**, or a breaking up of a region into smaller units.

Bulgaria

Bulgaria is part of the Balkan Peninsula. Its fertile soil and moderate climate have helped the country produce export grains, tobacco, potatoes, and fruit. Bulgaria remains primarily an underdeveloped agricultural nation, but it is attempting to build up its industry. The population is 9 million.

The country takes its name from an Asiatic people known as the Bulgars. They invaded the country during the A.D. 600s and mixed with the Slavic people already living there. The Slavs and Bulgars formed the first Bulgarian Empire around 680. The Byzantine Empire ruled the Bulgars from 1018 to 1185. Then the Ottoman Turks conquered a second Bulgarian Empire in 1396. The area remained part of the Ottoman Empire for the next 500 years.

Farming conditions are good in Bulgaria's fertile valleys and lowlands, where some farm workers still tend crops by hand.

Historically, the Bulgarians got along better with the Russians than any other Eastern European peoples. During the late 1800s, it was the Russians who helped the Bulgarians to overthrow the Turks. The Bulgarians also practiced the same Orthodox Christianity as the Russians. Because of the long Turkish rule, however, a large Muslim minority lives in the country. The Communist regime forced many of them to take Slavic names. Those who refused fled to neighboring Turkey.

In 1908 Bulgaria became an independent country with its own tsar. Independent Bulgaria was often at war with its neighbors. It lost two wars in 1912 and 1913 in an effort to gain an outlet on the Aegean Sea. During both world wars, Bulgaria sided with Germany and lost considerable territory as a result. At the end of World War II, Soviet troops occupied the country. The monarchy was abolished and a Communist government was established. It closely followed the lead of the Soviet Union in foreign policy. Bulgaria joined the Soviet Union in many economic ventures and is a member of the Warsaw Pact.

Bulgaria was one of the last Soviet satellites to feel the effects of Gorbachev's new policies. But the Communist regime fell when large crowds demonstrated in Sofia, the capital, demanding change. The Bulgarian Communist dictator, Todor Zhivkov, resigned and was jailed in 1989. Subsequent elections have returned the reformed Communists (socialists) to power.

Romania

Romania is part of the Danube River Basin. It is a mountainous region crisscrossed by the Carpathian Mountains and the Transylvanian Alps. Romania has some excellent natural resources, including oil. Nevertheless, it remains an economically underdeveloped country. The population numbers more than 23 million.

Romania was first inhabited by an ancient people known as the Dacians. Dacia was a province of the Roman Empire from about A.D. 101 to 274. Its name and its Romance language derive from this period of its history. Romania was also on the path of invaders: Goths, Huns, Avars, Slavs, and Magyars. These people as well as the Greeks and the Turks influenced the Romanian language.

During the Middle Ages, the Romanian provinces of Moldavia and Walachia (wah-LAY-kee-uh) formed independent nations. By the 1500s, however, the expanding Ottoman Empire controlled all of Romania. Prior to independence in 1878, Romania was the scene of repeated conflicts between Turks and Russians. When the Turks were pushed back, the Romanians had to contend with Russians who periodically pushed into Romanian territory.

At the beginning of World War I, Romania declared itself neutral. Eventually, it joined the Allies against Germany. It made great territorial gains in the peace settlement and became one of the largest countries in Europe. In World War II, Romania fought on the side of Germany and was later occupied by the Red Army. It had to give up its territorial gains and the monarchy. A Communist regime took over.

Romania had very close economic, political, and military ties with the Soviet Union until the 1960s. Then it became more independent. Under its Communist leader, Nicolae Ceausescu (chow-SHES-kyoo), Romania resumed relations with the United States and West Germany. Ceaucescu was the only leader in Eastern Europe to protest the Soviet invasion of Afghanistan. At the same time, Ceaucescu built up his power with the help of a large secret police.

Romania faced serious economic problems beginning in the late 1970s. Poor harvests and the decline in farm output led to food shortages. Food prices rose twice as fast as wages. Worldwide inflation hurt all the Eastern European nations, including Romania. The standard of living of the Romanian people fell. They had to pay more for their imports and found less demand for their exports. And Romania did not even produce enough oil to meet its own needs. It became dependent on oil imports, and less money was available for industrial growth.

During the turbulence that shook Eastern Europe in late 1989, Romania seemed untouched. The dictator Ceaucescu even went on a state visit to Iran. When he returned, the people rose up in revolt. Ceaucescu and his wife tried to flee, but Army troops captured the two and executed them by firing squad. The horrors committed by Ceausescu's police state were then revealed. The 1990 elections brought Ion Iliescu (i-lee-ES-cu), a former Communist official, to power.

With no experience in democratic leadership, Romania faces an unstable future. The country is also disturbed by conflict between Romanians and a large Hungarian minority who get support from Hungary.

Hungary

Hungary, a nation of 10.5 million inhabitants, lies on the western edge of the Danube River Basin. Like Czechoslovakia, Hungary is a landlocked nation. It is primarily an agricultural land. In recent years, however, industry has expanded and industrial exports have become increasingly important.

Hungary's location in the center of Europe placed it directly on the invasion route from east to west. Slavs and Germans first settled Hungary. They were overcome in the late 800s by the Magyars, who had originally come from the steppe of Central Asia. In 1001 King Stephen I united Hungary.

In the 1200s, the Mongols invaded Hungary. They were driven out with the aid of the Holy Roman Emperor. Between 1458 and 1490, Hungary again achieved unity under Matthias Corvinus. Then the Ottoman Turks conquered the country during the 1500s. Following the eviction of the Turks, Hungary became part of the Hapsburg Empire. Neither Slavic nor German, the Hungarians were unhappy within that empire.

During the Revolution of 1848, the Hungarians set up a republic under Lajos Kossuth (LAW-ohsh KAH-sooth). The Russians helped crush the uprising. In 1867 Hungary became an equal partner with Austria in establishing the Dual Monarchy of Austria-Hungary.

In World War I, Austria-Hungary was Germany's ally. With defeat, the empire and its many nationalities fell apart. Hungary lost large amounts of territory as a result of the peace settlement. Control of Hungary passed to revolutionaries. For a few brief months in 1919, Hungary was ruled by Communists led by Bela Kun. They were ousted by Admiral Miklos Horthy (HOR-tee), who set up a monarchy for the absent Hapsburgs with himself as regent.

In World War II, Hungary became an ally of Hitler's Germany and was more than willing to take lands belonging to its neighbors. By 1945 the Soviet Union had conquered all of Hungary. As in other Eastern European countries where Soviet troops were present, the Communists seized complete control in a relatively short time. By 1947 Hungary had a government patterned after that of Soviet Union.

Through the early 1950s, Hungary experienced serious economic problems. Dissatisfaction reached a crisis stage in 1956. The Hungarians rebelled. The rebels gained control for a short time and made Imre Nagy (NOJ) premier. Nagy promised free elections and planned to take Hungary out of the Warsaw Pact.

Soviet tanks and troops sped into Hungary to put down the revolution. Nagy was imprisoned and later executed. Thousands were imprisoned. Almost 200,000 people fled. The rebels were brave, daring, and almost successful, but they were poorly armed and could not withstand the overwhelming power of the Soviet army. The United Nations condemned the Soviet invasion, but this had no effect. The Communist government was reorganized under Janos Kadar. The Soviets were angered by the Hungarian revolution because it revealed the force they were compelled to use to control their satellites.

Despite the rebellion, Hungary was the first satellite to embark upon a new course. It allowed some changes in economic policy that varied considerably from that of the Soviet Union. In the late 1960s, Hungary began its New Economic Mechanism. Managers were given more authority. Workers and managers got pay incentives to increase production. Living conditions improved. Elements of the free enterprise system were

Since Tito's death, the top positions in Yugoslavia's government are rotated. Under this new plan, Milka Planinc was elected the first President of the Federal Executive Council that rules Yugoslavia.

encouraged. Farmers were allowed to grow whatever they wished and sell it. Food production rose and consumer goods became plentiful.

By 1990, Hungary's Communist party changed its name and allowed opposition parties to participate in politics. Because its path to democracy had evolved slowly, Hungary's changes appeared less dramatic than those that took place in Czechoslovakia, Poland, or Romania.

Yugoslavia

Yugoslavia is a federation of republics like that of the Soviet Union. The country lies on the Balkan Peninsula along the Adriatic Sea. It forms part of the Danube River Basin but is essentially a mountainous area. It has rich mineral resources and large forest lands. Today about two-thirds of the labor force works in industry and nonfarming jobs.

The 28 million Yugoslavs are a mix of various ethnic groups. Chief among them are the Serbs, Croats, Slovenes, Montenegrins, Macedonians, and Albanians. The ethnic mix is reflected in three official languages: Serbo-Croatian, Slovenian, and Macedonian. The major religions are Serbian Orthodox (41 percent), Roman Catholic (12 percent), and Islam (3 percent).

The nation has been divided and ruled by the Ottoman Empire, Austria-Hungary, Bulgaria, Montenegro, and Serbia. The latter two are now Yugoslavian republics. Yugoslavia was not formed as an independent nation until after World War I. Then it became a monarchy ruled by the royal family of Serbia. The young nation had a difficult time as each group jealously guarded its own ethnic, religious, and linguistic identity.

In 1941 the Germans invaded and occupied the country. Bitter guerrilla warfare took place against not only the Germans but also among factions representing particular ethnic groups. The Communist Josip Broz (YOH-sef BROHZ), later known as Marshal Tito, formed a national liberation movement which abolished the monarchy and proclaimed Yugoslavia a republic in 1945.

Yugoslavia was in ruins. Tito attempted to reorganize and rebuilt it into a Communist state. He later revised his thinking. He put most operations on a profit basis and eventually did away with collective farms. Yugoslavia was never conquered by the Red Army. Tito was determined to keep the country from becoming a Soviet satellite. In 1948 he broke with the Soviet bloc. The Soviet Union denounced him for his independence and expelled Yugoslavia from the Cominform—the Communist Information Bureau. It organized an international Communist effort to unseat Tito and destroy the Yugoslavian economy by a trade blockade. Tito survived these attacks and adopted a neutralist policy in the cold war. He accepted aid from the United States and other non-Communist countries.

When Khrushchev came to power in the Soviet Union, he tried to win Tito back into the Communist bloc. He apologized for Stalin's policies and offered to work more cooperatively. Relations improved between the two countries, but Tito kept Yugoslavia's policy of **nonalignment**.

Sarajevo was the site of the assassination of Archduke Franz Ferdinand in 1914, which started World War I. The city's many mosques were built under Turkish rule, from the 1400s to the 1800s.

After Tito died in 1980, the Communist government continued his policies. Gradually Yugoslavia's economy became more balanced between agriculture and industry. The standard of living has improved.

Because it was not a dictatorship within the Communist bloc like other Eastern European countries, Yugoslavia did not undergo the upheavals of 1989. Nevertheless, it has been subject to ethnic violence, particularly among Albanians and Macedonians living in the south and Croatians in the north who want to create an independent state.

Albania

The People's Socialist Republic of Albania is the smallest of the Communist countries. The 3.2 million Albanians live in a mountainous land on the Balkan Peninsula, isolated on the eastern shore of the Adriatic Sea. Albania's three different climates allow it to raise a variety of crops. However, the country has little industry and the nation is the poorest in Europe.

Albania has been a battleground for many centuries. The Greeks and the Romans conquered it. During the Middle Ages, it was invaded by the Goths, Bulgarians, Slavs, and Normans. For a time it belonged to the Byzantine Empire. The Albanian chieftain and national hero Scanderbeg tried to unify the country, but he was defeated by the Turks. Albania remained a Turkish possession for more than 400 years. During that time most of the people became Muslims. The country did not become an independent nation until 1912.

In 1925 Ahmed Bey Zogu took power and made himself King Zog I. The monarchy was short-lived. In 1939 Mussolini's Italy invaded and occupied the country. In the middle of the war, fighting broke out

NATIONAL PROFILES/THE SOVIET UNION AND EASTERN EUROPE						
Nation/Capital	Population/ Area (in sq mi)	Urban Population (as % of total)	Per Capita GNP (in U.S. $)	Adult Literacy Rate (%)	Life Expectancy	Population Growth Rate* (%)
Albania/Tiranë	3,273,000/11,100	35	**	75	71	2.0
Bulgaria/Sofia	8,934,000/42,823	67	**	98	72	0.1
Czechoslovakia/Prague	15,683,000/49,370	75	**	100	71	0.2
Hungary/Budapest	10,569,000/35,919	60	2,460	99	70	-0.2
Poland/Warsaw	37,777,000/120,725	61	1,850	98	71	0.6
Romania/Bucharest	23,273,000/91,699	54	**	98	70	0.5
Soviet Union/Moscow	290,938,000/ 8,649,496	66	**	99	69	0.9
Yugoslavia/Belgrade	23,842,000/98,766	46	2,680	90	71	0.6

Sources: *The 1990 Information Please Almanac* (Houghton Mifflin Company); *1990 World Population Data Sheet* (Population Reference Bureau, Inc., Washington D.C.)
 *A nation with a population growth rate of 2% or more doubles its population within 35 years or less.
**Not available.

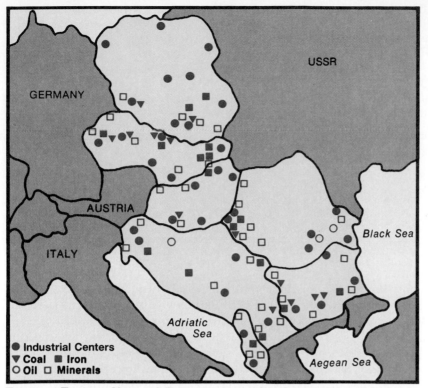

Eastern Europe Natural Resources and Industrial Centers

Legend:
- ● Industrial Centers
- ▼ Coal ■ Iron
- ○ Oil □ Minerals

Map labels: GERMANY, USSR, AUSTRIA, ITALY, Black Sea, Adriatic Sea, Aegean Sea

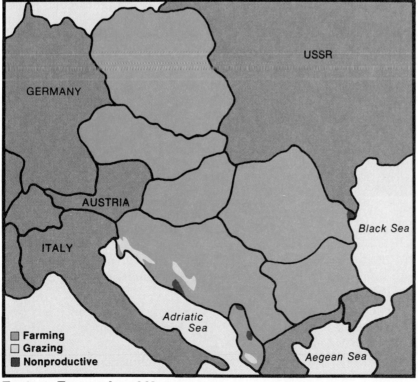

Eastern Europe Land Use

Legend:
- ▢ Farming
- □ Grazing
- ■ Nonproductive

Map labels: GERMANY, USSR, AUSTRIA, ITALY, Black Sea, Adriatic Sea, Aegean Sea

Workers on an Albanian collective pick tobacco. How can a surplus agricultural economy help a country to industrialize?

between non-Communist forces and Communist partisans led by Enver Hoxha. With the defeat of Italy and Germany, Albania became a Communist dictatorship under General Hoxha's control.

Initially, Albania allied itself with the Soviet Union. However, it broke off relations with the Soviet Union in 1961. Albanian leaders condemned Khrushchev's policies of de-Stalinization and peaceful coexistence. They insisted that war with the capitalist countries was inevitable. Albania withdrew from the Warsaw Pact. Its isolation from the rest of the Communist bloc and Yugoslavia's presence between it and the rest of the Soviet bloc permitted the Albanians to pursue their independent course of action. No Soviet tanks arrived to force the Albanians into line. For a time Albania's only ally in the Communist world was the People's Republic of China. But in 1978 Mao Zedong's successors broke off all military and economic ties with Albania when Albania criticized China's new policies.

Hoxha died in 1985, but his Communist successors seemed as determined as he was to keep Albania shut off from the rest of the world. Albania has so far been immune to the great changes sweeping the other nations of Eastern Europe.

SECTION 2 REVIEW

1. **Recall**   What national political institution did not survive the Communist takeovers in Bulgaria, Albania, Romania, and Yugoslavia?
2. **How and Why**   Which two countries of Eastern Europe had the most success in creating their own brands of communism? How did they do it?
3. **Critical Thinking**   How have ethnic groups made governing difficult in Yugoslavia and Romania?

Eastern Europe has a rich heritage of achievement in the arts and sciences. This excellence continued despite the long-term presence of Communist governments and censorship in the region. Those governments insisted on art and science in the service of the state. The removal of Communist regimes in the 1990s has allowed for the rebirth of freedom of expression.

The Arts

Folklore was and is the core of Eastern European culture. It includes the folk dances, songs, stories, dress, art, and handicrafts that characterize the various peoples of Eastern Europe. With the rise of nationalism (the awareness of and sense of loyalty to one nation above all others) and romanticism many Eastern European writers and composers turned to their native folklore for inspiration. They emphasized patriotic values and pride in their nations in a moving and emotional style. This period produced an outpouring of literature and music that expressed the desire of Eastern Europeans for independence. All countries produced noted artists.

Music Inspired by Polish folk music and dances, the pianist and composer Frederic Chopin (SHOH-pan), who lived from 1810 to 1849, expressed Polish nationalism in his *polonaises* and *mazurkas*. The Bohemian composer Antonin Dvořák (duh-VOR-zhahk) wrote a wide range of operas and symphonies based on folk materials. He gained fame for *From the New World*, a symphony that he composed while in the United States. For the piano he composed *Humoresque*. Two Hungarian composers also

Folk music is still a vital part of the cultures of many countries. Here, Romanian musicians entertain at a festival. Why do you think ethnic heritage and tradition remain important to so many people?

used their music to express nationalist feelings. Franz Liszt is famous for his *Hungarian Rhapsodies*. He toured Europe giving piano concerts, composed large numbers of secular and religious works, and conducted orchestras. His compatriot, Bela Bartok, who lived from 1881 to 1945, composed a wide range of music from symphonic poems to piano pieces and opera. He is one of the most influential composers of modern music.

Literature   Writers in Eastern Europe always played a more prominent role in politics than their counterparts in Western Europe. During the 1800s, most Eastern European countries were occupied by foreign powers and had no independence. In those countries, poets took the lead in arousing national feeling. Theirs were the only voices raised in opposition to tyranny and foreign occupation.

Adam Mickiewicz (mits-KYAY-vich), a romantic poet (1798–1855), was the foremost spokesman for nationalism in Poland. Mickiewicz organized military units to fight both the Austrians and Russians who occupied partitioned Poland. He eventually moved to Paris, where he became the leader of a large group of exiled patriots. He wrote *Pan Tadeusz* (1834), an epic poem about Poland during the Napoleonic wars.

At this time, the use of the written word in the national language gave prestige to the writers. In Poland, the importance of writers carried over to the period of Nazi occupation. Consequently, when the Nazis closed the universities and banned publishing in the Polish language, writers kept the flame of free Poland burning. Later, during the 1960s, the government's ban on a production of Mickiewicz's drama, *The Forefathers Eve* (1823), triggered student protests.

The Hungarians also demanded independence and social reform during the 1800s. Their chief poet was Sandor Petofi (PET-uh-fee), who fought in and was killed in the Revolution of 1848. His name became a rallying cry for political **activists** in the next century. During the 1956 rebellion in Hungary, the Petofi Circle of young intellectuals attacked the Communist regime and its supporters.

However, not all literature in Eastern Europe before the Communist period centered on nationalist themes. The well-known Joseph Conrad (1857–1924) penned novels that drew upon his personal experiences. Born in Poland, he was the son of a nobleman. He was a militant nationalist before leaving Poland to make a living in the British merchant marine. His experiences at sea greatly influenced his novel *Lord Jim* (1900). Conrad's characters are faced with inner urges and moral dilemmas that arise under great adversity. Set in the Belgian Congo where Conrad once worked, *The Heart of Darkness* (1902) examines the character of European colonials engaged in the exploitation of the region and its peoples.

Censorship and Dissidence   Wherever the Communists seized power in Eastern Europe, they imposed their concept of socialist realism on the arts. All art and literature was supposed to satisfy the needs of the Communist party. The party controlled all the publishing houses and art galleries. More important, it controlled the purse strings and therefore the livelihood of artists and writers. In a totalitarian police state, censorship—developed by Stalin in the Soviet Union and imposed on the satellites—stifled creative expression. It put walls around free thought.

Czeslaw Milosz (CHEZ-law MEE-lawsh), a Polish poet and essayist, was one of the first writers to escape totalitarianism. He fled Poland in 1951, taking up residence in the United States. During the German occupation of his homeland in World War II, he fought with the Polish underground. The experience of living under communism led him to focus on ideology in all his works. Milosz won the Nobel Prize for Literature in 1980.

In the late 1950s and 1960s, however, a revival of nationalism occurred. The revolts that shook Eastern Europe were followed by a great rebirth in the arts. Often writers and artists were the leaders of rebellion.

In Czechoslovakia censorship was lifted and writers had complete freedom for about three months in early 1968. The novelist Milan Kundera and the playwright Vaclav Havel played a prominent part in what is known as the Prague Spring. Then hard-line Communists returned to power and cracked down on all writers. Kundera ultimately left the country for France, and all his works were thereafter published first in French. His highly successful novel, *The Unbearable Lightness of Being* (1984), follows the relationships of two couples who live in a dreary totalitarian state. One of its many themes concerns the great weightlessness, or lightness, that people feel when they discover that life has no meaning.

Although Kundera left Czechoslovakia, others chose to remain there. Many who stayed became **apolitical**. Those who continued to fight the party line faced imprisonment. Havel encountered continuous police pressure and served terms of imprisonment. In his plays, Havel satirizes the failure of people to communicate as a sign of social decay. This theme is seen in his satire, *The Memorandum* (1965), in which the government makes up a new language, *Ptydepe*, which is too difficult for anyone to learn. With the ouster of the Communists in 1989, the widely respected Havel became president of Czechoslovakia.

In Eastern Europe, the arts had gradually become vehicles for protest rather than for Communist propaganda. Sensing this development, Communist governments tried to channel the call for change in a safe direction. They began to cultivate the theory of nationalist realism—an emphasis on the national interest. They allowed writers and artists to experiment as long as the needs of the party were satisfied. But a growing voice for democracy demanded to be heard too.

In Yugoslavia, nationalist realism had unfortunate results. In this federation of several ethnic groups, the ruling Communist party feared national self-determination. Each national group within Yugoslavia— Croatian, Slovene, Macedonian, Albanian, and so forth—might demand independence and break up the federation. For this reason, Yugoslav leaders imprisoned several prominent dissident Albanians from the Kossovo area and Croatians.

Under the Nicolae Ceausescu dictatorship, Romanian writers faced Eastern Europe's most severe censorship. Novelists and poets could

This polished bronze sculpture, called Bird in Space, *was made by Romanian Constantin Brancusi.*

produce either works praising Ceausescu and the Communist party or nationalistic novels and poems on subjects the party permitted. Romania was the only Soviet satellite that sent dissidents to psychiatric clinics and, in 1983, forced people to register typewriters.

Bulgaria, always close to the Soviet Union, long supported Soviet socialist realism. However, Todor Zhivkov's regime took a pragmatic approach and relaxed some of the rules governing censorship. Nevertheless, *samizdat* works led to imprisonment. Some dissidents emigrated. In Albania, Enver Hoxha and his successors continued heavy censorship.

Coinciding with Brezhnev's get-tough policies in the Soviet Union, Communist regimes placed stricter controls on writers in the 1970s. This continued until 1989, when the Soviet Union allowed Eastern Europeans to choose their own governments.

Science

Born in Warsaw in 1867, Marie Sklodowska (sklaw-DAWF-skah), better known as Marie Curie, had such an outstanding record in her studies that she won a gold medal when she graduated from the Russian secondary school at age 16. She taught school and participated in the nationalist movement by reading in Polish to women workers in one of the free, underground universities. Because her family needed money, Marie went to Paris to work as a governess. She lived in a tiny room on a meager diet of bread and tea. Marie still managed to continue her education, attending lectures at the Sorbonne. She began working in a scientific laboratory and there met Pierre Curie. They were married in 1895.

The Curies worked as a team trying to find the source of radioactivity in uranium ore called pitchblende. After going through tons of pitchblende, the Curies discovered two new radioactive chemical elements. They named these elements polonium—in honor of Marie's homeland— and radium. In 1903 they were awarded a Nobel Prize for Physics for their research in radioactivity. Three years later Pierre was killed instantly when run over by a horse-drawn cart. The Sorbonne appointed Madame Curie to take her husband's professorship. She became the first woman to teach there and continued her research alone. In 1911 Madame Curie received the Nobel Prize for Chemistry for discovering radium and polonium.

SECTION 3 REVIEW

1. **Recall**   How did poets inspire nationalism in Eastern Europe in the 1800s?
2. **How and Why**   Why did the Communist governments of Eastern Europe cultivate nationalist realism?
3. **Critical Thinking**   Why have writers played a particularly important political role in Eastern European countries?

R E V I E W

Reviewing People, Places, and Things

Identify, define, or explain each of the following:

Oder River	nonalignment
Silesia	Frederic Chopin
Thaddeus Kosciusko	Antonin Dvořák
Danzig	Franz Liszt
Polish Corridor	Adam Mickiewicz
Lech Walesa	Petofi Circle
Thomas G. Masaryk	Joseph Conrad
Alexander Dubček	Czeslaw Milosz
Tito	Marie Curie

Map Study

Using the maps on page 845, determine the answers to the following questions:

1. Which countries of Eastern Europe have oil resources?
2. Which countries are landlocked?
3. Which countries border both Western Europe and the USSR?

Understanding Facts and Ideas

1. What are the three geographic divisions of Eastern Europe?
2. **a.** What is Solidarity? **b.** What role did it play in the history of Poland?
3. What are the three chief regions of Czechoslovakia?
4. What other region of Czechoslovakia played an important part in the events leading up to World War II?
5. Which country in Eastern Europe developed the best relationship with the Russians? Why?
6. **a.** Which country has a Muslim majority? **b.** What other two countries have significant Muslim minorities?
7. Which countries in 1867 made up the Dual Monarchy?

8. What are the three official languages of Yugoslavia?
9. What was the Communist goal of socialist realism in the arts?
10. In which Eastern European country did writers face the most severe censorship?

Developing Critical Thinking

Relating Literature to History   a. How did folklore figure in the rise of nationalism in the countries of Eastern Europe? **b.** Why were the works of the Czech writers Milan Kundera and Vaclav Havel likely to disturb Communist censors?

Writing About History

Relating Past to Present   Select one of the Eastern European nations and make a current events scrapbook on it. Next to each news story write a caption explaining how the event relates to what you have learned in this chapter about that nation.

Applying Your Skills to History

Preparing a Chart   A chart arranges material in rows and columns according to subject. Each column and each row has only one topic. The chart allows the reader to compare and contrast material more quickly than by reading several pages of text.

Activity: Using the material in your text and library reference books, prepare a chart on the eight Eastern European countries. Write their names in rows along the left side of your paper. As column headings across the top write: **Date of Independence, Year of Communist Takeover, Major Political Figures, Major Historical Events, Major Artists and Writers, Recent Developments.** Fill in the blanks with the findings of your research.

THE SOVIET UNION AND EASTERN EUROPE

Reviewing Facts

1. Which country in Eastern Europe is at the greatest geographical disadvantage when invaded by its neighbors? Why?

2. Who prevented Russia from taking part in the Renaissance of Western Europe?

3. Which three countries partitioned Poland?

4. **a.** Why did Napoleon try to conquer Russia? **b.** What elements defeated him?

5. Which country lost territory by the Munich Pact? When did this occur?

6. How did the Soviet Union manage to dominate the countries of Eastern Europe after World War II?

7. Why do Soviet authorities fear the peoples of Soviet Central Asia?

8. Which countries of Eastern Europe first gained freedom from Soviet control in the late 1980s?

Understanding Main Ideas

1. **a.** What country long prevented Russia from achieving its goal of a warm-water port on the Black Sea? **b.** How did this country also hinder national self-determination in Eastern Europe?

2. Why was St. Petersburg truly Russia's "window to the West"? Why do you think the Communists moved the capital to Moscow?

3. **a.** How would you describe Russia's status in the eyes of the world in 1815? **b.** How and why had this changed by 1855?

4. How did Russia at the end of World War I differ from the Soviet Union at the end of World War II?

Applying Chronology Skills

1917	October Revolution
1921	New Economic Policy
1928	First Five Year plan
1936–1938	Stalin's purges of Communist party
1939	Nazi-Soviet Pact
1941	Nazi invasion of Soviet Union
1953	Stalin's death
1957	*Sputnik I* launched into orbit
1961	Yuri Gagarin, first man to orbit earth
1962	Cuban missile crisis
1964	Khrushchev ousted, Brezhnev general secretary
1975	Andrei Sakharov wins Nobel Peace Prize
1982	Brezhnev dies
1986	Gorbachev becomes general secretary
1989	Upheaval in Eastern Europe

1. How many years did Stalin dominate the Soviet Union?

2. How long was the Brezhnev era?

3. What event occurred about halfway through the Communist period?

Making Connections

Understanding Humanities Many of Russia's writers have suffered persecution and censorship. Select one dissident writer, describe his or her works, and relate how these works might have led to censorship.

Developing Critical Thinking

Making Comparisons   What are some of the religious, social, and economic forces that make the countries of Eastern Europe different from one another and different from the countries of Western Europe?

Using Sources

Lenin's Testament

I have in mind stability as a guarantee against a split [in the Communist party leadership] in the near future, and I intend to examine here a series of considerations of a purely personal character.

I think that the fundamental factor in the matter of stability [is] Stalin and Trotsky. The relation between them constitutes...a big half of the danger of that split, which might be avoided...by raising the number of members of the Central Committee to 50 or 100.

Comrade Stalin, having become General Secretary, has concentrated an enormous power in his hands; and I am not sure that he always knows how to use that power with sufficient caution. On the other hand, comrade Trotsky...is distinguished not only by his exceptional ability—personally, he is...the most able man in the present Central Committee—but also by his too far-reaching self-confidence and a disposition to be far too much attracted by the purely administrative side of affairs. —December 25, 1922

Postscript: Stalin is too rude, and this fault, entirely supportable in relations among us Communists, becomes unsupportable in the office of General Secretary. Therefore, I propose to the comrades to

find a way to remove Stalin from that position and appoint another man who in all respects differs from Stalin only in superiority—namely, more patient, more loyal, more polite and more attentive to comrades....[This matter] is not a trifle.

—LENIN

January 4, 1923

From *The Suppressed Testament of Lenin* (New York: Pioneer Publishers, n.d.), pp. 5–7.

1.   What does Lenin say about Stalin's ability to govern the Soviet Union?

2.   What criticism does Lenin make of Trotsky?

Extension Activities

Developing Historical Empathy   Imagine that you are a citizen of one of the republics in the Soviet Union. *Glasnost* allows you to speak your mind. *Perestroika* could let you determine the future of your republic. Study works in the library on this republic. Write an essay on your concerns as a member of a nationality. How do conditions appear at present? What hopes do you have for the future of your republic?

Read More About History and Culture

Abel, Elie. *The Shattered Bloc: Behind the Upheaval in Eastern Europe.* Boston: Houghton Mifflin, 1990.

Chesler, Evan R. *The Russian Jewry Reader.* New York: Behrman, 1974. History of Jews in Russia from the 700s.

Gray, Francine du Plessix. *Soviet Women: Walking the Tightrope.* New York: Doubleday, 1989.

Watt, Richard M. *Bitter Glory: Poland and Its Fate, 1918 to 1939.* New York: Simon and Schuster, 1979.

EPILOGUE

Today we live in a global village. Technological advances have made the world seem smaller. The time it

The World Today

India's first prime minister, Jawaharlal Nehru, once wrote, "Everything changes continually. What is history, indeed, but a record of change." He continued by saying, "And if there had been very few changes in the past, there would have been little of history to write."

As you have learned throughout this book, the history of humankind has indeed been a story of change. But human history has also been marked by adaptation. From the time of the last Ice Age to the present, people around the world have learned to live with changing conditions. Two great revolutions—the agricultural revolution and the industrial revolution—reshaped human life. Today, humankind faces a third great revolution: a change in its way of life in order to preserve the planet on which we live.

As you study the epilogue, think about these questions:

- What are some of the far-reaching effects of environmental pollution?

- Why are some world leaders concerned about the earth's ability to support its expanding population?

Landfills in many countries throughout the world are full. This barge had trouble finding a place that would take the garbage it carried. What does the banner on the garbage say?

When astronauts first went into space in the 1960s, their view of the earth showed a beautiful blue planet girdled with wide bands of green. Today, pictures taken by satellites show a brownish planet with very little green remaining. In the past 30 years, the earth's soil, water, and air have become seriously polluted.

Soil Pollution

Soil pollution involves damage to the thin layer of fertile soil that covers a large portion of the earth's land surface. The main cause of soil pollution is the use of large quantities of chemical fertilizers and pesticides. Another cause is the building of dams and canals for irrigation. Salts and minerals accumulate in the stored water. After the water is released, it spreads over the land and then begins to evaporate. As it evaporates, it leaves behind the stored salts and minerals. Eventually, these destroy the soil's fertility, making it useless for farming.

Solid wastes are also a major form of soil pollution. People in industrialized countries throw out billions of tons of solid wastes each year. Examples are plastic and paper bags and boxes, junked tires, cans, and bottles. Many solid wastes end up in open dumps or in landfills that pollute the soil.

Many industrial processes produce toxic or hazardous wastes. The radioactive wastes from nuclear power plants, for example, must be stored properly if they are not to become a threat to society.

Water Pollution

Throughout history, people have dumped their garbage into nearby rivers, lakes, and seas. Before the industrial revolution, they dumped only organic wastes that were soon degraded, or broken down. Since the industrial revolution, however, the situation has changed. Today, pesticides and chemical fertilizers from farms and lawns run off into the rivers, lakes, and oceans. Oil spills from tankers and offshore drilling accidents are common occurrences. Some industries dump inorganic chemicals that do not break down but remain to foul the bottom of rivers, lakes, and oceans. The water used to cool nuclear reactors in power stations sometimes raises water temperatures of the body of water into which it empties. Untreated sewage, which contains people's wastes and garbage, is another source of water pollution.

Air Pollution

Most air pollution is caused by the burning of fossil fuels—coal, oil, and natural gas. Burning fuels give off poisonous gases as well as particulates, or tiny particles of solid or liquid matter. The major sources of pollutants are car exhausts and factory fumes. The burning of garbage and trash also contributes to air pollution.

Automobile exhaust is the key component of the smog that blankets major cities.

Air pollution in Eastern Europe is a serious health problem. Workers in the industrial area of southern Poland have a life expectancy that is four years less than in the rest of the country. Almost half of the area's children suffer from hearing and seeing disabilities. Budapest, Hungary, maintains a lung clinic where people come to spend fifteen minutes at a time breathing oxygen. In industrial areas of northern Czechoslovakia, schoolchildren and their teachers have to be sent to the mountains for at least one month a year.

Other culture regions suffer from air pollution too. In Tokyo, many people cover their faces with surgical masks when they walk outdoors. Visitors to Beijing and other northern Chinese cities frequently develop respiratory diseases. On many days in Mexico City, a person can see no farther than two city blocks.

Another widespread problem caused by air pollution is acid rain. When the pollution in the air mixes with water vapor, acid forms and then falls to the earth in rain or snow. As a result, in hundreds of small lakes in many parts of the United States, Canada, and Europe, fish are dying. In some lakes no fish can be found at all.

National borders do not stop acid rain. Therefore pollution from Great Britain, France, or Eastern European countries can cause acid rain in Germany or in Sweden. In many mountain forests of the world, trees are deformed and twisted, and in some places they have stopped growing altogether. About half of West Germany's famous Black Forest is dead. The forests in the western United States are also becoming affected by acid rain.

Acid rain also affects art and architecture. The stained-glass windows in many European cathedrals are pitted with acid spots. The marble statues that fill the streets of many Greek and Italian cities are being eaten away. Such historic buildings as the Parthenon, the Tower of London, and Cologne Cathedral are, in the words of a Danish architect, "melting away like sugar candy."

The Greenhouse Effect

In recent years, people have become aware of a new ecological problem. The overcutting of trees and the increased use of fossil fuels for industry and transportation have caused a buildup of carbon dioxide in the atmosphere. In what is known as the **greenhouse effect**, the ever-increasing layer of carbon dioxide traps heat from the earth's surface.

Increasing numbers of scientists believe that because of the heat buildup, the earth is growing warmer. By 2050, they say, worldwide temperatures will have risen from 3 to 9 degrees Fahrenheit (2 to 5°C). If the increase is only 3 degrees, the climatic changes will be fairly mild. But if the increase is 9 degrees, the climatic changes will be major—as they were after the last Ice Age, when worldwide temperatures increased by 7 degrees Fahrenheit (3°C).

The warmer temperatures will cause ice caps in the Arctic and Antarctic to melt faster. Low-lying coastal areas around the world will be flooded, forcing some 2 billion people to move inland. People will have to build dikes to keep the salt water from penetrating the soil and ruining both freshwater supplies and farmland. Farmers will have to use different crops that are more suited to the changed climate. Thousands of species of plants and animals will disappear. There will be no more redwoods, no more seals or polar bears. But other species, such as the African tsetse fly that causes sleeping sickness, will expand into a much larger range.

"The Lungs of the Earth"

Trees serve many ecological functions. They prevent soil erosion and flooding. They provide fruits and other foods for people and animals. Most important of all, perhaps, they remove carbon dioxide from the atmosphere and release oxygen. In other words, they act as "the lungs of the earth." The more effective forests are, the less the greenhouse effect.

The largest remaining "lung" in the world is the rainforest of the Amazon, most of which lies in Brazil. This forest contains about one-fourth of the world's forest area and provides about one-half of its oxygen. Since 1965, however, it has been subject to massive deforestation. First, the government built roads into the interior and provided billions in tax incentives for cattle grazers. Hundreds of thousands of ranchers moved in and cleared the land, only to find that they could plant grasses for at most three years before the soil wore out. Then came the timber industry,

Growing concern over the long-range effects of pollution has led to increasing media attention to the problem.

"I knew there'd be a catch in it when they said the meek would inherit the earth."

searching for tropical hardwoods. Gold prospectors polluted the Amazon's tributaries with mercury, used in processing gold. Landless peasants burned millions of acres of timber to clear land for farming. The Brazilian government is building hydroelectric dams that will flood vast areas of the Amazon basin.

As a result, each year the Amazon's rainforest loses an area bigger than the Netherlands. As one scientist put it, "It's equivalent to clearing a football field every five seconds." If the destruction continues at the present rate, the entire rainforest will be gone in 25 to 30 years.

Some international lending institutions have suggested "debt for nature" swaps in which Brazil's foreign debt would be reduced in exchange for protection of the rainforest. But this idea has been rejected by the Brazilian government. "It would be giving a great measure of control over our national territory to other countries," said one official. "Brazil will never, never, never accept that." Besides, the official added, such industrial nations as Great Britain, the United States, France, West Germany, and Japan cut down their own forests and devastated the environment in order to develop. "Now you have the goodies, and you want to keep us from getting ours. You want to keep us down."

One possible solution might be to treat oxygen as a commodity. After all, oxygen—like oil—is a fuel. Why not buy the oxygen the rainforest produces? However, any international oxygen tax would have to be large enough to make it worthwhile for Brazil's government and people to shift from cattle ranching, mineral prospecting, lumbering, and farming to forest conservation.

Attempts to Control Pollution

Paying an international oxygen tax is one way to combat pollution. There are many others. One is using energy more efficiently. For example, coal-burning plants can install new smokestack equipment called "scrubbers" to remove sulfur compounds from the smoke before they escape into the atmosphere. Automobile manufacturers can build cars with smog-control devices and with engines that use lead-free gasoline.

Then, too, governments can build new sewage and waste treatment systems. Oil companies can stop using single-hulled tankers to ship oil and can substitute double-hulled tankers that are able to contain oil spills. Everyone can recycle paper, glass, aluminum, tin cans, wire hangers, and other throwaway products.

Such methods, however, only modify pollution. Much more effective would be abandoning technologies that create pollutants in the first place. For example, parents can give up using disposable diapers for babies and go back to old-fashioned but reusable cloth diapers. Poisonous compounds such as asbestos and DDT can be banned worldwide. Factories can stop using fossil fuels and substitute nuclear energy or, better yet, solar, wind, and biomass energy. They are renewable fuels, and they do not have the safety problems associated with nuclear energy. They are also cheaper and more efficient than nuclear power.

Farmers use modern machinery, but farming problems still exist in India.

One area that lends itself to an alternative technology is agriculture. Especially in the United States, farmers are beginning to limit their use of chemicals and are going back to organic methods. A few have gone all the way. They use no agrichemicals at all. Instead, they fertilize with cow manure, plant winter cover crops that they plow into the soil in spring, and rotate their crops to keep insect pests from multiplying. Other farms combine manure, cover crops, and crop rotation with a limited use of chemical fertilizers and herbicides.

The results to date have been impressive. Although the crop yield sometimes goes down a bit at first, there is no soil erosion. Also, the soil retains its moisture and is less damaged by drought. Farmers do not have to worry about increases in the resistance of insects to pesticides. Nor do they have to spend money on agrichemicals. In the long run, production remains constant, while profits are higher—and there is no damage to the environment.

Obstacles to Controlling Pollution

All over the world, demands for a cleaner environment are growing. But these demands must confront the basic economic factor of scarcity and the need to make trade-offs. In other words, clean water, clean soil, and clean air are not free. The price for protecting and improving the environment is slower economic growth and a higher cost of living.

Paying the price is, of course, much easier for rich, industrialized nations than it is for developing ones. But even rich nations have so far been reluctant to do what needs to be done.

Take the problem of chlorofluorocarbons (CFCs), for example. These gases are used as coolants in refrigerators and air conditioners, and as industrial cleaning solvents. Unfortunately, their use destroys the ozone layer, which screens out much of the harmful ultraviolet radiation from the sun and thus helps to provide the conditions under which life on the earth can exist.

In 1987 more than three dozen countries signed an agreement promising to ban the use of CFCs by the year 2000. But it took ten years of negotiations to complete the agreement, and even then, nations were reluctant to move until a gaping hole in the ozone layer over Antarctica showed how serious the situation was.

Air and water pollution have become increasingly serious problems in Japan in recent years. This photograph shows how industrial wastes are carried along a river near Tokyo.

SECTION 1 REVIEW

1. **Recall**   What are some causes of air and water pollution?
2. **How and Why**   Why are scientists concerned about the greenhouse effect?
3. **Critical Thinking**   Why do you think it will be difficult to control pollution in the world?

People have always worried about getting enough food to survive. One side of the equation is population, the number of mouths that must be fed. The other side of the equation is food production, the amount of food that is available. It is the balance between the two sides that determines whether, and how well, people live. In recent years, world leaders have become increasingly concerned about the earth's ability to support its expanding population.

The Population Explosion

When the agricultural revolution began, scholars estimate that there were about 10 million people on the earth. Today there are approximately 5.2 billion people, and the most common forecast for the year 2000 is 6.2 billion.

Even more dramatic than the total increase in numbers is the change in the rate of increase. It took 4 million years for the population to reach 2 billion people. It took only 45 years to reach 4 billion people. And another 2 billion people will arrive in just 22 more years. This rapid increase is known as the **population explosion**.

For most of humankind's existence, birth rates were high. But the population grew very slowly because death rates were likewise high. A family had to have five to seven children in order for two to reach adulthood. Also, life expectancy was comparatively short. An individual over 35 was considered old.

Population began surging in the late 1700s. The explosion originated in Western Europe. From there it spread first to North America and, later, to other parts of the world.

The reason for the population explosion was a drop in the death rate. The major factors were the construction of public water and sewage systems, vaccinations against disease, and the manufacture of cheap soap. These helped bring such killers as cholera, smallpox, typhoid, tuberculosis, and yellow fever under control. Another factor was an improvement in the amount and variety of food resulting from better farming and processing methods and from the interregional exchange of crops. With enough and better food to eat, people lived healthier and longer lives.

After World War I, modernization hit the nations of Africa, Asia, and Latin America, and their death rates likewise began to tumble. However, because sanitation and medical care improved much faster than it had in nineteenth-century Western Europe and the United States, the population of these nations grew much faster. But most developing nations do not have enough industrial jobs to support their people. There are no more frontier areas where people can go. Food production—as you will read later—is not keeping pace with the increases in population.

As a result, unemployment, poverty, and malnutrition in the developing nations of Africa, Asia, and Latin America is staggeringly high. For example, India has about 50 million persons without jobs. The per-capita income in developing countries is about $800 compared to $19,780 in the

United States. About two out of three persons worldwide go to bed hungry each night. More than 40,000 children starve to death each day.

Family Planning

During the late 1800s and 1900s, the birthrate in the industrialized nations of Western Europe and North America declined. Part of the reason was higher incomes and the passage of social security laws. People no longer had to depend on their children to take care of them when they grew old, so they had fewer children. Another part of the reason was female education and equal rights for women. Most educated women know how to use birth control methods properly. Family size also declines when women gain sources of status other than children and when they are prepared for employment opportunities outside the home.

Many cultures and religions favor large families. In some societies, manhood depends on the number of children a man fathers, while women are not considered responsible persons unless they are mothers. Muhammad taught that "Wealth and children are the ornament of this life." Hinduism admonishes its followers to have eight sons. The Roman Catholic Church considers artificial methods of birth control to be immoral. Some people look on birth control as a device for racist or imperialist oppression.

Nevertheless, about 80 countries have national birth control programs today. The first nation to adopt such a program was Japan, which legalized abortion and contraception in 1948. As you know, China began a strong campaign for family planning in 1976, with the goal of zero population growth. The Chinese government stressed economic incentives to promote its policy.

Other nations have emphasized different techniques. The government of Egypt sends social workers door-to-door to educate people on birth control. Bangladesh's government hands out contraceptive information to groups of rural village women along with loans for starting small businesses. The government of Kenya has set up rural health clinics that distribute free contraceptives. As a result, in the last five years Kenya's rate of population growth—the highest in the world—has been declining.

Yet despite these developments, the number of people in the world will continue to soar for at least another 100 or so years. There are three main reasons. One is the difficulty of changing cultural values that favor large families. The second is the cost of shifting from an agricultural to an industrial economy. The third is the fact that developing countries contain huge numbers of young people. Between 40 and 50 percent of their population is under 15 years. With such an age distribution, the total number of births will be high even though the birthrate declines.

Increasing the Food Supply

Farmers can increase output in four ways. They can develop new farmland, increase the productivity of existing farmland, develop new sources of food, and shift from wasteful crops to more efficient ones.

This sign is located on The Family Planning Center in Darima, India. The sign reads "A small family is a happy family. For free advice and help, go to the nearest family planning center."

When the United States was being settled by Western Europeans, it was easy to develop new farmland. The settlers simply cut down the forests and plowed the prairies. Today the only large areas of land that might be developed for farming lie in the jungles of Sub-Saharan Africa and in the rainforest of Brazil. However, the soil in these areas loses its fertility quickly when it is cultivated for crops, while the tropical climate is extremely uncomfortable. So this option is not practical.

Much more practical is increasing the productivity of existing farmland. One method is the Green Revolution that began in the 1960s. Geneticists developed new varieties of wheat and rice that resisted disease and yielded from two to four times as much per acre as natural varieties. Wheat and rice harvests soared. However, the new seeds required the use of large amounts of irrigation water and fertilizer. This was no problem for farmers in developed countries. But most farmers in developing nations could not afford to buy chemical fertilizers or to install electric or diesel-powered pumps to bring water to their land. Nor could poor people afford to buy the additional food that was grown because the cost of fertilizer and energy drove the price of the food too high. Unless the problem of poverty is solved, the Green Revolution does not provide enough of an answer.

Shifting from wasteful crops to more efficient crops essentially means shifting from beef consumption to grain consumption. Raising cattle for beef is a very inefficient use of land. It takes 8 pounds (3.6 kilograms) of grain feed to produce 1 pound (.45 kilograms) of beef. But you get about 10 times as many calories and more than four times as much protein from the eight pounds of grain as you do from the one pound of beef. In other words, if people—especially in developed countries—were to lower their meat consumption, there would be more grain available to feed people.

In addition to not producing enough food, many developing nations are unable to store and transport properly what food they have. They lack modern warehouses, railroads, and even paved roads. As a result, as much as one-fifth of their farm output either spoils or is consumed by rats and insects. Improving storage and transportation facilities would go a long way toward improving the health of their people.

Changing Government Policies

There are additional options available to developing nations with high birthrates. The first is giving priority to agriculture rather than industry. Instead of building steel mills and educating people for white-collar jobs, the governments of developing nations could pour their limited resources into digging wells, building rural roads, and training carpenters, electricians, tractor drivers, and other blue-collar workers. People could be encouraged to stay on the farms instead of migrating to overcrowded cities.

Emphasizing agriculture includes training people to employ more effective farming techniques. There are literally dozens of things already being done on a small scale that could be expanded. For example, farmers in Burkina Faso are able to catch more rainwater by placing stones along the contour lines of a field. The Chinese are planting a 4,300-mile-long (6 920-kilometer-long) ''green Great Wall'' of shrubs and trees across the northern part of their country to prevent the Gobi Desert from moving south. The Israelis have made the desert bloom through the use of ''fertigation''—dropping precise amounts of nutrients and water at the base of each plant.

A second option available to developing nations with high birthrates is reducing their purchases of military equipment. In 1984, for example, Sub-Saharan Africa was hit by widespread drought and famine. Yet most of the nations in the culture region spent more money on importing weapons than on importing food. Ethiopia, for example, spent six times as much. Unfortunately, since the governments of most of these nations depend on the military to remain in power, they are unlikely to reduce their arms purchases in the near future.

Coping with Water Shortages

Increasing food production is, in many instances, closely linked with irrigation. Yet in some of the world's most populous countries, water shortages loom on the horizon.

The demand for limited water supplies will probably be felt first in Egypt. All of its arable land is irrigated. But the country is the last in line to draw water from the Nile. As upper basin countries such as Uganda, Ethiopia, and Sudan develop the river's headwaters, less water will be available downstream. Yet Egypt's population keeps increasing at the rate of 1.5 million people a year.

Countries in other culture regions also face water shortages. In China, for example, the water table beneath Beijing is falling as much as 6.5 feet (2 meters) each year. But the country's growing industries demand more and more water. Some scholars fear that farmers in China's drier areas may lose up to 40 percent of their irrigation water to factories. Already people in such western cities as Ürümqi (uh-RUHM-chee) and Kashgar can turn on their water taps only a few hours a day. Irrigating farmland is more important than washing clothes or keeping clean.

Many Sub-Saharan nations are dependent on scarce water supplies as they strive to meet the food needs of their rapidly growing populations.

SECTION 2 REVIEW

1. **Recall**   What is the population explosion?
2. **How and Why**   Why are many countries encouraging people to limit the number of children they have?
3. **Critical Thinking**   Why is the problem of providing adequate food supplies greater in developing countries than in developed countries?

865

Reviewing People, Places, and Things

Identify, define, or explain each of the following:

pollution	DDT
solid waste	renewable fuels
toxic waste	CFCs
fossil fuels	population explosion
acid rain	malnutrition
greenhouse effect	productivity
deforestation	family planning
scrubber	Green Revolution
double-hulled tanker	consumption
recycle	fertigation

Understanding Facts and Ideas

1. What are five causes of soil pollution?

2. How has the pollution of water changed since the industrial revolution?

3. How has air pollution affected Tokyo, Beijing, and Mexico City?

4. Why can air pollution in one culture region have such a great effect on people in another culture region?

5. What are some problems that many scientists believe the greenhouse effect will cause?

6. Why are rainforests important to the environment?

7. How can people help control pollution?

8. What is the price to pay for protecting and improving the environment?

9. Why did the populations of many nations grow much faster after World War I than they had before?

10. Why did the passage of social security laws result in a decline in the birthrate?

11. What are four ways in which farmers can increase productivity?

12. How might the changing of government policies help food shortages?

Developing Critical Thinking

Choosing Alternative Solutions To choose an alternative solution to a problem, you must look at the solutions that have been attempted and then use creative thinking to find a new solution to help alleviate the problem. Making a chart to show the causes of the problem and some possible solutions helps to analyze the situation and to reach a decision as to what might be done to solve the problem.

Activity: Using the information in the text and other information you can gather about pollution of the environment, make a chart to show the causes of pollution and some solutions that have been attempted. Then suggest a creative solution to the pollution problem.

Writing About History

Citizenship in Action Do research to find out about the industries that produce large amounts of pollution. Then choose one manufacturer among those industries. Make a list of ways that manufacturers can cut down on pollution. Next, write a letter explaining how the company you chose can cut down on pollution. Address the letter to the president of the company.

Applying Your Skills

Making a Graph You can compute the population density per square mile by dividing the population in a location by the location's area. Use the National Profiles chart for each region in this textbook to determine the population density per square mile for the following countries: Kenya, India, Japan, Mexico, Iraq, France, and the Soviet Union. Graph your results.

CONTENTS

THE HUMAN EXPRESSION TIME LINE

Time scale (BC): 10000, 9500, 9000, 8500, 8000, 7500, 7000, 6500, 6000, 5500, 5000, 4800, 4600, 4400, 4200, 4000, 3800, 3600, 3400, 3200, 3000, 2800

The Middle East
- Domestication of plants and animals
- Earliest remains of towns
- Farming on Nile Delta in Egypt
- First and Second Dynasties (Egypt)
- Sumerian civilization (Mesopotamia)

Asia
- Domestication of plants (Southeast Asia)
- Pottery in Hoabinhian culture
- Asians settle in Philippines

Sub-Saharan Africa
- People in West Africa
- Green Sahara inhabited
- Farming in West Africa
- Farming in the Sudan

Western Europe
- Cro-Magnon people
- Domestication of plants and animals
- Megaliths

The Soviet Union and Eastern Europe
- Village life in eastern Russia
- Cro-Magnon people (Siberia)

Latin America
- Plants domesticated (Mexico)
- Asian hunters migrate
- Plants domesticated (South America)

The United States
- Food gathering begins

Timeline dates (top): 2800 · 2600 · 2400 · 2200 · 2000 · 1900 · 1800 · 1700 · 1600 · 1500 · 1400 · 1300 · 1200 · 1100 · 1000 · 900 · 800 · 700

Old Kingdom in Egypt

● Judaism begins

Kyksos era (Egypt)

Exodus

Kingdom of David and Solomon

Middle Kingdom (Egypt)

Aramaen trading centers dominate Middle East

Akkadian Empire (Mesopotamia)

● Kingdom of Judah and Kingdom of Israel

Mesopotamia becomes Babylonia

Hebrews settle Canaan

Empire Period (Egypt)

New Babylonian Empire (Mesopotamia)

Phoenicians dominate Mediterranean trade

Southeast Asians sail to Taiwan and Japan

Shang dynasty (China)

Xia dynasty (China)

Vedic period (India)

● Hinduism begins in India

Indus Valley civilization (India)

Asians migrate to India; Caste system

Jomon period (Japan)

● Plants, animals domesticated in the Sudan

Nubia part of the Egyptian Empire

Sahara dries up

Bantu migrations

Minoan civilization (Crete)

Greeks bring Phoenician alphabet to Italy ●

Mycenaean civilization (Greece)

First Olympic games in Greece ●

● Stonehenge (England)

Wide trading contacts in Russia

Olmec civilization (Mexico)
Base culture of Mesoamerica

● Villages in Middle and
South America

Mound cultures in Midwest

● Farming begins

869

700 600 500 400 300 200 100 B.C. 0 A.D. 100 200 300 400 500 600 700 800 900

Assyrian Empire

Persian Empire

Ptolemaic dynasty (Egypt)

● Christianity begins

● Diaspora

Sassanian dynasty (Persia)

Umayyad dynasty

● Assyrians scatter Ten Lost Tribes of Israel

● Hasmonean dynasty founded among Israelites

● Roman Empire divides

● Isalm begins

● Alexander the Great conquers Egypt

● Edict of Milan

Byzantine rule and/or influence

Roman Empire controls Middle East

Pathian rule (Persia)

Vandal invasions

Zhou dynasty (China)

● Daoism (China)

Dark Ages in China

● Confucianism (Korea)

Legalism (China) ●

Malays occupy Philippines

● India traders in Southeast Asia

Gupta dynasty (India)

● Shinto (Japan)

Maurya dynasty (India)

● Legendary beginning of Japanese empire

● China colonizes Korea

● Japan invades Korea

Chinese culture influences Japan

Warring States Period in China

Vietnam joins Han Dynasty

Buddhism (Japan) ●

● Buddhism (Korea)

Tang dynasty (China)

Great Wall of China begun

● Buddhism (China)

Lao people move into Laos ●

Qin dynasty (China) ●

Han dynasty (China)

Yamato clan (Japan)

Sui dynasty (China)

● Iron Age in northeast

● Christianity spreads

● Jews settle in Ethiopia

Migrations from Arabian Peninsula to Ethiopia

● Coptic Christianity (Egypt)

● Islam founded

Kingdom of Kush

Empire of Ghana

Nok culture (Nigeria)

Kingdom of Axum

Bantu migrations

● Hausa

Muslim influence (East Coast) ●

Etruscans (Italy)

Roman Republic

● Roman Empire splits into East and West

Hellenistic Age
Greek culture spreads into Middle East

Invasions
Ostrogoths, Vandals, Angles, Saxons, Jutes, Burgundians, Lombards

Viking Invasions

Socrates, Plato, Aristotle
Age of Pericles (Athens)

Roman Empire

● St. Patrick brings Christianity to Ireland

Greek city-states

● La Tene Culture (Celts) in west

● Christianity spreads

● Edict of Milan

Islam spreads ●

Byzantine Empire

Early Middle Ages

● Slavs in Russia

Roman civilization in Albania

Hun invasions ●

● Bulgar invasions

● Magyars conquer Slavs and Germans in Hungary

Scythians rule Russia
Greek culture introduced

● Christianity spreads

● Albania becomes part of Eastern Roman Empire

Goths invade Russia

● Slavs settle Balkan Peninsula

Roman rule in Romania

Eastern Slavs migrate to Russian steppes
Byzantine culture introduced

Invasions of Albania

Sarmatians rule Russia

Slavs migrate east, west, south ●

Invasions of Romania

Paracas culture (southern Peru) Various peoples compete for power in Andes

Teotihuacán (Mexico)

Huari empire (Peru)

Nazca culture (southern Peru)

Chavin culture (Peru)

Tiahuanaco (Mexico)

Mochica culture (northern Peru)

Mayan civilization

● Local cultures in California

Southwest cultures

Timeline (900–1700)

Dates across top: 900 1000 1050 1100 1150 1200 1250 1300 1350 1400 1450 1500 1550 1600 1650 1700

- Mongol invasions
- Safavid dynasty (Persia)
- Barbary States (North Africa)
- Moors rule Spain
- Crusades Islamic and Byzantine cultures influence Europe
- Abbasid dynasty
- Spain is center of Jewish learning and culture
- Khmer empire (Cambodia)
- da Gama finds route to Asia
- Invasions of India
- Arabs bring Islam to Malaysia
- Mongols rule Korea
- Ming dynasty (China)
- British East India Co. chartered
- Thais enter Thailand
- Yuan dynasty (China)
- Spain rules Philippines
- Heian period (Japan)
- Kamakura shōgunate (Japan)
- Mogul Empire (India)
- Mongols defeated in Vietnam
- Ashikaga shōgunate (Japan)
- Portugal controls Malaysia and Indonesia
- Vietnam expels Chinese
- Song dynasty (China)
- Great Wall completed
- Turkish Mongols rule India
- Japan closed to outsiders except Dutch traders
- State of Kanem
- da Gama reaches east coast of Africa
- Ife
- Empire of Kanem-Bornu 1350-1845
- Slave trade begins
- Kingdom of Lunda
- Empire of Songhai
- Empire of Mali
- Kingdom of Dahomey 1600-1904
- Christian kingdoms (Nubia)
- Monomotapa Empire
- Kingdom of Congo
- Zimbabwe
- Yoruba city-states (Nigeria)
- Muslim influence (West Africa)
- Bantu migrations
- Portuguese in Senegal, Cape Verde
- Kingdom of Burundi
- Vernacular languages develop
- Later Middle Ages
- Rise of middle class
- Age of Exploration
- Rise of English Parliament
- Counter-Reformation
- Magna Carta
- Hundred Years' War
- Holy Roman Empire
- Reformation
- Crusades
- Renaissance
- Feudalism; Manorialism
- Gothic architecture
- Movable type and printing press
- Roman Empire
- Thirty Years' War
- Hungary unites
- Albania joins Serbian Empire
- Jews settle in Ukraine
- Austria dominates Hungary;
- Eastern Orthodox Church becomes official religion of Russia
- Poles capture Moscow
- Jagellon dynasty unites Poland and Lithuania
- Slav, Varangian cultures merge into Russian
- Piast dynasty (Poland)
- Czechs, Slovaks form Czechoslovakia
- Renaissance in Eastern Europe
- Middle Ages in Eastern Europe
- Counter-Reformation in Eastern Europe
- Byzantine Empire
- Reformation (Eastern Europe)
- Serbs unite (Yugoslavia)
- Mongols invade Hungary and Russia
- Holy Roman Empire (Eastern Europe)
- Captaincy—generals (Brazil)
- Aztec (Mexico)
- Maize, potatoes introduced into Europe
- Conquistadores
- Columbus lands on San Salvador
- Incas
- Encomienda system (Spanish colonies)
- Various peoples compete for power in Mesoamerica
- Treaty of Tordesillas
- Viceroyalties (Spanish America)
- Chimú culture (Peru, Ecuador)
- Portugal claims Brazil
- Diamond boom (Brazil)
- 13 original colonies settled
- Woodlands culture
- Spanish begin to settle
- First black Africans
- Vikings land
- Age of Exploration

1700 1750 1800 1810 1820 1830 1840 1850 1860 1870 1880 1890 1900 1910

● French invade Egypt

● Russo-Turkish War

Qajar dynasty (Iran)

Suez Canal

Ottoman Empire rules most of the Middle East

N. Africa under Western domination ●

Crimean War

World Zionist Organization formed ●

Muhammad Ali's dynasty (Egypt)

● Britain gains control of Suez Canal

French control Indochina

Korea closed to outsiders

British control Burma

● Boxer Uprising

Tokugawa shōgunate (Japan)

● Chinese open five ports to British

Yi dynasty (Korea)

Perry opens Japan ●

British control Malaysia

Dutch govern Indonesia

U.S. takes Philippines ●

Laos splits into small kingdoms

● Vietnam unites   Ming or Qing dynasty (China)

● Meiji Restoration (Japan)

● British seize South Africa Dutch Colony

Ashanti Union

● Ethiopia united

Hausaland

● School of Negritude in French African literature

Slave trade ends ●

● Liberia independent

Empire of Malawi   Luba Kingdom

Africans resist European rule

Kingdom of Buganda

British in S. Africa ●   ● Europeans explore interior   ● Freed slaves settle Liberia

● Berlin Conference

Baroque movement   ● French Revolution

● Second French Empire

Olympic Games revived ●

Rococo movement

● Italy unified

Romanticism

Impressionism

● Congress of Vienna

● Realism

Materialism (in the arts and philosophy)

Neoclassicism

● Napoleon proclaims self emperor

● Third French Republic

● Fauvism

Industrial revolution

● Germany unified   Spanish-American War ●

Age of Reason   ● Era of nationalism begins

● First division of Poland   ● Napolean invades Russia

● Austro-Hungarian Monarchy   Revolution of 1905 ●

● Congress of Vienna unites Poland and Russia

● Sobieski of Poland saves Europe from Turks

Ottoman Empire (Eastern Europe)

● Second division of Poland

Alexander I makes
Russia a European power   Romanticism (in Eastern European arts)

Romania independent 1878-1946

● Third division of Poland

Emancipation Act frees Russian serfs ●

● Independence (Cuba)

Gold rush   ● Toussaint L'Ouverture heads Saint-Domingue

Pedro II rules Brazil   Republic (Brazil) ● ● Roosevelt Corollary to Monroe

● Gran Colombia collapses

Doctrine

Independence (Spanish South America)   ● Santa Anna president (Mexico)

Charter of Autonomy (Puerto Rico) ●

Baroque influence in arts

Ten Years' War (Cuba)   ● First International Conference
of American States

Bolívar president (Gran Colombia) ● ● Brazil independent

● Mexican-American War
Treaty of Guadalupe-Hidalgo

Slavery 1501-1889   ● Monroe Doctrine   Juárez president (Mexico) ●

Díaz dictator (Mexico) ●

● Creole revolt (Saint-Domingue)   United Provinces of Central America 1823-1838

Spanish-American War ●

● Independence (Saint Domingue (Haiti))

● Gadsden Purchase

Cuban revolt ●

● Declaration of Independence   ● Monroe Doctrine   Gadsden Purchase

Platt Amendment ●

● Revolutionary War 1776-1781

● Civil War 1861-1865

Open Door policy ●

● War of 1812—1812-1815   ● Texas declares independence from Mexico

Reconstruction

Industrial revolution ●   ● U.S. outlaws African slave trade

Spanish-American War ●

● Mexican War 1846-1848

● Statehood 1791-1959

● European immigration 1820-1860

Hawaii annexed ●

European Wars in N. America ● ● Lousiana Purchase

Timeline with date axis: 1910, 1920, 1930, 1940, 1945, 1950, 1955, 1960, 1965, 1970, 1975, 1980, 1985, 1990

(Middle East / Ottoman band)
- Young Turks gain control of Ottoman government
- 1912 Balkan Wars
- World War II
- State of Israel founded
- Arab oil embargo •
- • Israeli-Egyptian Peace Treaty
- Palestinian Arabs gain recognition •
- Israel withdraws from Sinai
- Iraq invades Kuwait •
- • Balfour Declaration
- Suez Canal nationalized
- Civil war in Lebanon
- • League of Nations
- Green Revolution
- OPEC increases oil prices
- UN peacekeeping force in Lebanon; PLO in chaos
- World War I
- • Ataturk takes over Turkey
- • OPEC
- Revolt in Iran, Shah overthrown •
- • Era of independence begins
- • Arab League formed
- Arab-Israeli conflicts flare with uneasy truces
- Iran-Soviet ties renewed •

(East Asia / South Asia band)
- • Japan bombs Pearl Harbor
- Korean War
- • Economic boom begins in Japan
- • Cultural Revolution (China)
- • Vietnamese boat people flee
- Japan controls Korea
- Mao Zedong in power in China
- Nationalist Chinese set up government on Taiwan
- Chinese student democracy protest ends in violence
- World War I
- • Korea divided
- East Pakistan becomes Bangladesh
- U.S.-PRC diplomatic relations
- India-Sri Lanka pact •
- Cambodia is a French protectorate
- Green Revolution
- Vietnam War
- Civil war in Cambodia
- • Intelstat
- • Gandhi
- Association of Southeast Asian Nations
- Economic control by communes abolished •
- • Japan expands in Asia
- World War II
- French-Indochinese War
- British control India
- Pakistan
- Era of Independence (Southeast Asia)
- • PRC admitted to UN
- Two Koreas join in project •
- Chiang Kaishek breaks with Communists and unites most of China
- British leave India
- • Taiwan removed from UN
- China republic under Sun Yatsen
- • A-bombs dropped
- • Vietnam divided into North and South
- Chinese and Soviets end hostility •

(Africa band)
- African socialism in Tanzania •
- Eight-month War between Somalia and Ethiopia
- World War I
- Apartheid in South Africa
- • Economic Community of African States (16 nations)
- • Congo Free State given to Belgium
- World War II
- OAU •
- Civil war (Nigeria)
- Namibia created •
- United Nations
- Rhodesia becomes Zimbabwe following independence
- Drought
- • Arab League
- Effort to oust South Africa from UN
- • Civil war (Chad)
- Green Revolution
- • Union of South Africa
- • Civil war (Angola)
- Bantustans (South Africa)
- • Biafra surrenders
- Cease fire in Angola •

(Europe / culture band)
- • Abstract expressionism
- • Council of Europe: NATO European Convention on Human Rights
- Movement for united Europe
- • Futurism
- • League of Nations
- West German-Soviet Accord •
- • Nazi party (Germany)
- World War II
- Hungary passageway for East Germans
- Mussolini and fascism rule (Italy)
- Franco rules Spain
- • Nuclear Test Ban Treaty
- • Cubism
- • Dadaism
- NATO deploys U.S.-built missiles in Europe •
- Common Market formed •
- Spain and Portugal join Common Market •
- World War I
- • International school of architecture
- Movements for ethnic identity
- East and West Germany reunited •
- • Surrealism
- Munich Pact •
- • Existentialism
- Constitution Act cuts Canada's last legal ties to Great Britain
- • Berlin Wall removed •
- • Penicillin begins wonder drug era

(USSR / Eastern Europe band)
- Russian Revolution ••
- • Russia gives Poland limited independence
- • USSR and communism dominate Eastern Europe
- • Soviets destroy Czechoslovakian revolution
- • Gorbachev comes to power
- •• Yugoslavia independent 1918-1945
- • Germany divided into East and West
- • Sputnik launched
- Brezhnev and Kosygin 1964-mid 1970s
- Brezhnev mid 1970s-1982
- • Bulgaria independent 1908-1946
- • Collective leadership of the USSR 1953
- • Nuclear Test Ban Treaty
- Andropov comes to power
- • Czechoslovakia independent 1918-1938
- • Nonproliferation Treaty
- Soviets introduce free market reforms •
- World War I
- • Communist dictatorship (Russia)
- Stalin takes over USSR
- Khruschev in power 1953-1964
- • SALT I
- • Balkan Wars
- World War II
- • USSR enters Olympic Games
- Strategic Arms Reduction Talks (START)
- • Solidarity (Poland)
- • Monarchy in Hungary 1919-1947
- • Cold War begins
- • Berlin Wall
- Detente
- SALT II (not ratified by U.S.) •
- • Albania independent 1912-1939
- • Hitler invades Poland
- • COMECON
- • Soviet troops destroy Hungarian revolution
- Afghan War

(Latin America band)
- World War I
- • Inter-American Commission on Women
- • Cuba allies with USSR
- Rise of middle class
- • Civil War (Mexico)
- • OAS
- • Puerto Rico becomes self-governing U.S. territory
- Fighting in Central America
- Uruguay and Brazil free
- • Panama Canal opens
- • Alliance for Progress
- Argentina invades Falkland Islands; British keep control •
- Women's suffrage 1940-1961
- World War II
- Cuban missile crisis •
- Castro rules Cuba
- Argentina votes out Peronists •
- Sandinistas in power in Nicaragua
- Realism (in the arts)
- • Good Neighbor Policy
- Bay of Pigs
- Land reform
- • Independence (Mexico)
- Invasion of Cuba
- • Puerto Ricans gain U.S. citizenship
- Age of Caudillos
- Cuba-U.S. agreements •
- • Panama Canal Treaties

(United States band)
- World War I
- • New Deal begins
- • Marshall Plan
- First astronaut in space •
- • Nuclear Test Ban Treaty
- • SALT I
- START •
- Reagan-Gorbachev talks
- Good Neighbor Policy •
- Peace Corps •
- U.S. missiles deployed by NATO
- Stock market crash •
- • OAS
- Nonproliferation Treaty •
- U.S. invades Panama •
- Japanese attack Pearl Harbor •
- World War II
- NATO •
- Cuban missile crisis •
- Full diplomatic relations with PRC; SALT II •
- Bush attends drug conference in Colombia
- • Korean War 1950-1953
- Astronauts on the moon •
- Camp David Accords •
- • Iranian crisis
- • Treaty of Versailles; League of Nations
- • U.S. drops A-bombs on Hiroshima, Nagasaki
- • U.S. in Vietnam 1964-1973
- • Panama Canal Treaties

873

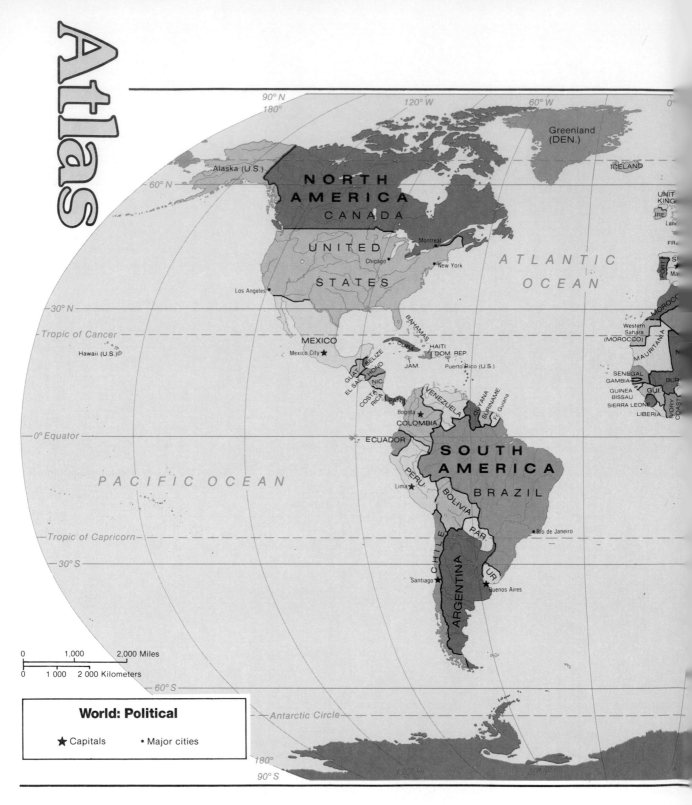

90° N
180°
120° W
60° W
0°

Greenland
(DEN.)

ICELAND

60° N
Alaska (U.S.)

NORTH
AMERICA
CANADA

UNIT
KING

IRE

Lond

UNITED

Montreal

Chicago

New York

STATES

ATLANTIC
OCEAN

FR

S
Ma

Los Angeles

30° N

PORT

Tropic of Cancer

BAHAMAS

Western
Sahara
(MOROCCO)

MOROCCO

MAURITANIA

Hawaii (U.S.)

MEXICO

Mexico City ★

CUBA

HAITI
DOM. REP.

JAM.

Puerto Rico (U.S.)

SENEGAL
GAMBIA

GUINEA
BISSAU
SIERRA LEONE

BUR

GUI.

GUAT.

BELIZE

HOND.

EL SAL.

NIC.

COSTA
RICA

PAN.

VENEZUELA

GUYANA

SURINAME

Fr. Guiana

IVORY
COAST

LIBERIA

Bogotá ★

COLOMBIA

0° Equator

ECUADOR

SOUTH
AMERICA

PACIFIC OCEAN

PERU

Lima ★

BRAZIL

BOLIVIA

Tropic of Capricorn

Río de Janeiro

PAR.

30° S

CHILE

Santiago ★

ARGENTINA

UR.

Buenos Aires ★

0   1,000   2,000 Miles

0   1 000   2 000 Kilometers

60° S

Antarctic Circle

World: Political

★ Capitals   • Major cities

180°

90° S

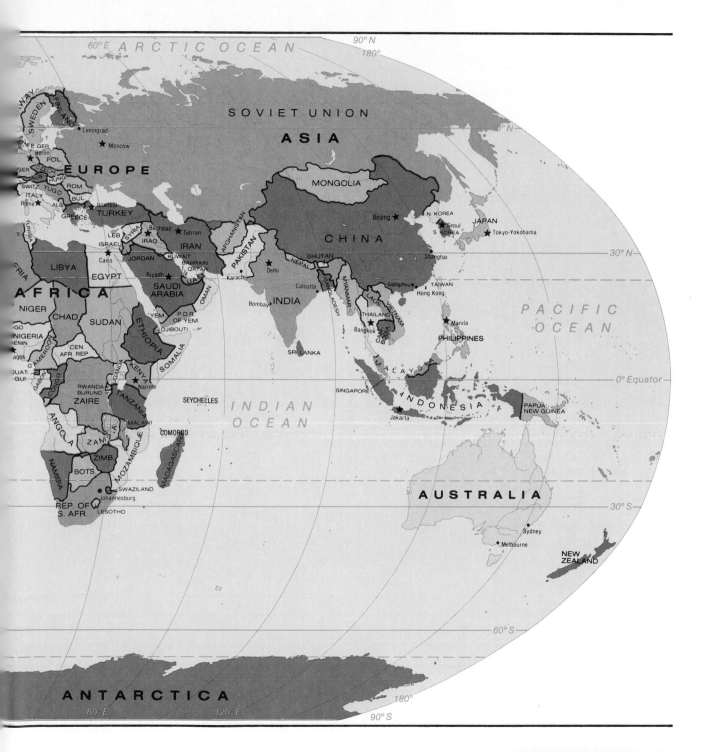

ARCTIC OCEAN

60°E
90°N
180°

SOVIET UNION

ASIA

• Leningrad

★ Moscow

EUROPE

MONGOLIA

N. KOREA
Beijing ★
★ Seoul
S. KOREA
JAPAN
★ Tokyo-Yokohama

Istanbul
TURKEY

Baghdad ★
★ Tehran

CHINA

AFGHANISTAN

PAKISTAN

Shanghai

30°N

LEB
SYRIA
ISRAEL
IRAQ

IRAN

BHUTAN

NEPAL

Cairo

JORDAN

KUWAIT
BAHRAIN
QATAR

Delhi

TAIWAN

MYANMAR

Guangzhou

Hong Kong

LIBYA

Riyadh ★

OMAN

Karachi

BANGLADESH

EGYPT

U.A.E.

Calcutta

LAOS
VIETNAM

AFRICA

SAUDI
ARABIA

P.D.R.
OF YEM.

Bombay

INDIA

THAILAND

★ Manila

NIGER

CHAD

SUDAN

'YEM.'

Bangkok ★

CAMBODIA

PHILIPPINES

PACIFIC
OCEAN

ETHIOPIA

DJIBOUTI

NIGERIA

CEN.
AFR. REP.

SRI LANKA

SOMALIA

agos

CAMEROON

UGANDA
KENYA

MALAYSIA

QUAT.
GUI

GABON
CONGO

RWANDA
BURUND
Nairobi

SINGAPORE

0° Equator

SEYCHELLES

INDONESIA

PAPUA
NEW GUINEA

ZAIRE

TANZANIA

INDIAN
OCEAN

Jakarta

ANGOLA

MALAWI

COMOROS

ZAMBIA

ZIMB

MOZAMBIQUE

MADAGASCAR

NAMIBIA

BOTS

AUSTRALIA

SWAZILAND

Johannesburg

REP. OF
S. AFR.

LESOTHO

30°S

Sydney

• Melbourne

NEW
ZEALAND

60°S

ANTARCTICA

60°E
120°E

180°

90°S

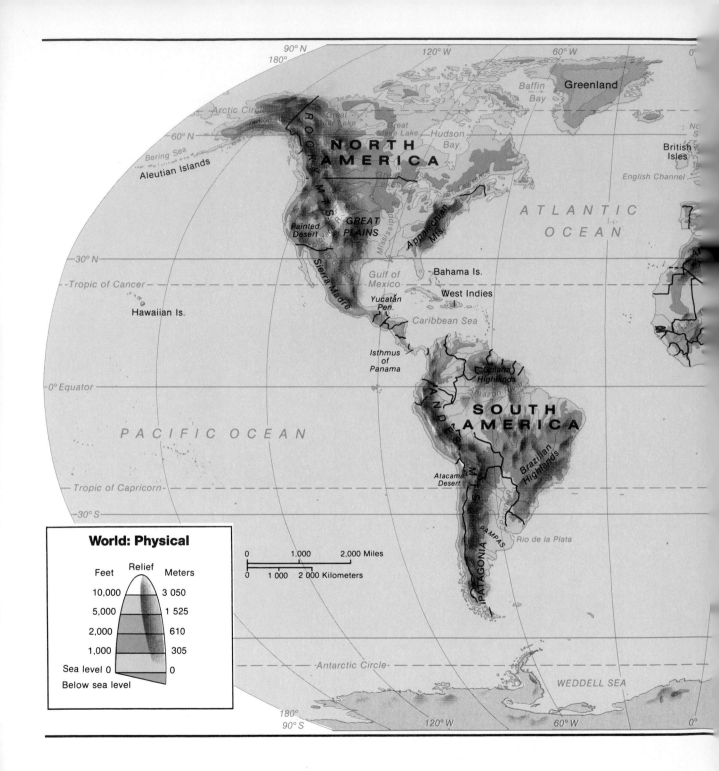

World: Physical

Feet	Relief	Meters
10,000		3 050
5,000		1 525
2,000		610
1,000		305
Sea level 0		0
Below sea level		

0   1,000   2,000 Miles

0   1 000   2 000 Kilometers

NORTH AMERICA

SOUTH AMERICA

ATLANTIC OCEAN

PACIFIC OCEAN

Greenland

Baffin Bay

Hudson Bay

British Isles

English Channel

Bering Sea

Aleutian Islands

Arctic Circle

Great Bear Lake

Great Slave Lake

Great Lakes

ROCKY MTS.

GREAT PLAINS

Painted Desert

Sierra Madre

Mississippi

Appalachian Mts.

Gulf of Mexico

Bahama Is.

West Indies

Caribbean Sea

Yucatán Pen.

Isthmus of Panama

Hawaiian Is.

Guiana Highlands

Amazon

Brazilian Highlands

ANDES

Atacama Desert

PAMPAS

Rio de la Plata

PATAGONIA

Weddell Sea

90° N
180°

120° W

60° W

0°

60° N

30° N

Tropic of Cancer

0° Equator

Tropic of Capricorn

30° S

Antarctic Circle

180°
90° S

120° W

60° W

0°

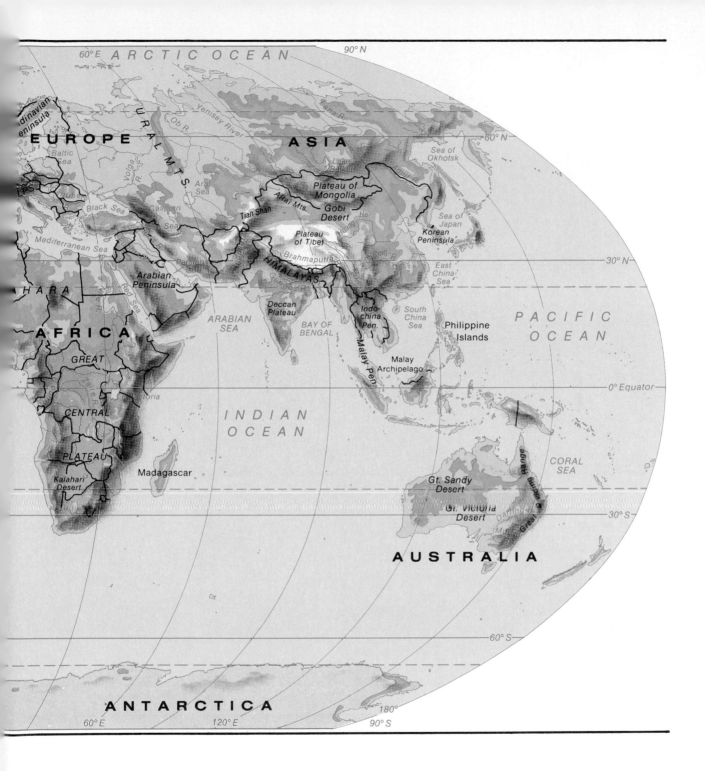

ARCTIC OCEAN
60° E
90° N
60° N

EUROPE
Scandinavian Peninsula
Baltic Sea
ALPS
Danube
Black Sea
Volga
Caspian Sea
Mediterranean Sea
SAHARA
Red Sea
Arabian Peninsula
Persian Gulf

U R A L   M T S.
Ob R.
Yenisey River
Lena R.

ASIA
Lake Baikal
Altai Mts.
Plateau of Mongolia
Gobi Desert
Tian Shan
Plateau of Tibet
Aral Sea
Amur R.
Hwang He
Chang R.

Sea of Okhotsk
Sea of Japan
Korean Peninsula
East China Sea
South China Sea

HIMALAYAS
Brahmaputra
Ganges R.
Indus R.

AFRICA
GREAT
Zaire R.
Victoria
CENTRAL
PLATEAU
Kalahari Desert

ARABIAN SEA
Deccan Plateau
BAY OF BENGAL
INDO-china Pen.
Malay Pen.
Malay Archipelago

Philippine Islands

PACIFIC OCEAN

30° N

INDIAN OCEAN
Madagascar

0° Equator

Gt. Sandy Desert
Gt. Victoria Desert
Darling R.
Murray
Great Dividing Range

CORAL SEA

30° S

AUSTRALIA

60° S

ANTARCTICA
60° E
120° E
180°
90° S

877

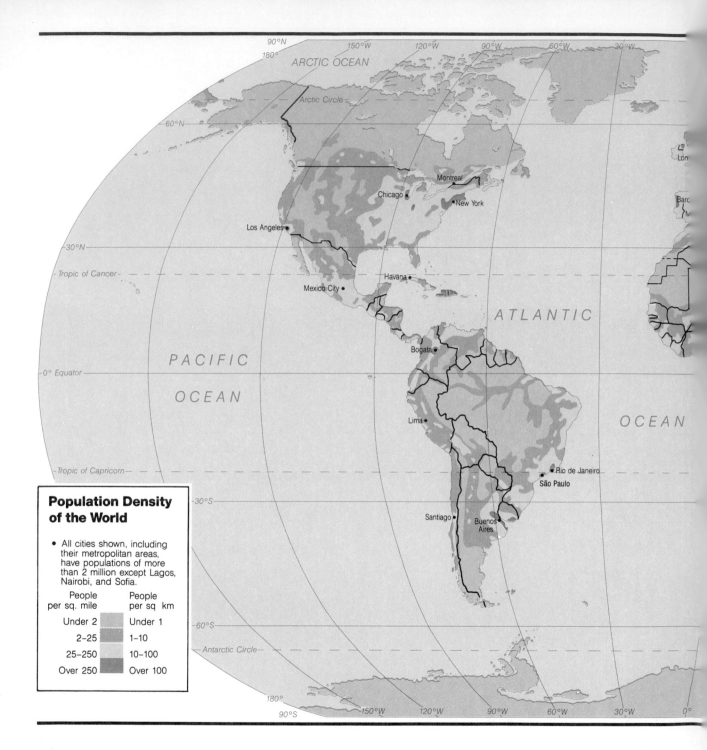

Population Density of the World

- All cities shown, including their metropolitan areas, have populations of more than 2 million except Lagos, Nairobi, and Sofia.

People per sq. mile		People per sq km
Under 2		Under 1
2–25		1–10
25–250		10–100
Over 250		Over 100

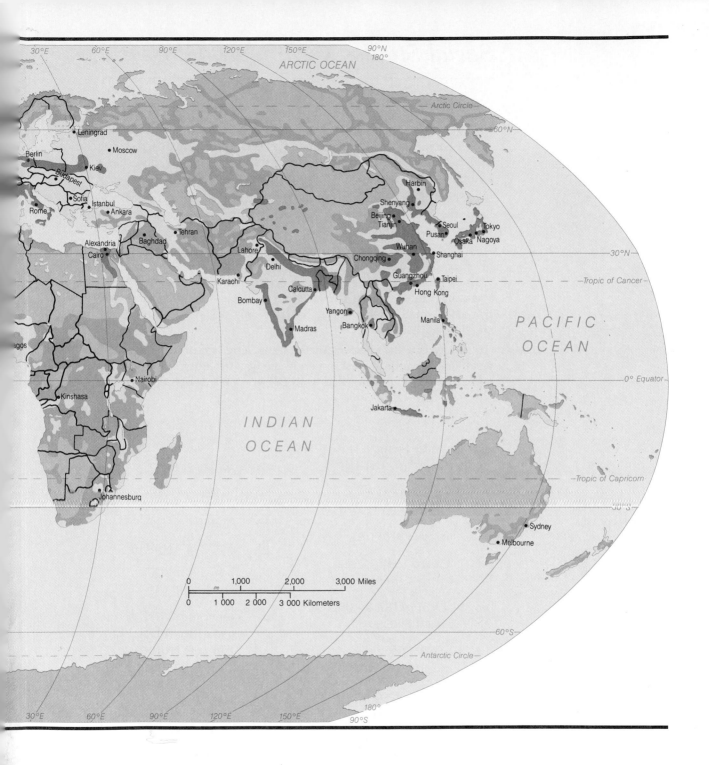

ARCTIC OCEAN

Arctic Circle

60°N

- Leningrad
- Moscow
Berlin
Kiev
Budapest
Sofia
Istanbul
Rome
Ankara

Harbin
Shenyang
Beijing
Tianjin
Seoul
Tokyo
Pusan
Osaka
Nagoya
Wuhan
Shanghai

Tehran
Alexandria
Baghdad
Cairo
Lahore
Delhi
Chongqing
Karachi
Guangzhou
Taipei
Calcutta
Hong Kong
Bombay
Madras
Yangon
Bangkok
Manila

30°N

Tropic of Cancer

PACIFIC
OCEAN

agos

Nairobi
Kinshasa

0° Equator

Jakarta

INDIAN
OCEAN

Tropic of Capricorn

Johannesburg

30°S

Sydney
Melbourne

0   1,000   2,000   3,000 Miles
0   1 000   2 000   3 000 Kilometers

60°S

Antarctic Circle

180°

30°E   60°E   90°E   120°E   150°E   90°S

30°E   60°E   90°E   120°E   150°E

Social Studies Vocabulary/Glossary

This glossary contains brief definitions of certain words and terms used in this book. The boldface number, e.g. (**123**), listed after each definition indicates the page where the word or term is first used. You may find additional meanings of words by using your dictionaries.

Some of the words in this glossary are respelled in a special way to help the reader say them. The respelling of a word appears in parentheses.

When a word has two or more syllables, the syllables are not usually given equal stress. In the respelling of a word, the syllable or syllables with the most stress are printed in large capital letters. Syllables with less stress are printed in small capital letters. Syllables that are not stressed are printed in small letters. Words that have only one syllable are printed in small capital letters.

Below is a list of special letters and letter groupings used for the respelling of words. A description of the way the letter or letters are said and an example of a respelled word follow each letter or letter grouping.

a	*a* in *trap* [TRAP]		**oo**	*oo* in *food* [FOOD]
ah	*a* in *far* [FAHR]			*u* in *rule* [ROOL]
	o in *hot* [HAHT]		**ow**	*ou* in *out* [OWT]
aw	*a* in *all* [AWL]		**oy**	*oi* in *voice* [VOYS]
	o in *order* [AWRD-uhr]		**th**	*th* in *thin* [THIN]
ay	*a* in *face* [FAYS]		**th**	*th* in *that* [THAT]
e	*e* in *let* [LET]		**u**	*u* in *put* [PUT]
	a in *care* [KER]			*oo* in *foot* [FUT]
ee	*e* in *equal* [EE-kwuhl]		**uh**	*u* in *cup* [KUHP]
	i in *ski* [SKEE]			*a* in *asleep* [uh-SLEEP]
i	*i* in *trip* [TRIP]			*e* in *term* [TUHRM]
	e in *erase* [i-RAYS]			*i* in *bird* [BUHRD]
iy	*i* in *kite* [KIYT]			*o* in *word* [WUHRD]
	y in *sky* [SKIY]		**z**	*s* in *atoms* [AT-uhmz]
oh	*o* in *rodeo* [ROHD-ee-OH]		**zh**	*s* in *measure* [MEZH-uhr]
	ow in *slow* [SLOH]			*z* in *azure* [AZH-uhr]

A

Absolute monarchy. A government in which power rests completely in the hands of a king or queen. **(645)**

Acculturation (uh-KUHL-chuh-RAY-shuhn). The process by which two cultural groups have contact over a long period of time and influence each other. **(7)**

Acid rain. Rainwater or other precipitation that has a high acid content because of pollutants such as sulfur dioxide and nitrogen dioxide. **(732)**

Alliance. A joining together of groups by a formal agreement to promote their mutual interests. **(687)**

Amnesty (AM-nuh-stee). An act of a government by which a pardon is offered to a large group of individuals, such as delinquent taxpayers. **(785)**

Animism (AN-uh-MIZ-uhm). A belief that all natural objects have a living soul. **(177)**

Annexation. The addition of territory to a nation or state. **(806)**

Anthropologist (AN-thruh-PAHL-uh-juhst). One who studies anthropology. **(5)**

Anthropology (AN-thruh-PAHL-uh-jee). The study of people, their place in the natural world, their cultural development, and their differing ways of living and behaving. **(5)**

Anti-Semitism (ANT-i-SEM-uh-TIZ-uhm). Hostility and prejudice against Jews. **(468)**

Apartheid (uh-PAHR-TAYT). A policy of racial segregation and economic and political discrimination against non-Europeans in the Republic of South Africa. **(88)**

Apolitical. Not concerned with or active in political life. **(849)**

Archaeologist (AHR-kee-AHL-uh-juhst). One who studies archaeology. **(6)**

Archaeology (AHR-kee-AHL-uh-jee). The study of the cultures of prehistoric and historic peoples through their remains, such as tools, weapons, pottery, buildings, and writings. **(6)**

Architecture (AHR-kuh-TEK-chuhr). The planning and construction of buildings. **(52)**

Arms race. Competition among nations to develop more and better weapons. **(66)**

Artifact (AHRT-i-FAKT). An object made by humans, either by hand or by machine. **(6)**

Artisan. A trained or skilled worker; a craftworker. **(645)**

Arts, the. Music, literature, painting, sculpture, dance, and so on. **(117)**

Assembly. A meeting of people for a specific purpose; often, a lawmaking body. **(646)**

Assimilation (uh-SIM-uh-LAY-shuhn). The act of becoming like others in customs and attitudes. **(150)**

Astronomical observatory. A structure used to observe heavenly bodies and to make celestial measurements. **(514)**

Astronomy. The science that studies the sun, moon, stars, planets, and other heavenly bodies. **(149)**

Authoritarian (aw-THAWR-uh-TER-ee-uhn). Believing in complete obedience to authority—for example, a government—instead of personal freedom. **(83)**

Autonomous (aw-TAHN-uh-muhs). Having the right of self-government. **(810)**

B

Balkanization (BAWL-kuh-nuh-ZAY-shuhn). The fragmentation of a region into smaller, often hostile, groups. **(839)**

Barter. The exchange of one kind of goods for another. **(415)**

Basin. A large or small depression, or low spot, in the land surface. **(28)**

Bloc. A combination of nations forming a group with common interests. **(789)**

Bourgeoisie (BOORZH-WAH-ZEE). The middle class. **(645)**

Buffer zone. A neutral or demilitarized zone between two hostile powers. **(787)**

Bureaucracy (byoo-RAHK-ruh-see). Together, all the departments or bureaus that administer a government. **(57)**

C

Cabinet. A group of advisers that helps a chief executive or monarch in administering a government. **(165)**

Capital. All property—machines, buildings, tools, and money—used to produce goods and services. **(20)**

Capitalism. An economic system in which land, machines, factories, and other means of production are privately owned. Goods and services are produced for profit in a free, usually competitive, market. **(665)**

Capitalist. One who supports capitalism. **(773)**

Cash crop. A crop that is raised to sell rather than for one's own use. **(31)**

Cash economy. An economic system in which money is used to buy goods and services. **(135)**

Caste (KAST) **system.** A social system in which people are grouped according to occupation, wealth, heredity, religion, or some other characteristic. **(154)**

Caudillo (kaw-THEE-yoh). Spanish for "chieftain"; a single, strong leader, usually a member of the military. **(340)**

Censor. An official of the Roman republic charged with taking the census and monitoring morals and conduct. **(541)**

Central planning. The setting of economic, social, or political goals by a national government. **(783)**

Chiefdom. A region or a people ruled by a chief. **(45)**

Chlorofluorocarbons (KLOHR-oh-FLUR-oh-KAHR-buhnz). Gases containing chlorine, fluorine, and carbon that are used in industrial products and processes and that contribute to the destruction of ozone high in the atmosphere. **(861)**

City-state. An independent community made up of a city and its surrounding area. **(50)**

Civil disobedience. A form of protest against government in which people use nonviolent means to resist authority. **(162)**

Civilization. The level of development that includes a food-producing base, increasing centralization of political and religious authority, large buildings, and often, but not always, the development of writing and written records. **(18)**

Civil rights. The rights of people to act and speak as they wish without government interference, providing they do not harm others. **(156)**

Civil servant. A nonmilitary person employed in government service. **(57)**

Civil war. A war between sections of the same state or nation. **(61)**

Clan. People within an ethnic group who claim to be descended from a common ancestor. **(9)**

Class. A grouping of persons according to similar social and economic levels. **(140)**

Class structure. The organization of social classes in a society, from the highest to the lowest class. **(140)**

Climate. The generally existing weather conditions of a region. **(30)**

Coalition (KOH-uh-LISH-uhn). A voluntary joining together of interest groups, political parties, or nations. **(164)**

Cold war. A conflict between nations using diplomatic, economic, or psychological means rather than military force. **(708)**

Collective farm. A large farm on which many people work together and share the profits. **(783)**

Colonial empire. An empire consisting of foreign territories, often overseas, that are exploited for their natural resources. **(64)**

Colonialism. A national policy that approves of taking control of the politics and economies of weaker peoples. **(182)**

Colony. A territory over which a nation claims the right of possession and over which that nation exercises political and economic control. **(64)**

Commerce (KAHM-ers). Large-scale buying, selling, or exchanging of goods. **(50)**

Communism. An economic system in which the community or government owns the means of

882

Direct rule. Rule by a central authority rather than by local officials. **(808)**

Dissident (DIS-uhd-uhnt). A person who disagrees with the policies of a government or with the prevailing ideas of his or her society. **(830)**

Divestment (diy-VEST-muhnt). The act of getting rid of something that is no longer wanted. **(92)**

Division of labor. The assigning of separate tasks to different groups, such as men and women or parents and children. **(665)**

Doctrine (DAHK-truhn). A position or principle taught by a church, government, or other group. **(108)**

Domesticate (duh-MES-ti-KAYT). To tame an animal; to refine a wild plant into one that can be cultivated as a crop. **(14)**

Dynasty (DIY-nuh-stee). A series of rulers who belong to the same family. **(147)**

─────── **E** ───────

Ecology (i-KAHL-uh-jee). The study of living things and their relationships to the environment. **(474)**

Economic development. The way a nation expands its economy to produce more jobs, goods, and services for the people to improve their standard of living. **(96)**

Economics. The study of how individuals and nations make choices about ways to use their scarce resources to fill their needs and wants. **(773)**

Economy. A system for producing, distributing, and consuming goods and for supplying services. **(164)**

Emissary (EM-uh-SER-ee). A representative of a monarch or government sent to another country on a special mission. **(315)**

Empire. A group of countries and territories united under one rule, as the Roman Empire. **(140)**

Entente (ahn-TAHNT). An agreement or understanding between two or more nations. **(687)**

Environment. All the outside influences and conditions, such as climate and geography, that affect the continuing development of a people. **(24)**

Erosion (i-ROH-zhuhn). The wearing away of the land by the action of wind, ice, or water. **(141)**

Ethnic (ETH-nik) group. A group of people who share a common culture, social and political ties, and/or language and geographic region. **(9)**

Export. Something sent to another country or place; to send goods to another country or place. **(57)**

Extended family. A family that includes father, mother, unmarried and married children and their families, grandparents, uncles, aunts, and cousins. **(9)**

─────── **F** ───────

Faction. A group of people within a larger organization whose opinions and goals are different from those of the larger group. **(775)**

Fascism (FASH-IZ-uhm). A political movement that places the interests of the nation above those of the individual and advocates a central government headed by a dictatorial leader and economic and social regimentation. **(693)**

Federation. A union of several separate states in which each state keeps its own sovereignty, or authority. **(84)**

Feudal (FYOOD-uhl) **system**. An economic, social, and political system in which upper-class landowners give to lower-class laborers protection and the use of their lands. In return, the laborers give military or other service to the landowner. **(49)**

Folklore. The tales, legends, beliefs, customs, and traditions of a people. **(150)**

Foreign policy. The policy of a government that governs its relations with foreign nations. **(160)**

Frescoes (FRES-kohz). Paintings made on walls by applying pigment to wet plaster. **(517)**

Front. A group formed to fight for political or economic goals. **(837)**

G

General Assembly. A lawmaking body. **(469)**

General strike. The simultaneous striking of workers in many different industries. **(776)**

Geocentric (JEE-oh-SEN-trik). Having the earth as its center. **(534)**

Geography. The study of the earth's surface, its physical features, political and natural divisions, natural resources, climates, peoples, land use, industries, and products. **(18)**

Glasnost (GLAHZ-nohst). Russian for "openness." The term describes the Soviet leader Mikhail Gorbachev's policy of open information, which allows the Soviet media to report fully about events at home and abroad and to criticize the government. **(794)**

Government. The exercise of authority over a state, district, organization, or institution. **(57)**

Graft. The acquisition of money or other gain through dishonest means, especially by corrupt practices in political office. **(545)**

Greenhouse effect. The warming of the earth that occurs when abnormal amounts of "greenhouse gases" such as carbon dioxide are present in the atmosphere. The gases trap the heat that would normally radiate into space. **(858)**

Gross national product (GNP). The total monetary value of all the goods and services produced by a nation during a given period. **(137)**

Guerrilla (guh-RIL-uh) **warfare.** Fighting by small groups that carry out raids against and harass an enemy. **(71)**

Guild (GILD). An association of workers who practice a common profession or craft. **(561)**

H

Heavy industry. The manufacture of steel, machines, transportation equipment, and the machinery used for making machines. **(783)**

Hereditary (huh-RED-uh-TER-ee). Passed on from one generation to the next. **(54)**

Heresy (HER-uh-see). An opinion that is contrary to the accepted doctrine of a religion or political party. **(573)**

Heretic (HER-uh-tik). A person that holds ideas that are considered heresy. **(438)**

Heritage. Inheritance; that which is passed on from one generation to the next. **(128)**

Hierarchy (HIY-uh-RAHR-kee). A group that is organized into ranks, one above the other. **(434)**

I

Imperialism. A nation's policy of extending its economic and political control over other nations, sometimes by force. **(180)**

Imports. Goods brought into a country to be sold. **(57)**

Industrialization. The change of an area's economic system from one based on agriculture or trade to one based on industry. **(7)**

Industrial revolution. The change from a farming to an industrial economy that began in England from the mid-1700s to the mid-1800s. **(64)**

Industry. A branch of economic activity, such as business, finance, or manufacturing. **(285)**

Inflation. An increase in the price of all goods and services over an extended period of time. **(551)**

Institution. Any established organization, law, custom, or practice. **(525)**

Interdependence. The dependence of nations on one another for social, economic, technological, or environmental help; sharing of resources and efforts to benefit many groups or nations. **(6)**

Isthmus (ISTH-muhs). A narrow piece of land that connects two large landmasses. **(619)**

J

Joint-stock company. A company with the right to sell stock, or shares, in the company. **(622)**

Junta (HUN-tuh). A group of people, often military, who join to control a government. **(350)**

K

Kibbutz (kib-UTS). A collective farming community or other collective settlement in Israel. **(479)**

Kinfolk. Relatives. **(88)**

L

Laissez-faire (LES-AY-FER) **capitalism**. An economic policy that claims the government should not use economic controls or interfere in any way between workers and employees. **(665)**

Language family. Languages that have their roots, or base, in the same source. **(8)**

Leaching. A process by which minerals in the soil are carried by water to great depths in the ground, where they cannot be taken up by plant roots. **(30)**

League. A union of two or more peoples, groups, or nations to promote matters of mutual interest. **(464)**

Left-wing. Supporting complete and sometimes sudden social, political, and/or economic change; opposite of right-wing. **(359)**

Legend. A story passed from one generation to the next; it may or may not be true. **(150)**

Liberal. A person, group, or party that is not bound by tradition and believes it is the responsibility of government to deal with social and economic problems. **(343)**

Lifestyle. The way a person lives. **(110)**

Linguistics (ling-GWIS-tiks). The scientific study of languages. **(7)**

M

Mandate (MAN-DAYT). An order or command; a League of Nations commission to a member nation to govern a colony or territory. **(458)**

Martial (MAHR-shuhl) **law**. Rule by the army with special military courts instead of the regular civil authority. **(185)**

Matrilineal (MA-truh-LIN-ee-uhl). Tracing descent through the mother's side of the family. **(101)**

Means of production. Factories, railroads and other transportation systems, machines, mines, land, and other things needed to produce goods. **(96)**

Megalith (MEG-uh-LITH). A large block of stone set into the earth in a standing position. **(514)**

Mercenaries. Soldiers who are hired by a foreign country for military service. **(627)**

Middle Ages. In European history, the centuries between about A.D. 500 and 1500. **(566)**

Migration. The movement of people from one country or region to another. **(44)**

Minority. A group within a country that differs in race, religion, language, or some other characteristic from the larger part of the population. **(169)**

Mixed economy. An economy in which some industries are privately owned and others are publicly owned. **(164)**

Monarchy (MAHN-uhr-kee). A form of government headed by one person, usually a hereditary ruler such as a king or queen. **(140)**

Monotheism (MAHN-uh-thee-IZ-uhm). The belief that there exists only one god. **(150)**

Multinational. A company that does business in more than one country. **(358)**

N

Nation. A grouping of peoples within specific boundaries into a single political, economic, and social unit. **(6)**

National identity. The sense of unity of a people who share the same land, economy, culture, and language. **(165)**

Nationalism. Loyal or patriotic feeling for one's own country. **(161)**

Nationality. A group of people who share a language and customs and either live in or have ancestors who came from the same country. **(165)**

Nationalize. To transfer control or ownership of private land or industry to the national government for the benefit of its citizens. **(96)**

Natural resources. Materials in nature such as

minerals, land, and water. **(138)**

Neolithic (NEE-oh-LITH-ik) **Period**. The period of prehistory when people began farming and raising domestic animals. **(15)**

Nonalignment. A policy of remaining neutral in disputes between larger powers. **(843)**

Nuclear (NOO-klee-uhr) **family**. Family that includes only a father, a mother, and their children. **(9)**

———— O ————

Open market. The part of an economy that is not controlled or regulated by the state. **(797)**

Opportunity cost. The things a nation is willing to give up or the amount it is willing to pay to reach its goals. **(20)**

———— P ————

Paleolithic (PAY-lee-uh-LITH-ik) **Period**. The period of prehistory when humans lived as hunter-gatherers and had not yet learned to farm. **(15)**

Pan-Arabism. A movement toward the unification of all Arab countries into one nation. **(464)**

Papyrus (puh-PIY-ruhs). A paperlike writing material used by the ancient Egyptians. **(418)**

Parliament (PAHR-luh-muhnt). A lawmaking body made up of elected representatives. **(332)**

Partisan. One who strongly supports a cause, faction, or party. **(699)**

Patrilineal (PA-truh-LIN-ee-uhl). Tracing descent through the father's side of the family. **(102)**

Peninsula. A piece of land that extends from a large landmass and that is mostly surrounded by water. **(129)**

Peonage (PEE-uh-nij). A system under which workers are held to service by debt. **(346)**

Perestroika (PER-uh-STROY-kuh). A Russian word for "restructuring." The term describes the economic and political reforms begun by Mikhail Gorbachev to make the Soviet economy more productive and the government more democratic. **(794)**

Permafrost (PUHR-muh-FRAWST). Permanently frozen subsoil. **(744)**

Pharaoh (FER-oh). A ruler of ancient Egypt. **(418)**

Politics. The art and science of government; the activities and organizations through which people and political parties seek power and control of a government. **(42)**

Pollution. The dirtying of the environment. **(857)**

Polytheism (PAHL-i-thee-IZ-uhm). The belief in many gods. **(17)**

Population explosion. A great increase in human population. **(862)**

Prehistory. The time before writing was developed. **(5)**

Prejudice (PREJ-uhd-uhs). Intolerance of others; an unfavorable opinion formed without knowledge. **(69)**

Prime minister. The leader of a parliamentary government. **(82)**

Proletariat (PROH-luh-TER-ee-uht). The masses of industrial workers, who own no land or other capital. **(773)**

Propaganda (PRAHP-uh-GAN-duh). Information or news used by a government, person, or group to influence the opinions and beliefs of others; often based on half-truths. **(831)**

Prophet (PRAHF-uht). A person who foretells future events. **(432)**

Proselytization (PRAHS-uh-luht-uh-ZAY-shuhn). Attempting to convince others to convert to one's religion or political point of view. **(819)**

Protectorate (pruh-TEK-tuh-ruht). A nation or state that depends on a stronger country for its defense and the conduct of its foreign affairs; not a possession of the more powerful country. **(457)**

Proverb (PRAHV-uhrb). A wise or useful saying. **(120)**

Province (PRAHV-uhns). A division of a country, somewhat like a state in the United States. **(147)**

Psychology (siy-KAHL-uh-jee). The study of the mind and its activities. **(672)**

Puppet government. A government whose

actions are prompted or controlled by outside entities. **(188)**

R

Racism. Racial discrimination or prejudice. **(670)**

Radical. One who favors extreme changes in government or society. **(645)**

Rationing. The control of the amounts of scarce goods available to individual members of the public. **(788)**

Raw materials. Materials such as iron, wood, or coal that are used in the manufacture of other goods. **(64)**

Reforestation. The planting of forest trees to replace those that have been harvested for lumber or other uses. **(292)**

Reform. A change for the better. **(766)**

Republic. A nation in which citizens elect representatives to administer the government. **(68)**

Revolution. A basic change in or complete overthrow of an existing government, political system, or society. **(14)**

Right-wing. Resisting change and favoring a return to what existed in the past; conservative. **(359)**

S

Satellite. A small country that follows a more important one in matters of policy. **(789)**

Savannah (suh-VAN-uh). An area of grassland with scattered trees and shrubs. **(30)**

Scarcity (SKER-suht-ee). A condition in which people do not have enough income or resources to satisfy their everyday needs. **(96)**

Schism (SIZ-uhm). A formal division, especially within a church. **(563)**

Script. A form of writing. **(43)**

Sculpture. A piece of art carved, cast, or modeled with material such as stone, clay, metal, or wood. **(42)**

Sect. A group of people who are united by certain ideas, beliefs, and opinions; often a religious group. **(55)**

Sedentary (SED-uhn-TER-ee) **agriculture.** Farming in one place, not moving along as the fertility of the fields becomes exhausted. **(31)**

Self-determination. The right of a people to decide for themselves what kind of government they want. **(186)**

Self-government. Government of, by, and for the people. **(80)**

Serf. A low-ranking person who is bound to the land and who must work for the landowners. **(53)**

Slash-and-burn agriculture. A farming system in which land is cleared and then burned to make it workable. **(31)**

Social Darwinism. A social theory that maintained that only the strongest nations could survive; it was derived from Darwinian ideas of survival of the fittest in nature. **(669)**

Socialism. A system in which the government owns the means of production and controls how they are used. **(96)**

Social structure. The system of classes and ranks in a society. **(180)**

Society. Any group of people who have a shared culture and identity. **(9)**

Socioeconomic (SOH-see-oh-EK-uh-NAHM-ik). Combining social and economic factors. **(665)**

Sociology (SOH-see-AHL-uh-jee). The study of the development, organization, and functioning of human society. **(8)**

Sphere of influence. An area in which a powerful nation exercises political and economic control over less powerful nations. **(235)**

Standard of living. The average level of goods, services, luxuries, and so on, that a person or group uses in daily living. **(135)**

State. A group of people organized under one government and living within a definite territory. **(147)**

State religion. A religion supported by the government. **(429)**

Status (STAT-uhs). The rank or standing of a

person or group in relation to other persons or groups. **(53)**

Steppe (STEP). A large area of level grassland. **(744)**

Subcontinent. A large landmass that is attached to a larger continent. **(129)**

Subsistence farmers. Farmers who raise enough for their own needs but have no surplus to send to market. **(31)**

Suffrage (SUHF-rij). The right to vote. **(663)**

Superpower. One of the most powerful nations in the world. **(164)**

——— T ———

Tariff (TAR-uhf). A tax on imports. **(381)**

Technology (tek-NAHL-uh-jee). The practical and industrial arts and the applied sciences of a society. **(6)**

Telecommunications (TEL-i-kuh-MYOO-nuh-KAY-shuhns). Communications transmitted by radio, television, telegraph, and so on. **(135)**

Territory. The area under the administration of a ruler, nation, state, and so on. **(161)**

Terrorism. The use of violence and the fear of violence to gain political or ideological ends. **(164)**

Third World. A cold-war term used to describe developing nations not on the side of either the major Communist or capitalist nations. **(792)**

Totalitarian (toh-TAL-uh-TER-ee-uhn) regime. A government under which every part of life—economic, religious, social, educational, etc.—is controlled by the government. **(693)**

Town. A settled area larger in size and population than a village but smaller than a city. **(110)**

Trade-off. The exchanging of one thing in return for another; the balancing of goals that are not all obtainable at the same time. **(20)**

Tradition. A custom, practice, or way of doing something that is handed down from one generation to the next. **(160)**

Treaty. A formal agreement between nations. **(267)**

Tribunal (triy-BYOON-uhl). A court of justice. **(707)**

Tribute. A forced payment of money by one nation, ruler, or group to another in return for protection or as a guarantee of peace. **(53)**

Tundra (TUHN-druh). Land in the far north that has a thin layer of soil over the permafrost and that supports only sparse vegetation such as mosses and lichens. **(744)**

Tyrant (TIY-ruhnt). In ancient Greece, a military leader supported by the people who seized power and ruled as a dictator. **(521)**

——— U ———

Unilateral (YOO-ni-LAT-uh-ruhl). Undertaken or done by one party without regard to the other party; one-sided. **(800)**

Union. A grouping together of nations, states, or individuals for a particular purpose. **(61)**

Urban (UHR-buhn). Of the city. **(135)**

Urbanization (UHR-buh-nuh-ZAY-shuhn). The change of an area from a rural to an urban environment. **(110)**

——— V ———

Values. Attitudes or beliefs a group holds to be important. **(106)**

Vassal (VAS-uhl). One who, in exchange for land and protection, promised loyalty and military or other services to a lord or lady. **(49)**

Vernacular (vuhr-NAK-yuh-luhr). Language of a particular region; the language of the common people as opposed to a literary language. **(434)**

——— W ———

Welfare state. A government that provides security in the form of such benefits as free medical care, unemployment insurance, and pensions for all its citizens. **(309)**

Westernization. The adoption of the culture, governmental forms, languages, or technological innovations of European countries by peoples in Asia or Africa. **(160)**

Albright-Knox Art Gallery, Buffalo, New York: Charles Clifton Fund 429; Bequest of Arthur Michael 180. Courtesy of American Honda Corporation 275. Courtesy of the American Numismatic Society, New York 316T, B, 523. AP/Wide World Photos—81, 84, 85, 86, 87, 88, 89, 121, 165, 188, 237T, B, 264, 348, 353, 361, 362, 378, 463, 672, 684, 689, 693, 709, 806, 837, 838. Archives Photographiques—Paris 421T. Courtesy of the Art Institute of Chicago 677. Art Reference Bureau 610, 627, 673, 676B; Scala Art Reference Bureau 594. Art Resource: 642C; Andrew Sacks 358. Ann Atene 226. Reproduced by kind permission of His Grace the Duke of Bedford 625. Henry D. Meyer/Berg & Associates 721. The Bettman Archive 38, 77, 117L, 267, 321, 329, 334, 342, 346, 347, 431, 486, 571, 573T, 576, 585T, 588, 591, 607, 613, 621, 635, 636, 639L, 640, 647, 649, 653, 659, 664L, R, 666, 669, 671T, B, 674, 676T, 694, 703, 711. UPI/Bettman: 702, 824. Reuters/Bettman, 243. Photo Bibliotheque Nationale Paris 314, 618. Copyright Bibliotheque Royale Albert ler, Brussels 582. Black Star: Yves de Braine 724; Dennis Capolongo 856; Cindy Karp 367; Claus Meyer 373; Anthony Suau 171, 172; Peter Tunley 245. Bodleian Library colour filmstrip 113D: 303; 161C: 580. Lee Boltin 308L, R, 437. Greta and Norman Britan 284, 301. Photo John Webb, Brompton Studio 634. Chiaroscuro/S. Kessler 390. Courtesy of *China Pictorial,* People's Republic of China 219, 222. Cincinnati Art Museum: J.J. Emery Fund 558. The John Omwake Playing Card Collection on permanent loan to the Cincinnati Art Museum from The United States Playing Card Company 586T. Bruce Coleman, Inc.: Nicholas DeVore 375; John Flannery 80; Jackie Foryst 310; J. Hesserschmidt 181; Elisa Leonelli 340. Columbian Information Service 371. Compix 698, 699. Culver Pictures 67, 73, 455, 457, 608, 682, 687, 688. DPI, Inc.: Jerry Frank 59, 100, 101, 109. George M. Davis 192, 257. John B. Davis 51. Leo de Wys Inc.: J.M. Bertrand 122; Peter Dublin 120; Victor Englebert 43; Helmut Oizinger; Andre Picou 24; Reininger 359. EASTFOTO: 202, 215, 236, 238, 246, 251. *Ebony* Magazine 58. Edison National Historic Society (photo provided by Edison Electric Institute) 660. Editorial Photocolor Archives (Art Resource) 16B, 402, 408, 417, 446, 451, 479, 491, 530, 544, 556, 573B, 586B, 597T, B, 626; Bruce Anspach 439L; D.W. Funt 432; Susan McKinney 439R. Eliot Elisofon Archives, Museum of African Art: Courtesy of the Nigerian Government, Department of Antiquities 60L; Courtesy of Paul and Ruth Tishman 55. FPG/Joan Kugler 205; Terry Qing 242. Courtesy of the Field Museum of Natural History, Chicago 60R. By permission of the Folger Shakespeare Library, Washington, D.C. 601, 603; Model by John Cranford Adams and Irving Smith on loan to the Folger Shakespeare Library 602, 606, 609. Rare Book Department, Free Library of Philadelphia 644. French Government Tourist Office 584. S.L.H. Fuller 64. Gamma-Liaison/J.C. Francolon 12. Gold Museum of Peru-Foundation Miguel Mujica Gallo 307. THE GRANGER COLLECTION, New York 335, 496, 562, 616. David Hallinger 366. The Robert Harding Picture Collection, London 132. Photograph Courtesy of the American Indian. Heye Foundation 313. The Higgins Armory Museum, Worcester, Massachusetts 524T, 578. Hirshhorn Museum and Sculpture Garden, Smithsonian Institution 728. Information Service of India 148, 162, 168R. Interfoto M TI, Hungary 216. *Israel Sun,* Ltd. 473. Italian Government Travel Office 599L, R. Courtesy of Janus Films 745 Fifth Avenue, New York, N.Y. 10022 (212-753-7100) and Museum of Modern Art/Film Stills Archive 261. Consulate General of Japan, N.Y. 277L. Japan National Tourist Association 265. Russell Jong 841. Don Klumpp Productions, Inc./Anne Rippy 229. Konran/Media, Inc. 113, 119, 380L. Kunsthistorische Museum, Vienna 598, 643R. Library of Congress 357, 656. Magnum: 374; Robert Azzi 401, 470; Bruno Barbey 385, 444, 641; Ian Berry 56, 107, 400; Werner Bischoff 384T; Rene Burri 13BL; Robert Capa 469; Elliott Erwitt 418; Burt Glinn 140, 495; Mark Godfrey 177; Charles Harbutt 383B; Eric Hartmann 11; Erich Lessing 37, 16B, 394-395, 412, 422, 502, 519, 538, 561L, 570, 605; Ingeborg Lippman 360; Bernard Lipnitzsky 464; Rick Merrons 380R; Inge Morath 448, 488; Chris Steele Perkins 716; Marc Ribound 187; Sepp Seitz 435; David Seymour 430. Ray Manley Photo 94. Milt

Index

The following abbreviations are used in this index: *c.,* chart; *cart.,* cartoon; *exc.,* excerpt; *g.,* graph; *ill.,* illustration; *m.,* map; *q.,* quotation; and *t.,* table.

51, 60; in Western Europe, 513, 728–729

Archimedes, 535

Architecture: of Andean cultures, 305; in China, 217, 219; Gothic, 585–586, *ill.* 584, 585; Greek, 531, 533; in India, 148; in Japan, *ill.* 263; in Latin America, 389–390, *ill.* 371, 389, 390; in Mesoamerica, 297, 298, 300; in Middle East, 424, 486, 490–491; Renaissance, 599, *ill.* 599; Roman, 555–556, *ill.* 557; romanticism and, 675; in Southeast Asia, 180; in Sub-Saharan Africa, 48, 52, 56, 119, *ill.* 119; in Western Europe, 585–586, 640, 641–642, *ill.* 500–501, 640, 675, 729

Argentina, 289, 290, 292, 367, 368, 370, *ill.* 289; economic development, 349, 379, 381, 382; independence movement, 328–329; politics, 349–351

Arias plan, 360, 362

Aristarchus, 534

Aristophanes, 532

Aristotle, 528, 529–530, 603, 604, *ill.* 530

Arkwright, Richard, 658

Armenia and Armenians, 807, 808

Arms race: nineteenth-century Europe, 686–687; cold war, 799

Arts: in Byzantine Empire, 562; in China, 215, 217, 218, 219–220, 247, *ill.* 208, 211, 219, 220, 221, 227, 229, 246; in Eastern Europe, 847–850, *ill.* 847, 850; in Greece, 527, 531–532, *ill.* 519, 534; in India, 146, 148, 153, 165–166; in Japan, 265–266, *ill.* 258; in Latin America, 382–390, *ill.* 322, 387, 388; in Mesoamerica, 297; in Middle East, 430, *ill.* 491, 495, 496; in Renaissance, 595–598, *ill.* 594, 596, 597, 598; in Southeast Asia, 180, 189, 191, *ill.* 176,

180; in Sub-Saharan Africa, 42, 43, 60–61, 117–122, *ill.* 24, 40, 117, 118, 122; in USSR, 828–832, *ill.* 738–739, 832; in Western Europe, 517, 638–643, 673–678, 723, 724–730, *ill.* 4, 571, 573, 576, 585, 586, 642, 643, 673, 675, 676, 677, 678, 680, 725, 726, 727, 728

Aryans (people), 142, 147, 150, 155

Ashanti (people), 61, 62, 74, 118

Ashanti Union of Akan States, 61, 66, 68, *ill.* 61, 62, *m.* 61

Ashikaga shogunate, 262–263

Asia. *See* East Asia; South and Southeast Asia.

Askia Mohammed, 57

Asoka, 147

As-Saheli, 56

Assyria (and Assyrians), 38, 41, 412–413, 424, 425, *ill.* 412, *m.* 413

Astronomy: Chaldean, 414; in ancient Egypt, 419; Greek, 534; in India, 149; in Western Europe, 514, 603–604

Aswan, 41

Aswan High Dam, 464, 475

Atacama Desert, 290, 329, *ill.* 290

Atahuallpa, 315, *ill.* 315

Ataturk, Mustafa Kemal, 461, 489

Athens, 521–522, 523–524, 525, 531, *m.* 523

Atlantic Ocean, 29, 45, 47

Atomic bomb, 271, 704, 723, *ill.* 270, 704. *See also* Nuclear arms.

Atomic theory, 670

Attila the Hun, 750

Australia, 620, 715

Austria, 506, 510, 514, 712, 723, 747; France and, 648; Germany and, 699; Hapsburg rule, 682; Napoleon and, 650, 652; Ottoman Empire and, 454; Poland and, 766; Prussia

and, 683, 684; World War II and, 699

Austria-Hungary, 684; alliances, 687; arms race and, 687; creation of, 684–685; France and, 682, 683; Italy and, 682, 683, 684; nationalism and, 684–685; nationalities under, 684–685; Triple Alliance, 687; World War I and, 688, 692

Avicenna, 494

Axis powers (World War II), 270

Axum, Kingdom of, 42, 43, *ill.* 43, *m.* 43

Azania, 50

Azerbaijan, 807–808

Aztecs, 302–304, 313–314, *ill.* 303, *m.* 302

B

Babylonia (and Babylonians), 411–412, 413, 414, 426, 429, 433, *ill.* 414, *m.* 411

Babylonian Captivity, 426, 433

Bach, Johann Sebastian, 639

Bacon, Roger, 586

Baghdad, 449, 450, 452, 486, 494

Baker, Samuel, 72

Balboa, 619

Balfour Declaration, 468

Balkans: nations of, 839–841, 843–846; and Ottoman Empire, 839, 840; and Russia, 768; World War I and, 840; World War II and, 840, 841. *See also* Greece; Turkey.

Baltic republics, 786, 805–806

Bandeirantes, 321–322

Bangladesh, 129, 132, 134, 151; creation of, 170, 171, 173; population, 173. *See also* India; Pakistan.

Banking, medieval Europe and, 580, *ill.* 580

Bantu-speaking peoples: kingdoms of, 46–49; languages of, 25, 36, 45; migrations of, 25, 44–45, 48, 52–53, *ill.* 45, *m.* 44

Communism: in Albania, 845–846; and the arts, 828, 830, 848–849; and capitalism, 667, 668, 773; in China, 237, 238–239, 242–247, 251, 792; in Cuba, 353–354; development of, 667–668, 773; in East Asia, 249, 250; in Eastern Europe, 836–837, 838, 840, 841, 842–843, 843–844; in Latin America, 359, 360, 362; Marx and, 667, 773; nationalism and, 803; religion and, 814–819; in Southeast Asia, 184, 185, 186, 188; in Sub-Saharan Africa, 94; in Western Europe, 693, 694, 695, 696, 711, 718, 719, 721; workers and, 667, 668, 773, 778, 781; world, 667, 791, 792. *See also* Communist party.

Communist Manifesto, 667

Communist party (Chinese): 237, 238, 247

Communist party (Soviet): Brezhnev and, 792–793; government and, 793–794; Gorbachev and, 793–794; Khrushchev and, 791–792; Lenin and, 778, 781, 782; organization of, 780, 790, 820; Stalin and, 781–786; Trotsky and, 781–782

Concordat of 1801, 651

Confucianism, 213, 223–225, 230, 234, 235

Confucius, 223, 224, 225, 226, 228, *ill.* 225

Congo, Kingdom of the, 47, *m.* 47

Congo Basin, 29, 45; Belgium and, 73, 74, 76

Congo River. *See* Zaire River.

Congress of Vienna, 767, 836, *m.* 654

Congress party (India), 169

Constantine I, 439, 551, 559

Constantinople, 42, 453, 461, 559, 564, 578, 754

Copernicus, Nicolaus, 603, 604

Coptic Christianity, 42, 43

Corinth, 522, *ill.* 524

Corneille, 643

Cortés, Hernán, 301, 313, 314, 315, *ill.* 314

Cossacks, 760

Costa Rica, 288, 331, *ill.* 288

Council of Chalcedon, 42

Council of Trent, 612

Counter-Reformation, 611–612

Crassus, 546

Crecy, battle of, 590

Crete, 418, 517

Crimea, 810

Crimean War, 455, 681, 768, 823

Croats (people), 748

Cro-Magnon people, 13–14, *ill.* 13

Cromwell, Oliver, 630–631, *ill.* 631

Crusades, 451–452, 564, *ill.* 566, 578; trade and, 578–579

Cuba, 288, 313, 619, 792; communism in, 353–354; independence, 334–335; land reform, 353, 375; revolution in, 353–354; U.S. and, 334, 335, 336, 352, 353, 354, 356, *cart.* 335

Cubism, 726

Cultural diffusion: 6, *ill.* 7; crusades and, 452, 579; South and Southeast Asia, 150, 177, 178, 179; Sub-Saharan Africa, 120

Cultural Revolution (China), 243–244, 247

Culture: anthropology and, 5–6; change and, 6–7; dating remains of, 10–11, 12; language and, 7–8

Cuneiform, 410, 413

Curie, Marie, 670, 850, *ill.* 671

Curie, Pierre, 670

Cuzco, 308

Cynics, 530

Cyrus of Persia, 414, 426

Czechoslovakia, 684, 692, 699, 702, 786; created, 837; history, 837–838; USSR and, 792–793, 838

Czechs (people), 748

—— D ——

Dadaism, 727

Da Gama, Vasco, 65, 159, 618, *m.* 617

Dahomey, Kingdom of, 62, 65, 66, 68

Dalai Lama, 248

Dalton, John, 670

Danes, 569, *ill.* 502

Dante Alighieri, 600

Danube River, 507, 747

Daoism, 213, 223, 226, 228, *ill.* 226

Darius the Great, 414, 415, 523, *ill.* 408

Darwin, Charles, 668, 669

Da Vinci, Leonardo, 597

Deccan Plateau, 129, 132

Declaration of the Rights of Man, 646

De Gaulle, Charles, 465, 716, 717

De Gobineau, Arthur, 669–670

Deism, 636

Deities: Aryan, 142, ancient Greek, 519–520, 527, *ill.* 532; early Middle East, 429; Egyptian, 429–430; Hindu, 144, 150, 180, *ill.* 149; Persian, 430; Roman, 553

De Klerk, F. W., 92

Delhi Sultanate, 151–152

Delian League, 523–524

Democritus, 670

Deng Xiaoping, 244, 245, 246, 247, 250, *ill.* 244

Denmark, 503, 507, 510, 514, 570, 710, 712, 721, *ill.* 721; World War II and, 700

Depressions, 380

Descartes, Rene, 636, *ill.* 636

Desertification, 32

Diaspora, 426, 433, 435, 467

Díaz, Bartholomew, 65, 618, *m.* 617

Díaz, Porfirio, 344–346

Dickens, Charles, 676

Dictatorship of the proletariat, 667, 773, 780

Diderot, Denis, 638

Dinka (people), 87

Diocletian, 550–551

Disease: in Sub-Saharan Africa, 34

Divine Comedy, 600

Dominican Republic, 357–358, 359

Don Quixote de la Mancha, 601

Dostoevski, Feodor, 829, *ill.* 828

Draco, 521

Drake, Francis, 621, 625

Drakensburg Mountains, 28

Drama: in China, 220–221; Greek, 532, *ill.* 533; in India, 143; in Israel, 496; in Japan, 262, 266; Renaissance, 602, *ill.* 602; Russian, 832; in Western Europe, 584, 676, 725

Dreyfus, Alfred, 467, 468

Dual Alliance, 687

Dubček, Alexander, 838

Du Bois, W. E. B., 81

Duma, 766, 778

Dutch East India Company, 69, 70

———— E ————

East Africa, 25, 37, 50–53

East Asia, *m.* 199, 200, 201; environment, 198–205; industry, 206, 207, 208; national profiles, 206; population, 198, 207, 210; resources, 204; standard of living, 208; transportation, 206, 207, 214; villages in, 205–206; Western Europeans and, 210. *See also* individual countries.

Eastern Orthodox Church, 440, 451, 563; in Russia, 754–755, 756, 764, 766, 768, 769, 812–815, 816, 828

East Germany. *See* Germany.

East India Company (British), 159–160, 161, 621–622

East Pakistan, 169, 170, 172, 173

Ecology: Middle East, 474–475; pollution and, 857–861

Economic development: in China, 244–245; in Japan, 268–269, 270, 272, 273–274; in Middle East, 474–475, 477–482; in Russia, 763, 770; in South and Southeast Asia, 135; in Sub-Saharan Africa, 93–98; in Western Europe, 622–623, 711–712, 717–718

Economics, 19–20; industrial revolution and, 665; Marxism and, 667, 668, 773; theories of, 665–668

Ecuador, 294, 329; independence, 328

Edict of Nantes, 612, 626, 628

Education: in Byzantine Empire, 562; in China, 224, 229, 244; Greek, 536; in India, 160, 164; in Japan, 260, 269, 276, 277, 278; in Latin America, 368, *ill.* 367; Nazis and, 696; in Middle East, 482; in Roman Empire, 558; in Russia, 755, 756; in Sub-Saharan Africa, 55, 56–57, 110–112, *ill.* 104, 110, 111; in USSR, 803, 821–823; in Western Europe, 586, 652, *ill.* 609

Edward I (king of England), 589

Edward VI (king of England), 610

Egypt, 403, 650; ancient, 41, 42, 50, 401, 417–422, 424, *ill.* 417, 418, 420, 421, 422, 430, 431, *m.* 418, 419; economic development, 457; European domination of, 456–457, 464; Greece and, 415, 416; Israel and, 464, 466, 470–472; Mamluks in, 452, 456; nationalism in, 464; Persians in, 414; Ptolemaic dynasty, 416; religion in, 429–430; Romans in, 416

Egyptian Feminist Union, 489

Einstein, Albert, 670–671, *ill.* 670

Eisenhower, Dwight D., 703, *ill.* 702

Elizabeth (tsarina), 765, 766

Elizabeth I (queen of England), 609, 610–611, 613, 621, 625, 628, *ill.* 625

El Salvador, 288, 331, 359, 362, *ill.* 359

Encyclopédie (Diderot), 638

Engels, Friedrich, 667, 773

England, 503, 570, 572; Anglo-Saxons in, 569; civil war in, 630–631; evolution of rights in, 589, 629–630, 632; explorations of, 617, 618, 621–622; France and, 562, 563, 590, 622, 717; Glorious Revolution, 632; Hundred Years' War, 590; Magna Carta, 588–589; in Middle Ages, 569, 579, 587–588; monarchy in, 587, 588, 589, 590, 624–625, 628–630, 631–632; in North America, 621, 622; Parliament develops, 589, 628, 630; Reformation in, 609–611; Renaissance in, 600, 602; Restoration in, 631–632; Spain and, 621, 624–625; Vikings in, 569

English Channel, 508, 732

English language, 37, 121–122, 161, 166

Enlightenment, 635, 636, 638, 643, 665

Enver Pasha, 455

Epicureans, 530

Erasmus, Desiderius, 601, *ill.* 601

Eratosthenes, 534

Eric the Red, 569

Eritrea, 87

Estates General, 645–646

Estonia and Estonians, 702, 764, 786, 805–806

Ethiopia, 29, 38, 74, 82, 87, *m.* 50; early history, 42, 43, 50, 52, 88, 109

Etruscans, 539–540, 542, 556, *ill.* 540

Euclid, 535

Euphrates River, 401, 413

Euripedes, 532

European Coal and Steel Community (ECSC), 711

Renaissance, 600–601; Roman, 557; romanticism in, 674; of Russia, 829; of Sub-Saharan Africa, 120–122; of USSR, 830–831; of Western Europe, 583–584, 643–644, 674, 724–725, *ill.* 644

Lithuania and Lithuanians, 702, 754, 760, 766, 786, 805, 806, 818, *ill.* 806

Livingstone, David, 72–73, 108

Livy, 557

Locke, John, 636–637

Lombards, 567

London, 507, 548

Long March (China), 238

Lost-wax process, 60

Louis XIII (king of France), 626

Louis XIV (king of France), 626–628, 641, 683, 764, *ill.* 627

Louis XVI (king of France), 645, 646, 648

Louis XVIII (king of France), 681

Louis Napoleon. *See* Napoleon III.

Louis Philippe (king of France), 681

Loyola, Ignatius, 611

Luba, Kingdom of, 46, *m.* 46

Lunda, Kingdom of, 46, 47, *m.* 46

Luo (people), 53

Luther, Martin, 607–608, 611, *ill.* 606

Lutheranism, 607–608, 819

Luthuli, Albert John, 89

Luxembourg, 509, 700, 710, 711

——M——

Macabees, 426

Mac Arthur, Douglas, 249, 272, 273

Macedonians, 525

Machiavelli, Niccolo, 601

Madagascar, 25, 37, *m.* 50

Madero, Francisco, 346

Madras, India, 159, *ill.* 128

Magellan, Ferdinand, 181, 619, *m.* 617

Magna Carta, 588–589, *ill.* 588

Magsaysay, Ramon, 184–185

Magyars, 684, 685

Mahabharata, 142, 143, 166

Maimonides, Moses, 435–436

Makuria, 42

Malawi, 46, 84, 94

Malawi, Lake, 46

Malayo-Polynesian languages, 36, 37

Malay Peninsula, 181, 185

Malays (people), 177; migrations of, *m.* 178

Malaysia, 129, 178, 180, 185

Maldives, 129

Mali, 111; early history, 54

Mali, Empire of, 56, 57, 62, *ill.* 56, *m.* 56

Malinche, 313, *ill.* 314

Malindi, 51, *ill.* 51, *m.* 50

Mamluks, 452, 456

Manchu dynasty. *See* Qing dynasty.

Manchuria, 233, 235, 238, 239, 270, 271, 775

Manchurian Plain, 199, 206

Mandela, Nelson, 90–91, 92, *ill.* 91

Mangosuthu Gatsha Buthelezi, 92

Mansa Musa, 56

Mao Zedong, 238, 241, 242, 243, 244, 245, 248, *ill.* 238

Marconi, Guglielmo, 661

Marco Polo, 217

Marcos, Ferdinand, 185

Marcus Aurelius, 555, *ill.* 554

Marie Antoinette, 646, 648, *ill.* 649

Marlowe, Christopher, 602

Marriage: in Japan, 276; in Latin America, 372; in Middle East, 487; in Roman Empire, 558; in South and Southeast Asia, 167, 168, *ill.* 167; in Sub-Saharan Africa, 103–104, 112

Marshall, George C., 710

Marshall Plan, 710–711, 789

Martel, Charles, 567

Martí, Jose, 335, *ill.* 334

Martinique, 288

Marx, Karl, 667, 668, 773, 775, 779, 781, *ill.* 667

Marxism, 773, 775, 778

Mary Tudor (queen of England), 610, 624

Masada, 496, *ill.* 425

Masai (people), 77

Masaryk, Thomas, 837, *ill.* 837

Mathematics: Greek, 535; in India, 149; in Middle East, 494

Mato Grosso, 289

Matope, 49

Mau Mau, 83

Mauritania, 54

Maurya dynasty, 147–148, *ill.* 148, *m.* 147

Maximilian (archduke), 344, 681

Mayas, 298–300, 301, *ill.* 296, 299, 300, *m.* 298

Mazzini, Giuseppe, 682

Mecca, 55, 56, 441, 442, 444, 454, 465, *ill.* 442

Medes, 413

Medicine: in China, 222, *ill.* 222; in ancient Egypt, 420; in Greece, 533–534; in India, 149–150; Islamic, 494; Middle Ages and, 604; Renaissance and, 604; in Sub-Saharan Africa, 107; UN and, 714; in USSR, 826; in Western Europe, 636, 671–672, 730, *ill.* 604

Mediterranean Sea, 29, 41, 43, 401, 404, 410, 417, 457, 481, 503, 522, 548; early states, 422–426, 454

Megalith builders, 514

Mehmet the Conqueror, 453

Meiji Restoration, 267–269, 277

Mein Kampf, 695

Mekong River, 132

Men: in China, 229, 242; in Greece, 535; in India, 166–167; in Japan, 276, 277; in Latin America, 372, 379; in Middle East, 487; in Roman Empire, 558; in Sub-Saharan Africa, 37, 102, 107; in USSR, 825

Mendel, Gregor, 669

Mendeleyev, Dmitri, 823, *ill.* 823

Menelik II (emperor of Ethiopia), 43, 74

Mensheviks, 775

Meroe, 41, 42

Mesoamerica, 297–304

Mesopotamia, 401, 411, 424

Metals and metalworking: in East Asia, 212; in Latin America, 306, 383, *ill.* 307, 313; in Middle East, 412; in South and Southeast Asia, 141, 177, 180; in Sub-Saharan Africa, 38, 42, 44, 51, 54; in Western Europe, 514

Mexican-American War, 343, 356, *ill.* 342

Mexico, 285, 288, 368, 370; caudillos and, 342–346; early cultures, 293–294, 297–304; economic development, 345, 381, 382; France and, 344, 681; independence, 329–331; land reform, 375, 378; revolutions, 346–348, *ill.* 346, 347; Spanish in, 313–314, 318; U.S. and, 343, 344, 347

Mexico City, 285, 302, 329, 330, 343, 379

Michelangelo, 598, *ill.* 594

Middle Ages: art and architecture in, 583–586; banking in, 580; Roman Catholic Church in, 571–574, 580; craft guilds in, 581; education in, 568, 586; feudalism, 571–574, 577; languages in, 583; literature of, 583–584; manorialism in, 575–576; philosophy in, 586–587; political life in, 581–582; towns and cities of, 579, 580–581, 582, *ill.* 582

Middle class: industrial revolution and, 657, 663; in Western Europe, 623

Middle East, 41, 55, *ill.* 404, *m.* 397, 398, 399; ancient kingdoms and empires of, 408–416; cities in, 486, *ill.* 486, *m.* 406; creativity, 490–496; early peoples, 403–404; economic development, 474–475, 477–482; education, 482; environment, 397–402, 474–475, *ill.* 401; European domination, *m.* 456, 458; land use, *m.* 476; nationalism in, 461, 462, 463, 464, 465; national profiles, 480; natural resources, *m.* 476; religions of, 409, 425, 426, 428–444; Roman Empire and, 416; transportation, 480–481; water and, 474–475. *See also* names of individual countries.

Milan, 592, 595

Mill, John Stuart, 665, 672

Milton, John, 643

Minamoto clan, 259

Ming dynasty, 217

Minoans, 517

Miranda, Francisco de, 326, 327, *ill.* 326

Mitterand, François, 717

Mixtecs (people), 300

Mobutu Sese Seko (Joseph Mobutu), 87, *ill.* 87

Mochica culture, 306, *ill.* 308, *m.* 306

Modernism, 386

Mogadishu, 51, *m.* 50

Mogul Empire, 152–153, 160, 169, *ill.* 152

Mohammed Riza Pahlavi, 462, 463

Mohenjo-Daro, 141

Moldavia, 806, 807

Molière, 643

Monaco, 512

Mongkut (king of Thailand), 182

Mongolia, 198, 199, 207, 208, 216, 250, *ill.* 251

Mongols, 250; in China, 216, 217, 221; in India, 152–153; Japan and, 261; in Middle East, 452–453, 454, *m.* 453; in Russia, 750, 756, 757, 759, 762, 766, 808, 811

Monomotapa Empire, 48, 49, *m.* 49

Monroe, James, 355

Monroe Doctrine, 355, 356, 357

Monrovia, Liberia, 68

Monsoons, 134, 180

Montagu, Mary Wortley, 636

Montesquieu, Baron de, 637, 644

Monteverdi, Claudio, 639

Montezuma II, 313

Moors, 313, 449, 591

More, Thomas, 601

Morelos, José María, 330

Morocco, 435, 457, 458; early history, 57

Morse, Samuel F. B., 660

Moscow, 654, 701, 757, 760, 780, *ill.* 747, 821

Moses, 424, 432

Mossi (people), 57, 62

Mozambique (port), 51, 66, *c.* 50

Mozambique (nation), 28, *m.* 50; early history, 46

Mozart, Wolfgang Amadeus, 640

Mugabe, Robert, 85, *ill.* 84

Muhammad, 441–443, 447

Muhammad Ali, 456

Muscovy. *See* Russia.

Music: of Eastern Europe, 847; of India, 165–166, *ill.* 166; of Japan, 278; of Latin America, 321, 383–384, *ill.* 383; of Middle East, 495, *ill.* 493, 495; Renaissance, 599; romanticism and, 674–675; Russian, 832; of Southeast Asia, 191; of Sub-Saharan Africa, 119–120, *ill.* 120; of Western Europe, 585, 638–640, 729–730, *ill.* 639

Muslims: in China, 243; in

India, 150–153, 162, 165, 169; in Southeast Asia, 185; in Sub-Saharan Africa, 42–43, 50, 52, 55, 56, 57. *See also* Islam.

Mussolini, Benito, 693–695, 703, *ill.* 693

Mutota, 49

Myanmar (Burma), 129, 178, 715; early history, 180, 181; ethnic minorities and, 189

Myceneans, 517

————N————

Namibia, 92

Nanjing, China, 237

Napoleon I, 420, 649, *ill.* 650, 653; career of, 650–651; empire of, 652–653, *m.* 651; Haiti and, 333, 652; Portugal and, 653; reforms of, 651–652; Russia and, 653–654, 767; Spain and, 325, 327, 330, 653; wars of, 332, 333, 650, 652–654

Napoleon III, 344, 681–682, 683, *ill.* 682

Narmer (Menes), 417

Nasser, Gamal Abdel, 464, 465, 470, 471, *ill.* 464

National Assembly (France), 646

Nationalism: communism and, 803; Japan and, 270; in Latin America, 349; in Middle East, 461, 462, 463, 464, 465; in South and Southeast Asia, 161–163, 183, 186; in Sub-Saharan Africa, 78, 81–85; in USSR, 804–810; in Western Europe, 681–685

Naturalism, 635

Nazca culture, 305, *ill.* 308

Nazism and Nazi party, 695–696, 703, 707, *ill.* 694

Nazi-Soviet Pact, 786, 806

Neanderthal people, 12–18, 404

Nebuchadnezzar, 413, 414, 425

Negritude, 121

Nehru, Jawaharlal, 163, 164, *ill.* 164

Nelson, Horatio, 652

Neolithic period, 16–17

Nepal, 129

Netherlands (Dutch), 507, 508, 509, 710, 711, 722; explorations of, 617, 618, 620–621, *ill.* 621; in Southeast Asia, 181, 620; in North America, 620; in Sub-Saharan Africa, 69–71, 620–621; World War II and, 700

New Babylonian Empire, 413–414, 424, *m.* 413

New Delhi, 136

New Economic Policy (USSR), 781, 783

New Granada, Viceroyalty of, 316, 328, *m.* 317

New Spain, Viceroyalty of, 316, *m.* 317

New Testament, 432, 436, 437, 438

Newton, Isaac, 635, 636, 671

New Zealand, 620, 715

Ngo Dinh Diem, 186

Nicaragua, 288, 331, 359, 360, 375

Nicholas I (tsar), 768, *ill.* 770

Nicholas II (tsar), 770, 773, 774, 776, 778

Nietzche, Friedrich, 669

Niger, 30, 94, 96, 111

Nigeria, 30, 94, 101, 112, 116, 117, 121; civil war, 86–87; early history, 60; resources, 34

Niger-Kordofanian languages, 36

Niger River, 29, 57, 60, 72

Nikon, Patriarch, 813

Nile River and Valley, 29, 38, 41, 42, 72, 74; ancient Egypt and, 401, 417, 421, 475. *See also* Egypt.

Nilo-Saharan languages, 36

Nineveh, 413

Nkrumah, Kwame, 82–83

Nō (drama), 262

Noba (people), 42

Nobatia, 42

Nok culture, 54, 60, 118, *ill.* 118

Nomads, 485, 750, *ill.* 402, 488

Noriega, Manuel, 363

Normandy, 569

Normans, 569

North Africa, 54, 55, 57, 402; Barbary States, 457–458. *See also* Middle East.

North Atlantic Treaty Organization (NATO), 710, 720, 722, 789, 790

North China Plain, 199

Northern Ireland, 506, 715–716

Northern Rhodesia, 84

North Korea, 198, 199, 207, 208, 249, 250. *See also* Korea.

Norway, 503, 508, 510, 570, 710, 712, 720; World War II and, 700, 702

Nubia, 41, 42, 419

Nuclear arms, 799, 800, 824–825

Nuclear power, 746

Nuremberg Trials, 707

Nyasaland, 84

Nyerere, Julius K., 96

————O————

Octavian, 547, 548

Odoacer, 552

O'Higgins, Bernardo, 329

Oil, 186, 204, 285, 288, 402, 458, 463, 465, 466, 477–478, 481, *g.* 402, 481, 720, 808, 809, *ill.* 403, 477

Old Testament, 432, 436

Olmecs, 297–298, *m.* 297

Olympic games, 519–520, *ill.* 520

Oman, 66

Omdurman, battle of, 74

Opera, 639, 675

Operation Bootstrap, 338, *ill.* 337

Opium War, 233, 234

Orange Free State, 71

Organization of Petroleum Exporting Countries (OPEC), 477–478, *m.* 478

Ortíz de Dominquez, Maria, 372

Osman I, 453

Ottoman Empire, 67, *m.* 454; Armenians and, 807; Balkans and, 839, 840; Byzantine Empire and, 453, 564; decline of, 454–455; Eastern Europe and, 454, 455; in Egypt, 454; expansion of, 453–454; in North Africa, 454; Poland and, 835; rise of, 453–454; Russia and, 455, 760, 765, 768; World War I and, 455, 458, 688, 692; Young Turks, 455. *See also* Turkey.

Ouagadougou (state), 62

Owen, Robert, 666

Oyo (city), 60

―――― P ――――――

Pachacuti, 308

Pacific Ring of Fire, 205

Pahlavi dynasty, 462

Pakistan, 129, 136, 151, 153, 163, 171, 715; civil war, 172–173; creation of, 169; recent developments, 170, 171. *See also* Bangladesh.

Palestine, 418, 419, 425–426, 436, 447, 466, 467, 468, *ill.* 470; partition of, 469–470

Palestine Liberation Organization (PLO), 472

Pan-Africanism, 81

Panama, 288, 299, 356, 362, 619, *m.* 363

Panama Canal, 356, 359, 362, *ill.* 364, *m.* 363

Papacy (and popes): Byzantine Empire and, 440, 563; created, 439; divisions within, 606–607; England and, 609; Luther and, 608; in Middle Ages, 571–572, 573, 574; Reformation and, 608, 609. *See also* names of popes.

Papal States, 567, 682, 683

Paracas culture, 306

Paraguay: independence, 329; modern, 374

Paris, 507

Park, Mungo, 72

Paris, Treaty of (Crimean War), 681

Parsis, 431

Pasteur, Louis, 671

Pathet Lao, 188

Patricians, 541

Pavlov, Ivan, 824

Pax Romana, 548–549

Peace of Augsburg, 624

Pedro I (emperor of Brazil), 332, 351

Pedro II (emperor of Brazil), 351, *ill.* 351

Peloponnesian War, 524, 533

Peninsula War, 653

Pentecostalists, 819

People's Republic of China. *See* China.

Pepin III, 567

Perestroika, 794, 803, 806, 809

Pericles, 527, 531

Perón, Eva, 349–350, 373

Perón, Juan D., 349, 350, *ill.* 350

Perry, Matthew, 267, *ill.* 267

Persian Empire (and Persians), 43, 414–415, *ill.* 446, *m.* 415; Arab Muslims overthrow, 447; Byzantine Empire and, 447; in Egypt, 414; Greece and, 415, 523–524, 525; Islam and, 431, 450; Phoenicians and, 424; Seleucid rule, 416. *See also* Iran.

Persian Wars, 523–524

Peru, 290, 292, 368, *ill.* 384; early cultures, 294, 305–310; independence, 328, 329; land reform, 375; Spanish in, 315

Peter I (the Great, tsar), 762–764, 765, 813, 828, *ill.* 763

Petition of Right, 628

Petrarch, 600

Pharaoh, 41

Phidias, 531

Philip of Macedon, 525

Philip II (king of France), 590

Philip IV (king of France), 590

Philip II (king of Spain), 624–625

Philippines, 129, 184–185; early history, 178; Spain and, 181, 619; United States and, 182, 185

Philistines, 425

Philo of Alexandria, 435

Philosophes, 329, 637–638

Philosophy: in China, 213, 217, 223–227, 228; in Greece, 528–530, 532; in India, 166; Jewish, 435–436; political, 601–602; Renaissance and, 595; in Roman Empire, 554–555; in Western Europe, 586, 636–638, 723–724

Phnom Penh, Cambodia, 180

Phoenicians, 38, 422–424, *m.* 423

Pisa, 595

Pizarro, Francisco, 315, *ill.* 315

Plato, 528–529

Platt Amendment, 356

Plebeians, 541

Poland, 707, 747, 748; communism and, 836, 837; early history, 748, 835; modern, 836–837; religion, 835; Russia and, 760, 764, 766; Solidarity, 837; USSR and, 786, 787, 836; World War II and, 700, 702, 703, 786, 788, 836

Poles (people), 684, 748, 760, 818

Political parties: in South and Southeast Asia, 169; in Sub-Saharan Africa, 88

Pollution, *cart.* 859, *ill.* 856, 858, 861; controlling, 860–861; East Asia and, 206; industrial revolution and, 662; Japan and, 276; air, 857–858; soil, 857; water, 857

Polo, Marco, 217, *ill.* 580

Pompey, 546

Pompidou, Georges, 717

Population: controlling, 862, *ill.* 863; explosion of, 862; govern-

438–439, 440, 551, 554, 812; decline of, 214, 549–550, 551–552; in Egypt, 416, 543; expansion of, 542–543, 548; Germanic invasions, 550–551; influenced by Greeks, 553–554; Julius Caesar and, 546–547; Middle East and, 416, 543; Octavian and, 548; Pax Romana, 548–549; Senate, 541, 542, 545, 546; philosophy, 554; religion, 553–554; society, 558; wars and conquests, 542–543. *See also* Byzantine Empire.

Romania, 747, 807, *ill.* 841; early history, 840; economic development, 841; USSR and, 840–841; World War I and, 688, 840; World War II and, 840

Romanov family, 758, 761, 774, 778, 813, *ill.* 774

Roman Republic, 540–543, 544–547, *m.* 539, 541

Romanticism, 386, 673–675

Rome, 507. *See also* Roman Empire.

Romero, Oscar, 361

Roosevelt, Franklin D., 358, 703, 707, 789

Roosevelt, Theodore, 356, 357, *ill.* 357

Roosevelt Corollary, 357

Rosetta Stone, 421

Roundheads, 630

Rousseau, Jean-Jacques, 329, 638, 643, 644, *ill.* 638

Rozwi (people), 49

Rubaiyat, 444

Rub' al Khali, 400

Rubens, Peter Paul, 642

Russia, *ill.* 804, *m.* 761, 777: Afghanistan and, 769; Alexander I and, 767, 768; Byzantine Empire and, 758, 813, *ill.* 755; under Catherine the Great, 765–767; civil war in, 780, 792, 799; communism in, 773, 778–782; early history, 748, 750, 753; Eastern Europe and, 760, 764; Europeanization of, 762–763; Finland and,

787; under Ivan IV, 758–759; Japan and, 271, 775; Kievan, 753–756; Mongols in, 750, 756, 757, 759, 762, 766, 808, 811; Moscow's rise, 757; Napoleon and, 653–654, 767; Nicholas II and, 770, 773, 774, 776, 778; Ottoman Empire and, 455, 765, 768; Peter the Great and, 762–764, 765; religion in, 754, 758, 764, 766, 768, 769, 812–813; repression and rebellion in, 766, 768, 775–776; revolution in, 776, 778–780; Romanov rule, 761–770, 773–778; Time of Troubles, 760; Varangians in, 570, 753; World War I and, 688, 774, 777–778, 779, 780. *See also* Union of Soviet Socialist Republics.

Russian Orthodox Church. *See* Eastern Orthodox Church.

Russo-Japanese War, 270, 775

Ruwenzori Mountains, 28, 72

Rwanda, Kingdom of, 53

——— **S** ———

Saadia Gaon, 435

Sadat, Anwar, 464, 472, *ill.* 472

Sahara Desert, 25, 30, 34, 37, 54, 400; once green, 37–38; rock paintings in, 37, 118, *ill.* 37

St. Petersburg, 764

Sakharov, Andrei, 825, *ill.* 824

Salamis, 523

Salinas de Gortari, Carlos, 348, *ill.* 348

Samarkand, 449, 453

Samurai, 259, 260–261, 262, 264, 268, 269, 276, *ill.* 261

Sandinistas, 360

San Marino, 512

San Martín, José de, 328–329

Sanskrit (language), 142

Santa Anna, 342, 343

Sappho, 536

Sardinia, Kingdom of, 682, 683

Sargon I (king of Akkad), 410

Sargon II (king of Assyria), 413

Sartre, Jean Paul, 724

Saud family, 465, *ill.* 465

Saudi Arabia, 400, 402, 441, 465, *ill.* 466; oil and, 477

Saul of Tarsus (Paul), 438

Savannahs, 30, 31

Schmidt, Helmut, 718

Schuman, Robert, 709, *ill.* 709

Science and technology: in Andean cultures, 310; in China, 221–222, 244; in ancient Egypt, 419–420; in Eastern Europe, 850; Greek, 533, *ill.* 534; in India, 149–150; industrial revolution and, 668; in Japan, 274; in Mesoamerica, 298; in Middle East, 493–494, *ill.* 493; Renaissance and, 603–604; in USSR, 823–825; in Western Europe, 617–618, 635–636, 658–661, 668–672, 723, *ill.* 605, 634, 635, 636, 656, 657, 658, 659, 671

Scipio, 543

Scotland, 506, 571, 609, 628, 630

Scott, Walter, 674

Scythians, 750, *ill.* 740

Sefuwa clan, 58

Seleucid rulers, 416, 425, *m.* 416

Seljuk Turks, 450–451, 578

Senegal, 96, 101, 111, 121; early history, 54, 62, 76

Senegal River, 60

Senghor, Leopold Sedar, 121, *ill.* 121

Seoul, South Korea, 207

Serbia, 688

Serbs (people), 684, 688, 748

Serfs and serfdom: in Sub-Saharan Africa, 53; in Russia, 761–762, 766, 767, 768–769, 777; in Western Europe, 576

Shabaka (king of Kush), 41

Shakespeare, William, 602, *ill.* 603

Shamir, Yitzhak, 474

Shang dynasty, 211–212, 218, 221, 247